Poland

Neil Wilson, Tom Parkinson, Richard Watkins

Contents

Pomerania p351
Warmia & Masuria p425
Wielkopolska p319
Mazovia & Podlasie p94
Warsaw p55
Silesia p260
Małopolska p161
Kraków p125
The Carpathian Mountains p207

Destination Poland

In Poland, the past is not another country – in fact, it's just along the road. Although Poland has emerged from the grim, grey decades of communism to rebuild itself as a proud and independent member of the New Europe, there are few places where history feels as close as it does here.

Only a few hours' drive from Kraków's bustling, medieval market square or the gleaming skyscrapers and gourmet restaurants of Warsaw's new financial district you can still find rural landscapes of wooden cottages and narrow fields, roadside shrines bedecked with flowers, and storks' nests perched on telegraph poles. Here, the fields are turned by horse-drawn plough, the hay is cut and stacked by hand, and families dressed in their Sunday best cram into tiny, 16th-century timber churches.

And the Polish landscape, as vast and varied as the thousand years of history that have unrolled across it, still offers a range of timeless sights for the patient traveller prepared to venture off the beaten track – a white-tailed eagle soaring the updraughts above Słowiński's shifting sand dunes; a summer sunset gilding the serrated, snow-patched peaks of the Tatra Mountains; a canoeist trailing a wake through the early morning mists that curl over a tree-fringed Masurian lake; and shaggy-shouldered bison snorting plumes of vapour into the crisp December air of the Białowieża Forest.

KRZYSZTOF DYDYŃSKI

SŁOWIŃSKI NATIONAL PARK (p403)
The finest and most unusual section of the Polish Baltic coast

GDAŃSK (p354)
A rich old Hanseatic city with much charm and character

TORUŃ (p385)
A Gothic city of mighty churches and the birthplace of Copernicus

AUSCHWITZ (p304)
The Nazis' largest extermination camp is Poland's most moving sight

BALTIC SEA

Zatoka Gdańska

Zatoka Pomorska

Zalew Szczeciński

GERMANY

BERLIN

COTTBUS

DRESDEN

PRAGUE

CZECH REPUBLIC

HRADEC KRÁLOVÉ

OLOMOUC

OSTRAVA

Łeba
Puck
Wejherowo
GDYNIA
SOPOT
GDAŃSK
Ustka
Lębork
Darłowo
SŁUPSK
Sławno
Kartuzy
KOŁOBRZEG
KOSZALIN
Bytów
Kościerzyna
Tczew
Białogard
Miastko
Starogard Gdański
Malbork
Gryfice
Szczecinek
Chojnice
Tuchola
Kwidzyń
Świnoujście
Połczyn Zdrój
Czaplinek
Grudziądz
Świecie
Goleniów
Złocieniec
Złotów
Chełmno
SZCZECIN
Stargard Szczecin
Wałcz
PIŁA
BYDGOSZCZ
TORUŃ
Choszczno
Chodzież
Myślibórz
Strzelce Kraj
Znin
Inowrocław
GORZÓW WLKP
Wronki
Strzelno
Oborniki
Gniezno
Kostrzyn
Skwierzyna
Szamotuły
POZNAŃ
Świebodzin
Września
KONIN
Koło
Środa
Śrem
Jarocin
Turek
Gubin
ZIELONA GÓRA
LESZNO
Gostyń
KALISZ
Lubsko
Nowa Sól
Krotoszyn
Żary
Zagań
Głogów
Ostrów Wlkp
SIERADZ
Rawicz
Lubin
Brzeg Dln
Trzebnica
Wieluń
Zgorzelec
Bolesławiec
Oleśnica
Kępno
Lubań
LEGNICA
Jawor
WROCŁAW
Namysłów
Kluczbork
Bogatynia
JELENIA GÓRA
Strzegom
Oława
Brzeg
OPOLE
Świdnica
Lubliniec
WAŁBRZYCH
Dzierżoniów
Strzelin
Strzelce Opole
Ząbkowice Śl
Nysa
Kędzierzyn
Kłodzko
Paczków
Prudnik
GLIWICE
Głuchołazy
Głubczyce
Racibórz
Rybnik
Jastrzębie
Cieszyn

ELEVATION

	1500 m
	1200 m
	900 m
	600 m
	300 m
	150 m
	0

0   60 km
0   40 miles

lp

MALBORK (p396)
The largest and arguably the best castle in Poland

THE GREAT MASURIAN LAKES (p438)
A beautiful world of lakes and forests and a favourite haunt of sailors and kayakers

BIAŁOWIEŻA NATIONAL PARK (p121)
Europe's largest original lowland forest – a place of primeval plant and animal life

ZAMOŚĆ (p200)
A jewel of Renaissance architecture; its city walls encircle more than 100 World Heritage Listed monuments

TATRA MOUNTAINS (p252)
An amazing alpine range with much to delight hikers and nature-lovers

KRAKÓW (p125)
Poland's most important historic city, this was the royal capital for over 500 years

RUSSIA
(KALININGRAD REGION)

LITHUANIA

BELARUS

UKRAINE

SLOVAKIA

To Vilno
(Wilno)

KALININGRAD
(KRÓLEWIEC)

Braniewo
Bartoszyce
ELBLĄG
Zalew Wiślany
SUWAŁKI
Lida
Kętrzyn
Gizycko
Olecko
Lidzbark Warm
Augustów
GRODNO
Ostróda
OLSZTYN
Mrągowo
Ełk
Grajewo
Iława
Szczytno
Nidzica
ŁOMŻA
BIAŁYSTOK
Brodnica
Mława
OSTROŁĘKA
Zambrów
Łapy
Golub-Dobrzyń
Hajnówka
Sierpc
CIECHANÓW
Ostrów Maz
Bielsk Podl
Białowieża
WŁOCŁAWEK
Płońsk
Nasielsk
Wyszków
BRIEST
(BRZEŚĆ)
PŁOCK
Wyszogród
Nowy Dwór Maz
Sokołów Podl
SIEDLCE
Gostynin
WARSAW
Otwock
Mińsk Maz
Biała Podlaska
Kutno
Sochaczew
Pruszków
To Minsk
Łowicz
Żyrardów
Góra Kalwaria
Łuków
Międzyrzec Podl
Zgierz
SKIERNIEWICE
Grójec
ŁÓDŹ
Pabianice
Włodawa
Zduńska Wola
Tomaszów Maz
Dęblin
To Łuck
PIOTRKÓW
TRYB
Opoczno
RADOM
Puławy
LUBLIN
Bełchatów
CHEŁM
Radomsko
Skarżysko Kam
Starachowice
Krasnystaw
Kłobuck
Ostrowiec Św
Kraśnik
Hrubieszów
KIELCE
ZAMOŚĆ
CZĘSTOCHOWA
Sandomierz
Stalowa Wola
Jędrzejów
Biłgoraj
Tomaszów Lub
BYTOM
Zawiercie
Mielec
Tarnobrzeg
KATOWICE
Olkusz
Chorzów
Chrzanów
Dębica
RZESZÓW
Jarosław
Oświęcim
KRAKÓW
Bochnia
TARNÓW
PRZEMYŚL
Pszczyna
Myślenice
BIELSKO-BIAŁA
Jasło
KROSNO
Żywiec
NOWY SĄCZ
Gorlice
Sanok
Nowy Targ
Krynica
Rysy
(2499m)
Zakopane

The cream of Poland's attractions range from the imposing medieval castles of the Teutonic Knights to the dinky little timber churches of the Carpathian Foothills, and from the shifting sand dunes of the Baltic coast to the jagged alpine peaks of the Tatra Mountains. Picturesque medieval towns and stunning national park scenery are all well represented in these highlights.

Stroll through the charming landscaped gardens of Łazienki Park (p74) in Warsaw

Admire the meticulously rebuilt medieval buildings of Warsaw's Old Town (p63)

Wander among the romantic 18th-century follies of Arkadia (p104)

KRZYSZTOF DYDYŃSKI

Take a trip back in time to the unique Renaissance town of Zamość (p200)

Observe a centuries-old religious tradition at the colourful Corpus Christi procession (p104) in Łowicz

KRZYSZTOF DYDYŃSKI

Explore the wealth of Polish history at Kraków's magnificent Wawel Castle (p134)

KRZYSZTOF DYDYŃSKI

Follow the mysterious Easter Passion Plays (p210) at the pilgrimage centre of Kalwaria Zebrzydowska

KRZYSZTOF DYDYŃSKI

KRZYSZTOF DYDY

Swim or sunbathe on the sandy beaches of Świnoujście (p415)

Relax among the shifting dunes of Słowiński National Park (p403)

KRZYSZTOF DYDYNSKI

Marvel at the weirdness of the Chapel of Skulls (p292) near Kudowa-Zdrój

KRZYSZTOF DYDY

KRZYSZTOF DYDYNSKI

Promenade through the medieval streets of Toruń's riverside Old Town (p387)

Getting Started

Poland is a pretty easy destination for the disorganised or last-minute traveller. No huge amount of advance planning is needed, anything you forget to pack can be picked up from its well-stocked shops, and English is widely spoken in the main tourist areas.

WHEN TO GO

The tourist season runs roughly from May to September, that is, from mid-spring to early autumn. Its peak is in July and August, the months of school and university holidays, and also the time when most Polish workers and employees take their annual leave. The Baltic beaches are taken over by swarms of holiday makers, resorts and spas are invaded by travellers, the Masurian lakes are crowded with hundreds of sailing boats, and mountains can hardly be seen for walkers.

In that period, transport becomes more crowded than usual, and can get booked out in advance. Accommodation may be harder to find, and sometimes more expensive. Fortunately, a lot of schools, which are empty during the holidays, double as youth hostels, as do student dormitories in major cities. This roughly meets the demand for budget accommodation. Most theatres are closed in July and August.

See Climate Charts (p463) for more information.

If you want to escape the crowds, the best time to come is either late spring/early summer (mid-May to June) or the turn of summer and autumn (September to mid-October), when tourism is under way but not in full flood. These are pleasantly warm periods, ideal for general sightseeing and outdoor activities such as walking, biking, horse riding and canoeing. Many cultural events take place in both these periods.

The rest of the year, from mid-autumn to mid-spring, is colder, darker and perhaps less attractive for visitors. This doesn't mean that it's a bad time for visiting city sights and enjoying the cultural life as it's no less active than during the tourist season. Understandably, hiking and other outdoor activities (apart from skiing) are less prominent in this period. Most camp sites and youth hostels are closed at this time.

The ski season runs from December to March. The Polish mountains are spectacular, but the infrastructure (hotels and chalets, lifts and tows, cable cars, transport etc) is still not well developed. Zakopane (p255), Poland's winter capital, and the nearby Tatra Mountains have some of the best ski facilities.

COSTS & MONEY

Though not the bargain it used to be, Poland is still a relatively inexpensive country for travellers. Just how inexpensive, of course, depends largely on what degree of comfort you need, what hotel standards you are used

---

DON'T LEAVE HOME WITHOUT...

- your travel-insurance policy details (p469)
- binoculars for bird- (and bison-) watching (p45)
- hiking boots (p462)
- a hangover remedy
- insect repellent (p490)

to, what kind of food you eat, where you go, how fast you travel and the means of transport you use. If, for example, you are accustomed to hire cars and plush hotels, you can spend as much as you would in the West.

If you are a budget traveller, however, prepared for basic conditions and willing to endure some discomfort on the road, a daily average of around US$30 to US$35 should be sufficient. This amount would cover accommodation in cheap hotels and hostels, food in budget restaurants,

---

TOP TENS

Historic Castles

Poland has more than 100 castles, some of them among the most impressive in Europe. Here's our top 10.

- Malbork (p396)
- Lidzbark Warmiński (p435)
- Kwidzyn (p394)
- Wawel (p134)
- Pieskowa Skała (p164)

- Baranów Sandomierski (p179)
- Niedzica (p251)
- Książ (p280)
- Gołuchów (p347)
- Krzyżtopór (p180)

Must-See Movies

Head down to the local video store or browse the DVDs on www.amazon.com to pick up our choice of the 10 best films by Polish directors. Most are in Polish (except for *The Pianist* and *Three Colours: Blue*), but are available with English subtitles. See p36 for more on Polish cinema.

- *Nóż w wodzie* (Knife in the Water; 1962)
  Director: Roman Polański
- *Kanał* (Sewer; 1957)
  Director: Andrzej Wajda
- *Człowiek z marmuru* (Man of Marble; 1976)
  Director: Andrzej Wajda
- *Miś* (Teddy Bear; 1981)
  Director: Stanisław Bareja
- *Przesłuchanie* (Interrogation; 1982)
  Director: Ryszard Bugajski

- *Seksmisja* (Sexmission; 1984)
  Director: Juliusz Machilski
- *Dekalog* (The Decalogue; 1987)
  Director: Krzysztof Kieślowski
- *Three Colours: Blue* (1993)
  Director: Krzysztof Kieślowski
- *Dług* (Debt; 1999)
  Director: Krzysztof Krauze
- *The Pianist* (2003)
  Director: Roman Polański

Novels

The following novels are mostly classics by leading Polish authors, except for *The Polish Officer*, which is by an American novelist but lends some insight into the Polish experience of WWII. All are available in English translation. See p35 for more on Polish literature.

- *Quo Vadis* (1905)
  Henryk Sienkiewicz
- *Under Western Eyes* (1911)
  Joseph Conrad
- *Ashes and Diamonds* (1958)
  Jerzy Andrzejewski
- *Solaris* (1961)
  Stanisław Lem
- *A Minor Apocalypse* (1984)
  Tadeusz Konwicki

- *Who Was David Weiser?* (1987)
  Pawel Huelle
- *The Polish Officer* (1995)
  Alan Furst
- *Prawiek and Other Times* (1996)
  Olga Tokarczuk
- *Never Again!* (2001)
  Katarzyna Grochola
- *Dreams and Stones* (2004)
  Magdalena Tulli

and travel at a reasonable pace by train or bus, and would still leave you a margin for some cultural events, a few beers and occasional taxis. If you plan on camping or staying in youth hostels and eating in cheap bistros and other self-services, it's feasible to cut this average down to US$20 to US$25 per day, without experiencing too much suffering. It's important to remember that cities are more expensive than the rural areas, with Warsaw being the most expensive.

Polish currency (the złoty; abbreviated to zł or, sometimes, PLN) is convertible and easy to change either way. There's no longer a currency black market in Poland.

TRAVEL LITERATURE

You will get far more out of your visit if you read up on the country before you go. There's no shortage of English-language books about Poland, though most deal with language, culture and customs rather than actual travel experiences.

In *The Bronski House,* accomplished travel writer Philip Marsden accompanies exiled poet Zofia Hinska on a return to the village, now in Belarus, where she spent her childhood. It is a magical evocation of life among the landed gentry of eastern Poland between the wars.

Holocaust Journey: Travelling In Search of the Past, by Martin Gilbert, is the thought-provoking diary of the famous 20th-century historian's travels to Holocaust sites such as the Warsaw Ghetto, Auschwitz and Treblinka, interwoven with the stories of survivors and their experiences.

The account of a 2400km walk through Germany, Poland, Russia, the Ukraine and Romania, *The Gypsy In Me,* by Ted Simon, begins as a tale of travelling through the aftermath of communism in Eastern Europe, and ends as a fascinating and moving personal quest for family origins.

For further background literature, look out for bookshops specialising in Eastern Europe; they exist in major cities around the world that have significant Polish communities. You can also contact **Hippocrene Books** (☎ 718-454 2366; www.hippocrenebooks.com; 171 Madison Ave, New York, NY 10016, USA) for its catalogue. It has a variety of books on Poland ranging from guidebooks and dictionaries to various translations of Polish literature.

INTERNET RESOURCES

Ministry of Foreign Affairs (www.msz.gov.pl) Information on embassies, visa requirements etc.

Pilot.pl (www.pilot.pl) Clickable, zoomable online maps and city plans.

Poland.pl (www.poland.pl) General directory site, an excellent place to start surfing.

Poland: What Where When (www.what-where-when.pl) Online version of the handy tourist magazine.

Polish Culture (www.culture.pl) News, profiles, essays, articles and listings on Polish culture.

Polish National Tourist Office (www.polandtour.org) Official site for general tourist information.

Polish Vodka (www.polishvodka.com.pl) All you ever wanted to know about the Polish spirit.

Travel Poland (www.travelpoland.com) Reliable online accommodation booking service.

HOW MUCH?

Double room in mid-range hotel
200zł

Cinema ticket
16zł

Litre of vodka
40zł

Tram ticket in Warsaw
2.40zł

100km bus trip
14zł

LONELY PLANET INDEX

Litre of petrol
3.85zł

1.5L of bottled water
2.50zł

0.5L of Żywiec beer
6zł

Souvenir T-shirt
12zł

Zapiekanki (Polish pizza)
3zł

Itineraries

CLASSIC ROUTES

BEST OF POLAND
Two Weeks / Gdańsk to Kraków

Poland's top attractions offer an appealing blend of town and country, a mix of indoor and outdoor pursuits. This north–south tour takes in the country's main highlights.

Begin with a day in the grand old port city of **Gdańsk** (p354), then head east to the **Great Masurian Lakes** (p438) for some water-based exploration (or relaxation), stopping at **Malbork** (p396) on the way to see the castle.

From here, it's not too long a drive to **Białowieża National Park** (p121), where you can ride a horse-drawn cart through primeval forest to see the bison herds, before heading to **Warsaw** (p55). Spend at least two days discovering the capital city, then turn south to Poland's 'other capital', **Kraków** (p125), which merits at least another two days of exploration.

Kraków is a convenient base for day trips to two more top sights – the strange, subterranean world of the **Wieliczka Salt Mine** (p147), and the chilling Nazi extermination camp at **Auschwitz** (p304) in Oświęcim, 60km to the west. Finally, head south again for two or three days of hiking amid the stunning scenery of the **Tatra National Park** (p252).

This 1250km route can be fitted comfortably into a two-week visit if you have a car, three weeks if using public transport. If you're pushed for time, do the southern half only, from Warsaw on, which can be squeezed into a week or 10 days.

TOWN, CHURCH & CASTLE Four Weeks / Gdańsk to Wrocław

This route meanders through central Poland, taking in the best of the country's historical sites, which range from medieval towns to imposing castles.

Begin in the port city of **Gdańsk** (p354), then head southeast to the grand castle of the Teutonic Knights at **Malbork** (p396). From here you can make a side trip to another fine castle at **Lidzbark Warmiński** (p435), before continuing south to the medieval town of **Toruń** (p385).

The route now leads southwest to **Gniezno** (p338), the cradle of the Polish state, and **Poznań** (p322), with its attractive Old Town. Next stop is **Warsaw** (p55), stopping to visit the old religious centre of **Łowicz** (p103) along the way.

After a few days in the capital, head southeast to picturesque **Kazimierz Dolny** (p192), **Lublin** (p183), with its small but attractive Old Town, and the Renaissance masterpiece of **Zamość** (p200), one of Poland's finest historic towns, before turning back west to the magnificent former capital city of **Kraków** (p125), taking in the beautiful castle of **Baranów Sandomierski** (p179) on the way.

After a few days of exploration, use the city as a base for day trips to the pilgrimage centre of **Kalwaria Zebrzydowska** (p210) and the imposing Monastery of Jasna Góra at **Częstochowa** (p166) before making a final trip westward to the delightful old city of **Wrocław** (p263).

Taking in every town mentioned here would involve a road trip of around 2000km, or three to four weeks travelling at a comfortable sightseeing pace.

ROADS LESS TRAVELLED

THE EASTERN MARCHES
Three Weeks / Kraków to Suwałki

Poland's most popular sights lie along the Gdańsk–Warsaw–Kraków–Tatra axis, that runs north–south through the country. To get off the beaten track, head for the eastern marches, borderlands running along the frontier with Ukraine and Belarus, where few visitors venture.

From **Kraków** (p125) head towards the southeastern corner of the country, stopping off at **Bóbrka** (p236), home to the world's earliest oil well. Make for **Sanok** (p225), with its skansen and icon museum, and devote a couple of days to exploring the remote **Bieszczady National Park** (p225).

Turn north, and take the back roads to the Renaissance town of **Zamość** (p200), by way of **Przemyśl** (p221) and its quirky Museum of Bells & Pipes. Continue to **Chełm** (p197), where you can explore the chalk tunnels beneath the town square, and then on to **Lublin** (p183).

Strike out north through the rural backwaters of eastern Poland to the pilgrimage site of **Grabarka** (p124), with its hill of 20,000 crosses, before making for **Hajnówka** (p120) and **Białowieża National Park** (p121).

Then it's north again to the provincial city of **Białystok** (p112), which provides a base for visiting the wooden mosques near the Belarusian border and the mysterious wetlands of **Biebrza National Park** (p117).

Finish with a short trip to the lake resort of **Augustów** (p449). From nearby **Suwałki** (p453) catch a train back to Warsaw, or on to Vilnius.

This 1200km trip is most easily done by car (allow two to three weeks), but it's also possible by public transport (which will take about four weeks). It would also make an interesting bicycle tour (six weeks for the whole route).

TAILORED TRIPS

UNESCO WORLD HERITAGE SITES

Poland has no fewer than 12 sites on the Unesco World Heritage List. Visiting all of them in one trip would take around two weeks.

Start at the magnificent castle of **Malbork** (p396), then go south to the medieval town of **Toruń** (p385), both legacies of the Teutonic Knights. Next stop is **Warsaw** (p55), where the painstakingly reconstructed Old Town was given World Heritage status in 1980.

If you have time, take a side trip to **Białowieża National Park** (p121) before heading to **Zamość** (p200). Then head to Kraków via the wooden churches of the Carpathian Foothills, including **Binarowa** (p239), **Dębno Podhalańskie** (p252), **Haczów** (p236) and **Sękowa** (p240).

The greatest concentration of Unesco sites is around **Kraków** (p125), including Kraków's own historic centre. There are other sites within an easy day trip of the city: the pilgrimage site of **Kalwaria Zebrzydowska** (p210), the weird and wonderful **Wieliczka Salt Mine** (p147) and the Nazi extermination camp at **Auschwitz** (p304).

Heading towards the Sudeten Mountains, you'll find the timber-and-clay Church of Peace at **Świdnica** (p277). Finally, it's west again to Łęknica and the lovely landscaped Park Mużakowski on the Nysa River.

NATIONAL PARKS

Poland is something of a paradise for wildlife enthusiasts, with a range of unspoiled habitats that have almost disappeared from the rest of Europe. A tour of all 23 national parks would take six weeks; this trip around the top 10 can be done in three weeks, two at a push.

From Gdańsk, head west along the coast in the hope of spotting white-tailed eagles above the dunes of **Słowiński National Park** (p403) or the cliffs and lagoons of **Wolin National Park** (p414). Then it's a long slog to **Karkonosze National Park** (p287) for alpine flora, black grouse and mouflon.

From here you can work your way east along the Carpathian Mountains, taking in the sandstone rock formations of the **Góry Stołowe National Park** (p293) and the bat caves of **Ojców National Park** (p164) before reaching the cream of Poland's national parks – the alpine mountains of the **Tatra National Park** (p252), and the scenic river gorge of **Pieniny National Park** (p249).

East again lie the wooded hills and mountain meadows of **Bieszczady National Park** (p225), one of the last corners of Europe where wolf, bear and lynx survive in the wild. If time allows, visit the primeval forest of **Białowieża National Park** (p121), famed for its bison, and the vast wetlands of **Biebrza National Park** (p117).

The Authors

NEIL WILSON · Coordinating Author, Warsaw, Mazovia & Podlasie

Neil's first guidebook gig in Eastern Europe was back in 1992, when he developed a fascination for foil-topped vodka bottles, prefabricated concrete buildings and words ending in '-ski'. He has returned on research trips every couple of years since then, and never fails to be impressed by the pace of change. A full-time freelance writer since 1988, Neil has written around 40 travel and walking guides for various publishers, working in recent years on Lonely Planet's *Eastern Europe* and *Prague* guides. He is based in Edinburgh, Scotland.

The Coordinating Author's Favourite Trip

There's nowhere quite like the national parks in the northeastern corner of Poland, one of the last places in Europe where primeval landscapes such as the vast reed beds of the Narew River (p117), the Biebrza marshes (p118), and the ancient forest of Białowieża (p121) still survive. I can still feel the gnarled bark of a huge, 500-year-old oak tree beneath my fingertips, no sound except the wind in the leaves and a woodpecker's occasional rat-a-tat-tat, and the knowledge that lurking out there in the woods are wild beasts – bison, elk and wolf. Stirring stuff.

Biebrza National Park
Narew National Park
Białowieża National Park

TOM PARKINSON · Silesia, Wielkopolska, Pomerania, Warmia & Masuria

A modern-languages graduate, Tom first discovered Eastern Europe on a transcontinental trip in an otherwise wasted gap year. He was quickly taken in by the charms of a region that still seemed to be in the process of opening up, and he has returned often ever since. Revisiting the newly EU'd Poland for this book brought a host of intriguing experiences: dodging sunburn by the Baltic and rainstorms in Toruń, fine dining and dancing in historic Gdańsk, learning Polish swear words in between scrambling the Sudeten Mountains, absorbing sombre monuments and batty modern art, battling a żurek (sour rye soup) addiction and visiting more churches than the pope.

RICHARD WATKINS · Kraków, Małopolska, The Carpathian Mountains

Richard was born in Wales and studied ancient history at Cardiff and Oxford Universities. His first paid job after leaving the academic world was teaching conversational English to college students in Bulgaria. Since then the travel bug has well and truly caught hold, and Richard has wandered the globe as a backpacker, English teacher and more recently, as a travel guidebook writer. Richard has written for several other Lonely Planet titles, including *Eastern Europe* and *Best of Prague*.

Snapshot

On 1 May 2004 Poland became a fully signed-up member of the EU. Many Poles feared that the new freedom of movement that came with EU membership would provoke a wave of emigration, with the young and well-educated leaving their homes for better-paid jobs in the West. But these fears appear to have been unfounded – instead, the younger generation feel optimistic that European integration will improve their chances of finding a good job in Poland.

In a 2003 poll taken by the **Public Opinion Research Centre** (www.cbos.pl), 62% of Poles said they were 'fairly satisfied' or 'very satisfied' with life in general; only 6% were 'fairly' or 'very unsatisfied'. On the other hand, when asked whether corruption was a problem in Poland, a whopping 65% said that it was a 'very big' problem, and another 25% said 'fairly big'.

Fifteen years after the collapse of communism, corruption and political instability remain the bugbear of Polish political life. Former Democratic Left Alliance (SLD) leader Leszek Miller resigned as prime minister on 2 May 2004 in the wake of a string of corruption scandals, leaving his party in disarray (though he hung around long enough to go down in the history books as being PM on the day of EU accession).

With unemployment running at around 20% (and a youth unemployment rate of 35%), a stagnating economy and the taint of corruption and mismanagement hanging over the government, the future for Polish politics looks far from settled. Following Miller's resignation, 24 of his MPs deserted from the SLD and formed a new political party called Polish Social Democracy – with elections looming in 2005, the increasingly battered and leaky hulk of the SLD appeared to be heading for the rocks.

The names to look out for in the next few years are Andrzej Lepper and Jan Rokita. Lepper, leader of the populist, left-wing, anti-EU party Samoobrona (Self-Defence), has struck a chord with the millions of Poles who feel they have been left behind in the transition to capitalism. Rokita heads the centre-right Platforma Obywatelska (Civic Platform) party, which is liberal on the economy and conservative on social issues.

A recent hot political potato is the issue of claims for reparations from expelled ethnic Germans who lost land and property when Poland's borders were moved to the west in the wake of WWII. In 2004 the Prussian Claims Society launched a legal campaign with the aim of reclaiming ancestral property on what is now Polish territory – a very touchy subject in Poland.

In a retaliatory move, the Polish parliament voted unanimously in September 2004 for a resolution calling for reparations for 'the enormous material and spiritual destruction caused by German aggression, occupation and genocide' in WWII (despite that fact that Poland officially dropped all demands for reparations in the 1950s). At a meeting in November 2004, the Polish prime minister and the German chancellor made a joint declaration that there was no legal basis for reparation claims, but the issue still has the potential to poison relations between the two countries.

FAST FACTS

Population: 38.63 million (July 2004)

Area: 312, 685 sq km

GDP (per head): US$11,100 (2003)

Inflation: 0.7% (2003)

Unemployment: 20% (2003)

Number of lakes: 9000

Number of bison in the wild: 350

Proportion of population who are practising Roman Catholics: 75%

Annual vodka consumption: 5.7L per head (in Russia, 15L)

Proportion of population who died in WWII: 20% (UK 0.9%; USA 0.2%)

History

Poland has not perished yet
As long as we (Poles) still live.
That which foreign force has seized
We at swordpoint shall retrieve.

The first lines of the national anthem reflect the proud and irrepressible nature of the Polish nation. One of the most patriotic, independent and rebellious of peoples, Poles have had innumerable occasions to defend their freedom and sovereignty throughout more than 1000 years of turbulent history.

Sandwiched between the aggressive powers of Germany and Russia, Poland has been repeatedly invaded and fought over. Its boundaries have shifted east and west as its power waxed and waned, from being the largest country in Europe in the 17th century, to being completely wiped off the map at the end of the 18th. An independent Poland re-emerged following WWI, only to be devastated again in WWII when it lost six million people, 18% of its population.

Poland changed the course of history in 1989 by becoming the first Eastern European state to break free of communism, proving the truth of Stalin's comment in 1944 that fitting communism onto Poland was like putting a saddle on a cow. Since then, the economic, social and psychological changes in the country have been tremendous.

ORIGINS

Poland takes its name from the Polanie (literally, the people of the fields, open-country dwellers), one of the Slavonic tribes who settled on the banks of the Warta River, near present-day Poznań, in the 10th century. Their tribal chief, the legendary Piast, managed to unite the scattered groups of the surrounding areas into a single political unit, and gave it the name Polska (later Wielkopolska, meaning Great Poland). Its first recorded ruler, Duke Mieszko I, was converted to Christianity in 966, the date that marks the formal birth of the Polish state.

Norman Davies' two-volume *God's Playground: a History of Poland* is beautifully written, easy to read and a perfect key to understanding 1000 years of the Polish nation.

Duke Mieszko I conquered the entire coastal region of Pomerania (Pomorze) and soon thereafter extended his sovereignty to include Śląsk (Silesia) to the south and Małopolska (Little Poland) to the southeast. By the time of his death in 992, the Polish state was established within boundaries similar to those of Poland today, and the first capital and archbishopric were established in Gniezno. By that time, towns such as Gdańsk, Szczecin, Poznań, Wrocław and Kraków already existed. But wars continued unabated in the north and the administrative centre of the country was moved from Wielkopolska to the less vulnerable Małopolska. By the middle of the 11th century, Kraków was established as the royal seat.

When pagan Prussians, from the region that is now the northeastern tip of Poland, attacked the central province of Mazovia in 1226, Duke Konrad of Mazovia called for help from the Teutonic Knights, a Germanic

TIMELINE	966	970s
	Birth of the Polish state	Gniezno's first cathedral built

military and religious order that had made its historic mark during the Crusades. Once the knights had subjugated the pagan tribes, they set up a state on the conquered territories that they ruled from their castle at Malbork. The knights soon became a major European military power and captured all of northern Poland.

Not until 1320 was the Polish crown restored and the state reunified. Under the rule of Kazimierz III Wielki (Casimir III the Great; 1333–70), Poland gradually became a prosperous and powerful state. Kazimierz Wielki regained suzerainty over Mazovia, then captured vast areas of Ruthenia (today's Ukraine) and Podolia, thus greatly expanding his monarchy towards the southeast.

Kazimierz Wielki was also an enlightened and energetic ruler on the domestic front. Promoting and instituting reforms, he laid down solid legal, economic, commercial and educational foundations. Over 70 new towns were founded, and the royal capital of Kraków flourished. In 1364 one of Europe's first universities was established at Kraków, and an extensive network of castles and fortifications was constructed to improve the nation's defences. There is a saying stating that Kazimierz Wielki 'found Poland built of wood and left it built of stone'.

Nicolaus Copernicus (1473–1543), the astronomer who first proposed that the earth orbits the sun, studied at the university of Kraków, founded by King Kazimierz III Wielki. Poles say that Copernicus 'stopped the sun and moved the earth'.

THE JAGIELLONIAN DYNASTY (1382–1572)

The close of the 14th century saw Poland forge a dynastic alliance with Lithuania, a political marriage that increased Poland's territory fivefold overnight and which would last for the next four centuries. Under Władysław II Jagiełło (1386–1434) Poland recovered eastern Pomerania, part of Prussia and the port of Gdańsk, and for 30 years the Polish empire was Europe's largest state, extending from the Baltic to the Black Sea.

But it was not to last. Another period of invasions began in 1475. This time the main instigators were the Ottomans, the Tatars of Crimea and the tsars of Moscow. Independently or together, they repeatedly invaded and raided the eastern and southern Polish territories, and on one occasion managed to penetrate as far as Kraków.

Despite the wars, the Polish kingdom's power was firmly established. In addition to prospering economically, the country advanced both culturally and spiritually as the early 16th century brought the Renaissance to Poland. During the reigns of Zygmunt I Stary (Sigismund I the Old; 1506–48) and his son Zygmunt II August (Sigismund II Augustus; 1548–72) the arts and sciences flourished, in a period that came to be referred to as Poland's golden age.

The bulk of Poland's population at that time was made up of Poles and Lithuanians, but included significant minorities of Germans, Ruthenians (Ukrainians), Tatars, Armenians and Livonians (Latvians). Jews constituted an important and steadily growing part of the community and by the end of the 16th century Poland had a larger Jewish population than the rest of Europe combined.

Religious freedom was constitutionally established by the Sejm (also known as the Diet; the lower house of Polish parliament) in 1573 and the equality of creeds officially guaranteed. Such diverse faiths as Roman Catholicism, Eastern Orthodoxy, Protestantism, Judaism and Islam were able to coexist relatively peacefully.

1038	1364
Kraków becomes Polish capital	Kraków university established

On the political front, Poland evolved during the 16th century into a parliamentary monarchy with most of the privileges going to the *szlachta* (gentry, the feudal nobility), who comprised roughly 10% of the population. In contrast, the status of the peasants declined, and they gradually found themselves falling into a state of virtual slavery.

ROYAL REPUBLIC (1573–1795)

During the reign of Zygmunt August, the threat of Russian expansionism increased. Hoping to strengthen the monarchy, the Sejm convened in Lublin in 1569 and unified Poland and Lithuania into a single state. It also made Warsaw the seat of the Sejm's future debates. Since there was no heir apparent to the throne, it also established a system of royal succession based on direct voting in popular elections by the nobility, who would all come to Warsaw to vote. In the absence of a serious Polish contender, a foreign candidate would be considered.

The experiment proved disastrous. For each royal election, foreign powers promoted their candidates by bargaining and bribing voters. During the period of the Royal Republic, Poland was ruled by 11 kings, only four of whom were native Poles.

The first elected king, Henri de Valois, retreated to France after only a year on the Polish throne. His successor, Stefan Batory (Stephen Bathory; 1576–86), prince of Transylvania, was fortunately a much wiser choice. Batory, together with his gifted commander and chancellor Jan Zamoyski, conducted a series of successful battles against Tsar Ivan the Terrible.

After Batory's premature death, the crown was offered to the Swede Zygmunt III Waza (Sigismund III Vasa; 1587–1632), during whose reign Poland achieved its greatest ever extent, more than three times the size of present-day Poland. Despite this, Zygmunt is best remembered for moving the Polish capital from Kraków to Warsaw between 1596 and 1609.

The beginning of the 17th century marked a turning point in Poland's fortunes. The increasing political power of the Polish nobility undermined the authority of the Sejm; the country was split up into several huge private estates, and nobles, frustrated by ineffective government, resorted to armed rebellion.

Meanwhile, foreign invaders were systematically carving up the land. Jan II Kazimierz Waza (John II Casimir Vasa; 1648–68), the last of the Vasa dynasty on the Polish throne, was unable to resist the aggressors – Russians, Tatars, Ukrainians, Cossacks, Ottomans and Swedes – who were moving in on all fronts. The Swedish invasion of 1655–60, known as the Deluge, was particularly disastrous. During the rule of Kazimierz Waza, the country lost over a quarter of its national territory, cities were burned and plundered, the countryside was devastated and the economy destroyed. From a population of 10 million, four million succumbed to war, famine and bubonic plague.

The last bright moment in the long decline of the Royal Republic was the reign of Jan III Sobieski (John III Sobieski; 1674–96), a brilliant commander who led several victorious battles against the Ottomans. The most famous of these was the Battle of Vienna in 1683, in which he defeated the Turks and forced their retreat from Europe.

By the start of the 18th century, Russia had evolved into a mighty, expansive empire that systematically strengthened its grip over Poland.

Legendary lover Casanova spent some time in Warsaw in the 1760s, but was forced to flee following a duel with a Polish aristocrat.

1569

Poland and Lithuania united as a single state

1596–1609

Capital moves from Kraków to Warsaw

Although Stanisław August Poniatowski (Stanislaus August Poniatowski; 1764–95), was a patron of literature and the arts, and presided over the restoration and baroque decoration of Warsaw's Royal Castle, he was essentially a puppet of the Russian regime. It was only during his reign that the Poles became aware of the severity of their country's situation, with direct intervention in Poland's affairs from Catherine the Great, empress of Russia.

PARTITION

A famous picture in the Historical Museum of Warsaw, entitled 'The Royal Cake', shows the rulers of Russia, Prussia and Austria tearing apart a map of Poland while the crown topples from the head of Stanisław August Poniatowski, who is remembered in history as 'the last king of Poland'.

The three countries agreed to annex substantial chunks of Poland, amounting to roughly 30% of Polish territory. The First Partition led to immediate reforms, and in 1791 the new, liberal Constitution of the 3rd of May was passed – the world's second written constitution (the first was that of the USA).

Catherine the Great, however, could tolerate no more of this dangerous democracy. Russian troops were sent into Poland, and despite fierce resistance the reforms were abolished by force. The Second Partition came in 1793, with Russia and Prussia strengthening their grip by grabbing over half the remaining Polish territory.

In response to this, patriotic forces under the leadership of Tadeusz Kościuszko, a hero of the American War of Independence, launched an armed rebellion in 1794. The campaign soon gained popular support and the rebels won some early victories, but the Russian troops, stronger and better armed, finally defeated the Polish forces.

This time the three occupying powers decided to eradicate the troublesome nation altogether, and in the Third Partition, effected in 1795, they divided the rest of Poland's territory among themselves. Poland disappeared from the map for the next 123 years.

Despite the partitions, Poland continued to exist as a spiritual and cultural community, and a number of secret nationalist societies was created. Since revolutionary France was seen as their major ally in the struggle, some leaders fled to Paris and established their headquarters there.

In 1815 the Congress of Vienna established the Congress Kingdom of Poland, a supposedly autonomous Polish state that nevertheless had the Russian tsar as its king. From its inception, its liberal constitution was violated by Tsar Alexander and his successors.

In response to Russian oppression, armed uprisings broke out. The most significant were the November Insurrection of 1830 and the January Insurrection of 1863, both of which were crushed by the Russians and followed by harsh repression, executions and deportations to Siberia.

In the 1870s Russia dramatically stepped up its efforts to eradicate Polish culture, suppressing the Polish language in education, administration and commerce, and replacing it with Russian. This was also a time of mass emigration – by the outbreak of WWI, about four million Poles, out of a total population of 20 to 25 million, had emigrated, primarily to the USA.

The website www.polish roots.org/genpoland /polhistory.htm shows how Poland's borders have shifted over the past 200 years since Partition.

DID YOU KNOW?

The Ottoman Empire, though an ancient enemy of the Poles, was the only European power that never recognised the partition of Poland.

1655–60	3 May 1791
Swedish invasion (the Deluge)	Poland gets a written constitution

WWI (1914–18)

WWI broke out in August 1914. On one side were the Central Powers, Austria-Hungary and Germany (including Prussia); on the other, Russia and its Western allies. With Poland's three occupying powers at war, most of the fighting was staged on the territories inhabited by the Poles, resulting in staggering losses of life and livelihood. Since no formal Polish state existed, there was no Polish army to fight for the national cause. Even worse, some two million Poles were conscripted into the Russian, German or Austrian armies, and were obliged to fight one another.

Paradoxically, the war eventually brought about Polish independence. After the October Revolution in 1917, Russia plunged into civil war and no longer had the power to oversee Polish affairs. The final collapse of the Austrian empire in October 1918 and the withdrawal of the German army from Warsaw in November brought the opportune moment. Marshal Józef Piłsudski took command of Warsaw on 11 November 1918, declared Polish sovereignty, and usurped power as the head of state. This date is recognised as the day of the founding of the Second Republic, so named to create a symbolic bridge between itself and the Royal Republic that existed before the partitions.

PIŁSUDSKI – PATRIOT, SOLDIER, STATESMAN

Father of the Polish republic, military mastermind of the Miracle on the Vistula, and victor over the might of the Soviet army, Marshal Józef Piłsudski is revered in Poland as a patriot, soldier and statesman.

Piłsudski was born in 1867 in the Russian-occupied Vilnius region and joined the antitsarist movement while still a teenager. Arrested in 1887 and sent to a prison in Siberia for five years, he returned to Poland and joined the newly founded Polish Socialist Party (PPS) in Warsaw. He was arrested again in 1900 and was briefly incarcerated in Warsaw's Citadel before being sent to a jail in St Petersburg. He escaped the following year and took refuge in Kraków.

In 1908 the PPS formed paramilitary squads that developed into the Polish Legions, the military force that fought under Piłsudski's leadership for Poland's independence during WWI. Following Germany's capitulation in 1918, Marshal Piłsudski came to Warsaw, took power on 11 November and proclaimed Poland a sovereign state. The Russian Revolution, however, had created a new enemy in the east.

In 1919 Piłsudski launched a massive offensive towards the east, capturing vast territories that had been Polish before the 18th-century partitions. A Soviet counteroffensive reached as far as Warsaw, but in the Battle of Warsaw in August 1920 (known as the Miracle on the Vistula), the Polish army, under Piłsudski, outmanoeuvred and defeated the Red Army.

Once an independent Poland was safely back on the map and a modern democratic constitution had been adopted in 1921, Piłsudski stepped down. Disillusioned with economic recession and governmental crisis, however, he reappeared on the political scene in May 1926. In a classic coup d'etat, he marched on Warsaw at the head of the army, resulting in three days of street fighting that left 400 dead and over 1000 wounded. After the government resigned, the National Assembly elected Piłsudski as president but he refused to take the post, opting instead for the office of defence minister, which he maintained until his death. There are few doubts, though, that it was Piłsudski who ran the country behind the scenes until he died of cancer in 1935. Despite his dictatorial style, he was buried with ceremony among Polish kings in the crypt of Kraków's Wawel Cathedral.

1793	1795
Second Partition of Poland	Third Partition of Poland

BETWEEN THE WARS (1918–39)

Poland began its new incarnation in a desperate position. After the war, the country and its economy were in ruins. It's estimated that over one million Poles lost their lives in WWI. All state institutions – including the army, which hadn't existed for over a century – had to be built up from scratch. Even the borders, which had been obliterated in the partitions, had to be redefined, and weren't made official until 1923.

The Treaty of Versailles in 1919 awarded Poland the western part of Prussia, providing access to the Baltic Sea. The city of Gdańsk, however, was omitted and became the Free City of Danzig. The rest of Poland's western border was drawn up in a series of plebiscites, which resulted in Poland acquiring some significant industrial regions of Upper Silesia. The eastern boundaries were established when Polish forces, led by Piłsudski, defeated the Red Army during the Polish-Soviet war of 1919–20. The victory brought Poland vast areas of what are now western Ukraine and Belarus.

When Poland's territorial struggle ended, the Second Republic covered nearly 400,000 sq km and was populated by 26 million people. One-third of the population was of non-Polish ethnic background, mainly Jews, Ukrainians, Belarusians and Germans.

Piłsudski retired from political life in 1922, giving way to a series of unstable parliamentary governments. For the next four years, frequently changing coalition cabinets struggled to overcome enormous economic and social problems.

Quite unexpectedly, Piłsudski seized power in a military coup in May 1926, and then held on to the reins of power until his death in 1935. Parliament was gradually phased out. Despite the dictatorial regime, political repression had little effect on ordinary people. The economic situation was relatively stable, and cultural and intellectual life prospered.

On the international front, Poland's situation in the 1930s was unenviable. In an attempt to regulate relations with its two inexorably hostile neighbours, Poland signed nonaggression pacts with both the Soviet Union and Germany. Nevertheless, it soon became clear that the pacts didn't offer any real guarantee of safety.

On 23 August 1939 a pact of nonaggression between Germany and the Soviet Union was signed in Moscow by their foreign ministers, Ribbentrop and Molotov. This pact contained a secret protocol defining the prospective partition of Eastern Europe between the two great powers. Stalin and Hitler planned to carve up the Polish state between themselves.

WWII (1939–45)

WWII began at dawn on 1 September 1939 with a massive German invasion of Poland. Fighting began in Gdańsk (at that time the Free City of Danzig) when German forces encountered a stubborn handful of Polish resisters at Westerplatte. The battle lasted a week. Simultaneously, another German line stormed Warsaw, which finally surrendered on 28 September. Despite valiant resistance there was simply no hope of withstanding the numerically overwhelming and well-armed German forces; the last resistance groups were quelled by early October. Hitler intended to create a Polish puppet state on the newly acquired territory, but since

White Eagle, Red Star, by Norman Davies, is a dramatic account of the Polish-Soviet war of 1919–20, when Poland prevented the Red Army from carrying the Russian Revolution into Germany

The Heart of Europe: a Short History of Poland, by Norman Davies, is a condensed version of *God's Playground* (see p18), with a greater emphasis on the 20th century.

Winston Churchill observed that 'Poland was the only country which never collaborated with the Nazis in any form and no Polish units fought alongside the German army'.

1810	1815
Birth of Frédéric Chopin	Congress Kingdom of Poland established

MASSACRE AT KATYŃ

In April 1943, German troops fighting Soviet forces on the eastern front came across extensive mass graves in the forest of Katyń, near Smolensk, in present-day Belarus. Exploratory excavations revealed the remains of several thousand Polish soldiers and civilians who had been shot in the head, execution-style. The Soviet government denied all responsibility and accused the Nazis of the crime. Two years later the war ended, the communists took power in Poland and the subject of Katyń remained taboo for decades, even though most Poles were aware of the tragic events.

It wasn't until 1990 that the Soviets admitted their 'mistake', without revealing any details of what had happened. In October 1992 the Russian government finally made public secret documents showing that Stalin's Politburo was responsible for the massacre at Katyń. Meanwhile, in the summer of 1991, further mass graves of Polish soldiers were discovered in Myednoye and Kharkov, both in central Russia.

During the late 1990s the picture became more complete. Soon after their invasion of Poland in September 1939, the Soviets took an estimated 180,000 prisoners, comprising Polish soldiers, police officers, judges, politicians, intellectuals, scientists, teachers, professors, writers and priests, and crammed them into various camps throughout the Soviet Union and the invaded territories. On Stalin's order, signed in March 1940, about 21,800 of these prisoners, including many high-ranking officers and intellectuals, were transported from the camps to the forests of Katyń, Myednoye and Kharkov, shot dead and buried in mass graves.

The Soviet intention was to exterminate the intellectual elite of Polish society, and eliminate the driving force and the leadership of the nation. Statistics confirm that in WWII Poland lost 21% of its prewar judges, 30% of university teachers, 40% of physicians and 57% of lawyers, some of them in Katyń and the other two massacre sites.

The full horror of the Katyń massacre was finally revealed during exhumations of the mass graves by Polish archaeologists in 1995–96; their findings can be seen in the Katyń Museum (p76) in Warsaw.

---

no collaborators could be found, western Poland was directly annexed to Germany, while the central regions became the so-called General Government, ruled by the Nazi governor from Kraków.

On 17 September eastern Poland was invaded by the Soviet Union, and by November had been swallowed up. Thus within two months Poland was yet again partitioned. Mass arrests, exile and executions followed in both invaded parts. It's estimated that between one and two million Poles were sent by the Soviets to Siberia, the Soviet Arctic and Kazakhstan in 1939–40. Many of them never returned.

Jews in Poland: a Documentary History, by Iwo Cyprian Pogonowski, provides a comprehensive record of half a millennium of Polish-Jewish relations in Poland.

Soon after the outbreak of the war, a Polish government-in-exile was formed in France under General Władysław Sikorski. It was shifted to London in June 1940. In July 1943 Sikorski died in an aircraft crash in Gibraltar, and Stanisław Mikołajczyk succeeded him as prime minister.

The course of the war changed dramatically when Hitler unexpectedly attacked the Soviet Union on 22 June 1941. The Germans pushed the Soviets out of eastern Poland and extended their power deep into Russia. For over three years, the whole of Poland lay under Nazi occupation. Hitler's policy was to eradicate the Polish nation and Germanise the territory. Hundreds of thousands of Poles were deported en masse to forced-labour camps in Germany, while others, primarily the intelligentsia, were

1830	1863
November Insurrection against Russian rule	January Insurrection against Russian rule

executed in an attempt to exterminate spiritual and intellectual leadership (see the boxed text opposite for more information).

The Jews were to be eliminated completely. At first they were segregated and confined in ghettos until a more efficient method was applied – the death camps. Almost the whole of Poland's Jewish population (three million) and roughly one million Poles died in the camps. In the Polish capital, the Jewish population was herded into the cramped confines of the Warsaw Ghetto, where organised resistance erupted in the Ghetto Uprising of 1943 (see the boxed text on p76).

A nationwide resistance movement, concentrated in the cities, had been put in place soon after the start of the war, to operate the Polish educational, communications and judicial systems. Armed squads were set up in 1940 by the government-in-exile, and these evolved into the Armia Krajowa (AK; Home Army), which was to figure prominently in the Warsaw Uprising (see the boxed text on p26).

Meanwhile, Stalin turned to Poland for help in the war effort against the German forces advancing eastwards towards Moscow. The official Polish army was re-formed late in 1941, but was largely under Soviet control. Nevertheless its Polish commander, General Anders, managed to have the majority of his troops diverted to North Africa, where they distinguished themselves at Tobruk, and later at Monte Cassino in Italy.

Hitler's defeat at Stalingrad in 1943 marked the turning point of the war on the eastern front, and from then on the Red Army successfully pushed westwards. After the Soviets liberated the Polish city of Lublin, the procommunist Polish Committee of National Liberation (PKWN) was installed on 22 July 1944 and assumed the functions of a provisional government. A week later the Red Army reached the outskirts of Warsaw.

Warsaw at that time remained under Nazi occupation. In a last-ditch attempt to establish an independent Polish administration, the resistance forces decided to gain control of the city before the arrival of the Soviet troops. For the outcome of the tragic Warsaw Uprising, see the boxed text on p26. Through the winter, the Red Army continued its westward advance across Poland, and after a few months reached Berlin. The Nazi Reich capitulated on 8 May 1945.

The impact of the war on Poland was staggering. The country had lost over six million people, about 20% of its prewar population. Out of three million Polish Jews in 1939, only 80,000 to 90,000 survived the war. The country and its cities lay in ruins; only 15% of Warsaw's buildings survived. Many Poles who had seen out the war in foreign countries opted not to return to the new political order.

COMMUNIST RULE

At the Yalta Conference in February 1945, Roosevelt, Churchill and Stalin decided to leave Poland under Soviet control. They agreed that Poland's eastern frontier would roughly follow the Nazi-Soviet demarcation line of 1939. In effect, the Soviet Union annexed 180,000 sq km of prewar Polish territory. In August 1945 at Potsdam, Allied leaders established Poland's western boundary along the Odra (Oder) and the Nysa (Neisse) Rivers, thereby reinstating about 100,000 sq km of Poland's western provinces after centuries of German rule.

DID YOU KNOW?

One of the great myths of WWII is that Polish cavalry charged against German tanks in the opening stages. In reality a Polish cavalry regiment destroyed a German infantry division, and was then counter-attacked by German armour. Nazi propaganda tried to twist the event into a symbol of Polish backwardness.

A Surplus of Memory: Chronicle of the Warsaw Ghetto Uprising, by Yitzhak Zuckerman, is a detailed narrative of this heroic act of Jewish resistance.

Rising '44, by Norman Davies, is a brilliant and very readable account of the heroic but doomed Warsaw Uprising of 1944.

11 November 1918	1920
Founding of the Second Republic	Poland defeats Red Army in Battle of Warsaw

THE WARSAW UPRISING

In the summer of 1944, with German forces retreating across Poland in the face of an advancing Soviet army, the Polish resistance in Warsaw was preparing for the liberation of their city. On 1 August 1944, orders were given for a general anti-German uprising, with the intention of establishing a Polish command in the city before the Red Army swept through. Though poorly armed and outnumbered, the Armia Krajowa (AK; Home Army) hoped that they might take control of the city centre and hold out for a week at most until airborne support from the Allies and the advancing Soviets finally drove the Nazis out of the capital.

The initial uprising was remarkably successful and the AK, creating barricades from ripped-up paving slabs and using the Warsaw sewers as underground communication lines, took over large parts of the city. But no help ever came. The Allies were preoccupied with breaking out of their beachhead in Normandy after the D-day landings, and sending airdrops to Warsaw was logistically complicated. The Red Army, which was camped just across the Vistula River in Praga, didn't lift a finger. On learning of the uprising, Stalin halted the offensive and ordered his generals not to intervene or provide any assistance in the fighting, instead allowing the Germans to break the back of any potential Polish resistance to a communist takeover of the country.

For 63 days the Warsaw Uprising raged with unprecedented savagery before the insurgents were ultimately forced to surrender; around 200,000 Poles were killed. The Nazi revenge was brutal – on Hitler's orders, every inhabitant of Warsaw was to be killed, no prisoners taken, and every single house was to be blown up and burned. Warsaw was literally razed to the ground. It wasn't until 17 January 1945 that the Soviet army finally marched in to 'liberate' Warsaw, which by that time was little more than a heap of empty ruins.

For the Poles, the Warsaw Uprising was one of the most heroic – and most tragic – engagements of the war. The events of the uprising are commemorated in the Museum of the Warsaw Uprising (p73) and the Monument to the Warsaw Uprising (p67).

The radical boundary changes were followed by population transfers of some 10 million people: Poles were moved into the newly defined Poland while Germans, Ukrainians and Belarusians were resettled outside its boundaries. In the end, 98% of Poland's population was ethnically Polish.

As soon as Poland formally fell under Soviet control, Stalin launched an intensive Sovietisation campaign. Wartime resistance leaders were charged with Nazi collaboration, tried in Moscow and summarily shot or sentenced to arbitrary prison terms. A provisional Polish government was set up in Moscow in June 1945 and then transferred to Warsaw. General elections were postponed until 1947 to allow time for the arrest of prominent Polish political figures by the secret police. Even so, Stanisław Mikołajczyk, the government-in-exile's only representative to return to Poland, received over 80% of the popular vote.

The 'official' figures, however, revealed a majority vote for the communists. The new Sejm elected Bolesław Bierut president; Mikołajczyk, accused of espionage, fled back to England.

In 1948 the Polish United Workers' Party (PZPR), henceforth referred to as 'the Party', was formed to monopolise power. In 1952 a Soviet-style constitution was adopted. The office of president was abolished and effective power passed to the first secretary of the Party Central Committee. Poland became an affiliate of the Warsaw Pact.

1 September 1939	19 April 1943
German invasion of Poland starts WWII	Start of Ghetto Uprising in Warsaw

Despite all its horrors, Stalinist fanaticism never gained as much influence in Poland as in neighbouring countries and it subsided fairly soon after Stalin's death in 1953. The powers of the secret police were eroded and some concessions were made to popular demands. The press was liberalised and Polish cultural values were resuscitated. In 1956, when Nikita Khrushchev denounced Stalin at the Soviet 20th Party Congress, Bierut died of a heart attack!

In June 1956 a massive industrial strike demanding 'bread and freedom' broke out in Poznań. Tanks rolled in and crushed the revolt, leaving 76 dead and over 900 wounded. Soon afterward, Władysław Gomułka, a former political prisoner of the Stalin era, was appointed first secretary of the Party. At first he commanded popular support, but later in his term he displayed an increasingly rigid and authoritarian attitude, putting pressure on the Church and intensifying persecution of the intelligentsia. It was ultimately an economic crisis, however, that brought about his downfall; when he announced official price increases in 1970, a wave of mass strikes erupted in Gdańsk, Gdynia and Szczecin. Again, the violence was put down by force, resulting in 44 deaths. The Party, to save face, ejected Gomułka from office and replaced him with Edward Gierek.

> You can find a library of wartime photographs chronicling the horror and destruction of the Warsaw Uprising at www .warsawuprising.com.

Another attempt to raise prices in 1976 incited labour protests, and again workers walked off the job, this time in Radom and Warsaw. Caught in a downward spiral, Gierek took out more foreign loans, but to earn hard currency with which to pay the interest, he was forced to divert consumer goods away from the domestic market and sell them abroad. By 1980 the external debt stood at US$21 billion and the economy had slumped disastrously.

By then, the opposition had grown into a significant force, backed by numerous advisers from the intellectual circles. The election of Karol Wojtyła, the archbishop of Kraków, as Pope John Paul II in 1978 and his triumphal visit to his homeland a year later dramatically increased political ferment. When, in July 1980, the government again announced food-price increases, the outcome was predictable: fervent and well-organised strikes and riots spread like wildfire throughout the country. In August, they paralysed major ports, the Silesian coal mines and the Lenin Shipyard in Gdańsk.

Unlike most previous popular protests, the 1980 strikes were nonviolent; the strikers did not take to the streets, but stayed in their factories.

SOLIDARITY

After long, drawn-out negotiations in the Lenin Shipyard in Gdańsk, an agreement was eventually reached on 31 August 1980. The government was forced to accept most of the strikers' demands. The most significant of these was recognition of the workers' right to organise independent trade unions, and to strike. In return, workers agreed to adhere to the constitution and to accept the Party's power as supreme.

> *The Polish Revolution: Solidarity 1980–82*, by Timothy Garton Ash, is an entertainingly written insight into a 16-month period that undermined the whole communist system.

Workers' delegations from around the country convened and founded Solidarity (Solidarność), a nationwide independent and self-governing trade union. Lech Wałęsa, who led the Gdańsk strike, was elected chair. In November, the Solidarity movement, which by then had gathered nearly 10 million members (60% of the workforce), was formally recognised by

1 August 1944	1947
Start of the Warsaw Uprising	Communist government 'elected'

the government. Amazingly, one million Solidarity members had come from the Party's ranks!

Gierek was ejected from office and his post taken over by Stanisław Kania; in October 1981 Kania was replaced by General Wojciech Jaruzelski, who continued to serve as prime minister and minister of defence, posts he had held prior to his new appointment.

Solidarity had a dramatic effect on the whole of Polish society. After 35 years of restraint, the Poles launched themselves into a spontaneous and chaotic sort of democracy. Wide-ranging debates over the process of reform were led by Solidarity, and the independent press flourished. Such taboo historical subjects as the Stalin-Hitler pact and the Katyń massacre could for the first time be openly discussed.

Not surprisingly, the 10 million Solidarity members represented a wide range of attitudes: from confrontational to conciliatory. By and large, it was Wałęsa's charismatic authority that kept the union on a moderate and balanced course in its struggle to achieve some degree of political harmony with the government.

The government, however, under pressure from both the Soviets and local hardliners, became increasingly reluctant to introduce any significant reforms and systematically rejected Solidarity's proposals. This only led to further discontent, and, in the absence of other legal options, strikes became Solidarity's main political weapon. Amid fruitless wrangling, the economic crisis grew more severe. After the unsuccessful talks of November 1981 between the government, Solidarity and the Church, social tensions increased and led to a political stalemate.

MARTIAL LAW & ITS AFTERMATH

When General Jaruzelski unexpectedly appeared on TV in the early hours of the morning of 13 December 1981 to declare martial law, tanks were already on the streets, army checkpoints had been set up on every corner, and paramilitary squads had been posted to possible trouble spots. Power was placed in the hands of the Military Council of National Salvation (WRON), a group of military officers under the command of Jaruzelski himself.

Mad Dreams, Saving Graces: Poland, a Nation in Conspiracy, by Michael T Kaufman, is a trip through the dark times of martial law and the gloomy period up till 1988 – as readable as it is informative.

Solidarity was suspended and all public gatherings, demonstrations and strikes were banned. Several thousand people, including most Solidarity leaders and Wałęsa himself, were interned. The spontaneous demonstrations and strikes that followed were crushed, and military rule was effectively imposed all over Poland within two weeks of its declaration.

Whether the coup was a Soviet decision or simply Jaruzelski's attempt to prevent Soviet military intervention, it attained its goal: reform was crushed and life in the Soviet bloc returned to the pre-Solidarity norm.

But Jaruzelski had no popular support and most Poles were hostile to the government. In October 1982 the government formally dissolved Solidarity and released Wałęsa from detention. Martial law was officially lifted in July 1983.

Solidarity continued underground on a much smaller scale, and enjoyed widespread sympathy and support. In July 1984 a limited amnesty was announced and some members of the political opposition were released from prison. But further arrests continued, following every public protest, and it was not until 1986 that all political prisoners were freed.

1978	1980
Karol Wojtyła, archbishop of Kraków, becomes Pope John Paul II	Solidarity trade union established

COLLAPSE OF COMMUNISM

The election of Gorbachov in the Soviet Union in 1985 and his *glasnost* and *perestroika* programmes gave an important stimulus to democratic reforms all through Eastern Europe. Again, Poland undertook the role of guinea pig. Jaruzelski softened his position and became willing to compromise over the democratisation of the system. In April 1989, in so-called round-table agreements between the government, the opposition and the Church, Solidarity was re-established and the opposition was allowed to stand for parliament.

In the consequent semifree elections in June 1989, Solidarity succeeded in getting an overwhelming majority of its supporters elected to the Senat, the upper house of parliament. The communists, however, reserved for themselves 65% of seats in the Sejm. Jaruzelski was placed in the presidency as a stabilising guarantor of political changes for both Moscow and the local communists, but the noncommunist prime minister, Tadeusz Mazowiecki, was installed as a result of personal pressure from Wałęsa. This power-sharing deal, with the first noncommunist prime minister in Eastern Europe since WWII, paved the way for the dominolike collapse of communism throughout the Soviet bloc. The Party, haemorrhaging members and confidence, dissolved itself in 1990.

'the Party, haemorrhaging members and confidence, dissolved itself in 1990'

In January 1990 the government introduced a package of reforms to change the centrally planned communist system into a free-market economy. The brain behind the radical plan was finance minister Leszek Balcerowicz. In a shock-therapy transition, all prices were permitted to move freely, subsidies were abolished, the money supply was tightened and the currency was sharply devalued and made fully convertible with Western currencies.

Within a few months the economy appeared to have stabilised, food shortages were no longer the norm and the shelves of shops filled up with goods. Meanwhile, however, prices skyrocketed and unemployment exploded. Not surprisingly, an initial wave of optimism and forbearance turned into uncertainty and discontent, and the tough austerity measures caused the popularity of the government to decline.

In the mid-1990 differences over the pace of political reform emerged between Mazowiecki and Wałęsa. Wałęsa complained that the government was too slow in removing old communists, the former members of the already nonexistent Party, from their political and economic posts. Mazowiecki, on the other hand, wary of political purges during a period of intense hardship, preferred instead to concentrate on the economic programme. A bitter rivalry continued until the presidential elections in November 1990. The first fully free elections were eventually won by Wałęsa. The Third Republic came into being.

LECH WAŁĘSA'S PRESIDENCY

During Wałęsa's statutory five-year term in office, Poland witnessed no fewer than five governments and five prime ministers, each struggling to put the newborn democracy on wheels and each doing it differently.

After his election, Wałęsa appointed Jan Krzysztof Bielecki, an economist and his former adviser, to serve as prime minister. His cabinet attempted to continue the austere economic policies introduced by the former government but was unable to retain parliamentary support

13 December 1981

Martial law declared in Poland

1990

Polish Communist Party dissolved

and resigned after a year in office. The next government, under Prime Minister Jan Olszewski, was, like its predecessor, plagued by discord, and collapsed after only five months of existence.

In June 1992 Wałęsa gave his consent to the formation of a government led by Hanna Suchocka of the Democratic Union. An independent and articulate university professor specialising in constitutional law, she was the nation's first woman prime minister, and became known as the Polish Margaret Thatcher. Suchocka's coalition government managed to command parliamentary majority, but was in increasing discord over many issues, and failed to survive a vote of no confidence in June 1993.

The impatient Wałęsa stepped in. Instead of asking another Solidarity politician to form a government, he decided to dissolve the parliament and call a general election. This was a gross miscalculation. The postcommunist opposition parties accused the parties of the outgoing Solidarity-led coalition of mismanagement and indifference to the painful social cost of their radical reforms, and promised a more balanced programme offering growth but focused on the people's needs. They succeeded in swaying public opinion and the pendulum swung to the left.

'they succeeded in swaying public opinion and the pendulum swung to the left'

The election resulted in a leftist government based on two parties – the Democratic Left Alliance (SLD) and the Polish Peasant Party (PSL) – both of which were reformed communist parties from the pre-1989 era. The two parties commanded almost a two-thirds majority in the 460-strong Sejm. The new coalition government was headed by PSL leader Waldemar Pawlak. The general direction of transformation to a market economy slowed down, particularly in the area of privatisation and foreign investment.

The continuous tensions within the coalition and its running battles with the president brought about a change in February 1995, following Wałęsa's threats to dissolve the parliament again unless Pawlak was replaced by a more proreform leader. The parliament came up with Józef Oleksy, another former Communist Party official, yet the quarrels with the president continued unabated.

Wałęsa's presidential style and his accomplishments were repeatedly questioned by practically all political parties and the majority of the electorate. His quirky behaviour and his capricious use of power prompted a slide from the favour he had enjoyed in 1990 to his lowest-ever level of popular support in early 1995, when polls indicated that only 8% of Poles preferred him as president for the next term. Despite this, Wałęsa manoeuvred vigorously towards his goal of another five years in office and, in a miraculous comeback, went close to achieving it.

ALEKSANDER KWAŚNIEWSKI'S PRESIDENCY

The November 1995 election was essentially a tight duel between the anticommunist folk figure, Lech Wałęsa, and the much younger, one-time communist technocrat and SLD leader, Aleksander Kwaśniewski. They finished nearly neck and neck: Wałęsa with 33% of the vote and Kwaśniewski with 35%. As neither gained more than 50% of the vote, a second round was held two weeks later. Again, Kwaśniewski won by a narrow margin (51.7% against 48.3%).

Włodzimierz Cimoszewicz, another former Communist Party official, took the post of prime minister. In effect, the postcommunists gained a stranglehold on power, controlling the presidency, government and parliament – a 'red triangle', as Wałęsa warned. The centre and the right – almost half of the political nation – effectively lost control over the decision-making process. Another loser was the Church, much favoured by Wałęsa during his term in the saddle. The Church didn't fail to caution the faithful against the danger of 'neopaganism' under the new regime.

By 1997 the electorate had apparently realised that the pendulum went too much to the left. The parliamentary elections, held in September 1997, were won by an alliance of about 40 small Solidarity offshoot parties, collectively named the Solidarity Electoral Action (AWS). The alliance formed a coalition with the centrist liberal Freedom Union (UW), pushing ex-communists into opposition. Jerzy Buzek of AWS, a professor in chemistry, became prime minister, and the new government accelerated the privatisation programme.

A completely new constitution was finally passed in October 1997, to replace the Soviet-style document in force since 1952 (though it had been amended to correspond with the postcommunist status quo).

President Kwaśniewski's political style sharply contrasted with the abrasive and unpredictable style of his predecessor, Wałęsa, which was marked by constant quarrels and backroom manoeuvring. Kwaśniewski brought political calm to his term in post, and was able to cooperate successfully with both the left and right wings of the political establishment. This gained him a remarkable degree of popular support, and paved the way to another five-year term in office.

On the international front, in March 1999 Poland was granted full membership of NATO (along with the Czech Republic and Hungary), and joined the EU on 1 May 2004.

RECENT DEVELOPMENTS

No fewer than 13 contenders went into the presidential race in the October 2000 election, but this time there were few doubts about who would be the winner. Kwaśniewski, who consistently led the polls throughout the presidential campaign, won a sweeping victory, capturing 54% of the vote. The centrist businessman Andrzej Olechowski came a distant second, with 17% support. Wałęsa, who again tried his luck, suffered a disastrous defeat, collecting just 1% of the vote. The political life of the legendary Solidarity leader ended in humiliation.

The September 2001 parliamentary election changed the political axis altogether. The major winner was the ex-communist SLD, which staged its great second comeback, taking 216 seats in the Sejm, just 15 short of an outright majority. The party formed a coalition with the PSL, repeating the pattern of the shaky alliance of 1993. The former senior Communist Party official Leszek Miller became prime minister.

Miller resigned on 2 May 2004, the day after Poland joined the EU, amid mounting popular unrest over high unemployment and poor living standards. He was replaced by the respected economist and Democratic Left Alliance member Marek Belka.

Fifteen years after the collapse of communism, with the economy in stagnation and the taint of corruption hanging over the government, the future for Polish politics looks far from settled.

'no fewer than 13 contenders went into the presidential race in the October 2000 election'

1999	1 May 2004
Poland becomes a member of NATO	Poland joins the EU

The Culture

THE NATIONAL PSYCHE

The Poles are a remarkably adaptable and inventive people, each person with their own solution for any dilemma, whether within the family or within the nation; history proves well enough that there has rarely been a consensus over crucial national questions. On the other hand, Poles possess an amazing ability to mobilise themselves at critical moments. Not always realistic, they can sometimes be charmingly irrational and romantic. While they love jokes and are generally easy-going, they may suddenly turn serious and hot-blooded when it comes to an argument.

By and large, Poles are more conservative and traditional than Westerners. The Roman Catholic religion plays an important role in this conservatism; the other factor is the limited and antiquated communications and services infrastructure in certain parts of the country.

Not surprisingly, given Poland's history, the past, especially the events of WWII, still has a firm grip on the Polish national psyche.

It is difficult for Western Europeans to grasp the effect that joining the EU has had on Poland, and the divisions it has engendered. While the majority see it as a positive guarantee of Poland's continuing independence (and, indeed, existence – many banners on 1 May 2004 declared Poland's entry into the EU as 'The End of Yalta'), there are others who see EU accession as a surrender of hard-won Polish independence to the bureaucrats of Brussels.

Poles are generally friendly and hospitable – there's a traditional saying that 'a guest in the house is God in the house'. If you're lucky enough to make some Polish friends, they are likely to be extremely generous and open-handed, reflecting another popular unwritten rule – 'get in debt but show your best'.

In greetings, Polish men are passionate about handshaking. Women, too, often shake hands with men, but the man should always wait for the woman to offer her hand first. You may often see the traditional, polite way of greeting when a man kisses the hand of a woman. Here, again, it's the woman who suggests such a form by a perceptible rise of her hand.

Polish men are also passionate about giving flowers to women. The rose was traditionally the flower reserved for special occasions, but there're no strict rules these days. What does still seem to be widely observed, however, is the superstition of presenting an odd, not an even, number of flowers.

Poles don't keep as strictly to the clock as people do in the West. You may have to wait a bit until your friend arrives for an appointed meeting. Likewise, if you are invited to dinner or a party in someone's home, don't arrive exactly on time or, God forbid, turn up early.

LIFESTYLE

Since capitalism replaced communism in the 1990s, the way of life in Poland's towns and cities has been rapidly converging with Western European and North American patterns. Shopping streets are lined with globalised brand names, TVs blare out the latest American and German dramas and sitcoms, and no-one leaves home without their *komórka* (mobile phone). Average monthly earnings rose from US$45 in 1989 to US$603 in 2003; during the same period, inflation fell from 250% to 2%. There is a huge appetite for self-improvement, and plenty of ambition

The Polish Way: a Thousand-Year History of the Poles and their Culture (1988), by Adam Zamoyski, is one of the best accounts of the culture of Poland from its birth to its recent past. Fully illustrated and exquisitely written, the book is an excellent introduction to the subject.

to take advantage of the new opportunities offered by EU membership. City walls and lampposts are plastered with posters advertising courses in English, German and Russian, and diplomas in business studies and computer programming.

Old habits die hard, however, and traditional ways of doing business persist in the unlikeliest of places. A 2004 TV advertising campaign promoting tourism in Warsaw was paid for not with money, but in free use of hotel rooms – a typically Polish barter arrangement.

There is a widening culture gap between the urban and rural communities. The old country ways are still very much alive in rural areas, and travelling in the remoter corners of Poland can sometimes feel like stepping back in time. Here you will see the family milk cow grazing by the roadside, people cutting and stacking hay by hand, and making their way home from the fields by horse and cart. No matter how high-powered their lives, city folk still feel a hankering for the country life, and many escape at weekends to go hunting for wild mushrooms and berries in the fields and forests.

The Roman Catholic Church plays a prominent role in the lives of most Poles – Poland is one of Europe's most religious countries, with 75% of the population describing themselves as practising Catholics (the corresponding figure for France is 12%). On Sunday mornings, from central Warsaw to the smallest rural village, you will see entire families out together, all dressed in their Sunday best, on their way to hear Mass.

POPULATION

Poland's population in 2004 stood at about 38.6 million. The population growth rate, which was pretty high in the postwar period, has dropped gradually over the last two decades to about 0.02%, a figure comparable to that of Germany.

There were massive migratory movements in Poland in the aftermath of WWII, and the ethnic make-up of the nation is now almost entirely homogeneous. According to the official statistics, Poles make up 96.7% of the population, Germans 0.4%, Ukrainians and Belarusians about 0.1% each, with the remaining 2.7% composed of other minorities – Jews, Lithuanians, Tatars, Roma (Gypsies), Lemks, Boyks and a dozen other groups.

Today's ethnic composition differs significantly from that before the war. Poland was for centuries one of Europe's most cosmopolitan countries, and was home to the continent's largest Jewish community. Just before the outbreak of WWII, Polish Jews numbered around three million; only 5000 to 10,000 Jews remain in Poland today.

Population density varies considerably throughout the country, with Upper Silesia being the most densely inhabited area, while the northeastern border regions remain the least populated. Over 70% of the country's inhabitants now live in towns and cities, compared with the 30% who did so in the 1930s. Warsaw is by far the largest Polish city (1.75 million), followed by Łódź (793,200) and Kraków (770,000).

According to rough estimates, between five and 10 million Poles live abroad, the result of two major episodes of emigration – one at the beginning of the 20th century and another during WWII. Emigration continued on a smaller scale after the war, particularly during the economic hardships of the 1980s and '90s. The largest Polish émigré community lives in the USA.

There were fears that widespread emigration would follow Poland's accession to the EU in 2004, but recent surveys suggest that those fears are unfounded, provided that the country's economy continues to improve.

DID YOU KNOW?

Chicago, with nearly a million residents of Polish extraction, is often cited as the world's second-largest Polish city after Warsaw.

DID YOU KNOW?

The most popular first names in Poland are Piotr, Jan and Andrzej for boys, and Anna, Maria and Katarzyna for girls.

SPORT

Piłka nożna (soccer) is Poland's most popular spectator sport, and national league matches invariably draw capacity crowds. The most successful and popular teams include Wisła Kraków (www.wisla.krakow.pl) and Legia Warszawa (www.legia.pl in Polish). Poland's national team was quite strong in the 1970s, taking third place in the World Cup competitions of 1974 and 1982, but its fortunes have fallen during the last 20 years.

Other popular spectator sports include basketball and volleyball. Cycling is reasonably popular, and Poland has had international successes in athletics, kayaking and rowing. More recently, tennis and skiing have become popular, as both spectator and participator sports, though Poland has no international stars in either. With a few racetracks in the country, including in both Warsaw and Sopot, horse racing has its small group of devotees.

RELIGION

Poland is a deeply religious country, with 95% of the population claiming to be Roman Catholics. Needless to say, the 'Polish pope', John Paul II, has strengthened the position of the Church in his homeland. Minority faiths, including the Orthodox Church, Protestantism and Judaism, make up the remaining 5%.

POLAND'S CATHOLIC CHURCH TODAY

Following the collapse of communism in 1989, Poland's Roman Catholic Church moved swiftly to fill the vacuum left by the communist government, claiming land, power and the role of moral arbiter of the nation. When Lech Wałęsa became president he was the Church's most prominent supporter, and never went anywhere without a priest at his side.

The Church's interference in politics created marked changes in political priorities. In the early 1990s the crusade against abortion soared to the top of the agenda and pushed economic issues into the background. Abortion had been legalised in 1956 during the communist era, and served, in practice, as a common form of birth control. Even though only about 10% of the population supported a total ban on abortion, the Church achieved its aim and the parliament duly voted for an antiabortion law, which was introduced in 1993. Moderates did manage to have amendments attached requiring that contraceptives be made available and that Polish schools begin providing sex education for the first time.

The Church also turned its attention to the younger generation, pressing for the reintroduction of religious instruction in schools. Voluntary religious education was introduced in primary schools in 1990 and became mandatory in 1992. A glut of young men studying for the priesthood led to a surplus of clergy, and priests became a new export item – many Catholic priests throughout Europe today are of Polish origin.

From around 1994, however, the Church began to lose some of its popular support as a result of a gathering backlash against its early successes. The more liberal segments of the population began to feel a growing resentment at the compulsory religious instruction in public schools, the strong antiabortion laws and the numerous privileges accorded to the Church, such as special treatment in the granting of electronic-media licences.

This unpopularity was compounded when the Church contributed to the return to power in 1995 of former communist politicians. This alienated a fair number of voters, who turned against the clerical militancy backed by Lech Wałęsa and voted instead for Aleksander Kwaśniewski in presidential elections that took place in 1995.

It took a long time for the Polish Church to make up its mind about Poland's accession to the EU. Despite the Polish Pope John Paul II being in favour, the Church only lent its support to the government campaign to promote EU membership on condition that Poland's existing abortion law remained in place.

In past times, Polish territory spanned the borders between Rome and Byzantium, and the Catholic Church (Kościół Katolicki) had to share its influence with other creeds, particularly the Orthodox Church (Kościół Prawosławny). In 1596 the Orthodox hierarchy in Poland split with Russian Orthodoxy and accepted the supremacy of the pope in Rome. This created the so-called Uniat Church (Kościół Unicki), often referred to as the Greek-Catholic Church (Kościół Greko-Katolicki). Despite the doctrinal change, the Uniat Church retained its traditional Eastern rites and liturgical language.

After WWII Poland's borders shifted towards the west, and consequently the Orthodox Church is now present only along a narrow strip on the eastern frontier; its adherents number a little over 1% of the country's population, yet it is the second-largest creed after Roman Catholicism. Orthodox churches are recognisable by their characteristic onion-shaped domes.

The Uniat Church has an even smaller number of believers (at most 0.5%), mostly Ukrainians and Lemks scattered throughout the country as a result of forced resettlement imposed by the communist authorities in the aftermath of WWII.

The hero of *A Minor Apocalypse* (1979), by Tadeusz Konwicki, is asked to burn himself alive in front of the Communist Party headquarters. The novel follows him around the city as he debates whether to go through with this act of self-destructive protest.

ARTS
Literature

The greatest name in 19th-century Polish literature is that of the Romantic poet Adam Mickiewicz (1798–1855). Mickiewicz is to the Poles what Shakespeare is to the British, and is as much a cultural icon as a historical and creative figure. Born in Novogrodek, in what is now Belarus, he was a political activist in his youth, and was deported to central Russia for five years. He left Poland in the 1830s, never to return, and served as professor of literature in Lausanne and Paris. His best works, written while he was in exile, have, not surprisingly, a strongly patriotic theme; his most famous poem, know to all Polish schoolchildren, is the epic, book-length *Pan Tadeusz* (1834), a romantic evocation of a lost world of 18th-century Polish-Lithuanian gentry, torn apart by the Partition of 1795. There is an exhibition dedicated to Mickiewicz in Warsaw's Literature Museum (p66).

You can read or download the entire text of Henryk Sienkiewicz' novel *Quo Vadis?* at www.gutenberg.net.

Two other great Romantic poets of the 19th century were Juliusz Słowacki (1809–49) and Zygmunt Krasiński (1812–59), who were also patriots writing in exile; you'll find their names on monuments, streets and squares all over Poland.

The Nobel prize for literature was first awarded in 1901, and it was only four years later that Henryk Sienkiewicz (1846–1916) became the first of several Polish writers to be so honoured. Sienkiewicz took the 1905 prize for *Quo Vadis?*, an epic novel set in ancient Rome. Chronicling the love affair between a pagan Roman and a young Christian girl, it is a clever exploration of what it means to be a Christian. The book was the world's first 'bestseller' and has been translated into dozens of languages; 100 years after its first publication it is still in print. Novelist and short-story writer Władysław Reymont (1867–1925) became another Nobel prize winner in 1924 for *The Peasants* (Chłopi), a four-volume epic about Polish village life.

In *Solaris* (1961), by Stanisław Lem, a psychologist is sent to investigate a space station where the crew are haunted by figures from their past. Like all the best sci-fi, the story uses the futuristic setting to explore what it is to be human – in this case the impossibility of truly knowing what is going on in someone else's mind.

Józef Teodor Konrad Nałęcz Korzeniowski (1857–1924) was born into a family of impoverished but patriotic gentry in Berdichev, in what is now western Ukraine. He left the country in 1874 and, after 20 years travelling the world as a sailor, settled in England. Though fluent in his native Polish, he dedicated himself to writing in English. He is known throughout the world by his adopted name of Joseph Conrad, and his novels (*Heart of Darkness* and *Lord Jim*, to name but two) are considered classics of English literature.

Between the wars several brilliant avant-garde writers emerged, who were only fully appreciated after WWII. They included Bruno Schulz (1892–1942), Witold Gombrowicz (1904–69) and Stanisław Ignacy Witkiewicz (also known as Witkacy; 1885–1939). Witkacy, an unusual talent in many fields (including painting, literature and photography) was the originator of unconventional philosophical concepts, the most notable being the 'theory of pure form'. He was also the creator of the theatre of the absurd long before Ionesco made it famous. Only in the 1960s were Witkacy's plays, such as *Mother* (Matka), *Cobblers* (Szewcy) and *New Deliverance* (Nowe Wyzwolenie), discovered internationally. He committed suicide soon after the outbreak of WWII as an expression of his belief in 'catastrophism', the disintegration of civilisation.

The postwar period presented Polish writers with a conundrum: adopt communism and effectively sell out, or take a more independent path and risk persecution. Czesław Miłosz (1911–2004), who broke with the communist regime, offered an analysis of this problem in *The Captive Mind* (Zniewolony Umysł). Miłosz, a long-time émigré who spent most of his life in the USA, occupies the prime position in Polish postwar literature, and the Nobel prize awarded to him in 1980 was recognition of his achievements.

One of the most remarkable figures of the postwar literary scene is novelist, screenwriter and film director Tadeusz Konwicki (b 1926). A teenage resistance fighter during WWII, Konwicki's pre-1989 works had the communist censors tearing their hair out; he has been described (on www.culture.pl) as 'the conscience of Polish society and the crazed mirror in which it is reflected'. He has written more than 20 novels, among which the best known are the brilliant *A Minor Apocalypse* (Mała Apokalipsa) and *The Polish Complex* (Kompleks Polski).

Polish literature's most recent Nobel prize went, in 1996, to Wisława Szymborska (b 1923), a Kraków poet little known beyond the borders of her motherland. The Swedish academy described her as 'the Mozart of poetry' with 'something of the fury of Beethoven'. For those intending to sample her work, a good introduction is the volume entitled *View with a Grain of Sand*, published in 1995. It's a selection of 100 poems, translated into English, that span nearly 40 years of her work.

Stanisław Lem (b 1921) is without doubt Poland's premier writer of science fiction. Around 27 million of his books, translated into 41 languages, have been sold around the world. Of the more than 30 novels he has written, the most famous is *Solaris*, which was made into a movie starring George Clooney in 2002.

Look in the window of any large Polish bookshop and you will see the latest best-selling offerings from a younger generation of writers that includes Gdańsk-based journalist and novelist Pawel Huelle (b 1957), Olga Tokarczuk (b 1962) and psychologist and translator Magdalena Tulli (b 1955). Katarzyna Grochola, whose pointedly humorous novels are about a woman's life in modern Poland, has been compared to Helen Fielding, author of *Bridget Jones's Diary*.

Cinema

Though the invention of the cinema is attributed to the Lumière brothers, some sources claim that a Pole, Piotr Lebiedziński, should take some of the credit; he built a film camera in 1893, two years before the movie craze took off.

The website www.polishwriting.net is a guide to around 20 contemporary Polish novelists whose works are available in English, and includes short biographies, interviews, articles and extracts from their works.

Who Was David Weiser?, by Pawel Huelle, is part thriller, part parable, and an intriguing multilayered story about a 13-year-old Jewish boy with supernatural powers who mysteriously disappears during an idyllic summer holiday.

Olga Tokarczuk is one of Poland's most popular authors. Her first novel, *House of Day, House of Night*, tells the story of a Polish village near the Czech border and its eccentric inhabitants, by turns witty and wise, tragic and comical.

The first Polish film was shot in 1908, but it was only after WWI that film production began on a larger scale. Until the mid-1930s Polish films were largely banal comedies or adaptations of the more-popular novels, and were hardly recognised beyond the country's borders. The biggest Polish contribution to international film in that period was that of actress Pola Negri, who was born in Poland and made her debut in Polish film before gaining worldwide fame.

During the first 10 years following WWII, Polish cinematography didn't register many significant achievements, apart from some semi-documentaries depicting the cruelties of the war. One such remarkable example is *The Last Stage* (Ostatni Etap), a moving documentary-drama directed by Wanda Jakubowska, an Auschwitz survivor.

The period that followed (1955–63) was unprecedentedly fruitful, so much so that it's referred to as the Polish School. Beginning with the debut of Andrzej Wajda, the school drew heavily on literature and dealt with moral evaluations of the war – its common denominator was heroism. A dozen remarkable films were made in that period, including Wajda's famous trilogy: *A Generation* (Pokolenie), *Canal* (Kanał) and *Ashes and Diamonds* (Popiół i Diament). Since then, the tireless Wajda has produced a film every couple of years; the ones that have gained possibly the widest recognition are *Man of Marble* (Człowiek z Marmuru), its sequel *Man of Iron* (Człowiek z Żelaza), and *Danton*.

In the early 1960s two young talents Roman Polański and Jerzy Skolimowski appeared on the scene. The former made only one feature film in Poland, *Nóż w wodzie* (Knife in the Water), and then decided to continue his career in the West. The latter shot four films, of which the last, *Ręce do Góry* (Hands Up), made in 1967, was kept on the shelf until 1985. He also left Poland. Whereas Skolimowski's work abroad has not gained widespread recognition, Polański has made it to the top. His career includes such remarkable films as *Cul-de-Sac, Rosemary's Baby, Chinatown, Macbeth, Bitter Moon* and *Death and the Maiden*.

Another ambassador of Polish cinema, Krzysztof Kieślowski, started in 1977 with *Blizna* (Scar), but his first widely acclaimed feature was *Amator* (Amateur). After several mature films, he undertook the challenge of making the *Dekalog* (Decalogue), a 10-part TV series that was broadcast all over the world. He then made another noteworthy production *The Double Life of Veronique* and confirmed his extraordinary abilities as a film maker with the trilogy *Three Colours: Blue/White/Red*. The last project won him important international film awards and critical acclaim as one of Europe's best directors. He died during heart surgery in March 1996.

Other important directors who started their careers during communist times include Krzysztof Zanussi, Andrzej Żuławski and Agnieszka Holland. The postcommunist period has witnessed a rash of young directors, but none has yet proved to be of the class of Polański or Wajda.

Poland has produced a number of world-class cinematographers, including Janusz Kamiński, who was awarded with two Oscars for his work on Steven Spielberg's *Schindler's List* and *Saving Private Ryan*. He also directed photography in *Jurassic Park: the Lost World*.

Less known but perhaps no less talented are several other Polish cinematographers responsible for various acclaimed Hollywood productions, including Adam Holender (*Midnight Cowboy*), Andrzej Bartkowiak (*Verdict, Jade, Terms of Endearment, Prizzi's Honor*), Andrzej Sekuła (*Pulp Fiction*) and Piotr Sobociński (*Marvin's Room, Ransom*).

Roman Polański's debut feature *Nóż w wodzie* (Knife In the Water; 1963) is a consummate piece of film-making, a tense battle of wits between two men – one older, one younger – over a pretty woman, and set on a yacht on the Great Masurian Lakes. It won an Oscar nomination for Best Foreign Film.

The Pianist (2003), the harrowing true story of a Warsaw Ghetto survivor, won three Oscars (including Best Actor and Best Director) and two Baftas for Roman Polański.

Krzysztof Kieślowski's *Three Colours* trilogy (1993–94) explores the French Revolution's ideals of *liberté, égalité* and *fraternité* as they apply in modern life. *Blue*, which deals with liberty and is widely regarded as the best, is the tale of a woman who attempts to free herself of all commitments following the death of her husband.

Music

The foremost figure in the history of Polish music is of course Frédéric Chopin (1810–49), who crystallised the national style, taking inspiration from folk or court dances and tunes such as *polonez* (polonaise), *mazurek* (mazurka), *oberek* and *kujawiak*. No-one else in the history of Polish music has so creatively used folk rhythms for concert pieces, nor achieved such international recognition. Chopin has become the very symbol of Polish music.

Overshadowed by Chopin's fame, another composer inspired by folk dances was Stanisław Moniuszko (1819–72) who created Polish national opera. Two of his best-known operas, *Halka* and *Straszny Dwór,* are staples of the national opera-house repertoire. Also eclipsed by Chopin's achievements was Henryk Wieniawski (1835–80), another remarkable 19th-century composer, who was also a great violinist.

By the beginning of the 20th century, Polish artists were starting to make their way onto the world stage. The first to do so were the piano virtuosos Ignacy Paderewski (1860–1941) and Artur Rubinstein (1886–1982), the latter performing right up until his death.

The premier musical personality of the first half of the 20th century was Karol Szymanowski (1882–1937). His best-known composition, the ballet *Harnasie,* was influenced by folk music from the Tatra Mountains, which he transformed into the contemporary musical idiom.

In the field of more-modern music, Poland is up there with the world's best. In the 1950s and 1960s a wealth of talent emerged, including Witold Lutosławski, with his *Musique Funèbre* and *Jeux Vénitiens,* and Krzysztof Penderecki, with his monumental dramatic forms such as *Dies Irae, Ubu Rex, Devils of Loudun, Seven Gates of Jerusalem* and *Credo.*

Originally eclipsed by the aforementioned masters, Henryk Górecki developed his own musical language. His Symphony No 3 was written in 1976, but it wasn't until the early 1990s that the second recording of this work hit musical audiences worldwide. The phenomenal success of the third symphony shed light on the other compositions of Górecki, notably his String Quartets Nos 1 and 2, written for, and exquisitely performed by, the Kronos Quartet.

Jazz took off in the 1950s (at that time it was an underground movement) around the legendary pianist Krzysztof Komeda, who later composed the music to most of the early Polański films, before his tragic death. Komeda inspired and influenced many jazz musicians, such as Michał Urbaniak (violin, saxophone), Zbigniew Namysłowski (saxophone) and Tomasz Stańko (trumpet), all of whom became pillars of

The website of the Narodowy Instytut Fryderyka Chopina (National Frédéric Chopin Institute; www.nifc.pl) contains a vast amount of information on Poland's most famous composer, much of it translated into English.

THE CHOPIN TRAIL

There are several places in and around Warsaw that are associated with Poland's national composer, Frédéric Chopin.

- Chopin Monument (p75) – piano recitals of Chopin's music are held on Sunday afternoons in summer (see p87)
- Chopin Museum (p70) – a small museum housed in the headquarters of the Chopin Society
- Holy Cross Church (p70) – where Chopin's heart is buried
- Warsaw University (p70) – from 1826 to 1829 Chopin studied at the school of music here
- Żelazowa Wola (p92) – Chopin's birthplace; the house where he was born has been restored as a museum

POLISH HIP-HOP

Poland's musical scene encompasses a broad spectrum of artists, playing everything from folk and jazz to punk and rock, but turn on any music TV and all you'll see is home-grown hip-hop. Whether it's thanks to the restrictions of the communist era or the current high levels of youth unemployment, since 1990 a whole generation has enthusiastically embraced the 'money, guns and hos' gangsta philosophy, and the recent worldwide commercial explosion of the genre has opened things up wide for Poland's many urban crews and posses.

Little of what you'll hear is revolutionary in a musical sense, but the point is that you'll hear it – hip-hop is firmly ensconced in the mainstream in Poland. It's also virtually the only form of Polish-language music to make it out of the country, and while it's never going to outsell Eminem, you can already find Polish rap nights in clubs as far afield as London. Unsurprisingly, the heaviest presence is in Germany, where a large expat population and an equally active hip-hop scene provide a booming market.

Names to look out for include 52 Dębiec, Ascetoholix, Zipera, Jeden Osiem L, Slums Attack, Grammatik, Fisz, Kaliber 44 and Kodex II; tune into radiostacja (101.5FM in Warsaw) or pick up one of its compilation CDs to get a taste of what's hot in the scene. If you don't speak any Polish you won't make much sense of anything, but there's the usual sprinkling of American slang and you should at least recognise the term *kurwa* after a while – it is of course the f-word, proving that some things in hip-hop transcend national boundaries.

Polish jazz in the 1960s and remain active today. Urbaniak opted to pursue his career in the USA, and is the best-known Polish jazz musician on the international scene.

Of the younger generation, Leszek Możdżer (piano) is possibly the biggest revelation thus far, followed by several other exceptionally skilled pianists such as Andrzej Jagodziński and Włodzimierz Pawlik. Other young jazz talents to watch out for include Piotr Wojtasik (trumpet), Maciej Sikała (saxophone), Adam Pierończyk (saxophone), Piotr Baron (saxophone) and Cezary Konrad (drums).

While Polish pop has mirrored the major Western fashions, it has added local colour and language. The best known rock-pop veteran groups include Lady Punk, Republika, Budka Suflera, Manaam and Bajm. Recent years have seen a rash of productions covering just about every musical genre and style from salsa to rap. Brathanki and Golec u Orkiestra are both popular groups that creatively mix folk and pop rhythms.

Warsaw was the first European capital to fall in love with opera – the city's first opera performance was staged in the Royal Castle in 1628, just 28 years after the first ever opera was performed in Florence.

Architecture

Over the centuries Poland has followed the main Western European architectural styles, with some local variations. The earliest, the Romanesque style, which dominated from the late 10th to the mid-13th centuries, used mainly stone and was austere, functional and simple. Round-headed arches, semicircular apses and symmetrical layouts were almost universal. The remnants of the Romanesque style in Poland are few but there are some precious examples, including the collegiate church at Tum (p106).

The Gothic style made its way into Poland in the first half of the 13th century but it was not until the early 14th century that the so-called High Gothic became universally adopted. Elongated, pointed arches and ribbed vaults were characteristic of the style. Brick came into common use instead of stone, and the buildings, particularly churches, tended to reach impressive loftiness and monumental size. Gothic established itself for a long time in Poland and left behind countless churches, castles, town halls and burghers' houses, and the mighty Gothic fortress of Malbork castle (p396). Polish towns with a fine legacy of Gothic architecture include Kraków (p125), Lublin (p183), Wrocław (p263), Gniezno (p338) and Toruń (p385).

In the 16th century a new fashion transplanted from Italy started to supersede Gothic as the dominant style. More delicate and decorative, Renaissance architecture didn't go for verticality and large volume but instead focused on perfect proportions and a handsome visual appearance. In contrast to Gothic, brickwork was almost never allowed to go uncovered. Much attention was paid to both detail and decoration, which included bas-reliefs, gables, parapets, galleries, round arches and stucco work. There are a number of Renaissance buildings in Poland – notably Wawel Castle and the Sigismund Chapel in Kraków (p130), and the castles at Baranów Sandomierski (p179) and Ogrodzeniec (p166) – though many of them were later 'adorned' by the subsequent architectural fashion, the baroque.

Baroque appeared on Polish soil in the 17th century and soon became ubiquitous. A lavish, highly decorative style, it placed a strong imprint on existing architecture by adding its sumptuous décor, which is particularly evident in church interiors and the palaces of the aristocracy. The most prominent figure of the baroque period in Poland was Tylman van Gameren, a Dutch architect who settled in Poland and designed countless buildings; his finest masterpieces include Warsaw's Krasiński Palace (p68), Palace of Nieborów (p104), St Anne's Church in Kraków (p139) and the Royal Chapel in Gdańsk (p363). In the 18th century baroque culminated in French-originated rococo, but it didn't make much of a mark on Poland, which by then was swiftly sliding into economic and political chaos.

At the beginning of the 19th century, a more complex phase of architectural development started in Poland, which might be characterised as a period of the 'neo', or a general turn back towards the past. This phase comprised neo-Renaissance, neo-Gothic and even neo-Romanesque styles. The most important of all the 'neo' fashions, though, was neoclassicism, which used ancient Greek and Roman elements as an antidote to the overloaded baroque and rococo opulence. Monumental palaces adorned with columned porticoes were erected in this period, as well as churches that looked like Roman pantheons. Italian architect Antonio Corazzi was very active in Poland in this period, and designed several massive neoclassical buildings, including the Teatr Wielki (Grand Theatre; see p69) in Warsaw, the town where neoclassicism left its strongest mark.

The second half of the 19th century was dominated by eclecticism – the style that profited from all the previous trends – but it didn't produce any architectural gems. More innovative was Art Nouveau, which developed in England, France, Austria and Germany, and made its entrance into Poland (still under Partition) at the beginning of the 20th century. It left behind some fresh decorative marks, especially in Kraków (p125) and Łódź (p97). After WWI, neoclassicism took over again but lost out to functionalism just before WWII.

The postwar period started with a heroic effort to reconstruct destroyed towns and cities, and the result, given the level of destruction, is really impressive. Meanwhile, one more architectural style, socialist realism, was imposed by the communist regime. The most spectacular building in this style is the Palace of Culture & Science (p70) in Warsaw, a gift from the Soviet Union.

Since the 1960s Polish architecture has followed more general European styles, though with one important local distinction: almost all major cities have been ringed by vast suburbs of anonymous concrete apartment blocks, a sad consequence of massive urbanisation and the architects' lack of imagination. In Poland's defence, it didn't have the necessary cash flow to accommodate aesthetic values. Nor did Poland receive external assistance from the Marshall Plan, which helped other Western European nations to rebuild after the war. Only after the fall of communism was there a trend towards the construction of homes on a more human scale.

Painting

Bernardo Bellotto (c 1720–80) was born in Venice, the nephew (and pupil) of that quintessential Venetian artist, Canaletto. He specialised in *vedute* (town views) and travelled widely in Europe, becoming court painter in Warsaw during the reign of King Stanisław August Poniatowski (1764–95). An entire room in Warsaw's Royal Castle (p65) is devoted to his detailed views of the city, which proved invaluable as references during the reconstruction of the Old Town after WWII. Bellotto often signed his canvases 'de Canaletto', and as a result is commonly known in Poland simply as Canaletto. Also on display in the castle are works by Marcello Bacciarelli (1731–1818), the king's favourite portraitist, who also produced a set of paintings depicting important moments in Polish history.

It's almost impossible to enter a major Polish museum without seeing at least one painting by Jan Matejko (1838–93). Born in Kraków, Matejko created stirring canvases that glorified Poland's past achievements, aiming to keep alive in the minds of his viewers the notion of a proud and independent Polish nation, during a time when Poland had ceased to exist as a political entity. His best-known work is the huge tableau *The Battle of Grünwald* (1878), which is on display in Warsaw's National Museum (p73). It took three years to complete, and depicts the famous victory of the united Polish, Lithuanian and Ruthenian forces, led by King Władysław II Jagiełło, over the Teutonic Knights in 1410 (p19).

Other painters of the period who documented Polish history, especially battle scenes, include Józef Brandt (1841–1915) and Wojciech Kossak (1857–1942), the latter particularly remembered as co-creator of the colossal *Racławicka Panorama,* which is on display in Wrocław (p265).

The closing decades of the 19th century saw the development of Impressionism in Europe, but it was met with much reserve by Polish artists. Even though many of the first-rank national painters of this period, such as Aleksander Gierymski (1850–1901), Józef Chełmoński (1849–1914), Władysław Podkowiński (1866–95), Leon Wyczółkowski (1852–1936) and Julian Fałat (1853–1929) were in some way, or for some time, influenced by the new style, they preferred to express themselves in traditional forms and never completely gave up realism. This is particularly true of their Polish landscapes, an important part of their work.

On the other hand, the revolution in European painting influenced those Polish artists who lived and worked outside Poland, particularly those in Paris. Among them were Olga Boznańska (1865–1940), whose delicate portraits were painted with notable hints of Impressionism, and Tadeusz Makowski (1882–1932), who adopted elements of Cubism and developed an individual, easily recognisable style.

After WWII and up until 1955, the visual arts were dominated by socialist realism, but later they developed with increasing freedom, expanding in a variety of forms, trends and techniques. Among the outstanding figures of the 20th-century generation are: Tadeusz Kulisiewicz (1899–1988), who started his career before WWII but reached mastery in his delicate drawings in the postwar period; Tadeusz Kantor (1915–90),

DID YOU KNOW?

Jan Matejko painted portraits of every Polish king from 960 to 1790, and scenes of every major event or battle in Polish history. Images of many of his paintings can be found on the website www.malarze.com.

who was renowned mainly for his famous Cricot 2 Theatre but who was also very creative in painting, drawing and other experimental forms; Jerzy Nowosielski (b 1923), whose painting is strongly inspired by the iconography of the Orthodox Church and who has decorated the interiors of several churches (including the Orthodox Church of the Holy Trinity, (p120) in Hajnówka; and Zdzisław Beksiński (b 1929), who is considered one of the best contemporary painters Poland has produced, and has created a unique, mysterious and striking world of dreams in his art.

Folk Arts & Crafts

Poland has long and rich traditions in folk arts and crafts, and there are significant regional distinctions. Folk culture is strongest in the mountainous regions, especially in the Podhale at the foot of the Tatras, but other relatively small enclaves, such as Kurpie and Łowicz (both in Mazovia), help to keep traditions alive.

Industrialisation and urbanisation increasingly encroach on traditional customs. People no longer wear folk dress except for special occasions, and the artefacts they make are mostly for sale as either tourist souvenirs or museum pieces; in any case, they are not used for their original purposes. The growing number of ethnographic museums is an indicator of the decline of traditional folk art; these museums are the best places to see what is left. One interesting type of ethnographic museum is the skansen (open-air museum; see the boxed text below), created to preserve traditional rural architecture.

Despite the decline there's still a lot to see outside the museums and skansens. The Polish rural population is conservative and religious, which means that traditions don't die overnight. The further off the

---

POLAND'S SKANSENS

'Skansen' is a Scandinavian word referring to an open-air ethnographic museum. Aimed at preserving traditional folk culture and architecture, a skansen gathers together a selection of typical, mostly wooden, rural buildings (dwellings, barns, churches, mills) collected from the region, and often reassembles them to look like a natural village. The buildings are furnished and decorated in their original style, incorporating a range of traditional household equipment, tools, crafts and artefacts, and offer an insight into the life, work and customs of the period.

The concept of open-air museums emerged in the late 19th century in Scandinavia. In the interwar period, interest in skansens spread all over Europe and beyond, to Austria, Germany, the UK and the USA, although most are concentrated in Scandinavia and Central Europe. The largest existing open-air museum is the Muzeul Satului in Bucharest.

Poland's first skansen was established in 1906 in Wdzydze Kiszewskie (p383), near Gdańsk, and focussed on Kashubian folk culture. The next one appeared in 1927 in Nowogród (p110), in northern Mazovia, dedicated to traditional Kurpie culture. Both were almost totally destroyed during WWII but were later reconstructed.

There are currently about 35 museums of this kind that are scattered all over Poland and feature distinctive regional traits. They are usually called *muzeum budownictwa ludowego* (museum of folk architecture), *muzeum wsi* (museums of the village) or *park etnograficzny* (ethnographic park), but the term 'skansen' is universally applied to all of them.

Although most skansens have been established by reassembling regional buildings on the site of the museum, there are also some small *in situ* skansens, including the one in Kluki (p404), and some specialist ones, notably the oil-industry skansen in Bóbrka (p236). It's hard to form a hard-and-fast 'skansen top 10' list, but at the very least you shouldn't miss the ones in Sanok (p227) and Nowy Sącz (p243).

beaten track you get, the more you'll see. Traditions periodically spring to life around religious feasts and folk festivals, and these events offer the best opportunity to get a feel for how deep the folk roots remain.

Theatre & Dance

Although theatrical traditions in Poland go back to the Middle Ages, theatre in the proper sense of the word didn't develop until the Renaissance period and initially followed the styles of major centres in France and Italy. By the 17th century the first original Polish plays were being performed on stage. In 1765 the first permanent theatre company was founded in Warsaw and its later director, Wojciech Bogusławski, came to be known as the father of the national theatre.

Theatre development was hindered during Partition. Only the Kraków and Lviv theatres enjoyed relative freedom, but even they were unable to stage the great Romantic dramas, which were not performed until the beginning of the 20th century. By the outbreak of WWI, 10 permanent Polish theatres were operating. The interwar period witnessed a lively theatrical scene with the main centres situated in Warsaw and Kraków.

'the interwar period witnessed a lively theatrical scene'

After WWII Polish theatre acquired an international reputation. Some of the highest international recognition was gained by the Teatr Laboratorium (Laboratory Theatre), which was created in 1965, and led by Jerzy Grotowski in Wrocław. This unique experimental theatre, remembered particularly for *Apocalypsis cum Figuris,* was dissolved in 1984, and Grotowski concentrated on conducting theatrical classes abroad until his death in early 1999. Another remarkable international success was Tadeusz Kantor's Cricot 2 Theatre of Kraków, formed in 1956. Unfortunately, his best creations, *The Dead Class* (Umarła Klasa) and *Wielopole, Wielopole,* will never be seen again; Kantor died in 1990 and the theatre was dissolved a few years later.

Among existing experimental theatres, the most powerful and expressive include the Gardzienice, based in the village of the same name near Lublin, the Teatr Witkacego (Witkacy Theatre) in Zakopane, and the Wierszalin in Białystok.

In the mainstream, the most outstanding theatre company in Kraków is the Teatr Stary (Old Theatre). There are several top-ranking theatres in Warsaw, including the Centrum Sztuki Studio (Studio Art Centre), Teatr Polski (Polish Theatre), Teatr Ateneum, Teatr Powszechny and Teatr Współczesny.

Polish theatre directors to watch out for include Jerzy Jarocki, Jerzy Grzegorzewski, Kazimierz Dejmek, Andrzej Wajda, Krystian Lupa and Maciej Prus.

Prominent among other forms of theatre are Wrocławski Teatr Pantomimy (Pantomime Theatre of Wrocław) and Polski Teatr Tańca (Polish Dance Theatre) based in Poznań.

Environment

THE LAND

Poland covers an area about as big as the UK and Ireland put together, or a bit less than half the size of Texas. The territory is roughly square in shape, reaching a maximum of about 680km from west to east and 650km from north to south. It is bordered by the Baltic Sea to the northwest along a 524km coastline; by Germany to the west (along a 460km border); both the Czech and Slovak republics to the south (1310km); and Ukraine, Belarus, Lithuania and Russia to the east and northeast (1244km).

A quick glance at the map suggests that Poland is a vast, flat, low-lying plain – 75% of Poland is less than 200m above sea level – but a closer look reveals a more complex topography. Poland's landscape is largely a legacy of the last ice age, when the Scandinavian ice sheet advanced southward across the Polish plains and then receded again about 10,000 years ago. Four landscapes zones are recognisable, running east–west across the country: the southern mountains; the central lowlands; the lake belt; and the Baltic coast.

The southern mountains stretch from the Sudeten Mountains, in the southwest, through the Tatra to the Beskidy in the southeast. The Sudeten are geologically ancient hills, their rounded forms reaching their highest point at the summit of Śnieżka (1602m) in the Karkonosze range. Poland's highest point is Rysy (2499m) in the Tatra, a jagged, alpine range of mountains on the border with Slovakia.

To the north of the Tatra lies the lower but much larger and densely forested range of the Beskids (Beskidy), with its highest peak being Babia Góra (1725m). The southeastern extremity of Poland is taken up by the Bieszczady, which is part of the Carpathians; the highest summit is Tarnica (1343m).

The rolling, agricultural landscapes of the central lowlands stretch from west to east across the middle of the country, comprising the historic regions of Lower Silesia (Dolny Śląsk), Greater Poland (Wielkopolska), Mazovia (Mazowsze) and Podlasie. This is where streams flowing south from the melting glaciers deposited thick layers of sand and mud that, along with returning vegetation, helped produce some of the country's most fertile soils – the land here is mostly farmland, and the central lowlands are Poland's main grain-producing region.

In places, notably in Kampinos National Park (p92) to the west of Warsaw, these fluvioglacial sand deposits have been blown by the wind into sand dunes up to 30m in height, some of the largest inland dune complexes in Europe. In Silesia, in the western part of the lowlands, vast coal deposits provided the fuel for the industrial revolution of the 19th century.

The southern edge of the ice sheet left behind a broad belt of moraines – hummocky deposits of sticky clay mixed with stones and boulders that had been carried down by the glaciers, then dumped as the fringes of the ice sheet began to melt. This lake zone, which takes in the regions of Pomerania (Pomorze), Warmia and Masuria (Mazury), consists of gently undulating plains. It's forested rather than farmed (the acid, clay-rich soils are much less fertile than those to the south) and dotted with thousands of postglacial lakes, most of which are in the northeastern region of Masuria. Poland has over 9000 lakes, more than any other country in Europe except Finland.

DID YOU KNOW?

Legend has it that Lenin himself climbed Rysy back in 1912 or 1914; a rock near the summit where he is said to have sat and rested is painted with a red hammer and sickle.

The fourth zone is the coastal plain that fringes the Baltic Sea, and is characterised by sand dunes and swamps, the sand again having been deposited by the melting ice sheet. These sand and gravel deposits not only form the beaches of Poland's seaside resorts, but also the shifting dunes of Słowiński National Park (p403) and the sand bars and gravel spits of Hel (p381) and the Vistula Lagoon.

All Poland's rivers drain northwards into the Baltic Sea. The longest (1090km) is the mighty Vistula (Wisła), which runs through the middle of the country, with its important right-bank tributaries, the Bug and the Narew. It is known as the mother river of Poland because it passes through the historically important cities of Kraków and Warsaw, and its entire basin lies within the country's boundaries. The second longest is the Odra (Oder), which forms part of Poland's western border.

DID YOU KNOW?

The 1090km Vistula River, rising from pristine springs in the Carpathian Mountains and flowing into the sea to the east of Gdańsk, is the seventh-longest river in Europe (excluding Russia).

WILDLIFE
Animals

Poland offers some of Central Europe's best opportunities for watching wildlife, and is one of the few places on the continent where you can see large mammals such as elk and bison in the wild. The country's forests, plains, swamps and mountains are home to some 90 species of mammal, of which the most common include hare, red deer, wild boar and fox. Elk and lynx live in the woods of the far northeast, while brown bears and wildcats can be found in the mountain forests.

Several hundred European bison live in the Białowieża National Park (p121), which is in Podlasie. These massive animals once inhabited the continent in large numbers, but were brought to the brink of extinction early in the 20th century, before being successfully reintroduced into the wild.

Wolves are found in several areas, especially the Bieszczady and other parts of the Carpathians Mountains, and in the forests on the eastern borders of Poland, notably in the Białowieża National Park. They are in serious decline, however, and have been persecuted by hunters and shepherds; special legislation was passed to protect them in 1998. The total wolf population of the country is estimated to be around 750.

The Polish plains were once home to wild horses, several species of which have been preserved in zoos; one of them, the tarpan, can be seen in Białowieża National Park. Poland has a long tradition of breeding Arabian horses, which are much appreciated on world markets. Many important international championships have been won by Polish-bred Arabians. There are a number of stud farms and horse riding is popular.

DID YOU KNOW?

Polish peasants once believed that a stork's nest on the roof of a building would protect it from lightening strikes.

Poland is also a bird-watcher's paradise. The vast areas of lake, marsh and reed-bed along the Baltic coast, and in the swampy basins of the Narew and Biebrza Rivers, are home to many species of waterfowl, and are visited by huge flocks of migrating geese, ducks and waders in spring and autumn, while a small community of cormorants lives in the Masurian lakes. Storks, which arrive from Africa in spring to build their nests on the roofs and chimneys of houses in the countryside, are a much loved part of the rural scene.

The *orzeł* (eagle) is the national symbol of Poland, and was adopted as a royal emblem in the 12th century. Several species can be spotted in Poland, mostly in the southern mountains, including golden eagle and short-toed eagle, plus the rare booted eagle, greater spotted eagle and lesser spotted eagle. The white-tailed eagle, supposedly the species on which the national emblem is based, lives in the Słowiński (p403) and Wolin (p414) National Parks.

Plants

In prehistoric times pretty much all of Poland would have been covered by the great primeval forest that once spread across most of lowland Europe. Today, only a single fragment of that ancient lowland mixed forest remains, protected in the heart of Białowieża National Park (p112), where five-century-old oak trees survive.

The website of the Board of Polish National Parks (www.mos.gov.pl/kzpn) provides details on all of Poland's national parks.

Forests cover just over a quarter of Poland's territory. This area is increasing – every year some 100 to 130 sq km of new forest is planted, with a goal of achieving 30% forest coverage by 2025. Over 80% of the forest area is administered by the state, about 2% of which is protected by national parks. By far the most common species is pine (70% of the total area), but the share of deciduous species such as oak, beech, birch and linden (which dominated the ancient woodlands) is on the increase, enriching the forest's biological diversity and its natural resistance.

Forests provide timber (about 20 million cu metres a year), wild mushrooms and fruit, habitat for wildlife, a playground for hunting (now largely restricted) and a base for recreation and activities.

The mountains of southern Poland harbour alpine flowers such as saxifrage, larkspur and *Poa granitica*, as well as around 700 species of lichen.

CONSERVATION AREAS

About 23% of the country's territory is currently under some sort of protection (in national or landscape parks or other protected areas), and the goal is to achieve a total of 30%.

Poland has 23 *parki narodowe* (national parks), covering about 3200 sq km, a mere 1% of the country's surface area. The parks are scattered

Park	Features	Activities	Best time to visit	Page
Białowieża NP	primeval forest; bison, elk, lynx, wolf	wildlife-watching, hiking	spring, summer	p121
Biebrza NP	river, wetland, forest; elk, great snipe, aquatic warbler	bird-watching, canoeing	spring, autumn	p117
Kampinos NP	forest, sand dunes	hiking, mountain-biking	summer	p92
Karkonosze NP	mountains; dwarf pine, alpine flora	hiking, mountain-biking, skiing	summer, winter	p287
Narew NP	river, bog, reed-beds; beaver, waterfowl	bird-watching, canoeing	spring, autumn	p118
Ojców NP	forest, rock formations, caves; eagles, bats	hiking	autumn	p164
Roztocze NP	forest; elk, wolf, beaver, tarpan	hiking	spring, autumn	p206
Słowiński NP	forest, bog, sand dunes; white-tailed eagle, waterfowl	hiking, bird-watching	all year	p403
Tatra NP	alpine mountains; chamois, eagle	hiking, climbing, skiing	all year	p254
Wolin NP	forest, lake, coast; white-tailed eagle, bison	hiking, bird-watching	spring, autumn	p414

fairly evenly throughout the country, except in the Carpathian Mountains where there are six. One Polish national park, Białowieża (p121), is on the Unesco World Heritage List.

About 85% of the area of all parks is state owned, whereas the remaining 15% is in private hands. The state is gradually acquiring the private land, a process that will take a decade or two to complete. The parks are administered by a special department of the Ministry of Environment; park maintenance is financed from the state budget.

No permit is necessary to visit the parks, but most have introduced entry fees (of around 5zł), which you must pay at the park office or an entry point. Camping in the parks is not allowed except on specified sites.

Apart from the national parks, a network of other areas called *parki krajobrazowe* (landscape parks), has been established. As the name suggests, their scenery is the major attraction and they are accordingly picturesque and not so strictly preserved. The first landscape park was created in 1976 and today there are 105 of them. They are found in all regions and together cover about 20,000 sq km, or 6% of the country's area.

There are also the *rezerwaty* (reserves). These are usually small areas that contain a particular natural feature such as a cluster of old trees, a lake with valuable flora or an interesting rock formation.

ENVIRONMENTAL ISSUES

Environmental issues that have been hitting the headlines in recent years include the development of the Via Baltica Expressway and logging threats to the Białowieża Forest.

The Via Baltica is a road-transport project that plans to build a multi-lane freeway linking Warsaw to Helsinki by way of the Baltic states. The problem is that the preferred route through northeastern Poland (approved by the Ministry of the Environment) will impact on the Biebrza and Narew National Parks, and the Augustów and Knyszyn Forests. However, the alternative route, which avoids conservation areas, also bypasses the city of Białystok, which is badly in need of the economic boost that the new highway would provide; hence the standoff.

You can find information on various environmental campaigns on the Worldwide Fund for Nature's Polish website (www.wwf.pl).

Only 16% of the huge Białowieża Forest in Podlasie is protected by the Białowieża National Park. The rest of the forest has only limited protection (eg it is illegal to fell trees that are more than 100 years old), but there is economic pressure in this relatively poor region of Poland for commercial logging to be increased. As a result, the Worldwide Fund for Nature in Poland has launched a campaign to extend the area of the national park.

The communist regime in Poland spent virtually nothing on protecting the country's environment. Decades of intensive industrialisation without even the most elementary protection turned rivers into sewers and air into smog. It wasn't until 1990, after the regime crumbled, that the Ministry of Environmental Protection was set up and began to develop an environmental policy to try to clean up the mess left by the communists. Today, 15 years down the track, Poland's environment is improving but it's still in an unenviable state.

Poland has a number of seriously polluted urban and industrial areas (called 'ecological hazard zones'), which account for about 10% of the country's territory. Their treatment is a priority of the government's current environmental policy.

Air pollution continues to be one of Poland's most serious problems. The major pollutant is the energy sector, which uses outdated technologies and highly polluting fuels, such as coal and lignite. The situation

THE WHITE STORK – A BIRD OF GOOD LUCK

Everybody knows that storks *(bocian)* bring babies, right? In many countries, including Poland, it's also believed that storks drop off not only little bundles of joy but also healthy doses of good luck. As a result, storks are much loved and special efforts are made to encourage them to nest.

The most commonly seen species of stork in Poland is the white stork *(Ciconia ciconia)*, a large bird, about 1m tall and with a wingspan of up to 2m, with a white body and black flight feathers, a red bill and long red legs. It is voiceless, but is capable of clattering its bill loudly.

Each summer, Poland becomes home to one in three of Europe's white stork population, attracting around 30,000 stork couples. They are most numerous in Masuria and Podlasie in northeastern Poland.

Every spring storks migrate to Poland from as far away as South Africa, and return to the same nests, which were built many years ago. Favourite locations for nests include the rooftops of countryside cottages, particularly chimney stacks, and the tops of churches and castle towers, telephone poles and electricity pylons.

The white stork population in Poland is diminishing, mostly because of human impact on its habitat, including the draining of wetlands, the spread of intensive agriculture, and the felling of old, tall trees that once served as nesting sites. Many storks die from electrocution, while nesting in electricity pylons or attempting to perch on power lines.

is worst in large industrial cities, and especially in Upper Silesia, which occupies just 2% of the country's territory but produces nearly 20% of sulphur dioxide emissions.

With the sixth-highest level of carbon dioxide emissions in Europe, Poland is a significant contributor to global warming. Its goal of reducing emissions is still a long way ahead. So far the country has managed to stabilise them at the (alarmingly high) 1990 level, which is already a significant achievement. Poland now receives World Bank assistance to reduce carbon dioxide emissions. Ironically, the main benefactors are the major polluters themselves, the huge, belching plants that have been going bankrupt and closing.

Poland's natural water supplies are limited, with the figures for available water per capita among the lowest in Europe. At the same time, the utilisation of the country's water resources is inefficient, with high per capita consumption. To make matters worse, a great deal of the water available – that received by over half the population – is polluted, largely because of poor waste-water treatment. Poland has upgraded or constructed about 350 waste-water treatment plants over the past decade, yet many more are needed. Another aspect of the problem is that virtually all Polish rivers flow into the Baltic Sea, a shallow and tideless body of water that has weak circulation and is highly sensitive to pollution.

Poland is one of Europe's largest sources of industrial waste (mainly from coal mining and heavy industry), and only about 1% of it is treated. Treatment of municipal waste is also minimal, and it virtually all of it ends up in landfills without sorting.

Food & Drink

For centuries Poland has been a cosmopolitan country and its food has been influenced by various cuisines. The Jewish, Lithuanian, Belarusian, Ukrainian, Russian, Hungarian and German traditions have all made their mark. Polish food is hearty and filling – a favourite saying is *'Jedzcie, pijcie, i popuszczajcie pasa'* (Eat, drink, and loosen your belt) – rich in meat and game, thick soups and sauces, and abundant in potatoes and dumplings.

Poland's best-known dishes are *bigos* (sauerkraut with a variety of meats), *pierogi* (dumplings) and *barszcz* (red beetroot soup, originating from Russian borscht). Favourite Polish seasonings include marjoram, dill and caraway seeds.

STAPLES & SPECIALITIES

In Polish culture, *chleb* (bread) has always meant more than mere sustenance. It is a symbol of fertility and good fortune, and still plays an important part in traditional Polish weddings. After the ceremony, the happy couple visit the bride's parents to receive their blessing, and are welcomed with the gift of bread and salt. Traditional Polish bread is generally made using rye flour, but Polish bakeries turn out a bewildering variety of different breads, including loaves flavoured with sunflower, poppy and sesame seeds, raisins and nuts.

Rye is a staple ingredient of another favourite Polish dish, *żurek*. This traditional soup is made with beef or chicken stock, bacon, onion, mushrooms and sour cream, and is given a distinctive, tart flavour with the addition of *kwas* (a mixture of rye flour and water that has been left to ferment for several days). It's often accompanied by *z jajkiem* (hard-boiled egg) or *z kiełbasą* (Polish sausage).

Another traditional Polish grain is buckwheat, which is often served as a side dish in the form of *kasza gryczana* (buckwheat grits).

DID YOU KNOW?

The Polish street snack of choice is *zapiekanki*, also known as 'Polish pizza' – a half baguette split lengthwise and topped with melted cheese, chopped mushrooms and ketchup.

TRAVEL YOUR TASTEBUDS

If there's a genuinely traditional Polish dish, it's *bigos*. It's made with sauerkraut, fresh chopped cabbage and meat, including one or more of pork, beef, game, sausage and bacon. All the ingredients are mixed together and cooked over a low flame for several hours, then put aside to be reheated a few times, a process that allegedly enhances the flavour. The whole operation takes a couple of days but the effect can be impressive – a well-cooked, several-days-old *bigos* is mouthwatering. Every family has its own well-guarded recipe as far as the ingredients, seasonings and cooking time are concerned, and you will never find two identical dishes.

Because it's so time-consuming, *bigos* does not often appear on a restaurant menu and the dish served under this name in cheap bars and other seedy eateries is a far cry from the real thing. The best place to try *bigos* is at someone's kitchen table – if you ever happen to get such an invitation, don't pass it up. *Bigos* is at its most delicious when washed down with liberal quantities of vodka, so bring along a bottle.

We Dare You...

Adventurous diners may want to look out for some of the less appetising-sounding entries on the menu, most of which, nonetheless, are absolutely delicious. These include *nóżki w galarecie* (jellied pigs' knuckles), *flaki* (seasoned tripe cooked in bouillon with vegetables), *karp w galarecie* (jellied carp) and *czernina* (ducks'-blood soup).

Pierogi (often flagged on English-language menus as 'Polish ravioli') are square- or crescent-shaped dumplings made with unleavened noodle dough, which is similar to the dough used in Chinese dim sum dumplings, and stuffed with a whole range of fillings. The most popular of these being cottage cheese, potato, minced meat, sauerkraut and wild mushrooms. To serve, they are usually boiled and then doused in melted butter.

Favourite main dishes include *schab wieprzowy* (roast loin of pork) – or preferably *dzik* (wild boar) – with caraway seeds and chopped marjoram rubbed into the skin before roasting, *golonka* (boiled pigs' knuckles) served with horseradish and sauerkraut, and *kaczka z jabłkami* (roast duck with apples). The main course is usually accompanied by *ziemniaki* (potatoes), which are served in many forms – boiled, roasted, fried, or mashed. One of the more distinctively Polish recipes is *placki ziemniaczane* (potato fritters) – patties of grated potato and onion fried until crisp and often served with sour cream.

Poles have always taken advantage of the abundant wild food that grows in field and forest and a favourite summer pastime, even for city folk, is gathering wild mushrooms and berries. The necessity in times past of making abundant summer food last through the long, cold winters means that Polish cuisine is rich in pickles, preserves and smoked fish and meat. The most famous Polish preserves are sweet and fragrant *ogórki kiszone* (dill-pickled cucumbers), often sold from wooden barrels at fruit and vegetable markets.

DRINKS
Tea & Coffee

Poles are passionate tea drinkers. *Herbata* (tea) is served in a glass, rarely in a cup, and is never drunk with milk. Instead, a slice of lemon is a fairly popular addition, plus a lot of sugar. In restaurants you usually get a glass of boiling water and a tea bag on the side.

Kawa (coffee) is another popular drink, and here too the Polish way of preparing it probably differs from what you are used to. The most common form is *kawa parzona*, a concoction made by putting a couple of teaspoons of ground coffee beans directly into a glass and topping it with boiling water.

The Western world's love affair with double-decaf skinny latte and the like, however, has spread to Poland, and an increasing number of Starbucks-style cafés have hit the streets of Warsaw and other cities.

Beer & Wine

There are several brands of locally brewed Polish *piwo* (beer), the best of which includes Żywiec, Okocim and EB. Beer is readily available in shops, cafés, bars, pubs and restaurants – virtually everywhere. Not all bars chill their beer, so if you want a cold one ask for *zimne piwo* (cold beer).

Poland doesn't have much of a tradition of wine drinking. In fact, the average annual wine consumption is just 1L per head of population (compared with 56L for France). The country doesn't produce its own *wino* (wine), apart from a suspicious alcoholic liquid made using apples and God knows what else, nicknamed *wino-wino* or *bełt* and consumed by those on the darker margins of society who either can't afford or can't find a bottle of vodka.

Imported wines have traditionally come from the former eastern bloc, mostly from Hungary and Bulgaria, and if you're not too fussy they're acceptable and cheap. Western European wines, particularly French, German and Spanish, are now widely available in shops and restaurants.

DRINKING VODKA POLISH-STYLE

To begin with, forget about vodka-based cocktails. In Poland vodka is drunk neat, usually in 50mL shot glasses, though measures can range from 25mL to 100mL. Regardless of the size of the glass, it's downed in a single gulp, or *do dna* (to the bottom), as Poles say. A piece of a snack or a sip of mineral water is consumed just after drinking to give some relief to the throat and glasses are immediately refilled for the next drink.

As you may expect, at this rate you won't be able to keep up with your fellow drinkers for long, and will soon end up well out of touch with the real world. Go easy and either miss a few turns or sip your drink in stages. Though this will be beyond the comprehension of a 'normal' Polish drinker, you, as a foreigner and guest, will be treated with due indulgence. Whatever you do, don't try to outdrink a Pole. *Na zdrowie* (Cheers)!

Spirits

Wódka (vodka) is the No 1 Polish tipple and is consumed in large quantities. Vodka is every bit as much the Polish national drink as it is the Russian, and the Poles claim it was they who invented it, not their old enemies to the east.

These days drinking habits in the cities are changing, with Poles increasingly turning to beer instead of vodka. Yet, as soon as you go to a small town and enter the only local restaurant, you'll see those same tipsy folk debating jovially over bottles of vodka. Old habits die hard.

Polish vodka comes in a number of colours and flavours. Clear vodka is not, as is often thought in the West, the only species of the family. Though it does form the basic 'fuel' for seasoned drinkers, there's a whole spectrum of vodka varieties, from very sweet to extra dry, including *myśliwska* (flavoured with juniper berries), *wiśniówka* (flavoured with cherries), *żubrówka* ('bison vodka', which is flavoured with grass from the Białowieża Forest on which the bison feed) and *jarzębiak* (flavoured with rowan berry). Other notable spirits include *krupnik* (honey liqueur), *śliwowica* (plum brandy), *winiak* (grape brandy) and Goldwasser (a thick liqueur laced with flakes of real gold leaf). Finally, there's *bimber*, a home-made spirit, which ranges in quality from very poor to excellent. Clear vodka should be served well chilled. Flavoured vodkas don't need much cooling, and some are best drunk at room temperature.

Vodka is traditionally sold in half-litre or quarter-litre bottles, but EU regulations mean that the much-loved *ćwiartka* (quarter) will have to be phased out and replaced with a standard 0.2L bottle. As a result, there has been a huge increase in sales of quarters as people buy them up as souvenirs.

WHERE TO EAT & DRINK

A *restauracja* (restaurant) is the main place for a meal with table service. They range from unpretentious eateries where you can have a filling meal for less than 20zł all the way up to luxurious establishments that may leave a sizable hole in your wallet. The former type is mostly to be found in smaller towns and the back streets of city suburbs, while the latter is almost exclusively confined to the largest cities. The menus of most top-class restaurants are in Polish with English and/or German translations, but don't expect foreign-language listings in cheaper eateries, nor waiters speaking anything but Polish.

Restaurants generally open around 9am or 10am (usually with a breakfast menu) or at about noon. Closing time varies greatly from place to place and from city to province. In smaller towns it may be pretty hard to find somewhere to eat after 9pm, whereas in big cities there are always places that stay open until 11pm or midnight.

A Polish *bar mleczny* (milk bar) is a no-frills, self-service cafeteria that serves mostly meat-free dishes at ultralow prices. The 'milk' part of the name reflects the fact that a good part of the menu is based on dairy products. You can fill up for about 8zł to 12zł. Milk bars were created to provide cheap food for the less affluent and were subsidised by the state. The free-market economy forced many to close, but a number have survived by introducing meat dishes, upgrading standards and raising their prices.

Milk bars open around 7am to 8am and close at 6pm to 8pm (earlier on Saturday); only a handful are open on Sunday. The menu is posted on the wall. You tell the cashier what you want, then pay in advance; the cashier gives you a receipt, which you hand to the person dispensing the food. Once you've finished your meal, return your dirty dishes (watch where other diners put theirs). Milk bars are very popular and there are usually queues, but they move quickly. Smoking is not permitted and no alcoholic beverages are served.

DID YOU KNOW?

The Polish equivalent of *bon appetit* is *smacznego* (pronounced smach-*nay*-go).

A *kawiarnia* (café) in communist Poland was essentially a meeting place rather than an eating place. They offered coffee, tea, sweets and a choice of drinks, but hardly anything more substantial. Now most cafés have introduced snacks and light meals. Generally speaking, the borderline between a café and a restaurant has become blurred. Cafés tend to open around 10am and close at any time between 9pm and midnight. Most cafés are smokers' territory and, given Polish smoking habits, the atmosphere can be really dense.

VEGETARIANS & VEGANS

Vegetarians won't starve in Poland – the cheapest place to look is a milk bar, but many new restaurants and salad bars have vegetarian dishes on the menu. On the whole, vegetarian food is cheaper than meat; it's varied and usually well prepared. Typical Polish vegetarian fare:

knedle – dumplings stuffed with plums or apples
kopytka – Polish gnocchi; noodles made from flour and boiled potatoes
leniwe pierogi – boiled noodles served with cottage cheese
naleśniki – crepes; fried pancakes, most commonly *z serem* (with cottage cheese) or *z dżemem* (with jam), and served with sour cream and sugar
pierogi – dumplings made from noodle dough, stuffed and boiled; the most popular are *z serem* (with cottage cheese), *z jagodami* (with blueberries) and *z kapustą i grzybami* (with cabbage and wild mushrooms)
placki ziemniaczane – fried pancakes made from grated raw potatoes with egg and flour; served *ze śmietaną* (with sour cream) or *z cukrem* (with sugar)
pyzy – ball-shaped steamed dumplings made of potato flour

Accompaniments & Salads

Potatoes are the most common accompaniment to the main course and they are usually boiled or mashed. *Frytki* (chips) are also popular, as are steamed buckwheat grits. *Surówki* (*sałatki*; salads) can come as a light dish on their own or as a side dish to the main course. The latter variety includes:

ćwikła z chrzanem – boiled and grated beetroot with horseradish
mizeria ze śmietaną – sliced fresh cucumber in sour cream
sałatka z pomidorów – tomato salad, often served with onion
surówka z kiszonej kapusty – sauerkraut, sometimes served with apple and onion

---

THE ART OF READING POLISH MENUS

The menu is normally split into several sections, including *przekąski* (starters), *zupy* (soups), *dania drugie* (main courses), *dodatki* (side dishes), *desery* (desserts) and *napoje* (drinks). The main courses are often further split into *dania mięsne* (meat dishes), *dania rybne* (fish dishes), *drób* (poultry) and *dania jarskie* (vegetarian dishes).

The name of the dish on the menu is accompanied by its price and, usually, by its weight or other quantity. The price of the main course doesn't normally include side orders such as potatoes, chips, salads etc, which you choose from the *dodatki* section. You then have to tally up the price of the components to get the complete cost of the dish. Only when all these items are listed together is the price that follows for the whole plate of food.

Also note that for menu items that do not have a standard portion size – most commonly fish – the price given is often per 100g. When ordering, make sure you know how big a fish (or piece of fish) you're getting. To avoid surprises in the bill, study the menu carefully and make things clear to the waiter.

WHINING & DINING

Children are welcome in most restaurants, but it's rare to find a special children's menu – you'll have to make do with smaller portions of the adult menu. For more information on travelling with children, see p463.

HABITS & CUSTOMS

Poles start off their day with *śniadanie* (breakfast), which is broadly similar to its Western counterpart and may include *chleb z masłem* (bread and butter), *ser* (cheese), *szynka* (ham), *jajka* (eggs), and *herbata* or *kawa*.

The most important and substantial meal of the day is *obiad* (lunch), usually eaten somewhere between 1pm and 5pm, either at home or in the *stołówka* (workplace canteen) or in a milk bar. Judging by its size, it's closer to a Western dinner, but the timing is more like lunch. You could say it's a dinner at lunch time.

The evening meal is *kolacja* (supper). The time and menu vary greatly: sometimes it can be nearly as substantial as *obiad*; more often it's similar to *śniadanie*, or even as light as just a pastry and a glass of tea.

Etiquette and table manners are more or less the same as in the West. When beginning a meal, whether it's in a restaurant or at home, it's good manners to wish your fellow diners *smacznego* (bon appetit). When drinking a toast, the Polish equivalent of 'cheers' is *na zdrowie* (literally, 'to health').

EAT YOUR WORDS

If you want to twist your tongue around a little Polish as well as some *pierogi*, turn to the Language chapter on p493 for a bit of pronunciation practice.

Useful Phrases
Table for (four), please.
  Poproszę stolik dla (czterech osób).   po-*pro*-she *sto*-leek dla (*chte*-reh o-soop)
May I/we see the menu?
  Czy można prosić o kartę?   chi *mozh*-na pro-sheech o *kar*-te
What's the speciality here?
  Jaka jest specjalność zakładu?   ya-ka yest spe-*tsyal*-noshch zak-*wa*-doo
What do you recommend?
  Co pan/pani poleca?   tso pan/*pa*-nee po-*le*-tsa

Are the side dishes included in the price?
  Czy dodatki są wliczone w cenę?   chi do-*dat*-ki som vlee-*cho*-ne *ftse*-ne
Can I have the bill, please?
  Poproszę o rachunek?   po-*pro*-she o ra-*hoo*-nek

Menu Decoder

barszcz czerwony – beetroot broth; can be served *barszcz czysty* (clear), *barszcz z uszkami* (with tiny ravioli-type dumplings stuffed with meat), or accompanied by *barszcz z pasztecikiem* (a hot pastry filled with meat)

befsztyk tatarski – raw minced beef accompanied by chopped onion, raw egg yolk and often chopped dill cucumber; eat it only in reputable restaurants

botwinka – soup made from the stems and leaves of baby beetroots; often includes a hard-boiled egg

bryzol – grilled beef steak

chłodnik – cold beetroot soup with sour cream and fresh vegetables; served in summer only

gołąbki – cabbage leaves stuffed with minced beef and rice, sometimes also with mushrooms

grochówka – pea soup, sometimes served *z grzankami* (with croutons)

kapuśniak – sauerkraut soup with potatoes

kotlet schabowy – a fried pork cutlet coated in breadcrumbs, flour and egg, found on nearly every menu

krupnik – thick barley soup containing a variety of vegetables and occasionally small chunks of meat

łosoś wędzony – smoked salmon

melba – ice cream with whipped cream and fruit

pieczeń wieprzowa – roast pork

pieczeń wołowa – roast beef

polędwica pieczona – roast fillet of beef

rosół – beef or chicken bouillon, usually served *z makaronem* (with noodles)

rumsztyk – rump steak

sałatka jarzynowa – vegetable salad, commonly known as Russian salad

schab pieczony – roast loin of pork seasoned with prunes and herbs

sztuka mięsa – boiled beef with horseradish

śledź w oleju – herring in oil with chopped onion

śledź w śmietanie – herring in sour cream

zraz zawijany – stewed beef rolls stuffed with mushrooms and/or bacon and served in a sour-cream sauce

zupa grzybowa – mushroom soup

zupa jarzynowa – mixed vegetable soup

zupa ogórkowa – dill cucumber soup, usually with.potatoes and other vegetables

zupa pomidorowa – tomato soup, usually served either *z makaronem* (with noodles) or *z ryżem* (with rice)

zupa szczawiowa – sorrel soup, usually served with hard-boiled egg

Food Glossary

bażant – pheasant
befsztyk – beef steak
budyń – milk pudding
ciastko – pastry, cake
dorsz – cod
dzik – wild boar
gęś – goose
indyk – turkey

kaczka – duck
karp – carp
kurczak – chicken
lody – ice cream
pstrąg – trout
sarna – roe deer
stek – steak
zając – hare

Warsaw

Warsaw ✪

Like a phoenix rising from the ashes, Warsaw has rebuilt itself from the rubble of WWII to once again become a thrusting, thriving capital city on the banks of the Vistula. It's Poland's most cosmopolitan, dynamic and progressive urban centre, dotted with luxury hotels, gourmet restaurants and elegant shops, and home to a rich and varied cultural scene. Whether you're interested in fine dining, museums, theatre, opera or bazaars, you will find more to choose from here than in any other Polish city.

It's true that first impressions of Warsaw are not always favourable, especially as you emerge from Warszawa Centralna train station onto the soot-streaked concrete and potholed pavements of Al Jerozolimskie. And word association doesn't help – the name Warsaw conjures up negative images such as 'Ghetto' and 'Pact', and Vistula sounds like a painful medical condition. Even expats who love the place refer to the city as the 'Big Potato'.

But don't be put off. The Old Town and Royal Castle have been restored to postcard perfection, and the park-and-palace complexes of Łazienki and Wilanów are as pretty as any in Poland. The city's restaurants and nightlife are the best in the country, and its many historical museums and monuments provide a sobering insight into the suffering of the Poles during WWII.

In a way, Warsaw epitomises the Polish nation – a blend of old and new both in spirit and appearance, respecting tradition but racing towards the future.

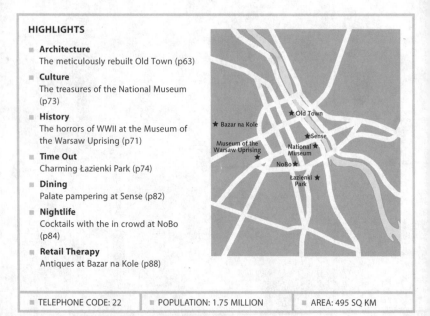

HIGHLIGHTS

- **Architecture**
  The meticulously rebuilt Old Town (p63)

- **Culture**
  The treasures of the National Museum (p73)

- **History**
  The horrors of WWII at the Museum of the Warsaw Uprising (p71)

- **Time Out**
  Charming Łazienki Park (p74)

- **Dining**
  Palate pampering at Sense (p82)

- **Nightlife**
  Cocktails with the in crowd at NoBo (p84)

- **Retail Therapy**
  Antiques at Bazar na Kole (p88)

★ Old Town
★ Bazar na Kole
★ Sense
Museum of the Warsaw Uprising ★
National ★ Museum
NoBo ★
Łazienki ★ Park

■ TELEPHONE CODE: 22   ■ POPULATION: 1.75 MILLION   ■ AREA: 495 SQ KM

HISTORY

By Polish standards, Warsaw is a young whippersnapper of a city. While some other towns such as Kraków, Poznań, Wrocław or Gdańsk were close to celebrating their quincentenaries, the present-day capital was just beginning to emerge from the obscurity of the Mazovian forests.

It was not until the beginning of the 14th century that the dukes of Mazovia built a stronghold on the site where the Royal Castle stands today, and in 1413 the dukes made Warsaw their seat. Like most medieval Polish towns, it was planned on a grid around a central square and surrounded with fortified walls. In 1526, after the last duke died without an heir, Warsaw and the whole of Mazovia came under the direct rule of the king in Kraków.

Warsaw's fortunes took a turn for the better after the unification of Poland and Lithuania in 1569, when the Sejm (the lower house of parliament) voted to make Warsaw the seat of its debates, because of its central position. The ultimate ennoblement came in 1596 when King Zygmunt III Waza decided to move his capital from Kraków to Warsaw.

Like the rest of Poland, Warsaw fell prey to the Swedish invasion of 1655 to 1660, but soon recovered and continued to develop. Paradoxically, the 18th century – a period of catastrophic decline for the Polish state – witnessed Warsaw's greatest prosperity, when a wealth of great palaces and churches was erected. Cultural and artistic life flourished, particularly during the reign of the last Polish king, Stanisław August Poniatowski. In 1791 the first constitution in Europe was signed in Warsaw, by then a city of 120,000 inhabitants.

Reduced to the status of a provincial town following the partition of Poland in 1795, Warsaw became a capital once more in 1807 when Napoleon created the Duchy of Warsaw, and it continued as capital of the Congress Kingdom of Poland. In 1830, however, Poland fell under Russian rule and remained so until WWI. The second half of the 19th century saw steady urban development and industrialisation, including a railway linking Warsaw with Vienna and St Petersburg.

After WWI Warsaw was reinstated as the capital of independent Poland and within 20 years made considerable advances in the fields of industry, education, science and culture. The population increased from about 750,000 in 1918 to nearly 1.3 million in 1939, of whom 380,000 were Jews who had traditionally made up a significant part of Warsaw's community.

Nazi bombs began to fall on 1 September 1939 and a week later the city was besieged. Despite brave resistance, Warsaw fell to the enemy on 28 September. This, however, turned out to be only the beginning of the tragedy. The five-year Nazi occupation, marked by constant arrests, executions and deportations, triggered two acts of heroic armed resistance, both cruelly crushed.

The first was the Ghetto Uprising (p72) in April 1943, when heavily outnumbered and largely unarmed Jewish civilians fought fiercely for almost a month against overwhelming Nazi forces.

The second was the Warsaw Uprising (p26) of 1944 that hoped to liberate the capital and set up an independent government before the arrival of the Red Army (which was already camped on the eastern bank of the Vistula River). Street fighting began on 1 August, but after 63 days the insurgents were forced to capitulate. For the next three months the Nazis methodically razed the city to the ground. Only on 17 January 1945 did Soviet forces cross the river to 'liberate' Warsaw.

About 85% of Warsaw's buildings were destroyed and 800,000 people – more than half of the prewar population – perished. (For comparison, the total military casualties for US forces in WWII was 400,000, for UK forces 280,000.) No other Polish city suffered such immense loss of life or such devastation in the war. Given the level of destruction, there were even suggestions that the capital should be moved elsewhere, but instead it was decided to rebuild parts of the prewar urban fabric. According to the plan, the most valuable historic monuments, most notably the Old Town, would be restored to their previous appearance based on original drawings and photographs.

The authorities also had to build, from scratch, a whole new city capable of providing housing and services to its inhabitants. This communist legacy is less impressive. The city centre was, until quite recently, a blend of bunkerlike Stalinist structures and

WARSAW

0 — 2 km
0 — 1 mile

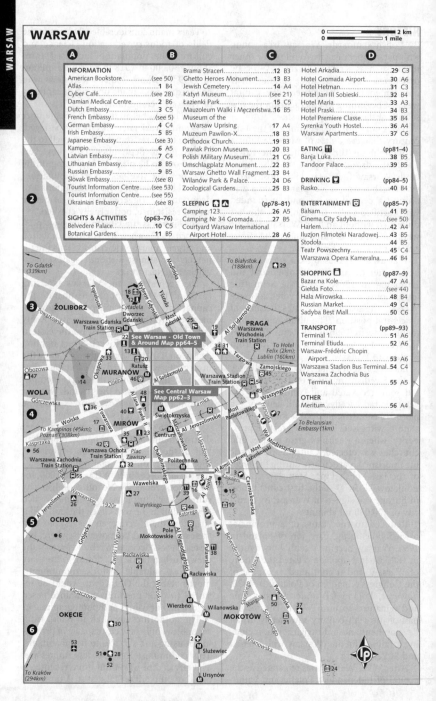

INFORMATION
American Bookstore..................(see 50)
Atlas....................................**1** B4
Cyber Café.........................(see 28)
Damian Medical Centre............**2** B6
Dutch Embassy......................**3** C5
French Embassy....................(see 5)
German Embassy....................**4** C4
Irish Embassy........................**5** B5
Japanese Embassy..................(see 3)
Kampio................................**6** A5
Latvian Embassy....................**7** C4
Lithuanian Embassy................**8** B5
Russian Embassy....................**9** B5
Slovak Embassy.....................(see 8)
Tourist Information Centre.......(see 53)
Tourist Information Centre.......(see 55)
Ukrainian Embassy.................(see 8)

SIGHTS & ACTIVITIES (pp63–76)
Belvedere Palace....................**10** C5
Botanical Gardens..................**11** B5

Brama Straceń.......................**12** B3
Ghetto Heroes Monument.......**13** B3
Jewish Cemetery....................**14** A4
Katyń Museum.......................(see 21)
Łazienki Park.........................**15** C5
Mauzoleum Walki i Męczeństwa.**16** B5
Museum of the
  Warsaw Uprising.................**17** A4
Muzeum Pawilon-X.................**18** B3
Orthodox Church...................**19** B3
Pawiak Prison Museum............**20** B3
Polish Military Museum............**21** C6
Umschlagplatz Monument........**22** C5
Warsaw Ghetto Wall Fragment..**23** B4
Wilanów Park & Palace............**24** D6
Zoological Gardens.................**25** B3

SLEEPING (pp78–81)
Camping 123.........................**26** A5
Camping Nr 34 Gromada.........**27** B5
Courtyard Warsaw International
  Airport Hotel......................**28** A6

Hotel Arkadia.......................**29** C3
Hotel Gromada Airport............**30** A6
Hotel Hetman.......................**31** C3
Hotel Jan III Sobieski..............**32** B4
Hotel Maria..........................**33** A3
Hotel Praski..........................**34** B3
Hotel Premiere Classe.............**35** B4
Syrenka Youth Hostel..............**36** A4
Warsaw Apartments................**37** C6

EATING (pp81–4)
Banja Luka...........................**38** B5
Tandoor Palace.....................**39** B5

DRINKING (pp84–5)
Rasko..................................**40** B4

ENTERTAINMENT (pp85–7)
Balsam................................**41** B5
Cinema City Sadyba................(see 50)
Harlem................................**42** A4
Iluzjon Filmoteki Narodowej.....**43** B5
Stodoła...............................**44** B5
Teatr Powszechny..................**45** C4
Warszawa Opera Kameralna.....**46** B4

SHOPPING (pp87–9)
Bazar na Kole.......................**47** A4
Giełda Foto..........................(see 44)
Hala Mirowska......................**48** B5
Russian Market.....................**49** C4
Sadyba Best Mall...................**50** C6

TRANSPORT (pp89–93)
Terminal 1...........................**51** A6
Terminal Etiuda.....................**52** A6
Warsaw-Frédéric Chopin
  Airport.............................**53** A6
Warszawa Stadion Bus Terminal.**54** C4
Warszawa Zachodnia Bus
  Terminal............................**55** A5

OTHER
Meritum...............................**56** A4

WARSAW IN...

One Day
Start the day with a coffee at one of the cafés along ul Nowy Świat before heading to the **Royal Castle** (p65) for a taste of Warsaw's past glory. Spend the rest of the morning exploring the back streets of the **Old Town** (p66), then have lunch at a restaurant on Old Town Sq; **Dom Restauracyjny Gessler** (p82) is good. In the afternoon, take a look at the **Historical Museum of Warsaw** (p66). Head across town to the **Museum of the Warsaw Uprising** (p73). Wait until late afternoon before visiting the viewing terrace of the **Palace of Culture & Science** (p70). Round off the day with dinner at one of the appealing restaurants south of Al Jerozolimskie; try **Banja Luka** (p84) for a spot of rustic charm.

Two Days
With a second day to play with, you can pass the morning exploring beautiful **Łazienki Park** (p74), and perhaps head further south to call into either the **Katyń Museum** (p76) or **Wilanów** (p75). In the afternoon, depending on your tastes, you can enjoy the cultural highlights of the **National Museum** (p73), or get a taste of bargain shopping, Warsaw-style, at the **Russian Market** (p88). If your budget will stretch to it, cap your visit with a truly memorable dinner at **Kurt Scheller's Restaurant** (p84).

equally dull edifices of a later era, while the outer suburbs, home to the majority of Warsaw's inhabitants, were composed almost exclusively of anonymous, prefabricated concrete blocks.

With the arrival of a market economy in 1989, the face of Warsaw started changing rapidly. Newly constructed steel-and-glass towers have broken the monotony of the grey landscape, shop windows catch the eye with innovative designs and colour, and the city outskirts are steadily filling up with villas and family houses on a more human scale than the monstrous slabs of yesterday.

ORIENTATION

Warsaw is divided into two very different parts by the Vistula (Wisła) River. The city centre, including the Old Town, lies on the western side of the river. The smaller, east-bank sector is called Praga; it has few sights but has begun to be colonised by new tourist hotels.

The west-bank city centre is a huge, sprawling area that can be confusing to the first-time visitor. It helps to imagine the city as a noughts-and-crosses (tick-tacktoe) grid – the two east–west lines are the major traffic arteries of Al Solidarności and Al Jerozolimskie, the north–south lines are ul Towarowa (plus its extensions ul Okopowa and ul Żwirki i Wigury) and ul Marszałkowska.

Within this grid, the historic districts of the Old Town and New Town lie in the top-right square, while the heart of 19th-century Warsaw is to the south, in the centre-right square. The central square holds the modern financial district, which is home to the prominent landmark of the Palace of Culture & Science, and part of the former Jewish Ghetto, which extends northward into the top-centre square. The rest of the post-WWII city centre spreads south of Al Jerozolimskie in the bottom-centre and bottom-right squares.

The Royal Way (Trakt Królewski; an ancient processional route) leads south from the Old Town for 4km (through the centre-right and bottom-right squares) along ul Krakowskie Przedmieście, ul Nowy Świat and Al Ujazdowskie all the way to Łazienki Park; Wilanów, another royal retreat, lies on the southern outskirts of the city.

Warszawa Centralna train station (also known as Dworzec Centralny) is on Al Jerozolimskie at the bottom edge of the central square, and Warszawa Zachodnia bus terminal is 3km to its west, also on Al Jerozolimskie. Warsaw's international airport lies on the southwestern edge of the city.

INFORMATION
Bookshops
American Bookstore (www.americanbookstore.pl) Sadyba Best Mall (Map p58; ☎ 550 31 73; ul Powsińska 31); ul Koszykowa (Map pp62-3; ☎ 660 56 37;

ul Koszykowa 55); ul Nowy Świat (Map pp62-3; ☎ 827 48 52; ul Nowy Świat 61; ☯ 10am-7pm Mon-Sat, 10am-6pm Sun) English-language publications, including classic and contemporary literature, history, coffee-table books and magazines. Also has a choice of travel guidebooks, including Lonely Planet titles.

Atlas (Map p58; ☎ 620 36 39; Al Jana Pawła II 26; ☯ 10am-7pm Mon-Fri, 10am-4pm Sat) Specialises in maps, atlases and travel guides; the best place in town for hiking and national park maps.

EMPiK Megastore ul Marszałkowska (Map pp62-3; ☎ 827 82 96; ul Marszałkowska 116/122); ul Nowy Świat (Map pp62-3; ☎ 827 06 50; ul Nowy Świat 15/17) Stocks a wide selection of British, German, French and US newspapers and magazines; the Marszałkowska branch has a good selection of maps, guidebooks and coffee-table books.

Marjanna (Map pp64-5; ☎ 826 62 71; ul Senatorska 38; ☯ 11am-6pm Mon-Fri, 10am-2pm Sat) Located in the Institut Français Varsovie. The city's best French-language bookshop. Also has a decent selection of French press.

Traffic Club (Map pp62-3; ☎ 692 14 54; ul Bracka 25; ☯ 10am-10pm Mon-Sat, 10am-7pm Sun) Large, laid-back bookshop with armchairs and tables, set in a beautifully converted early-20th-century department store with huge stained-glass windows. Wide range of city maps on the 1st floor. Good selection of fiction in English and German on the 2nd.

Cultural Centres

All these cultural centres have their own libraries with a selection of books and press from their own country.

British Council (Map pp62-3; ☎ 695 59 00; www .britishcouncil.pl; Al Jerozolimskie 59)

Goethe Institut Warschau (German Cultural Institute; Map pp62-3; ☎ 505 90 00; www.goethe.de/warschau in German & Polish; ul Chmielna 11a)

Institut Français Varsovie (French Cultural Institute; Map pp64-5; ☎ 826 62 71; www.ifv.pl in French & Polish; ul Senatorska 38)

Istituto Italiano di Cultura (Italian Institute; Map pp62-3; ☎ 628 06 18; www.iic.pl in Italian; ul Marszałkowska 72)

Emergency

The general emergency number if dialling from a mobile phone is ☎ 112. See also Medical Services, right.

Ambulance (☎ 999)
Car breakdown (☎ 981)
Fire brigade (☎ 998)
Municipal police (☎ 986)
Police (☎ 997)
Tourist police (☎ 0800 200 300)

Internet Access

There are several hot and dingy 24-hour Internet cafés located in the shopping arcades beneath Warszawa Centralna train station; the following places are much more comfortable.

Casablanca (Map pp64-5; ☎ 828 14 47; ul Krakowskie Przedmieście 4/6; per 10 min 1.50zł; ☯ 9-1am)

Cyber Café (Map p58; ☎ 650 01 72; Courtyard Warsaw International Airport Hotel, ul Żwirki i Wigury 1; per hr from 25zł; ☯ 24hr) Plush café in a hotel lobby with wireless access for WiFi enabled laptops, plus three terminals for those without. Ask the waiting staff for a code.

Internet Café (Map pp62-3; ☎ 826 60 62; ul Nowy Świat 18/20; per hr 4zł; ☯ 9am-11pm Mon-Fri, 10am-10pm Sat & Sun)

Pub Internetowy Piękna (Map pp62-3; ☎ 622 33 77; ul Piękna 68a; per hr 4zł; ☯ 9am-midnight Mon-Fri, noon-midnight Sat & Sun)

Simple Internet Café (Map pp62-3; ☎ 628 31 90; ul Marszałkowska 99/101; per hr 1-4zł; ☯ 24hr) Warsaw's biggest, with 150 terminals; highest rates 7pm to 11pm, cheapest 2am to 7am. Buy a password from the counter; unused credit remains valid for subsequent visits.

Verso Internet (Map pp64-5; ☎ 831 28 54; ul Freta 17; per hr 5zł; ☯ 8am-8pm Mon-Fri, 9am-5pm Sat, 10am-4pm Sun)

Medical Services

The city's ambulance service can be contacted on ☎ 999, ☎ 112 and ☎ 628 24 24, but don't count on the dispatcher being able to speak English; in an emergency, it's better to get in touch with Falck or LIM Medical Centers. For nonurgent treatment, you can go to one of the city's many *przychodnia* (outpatient clinics). Your hotel or your embassy (see p466) in Warsaw can provide recommendations.

There are plenty of pharmacies in Warsaw where you can get medical advice; look or ask for an *apteka*. There are always several pharmacies that stay open all night; a list is provided (in Polish) in the *Gazeta Wyborcza* newspaper (in the Supermarket section).

Apteka 21 (Map pp62-3; ☎ 825 31 28; Warszawa Centralna train station, Al Jerozolimskie 54; ☯ 24hr) An all-night pharmacy at the central train station.

Damian Medical Centre (Map p58; ☎ 847 33 13, 853 16 44; www.damian.com.pl; ul Wałbrzyska 46; ☯ 7am-9pm Mon-Fri, 8am-4pm Sat, 10am-3pm Sun) A reputable private outpatient clinic with hospital facilities.

EuroDental (Map pp62-3; ☎ 627 58 88; www.euro dental.com.pl; ul Śniadeckich 12/16; ☯ 8am-8pm

Mon-Sat, 10am-6pm Sun) Private dental clinic with English-, French- and German-speaking staff.

Falck Medical Center (Map pp64-5; ☎ 536 97 40, 24hr emergency ☎ 96 75; ul Sapieżyńska 10; ☒ 7.30am-8pm Mon-Fri, 8am-2pm Sat) Danish company with its own outpatient clinic, 24-hour ambulance service, and English-speaking doctors and paramedics; it can also arrange house calls. An ambulance call out costs 360zł (can be reclaimed through insurance).

LIM Medical Center (Map pp62-3; ☎ 458 70 00, 630 30 30; www.cm-lim.com.pl; Marriott Hotel Bldg, Al Jerozolimskie 65/79; ☒ 7am-9pm Mon-Fri, 8am-8pm Sat, 9am-1pm Sun) Private clinic with English-speaking specialist doctors and its own ambulance service; carries out laboratory tests and arranges house calls.

Money

Currency-exchange offices, known as *kantors*, and ATMs are easy to find around the city centre. *Kantors* open 24 hours can be found at the Warszawa Centralna train station and either side of the immigration counters at the airport, but exchange rates at these places are about 10% lower than in the city centre. Avoid changing money in the Old Town where the rates are even worse.

The banks listed here exchange major-brand travellers cheques, offer cash advances on Visa and MasterCard and have ATMs that take just about every known credit card.

Amex Marriott Hotel (Map pp62-3; ☎ 630 69 52; Al Jerozolimskie 65/79; ☒ 8am-8pm Mon-Fri, 10am-6pm Sat & Sun); ul Sienna (Map pp62-3; ☎ 581 51 15; ul Sienna 39; ☒ 9am-6pm Mon-Fri) Cashes its own travellers cheques as well as those of other major banks, but the rate may be lower than Bank Pekao. Staff speak English and there are no long lines. Main branch is on ul Sienna. Marriott Hotel branch changes travellers cheques but doesn't have a poste restante service.

Bank Pekao Marriott Hotel (Map pp62-3; ☎ 630 53 03; Al Jerozolimskie 65/79); Plac Bankowy (Map pp64-5; ☎ 531 10 00; Plac Bankowy 2); ul Krakowskie Przedmieście (Map pp62-3; ☎ 828 42 00; ul Krakowskie Przedmieście 1); ul Wilcza (Map pp62-3; ☎ 625 76 13; ul Wilcza 70) Cashes travellers cheques and has more than a dozen offices in the city centre. Cash advances on Visa and Master-Card, either from the cashier or ATM.

Western Union (Map pp62-3; general info ☎ 636 56 88, toll-free ☎ 0800 120 224; Bank BPH, Al Jerozolimskie 27; ☒ 9am-5pm Mon-Fri) Money-transfer service, with branches at a number of locations; this is the main central office.

Post & Telephone

Warsaw has over 100 post offices; the main one is listed here. If you want letters sent to you, the address is c/o Poste Restante, Poczta Główna, ul Świętokrzyska 31/33, 00-001 Warszawa; the mail is kept for 14 working days. Amex card holders can also receive poste restante mail through the Amex office (left); letters should be addressed c/o American Express Poland, ul Sienna 39, 00-121 Warszawa. Mail is kept for three months.

There are public telephones all over the city; almost all run on phonecards only. You can also make calls (and pay in cash) at the main post office.

Main post office (Poczta Główna; Map pp62-3; ☎ 826 03 03; ul Świętokrzyska 31/33; ☒ 24hr) Sells stamps, deals with parcels, and offers a packing service. Poste restante is at window No 12.

Tourist Information

The various branches of the city's official Tourist Information Centre provide free city maps and booklets, such as the handy *Warsaw in Short* and the *Visitor*, sell maps of other Polish cities, and will help you book a hotel room. They also sell the Warsaw Tourist Card, which gives free or discounted access to most of the main museums, free public transport and discounts at some theatres, sports centres and restaurants. Cards valid for 24 hours/three days cost 35zł/65zł.

Free monthly tourist magazines worth seeking out include *Poland: What, Where, When; What's Up in Warsaw* and *Welcome to Warsaw*. All are mines of information about cultural events and provide reviews of new restaurants, bars and nightclubs. They're available in the lobbies of most top-end hotels. The comprehensive monthlies *Warsaw Insider* (8zł) and *Warsaw in Your Pocket* (5zł) are also useful.

Tourist Information Centre (Centrum Informacji Turystycznej; ☎ 94 31; www.warsawtour.pl) Airport (Map p58; ☒ 8am-8pm May-Sep, 8am-6pm Oct-Apr); Old Town (Map pp64-5; ul Krakowskie Przedmieście 89; ☒ 9am-8pm May-Sep, 9am-6pm Oct-Apr); Warszawa Centralna train station (Map pp62-3; ☒ 8am-8pm May-Sep, 8am-6pm Oct-Apr); Warszawa Zachodnia bus terminal (Map p58; ☒ 9am-5pm)

Warsaw Tourist & Cultural Information Centre (Map pp62-3; ☎ 656 68 54; www.e-warsaw.pl; Palace of Culture & Science, Plac Defilad 1; ☒ 9am-5pm Mon-Fri, 9am-3pm Sat & Sun) Information on cultural events.

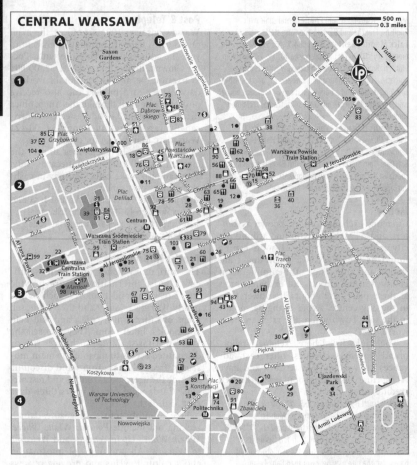

CENTRAL WARSAW

0 — 500 m
0 — 0.3 miles

Travel Agencies

Almatur (Map pp62-3; ☎ 826 35 12, 826 26 39; www
.almatur.com.pl; ul Kopernika 23; 🕑 9am-7pm Mon-Fri,
10am-3pm Sat) Handles student travel. Sells international
air, bus and ferry tickets. Also offers sailing, kayaking and
horse-riding holidays.

Kampio (Map p58; ☎ 823 70 70; www.kampio.com.pl;
ul Maszynowa 9/2; 🕑 10am-5pm Mon-Fri) Focuses on
ecotourism, organising kayaking, biking and bird-watching
trips to out-of-the-way areas. Biking trips in Masuria and
bird-watching in Białowieża and Biebrza National Parks are
on the tour list.

Orbis Travel (www.pbp.com.pl in Polish) Plac Konstytucji
(Map pp62-3; ☎ 629 92 01; Plac Konstytucji 4; 🕑 10am-
6pm Mon-Fri); ul Bracka (Map pp62-3; ☎ 827 72 65; ul
Bracka 16; 🕑 10am-6pm Mon-Fri) The largest agency in
Poland, with offices all over town.

Pekaes Bus (www.pekaesbus.com.pl) ul Żurawia (Map
pp62-3; ☎ 621 34 69; ul Żurawia 26; 🕑 8.30am-6pm
Mon-Fri, 9am-2pm Sat); Warszawa Centralna (Map pp62-3;
northern underground arcade, Warszawa Centralna train
station) Official Eurolines agent in Warsaw, sells bus tickets
to European destinations.

STA Travel (Map pp62-3; ☎ 626 00 80; www.sonata
travel.com.pl; ul Krucza 41/43; 🕑 10am-6pm Mon-Fri)
Specialises in cheap international air fares for particular
age groups and for students, but also provides general
travel agency services for all.

Wasteels (Map pp62-3; ☎ 825 50 09; www.wasteels
.com.pl in Polish; Warszawa Centralna train station, Al
Jerozolimskie 54; 🕑 8.30am-7.30pm Mon-Sat, 10am-
7pm Sun) Sells bus tickets to various European cities,
including an express service to Berlin, with discounts for
students and those under 26. Also sells EuroDomino passes.

DANGERS & ANNOYANCES

Warsaw is no mare dangerous than any other European capital city, but you should take precautions while strolling about the streets at night, and watch your possessions on public transport and in other crowded places. Pickpockets are especially active on bus 175 (between the airport and the city centre), on the trams that run along Al Jerozolimskie, and in and around the central train station. Beware also of 'mafia taxis' (see p92).

Mosquitoes can be irritating in summer, especially at sights close to the river such as Łazienki Park and Wilanów.

SIGHTS
Old Town & Around

Warsaw's Old Town (Stare Miasto) was rebuilt from the foundations up on what was, after WWII, nothing but a heap of rubble; around 90% of the houses were destroyed. The monumental reconstruction took place between 1949 and 1963 with the aim of restoring the town to its 17th- and 18th-century appearance – today there is not a single building in the area that looks less than 200 years old. Unesco's decision to include Warsaw's Old Town on the World Heritage List is testament to the quality of the work done by the Polish restorers.

CASTLE SQUARE

Triangular Castle Sq (Plac Zamkowy) is where most visitors begin their exploration of the Old Town. In its centre rises the lofty 22m-high **Sigismund III Vasa Column** (Kolumna Zygmunta III Wazy; Map pp62–3), a monument to the king who moved the capital from Kraków to Warsaw. Erected by the king's son in 1644, it's Poland's second-oldest secular monument (after Gdańsk's Neptune). It was knocked down during WWII, but the statue survived and was placed on a new column four years after the war. The original, shrapnel-scarred granite column now lies along the south wall of the Royal Castle.

WARSAW

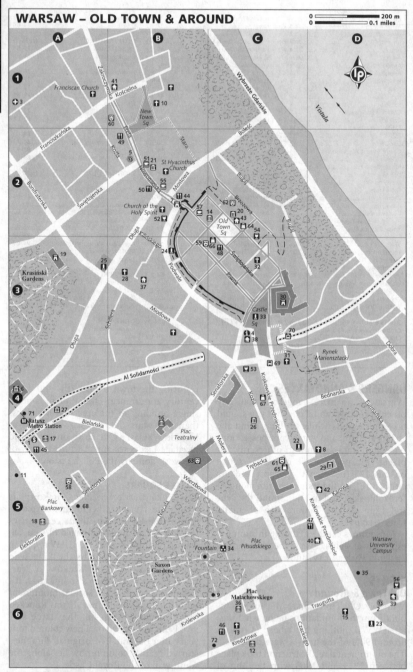

WARSAW – OLD TOWN & AROUND

0   200 m
0   0.1 miles

ROYAL CASTLE

The eastern side of the square is dominated by the **Royal Castle** (Zamek Królewski; Map pp64-5; ☎ 657 21 70; www.zamek-krolewski.art.pl; Castle Sq 4; Route I adult/student 10/5zł, Route II 18/12zł, free Sun; ☺ 10am-6pm Tue-Sat, 11am-6pm Sun & Mon mid-Apr–Sep, 10am-4pm Tue-Sat, 11am-4pm Sun Oct–mid-Apr). It was founded in the 14th century, but its heyday was in the mid-17th century, when it became one of Europe's most splendid royal residences, and during the reign of Stanisław August Poniatowski (1764–95) when its grand baroque apartments were created. During WWII the castle was deliberately destroyed on Hitler's orders, but it was entirely rebuilt from scratch between 1971 and 1984, incorporating surviving works of art and thousands of original architectural fragments.

The most impressive part of the castle is the Great Apartment on the 1st floor, dominated by the magnificent **Great Assembly Hall**. Restored to its 1781 décor of dazzling gilded stucco and golden columns, it once served as an audience room, concert hall and venue for important court meetings. The enormous ceiling painting, *The Disentanglement of Chaos*, is a postwar re-creation of a work by Marcello Bacciarelli showing King Stanisław bringing order to the world. The king's face also appears in a marble medallion above the main door, flanked by the allegorical figures of Peace and Justice.

The neighbouring **Knight's Hall** was conceived by the king as a national pantheon; the six huge canvases (surviving originals) depict pivotal scenes from Polish history. A door leads off the hall into the smaller **Marble Room**, decorated in 16th-century style with coloured marble and trompe l'œil painting. The room houses 22 portraits of Polish kings, from Bolesław Chrobry to a large gilt-framed image of Stanisław August Poniatowski himself.

The lavishly decorated **Throne Room**, its rich red and gold décor set off with 86 Polish eagles worked from silver wire, leads through to the **King's Apartment**. At its far end is the **Canaletto Room**, which holds 23 paintings by Bernardo Bellotto (1721–80), better known in Poland as Canaletto (he used the name of his more famous uncle). Bellotto's many paintings recorded Warsaw's architecture with amazing detail and these works, which survived WWII, were of great help in reconstructing the city's historic monuments.

Also on the 1st floor, the **Crown Prince's Apartment** houses a collection of historical paintings by Jan Matejko, including one of his most famous works, *The Constitution of the 3rd of May 1791*, showing King Stanisław being borne into the castle on the shoulders of a jubilant crowd. Labels in English explain the rich symbolism of these canvases.

BEHOLD, A CASTLE REBORN

The Royal Castle's history goes back to the 14th century, when a wooden stronghold was built by the dukes of Mazovia. It was later rebuilt in brick. Greatly extended when the capital was moved to Warsaw, the castle became the seat of the king and the Sejm and remained so until the fall of the Republic in 1795. It then served the tsars, and in 1918, after Poland had regained its independence, it became the residence of the president. The castle survived most of WWII without major damage, but after the Warsaw Uprising in 1944 it was blown up by the Nazis.

It wasn't until 1971 that reconstruction began, and by 1984 the splendid baroque castle stood again as if nothing had happened. Given its spiritual importance as the very symbol of Warsaw, thousands of Poles living all over the world donated funds for the castle's rebirth, and many volunteers participated in the building's re-creation. Although the brick structure is a copy, many original architectural fragments have been incorporated into the walls. The castle's 300 rooms have been filled with period furniture and works of art, some of which had been hidden elsewhere and survived WWII. Most were collected from other historic buildings.

A good part of the castle's interior is now a museum, providing an insight into how royalty once lived. The rooms are once again richly decorated and crammed with *objets d'art* as they were two centuries ago, and it's hard to believe that the building is actually less than 40 years old.

A **guided tour** (☎ 657 23 38) of the castle in English, French, German, Spanish, Italian or Russian costs 45zł extra per group; book in advance, though English- and German-speaking guides can usually be obtained at short notice. Route I takes in the cellars, the Court Apartments, the Parliament Chambers and the Crown Prince's Apartment; Route II covers the Great Apartment and the King's Apartment. A Sunday visit is recommended as you are free to wander at leisure, rather than having to move along with a tour group.

OLD TOWN

Ul Świętojańska (St John St) leads from Castle Sq towards Old Town Sq past the restored neo-Gothic façade of **St John's Cathedral** (Katedra Św Jana; Map pp64–5; ☎ 831 02 89; ul Świętojańska 8; admission free; ◷ 10am-1pm & 3-6pm Mon-Sat, 3-6pm Sun). The oldest of Warsaw's churches, it was built at the beginning of the 15th century on the site of a wooden church, and subsequently remodelled several times. Razed during WWII, it regained its Gothic shape through postwar reconstruction. Look for the red-marble Renaissance tomb of the last dukes of Mazovia in the right-hand aisle, then go downstairs to the **crypt** (admission 1zł) to see more tombstones, including that of Nobel prize–winning writer Henryk Sienkiewicz.

Old Town Sq (Rynek Starego Miasta) is the loveliest square in Warsaw, lined with open-air cafés and stalls selling paintings and drawings – it is hard to believe that in 1945 it was nothing more than a sea of rubble with the walls of just two houses (Nos 34 and 36) protruding. Today the Rynek is a fine blend of Renaissance and baroque with Gothic and neoclassical elements. In the middle is a statue of the **Mermaid** (Syrena), the symbol of Warsaw, cast in 1855. It stands on the site of the city's original town hall, which was demolished in 1817 when the administration moved to Plac Teatralny.

The **Historical Museum of Warsaw** (Muzeum Historyczne Warszawy; Map pp64–5; ☎ 635 16 25; Old Town Sq 42; adult/student 5/2.50zł, free Sun; ◷ 11am-6pm Tue & Thu, 10am-3.30pm Wed & Fri, 10.30am-4.30pm Sat & Sun) occupies the entire northern side of the Rynek. Its extensive collection illustrates the history of Warsaw from its beginnings until the present day, including chilling photographs of the destruction and suffering of WWII. Don't miss the documentary film, screened several times daily, about the reconstruction of the city; the English version is usually at noon.

The nearby **Literature Museum** (Muzeum Literatury; Map pp64–5; ☎ 831 40 61; Old Town Sq 20; adult/student 5/4zł, free Sun; ◷ 10am-3pm Mon, Tue & Fri, 11am-6pm Wed & Thu, 11am-5pm Sun) features a permanent exhibition dedicated to Adam Mickiewicz, Poland's most famous poet.

Ul Nowomiejska leads northwest to the red-brick **Barbican** (Barbakan; Map pp64–5), a semicircular defensive tower topped with a decorative Renaissance parapet. It was partially dismantled in the 19th century, but reconstructed after WWII.

NEW TOWN

The New Town (Nowe Miasto) was founded at the end of the 14th century, not long after the Old Town, and in 1408 was granted its own jurisdiction and administration. Since then, there have been two towns half a kilometre apart, each with its own main square, town hall and parish church. The New Town was inhabited mostly by people of lower social standing, and never had fortifications like those around the Old Town.

Ul Freta, the New Town's main street, leads north from the Barbican towards **New Town Sq** (Rynek Nowego Miasta), passing the former family home of Marie Curie (see the boxed text below). The **Maria Skłodowska-Curie Museum** (Map pp64-5; ☎ 831 80 92; ul Freta 16; adult/student 6/3zł, free Thu; ☷ 10am-4pm Tue-Sat, 10am-2pm Sun) hosts a modest exhibition on the life and work of this distinguished scientist, who was born here in 1867.

The **Church of the Nuns of the Holy Sacrament** (Kościół Sakramentek; Map pp64-5; ☎ 635 71 13; New Town Sq 2) is the work of the most prominent architect of the baroque period in Poland, Tylman van Gameren. During the 1944 Warsaw Uprising the church was used as a hospital, and several hundred people died inside it when it was bombed.

UL DŁUGA

Ul Długa leads southwest from ul Freta past the **Polish Army Field Cathedral** (Katedra Polowa Wojska Polskiego; ul Długa 13/15), the soldiers' place of worship. A large anchor and aeroplane propeller in front of the church pay homage to the sailors of the navy and pilots of the air force, and the main door features bas-reliefs of major battles fought by Polish forces. Inside are numerous commemorative plaques in memory of Polish soldiers who perished on various fronts all over the world.

At the intersection of ul Długa and ul Bonifraterska stands the dramatic **Monument to the Warsaw Uprising** (Pomnik Powstania

---

MARIE CURIE

In 1995 the remains of Marie Curie (1867–1934) were reinterred in the Panthéon in Paris, making her the first woman to receive this honour in recognition of her own achievements. Those accomplishments included the discovery of the chemical elements radium and polonium, work that laid the foundations of radiography, nuclear physics and cancer therapy. She was the first woman to be awarded a Nobel prize and the first person ever to win two Nobel prizes.

Born in Warsaw (then under Russian partition) into a family of Polish teachers, Maria Skłodowska lived here for the first 24 years of her life. She developed a strong fascination for science and decided to pursue a scientific career, but under Russian rule women were not allowed to enter institutions of higher education.

Maria therefore went to Paris in 1891 to study physics and mathematics at the Sorbonne, earning degrees in both subjects. In 1895 she married French physical chemist Pierre Curie (1859–1906), and changed her Polish name Maria to the French Marie. Their scientific partnership proved to be extremely fruitful, even though their living conditions were extremely poor – their laboratory was not much more than a barn.

Their investigation of the radiation of uranium ore resulted in the discovery in 1898 of two new radioactive elements, polonium (named after Marie's homeland) and radium. In 1903, they, together with Antoine Henri Becquerel, were awarded the Nobel prize for physics, for the discovery of natural radioactivity.

After Pierre's tragic death in a traffic accident in 1906, Marie devoted all her energy to the research work they had begun together. She succeeded him as lecturer and head of physics at the Sorbonne – the first woman ever to teach at this 650-year-old university. Two years later she became a professor and in 1911 was awarded the Nobel prize for chemistry, for the isolation of pure radium.

Marie Curie was instrumental in founding the Radium Institute in Paris in 1914, which later became a universal centre for nuclear physics and chemistry. She also helped establish the Radium Institute in Warsaw in 1932. She died in 1934 of leukaemia caused by prolonged exposure to radiation.

SYMBOL OF FAITH

All over Warsaw, on monuments and memorials, in museums and old photographs, you will see a distinctive monogram in the form of a 'P' stuck atop a 'W' in the shape of an anchor, the Catholic symbol of faith. This monogram – 'PW' stands for 'Polska Walczy' (Poland Fights) – was the symbol of the Armia Krajowa (AK; Home Army), the Polish resistance army that led the Warsaw Uprising in 1944. Fortuitously, 'PW' can also stand from 'Powstanie Warszawskie' (Warsaw Uprising), and the monogram has come to serve as a symbol of that tragic but heroic struggle.

Warszawskiego; see the boxed text on p26), a bronze tableau depicting Armia Krajowa (AK; Home Army) fighters emerging ghost-like from the shattered brickwork of their ruined city, while others descend through a manhole into the network of sewers. The monument was unveiled on 1 August 1989, the 45th anniversary of the uprising.

On the opposite side of ul Bonifraterska is the **Krasiński Palace** (Pałac Krasińskich; 1677), designed by the ubiquitous Tylman van Gameren and considered one of the most splendid baroque palaces in Warsaw.

CITADEL

The west bank of the Vistula, to the north of the New Town, is dominated by a massive 19th-century fortress known as the **Citadel** (Cytadela; Map p58). It was built by the Russian tsar following the November Insurrection of 1830 (see p21), not as a defensive structure but to intimidate the population of Warsaw. It also served as a notorious political prison.

The huge gate overlooking the river is known as **Brama Straceń** (Gate of Execution; Map p58), and houses a memorial to the political prisoners who were executed on this spot. From the gate, a short cobbled road leads to the **Muzeum Pawilon-X** (Block 10 Museum; Map p58; ☎ 839 23 83; ul Skazańców 25; admission free; ☪ 9am-4pm Wed-Sun), which preserves a wing of the old political prison. The cells are labelled with the names of the more famous prisoners who were incarcerated here, the best known being Józef Piłsudksi who did time in cell No 25 on the 1st floor; another cell

contains the anvil on which prisoners were made to forge their own shackles.

The museum displays a remarkable collection of paintings by Alexander Sochaczewski (1843–1923) who, along with 20,000 other anti-Russian insurgents, was imprisoned here before being transported to the labour camps of Siberia in 1866. The paintings depict the suffering of his fellow prisoners; one huge canvas titled *Pożegnanie Europy* (Farewell to Europe) shows a convoy of despairing deportees (including the artist himself) at a snow-swept stone obelisk in the Urals marking the boundary between Europe and Asia. In the museum grounds is an original *kibitka,* the closed prison carriage that was used to transport high-security prisoners to the east.

South of the Old Town

The district to the south of the Old Town – from Al Solidarności south to Al Jerozolimskie, and from ul Krakowskie Przedmieście west to ul Marszałkowska – was the commercial and cultural heart of 19th-century Warsaw. Its main street, ul Krakowskie Przedmieście, marks the start of the Royal Way (Trakt Królewski), a 4km processional route from the Royal Castle to the king's summer residence at Łazienki Park (see p74) via ul Nowy Świat and Al Ujazdowskie.

PLAC BANKOWY

Plac Bankowy (Bank Sq) was once the financial district of 19th-century Warsaw. Along its western side is a series of grand neoclassical buildings designed by Antonio Corazzi in the 1820s, including the imposing **City Hall** (Ratusz; Map pp64–5), originally a ducal palace though it has housed the city authorities since 1947, and the former stock exchange and Bank of Poland building, now home to the **John Paul II Collection** (Kolekcja im Jana Pawła II; Map pp64–5; ☎ 620 27 25; Plac Bankowy 1; adult/student 5/2.50zł; ☪ 10am-4pm Tue-Sun). The art collection was donated to the Catholic Church by the Carrol-Porczyński family, and includes works by some of the best European painters – Cranach, Rubens, Velázquez, Goya, Renoir, Sisley, Van Gogh and Chirico.

The eastern side of the square was redeveloped after WWII and is now dominated by a blue skyscraper built on the site of a synagogue destroyed by the Nazis. The story goes that a local rabbi placed a curse on the site and, sure enough, the skyscraper was dogged by problems and took 30 years to build. Just behind it is the **Jewish Historical Institute** (Żydowski Instytut Historyczny; Map pp64-5; ☎ 827 92 21; www.jewishinstitute.org.pl; ul Tłomackie 3/5; adult/student 10/5zł; ☉ 9am-4pm Mon-Wed & Fri, 11am-6pm Thu), housing a library and museum featuring paintings, sculptures, old religious objects related to Jewish culture, and photos from the Warsaw Ghetto of 1940 to 1943.

The north end of the square is a busy intersection overlooked by the former Arsenal, a massive 17th-century building that now houses the **Archaeological Museum** (Muzeum Archeologiczne; Map pp64-5; ☎ 831 15 37; ul Długa 52; adult/student 6/3zł, free Sun; ☉ 9am-4pm Mon-Thu, 11am-6pm Fri, 10am-4pm Sun), where the permanent exhibition on the prehistory of Poland is periodically enlivened by temporary displays.

Stranded on a nearby traffic island in the middle of Al Solidarności is the **Museum of Independence** (Muzeum Niepodległości; Map pp64-5; ☎ 826 90 91; Al Solidarności 62; adult/student 5/2zł, free Sun; ☉ 10am-5pm Tue-Fri, 10am-4pm Sat & Sun), which stages temporary exhibitions related to Poland's struggles for independence.

PLAC TEATRALNY

The broad expanse of Plac Teatralny (Theatre Sq) is bordered on the south by the colossal **Teatr Wielki** (Grand Theatre; Map pp64-5; ☎ 826 50 19; Plac Teatralny 1). This neoclassical edifice, thought to be the largest theatre building in Europe, was designed by Antonio Corazzi and constructed between 1825 and 1833. After it was burnt out during WWII, only the façade was restored; the rest was reshaped to suit modern needs. Inside is a 1900-seat auditorium and two smaller stages. The **Jabłonowski Palace** (Pałac Jabłonowskich; Map pp64-5) is opposite the theatre. It served as the town hall from 1817 until WWII.

SAXON GARDENS & AROUND

The magnificent **Saxon Gardens** (Ogród Saski; Map pp64-5; admission free; ☉ 24hr) were laid out in the early 18th century as the city's first public park, modelled on the French gardens at Versailles. The main avenue is lined with chestnut trees and baroque **statues** (allegories of the Virtues, the Sciences and the Elements) and there's an ornamental **lake** overlooked by a 19th-century **water tower** in the form of a circular Greek temple.

The eastern end of the gardens, on Plac Piłsudskiego (Piłsudski Sq), was once dominated by the 18th-century Saxon Palace (Pałac Saski), which served as a royal residence. It was demolished by the Wehrmacht (the armed services of the German Third Reich) during WWII and all that survived were three arches of a colonnade, which had sheltered the **Tomb of the Unknown Soldier** (Grób Nieznanego Żołnierza; Map pp64-5) since 1925. The guard is changed every hour, and groups of soldiers marching back and forth between the tomb and the Radziwiłł Palace (pausing to wait for a green light at pedestrian crossings!) are a regular sight, though the big event is the ceremonial changing of the guard that takes place every Sunday at noon.

South across ul Królewska is the **Zachęta Gallery of Modern Art** (Map pp64-5; ☎ 827 58 54; Plac Małachowskiego 3; adult/student 10/7zł, free Thu; ☉ noon-8pm Tue-Sun), a beautiful neoclassical temple that stages temporary exhibitions of contemporary art. Nearby is the 18th-century **Evangelical Church** (Map pp64-5; ☎ 827 68 17; Plac Małachowskiego 3). A circular edifice topped with the largest dome in Warsaw, the church is renowned for its excellent acoustics and is the venue for a variety of musical events.

Across the street is the **Ethnographic Museum** (Muzeum Etnograficzne; Map pp64-5; ☎ 827 76 41; ul Kredytowa 1; adult/student 8/4zł, free Wed; ☉ 9.30am-4pm Tue, Thu & Fri, 11am-6pm Wed, 10am-5pm Sat & Sun), which provides an insight into Polish folklore and crafts. It also has a collection of tribal art from Africa, Oceania and Latin America.

UL KRAKOWSKIE PRZEDMIEŚCIE

The north end of ul Krakowskie Przedmieście (Krakow Suburb St), adjoining Castle Sq, is dominated by **St Anne's Church** (Kościół Św Anny; Map pp64-5; ☎ 826 89 91; ul Krakowskie Przedmieście 68), erected in 1454 but burnt down by the Swedes and rebuilt in the 1660s in baroque style. Further alterations gave it a neoclassical façade, while the freestanding belfry acquired a neo-Renaissance look; miraculously it escaped major damage during WWII. The interior boasts baroque murals and a trompe l'œil–painted ceiling, a rococo high altar and ornate organ pipes. The **viewing terrace** (adult/child 2/1zł; ☉ 10am-8pm Mon-Fri, 10am-9pm Sat & Sun), atop the belfry, offers a superb view over the Old Town.

Heading south you pass the **Monument to Adam Mickiewicz** (Map pp64–5), before reaching the former **Carmelite Church** (Kościół Karmelitów; Map pp64-5; ☎ 826 05 31; ul Krakowskie Przedmieście 52/54). This church, too, escaped the ravages of war and, like St Anne's, has 18th-century fittings, including the high altar designed by Tylman van Gameren.

Set next to the church is the neoclassical **Radziwiłł Palace** (Pałac Radziwiłłów; Map pp64–5), which is guarded by four stone lions and an equestrian **Statue of Prince Józef Poniatowski**. The prince was the nephew of the last Polish king, Stanisław August, and commander in chief of the Polish army of the Duchy of Warsaw created by Napoleon. Today the palace is the official residence of the president, the Polish equivalent of the US White House.

A short detour along ul Kozia leads to the **Museum of Caricature** (Muzeum Karykatury; Map pp64-5; ☎ 827 88 95; ul Kozia 11; adult/student 5/2.50zł, free Sat; ⏰ 11am-5pm Tue, Wed & Fri-Sun, 11am-6pm Thu), a collection of some 15,000 original works by Polish and foreign caricaturists, plus satirical and humorous books, magazines and the like.

A decorative gate topped with the Polish eagle marks the entrance to the central campus of **Warsaw University** (Uniwersytet Warszawski; ☎ 620 03 81; ul Krakowskie Przedmieście 26/28). The oldest building here is the Kazimierz Palace (Pałac Kazimierzowski; 1634), at the far eastern end of the campus, now the office of the rector. Since its founding in 1816, Warsaw University has always been a focus for independent political thought, a thorn in the flesh of both the tsarist regime and communist government. In the postwar period, many student protests started here.

Because it's so close to the university, the **Holy Cross Church** (Kościół Św Krzyża; ☎ 826 89 10; ul Krakowskie Przedmieście 3) has witnessed more student demonstrations and tear gas than any other church in Poland. During the Warsaw Uprising, it was the site of heavy fighting between the insurgents and the Nazis. It was seriously damaged, but some original baroque altarpieces have survived and adorn its interior. Note the epitaph to Frédéric Chopin on the second pillar on the left-hand side of the nave. It covers an urn containing the composer's heart, brought from Paris after Chopin's death and placed here in accordance with his will.

The contemplative figure sitting on a plinth south of the university is a **Monument to Nicolaus Copernicus** (Pomnik Mikołaja Kopernika; Map pp64–5), the great Polish astronomer who, as Poles often say, 'stopped the sun and moved the earth'. During WWII, the Nazis replaced the Polish plaque with a German one and later removed the statue. After the war it was found on a scrapheap in Silesia and was returned to its site.

UL NOWY ŚWIAT

At the intersection with ul Świętokrzyska, ul Krakowskie Przedmieście changes name to **ul Nowy Świat** (New World St). From the 19th century until WWII this was the city's main shopping street, lined with posh shops and fashionable cafés. Though the destruction of 1944 was almost total, the reconstruction here was as meticulous as in the Old Town and has restored the street's 19th-century neoclassical appearance, characterised by a remarkable stylistic unity. Architecture apart, it is again one of the busiest commercial streets in the city, lined with shops, boutiques, bookshops and cafés.

A short detour east along ul Ordynacka leads to **Ostrogski Palace** (Map pp62–3). Situated on a high fortified platform on the Vistula escarpment, the small baroque palace (again designed by Tylman van Gameren) is today the seat of the Chopin Society, which hosts recitals and chamber music concerts in a lovely concert hall inside. There is also a small **Chopin Museum** (Map pp62-3; ☎ 827 54 71; ul Okólnik 1; adult/student 10/5zł, free Wed; ⏰ 10am-5pm Mon, Wed & Fri, 10am-6pm Thu, 10am-2pm Sat & Sun May-Sep, closed Oct-Apr) related to the artist's life and work.

Financial District

Warsaw's burgeoning financial and business district lies southwest of the Old Town, and is bounded roughly by ul Marszałkowska, Al Jerozolimskie, ul Jana Pawła II and Al Solidarności. The last 10 years have seen a frenzy of building activity here, with shiny new towers rising amid the communist-era, low-rise, concrete apartment blocks.

Ironically, the focal point for the financial district's forest of newly sprouted skyscrapers is a legacy of communism, the imposing **Palace of Culture & Science** (Pałac Kultury i Nauki, PKiN; Map pp62-3; ☎ 656 71 36; www.pkin.pl; Plac Defilad 1; admission free; ⏰ 9am-8pm Sun-Thu, 9am-11pm Fri & Sat). Still the

AN ELEPHANT IN LACY UNDERWEAR

A 'gift of friendship' from the Soviet Union, Warsaw's most prominent landmark dominates the city centre like a socialist-realist rocket ship.

Built between 1952 and 1955 and officially christened the Palace of Culture & Science (Pałac Kultury i Nauki, or just PKiN), it was then Europe's tallest building (231m) outside Moscow and is still the tallest in Poland (and now fifth-tallest in Europe). The palace was immediately hated by most of the city's residents and soon garnered a whole string of nicknames, from Stalin's Palace to Russian Wedding Cake to Vertical Barracks; the best of them makes reference both to the building's size and to the fussy sculptures that frill the parapets – the Elephant in Lacy Underwear.

It houses a huge congress hall – not only the former meeting place of the Polish Communist Party, but also a concert venue once graced by the Rolling Stones – three theatres, a multiplex cinema and two museums, as well as hectares of office space. The basement levels are patrolled by a 50-strong pride of feral cats, who keep the building clear of rats and in return receive pampering from an official vet.

After the fall of communism there were debates about what should be done with the unloved colossus, with ideas ranged from demolishing the whole thing to hiding it behind a screen of surrounding skyscrapers. The huge empty area around the PKiN is now earmarked for redevelopment, with construction due to begin in 2005. At the time of writing, work had already begun on the Złote Tarasy (Golden Terraces) project, to the west of the palace, which will include a retail and leisure complex and a new bus station.

tallest building in Warsaw (and in Poland), and the city's most prominent landmark, it was built in the early 1950s as a 'gift of friendship' from the Soviet Union to the Polish nation (see the boxed text above). An ear-popping high-speed lift will whisk you to the palace's 30th floor (115m up) where there's a **viewing terrace** (adult/student 18/12zł; ☾ 9am-6pm) offering a bird's-eye view of the city. Poles often joke that this is the best view of the city because it's the only one that doesn't include the Palace of Culture & Science itself! Enter via the main entrance (facing ul Marszałkowska) and continue straight ahead up the stairs to the ticket office. One-hour **guided tours** (☎ 656 63 45; wycieczka@pkin .pl; per person 40zł; ☾ 10am & 2pm Mon-Sat) of the palace allow you to visit the 2800-seat Congress Hall, former gathering place of the Communist Party faithful, impressive marble-lined chambers and meeting rooms, and former Soviet president Brezhnev's favourite chill-out room. Tours must be booked in advance, and there's a five-person minimum.

Just south of the palace is the **Fotoplastikon** (Map pp62-3; ☎ 625 35 52; Al Jerozolimskie 51; adult/student 8/5zł; ☾ noon-5pm Mon-Fri, 11am-2pm Sat), reputedly the last working example of its kind in Europe. A large rotating drum set with individual eyepieces displays stereoscopic 3D photos dating from the early 20th century, some of them in colour. Each session consists of 48 pictures and takes about 20 minutes. The entrance is in the courtyard off the street. The family-run business has been operating here since 1901.

Former Jewish Ghetto

Before WWII the Mirów and Muranów districts, stretching north from the new financial district to ul Zygmunta Słomińskiego and west to ul Towarowa and ul Okopowa, were home to a thriving Jewish community of around 380,000 people. It was here that the Nazis created the horrific Warsaw Ghetto in 1940 (see the boxed text on p72). But after crushing the 1943 Ghetto Uprising the Nazis razed the quarter to the ground and only a few remnants of Jewish Warsaw survive today.

It is a large area to try to cover on foot, but fortunately the main sights are clustered together in the northern part. Take tram 16, 17, 19, 29 or 33 northbound on Al Jana Pawła II to the Anielewicza stop, and walk back south one block to the **Pawiak Prison Museum** (Map p58; ☎ 831 13 17; ul Dzielna 24/26; admission free; ☾ 9am-5pm Wed & Fri, 9am-4pm Thu & Sat, 10am-4pm Sun). Built in 1830, Pawiak was Poland's most notorious political prison, once used for incarcerating the enemies of the Russian tsar. During WWII it became even more notorious as the Gestapo's main prison facility – between 1939 and 1944 around 100,000

THE WARSAW GHETTO

At the outbreak of WWII Warsaw was home to about 380,000 Jews (almost 30% of the city's total population), more than any other city in the world except New York.

In November 1940 the Nazis established a ghetto in the predominantly Jewish districts of Muranów and Mirów, west of the city centre, sealed off by a 3m-high brick wall. In the following months about 450,000 Jews from the city and its surroundings were crammed into the area within the walls, creating the largest and most overcrowded ghetto in Europe. By mid-1942 as many as 100,000 people had died of starvation and epidemic diseases, even before deportation to the concentration camps had begun.

In a massive liquidation campaign in the summer of 1942, about 300,000 Jews were transported from the ghetto to the death camp at Treblinka (p111). Then in April 1943, when only 50,000 people were left, the Nazis began the final liquidation of the ghetto. In a desperate act of defiance, the survivors took up arms in a spontaneous uprising.

From the outbreak of the uprising on 19 April it was clear that the Jews had little chance of victory against the heavily armed Nazis. German planes dropped incendiary bombs, turning the entire district into a chaos of burning ruins. Fierce fighting lasted for almost three weeks until, on 8 May, the Nazis surrounded the Jewish command bunker and tossed in a gas bomb. The members of the command, including the commander in chief Mordechaj Anielewicz, took their own lives instead of surrendering.

Around 7000 Jews were killed in the fighting and another 6000 perished in fires and bombed buildings. The Nazis lost 300 men with another 1000 injured. The ghetto was razed to the ground except for a few scraps of wall which survive to this day.

prisoners passed through its gates, of whom around 37,000 were executed on site and 60,000 transported to the gas chambers. It was blown up by the Nazis in 1944, but half of the mangled gateway, complete with rusting, original barbed wire, and three detention cells survive (which you can visit), along with chilling memoirs of the horrors suffered by the inmates.

About 200m north of Pawiak, on the corner of ul Anielewicza and ul Zamenhofa, is a tree-lined park, which in summer is dotted with sunbathers. It's an incongruously peaceful setting for the **Ghetto Heroes Monument** (Map p58), a memorial to the thousands who lost their lives in the ill-fated Ghetto Uprising of 1943. The grey stone tower is built of Swedish granite, originally imported by the Nazis to build their own victory monument. On one side a bronze relief depicts a crush of doomed but defiant insurgents; on the other is a scene of martyrdom – a Jewish elder clutching a Torah scroll leads a group of his people, the sinister outlines of Nazi helmets and bayonets visible in the background. In the northwest corner of the park is **Skwer Willy Brandta** (Willy Brandt Sq), with another memorial marking the visit of German Chancellor Willy Brandt to this spot on 7 December

1970, when he famously fell to his knees in a gesture of contrition for Germany's crimes against Poland.

From the Ghetto Heroes Monument head north along ul Zamenhofa, past a garden with a little mound topped by a simple limestone block, a **Monument to Mordechaj Anielewicz**, leader of the Ghetto Uprising, who perished in a bunker on this site in 1943. At the north end of ul Zamenhofa turn left along ul Stawki and cross the street at the tram stop. A little further along is the **Umschlagplatz Monument**, marking the site of the *umschlagplatz* (literally, 'taking-away place'), the railway terminus from which Warsaw's Jews were transported to Treblinka (p111). The four marble walls, symbolic of the cattle trucks into which the prisoners were herded, are carved with more than 3000 Jewish forenames, from Aba to Zygmunt, and the stark message: 'Along this path of suffering and death over 300,000 Jews were driven in 1942–43 from the Warsaw Ghetto to the gas chambers of the Nazi death camps'.

It's a 15-minute walk west along ul Stawki and then south on ul Okopowa to the **Jewish Cemetery** (Cmentarz Żydowski; Map p58; ☎ 838 26 22; ul Okopowa 49/51; adult/student 4/2zł; ☟ 10am-4pm Mon-Thu, 9am-1pm Fri, 9am-4pm Sun). Founded in

1806, it suffered little during the war and still boasts more than 150,000 tombstones – the largest collection of its kind in Europe – though large parts are neglected and very overgrown. A notice near the entrance lists the graves of many eminent Polish Jews, including Ludwik Zamenhof, creator of the international artificial language Esperanto. Look also for the **tomb of Ber Sonnenberg** (1764–1822), one of Europe's finest funerary monuments; take the first paved path on the left beyond the ticket office and when you arrive at a junction on your right, look left: it's the roofed structure over by the wall. The marble relief on one side shows a walled city by a river and a Jewish cemetery; on the other side is the Tower of Babel and a forest hung with musical instruments, as well as a ship sinking in the river.

A five-minute walk northwest from the Palace of Culture & Science leads to Plac Grzybowski. Here, behind the **Teatr Żydowski** (Jewish Theatre; Map p62-3; ☎ 620 70 25; www.teatr -zydowski.art.pl; Plac Grzybowski 12/16) is the **Nożyk Synagogue** (Map p62-3; ☎ 620 43 24; ul Twarda 6; admission 3.50zł; ⏱ 10am-8pm Sun-Thu, 10am-4pm Fri). Built in 1902 in neo-Romanesque style and named after its founder, it was the only one of Warsaw's synagogues to survive WWII, albeit in a sorry state. It was restored and is once again open for religious services.

Ul Próżna, a short street leading off Plac Grzybowski, opposite the Teatr Żydowski, is an eerie and incongruous survivor of WWII. Its crumbling, unrestored red-brick façades, the ornamental stucco long since ripped away by bomb blasts, are still pock-marked with bullet and shrapnel scars. A few blocks to the south, in the courtyard of an apartment building at ul Sienna 55, stands one of the few surviving fragments of the red-brick **wall** (Map p58) that once surrounded the Warsaw Ghetto.

On the southwestern edge of the former ghetto, housed in a restored red-brick power station, stands the new **Museum of the Warsaw Uprising** (Muzeum Powstania Warszawskiego; Map p58; ☎ 626 95 06; www.1944.pl; ul Przyokopowej 28; admission free; ⏱ 10am-8pm Thu, 10am-6pm Fri-Sun). Officially opened on 1 August 2004, the 60th anniversary of the uprising, the museum charts the history of that tragic conflict (see the boxed text on p26) by means of photographs, film archives and the recollections of those who survived.

South of Al Jerozolimskie

Al Jerozolimskie is Warsaw's main east–west traffic artery, which is named after an 18th-century Jewish settlement, Nowa Jerozolima (New Jerusalem), that once lay on the western edge of Warsaw. The region to its south, centred on the broad avenue of ul Marszałkowska, is the post-WWII city centre built by the communist regime in the 1950s. The early postwar architecture that lines this major thoroughfare reaches its peak at **Plac Konstytucji** (Constitution Sq). A showpiece of socialist-realist architecture, the square is adorned with three huge stone lampposts and two giant colonnades, and the southern approach is lined with arcades bearing giant reliefs of heroic workers – the imposing scale and rigid, rectilinear forms are pinnacles of conformity and control. The square was designed as the focal point of the Marszałkowska Dzielnica Mieszkaniowa (Marszałkowska Residential Area, better known as 'MDM'), a model socialist housing development.

NATIONAL & POLISH ARMY MUSEUMS

To the east of the Al Ujazdowskie and Al Jerozolimskie junction lies the huge building that houses the **National Museum** (Muzeum Narodowe; Map p62-3; ☎ 621 10 31; www.mnw.art.pl; Al Jerozolimskie 3; adult/student 12/7zł, free Sat; ⏱ 10am-4pm Tue, Wed & Fri-Sun, 10am-6pm Thu), which holds exhibits ranging from archaeology to 20th-century Polish art. The museum is wheelchair accessible.

The museum's greatest treasure is the **Faras Collection**, a display of early-Christian art from a town on the banks of the Nile in what is now Sudan, rescued by Polish archaeologists from the rising waters of the Aswan High Dam. Frescoes and architectural fragments, dating from the 8th to 12th centuries, combine ancient Egyptian symbolism (winged sun discs and lotus flowers, for example) with Christian iconography, and include beautiful, expressive and often colourful images such as those of St Anna, finger pressed against her lips, and the Virgin and Child against a starry blue background, flanked by the archangels Michael and Gabriel. A scale model of Faras' ruined cathedral helps put the salvaged frescoes in context.

The gallery of **Medieval Art** features a superb collection of religious painting and sculpture from all over Poland, with many gruesome renditions of the Crucifixion and scenes of grisly martyrdom. Most impressive is the huge Wrocław triptych depicting the *Martyrdom of St Barbara* (1447). The carved reliefs show scenes from the saint's life and death – at top right she is spirited through a wall by an angel; at bottom left she is tortured; and at bottom right she is dragged behind a horse while an angel bears her shroud above.

The upper floors are given over to **Polish Art** from the 16th to mid-20th centuries. Highlights include the gallery devoted to the historical paintings of Jan Matejko, notably his huge epic canvas *The Battle of Grunwald* (1878). The two main figures are the white-clad Ulric, grand master of the Teutonic Knights, to the left; and Witold, grand duke of Lithuania, dressed in red and sword raised in victory, perched atop a wild-eyed steed on the right. In the same room is Matejko's famous painting of *Stańczyk* (1862), the 16th-century court jester of King Sigismund the Old; here he represents the nation's conscience, meditating sadly on a major military defeat while the king and queen dance in the background.

Next door, and housed in the same building, is the **Polish Army Museum** (Muzeum Wojska Polskiego; Map p62-3; ☎ 629 52 71; Al Jerozolimskie 3; adult/student 12/7zł, free Wed; ☸ 10am-4pm Wed-Sun). It's one of two army museums in the city (see also p76), and presents the history of the Polish army from the creation of the Polish state until WWII. Heavy armour, tanks and fighter planes from WWII are displayed in the park adjoining the museum.

AL UJAZDOWSKIE & AROUND

From ul Nowy Świat, the Royal Way continues south to Łazienki Park along Al Ujazdowskie, a pleasant avenue bordered by old mansions and parks, and home to Warsaw's embassy quarter. It passes through Plac Trzech Krzyży (Three Crosses Sq), with the 19th-century **St Alexander's Church** (Kościół Św Aleksandra; Map pp62-3), modelled on the Roman Pantheon, in the middle.

Just over 1km south of Al Jerozolimskie, on the east side of Al Ujazdowskie, stands stately **Ujazdów Castle** (Zamek Ujazdowski; Map pp62-3). Erected in the 1620s for King Zygmunt III Waza as his summer residence, it was burned down by the Nazis in 1944, blown up by the communists in

1954 and eventually rebuilt in the 1970s. It now houses the **Centre for Contemporary Art** (Centrum Sztuki Współczesnej; Map p62-3; ☎ 628 12 71; www.csw.art.pl; Al Ujazdowskie 6; adult/student 10/5zł, free Thu; ☸ 11am-5pm Tue-Thu, Sat & Sun, 11am-9pm Fri), which features changing exhibitions of modern art.

Immediately to the south of the castle are the **Botanical Gardens** (Ogród Botaniczny; Map p58; ☎ 628 75 14; Al Ujazdowskie 4; adult/student 4.50/2.50zł; ☸ 10am-7pm Apr-Oct), established in 1818.

Nearby is the **Mauzoleum Walki i Męczeństwa** (Mausoleum of Struggle & Martyrdom; Map p58; ☎ 629 49 19; Al Szucha 25; admission free; ☸ 9am-5pm Wed, 9am-4pm Thu & Sat, 10am-5pm Fri, 10am-4pm Sun), entered through a door on the left of the main entrance to the imposing Ministry of Education & Religious Affairs. During WWII this building served as the Gestapo headquarters, and this little museum is a memorial to the thousands of Poles who were interrogated, tortured and murdered here. The basement corridor contains three holding cells (known as 'trams' because of the seating arrangement), a Gestapo officer's interrogation room (complete with original bullwhips, coshes, knuckledusters etc), and several prison cells. Look through the peephole of cell No 3 and you'll see a bullet scar on the back wall. The radio in the corridor was turned up loud to drown out the screams during torture sessions.

ŁAZIENKI PARK

A former summer home of King Stanisław August Poniatowski, the **Łazienki Park** (Park Łazienkowski; Map p58; ☎ 625 79 44; ul Agrykola 1; admission free; ☸ dawn-sunset) – pronounced *wah-zhen-kee* – was once a hunting ground attached to Ujazdów Castle. The area was acquired by the king in 1776 and within a short time transformed into a splendid park complete with a palace, an amphitheatre and various follies and other buildings. There are several entrances to the park, the most popular being from Al Ujazdowskie.

A path leads downhill from the gate, passing the circular **Water Reservoir** (Wodozbiór; admission free; ☸ 9am-4pm Tue-Sun), which stored water for distribution through wooden pipes to the palace and its fountain; it now houses an art gallery. Further down is the pretty little **White House** (Biały Dom; adult/student 5/3zł; ☸ 9am-4pm Tue-Sun), the first building to be erected in the park (1776). It was used by the king until the palace proper was completed, and retains most of its original 18th-century interior decoration.

At the foot of the hill is an ornamental lake straddled by the beautiful, neoclassical **Palace on the Water** (Pałac na Wodzie; ☎ 625 79 44; adult/concession 12/9zł, free Thu; ☺ 9am-4pm Tue-Sun), the former residence of the king. Like most other Łazienki buildings, it was designed by the court architect Domenico Merlini, and incorporated an existing bathhouse (*łazienki* in Polish, hence the name). During WWII the Nazis attempted to blow it up, but succeeded only in starting a fire that destroyed much of the 1st floor. Renovated and refurbished, the palace is now open to guided tours – highlights include the 17th-century marble reliefs depicting scenes from Ovid's *Metamorphoses* gracing the original bathhouse, and the ornate ballroom.

Near the palace is the **Island Amphitheatre** (Amfiteatr na Wyspie), built in 1790 and based on the appearance of the Roman theatre at Herculaneum. It is set on an islet in the lake, allowing part of the action to take place on the water; plays are occasionally performed here in summer.

The **Chopin Monument** (Pomnik Chopina), near the middle entrance to the park on Al Ujazdowskie, was unveiled in 1926 and depicts the composer in a moment of inspiration. Rows of benches set among beds of roses provide seating for open-air concerts of Chopin's music, staged here on Sunday (at noon and 4pm) from May to September.

At the southern limit of Al Ujazdowskie is the 18th-century **Belvedere Palace** (Pałac Belweder; Map p58; ul Belwederska 52), which served as the official residence of Marshal Józef Piłsudski (from 1926 to 1935) and of later Polish presidents from 1945 to 1952 and 1989 to 1994.

WILANÓW

On the city limits, 6km south of Łazienki, is another park-and-palace complex, Wilanów (vee-*lah*-noof), which served as the royal summer residence for Jan III Sobieski, remembered for his victory over the Turks in the Battle of Vienna in 1683.

The king acquired the land in 1677, and within 20 years managed to transform the simple existing manor house into a splendid Italian baroque villa (calling it in Italian '*villa nuova*' from which the Polish name is derived). After the king's death, Wilanów changed hands several times, with each new owner extending and remodelling it, adding a range of styles from baroque to neoclassical. During WWII, the Nazis plundered it, but the building itself didn't suffer major damage. Most of the furnishings and art were retrieved after the war, and after a decade-long restoration the palace regained its former splendour.

A guided tour of **Wilanów Palace** (Map p58; ☎ 842 07 95; ul Wiertnicza 1; ☺ 9.30am-4pm Mon & Thu-Sat, 9.30am-6pm Wed, 9.30am-7pm Sun mid-May–mid-Sep, 9.30am-4pm Wed-Mon) will lead you through many rooms fitted out with period furniture and decoration in various styles. Tours in Polish cost 20zł/10zł for adults/students, tours for groups of up to five in English, French, German, Russian or Spanish cost 135zł. The last admission is 90 minutes before closing. Highlights include the two-storey Grand Entrance Hall, the Grand Dining Room, and the Gallery of Polish Portraits, featuring a collection of paintings from the 16th to 19th centuries. Note the so-called coffin portraits – a very Polish feature – that are images painted on a piece of tin or copper plate personifying the deceased, then attached to the coffin during the funeral. The exterior of the palace is adorned with impressive murals, including a 17th-century sundial with a bas-relief of Chronos, god of time.

The side gate next to the northern wing of the palace leads to the **gardens and parks** (adult/student 4.50/2.50zł, free Thu; ☺ 9.30am-sunset), which, like the palace itself, display a variety of styles. The central part comprises a manicured, two-level baroque Italian garden, which extends from the rear façade of the palace down to the lake. South of it is the Anglo-Chinese park, and in the northern part of the grounds is the English landscape park. You can take a **boat trip** (trips per person 8zł) on the lake, but remember to take mosquito repellent in summer.

The **Orangery** (Oranżeria; adult/student 6/3zł, free Thu; ☺ 9.30am-2.30pm Wed-Mon), off the northern wing of the palace, features decorative art and sculpture from the 16th to 19th centuries.

Just outside the main gateway to the palace grounds is the **Poster Museum** (Muzeum Plakatu; ☎ 842 26 06; ul Kostki Potockiego 10/16; adult/student 8/5zł, free Wed; ☺ 10am-3.30pm Tue-Sun), the only institution of its kind in Poland and probably one of the few in the world. It displays just what it says – posters – and the exhibits are changed regularly. The International Poster Biennial (which was established in 1966) is held here for a few summer months in even-numbered years.

Get to Wilanów on bus 116 or 180 from any stop on ul Krakowskie Przedmieście, ul Nowy Świat or Al Ujazdowskie.

SADYBA FORT
On the way to Wilanów you'll pass the red-brick walls of 19th-century Sadyba Fort, which now houses a branch of the **Polish Military Museum** (Muzeum Wojska Polskiego; Map p58; ☎ 842 66 11; ul Powsińska 13; admission free; ☉ 10am-4pm Wed-Sun). There are exhibitions dedicated to the Polish army and air force, and an extensive outdoor collection of tanks, heavy guns, armoured vehicles, aircraft, helicopters, missiles and other military hardware.

Just inside the entrance is the grim but moving **Katyń Museum** (Muzeum Katyńskie; Map p58), which reveals details of the massacre of Polish officers and intellectuals by the Soviets in 1940 (see the boxed text on p24). There is a copy of a chilling, top-secret letter from Beria, the chief of the secret police, to Stalin advising that the Soviet authorities 'apply towards [the Polish officers] the punishment of the highest order – shooting…without summoning the arrested and without presentation of evidence'.

There are only a few basic labels in English, but the mute testimony of the piles of personal items – combs, spectacles, coins, cigarette lighters, pipes, belt buckles, boots – recovered during exhumation of the mass graves in 1995 and 1996, and the photographs of rows of skulls, each with a single bullet hole, needs no translation.

Take bus 131 from Warszawa Centralna train station to the line's end, or 180 from any stop on ul Krakowskie Przedmieście, ul Nowy Świat or Al Ujazdowskie and get off at the Sadyba stop.

Praga
Founded in the 15th century on the right bank of the Vistula, Praga is Warsaw's eastern suburb. It began life as a separate village but was eventually incorporated into Warsaw in 1791, and by the outbreak of WWII it had become a large, working-class district. As it was not directly involved in the battles of 1944, Praga didn't suffer

much damage and retains some of its pre-war architecture. The most interesting area lies just across the Vistula from the Old Town. It's a 15-minute walk or a short trip by any tram heading east over the Śląsko-Dąbrowski Bridge.

Just beyond the Śląsko-Dąbrowski Bridge are the **Zoological Gardens** (Ogród Zoologiczny; Map p58; ☎ 619 40 41; ul Ratuszowa 1/3; adult/student 12/6zł; ☉ 9am-6pm). Established in 1928, the zoo has some 3000 animals representing 280 species from around the world. Further down Al Solidarności, at the intersection with ul Targowa, is the **Orthodox Church** (Cerkiew Prawosławna; ☎ 619 08 86; Al Solidarności 52), topped with five onion-shaped domes. Built in the 1860s in Russo-Byzantine style, it retains its original interior decoration.

The biggest attraction on the east bank is the **Russian Market** (see p88), which crowds into the disused **Stadion Dziesięciolecia** (10th Anniversary Stadium), built in 1957 and named for the 10th anniversary of Poland becoming a communist state.

WALKING TOUR
Warsaw's compact Old Town is full of interesting little nooks and crannies linked by paths and alleyways. This walk will lead you off the main tourist routes and into the back streets.

Start at Plac Krasińskich, accessible by bus No 175. After looking at the **Monument to the Warsaw Uprising** (1; p67), head northeast along ul Długa and take the first right into ul Kilińskiego. At the far end you will see the red-brick fortifications of the Old Town; go right and then left into the garden below the walls to see the **Monument to the Little Insurgent (2)**, a memorial to the children who died in the Warsaw Uprising. Follow the path northwards along the inside of the walls to the **Barbican (3)**, where there is often an outdoor art exhibition in summer.

Turn right and follow ul Nowomiejska to the **Old Town Sq** (4; p66) and, after stopping for a drink at one of the outdoor cafés, head diagonally across the square and go left down ul Celna, then right to a **viewpoint (5)**

Start/Finish: Plac Krasińskich/Royal Way
Distance: 2km
Duration: one hour

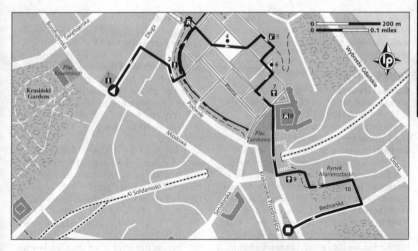

looking across the river to Praga. Go up the stairs to the left of the rear entrance to the John Bull Pub to reach the picturesque little square called **Plac Kanonia (6)**; the cracked 17th-century bell in the middle was rescued from the WWII ruins of **St John's Cathedral (7**; p66). Beyond the bell, go through the arch on the right – the gallery above the arch was once a private passage linking the cathedral to the king's residence in the Royal Castle – and along the alley beside the cathedral, then left at the end to reach Castle Sq and the **Royal Castle (8**; p65).

At the southern end of Castle Sq, turn left immediately before the bell tower of **St Anne's Church (9**; p69). Start down the steps, then bear right along the cobbled path that slopes down and around behind the church, then continue downhill into the little square of Rynek Mariensztacki, which lies at the heart of the attractive **Mariensztat (10)** district. Rebuilt in 1948, with buildings inspired by Warsaw's 18th-century architecture, it was the city's first socialist housing development. Turn right along ul Sowia, and then climb up the picturesque cobbled lane of ul Bednarska to finish on the Royal Way at ul Krakowskie Przedmieście.

COURSES

There are many private schools that offer courses for foreigners in Polish language. Three-week intensive courses cost around 1400zł to 1800zł, while personalised lessons cost around 25zł to 50zł an hour.

Academia Polonica (Map p62-3; ☎ 629 93 11; www .academiapolonica.com; Al Jerozolimskie 55/14)

IKO (Map p62-3; ☎ 826 22 59; www.iko.com.pl; ul Kopernika 3)

Meritum (Map p58; ☎ 314 44 88; www.meritum .com.pl; ul Gizów 6)

Polonicum (Institute of Polish Language & Culture for Foreigners at Warsaw University; Map p64-5; ☎ 552 15 55; www.polonicum.uw.edu.pl; ul Krakowskie Przedmieście 26/28)

Schola Polonica (Map p62-3; ☎ 625 26 52; www .schola.pl; ul Jaracza 3/19)

WARSAW FOR CHILDREN

It's not too much of a challenge to keep the kids amused in Warsaw, with attractions ranging from the Zoological Gardens (opposite) to the viewing terrace at the top of the Palace of Culture & Science (p70). Alternatively, you can explore Łazienki Park (p74), keeping an eye out for the peacocks that wander freely on the grounds, and go for a boat trip on the lake beside the Palace on the Water; there are boat trips at Wilanów (p75) too.

Both branches of the Polish Military Museum (p73 and opposite) have exciting collections of tanks, planes and helicopters, some of which you can climb into, and there are good, safe children's playgrounds in the Saxon Gardens (Map pp64–5) and Ujazdowski Park (Map pp62–3).

A useful English-language guidebook aimed at expat families in Warsaw, *The Capital For Children* (28zł), is available from branches of EMPiK and American Bookstore (p59). Lonely Planet's *Travel with Children*, by Cathy Lanigan, is also a useful resource.

TOURS

Mazurkas Travel (Map p62-3; ☎ 629 18 78; www .mazurkas.com.pl; lobby, Novotel Centrum, ul Nowogrodzka 24/26; ☒ 9am-6pm Mon-Fri) Warsaw's major tour operator can organise five-hour city tours (90zł per person) as well as longer trips to Kraków and Gdańsk.

Our Roots (Map p62-3; ☎ /fax 620 05 56; ul Twarda 6; ☒ 10am-2pm Mon-Fri) Specialises in tours of Jewish sites. Stocks some guidebooks and general publications on Jewish issues, and offers daily tours around Jewish monuments in Warsaw. Other tours can be organised on request.

Trakt (Map p64-5; ☎ 827 80 68; www.trakt.com.pl; ul Kredytowa 6; ☒ 8am-7pm Mon-Fri, 9am-1pm Sat & Sun) Offers guided tours in several major languages, including English and German (400zł per group for up to five hours).

FESTIVALS & EVENTS

Mozart Festival (www.wok.pol.pl) Staged annually from mid-June to end of July and organised by the Warsaw Opera Kameralna. Features performances of all 26 of Mozart's stage productions plus a selection of his other works.

Art of the Street Festival (Festiwal Sztuka Ulicy; www .sztukaulicy.pl) Held in early July, this five-day festival features street theatre, open-air art installations and 'happenings' staged unpredictably in public places such as Old Town Sq, the Royal Way, public parks, and even bus stops.

Warsaw Summer Jazz Days (www.adamiakjazz.pl in Polish) This series of concerts, throughout July and August, brings leading international jazz stars to town, mixed in with performances by local talent. Major gigs are held in Congress Hall at the Palace of Culture & Science.

Warsaw Autumn International Festival of Contemporary Music (www.warsaw-autumn.art.pl) This 40-year-old festival, held over 10 days in September, is the city's pride and joy and offers a chance to hear the world's best avant-garde music, including new works by major Polish composers.

Frédéric Chopin International Piano Competition (www.konkurs.chopin.pl) This much-acclaimed competition takes place every five years; the next one is in September and October 2005.

Warsaw International Film Festival (www.wff.pl) A major 10-day festival held in October, with a packed programme of art-house film premieres, lectures and screen-writing workshops. Films have English subtitles.

JVC Jazz Festival Warsaw (www.festivalproductions .net) One of the most prestigious jazz festivals in Europe, this three-day event takes place in late October. Has already played host to most of the jazz greats, from Dizzy Gillespie to Miles Davis and Wynton Marsalis.

SLEEPING

Warsaw today sports an ever-increasing range of upmarket hotels, to the point where supply has begun to outstrip demand – it's worth asking for a discount when booking top-end hotels here. Recent years have also seen the arrival of modern, independent backpacker hostels. Unfortunately, there are still very few budget and mid-range hotels that can boast an ounce of character or atmosphere.

Apart from the cluster of five-star hotels in and around the financial district, Warsaw has no particular 'hotel district'. Accommodation is scattered widely across the city, but there is a scarcity of good-quality, mid-range places in and around the Old Town. The up-and-coming area for tourist hotels is Praga, which is just a short tram ride across the river from the Old Town.

The city's tourist information offices (p611), including the two convenient desks at the airport and Warszawa Centralna train station, can help you to find and book accommodation.

Old Town & Around
MID-RANGE

Old Town Apartments (Map p64-5; ☎ 887 98 00; www.warsawshotel.com; Old Town Sq 12/14; 1-/2-bedroom apt from 240/370zł) This agency rents out a range of apartments sleeping from one to six people, with superb central locations on and around the Old Town's main square. All are attractively furnished and include bathroom and kitchen with cooker and fridge, but no phone. The one-bedroom apartments can sleep up to four people, with two sleeping on a sofa bed in the living room.

TOP END

Le Regina (Map p64-5; ☎ 531 60 00; www.leregina .com; ul Kościelna 12; s & d 650-960zł, ste 1500-3500zł; ☒ ☐ ☎) Housed in a lovely arcaded 18th-century-style palace just a few minutes' walk from the Old Town, the Regina manages a successful combination of traditional architecture and contemporary design – the reception lobby is a strikingly modern take on a medieval knights' hall. Rooms are light and airy, decorated in shades of chocolate and vanilla, with lots of polished walnut, gleaming chrome and marble in the more expensive rooms.

Dom Literatury (House of Literature; Map p64-5;
☎ 635 04 04, ☎ /fax 828 39 20; fundacja@fundacjadl
.com; ul Krakowskie Przedmieście 87/89; s/d/tr 220/370/
450zł; P) Ideally located opposite the Royal
Castle, Dom Literatury is the headquarters
of the Polish PEN Club, a writers' organisation. It offers 13 plush rooms featuring formal décor, deep sofas and wooden beams
on the ceiling; all are on the 3rd floor, some
with superb views over the Old Town, but
there's no lift. Used to dealing with a mainly
domestic clientele, the reception staff aren't
always that fluent in English.

South of the Old Town
BUDGET
Smolna Youth Hostel (Map p62-3; ☎ /fax 827 89 52; ul
Smolna 30; dm/s/d 35/62/114zł) Central and popular, with 110 beds in singles, doubles and
12-bed dorms. The basic rooms are kept
scrupulously clean, but there's a somewhat
regimented atmosphere – an 11pm curfew
and strict no-alcohol rule. Take bus 175
from the airport, or any eastbound tram
from the main train station.

Oki Doki Hostel (Map p62-3; ☎ 826 51 12; www
.okidoki.pl; Plac Dąbrowskiego 3; dm/s/d 45/110/130zł;
▯) A stylish new hostel in a conveniently
central location, the Oki Doki has colourful, individually decorated rooms sporting
arty themes and a maximum of only four
beds per dorm. There's a late-opening bar
(where you can buy breakfast in the morn-

ing), a self-service laundry and no curfew.
The Old Town is only 10 minutes' walk
away, as is the central train station.

Bursa Szkolnictwa Artystycznego (Map p64-5;
☎ 635 41 74; fax 635 36 31; ul Miodowa 24a; dm 36zł;
☺ Jul & Aug) This art-school dorm is clean
and quiet, and only 200m from the Old
Town. The entrance is from ul Kilińskiego –
follow the 'Bursa' signs around to the back
of the building.

MID-RANGE
Hotel Mazowiecki (Map p62-3; ☎ 827 23 65; www
.hotelbelwederski.pl; ul Mazowiecka 10; s/d with shared
bathroom 150/200zł, with private bathroom 200/250zł)
The Hotel Mazowiecki once housed mili-
tary accommodation reserved for army officers, but is now open to all. The original
communist-era brown drab décor has been
brightened up with fresh paint, yellow curtains, green carpets and new furniture, and
it is now a pleasant mid-range hotel with a
superb central location.

Hotel Gromada (Map p62-3; ☎ 582 99 90; www
.hotels.gromada.pl; Plac Powstańców Warszawy 2; s/d
with shared bathroom 200/230zł, with private bathroom
320/350zł; P ✗) The 300-bed Hotel Gromada
doesn't look too inspiring from the outside – two big, blocky glass-and-concrete
boxes – but its rooms are comfortable, attractive and excellent value considering the
central location.

TOP END
Le Royal Méridien Bristol Hotel (Map p64-5; ☎ 551
10 00; www.warsaw.lemeridien.com; ul Krakowskie
Przedmieście 42/44; s & d from 750zł; P ✗ ▯ ▮)
Established in 1899 and restored to its former
glory after a US$36 million renovation, the
Bristol is touted as Poland's most luxurious
hotel. Its neoclassical façade, spectacularly
floodlit at night, conceals a feast of original
Art Nouveau features, and huge rooms that
are both traditional and homy. Attentive
staff cater to your every whim, and the Old
Town is only a few minutes' walk away.

Hotel Orbis Europejski (Map p64-5; ☎ 826 50
51; www.orbis.pl; ul Krakowskie Przedmieście 13; s/d/ste
400/460/870zł; P ✗) This historic hotel has
an atmosphere of elegance and grandeur,
with an Art Nouveau façade and spacious,
old-fashioned rooms. It is well placed near
the Saxon Gardens and its location and
sense of tradition make it an appealing
choice.

Hotel Harenda (Map p64-5; ☎ 826 00 71; www .hotelharenda.com.pl; ul Krakowskie Przedmieście 4/6; s/d/ ste 325/360/500zł; P ⌨) Housed in an elegant neoclassical building, the Harenda boasts a quiet location close to the Old Town and an appealingly old-fashioned ambience. The single rooms are on the small side but the bathrooms are spotless; you're paying for the location here.

Financial District
MID-RANGE

Premiere Classe (Map p58; ☎ 624 08 00; www.premiere classe.com.pl; ul Towarowa 2; s/d 175/200zł; P ✕) The cheapest part of a brand-new complex of three French chain hotels just west of the city centre, this place offers bland, modern rooms with slightly cramped modular bathrooms at a very reasonable price. Bus 175 stops outside, linking the hotel with both the airport and the Old Town; look for the Hotel Campanile building – the entrance to the Premiere Classe is hidden around the corner on the north side. Breakfast is 18zł extra.

Friends Guesthouse (Map p62-3; ☎ 601 24 34 44; www.friends-poland.com; ul Sienkiewicza 4; s/d 190/240zł) This gay-friendly guesthouse offers three compact but smartly decorated rooms, each with a private shower, and shared toilet and kitchenette. Staff are friendly and professional, and the location is ideal.

TOP END

Hotel Maria (Map p58; ☎ 838 40 62; www.hotel maria.pl; Al Jana Pawła II 71; s/d 340/400zł; P ⌨) The family-friendly Maria is a modern, low-rise, 22-room hotel with spacious, bright and cheerful rooms, conveniently located for visiting the city's Jewish sights; the Old Town is a 10-minute bus ride away.

NEAR THE AIRPORT

Courtyard Warsaw International Airport Hotel (Map p58; ☎ 650 01 00; www.marriott .com; ul Żwirki i Wigury 1; s & d from 430zł; P ✕ ⌨ ⌨) Right across the street from airport Departures – you couldn't get any closer unless you slept in the terminal.

Hotel Gromada Airport (Map p58; ☎ 576 46 00; www.hotele.gromada.pl; ul 17 Stycznia 32; s/d from 200/230zł; P) Just 800m north of the airport, two stops away on bus 175 or 188.

Hotel Jan III Sobieski (Map p58; ☎ 579 10 00; www.sobieski.com.pl; Plac Zawisy 1; s/d 900/1050zł; P ✕ ⌨) Looking like a giant block of Neapolitan ice cream in swirling pink, yellow and red, the Sobieski's colourful façade is an unmissable landmark at the western end of Al Jerozolimskie. A top business hotel with helpful staff and all the mod cons and facilities you could wish for, the hotel is located halfway between the airport and the Old Town, and close to the city's financial district.

South of Al Jerozolimskie
BUDGET

Nathan's Villa Hostel (Map p62-3; ☎ 622 29 46; www.nathansvilla.com; ul Piękna 24/26; dm/s/d 50/ 120/140zł; ✕ ⌨) A spotless new backpackers hostel set in a quiet courtyard, south of the centre, and offering the same high standards as its sister establishment in Kraków. There's a kitchen, common room, reading room, free laundry and no curfew. It's hugely popular, so book well in advance. Take bus 131, 501, 505 or 525 from Warszawa Centralna train station to the Plac Konstytucji stop.

Dizzy Daisy Hostel (Map p62-3; ☎ 660 67 12; www .hostel.pl; ul Górnośląska 14; s/d/tr 80/100/135zł; ☼ Jul & Aug) Offers basic, decent rooms (no dorms) in a renovated old building near the river, south of the centre, with kitchen facilities, common room, 24-hour reception and no curfew. Doubles with private bathroom (120zł) are also available. Take bus 107 from Al Jerozolimskie (the stop outside the Novotel, a block east of the central train station) to the Wiejska stop; continue under the bridge and down the stairs across the street.

Hotel Agrykola (Map p62-3; ☎ 622 91 10; www .hotelagrykola.pl in Polish; ul Myśliwiecka 9; dm from 20zł, s/d 270/320zł; P) Halfway between hostel and hotel, the Agrykola is a bright, modern place incorporating a sports centre. It has a restaurant, sauna and solarium, and there's no curfew. It's a little off the beaten track; take bus 107 from Al Jerozolimskie (the stop outside the Novotel, a block east of the central train station) to the Rozbrat stop; the entrance is back on the other side of the roundabout, beneath the overpass.

Biuro Podróży Syrena (Map p62-3; ☎ 628 75 40; www.kwatery-prywatne.pl; ul Krucza 17; s/d from 70/100zł, 4-bed apt from 200zł; ☼ office 9am-7pm Mon-Fri, 11am-7pm Sat, 2-7pm Sun) This agency offers rooms in private apartments, as well as whole apartments, for short-term rental. All the accommodation is in the city centre and one-night rental is accepted.

Camping 123 (Map p58; ☎ 823 37 48; ul Warszawskiej 1920r 15/17; per tent 10zł; P ⛾) Set in extensive grounds near the Warszawa Zachodnia bus terminal, Camping 123 has well-tended grass, tree-shaded areas and a tennis court. There are also wood-panelled, two-person bungalows (84zł) to rent, though beware – the walls are very thin, so you can hear your neighbours' every movement.

Camping Nr 34 Gromada (Map p58; ☎ 825 43 91; ul Żwirki i Wigury 32; per tent 10zł, plus per person 10zł; ⛾ May-Sep; P) Gromada is the most central and popular camp site for visiting backpackers, and is easily accessible from both the airport (bus 175 and 188) and the central train station (bus 136 and 175).

MID-RANGE

Warsaw Apartments (Map p58; ☎ 550 45 50; www.warsaw-apartments.com.pl; ul Augustówka 9; 1-/2-person apt 220/250zł; P) This modern apartment block, a 15-minute bus ride south of the city centre, offers serviced one- and two-bedroom apartments that have phone, TV, cooker and refrigerator, which can be rented by the night; for stays of over a month the nightly rate falls by almost 50%.

Praga
MID-RANGE

Hotel Praski (Map p58; ☎ 818 49 89; www.praski.pl; Al Solidarności 61; s/d 240/300zł; P) Little more than 1km from the Old Town, the Praski is set in an attractively refurbished apartment block overlooking a park. It has smallish but comfortable, modern rooms decorated in burgundy, rose and green, and there are cheaper rooms with shared bathrooms (single 160zł, double 220zł) on offer.

Hotel Arkadia (Map p58; ☎ 678 50 55; www.hotel arkadia.pl; ul Radzymińska 182; s/d/ste 190/260/390zł; P) An attractive modern hotel with a family atmosphere, spacious rooms and friendly service, the Arkadia is another good-value, east-bank alternative. It's about 10 minutes from the Old Town on bus 190 or 512.

Hotel Felix (☎ 610 21 82; www.felix.com.pl; ul Omulewska 24; s & d from 175zł; P) Set in an unexciting Soviet-style block that has been cheered up with contemporary furniture and colourful fabrics, the Felix offers spotlessly clean,

good-value accommodation. Rates decrease at weekends, in July and August and in winter, but breakfast is 20zł extra. Take tram 9, 24 or 44 from the Warszawa Centralna train station to the Wspólna Droga stop.

TOP END

Hotel Hetman (Map p58; ☎ 511 98 00; www.hotelhet man.pl; ul Kłopotowskiego 36; s/d 300/360zł; P) Across the river but only just over 1km's walk or bus ride from the Old Town, the Hetman sports English-speaking staff, brand-new rooms decked out in soothing shades of pink and green, gleaming bathrooms, and a fitness room with Jacuzzi. It's in a quiet location, but buses and trams to all parts of the city stop nearby.

Western Suburbs
BUDGET

Syrenka Youth Hostel (Map p58; ☎ 632 88 29; www.ptsm.com.pl/ssmnr6; ul Karolkowa 53a; dm/s/d 36/160/260zł; P ⛾) This friendly and cheerful place has a wide range of hostel and hotel rooms with shiny new bathrooms, a café and a self-catering kitchen. Dorms have to be vacated between 11am and 5pm and there's an 11pm curfew. It's in Wola, 2km west of the train station; take tram 12 or 24 westbound to the DT Wola stop, and go through the passage under the Centrum Wola department store.

EATING

Warsaw has a wider choice of restaurants than any other Polish city, and these accommodate every price bracket. The capital offers some of Poland's classiest eateries, and its greatest range of ethnic cuisines. You can assume that most upmarket restaurants have foreign-language menus and accept credit cards.

As Warsaw restaurants are a little pricier than other Polish cities, the price breakdown (based on the average cost of a main course) in this chapter is: budget (less than 20zł), mid-range (20zł to 40zł) and top end (more than 40zł).

Old Town & Around
BUDGET

Bar Mleczny Pod Barbakanem (Map pp64-5; ☎ 831 47 37; ul Mostowa 27/29; mains 2-7zł; ⛾ 8am-5pm Mon-Fri, 9am-5pm Sat & Sun) Just outside the Barbican, this popular milk bar has survived the fall of the Iron Curtain and continues to serve cheap, unpretentious food in a location that would be the envy of many upmarket eateries.

MID-RANGE

Fret á Porter (Map pp64-5; ☎ 635 37 54; ul Freta 37; mains 30-60zł; ☺ noon-midnight) Choose between the pavement terrace, with views of tree-lined New Town Sq, and the eccentric dining room with its modern art on rag-rolled brick walls and multicoloured napkins clashing with Regency-striped upholstery. The menu also indulges in bold contrasts, ranging from traditional Polish dishes (green lentil soup with mint, roast duck and grilled pork) to exotic offerings such as kangaroo and emu steaks.

Restauracja Pod Samsonem (Map pp64-5; ☎ 831 17 88; ul Freta 3/5; mains 15-25zł; ☺ 10am-11pm) Situated in the New Town, Pod Samsonem is frequented by locals and tourists looking for inexpensive and tasty Polish food infused with a Jewish flavour – marinated herring, gefilte fish and *kawior po żydowsku* ('Jewish caviar' – chopped chicken liver with garlic). It's always busy and you may have to wait, especially for the popular outdoor tables.

TOP END

Dom Restauracyjny Gessler (Map pp64-5; ☎ 831 44 27; Old Town Sq 21/21a; mains 50-100zł; ☺ 11am-midnight) The Gessler house offers a choice of two dining areas: an elegant, formal restaurant on the ground floor, and a rustic country inn, arranged in labyrinthine brick-vaulted cellars down below. The menu is dominated by traditional Polish dishes, ranging from borscht and *żurek* (traditional

---

THE AUTHOR'S CHOICE

Sense (Map pp62-3; ☎ 826 65 70; ul Nowy Świat 19; mains 20-55zł; ☺ noon-11pm Mon-Thu, noon-12.30am Fri & Sat, noon-10pm Sun) Red-brick, teak and terracotta décor along with dark-brown leather benches, lazy ceiling fans and a garden terrace make for a laid-back atmosphere at this deeply cool restaurant and bar. The menu has an oriental vibe, featuring Malaysian, Thai and Indonesian specialities such as succulent satay and nasi goreng, as wells as steak and seafood.

---

sour rye soup) to roast venison with cranberries and roast duck stuffed with apples. Reservations are recommended.

South of the Old Town
BUDGET

Bar Krokiecik (Map pp62-3; ☎ 827 30 37; ul Zgoda 1; mains 8-17zł; ☺ 9am-8pm) The self-service Bar Krokiecik is deservedly popular. It's an attractive, modern version of the traditional Polish milk bar serving soups (borscht and *żurek*), salads and hot dishes such as *fasolka po bretońsku* (sausage and bean casserole), *strogonow z wołowiny* (beef stroganoff) and *ragout z kurczaka* (chicken ragout).

Bar Sałatkowy z Tukanem Plac Bankowy (Map pp64-5; ☎ 531 25 20; Plac Bankowy 2; salad portions 2-5zł; ☺ 8am-8pm Mon-Fri, 10am-5pm Sat); ul Koszykowa (Map pp62-3; ☎ 630 88 20; ul Koszykowa 54; ☺ 8am-7pm Mon-Fri, 10am-4pm Sat); ul Kredytowa (Map pp64-5; ☎ 827 71 19; ul Kredytowa 2; ☺ 10am-7pm Mon-Fri, 10am-5pm Sat) The 'Toucan' offers a wide choice of fresh and inventive salads – choose from the likes of *bałkańska* (tomato, cucumber, capsicum, olives and feta cheese), *kukurydziana* (sweet corn, hazelnut and prune) and *mamut* (runner beans, almonds and vinaigrette). The main branch is a gleaming self-service salad bar set on the ground-floor mall of the prominent blue skyscraper on Plac Bankowy.

Melon (Map pp62-3; ☎ 828 64 28; ul Nowy Świat 52; mains 8-17zł; ☺ noon-8pm Mon-Sat) Formerly known as Mata Hari (the sign still hangs in the entrance alley), this cheap and cheerful little café-bar, tucked away in a courtyard, serves delicious vegetarian food to eat in or take away. Dishes range from soups (mung bean, cream of broccoli) and salads (spinach, chickpea and tofu) to veggie burgers, samosas and dumplings.

Między Nami (Between You & Me; Map pp62-3; ☎ 827 94 41; ul Bracka 20; mains 10-20zł; ☺ 10am-11pm Mon-Sat, 4-10pm Sun) Między Nami is a trendy little café-bar with bleached wood furniture, white walls, designer lamps, and outdoor tables cordoned off by a potted-plant jungle. It serves tasty set vegetarian dishes, with a different menu each day – the homemade tomato soup is delicious. There's no sign over the door; look for the Gauloises Blondes awnings.

Other good options for a fast, inexpensive meal include the conveniently located, canteen-style **Bar Mleczny Familijny** (Map pp62-3;

☎ 826 45 79; ul Nowy Świat 39; mains 2-6zł; ⏱ 7am-8pm Mon-Fri, 9am-5pm Sat & Sun) and the tiny **Bar Aysza Tripolis** (Map pp62-3; ☎ 621 67 23; ul Wspólna 65a; mains 5-10zł; ⏱ 11am-midnight), which serves some of the tastiest Middle Eastern food in town.

MID-RANGE

Café Design (Map pp64-5; ☎ 828 57 03; ul Krakowskie Przedmieście 11; mains 28-38zł; ⏱ 10am-midnight Mon-Sat, 11am-midnight Sun) Choose between the stylish dining room decked out in cream linen and mahogany, or the little outdoor terrace with comfy cane chairs and a view of the imposing Bristol Hotel. The international menu is dotted with light but tasty offerings such as goat's cheese, rocket and walnut salad, and (in late summer) fragrant *kurki* (wild chanterelles) stewed in butter and served with toast.

Restauracja Polska (Map pp62-3; ☎ 826 38 77; ul Nowy Świat 21; mains 25-50zł; ⏱ noon-11pm) The Polska is a classic old-fashioned Polish restaurant of the type that Polish families favour for special occasions – folksy farmhouse décor, lacy tablecloths, bouquets of flowers everywhere, and smartly dressed, attentive staff. The menu is devoted to hearty home cooking – this is the place to try authentic *pierogi* (dumplings), *żurek, schab z dziku* (roast wild boar with crispy dumplings) and other *dania staropolskie* (old Polish dishes). The restaurant is set well back from the street – enter the gate at No 21 and go straight ahead until you see it on your right. Don't be put off by the scruffy exterior.

Chianti (Map pp62-3; ☎ 828 02 22; ul Foksal 17; mains 30-50zł; ⏱ noon-11pm) A rustic, candlelit cellar with rough stone walls, wooden floors and ceilings, and wrought-iron lamp stands, Chianti is a popular venue for a romantic tête-à-tête over an Italian dinner – choose from the likes of carpaccio, home-made pasta, veal, salmon, and wild mushrooms in late summer – washed down with a bottle of the eponymous vino.

Arsenał (Map pp64-5; ☎ 635 83 77; ul Długa 52; mains 15-35zł; ⏱ 9am-11pm) Set in the same 17th-century building that houses the Archaeological Museum, this place dishes up home-made pasta with a range of sauces, crisp salads, crunchy pizzas and Italian ice cream, which makes it very popular with parents who can eat their fill while kids make use of the playroom, sandpit and climbing frame.

TOP END

Deco Kredens (Map pp62-3; ☎ 826 06 60; ul Ordynacka 13; mains 30-60zł; ⏱ 10am-11pm Mon-Fri, 11am-11pm Sat & Sun) This place flaunts an appealingly over-the-top Art Deco dining room, dressed in red and gold and crammed with mirrors, marble, stained glass and Man Ray photographs; two curvaceous, black-onyx nymphs clad in gold bikinis frame the studded-leather bar. Fat armchairs tempt you to linger over a menu of Polish and international cuisine – the crispy roast duck, served on a wooden platter with potato pancakes, beetroot and baked apple, is superb.

London Steak House (Map pp62-3; ☎ 827 00 20; Al Jerozolimskie 42; mains 40-70zł; ⏱ 11am-midnight) The English theme runs from the red telephone kiosk and pillar box at the entrance, to the dummy dressed in a bobby's uniform, the telephone kiosk salt-and-pepper shakers, and the roses that dominate the décor. But what you come for are the steaks – the best British beef ranging from sirloin with onions, pepper, mustard or mushroom sauce to T-bone with all the trimmings.

South of Al Jerozolimskie

BUDGET

Warsaw Tortilla Factory (Map pp62-3; ☎ 621 86 22; ul Wilcza 46; mains 12-24zł; ⏱ noon-1am Sun-Thu, noon-2am Fri & Sat) One of the most authentic Mexican restaurants in town and hugely popular with expats, the Factory sports a trendy blend of red brick, dark wood and steel and a menu that packs a punch in both the hunger-quenching and hot-chilli departments. There's a special 'hangover brunch' served till 5pm at weekends, accompanied by spiced-up Bloody Marys.

MID-RANGE

India Curry (Map pp62-3; ☎ 816 13 50; ul Żurawia 22; mains 30-46zł; ⏱ 11am-11pm) A candlelit dining area dotted with Indian art, woodcarvings and floral garlands is a relaxed setting in which to enjoy some excellent Indian cuisine, ranging from crispy prawns served with a fiery red chilli paste, to classics such as tandoori chicken and rogan josh. The menu boasts as many vegetarian dishes as meat ones, such as *malai kofta* (balls of cottage cheese stuffed with nuts in a coconut, herb and cashew sauce) and *aloo bhindi bhaji* (curried potato and okra).

Banja Luka (Map p58; ☎ 854 07 82; ul Puławska 101; mains 18-35zł; ☻ noon-midnight) This welcoming, child-friendly, Balkan-themed restaurant has a rustic cottage atmosphere with pine tables, stone walls draped with fishing nets, lots of fresh flowers and a garden terrace with a tinkling fountain. The menu consists of Serbian and Croatian specialities such as *čevapčiči* (spicy kebabs of minced meat with sweet pepper sauce) and *penjene palačinky* (cheese-and-spinach fritters doused in dill and cream).

Bacio (Kiss; Map pp62-3; ☎ 626 83 03; ul Wilcza 43; mains 25-50zł; ☻ noon-midnight Mon-Fri, 1pm-midnight Sat & Sun) A flowery, flouncy, romantic little restaurant, crammed to the ceiling beams with all kinds of art, mismatched furniture, candles, bunches of herbs and evidence of a serious cat fetish. Bacio specialises in hearty helpings of authentic Italian home cooking, from melt-in-the-mouth carpaccio to linguine in truffle sauce.

Tandoor Palace (Map p58; ☎ 825 23 75; ul Marszałkowska 21/25; mains 25-50zł; ☻ noon-10.30pm) Billed as the best Indian restaurant in Poland, the Palace's food is prepared by experienced North Indian chefs using a genuine *tandoor* (clay oven). The extensive menu ranges from classics such as butter chicken, *shahi korma* (chicken or lamb in a mild, creamy sauce with crushed almonds) and biryani to Kashmiri balti dishes and sizzling platters.

Restauracja Adler (Map pp62-3; ☎ 628 73 84; ul Mokotowska 69; mains 28-48zł; ☻ 8am-midnight Mon-Fri, 1pm-midnight Sat & Sun) A tiny oasis of beer-hall bonhomie amid the concrete jungle of Plac Trzech Krzyży, the Adler has a rustic dining room and tree-shaded garden tables serviced by staff bearing foaming glasses of Erdinger wheat beer. Service is impeccable and the Bavarian menu includes roast pork knuckle with dumplings and sauerkraut, and apple strudel with ice cream.

TOP END

Kurt Scheller's Restaurant (Map pp62-3; ☎ 584 87 71; Hotel Rialto, ul Wilcza 73; mains 50-150zł; ☻ noon-10.30pm Sun-Fri, 5.30-10.30pm Sat) The elaborately moustached Mr Scheller is Poland's most famous chef, and this beautiful Art Deco restaurant is widely regarded as Warsaw's finest. The international fusion menu ranges from smoked sturgeon to honey-marinated veal by way of spicy Thai soup

and seared tuna with sun-dried tomato purée. Traditional Polish dishes are given a modern twist, with offerings such as duck borscht with coriander, and pan-fried *sandacz* (pike-perch) with tomato jam and *rucola* (rocket) pesto.

DRINKING
Bars

Most drinking establishments open at 11am or noon and close only when *ostatniego gościa* (the last guest) leaves – in practice, any time between midnight and 4am.

Chimera (Map pp64-5; ☎ 635 69 19; ul Podwale 29) Chimera's lovely, shady courtyard bar offers a peaceful afternoon retreat that's a million miles away from the crowds on nearby Old Town Sq. In contrast, the basement bar is a bohemian cavern of junk-shop furniture, weird art, cool tunes and a twenty-something crowd in party mood.

Irish Pub (Map pp64-5; ☎ 826 25 33; ul Miodowa 3) Warsaw's original Irish pub is still one of the busier drinking haunts in the Old Town area, with a dark, crowded crush of tables, sticky wooden floor, raucous conversation and Guinness, Kilkenny and Belfast Ale on tap. There's live music (Celtic, country, folk, blues) most nights.

John Bull Pub (Map pp64-5; ☎ 831 03 67; ul Jezuicka 4) Perhaps the first English-style watering hole to cross the Iron Curtain, the John Bull is an elegant and comfortable shrine to polished brass, mahogany and brown beer, but the main attraction on a summer's day is the outdoor tables on the terrace out back, with a view across the Vistula.

Pub Harenda (Map pp64-5; ☎ 826 29 00; ul Krakowskie Przedmieście 4/6) The downstairs bar here is a serious, smoky drinking establishment of the central European beer-hall variety, with serried ranks of wooden benches jammed belly to belly with dedicated drinkers bending the elbow well into the small hours of the morning. There's also a summer beer garden where the air is fresher, regular live jazz and jam sessions through the week, and hip-hop parties on Saturday night.

Paparazzi (Map pp62-3; ☎ 828 42 19; ul Mazowiecka 12) A sleekly styled and seriously trendy café-bar lined with framed photos of local celebrities and frequented in the evenings by sharp suits eyeing up short skirts as they work their way through a bewildering menu of cocktails. There's a more laid-back atmosphere in the afternoons, when you can flick through a fashion mag over a caffe latte or a glass of Zinfandel.

NoBo (Map pp62-3; ☎ 622 40 07; ul Wilcza 58a) The coolest pre- and postclub bar in town, NoBo has a pleasantly exotic colour scheme of scarlet, maroon and chocolate brown, combined with comfy sofas and chilled-out tunes. It's famed for its fine cocktails and a tempting menu of fusion food, and has hosted many of Europe's top DJs.

U Szwejka (Map pp62-3; ☎ 621 62 11; Plac Konstytucji 1) Named after that famous fictional Czech, *The Good Soldier Švejk*, this homely pub serves up foaming jars of the Czech Republic's finest beer, Pilsner Urquell, and a range of tasty food to whet your thirst. Outdoor tables offer a grandstand view of Constitution Sq's imposing socialist-realist architecture.

Cafés

Pożegnanie z Afryką (Map pp64-5; ☎ 831 44 20; ul Freta 4/6; coffee 8-10zł, snacks 8-12zł; ☼ 11am-9pm) 'Out of Africa' is a tiny café offering nothing but coffee – but what coffee! There are about 50 varieties to choose from, served in a little pot, and a range of tempting cakes. This is the original shop in a chain of about 20 branches scattered around Poland's major cities. You can buy coffee beans whole or freshly ground to take away.

Café Belle Epoque (Map pp64-5; ☎ 635 41 05; ul Freta 18; tea 10zł, mains 10-20zł; ☼ noon-10pm) This atmospheric café is a fairyland of chiffon, velvet and lacy lampshades, crammed with bric-a-brac and dusty antiques – you can buy pretty much anything you see here. An excellent range of speciality teas is accompanied by a menu of cakes, snacks and light meals.

Antykwariat (Map pp62-3; ☎ 629 99 29; ul Żurawia 45; coffee 8zł; ☼ 11am-11pm Mon-Fri, 1-11pm Sat & Sun) This quaint café has a lovely sepia-tinted atmosphere, all scuffed wood, mismatched furniture and old cushions, crammed with creaking chairs, knick-knacks and framed postcards of old Warsaw. You can choose a book from the overflowing shelves to accompany your tea or coffee, though the warren of little rooms can get a bit smoky when it fills up with postclass students later in the day.

Green Coffee (Map pp62-3; ☎ 629 83 73; ul Marszałkowska 84/92; coffee 9zł, snacks 7-15zł; ☼ 7am-11pm) An upmarket coffee shop with clean, modern lines, smiling English-speaking staff and some of the best coffee in Warsaw, Green Coffee is a peaceful haven amid the high-rises and hectic traffic of busy ul Marszałkowska.

Cava (Map pp62-3; ☎ 826 64 27; ul Nowy Świat 30; coffee 7-12zł, snacks 15-25zł; ☼ 9am-midnight Mon-Fri, 10am-midnight Sat & Sun) With dark, designer wood counters and suede-topped stools inside, and canvas-backed director's chairs on the outdoor terrace, Cava makes a comfortable hang-out for some coffee-fuelled people-watching. The munchies menu includes salads, ciabatta sandwiches and lovely sticky cakes and pastries.

Same Fusy (Only Tea Leaves; Map pp64-5; ☎ 831 99 36; ul Nowomiejska 10; tea 12-19zł, snacks 8-12zł; ☼ 1-11pm) This teahouse, just off Old Town Sq, cultivates an exotic atmosphere, with leopard-print seats, African bongo stools and huge papier-mâché snails on the wall. It offers 150 varieties of tea, from Indian Darjeeling to Argentinean *yerba mate*, thick slices of carrot cake, and Celtic tunes on the sound system.

ENTERTAINMENT

Warsaw has a rich and varied cultural life, particularly in the fields of classical music, opera and theatre. The city also offers plenty of lighter entertainment in the form of bars, clubs, cinemas and jazz spots.

You can find detailed listings of museums, art galleries, cinemas, theatres, musical events and festivals (in Polish only) in the Friday edition of *Gazeta Wyborcza* and in the monthly cultural magazine *WiK* (Warszawa i Kultura). The free what's-on monthly *Aktivist* is distributed through restaurants, bars and clubs.

As for useful English-language listings, the monthly *Warsaw Insider* and the entertainment columns of the weekly *Warsaw Voice* provide some information on cultural events, as well as on bars, pubs and other nightspots.

You can buy tickets for theatre, opera, musical events and visiting shows at **Kasy ZASP** (Map pp62-3; ☎ 621 94 54, 621 93 83; Al Jerozolimskie 25; ☼ 11am-6.30pm Mon-Fri) and **Bileteria Rondo** (Map pp62-3; Underground Arcade Nos 1 & 36, cnr Al Jerozolimskie & ul Marszałkowska; ☼ 8am-8pm Mon-Fri, 9am-8pm Sat, 11am-7pm Sun). You can buy tickets for some major events at the Bileteria desk in EMPiK Megastores (see p60);

tickets for particular events can also be bought directly from theatre box offices.

Clubs & Discos

Stodoła (Map p58; ☎ 825 60 31; ul Batorego 10; adult/student 15/10zł; ☽ 7pm-4am) One of Warsaw's biggest and the longest-running student club in Poland (on the go since 1956, in its current location since 1972), Stodoła hosts club sessions offering eurodance, techno, house, R & B, soul, hip-hop and frequent live bands.

Balsam (Map p58; ☎ 844 74 85; ul Racławiska 99; ☽ 6pm-4am) The latest place to hit the capital's clubbing scene, Balsam is set in a series of vaulted caverns within 19th-century Fort Mokotów. There are DJ nights when the fortress walls quiver to the beat of hiphop, ragga and dance, and there are regular live bands playing music ranging from rock and jazz to folk.

Punkt (Map pp62-3; ☎ 502 62 75 81; ul Koszykowa 55; admission 10-20zł; ☽ 9pm-4am Wed & Thu, 9pm-6am Fri & Sat) Small, crowded and loud, Punkt pulls in a hard-drinking, up-for-it crowd with a mix of DJs and live local bands.

Underground Music Café (Map pp62-3; ☎ 826 70 48; ul Marszałkowska 126/134; adult/student 10/5zł; ☽ 1pm-4am Mon-Sat, 4pm-4am Sun) Low ceilings, low lighting, low prices – this dark and crowded basement is frequented by hordes of students and backpackers bopping along to resident DJs playing house, pop, R & B, soul, funk and hip-hop. Thursday is disco night with 1970s' and 1980s' chart hits.

Hybrydy (Map pp62-3; ☎ 822 30 03; ul Złota 7/9; adult/student 12/6zł, Fri & Sat 22/12zł; ☽ 9pm-3am Tue-Sat) This long-standing student club has a great main room with circular stage and a long, wavy, up-lit bar. It hosts regular DJ nights as well as live gigs.

Ground Zero (Map pp62-3; ☎ 625 39 76; ul Wspólna 62; admission 20zł; ☽ 9pm-4am Wed-Sat) Housed in a building that was supposedly designed as a nuclear bomb shelter, connected to the Palace of Culture & Science by an underground passage, Ground Zero is a huge dance club that attracts a mainstream clientele of lads on the pull and girls out for the night. Friday night is Ladies Night (women get in free), and Saturday is when the disco classics get an airing.

Harlem (Map p58; ☎ 435 56 67; ul Kolejowa 8/10; admission 15zł; ☽ 9pm-6am Wed, Fri & Sat) A grungy factory warehouse has been converted into one of Warsaw's most popular clubs, with DJs pumping out urban music, hip-hop, R & B and gangsta rap – expect lots of boys in back-to-front baseball caps and glam ladies in tight tops sipping beer through a straw from plastic glasses.

Jazz

Jazz Café Helicon (Map pp64-5; ☎ 635 95 05; ul Freta 45/47) A small café-bar done up in smart black-and-white tile, which has occasional exhibitions of photography adorning the walls, Helicon is set in a former music shop and indeed still sells jazz and blues CDs – you can ask the owner to play a disc before you buy. There's live jazz on Tuesday, Thursday and Sunday (admission free).

Klub Tygmont (Map pp62-3; ☎ 828 34 09; ul Mazowiecka 6/8; admission Fri & Sat 10zł, free Sun-Thu; ☽ 3pm-1am Mon-Thu, 3pm-4am Fri, 6pm-4am Sat & Sun) Tygmont is an old-style jazz club – dark and

---

GAY & LESBIAN WARSAW

Warsaw's gay nightlife has been inching out of the closet since the mid-1990s, and there is now a fair selection of gay and lesbian venues. For a guide to all the latest places and events, check out the websites www.innastrona.pl, www.gay.pl and www.warsaw.gayguide.net.

Rasko (Map p58; ☎ 890 02 99; ul Krochmalna 32a; ☽ 5pm-3am) Warsaw's most popular gay and lesbian bar, Rasko is a cosy and welcoming little pub with regular karaoke and drag nights.

Kokon (Map pp64-5; ☎ 831 95 39; ul Brzozowa 37; admission 9zł; ☽ 4pm-3am) The Kokon is a four-floor gay club in the heart of the Old Town, done up with designer chic and featuring 1970s' and 1980s' hits, 'gay house' music and a weekly drag show.

Fantom (Map pp62-3; ☎ 828 54 09; ul Bracka 20a; admission 15zł; ☽ 2pm-2am Mon-Fri, 2pm-4am Sat, 4pm-1am Sun) Poland's longest-running gay club, Fantom has been on the go since 1994 and stages a huge party starting every Saturday at 10pm. It's a steamy, full-on experience, complete with sauna, Jacuzzi, sex shop and video lounge; the inconspicuous entrance (a black door with 'Fantom' stencilled on it) is in the courtyard behind Między Nami.

smoky – and offers a dinner menu served till 12.30am. There's live jazz on weekday nights, and Latino dance classes followed by a Latino disco on Saturday.

Jazz Bistro Gwiazdeczka (Map pp64-5; ☎ 887 87 65; ul Piwna 40; admission free; ☺ 10am-midnight) An elegant, modern club of bare brick walls, white arcades and a beautiful glass-roofed atrium, the Jazz Bistro serves up laid-back live jazz of the piano-plus-vocalist variety from 7pm to 10pm most evenings.

Classical Music & Opera

Filharmonia Narodowa (National Philharmonic; Map pp62-3; ☎ 826 72 81, box office ☎ 551 71 28; www .filharmonia.pl; ul Jasna 5; ☺ 10am-2pm & 3-7pm Mon-Sat) The home of the world-famous National Philharmonic Orchestra and Choir of Poland, founded in 1901, this venue has a concert hall (enter from ul Sienkiewicza 10) and a chamber-music hall (enter from ul Moniuszki 5), both of which stage regular concerts. The box office entrance is on ul Sienkiewicza.

Warszawa Opera Kameralna (Warsaw Chamber Opera; Map p58; ☎ 831 22 40; www.wok.pol.pl; Al Solidarności 76b; ☺ box office 10am-7pm) This Warszawa Opera's repertoire ranges from medieval mystery plays to contemporary works, but it's most famous for its performances of Mozart's operas – the annual Mozart Festival (p78) is staged here.

Teatr Wielki (Grand Theatre; Map pp64-5; ☎ 692 02 08; www.teatrwielki.pl; Plac Teatralny 1; ☺ box office 9am-7pm Mon-Fri) This magnificent neoclassical theatre, dating from 1833 and rebuilt after WWII, is the city's main stage for opera and ballet, with a repertoire of international classics and works by Polish composers, notably Stanisław Moniuszko.

Chopin Society (Map pp62-3; ☎ 827 54 71; Ostrogski Palace, ul Okólnik 1) The society organises piano recitals in the beautiful auditorium within the Ostrogski Palace (also home to the Chopin Museum; p70). Every Sunday from May to September, piano recitals are held next to the Chopin monument in Łazienki Park (p74) and at Chopin's birthplace in Żelazowa Wola (p92).

Cinemas

Most films (except for children's films, which are dubbed into Polish) are screened in their original language with Polish subtitles. You can check listings on www.kino .pl (in Polish only, but decipherable – click on 'Repertuar', then 'Warszawa', then the name of the cinema). Some good cinemas:

Cinema City Sadyba (Map p58; ☎ 550 33 33; ul Powsińska 31; admission 22zł) Modern 12-screen multiplex with wheelchair access.

Iluzjon Filmoteki Narodowej (Map p58; ☎ 646 12 60; www.fn.org.pl; ul Narbutta 50a; admission 10-16zł) Home to the national film archive, and also Warsaw's main art-house cinema.

Kino Luna (Map pp62-3; ☎ 621 78 28; www.kino luna.pl in Polish; ul Marszałkowska 28; admission 5-16zł) Mainly art-house films from all over the world.

Kino Rejs (Map pp64-5; ☎ 826 33 35; ul Krakowskie Przedmieście 21/23; admission 5-15zł) Mainstream movies.

Kinoteka (Map pp62-3; ☎ 826 19 61; www.kinoteka .pl; Plac Defilad 1; admission 18zł) Multiplex housed in the Palace of Culture & Science; entrance faces Al Jerozolimskie.

Theatre

Polish theatre has long had a high profile and continues to do so. Warsaw has about 20 theatres, including some of the best in the country. Most theatres close in July and August for their annual holidays. The leading playhouses, all of which lean towards contemporary productions:

Teatr Ateneum (Map pp62-3; ☎ 625 73 30; ul Jaracza 2)

Teatr Dramatyczny (Map pp62-3; ☎ 620 21 02; www .teatrdramatyczny.pl; Palace of Culture & Science, Plac Defilad 1)

Teatr Powszechny (Map p58; ☎ 818 25 16; ul Zamojskiego 20)

The **Teatr Żydowski** (Jewish Theatre; Map pp62-3; ☎ 620 70 25; www.teatr-zydowski.art.pl; Plac Grzybowski 12/16) derives its inspiration from Jewish culture and traditions, and some of its productions are performed in Yiddish – Polish and English translations provided through headphones.

SHOPPING

Warsaw's shopping scene has changed enormously over the past decade. Western brand names have overrun the city, and the old run-down establishments of the communist era have almost completely disappeared – a case of goodbye Marx, hello Marks & Spencer. There are Western-style shopping malls and supermarkets everywhere, the shops are well stocked and the assistants are much more polite than they used to be.

The main shopping area lies in the maze of streets between the Palace of Culture & Science and ul Nowy Świat, and along the eastern part of Al Jerozolimskie and the southern part of ul Marszałkowska.

Arts, Crafts & Souvenirs

Cepelia Plac Konstytucji (Map pp62-3; Plac Konstytucji 5); ul Chmielna (Map pp62-3; ul Chmielna 8); ul Krucza (Map pp62-3; ul Krucza 23); ul Marszałkowska (Map pp62-3; ☎ 628 77 57; ul Marszałkowska 99/101) An established organisation dedicated to promoting Polish arts and crafts, Cepelia stocks its shops with woodwork, pottery, sculpture, fabrics, embroidery, lace, paintings and traditional costumes from various Polish regions.

Neptunea (Map pp64-5; ☎ 826 02 47; ul Krakowskie Przedmieście 47/51; ☒ 11am-7pm Mon-Fri, 11am-5pm Sat) Amid a huge range of crafts, furniture and musical instruments from all over the world, Neptunea carries Polish jewellery in silver and amber, carved stoneware, minerals and crystals.

Desa Unicum Old Town Sq (Map pp64-5; ☎ 621 66 15; Old Town Sq 4/6; ☒ 11am-7pm Mon-Fri, 11am-4pm Sat & Sun); ul Marszałkowska (Map pp62-3; ul Marszałkowska 34/50, near Plac Zbawiciela); ul Nowy Świat (Map pp62-3; ul Nowy Świat 51, on cnr of ul Warecka) Desa Unicum is an art and antiques dealership that sells a range of old furniture, silverware, watches, paintings, icons and jewellery. Note that it's officially forbidden to export products manufactured before 1945, unless you have authorisation (see p464).

Galeria Plakatu (Map pp64-5; ☎ 831 93 06; Old Town Sq 23; ☒ 10am-7pm) Stocks over 2000 art posters, ranging from vintage film and theatre posters to works by contemporary Polish graphic artists. Popular buys include Polish circus posters from the 1960s and '70s, and political and propaganda posters, notably the Solidarność posters of 1989.

Galeria Grafiki i Plakatu (Map pp62-3; ☎ 621 40 77; ul Hoża 40; ☒ 11am-6pm Mon-Fri, 10am-3pm Sat) This gallery stocks what is unquestionably the best selection of original prints and graphic art in Poland. It also has a good range of posters.

Galeria Art (Map pp64-5; ☎ 828 51 70; ul Krakowskie Przedmieście 17) Owned by the Union of Polish Artists, this gallery offers a broad range of contemporary Polish art for sale, and a knowledgeable English-speaking manager who will talk you through the works on display.

Księgarnia Muzyczna Odeon (Map pp62-3; ☎ 621 80 69; ul Hoża 19; ☒ 10am-6pm Mon-Fri, 10am-3pm Sat) A specialist music bookshop stocking a reasonable range of CDs covering works by national composers from Chopin to Penderecki, as well as a selection of Polish jazz.

Markets

Russian Market (Map p58; Stadion Dziesięciolecia, entrances on ul Waszyngtona & Al Zieleniecka; ☒ 6am-1pm) This is Europe's biggest flea market, with thousands of stalls crowded around the disused '10th Anniversary' (sometimes written X-lecia) soccer stadium. Like Dante's image of hell, the stalls are ranged in concentric rings surrounding the eerily empty stadium; the deeper you penetrate, the more sinister goods become. Shoes and clothing in the outer parts, pirated *kompakty* (CDs and DVDs), ex-Soviet military items (including guns, allegedly) and illegal booze (whispered offerings of '*spirytus, spirytus*' as you pass by) in the inner rings. In between you'll find everything from fake furs, perfumes and handbags to fishing tackle, binoculars and power tools. Beware of pickpockets.

Bazar na Kole (Map p58; ul Obozowa; ☒ early morning-2pm Sat & Sun) This huge and fascinating antiques and bric-a-brac market, located in the western suburb of Koło, offers everything from old farm implements and furniture to WWII relics such as rusted German helmets, ammo boxes and shell casings. In between are brass plates engraved with the Polish eagle, lovely 1930s lamps and light fittings, old clocks by the carriage load, cast-iron keys from long-lost doors, jewellery, lapel pins, badges, broken dolls and lots of bad art. Take tram 12, 13 or 24 to the Dalibora stop.

Hala Mirowska (Map p58; Al Jana Pawła II; ☒ dawn-dusk) The original brick pavilions of this 19th-century marketplace have been converted into modern supermarkets, but the stalls arranged around the south and west sides are crammed with fresh flowers, fruit and vegetables, wild mushrooms, berries, pigs' trotters, sausages, smoked fish, live carp, and pickled gherkins sold from wooden barrels.

Giełda Foto (Map p58; ☎ 825 60 31; ul Batorego 10; ☒ 10am-2pm Sun) This photo market, in the Stodoła student club, offers an amazing variety of cameras and accessories, ranging from prewar goods to the newest equipment; people from other cities come here to buy and sell photo gear. Film, cameras and accessories can be bought at cheaper prices than in shops. If you are a camera buff it's worth a visit even if only to look.

Shopping Centres & Department Stores

Galeria Centrum (Map pp62-3; ☎ 551 45 17; ul Marszałkowska 104/122; ⏰ 9.30am-9pm Mon-Fri, 9.30am-8.30pm Sat, 10.30am-5pm Sun) A privatised version of the formerly state-owned chain of Dom Towarowe shops, this department store sells good-value, mass-market men's, women's and children's clothing, accessories, shoes, cosmetics and jewellery.

Marks & Spencer (Map pp62-3; ☎ 652 05 24; Al Jerozolimskie 52; ⏰ 10am-8pm Mon-Fri, 10am-6pm Sat, 10am-4pm Sun) The famous British department store comes to Warsaw, offering fashion and cosmetics. If the building looks a little temporary, that's because it is, until the city's planning department makes a final decision on the use of the land here.

Smyk (Map pp62-3; ☎ 551 43 00; cnr Al Jerozolimskie & ul Krucza; ⏰ 9.30am-8.30pm Mon-Fri, 9am-8pm Sat, 10am-4pm Sun) The name is Polish slang for 'small child' and the store's motto is 'cały dla małych' (everything for the little ones) – here you can find all from children's clothes and shoes to pushchairs, baby articles, toys, books and stationery.

Sadyba Best Mall (Map p58; ☎ 550 30 00; ul Powsińska 31) A shiny modern mall, south of the city centre, housing a wide range of fashion stores (Levi's, Pietro Filipi, Andriotti), shoe shops (Gino Rossi and Max&Max), jewellery and perfume stores, an American Bookstore branch, a multiplex cinema and a dozen different eating places.

GETTING THERE & AWAY

Air

AIRPORT

Warsaw-Frédéric Chopin Airport (Port Lotniczy im F Chopina; Map p58; ☎ 650 41 00; www.lotnisko-chopina .pl) lies in the suburb of Okęcie, at the southern end of ul Żwirki i Wigury, 10km south of the city centre; it handles all domestic and international flights.

In the Terminal 1 international arrivals (odloty) hall, there's a **tourist information desk** (⏰ 8am-8pm), which sells city maps and can help find accommodation. You will also find some **currency-exchange counters** (⏰ 24hr),

a couple of ATMs, several car-hire agencies and a **left-luggage office** (per bag per day 5zł; ⏰ 24hr). You can buy tickets for public transport from **Ruch newsagency** (⏰ 5am-10pm).

The upper level of Terminal 1 houses international departures (przyloty), which has airline offices, a **bank** (⏰ 8am-6pm Mon-Fri, 8am-1pm Sat), and a **post office** (⏰ 8am-8pm Mon-Fri, 8am-2pm Sat).

Budget airlines, including Wizz, Germanwings and SkyEurope, use Terminal Etiuda (Map p58), a separate building that's a few minutes' walk south of the main terminal building. It's a basic, overcrowded place with no amenities – no computerised check-in, no bars or restaurants, no shopping, and no conveyor belts – you have to carry your own checked baggage through security.

Terminal 2 was under construction at the time of writing, and is due to open by the end of 2006.

FLIGHTS

You'll find information about domestic routes and fares on p480. Tickets can be booked at **LOT** (Polish Airlines; Map pp62-3; ☎ 0801 300 952; www.lot.com.pl; Marriott Hotel, Al Jerozolimskie 65/79; ⏰ 9am-7pm Mon-Fri, 9am-3pm Sat) or at most travel agencies. The LOT timetable lists international flights to and from Poland on various airlines, along with LOT's own international and domestic flights.

Bus

Warsaw is home to two Państwowa Komunikacja Samochodowa (PKS) bus terminals. **Warszawa Zachodnia bus terminal** (Map p58; ☎ 822 48 11; Al Jerozolimskie 144), west of the city centre, serves international routes and domestic routes towards the south and west. **Dworzec Warszawa Stadion** (Stadium Bus Terminal; ☎ 818 15 89; cnr ul Zamojskiego & ul Targowa), on the east side of the river, handles all domestic bus traffic to the north, east and southeast. Bus tickets are sold at the respective terminals. Some international services depart from the Warszawa Centralna bus terminal on the north side of Warszawa Centralna train station.

PKS operates several buses a day from Warszawa Zachodnia to Gdańsk (50zł, 6½ hours), Częstochowa (35zł, 3½ hours), Kazimierz Dolny (22zł, 3½ hours), Kraków (39zł, 5½ hours), Olsztyn (32zł, four hours), Toruń (35zł, four hours), Wrocław (45zł,

WARSAW

6½ hours) and Zakopane (53zł, 7½ hours). Services from Warszawa Stadion include a few daily buses to Lublin (25zł, 3½ hours), Białystok (24zł, 3¾ hours) and Zamość (37zł, 4¾ hours).

Polski Express coaches depart from Warsaw's Frédéric Chopin airport and pick up passengers at its own **bus stop** (Map pp62-3; Al Jana Pawła II), to Warszawa Centralna train station. Tickets for Polski Express routes are available from either of its offices – the main office **Centralny Punkt Informacji i Sprzedaży Biletów** (Central Information & Ticket Sales Point; ☎ 844 55 55; ❤ 6.30am-9.30pm) is beside the bus stop – and from selected Orbis Travel outlets and **Almatur** (Map pp62-3; ☎ 826 35 12, 826 26 39; www .almatur.com.pl; ul Kopernika 23; ❤ 9am-7pm Mon-Fri, 10am-3pm Sat), but they cannot be bought at PKS terminals. Polski Express buses travel to Białystok (34zł, 3¾ hours; one daily), Gdynia via Gdańsk (72zł, 7½ hours, two daily), Kraków (67zł, eight hours, two daily), Lublin (34zł, 3¼ hours, six daily), Szczecin (80zł, 11 hours, two daily) and Łódź (30zł, 2½ hours, three daily).

For information on international bus routes, see the Land section of the Transport chapter (p478).

Car

All the major international car-hire companies have offices in Warsaw (see p483). Polish companies offer cheaper rates, but may have fewer English-speaking staff. Dependable local operators include **Local Rent-a-Car** (☎ 826 71 00; www.lrc.com.pl; ul Marszałkowska 140), which offers an Opel Corsa for €31 a day, or €231 a week, including tax, collision damage waiver (CDW), theft protection and unlimited mileage.

Train

Warsaw has several train stations, but the one that most travellers use almost exclusively is **Warszawa Centralna train station** (Dworzec Centralny, Warsaw Central; Map pp62-3; Al Jerozolimskie 54); it handles the overwhelming majority of domestic trains and all international services. Refer to the relevant town's Getting There & Away section for information about services to/from Warsaw. For details of international trains, see p478.

Remember, Warszawa Centralna is not always where domestic and international trains terminate, so make sure you get off the train sharply when it arrives. And watch your belongings closely as pickpocketing and theft are on the increase.

The station's spacious main hall houses ticket counters, ATMs and snack bars, as well as a post office, newsagents (where you can buy public-transport tickets) and a tourist information desk. Along the underground passages leading to the tracks and platforms are a dozen *kantors* (one of which is open 24 hours), a **left-luggage office** (❤ 7am-9pm), luggage lockers, eateries, several other places to buy tickets for local public transport, Internet cafés and bookshops.

Tickets for domestic trains are available from counters at the east end of the main hall (but allow at least an hour for possible queuing), and international train tickets are available from the office at the west end, or can be bought in advance from any major Orbis Travel office. Tickets for immediate departures on domestic and international trains are also available from numerous, well-signed booths in the underpasses leading to Warszawa Centralna.

Some domestic trains also stop at **Warszawa Śródmieście train station** (Map pp62-3; Al Jerozolimskie), which is 300m east of Warszawa Centralna, at **Warszawa Zachodnia train station** (Map p58; Al Jerozolimskie), next to Warszawa Zachodnia bus terminal, and at Warszawa Wschodnia, in Praga, on the east bank of the Vistula.

GETTING AROUND
To/From the Airport

The cheapest way of getting from the airport to the city (and vice versa) is by city bus 175 (2.40zł, every eight to 15 minutes, 5am to 11pm), which will take you all the way to the Miodowa stop (Map pp64-5; 30 to 40 minutes) in the Old Town, passing en route along Al Jerozolimskie, ul Nowy Świat and ul Krakowskie Przedmieście.

If you arrive in the wee hours, night bus 611 links the airport with Warszawa Centralna train station every 30 minutes between 11pm and 5am. The bus stop is on a traffic island outside the international arrivals hall – look for the red-and-yellow bus shelter. There's a second stop outside Terminal Etiuda. Watch your bags closely – this line is a favourite playground for thieves and pickpockets. Don't forget to buy tickets at the airport's Ruch newsagency, located in the arrivals hall, and to validate them in one of the ticket machines when you board the bus.

The taxi stand is right outside the door of the arrivals hall and handles taxis run by MPT Radio Taxi, Sawa Taxi and Taxi Merc. They all have desks inside the terminal, so you can ask about the fare to your destination – it shouldn't be more than about 20zł to the Hotel Premiere Classe and 30zł to the Old Town. Ignore the unlicensed drivers who tout for business in the arrivals hall.

Car & Motorcycle

Warsaw's streets are full of potholes – some more dangerous than others – so driving demands constant attention.

The local government has introduced paid parking on central streets. You pay using coins in the nearest ticket machine (*parkomat*) and get a receipt that you display in the windscreen. For security, try to park your car in a guarded car park (*parking strzeżony*). There are some in central Warsaw, including one on ul Parkingowa, behind the Novotel (Map pp62–3).

PZM (☎ 981, 96 37; ul Kaszubska 2) operates a 24-hour road breakdown service (*pomoc drogowa*).

Public Transport

Warsaw's integrated public transport system is operated by **Zarząd Transportu Miejskiego** (City Transportation Board; 24hr info line ☎ 94 84; www.ztm .waw.pl) and consists of a network of tram, bus and metro lines, all using the same ticketing system. The main routes operate from about 5am to about 11pm, and services are frequent and pretty reliable, though it's often crowded during rush hours (7am till 9am and 4.30pm till 6.30pm Monday to Friday). After 11pm several night bus routes link major suburbs to the city centre. The night-service 'hub' is at ul Emilii Plater, next to the Palace of Culture & Science, from where buses depart every half-hour.

It's best to buy a ticket before you board a bus, tram or metro. Tickets are sold at Ruch and Relay newsstands, hotels, post offices, metro stations and various general stores – look for a sign saying 'Sprzedaż Biletów ZTM'.

Tickets, timetables and information are available at the following ZTM information desks:

Hala sprzedaż biletów ZTM (Map pp64–5; ul Senatorska 37; ⏰ 7am-5pm Mon-Fri)
Punkt informacji ZTM (Map pp64–5; Pawilon 09, Ratusz metro station; ⏰ 7am-7pm Mon-Fri)
Punkt informacji ZTM (Map pp62–3; Pawilon 1000G, Świętokrzyska metro station; ⏰ 7am-7pm Mon-Fri)

A *jednorazowy bilet* (single-journey ticket) costs 2.40zł (1.25zł for school children aged four or over; kids under four ride free); these tickets are not valid for transferring between services. A *90-minutowy bilet* (90-minute ticket) costs 6zł, and is valid for 90 minutes from the time of validation, with unlimited transfers. Also available are one-/three-/seven-day unlimited transfer tickets (9.60zł/14.40zł/32zł). A single-fare night-bus ticket costs 4.80zł. You can also buy a ticket from a bus or tram driver, but it's more expensive (single-journey ticket 3zł) and you have to provide the exact fare. Foreign students under 26 years of age who have an International Student Identity Card (ISIC) get a discount of 48% (in Warsaw only; no other Polish city gives ISIC student concessions).

There are no conductors on board vehicles. Validate your ticket by feeding it (magnetic stripe facing down) into the little yellow machine on the bus or tram or in the metro-station lobby the first time you board; this stamps the time and date on it (or the route number for single-fare tickets). Inspections are common and fines are high (120zł for travel without a validated ticket) and there's a new breed of tough and rude plain-clothes inspectors who literally hunt for foreign tourists. Watch out for pickpockets on crowded buses and trams (especially the notorious bus 175 and trams running along Al Jerozolimskie).

The construction of Warsaw's metro system began in 1983 and so far only a single line is in operation, running from the southern suburb of Ursynów (Kabaty station) to Dworzec Gdański via the city centre. A northern extension to Młociny should be completed by 2007, and there are long-term plans to build a second, east–west line. Yellow signs with a big red letter 'M' indicate the entrances to metro stations. Every station has a public toilet and there are lifts for disabled passengers. You use the same tickets as on trams and buses, but you validate the ticket at the gate at the entrance to the platform, not inside the vehicle. Trains run every eight minutes (every four minutes during rush hours).

Taxi

Taxis in Warsaw are easily available and not too expensive by Western standards: around 6zł flag fall and 1.30zł to 2zł per kilometre (50% higher after 10pm). Reliable companies include **MPT Radio Taxi** (☎ 919), which has English-speaking dispatchers, **Partner Taxi** (☎ 96 69), **Super Taxi** (☎ 96 22), **Tele Taxi** (☎ 96 27) and **OK! Taxi** (☎ 96 28).

All are recognisable by signs on the taxi's roof with the company name and phone number. Beware of 'pirate' or 'mafia' taxis, which do not display a phone number or company logo – the drivers may try to overcharge you and turn rude and aggressive if you question the fare. They hang out at central taxi ranks and in the vicinity of luxury hotels and tourist sights, and may approach you in the arrivals hall at the airport.

All official taxis in Warsaw have their meters adjusted to the appropriate tariff, so you just pay what the meter says. When you board a taxi, make sure the meter is turned on in your presence, which ensures you don't have the previous passenger's fare added to yours. Taxis can be waved down on the street, but it is better to order a taxi by phone; there's no extra charge for this service.

AROUND WARSAW

KAMPINOS NATIONAL PARK

☎ 22

Popularly known as the Puszcza Kampinoska, the **Kampinos National Park** (Kampinoski Park Narodowy; ☎ 722 60 01) begins just outside Warsaw's northwestern administrative boundaries and stretches west for about 40km. It's one of the largest national parks in Poland, with around three-quarters of its area covered by forest, mainly pine and oak.

The park includes Europe's largest area of inland sand dunes, mostly tree-covered and up to 30m high, and some barely accessible peat bogs that shelter much of its animal life. Elks, beavers and lynxes live in the park but are hard to spot; you are more likely to see other animals such as hares, foxes, deer and, occasionally, wild boars. The park is home to some bird life,

including black storks, cranes, herons and marsh harriers.

The **Muzeum Puszczy Kampinoskiej** (Kampinos Forest Museum; ☎ 725 01 23; Granica; admission free; ⏰ 9am-4pm Tue-Sun) is 1km west of the village of Kampinos on the southern boundary of the park, and has an exhibition on Poland's national parks as well as a small skansen (open-air museum of traditional architecture) of forest buildings.

The park is popular with hikers from the capital, who take advantage of its 300km of marked walking and cycling trails. The eastern part of the park, closer to the city, is more favoured by walkers as it's accessible by public transport; the western part is less visited. As well as half- and one-day hikes, there are two long trails that traverse the entire length of the park, both starting from Dziekanów Leśny on the eastern edge of the park. The red trail (54km) ends in Brochów, and the green one (51km) in Żelazowa Wola.

If you plan on hiking in the park, buy a copy of the Compass *Kampinoski Park Narodowy* map (scale 1:30,000), available from bookshops in Warsaw (see p59).

There are no hotels within the park but there are several bivouac sites designated for camping. There are hotels just outside the park's boundaries in Czosnów, Laski, Leszno, Tułowice and Zaborów. Ask at one of Warsaw's tourist information centres (p61) for a full list of places to stay near the park.

Getting There & Away

The most popular jumping-off point for walks in the eastern part of the park is the village of Truskaw. To get there from central Warsaw, take tram 4 or 36 northbound on ul Marszałkowska to Plac Wilsona, then city bus 708 (two or three an hour on weekdays, hourly on Saturday).

PKS buses run from Warszawa Zachodnia bus terminal to Kampinos (8zł, one hour, three daily).

ŻELAZOWA WOLA

☎ 46

Frédéric Chopin was born on 22 February 1810 in the tiny village of Żelazowa Wola (zheh-lah-*zo*-vah *vo*-lah), 53km west of Warsaw on the edge of the Kampinos National Park. The house where he was born has been restored and furnished in period style, and is now a **museum** (☎ 863

33 00; adult/student museum & park ticket 12/6zł, park only 4/2zł; ☻ 9.30am-5.30pm Tue-Sun May-Sep, 10am-4pm Tue-Sun Oct-Apr). It's a lovely little country house with beautiful gardens, but there is little in the way of original memorabilia. Nonetheless, the tranquillity and charm of the place make it a pleasant stop.

Piano recitals, often performed by top-rank virtuosos, are held here each Sunday from the first Sunday in May to the last Sunday before 17 October, the anniversary of Chopin's death. There are usually two concerts, up to an hour long, at 11am and 3pm; there's no fee other than the park-only entrance ticket. Check the programme in Warsaw (at the tourist information centre, p61, or the Chopin Museum, p70) before setting off.

There's a restaurant opposite the entrance to the museum, but nowhere to stay overnight. The nearest accommodation is in Sochaczew, 6km away.

Getting There & Away

PKS buses run from the Warszawa Zachodnia bus terminal to Żelazowa Wola (10zł, 1¼ hours, three a day). There's a morning departure from Warsaw at 9.45am; a bus returning to Warsaw leaves Żelazowa Wola at 4.38pm.

Several travel agencies in Warsaw put together organised tours for the Sunday concerts – a more comfortable option. The tourist information office of the Chopin Museum can provide a list.

Mazovia & Podlasie

If Poland is at the heart of Europe, then Mazovia lies at the heart of Poland. The former duchy of Mazovia (Mazowsze in Polish) is Warsaw's ancient hinterland, a rolling agricultural landscape dotted with castles and cathedrals and riven by three mighty rivers – the Vistula, the Narew and the Bug. It's a largely rural region, save for Łódź – Poland's top textile town, film capital and second-largest city, famed for its golden mile of restaurants, bars and Art Nouveau buildings on ul Piotrkowska. Mazovia's other sights are mainly palaces, parks, castles and churches, along with the historic riverside towns of Płock and Pułtusk.

Podlasie lies to the east, stretching away towards the border with Belarus. As you head into its wooded plains the landscape becomes more rustic, its villages made up of traditional wooden houses, with milk cows grazing by the roadside, turf-roofed potato stores in the gardens, and old ladies on bicycles wobbling along the narrow, potholed roads. The main attraction here is the great outdoors – spotting wild European bison through the moss-draped boughs of Białowieża's primeval forest, paddling a canoe through the 'African Queen' reedscapes of the Biebrza River basin, or cuddling up on a winter sledge ride through the Białowieża woods.

MAZOVIA & PODLASIE

HIGHLIGHTS

- **Dining Out**
  The restaurants along Łódź' ul Piotrkowska (p101)

- **Sleeping In**
  Castle comforts at Pułtusk's Dom Polonii (p110)

- **Architecture**
  Nieborów's aristocratic palace (p104)

- **Offbeat**
  The romantic follies of Arkadia (p104)

- **Timber Technology**
  The working water mill at Ciechanowiec (p112)

- **About in a Boat**
  A kayak tour in Biebrza National Park (p117)

- **Wildlife**
  Bison-spotting in Białowieża National Park (p121)

- **Religious Tradition**
  The colourful Corpus Christi procession in Łowicz (p104)

★ Biebrza National Park
★ Białowieża National Park
★ Pułtusk
★ Ciechanowiec
★ Arkadia
★ Łowicz ★ Nieborów
★ Łódź

| ■ TELEPHONE CODES: 23, 24, 25, 42, 46, 85, 86 | ■ POPULATION: 8,986,000 (including Warsaw) | ■ AREA: 76,118 SQ KM |

MAZOVIA & PODLASIE

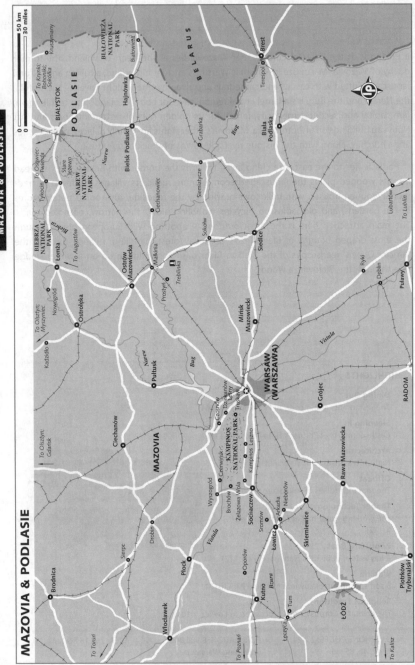

WESTERN MAZOVIA

ŁÓDŹ

☎ 42 / pop 793,200

Łódź (pronounced woodge) is a lively, likeable city, well off the usual tourist trail, and has some attractive Art Nouveau architecture at its heart. The city is also home to Poland's biggest film studios and one of Europe's most famous film schools (established 1948), whose alumni include most of the great figures of Polish cinema, such as Polański, Wajda and Kieślowski (it was only a matter of time before someone dreamed up the groan-inducing nickname 'Holly-Łódź').

At first sight Łódź can appear sprawling, grubby and run-down, but this is only half the picture. Although there isn't a single city building more than 200 years old, there is an enormous wealth of 19th- and early-20th-century architecture, and in recent years there has been a concerted effort from the authorities to brighten up the city centre.

History

By Polish standards Łódź is a relatively young place, but rapid industrial development in the 19th and 20th centuries saw it grow to become Poland's second-largest city, its fortune founded on the textile industry – it has been called the Polish Manchester. Although the first account of its existence dates from the 14th century, it remained an obscure settlement until the beginning of the 19th century. In the 1820s the government of the Congress Kingdom of Poland embarked on a programme to industrialise the country, and Łódź was selected to be a new textile centre. It subsequently underwent an unprecedented economic boom.

Enterprising industrialists – Poles, Jews and Germans alike – rushed in to build textile mills, closely followed by workers flooding into the city. The arrival of the steam engine in 1838 and the abolition of customs barriers to Russia in 1850 only increased the city's prosperity. Wealthy mill owners built opulent palaces while drab proletarian suburbs spread out around the centre. By the outbreak of WWI, Łódź had grown a thousandfold, reaching a population of half a million.

Following WWI the city's growth slowed, mainly because of the loss of the huge Russian market, but industrial sectors such as machinery and chemistry continued to expand. In the 1930s ethnic Poles made up only half the population; the rest were mostly Jews and Germans. During WWII the Nazi occupiers created a Jewish ghetto in Łódź, as they did in the capital – around 200,000 Jews from Greater Poland, Germany, Austria, Czechoslovakia and Luxembourg passed through the Łódź ghetto. Unlike Warsaw, however, the city escaped major destruction during WWII, and Łódź continued as Poland's textile capital, responsible for nearly half of Poland's textile production, though this figure has dropped in recent years.

Orientation

Ul Piotrkowska is Łódź' 3.6km-long north–south backbone. Most of the city's tourist sights, hotels and restaurants are on or near this street. The main train station, Łódź Fabryczna, and the Dworzec Centralny PKS (Państwowa Komunikacja Samochodowa) bus station are next to each other, two blocks east of the northern end of ul Piotrkowska. A second train station, Łódź Kaliska, lies 1.5km west of Piotrkowska.

Information

BOOKSHOPS

EMPiK ul Narutowicza (ul Narutowicza 8/10; ☺ 10am-7pm Mon-Fri, 10am-3pm Sat); ul Piotrkowska (ul Piotrkowska 81; ☺ 9am-9pm Mon-Sat, 11am-7pm Sun) Good range of foreign newspapers and magazines at the ul Piotrkowska branch.

Księgarnia Oxpol (☎ 630 20 13; ul Piotrkowska 63; ☺ 10am-6pm Mon-Fri, 10am-3pm Sat) English-language books.

INTERNET ACCESS

C@fé del Mundo (☎ 633 68 67; 2nd fl, ul Piotrkowska 53; per hr 1.50zł ; ☺ 9am-midnight) Attractive place with 45 computers.

Internet Matrix Caffé (☎ 632 68 06; ul Piotrkowska 83; per hr 2zł; ☺ 9am-midnight) Grungy basement café full of teenage gamers.

Silver Zone (☎ 639 58 00; Al Piłsudskiego 5; per hr 6zł; ☺ 10am-11pm) Comfy seats and fast connections.

MONEY

There are many *kantors* (private currency-exchange offices) and ATMs along ul Piotrkowska and on the adjacent streets. The

MAZOVIA & PODLASIE

ŁÓDŹ

0 — 300 m
0 — 0.2 miles

To Dworzec Północny (300m),
Hotel Urzędu
Miasta (400m)

To Teatr
Muzyczny
(200m)

Plac Wolności

To Plac
Dąbrowskiego

To Camping
Nr 167 Na
Rogach
(5km)

Łódź Fabryczna
Train Station

Łódź Kaliska
Train Station

Galeria Łódzka
Shopping Centre

To Priest's Mill
(1km)

To Hotel Boss
(1.5km)

To Camping Stawy
Jana (4km)

INFORMATION	
Bank Pekao	1 C2
C@fé del Mundo	2 C2
Centrum Informacji Kulturalnej	3 C4
Centrum Informacji Turystycznej	4 C4
EMPiK	5 C2
EMPiK	6 C3
Eurotravel	7 C3
Internet Matrix Caffé	8 C3
Księgarnia Oxpol	9 C3
Main Post Office	10 D3
Orbis Travel	11 C3
Silver Zone	(see 41)

SIGHTS & ACTIVITIES	(pp99–100)
Cathedral	12 C6
City Art Gallery	13 C3
Historical Museum of Łódź	14 C1
Modern Art Museum	15 B2
Museum of Ethnography & Archaeology	16 C1
Textile Museum	17 D6

SLEEPING	(p101)
Hotel Grand	18 C3
Hotel Polonia	19 D2
Hotel Savoy	20 C3
Pensjonat Déjà Vu	21 D5
Youth Hostel Legionów	22 B1
Youth Hostel Zamenhofa	23 C4

EATING	(pp101–2)
Bar Kaskada	24 C3
Greenway	25 C3
Hort-Café	26 C3
Karczma u Chochoła	27 C5
Karczma u Chochoła	28 C3
Mexican	(see 37)
Restauracja Krokodyl	29 D6
Restauracja Sphinx	30 D6
Restauracja Sphinx	31 C4
Restauracja Sphinx	32 C3
Tesco	33 D4

DRINKING	(p102)
Bufet Łódź Kaliska	34 C3
Irish Pub 77	35 C3
Piotrkowska Klub	36 C3
Prêt á Café	37 C3

ENTERTAINMENT	(pp102–3)
Filharmonia Łódzka	38 C5
Kino Cytryna	39 C2
Łódzki Dom Kultury	40 D2
Silver Screen	41 C4
Teatr im Stefana Jaracza	42 D2
Teatr Powszechny	43 B1
Teatr Wielki	44 D2

TRANSPORT	(p103)
Dworzec Centralny PKS	45 D2

main branch of **Bank Pekao** (☎ 637 03 33; Al Kościuszki 47; ☼ 8am-6pm Mon-Fri, 10am-2pm Sat), which has a dozen branch offices around town, cashes American Express travellers cheques and gives cash advances on Visa and MasterCard.

POST
Main post office (☎ 633 94 52; ul Tuwima 38; ☼ 24hr)

TOURIST INFORMATION
Centrum Informacji Kulturalnej (Cultural Information Centre; ☎ 633 92 21; www.cik.lodz.pl in Polish; ul Zamenhofa 1/3; ☼ 10am-6pm Mon-Fri, 10am-2pm Sat) Info on cultural events and what's on.

Centrum Informacji Turystycznej (Tourist Information Centre; ☎ 638 59 56; www.uml.lodz.pl; Al Kościuszki 88; ☼ 8am-6pm Mon-Fri, 9am-1pm Sat) General tourist information; pick up the free magazine *Welcome to Łódź*.

TRAVEL AGENCIES
Eurotravel (☎ 630 44 88; Al Kościuszki 22; ☼ 9.30am-5.30pm Mon-Fri, 10am-1pm Sat) Youth travel, domestic and international bus tickets, Eurolines.

Orbis Travel (☎ 636 61 26; ul Piotrkowska 68; ☼ 9am-6pm Mon-Fri, 10am-2pm Sat) General travel.

Sights
UL PIOTRKOWSKA
The backbone of the city is the ramrod-straight, 3.6km-long, mostly pedestrianised thoroughfare of ul Piotrkowska, a vibrant avenue lined with restaurants, pubs, open-air cafés, art galleries and elegant shops, and a stage for festivals, buskers, happenings and street theatre. Many historical façades have been restored, making this Poland's finest Art Nouveau street. Most of Łódź' sights lie within a few blocks of Piotrkowska.

HISTORICAL MUSEUM OF ŁÓDŹ
A good starting point for your explorations is the **Historical Museum of Łódź** (Muzeum Historii Miasta Łodzi; ☎ 654 03 23; ul Ogrodowa 15; adult/concession 6/3zł, free Wed; ☼ 10am-4pm Tue & Thu, 10am-2pm Fri-Sun, 2-6pm Wed), near the northern extremity of ul Piotrkowska. It's housed in the magnificent palace of the Poznański family, who were among the wealthiest of the city's Jewish textile magnates. The main attraction is the ornately decorated interior – more like a prince's palace than a businessperson's – but the museum also features

exhibitions on Łódź' history, the Łódź ghetto, and famous citizens including pianist Artur Rubinstein, writer Jerzy Kosiński and poet Julian Tuwim. All three, of Jewish origin, were born in Łódź.

MUSEUM OF ETHNOGRAPHY & ARCHAEOLOGY
Nearby, on the former market place of Plac Wolności (Liberty Sq), is the **Museum of Ethnography & Archaeology** (Muzeum Archeologiczne i Etnograficzne; ☎ 632 84 40; Plac Wolności 14; adult/concession 6/4zł, free Tue; ☼ 10am-5pm Tue, Thu & Fri, 9am-4pm Wed, 9am-3pm Sat, 10am-3pm Sun), which features archaeological finds from central Poland, dating from the Stone Age to the Middle Ages, and regional ethnographic exhibitions.

MODERN ART MUSEUM
Two blocks west of ul Piotrkowska, the **Modern Art Museum** (Muzeum Sztuki; ☎ 633 97 90; ul Więckowskiego 36; adult/concession 6/4zł, free Thu; ☼ 10am-5pm Tue, 11am-5pm Wed & Fri, noon-7pm Thu, 10am-4pm Sat & Sun) contains an extensive collection of 20th-century paintings, drawings, sculpture and photography from Poland and abroad, as well as many works by contemporary artists. There are also works by Picasso, Chagall and Ernst (not always on display).

CITY ART GALLERY
Nearby is the **City Art Gallery** (Miejska Galeria Sztuki; ☎ 632 79 95; ul Wólczańska 31/33; adult/concession 4/2zł; ☼ noon-5pm Tue-Fri, noon-4pm Sat & Sun), housed in a handsome 1903 Art Nouveau villa that once belonged to a German industrialist, Leopold Kindermann. It hosts temporary exhibitions, usually by contemporary Polish artists, and the building itself is well worth a look for its own sake.

TEXTILE MUSEUM
Near the southern end of ul Piotrkowska stands the **Textile Museum** (Centralne Muzeum Włókiennictwa; ☎ 683 26 84; ul Piotrkowska 282; adult/concession 6/4zł, free Fri; ☼ 9am-5pm Tue, Wed & Fri, 11am-7pm Thu, 11am-4pm Sat & Sun). Located inside one of the city's oldest textile mills, dating from the 1830s, it houses a collection of machinery ranging from early looms to contemporary devices. Fabrics, clothing and other objects related to the industry are on the 1st floor.

MAZOVIA & PODLASIE

PRIEST'S MILL

A grand villa dating from 1875, the **Priest's Mill** (Księży Młyn; ☎ 674 96 98; ul Przędzalniana 72; adult/concession 6/3zł; ⏰ 10am-5pm Tue, noon-5pm Wed & Fri, noon-7pm Thu, 11am-4pm Sat & Sun) is the former residence of the wealthy Herbst family, and is now a museum showing how the pre-WWII barons of industry lived. Although the owners fled abroad before the war, taking all the furnishings and works of art with them, the interior has been restored and furnished like the original. It's 1.5km east of the Textile Museum (a 20-minute walk along ul Tymienieckiego, or take bus 55).

JEWISH GHETTO

In May 1940 the Nazis sealed off the northern part of Łódź city centre to create a Jewish ghetto (called the Litzmannstadt Ghetto, after the German name for Łódź). Between then and August 1944 around 200,000 Jews passed through its gates; when the Red Army liberated Łódź in 1945, fewer than 900 Jewish survivors remained. The tourist information centre provides a leaflet outlining a guided walk through the former ghetto.

JEWISH CEMETERY

In 1892 the **Jewish Cemetery** (Cmentarz Żydowski; ☎ 656 70 19; ul Bracka 40; admission 4zł; ⏰ 9am-5pm Sun-Thu, 9am-3pm Fri) was founded to provide a final resting place for members of the large and steadily growing Jewish community. Covering an area of about 40 hectares, this is the largest Jewish graveyard in Europe, with around 68,000 surviving tombstones, some of which are very beautiful. The cemetery is about 3km northeast of the centre. Take tram 1 from ul Kilińskiego or 6 from Al Kościuszki. The cemetery's entrance is from ul Zmienna, close to the tram terminus; men will need a head cover to get in.

Festivals & Events

Łódź Ballet Meetings A dance and ballet festival that includes both Polish and foreign groups, and runs for two weeks in May of every odd-numbered year. Performances are staged in the Teatr Wielki.

International Tapestry Triennial International exhibition of the art of tapestry and other textile art. The main exhibition is held in the Textile Museum from June to October, and is accompanied by other displays in private art galleries. The 12th triennial will be held in 2007.

Camerimage (www.camerimage.pl) Held over seven days in late November/early December. An international

---

HOLLY-ŁÓDŹ BOULEVARD

Running right through the heart of the city, ul Piotrkowska is Łódź' main commercial artery, feeding crowds of shoppers, tourists, diners and drinkers into its surrounding network of shops, restaurants, cafés and bars.

Ul Piotrkowska started life in the 19th century as the road to Piotrków Trybunalski (hence its name), then the major town of the region. By the beginning of the 20th century Piotrkowska was an elegant boulevard, lined with Art Nouveau buildings and expensive restaurants, but in the wake of WWII it became a gloomy, grey street of soot-blackened façades and a handful of half-empty shops, much the same as city streets all over communist Poland. Its revival began in the 1990s, when the Piotrkowska Street Foundation was created by a group of local artists and architects with the aim of turning the derelict street into a lively European city mall.

In front of the famous **Hotel Grand** at No 72, which has been in business since 1888, is the **Aleja Gwiazd** (Ave of the Stars), a series of bronze stars set in the pavement in imitation of Los Angeles' Hollywood Blvd, each dedicated to a well-known name in Polish film. Nearby, in front of the house (No 78) where the eminent Polish pianist once lived, is **Rubinstein's Piano**, a bronze monument much loved by tourists who have their photo taken sitting next to the great man's image. A few paces down the street is **Tuwim's Bench** (at No 104), another unusual monument, this one created in memory of local poet Julian Tuwim. Touch his nose – it's supposed to bring good luck. The last of the series is **Reymont's Chest** (at No 135), showing the Nobel prize winner in literature, Władysław Reymont, sitting on a large travel trunk.

Although the northern half of ul Piotrkowska is pedestrianised, public transport is provided by a fleet of **bicycle rickshaws** (rikszą; ☎ 919, from a mobile phone ☎ 0800 500 919); for a small fee they will whisk you from one end to the other, and you can even order one by phone, as you would a taxi.

festival celebrating the art of cinematography. Screenings are staged in the Teatr Wielki.

Sleeping

The low number of foreign tourists visiting the city means that Łódź' hotel scene is aimed mainly at the business and trade fair market, and few places have anything in the way of character.

BUDGET

Youth Hostel Legionów (☎ 630 66 80; www.ptsm.pl /lodz; ul Legionów 27; dm 18-30zł, s/d from 45/70zł; P X) With hotel-quality singles and doubles equipped with radio, TV and private bathroom, plus a café and a gym on the premises, this place is one of Poland's best youth hostels. There's a 24-hour reception but a 10pm curfew, and alcohol is banned. It's often full so it pays to book ahead.

Youth Hostel Zamenhofa (☎ 636 65 99; ul Zamenhofa 13; dm 18-30zł, s/d 45/70zł) The city's second hostel is not quite as spiffy as the Legionów one, having fewer and smaller rooms with shared facilities. It's normally open Thursday to Monday unless booked in advance by groups, or if the other hostel is full.

Camping Nr 167 Na Rogach (☎ 659 70 13; ul Łupkowa 10/16; tent site 8-10zł, car 12zł, d 68-98zł; P) This camping ground is about 5km northeast of the city centre, on the Łowicz road. It has heated wooden chalets available year-round, and attractive, sheltered tent pitches. It's accessible by bus 56 or 60 from ul Narutowicza near Łódź Fabryczna train station.

Camping Stawy Jana (☎ 646 15 51; ul Rzgowska 247; tent site per person 5zł, car 5zł, s/d 35/70zł; P) Stawy Jana is part of a sports centre, and offers a choice between your own tent or heated chalets. It's 5km south of the centre on the Piotrków Trybunalski road. Take tram 5 from ul Kilińskiego near Łódź Fabryczna station to the end of the line and continue walking south for 500m.

MID-RANGE

Hotel Boss (☎ 672 48 89; www.hotel-boss.pl; ul Tatrzańska 11; s/d from 80/110zł; P X) Looks a bit of a soulless concrete box from the outside, but some effort has been made to make the rooms feel homy. It's a bit of a hike from the centre – 10 minutes from central ul Piotrkowska on tram 7 or 13 – but comfortable and good value.

Hotel Polonia (☎ 632 87 73; www.hotelspt.com .pl; ul Narutowicza 38; s/d 75/110zł, with private bathroom 125/140zł) The ageing Polonia (built in 1932) is badly in need of a makeover – the standard rooms are stuck in the 1970s, as are the cheaper rooms with shared bathrooms. But the main attraction is the plum location, just a few minutes' walk from both ul Piotrkowska and the train and bus stations.

Hotel Urzędu Miasta (☎ 640 66 09; fax 640 66 45; ul Bojowników Getta Warszawskiego 9; s/d/tr 100/144/180zł) This hotel is run by the city council and provides basic, characterless accommodation, but at just 500m north of Plac Wolności it's not a bad trade-off of price versus location.

TOP END

Pensjonat Déjà Vu (☎ 636 20 60; ziemiaobiecana@lodz online.com; ul Wigury 4/6; d 260zł; P) This charming guesthouse, set in a grand villa dating from 1925, has preserved the style and décor of the original house, with dark wood panelling, brass bedsteads, stained glass and period furniture; even the receptionist is dressed in 1920s style! There are just six double rooms, so advance booking is essential.

Hotel Grand (☎ 633 99 20; www.orbis.pl; ul Piotrkowska 72; s 190-348zł, d 190-433zł; P X) The old-fashioned Grand is the city's longest-running hotel, slap bang in the middle of all the action on ul Piotrkowska. Opened in 1888 at the peak of the textile boom, it was for a long time the city's top hotel, hosting such distinctive guests as Pablo Casals and Isadora Duncan. The public areas still retain a turn-of-the-century atmosphere, but the rooms, while comfortable, are mostly modern and bland.

Hotel Savoy (☎ 632 93 60; fax 632 93 68; ul Traugutta 6; s/d 150/220zł) The Savoy is not as dignified as the Grand, but still has a great location, a five-minute walk from both the train station and ul Piotrkowska. Standard rooms are communist brown-and-beige in both colour and character, but there are also 'retro style' rooms (235zł for a single, 310zł for a double) where new carpets, wallpaper and 'old style' furniture try to create some period atmosphere.

Eating

Karczma U Chochoła (☎ 632 51 38; ul Traugutta 3; mains 18-46zł; ☉ noon-11pm Sun-Thu, noon-midnight Fri & Sat) U Chochoła is a family restaurant

MAZOVIA & PODLASIE

dressed up like a traditional country inn, with timber beams, chunky wooden tables and chairs, and folksy art on the walls. It serves typical old-style Polish farmhouse fare, such as borscht and roast pork, and has an outdoor dining area at the back. There's a second branch at ul Piotrkowska 200 (same hours and prices), holding live jazz on Friday at 9pm.

Mexican (☎ 633 68 68; ul Piotrkowska 67; mains 15-30zł; ◷ 11.30-2am) Waitresses in not-quite-flamenco dresses (is the bare midriff traditional?) and waiters in not-quite-sombreros try to inject some Latin atmosphere into this bright and lively courtyard restaurant set around a tinkling fountain. Reasonable margaritas, tasty fajitas, and Latino music from 7pm Tuesday to Saturday.

Restauracja Krokodyl (☎ 630 52 62; ul Piotrkowska 88; mains 25-40zł; ◷ 9am-midnight) Dark wood and cream linen lend a clean, minimalist feel to this posh bar and restaurant. The menu is international, but includes a good selection of Polish country classics including sharp, tangy żurek (traditional sour rye soup), roast duck and saddle of lamb.

Greenway (☎ 632 08 52; ul Piotrkowska 80; mains 6.50-8zł; ◷ 10-1am) An attractive, modern vegetarian café-bar serving a range of appealing dishes such as Mexican goulash (with beans and sweet corn), Indian vegetable kofta and spinach dumplings.

Restauracja Sphinx (☎ 632 23 68; ul Piotrkowska 93; mains 10-20zł; ◷ noon-11pm Sun-Thu, noon-midnight Fri & Sat) Part of a chain that was born in Łódź but now has branches all over Poland, this strangely Egyptian-themed place (palm trees, pyramids and sphinxes) offers a choice of Middle Eastern (shawarma, shashlik and doner kebab) or Polish (grilled chicken, steak and pork) fast food, generous portions and fast service. There are other branches at ul Piotrkowska 175a and 270.

Hort-Café (☎ 636 63 77; ul Piotrkowska 106/110; mains 8-20zł; ◷ 9am-8pm Mon-Sat, 11am-8pm Sun) Part bakery and part café, this homy little place serves pastries, cream cakes, milk shakes, ice cream, light meals, salads and crepes in a pot plant– and flower-bedecked space. There's an outdoor summer terrace (and two trees growing right through the roof!).

For a quick, cafeteria-style meal, try **Bar Kaskada** (☎ 633 50 92; ul Narutowicza 7/9; mains 2-5zł; ◷ 10am-6pm Mon-Fri, 10am-4pm Sat & Sun). Self-caterers can head for the **Tesco supermarket** (☎ 635 70 00; Al Piłsudskiego 15; ◷ 8am-9pm Mon-Sat, 9am-8pm Sun) in the huge Galeria Łódźa shopping centre.

Drinking

Pret á Café (☎ 632 92 03; ul Piotrkowska 67; ◷ 9am-1pm Mon-Fri, 11am-10pm Sat, noon-10pm Sun) Half café-bar and half boutique, this cool little corner of minimalist chic, in an alley off ul Piotrkowska, has framed designer dresses on the wall, fashion mags lying on the taupe leather banquettes, a mini-catwalk for impromptu fashion shows and a rack of fancy frocks to flick through.

Bufet Łódź Kaliska (☎ 630 69 55; ul Piotrkowska 102) A spacious but smoky two-level club done up in a grungy décor of overlapping concert posters and scuffed café tables, Łódź Kaliska is an energetic drinking den and live music venue that pulls in a broad cross-section of Łódź society. In summer the crowds spill out onto an outdoor terrace in the street.

Piotrkowska Klub (☎ 632 24 78; ul Piotrkowska 97) This place is easily recognisable by the two-storey, wrought-iron and glass drinking area that stands outside the front door. Looking a bit like a flower-festooned tram and offering great views up and down ul Piotrkowska, it's called the Akwarium and is the most popular part of a pub that includes a retro-style, wood-panelled and studded-leather bar and an intimate club room with low lighting and cosy booths.

Irish Pub 77 (☎ 632 48 76; ul Piotrkowska 77) Brick and tile floors, wood panelling and pub mirrors on the wall, polished glasses above the bar and a young, smartly dressed staff – all the usual 'Irish pub' boxes are ticked here, including Guinness and Kilkenny on tap. There's a big beer garden out back and a menu of hearty pub grub, such as grilled pork and roast veg served on a wooden platter.

Entertainment

The **Centrum Informacji Kulturalnej** (Cultural Information Centre; ☎ 633 92 21; www.cik.lodz.pl in Polish; ul Zamenhofa 1/3; ◷ 10am-6pm Mon-Fri, 10am-2pm Sat) is the best place to find out what's on, and also sells tickets for some shows. You can pick up the monthly *Kalejdoskop*, which details (in Polish) what's going on in local theatres, cinemas, art galleries and museums, or check out the website www.reymont.pl.

CINEMAS

As home to Poland's film industry, Łódź is well supplied with cinemas. The most convenient city centre ones:

Łódzki Dom Kultury (Łódź Cultural Centre; ☎ 633 98 00; ul Traugutta 18; admission 10-12zł) Two screens mostly showing box-office hits.

Kino Cytryna (☎ 632 18 59; ul Zachodnia 81/83; admission 10-12zł) Mix of Hollywood and art-house cinema.

Silver Screen (☎ 639 58 58; Al Piłsudskiego 5; admission 14-18zł) Ten-screen multiplex.

OPERA, THEATRE & CLASSICAL MUSIC

Teatr Wielki (Grand Theatre; ☎ 633 99 60; Plac Dąbrowskiego; ☿ box office noon-7pm Tue-Sat, 3-7pm Sun) The city's main venue for opera and ballet also stages festival events and visiting shows.

Filharmonia Łódzka (Łódź Philharmonic; ☎ 637 14 82; www.filharmonia.lodz.pl; ul Piotrkowska 243; ☿ box office noon-4pm Mon-Thu, from 3pm on performance days) Stages regular concerts of classical music every Friday and occasionally on other days of the week.

Some of the city's other theatre venues:

Teatr Muzyczny (Music Theatre; ☎ 678 19 68; ul Północna 47/51) Stages mostly operettas and musicals.

Teatr im Stefana Jaracza (☎ 632 66 18; ul Jaracza 27) Among the most respected drama theatres in Poland.

Teatr Powszechny (☎ 633 50 36; ul Legionów 21) Polish drama.

Getting There & Away

BUS

The **Dworzec Centralny PKS** (central bus station; ☎ 631 97 06; Plac Sałacińskiego 1) is right outside Łódź Fabryczna train station. There are buses to Warsaw (23zł, 2½ hours, seven daily), Płock (22zł, three hours, five daily), Kielce and Radom. Polski Express buses run to Warsaw airport (30zł, 2½ hours, three daily), Gdańsk (60zł, 6¼ hours, one daily) and Kraków (57zł, six hours, two daily) via Częstochowa and Katowice.

Buses to Łowicz depart from the **Dworzec Północny** (northern bus terminal; ☎ 616 04 33; ul Smugowa 30/32), 1km north of Dworzec Centralny.

TRAIN

The city has two train stations. **Łódź Fabryczna** (station ☎ 636 55 55, train info ☎ 94 36; Plac Sałacińskiego 1), which is a few blocks east of ul Piotrkowska, is the main station for Warsaw (29zł, 1¾ hours, at least hourly) and Kraków (38zł, 3½ hours, one daily). **Łódź**

Kaliska (station ☎ 664 44 04, train info ☎ 93 14; Al Unii Lubelskiej 3/5), to the west of the city centre, handles trains to Wrocław (42zł, four hours, three daily), Poznań (40zł, 3½ hours, four daily) and Łowicz (11zł, 1¾ hours, six daily). You also use this station for Toruń, Bydgoszcz, Kalisz and Gdańsk.

Getting Around

Łódź' public transport system is operated by **Miejskie Przedsiębiorstwo Komunikacyjne** (MPK; info ☎ 672 11 12), and includes trams and buses, both of which use the same ticket system. A ticket becomes valid for a set length of time after you validate it in the machine on board, and remains valid for unlimited transfers between bus and tram lines. There are 10-, 30-, 60- and 120-minute tickets available, which cost 1.50zł, 2.20zł, 3.30zł and 4.40zł respectively; A 24-hour ticket costs 8.80zł.

You can order a taxi from **Euro Taxi** (☎ 646 46 46, 96 67). The **bicycle rickshaws** (☎ 919, from a mobile phone ☎ 0800 515 919) that ply ul Piotrkowska can be ordered by phone, and cost around 5zł to 10zł per trip (two passengers maximum).

ŁOWICZ

☎ 46 / pop 32,000

Founded in the 12th century, Łowicz (*wo-veech*) was the seat of the archbishops of Gniezno – the supreme Church authority in Poland – for over 600 years. Best known for the massive cathedral overlooking its central square, Łowicz is also a regional centre for folk arts and crafts, best seen during the elaborate celebrations of Corpus Christi (Boże Ciało).

Information

Polskie Towarzystwo Turystyczno-Krajoznawcze (PTTK; Polish Tourist & Countryside Association; ☎ 837 32 69; Stary Rynek 3; ☿ 9am-4pm Mon-Fri) On the main square. Provides tourist information.

Sights

The vast 15th-century **Łowicz Cathedral** (☎ 837 62 66; Stary Rynek 24/30) dominates Stary Rynek (Old Town Sq). Originally Gothic, it underwent several renovations and now reflects a mishmash of styles, including Renaissance, baroque and rococo. Twelve archbishops of Gniezno and primates of Poland are buried in the church.

MAZOVIA & PODLASIE

On the opposite side of the square is **Łowicz Museum** (☎ 837 39 28; Stary Rynek 5/7; adult/concession 7/4zł, free Sat; ☯ 10am-4pm Tue-Sun, closed days following public holidays), housed in a 17th-century missionary college designed by prolific Dutch architect Tylman van Gameren. The former priests' chapel, its vault decorated with baroque frescoes (1695) by Italian artist Michelangelo Palloni, houses the baroque art section. The 1st floor is devoted to the archaeology of the region and the history of Łowicz. The 2nd floor boasts a collection of local folk costumes, decorated wooden furniture, coloured paper cutouts, painted Easter eggs, pottery and woodcarving. In the back garden of the museum are two old **farmsteads** from the region, complete with original furnishings, implements and decoration.

Festivals & Events

Łowicz' main religious event is **Corpus Christi** (which falls on a Thursday in May or June) during which a procession, with most of its participants dressed in brightly coloured and embroidered traditional costumes, circles the main square and the cathedral. This is the most solemn celebration of Corpus Christi in the country, and it's the best time to visit Łowicz and get a real feel for the devout Catholicism of rural Poland. The procession starts at around noon and takes roughly two hours to complete the whole circuit.

Sleeping & Eating

Youth hostel (☎ 837 37 03; ul Grunwaldzka 9; dm 8-12zł; ☯ Jul & Aug) This basic, summer-only hostel is housed in a primary school next to the Warsaw–Poznań highway, 1.5km north of Stary Rynek.

Hotel Aneta (☎ 837 04 48; hotel_aneta@lowicz .com.pl; ul Powstańców 1883r 12; d/tr 45/60zł, d with bathroom 80zł) A former workers' dormitory built from prefabricated panels, the small, basic rooms of this hotel are not the stuff of luxury, but will do in a pinch. It's about 1.5km south of the centre.

Hotel Zacisze (☎ 837 33 26; odidk@2com.pl; ul Kaliska 5; s/d/tr 85/110/170zł; ⓟ ⓘ) Located 300m south of Stary Rynek, this is a comfortable, modern place with a 1970s motel feel. It has its own reasonably priced restaurant and a covered swimming pool.

Getting There & Away

The bus and train stations are side by side, about a five-minute walk east from Stary Rynek. There are regular fast trains to Warsaw (22zł, one hour, every two hours) to and Kutno (14zł, ½ hour, hourly), and slow trains to Łódź (11zł, 1¾ hours, six daily).

AROUND ŁOWICZ
Nieborów & Arkadia
☎ 46 / pop 1500

Designed by Tylman van Gameren for Cardinal Radziejowski, archbishop of Gniezno and primate of Poland, the baroque, late-17th-century **Palace of Nieborów** (nyeh-*bo*-roof) lies 10km southeast of Łowicz.

After changing hands several times, the palace was eventually bought by Prince Michał Hieronim Radziwiłł in 1774. He and his wife Helena crammed it with valuable furniture and works of art, including paintings, antique sculptures and an imposing library. An informal, English-style landscaped park, designed by Szymon Bogumił Zug, was laid out next to the old baroque garden. A majolica (a type of porous pottery) factory, the only one in Poland at the time, was established on the grounds in 1881 and operated on and off until 1906.

In the 1920s the palace underwent its last important transformation, when a mansard storey was added to the building. The palace remained in the possession of the Radziwiłł family right up to WWII, after which, fortunately undamaged, it was taken over by the state and converted into a museum.

More than half of the palace rooms are now occupied by the **Nieborów Museum** (☎ 838 56 35; adult/concession 10/5zł, park only 5/3zł, free Mon; ☯ 10am-4pm daily Mar & Apr, 10am-6pm daily May & Jun, 10am-4pm Mon-Fri, 10am-6pm Sat & Sun Jul-Sep, 10am-3.30pm Tue-Sun Oct). Part of the ground floor features Roman sculpture and bas-reliefs, most of which date from the first centuries AD. To reach the upstairs, go up the unusual staircase clad with ornamental Dutch tiles dating from around 1700.

The whole 1st floor was restored and furnished according to the original style and contains a wealth of *objets d'art*. Take note of the tiled stoves, each one different, made in the local majolica factory, and don't miss the two late-17th-century globes in the library, the work of Venetian geographer Vincenzo Coronelli.

Warsaw's Old Town and the Sigismund III Vasa Column (p63)

Palace of Culture & Science (p70), Warsaw

Łazienki Park and the Palace
on the Water (p74), Warsaw

Streetcar, Warsaw (p91)

Women in traditional dress, Corpus Christi celebrations (p104), Łowicz

Rural architecture, Nowogród (p110)

Ruins of Arkadia (p104)

War memorial, Treblinka II, Treblinka (p111)

The **French garden** (⊙ 10am-dusk), on the southern side of the palace, has a wide central alley lined with old lime trees and is dotted with sculptures, statues, tombstones, sarcophagi, pillars, columns and other stone fragments dating from various periods. Many of them were brought from Arkadia. The **English landscaped park** (⊙ 10am-dusk), complete with stream, lake and ponds, is to the west of the garden, behind an L-shaped reservoir.

Princess Helena Radziwiłł of Nieborów palace laid out the romantic landscape park of **Arkadia** (adult/concession 5/2zł, free Mon, parking 8zł; ⊙ 10am-dusk) in the 1770s to be an 'idyllic land of peace and happiness', but after the princess' death, the park fell into decay. Most of the works of art were taken to Nieborów's palace and can be seen there today, and the abandoned buildings fell gradually into ruin. Today it is a charming, tree-shrouded secret world of ruins, peeling pavilions, temples and follies, including a red-brick **Gothic House** (Domek Gotycki) perched above **Sybil's Grotto**, a 'Roman' aqueduct, and the impressive **Archpriest's Sanctuary** (Przybytek Arcykapłana), a fanciful mock ruin dominated by a classical bas-relief of Hope feeding a Chimera. The focus of the park is **Diana's Temple** (Świątynia Diany), which overlooks the lake and houses a display of Roman sculpture and funerary monuments.

Only recently has some conservation work been carried out with the restoration of Diana's Temple and the Archpriest's Sanctuary, while most other structures and the park itself have been left virtually untouched. Paradoxically, the air of decay adds to the charm and romantic atmosphere of the place.

SLEEPING
There are no hotels in or around Nieborów, only a **Youth Hostel** (☎ /fax 838 56 94; Al Legionów Polskich 92; dm 8-12zł; ⊙ Jul & Aug), 1.5km north of the palace, on the road towards Bednary, and a camping ground, **Camping Nr 77** (☎ 838 56 92; tent site 6zł, plus per person 6zł, cabins from 45zł; ⊙ May-Oct), west of the palace park, off the Skierniewice road (an 800m walk from the park's main gate).

GETTING THERE & AWAY
Arkadia is on the south side of the Łowicz–Skierniewice road (No 70), 4km southeast

of Łowicz; Nieborów is on the same road, a further 5km beyond Arkadia. Where the main road bends sharply to the right at Nieborów, keep straight on – the palace is 300m ahead, on the right.

Slow trains from Warsaw (Warszawa Śródmieście, Warszawa Zachodnia and other commuter stations only, not Warszawa Centralna) to Łowicz stop at Mysłaków (12zł, 1¾ hours, five or six daily), the last stop before reaching Łowicz. From the station it's a 10-minute walk to Arkadia, and another 5km (around 50 minutes' walk) to Nieborów. Warsaw–Łowicz trains also stop at Bednary, which is 4km from Nieborów.

There are five or six buses daily between Łowicz and Skierniewice, stopping at both Arkadia and Nieborów.

Sromów
☎ 46 / pop 800
Sromów (*sro*-moof) is a tiny rural hamlet with one great attraction – a private **Folk Museum** (Muzeum Ludowe; ☎ 838 44 72; admission 6zł; ⊙ 9am-7pm Mon-Sat, noon-7pm Sun), founded by skilled artisan and passionate crafts collector Julian Brzozowski.

Set in a garden full of folksy statues, the museum is housed in four buildings, two of which feature animated tableaux of historic scenes and village life – a country wedding, a pageant of kings, a Corpus Christi procession in Łowicz, the four seasons on the farm, and a chapel featuring a dozen life-sized figures, built next to the museum to commemorate the pope's visit to the region in 1999. The figures are all carved from wood and painstakingly painted and costumed. The animation, with synchronised music, is driven by concealed rods and shafts powered by 28 electric motors. All this is the result of 50 years of work by Mr Brzozowski and his family. Although a little kitsch, it is unique and fascinating.

The other buildings house a collection of about 30 old horse carts and carriages, assembled by the owner from the surrounding villages. Other exhibits include traditional paper cutouts, regional costumes, folk paintings, decorated wooden chests and embroidery. If the museum appears closed (as it sometimes is during quiet seasons), ask at Mr Brzozowski's house across the road, and he or someone from the family will open it and show you around.

Though only 65km from Warsaw, the village and surrounding area are very rural – there are old wooden houses, a few thatched roofs, cows grazing on the roadside and chickens foraging everywhere.

GETTING THERE & AWAY

Sromów, 10km northeast of Łowicz, is hard to find even on detailed, large-scale maps. Driving from Warsaw, follow road No 2 (E30) towards Poznań. The minor road to Sromów is on the right, about 16km after Sochaczew, and 8km before Łowicz; there is a small sign ('Sromów – Muzeum') about 1km before the turn-off, which also has a signpost for Rybno. The museum itself is about 2km from the main road; take the first turn on the left.

Public transport is difficult. Sporadic buses from Łowicz to Rybno will let you off on the Rybno road, 1km from the museum.

ŁĘCZYCA & TUM

☎ 24 / pop 17,000 & 500

Set amid the marshes in the valley of the Bzura River, Łęczyca (wen-*chi*-tsah) is an ordinary town with a 1500-year history. It began in the 6th century when a stronghold was built 2km east of the present town site. By the 10th century a Benedictine abbey was established, and one of the first Christian churches in Poland was built. In the 12th century a monumental Romanesque collegiate church replaced the former one, and the settlement expanded. It was burnt down by the Teutonic Knights in the early 14th century, and the town was then moved to its present location, where a castle and defensive walls were erected.

During the next two centuries Łęczyca prospered, becoming the regional centre and the seat of numerous ecclesiastical synods. Later on, however, due to wars, fires and plagues, the town lost its importance. In the 19th century the defensive walls and most of the castle were sold for building material. The surviving part of the castle was restored after WWII and turned into a museum.

The focus of interest here is the **Łęczyca Museum** (☎ 721 24 49; ul Zamkowa 1; adult/concession 4/2zł; ⊙ 10am-4pm Tue-Fri, 10am-3pm Sat & Sun), set in what is left of the castle. There are modest archaeological and historical collections, and an ethnographic section that features regional artefacts, mostly woodcarving.

The original site of Łęczyca grew into an independent village and was named **Tum**. The stronghold fell into ruin but the collegiate **church** was rebuilt. It's Poland's largest Romanesque church and a fine example of the architecture from that period. Although rebuilt several times, it has essentially preserved its original 12th-century form. It's a sizable defensive construction with two circular and two square towers, and two semicircular apses on each end, all built from granite and sandstone. The interior retains Romanesque features but is influenced by later Gothic remodelling, especially in the aisles. The Romanesque portal in the porch (the entrance to the church) is one of the finest in Poland. From the same period are the fragments of the frescoes in the western apse. If the church is locked, get the keys from the priest's house, 100m east of the church, on the opposite side of the road.

Sleeping

The only reliable accommodation option is the **Zajazd Senator** (☎ /fax 721 24 04; ul Ozorkowskie Przedmieście 47, Łęczyca; d/tr 100/130zł), on the Łódź road, 3km from the centre. There's nowhere to stay or eat in Tum.

Getting There & Away

The train station is on the southern outskirts of Łęczyca. Several trains daily run north to Kutno (6zł, 40 minutes) and south to Łódź (8zł, one hour).

The bus terminal is close to the castle. There are plenty of buses to Łódź (35km), and several to Kutno (25km). Tum is only 30 minutes' walk from Łęczyca.

OPORÓW

☎ 24 / pop 1000

Lying well off the main tourist routes, the village of Oporów (oh-*po*-roof) is rarely visited, even though it may be worth a detour for its Gothic **castle**. Although it's a fairly small and not particularly elaborate construction, this is one of the few castles in Poland to have survived almost in its original form.

The fortified residence was built in the mid-15th century for Władysław Oporowski, the archbishop of Gniezno. Though it changed owners several times during its history, it underwent only a few alterations. The more important changes were the 17th-century wooden ceilings on the 1st floor, covered with Renaissance decoration, the enlargement of the windows and the construction of the terrace at the entrance.

Restored after WWII, today it houses the **Oporów Museum** (☎ 285 91 22; adult/concession 4/2zł, free Sat; ☺ 10am-4pm Tue-Sun), which features a collection of furniture, paintings, weapons and other objects dating from the 15th to the 19th centuries. The majority of the exhibits are not directly connected with the castle's history, but were acquired from old palaces and residences of the region. The castle is surrounded by a moat and a fine **park** (admission free; ☺ 8am-6pm).

Oporów is best visited using your own transport.

PŁOCK

☎ 24 / pop 130,000

Perched on a cliff high above the Vistula, Płock (pronounced pwotsk) is one of the oldest settlements in Poland. Having been neglected for decades, the Old Town has seen some restoration work in recent years, though much of the place still looks pretty run down. All the same, a couple of museums, a cathedral and a dramatic riverside setting make it worth a stop if you're in the area.

Płock was a royal residence between 1079 and 1138 and the first Mazovian town to be given a municipal charter (in 1237). Its city walls were built in the 14th century and the town developed as a wealthy trading centre until the 16th century. The flooding of the Vistula in 1532, when half the castle and part of the defensive walls slid into the river, was merely a portent of further disasters to come, and the wars, fires and plagues that struck the town in the following centuries brought its prosperity to an end. Płock never regained its former glory and failed to develop into a major city.

After WWII the new regime made Płock an industrial centre by building a large oil refinery and petrochemical plant just 2km north of the historic centre.

Information

Bank Pekao (☎ 262 77 08; ul Kwiatka 6; ☺ 8am-6pm Mon-Fri, 10am-2pm Sat) Cashes travellers cheques.
Centrum Informacji Turystycznej (Tourist Information Centre; ☎ 367 19 44; Dom Darmstadt, Stary Rynek 8; ☺ 9am-5pm Mon-Fri, 10am-2pm Sat May-Sep, 8am-4pm Mon-Fri Oct-Apr)

EMPiK (☎ 262 49 16; Plac Narutowicza 5; ☺ 9am-6pm Mon-Fri, 9am-2pm Sat) Bookstore.
Klub Internetowy Intercafé (☎ 266 45 73; ul Rembielińskiego 6a; per hr 6zł; ☺ 8am-10pm Mon-Thu, 8am-midnight Fri & Sat, 10am-11pm Sun)
Main post office (☎ 262 57 54; ul Bielska 14b; ☺ 8am-8pm Mon-Fri, 8am-2pm Sat)

Sights

The only substantial vestiges of the original Gothic **castle** are its two red-brick towers: the **Clock Tower** (Wieża Zegarowa) and the **Noblemen's Tower** (Wieża Szlachecka). The adjacent 16th-century Benedictine abbey has been extensively reconstructed and now houses the **Mazovian Museum** (Muzeum Mazowieckie; ☎ 262 44 91; ul Tumska 2; adult/concession 5/2zł, free Thu; ☺ 9am-4pm Tue-Thu & Sun, 10am-5pm Fri & Sat mid-May–Sep, 9am-3pm Wed-Fri, 9am-4pm Sat & Sun Oct–mid-May). It features exhibits on the history of the town and the castle, and houses Poland's best Art Nouveau collection, which includes furniture, paintings, sculptures, glass, ceramics and everyday utensils from Poland and beyond.

The mighty **cathedral** (admission free; ☺ 10am-5pm Mon-Sat, 2-5.30pm Sun & public holidays) was built in the 12th century, and although it lost its original Romanesque character during numerous transformations, it remains an imposing structure. Note the main doors made of sculptured bronze – copies of the original 12th-century doors commissioned by the local bishops. The originals disappeared in mysterious circumstances and reappeared in Novgorod, Russia, where they are now. The bronze relief in the tympanum above the door shows the Adoration of the Magi, with a model of the cathedral (symbolically offered as a gift) below.

The interior, topped with a Renaissance dome added in the mid-16th century, boasts a number of tombstones and altarpieces from various periods. The frescoes date from the early 20th century. The royal chapel (at the back of the north aisle) holds the sarcophagi of two Polish kings, Władysław Herman and his son Bolesław Krzywousty, who lived in Płock during their reigns.

Next to the cathedral is the **Diocesan Museum** (Muzeum Diecezjalne; ☎ 262 26 23; ul Tumska 3a; adult/concession 4/2zł; ☺ 10am-3pm Tue-Sat, 11am-4pm Sun May-Sep, 10am-1pm Wed-Sat, 11am-2pm Sun Oct-Apr), which has a collection of paintings, religious art and folk woodcarving.

MAZOVIA & PODLASIE

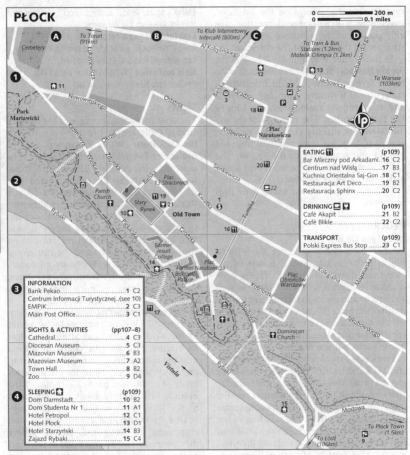

PŁOCK

0 _____ 200 m
0 _____ 0.1 miles

To the northwest of the castle and the cathedral stretches the **Old Town**. Although the street layout has been preserved largely unmodified, the architecture has changed over the centuries. Today it's the neoclassical style of the 19th century that is most noticeable, particularly on the façades of the houses lining ul Grodzka, the Old Town's main thoroughfare.

Stary Rynek (Old Town Sq) was the heart of 14th-century Płock, though today it is lined with renovated 18th- and 19th-century houses. The western side is occupied by the neoclassical **town hall** (Ratusz), built in the 1820s after the old Gothic town hall, which once sat in the middle of the square, was pulled down.

Further west are two large, recently restored 19th-century **granaries**. One of them houses an extension of the **Mazovian Museum** (☎ 262 25 95; ul Kazimierza Wielkiego 11b; adult/concession 2/1zł, free Sat; ⊗ 9am-4pm Tue-Thu & Sun, 10am-5pm Fri & Sat mid-May–Sep, 9am-3pm Wed-Fri, 9am-4pm Sat & Sun Oct–mid-May). It features temporary exhibitions of ethnographic and folk art.

From the granaries, you can return to the cathedral by a path that follows the clifftop – a pleasant walk with great views over the Vistula all the way along. To the east of the road bridge is the **Zoo** (Ogród Zoologiczny; ☎ 262 32 72; ul Norbertańska 2; adult/concession 6/3zł; ⊗ 9am-8pm May-Sep, 9am-3pm Oct-Apr), which has a picturesque wooded setting above the river. It's home to Poland's largest snake collection.

Sleeping

Dom Studenta Nr 1 (☎ 262 43 40, 262 43 58; ul Nowowiejskiego 6; dm 28zł) This year-round student hostel is the most convenient of several dorms of that type scattered across town (most others are seasonal and/or a long way from the centre). Accommodation is in four-bed rooms with shared facilities.

Motelik Olimpia (☎ 262 04 07; olimpia46@poczta .onet.pl; ul Dworcowa 46; s/d 60/80zł, with private bathroom 80/100zł; P) This is a basic little 11-room motel, with garden and barbecue, handily located directly opposite the train and bus stations.

Dom Darmstadt (☎ 264 11 11; fax 262 20 00; Stary Rynek 8; d 120zł) Ideally situated on the top floor of a historic townhouse overlooking the Rynek (the Tourist Information Centre is on the ground floor), Dom Darmstadt is a quiet, cosy place that has just three double rooms sharing one bathroom and a kitchen. Book well in advance.

Hotel Płock (☎ 262 93 93; www.hplock.plocman.pl; Al Jachowicza 38; s/d 135/150zł; P) A big, boxy modern place located on the main drag of the new town, 1km north of the old, the Hotel Płock is one of those time-warp places where the rooms may be newly decorated but still feel trapped in a time of flock wallpaper, satinet and plush upholstery. Perfectly fine, as long as you like the chintzy look.

Zajazd Rybaki (☎ /fax 264 56 57; ul Mostowa 5/7; s/d/tr 140/160/200zł; P) Set in a restored and refurbished 19th-century house near the Vistula, the 'Fisherman's Inn' provides accommodation with a bit of atmosphere, in rooms with wooden beams and river views. It has its own restaurant serving traditional Polish cooking.

Hotel Starzyński (☎ 262 40 61; www.starzynski.com .pl; ul Piekarska 1; s 190-280zł, d 250-330zł, ste 350-450zł; P) This communist-era hotel sports 'interesting' architecture – a huge lozenge-shaped block perched on the edge of the cliff above the Vistula. The décor is quirky but appealing, reminiscent of, but not quite, Art Deco. The more-expensive rooms have superb views over the river, as does the hotel restaurant.

Hotel Petropol (☎ 262 44 51; www.orbis.pl; Al Jachowicza 49; s/d 200/260zł; P ✗) The business-oriented Petropol is big, bland and very comfortable, with spacious rooms (including one adapted for wheelchair users), a small gym and English-speaking staff. The restaurant is a bit soulless though.

Eating & Drinking

Restauracja Art Deco (☎ 268 57 51; Stary Rynek 17; mains 15-40zł; ☺ 11am-11pm) Set in the middle of the sunny side of Stary Rynek, this place has the comfiest outdoor tables on the square, and a menu of Polish favourites ranging from *czernina staropolska* (ducks'-blood soup) and a *pierogi* (dumpling) platter to roast duck, roast pork, and potato dumplings with pork crackling.

Centrum nad Wisłą (ul Rybaki; mains 3.5-5zł; ☺ 11am-9pm) Wooden pavilions in the park, down near the river, shelter this family-oriented eatery, which serves beer and soft drinks, and rustles up grilled fish, chicken and steak on a big outdoor barbecue. There's a kids' play area too.

Bar Mleczny Pod Arkadami (☎ 262 95 21; ul Tumska 5; mains 4-8zł; ☺ 9am-6pm Mon-Fri, 9am-4pm Sat & Sun) A basic canteen and survivor of all the political and economic changes of recent decades. It's barely changed since the communist era and provides a rare insight into an archetypal milk bar of that period.

For a quick snack, try **Kuchnia Orientalna Saj-Gon** (☎ 268 77 00; Plac Narutowicza 1, Nowy Rynek 9) for Asian food, or **Restauracja Sphinx** (☎ 262 84 81; ul Tumska 13) for big portions of Polish or Middle Eastern fast food.

Café Blikle (☎ 268 34 57; ul Tumska) is a good place for cakes, coffee and ice cream, while **Café Akapit** (☎ 262 97 73; Stary Rynek 27) has cheap beer and a prime people-watching spot on the Old Town Sq.

Getting There & Away

The train and bus stations are nearly 2km northeast of the Old Town. There are no direct trains to Toruń and only one a day to Warsaw.

There are regular PKS buses to Warsaw (21zł, two hours, 10 daily), two a day to Gdańsk and one a day to Toruń. Polski Express buses run to Warsaw and Bydgoszcz (six a day); the **Polski Express bus stop** (ul Nowy Rynek) is opposite the Hotel Płock, in the new town centre.

SIERPC

☎ 24 / pop 20,000

The town of Sierpc (pronounced shehrpts) has an interesting **skansen** (Muzeum Wsi Mazowieckiej; ☎ 275 28 83; ul Narutowicza 64; adult/concession 9/6zł; ☺ 8am-5pm Mon-Fri, 9am-4pm Sat & Sun May-Sep, 9am-3pm Tue-Sun Oct-Apr). A typical north Mazovian village of a dozen farms has been reproduced in the grounds using old buildings collected from the region. As in most skansens (open-air museums of traditional architecture), the cottages have traditional furnishings, implements and decoration.

The skansen is 3km west of Sierpc, and is signposted from the junction in the town centre; the last 2km is on a dirt road.

NORTHERN & EASTERN MAZOVIA

PUŁTUSK

☎ 23 / pop 19,000

With a history going back to the 10th century, Pułtusk (poow-toosk) is one of Mazovia's oldest towns. It enjoyed its golden age in the 15th and 16th centuries when it was the residence of the bishops of Płock and an important trade and cultural centre. Later on, however, serious fires devastated the town several times, as did repeated invasions, for Pułtusk often found itself at the centre of conflict. In 1806 Napoleon's army fought one of its toughest battles in the campaign against Russia here, and in 1944 Pułtusk was in the front line for several months during which time 80% of its buildings were destroyed.

Sights & Activities

The town's historic core, set on an island, is laid out around a 400m-long cobbled **Rynek**, the longest market square in the country. In its middle stands the 15th-century brick tower of the town hall, today a **Regional Museum** (☎ 692 51 32; Rynek; adult/concession 5/3zł; ⏰ 10am-4pm Tue-Sat, 10am-2pm Sun), which features the history of the town and archaeology of the region. The green **house** (No 29) nearby, on the east side of the square, is where Napoleon stayed after the Battle of Pułtusk.

The northern end of the square is bordered by the **collegiate church** (kolegiata). Erected in the 1440s, the church received a Renaissance touch a century later. Its interior, crammed with a dozen baroque altars, has Renaissance stucco decoration on the nave's vault, but the aisles have retained their original Gothic features. Note the 16th-century wall paintings in the chapel at the head of the right-hand aisle.

At the opposite end of the square stands the **castle**. Built in the late 14th century as an abode for bishops, it was rebuilt several times in later periods. It's now a plush hotel and conference centre.

A cobbled road leads around the north side of the castle to a little harbour on the river where you can hire **rowing boats** and **kayaks** (6zł per hour).

Sleeping & Eating

Dom Polonii (☎ 692 90 00; www.dompolonii.pultusk .pl; ul Szkolna 11; s/d/tr/ste 250/330/390/530zł; P) Housed in the restored and much-converted castle, Dom Polonii offers atmospheric accommodation in sepia-tinted rooms redolent of past elegance, with creaky parquet flooring and archaic plumbing. There are cheaper rooms in other buildings in and around the castle grounds (doubles 110zł to 240zł). The hotel has several places to eat.

Hotel Baltazar (☎ 692 04 75; www.hotel-baltazar .com.pl; ul Baltazara 41; d/tr 120/150zł; P) Hidden away at the end of a minor road, 1km north of the Rynek (signposted), is an attractive modern alternative to the Dom Polonii with bright, spacious rooms and friendly service.

Hotel Zalewski (☎ 692 05 23; zalewski@post.pl; ul Jana Pawła II 19; s/d 100/120zł; P) An ageing, motel-style place on the southern edge of town, whose main attraction is its convenient location close to the bus terminal.

Restauracja Karmazynowa (mains 30-70zł; ⏰ 11am-11pm) An old-fashioned dining room, in the Dom Polonii, with wood panelling, gilt-framed mirrors and Persian rugs, offering a classic Polish menu of stuffed pike, pierogi, pork, venison and veal.

Getting There & Away

Pułtusk lies on the road from Warsaw to the Great Masurian Lakes. There's no railway in town, but there are regular buses to and from Warsaw (12zł, 1½ hours, half-hourly). **Pułtusk bus station** (ul Nowy Rynek) is just off the main road through town, and about 600m southwest of the Rynek.

NOWOGRÓD

☎ 86 / pop 1800

Nowogród (no-vo-groot) is a small town on the Narew River, on the eastern edge of the Puszcza Zielona (Green Forest). It was one of the early strongholds of the Mazovian dukes and traditionally one of the craft centres of this part of northern Mazovia. Its inhabitants, known as the Kurpie, have developed a distinctive style of dress, music and house decoration, but are best known in Poland for their paper cutouts and weaving.

Founded in 1927, the **Skansen Kurpiowski** (☎ 217 55 62; ul Zamkowa 25; adult/concession 5.50/3zł; ☽ 8am-4pm Mon-Fri, 10am-5pm Sat & Sun May-Sep, 9am-2pm Mon-Fri Oct-Apr) is the second-oldest museum of its kind in Poland, spectacularly located on a steep bank overlooking the Narew. Like the rest of the town, it was completely destroyed during WWII and rebuilt from scratch. Most of the buildings, however, are genuine 19th-century pieces of rural wooden architecture collected from all over the Kurpie region. There are about 30 buildings including cottages, barns, granaries and mills with fine architectural detail and elaborate decoration. There's also a collection of charming beehives, including some fashioned from hollow tree trunks.

Sleeping options include a summer-only **Youth Hostel** (☎ 217 55 17; ul 11 Listopada 12; dm 12-16zł; ☽ Jul & Aug), two blocks south of the Rynek, and the modern **Hotel Zbyszko** (☎ /fax 217 55 18; ul Obrońców Nowogrodu 2; s/d/tr 110/150/190zł; P), on the bank of the Narew, on the western edge of town.

The skansen is best visited with your own transport as there's only one bus a day, on Friday, Saturday and Sunday only, from Warsaw to Nowogród (20zł, 3½ hours); the bus stop is on the Rynek, a few minutes' walk from the skansen.

TREBLINKA
☎ 25
In a peaceful clearing, hidden deep in the Mazovian pine forest, stands a granite monolith; around it is a field of 17,000 jagged, upright stones, many engraved with the name of a town or village. Beneath the grass, mingled with the sand, lie the ashes of some 800,000 human beings.

Treblinka, the site of the Nazis' second-largest extermination camp after Auschwitz, is another name that will forever be associated with the horror of the Holocaust. Between July 1942 and August 1943 an average of more than 2000 people a day, mostly Jews, were murdered in the camp's gas chambers and their bodies burnt on huge, open-air cremation pyres.

Following an insurrection by the inmates in August 1943, the death camp was completely demolished and the area ploughed over and abandoned. The site of the camp is now the **Museum of Struggle & Martyrdom** (Muzeum Walki i Męczeństwa; ☎ 787 90 76; admission 2zł; ☽ 24hr). Access is by a short road that branches off the Małkinia–Sokołów Podlaski road and leads to a car park and a **kiosk** (☽ 9am-7pm Apr-Oct, 9am-4pm Nov-Mar) that provides information and sells guidebooks.

It's a 10-minute walk from the car park to the site of the **Treblinka II** extermination camp, alongside a symbolic railway representing the now-vanished line that brought the cattle trucks full of Jews from the Warsaw Ghetto. The huge granite monument, 200m east of the ramp, stands on the site where the gas chambers were located. Around it is a vast symbolic cemetery in the form of a forest of granite stones representing the towns and villages where the camp's victims came from. Unlike Auschwitz, nothing remains of the extermination camp, but the labels on the plan showing the original layout are chilling enough – 'Building for Sorting Gold and Valuables'; 'Storehouse for Victims' Property (Disguised As Train Station)'; 'Barracks Where Women Undressed, Surrendered Valuables and Had Heads Shaven'; 'Approach to Gas Chambers'.

A further 20-minute walk leads to another clearing and the site of **Treblinka I**, a penal labour camp that was set up before Treblinka II, where remains of the camp, including the concrete foundations of the demolished barracks, have been preserved.

Getting There & Away
Treblinka is about 100km northeast of Warsaw, a two-hour drive away. Take route 8 towards Białystok and 15km north of Wyszków turn right on road No 694 (signposted Ciechanowiec). When you reach Małkinia (26km from the main road) take the first turn on the right (again signposted Ciechanowiec), then go right again immediately after the railway (road No 677 to Przewóz). You cross a rickety wooden bridge over the Bug River, then cross a railway line to reach Treblinka village (4km from Małkinia). Continue for another 4km through the hamlet of Poniatowo; the entrance to the site is the first turn on the right after you cross the railway line again.

Małkinia lies on the Warsaw–Białystok railway line; there are trains from Warszawa Centralna every two hours, and more frequent ones from Warszawa Wileńska station (15zł to 25zł, 1¾ hours). There are no buses to Treblinka so your only option (other than an 8km walk) is to take a taxi from the train station; reckon on paying between 50zł and 100zł, depending on how long you want the taxi to wait.

CIECHANOWIEC
☎ 86 / pop 4800

Ciechanowiec (chekha-*no*-vyets), on the borderland between Mazovia and Podlasie, is famous for its **Museum of Agriculture** (Muzeum Rolnictwa; ☎ 277 13 28; ul Pałacowa 5; adult/concession 6/3zł; ◷ 9am-4pm Mon-Sat, 9am-6pm Sun May-Sep, 9am-4pm daily Oct-Apr). Set in the grounds of a former estate, it consists of an early-19th-century palace, stables, coach house and other outbuildings that are now exhibition halls. The grounds are occupied by a **skansen**, showing 40 examples of wooden architecture from all over Mazovia and Podlasie, including dwellings representing different social classes, from simple peasant cottages to manor houses of the nobility, and has a variety of granaries, barns and mills. There's a 19th-century water mill in working order, and plenty of old beehives.

The guided tour takes you through the interior of several wooden houses, and you'll also be shown exhibitions featuring items such as old agricultural machinery, archaic tractors, primitive steam engines, peasants' horse-drawn carts and rudimentary tools. There's also a small botanic garden growing medicinal plants and a veterinary exhibition. The tour takes about two hours.

English- and German-speaking guides (40zł per group) may be available on the spot, but if you want to be sure call the museum in advance and book.

Sleeping
The **museum** (☎ 277 13 28; r per person 25zł) itself offers accommodation, with 45 beds available in various rooms in the palace and several other buildings. These include some attractive places, such as the 1858 hunting lodge and the water mill, both of which are part of the skansen's collection. The standard varies depending on where you stay, but the price remains the same.

Getting There & Away
The bus station is a few minutes' walk from the museum. There are half a dozen buses daily from Białystok (13zł, 2½ hours), while from Warsaw (Dworzec Warszawa Stadion), there are two fast buses (24zł, 2¾ hours) in the afternoon and one ordinary bus (20zł, 3½ hours) in the morning.

PODLASIE

Podlasie (pod-*lah*-sheh, literally 'the land close to the forest') owes its name to the vicinity of the vast forests that once covered much of that part of Poland. The best preserved of these, the Białowieża Forest, now boasts the Białowieża National Park, which is the major attraction in the region.

There's also much more to see and do here. Other attractions of the region include the national parks of the Biebrza and Narew Rivers. They both protect extensive lowland marshes of the river valleys.

Stretching along the border of Poland and Belarus, Podlasie has for centuries been influenced by these two cultures. With its blend of West and East, Catholicism and Orthodoxy, you may at times feel as though you're travelling in a completely different country. The further off the main track you go, the more onion-shaped Orthodox domes you'll see and the more Belarusian language you'll hear.

The Tatars settled in Podlasie in the 17th century, giving the region a Muslim touch, and their legacy survives to this day (see p119). There were also Jews living here and they too have left traces of their presence (see p116).

Except for the Białowieża National Park, Podlasie is not a touristy area and seldom sees foreign visitors. The only city is Białystok; everything else, particularly the countryside, seems to be half asleep, enjoying the unhurried life of bygone days, as it has for centuries.

BIAŁYSTOK
☎ 85 / pop 280,000

Founded in the 16th century, Białystok (byah-*wis*-tok) really began to develop in the mid-18th century, when Jan Klemens Branicki, the commander of the Polish armed forces and owner of vast estates –

including the town – established his residence here and built a palace. A century later the town received a new impetus from the textile industry, and eventually became Poland's largest textile centre after Łódź.

During the textile boom, Białystok attracted an ethnic mix of entrepreneurs, including Poles, Jews, Russians, Belarusians and Germans, and simultaneously drew in a sizable urban proletariat. The town grew in a spontaneous and chaotic manner (still visible today) and by the outbreak of WWI had some 80,000 inhabitants and over 250 textile factories.

In 1920, during the Polish-Soviet war, the Bolsheviks installed a provisional communist government in the Branicki Palace, its leaders Julian Marchlewski and Feliks Dzierżyński calling for the formation of a Polish Soviet Republic. It lasted no longer than a month.

WWII was not kind to Białystok. The Nazis murdered half the city's population, including almost all the Jews, destroyed most of the industrial base and razed the central district. Postwar reconstruction concentrated on tangible issues such as the recovery of industry, infrastructure and state administration, together with the provision of basic necessities. As you can still see today, historic and aesthetic values receded into the background.

Białystok doesn't have many great attractions and is not a prime travel destination. But the mix of Polish and Belarusian

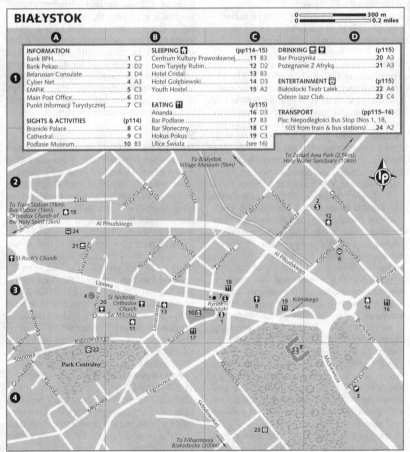

BIAŁYSTOK

0 — 300 m
0 — 0.2 miles

INFORMATION		SLEEPING 🏠	(pp114–15)	DRINKING 🍺	(p115)
Bank BPH	1 C3	Centrum Kultury Prawosławnej	11 B3	Bar Pruszynka	20 A3
Bank Pekao	2 D2	Dom Turysty Rubin	12 D2	Pożegnanie Z Afryką	21 A3
Belarusian Consulate	3 D4	Hotel Cristal	13 B3		
Cyber Net	4 A3	Hotel Gołębiewski	14 D3	ENTERTAINMENT	(p115)
EMPiK	5 C3	Youth Hostel	15 A2	Białostocki Teatr Lalek	22 A4
Main Post Office	6 D3			Odeon Jazz Club	23 C4
Punkt Informacji Turystycznej	7 C3	EATING 🍴	(p115)		
		Ananda	16 D3	TRANSPORT	(pp115–16)
SIGHTS & ACTIVITIES	(p114)	Bar Podlasie	17 B3	Plac Niepodległości Bus Stop (Nos 1, 18,	
Branicki Palace	8 C4	Bar Słoneczny	18 C3	103 from train & bus stations)	24 A2
Cathedral	9 C3	Hokus Pokus	19 C3		
Podlasie Museum	10 B3	Ulice Świata	(see 16)		

cultures gives it a special atmosphere not found in other Polish cities. Białystok is also a jumping-off point for excursions to Tykocin, Kruszyniany and Bohoniki.

Information

Bank BPH (☎ 664 61 11; Rynek Kościuszki 7; ⏰ 8am-6pm Mon-Fri)

Bank Pekao (☎ 664 88 00; ul Sienkiewicza 40; ⏰ 8am-6pm Mon-Fri, 9am-1pm Sat) Cashes Amex travellers cheques.

Cyber Net (☎ 742 33 11; ul Grochowa 2; per hr 1.5zł; ⏰ 9am-midnight)

EMPiK (☎ 743 50 68; ul Sienkewicza 3; ⏰ 9.30am-6.30pm Mon-Fri, 9.30am-3pm Sat) Some English-language books, magazines and newspapers.

Main post office (☎ 732 87 64; ul Warszawska 10; ⏰ 8am-8pm Mon-Fri, 8am-2pm Sat)

Punkt Informacji Turystycznej (Tourist Information Point; ☎ 653 79 50; 1st fl, ul Sienkiewicza 3; ⏰ 10am-6pm Mon-Fri) Situated in the Holiday Travel office.

Sights

The centre of the city is marked by the triangular Rynek Kościuszki, the former market square, with its 18th-century **town hall** in the middle. The town hall was rebuilt from scratch after the war and now houses the **Podlasie Museum** (Muzeum Podlaskie; ☎ 742 14 73; Rynek Kościuszki 10; adult/concession 4/2zł; ⏰ 10am-5pm Tue-Sun), which features a modest collection of Polish painting, including some important names such as Malczewski and Witkacy.

In the park to the east of the square stands the **Branicki Palace** (Pałac Branickich). Eminent in Polish political life, Jan Klemens Branicki was a contender for the Polish crown, but after Stanisław August Poniatowski was elected Branicki left the court, moved to Białystok and set about building a residence that would rival the king's in importance and luxury. The mighty, horseshoe-shaped baroque palace used to be referred to as the Versailles of the North, but it was burnt down in 1944 by the retreating Nazis. After the war, its exterior was restored to the original 18th-century shape, but the interior, except for the central ballroom, was largely modernised. Today it's the seat of the Academy of Medicine and is not open to tourists, though you're free to wander through the landscaped gardens and admire the exterior murals.

Across the road from the palace is a strange merger of two churches: a small 17th-century **old parish church** and, attached to it, a huge mock-Gothic **cathedral**. The latter was constructed at the beginning of the 20th century as an 'extension' of the former, the only way to bypass the tsarist bureaucracy that officially forbade Poles to build new Catholic churches.

It's worth making a detour outside the central area to the modern **Orthodox Church of the Holy Spirit** (Cerkiew Św Ducha; ☎ 653 28 54; ul Antoniuk Fabryczny 13), 3km northwest of the centre (bus No 5 from ul Lipowa in the centre will let you off nearby). Begun in the early 1980s, this monumental building is the largest Orthodox church in Poland. The huge, central, onion-shaped dome is topped with a large cross (weighing 1500kg) symbolising Christ, while 12 smaller crosses around it represent the apostles. The spacious interior boasts a spectacular main iconostasis and two smaller ones on either side, and a fantastic giant chandelier. The church is locked, except for daily morning services and the Sunday Mass, but inquire at the **Kancelaria** (church office; ⏰ 8-11am & 3-5pm Mon-Fri) in the house behind the church, and somebody may open it for you.

Sleeping

Youth Hostel (☎ 652 60 69; www.ssm.bialystok.ids.pl; Al Piłsudskiego 7b; dm 19-25zł; ⏰ year-round) This modern hostel is housed in an old-style villa, incongruously set amid concrete apartment blocks (it's tucked away from the street behind block No 7), and offers accommodation in pine bunk beds in wood-panelled dorms of six to 16 beds, with kitchen and 24-hour reception. It's a 1.5km trek across the flyover from the train station, or take bus 1 or 18 and get off at the first stop.

Zajazd Awa Park (☎ 675 05 86; www.awapark.pl; ul 27 lipca 24/1; r 50-100zł; 🅿 🖭) About 2.5km northeast of the centre, this is a new hotel with crisp, modern rooms and no-nonsense functional décor. The accommodation is great value, but it's a bit far out of the city; take bus 3, 6 or 18 northbound from ul Sienkiewicza, or 18 from the train station.

Dom Turysty Rubin (☎ 677 23 35; rubin@puszcza.pl; ul Warszawska 7; d/tr 70/90zł, with private bathroom 120/150zł) The grand 19th-century façade is in need of a makeover, as are the somewhat faded rooms, but it's clean and comfortable and the location good, an easy walk from the city centre.

Centrum Kultury Prawosławnej (☎ 744 30 10; ckp@orthodox.bialystok.pl; ul Św Mikołaja 5; s/d 90/150zł; ✗) This cultural centre, run by the Orthodox Church community, offers quiet, nonsmoking guest rooms, all with private bathrooms, to all-comers. Great location just a few minutes' stroll from the city centre.

Hotel Cristal (☎ 742 50 61; www.cristal.com.pl; ul Lipowa 3; s 230-270zł, d 250-300zł; **P**) Located right in the centre of town, the Best Western Cristal has plush, international-standard rooms aimed at business travellers. Rates fall by 20% to 30% on weekends. Guests have free access to the hotel's sauna, Jacuzzi and gym.

Hotel Gołębiewski (☎ 743 54 35; www.golebiewski .pl; ul Pałacowa 7; s/d 260/280zł; **P** 🏊) The almost unpronounceable Gołębiewski is another business-oriented hotel, a faceless multistorey block concealing spacious modern rooms and a swimming pool, sauna and Jacuzzi complex.

Eating & Drinking

Hokus Pokus (☎ 741 63 48; ul Kilińskiego 12; mains 8-18zł; ☾ 10am-11pm Mon-Sat, noon-11pm Sun) A smart, stylish bar and restaurant in an anonymous little back street that seems to be on its way to becoming the trendiest spot in town. The retro décor blends russet upholstery, chrome, sheepskin and stainless steel, while the menu mixes Italian and American – excellent pizza, pasta, steaks and burgers.

Ananda (☎ 741 33 36; ul Warszawska 30; mains 10-16zł; ☾ noon-10pm) Hidden away behind the Hotel Gołębiewski, this place features old-fashioned looks and an arty interior. The very modern menu of mostly vegetarian food includes Chinese and Thai dishes as well as Polish fish dishes. There's a little garden for outdoor dining in summer.

Ulice Świata (☎ 740 41 61; ul Warszawska 30a; mains 12-20zł; ☾ 1-11pm) Next door to the Ananda, is an attractive two-level place whose menu offers a huge range of dishes from all over the world, from African and American to Mexican and Mediterranean.

Pożegnanie Z Afryką (☎ 625 55 05; ul Waryńskiego 3/5; ☾ 10am-8pm) This branch of the famous Warsaw coffee shop is the best place for a cup of real coffee, with its 30-odd blends.

Bar Pruszynka (☎ 744 63 14; ul Grochowa 3; mains 4-8zł; ☾ 10-1am Mon-Thu, 10-3am Fri & Sat, noon-midnight Sun) One of Białystok's liveliest and most popular bars – walk past on any summer evening and the buzz of conversation will

be spilling off the outdoor terrace from 5pm onwards. Pruszynka pulls in a young party crowd on weekends with a programme of live bands, discos and karaoke nights.

For a fast, cheap meal, the **Bar Podlasie** (☎ 742 25 04; Rynek Kościuszki 15; mains 6-10zł; ☾ 8am-8pm) and **Bar Słoneczny** (☎ 743 58 15; ul Sienkiewicza 5; mains 6-10zł) are the places to go.

Entertainment

Białystok does its best to provide a full cultural programme.

Filharmonia Białostocka (☎ 732 23 31; ul Podleśna 2) Holds concerts of classical music every Friday, as well as hosting special events and visiting orchestras.

Białostocki Teatr Lalek (☎ 742 50 31; ul Kalinowskiego 1) One of Poland's best puppet theatres, and stages children's shows, such as *Pinocchio* or *Punch and Judy* as well as traditional Polish stories, at least three or four times a week.

Odeon Jazz Club (☎ 742 49 88; ul Akademicka 10/1; ☾ noon-1am) The city doesn't have a big jazz scene, but this is a long-standing venue where you can listen to live jazz and blues, mostly on weekends.

Getting There & Away

The **Dworzec PKS bus station** (☎ 745 80 18; ul Bohaterów Monte Cassino 10) and **Dworzec PKP train station** (☎ 682 42 12; ul Dworcowa 1) are next to each other, about 2km west of the central area. You can walk to the centre in 20 minutes, or take bus 2, 4 or 28 to Rynek Kościuszki.

BUS

There are regular PKS buses from Warsaw (Dworzec Warszawa Stadion) to Białystok (24zł, 3¾ hours, four daily), and Polski Express buses from Warsaw airport (one daily). Buses to Olsztyn (28zł, five hours) run three times a day, and to Gdańsk (44zł, nine hours) once a day.

On the international routes, there's one departure a day to Minsk (50zł, 10 hours) in Belarus and one a week (on Friday) to Vilnius (40zł, eight hours) in Lithuania.

TRAIN

The main intercity rail services are to Warsaw (Warszawa Wschodnia station; 34zł, 2½ hours, every two hours), to Kraków (60zł, 4¾ hours, one daily) and to Gdańsk (49zł, 7½ hours, two daily) via Olsztyn.

MAZOVIA & PODLASIE

International trains from Warsaw to Vilnius (241km) and St Petersburg in Russia (948km) stop at Białystok. If you plan on taking this route, check in advance whether you need a Belarusian transit visa, because the railway cuts through a short stretch of Belarus, passing through Hrodna.

AROUND BIAŁYSTOK

About 10km north of Białystok is the **Holy Water Sanctuary** (Sanktuarium Święta Woda) where a miraculous spring has been a site of pilgrimage since the early 18th century. Then in 1997 the nearby hill was declared a Monument to the 3rd Millennium, or the Mountain of Crosses, and the place began to change dramatically. Since then, crowds of pilgrims have rushed to visit the site, leaving crosses of every shape and size. There are now more than 10,000 crosses and the number grows with every year.

The site is next to the road to Sokółka, 2km north of Wasilków, opposite a yellow Pronar petrol station. To get there, take bus 100 from ul Bohaterów Monte Cassino opposite the PKS bus terminal in Białystok.

TYKOCIN

☎ 85 / pop 2100

Tykocin (ti-*ko*-cheen) came into being in the 13th century as one of the strongholds of the Mazovian dukes. Its real growth began in the 15th century and was further accelerated after the town became the property of King Zygmunt II August in 1543. It was during this period that Jews started to settle in Tykocin, their community growing rapidly to define the town's character for the next four centuries.

Located on the Warsaw–Vilnius trade route and enjoying numerous royal privileges, Tykocin developed into the commercial centre of the region, to be surpassed by Białystok only at the end of the 18th century. This marked the turning point of Tykocin's fortunes and from then on the town gradually slid into decline. During WWII it lost all its Jews – half of the town's population – and in 1950 it was deprived of its town charter to become an ordinary village. It recovered its charter in 1994, but otherwise nothing has changed. It remains a small, sleepy place, where not much goes on, but several historic buildings survive as evidence of the town's illustrious past.

Sights

Tykocin's 17th-century **synagogue** is one of the best-preserved of its kind in Poland, its four-square form dominating the western part of town, which was traditionally the Jewish quarter. This sober-looking edifice, erected in 1642, remained in use for religious services right up till WWII.

Renovated after the war, the synagogue is now the **Tykocin Museum** (☎ 718 16 13; ul Kozia 2; adult/concession 5/3zł; ⏱ 10am-5pm Tue-Sun). The interior, with a massive almemar (raised platform on which the reading desk stands) in the centre and an elaborate Aron Kodesh (the Holy Ark where the Torah scrolls are kept) in the eastern wall, has preserved many of the original wall paintings including Hebraic inscriptions. The exhibition features Talmudic books, liturgical equipment and other objects related to religious ritual. There's an extension of the museum in the **Talmudic house**, right behind the synagogue, which is used mostly for temporary exhibitions.

At the opposite end of the town stands the 18th-century baroque **Holy Trinity Church** (Kościół Św Trójcy). Two symmetrical towers linked to the main building by arcaded galleries overlook the spacious **Rynek** (called Plac Czanieckiego). In the middle of the square stands the **Monument to Stefan Czarniecki**, a national hero who distinguished himself in battles against the Swedes. The statue, from the 1760s, is one of the oldest secular monuments in Poland.

Sleeping & Eating

Dom Pod Czarnym Bocianem (House Beneath the Black Stork; ☎ 718 74 08; www.czarnybocian.prv.pl; ul Poświętna 16; d 80zł) A pleasant, modern villa on the bank of the Narew River, run as a guesthouse by a local couple, both teachers. There are five double rooms with en suite bathrooms. Guests have use of the kitchen for fixing snacks and meals and can use kayaks free of charge.

Dworek Nad Łąkami (☎ 718 74 44, in Białystok ☎ 742 16 70; dworek@dworek.com.pl; Kiermusy; s/d 190/250zł; P) An impressive manor house decorated in traditional Polish style, this is part of a complex that includes a countryside inn (Karczma Rzym) and a faux-medieval castle and banqueting hall (Jantarowy Kasztel). It is 3km northwest of Tykocin, on the road towards the village of Nieciece.

Tykocin also has a basic summer **Youth Hostel** (☎ 718 16 85; ul Kochanowskiego 1; dm 12-16zł; Jul & Aug) in the local school, and the **Restauracja Tejsza** (☎ 718 77 50; ul Kozia 2; mains 10-20zł; 10am-8pm), in the basement of the Talmudic house (enter from the back), which serves inexpensive kosher meals.

Getting There & Away

Tykocin is 38km west of Białystok. There are about 20 buses daily between Białystok and Tykocin (8zł, one hour); buses stop at Stary Rynek, 100m from the synagogue.

BIEBRZA NATIONAL PARK

☎ 86

The Biebrza (*byehb*-zhah) National Park (Biebrzański Park Narodowy) encompasses almost the entire basin of the Biebrza River along its course of more than 100km, from its source near the Belarusian border to where it joins the Narew River. Established in 1994, it is Poland's largest national park.

The **Biebrza Valley** is Central Europe's largest area of natural bog. The varied landscape consists of river sprawls, peat bogs, marshes and damp forests. Typical local flora includes numerous species of moss, reed grass and a range of medicinal herbs. The fauna is rich and diverse and features mammals such as wolf, wild boar, fox, roe deer, otter and beaver. The king of the park, however, is the elk; a population of about 500 lives here.

The park, which boasts a total of about 270 bird species (more than half of all species recorded in Poland), is a favourite destination for bird-watchers. You'll find storks, cranes, hawks, curlews, snipe, ruffs, egrets, harriers, crakes, sandpipers, owls, shrikes and at least half a dozen species of warblers. Among the less common varieties are the great snipe, the white-winged black tern and the aquatic warbler.

Information

The place to go before any exploration of the park is the **visitors information centre** (☎ 272 06 20; www.biebrza.org.pl; Osowiec-Twierdza; adult/concession 4/2zł; 7.30am-7.30pm May-Sep, 7.30am-3.30pm Mon-Fri Oct-Apr) at the park's headquarters, just along the road from Osowiec-Twierdza train station. You pay the park admission fee here.

The helpful English-speaking staff will provide information about the park and its facilities. You'll be able to get details of where to stay and eat (or to buy food), and advice on the best watching spots for different bird species and how to get there. The centre provides information on where to find guides (40zł an hour per group) and hires out kayaks (4zł an hour or 20zł a day). The office is stocked with maps and brochures on the park, some of which are in English.

Sights & Activities

The park can be broadly divided into three areas: the **Northern Basin** (Basen Północny), the smallest and least-visited area of the park; the **Middle Basin** (Basen Środkowy), stretching along the river's broad middle course and featuring a combination of wet forests and boglands; and the equally extensive **Southern Basin** (Basen Południowy) where most of the terrain is taken up by marshes and peat bogs. The showpiece is the **Red Marsh** (Czerwone Bagno), in the middle basin, a strictly protected nature reserve encompassing a wet alder forest that is inhabited by about 400 elks.

Despite its overall marshy character, large parts of the park can be explored relatively easily on foot. About 200km of signposted trails have been tracked through the most interesting areas, including nearly 50km through the Red Marsh alone. Dikes, boulders and dunes among the bogs provide access to some splendid bird-watching sites. Several viewing towers on the edge of the marshland allow for more general views of the park.

Another way of exploring the park is by **boat**. The principal water route in the park goes from the town of Lipsk downstream along the Biebrza to the village of Wizna. This 139km stretch can be paddled at a leisurely pace in seven to nine days. Bivouac sites along the river allow for overnight stops and food is available in towns on the way. The visitors information centre in Osowiec-Twierdza can provide maps and information. You can also hire a kayak for just a few hours or a day and cover part of the route; the staff will advise you. Access to kayak trails costs 5.50zł for adults and 3.50zł concession per day on top of hire charges.

Sleeping

There are several bivouac sites within the park and more outside its boundaries. The three most strategically located sites are in Osowiec-Twierdza (2km from the office), Grzędy (a gateway to the Red Marsh) and Barwik (close to the great snipe's habitat). All three are accessible by road and have car parks. You'll pay about 5zł per person per night to pitch your tent. There are also five rooms (for up to 16 people) in the **hunting lodge** (per person 30zł) in Grzędy.

The nearest hotels to the park are in Goniądz, Mońki and Rajgród. Youth hostels in the region include ones in Goniądz, Grajewo, Osowiec-Twierdza and Wizna; all are open in July and August only. There are also about 70 agrotourist farms in the region – the park's visitor information centre can provide details.

Getting There & Around

Osowiec-Twierdza is 50km northwest of Białystok, and sits on the railway between Białystok (16zł, one hour, six daily) and Ełk. The park office is just 200m from Osowiec-Twierdza station, and there are hiking trails and lookout towers within a few kilometres.

Having your own transport is a huge advantage, as you can easily access most of the park's major attractions.

NAREW NATIONAL PARK

Another marshland nature reserve, the Narew (*nah*-ref) National Park (Narwiański Park Narodowy) is just as interesting as the Biebrza park but not as geared up for visitors. The park protects an unusual stretch of the Narew River that's nicknamed the 'Polish Amazon', where the river splits into dozens of channels that spread out across a 2km-wide valley, forming a constellation of swampy islets in-between.

The park encompasses an area of about 73 sq km, 25% of which is bog and a further 3% water. Predictably, the most abundant flora and fauna species are those accustomed to aquatic conditions, including the omnipresent white-and-yellow water lilies. Among mammals, the beaver is the most characteristic inhabitant, numbering at least 250 individuals living in about 70 lodges. The area is a favourite ground for birds, with as many as 200 species identified in the park, including about 150 species that breed here.

Sights & Activities

The most interesting area is the northwestern part of the park, where the watery labyrinth of channels is most extensive. The best way to get a taste of the marshland is by **boat**, paddling through narrow, snaking channels and ponds with water so crystal clear you can see fish and plants to a depth of 2m. The best time for bird-watching is either early morning or late afternoon, when water birds are most active.

The main starting points for exploring the park are the tiny hamlet of Kurowo and the village of Uhowo. **Kurowo** sits on the left (western) bank of the Narew, connected to the outer world only by a rough road, which rarely sees a passing car. The central point of this tiny hamlet is a late-19th-century country mansion surrounded by a 10-hectare park. The building houses the **Narew National Park Headquarters** (☎ 85-718 14 17; www.npn.pl in Polish; ☒ 7.30am-3.30pm Mon-Fri) and a small exhibition on the park's natural history. You can camp near the building and use the toilets but there are no showers. There's no restaurant so bring your own food. Kayaks are available for 4zł an hour.

Uhowo, near Łapy at the southern end of the park, is larger. This is the home base of **Kaylon** (☎ 85-715 53 08; www.kaylon.pl; ul Kolejowa 8), an agency that organises canoeing expeditions through the park from May to September. Three-/five-day trips cost 270zł/430zł per person, plus 22zł a day for kayak hire, or 32zł a day for a three-person Canadian canoe.

Getting There & Around

There's no public transport to Kurowo, so without a car or bike you'll have a bit of a walk. The starting point is the village of Stare Jeżewo, 28km west of Białystok, on the main road (No 8) towards Warsaw. It's serviced by frequent buses from Białystok. From Stare Jeżewo, walk 500m south on the road to Sokoły, and turn left at the first (unsigned) crossroads. Follow this side road for 3km until you reach another crossroads where the seal ends. Take the road to the right (south) for another 1km until you see a large brick granary where the road divides. Take the left-hand fork for the last 1km to Kurowo. It takes a bit over an hour, but it's a pleasant walk through a bucolic landscape.

KRUSZYNIANY & BOHONIKI

☎ 85

These two small villages, close to the Belarusian border to the east of Białystok, are noted for their timber mosques, the only surviving historic mosques in Poland. They were built by the Muslim Tatars, who settled here at the end of the 17th century.

Spreading for over 2km along the road, **Kruszyniany** looks much larger than it really is. The green-painted **mosque**, hidden in a cluster of trees set back from the main road, is in the central part of the village. It's an 18th-century rustic wooden construction, in many ways similar to old timber Christian churches.

The mosque's modest interior, made entirely from pine, is divided into two rooms, the smaller one designed for women, who are not allowed into the main prayer hall. The latter, with carpets covering the floor, has a small recess in the wall, the mihrab, in the direction of Mecca. Next to it is the minbar, a pulpit from which the imam says prayers. The painted texts hanging on the walls, the Muhirs, are verses from the Quran.

The mosque is used for worship, and on the most solemn holy days there may not be enough room inside for all the congregation. At other times it's locked, but go to house No 57, next to the mosque on the same side of the road, and someone will open it for you. Be properly dressed (no bare legs) and take off your shoes before entering the prayer hall.

The **Mizar** (Muslim cemetery) is located in the patch of woodland 300m beyond the

MAZOVIA & PODLASIE

THE TATARS OF POLAND

In the 13th century large parts of Eastern Europe were ravaged by hordes of fierce Mongol horsemen from Central Asia. These savage nomadic warriors (commonly, though confusingly, referred to in Europe as the Tatars) came from the great Mongol empire of Genghis Khan, which at its peak stretched from the Black Sea to the Pacific. They first invaded Poland in 1241 and repeatedly overran and destroyed most of Silesia and Małopolska, the royal city of Kraków included. They withdrew from Europe as fast as they came, leaving few traces other than some folk stories (such as Kraków's Lajkonik; see p150). Not long after, the empire broke up into various independent khanates.

By the end of the 14th century, Poland and Lithuania faced an increasing threat from the north, from where the Teutonic order swiftly expanded southwards and eastwards over their territories. As a measure of protection, Lithuania (which was soon to enter into a political alliance with Poland) began looking for migrants eager to settle its almost uninhabited borderland fringes. It welcomed the refugees and prisoners of war from the Crimean and Volgan khanates, offspring of the once powerful Golden Horde state ruled by the heirs of Genghis Khan. The new settlers were Muslim Tatars of a different tribal background.

The Tatars' military involvement in Polish affairs began in 1410 at the Battle of Grunwald, where King Jagiełło defeated the Teutonic Knights; in this battle a small unit of Tatar horsemen fought alongside the Polish-Lithuanian forces. From that time the numbers of Tatar settlers grew, and so did their participation in battles in defence of their adopted homeland. By the 17th century, they had several cavalry formations reinforcing Polish troops in the wars, which were particularly frequent at that time.

In 1683, after the victory over the Turks at the Battle of Vienna, King Jan Sobieski granted land in the eastern strip of Poland to those who had fought under the Polish flag. The Tatars founded new settlements here and built their mosques. Of all these villages, only Kruszyniany and Bohoniki have preserved some of their Tatar inheritance, though apart from their mosques and cemeteries not much else remains. The original population either integrated or left, and there are only a few families living here today that are true descendants of the Tatars.

Of a total of some 3000 people of Tatar origin in Poland, the majority found homes in large cities such as Warsaw, Białystok and Gdańsk. Nonetheless, they flock together in Kruszyniany and Bohoniki for important holy days, as Poland's only mosques (apart from one built in Gdańsk in the 1990s) are here. And they usually end up here at the local Tatar graveyards, two of only three still in use in the country (the other is in Warsaw).

mosque. The recent gravestones are Christian in style, showing the extent of cultural assimilation that has taken place, and are on the edge of the graveyard. Go deeper into the wood, where you'll find old tombstones hidden in the undergrowth. Some of them are inscribed in Russian, a legacy of tsarist times.

The village of **Bohoniki** is smaller and so is its **mosque**. Its interior is similar in its decoration and atmosphere to that of Kruszyniany, though it's more modest. It, too, can be visited; the keys are kept at the house across the road from the mosque.

The **Muslim cemetery** is about 1km north of the mosque. Walk to the outskirts of the village then turn left up to a small forested area. As in Kruszyniany, the old tombstones are further afield, overgrown by bushes and grass.

There are no accommodation options in either village, but Kruszyniany has an unusual place to eat in the canvas-roofed **Tartar Yurt** (☎ 710 84 60; ul Słowackiego 26; mains 10-20zł; ☯ 10am-8pm), a restaurant that serves traditional Tatar dishes such as *babka ziemniaczana* (potato cakes); you can even watch as your host does the preparation and cooking.

The two villages are 37km apart, each about 50km from Białystok, and are best reached by car. Visiting by public transport is not feasible.

HAJNÓWKA
☎ 85 / pop 25,000

Set on the edge of the Białowieża Forest, Hajnówka (high-*noof*-kah) is the main gateway for the Białowieża National Park. The town was founded in the 18th century as a guard post to protect the Białowieża Forest, which was used as a hunting ground by the Polish kings, and also later by the tsars. Early last century, when the tsars were busy dealing with domestic problems, the exploitation of the forest began in earnest, which is how the town came to grow. Today, Hajnówka is a local centre of the timber industry, and has a mixed Polish-Belarusian population.

Information
PTTK Office (☎ 682 27 85; ul 3 Maja 37; ☯ 9am-5pm Mon-Fri, 9am-1pm Sat) Can provide tourist information and sells maps of the Białowieża National Park.

Sights
The **Orthodox Church of the Holy Trinity** (Cerkiew Św Trójcy; ☎ 873 29 71; ul Dziewiatowskiego 13) is the town's major (well, only) sight and arguably one of the most beautiful modern Orthodox churches in Poland. Begun in the early 1970s and fully completed two decades later, the irregular structure, covered by an undulating roof, supports two slender towers, the main one 50m high. The bold, unconventional design, the work of Polish architect Aleksander Grygorowicz, has resulted in a powerful and impressive building.

Its creators have done a good job inside. The icons and frescoes include the work of Jerzy Nowosielski, and the stained-glass windows are from a Kraków workshop. Look out for the chandelier and iconostasis.

The **Kancelaria** (☯ 10am-1pm & 2-5pm Mon-Sat) is in the house next to the church. If you inquire there during opening hours one of the priests will show you around the church. Otherwise try to coincide your visit with the services (10am Sunday, 8am weekdays).

Hajnówka's only other attraction is somewhat less spiritual, but probably more famous. **Bar U Wołodzi** (☎ 682 46 26; ul 3 Maja 34a) is known throughout Poland for its bizarre collection of communist memorabilia. Ask to be let into the VIP room, where you can try on any of the dozens of Soviet uniforms and take as many snaps as you wish.

Sleeping
Most people simply pass through Hajnówka on their way to or from Białowieża, but if you have to stay the night you have the choice of the bright and modern **Hotelik Orzechowski** (☎ 682 27 58; www.hotel-orzechowski .com.pl; ul Piłsudskiego 14; s/d/tr 100/140/180zł), or the drab **Dom Nauczyciela** (☎ /fax 682 25 85; ul Piłsudskiego 6; s/d/tr 60/80/100zł).

Getting There & Away
The train and bus stations are next to each other, south of the main road junction and roundabout in the middle of town. There are frequent buses from Białystok to Hajnówka (12zł, two hours, 12 daily).

From Warsaw, you can take a fast train from Warszawa Wschodnia to Siedlce, and connect with the slow train to Hajnówka (40zł, 4½ hours, two daily). There's also one direct train from Warsaw to Hajnówka each day (four hours).

BIAŁOWIEŻA NATIONAL PARK

☎ 85

The Białowieża (byah-wo-*vyeh*-zhah) National Park (Białowieski Park Narodowy) is the oldest national park in the country, and is famous as the place where the European bison was successfully reintroduced into the wild. The park protects a small part of a much bigger forest known as the Puszcza Białowieska (Białowieża Forest) which straddles the border between Poland and Belarus.

The *puszcza* (primeval forest) was once an immense and barely accessible forest stretching for hundreds of kilometres, but is now reduced to an area of about 1200 sq km, distributed approximately evenly between Poland and Belarus. In the 15th century it became a private hunting ground for Polish monarchs and later for Russian tsars. During WWI the Germans exploited it intensively, felling around 5 million cu metres of timber. The gradual colonisation and exploitation of its margins has also diminished the forest's area and altered its ecosystem. Even so this vast forest, protected for so long by royal patronage, has preserved its primeval core largely untouched, and is the largest area of original lowland forest left in Europe.

Soon after WWI the central part of the *puszcza* was made a nature reserve, and in 1932 it was formally converted into a national park. Today the total area of the park is 105 sq km, of which 47 sq km is strictly protected. It is included on Unesco's World Heritage List.

Orientation

The starting point for excursions into the national park is the village of Białowieża, 85km southeast of Białystok. It has accommodation, food and several travel agencies who can organise visits to the Strictly Protected Area of the park.

The village straggles along for about 3km on the southern edge of the national park, centred on the rectangular Park Pałacowy (Palace Park), which contains the Natural History Museum. The tourist office and Hotel Żubrówka are at the southern entrance to the Park Pałacowy; the youth hostel is near its eastern entrance.

Arriving by bus from Hajnówka, there are three bus stops in Białowieża: one at the entrance to the village (opposite the camping ground), one just after the Hotel Żubrówka (closest to the PTTK office), and one at the post office (closest to the youth hostel and museum).

Soon after your arrival check with a travel agency about visiting the Strictly Protected Area, as all visits must be accompanied by a guide and it may take a while to arrange one or to gather a group to share the costs. If you have some time before your tour, visit the museum, which will introduce you to the local habitat and its wildlife.

MAPS
Try to get hold of the 1:85,000 *Białowieża Forest & Neighbourhood* map by ATI Kart, which has English-language information and street plans of Hajnówka and Białowieża. It's on sale in bookshops in Warsaw and Białystok, and at the PTTK offices in Hajnówka and Białowieża.

Information
MONEY
You can change money and cash travellers cheques at the reception desk of the **Hotel Żubrówka** (☎ 681 23 03; www.hotel-zubrowka .pl; ul Olgi Gabiec 6), and there's an ATM right outside the hotel entrance.

TOURIST INFORMATION
National Park Information Centre (☎ 681 29 01; www.bpn.com.pl; Park Pałacowy; ⊙ 8am-4pm Tue-Sun) A small wooden hut at the eastern entrance to the Park Pałacowy; you can also get park information at the Natural History Museum.

PTTK Tourist Service (Biuro Usług Turystycznych PTTK; ☎ 681 22 95; www.pttk.bialowieza.pl; ul Kolejowa 17; ⊙ 8am-4pm Mon-Fri, 8am-3pm Sat) Can arrange accommodation, guides, bike hire.

TRAVEL AGENCIES
There are several agencies that organise trips into the national park. The major operator is PTTK Tourist Service, which can organise English-, German- or Russian-speaking guides (180zł for up to three hours, 60zł per hour thereafter) for visits to the Strictly Protected Area of the park, and trips by *britzka* (horse-drawn cart) or sledge in winter into the national park (from 125zł for four people); and bike hire (5zł an hour, 25zł a day).

MAZOVIA & PODLASIE

Other agencies with English-speaking guides:

Biuro Turystyki Ryś (☎ 681 22 49, 0608 582 840; ul Krzyże 22)

Nature Tour (☎ 681 20 07, 0606 443 007; naturetour@wp.pl; Park Dyrekcyjny 4/1)

Sights

PARK PAŁACOWY

At the end of the 19th century, the **Park Pałacowy** (Palace Park; admission free; ☉ 24hr) was laid out around a splendid palace built for the Russian tsar in 1894 on the site of an ancient royal hunting lodge once used by Polish kings. The **Russian Orthodox Church**, outside the eastern entrance to the park, was built at the same time. The southern entrance to Park Pałacowy, beside the PTTK office, leads across a fish pond past a stone **obelisk**, which commemorates a bison hunt led by King August III Saxon in 1752. The royal bag that day was 42 bison, 13 elks and two roe deer.

The avenue leads uphill past a red-brick **gate**, all that remains of the tsar's palace – it was burnt to the ground by retreating Nazis in 1944. Its site is now occupied by the **Natural History Museum** (Muzeum Przyrodniczo-Leśne; ☎ 681 22 75; Park Pałacowy; adult/concession 10/5zł, viewing tower 5/2.50zł; ☉ 9am-4.30pm Mon-Fri, 9am-5pm Sat & Sun mid-Apr–Sep, 9am-4pm Tue-Sun Oct–mid-Apr), which features exhibitions devoted to the park's history, the archaeology and ethnography of the region, and a collection of plants and animals that grow or live in the forest, including the famous bison. There's also a viewing tower that gives a great view over the village. Just north of the museum is a grove of 250-year-old oaks.

The main entrance to the Strictly Protected Area of the national park leads off the northwest corner of the Park Pałacowy.

STRICTLY PROTECTED AREA

Dating from 1921, the **Strictly Protected Area** (SPA, Obszar Ochrony Ścisłej; adult/child 10zł/5zł) is the oldest section of the national park, covering an area of around 4750 hectares, bordered on the north and west by the marshy Hwoźna and Narewka Rivers, and on the east by the Bielawiezskaja Primeval Forest National Park in Belarus.

The terrain is mostly flat, swampy in parts, and covered with mixed forest of oak, hornbeam, spruce and pine. Ancient trees reach spectacular sizes uncommon else-

where, with spruce 50m high and oak trunks 2m in diameter; some of the oak trees are more than 500 years old. The forest is home to a variety of large mammals, including elk, stag, roe deer, wild boar, lynx, wolf, beaver and the uncontested king of the *puszcza*, the bison. There are about 120 species of birds including owls, cranes, storks, hazelhens and nine species of woodpecker.

The SPA can only be entered in the company of an official guide, who can be hired through the travel agencies listed on p121. You can hike, travel by horse-drawn cart or, in winter, horse-drawn sledge. The standard tour takes about three hours, but longer routes including some of the more remote areas are also available (five hours or more).

Hiking is probably the best way to get a close feel for the forest, and the most popular with visitors. The normal route follows an 8km trail, which takes about four hours. The reserve gets pretty swampy in spring (March to April) and may at times be closed to visitors.

BISON RESERVE

If you don't have time for a guided tour of the SPA, get a close look at some of the wildlife in the **Bison Reserve** (Rezerwat Żubrów; ☎ 681 23 98; adult/concession 6/3zł; ☉ 9am-5pm May-Sep, 8am-4pm Tue-Sun Oct-Apr), a park where animals typical of the *puszcza*, including bison, elk, wild boar, wolf, stag and roe deer, are kept in large, ranch-style enclosures. You can also see the *żubroń*, a cross between a bison and cow, which has been bred so successfully in Białowieża that it is even larger than the bison itself, reaching up to 1200kg.

Another peculiarity is the tarpan (*Equus caballus gomelini*), a small, stumpy, mouse-coloured horse with a dark stripe running along its back from head to tail. The tarpan is a Polish cousin of the wild horse (*Equus ferus silvestris*) that once populated the Ukrainian steppes but became extinct in the 19th century. The horse you see is the product of selective breeding in the 1930s, which preserved the creature's original traits.

The reserve is 3km west of the Park Pałacowy (4.5km by road). You can get here on foot by the green- or yellow-marked trails, both starting from the PTTK office, or by the trail called Żebra Żubra (Bison's Ribs). You can also get there by horse-drawn cart – ask at the PTTK office for details.

THE BISON – BACK FROM THE BRINK

The European bison (*Bison bonasus*; żubr in Polish) is the biggest European mammal, its weight occasionally exceeding 1000kg. These large cattle, which live for as long as 25 years, look pretty clumsy but can move at 50km/h when they need to.

Bison were once found all over the continent, but the increasing exploitation of forests in Western Europe began to push them eastwards. In the 19th century the last few hundred bison lived in freedom in the Białowieża Forest. In 1916 there were still 150 of them here but three years later they were totally wiped out. By then, only about 50 bison survived in zoos throughout the world.

It was in Białowieża that an attempt to prevent the extinction of the bison began in 1929, by bringing several animals from zoos and breeding them in their natural habitat. The result is that today there are more than 300 bison living in freedom in the Białowieża Forest alone and about 350 more have been sent to a dozen other places in Poland. Many bison from Białowieża have been distributed among European zoos and forests, and their total current population is estimated at about 2500.

ROYAL OAKS

About 3km north of the Bison Reserve are the Royal Oaks (Dęby Królewskie), a score of ancient trees, some over four centuries old. There's a short walking trail that winds its way among them. Each of the trees is named after a Lithuanian or Polish monarch; biggest of the lot is Stefan Batory, 5.1m in circumference, 40m tall, and 450 years old.

To get here, take the motor road from Białowieża towards Narewka (it begins beside the PTTK office, and has blue trail marks) for 5km to a crossroads. Turn right; the oaks are 200m along the dirt road. You can also hike north from the Bison Reserve on a yellow-marked trail (3km). If you take a cart to the Bison Reserve, you can visit the oaks on the same trip.

Sleeping & Eating

Białowieża has a fair choice of accommodation options, most of which are inexpensive. Apart from the places listed here, the road approaching the village is lined with dozens of signs advertising *pokoj gościnne* (guest rooms) in private homes (25zł to 35zł per person).

Youth Hostel Paprotka (☎ 681 25 60; www .paprotka.com.pl; ul Waszkiewicza 6; dm 14-19zł, d 50zł) This friendly hostel is set in an old timber house, behind the mustard-coloured school building. There are dormitories of six to 12 beds each, a couple of doubles and quads, a kitchen and a nice big common room with a roaring fire at one end.

Pensjonat Unikat (☎ 681 27 74; www.unikat.bialo wieza.com; ul Waszkiewicza 39; d/tr/q 100/120/140zł; **P**) About 300m beyond the youth hostel, the Unikat is a rustic, 50-bed timber guesthouse done up like a hunting lodge – lots of wood panelling, a bison's head above the fireplace and a deerskin nailed to the wall above your bed.

Dom Turysty PTTK (☎ 681 25 05; Park Pałacowy; d/tr/q 80/96/120zł) This 19th-century, red-brick pavilion in the Park Pałacowy, is operated by PTTK, and offers small, basic rooms with private bathrooms, and a bistro serving cheap meals. It's popular with school and student groups, so it can occasionally be busy and noisy.

Hotel Żubrówka (☎ 681 23 03; www.hotel-zubrowka .pl; ul Olgi Gabiec 6; s 260-290zł, d 290-320zł, ste 380-900zł; **P** 💻) The Best Western–owned hotel is the plushest in town, continuing the hunting lodge theme with lots of red brick, timber beams, bison heads behind the reception desk and dark wood furniture in the rooms; the suites have open fireplaces too.

Hotel Białowieski (☎ 681 20 22; www.hotel .bialowieza.pl; ul Waszkiewicza 218b; s 140-170zł, d 170-200zł, ste 390zł; **P** 💻) The rooms at the child-friendly Białowieski are bright and modern and offer the same comfort level as the Żubrówka, but with a little less atmosphere; many have balconies overlooking the garden. There's a play area at the back.

Camping U Michała (☎ 681 27 03; ul Krzyże 11; per person 14-16zł) The well-equipped and comfortable camping ground is right beside the main road, at the entrance to Białowieża village, just five minutes' walk from the PTTK office. Facilities include hot showers, barbecue areas and electricity hook-ups for campervans.

MAZOVIA & PODLASIE

There are pretty good restaurants at the Białowieski and Żubrówka hotels, a pizzeria across the road from the latter, and a grill-bar beside the car park, behind the PTTK office. For self-caterers there is a grocery shop **Sklep Jarzębinka** (7am-10pm Mon-Sat, 8am-10pm Sun Jul & Aug, 7am-9pm Mon-Sat, 11am-7pm Sep-Jun), opposite the Hotel Żubrówka.

Getting There & Away

PKS buses run from stance No 2 at Hajnówka bus station (outside the train station) to Białowieża (4.40zł, one hour, eight daily). The private company Oktobus also runs buses (seven daily) to Białowieża from the bus stop outside the prominent CTO store on Hajnówka's main street, ul 3 Maja.

There are also two or three buses a day direct from Białystok to Białowieża (13zł, two hours).

GRABARKA

The **Holy Mountain of Grabarka** hardly means a thing to the average Roman Catholic Pole, yet it's a major place of pilgrimage for the Orthodox Church community. Remote from main roads and important urban centres, the 'mountain' (more of a wooded mound, really) lies 1km east of the obscure hamlet of Grabarka. The only town of any size in the region is Siemiatycze, 9km to the west.

A **convent** and a **church** are hidden among woods on top of the hill. The 18th-century timber church went up in flames in 1990, but it was rebuilt in a similar shape to the previous one. The convent was established in the aftermath of WWII, in an effort to gather all the nuns, scattered throughout the country, from the five convents that had existed before the war. Since then Grabarka has become the largest Orthodox pilgrimage centre in Poland.

The most striking thing about the place is that the hill is covered with around 20,000 **crosses** of different shapes and sizes ranging from 5cm miniatures to structures several metres tall. The story of the Grabarka crosses goes back to 1710, when an epidemic of cholera broke out in the region and decimated the population. Amid utter despair, a mysterious sign came from the heavens, which indicated that a cross should be built and carried to a nearby hill. Those who reached the top escaped death, and soon afterwards the epidemic disappeared.

The hill became a miraculous site and the thanksgiving church was erected. Since then pilgrims have been bringing crosses here to place alongside the first one.

Grabarka's biggest feast is the **Spas** (Day of Transfiguration of the Saviour) on 19 August. The ceremony begins the day before at 6pm and continues with Masses and prayers throughout the night, culminating at 10am with the Great Liturgy, celebrated by the metropolitan of the Orthodox Church in Poland. Up to 50,000 people may come from all over the country to participate.

Before climbing the holy mountain, the pilgrims perform ritual ablutions in the stream at the foot of the hill and drink water from the holy well, which supposedly has miraculous properties. The more fervent of them fill large bottles with the wonder-working liquid to take back home to prevent misfortune or heal the ill. Those who bring crosses have them blessed before adding them to the spectacular collection.

On that night, the surrounding forest turns into a car park and camping ground. Cars and tents fill every space between the trees. Despite this wave of modernity, the older, more traditional generation comes on foot without any camping gear and keeps watch all night. The light of the thin candles adds to the mysterious atmosphere.

If you wish to experience this magical night, you have the same options – to pitch your tent or to stay awake. The commercial community is well represented with plenty of stalls selling food and drink and a variety of religious goods, including CDs and cassettes of Orthodox church music.

Getting There & Away

Sycze train station (more of a halt with an empty platform) is a short walk from the hill. Trains run to Sycze from Siedlce (10zł, 1¼ hours, five daily) and Hajnówka (10zł, 1½ hours, four daily). There is one train daily direct from Warsaw (30zł, three hours).

From the Sycze train platform, it's a little over 1km to the holy mountain. There are no obvious signs to indicate the direction but the yellow trail heading south will get you there. If you are coming from Hajnówka, go left from the platform down the road. From there the road veers right, but follow the track straight into the forest – you'll come across the trail and signs as you go.

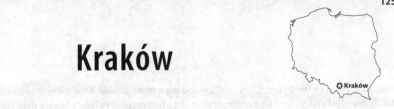

Kraków

CONTENTS

Kraków is Poland's third-largest city and the country's most popular tourist destination by far. As the royal capital for half a millennium, it absorbed more of Poland's history than any other city, and, miraculously, Kraków was the only large Polish city to emerge from WWII unscathed. Its stunning, well-preserved collection of medieval and Renaissance architecture is unrivalled, from the Old Town with its soaring Gothic churches, to the splendid Wawel Castle and Cathedral, and the former Jewish district of Kazimierz, with its poignant, silent synagogues.

No other city in Poland has so many historic buildings and monuments, and nowhere else will you encounter such a vast collection of works of art (2.5 million). In appreciation of the town's exceptional historic and artistic values, in 1978 Unesco included the centre of Kraków on its first World Heritage List. Kraków has traditionally been one of the major centres of Polish culture, and its status remains very high. Many leading figures of contemporary arts and culture – Andrzej Wajda, Roman Polański and Krzysztof Penderecki, to name just a few – are associated with Kraków, and two winners of the Nobel prize for literature, Czesław Miłosz and Wisława Szymborska, live here. The city also produced the first Polish pope.

Give yourself at least several days or even a full week for Kraków. This is not a place to rush through. The longer you stay, the more captivating you'll find it and there's almost always a festival or some other special event going on.

KRAKÓW

HIGHLIGHTS

■ **History**
A wealth of Polish history at the magnificent Wawel Castle (p134)

■ **Culture**
Leonardo da Vinci's *Lady with an Ermine* at the Czartoryski Museum (p138)

■ **Time Out**
The many cafés around Rynek Główny (p136)

■ **Offbeat**
The unique atmosphere of the Wieliczka Salt Mine (p147)

■ **Dining**
No chance of dumplings and cabbage with a gourmet meal at Paese (p155) or Copernicus (p156)

■ **Get Physical**
The ultramodern Park Wodny swimming pool complex (p147)

■ **Relaxing**
A canter round the Old Town in the back of a horse-driven carriage (p147)

| ■ TELEPHONE CODE: 12 | ■ POPULATION: 770,000 | ■ AREA: 327 SQ KM |

HISTORY

The first traces of the town's existence date from around the 7th century. In the 8th and 9th centuries Kraków was one of the main settlements of the Vistulans (Wiślanie), the tribe that several centuries earlier had spread around the region known as Little Poland or Małopolska. The earliest written record of Kraków dates from 965, when an Arabian traveller and merchant of Jewish descent, Ibrahim ibn Yaqub from Cordova, visited the town and referred to it in his account as a trade centre called Krakwa.

In 1000 the bishopric of Kraków was established, and in 1038 Kraków became the capital of the Piast kingdom. Wawel Castle and several churches were built in the 11th century and the town, initially gathered around Wawel Hill, grew in size and power.

In 1241 the Tatars overran Kraków and burned down the largely timber-built town. In 1257 the new town's centre was designed on a grid pattern, with a market square in the middle, and brick and stone largely replacing wood; Gothic became the dominant architectural style.

Good times came with the reign of King Kazimierz Wielki, a generous patron of art and scholarship. In 1364 he founded the Kraków Academy (later renamed the Jagiellonian University), the second university in central Europe after Prague's. Nicolaus Copernicus, who would later develop his heliocentric view of the universe, studied here in the 1490s.

Kraków's economic and cultural expansion reached a peak in the 16th century. The medieval Wawel castle gave way to a mighty palace, learning and science prospered, and the population passed the 30,000 mark.

It was not to last, however. The capital was moved to Warsaw in 1596, and although Kraków remained the place of coronations and burials, the king and the court resided in Warsaw, and political and cultural life was centred there. The Swedish invasion of 1655 did a lot of damage, and the 18th century, with its numerous invasions, accelerated the decline. By the end of the century the city's population had dropped to 10,000. Following the final Third Partition of Poland, Kraków fell under Austrian rule.

Austria proved to be the least oppressive of the three occupants, and the city enjoyed a reasonable and steadily increasing cultural and political freedom. By the closing decades of the 19th century it had become a major centre for Polish culture and the spiritual capital of the formally nonexistent country – a focus for intellectual life and theatre. The avant-garde artistic and literary movement known as Młoda Polska (Young Poland) was born here in the 1890s. It was also here that a national independence movement originated, which later produced the Polish Legions under the command of Józef Piłsudski.

By the outbreak of WWII the city had 260,000 inhabitants, 65,000 of whom were Jews. During the war, Kraków, like all other Polish cities, witnessed the silent departures of Jews who were never to be seen again. The city was thoroughly looted by Nazis but didn't experience major combat or bombing. As such, Kraków is virtually the only large Polish city that has its old architecture almost intact.

After the liberation, the communist government was quick to present the city with a huge steelworks at Nowa Huta, just a few miles away from the historic quarter, in an attempt to break the traditional intellectual and religious framework of the city. The social engineering proved less successful than its unanticipated by-product – ecological disaster. Monuments that had somehow survived Tatars, Swedes and Nazis plus numerous natural misfortunes have been gradually and methodically eaten away by acid rain and toxic gas.

With the creation of Nowa Huta and other new suburbs after the war, Kraków trebled in size to become the country's third-largest city, after Warsaw and Łódź. The historic core, though, has changed little and continues to be the political, administrative and cultural centre.

ORIENTATION

The great thing about Kraków is that almost all you need is at hand, and conveniently squeezed into the compact area of the Old Town. Even consulates, which normally prefer quiet, residential districts outside central areas, have gathered right in the heart of the historic quarter.

The Old Town, about 800m wide and 1200m long, has the Main Market Sq in the middle, and is encircled by the green park of the Planty, which was once a moat. On the southern tip of the Old Town sits the

Wawel castle, and further south stretches the district of Kazimierz.

The bus and train stations – where you're most likely to arrive – are next to each other on the northeastern rim of the Old Town. Rynek Główny, the heart of the city, is about 600m from the station. Balice Airport, also known as John Paul II International Airport, is about 12km west of the city centre, to which it is linked by regular bus service. If using a taxi, make sure you use a licensed operator with a meter. See p160 for information on getting to and from the airport.

Maps
Tourist offices have an ample supply of good, free maps of the city, and they should suffice for a short visit. If you want something more detailed, one of the best is the 1:20,000 scale *Falk Kraków* produced by **Pascal** (www.pascal.onet.pl in Polish), which also includes a 1:10,000 scale map of the Old Town and a 1:30,000 scale map of Nowa Huta. It costs around 6zł and is widely available at bookshops such as EMPiK.

INFORMATION
Bookshops
Columbus (Map pp132-3; ☎ 431 20 98; ul Grodzka 60)
EMPiK (Map pp132-3; ☎ 429 45 77; Rynek Główny 5) Has a good selection of English-language novels, plus international newspapers and magazines. It also has a good map section.
English Book Centre (Map pp132-3; ☎ 422 62 00; Plac Matejki 5)
Inter Book (Map pp132-3; ☎ 632 10 08; ul Karmelicka 27)
Jarden Jewish Bookshop (Map p141; ☎ 421 71 66; ul Szeroka 2) The widest choice of publications related to Jewish issues can be found at this bookshop in Kazimierz.
Massolit Books & Cafe (☎ 432 41 50; ul Felicjanek 4) Sells new and second-hand English-language fiction and nonfiction, including Polish history and literature.
Sklep Podróżnika (Map pp132-3; ☎ 429 14 85; ul Jagiellońska 6) Has some of the best selection of regional and city maps.
Szawal (Map pp132-3; ☎ 421 53 61; ul Długa 1)

Cultural Centres
British Council (Map pp132-3; ☎ 428 59 32; Rynek Główny 26)
French Institute (Map pp132-3; ☎ 424 53 50; www.ifcracovie.org.pl in Polish; ul Stolarska 15)
Goethe Institute (Map pp132-3; German; ☎ 422 69 02; Rynek Główny 20)

Italian Institute of Culture (Map pp132-3; ☎ 421 89 43; ul Grodzka 49)
Judaica Foundation (Map p141; ☎ 430 64 49; www.judaica.pl; ul Meiselsa 17)
Manggha Centre of Japanese Art & Technology (Map p129; ☎ 267 27 03; ul Konopnickiej 26)

Emergency
Ambulance (☎ 999)
Fire brigade (☎ 998)
Medical information (☎ 9439)
Police (☎ 997)
Public safety & tourist assistance information (☎ 0800 200 300, from a mobile phone ☎ 601 55 55; ✆ 8am-midnight) English and German.

Internet Access
There are plenty of Internet cafés all around town. All the places listed below are within 100m of the main square, and all open till at least 10pm, some until midnight. Prices vary, but you can expect to pay around 5zł per hour.
Cafe Internet br@cka (Map pp132-3; ☎ 421 78 52; ul Bracka 3-5)
Cafe Internet Citiplex Ars (Map pp132-3; ☎ 421 41 99; ul Św Jana 6)
Cafe Internet e-network (Map pp132-3; ☎ 431 23 94; ul Sienna 14)
Cyber Café U Luisa (Map pp132-3; ☎ 421 90 92; Rynek Główny 13)
InterMark Internet Club (Map pp132-3; ☎ 422 03 19; ul Floriańska 30)
Klub Garinet (Map pp132-3; ☎ 423 22 33; ul Floriańska 18)
Klub Internetowy Pl@net (Map pp132-3; ☎ 292 76 85; Rynek Główny 24) One of the handiest, right on the main square.
Looz Internet Café (Map pp132-3; ☎ 428 42 10; ul Mikołajska 13)

Internet Resources
www.cracow-life.com Lots of hints on eating, drinking and entertainment.
www.explore-krakow.com More information on sights and activities.
www.krakow-info.com An excellent introduction to the city.
www.krakow.pl Good general information.

Medical Services
Pharmacies are everywhere – the city has more than 200 of them. The **US Consulate Department of Citizen Services** (☎ 429 66 55) can provide a list of doctors who speak English.

GREATER KRAKÓW

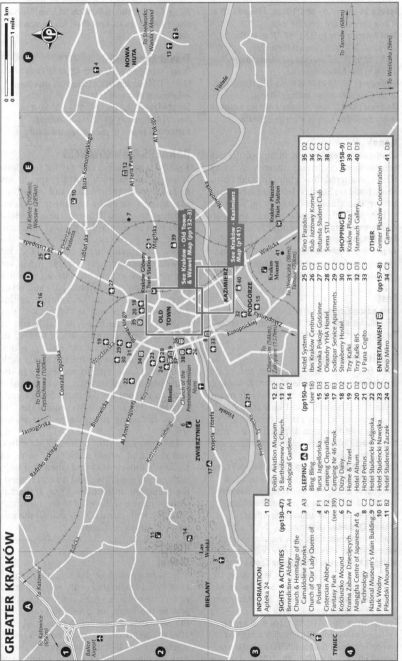

Apteka 24 (Map p129; ☎ 411 01 26; ul Mogilska 21) A 24-hour pharmacy east of the Old Town.

Dent America (Map pp132-3; ☎ 421 89 48; Plac Szczepański 3) A Polish-American dental clinic.

Falck (☎ 96 75; ul Racławicka 26) Attends house calls and has its own ambulance service.

Medicover (☎ 430 00 34; ul Krótka 1) Has English-speaking specialist doctors and does lab tests.

Mediprof (☎ 421 79 97; ul Szpitalna 38) Has doctors of various specialities, many of whom speak English.

Money

Cash can be exchanged in any of the numerous *kantors* (private currency-exchange offices) scattered throughout the Old Town. Some trade on Sunday, but rates are usually poorer; change enough money on Saturday to last you until Monday. There are many ATMs throughout the central area.

Bank Pekao (Map pp132-3; Rynek Główny 31) Travellers cheques are probably best changed here. Cash advances on Visa and MasterCard are also obtainable here, either from the cashier inside or the ATM outside.

Post

Main post office (Map pp132-3; ul Westerplatte 20; ☽ 7.30am-8.30pm Mon-Fri, 8am-2pm Sat, 9-11am Sun) The place to post your epistles.

Tourist Information

Two free magazines, *Welcome to Craców & Małopolska* and *The Visitor: Kraków & Zakopane* are available at tourist offices and some travel agencies and upmarket hotels. The *Kraków in Your Pocket* booklet (5zł) is a more useful source of practical information, particularly on eating, drinking and accommodation.

Cultural Information Centre (Centrum Informacji Kulturalnej; Map pp132-3; ☎ 421 77 87; www.karnet.krakow 2000.pl; ul Św Jana 2; ☽ 10am-6pm Mon-Fri, 11am-4pm Sat) This is the best place to get information about (and tickets for) the plethora of cultural events in the city.

Kraków Card (www.krakowcard.com; 2-/3-day 45/65zł) Available from tourist offices; gives free travel on public transport and free entry to many of the city's museums.

Małopolska Tourism Information Centre (Map pp132-3; ☎ 421 77 06; www.mcit.pl; Rynek Główny 1/3; ☽ 9am-7pm Mon-Fri, 9am-4pm Sat & Sun Apr-Sep, 9am-5pm Mon-Fri, 9am-2pm Sat Oct-Mar) The ever-busy main tourist office is inside the Cloth Hall.

Tourist office (Map p141; ☎ 432 08 40; ul Józefa 7; ☽ 9am-4pm Mon-Fri) This tourist office in Kazimierz provides information about Jewish heritage in that area.

Tourist office (Map pp132-3; ☎ 432 01 10; ul Szpitalna 25; ☽ 8am-8pm Mon-Fri, 9am-5pm Sat & Sun) This is a smaller and less harried tourist office, near the main train station.

Travel Agencies

Orbis Travel (Map pp132-3; ☎ 422 40 35; Rynek Główny 41) Sells transportation tickets (air, train, ferry) and organises tours – see p149.

Sonata Travel (Map pp132-3; ☎ 429 51 65; ul Św Tomasza 4) Represents STA Travel and has cheap international air fares for young people and students.

DANGERS & ANNOYANCES

Kraków is generally a safe city for travellers, although as a major tourist hot spot, it has its fair share of pickpockets and opportunistic thieves, so do be vigilant in crowded public areas. If you have a car, be sure not to leave it in an unguarded spot, as car crime is a growing problem.

If you're staying in the centre of the Old Town, especially near the Main Market Sq, you may experience late-night noise from the many restaurants, bars and other entertainment venues that cluster in this area; ask for a room at the back if this is going to be an issue. At the height of summer, the sheer numbers of tourists in town can be a little overwhelming, which can mean long queues for top sights such as Wawel Castle, and scarce seating in the more popular restaurants. You should also keep an eye out for the many horses-and-carriages that cart tourists around the Old Town, including along the pedestrianised streets.

In common with other Polish cities, you may find whole sections of some of Kraków's museums closed when you visit, with no prior warning and no corresponding reduction in the ticket price. If there is something you really want to see, it's worth checking with counter staff that all the galleries are open on the day.

SIGHTS
Wawel

The very symbol of Poland, the Wawel (*vah*-vel) is saturated with Polish history as no other place in the country. It was the seat of the kings for over 500 years from the early days of the Polish state, and even after the centre of power moved to Warsaw, it retained much of its symbolic and almost magical power. Today a silent guardian of a millennium of national history, Wawel is about the most visited sight in Poland.

The way up the Wawel Hill begins at the end of ul Kanonicza, from where a lane leads uphill. Past the equestrian statue of Tadeusz Kościuszko, it turns to the left leading to a vast open central square surrounded by several buildings, of which the cathedral and the castle are the major attractions.

Plan on at least four hours if you want anything more than just a general glance over the place. Note the different opening hours of the cathedral and the castle exhibitions (see the following sections). In summer, it's best to come early as there may be long queues for tickets later in the day. Alternatively, you can prebook your tickets by phoning at least one day ahead (☎ 422 16 97). Avoid weekends, when Wawel is besieged by visitors.

WAWEL CATHEDRAL

The national temple, the **Wawel Royal Cathedral** (Map pp132-3; royal tombs & bell tower adult/concession 8/4zł; 9am-3.45pm Mon-Sat, 12.15-3.45pm Sun) has witnessed most of the coronations, funerals and entombments of Poland's monarchs; wandering around the numerous, grandiose royal sarcophagi is like a tour through Polish history itself. Many outstanding artists had a hand in the gradual

creation of the cathedral, and have left behind a wealth of magnificent works of art. It's both an extraordinary artistic achievement and Poland's spiritual sanctuary.

The building you see is the third church on this site, erected between 1320 and 1364. The original cathedral (known as St Gereon's Church) was founded around 1020 by the first Polish king, Bolesław Chrobry, and was replaced with a larger Romanesque construction some 100 years later. When it was burnt down in 1305, only a crypt, known as St Leonard's Crypt, survived.

The present-day cathedral is basically a Gothic structure but chapels in different styles were later built all round it. Before you enter, note the massive iron door and, hanging on a chain to the left, huge prehistoric animal bones. They are believed to have magical powers; as long as they are here, the cathedral will remain too. The bones were excavated on the grounds at the beginning of the 20th century.

Once inside, you'll get lost in a maze of sarcophagi, tombstones and altarpieces scattered throughout the nave, chancel and ambulatory. Among a score of chapels, the showpiece is the **Sigismund Chapel** (Kaplica Zygmuntowska) on the southern wall, often referred to in tourist brochures as 'the most beautiful Renaissance chapel north of the

ST STANISLAUS – THE PATRON SAINT OF POLAND

St Stanislaus, Poland's first saint, was Kraków's bishop, Stanisław Szczepanowski in his real life. In 1079 he was condemned to death by King Bolesław Śmiały (Boleslaus the Bold) for joining the opposition against the king and excommunicating him. According to the legend, the king himself carried out the sentence by beheading the bishop.

The murder not only got the bishop canonised as patron saint of Poland, but it also cast a curse on the whole royal line. The first victim of the spiteful saint was the executioner himself, who was forced into exile. Successive kings built a commemorative church on the site of the crime (known as Skałka Church) and made penitential pilgrimages to it, but it didn't seem to help. In another effort, a sumptuous mausoleum to the saint was erected in the very centre of the Wawel Cathedral, yet the curse continued to hang over the throne. It was believed, for example, that no king named Stanisław could be crowned and buried at Wawel, and indeed, two Polish monarchs bearing this name, Stanisław Leszczyński and Stanisław August Poniatowski, were crowned and buried elsewhere.

The curse went even further: no clergyman named Stanisław could become Kraków's bishop. The only one of that name in the town's history, Stanisław Dąbski, was elected in 1699, but fell ill and died just a few months later. The Church authorities apparently didn't risk election of another Stanisław after that. Meanwhile, they have desperately tried to conciliate the saint. Every year, on the Sunday following 8 May (the saint's holy day), a procession attended by the Church's top hierarchy, with almost all the episcopate present, proceeds from the Wawel Cathedral to the Skałka Church.

KRAKÓW

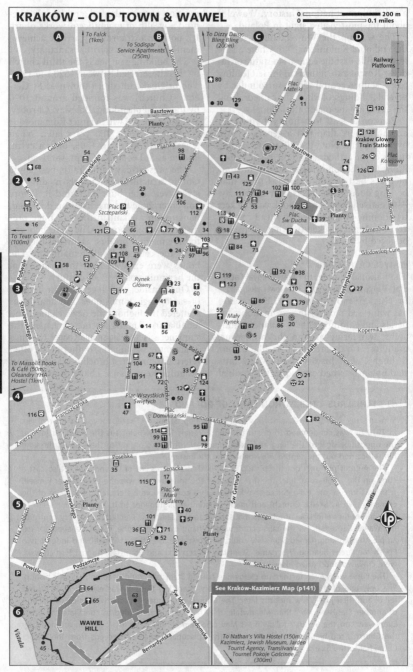

KRAKÓW – OLD TOWN & WAWEL

0 ————— 200 m
0 ————— 0.1 miles

To Falck
(1km)

To Sodispar
Service Apartments
(250m)

To Dizzy Daisy;
Bling Bling
(200m)

Railway
Platforms

127

Plac
Matejki

80

30   129   11

130

Basztowa

Planty

Krakóv Głowny
Train Station

Kraków Głowny
Train Station

128

Plac
Kolejowy

26

126

Lubicz

Garbarska

54

Pijarska   98

37

Basztowa

74

68

15

Reformacka

29

Sw. Jana   43

125

46

31

113

Plac
Szczepański

106

112

118

90

111

94

102   100

53

122

Sw. Ducha   39

Planty

Zamenhofa

9

107

4

34

Sw. Marka

18

Sw. Tomasza

121

66

77

103

Szczepańska

7

24

97   96

55

84

73

28

108

49

Sw. Krzyza

92   38

Kanonicza

120

Sw. Tomasza

32

109

119   123

110   70

58

Rynek
Głowny

25

117

23

48

60

89   69

79

27

62

41

61

10

Mikolajska   86   20

2

59

Mały
Rynek   87

5

3

19

14

56

Sw. Tomasza

Golebia

Wislna

88

Pasaz Bielaka   Sienna

93

67   8   13

21

104

75

33

22

72

124

12

44

51

Plac Wszystkich
Świętych

50

82

47

Plac
Dominikański

Wislopole

116

114

95

Dominikańska

99

78

83

85

Poselska

35

Senacka

17

115

Plac Sw.
Marii
Magdaleny

101   40

36   71   57

52

105   6

Podzamcze

Powisle

64

63

76

65

WAWEL
HILL

45

Vistula

Bernardyńska

See Kraków-Kazimierz Map (p141)

To Nathan's Villa Hostel (150m);
Kazimierz, Jewish Museum, Jarden
Tourist Agency, Transilvania,
Tournel Pokoje Gościnne
(300m)

Alps'. From the outside, it's easily recognised by its gilded dome. At the time of research, it was undergoing complete renovation and its magnificent silver panels were on show in the Cathedral Museum (p134). Another highlight is the **Holy Cross Chapel** (Kaplica Świętokrzyska) in the southwestern corner of the church, distinguished by the unique 1470 Byzantine frescoes and marble sarcophagus from 1492 by Veit Stoss.

Right in the middle of the church stands the flamboyantly baroque **Shrine of St Stanislaus** (Mauzoleum Św Stanisława), dedicated to the bishop of Kraków, who was canonised in 1253 to become the patron saint of Poland (see the boxed text on p131). The silver sarcophagus, adorned with 12 relief scenes from the saint's life, was made in Gdańsk between 1669 and 1671; the ornamented baldachin over it is about 40 years older.

Ascend the **Sigismund Tower** (accessible through the sacristy) to see the Sigismund Bell, popularly called 'Zygmunt'. Cast in 1520, it's 2m high and 2.5m in diameter, and weighs 11 tonnes, making it the largest historic bell in Poland. Its clapper weighs 350kg, and six strong men are needed to ring the bell, which happens only on the most important church holidays and for significant state events.

Back down in the church, go downstairs (from the left-hand aisle) to the **Poets' Crypt**, where three great Romantic poets, Adam Mickiewicz, Juliusz Słowacki and Cyprian Kamil Norwid, are buried.

Further towards the back of the church in the same aisle you'll find the entrance to **St Leonard's Crypt**, the only remnant of the 12th-century Romanesque cathedral. Follow through and you will get to the dank **Royal Crypts**, where, apart from kings, several national heroes, including Tadeusz Kościuszko and Józef Piłsudski, are buried. Visit the Royal Crypts at the end of your cathedral tour, because the exit is outside the cathedral.

Diagonally opposite the cathedral is the **Cathedral Museum** (Muzeum Katedralne; Map pp132-3; adult/concession 5/2zł; 10am-3pm Tue-Sun), which holds historical and religious objects from the cathedral. There are plenty of exhibits, including church plate and royal funerary regalia, but not a single crown. They were all stolen from the treasury by the Prussians in 1795 and reputedly melted down. Each crown could have easily contained 1kg of pure gold, not to mention the artistic value.

WAWEL CASTLE

The political and cultural centre of Poland until the early 17th century, **Wawel Royal Castle** (Map pp132-3; ☎ 422 51 55; www.wawel.krakow.pl) is, like the cathedral, the very symbol of Poland's national identity.

The original small residence was built in the early 11th century by King Bolesław Chrobry, beside the chapel dedicated to the Virgin Mary (known as the Rotunda of SS Felix and Adauctus). King Kazimierz Wielki turned it into a formidable Gothic castle. It was burnt down in 1499, and King Zygmunt Stary commissioned a new residence. Within 30 years a splendid Renaissance palace, designed by Italian architects, had been built. Despite further extensions and alterations, the Renaissance structure, complete with a spacious arcaded courtyard, has been preserved to this day.

Repeatedly sacked and devastated by Swedes and Prussians, the castle was occupied after the last Partition by the Austrians, who intended to make Wawel a citadel. Their plan included turning the castle into barracks, and the cathedral into a garrison church, moving the royal tombs elsewhere. They succeeded in realising some of their projects. They turned the royal kitchen and the coach house into a military hospital, and razed two churches standing at the outer courtyard to make room for a parade ground. During the work, they stumbled upon a perfectly preserved pre-Romanesque Rotunda of SS Felix and Adauctus and pulled down a good part of it. They also enveloped the whole hill with a new ring of massive brick walls, largely ruining the original Gothic fortifications.

Only in 1918 was the castle recovered by Poles and restoration work begun. It was continued after WWII and succeeded in recovering a good deal of the castle's earlier external form and its interior decoration.

The castle is now a museum containing five separate sections, each requiring a separate ticket that's valid for a specific time. There's a limited daily quota of tickets for some parts, so arrive early if you want to see everything, or phone ahead to reserve. You will need a ticket even on 'free' days. There's a ticket office on the access lane to the Wawel Hill, opposite the statue of Kościuszko, and another inside the castle compound.

The **Royal Chambers** (Komnaty Królewskie; adult/concession 12/7zł, free Mon; 9.30am-noon Mon, 9.30am-4pm Tue & Fri, 9.30am-3pm Wed, Thu & Sat, 10am-3pm Sun) is the largest and most impressive exhibition; the entrance is in the southeastern corner of the courtyard. Proceed through the apparently never-ending chain of rooms and chambers of the castle, restored in their original Renaissance and early-baroque style and crammed with period furnishings and works of art.

The two biggest (and most spectacular) interiors are the **Senators' Hall**, originally used for the senate sessions, court ceremonies, balls and theatre performances, and housing a magnificent series of five 16th-century tapestries following the story of Adam and Eve, and the **Throne Hall**. Look at the coffered ceiling of the latter, with 30 individually carved and painted wooden heads staring back at you. Known as Wawel heads, these are all that have survived from a total of 194 heads, which were carved in around 1540 by Sebastian Tauerbach. They were meant to illustrate the Life of Man, from birth to death. Look out too for the huge Bruges tapestry depicting 'God speaking to Noah', dating from around 1550.

Another of the castle's showpieces is the **Royal Private Apartments** (Prywatne Apartamenty Królewskie; adult/concession 15/12zł; 9.30am-4pm Tue & Fri, 9.30am-3pm Wed, Thu & Sat, 10am-3pm Sun); the entrance is in the middle of the eastern side of the courtyard. In a way, it's a continuation of the previous trip, but leading through some more-intimate interiors, and thus giving an insight into how the monarchs and their families once lived. The apartments are

WAWEL CHAKRA

Once upon a time Lord Shiva threw seven magic stones towards seven parts of the world, and one of these landed in Kraków. The places that had been hit began to radiate the god's energy. That's what legend says, but according to Hindu esoteric thinkers, these seven sites are indeed centres of supernatural energy that is reputed to give exceptional spiritual strengths. The centres, known as chakras, are related to seven celestial bodies and include Delhi (Moon), Delphi (Venus), Jerusalem (Sun), Kraków (Jupiter), Mecca (Mercury), Rome (Mars) and Velehrad (Saturn). The seven earth chakras have their seven equivalent spiritual centres of power in the human body.

Kraków's chakra resides at Wawel, in the northwestern corner of the royal castle's courtyard. It's believed to be centred in the chancel of St Gereon's Church, considered Wawel's first cathedral and founded in around 1020. Only the foundations and crypt of this church have survived, but they are off-limits to tourists. The holy force that, as the legend has it, lies here, is said to not only produce energy that revives life-giving forces, but also protects the city from misfortunes (as it did by saving it from destruction in WWII).

The history of the Wawel chakra is as esoteric as the chakra itself. It's not known whether the kings had any idea about what they were living on – at least there are no historic records about it. In the 19th century, Wawel was becoming a legendary place, but this was due more to its significance as a spiritual symbol of Poland in the time when the country formally didn't exist, rather than as a source of a supernatural energy.

This Pandora's box of controversy was probably opened by a Hindu traveller, who visited Kraków in the early 1920s and, for some reason, expressed particular interest in the remains of St Gereon's Church. The following years witnessed a number of other Hindu visitors, all of whom came specifically to the ruined church, where they meditated for hours in deep silence, to the increasing astonishment of the Wawel management. The management was perhaps in for an even bigger shock when the Indian government delegation, led by Prime Minister Nehru, kindly asked if they could include the ruin in their official Wawel tour and be left alone inside.

The chakra drew in all sorts of dowsers, who came with divining rods and wands. According to their measurements, Wawel radiates stronger energy than any other known site in Poland. They also confirmed that the main source of radiation lies underneath the chancel of St Gereon's Church. The studies published by them, after a complex research of Wawel, are full of diagrams, figures and comments, all of which seem to confirm the uniqueness of the place and its supernatural properties.

visited with a guide (included in the ticket price); English tours depart on the hour.

As in the Royal Chambers, you'll see plenty of magnificent old tapestries hanging on the walls. The collection, largely assembled by King Zygmunt August, once numbered over 350 pieces, but only 138 survive. Even so, this is probably the largest collection of its kind in Europe, and one of Wawel's most precious possessions.

The **Crown Treasury & Armoury** (Skarbiec Koronny i Zbrojownia; adult/concession 12/7zł, free Mon; ☿ same as Royal Chambers) are housed in vaulted Gothic rooms surviving from the 14th-century castle, in the northeastern part of the castle. The most famous object in the treasury is the Szczerbiec (Jagged Sword; c 1250), which was used at all Polish coronations from 1320 onwards. The adjacent armoury features a collection of old weapons from

various epochs (mainly from the 15th to 17th centuries), as well as replicas of the banners of the Teutonic Knights captured at the Battle of Grunwald in 1410.

The **Museum of Oriental Art** (Sztuka Wschodu; adult/concession 6/4zł, free Mon; ☿ same as Royal Chambers) features a collection of 17th-century Turkish banners and weaponry, captured after the Battle of Vienna, displayed along with a variety of old Persian carpets, Chinese and Japanese ceramics, and other Asian antiques. The entrance is from the northwestern corner of the courtyard.

The **Lost Wawel** (Wawel Zaginiony; adult/concession 6/4zł, free Mon; ☿ 9.30am-4pm Tue & Fri, 9.30am-3pm Wed, Thu & Sat, 10am-3pm Sun) exhibition is accommodated in the old royal kitchen. Apart from the remnants of the late 10th-century Rotunda of SS Felix and Adauctus, which is reputedly the first church in Poland, you can see various archaeological finds (including colourful old ceramic tiles from the castle's stoves), as well as models of the previous Wawel churches. The entrance to the exhibition is from the outer side of the castle.

DRAGON'S CAVE

You can complete your Wawel trip with a visit to the **Dragon's Cave** (Smocza Jama; Map pp132-3; admission 3zł; ☺ 10am-5pm Apr-Oct), former home of the legendary Wawel Dragon (Smok Wawelski). The entrance to the cave is next to the **Thieves' Tower** (Baszta Złodziejska) at the western edge of the hill. From here you'll get a good panorama over the Wisła and the suburbs further to the west, including the Manggha Centre of Japanese Art & Technology on the opposite bank of the river, and the Kościuszko Mound far away on the horizon.

After you buy your ticket from the coin-operated machine at the entrance, you descend 135 steps to the cave, then stumble some 70m through its damp interior and emerge onto the bank of the Wisła next to the fire-spitting bronze dragon, the work of renowned contemporary sculptor Bronisław Chromy.

KRAKÓW'S DRAGON

According to legend, once upon a time there lived a powerful prince, Krak or Krakus, who built a castle on a hill named Wawel on the banks of the Vistula and founded a town named after himself. It would have been paradise if not for a dragon living in a cave underneath the castle. This fearsome and ever-hungry huge lizard decimated cattle and sheep, and was not averse to human beings, especially pretty maidens.

The wise prince ordered a sheep's hide to be filled with sulphur, which was set alight, and the whole thing was hurled into the cave. The voracious beast devoured the bait in one gulp, only then feeling the sulphur burning in its stomach. The dragon rushed to the river, and drank and drank and finally exploded, giving the citizens a spectacular fireworks display. The town was saved. The dragon has become the symbol of the city, immortalised in countless images, and the dragon's monument has been placed where the beast once lived.

Old Town

The Old Town developed gradually throughout the centuries. Its plan was drawn up in 1257 after the Tatar invasions, and has survived more or less in its original form. The construction of the fortifications began in the 13th century, and it took almost two centuries to envelop the town with a powerful, 3km-long chain of double defensive walls complete with 47 towers and eight main entrance gates, plus a wide moat.

With the development of military technology, the system lost its defensive capability and, apart from a small section to the north, was demolished at the beginning of the 19th century. The moat was filled up and a ring-shaped park, the Planty, was laid out on the site, surrounding the Old Town with parkland.

The Old Town has plenty of historical monuments, enough to keep you exploring for at least several days. There are a dozen museums and nearly 20 churches here, not to mention scores of other important sights.

Except for some enclaves, the sector is car-free or a car limited-access area, so you can stroll largely undisturbed by traffic noise and pollution. It's best explored casually and without a particular plan, savouring its architectural details, while dropping into art galleries and cosy cafés and bars along the way.

RYNEK GŁÓWNY

Measuring 200m by 200m, Kraków's **Main Market Sq** (Rynek Główny) is the largest medieval town square in Poland and reputedly in all of Europe. It's considered to be one of the finest urban designs of its kind. Its layout was drawn up in 1257 and has been retained to this day, though the buildings have changed over the centuries. Today most of them look neoclassical, but don't let the façades confuse you – the basic structures are older, sometimes considerably so, as can be seen in their doorways, architectural details and interiors. Their cellars date from medieval times.

Dominating the square is the centrally positioned **Cloth Hall** (Sukiennice; Map pp132-3). It was built in the 14th century as a centre for the cloth trade, but was gutted by fire in 1555 and rebuilt in Renaissance style. In the late 19th century arcades were added, giving the hall a more-decorative ap-

BRENT WINEBRENNER

The 16th-century Wawel Castle (p134), Kraków

KRZYSZTOF DYDYŃSKI

A colourful café, Kraków (p154)

Cloth Hall (p136), Kraków

KRZYSZTOF DYDYŃSKI

MANFRED GOTTSCHALK

Horse-drawn carriage (p147), Kraków

Krzyżtopór Castle (p180), Ujazd

Krzyżtopór Castle (p180), Ujazd

Rock formations, Kraków-Częstochowa Upland (p164)

Arcaded burghers' houses, Old Town Sq (p202), Zamość

pearance. The ground floor is still a trading centre for crafts and souvenirs, while the upper floor is taken over by the **Gallery of 19th-Century Polish Painting** (Map pp132-3; ☎ 422 11 66; adult/concession 5/2.50zł, free Sun; ⏰ 10am-3pm Tue, Wed & Fri-Sun, 10am-5.30pm Thu). It displays works by painters of the period, including Józef Chełmoński, Jacek Malczewski, Aleksander Gierymski and the leader of monumental historic painting, Jan Matejko.

The **Town Hall Tower** (Wieża Ratuszowa; Map pp132-3; ☎ 422 99 22, ext 218; admission 4zł; ⏰ 10am-4.30pm), next to the Cloth Hall, is all that is left of the 15th-century town hall dismantled in the 1820s. It has been extensively renovated over the past years and is open to visitors in summer.

At the northern corner of the Rynek, the Krzysztofory Palace is home to the **Historical Museum of Kraków** (Muzeum Historyczne Krakowa; Map pp132-3; ☎ 422 99 22; Rynek Główny 35; adult/concession 4/2.50zł; ⏰ 9am-3.30pm Tue, Wed & Fri, 11am-6pm Thu). It features a bit of everything related to the city's past, including old clocks, armour, paintings, *szopki* (Nativity scenes), and the costume of the Lajkonik (see the boxed text on p150).

In the southern corner of the square is the small, domed **St Adalbert's Church** (Kościół Św Wojciecha; Map pp132-3). One of the oldest churches in the town, its origins date from the 10th century. You can see the original foundations in the basement, where a small exhibition also presents archaeological finds excavated from the Rynek.

A few steps north from the church is the **Statue of Adam Mickiewicz** (Map pp132-3) surrounded by four allegorical figures: the Motherland, Learning, Poetry and Valour. It's here that the *szopki* competition is held in early December (see p150).

The flower stalls just to the north of the statue have reputedly been trading on this site from time immemorial. This area is also the 'pasture' for Kraków's population of pigeons, thought to be the second-largest in Europe after that of Venice.

ST MARY'S CHURCH

Overlooking the square from the east is **St Mary's Church** (Kościół Mariacki; Map pp132-3; Rynek Główny 4; adult/concession 4/2zł; ⏰ 11.30am-6pm Mon-Sat, 2-6pm Sun). The first church on this site was built in the 1220s and, typically for the period, was 'oriented' – that is, its presby-

tery pointed east. Following its destruction during the Tatar raids, the construction of a mighty basilica started, using the foundations of the previous church. That's why the church stands at an angle to the square.

The façade is dominated by two unequal towers. The lower one, 69m high and topped by a Renaissance dome, serves as a bell tower and holds five bells, while the taller one, 81m high, has traditionally been the city's property and functioned as a watchtower. It's topped with a spire surrounded by turrets – a good example of medieval craftsmanship – and in 1666 was given a 350kg gilded crown that's about 2.5m in diameter. The gilded ball higher up contains Kraków's written history.

The main church entrance, through a baroque porch added to the façade in the 1750s, is only used by worshippers; tourists enter through the side, southern door, which gives access to the chancel. The chancel is illuminated by the magnificent stained-glass windows dating from the late 14th century. On the opposite side of the church, above the organ loft, is a fine Art Nouveau stained-glass window by Stanisław Wyspiański and Józef Mehoffer. The colourful wall paintings, designed by Jan Matejko, harmonise beautifully with the medieval architecture and are an appropriate background for the grand high altar, which is acclaimed as the greatest masterpiece of Gothic art in Poland.

The altarpiece is a pentaptych (consisting of a central panel and two pairs of side wings), intricately carved in lime wood, painted and gilded. The main scene represents the Dormition of the Virgin, while the wings portray scenes from the life of Christ and the Virgin. The altarpiece is topped with the Coronation of the Virgin and, on both sides, the statues of the patron saints of Poland, St Stanislaus and St Adalbert.

Measuring about 13m high and 11m wide, the pentaptych is the largest piece of medieval art of its kind. It took 12 years for its maker, the Nuremberg sculptor Veit Stoss (known to Poles as Wit Stwosz), to complete this monumental work before it was solemnly consecrated and revealed in 1489.

The pentaptych is open daily at 11.50am and closed after the evening Mass, except for Saturday when it's left open for the Sunday morning Mass. The altarpiece apart,

KRAKÓW'S MUSICAL SYMBOL

Every hour the *hejnał* (bugle call) is played on a trumpet from the higher tower of St Mary's Church to the four quarters of the world in turn. Today a musical symbol of the city, this simple melody, based on only five notes, was played in medieval times as a warning call. Intriguingly, it breaks off abruptly in midbar. Legend links it to the Tatar invasions; when the watchman on duty spotted the enemy and sounded the alarm, a Tatar arrow pierced his throat midphrase, the tune has stayed this way thereafter. Since 1927, the *hejnał* has been broadcast on Polish Radio every day at noon.

don't miss the stone crucifix on the baroque altar in the head of the right-hand aisle, another work by Veit Stoss, and the still larger crucifix placed on the rood screen, attributed to pupils of the master.

To the south of the church is the small, charming **St Mary's Sq** (Plac Mariacki), which until the early 19th century was a parish cemetery. The 14th-century **St Barbara's Church** (Kościół Św Barbary; Map pp132–3), bordering the square on the east, was the cemetery chapel. Next to its entrance, there's an open chapel featuring stone sculptures of Christ and three apostles, also attributed to the Stoss school.

A passage adjoining the church will take you straight onto the **Little Market Sq** (Mały Rynek), which was once the second-largest marketplace in town and traded mainly in meat.

CZARTORYSKI MUSEUM

The **Czartoryski Museum** (Muzeum Czartoryskich; Map pp132-3; ☎ 422 55 66; ul Św Jana 19; adult/concession 7/4zł; ☯ 10am-3.30pm Tue-Thu & Sat & Sun, 10am-6pm Fri) is one of the best in town, and is itself something of a museum of a museum. Originally established in 1800 in Puławy by Princess Izabela Czartoryska as the first historical museum in Poland, the collection was secretly moved to Paris after the November Insurrection of 1830 (in which the family was implicated) and in the 1870s brought to Kraków. The collection experienced another 'excursion' during WWII when the Nazis seized it and took it to Ger-

many, and not all the exhibits were recovered. Even so, there's a lot to see, including a fascinating collection of European painting, mainly Italian, Dutch and Flemish. The stars of the show are Leonardo da Vinci's masterpiece, *Lady with an Ermine* (c 1482) and Rembrandt's *Landscape with the Good Samaritan*, also known as *Landscape before a Storm* (1638). Other exhibitions include Greek, Roman, Egyptian and Etruscan art and Turkish weapons and artefacts, such as carpets, saddles and a campaign tent, recovered after the 1683 Battle of Vienna. Much of the labelling is in French, though there are occasional English explanations too. Allow yourself at least an hour or two to view the collection.

COLLEGIUM MAIUS

The **Collegium Maius** (Map pp132-3; ☎ 422 05 49; ul Jagiellońska 15; adult/concession 10/5zł; ☯ 10am-3pm Mon-Wed & Fri, 10am-6pm Thu, 11am-2pm Sat), built as part of the Kraków Academy, is the oldest surviving university building in Poland, and one of the best examples of 15th-century Gothic architecture in the city. It has a magnificent arcaded courtyard and a fascinating university collection kept inside.

You will be shown around historic interiors where you'll find rare 16th-century astronomic instruments that were supposedly used by Copernicus, a bizarre alchemy room, old rectors' sceptres and, the highlight of the show, the oldest existing globe (c 1510) showing the American continent. You'll also visit an impressive Aula, a hall with an original Renaissance ceiling, crammed with portraits of kings, benefactors and professors of the university.

All visits are guided in groups; tours begin every half-hour and there's usually one tour daily in English. Tours in French and German can be arranged on request. In summer it's advisable to reserve in advance, either personally in the museum office (2nd floor) or by phone. The **courtyard** (☯ 7am-sunset) can be entered free of charge.

Also here is an interactive exhibition hall, **Ancient and Modern Sciences** (☎ 422 10 33, ext 1319; adult/concession 6/4zł; ☯ 10am-2.30pm Mon-Sat), which has hands-on displays and experiments covering topics such as acoustic waves, time measurements and alchemy, which children with a scientific bent might enjoy.

ST ANNE'S CHURCH

Around the corner from the Collegium Maius is the baroque **St Anne's Church** (Kościół Św Anny; Map pp132-3; ul Św Anny 11). Designed by the omnipresent Tylman van Gameren, and built in the late 17th century as a university church, it was long the site of inaugurations of the academic year, doctoral promotions, and a resting place for many eminent university professors. A spacious, bright interior fitted out with fine furnishings, gravestones and epitaphs, and embellished with superb stucco work and murals – all stylistically homogeneous – puts the church among the best classical baroque buildings in Poland.

MUSEUM OF PHARMACY

The **Museum of Pharmacy** (Muzeum Farmacji; Map pp132-3; ☎ 421 92 79; ul Floriańska 25; adult/concession 6/3zł; ☺ 3-7pm Tue, 11am-2pm Wed-Sun) is one of Europe's largest museums of its kind, and one of the best. Accommodated in a beautiful historic townhouse, it features a 22,000-piece collection, which includes old laboratory equipment, rare pharmaceutical instruments, heaps of glassware, stoneware, mortars, jars, barrels, medical books and documents.

MATEJKO HOUSE

Matejko House (Dom Matejki; Map pp132-3; ☎ 422 59 26; ul Floriańska 41; adult/concession 5/3zł, free Sun; ☺ 9am-3.30pm Tue, Thu, Sat & Sun, 11am-6pm Wed & Fri) is the place where Jan Matejko lived and worked for the 20 most fruitful years of his life (1873–93). Matejko, uncontested leader of national historical painting, was renowned for his powerful canvases documenting Polish history. His house is now a museum displaying memorabilia and some of his paintings and drawings (his larger paintings are in the Cloth Hall gallery). The house is a 16th-century structure, remodelled according to a design by Matejko himself.

FLORIAN GATE

The **Florian Gate** (Brama Floriańska; Map pp132-3) is the only one of the original eight gates that was not dismantled during the 19th-century 'modernisation'. It was built around 1300, although the top is a later addition. The adjoining walls, together with two towers, have also been left, and today host an outdoor art gallery, where you can peruse some distressingly kitsch artwork.

BARBICAN

The most intriguing remnant of the medieval fortifications, the **Barbican** (Barbakan; Map pp132-3; adult/concession 5/3zł; ☺ 10.30am-6pm in summer) is a powerful, circular brick bastion adorned with seven turrets. There are 130 loopholes in its 3m-thick walls. This curious piece of defensive art was built around 1498 as an additional protection of the Florian Gate, and was once connected to it by a narrow passage running over a moat. It's one of the very few surviving structures of its kind in Europe, and also the largest and perhaps the most beautiful.

ARCHAEOLOGICAL MUSEUM

The **Archaeological Museum** (Muzeum Archeologiczne; Map pp132-3; ☎ 422 75 60; ul Poselska 3; adult/concession 7/5zł; ☺ 9am-2pm Mon-Wed, 2-6pm Thu, 10am-2pm Fri & Sun) presents Małopolska's history from the Palaeolithic period up until the early Middle Ages. Also on show is an absorbing collection of ancient Egyptian artefacts, including both human and animal mummies. The gardens, laid out with rose bushes, magnolia trees and contemporary sculptures, are a lovely place for a stroll afterwards.

CHURCH OF THE HOLY CROSS

Undistinguished from the outside, the small 15th-century **Church of the Holy Cross** (Kościół Św Krzyża; Map pp132-3; ul Św Krzyża 23) deserves a visit for its Gothic vaulting, which is one of the most beautiful in the city. An unusual design with the palmlike vault supported on a single central column, it was constructed in 1528 and was recently thoroughly renovated.

FRANCISCAN CHURCH

The mighty **Franciscan Church** (Kościół Franciszkanów; Map pp132-3; ul Franciszkańska) was erected in the second half of the 13th century but repeatedly rebuilt and refurnished after at least four fires, the last and the most destructive being in 1850 when almost all the interior was burnt out. Of the present decorations, the most interesting are the Art Nouveau stained-glass windows in the chancel and above the organ loft, the latter regarded among the greatest in Poland. All were designed by Stanisław Wyspiański, who also executed most of the frescoes in the presbytery and the transept.

KRAKÓW

KRAKÓW

Adjoining the church from the south is the monastery, which preserved its original Gothic cloister complete with fragments of 15th-century frescoes. Portraits of Kraków's bishops adorn the cloister walls. The entrance to the cloister is from the transept of the church or from the outside next to the chancel.

DOMINICAN CHURCH
The equally powerful **Dominican Church** (Kościół Dominikanów; Map pp132-3; ul Stolarska 12) was also built in the 13th century and badly damaged in the 1850 fire, though its side chapels, dating mainly from the 16th and 17th centuries, have been preserved in reasonably good shape. Monumental neo-Gothic confessionals and stalls are a later adornment. Note the original 14th-century doorway at the main entrance to the church.

The monastery, just behind the northern wall of the church, is accessible from the street. The cloister there has retained its Gothic shape pretty well and boasts a number of fine epitaphs, tombs and paintings.

WYSPIAŃSKI MUSEUM
Dedicated to one of Kraków's most beloved sons and the key figure of the Młoda Polska (Young Poland) movement, the **Wyspiański Museum** (Muzeum Wyspiańskiego; Map pp132-3; ☎ 422 70 21; ul Szczepańska 11; adult/concession 7/5zł; ☼ 11am-6pm Tue-Fri, 10am-3pm Sat & Sun), on the 1st and 2nd floors of Szołayski House, reveals how many branches of art Stanisław Wyspiański explored. A painter, poet and playwright, he was also a designer particularly renowned for his stained-glass designs, some of which are in the exhibition.

His most unusual proposal, though, is the 'Acropolis', a project to reconstruct the Wawel as Poland's political, religious and cultural centre. There's a model made according to his design – an amazing mix of epochs and styles, a Greek amphitheatre and a Roman circus included. Wyspiański's vision has never been realised. Later calculations proved that the hill wouldn't support so many buildings squeezed onto its top.

CHURCH OF SS PETER & PAUL
The first baroque building in Kraków, the **Church of SS Peter & Paul** (Kościół Św Piotra i Pawła; Map pp132-3; ul Grodzka) was erected by the Jesuits, who had been brought to the city in 1583 to fight the Reformation. Designed on the Latin cross layout and topped with a large dome, the church has a refreshingly sober interior, apart from some fine stucco decoration on the vault. The figures of the Twelve Apostles standing on columns in front of the church are copies of the statues from 1723.

ST ANDREW'S CHURCH
Built towards the end of the 11th century, **St Andrew's Church** (Kościół Św Andrzeja; Map pp132-3; ul Grodzka) is one of Kraków's oldest, and has preserved much of its austere Romanesque stone exterior. As soon as you enter, though, you're in a totally different world; its small interior was subjected to a radical baroque overhaul in the 18th century.

ARCHDIOCESAN MUSEUM
Located in a 14th-century townhouse, the **Archdiocesan Museum** (Muzeum Archidiecezjalne; Map pp132-3; ☎ 421 89 63; ul Kanonicza 19; adult/concession 5/3zł; ☼ 10am-3pm Tue-Sat) presents a collection of religious sculpture and painting, dating from the 13th to 16th centuries. Also on display is the room where Karol Wojtyła (today's Pope John Paul II) lived from 1951 until 1958, complete with his furniture and belongings – including his skis.

MUSEUM OF INSURANCE
If you're really stuck for something to do, why not drop by the **Museum of Insurance** (☎ 422 88 11; Map pp132-3; ul Dunajewskiego 3; admission free; ☼ 9-11am Tue-Fri), the only one of its kind in Poland. Documents, policies, and 'documents related to insurance policies' are on display, alongside a few portraits and historical artefacts. For those keen to learn more, there's also a library.

Outside the Old Town
MANGGHA CENTRE OF JAPANESE ART & TECHNOLOGY
The **Manggha Centre** (Map p129; ☎ 267 27 03; www.manggha.krakow.pl in Polish; ul Konopnickiej 26; adult/concession 5/3zł, free Sun; ☼ 10am-6pm Tue-Sun), sitting on the southern bank of the Wisła, was the brainchild of the Polish film director Andrzej Wajda, who donated the US$340,000 Kyoto Prize money he received in 1987 for his artistic achievements to fund a permanent home for the National Museum's extensive collection of Japanese art,

ceramics, weapons, fabrics, scrolls, wood-cuts and comics. The building, opened in 1994, was designed by the Japanese architect Arata Isozaki. The bulk of the collection is made up of the 6500 or so pieces assembled by Feliks Jasieński (1861–1929), an avid traveller, art collector, literary critic and essayist, known by his pen name of Mangggha (which is where the centre's name comes from). He donated the collection to Kraków's National Museum, before it had the facilities to exhibit it. The centre also has a multifunctional high-tech auditorium where events presenting Japanese culture (film, theatre, traditional music) are held. Guided tours in foreign languages are also available (100zł).

POLISH AVIATION MUSEUM
On show at the **Polish Aviation Museum** (Muzeum Lotnictwa Polskiego; Map p129; ☎ 412 90 00; Al Jana Pawła II 39; adult/concession 7/4zł; ☻ 9am-4pm Tue-Fri, 10am-3pm Sat, 10am-4pm Sun May-Oct, 9am-3pm Mon-Fri Nov-Apr) is Poland's largest collection of flying machines, made up of over 100 aircraft. Rare examples of WWI British, German and Russian planes are here, as well as Polish aircraft from WWII to the present day. Entry to the grounds is free on Mondays.

Kazimierz
Today one of Kraków's inner suburbs and located within walking distance southeast of the Wawel, Kazimierz was for a long time an independent town with its own municipal

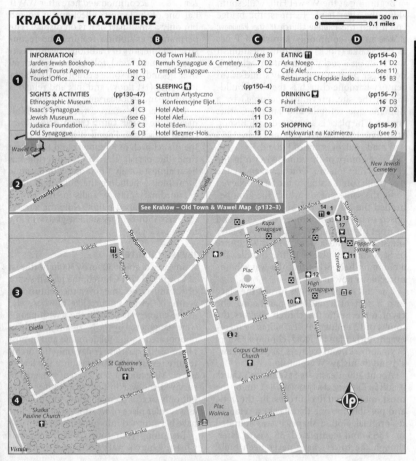

charter and laws. Its colourful history was determined by its mixed Jewish-Polish population, and though the ethnic structure is now wholly different, the architecture gives a good picture of its past, with clearly distinguishable sectors of what were Christian and Jewish quarters. The suburb is home to some important tourist sights, including churches, synagogues and museums.

WESTERN KAZIMIERZ

The western part of Kazimierz was traditionally Catholic, and although many Jews settled here from the early 19th century until WWII, the quarter preserved much of its original character, complete with its churches.

Beginning at the Wawel Hill, walk south along the river bank. Just past the bridge you'll find the **Pauline Church** (Kościół Paulinów; ul Skałeczna 15), commonly known to Poles as the Skałka (Rock) due to its location; it was built on a rocky promontory, which is no longer pronounced. Today's mid-18th-century baroque church is the third building on the site, previously occupied by a Romanesque rotunda and later a Gothic church. The place is associated with Bishop Stanisław (Stanislaus), canonised in 1253 and made patron saint of Poland.

The memory of the saint lives on in the church's dim interior. You can even see the tree trunk (on the altar to the left), believed to be the same one on which the king beheaded the bishop. The body is then supposed to have been dumped into the pond in front of the church. The pond was later transformed into a pool, with a sculpture of St Stanislaus placed in the middle. It's a common held belief that the water holds miraculous powers.

The cult of the saint has turned the place into a sort of a national pantheon. The crypt underneath the church shelters the tombs of 12 eminent Poles including medieval historian Jan Długosz, composer Karol Szymanowski, and painters Jacek Malczewski and Stanisław Wyspiański.

About 200m east sits **St Catherine's Church** (Kościół Św Katarzyny; ul Augustiańska 7). One of the most monumental churches in the city, and possibly the one that has best retained its original Gothic shape, it was founded in 1363 and completed 35 years later, though the towers have never been built.

The church was once on the corner of Kazimierz' market square but the area was built up in the 19th century. The lofty and spacious whitewashed interior boasts the imposing, richly gilded baroque high altar from 1634.

Continue east on ul Skałeczna, turn right into ul Krakowska, and you'll see the former **town hall** (Map p141) of Kazimierz in front of you. Built in the late 14th century in the middle of a vast market square (Plac Wolnica is all that's left), it was significantly extended in the 16th century, at which time it acquired its Renaissance appearance. The **Ethnographic Museum** (Muzeum Etnograficzne; Map p141; ☎ 430 55 63; Plac Wolnica 1; adult/concession 4/3zł, free Sun; ☉ 10am-6pm Mon, 10am-3pm Wed-Fri, 10am-2pm Sat & Sun) accommodated here after WWII has one of the largest collections in Poland but only a small part of it is on display. The permanent exhibition features the reconstructed interiors of traditional peasant cottages (ground floor), folk costumes from all over Poland and some extraordinary Nativity scenes (1st floor), and folk and religious painting and woodcarving (2nd floor).

In the northeastern corner of Plac Wolnica is the **Corpus Christi Church** (Kościół Bożego Ciała; ul Bożego Ciała). Founded in 1340, it was the first church in Kazimierz and for a long time the parish church. Its interior has been almost totally fitted out with baroque furnishings, including the huge high altar, extraordinary massive stalls in the chancel and a boat-shaped pulpit. Note the surviving early 15th-century stained-glass window in the presbytery.

JEWISH QUARTER

A tiny area of about 300m by 300m northeast of Corpus Christi Church, the Jewish sector of Kazimierz became, over the centuries, a centre of Jewish culture like nowhere else in the country. In WWII, the Jewish people were slaughtered by the Nazis and with them disappeared all the folklore, life and atmosphere of the quarter. Today only the architecture reveals that this was once the Jewish town. Miraculously, all seven synagogues survived the war in better or worse shape, but only one of them continues to function as a regular place of worship, and two more have been turned into museums.

Beginning your tour from the Corpus Christi Church, walk north and then east-

KAZIMIERZ' CHEQUERED JEWISH-POLISH HISTORY

Kazimierz was founded in 1335 by King Kazimierz Wielki (hence its name) just on the southern outskirts of Kraków. Thanks to numerous privileges granted by the king, it developed swiftly and soon had its own town hall and a market square almost as large as that of Kraków, and two huge churches. The town was encircled with defensive walls and by the end of the 14th century came to be Małopolska's most important and wealthiest city after Kraków.

The first Jews came to settle in Kazimierz soon after its foundation, but it wasn't until the end of the 15th century that their numbers began to grow quickly, following their expulsion from Kraków in 1494 by King Jan Olbracht. They settled in a relatively small prescribed area of Kazimierz, northeast of the Christian quarter, and the two sectors were separated by a wall.

The subsequent history of Kazimierz was punctuated by fires, floods and plagues, with both communities living side by side, confined to their own sectors. The Jewish quarter became home to Jews fleeing persecution from all corners of Europe, and it grew particularly quickly, gradually determining the character of the whole town.

At the end of the 18th century Kazimierz was administratively incorporated into Kraków, and in the 1820s the walls were pulled down. At the outbreak of WWII Kazimierz was a predominantly Jewish suburb, with a distinctive culture and atmosphere. But most Jews were exterminated by the Nazis in the death camps. Of 65,000 Kraków Jews (most of whom lived in Kazimierz) in 1939, only about 6000 survived the war. The current Jewish population in the city is estimated at between 100 and 150.

During the communist rule, Kazimierz was largely a forgotten place on Kraków's map, partly because the government didn't want to touch the sensitive Jewish question. In the early 1990s, the suburb slowly made its way onto the pages of tourist publications but its grubby appearance didn't help much to promote it. Then came Steven Spielberg to shoot *Schindler's List* and everything changed overnight.

Actually, Kazimierz was not the setting of the movie's plot – most of the events portrayed in the film took place in the Płaszów death camp, the Podgórze ghetto and Schindler's factory, all of which were further to the southeast, beyond the Vistula. Yet the film turned the world's attention to Kraków's Jewry as a whole, and since Kazimierz is the only substantial visual relic of Jewish heritage, it has benefited the most. 'Schindler's Tourism' now draws in crowds of visitors – Poles and foreigners alike – to the place, which hardly saw any tourists a decade ago. Isn't it a bitter irony that a couple of hours on screen can mean more than half a millennium of history?

As a result of the state's long neglect, the quarter still looks dilapidated, except for some of its small enclaves that have been restored and revitalised by private entrepreneurs. A more-comprehensive development programme is hindered by limited funds and, particularly, unsettled titles of real estate once belonging to Jews, while restoration work on the quarter's synagogues continues slowly.

ward along ul Józefa (historically the main entry to the Jewish town) to **Isaac's Synagogue** (Synagoga Izaaka; Map p141; ☎ 430 55 77; ul Kupa 18; admission 7zł; ☼ 9am-7pm Sun-Fri). Kraków's largest synagogue, built from 1640 to 1644, was returned to the Jewish community in 1989 and is today open as a museum. You can see the remains of the original stucco and wall-painting decoration, and watch two wordless historic documentary films on 'the Jewish District in 1936' and 'the Removal to the Kraków Ghetto', from 1941.

One block east is the **Old Synagogue** (Stara Synagoga; Map p141; ☎ 422 09 62; ul Szeroka 24; admission 6zł; ☼ 10am-2pm Mon, 9am-3.30pm Wed, Thu, Sat &

Sun, 10am-5pm Fri). The name refers to the fact that this is the oldest Jewish religious building in Poland, dating back to the end of the 15th century. Damaged by fire in 1557, it was reconstructed in Renaissance style by the Italian architect Matteo Gucci. It was plundered and partly destroyed by the Nazis, but later restored, and today houses the small **Jewish Museum** (Map p141). The prayer hall, complete with a reconstructed Bimah (raised platform at the centre of the synagogue where the Torah is read) and the original Aron Kodesh (the niche in the eastern wall where Torah scrolls are kept), houses an exhibition of liturgical objects related to Jewish culture. The adjacent rooms are dedicated to Jewish traditions and art.

To the north of the Old Synagogue stretches ul Szeroka, the central street of the Jewish quarter. Short and wide, it looks more like an elongated square than a street, and is often packed with tourist coaches and cars. Near its northern end are the **Remuh Synagogue and Cemetery** (Map p141; ☎ 422 12 74; ul Szeroka 40; adult/concession 5/2zł; ♥ 9am-4pm Sun-Fri). This is the smallest synagogue in Kazimierz and the only one regularly used for religious services. The synagogue was established in 1553 by a rich merchant, Israel Isserles, but associated with his son Rabbi Moses Isserles, a philosopher and scholar.

The cemetery is just behind the synagogue. Founded at the same time as the synagogue itself, it was closed for burials in the early 19th century, when a new, larger cemetery was established. During WWII Nazis razed the tombstones to the ground. During postwar conservation work, however, workers discovered some old tombstones under the layer of earth. Further systematic work uncovered about 700 gravestones, some of them outstanding Renaissance examples that were four centuries old. It seems that the Jews themselves buried the stones to avoid their desecration by foreign armies, which repeatedly invaded Kraków in the 18th century. The tombstones have been meticulously restored, making up one of the best-preserved Renaissance Jewish cemeteries anywhere in Europe. The tombstone of Rabbi Moses, dating from 1572, is right behind the synagogue. You can recognise it by the stones placed on top in an expression of respect.

Dating from 1862, the neo-Romanesque **Tempel Synagogue** (Map p141; ul Miodowa 24; adult/concession 5/2zł; ♥ 10am-6pm Sun-Fri) is Kazimierz' youngest synagogue. The large prayer hall, with a balcony running all around it, has walls and a ceiling decorated with colourful floral and geometric patterns, and beautiful stained-glass windows.

Much larger than the old Remuh graveyard is the **New Jewish Cemetery** (ul Miodowa 55), behind the railway bridge. It was established around 1800 and is the only current burial place for Jews in Kraków. Its size gives an idea of how large the Jewish population must have been. There are still about 9000 surviving tomb-

stones (the oldest dating from the 1840s), some of which are of great beauty. In contrast to the manicured Remuh cemetery, the newer one is completely unkempt, which makes it an eerie sight. The entrance to the cemetery is through the funeral building you'll see to your right or through the gate in the fence – whichever you find open.

You can return to the Old Town by tram from ul Starowiślna, or just walk. If you want to continue exploring the Jewish heritage, you can contact the Jarden Tourist Agency (p149), which offers a variety of tours, including their showpiece, the 'Retracing Schindler's List' tour.

Kraków's Suburbs & Outskirts
ZWIERZYNIEC

Zwierzyniec's prime attraction is the **Kościuszko Mound** (Kopiec Kościuszki; Map p129; Al Waszyngtona; adult/concession 5/2.50zł; ♥ 9am-sunset, exhibition 9.30am-3pm), erected between 1820 and 1823 soon after Kościuszko's death, to pay tribute to the man who embodied the dreams of independent Poland in times of foreign occupation. It sits on a natural hill, commanding spectacular views over the city.

The entrance is through a small neo-Gothic chapel, which has a small exhibition of memorabilia related to Kościuszko. The large brick fortification at the mound's foothill is a fortress built by the Austrians in the 1840s (and now a hotel).

Bus 100 will take you (every hour or so) directly to the mound from Plac Matejki opposite the Barbican.

When taking a trip to Zwierzyniec, you may visit the **National Museum's Main Building** (Map p129; Gmach Główny; ☎ 295 55 00; Al 3 Maja 1; adult/concession 8/5zł, free Sun; ♥ 9am-3.30pm Tue & Thu, 11am-6pm Wed & Fri, 10am-3.30pm Sat & Sun) on the way. It houses three permanent exhibitions: the Gallery of 20th-Century Polish Painting, the Gallery of Decorative Art, and Polish Arms and National Colours – plus various temporary exhibitions. The painting gallery features an extensive collection of Polish painting (and some sculpture) covering the period from 1890 until the present day. There are several stained-glass designs (including the ones for Wawel Cathedral) by Stanisław Wyspiański, and an impressive selection of Witkacy's paintings. Jacek Malczewski and Olga Boznańska are both well represented also. Of the postwar artists, take particular note of the works by Tadeusz Kantor, Jerzy Nowosielski and Władysław Hasior, to name just a few.

LAS WOLSKI

The 485-hectare **Las Wolski** (Wolski Forest; Map p129), west of the city centre and beyond Zwierzyniec, is the largest forested area within the city limits. It's a popular weekend destination among the city dwellers, thanks to the beauty of the forest and the attractions it shelters.

The forest's hilly southern part facing the Vistula, known as Srebrna Góra (Silver Mountain), is topped with the mighty **Church & Hermitage of the Camaldolese Monks** (Kościół i Erem Kamedułów; Map p129). The order was brought to Poland from Italy in 1603 and in time founded a dozen monasteries throughout the country; today only two have survived (the other is in Masuria).

The order, with its very strict rules, attracts curiosity – and a few ironic smiles, particularly for its Memento Mori ('remember you must die') motto – and its members' ascetic way of life. The monks live in seclusion in hermitages and contact each other only during prayers, and some have no contact with the outer world at all. They are vegetarian and have solitary meals in their 'homes', with only five common meals a year. There's no TV or radio, and the conditions of life are austere. The hermits don't sleep in coffins as rumoured, but they do keep the skulls of their predecessors in the hermitages.

Kraków was the first of the Camaldolese seats in Poland; a church and 20 hermitages were built between 1603 and 1642 and the whole complex was walled in. Not much has changed since. The place is spectacularly located and can be visited.

You approach it through a long walled alley that leads to the main gate. Once inside, you come to the massive white limestone façade of the church (50m high and 40m wide). A spacious, single-nave interior is covered by a barrel-shaped vault and lined on both sides with ornate baroque chapels.

Underneath the chancel of the church is a large chapel used for prayers and, to its right, the crypt of the hermits. Bodies are placed into niches without coffins and then sealed. Latin inscriptions state the age of the deceased and the period spent in the hermitage. The niches are opened after 80 years and the remains moved to a place of permanent rest. It's then that the hermits take the skulls to keep in their shelters.

In the garden behind the church are 14 surviving hermitages where several monks live (others live in the building next to the church), but the area is off-limits to tourists. You may occasionally see hermits in the church, wearing fine cream gowns.

Men can visit the church and crypt any day from 8am to 11am and 3pm to 5pm (till 4pm in autumn and winter), but women are allowed inside only on major holidays. There are 12 such days during the year: 7 February, 25 March, Easter Sunday, the Sunday and Monday of the Pentecost, Corpus Christi, 19 June, the Sunday after 19 June, 15 August, 8 September, 8 December and 25 December.

The hermitage is 7km west of the city centre. Take tram 1, 6 or 32 to the end of the line in Zwierzyniec and change for any westbound bus except No 100. The bus will let you off at the foot of Srebrna Góra, then it's a 200m walk up the hill to the church.

After visiting the church you can walk north for about 1km through the forest to the **Zoological Gardens** (Ogród Zoologiczny; Map p129; ☎ 425 35 51; ul Leśna 23; adult/concession 8/4zł; ☺ 9am-sunset). The 20-hectare zoo is home to about 2000 animals representing 300 species from around the world.

About 1km further north is the **Piłsudski Mound** (Kopiec Piłsudskiego; Map p129), the youngest and largest of the four city mounds, and erected in honour of the marshal after his death in 1935. Bus 134 from the zoo will bring you back to the city.

TYNIEC

A distant suburb of Kraków, 10km southwest of the centre, Tyniec is the site of the **Benedictine Abbey** (Klasztor Benedyktynów; Map p129) perched on a cliff above the Vistula. The Benedictines were brought to Poland in the second half of the 11th century, and it was in Tyniec that they established their first home. The original Romanesque church and the monastery were destroyed and rebuilt several times. Today, the church is essentially a baroque building though the stone foundations and the lower parts of the walls, partly uncovered, show its earlier origins.

You enter the complex through a pair of defensive gates, resembling the entrance to

KRAKÓW

a castle, and find yourself in a large court-yard. At its far end is an octagonal wooden pavilion, which protects a stone well dating from 1620.

The monastery cannot be visited but the church is open to all. Behind a sober façade, the dark interior is fitted out with a mix of baroque and rococo furnishings. The organ is plain but has a beautiful tone, and concerts are held here in summer. Check the current programme with the Cultural Information Centre (p130) and try to make your trip coincide with a concert – a much more attractive bet than just visiting the building. To get to the abbey take bus 112 from Rynek Dębnicki, near Rondo Grunwaldzkie.

NOWA HUTA

The youngest and largest of Kraków's suburbs, **Nowa Huta** (New Steelworks; Map p129; www .nh.pl in Polish) is a result of the postwar rush towards industrialisation. In the early 1950s a gigantic steelworks and a new town to serve as a dormitory for the workforce, were built 10km east of the city centre. The steel mill accounted for nearly half the national iron and steel output and the suburb has become a vast urban sprawl populated by over 200,000 people.

Because of increasing awareness of environmental issues, the industrial management was forced to cut production and reduce the workforce, yet the mammoth plant is still working despite the fact that it's unprofitable.

The steelworks can't be visited, but you may want to have a look around the suburb. Nowa Huta is a shock after the Old Town's medieval streets. Tram 4 or 15 from the central train station will drop you at Plac Centralny, the suburb's central square. It doesn't matter where you start your sightseeing as the landscape varies little throughout the district. Most of it is a grey concrete sea of Stalinist architecture, but fortunately, there are a few interesting sights in that sea.

In the northwestern part of the suburb, is the **Church of Our Lady Queen of Poland** (Map p129; ul Obrońców Krzyża), commonly known as the Arka Pana (Lord's Ark). This interesting though rather heavy, boat-shaped construction was the first new church permitted in Nowa Huta after WWII, and was completed in 1977. Up to that year, the inhabitants used the two historic churches, which somehow escaped the avalanche of concrete. They are both on the southeastern outskirts of Nowa Huta, in the Mogiła suburb, and are worth a visit if you are in the area. The small, shingled **St Bartholomew's Church** (Kościół Św Bartłomieja; Map p129; ul Klasztorna) dates from the mid-15th century, which makes it Poland's oldest surviving three-naved timber church. It's open only for the Sunday religious service. At other times, inquire in the house at the back, and a nun may open it for you.

Across the street is the **Cistercian Abbey** (Opactwo Cystersów; Map p129), which consists of a church and monastery with a large garden-park behind it. The Cistercians came to Poland in 1140 and founded their first monastery in Jędrzejów. They later established other abbeys around the country, including this one in Mogiła, in 1222.

The church, open most of the day, has a large three-naved interior with a balanced

---

NOWA HUTA – A COMMUNIST FANTASY

The postwar communist regime deliberately built Nowa Huta steelworks in Kraków to give a 'healthy' working-class and industrial injection to the strong aristocratic, cultural and religious traditions of the city. Other more-rational reasons counted less. It was not of any importance, for example, that Kraków had neither ores nor coal deposits and that virtually all raw materials had to be transported from often distant locations. The project didn't take into account that the site boasted one of the most fertile soils in the region, nor that construction of the complex would destroy villages with histories going back to the early Middle Ages.

The communist dream hasn't materialised exactly as planned. Nowa Huta hasn't in fact threatened the deep traditional roots of the city. Worse, it actually became a threat to its creators, with strikes breaking out here as frequently as anywhere else, paving the way for the eventual fall of communism. The steelworks did, however, affect the city in another way: it brought catastrophic environmental pollution that threatened people's health, the natural environment and the city's historical monuments.

mix of Gothic, Renaissance and baroque furnishings and decoration. Have a look at the Chapel of the Crucified Christ (in the left transept), the polyptych in the high altar, and beautiful stained-glass windows behind it.

WIELICZKA
Just outside the administrative boundaries of Kraków, about 15km southeast of the city centre, Wieliczka (vyeh-*leech*-kah) is famous for its **Salt Mine** (Kopalnia Soli; ☎ 278 73 02; www .kopalnia.pl; ul Daniłowicza 10; adult/concession 34/20zł, 20% discount after 6pm & Nov-Feb; ☼ 7.30am-7.30pm Apr-Oct, 8am-4pm Nov-Mar), which has been operating uninterrupted for at least 700 years, making it the oldest Polish industrial plant in continuous operation.

The mine is renowned for the preservative qualities of its microclimate, as well as for its health-giving properties. An underground sanatorium has been established at a depth of 211m, where chronic allergic diseases are treated.

The mine has a labyrinth of tunnels, about 300km distributed over nine levels, the deepest being 327m underground. A section of the mine is open to the public as a museum, and it's a fascinating trip. The Wieliczka mine is on Unesco's World Heritage List.

You visit three upper levels of the mine, from 64m to 135m below the ground, walking through an eerie world of pits and chambers, all hewn by hand from solid salt. Some have been made into chapels, with altarpieces and figures, others are adorned with statues and monuments – all carved out of salt – and there are even underground lakes.

The highlight is the ornamented **Chapel of the Blessed Kinga** (Kaplica Błogosławionej Kingi), which is actually a fair-sized church measuring 54m by 17m, and 12m high. Every single element here, from chandeliers to altarpieces, is of salt. It took over 30 years (1895–1927) to complete this underground temple, and about 20,000 tonnes of rock salt had to be removed. Occasional Masses and concerts are held here.

Visitors are guided in groups and the tour takes about two hours. You walk about 2km through the mine – wear comfortable shoes. The temperature in the mine is 14°C. In summer, when the mine is often overrun by visitors, tours start every five minutes or so, but in winter, tours depart every half-hour to an hour, when there are enough tourists.

Tours are in Polish, but in summer English tours (July to August) operate at 10am, 11.30am, 12.30pm, 1.45pm, 3pm and 5pm (three daily in June and September). Two tours a day (July to August) also run in German. Check with the tourist office before you visit, as these times are likely to change. English-language brochures are available at the souvenir kiosk by the mine entrance.

There's a **museum** (☎ 278 32 66; ☼ 8am-4pm) accommodated in 16 worked-out chambers on the 3rd level of the mine, where the tour ends. Entry is included in the price of the tour. It features a collection of objects related to the mine. From here a lift takes you back up to the outer world.

Minibuses to Wieliczka town depart every 10 minutes, between 6am and 8pm, from near the bus terminal in Kraków, and drop passengers outside the salt mine (2zł). Trains between Kraków and Wieliczka leave every 45 minutes throughout the day (3.5zł), but the train station in Wieliczka is a fair walk from the mine.

ACTIVITIES
See Kraków in style in one of the many **horse-drawn carriages**, which line the main market square. You decide which route you want to take, or leave it up to the driver to take you for a trot round the sights of the Old Town. Carriages cost 120zł per hour.

Those in search of something a little more active should head to **Park Wodny** (Map p129; ☎ 616 31 90; www.parkwodny.pl in Polish; ul Dobrego Pasterza 126; all-day tickets adult/concession Mon-Fri 41/33zł, Sat & Sun & public holidays 45/37zł; ☼ 8am-10.30pm Jun-Aug, 8.30am-10pm Sep-May), around 2.5km northeast of the Old Town. This huge, state-of-the-art water park boasts various pools, water chutes, Jacuzzis, climbing-walls and saunas, as well as video games, an Internet café, a restaurant and a bar. Tickets for one-hour (adult/concession from 15zł/12zł) and three hours (from 31zł/23zł) are also available. Entry is free for children under three years.

Roughly 2km east of the city centre, **Fantasy Park** (Map p129; ☎ 290 95 15; www.fantasypark .pl; Al Pokoju 44; ☼ 10am-2am), in the Kraków Plaza shopping centre, has 16 tenpin-bowling lanes (around 44zł per hour), plus pool tables, video games and a bar. There's also a supervised kids' play area, and discos on Friday and Saturday nights (over 21s only).

WALKING TOUR

Start/Finish: St Mary's Church/Wawel
Cathedral
Distance: approximately 1.5km
Duration: around 1½ hours

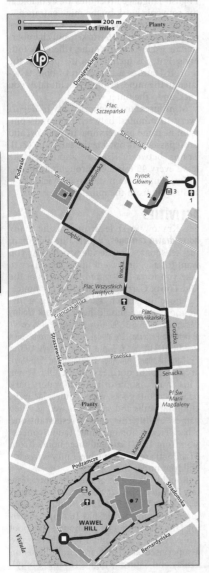

Start your tour outside **St Mary's Church (1)** in Rynek Główny. Take a leisurely stroll around the main square, passing through the **Cloth Hall (2)** to browse the craft stalls, then head upstairs to the **Gallery of 19th-century Polish Painting (3)**. Head west on ul Szewska as far as the junction with ul Jagiellońska, then follow this street south, stopping by the **Collegium Maius (4)** for a quick look round the courtyard. Carry on to the junction with ul Gołębia. Take this road as far as ul Bracka, then turn south past the **Franciscan Church (5)**, and join busy ul Grodzka, which is replete with eateries if you fancy a quick bite. Go as far as ul Senacka, and from there turn south onto the charming ul Kanonicza. This will lead you right to the foot of **Wawel Hill (6)**. Climb to the top to visit the stately **Wawel Royal Castle (7)** and **Wawel Cathedral (8)**, or just take in the stunning views across the river.

KRAKÓW FOR CHILDREN

Kraków isn't the most child-friendly of cities, but there's enough going on in the vicinity to keep kids amused for a few days. The main attraction for younger children is undoubtedly **Park Wodny** (p147), a very modern and well-equipped water-park complex, with three large pools and Poland's longest water chute (202m).

Fantasy Park (p147) has a supervised children's play area with climbing frames and the like to keep toddlers occupied, while older siblings can try their hand at tenpin bowling or pool.

Hands-on science is offered at the **Collegium Maius** (p138), where older children can experiment with light and sound waves and other academically oriented displays. Exhibitions at the **Manggha Centre of Japanese Art & Technology** (p140) and the **Polish Aviation Museum** (p141) might also catch their attention.

Away from the city centre, the **Zoological Gardens** (p145) are an obvious choice for a day out with the kids, and there are pleasant grounds for a walk afterwards.

The puppet show *Golem*, which plays regularly at **Teatr Groteska** (p158) is a big hit with kids and adults alike, but it's probably not appropriate for very young children.

Around 2km northeast of the centre, **Kraina Zabaw Dziecięcych** (Map p129; ☎ 411 30 07; ul Nieduża 4; ⊙ 9am-9pm), just off Al Jana Pawła II, is a supervised indoor play-area for toddlers, with prices starting at 6zł for the first hour.

Topolino (☎ 633 06 62) offers a babysitting service; phone for rates and availability. Tourist offices in Kraków don't keep any information about such services, but many top-end hotels offer babysitting for guests.

TOURS

Three travel agencies, **Orbis Travel** (Map pp132-3; ☎ 422 40 35; Rynek Główny 41), **Jan-Pol** (Map pp132-3; ☎ 421 42 06; ul Westerplatte 15/16) and **Intercrac Travel** (Map pp132-3; ☎ 422 58 40; ul Krupnicza 3), jointly operate a set programme of tours in and outside Kraków. They include city sightseeing by coach (110zł), the 'Traces of Jewish culture' tour (110zł), the Wieliczka salt mine (120zł), the Auschwitz-Birkenau death camps (120zł) and Zakopane (255zł). Students under 25 get 25% discount on the Wieliczka and Auschwitz tours, and there's a 10% discount if you book a second trip. Contact any of the three operators for their free *Cracow Tours* brochure with full descriptions.

Jarden Tourist Agency (Map p141; ☎ 421 71 66; www.jarden.pl; ul Szeroka 2), in Kazimierz' Jewish quarter, is the best-known agency offering a choice of tours discovering Jewish heritage. Guided walking tours around Kazimierz cost 35zł/45zł per person (two/three hours).

Its showpiece, 'Retracing Schindler's List', costs 65zł per person (two hours by car). All tours require a minimum of three people and must be arranged in advance. All tours are in English, but French- and German-speaking guides can be arranged. Jarden also does an Auschwitz-Birkenau tour (six to seven hours by car). A minimum group of four is required, and the cost is around 120zł per person.

Marco der Pole (Map pp132-3; ☎ 430 21 31; www.marcoderpole.com.pl; ul Kanonicza 15) organises walking tours of the Old Town and of Kazimierz between April and October. Both cost 70zł, or 50zł for students under 25 with valid ID, and children under 14. Tickets are available at tourist information offices, hotels or on the spot from the guide – tours start from the Cloth Hall, facing St Mary's Church.

Bird Service (Map pp132-3; ☎ 292 14 60; www.bird.pl; ul Św Krzyża 17) is one of Poland's best specialists in bird-watching tours. It organises birding trips in eastern Poland, including the Białowieża and Biebrza National Parks. It also offers week-long bicycle tours along the Dunajec River in the Carpathian Mountains.

Bird Service organises the Polish Bird Festival, held annually in the second week of May in northeastern Poland. This is a holiday package that covers eight nights accommodation in an optimal bird-watching location, half-board and information.

FESTIVALS & EVENTS

Kraków has one of the richest cycles of annual events in Poland. The Cultural Information Centre (p130) will give you programme details. There are some important events near Kraków, particularly the famous **Passion Play** (p210) on Maundy Thursday and Good Friday, during Easter week in Kalwaria Zebrzydowska.

Festival of Sailors' Songs 'Shanties' (February)

Organ Music Festival (March/April) With a tradition of over 30 years, this festival gives people a chance to listen to organ recitals, which take place in several city churches.

Student Song Festival (May) An event organised annually since the mid-1960s. Some concerts are staged on the Main Market Sq.

Juvenalia (May) During this student carnival, students receive symbolic keys to the town's gates and 'take power' over the city for four days and three nights. There's street dancing, fancy-dress parades, masquerades and lots of fun.

Cracovia Marathon (May) An increasingly popular international running event.

LAJKONIK – KRAKÓW'S LEGENDARY FIGURE

Lajkonik is a fairy-tale figure, performed by a disguised man who looks like a Tatar riding a little horse, and decked out in embroidered garments. He comes to life on the Thursday, seven days after Corpus Christi, and heads a joyful pageant from the Premonstratensian Convent in the suburb of Zwierzyniec to the Rynek Główny.

The pageant, accompanied by a musical band, takes at least six hours to complete the trip, while Lajkonik takes to dancing, jumping and running, greeting passers-by, popping into cafés en route, collecting donations and striking people with his mace, which is said to bring them good luck. Once the pageant reaches the main square, Lajkonik is greeted by the city mayor and presented with a symbolic ransom and a goblet of wine.

The event is believed to stem from the Tatar invasions of the 13th century. Legend has it that the headman of the local raftsmen defeated a Tatar khan, then put his robes on and triumphantly rode into the city. The Lajkonik festivities have taken place for at least two hundred years.

The horse's structure and garb used in the event were designed by Stanisław Wyspiański and the original is kept in the Historical Museum of Kraków. It consists of a wooden frame covered with leather and caparison, and embroidered with nearly a thousand pearls and coral breads. The whole outfit weighs about 40kg.

Polish & International Short Film Festivals
(May/June)

Pageant (a Thursday in May or June) Seven days after Corpus Christi, a colourful pageant headed by the Lajkonik, a comical figure disguised as a Tatar riding a horse, parades from Zwierzyniec to the main square.

Jewish Culture Festival (June/July) Features a variety of cultural events including theatre, film, music and art exhibitions, and concludes with a grand open-air *klezmer* (Jewish folk music) concert on ul Szeroka. It's reputedly the biggest festival of its kind in Europe.

Organ recitals (late June to late August) Held on Sunday in the Benedictine Abbey, Tyniec. There are also organ recitals in July and August in St Mary's Church.

International Festival of Street Theatre (July) Takes place on the Main Market Sq.

Summer Jazz Festival (July) Featuring the best of Polish modern jazz.

Old Jazz in Kraków Festival (July and August) Focuses on traditional jazz forms.

Music in Old Kraków International Festival (August) The most important musical event goes for two weeks, spans five centuries of musical tradition, from medieval to contemporary, and is presented in concert halls, churches and other historic interiors.

Competition of szopki (1st Thursday of December) Held on the main square beside the statue of Adam Mickiewicz and attracts crowds of spectators. A sort of Nativity scene, but very different from those elsewhere in the world, Kraków's *szopki* are elaborate compositions built in an architectural, usually churchlike form, and made in astonishing detail from cardboard, wood, tinfoil and the like – some are even mechanised. The prizewinning specimens are put on display until mid-

February at a special exhibition in the Historical Museum of Kraków. You can see some of the old Nativity scenes in the Ethnographic Museum.

SLEEPING

Kraków is Poland's premier tourist destination, with prices to match, and while there is an ever-increasing supply of accommodation options, advance booking during the busy summer season is recommended for the more-central places. The Old Town is the main area for mid-range and top-end hotels, as well as a few budget places, while cheaper, and sometimes better-value, options can be found outside the area bounded by the Planty.

Kazimierz also has a number of atmospheric mid-range and top-end hotels, in a quieter location. Note that some of the more-expensive hotels often quote prices in euros or US dollars.

Modern hostels, geared towards the needs (and expectations) of Western backpackers are springing up outside the city centre, while private rooms and apartments may be the answer, if you're intending to stay a bit longer. **Waweltur** (Map pp132-3; ☎ 422 19 21; www .waweltur.com.pl; ul Pawia 8; s/d/apt from 55/107/140zł; ☻ 8am-8pm Mon-Fri, 8am-2pm Sat) arranges accommodation in private rooms in family homes scattered around the city (so check the location carefully before deciding). The apartments are self-contained, and come with kitchens and bathrooms.

You may also be offered a private room by someone on the street. The tourist offices don't recommend these services, but if you decide to use them, ask to see the location on the map first, and pay only after you have seen the room and accepted it.

City Centre & Suburbs
BUDGET

Kraków has a good supply of budget places, though few of these are anywhere close to the centre and you will need to do some commuting. Bright, clean, modern hostels with multilingual staff are a relatively new, and very welcome, addition to the budget accommodation scene, while the older, cheaper, traditional youth hostels may be a bit basic for some. During holidays, they tend to fill up with noisy groups of schoolkids and readers have complained about standards of cleanliness. During the summer, several student hostels let out rooms on the outskirts of town, and these often have good on-site facilities.

Kraków has several camping grounds, all of which are pretty distant from the centre but are linked to it by public transport.

Nathan's Villa Hostel (☎ 422 35 45; www.nathans villa.com; ul Św Agnieszki 1; dm from 45zł; **P** 🖵) The best hostel in town, Nathan's is conveniently located roughly half-way between the Old Town and Kazimierz. Comfy rooms, sparkling bathrooms, free laundry, free breakfast and a friendly atmosphere make this place a big hit with backpackers.

Dizzy Daisy (Map p129; ☎ 292 01 71; www.hostel .pl; ul Pędzichów 9; dm/d/tr 35/100/135zł; 🖵) Another branch of the growing and well-regarded Poland-wide chain, this is a recently refurbished modern hostel with great facilities, and frequented by an international crowd of party people.

Bling Bling (Map p129; ☎ 634 05 32; www.bling bling.pl; ul Pędzichów 7; dm 45zł) This is another very modern hostel, a couple of doors down from Dizzy Daisy. It offers a similarly shining standard of accommodation.

Bursa Jagiellońska (Map p129; ☎ 656 12 66; www .bursa.krakow.pl; ul Śliska 14; s/d/tr/q 53/92/129/ 156zł; 🟡 Jul-Sep; **P** 🖵) Located in Podgórze, 2.5km south of the Old Town (and linked to it by tram 10), Bursa is one of the better student hostels, and belongs to the city's venerable university. It's a neat, well-equipped place offering free laundry

and Internet facilities and shared kitchens. There's a 10% discount for those with an International Student Identity Card (ISIC) or Euro<26 card.

Hotel Studencki Żaczek (Map p129; ☎ 633 19 14; www.zaczek.com.pl; Al 3 Maja 5; s/d/tr 85/120/150zł) Żaczek is very conveniently located just 1km west of the Old Town. It has a variety of accommodation on offer, including cheaper rooms with shared bathrooms and four- or five-bed rooms. Breakfast is 10zł extra.

Strawberry Hostel (Map p129; ☎ 636 15 00; ul Racławicka 9; dm/d 40/50zł; 🟡 Jul & Aug; **P**) Well-run and popular with travellers, this clean and cosy 200-bed hostel is 2km northwest of the Old Town and easily accessible by several tram lines.

Trzy Kafki BIS (Map p129; ☎ 263 20 10; www.trzy kafki.pl; ul Kawaryjska 42; s/d/tr 60/80/100zł) South of the River Wisła, this neat little guesthouse is a step up in quality from the original Trzy Kafki hostel, though again, there are only shared bathrooms. It's handy for exploring Kazimierz, but a long walk from the Old Town.

Hotel Studencki Nawojka (Map p129; ☎ 633 58 77; http://nawojka.bratniak.krakow.pl; ul Reymonta 11; s/d/tr from 80/85/100zł; 🖳) Located 2km west of the centre, Nawojka has a dozen clean and simple en-suite all-year rooms and many more, basic student rooms in summer. There's a grocery shop on site. Take bus 179 from the rail station.

Hotel Studencki Bydgoska (Map p129; ☎ 638 77 88; http://bydgorska.bratniak.krakow.pl; ul Bydgoska 19; s 50-90zł, d 70-110zł, tr 90-129zł; 🟡 Jul-Sep; 🖵) Bydgoska is a cheap and simple student hostel that's northwest of the centre and accessible via buses 501, 511 and 208 from the station. It has inexpensive beds for around 30 people during the academic year, and many more (with bathrooms and kitchens) during the summer months. There's a restaurant, a gym and a TV room on site.

Trzy Kafki (Map p129; ☎ 632 88 29; www.trzykafki .pl; Al Słowackiego 29; s/d/tr 50/70/90zł; 🖵) Roughly 1.5km northwest of the Old Town, this place is part of a chain of three establishments in Kraków, and has fairly simple rooms with modern shared bathrooms and kitchens. It offers a laundry service and breakfast is 9zł extra.

Oleandry YHA Hostel (Map p129; ☎ 633 88 22; fax 633 89 20; ul Oleandry 4; dm 28zł) Handily located around 1km west of the Old Town, this is a very big (and often very noisy) place with basic dorms in need of updating and a midnight curfew. Take tram 15 from outside the main train-station building and get off just past Hotel Cracovia.

Camping Nr 46 Smok (Map p129; ☎ 429 83 00; ul Kamedulska 18; camping per person/tent 15/19zł; P) This quiet camping ground is around 4km west of the Old Town. To get here from the Kraków Główny train station, take tram 2 to the end of the line in Zwierzyniec and change for any westbound bus (except bus 100).

Camping Clepardia (Map p129; ☎ 415 96 72; campclep@poczta.onet.pl; ul Pachońskiego 28A; camping per site/person 8/15zł, d/tr bungalows 80/100zł; Jun-Sep; P) Clepardia has tent space and several cabins with a bathroom, and guests have free access to the outdoor swimming pool next door. It's 4km north of the centre, and accessible by bus 115 from the main train station; get off at Billa Supermarket.

MID-RANGE

Most mid-range options are located away from the heart of the city, but there are many within easy walking distance of the Rynek and major sights. Others can be found slightly further out, mostly to the north and west.

Hotel Saski (Map pp132-3; ☎ 421 42 22; www .hotelsaski.com.pl; ul Sławkowska 3; s/d/ste 260/330/410zł;) If you're in the mood for a touch of *belle époque*, Central European style, but without the hefty price tag, the Saski may be the place for you. This grand old establishment occupies an historic mansion just off Rynek Główny. The uniformed doorman, rattling century-old lift and ornate furnishings lend the place a certain glamour, and though the rooms themselves are comparatively plain, they do have very modern bathrooms, and the double set of doors is an unusual feature. Breakfast in the adjoining restaurant, Metropolitan (p155), is excellent. On the downside, the hotel's very central location does mean that late-night noise from surrounding bars and cafés can be a problem.

Hotel Petrus (Map p129; ☎ 269 29 46; www.petrus .net.pl; ul Pietrusińskiego 12; s/d Mon-Fri 209/270zł, Sat & Sun 185/245zł; P) Get away from the crowds at this beautifully appointed place close to Park Skały Twardowskiego, about 2km southwest of the city centre. Rooms are cool and modern and there's a cosy

lounge with a log fire, as well as a sauna, gym, restaurant and beer garden.

U Pana Cogito (Map p129; ☎ 269 72 00; www .pcogito.pl; ul Bałuckiego 6; s/d/apt €42/54/61; P) Stark white seems to be the décor scheme of choice at this friendly and tiny (sixroom) hotel, about 1km southwest of the centre. All rooms have big bathrooms and refrigerators, and for extra privacy, the one apartment has a separate entrance; longstay rates are negotiable. The hotel also has its own restaurant, also done out in fresh, minimalist white.

Hotel Wawel-Tourist (Map pp132-3; ☎ 424 13 00; www.wawel-tourist.com.pl; ul Poselska 22; s 190-270zł, d 280-360zł;) Ideally located just off busy ul Grodzka, Wawel-Tourist offers reasonably good value and the pricier, newly renovated rooms are large and comfortable. It's set far enough back from the main drag to avoid most of the noise.

Hotel System (Map p129; ☎ 614 48 00; www .hotelsystem.pl; Al 29 Listopada 189; s/d from 99/198zł; P) Located roughly 3km northeast of the Old Town, Hotel System is a big and very modern place with stylish rooms and an excellent range of facilities for the price, including free Internet access, a gym, a sauna and a good restaurant.

Home & Travel (Map p129; ☎ 633 80 80; www.home travel.pl; ul Wrocławska 5a; s/d 120/180zł;) This is a newish place north of the Old Town, with a classy, contemporary feel. The spacious rooms all come with welcome extras such as refrigerators and tea- and coffeemaking machines, and some have modem connections.

Sodispar Service Apartments (Map p129; ☎ 0602 247 438; www.sodispar.pl; ul Lubelska 12; apt 100-480zł;) Sodispar, north of the Old Town, has several comfortable apartments sleeping up to four people, and is a good choice if you intend lingering in Kraków. There's a twonight minimum stay, and cheaper rates are available for longer stays. Rooms all have free Internet connection and computers can be hired for a small extra charge.

Wielopole Guest Rooms (Map pp132-3; ☎ 422 14 75; www.wielopole.pl; ul Wielopole 3; s/d from 150/225zł; P) Wielopole's bright and unfussy modern rooms are housed in a renovated block on the eastern edge of the Old Town, and all have spotless bathrooms. Breakfast (served in your room) is extra. It's great value for the fairly central location.

Hotel Jan (Map pp132-3; ☎ 430 19 92; www.hotel -jan.com.pl; ul Grodzka 11; s/d 275/360zł) Hotel Jan is a restored town house on a busy (and often noisy) pedestrian street, just a stone's throw from the main square. Rooms are pleasant and comfortable, and the chilly medieval cellar makes an atmospheric setting for breakfast (though the grey marble-clad hallways are decidedly gloomy).

Hotel Alexander (Map pp132-3; ☎ 422 96 60; www.alexhotel.pl; ul Gabarska 18; s/d 280/360zł; P ✗) Alexander is a modern, if slightly anonymous place, offering the usual standard of three-star comfort: perfectly acceptable but somewhat impersonal. It's on a shabby but quiet street, just west of the Old Town.

Dom Polonii (Map pp132-3; ☎ /fax 422 43 55; Rynek Główny 14; d/ste 235/348zł) You couldn't ask for a more-central location than this. The Dom has just two high-ceiling double rooms (overlooking the Rynek) and one double suite, all on the top floor. Predictably, it books up fast.

Hotel Royal (Map pp132-3; ☎ 421 35 00; www .royal.com.pl; ul Św Gertrudy 26-29; s 160-210zł, d 220-300zł, tr 300-330zł, ste 360zł; P) This impressive Art Nouveau edifice is one of the surprisingly few hotels close to Wawel Hill. It's split into two sections; the higher-priced two-star rooms are cosy and far preferable to the fairly drab one-star rooms at the back.

Hotel Polonia (Map pp132-3; ☎ 422 12 33; www .hotel-polonia.com.pl; ul Basztowa 25; s/d/ste 251/285/450zł) Polonia occupies a grand old building near the train and bus stations. The rooms are light and modern but many overlook the noisy main road. The suites are particularly spacious and attractive though.

Ibis Kraków Centrum (Map p129; ☎ 299 33 00; www.accorhotels.com; ul Syrokomli 2; s/d 199/249zł; P ✗) This unpretentious modern hotel, just west of the Old Town in Nowy Świat, offers the usual standard you would expect from the international Ibis chain, and represents good value. If it's character you're after, however, you'll be disappointed.

Monika Pokoje Gościnne (Map p129; ☎ 413 84 80; www.hotelmonika.pl; ul Langiewicza 6; s/d/tr/ste 150/215/290/430zł; P) Monika has a wide choice of neat and simple rooms, including large suites with kitchens, in a modern block north of the Old Town. Organised tours are arranged for guests and prices are slightly cheaper on weekends.

Pokoje Gościnne Jordan (Map pp132-3; ☎ 421 21 25; www.jordan.pl/informacja_turystyczna/index_eng; ul Długa 9; s/d/tr 140/210/280zł) Jordan is a small, reasonable place on the northern edge of the Old Town. The rooms are on the upper floors but you book through the travel agency downstairs.

TOP END

There are plenty of upmarket accommodation options in the Old Town and around, which is certainly Kraków's most atmospheric area in which to stay, though some are not such great value.

Hotel Copernicus (Map pp132-3; ☎ 424 34 00; copernicus@hotel.com.pl; ul Kanonicza 16; s/d/ste 650/750/1100zł; ✗ ⚑) Nestled in two beautifully restored buildings in one of Kraków's most picturesque and atmospheric streets, Copernicus is arguably the city's finest and most luxurious offering. The rooftop bar, with spectacular views over Wawel, and the swimming pool accommodated in medieval vaulted brick cellar, add to the hotel's class.

Hotel Wit Stwosz (Map pp132-3; ☎ 429 60 26; www.wit-stwosz.com.pl; ul Mikołajska 28; s/d/tr from 290/340/430zł) Wit Stwosz occupies a recently renovated 16th-century town house. Rooms are fully modernised, though some are rather plain. Overall it's comfortable, stylish and remarkably good value for a top-end hotel.

Hotel Campanile (Map pp132-3; ☎ 424 26 00; www.campanile.com.pl in Polish; ul Św Tomasza 34; d/ste 310/520zł; P ✗) Kraków's outlet of the French hotel chain, this large (106 rooms) and modern hotel has somehow succeeded in nestling in the Old Town, just a few blocks from the Rynek. It has attractive, bright rooms done out in corporate green and cream, some with disabled access.

Hotel Amadeus (Map pp132-3; ☎ 429 60 70; www .hotel-amadeus.pl; ul Mikołajska 20; s/d/ste US$160/170/240; ✗) Amadeus, with its Mozartian flair, is one of Kraków's most refined hotels. Rooms are tastefully furnished and service is of a high standard, but some rooms are a little small and ordinary. There's a sauna and a fitness centre, and a well-regarded gourmet restaurant.

Hotel Pollera (Map pp132-3; ☎ 422 10 44; www .pollera.com.pl; ul Szpitalna 30; s/d 295/345zł; P) Pollera is a classy place with large rooms that are crammed with elegant furniture. The singles are unexciting, but the doubles are far nicer, and it's central and quiet.

Hotel Rezydent (Map pp132-3; ☎ 429 54 95; www .rthotels.com.pl; ul Grodzka 9; s/d/tr €68/90/110; ⊠) Rezydent occupies a restored medieval house just a few steps south of the main square. Rooms are beautifully kept and some retain their historic charm, though perhaps less charming is its position above a kebab shop on the main drag.

Hotel Atrium (Map p129; ☎ 430 02 03; www.hotel atrium.pl; ul Krzywa 7; s/d/apt €77/97/147; Ⓟ ⊠) Clean, cool and contemporary, Atrium offers 50 understated and comfortable rooms close to the train station. It also has a good restaurant.

Kazimierz

MID-RANGE & TOP END

Kazimierz has a small but characterful selection of mid-range and top-end hotels, some with a distinct Jewish flavour. It's a pleasant, peaceful and fashionable place to stay.

Centrum Artystyczno Konferencyjne Eljot (Map p141; ☎ 430 66 06; www.eljotartcenter.com; ul Miodowa 15; s/d/ste 239/299/429zł; ⊠ 💻) The rooms at Eljot are large and stylish, and all come with the usual mod cons including modem connections. The building also hosts occasional dramatic and musical events, and its cellars double as conference rooms. Prices drop at weekends, and are significantly cheaper, and very good value, if you book via the website.

Hotel Klezmer-Hois (Map p141; ☎ /fax 411 12 45; www.klezmer.pl; ul Szeroka 6; s/d from €48/60) This uniquely stylish little hotel has been restored to its prewar, Jewish character, and has 10 airy rooms, each decorated differently, though the cheaper rooms do not have private bathrooms. There's a good-quality Jewish restaurant on site, as well as an art gallery, and concerts every evening.

Hotel Eden (Map p141; ☎ 430 65 65; www.hoteleden .pl; ul Ciemna 15; s/d/tr US$80/105/125; ⊠) Located in three meticulously restored 15th-century town houses, Eden has 27 comfortable rooms and comes complete with a pub, a sauna and the only mikvah (traditional Jewish bath) in Poland. Kosher meals are available on advance request.

Hotel Abel (Map p141; ☎ 411 87 36; www.hotelabel .pl; ul Józefa 30; s/d from 120/160zł; ⊠) The unassuming Abel has 15 clean, plain rooms in a 19th-century block in the heart of the Jewish quarter. It's a neat, friendly place and offers good value for this part of town.

Hotel Alef (Map p141; ☎ /fax 421 38 70; ul Szeroka 17; s/d/ste €46/62/78) Alef offers large, charming rooms, furnished with genuine antiques. It has a good Jewish restaurant downstairs, Café Alef (see p156) and some great views from the top floor.

EATING

By Polish standards, Kraków is a food paradise. The Old Town is tightly packed with gastronomic venues, serving a wide range of international cuisines and catering for every pocket.

Kraków has plenty of budget eateries called *jadłodajnia*. These small places offer hearty Polish home-style meals at very low cost. Cheap takeaway fare can be found along ul Grodzka, while better-quality restaurants line the streets away from the main square; some of the places here are overpriced tourist traps, clearly geared up for the passing tourist trade. Kazimierz has a number of small restaurants, which offer Jewish cuisine, and are definitely worth the walk.

City Centre

BUDGET

Smaki Świata (Map pp132-3; ☎ 428 27 70; ul Szpitalna 38; mains 10.50-16.80zł; ☼ lunch & dinner) This two-level restaurant not far from the railway station, offers hearty, international vegetarian dishes, including moussaka, pasta and chimichangas, plus cheaper snacks and a big list of teas.

Gruziński Chaczapuri (Map pp132-3; ☎ 604 508 380; cnr ul Floriańska & ul Św Marka; mains 8-20zł; ☼ 9am-midnight) If you have a hankering for something a little different, this cheap and cheerful place serving up Georgian dishes is the place to go to: cheese pie is the curious but tasty speciality of the house. Grills, salads and steaks fill out the menu, and the wine's not bad either.

Gospoda CK Dezerter (Map pp132-3; ☎ 422 79 31; ul Bracka 6; mains 10-25zł; ☼ lunch & dinner) Dezerter is a pleasantly decorated place that focuses on traditional, meaty Central European specialities, including Austro-Hungarian cuisine.

Green Way (Map pp132-3; ☎ 431 10 27; ul Mikołajska 14; mains 8-11zł; ☼ 10am-10pm Mon-Sat, 11am-9pm Sun) Some of Kraków's best-value vegetarian fare is on offer at Green Way, with veggie-burgers, enchiladas and salads on the menu.

Restauracja Sąsiedzi (Map pp132-3; ☎ 421 41 46; ul Szpitalna 40; mains 6-19.50zł; ☯ lunch & dinner) Marginally more expensive than most other *jadłodajnias*, but rather smarter and open longer, this two-level place has a beautiful cellar and good food, including fish and veggie options.

Bar Mleczny Dworzanin (Map pp132-3; ☎ 422 76 21; ul Floriańska 19; mains 5-15zł; ☯ lunch & dinner) A bargain-basement 'milk bar' or cafeteria, Dworzanin is one of the cheapest places in town, and is often full due to its tasty food and low prices; it also has a good salad bar.

Bar Wegetariański Vega (Map pp132-3; ☎ 422 34 94; ul Św Gertrudy 7; mains 5-10zł; ☯ lunch & dinner) Vega is an excellent, exclusively vegetarian place, serving tasty pierogi, crepes, tofu and salads in bright and pleasant surrounds.

Jadłodajnia (Map pp132-3; ☎ 421 14 44; ul Sienna 11; mains 5-15zł; ☯ 9am-5pm Mon-Fri, 10am-3pm Sat & Sun) Another old-style cheap-eats restaurant dating from 1934, and possibly still serving the same menu. Soups, salads and meat-and-potatoes dishes prevail.

Taco Mexicano (Map pp132-3; ☎ 421 54 41; ul Poselska 20; mains 10-15zł; ☯ lunch & dinner) Taco is popular among locals and visitors alike for its fairly authentic Mexican food at reasonable prices. You can have enchiladas, burritos and tacos and wash them down with *café carajillo* or tequila.

MID-RANGE

Bombaj Tandoori (Map pp132-3; ☎ 422 37 97; ul Mikołajska 11; mains 13-30zł; ☯ lunch & dinner) Bombaj is the best curry-house in Kraków, with friendly staff and a lengthy menu of Indian standards. The 13zł lunch specials are excellent value, while diners receive a 20% discount off their next evening meal.

Ipanema (Map pp132-3; ☎ 422 53 23; ul Św Tomasza 28; mains 15-120zł; ☯ lunch & dinner) This laid-back Brazilian restaurant is brightly adorned with bananas and coffee-grinders, and features steaks, grills, fish and a range of interesting 'Afro-Brazilian' dishes. Everything seems to come with a side-serving of good old Polish cabbage though.

Metropolitan (Map pp132-3; ☎ 421 98 03; ul Sławkowska 3; mains 20-50zł; ☯ 7.30am-midnight) Metropolitan, attached to Hotel Saski, is a snazzy modern restaurant with a cosmopolitan feel. It has photos of London plastering the walls and is a great place for breakfast. It also serves pasta, grills and steaks.

Smak Ukraiński (Map pp132-3; ☎ 421 92 94; ul Kanonicza 15; mains 15-50zł; ☯ lunch & dinner) Hidden away below one of Kraków's most attractive streets, this little place presents authentic Ukrainian edibles in a cosy little cellar decorated with predictably folksy flair. Expect lots of dumplings, borscht and waiters in waistcoats.

Jama Michalika (Map pp132-3; ☎ 422 15 61; ul Floriańska 45; mains 15-50zł; ☯ 8am-10pm) Jama Michalika, established in 1895, was traditionally a hang-out for writers, painters, actors and other artistic types. Today it's a grand, and somewhat touristy place with a very green interior and lots of puppets and theatrical etchings adorning the walls. The traditional Polish food is reasonable value but wait-staff seem very reluctant to show themselves. The compulsory coat-check and pay-toilets are an annoying extra expense too.

Casa della Pizza (Map pp132-3; ☎ 421 64 98; Mały Rynek 2; mains 15-30zł; ☯ lunch & dinner) As the name suggests, this is an amenable and unpretentious place, away from the bulk of the tourist traffic, and with a long menu of pizza and pasta. It's a nice spot for a drink as well.

Guliwer (Map pp132-3; ☎ 430 24 66; ul Bracka 6; mains 15-40zł; ☯ lunch & dinner Mon-Sat) Done out like a Provençal farmhouse kitchen, with dried herbs and flowers dangling from the ceiling, Guliwer is a reasonable spot for French food, though the service is a touch gloomy.

Balaton (Map pp132-3; ☎ 422 04 69; ul Grodzka 37; mains 20-40zł; ☯ lunch & dinner) Balaton, with its squeaky door and shabby exterior, may not look that inviting, but it's a very popular place for simple Hungarian food served at long tables, which seem to fill up very quickly. This is probably due more to its handy location than any culinary wizardry though.

Restauracja Cherubino (Map pp132-3; ☎ 429 40 07; ul Św Tomasza 15; mains 15-45zł; ☯ lunch & dinner) Cherubino offers hearty Tuscan and Polish cuisine in its charming, artsy interior, which features antique carriages and boats.

TOP END

Paese (Map pp132-3; ☎ 421 62 73; ul Poselska 24; mains 20-56zł; ☯ lunch & dinner) Paese offers Corsican and some mainland French cuisine, including such dishes as filet mignon, duck in lavender sauce and saddle of venison. Fish and vegetarian options are also on the menu. The food is good, the prices acceptable and the interior bright and cheerful.

Copernicus (Map pp132-3; ☎ 424 34 21; ul Kanonicza 16; mains 49-70zł; ☺ lunch & dinner) In the hotel of the same name, Copernicus is one of Kraków's classiest restaurants. Pigeon, rabbit, fish and game feature on the menu, and service is of a predictably high standard.

Restauracja Pod Aniołami (Map pp132-3; ☎ 421 39 99; ul Grodzka 35; mains 25-70zł; ☺ lunch & dinner) 'Under the Angels' occupies vaulted cellars decorated with traditional folksy knick-knacks, and offers excellent typical Polish food in an attractive subterranean atmosphere.

Restauracja Cyrano de Bergerac (Map pp132-3; ☎ 411 72 88; ul Sławkowska 26; mains 45-100zł; ☺ lunch & dinner) One of Kraków's top eateries, this restaurant serves fine, authentic French cuisine in one of the city's loveliest cellars. Prices are relatively high, and the portions are not overly copious, but the quality matches the price.

Kazimierz
MID-RANGE
Café Alef (Map p141; ☎ 421 38 70; ul Szeroka 17; mains 12-38zł; ☺ lunch & dinner) This self-consciously quaint place in the heart of Kazimierz offers a wide array of Jewish-inspired dishes, such as chicken *knedlach* and stuffed gooseneck, amongst a miscellany of antique furniture and paintings.

Restauracja Chłopskie Jadło (mains 20-50zł; ☺ lunch & dinner) ul Św Agnieszki 1 (Map p141; ☎ 421 85 20); ul Św Jana 3 (Map pp132-3; ☎ 429 51 57) This place, a short walk south of Wawel, looks like a rustic country inn somewhere at the crossroads in medieval Poland, and serves up traditional Polish 'peasant grub', as its name says. Live folk music is performed here on some evenings, adding to the rustic atmosphere. It's one of Kraków's most unusual culinary adventures, and has very reasonable prices. A smaller outlet of the same chain can be found in the Old Town.

You'll find similar food, décor and atmosphere (at similar prices) a few paces down the street at **Hotel Klezmer-Hois** (Map p141; ☎ 411 12 45; ul Szeroka 6) and at **Arka Noego** (Map p141; ☎ 429 15 28; ul Szeroka 2), where you can try kosher vodka and listen to occasional *klezmer* (Jewish folk) music.

DRINKING
There are more than 100 bars and pubs in the Old Town alone. Some offer snacks or meals but most are just watering holes. Many are in vaulted cellars, and are patronised by enthusiastically chain-smoking Poles. Some pubs are open until midnight, but many don't close until the wee hours of the morning. If beer and nicotine aren't your scene, there are plenty of tea- and coffee houses around town.

Pod Papugami (Map pp132-3; ☎ 422 82 99; ul Św Jana 18; ☺ 1pm-2am) 'Under the Parrots' is a vaguely 'Irish' cellar pub decorated with old motorcycles, street-signs and other junk, which is starting to seem a trifle dated.

Nic Nowego (Map pp132-3; ☎ 421 61 88; ul Św Krzyża 15; ☺ 7am-3am Mon-Fri, 10am-3am Sat & Sun) Nic Nowego, run by a genuine Irishman, is one of Kraków's more-authentic Irish pubs. It's a bright, modern place with a great atmosphere, and food is also on offer.

Transilvania (Map p141; ☎ 431 14 09; ul Szeroka 9; ☺ 10am-2am) Transilvania is a convivial and unusual place in Kazimierz, with a rather more-original vampire theme going on. Gothic imagery and occasional tarot-card readings add atmosphere to the beery scene.

Piwnica Pod Złotą Pipą (Map pp132-3; ☎ 421 94 66; ul Floriańska 30; ☺ noon-midnight) This is another inviting cellar bar. It's a more-sedate place that's better suited to conversation than listening to music, and serves light meals.

Free Pub & Dekafencja (Map pp132-3; ☎ 802 90 82; ul Sławkowska 4; ☺ 11am-last customer) An amenable blend of late-morning coffee house and late-night bar, the Free Pub is open longer than most. You could start your day here with a cappuccino and a muffin, and end it with a couple of beers.

Coffee Republic (Map pp132-3; ☎ 0605 403 382; ul Bracka 4; ☺ 8.30am-midnight) This pleasantly laid-back student hang-out is a relaxing place to linger over a café latte, while perusing the papers. It also serves cakes and snacks.

Wiśniowy Sad (Map pp132-3; ☎ 430 21 11; ul Grodzka 33; ☺ 10am-10pm) With its old furniture, lacy tablecloths and scattered antiques, the 'Cherry Orchard', evokes the world of Chekov, and serves Russian-style tea and pastries. Sip your Darjeeling to live piano recitals Thursday to Sunday – very civilized.

Demmers Teahouse (Map pp132-3; ☎ 423 16 60; ul Kanonicza 21) An outlet of the famous Viennese teahouse, this is possibly the best place in Kraków for a cup of tea. It sells around 100 varieties, many of which can be tried in an intimate tearoom in the 13th-century cellar.

TriBeCa Coffee (Map pp132-3; ☎ 421 30 85; ul Karmelicka 8; ☒ 9am-9pm Mon-Fri, 10am-3pm Sat & Sun) TriBeCa is a warm and inviting place that offers excellent coffee plus a choice of sandwiches and pastries.

Café Camelot (Map pp132-3; ☎ 421 01 23; ul Św Tomasza 17; ☒ 9am-midnight) Camelot is an amazing, bohemian café that's decorated with beautiful pieces of folk art, and apart from coffee, cakes and drinks, has a short menu of light dishes. There are occasional poetry readings and also live music downstairs.

ENTERTAINMENT

Kraków has a lively cultural life, particularly in the theatre, music and visual arts, and there are numerous annual festivals. The **Cultural Information Centre** (Centrum Informacji Kulturalnej; Map pp132-3; ☎ 421 77 87; www.karnet.krakow2000. pl in Polish; ul Św Jana 2; ☒ 10am-6pm Mon-Fri, 10am-4pm Sat), just off the main square, will provide detailed what's on information. It publishes a comprehensive Polish-English monthly magazine, *Karnet* (3zł), which lists cultural events, and sells tickets for some of them.

Another (free) local what's-on monthly magazine, *Weekend w Krakowie* (Weekend in Kraków), has less-detailed coverage. For some English-language help, get a copy of *Kraków In Your Pocket* (5zł), which has excellent coverage of entertainment, including bars, pubs and discos. The two leading local papers, *Gazeta Krakowska* and *Gazeta Wyborcza*, list programs of cinemas, theatres, concerts etc. The Friday edition of the latter has a more comprehensive what's-on section that includes information on museums, art galleries and activities.

Nightclubs

There are quite a number of nightclubs and discos in the Old Town. The following places are recommended.

Klub Pasja (Map pp132-3; ☎ 423 04 83; ul Szewska 5) Occupying vast brick cellars, Pasja is trendy and attractive, and is frequented by foreigners. It's open daily and has a billiard section.

Music Bar 9 (Map pp132-3; ☎ 422 25 46; ul Szewska 9) Close to Pasja, this complex, with a large bar in a covered courtyard and a disco in the cellar, mostly attracts a young crowd and operates Tuesday to Saturday.

Equinox (Map pp132-3; ☎ 421 17 71; ul Sławkowska 13/15) Equinox has long been one of the most popular haunts, and has discos nightly.

Fshut (Map p141; ☎ 429 26 09; ul Szeroka 10) One of Kraków's hippest new nightspots, Fshut is a subterranean club in Kazimierz that plays everything from R&B and reggae to house music every night of the week, with guest DJs on the weekend. Fashion shows, film screenings, exhibitions and other arty offerings take place here at irregular intervals.

Jazz

Kraków has a lively jazz life and a number of jazz clubs.

Jazz Club U Muniaka (Map pp132-3; ☎ 423 12 05; ul Floriańska 3; tickets 20zł; ☒ 6.30pm-2am) Housed in a fine cellar, this is one of the best-known jazz outlets, and was founded by the veteran saxophonist Janusz Muniak, who often performs here. There is usually live jazz from Thursday to Saturday nights.

Harris Piano Jazz Bar (Map pp132-3; ☎ 421 57 41; Rynek Główny 28; tickets 15-20zł; ☒ 1pm-2am) Another active jazz haunt, Harris hosts jazz and blues bands most days of the week.

Indigo Jazz Club (Map pp132-3; ☎ 429 17 43; ul Floriańska 26; ☒ 3pm-3am) Positioned in amazing vaulted cellars with beautiful acoustics, Indigo is a well-regarded place that doesn't seem to have a strict concert schedule, but does host live jazz once or twice a week.

Piec' Art (Map pp132-3; ☎ 429 64 25; ul Szewska 12; ☒ 3pm-midnight) This cosy cellar club tends to stage jazz on Wednesday and irregular gigs on other days.

Klub Jazzowy Kornet (Map p129; ☎ 427 02 44; Al Krasińskiego 19; ☒ 11am-11pm Mon-Sat, 3-11pm Sun) A bit out of the centre, Kornet has free concerts and/or jam sessions on Wednesday and Friday, and various jazz and blues acts on other nights.

Classical Music

The **Filharmonia Krakowska** (Kraków Philharmonic; Map pp132-3; ☎ 422 43 12; www.filharmonia.krakow .pl; ul Zwierzyniecka 1; tickets 6-20zł) is home to one of the best orchestras in the country. Concerts are held on Friday and Saturday and irregularly on other days.

Cinemas

Kraków has about 20 cinemas, with half of them in the centre. The cinemas that may have some art-house and quality mainstream movies on their programme include **Kino Mikro** (Map p129; ☎ 634 28 97; ul Lea 5), **Kino Paradox** (Map p129; ☎ 430 00 25; ul Krowoderska 8) and the cinema club in the **Rotunda Student Club** (Map p129; ☎ 634 34 12; ul Oleandry 1).

Theatre

Kraków has a dozen theatres (more than any other Polish city, except Warsaw), including some of Poland's best playhouses.

Cricoteka (Map pp132-3; ☎ 422 83 32; ul Kanonicza 5; ⊙ 10am-2pm Mon-Fri) Cricoteka is the centre that documents the avant-garde Cricot 2 theatre, created in 1955 by Tadeusz Kantor. Kraków's best-known theatre outside the national borders, Cricot 2 was dissolved after Kantor died in 1990. Theatre buffs may be interested in visiting this place.

Stary Teatr (Old Theatre; Map pp132-3; ☎ 422 85 66; ul Jagiellońska 5; tickets 20-30zł) This is the best-known city theatre and has attracted the cream of the city's actors.

Teatr im Słowackiego (Słowacki Theatre; Map pp132-3; ☎ 422 45 75; Plac Św Ducha 1; tickets 11-20zł) The theatre focuses on Polish classics and large-scale productions. It's in a large and opulent building (an historical monument in itself), patterned on the Paris Opera and built in 1893. It was totally renovated in 1991, and its interior is spectacular. Opera and ballet performances are also staged here, as there's no proper opera house in Kraków.

Teatr Groteska (☎ 632 92 00; ul Skarbowa 2; tickets 10-14zł) The 'Grotesque Theatre' is best-known for its creepy, wordless puppet-show, *Golem*, about the living clay-creature conjured up by a Prague rabbi. It also hosts the odd music performance.

Scena STU (Map p129; ☎ 422 27 44; Al Krasińskiego 16; tickets 15zł) STU started in the 1970s as an 'angry', politically involved, avant-garde student theatre and was immediately successful. Today it no longer deserves any of those adjectives, but nonetheless it's a solid professional troupe.

SHOPPING

Kraków's Old Town hosts a vast array of shops, selling everything from tacky T-shirts to exquisite crystal glassware, and all within a short walk from the Main Market Sq. Ul Grodzka and ul Floriańska are good places to start looking.

Antiques & Crafts

The most obvious place to start your shopping expedition is the arcaded **Cloth Hall** (p136), which houses dozens of little shops selling amber jewellery, wooden chess sets, glass, textiles, T-shirts and other reasonably priced souvenirs.

Alhena (Map pp132-3; ☎ 421 54 95; pl Mariacki 1) This small shop sells an attractive range of glassware, including pieces produced by Poland's famous Krosno factory.

Antykwariat na Kazimierzu (Map p141; ☎ 292 61 53; ul Meiselsa 17) In the basement of the Judaica centre, this intriguing place has a jumble of antique china, glass, paintings, books and other assorted stock.

In the summer season, an antique and bric-a-brac fair is held for one weekend a month at the main square. For the rest of the year, it's held on every second and fourth Saturday of the month at ul Siemiradzkiego 13.

Books & Music

EMPiK (Map pp132-3; ☎ 429 42 34; Rynek Główny 5) Like its other outlets, EMPiK has an extensive selection of music and books, including English novels, plus international newspapers and magazines. Internet access is also available here (4zł per hour)

Jarden Jewish Bookshop (Map p141; ☎ 421 71 66; ul Szeroka 2) This bookshop has the best selection of books referring to Jewish issues, as well as CDs of Jewish music.

Jazz Compact (☎ 422 26 53; Rynek Główny 28) This tiny shop has an extensive selection of jazz, including Polish jazz.

Contemporary Art

Kraków is a good place to get an insight into what's currently happening in Polish art and, if you wish, to buy some. The outdoor gallery at the Florian Gate is the place to go, if you're after amateur daubs of the 'vase of flowers' variety, and there are plenty of decent commercial art galleries in town.

Starmach Gallery (Map p129; ☎ 656 43 17; ul Węgierska 5) One of the most prestigious art galleries in town, Starmach has renowned contemporary painting, though perhaps it's not for everyone's pocket.

Labirynt (Map pp132-3; ☎ 292 60 80; ul Floriańska 36) A more-affordable place for art, Labirynt has a decent mix of painting and sculpture.

Jan Fejkiel Gallery (Map pp132-3; ☎ 429 15 53; ul Grodzka 25) Fejkiel has the best collection of contemporary prints and drawings in Kraków.

Andrzej Mleczko Gallery (Map pp132-3; ☎ 421 71 04; ul Św Jana 14) The gallery displays and sells comic drawings by one of the most popular Polish satirical cartoonists.

Galeria Plakatu (Poster Gallery; Map pp132-3; ☎ 421 26 40; ul Stolarska 8-10) Without any doubt, this is Kraków's best choice of posters, created by Poland's most prominent poster makers.

GETTING THERE & AWAY
Air
The airport, is in Balice, about 12km west of the city, and is accessible by bus 208 from just north of the PKS bus terminal, and by the more-frequent bus 152 from the bus stop at ul Lubicz, south of the train station. A taxi between the airport and the city centre shouldn't cost more than 60zł. The **LOT office** (Map pp132-3; ☎ 411 67 00; ul Basztowa 15) deals with tickets and reservations.

Within Poland, the only flights from here are to Warsaw, but you can get there much more cheaply, centre-to-centre, by train. Kraków has direct flight connections with Frankfurt/Main, London, Paris, Rome, Vienna and Chicago.

Bus
The PKS bus terminal is next to Kraków Główny train station. Travel by bus is particularly advisable to Zakopane (9zł, 2½ hours) as it's considerably shorter and faster than by train. Fast PKS buses go there roughly every hour. Two private companies, Trans-Frej and Szwagropol, also run buses to Zakopane, which are marginally faster (10zł, two hours). They depart from the front of the terminal. Tickets for Trans-Frej are available from **Waweltur** (Map pp132-3; ☎ 422 19 21; ul Pawia 8). For Szwagropol, tickets are sold by **Centrum Turystyki** (Map pp132-3; ☎ 422 29 04; ul Worcella 1).

There are three morning PKS departures to Częstochowa (11.50zł, 2½ hours) and three morning and two afternoon buses to Oświęcim (10zł, 1½ hours). Other destinations include two buses a day to Lublin

(28zł, 4½ hours), two to Zamość (30zł, five hours) and eight to Cieszyn at the Czech border (13.50zł, two hours). There are also several buses to Warsaw (39zł, five hours). For other destinations, it is better to take the train. Tickets are available directly from the bus terminal. Note that buses to Oświęcim don't depart from the terminal but from the bus stop on the opposite side of the train station, which is accessible by a passageway under the platforms.

There are plenty of international bus routes originating in Kraków, going to Amsterdam (311zł, 20½ hours), London (450zł, 27 hours), Munich (250zł, 19 hours), Paris (319zł, 24 hours), Riga (200zł, 20 hours), Rome (295zł, 25 hours), Vienna (140zł, 10½ hours) and many other destinations. Information and tickets are available from travel agencies throughout town, including **Sindbad** (☎ 421 02 40) in the bus terminal. Check the website www.eurolinespolska .com.pl for the latest prices and timetable information.

Train
The central train station, Kraków Główny, on the northeastern outskirts of the Old Town, handles all international and most domestic trains. The only other station of any significance is Kraków Płaszów, 4km southeast of the city centre, which operates some trains that don't call at Kraków Główny. Local trains between the two stations run every 15 to 30 minutes. All trains listed in this section depart from the central station.

Each day from Kraków, ten trains head to Warsaw (37zł, 2¾ hours). Also every day from Kraków there are several trains to Wrocław (40.20zł, 3¾ hours), two to Poznań (56zł, six hours) and two to Lublin (48zł, five hours).

To Częstochowa (30zł, two hours), there are two morning fast trains as well as several afternoon/evening trains. Trains to Katowice (20zł, 1½ hours) run every half-hour to an hour. There are plenty of trains daily to Tarnów (20zł, 1½ hours) that pass through Bośnia (a gateway to Nowy Wiśnicz). A dozen of these trains continue to Rzeszów (35zł, 3½ hours).

To Oświęcim (19zł, 1½ hours), you have a couple of trains early in the morning and then nothing until the afternoon. There are more trains to Oświęcim from Kraków

Płaszów station, though they don't depart regularly either; check the bus schedule before going to Płaszów.

Internationally, there are one or two direct trains daily to Berlin, Bratislava, Bucharest, Budapest, Hamburg, Kyiv, Odesa, Prague and Vienna.

Tickets and couchettes can be bought directly at Kraków Główny station or at **Orbis Travel** (Map pp132-3; Rynek Główny 41).

GETTING AROUND
To/From the Airport

Balice Airport, also known as John Paul II International Airport, is roughly 12km west of the city centre. Bus 208 links the airport with the Old Town and the railway station (2.60zł). Otherwise a taxi will cost you upwards of 30zł.

Car & Motorcycle

With limited parking, and with much of the Old Town a car-free zone, having a car may be more of a hindrance than a help. If you are travelling by car, the major route into the city is the A4; note that a 5zł toll is paid when you enter and exit it. The Old Town is closed to traffic, except for access to two guarded car parks on Plac Szczepański and Plac Św Ducha – the most convenient places to park (around 8zł to 10zł per hour), if you can find space. If not, use one of the guarded car parks in the surrounding area. Street parking in the area outside the Old Town, known as 'Zone C', requires special tickets (karta postojowâ), which you buy in a Ruch kiosk, mark with the correct month, day and time, and then display on your windscreen. Tickets cost 4zł for one hour or 55zł for 24 hours.

Public Transport

Most tourist attractions are in the Old Town or within easy walking distance, so you won't need buses or trams unless you're staying outside the centre. Kraków is served by both buses and trams, which run between 5am and 11pm. Some night buses run later. Single-journey (2.20zł), one-hour (2.80zł) and one-day (9zł) tickets can be bought at street kiosks, and must be stamped as soon as you board. Note that a single ticket is also required for bulky luggage such as backpacks. Tickets for night buses are 4.40zł.

Taxi

If travelling by taxi, be sure to choose a licensed operator with a meter. Should you need a taxi, these are some of the better-known companies:

Barbakan Taxi (☎ 0800 404 400)
Euro Taxi (☎ 96 64)
Express Taxi (☎ 0800 111 111)
Metro Taxi (☎ 96 67)
Radio Taxi (☎ 0800 500 919)

AROUND KRAKÓW

Kraków is a convenient jumping-off point for day trips to some nearby places of interest, of which the **Ojców National Park** (p164) and **Oświęcim** (Auschwitz-Birkenau death camps; p304) are two obvious destinations. **Kalwaria Zebrzydowska** (p210) is another, in particular if you happen to be there during Easter. You could also consider **Nowy Wiśnicz** (p211) and **Dębno** (p212), if you are not heading further east.

Małopolska

162

Małopolska (literally 'Little Poland') encompasses a sizeable chunk of southeastern Poland, bordering Ukraine to the east, Mazovia to the north and the Carpathian Mountains to the south. It's still a largely rural area, a land of rustic villages, picturesque countryside and rolling green hills, little explored by foreign tourists. The biggest city and main transport hub is Lublin, a place of great historical importance but little aesthetic merit. It does, however, have a small but appealing Old Town that's worth a wander. The region's major attraction is Częstochowa, Poland's spiritual heart and home to the country's most important Catholic shrine, which is dedicated to the *Black Madonna* and has been drawing countless pilgrims over the centuries.

No tour of Małopolska should bypass Zamość, the unique, and somewhat incongruous Renaissance-planned town that looks as if it might have been airlifted from northern Italy and dropped on the Lublin Upland. Other towns of interest include Chełm, with its intriguing chalk tunnels, and tiny Kazimierz Dolny, which is popular with weekenders from Warsaw, looking for a bit of tranquillity. Elsewhere, the Roztocze and Świętokrzyski National Parks are havens for wildlife and walkers.

Historically, together with Wielkopolska, Małopolska was the cradle of the Polish state. Settled by Slavs from the early Middle Ages, the region grew in importance after the kings chose Kraków as the royal seat in 1038. As a royal province, the region enjoyed the special attention of the kings, who built an array of castles to protect it. As a borderland, it also faced more than its share of unrest, invasion and war, but Małopolska was always one of the most 'Polish' regions of the country, and still retains much of that traditional flavour.

HIGHLIGHTS

▪ **Architectural Wonder**
The unique Renaissance-planned town of Zamość (p200) for a trip back in time

▪ **Follow the Pilgrims' Path**
The spiritual traditions of Poland's national shrine dedicated to the *Black Madonna* at Częstochowa (p169)

▪ **Culture**
The amazing Chapel of the Holy Trinity (p185) in Lublin Castle, with its colourful murals

▪ **Walking**
The trails in Roztocze National Park (p206)

▪ **Out and About**
Paradise Cave (p173) near Kielce

▪ **Off Beat**
Jędrzejów's unusual Sundial Museum (p173)

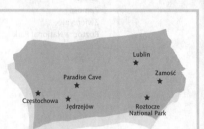

▪ TELEPHONE CODES: 12, 15, 32, 34, 41, 48, 81, 82, 84

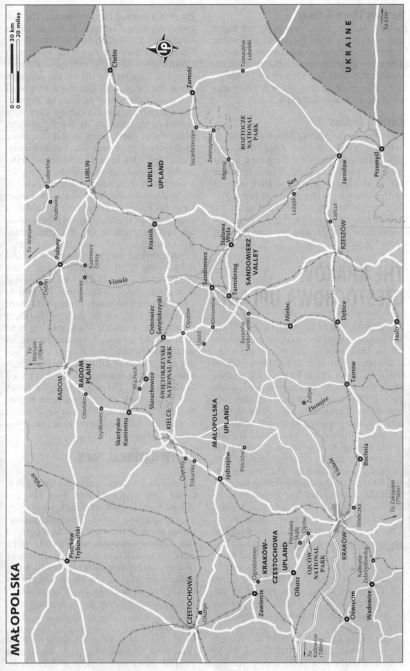

MAŁOPOLSKA

0 — 30 km
0 — 20 miles

UKRAINE

To Lviv

Chełm

Zamość

Tomaszów
Lubelski

ROZTOCZE
NATIONAL
PARK

Lubartów

LUBLIN

LUBLIN
UPLAND

Szczebrzeszyn

Zwierzyniec

Biłgoraj

San

Jarosław

Przemyśl

Kozłówka

To Warsaw

Puławy

Kazimierz
Dolny

Janowiec

Dęblin

Vistula

Kraśnik

Leżajsk

Łańcut

RZESZÓW

Stalowa
Wola

SANDOMIERZ
VALLEY

Sandomierz

Tarnobrzeg

Mielec

Dębica

Jasło

Ostrowiec
Świętokrzyski

Opatów

Klimontów

To
Warsaw (70km)

Ujazd

Baranów
Sandomierski

RADOM
PLAIN

Wąchock

ŚWIĘTOKRZYSKI
NATIONAL PARK

KIELCE

Starachowice

Ostrowiec

Oleśnica

MAŁOPOLSKA
UPLAND

Tarnów

Zalipie

Dunajec

RADOM

Skarżysko
Kamienna

Szydłowiec

Chęciny

Tokarnia

Jędrzejów

Pińczów

Bochnia

Vistula

Piotrków
Trybunalski

Pilica

To Zakopane
(75km)

Wieliczka

KRAKÓW–
CZĘSTOCHOWA
UPLAND

Pieskowa
Skała

Ojców

OJCÓW
NATIONAL
PARK

KRAKÓW

Ogrodzieniec

Olkusz

Kalwaria
Zebrzydowska

CZĘSTOCHOWA

Zawiercie

Olsztyn

Oświęcim

Wadowice

To
Katowice
(18km)

Getting There & Away

Lublin, Radom and Częstochowa are major transport hubs, both for trains and, more conveniently, for buses from all over Poland. There are frequent services between the region's main cities and Warsaw and Kraków. See the relevant Getting There & Away sections for each town for more details.

Getting Around

Most towns in Małopolska have reasonable bus links with their neighbours, and you'll probably find these the most efficient means of public transport. Trains are often slower and less frequent and train stations further away from the centre of town. Private minibuses are increasingly useful for getting around cheaply and quickly. See the relevant Getting Around sections for each town for more details.

THE KRAKÓW-CZĘSTOCHOWA UPLAND

The Kraków-Częstochowa Upland (Wyżyna Krakowsko-Częstochowska) is a picturesque belt of land, roughly 20km to 40km wide, that stretches for over 100km from Kraków to Częstochowa. It was formed of limestone some 150 million years ago in the Jurassic period (the name comes from the Jura mountains in France, and this Polish upland region is also popularly known as the Jura).

Erosion of the upland has left behind a variety of strange rock formations, taking, for example, the shapes of freestanding pillars, clubs and gates. There are also between 500 and 1000 caves, the overwhelming majority of all those in Poland. The largest concentrations are in the Ojców area and around the village of Olsztyn near Częstochowa. They are largely unexplored – the haunt of speleologists and other adventurers.

The flora and fauna of the upland is diverse. A good part of the region is covered by forest, mostly beech, pine and fir. There are 17 species of bat – the symbol of the Jura – living in the local caves, and you can occasionally come across hares, roe deer and even elk.

The region's great cultural attractions are the numerous castles. When Silesia fell to Bohemia in the mid-14th century, leaving the Jura a natural border between the two countries, King Kazimierz Wielki set about fortifying the frontier, and a chain of castles was built all the way from Kraków to Częstochowa. Taking advantage of the topography, they were built on the hill tops along the ridge and, like the Great Wall of China, were meant to form an impregnable barrier against the enemy. They were indeed never breached by the Bohemians, with whom there were simply no more major conflicts. It was the Swedish invasion of 1655 that brought destruction to the castles and successive invasions during the 18th century reduced most of them to ruins. Apart from the Pieskowa Skała, the castles were not rebuilt. Today there are a dozen ruined castles scattered around the upland; the most impressive are at Ogrodzieniec and Olsztyn.

An excellent way to explore the upland is by hiking the Trail of the Eagles' Nests (Szlak Orlich Gniazd). The trail, signposted in red, winds for 164km from Kraków to Częstochowa and passes through the most interesting parts of the Jura, including a dozen ruined castles. Total walking time is about 42 hours. Accommodation, in youth hostels (July and August only), hotels or agrotourist farms, is always within a day's walking distance, so you don't need camping gear. There are regional maps that give details of the route and tourist facilities. The tourist offices in Kraków and Częstochowa should have these maps and other information.

OJCÓW NATIONAL PARK
☎ 12

At only 21.5 sq km in size, the Ojców National Park (Ojcowski Park Narodowy) is Poland's smallest national park, yet it's very picturesque and varied. The park encompasses some of the most beautiful parts of the Kraków-Częstochowa Upland. In its small area you'll find two castles, a number of caves, impressive rock formations and a wide variety of plant life. Most of the park is beech, fir, oak and hornbeam forest, which is particularly photogenic in autumn.

Orientation

Most tourist attractions are along the road that runs through the park beside the Prądnik River with Ojców and Pieskowa

Skała, about 7km apart, being the main points of interest. Though buses run between these two localities, it's best to walk the whole stretch, enjoying the sights and scenery. The Trail of the Eagles' Nests also follows this road.

Give yourself plenty of time in the park – it's a captivating place. Buy the *Ojcowski Park Narodowy* map (scale 1: 22,500) in Kraków before setting off. The map includes all the marked trails, rocks, caves, gorges and the like.

Sights & Activities

Ojców is the only village in the park. Its predominantly wooden houses are scattered across a slope above the river. The hill at the northern end of the village is crowned with the ruins of **Ojców Castle**, with its original 14th-century entrance gate and an octagonal tower.

One of the two long buildings just south of the castle houses the **Natural History Museum** (Muzeum Przyrodnicze; ☎ 389 20 40; admission 2zł; ☿ 9am-4.30pm Tue-Sun mid-May–mid-Nov, 8am-3pm Tue-Fri mid-Nov–mid-May), which focuses on the geology, archaeology and flora and fauna of the park. A wooden mansion a few paces further south accommodates the **Regional Museum** (Muzeum Regionalne; ☎ 389 20 10; adult/concession 5/3zł; ☿ 10am-3.30pm Tue-Sun) which features the history and ethnography of the region.

The black trail, which heads southwards from Ojców Castle, takes you to the **Łokietek Cave** (Jaskinia Łokietka; admission 5zł; ☿ 9.30am-4.30pm Apr-Nov). About 250m long, this cave consists of one small and two large chambers. Guided tours take half an hour.

More interesting and larger is the **Wierzchowska Górna Cave** (☎ 411 07 21; adult/concession 6/4zł; ☿ 9am-5pm May-Aug, 9am-4pm Apr, Sep & Oct), in the village of Wierzchowie, outside the park boundaries, 5km southwest of Ojców; the yellow trail will take you there. It's the longest cave in the whole region – 1km long – and about 370m of its length can be visited. The 50-minute tours begin on the hour. The temperature inside is 7.5°C year-round.

Other caves open to the public (in summer) include the **Dark Cave** (Jaskinia Ciemna), close to Ojców and easily reached by the green trail, and the **Bat Cave** (Jaskinia Nietoperzowa), further away and accessible by the blue trail.

About 200m north of Ojców Castle is the **Chapel upon the Water** (Kaplica na Wodzie), positioned above the river bed where it was rebuilt from the former public baths. The chapel is open only for religious services on Sunday morning.

In the hamlet of Grodzisko, about 2km to the north, the road divides: take the left-hand fork skirting the river and look for the red trail that branches off the road to the right and heads uphill. It will take you to the small baroque **Church of the Blessed Salomea**, erected in the 17th century on the site of the former convent of Poor Clares. The stone wall encircling the church is adorned with statues representing Salomea and her family. Behind the church is an unusual carved stone elephant (1686) supporting an obelisk on its back.

Follow the red trail, which brings you back down to the road. Walk for several kilometres to an 18m-tall limestone pillar known as **Hercules' Club** (Maczuga Herkulesa). A short distance beyond it is the **Pieskowa Skała Castle**. The castle was erected in the 14th century but the mighty fortress you see is the result of major rebuilding in the 16th century. It's the best-preserved castle in the upland and it houses a **museum** (☎ 389 60 04; admission 4zł; ☿ 10am-3.30pm Tue-Sun).

You first enter a large outer courtyard, which is accessible free of charge. From here you get to the arcaded inner courtyard and the museum. On display is European art from the Middle Ages to the mid-19th century, including furniture, tapestries, sculpture, painting and ceramics.

There's a restaurant-café in the outer courtyard of the castle, a good place to finish your sightseeing with a beer, coffee or a meal. In summer they open the terrace on the roof, providing a good view over the castle and the surrounding forest.

Sleeping & Eating

Local people in Ojców rent out rooms in their homes for around 30zł to 60zł per person. The rooms can be arranged through the **Ojcowianin travel agency** (☎ 389 20 89) or the **PTTK office** (☎ 389 20 10; http://ojcow.pttk.pl), both in the building of the regional museum.

Camping Złota Góra (☎ 389 20 14; Złota Góra; bed in on-site tent 20zł; ☿ May-Sep) This camping ground has six large military tents with beds and a restaurant.

MAŁOPOLSKA

Dom Wycieczkowy Zosia (☎ 389 20 08; Złota Góra; bed in d, tr or q 26-30zł) About 500m down the road from the camping ground, this place is one of the few regular all-year hostels around. Zosia is 1km west of Ojców Castle.

Getting There & Away

There are a few morning buses from Kraków to Ojców (4.40zł, 1½ hours). You can then walk to Pieskowa Skała, from where you can take a bus back to Kraków (5zł, 1½ hours).

OGRODZIENIEC

☎ 32 / pop 4500

Perched on top of the highest hill of the whole upland (504m), the fairy-tale ruin of the **Ogrodzieniec Castle** (☎ 673 22 20; admission 3zł; ☉ 9am-sunset Apr-Oct) is among the most picturesque in the country. Using natural rock for the foundations and some parts of the walls (a feature typical of castles in the region) the fortress was built during the reign of King Kazimierz Wielki but enlarged and remodelled in the mid-16th century. The owner at the time, the wealthy Kraków banker Seweryn Boner, employed the best Italian masters from the royal court, and they turned the Gothic castle into a Renaissance residence, said to be almost as splendid as the Wawel castle. The castle fell prey to the Swedes in 1655 and never regained its grandeur. The last owners abandoned it in the 1810s, and since then the ruin has been untouched. It's now a tourist sight.

Getting There & Away

The castle is in Podzamcze, 2km east of Ogrodzieniec; the two places are linked by buses. Ogrodzieniec is on the Zawiercie–Olkusz road and buses run regularly between these towns. From Zawiercie, you can continue north on one of the frequent trains to Częstochowa, while buses from Olkusz can take you directly to Kraków.

CZĘSTOCHOWA

☎ 34 / pop 260,000

Częstochowa (chen-sto-*ho*-vah) is the spiritual heart of Poland and the country's national shrine. It owes its fame to the miraculous icon of the *Black Madonna*, kept in the Monastery of Jasna Góra (literally 'Bright Mountain'), which has been pulling in pilgrims from all corners of the country and beyond for centuries.

Today Częstochowa attracts some of the largest pilgrimages in the world (local sources put it fifth, after Varanasi, Mecca, Lourdes and Rome). Tourists and the faithful alike flock in large numbers throughout the year, with significant peaks on Marian feasts, particularly on the day of the Assumption on 15 August. You're likely to find yourself drawn to the city, whether through devotion or curiosity.

History

Though the earliest document mentioning Częstochowa's existence dates from 1220, the town's development really began with the arrival of the Paulite order from Hungary in 1382. The monks founded a monastery atop a hill known as Jasna Góra. The monastery probably would not have gained its exceptional fame if not for a painting of the Virgin Mary, commonly referred to as the *Black Madonna*, which was presented in 1384 to the order and soon began to attract crowds of believers, thanks to numerous miracles attributed to the image.

Growing in wealth and importance, the monastery was gradually extended and turned into a fortress surrounded by stout defensive walls with massive bastions. It was one of the few places in the country to withstand the Swedish sieges of 1655 to 1656, the 'miracle' naturally being attributed to the *Black Madonna* and contributing to still larger floods of pilgrims. Interestingly, before the siege the Madonna was transferred to Silesia for safekeeping, yet somehow she was still able to save the monastery.

The town of Częstochowa grew as a centre providing facilities for the pilgrims visiting the monastery. In the second half of the 19th century, the construction of the Warsaw–Vienna railway line stimulated the development of commerce and industry. By the outbreak of WWII the city had 140,000 inhabitants.

After the war, in an attempt to overshadow the town's religious status, the communists intensified the development of industry. Today Częstochowa has a large steelworks and a number of other factories complete with a forest of smoky chimneys. Amid them, however, the tower of the Paulite monastery still proudly overlooks the city, showing pilgrims the way to the end of their journey.

CZĘSTOCHOWA

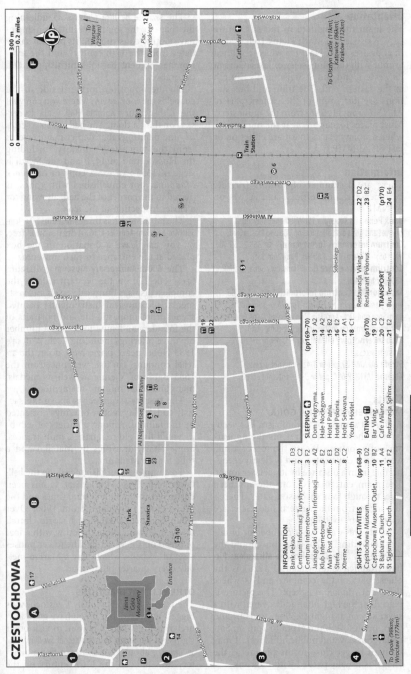

(pp169–70)

INFORMATION
Bank Pekao	1 D3
Centrum Informacji Turystycznej	2 C2
Centrum Internetowe	3 F2
Jasnogórski Centrum Informacji	4 A2
Klub Internetowy	5 E2
Main Post Office	6 E3
Strefa	7 D2
Xtreme	8 C2

SIGHTS & ACTIVITIES (pp168-9)
Częstochowa Museum	9 D2
Częstochowa Museum Outlet	10 B2
St Barbara's Church	11 A4
St Sigismund's Church	12 F2

SLEEPING (pp169–70)
Dom Pielgrzyma	13 A2
Hale Noclegowe	14 A2
Hotel Patria	15 E2
Hotel Polonia	16 E2
Hotel Sekwana	17 A1
Youth Hostel	18 C1

EATING (p170)
Bar Viking	19 D2
Cafe Milano	20 C2
Restauracja Sphinx	21 E2
Restauracja Viking	22 D2
Restaurant Polonus	23 B2

TRANSPORT (p170)
Bus Terminal	24 E4

MAŁOPOLSKA

Orientation

The main thoroughfare in the city centre is Al Najświętszej Marii Panny (referred to in addresses as Al NMP), a wide, tree-lined avenue with the Monastery of Jasna Góra at its western end and St Sigismund's Church at the eastern end. The train and bus stations are just south of the eastern part of Al NMP, roughly 2km from the monastery. Most places to stay are near the monastery, whereas many places to eat are either on or just off Al NMP.

Information

There are a number of *kantors* (private currency-exchange offices) and ATMs on Al NMP.

Bank Pekao (ul Kopernika 19) Will change travellers cheques and gives cash advances on Visa and MasterCard.

Centrum Informacji Turystycznej (☎ 368 22 60; Al NMP 65; 🕙 9am-5pm Mon-Fri, 9am-2pm Sat)

Centrum Internetowe (Dom Handlowy Seka, Al NMP 12D; per hr 3-4zł)

Jasnogórskie Centrum Informacji (☎ 365 38 88; www.jasnagora.pl; 🕙 7.30am-7pm May–mid-Oct, 8am-5pm mid-Oct–Apr) The Monastery of Jasna Góra has its own information centre, inside the compound.

Klub Internetowy (Al Wolności 11; per hr 3-4zł) Internet access.

Strefa (Al NMP 29; per hr 3-4zł) Internet access.

Xtreme (Al NMP 65A; per hr 3-4zł) Internet access.

Sights

MONASTERY OF JASNA GÓRA

A vibrant symbol of Catholicism in a secular sea, the monastery retains the appearance of a fortress. It's on the top of a hill, west of the city centre, and is clearly recognisable from a distance by its slender tower. The main entrance is from the southern side, through four successive gates. There's also a gate from the western side. Gates are open 5.30am to 9.30pm.

Inside the walls are a number of buildings, including a chapel, a church and the monastery. The **Chapel of the Miraculous Picture** (Kaplica Cudownego Obrazu) is the oldest part of the complex and is where the *Black Madonna* is kept. The picture is placed on the high altar and covered with a silver screen at night (9.30pm to 6am) and from noon to 1.30pm (1pm to 2pm on Saturday, Sunday and public holidays). It may be hard to get close to the picture as the chapel is usually packed with pilgrims.

The sizable **basilica** *(bazylika)*, adjoining the chapel to the south, was initially a single-nave Gothic construction. Its present shape dates from the 17th century and the interior has opulent baroque furnishings and decoration.

On the opposite, northern side of the chapel is the monastery, where you can visit the 17th-century **Knights' Hall** (Sala Rycerska) on the 1st floor. The hall boasts a series of nine paintings that depict major events from the monastery's history, including the Hussite raid of 1430 and the Swedish siege of 1655. An exact copy of the *Black Madonna*, not embellished with robes, is placed in the corner of the hall, allowing for a closer inspection of the icon.

The monastery has three **museums** (🕙 9am-5pm Apr-Sep, 9am-4pm Oct-Mar). Admission is free, or you can leave a donation in the box placed at the entrance to each museum.

The **600th-Anniversary Museum** (Muzeum Sześćsetlecia), on the western side of the complex, displays liturgical vessels and vestments, old musical instruments, painted scenes from monastic life and portraits of the founders and superiors, plus a number of votive offerings including Lech Wałęsa's 1983 Nobel peace prize. Next door, the **arsenal** contains Turkish weapons from the 1683 Battle of Vienna as well as medals, maps and other military mementoes.

The **treasury** *(skarbiec)* is above the sacristy and displays votive offerings presented by the faithful. Among a variety of exhibits you'll find old reliquaries, monstrances, home altars, drawings by Matejko and a robe for the Madonna.

To complete your visit, climb up the **bell-tower** (wieża; 🕙 8am-4pm Apr-Sep). It has been destroyed and rebuilt several times and the present one only dates from 1906. Over 106m high, it's the tallest historic church tower in Poland. Note the crow with a loaf of bread on the very top. The tower houses a set of 36 bells, which play a Marian melody every quarter of an hour.

OTHER CITY ATTRACTIONS

The monastery is obviously Częstochowa's biggest drawcard, but if you have got a leisurely itinerary, you may want to visit other sights. **St Barbara's Church** (Kościół Św Barbary; ul Św Barbary), about 1km south of the monastery, was built in the 17th century on the

THE BLACK MADONNA OF CZĘSTOCHOWA

The *Black Madonna* is a painting on a lime-tree timber panel (measuring 122cm by 82cm) that depicts the Virgin Mary with the Christ child. The picture looks like a Byzantine icon, but it's not known when and where the original was created: the time of its creation is put somewhere between the 6th and 14th centuries, and theories of its provenance range from Byzantium and Red Ruthenia to Italy and Hungary. What is known is that the icon was brought from Ruthenia in 1382 and offered to the Paulite order a couple of years later.

In 1430 the icon was damaged by the Hussites, who slashed the face of the Madonna and broke the panel. The picture was repainted afterwards in a workshop in Kraków, but the scars on the face of the Virgin Mary were left as a reminder of the sacrilegious attack.

In 1717 the *Black Madonna* was crowned 'Queen of Poland' in a ceremony attended by 200,000 of the faithful. This was the first ever painting crowned outside Italy. Since then the image has traditionally been crowned and dressed with richly ornamented robes, and these days the Madonna has a wardrobe of robes and crowns, which are changed on special occasions.

spot where the Hussites were thought to have slashed the icon and thrown it away. The monks who found the panel wanted to clean the mud off it, and a spring miraculously bubbled from the ground. The spring exists to this day in the chapel behind the church, and the water is supposed to have health-giving properties. The painting on the vault of the chapel depicts the story.

The **Częstochowa Museum** (Muzeum Częstochowskie; ☎ 324 32 75; Plac Biegańskiego 45; admission 3zł; ☷ 8.30am-4pm Wed-Sat, 10am-4pm Sun), in the late neoclassical town hall dating from 1828, features an ethnographic collection and modern Polish paintings, plus some temporary exhibitions. **Częstochowa Museum outlet** (Park Staszica; ☷ 8.30am-4pm Wed-Sat, 10am-4pm Sun) stages temporary exhibitions.

OLSZTYN CASTLE

A visit to the Olsztyn castle, 11km east of Częstochowa, is a refreshing trip out of the city. The castle is in ruins, but what a charming ruin it is. You can get to Olsztyn by city bus 58 or 67 from ul Piłsudskiego opposite the train station. Alternatively, you can walk along the Trail of the Eagles' Nests, which starts from Plac Daszyńskiego and leads via Olsztyn up to Kraków.

Festivals & Events

Marian feasts The major Marian feasts at Jasna Góra are on 3 May, 16 July, 15 August, 26 August, 8 September, 12 September and 8 December, and on these days the monastery is packed with pilgrims.

Assumption (15 August) The celebration of Assumption is particularly important, with pilgrims from all over Poland travelling to Jasna Góra on foot. The Warsaw pilgrims leave

the capital on 6 August every year for the 250km trip. Up to 250,000 faithful flock to the monastery for this feast.

'Gaude Mater' International Festival of Religious Music On a more artistic front, this is the city's main event, the held in May.

Sleeping

Bear in mind that Częstochowa gets lots of pilgrims, so finding a place to stay, especially a cheap one, may not be easy – particularly on and around Marian feast days. It may be best to avoid these periods or make a day trip to the city.

Hotel Sekwana (☎ 324 89 54, ☎ /fax 324 63 67; ul Wieluńska 24; s/d/apt 150/200/280zł; **P**) A comfortable place to stay in the monastery area, Sekwana has 20 rooms and its own restaurant specialising in Polish and French cuisine.

Hotel Patria (☎ 324 70 01; patria@orbis.pl; ul Popiełuszki 2; s/d/apt 344/448/680zł; **P** ✗) This Orbis-owned hotel is the top-end option in the monastery area. Like most Orbis stock, it's clean, modern and comfortable but hardly an inspiring choice. It can have attractive weekend discounts.

Hale Noclegowe (☎ 377 72 24; ul Klasztorna 1; dm 15-20zł; ☷ May–mid-Oct) This Church-run place, just next to the monastery, provides some of the cheapest accommodation in town. It's clean but basic; rooms have shared facilities and there's no hot water. There's a 10pm curfew.

Dom Pielgrzyma (☎ 324 70 11; ul Wyszyńskiego 1/31; dm/s/d from 20/60/90zł) Dom is another Church-operated lodging facility, right behind the monastery and is remarkably good value. Curfew here is also at 10pm. There's a cheap cafeteria on the premises.

MAŁOPOLSKA

Hotel Polonia (☎ 324 23 88; fax 365 11 05; ul Piłsudskiego 9; s/d/tr/q 100/120/150/180zł) Polonia is handily located opposite the station, and offers a reasonable standard of comfort for the price, though it's a little dated.

Youth hostel (☎ 324 31 21; ul Jasnogórska 84/90; dm 20zł; ☑ Jul & Aug) This modest 90-bed hostel is also close to the monastery, but it's only open during summer holidays.

Eating

As might be expected, there are plenty of budget eating outlets in the monastery area, apart from the above-mentioned cafeteria of Dom Pielgrzyma and the snack bar at the camping ground. There are also quite a number of eateries on and around Al NMP.

Restaurant Polonus (☎ 801 33 18; Al NMP 75; mains from 15zł; ☑ 10am-midnight) A decent option near the path up to the monastery, serving good quality Polish cuisine.

Bar Viking (☎ 324 57 68; ul Nowowiejskiego 10; mains 10-28zł; ☑ 10am-10pm) One of the cheapest eateries in the centre, Bar Viking serves tasty meals and has outdoor tables in summer. The adjacent restaurant of the same name is a more-upmarket proposition.

Cafe Milano (☎ 365 49 29; Al NMP 57/59; ☑ 7am-11pm) This Spanish-run café serves up the best espresso, cappuccino and ice cream in town – warmly recommended.

Restauracja Sphinx (☎ 366 41 85; Al Kościuszki 1; mains 15-35zł; ☑ lunch & dinner) Like elsewhere, Sphinx serves up standard kebab-and-salad-style dishes in various forms in an attractive, pseudo-oriental setting.

Getting There & Away
BUS

The bus terminal is close to the central train station and operates plenty of buses in the region. You may use it if going to Jędrzejów (10.50zł, two hours) or Opole (11.50zł, two hours). There's one direct bus to Ogrodzieniec at 2pm (7.80zł, one hour); if you don't want to wait for it, take any of the frequent trains to Katowice, get off in Zawiercie and change for a bus.

There are half a dozen buses to Kraków, going different ways and taking up to three hours. Alternatively, take the faster Polski Express bus (20zł, two hours, three daily). Polski Express buses also head to Warsaw (50zł, three hours, one daily).

TRAIN

The **train station** (Al Wolności) handles half a dozen daily fast trains to Warsaw (35zł, 3½ hours) and about the same number of fast trains to Kraków (25zł, two hours). Trains to Katowice (17zł, 1½ hours) run every hour or so, from where there are connections to Kraków and Wrocław.

THE MAŁOPOLSKA UPLAND

Occupying an area skirted by the Vistula and Pilica Rivers, the Małopolska Upland (Wyżyna Małopolska) culminates in the Holy Cross Mountains (Góry Świętokrzyskie), at the foot of which sits Kielce, the main urban centre. The upland offers a number of varied cultural attractions and wide stretches of beautiful landscape.

KIELCE
☎ 41 / pop 220,000

Kielce (*kyel*-tseh) is set in a valley amid gentle hills and consists of a compact centre with predominantly 19th-century architecture, and a ring of postwar suburbs perched on the surrounding slopes.

The city itself has little to merit much more than a quick look-over, but it lies close to a fine mountain range (p174) and might be a good base for visiting its national park. There are also some interesting places in Kielce's vicinity (p173).

Information

For changing cash, there are plenty of *kantors* on ul Sienkiewicza.

Arena (☎ 344 22 47; ul Piotrkowska 6; per hr 2-3zł) Internet access.

Bank Pekao (ul Sienkiewicza 18) Travellers cheques can be cashed at this bank, which also gives advances on Visa and MasterCard, and has an ATM.

Małpka (☎ 343 86 81; ul Słowackiego 8; per hr 2-3zł) Internet access.

Miejski Ośrodek Informacji Turystycznej (☎ 367 64 36; Rynek 1; ☑ 7.30am-5pm Mon-Fri Nov-Mar, 7.30am-7pm Mon-Fri & 10am-3pm Sat Apr-Oct) Located in the building of the city's municipal office.

Planetka (☎ 344 87 92; ul Planty 12; per hr 2-3zł) Internet access.

Strefa 51 (☎ 366 09 89; ul Paderewskiego 34; per hr 2-3zł) Internet access.

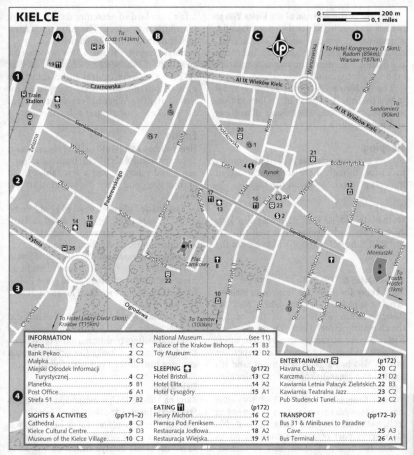

KIELCE

INFORMATION		
Arena	1	C2
Bank Pekao	2	C2
Małpka	3	C3
Miejski Ośrodek Informacji Turystycznej	4	C2
Planeta	5	B1
Post Office	6	A1
Strefa 51	7	B2

SIGHTS & ACTIVITIES	(pp171–2)	
Cathedral	8	C3
Kielce Cultural Centre	9	D3
Museum of the Kielce Village	10	C3

National Museum	(see 11)	
Palace of the Kraków Bishops	11	B3
Toy Museum	12	D2

SLEEPING	(p172)	
Hotel Bristol	13	C2
Hotel Elita	14	A2
Hotel Łysogóry	15	A1

EATING	(p172)	
Fleury Michon	16	C2
Piwnica Pod Feniksem	17	C2
Restauracja Jodłowa	18	A2
Restauracja Wiejska	19	A1

ENTERTAINMENT	(p172)	
Havana Club	20	C2
Karczma	21	D2
Kawiarnia Letnia Pałacyk Zielińskich	22	B3
Kawiarnia Teatralna Jazz	23	C2
Pub Studencki Tunel	24	C2

TRANSPORT	(pp172–3)	
Bus 31 & Minibuses to Paradise Cave	25	A3
Bus Terminal	26	A1

MAŁOPOLSKA

Sights

The most important city sight is the **Palace of the Kraków Bishops** (Pałac Biskupów Krakowskich), a sumptuous 17th-century baroque structure reflecting Kraków's wealth and prosperity. Kielce and its surroundings were the property of the Kraków bishops from the 12th century up to 1789, and they built the palace as one of their seats.

Today the palace houses the **National Museum** (☎ 344 40 14; Plac Zamkowy 1; adult/concession 10/5zł, free Sun; ⏰ 10am-6pm Tue, 9am-4pm Wed-Sun), where you can see authentic interiors from the 17th and 18th centuries. Of unique value are the three elaborate plafonds (ornamented ceilings) from around 1641, painted in the workshop of the Venetian Tommaso Dola-

bella. The whole clan of Kraków bishops look down on you from the murals in their former dining hall, the largest room in the palace: the upper strip was painted in the 1640s, and the lower one was added two centuries later.

The palace's side wing features a gallery of Polish painting from the 17th century to WWII, while the ground floor houses a collection of historic armour and temporary exhibitions.

The **cathedral** facing the palace was originally Romanesque, but the present-day building dates from the 17th century and has been altered several times since then; the opulent interior fittings reflect these transformations, though baroque decoration predominates.

Nearby is the **Museum of the Kielce Village** (Muzeum Wsi Kieleckiej; ☎ 344 92 97; ul Jana Pawła II 6; admission 6zł; 🕙 10am-3pm Mon-Fri & Sun). Accommodated in an 18th-century thatched country manor, the museum stages temporary ethnographic exhibitions.

The **Toy Museum** (Muzeum Zabawkarstwa; ☎ 344 40 78; ul Kościuszki 11; admission 2zł; 🕙 10am-5pm Tue-Sun) holds a unique assemblage of antique and modern toys.

Sleeping

Budget accommodation is hard to come by in Kielce, though there are several decent mid-range places to spend the night.

BUDGET

Youth hostel (☎ 342 37 35; ul Szymanowskiego 5; dm 25-30zł) This fairly average but well-run 67-bed PTTK hostel is about 1.5km east of the city centre.

MID-RANGE & TOP END

Hotel Leśny Dwór (☎ 362 10 88; www.lesnydwor .com.pl; ul Szczepaniaka 40; s/d/ste 160/220/350zł; P) Roughly 3km southwest of the centre, the charming Hotel Leśny Dwór is one of Kielce's more-attractive small hotels, offering neat and stylish rooms at a competitive rate. It also has a good restaurant, and it's located in a pleasant spot just opposite Park Baranowski.

Hotel Kongresowy (☎ 332 63 93; www.exbud .com.pl; ul Manifestu Lipcowego 34; s/d/ste Mon-Fri from 260/320/470zł, Sat & Sun from 156/192/282zł; P ✗) Occupying part of a huge complex about 1.5km northeast of town, this very modern top-end hotel has the best facilities in town. Rooms are stylish and spacious, and all come with modem connections and spotless bathrooms. There's a 'recreational centre' with a gym, a sauna, a Jacuzzi and a massage parlour, two very good restaurants and a conference centre. The weekend rates are great value. Catch bus 4 or 34 from the centre of town.

Hotel Elita (☎ 344 22 30; www.hotelelita.com.pl; ul Równa 4A; s/d/apt 200/260/360zł; P) This 11-room hotel is possibly the best central option, with clean, modern, and attractively furnished rooms. It's reasonable value by local standards.

Hotel Bristol (☎ 368 24 60; bristol@webmedia.pl; ul Sienkiewicza 21; s/d/tr 190/240/270zł; P) Central and convenient, the 45-bed Bristol offers a fair standard of accommodation, though it's a little overpriced. The entrance is from ul Kapitulna, not ul Sienkiewicza.

Hotel Łysogóry (☎ 366 55 00; www.lysogory.com .pl in Polish; ul Sienkiewicza 78; s/d/apt 240/330/450zł; P) Another very central and comfortable option, but it's somewhat overpriced for what's on offer. Weekend discounts of up to 50% make it much better value though.

Eating

Fleury Michon (☎ 344 63 11; ul Sienkiewicza 28; mains 5-10zł; 🕙 breakfast & lunch) With fresh rolls, croissants and pastries, and a few tables to sit at, this is a good place for breakfast or just a snack.

Restauracja Jodłowa (☎ 361 04 87; ul Paderewskiego 3/5; mains 5-13zł; 🕙 lunch & dinner) A typically cheap and cheerful budget place, serving simple, filling Polish food.

Piwnica Pod Feniksem (☎ 343 19 20; ul Sienkiewicza 25; mains 10-30zł; 🕙 lunch & dinner) This basement restaurant and bar serves good Polish food in plain surrounds. The speciality of the house is veal.

Restauracja Wiejska (☎ 366 05 45; ul Czarnowska 22; mains 10-60zł; 🕙 lunch & dinner) This split-level restaurant offers traditional old-Polish peasant food in what looks like an old timber country inn, decked out with folksy décor.

Drinking

Karczma (☎ 368 22 87; ul Bodzentyńska 9) and **Pub Studencki Tunel** (☎ 344 52 00; ul Duża 7) are among the best places for a beer or two. In summer, you can also try the open-air **Kawiarnia Letnia Pałacyk Zielińskich** (☎ 368 20 55; ul Zamkowa 5).

Entertainment

Havana Club (☎ 343 80 04; ul Piotrkowska 12) is one of the city's hippest discos, and **Kawiarnia Teatralna Jazz** (☎ 344 58 36; ul Duża 9) is Kielce's leading jazz club.

Getting There & Away

BUS

The strange UFO-shaped bus terminal, close to the train station, is relatively well organised. There are buses to Łódź (15.80zł, three hours, six to seven daily), Kraków (12.50zł, 1½ hours, five daily), Święty Krzyż (5.60zł, one hour, four to five daily) and Sandomierz (10.50zł, two hours, six daily). For Święta Katarzyna (4.40zł), take a bus going to Bodzentyn or Starachowice; and for Nowa Słupia (6.20zł), board a bus to Ostrowiec Świętokrzyski. For Tokarnia (4.40zł), there are buses every one to two hours – inquire at the information desk.

TRAIN

The train station is in the centre, at the western end of ul Sienkiewicza. Two dozen trains run to Radom (20zł, two hours) and half of them continue on to Warsaw (42zł, 3½ hours). Other trains go to Kraków (34zł, three hours, 10 daily), Lublin (45zł, four hours, five to six daily) and Częstochowa (22zł, 1½ hours, three daily).

AROUND KIELCE

☎ 41

Paradise Cave

Discovered in 1964, the **Paradise Cave** (Jaskinia Raj; ☎ 346 55 18; tours 10zł; ☷ 10am-5pm Tue-Sun May-Aug, 10am-4pm Tue-Sun Mar, Apr & Sep-Nov) is one of the better caves in Poland (the best one is arguably the Bear's Cave in the Sudeten Mountains – see p297). Although relatively small – only 8m high at its highest point – the cave has a couple of spectacular chambers complete with stalactites, stalagmites and columns.

A building at the entrance to the cave shelters a ticket office, a café and a museum. Some finds from the cave which are on display in the museum show that it was once used by animals and primitive humans as a shelter. You enter the cave and do a 180m-long loop through its chambers. All visits are guided (in Polish only) in groups of up to 15 people; the tour takes around half an hour. No photography is allowed inside.

The cave has become a major tourist attraction for school groups, with the result that, at times (particularly in May and June), little room is left for individual tourists. Owing to environmental factors, a limited number of people are allowed inside each day, so some days may be fully booked out. In order to be assured of a tour, book in advance on ☎ 346 55 18. Bring some warm clothes, as the temperature inside the cave is only 9°C year-round.

The cave is 600m off the Kraków road, about 10km from central Kielce. You can get close on city bus 31, which runs through to Chęciny every half-hour (every hour on Sunday). It departs from near the corner of ul

Żytnia and ul Paderewskiego in Kielce. Ask to be let off at the bus stop just before the turn-off to the cave; the next bus stop is a long way off. There are also private minibuses departing from the same place as buses, as soon as they fill up with passengers.

Near the cave beside the car park, **Zajazd Raj** (☎ 346 51 27; s/d/q 90/120/200zł) is a small, 11-room hotel with adequate facilities and a decent restaurant serving up Polish cuisine (mains 8zł to 38zł).

Tokarnia

The village of Tokarnia is home to the **Open-Air Museum of the Kielce Village** (Muzeum Wsi Kieleckiej; ☎ 315 41 71; adult/concession 6/4zł; ☷ 10am-5pm Tue-Sun Apr-Oct, 9am-2pm Mon-Fri Nov-Mar). Covering an area of 80 hectares (including 20 hectares of woodland), this is one of Poland's largest skansens (open-air museums of traditional architecture). About 30 structures have been completed, including interiors. A number of fine implements have been collected, and some are amazing (note the huge barrels carved out of a single tree trunk). Give yourself about two hours to see it all. In summer, a café opens in the house at the entrance to the museum.

The skansen is 20km from Kielce; buses ply this route roughly every hour. Get off at the bus stop in the village of Tokarnia and walk for around 1km up the road to the skansen's entrance.

JEDRZEJÓW

☎ 41 / pop 18,000

The pride of Jędrzejów (yend-*zheh*-yoof) is its **Sundial Museum** (Muzeum Zegarów Słonecznych; ☎ 386 24 45; Rynek 7/8; admission 5zł; ☷ 9am-4pm Tue-Sun May-Sep, 9am-3pm Oct-Apr, closed public holidays & day following). With more than 300 specimens, it's reputedly the world's third-largest sundial collection after Oxford and Chicago. Among the exhibits are the 16th- and 17th-century pocket sundials, which are made of ivory and are adjustable depending on the latitude; two intricate instruments capable of measuring time to within half a minute; and a range of sundials from the Far East. Strangest of all is the 18th-century apparatus equipped with a cannon, which used to fire at noon. The oldest instrument in the collection, dating from 1524, was designed for measuring time at night from the position of the stars. The museum also has an extensive gnomonics (the science of sundials) library, old clocks and watches, furniture and household implements.

All visitors are guided in groups; 50-minute tours begin on the hour. The last tour departs one hour before closing time.

Church buffs might be interested in visiting the **Cistercian Abbey** (Opactwo Cystersów; ul 11 Listopada) on the western outskirts of town, 2km from the Rynek, and on the road to Katowice. Founded in 1140, this was the first Cistercian abbey in Poland. For the Poles, the place is associated with Wincenty Kadłubek (1161–1223), Kraków's bishop and the first known Polish chronicler, author of *Chronica Polonorum*. He spent the last years of his life in the monastery and was buried here.

The original Romanesque church was repeatedly modified, most recently in the 18th century, when the twin towers were added and the interior acquired its baroque décor. The stucco walls resemble marble, and the rich interior furnishings include opulent altarpieces, stalls in the presbytery and a splendid organ. Kadłubek's remains repose in a small 17th-century baroque coffin in the side chapel off the left aisle. The monastery adjoining the church has a courtyard lined with 15th-century Gothic cloisters.

Sleeping & Eating

Apparently the only regular accommodation in town, **Noclegi Zacisze** (☎ 386 18 26; Al Piłsudskiego 4; s/d 35/45zł) is a large, uninspiring block, 800m west of the Rynek along ul 11 Listopada, and offers basic rooms and has its own restaurant. There are more places to eat in the town centre.

Getting There & Away

The bus and train stations are next to each other, 2km west of the Rynek and linked to it by urban buses. Since Jędrzejów lies on the Kraków–Kielce highway and railway line, there's sufficient transport to either destination and you shouldn't have to wait more than an hour for a bus or train.

ŚWIĘTOKRZYSKI NATIONAL PARK

☎ 41

The Góry Świętokrzyskie (literally, 'Holy Cross Mountains') run for 70km east–west across the Małopolska Upland. This is Poland's oldest mountainous geological formation, and consequently the lowest,

due to gradual erosion for over 300 million years. The highest peak is just 612m, and the whole outcrop is more a collection of gently rolling wooded hills rather than mountains in the real sense of the word. The region retains some of its primeval nature, and a national park has been set up to protect the best of what is left.

The Świętokrzyski (shfyen-to-*kshis*-kee) National Park protects the highest, 15km-long central range, known as the Łysogóry (Bald Mountains). It has a peak at each end: Mt Łysica (612m) in the west and Mt Łysa Góra (595m) in the east. Between them is a belt of forest, which is mostly fir and beech, and covers almost all the 60 sq km of the park. Watch out for the unusual *gołoborza*: heaps of broken quartzite rock on parts of the northern slopes below the two peaks.

Apart from these natural attractions, there's the Święty Krzyż abbey and adjacent museum on top of Mt Łysa Góra, and another museum at the foothill village of Nowa Słupia. The mountains make a pleasant half or full-day trip.

GETTING THERE & AROUND

The park is about 20km east of Kielce. You can get there by bus from the city to three different access points: the village of Święta Katarzyna on the western end, at the foot of Mt Łysica; the Święty Krzyż abbey on the top of Mt Łysa Góra; and the village of Nowa Słupia, 2km east from Święty Krzyż.

If you're not enthusiastic about walking, it's best to go by bus directly to Święty Krzyż, visit the place, then go down to Nowa Słupia to see the museum and take a bus back to Kielce or wherever else you want to go.

If you plan on hiking, there's an 18km marked trail between Święta Katarzyna and Nowa Słupia, via Święty Krzyż. It's best to set off from Nowa Słupia, as there are museums here and in nearby Święty Krzyż; if you start from the opposite end of the trail, you will have to get moving early to reach the museums before they close. The following description includes the whole route from Nowa Słupia to Święta Katarzyna.

Nowa Słupia

The village of Nowa Słupia is known for its **Museum of the Holy Cross Ancient Metallurgy**

(Muzeum Starożytnego Hutnictwa Świętokrzyskiego; ☎ 317 70 18; ul Świętokrzyska 59; adult/concession 4/2zł; ⏰ 9am-4pm Tue-Sun), on the road to Święty Krzyż. The museum has been established on the site where primitive smelting furnaces *(dymarki)*, dating from the 2nd century AD, were unearthed in 1955. A huge number of furnaces have been found in the surrounding area, indicating that the region was an important ancient metallurgical centre, the largest so far discovered in Europe.

From the museum, a 2km path called King Way (Droga Królewska) leads up to Święty Krzyż (by car, it's a 16km detour).

Nowa Słupia has a couple of budget accommodation options, and locals rent out rooms in their homes. The PTSM **Youth hostel** (☎ 317 70 16; ul Świętokrzyska 61; dm 25-30zł), next to the museum, offers 60 beds in doubles, quads and large dorms.

Buses from Nowa Słupia can take you to Kielce (6.20zł, 1½ hours). For Sandomierz, you have to change buses in either Ostrowiec Świętokrzyski or Łagów.

Święty Krzyż

Giving its name to the mountains, Święty Krzyż (Holy Cross) is a Benedictine **abbey** situated at the top of Mt Łysa Góra. The Święty Krzyż abbey was built in the early 12th century, on the site of a pagan place of worship that existed here during the 8th and 9th centuries. The abbey's **Holy Cross Church** (⏰ 9am-5pm Mon-Sat, noon-5pm Sun & holidays) was rebuilt several times over the years and the present-day church, and its mainly neoclassical interior, is a product of the late 18th century.

The monastery has retained more of its original shape, including its Gothic vaulted cloister. It shelters a small **Missionary Museum** (Muzeum Misyjne; ☎ 317 70 21; ⏰ 9am-noon & 1-4pm Mon-Sat, noon-4pm Sun) featuring some objects collected by the missionaries.

The **Natural History Museum** (Muzeum Przyrodniczo-Leśne; ☎ 317 70 87; admission 3zł; ⏰ 10am-4pm Tue-Sun Apr-Oct, 9am-3pm Tue-Sun Nov-Mar, closed public holidays & day following) is on the western side of the abbey, facing a huge TV mast. It focuses on the geology and the plant and animal life of the park.

The quartzite rocks are just past the TV mast to the right; a short side path will lead you there.

There are two budget places to stay next to each other, near the car park on the access road, 2km before Święty Krzyż. The first, **Jodłowy Dwór** (☎ 302 50 28; fax 302 61 46; d/tr 90/120zł), a large 160-bed hotel doesn't offer much luxury, but is reasonable and has a cheap restaurant, with breakfast included. Basic but acceptable, the **Almatur Jodłowy** (☎ 302 50 97; beds in r with/without private bathroom 50/40zł) has 50 beds and simple meals.

From Święty Krzyż you can take the bus straight to Kielce (32km, every three hours) or walk along the red trail to Święta Katarzyna.

The Trail

The 16km trail from Święty Krzyż to Święta Katarzyna is an easy four-hour walk. The trail follows the road for the first 2km to the car park (where the Jodłowy Dwór and Almatur hostel are), then branches off and runs west along the edge of the forest for about 9km. It then enters the woods, ascends the peak of Mt Łysica and winds down for 2km to Święta Katarzyna.

Święta Katarzyna

This small village is developing into a local holiday centre with several simple places to stay and eat including the **youth hostel** (☎ 311 20 88; ul Kielecka 45; dm 25-30zł), which is set in pleasant grounds and provides simple lodging in four- to eight-bed dorms for 45 guests.

The former Dom Wycieczkowy PTTK, **Ośrodek Wypoczynkowy Jodełka** (☎ 311 21 11; fax 311 21 12; ul Kielecka 3; s/d 45/78zł), has been extensively revamped and now offers excellent value and has its own restaurant.

Buses go regularly to Kielce (4.40zł), for those who don't want to stay in Swieta Katarzyna after the trek.

THE SANDOMIERZ VALLEY

The Sandomierz Valley (Kotlina Sandomierska) covers an extensive area in and around the fork of the Vistula and San Rivers. The region's major historic centre – and today its main tourist destination – is the town of Sandomierz. There are also some impressive castles in the region.

MAŁOPOLSKA

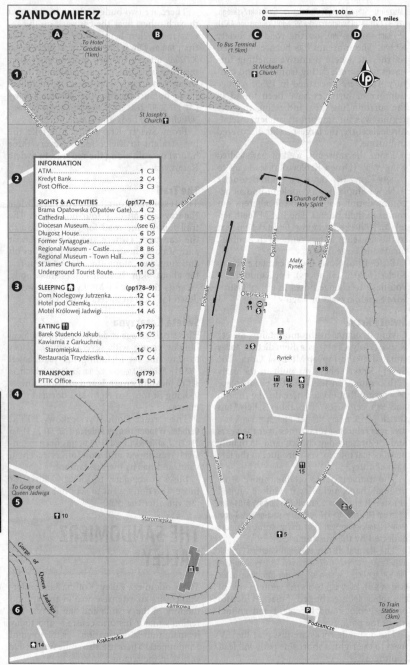

SANDOMIERZ

0 —— 100 m
0 —— 0.1 miles

To Hotel Grodzki (1km)

To Bus Terminal (1.5km)

St Michael's Church

Mickiewicza

St Joseph's Church

Church of the Holy Spirit

Tatarska

Mały Rynek

Oleśnickich

Rynek

Zamkowa

Zamkowa

To Gorge of Queen Jadwiga

Staromiejska

Gorge of Queen Jadwiga

Katedralna

Zamkowa

Krakowska

Podzamcze

To Train Station (3km)

MAŁOPOLSKA

SANDOMIERZ

☎ 15 / pop 27,000

Sandomierz is a small, pleasant town overlooking the Vistula River from a 40m hill. It preserves the yesteryear atmosphere typical of old country towns, and shelters some fine historic buildings, which are remnants of its illustrious past. Both its atmosphere and architecture make a visit worthwhile.

History

It's not exactly clear when the town sprang to life, but at the end of the 11th century the chronicler Gall Anonim classified Sandomierz, along with Kraków and Wrocław, as major settlements of the realm (*sedes regni principale*). Destroyed by Tatar raids in the year 1259, the town was moved uphill to its present location and fortified in the 14th century. A busy river port and trade centre on the Kraków–Kyiv route, Sandomierz grew and prospered until the mid-17th century. Its glory came to an abrupt end with the Swedish Deluge, after which the town never really revived. By the outbreak of WWII its inhabitants numbered 10,000, not many more than had lived here three centuries earlier.

The town came through the war unscathed and preserved its historic architecture intact, but ironically it nearly lost the whole lot in the 1960s when the soft loess soils on which Sandomierz sits began to dangerously slide down into the river. A large rescue operation was launched, and the city was again 'fortified', this time with substantial injections of concrete and steel into the slippery slopes. Today, safe and restored, the town still proudly boasts its historic gems.

Information

There's no genuine tourist office in town. Try the **PTTK office** (☎ 832 23 05; www.pttk-san domierz.pl in Polish; Rynek 12).

There are only a few *kantors* in the Old Town, including one in the **post office** (Rynek 10). The Kredyt Bank, a few doors south of the post office, also changes cash and may pay better than the *kantor*. There are also a few *kantors* on ul Mickiewicza close to the corner of ul 11 Listopada, about 1km northwest of the Old Town. One of the very few central ATMs is at Rynek 9.

Sights

The 14th-century **Opatów Gate** (Brama Opatowska; ul Opatowska; admission 1zł; ☉ 10am-5.30pm in summer) is the main entrance to the Old Town and the only surviving gate of the four that were built as part of the fortification system. The decorative Renaissance parapets were added in the 16th century. You can go to the top to look around, but the view of the Old Town is not that good.

The sloping **Rynek** is lined with houses dating from different periods, some of which were built after WWII. In the 16th century all the houses had arcades. Today only two of them, those at Nos 10 and 27, still have their arcades.

In the middle stands the **town hall**, the oldest building on the Rynek. Its main Gothic structure was adorned with decorative parapets and tower in the Renaissance period. Its ground floor houses a section of the **Regional Museum – Town Hall** (Muzeum Okręgowe – Ratusz; Ryne; adult/concession 4/3zł; ☉ 10am-5pm Tue-Sun May-Sep, 9am-4pm Tue-Fri & 10am-3pm Sat & Sun Oct-Apr) on the town's history and has a model of what it looked like three centuries ago.

One of the town's premier attractions is the **Underground Tourist Route** (Podziemna Trasa Turystyczna; ☎ 832 30 88; ul Oleśnickich; adult/concession 6.50/3.50zł; ☉ 10am-6pm May-Sep, 10am-5pm Oct-Apr). It leads through a chain of 30-odd cellars beneath the houses around the Rynek. Built mostly during boom times in the 15th and 16th centuries, these storage cellars gradually fell into disuse and were abandoned when trade declined. Dug out of soft soil and lacking proper reinforcements, they effectively undermined the city and contributed to the postwar near-disaster. In the complex restoration programme, carried out from 1964 to 1977, they were restored and linked to ensure the safety of the town and provide yet another attraction.

The entrance to the cellars is from ul Oleśnickich, just off the Rynek, and you finish the tour in the town hall. The route is about 500m long and the deepest cellars are 12m below the street level. It can only be visited on a guided tour (in Polish only); these leave approximately every hour and take 40 minutes to complete.

Nearby, the 18th-century **synagogue** (ul Żydowska) retains the remains of its decoration on the inside, but it houses the town's registry and cannot be visited.

From the Rynek, take ul Mariacka to the **cathedral** (☎ 832 73 43; ul Mariacka; ⓧ to visitors 10am-2pm & 3-5pm Tue-Sat, 3-5pm Sun & public holidays). Built in the 1360s, this massive church has preserved much of its Gothic exterior, apart from the baroque façade added in the 17th century. The baroque took hold more strongly inside the building, though some of the earlier decoration has survived, notably the Russo-Byzantine frescoes in the chancel. One of the few examples of such frescoes in Poland, they were painted in the 1420s but later whitewashed, and only revealed and restored at the beginning of the 20th century.

Nearby is the **Długosz House** (Dom Długosza) built for the medieval historian in 1476. It today houses the **Diocesan Museum** (Muzeum Diecezjalne; ☎ 832 23 04; ul Długosza 9; adult/concession 4/3zł; ⓧ 9am-4pm Tue-Sat & 1.30-4pm Sun & public holidays Apr-Oct, 9am-3pm Tue-Sat & 1.30-3pm Sun & public holidays Nov-Mar). It features furniture, tapestries, ceramics, crafts and archaeological artefacts, and a collection of religious art.

The **castle**, a few steps downhill from the cathedral, was built in the 14th century on the site of a previous wooden stronghold and gradually extended during the next three centuries. It now accommodates the **Regional Museum – Castle** (Muzeum Okręgowe – Zamek; ☎ 644 57 57; ul Zamkowa 14; adult/concession 3/2zł; ⓧ 10am-5pm Tue-Sun May-Sep, 9am-4pm Tue-Fri & 10am-3pm Sat & Sun Oct-Apr). It features small ethnographic, archaeological and art collections, the old castle kitchen, and temporary exhibitions.

St James' Church (Kościół Św Jakuba; ☎ 832 73 43; ul Staromiejska; ⓧ to visitors 10am-4pm) is the oldest monument in town. Dating from the 1230s, it's believed to be the first brick church in Poland and is particularly renowned for its Romanesque doorway. The church retains the austere exterior typical of the period, but the interior has been modernised. Among a few historic objects left is the sarcophagus in the presbytery, carved in 1676 out of a single oak trunk. The belfry beside the church holds two of the oldest bells in Poland, cast in 1314 and 1389. They can only be heard on very special occasions.

Continue up ul Staromiejska as far as St Paul's Church and turn left downhill into the **Gorge of Queen Jadwiga** (Wąwóz Królowej Jadwigi), the best of the gorges around the town. It will lead you down to ul Krakowska, or you can take the first path to the left and back to St James' Church.

MARTYROLOGIUM ROMANUM OF SANDOMIERZ' CATHEDRAL

One of the most unusual sights inside Sandomierz' cathedral is a series of 12 large paintings on the side walls, known as the *Martyrologium Romanum*. Look closely – they depict all imaginable methods of torture and just about all the horrific ways a human could die. You could spend hours examining the details.

This bizarre set of canvases is the early-18th-century work of Karol de Prevot. The paintings are supposed to symbolise the 12 months of the year. Next to each scene of torture on each painting is the ordinal number that reputedly represents the day of the month. Legend has it that if you find the month and the day on which you were born, you'll discover how you're going to die.

Prevot was also responsible for another four similarly macabre paintings on the back wall of the church under a sumptuous baroque organ. These pictures depict scenes from Sandomierz' history, including the Tatar massacre of 1259 and the blowing up of the castle by the Swedes in 1656.

Sleeping

Hotel Pod Ciżemką (☎ 832 05 50; www.sandomierz -hotel.com.pl in Polish; Rynek 27; d/ste 250/300zł) Extensively refurbished, Pod Ciżemką is the best place in the Old Town, offering six comfortable double rooms, three suites, and a good restaurant.

Motel Królowej Jadwigi (☎ /fax 832 29 88; www .motel.go3.pl; ul Krakowska 24; d/tr/q 150/170/220zł; Ⓟ) Located a little off the Old Town, this 14-room motel has neat rooms and a charming restaurant, all nicely decorated with antiques and paintings, and full of flowers. It also boasts a gym and a billiard room.

Hotel Grodzki (☎ 832 24 23; www.hotelgrodzki.pl; ul Mickiewicza 38; d/tr with bathroom 170/270zł, d without bathroom 120zł; Ⓟ) Grodzki is a large modern hotel 1km northwest of the Old Town. It offers satisfactory standards and reasonable Polish food in its own restaurant. Doubles without bathrooms are small yet they're not bad value for the price given the unlimited breakfast that's included.

Dom Noclegowy Jutrzenka (☎ 832 22 19; ul Zamkowa 1; s/d/tr 60/70/90zł; Ⓟ) Jutrzenka is one of the cheapest places to stay in Sandomierz'

Old Town. It only has six rooms, and all are with shared facilities, but it's clean and perfectly acceptable.

Eating

Barek Studencki Jakub (☎ 832 72 29; ul Mariacka 9l; mains 8-15zł; ☽ lunch & dinner) Jakub is a small basement cafeteria that serves some of the cheapest meals in town.

There are a few budget places to eat on the Rynek, including **Restauracja Trzydziestka** (☎ 644 53 12; Rynek 30; mains 10-15zł; ☽ lunch & dinner) and **Kawiarnia z Garkuchnią Staromiejska** (☎ 832 37 78; Rynek 28; mains 8-15zł; ☽ lunch & dinner), both of which serve simple but acceptable food.

For something more substantial, try the restaurants at **Hotel Pod Ciżemką** (☎ 832 05 50; Rynek 27), **Motel Królowej Jadwigi** (☎ /fax 832 29 88; ul Krakowska 24) and **Hotel Grodzki** (☎ 832 24 23; ul Mickiewicza 38).

Getting There & Away

BUS

The bus terminal is more centrally located but it's still 1.5km northwest of the Old Town; frequent urban buses go there from Brama Opatowska.

There are a dozen fast buses to Warsaw (50zł, three hours), which cost roughly the same as the train.

Buses to Tarnobrzeg (4zł, 45 minutes) depart roughly every half-hour but the suburban bus 11 from Brama Opatowska is more convenient, and just as frequent. From Tarnobrzeg, frequent buses will take you on to Baranów Sandomierski (4zł, 50 minutes).

For Ujazd, you need to go to Klimontów (buses roughly every hour) and change there.

TRAIN

The train station, 3km southeast of the Old Town, on the other side of the Vistula, is served by city buses to/from Brama Opatowska. Three fast trains run to Warsaw daily (55zł, 3½ hours) and two to Przemyśl (38zł, 2½ hours).

BARANÓW SANDOMIERSKI

☎ 15 / pop 1500

The village of Baranów Sandomierski lies on the edge of an area where huge sulphur deposits were discovered in the 1950s. Its fame, however, is based not on sulphur but

on its **castle** (☎ 811 80 40; ul Zamkowa 20; adult/concession 6/4zł; ☽ exhibitions 9am-2.30pm Tue-Sat, 9am-5pm Sun, closes 1 hr earlier Sat & Sun Oct-Apr, closed public holidays & day following).

The castle was built at the end of the 16th century for the Leszczyński family, the owners of large estates in Wielkopolska. It was encircled with powerful fortifications but they were dismantled in the 19th century. The whole structure is thought to have been designed by the talented Italian architect Santi Gucci, who was responsible for many other projects in Poland.

In the late 17th century, the new owners, the Lubomirski family, commissioned Tylman van Gameren for an enlargement of the western wing. Although the castle suffered two major fires in the 19th century, it was refurbished both times and was inhabited almost continuously until WWII. Damaged during the war, it was handed over into the care of the Siarkopol, a state-owned sulphur enterprise, which restored it and maintained it until recently.

The castle is considered one of the most beautiful Renaissance residences in Poland. Set in a pleasant, well-kept park, it has four corner towers and a lovely arcaded courtyard. The two-storeyed arcades, with their slender columns supporting graceful arches, are very Italianesque. Look out for the fanciful masks on the column plinths, the vault decoration, and the superb carved-stone portals.

Some of the castle's original rooms, complete with period furnishings, paintings and decoration, are open to visitors. The former chapel on the west side of the building is used for temporary exhibitions.

Another exhibition, a reminder of the castle's former patron, is in the basement and shows the achievements of the sulphur industry, plus some archaeological finds that include the remains of the Gothic stronghold discovered after WWII, during the process of the castle's restoration.

Sleeping & Eating

Housed in the building just to the west of the castle, **Hotel Zamkowy** (☎ /fax 811 80 39; ul Zamkowa 20; s/d/ste US$61/92/112; **P**) has been thoroughly renovated and offers a high standard of accommodation. It also offers a few rooms and one suite in the castle itself, and there's a restaurant in the basement.

MAŁOPOLSKA

Getting There & Away

The train station is well out of the village so it's much more convenient to travel by bus; the bus stop is close to the Rynek, roughly 1.5km from the castle.

There's no direct transport to Sandomierz but frequent buses run to Tarnobrzeg (4zł), where you catch another, equally frequent bus. Some of the buses to Tarnobrzeg depart from the entrance to the castle.

There are four fast buses to Kraków (19zł, two hours); the last one passes through just before 1pm. All Kraków-bound buses go via Tarnów (12zł, 1½ hours). Four buses a day run to Warsaw (26zł, four hours) and one to Zamość (17zł, three hours). There are also two buses a day to Zakopane via Tarnów and Nowy Sącz.

UJAZD

☎ 15 / pop 600

The small village of Ujazd (oo-yahst) is known for the ruined **Krzyżtopór Castle** (☎ 860 11 33; admission 4zł; ☼ till sunset) that dominates the area. Designed by Italian architect Lorenzo Muretto (Wawrzyniec Senes to the Poles) for the governor of the Sandomierz province, Krzysztof Ossoliński, this monumental building was erected between 1631 and 1644 and was one of the most unusual castles in Poland.

Built inside massive stone walls with bastions at the five corners, the castle was designed to embody a calendar. It had four towers symbolising the four seasons and 12 halls, one for each month. Exactly 52 rooms were built, one for each week in the year, and 365 windows. The designer didn't forget to provide an additional window, which was only to be used during the leap year, and was walled up the rest of the time.

The castle's great dining hall had a huge crystal aquarium built into its ceiling. An extensive system of cellars was built; some of them were used as stables for the owner's 370 white stallions, and are said to have been equipped with mirrors and black-marble mangers. Like every respectable castle, it had a tunnel, which linked Krzyżtopór to his brother's castle at Ossolin, 15km away. The tunnel's floor is said to have been covered with sugar, to allow the brothers to visit each other in horse-drawn sledges, while at the same time enjoying an impression of travelling on snow.

Nothing is left of the mangers or aquariums, yet these and other stories, merging fact with legend, have given the castle an other-worldly reputation. Ossoliński's personal interest in astrology and magic may also have had something to do with it.

Ossoliński didn't enjoy his home for long; he died in 1645, a year after the castle was completed. Only 10 years later, the Swedes did significant damage to the castle, and took away some of the most precious treasures. Though the subsequent owners lived in part of the castle till 1770, it was only a shadow of its former self and swiftly declined thereafter.

After WWII, plans to transform the castle into a military school were discussed but rejected and the ruins were left to their fate for four decades. In the early 1990s, restoration work started, aiming to rebuild the castle and perhaps make it into a hotel, but the plan was abandoned. So, until a new programme is launched, all you can see is a formidable ruin.

Miraculously, the castle's entrance gate still proudly bears the two massive stone symbols of the castle: the Krzyż (Cross), representing the religious devotion of the owner, and the Topór (Axe), the coat of arms of the Ossoliński family, are both still in good condition.

Don't miss this place: the longer you stay, the more it grows on you. The castle is off the beaten track so it doesn't get many tourists, particularly on weekdays. You may find you have the ruin all to yourself.

Sleeping & Eating

There are no hotels around but if you have a tent, you can camp right at the foot of the castle or even in its courtyard – an idyllic location, but perhaps not advisable for lone travellers. There doesn't seem to be anywhere to eat, except for a kiosk by the entrance to the castle, where you can buy some basic food and drink.

Getting There & Away

Ujazd lies on a side road and has no direct transport links with the major cities of the region. The only points of access are Opatów (3.80zł, 45 minutes) or Klimontów (3.20zł, 35 minutes), which are linked with Ujazd by several buses daily and also have onward transport to Sandomierz and Kielce.

THE RADOM PLAIN

The Radom Plain (Równina Radomska) stretches between Małopolska to the south and Mazovia to the north. It's a relatively small area, little visited by travellers, and dominated by bustling Radom. The skansen, just outside town, is reason enough to stop by, while other local highlights include the interesting Centre of Polish Sculpture at Orońsko and the pretty town of Szydłowiec, with its mediaeval church and the unique Museum of Polish Folk Instruments.

RADOM

☎ 48 / pop 250,000

Radom is an important industrial centre 100km south of Warsaw. Although it developed into a strong fortified town during the reign of King Kazimierz Wielki, little of its historical character is left. If you decide to stop here, visit the skansen.

Sights

The Miasto Kazimierzowskie (the historic town founded by Kazimierz Wielki in the mid-14th century) preserves its layout but not its urban fabric. Possibly the best reminder of those times is the Gothic **parish church**, built in the 1360s.

One block west is the Rynek, today lined with a hotchpotch of buildings, mostly from the 19th century. On its southern side is the **Radom Museum** (Muzeum im Jacka Malczewskiego; ☎ 362 43 29; Rynek 11; adult/concession 5/3zł; 🕑 9am-4pm Tue-Thu, 10am-5pm Fri, 10am-4pm Sun), which features a small permanent archaeological collection plus some temporary exhibitions.

East of the old quarter is Radom's new centre, which stretches along its main nerve, the 1km-long ul Żeromskiego. Partly closed to the traffic, the street boasts some 19th- century neoclassical houses.

The most interesting city sight is the **skansen** (Muzeum Wsi Radomskiej; ☎ 332 92 81; ul Szydłowiecka 30; adult/concession 5/3zł; 🕑 9am-5pm Tue-Fri & 10am-6pm Sat & Sun May-Sep, 10am-3pm Tue-Sun Oct-Apr), on the southwestern outskirts of the city, 9km outside the centre and 1km off the Kielce road. Urban buses 5, 17 and K from the city centre will let you off nearby.

The skansen has examples of traditional rural architecture brought together from all over the region. It has five charming windmills and a cluster of over 100 beehives. Some peasants' cottages have been furnished in original style, while other timber houses display exhibitions on local folklore.

Sleeping & Eating

Hotel Gromada (☎ 330 85 86; radom@gromada.pl; ul Bulwarowa 15; s/d Mon-Thu 220/250zł, Fri-Sun 190/219zł; Ⓟ) Roughly 2.5km west of the town centre, in a quiet location near the Borki reservoir, the Gromada offers the best facilities in town, with airy, spacious rooms that all have refrigerators. There's an on-site restaurant and bar, and a business centre.

Hotel Glass (☎ 340 25 85; www.hotelglass.radom.pl; ul Prażmowskiego 17; s/d/ste 108/160/215zł; Ⓟ 💻) With its striking mirrored façade, Hotel Glass has a clean, modern look, though rooms, by comparison, are fairly plain and functional. Nevertheless, it's central, convenient and comfortable, and also has a restaurant and a solarium.

Hotel Iskra (☎ 383 87 45; www.hoteliskra.radom.pl in Polish; ul Planty 4; s/d Mon-Fri from 110/120zł, Sat & Sun from 80/100zł; Ⓟ) Located opposite the train station, this is one of the cheapest central hotels. It's a pretty ordinary, unexciting place but it does have its own restaurant.

Youth hostel (☎ 360 05 14; ul Kilińskiego 20; dm 25-30zł) This central year-round hostel has 40 beds in six- to eight-bed dorms. Check-in time is from 5pm to 9pm.

Getting There & Away

The train and bus stations are next to each other, 2km south from the central city street, ul Żeromskiego. A dozen trains (18zł, three hours) and two dozen buses run to Warsaw (13.50zł, 2½ hours). Several daily buses also go to Lublin (12.50zł, 2½ hours) and Puławy (7.80zł, 1½ hours). It's better to travel to Kielce (30zł, two hours) by train (at least 15 daily). Buses to Szydłowiec (5.50zł, 50 minutes) run approximately every hour; the same buses, as well as the urban bus K, will take you to Orońsko (3.80zł, 30 minutes).

OROŃSKO

☎ 48 / pop 1200

A roadside village near Radom, Orońsko is the home of the **Centre of Polish Sculpture** (Centrum Rzeźby Polskiej; ☎ 618 45 16; www.rzezba-oronsko.pl; ul Topolowa 1; adult/concession 5/3zł; 🕑 indoor exhibitions & palace 8am-4pm Tue-Fri & 10am-6pm Sat & Sun May-Sep, 7am-3pm Tue-Fri & 8am-4pm Sat & Sun Oct-Apr, park till sunset), established in the grounds of a 19th-century estate complete with a palace, chapel, orangery, granary and coach house, all surrounded by a lovely landscaped park.

An exhibition hall was constructed in 1993 to present changing displays of some of Poland's best modern art. Temporary exhibitions are also held in the orangery and outbuildings. Some of the sculptures have been scattered throughout the park to make an outdoor display. This is also a working artistic centre and several workshops and studios for rented to artists.

You can also visit the palace; it has been left in late 19th-century style, exactly as it was during the time the Polish painter Józef Brandt (1841–1915) lived and worked here.

Sleeping & Eating

The centre has its own **hotel** (☎ /fax 618 45 16; ul Topolowa 1; s/d 43/60zł; P). Based in a former granary, it offers neat rooms and a café serving drinks and snacks. The centre's kitchen can provide meals for guests if requested, but you should let them know in advance. Three meals a day costs 26.50zł per person.

Getting There & Away

Orońsko lies on the Radom–Kielce highway and the bus service is frequent (there's no railway at all). To Radom (3.80zł, 30 minutes), you can go either on the Radom urban bus K or the PKS bus coming through from Szydłowiec. The same buses will let you off close to Radom's skansen (roughly halfway to Radom). To Szydłowiec (3.20zł, 30 minutes), PKS buses run every hour or so. There are no direct buses to Kielce; you will need to change in Skarżysko Kamienna.

SZYDŁOWIEC

☎ 48 / pop 14,000

Szydłowiec (shi-*dwo*-viets), on the Radom–Kielce highway, is an old town which got its municipal charter in 1470. It passed through the hands of some great aristocratic families, including the Sapieha and Radziwiłł, who made it a prosperous urban centre. Just before WWII, 70% of its population was Jewish. The town has some important sights that justify a visit.

Sights

The **town hall**, in the middle of the Rynek, is a handsome, castlelike structure complete with towers and decorative parapets, and whitewashed all over. Built in the early 17th century, it's a good example of Polish Renaissance architecture.

The **church**, shaded by tall trees on the southern side of the Rynek, dates from the end of the 15th century and its interior is living proof of its age. The original details include the wooden high altar, the polyptych in the presbytery, the panelled ceiling under the organ loft and the impressive flat wooden ceiling of the nave – all of which date from the beginning of the 16th century.

About 500m northwest of the Rynek is a large 16th-century **castle** encircled by a moat. It shelters the **Museum of Polish Folk Musical Instruments** (Muzeum Polskich Ludowych Instrumentów Muzycznych; ☎ 617 17 89; ul Sowińskiego 2; adult/concession 4/3zł; 🕑 9am-3.30pm Tue-Sun), the only one of its kind in the country. The museum has a collection of over 2000 instruments, but only a small selection is displayed due to limited space.

The town has a **Jewish cemetery**, one of the largest in Poland. What you see today is a quarter of the original graveyard – it was four times larger when founded in 1788 and right up to WWII. Over 2000 tombstones, mostly from the 19th century (the oldest dating from 1831), stand amid trees and undergrowth untouched for decades. To get there, take ul Kilińskiego east from the Rynek, turn left onto ul Kościuszki (the road to Radom), and after 250m turn right into ul Spółdzielcza. The cemetery is 100m ahead.

Sleeping & Eating

Just about the only place to stay in town, the **youth hostel** (☎ 617 59 55, 617 41 46; ul Kolejowa 16; dm 25-30zł) is in a nice house beyond a colony of dull apartment blocks, 1km southeast of the Rynek.

Sheltered in the cellars of the town hall, **Piwnica Szydłowiecka** (☎ 617 02 24; Rynek 1; mains 10-20zł; 🕑 lunch & dinner) is the most pleasant place to eat and drink in town.

Getting There & Away

The bus terminal is 1km north from the Rynek. There are plenty of buses to Radom (5.50zł, 50 minutes), passing Orońsko on their way. Only a few buses go straight to Kielce (6.80zł, 1½ hours).

The train station is 5km east of town – not worth the trip.

MAŁOPOLSKA

THE LUBLIN UPLAND

The Lublin Upland (Wyżyna Lubelska) stretches east of the Vistula and San Rivers, up to the Ukrainian border. The upland is largely unspoilt, with the only city of any size being Lublin. The closer to the eastern border you get, the stronger the Eastern Orthodox Church influence. Having private transport is useful for exploring remote areas. Otherwise, you'll probably visit the three important historic towns and the showpieces of the region – Lublin, Kazimierz Dolny and Zamość – and some of their environs.

LUBLIN

☎ 81 / pop 360,000

Lublin has always been one of Poland's most important cities. Probably due to its borderland location, it often took the lead at crucial historical moments when the country's fate hung in the balance. In 1569 the Lublin Union was signed here, uniting Poland and Lithuania to create the largest European state of the time, stretching from the Baltic almost to the Black Sea. In the dying days of WWI, in November 1918, it was in Lublin that the first government of independent Poland was formed, and soon handed power over to Józef Piłsudski. It was here again that the provisional communist government was installed by the Soviets in July 1944, during the last stages of WWII. Lublin is also considered by some to be the true birthplace of Solidarity, the avalanche of strikes that in 1980 spread throughout Poland and eventually led to the Gdańsk agreements.

Despite such historical prominence, Lublin has always lagged behind Poland's more-illustrious, progressive or simply more-attractive towns. Today, while parts of the city are looking pretty shabby and generally run-down, Lublin's small but well-preserved Old Town, with its elegant mix of Gothic, Renaissance and baroque architecture, is a pleasant place to wander. Good transport links also make it a handy base for exploring the surrounding country.

History

Lublin came to life as an outpost protecting Poland against repeated raids from the east by Tatars, Lithuanians and Ruthenians. In the 12th century, a stronghold was built

on the site where the castle stands today. In 1317 Lublin received a municipal charter and soon after the castle and fortified walls were built by Kazimierz Wielki. When the Polish kingdom expanded towards the southeast, Lublin became an important trading centre and continued to develop. In 1578 the Crown Tribunal, the highest law court of Małopolska, was established here. By the end of the 16th century the population passed the 10,000 mark and the town prospered.

The glorious times ended there. As elsewhere, from the mid-17th century Lublin slid into decline. It revived before WWI, and in 1918 the Lublin Catholic University (commonly known as KUL) was founded. It managed to operate throughout the time of communist rule. Right up until the collapse of communism in 1989, it was the only private university in Eastern Europe.

A Jewish community developed in Lublin in the mid-14th century, and grew so rapidly that some 200 years later the town had the third-largest Jewish population in Poland after Kraków and Lviv. In the mid-18th century Jews formed half the population, and just before WWII made up about 30%. Over three dozen synagogues and prayer houses, and four Jewish graveyards existed here. A visit to the Majdanek death camp will help you to understand what happened later.

Since WWII Lublin has expanded threefold and is the largest and most important industrial and educational centre in eastern Poland. Vast suburbs and factories have been built all around the historic town.

Luckily, Lublin didn't experience significant wartime damage, so its Old Town has retained much of its historic architectural fabric. Early postwar restoration was superficial, and, unfortunately, the quarter looks dilapidated and untidy. A more-thorough programme is currently underway, but it's progressing painfully slowly.

Orientation

Although Lublin is a fairly big, busy city, it's only the comparatively tiny Old Town that is likely to merit your attention. The New Town stretches to the west along its main thoroughfare, ul Krakowskie Przedmieście, which later turns into Al Racławickie, where you'll find the city park, Ogród Saski, a vast and welcome expanse of greenery in an otherwise scruffy, built-up area.

MAŁOPOLSKA

LUBLIN

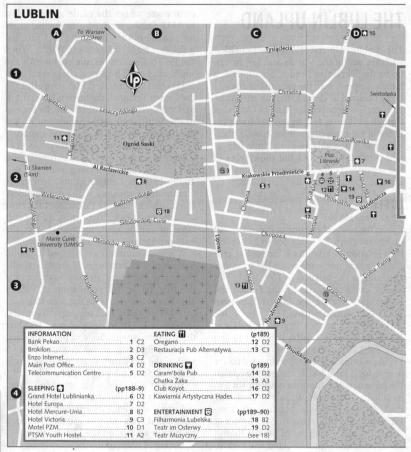

Coming by bus you arrive at the northern edge of the Old Town, while the train deposits you, less conveniently, 2km south of the town centre.

Information

Internet facilities are all open roughly 10am to 10pm or later daily, and charge about 5zł per hour. Plenty of *kantors* line ul Krakowskie Przedmieście and adjacent streets, and you'll also find several ATMs there.

Bank Pekao ul Krakowskie Przedmieście (Map pp184–5; ul Krakowskie Przedmieście 64); ul Królewska (Map p186; ul Królewska 1) Changes travellers cheques and gives cash advances on Visa and MasterCard.

Brokilon (Map pp184–5; ☎ 534 56 22; ul Graniczna 13) Internet access.

Enzo Internet (Map pp184–5; ☎ 534 75 25; 1st fl, ul Krakowskie Przedmieście 57) Internet access.

LOIT Tourist Information Centre (Map p186; ☎ 532 44 12; www.lublin.pl in Polish; ul Jezuicka 1/3; ⏲ 10am-6pm Mon-Sat May-Sep, 9am-5pm Mon-Sat Oct-Apr) Has helpful English-speaking staff, and lots of free brochures, including the city walking-route guides *Along the Multicultural Trail* and *Tourist Trail of Architectural Monuments* as well as *The Lublin Voivodship Tourist Guide*.

www café (Map p186; ☎ 442 35 80; 3rd fl, Rynek 8) Internet access.

Sights
CASTLE

The imposing **castle**, which started life in the 14th century, stands on a hill northeast of the Old Town. What remains was rebuilt as

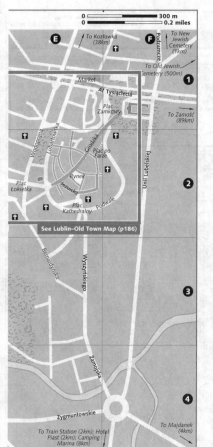

Zygmuntowskie

To Train Station (2km); Hotel
Piast (2km); Camping
Marina (8km)

a prison in the 1820s and remained as such until 1944. During the Nazi occupation, over 100,000 people passed through this prison before being deported to the death camps. Most of the edifice is now occupied by the **Lublin Museum** (Map p186; ☎ 532 50 01; www .zamek-lublin.pl; ul Zamkowa 9; adult/concession 10/6zł; free Sat; ☯ 9am-4pm Wed-Sat, 9am-5pm Sun). On show are paintings, silverware, porcelain, woodcarvings and weaponry, mostly labelled only in Polish. The Polish painting section covers works from the 18th century to the present and has several big names including Jacek Malczewski, Witkacy and Tadeusz Kantor, plus two important works by Jan Matejko: the giant *Lublin Union of 1569* and the smaller *Admission of the Jews to Poland in*

1096. While you're here, check out the alleged 'devil's paw-print' on the 17th-century table in the foyer, linked to an intriguing local legend involving a team of demons coming to the aid of a wronged widow.

At the eastern end of the castle – but only accessible through the museum entrance – is the exquisite 14th-century **Chapel of the Holy Trinity** (incl with museum ticket or adult/concession 6/4zł; ☯ 9am-3.45pm Mon-Sat, 9am-4.45pm Sun). Its interior is entirely covered with polychrome Russo-Byzantine frescoes painted in 1418. They were later plastered over and only discovered in 1897; the complex restoration took (with some breaks) exactly 100 years. They are possibly the finest medieval wall paintings in Poland.

OLD TOWN

The Old Town (Stare Miasto) is so small that it takes less than an hour to get to know its narrow, winding streets. It's a bit soulless, as there are few of the shops, cafés and restaurants (apart from some on the Rynek and ul Grodzka) that normally give life and atmosphere to a town. Most streets are unlit and deserted after 8pm or 9pm, and may be unsafe – avoid strolling at night around the back streets. This advice also applies to the environs of the castle and the bus terminal. The historic quarter is centred on the **Rynek**, the irregularly shaped main square surrounding the neoclassical **Old Town Hall** (1781; Map p186). The Old Town was once surrounded by fortified walls, of which the only significant remnant is the 14th-century **Kraków Gate** (Brama Krakowska; Map p186). Built in Gothic style, it received an octagonal Renaissance superstructure in the 16th century and a baroque topping in 1782. Inside, the **Historical Museum of Lublin** (Muzeum Historii Miasta Lublina; Map p186; ☎ 532 60 01; Plac Łokietka 3; adult/concession 3/1.50zł; ☯ 9am-4pm Wed-Sat, 9am-5pm Sun) has displays of old documents and photographs relating to civic history.

For an expansive **view** of the Old Town, climb to the top of the **Trinitarian Tower** (1819; Map p186), which houses the **Archdiocesan Museum** (Muzeum Archiecezjalne; Map p186; ☎ 743 73 92; Plac Katedralny; adult/concession 7/5zł; ☯ 10am-5pm Apr-Oct). Next to the tower is the 16th-century **cathedral** (Plac Katedralny; ☯ dawn-sunset), formerly a Jesuit church. Its impressive baroque trompe l'oeil frescoes were the work of Moravian artist Józef Majer. The

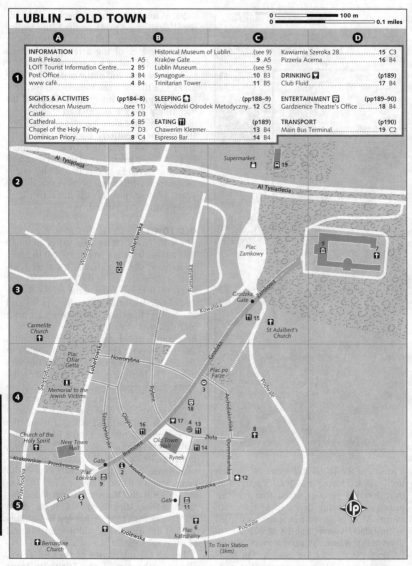

LUBLIN – OLD TOWN

INFORMATION	
Bank Pekao...................................**1** A5	
LOIT Tourist Information Centre....**2** B5	
Post Office...................................**3** B4	
www café.....................................**4** B4	
SIGHTS & ACTIVITIES (pp184–8)	
Archdiocesan Museum..................(see 11)	
Castle...**5** D3	
Cathedral.....................................**6** B5	
Chapel of the Holy Trinity.............**7** D3	
Dominican Priory..........................**8** C4	

Historical Museum of Lublin...........(see 9)	
Kraków Gate................................**9** A5	
Lublin Museum.............................(see 5)	
Synagogue...................................**10** B3	
Trinitarian Tower..........................**11** B5	
SLEEPING (pp188–9)	
Wojewódzki Ośrodek Metodyczny.. **12** C5	
EATING (p189)	
Chawerim Klezmer........................**13** B4	
Espresso Bar.................................**14** B4	

Kawiarnia Szeroka 28....................**15** C3	
Pizzeria Acerna.............................**16** B4	
DRINKING (p189)	
Club Fluid.....................................**17** B4	
ENTERTAINMENT (pp189–90)	
Gardzienice Theatre's Office **18** B4	
TRANSPORT (p190)	
Main Bus Terminal........................**19** C2	

painting of the Virgin Mary is said to have shed tears in 1945, so it's a source of pride and reverence for local believers.

Visit the **acoustic chapel** (kaplica akustyczna; ☼ 10am-2pm & 3-5pm Tue-Sun), so called because two people standing in opposite corners can whisper and still be heard. Behind the chapel is the **treasury** (skarbiec; ☼ 10am-2pm & 3-5pm Tue-

Sun), where you can inspect trompe l'oeil frescoes by Majer in more detail (those in the chapel are copies). The entrance to the chapel and the treasury is through the far end of the right-hand aisle of the cathedral.

Another remarkable religious building is the **Dominican Priory** (Kościół Dominikanów; Map p186; ul Złota 9). It was founded by King Kazimierz

Wielki in 1342 but was burnt down twice, rebuilt in Renaissance style and most of its internal fittings later replaced by baroque decoration. The Lublin Union was signed here in 1569. Closed by the Russians in 1886, the monks only returned less than a year before the outbreak of WWII. They were again expelled by the postwar communist regime and the building was finally returned to the Dominicans in 1993. Decades of neglect have taken their toll and renovation has been slow. Note the large historical painting by an unknown artist, which depicts the 1719 fire of the city. The painting is in the chapel just to the right as you enter the church.

MAJDANEK

Majdanek, 4km southeast of Lublin's centre, was one of the Nazis' largest death camps, and the site of the massacre of about 235,000 people, including over 100,000 Jews. Just four months after the camp's liberation, the **Majdanek State Museum** (Państwowe Muzeum na Majdanku; ☎ 744 19 55; admission free; ⏰ 8am-6pm May-Sep, 8am-3pm Oct-Apr) was founded on the site, thus making it the first memorial institution of its kind in the world. Barracks, guard towers and barbed-wire fences remain as they were during WWII; even more chilling are the crematorium and gas chambers.

At the entrance is a Visitors Centre where a short film (2zł) can be viewed. From the centre, the marked 'visiting route' (5km) passes the massive stone **Monument of Fight & Martyrdom** and finishes at the domed **mausoleum** holding the ashes of many victims.

Trolleybus 156, from near the Bank Pekao along ul Królewska, goes to the entrance of Majdanek.

Pick up the free *Heritage Trail of the Lublin Jews* pamphlet (in English) from the tourist office if you want to walk along the marked **Jewish Heritage Trail** around Lublin.

JEWISH RELICS

The first census of 1550 recorded 840 Jews in Lublin. In 1939, just before WWII, there were 42,830 Jews, about 8000 of whom survived the war. Today there are, at most, two dozen Jews living in the city.

There's only one surviving **synagogue** (Map p186; ☎ 532 09 22; ul Lubartowska 8; ⏰ exhibition 1-3pm Sun, other times by appointment) of the 38 that functioned before WWII. It's in an early 20th-century building, similar to many others on this street, without any apparent features of a synagogue. The synagogue occupies the 1st floor of the building, as it did before the war. Religious services are now sporadic. There's a modest exhibition of old photographs,

---

THE DEATH CAMP OF MAJDANEK

Established on the southeastern outskirts of Lublin, Majdanek was one of the Nazis' easternmost camps, and was purposely located in accord with Hitler's plans of easternward expansion. At the same time, the camp was set in the region populated by a sizable Jewish population.

According to initial plans, the camp was to cover 516 hectares and hold 250,000 prisoners at a time, but the defeat of the German army on the eastern front led to a change of plan. Only about 20% of the initial project was eventually built, yet it still came to be one of the Nazis' largest camps.

The camp began to operate in autumn 1941 and was gradually extended over the following years, using prisoners as a workforce. Gas chambers were built by mid-1942 and became the main means of extermination, along with mass executions, starvation and exhaustion. Cyklon B gas was the major factor used to put the victims to death – more than 7700kg of it was brought to the camp. The dead bodies were initially burned on open-air grates made of truck chassis, until a purpose-built crematorium, capable of cremating up to 1000 bodies a day, was completed in autumn 1943.

The Nazis kept anything of value that belonged to the victims. All clothing, personal possessions, jewellery and money were taken away from the prisoners on entering the camp. As if this was not horrific enough, each prisoner's hair was cut and sold to a textile company to add in manufacturing the fabrics – a total of 730kg of hair was sent out of Majdanek. Gold and silver teeth were removed from the dead bodies. The Nazis even used the ashes of the cremated bodies as a fertiliser in the camp's gardens and fields.

Majdanek was liberated by the Soviet Army in July 1944. During its nearly three-year period in operation some 235,000 people, representing 50-odd nationalities, were exterminated. Jews were the dominant group – some 110,000 perished here. About 75,000 Poles also perished.

books in Hebrew and ritual objects. Enter the gate from the street and you'll find the door leading upstairs to the synagogue on your right in the passageway.

The **old Jewish cemetery**, established in the first half of the 16th century, has 30-odd readable tombstones. The oldest dates from 1641 and is the oldest Jewish tombstone in Poland in its original location. The graveyard is on a hill between ul Sienna and ul Kalinowszczyzna, a short walk northeast from the castle. It is surrounded by a high brick wall so you can't see anything from the outside, and the gate is locked. Contact **Mrs Honig** (☎ 747 86 76; Apt 7, ul Dembowskiego 4) at her home, 200m north of the cemetery. She has the keys and lets visitors in (leave a donation).

The **new Jewish cemetery** was founded in 1828, and about 52,000 Jews were buried here until 1942. The cemetery was devastated by the Nazis and there are no tombs except for a few very damaged ones. In 1991 a modern concrete mausoleum was erected behind the entrance, and it houses a small museum dedicated to the history of the Lublin Jewry. The new graveyard is on ul Walecznych, about 1km north from the old one. The graveyard and the museum can be visited daily at any time during daylight hours – there is a 24-hour guard on duty.

SKANSEN

Lublin has an interesting **skansen** (Muzeum Wsi Lubelskiej; ☎ 533 85 13; ul Warszawska 96; adult/concession 6/4zł; ⏱ 9am-6pm), about 5km west of the centre, on the Warsaw road. Covering an undulating terrain of 25 hectares, it has half a dozen old farmsteads that are open to visitors and have fully equipped interiors. It all looks like a traditional village. There's also a fine manor house, a windmill, an Orthodox church and a carved timber gate (1903) designed by Stanisław Witkiewicz (see p255).

To get to the skansen from the centre, take bus 18, 20 or 5 from Al Racławickie.

Sleeping

Lublin has a fair choice of accommodation, from cheap and simple hostels to a couple of rather pricey top-end hotels. International tourists remain thin on the ground in Lublin, and it's Polish and Eastern European business travellers who seem to occupy the bulk of hotel beds. Consequently, many of these places are pretty ordinary and overpriced.

BUDGET
PTSM Youth Hostel (Map pp184-5; ☎ /fax 533 06 28; ul Długosza 6; dm/tr 24/28zł) This modest but well-run place is 2km west of the Old Town, and accessible by trolleybus 150 from the train station, and buses 5, 10, 18 and 57 from the bus terminal. It's 50m up a lane off ul Długosza, and in the heart of the university district. Bed clothes are 6zł extra.

Wojewódzki Ośrodek Metodyczny (Map p186; ☎ 532 92 41; www.wodn.lublin.pl in Polish; ul Dominikańska 5; beds 45zł) Rooms here have between two and five beds. It's good value and often busy, so book ahead. Look for the 'Wojewódzki Ośrodek Doskonalenia Nauczycieli' sign outside.

Hotel Piast (☎ 532 16 46; ul Pocztowa 2; s/d/tr 46/62/81zł) Opposite the train station, the Piast is OK for a late-night arrival or early-morning departure. It's a long way from anywhere and at the rougher end of town.

Camping Marina (☎ /fax 744 10 70; ul Krężnicka 6; camping per tent 8zł, cabins from 55zł; ⏱ May-Sep) The Marina camping ground is serenely located on a man-made lake, the Zalew Zemborzycki, about 8km south of the Old Town. Take bus 17, 20 or 21 from the train station to Stadion Sygnał and then catch bus 25.

MID-RANGE & TOP END
Grand Hotel Lublinianka (Map pp184-5; ☎ 446 61 00; www.lublinianka.com; ul Krakowskie Przedmieście 56; s €65-117, d €75-140; Ⓟ ✗) Housed in an imposing former bank, the Grand is the swankiest place in town. The cheaper 3rd-floor rooms are rather small, but 'standard' rooms are more acceptable and have glitzy marble bathrooms. Facilities include free use of a sauna and Turkish bath, and there's a good restaurant on site. The 30% weekend discount makes it rather more affordable.

Hotel Europa (Map pp184-5; ☎ 535 03 03; www .hoteleuropa.pl; ul Krakowskie Przedmieście 29; s/d 290/380zł; Ⓟ ✗) The squeaky-clean Europa is Lublin's most central hotel, offering thoroughly modernised rooms in a restored 19th-century building on the city's main shopping street. It's very popular and books up quickly.

Hotel Mercure-Unia (Map pp184-5; ☎ 533 72 12; www.orbis.pl; Al Racławickie 12; s/d from 320/380zł; Ⓟ ✗) Offering the usual upscale chain-hotel setup, this big, central place is very much geared towards the business-traveller market, and there's no real character here. But it's convenient, and rooms are light, comfortable and well maintained.

Hotel Victoria (Map pp184-5; ☎ 532 70 11; fax 532 90 26; ul Narutowicza 58/60; s/d from 190/290zł; **P** ✗) This gloomy concrete high-rise is away from the centre, but still within easy walking distance. Small rooms, glum service and a clientele largely made up of loud businesspeople are features unlikely to delight, though it's perfectly adequate for a night or two.

Motel PZM (Map pp184-5; ☎ 533 42 32; ul Prusa 8; s/d from 120/160zł; **P**) PZM is a typically unexciting modern complex, but it's clean, functional, very handy for the bus station, and represents good value.

Eating & Drinking

The Old Town, and the streets nearby, are the best places to look for a bite to eat, while there are many more restaurants scattered around the 'new' part of town too.

Kawiarnia Szeroka 28 (Map p186; ☎ 534 61 09, ul Grodzka 21; mains around 20zł; ☽ lunch & dinner) This is a charming, evocative place with a menu of good, if not exactly innovative, Jewish and Polish cuisine and, of course, plenty of beer and vodka. There's a terrace at the back and evenings are often enlivened by the presence of *klezmer* (Jewish folk-music) bands; if you choose to stay for the music, an extra 12zł will be added to your bill – it's well worth it.

Chawerim Klezmer (Map p186; ☎ 534 73 05; ul Złota 2; mains 12-19zł; ☽ 1-11pm Mon-Thu, 1pm-1am Fri & Sat, 1-10pm Sun) An intimate little place in a vaulted cellar off the main square, and decked out in Jewish artworks and photographs. It offers reasonably priced Polish and Jewish cuisine and a good wine list, including a number of Israeli wines. Be careful with the narrow spiral steps down from the square though!

Oregano (Map pp184-5; ☎ 442 55 30; ul Kościuszki 7; mains 27-45zł; ☽ lunch & dinner) This pleasant, upmarket restaurant specialises in Mediterranean cuisine, featuring pasta, paella and seafood on the menu.

Pizzeria Acerna (Map p186; ☎ 532 45 31, Rynek 2; pizza from 11zł; ☽ lunch & dinner) Acerna is a popular subterranean place on the main square, serving up cheap pizza and pasta.

Restauracja Pub Alternatywa (Map pp184-5; ☎ 532 48 46; ul Chopina 11; mains 10-20zł; ☽ 11am-midnight Mon-Sat, 2pm-midnight Sun) A busy cellar pub away from the hubbub of the centre, with regular live music, the ubiquitous pizza, and other light snacks and meals.

Espresso Bar (Map p186; ☎ 534 49 43; Rynek 9; ☽ noon-midnight) This is a cosy spot for a cappuccino or something stronger, and it's run by a friendly English-speaking couple. It also serves light meals and snacks. Unusually for Lublin, it's not in a cellar.

Caram'bola Pub (Map pp184-5; ☎ 534 63 80; ul Kościuszki 8; ☽ 11am-late) This little pub is a pleasant place for a beer or two. Again, it also serves inexpensive bar food.

Entertainment

The major local daily paper, the *Kurier Lubelski*, has listings of what's on. The free monthly *Lublin w Pigułce* covers cultural events. The tourist office may also be able to tell you what's going on around town.

NIGHTCLUBS

Club Koyot (Map pp184-5; ☎ 743 67 35; ul Krakowskie Przedmieście 26; ☽ noon-late Mon-Fri, 5pm-late Sat & Sun) Hidden away in a little courtyard, Club Koyot features live music most nights.

Club Fluid (Map p186; ☎ 607 689 383; ul Grodzka 1; ☽ noon-late) Also has various live acts; look out for posters around town.

Kawiarnia Artystyczna Hades (Map pp184-5; ☎ 532 56 41; ul Peowiaków 12) Hades has live music on some nights, and a disco usually on Friday. The annual three-day Hades Jazz Festival takes place here in October.

Chatka Żaka (Map pp184-5; ☎ 533 32 01; ul Radziszewskiego 16) This student club, of Marie Curie University, has a pool table and a beer garden, and live-music events on some nights.

THEATRES

Teatr im Osterwy (Map pp184-5; ☎ 532 42 44; ul Narutowicza 17) The main venue for drama features mostly classical plays with some emphasis on national drama.

Filharmonia Lubelska (Map pp184-5; ☎ 532 44 21; ul Skłodowskiej-Curie 5) The Philharmonic has a huge, new auditorium, where it stages concerts of classical and contemporary music.

Teatr Muzyczny (Map pp184-5; ☎ 532 25 21; ul Skłodowskiej-Curie 5) Sharing a building with the Philharmonic, the Musical Theatre presents operettas and various musical events.

Gardzienice Theatre (Map p186; ☎ 532 98 40, 532 96 37; ul Grodzka 5A) Theatre buffs may be interested in this experimental theatre company, one of the most outstanding companies currently performing in Poland. Each of its productions is a whirl of sights and sounds performed barefoot by candlelight, with reckless energy and at breakneck speed,

MAŁOPOLSKA

accompanied by music and singing by the actors themselves. Established in 1977 in the small village of Gardzienice, 28km southeast of Lublin, the theatre is based and performs there. The theatre is often abroad and, when at home, only performs on weekends to an audience small enough to be packed into its tiny theatre. You need to book well in advance.

Getting There & Away

BUS

The main bus terminal, Dworzec Główny PKS, is at the foot of the castle near the Old Town and handles most of the traffic. Private minibuses depart for numerous destinations around the country including Warsaw (25zł, 3½ hours, every 30 minutes), from a bus stop just behind the terminal. A few others, including buses to Zamość (9zł, two hours, every 20 minutes) leave from a less-organised route west of the terminal.

Buses to Kazimierz Dolny (8.10zł, two hours) run every hour or so (look for the Puławy bus via Nałęczów and Kazimierz). PKS buses run to Zamość (10zł, 2½ hours) every half-hour.

There are three buses to Sandomierz daily (12.50zł, 2½ hours) – look for the Tarnobrzeg bus in the timetable. Buses to Chełm (10zł, 1½ hours) run approximately every other hour. Every morning a fast bus goes directly to Kraków (25zł, four hours). A Polski Express bus goes to Warsaw every other hour (34zł, three hours).

There are two morning buses to Kozłówka (6.20zł, 1½ hours), and then nothing until about 3pm. They are hard to find in the timetable – ask at the information counter.

Six buses a day to Przemyśl (18.50zł, three hours) depart from the south terminal next to the train station.

TRAIN

The main station, Lublin Główny, is linked to the Old Town by trolleybus 160 and several buses including 13 and 17. There are at least half a dozen fast trains daily to Warsaw (34zł, 3½ hours) and Radom (25zł, 2½ hours), and two fast trains to Kraków (45zł, three hours). Tickets can be bought directly from the station or from **Orbis Travel** (ul Narutowicza 33A). Ordinary trains to Chełm (19zł, two hours) depart every one or two hours.

KOZŁÓWKA
☎ 81

The hamlet of Kozłówka (koz-*woof*-kah), 38km north of Lublin, is famous for its sumptuous late-baroque **palace**, built in the mid-18th century. The residence was acquired by the Zamoyski family in 1799, and today houses the **Museum of the Zamoyski Family** (☎ 852 83 00; www.muzeumzamoyskich.lublin.pl; adult/concession 10/5zł; ⊙ 10am-4pm Mon-Fri, 10am-5pm Sat & Sun Mar-Oct, 10am-3pm Nov & Dec). It features original furnishings, ceramic stoves and a large collection of paintings, mostly dating from the 17th to 19th centuries, though there are no great masterpieces on show here.

The palace is noted too for its **Socialist-Realist Art Gallery** (adult/concession 4/2zł; ⊙ 10am-4pm Mon-Fri, 10am-5pm Sat & Sun Mar-Oct, 10am-3pm Nov & Dec). It has an overwhelming number of portraits and statues of the revolutionary communist leaders, and also features many idealized proletarian scenes of farmers, factory workers and so on, striving for socialism.

You can stay in the palace rooms and at an 'agrotourist' **farm** (☎ 852 83 00), but contact staff ahead about availability and current costs.

From Lublin, two buses head to Kozłówka each morning, usually on the way to Michów. Only a few buses return directly to Lublin in the afternoon, so check the timetable before visiting the museum. Alternatively, you can catch one of the frequent buses to/from Lubartów, which is regularly connected by bus and minibus to Lublin.

Getting There & Away

The usual departure point for Kozłówka is Lublin – see p190 for transport details. Returning to Lublin, there are only a few direct buses in the afternoon, so check the timetable before visiting the museum, and plan your visit accordingly. There are more buses to Lubartów, from where buses and minibuses run regularly to Lublin. There are also a few afternoon buses from Kozłówka to Puławy.

PUŁAWY
☎ 81 / pop 55,000

The town of Puławy (poo-*wah*-vi) reached its golden age at the end of the 18th century when the Czartoryski family, one of the big aristocratic Polish clans, made it an important centre of political, cultural and intellectual life. Prince Adam Kazimierz Czartoryski

SOCIALIST REALISM – ART AS A POLITICAL TOOL

Socialist realism originated in the 1920s in the Soviet Union and became the only accepted style in visual arts, architecture, film, music and literature by the mid-1930s. After WWII, it spread widely throughout the countries of the eastern bloc, by then controlled by the Soviet Union.

In Poland, the new regime initially allowed for some ideological and cultural pluralism. Only in 1949, when the communists felt themselves sufficiently strong and safe in the saddle, was socialist realism formally implemented, and it came to be the official artistic doctrine until 1955. A huge body of paintings, sculptures, monuments, poems and songs was produced in that short period.

According to its official credo, socialist realism was 'a creative way of transferring Marxism into the realm of art'. It was a doctrine that was designed to develop a 'socialist culture' by artistic means. Its creators aimed to find an artistic vehicle to promote the communist ideology. In effect, art was reduced to the role of communist propaganda tool. The artists could no longer express themselves but were obliged to just transmit the official dogma in a determined pseudo-artistic form.

Since the new 'art' was intended to target the masses, not just an intellectual elite, it had to be easily understood by ordinary people. It therefore employed 19th-century realism and academism as the easiest way to promote the new ideas in painting and sculpture. Modern styles and artistic experiments were out of question, as were any independent creative attempts. The new art had to be optimistic and motivating, and promote the new order.

Images of communist leaders were probably the most common in the visual arts of the new artistic creation. These apart, the apotheosis of labour was very popular – happy bricklayers at work, smiling young women drivers on tractors ploughing the fields, or dockyard workers enthusiastically building a ship. Other common subjects included important historical and social events, communist-party meetings, congresses etc.

After Stalin's death in 1953, the lunacy began to subside fairly quickly in Poland. Socialist realism works were discreetly removed from public view and put into the confines of warehouses. Kozłówka, which was then the central storage facility of the Ministry of Culture and Art (the Kozłówka palace wasn't opened until 1977), was one of the major recipients. Today, they are all back on the walls and pedestals, but this time as museum pieces.

and his wife Izabela accumulated a large library and art collection, and surrounded themselves with artists and writers.

After the failure of the November Insurrection of 1830, which was strongly backed by the Czartoryskis, the whole estate was confiscated by the tsar, and the family had to flee the country. The art collection was secretly moved to Paris. In the 1870s it was brought back to Poland, but to Kraków, not Puławy, and today it constitutes the core of the Kraków Czartoryski Museum.

After WWII a huge nitrate combine was built near Puławy, and the town became a badly polluted industrial centre.

Information

There's no genuine tourist office in Puławy. If in need, try the **PTTK office** (☎ 886 47 56; ul Czartoryskich 8A) at the entrance to the Czartoryski park-and-palace complex.

The **Bank Pekao** (Al Królewska 11A) is close to the palace. There are several *kantors* in the centre, including a few on ul Piłsudskiego.

Sights

The **Czartoryski Palace**, designed by Tylman van Gameren and built in 1676 to 1679, has been altered substantially over the years and is now a sober, late-neoclassical building. It's home to an agricultural research institute, and is not a tourist sight but you can try to have a discreet look inside. Enter through the main central door, turn to the right and go up the staircase to the 1st floor to see the only two rooms worth a glimpse, the music hall and the Gothic hall.

The **landscape park** (admission free; ☉ till sunset) surrounding the palace was founded in the late 18th century by Princess Izabela. It's a typical romantic park of the era (similar to the Arkadia park in Mazovia) and incorporates several pavilions and buildings. The Temple of the Sybil (Świątynia Sybilli) and the Gothic House (Domek Gotycki) both date from the early 19th century and are used as exhibition grounds from May to October. A map showing the location of important sights is displayed at the entrance.

MAŁOPOLSKA

The **Regional Museum** (☎ 887 86 74; ul Czartoryskich 6A; admission 3zł; ☉ 10am-2pm Tue-Sun), 200m north of the palace, features ethnographic and archaeological exhibits, plus temporary displays, some of which are related to the Czartoryski family.

About 200m to the west, on ul Piłsudskiego, is the **Czartoryski Chapel**, modelled on the Roman Pantheon and built from 1801 to 1803. The circular, domed interior has lost its original furnishings and decoration. Today it's a parish church.

Sleeping & Eating

Puławy has a scattering of drab hotels of the concrete-box persuasion, though prices are reasonable. The hotel restaurants are the best places to have lunch and dinner.

Youth hostel (☎ 886 33 67; fax 888 36 56; ul Włostowicka 27; dm 30zł) This large, 118-bed hostel is 2km out of the centre on the Kazimierz Dolny road. Don't come back into the centre if you're heading for Kazimierz – catch the bus near the entrance of the youth hostel.

Hotel Wisła (☎ /fax 886 46 15, 886 27 37; ul Wróblewskiego 1; d/tr 120/140zł; P) An affordable, if slightly dated, central place, Wisła has airy rooms with bathrooms and its own restaurant.

Centrum Szkoleniowo-Kongresowe Instytutu Uprawy, Nawożenia i Gleboznawstwa (☎ /fax 887 73 06, 887 73 07; Al Królewska 17; s/d 108/146zł; P) Centrum is another uninspiring modern block in a quiet spot just 200m from the Czartoryski Palace. It's good value, though, and has its own restaurant.

Getting There & Around

BUS

The PKS bus terminal is in the city centre. PKS buses to Lublin (7zł, 90min) depart every half-hour, but the service to Warsaw (19zł, three hours) is less frequent. Both these destinations are also serviced by Polski Express, with seven departures a day to each. Other PKS buses run to Radom (7.80zł, two hours, four to five daily) and Łódź (16zł, 2½ hours, four daily). There are also three morning buses to Lubartów; they will let you off at Kozłówka.

For Kazimierz Dolny (3.20zł, one hour), PKS buses leave at least every hour, but also check the schedule of suburban bus 12 in front of the terminal and take the one that goes first. Do the same if you head for Janowiec (choosing between PKS and city bus 17).

TRAIN

The town has two train stations: Puławy and Puławy Miasto. The latter is the main one and is closer to the centre, yet it's still nearly 2km northeast of the central area. It is serviced by city buses; otherwise use taxis.

At least one train per hour leaves for Lublin (17zł, two hours) but it's more convenient to travel on the buses, which go centre-to-centre. Trains to Warsaw (25zł, 2½ hours) run roughly every other hour. For Kraków (36zł, four hours), there is only one morning and one evening train, but several fast trains go to Radom (18zł, two hours) and on to Kielce (22zł, three hours), from where the transport to Kraków is regular.

KAZIMIERZ DOLNY

☎ 81 / pop 4000

Positioned on the bank of the Vistula at the foot of wooded hills, Kazimierz Dolny is a charming, picturesque town. It has some fine historic architecture, interesting museums and is nestled in attractive countryside. For many years Kazimierz has attracted artists and intellectuals, and painters setting up their easels outdoors are a common sight in summer.

Kazimierz has become a fashionable weekend and holiday spot for tourists (mainly from Warsaw), which gives it something of a split personality – from a quiet, sleepy, old-fashioned village on weekdays and off season, it turns into a hive of activity on summer weekends.

History

The town was founded in the 14th century by King Kazimierz Wielki (hence its name), who built the castle and gave it a municipal charter with numerous privileges attached. The town was called Dolny (lower), to distinguish it from upriver Kazimierz, which is today part of Kraków.

Kazimierz Dolny soon became a thriving commercial centre. Merchandise from the whole region, principally grain and salt, was shipped down to Gdańsk and further on for export. Kazimierz enjoyed

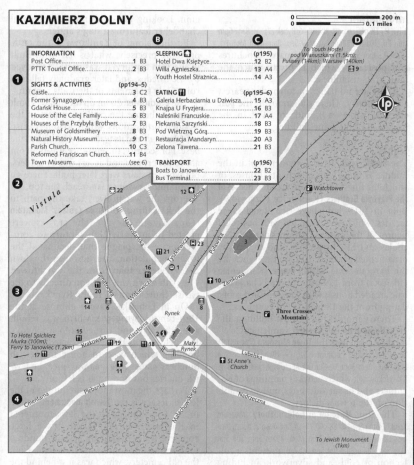

KAZIMIERZ DOLNY

INFORMATION	
Post Office	**1** B3
PTTK Tourist Office	**2** B3

SIGHTS & ACTIVITIES	(pp194–5)
Castle	**3** C2
Former Synagogue	**4** B3
Gdańsk House	**5** B3
House of the Celej Family	**6** B3
Houses of the Przybyła Brothers	**7** B3
Museum of Goldsmithery	**8** B3
Natural History Museum	**9** D1
Parish Church	**10** C3
Reformed Franciscan Church	**11** B4
Town Museum	(see 6)

SLEEPING	(p195)
Hotel Dwa Księżyce	**12** B2
Willa Agnieszka	**13** A4
Youth Hostel Strażnica	**14** A3

EATING	(pp195–6)
Galeria Herbaciarnia u Dziwisza	**15** A3
Knajpa U Fryzjera	**16** B3
Naleśniki Francuskie	**17** A4
Piekarnia Sarzyński	**18** B3
Pod Wietrzną Górą	**19** B3
Restauracja Mandaryn	**20** A3
Zielona Tawena	**21** B3

TRANSPORT	(p196)
Boats to Janowiec	**22** B2
Bus Terminal	**23** B3

particularly good times between the mid-16th and mid-17th centuries. A large port, a number of splendid burghers' mansions and nearly 50 granaries were built in that period, and the population passed the 2500 mark by 1630.

The Swedish Deluge, followed by the Northern War and the cholera epidemic of 1708, brought an end to the town's prosperity, and the displacement of the Vistula bed towards the west, away from the town, also accelerated its economic decline. By the 19th century, Puławy overshadowed Kazimierz as both a trade and a cultural centre. A small-scale revival as a tourist centre began at the end of the 19th century, but then came WWI and WWII, both of which caused serious damage to Kazimierz. Following WWII, a development plan aimed at preserving the town in line with its historical character was approved, and many of the old buildings have since been restored.

The history of Kazimierz, like that of the whole region, is intimately linked with Jewish culture. From the town's beginnings, Jews formed an important and expanding part of the community, becoming the majority during the 19th century. Before WWII they formed over half the town's population, but only a handful survived the war. About 3000 Jews from Kazimierz and its environs had their lives ended in the Nazi death camps.

Information

The **PTTK office** (☎ 881 00 46; Rynek 27; ☼ 8am-6pm Mon-Fri, 10am-5.30pm Sat May-Sep, 8am-4pm Mon-Fri, 10am-2.30pm Sat Oct-Apr) sells maps, brochures and postcards, which is pretty much the limit of its usefulness.

There are no banks in town; the nearest are in Puławy. There's a *kantor* in the **post office** (ul Tyszkiewicza 2), and an ATM in the back wall of the same building.

Sights

The **Rynek**, with an old wooden well in the middle, is lined with merchants' houses, of which the finest are the two arcaded **Houses of the Przybyła Brothers** (Kamienice Przybyłów). Built in 1615, both have rich Renaissance façades, which are decorated with bas-relief figures of the owners' patron saints, St Nicholas and St Christopher, and topped by ornamented parapets. Also on the Rynek are the baroque-style **Gdańsk House** (Kamienica Gdańska) from 1795, and several characteristic arcaded houses with wooden-tiled roofs, dating from the 18th and 19th centuries.

There's another fine historic building, the 1630 **House of the Celej Family** (Kamienica Celejowska). It shelters the **Town Museum** (☎ 881 01 04; ul Senatorska 11; admission 5zł; ☼ 10am-5pm Tue-Sun May-Sep, 10am-3pm Tue-Sun Oct-Apr, closed public holidays & day following), which features paintings of Kazimierz and its surroundings, and an exhibition on the town's history.

The tiny **Museum of Goldsmithery** (Muzeum Sztuki Złotniczej; ☎ 881 02 71; ul Zamkowa 2; adult/concession 6/4zł; ☼ 10am-5pm Mon, 10am-5pm Tue-Sun May-Sep, 10am-3pm Tue-Sun Oct-Apr) presents a collection of gold- and silverwork, including Judaic cult silverware and jewellery.

Set on the nearby hill is the **Reformed Franciscan Church** (Kościół Reformatów). It was built at the end of the 16th century but lost its original style with subsequent baroque and neoclassical decorations.

The Gothic **parish church**, on the opposite side of the Rynek, was built in the mid-14th century but was remodelled when Renaissance style flooded Poland. Of interest in its interior is the ornate carved organ from 1620, which sounds as good as it looks; organ recitals are held here. Also note the Renaissance stalls in the chancel and the stucco decoration of the nave's vault, a classic example of the so-called Lublin-Renaissance style that's typical of the re-

gion. Looking up, don't miss the unusual chandelier featuring a stag's antlers.

Further along ul Zamkowa is the **castle** or, more precisely, what is left of it. Built in the 14th century, it was partly destroyed by the Swedes, and later gradually fell into ruin. Only fragments of the walls remain.

The **watchtower**, 200m up the hill, was built a century before the castle as a part of the wooden fortifications, which no longer exist. It's 20m high and its walls are 4m thick at the base. For security, the entrance was built 6m above the ground and access was by ladders, but wooden stairs were later built. There's a panoramic view once you reach the top.

From the watchtower, take the path to the left leading to **Three Crosses' Mountain** (Góra Trzech Krzyży). The crosses were erected in the early 18th century to commemorate the plague that decimated the town's population. The view over the town is even better than from the watchtower. The path down will lead you directly to the parish church and on to the Rynek.

On ul Lubelska, have a glimpse at the 18th-century **synagogue**, which was rebuilt after the war and turned into a cinema. Just behind it is the reconstructed wooden building which used to house the Jewish butchers' stalls. This area was once the Jewish quarter but not much is left of it.

Perhaps the most moving reminder of the Jewish legacy is the **Jewish monument**, raised in 1984 in homage to the Jews murdered in Kazimierz during WWII. It's a large concrete wall covered by several hundred tombstones and tombstone fragments from the old cemetery, which was just behind the wall. There are still some finely carved tombstones in situ, that are worth looking around. The monument is a little over 1km from the Rynek, on the road to Opole Lubelskie.

On the opposite side of town, on the Puławy road, is the **Natural History Museum** (Muzeum Przyrodnicze; ☎ 881 03 26; ul Puławska 54; adult/concession 5/3zł; ☼ 10am-5pm Tue-Sun May-Sep, 10am-3pm Tue-Sun Oct-Apr, closed public holidays & day following). It is housed in a large, finely restored granary dating from 1591, and has mineralogy and flora-and-fauna sections. When you get to the top floor, look up at the intricate wooden structure supporting the roof, which is an exquisite example of 16th-century engineering. The massive beams have been joined by wooden pegs only – no nails were used.

Only a few **granaries** have survived out of a total of nearly 50. Most were built in the 16th and 17th centuries, during a boom in the grain trade. Apart from the one housing the National History Museum and its neighbour just 50m away, there's a good example on ul Krakowska, which is now the Hotel Spichlerz Murka.

Activities

The area around Kazimierz has been decreed the **Kazimierz Landscape Park** (Kazimierski Park Krajobrazowy). Many walking trails have been traced in the countryside, and in places they wind through the gorges that are a feature of the region.

There are three easy short trails known as *szlaki spacerowe* (walking routes) signposted in yellow, green and red, and three significantly longer treks called *szlaki turystyczne* (tourist routes) marked in blue, green and red. Almost all these routes originate in the Rynek. The tourist office sells maps of the park, which have trails marked on them.

Festivals & Events

The highly acclaimed **Festival of Folk Bands & Singers** takes place in the last week of June, from Friday to Sunday. Concerts are held on Mały Rynek, while the main Rynek fills up with handicraft stalls. The festival offers an opportunity to listen to music that you rarely hear nowadays. Dozens of amateur groups perform, ranging from soloists to large choirs, and they all wear the traditional costumes of their regions.

Kazimierz also hosts a more subdued **Film & Art Festival** in August, with classical music concerts, art exhibitions and outdoor film shows.

Sleeping

Kazimierz has plenty of places to stay. Particularly numerous are rooms for rent in private houses. The PTTK office on the Rynek can arrange rooms (30zł to 60zł per person) in some of the houses. Virtually every third house in town has some rooms for rent, and you'll easily recognise them by boards saying 'pokoje' (rooms) or 'noclegi' (accommodation). Aside from private rooms, there are several regular hostels and hotels to choose from, but many will be booked solid on weekends, especially in spring and summer, so advance reservations are essential.

BUDGET

Youth Hostel Pod Wianuszkami (☎ /fax 881 03 27; ul Puławska 80; dm/d 30/70zł) Located in a granary, 1.5km from the Rynek, this 68-bed hostel is pleasant and well run, and the price includes breakfast.

Youth Hostel Strażnica (☎ 881 04 27; ul Senatorska 25; dm 35zł) A bit smaller and more basic but very central, Strażnica hostel is tucked away in the building of the fire-brigade station. Breakfast is included.

MID-RANGE

Hotel Dwa Księżyce (☎ /fax 881 07 61; ul Sadowa 15; s/d/ste 140/180/300zł; P) The 'Two Moons' probably offers the best standard in town, and is located along a quiet lane not far from the centre. It has 16 fresh and stylish rooms and two apartments, most with balconies, plus a restaurant and a commercial art gallery.

Willa Agnieszka (☎ 882 03 56; willa_agnieszka@wp.pl; ul Krakowska 41a; s/d Mon-Fri 128/183zł, Sat & Sun 105/152zł; P) The 12-roomed Willa Agnieszka is a sparklingly modern and restful place with large, airy rooms. There's an on-site restaurant and conference facilities.

Hotel Spichlerz Murka (☎ /fax 881 00 36; ul Krakowska 59/61; s/d 90/160zł) Located in a former granary set back in its own grounds from a very quiet lane, Murka oozes character, though the rooms themselves are rather spartan. The owners run another stylish hotel nearby and a camping ground further along.

Eating & Drinking

Kazimierz certainly has no shortage of cafés and restaurants, which you'll find all around the centre of town.

Zielona Tawerna (☎ 881 03 08; ul Nadwiślańska 4; mains 15-30zł; lunch & dinner) Housed in an old wooden house, in an antique-filled suite of rooms, the 'Green Tavern' has a big menu of grilled meats, fish, salads and vegetarian options. There's also a pleasant garden where you can have a quiet drink.

Piekarnia Sarzyński (☎ 881 06 43; ul Nadrzeczna 6; mains from 6zł; breakfast & lunch) The Sarzyński bakery has delicious rolls, cakes and bread, including some unusual bread in the shape of roosters, crayfish and other animals. There's also a sit-down section where you can have light meals of salads, dumplings and the like.

Naleśniki Francuskie (☎ 882 03 35; ul Krakowska 26; crepes 4-5zł; 1-7pm Mon-Fri, 11am-8pm Sat,

10am-7pm Sun) This tiny, quaint café away from the centre is the place to head if you find yourself craving crepes. There's a huge variety on the menu, as well as plenty of teas.

Restauracja Mandaryn (☎ 881 02 20; ul Senatorska 17; mains 20-30zł; ☽ lunch & dinner) Serving Polish and international cuisine in vaguely Oriental surroundings, Mandaryn offers one of Kazimierz' more-varied menus, featuring omelettes, salads and steaks.

Galeria Herbaciarnia U Dziwisza (☎ 881 02 87; ul Krakowska 6; teas from 3zł; ☽ breakfast & lunch) An art gallery-cum-tea room, this is a charming olde-worlde place. There are around 100 types of tea to choose from.

Knajpa U Fryzjera (☎ 881 04 26; ul Witkiewicza 2; mains 19-25zł; ☽ lunch & dinner) This agreeable little place, set up in a former hairdresser's salon, serves up authentic Jewish specialities in a homely atmosphere.

Pod Wietrzną Górą (☎ 881 05 43; ul Krakowska 1; mains 11-23zł; ☽ breakfast, lunch & dinner) This bright and modern place offers the usual range of Polish specialities, including lots of grills, steaks and dumplings, as well as lighter snacks and pizza, and there's a beer-garden at the back.

Getting There & Around

Kazimierz can be conveniently visited as a stop on your Lublin–Warsaw route, or as a day trip from Lublin. There's no railway in Kazimierz but there's a decent bus service.

BOAT

If there are passengers interested in summer, a pleasure boat runs to Janowiec, on the opposite side of the Vistula – ask at the wharf at the end of ul Nadwiślańska.

There's also a car and passenger ferry from May to September. Its departure point is 1km west of Hotel Murka Spichlerz.

BUS

The PKS bus terminal is about 100m north of the Rynek and has a service to Puławy (3.20zł, 45 minutes) every half-hour or so. The similarly frequent Puławy urban bus 12 can take you directly to the Puławy train station. Buses to Lublin (8.10zł, two hours) go roughly every hour. There are about five fast buses straight to Warsaw daily (22zł, 3½ hours), or go to Puławy and change for the train.

JANOWIEC

☎ 81 / pop 1200

The village of Janowiec (yah-*no*-vyets), 2km upstream on the other side of the Vistula from Kazimierz Dolny, is known for its **castle**, which is now part of the **Janowiec Museum** (☎ 881 52 28; ul Lubelska 20; adult/concession 8/6zł; ☽ 10am-5pm Mon-Fri, 10am-2pm Sat & Sun May-Oct, 10am-2pm Mon, 10am-5pm Tue-Fri, 10am-7pm Sat & Sun Nov-Apr).

Built at the beginning of the 16th century by the Firlej family, and gradually extended during the next century by subsequent owners, the castle grew to have over 100 rooms and become one of the largest and most splendid castles in Poland. Many prominent architects, including Santi Gucci and Tylman van Gameren, had a hand in the castle's development.

The castle went into decline in the 19th century, and was largely destroyed during WWI and WWII. It was the only private castle in Poland under communist rule until its owner donated it to the state in 1975. By then, it was a genuine ruin.

While it's still a ruin, much has changed over recent years. Intensive work has been going on and has given the castle back some of its rooms and portions of the walls, complete with vaults, arcades and external painted decoration. The latter is possibly its most striking feature; the walls have been painted with horizontal white and red strips, and grotesque human figures. It all looks like a modern-art joke, but reputedly isn't; historians say that's how the original castle was adorned. Some of the restored rooms house an exhibition related to the castle.

In the park beside the castle is a **manor house** from the 1760s (another part of the museum), fitted out with period furnishings and decoration, and giving an insight into how Polish nobility once lived. Among the outbuildings surrounding the manor is an old two-storey granary, which has an interesting **ethnographic exhibition** that features old fishing boats, ceramics, tools and household implements.

It's also worth going downhill to the village of Janowiec, at the foot of the castle, to visit its mid-14th-century Gothic **parish church**, extensively rebuilt in Renaissance style in the 1530s. Inside is the tomb of the Firlej family, carved in the workshop of Santi Gucci from 1586 to 1587.

Sleeping & Eating

The PTTK office in Kazimierz (see p194) will be able to tell you about the availability of private rooms in town. For a meal, go to the **Restauracja Serokomla** (☎ 881 52 77; ul Sandomierska 24; mains 10-20zł; ⏰ lunch & dinner) or **Maćkowa Chata** (☎ 881 54 62; ul Sandomierska 2; mains 10-15zł; ⏰ lunch & dinner); both are close to Janowiec's Rynek.

Getting There & Away

You can visit Janowiec from Kazimierz Dolny, by pleasure boat or ferry. Alternatively, there is a regular service to/from Puławy (3.10zł, 30 minutes) by urban bus 17 and PKS buses.

CHEŁM

☎ 82 / pop 70,000

Chełm (pronounced hewm) is a mid-sized town about 70km east of Lublin, not far from the Ukrainian border. It's off the popular tourist track, but won't take you far off the Lublin–Zamość route; it's an easy daytrip from either. Interestingly, Chełm sits on an 800m-thick layer of almost pure chalk. Over the centuries Chełm's economic development has relied on rich chalk deposits. The old tunnels, below the ground, are the town's primary attraction. It also has an attractive enclosed cathedral sanctuary, which is a relaxing spot for a stroll.

History

Chełm was founded in the 10th century and, like most towns along the eastern border, it shifted between the Polish Piast crown and the Kyivan duchy on various occasions. King Kazimierz Wielki eventually got hold of the area in 1366 and King Władysław Jagiełło established a bishopric here some 50 years later.

Around this time Jews began to settle in the town, and swiftly grew in strength and numbers – by the end of the 18th century Jews accounted for 60% of the town's population. At that time there were 49 houses lining the market square, and 47 of them belonged to Jews.

As happened elsewhere in the country, Chełm's good times ended in the 17th century – the period of wars, ravages and Poland's general decline. Later came the Partitions, and the town fell under first Austrian then Russian occupation.

It wasn't until WWI that Chełm began to recover as part of independent Poland, only to experience the horrors of WWII two decades later, including the mass execution of Jews, whose population had grown by that time to about 17,000.

Information

Kantors are in reasonable supply; there are some on ul Lwowska.

Adyton (☎ 501 047 907; ul Lwowska 13P; per hr 2zł; ⏰ 10am-10pm) Reliable and central Internet café.

Bank Pekao (Al I Armii Wojska Polskiego 41) It's some distance from the centre, but there are several central ATMs, including ones at Lwowska 13 and ul Lubelska 65 and 69.

Chełm Public Library (☎ 563 95 92; ul Partyzantów 27)

Chełmski Ośrodek Informacji Turystycznej (☎ 565 36 67; itchelm@wp.pl; ul Lubelska 63; ⏰ 8am-4pm Mon-Fri, 9am-2pm Sat & Sun) The tourist office is an excellent source of local information, offering a number of useful free tourist brochures, including *Along the Route of Chełm's Old Architecture* and the comprehensive *Chełm Tourist Guide*.

Sights

The city's star attraction is the **Chełm Chalk Tunnels** (Chełmskie Podziemia Kredowe; ☎ 565 25 30; www.um.chelm.pl; ul Lubelska 55A; adult/concession 9/6zł; ⏰ 9am-4pm), an array of old chalk passages, hewn out by hand about 12m below ground level. Reputedly the world's only underground chalk mine, it started in medieval times, and by the 16th century was known nationally for the excellent quality of the local chalk. By 1939 a multilevel labyrinth of corridors grew to a total length of 15km. They effectively undermined the town and became a real danger. Following the collapse of a building and part of a street in 1965, the mine was closed and the voids were silted up – except for an 1800m stretch, which was strengthened and opened as a tourist attraction.

All visits are guided (in Polish only) in groups. Tours normally depart at 11am, 1pm and 4pm daily and take about 45 minutes. The temperature in the tunnels is 9°C year-round, so come prepared.

Chełm lies on a plain with a conspicuous hill right in the middle. The first settlement and stronghold were on top of the hill. Nothing is left of this apart from a distinctly recognisable artificial elevation, topped with a wooden crucifix.

MAŁOPOLSKA

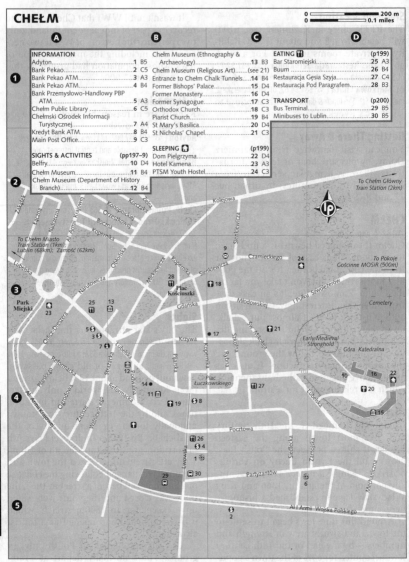

Today, the hill is crowned with the sparklingly white **St Mary's Basilica** (Bazylika Mariacka) surrounded by a complex of religious buildings that were once a bishops' palace and a monastery. The late-baroque basilica was remodelled from a Uniat church built here in the mid-18th century. The interior is sober and lacks much decoration, except

for the silver antependium at the high altar, which shows Polish knights paying homage to Our Lady of Chełm. The icon of the Madonna herself overlooks the altar. It's a replica; the original was removed by the Russians during WWI and is now in Ukraine. Just outside, the freestanding 40m-high **Belfry**, originally built in the 19th-century in the Orthodox style, was later given a partial neoclassical makeover.

More impressive is the former **Piarist Church** (Kościół Pijarski), off Plac Łuczkowskiego. This twin-towered late-baroque church was built on an oval plan in the mid-18th century. Once you enter through the massive ornamented doors, you'll find yourself enveloped in a colourful interior, with wall paintings covering every square centimetre of the walls and vaults. This trompe l'oeil decoration was executed in 1758 by Józef Mayer, the same artist who embellished Lublin's cathedral. The furnishings are all in rococo style. Today it's the parish church.

The former monastery next door houses the **Chełm Museum** (Muzeum Chełmskie; ☎ 565 26 93; ul Lubelska 55; adult/concession 3/2zł, free Thu; ◷ 10am-3.30pm Tue-Fri, 11am-3pm Sat & Sun), which features a collection of modern Polish painting, natural-history displays plus temporary exhibitions. The museum has three other outlets, which are open the same hours and charge the same admission, or you can buy a combined entry ticket to all four sites (adult/concession 6zł/4zł). The **ethnography and archaeology branch** (ul Lubelska 56a) displays the museum's collection of archaeological finds dating from the Stone Age onwards, and also stages ethnography and temporary exhibitions. The **Department of History branch** (ul Lubelska 57) houses documents and photographs relating to Chełm's past. The third one, **St Nicholas' Chapel branch** (ul Św Mikołaja 4), showcases religious art from the 18th to the 20th centuries. Concerts of classical music are held here at times.

Of the scarce relics of the Jewish legacy, you may want to have a look at the unspectacular **synagogue** of 1914, on the corner of ul Kopernika and ul Krzywa. It now houses offices and is not open to the public. A few steps north, on Plac Kościuszki, is the neoclassical **Orthodox church** built under tsarist rule in 1852.

Sleeping

Chełm doesn't have a great choice of accommodation options, and unless you're looking for a dorm room, it's probably best visited as a day trip from Lublin or Zamość. The tourist office will have details of seasonal youth hostels in the area.

Dom Pielgrzyma (☎ 565 36 56; ul Lubelska 2; dm/s/d 15/50/100zł) An interesting budget

option, the 'Pilgrim House' is a peaceful 18th-century church facility just behind the cathedral. It offers two singles and one double, all with bathrooms and two 25-bed dorms. Note, however, that the hostel is within the cathedral sanctuary, which closes at 9.30pm.

PTSM Youth Hostel (☎ 564 00 22; ul Czarnieckiego 8; dm 30zł) This 48-bed hostel, conveniently located in the centre, has clean and cosy dorms. The price is slightly cheaper for stays of more than one night.

Pokoje Gościnne MOSiR (☎ 563 02 86; ul I Pułku Szwoleżerów 15A; d/tr/q 60/58-90/77zł) MOSiR is a simple budget hotel next to the city stadium, beyond the Góra Katedralna. The cheaper triple rooms and quad rooms are basic affairs and don't have bathrooms.

Hotel Kamena (☎ 565 64 01; www.hotelkamena .pl; Al Armii Krajowej 50; s/d 115/150zł; ℗) The Kamena is a grim communist-era relic that time seems to have forgotten. The musty, somnolent, end-of-the-world aura is mildly depressing, and the cracked windows in reception don't exactly inspire confidence, but the rooms are clean, and it's central. It also has a restaurant.

Eating

Restaurants are scattered all around town, with a few in the area of Plac Łuczowskiego. The pedestrianised ul Lwowska has a few coffee bars, pizzerias and the like.

Bar Staromiejski (☎ 565 43 40; ul Lubelska 68; mains 5-10zł; ◷ 8am-6pm Mon-Fri, 8am-3pm Sat) One of the cheapest eateries in town, this milk bar has the usual budget Polish food. Apparently, the chef recommends the tripe. Get yours now!

Buum (☎ 565 84 62; ul Lwowska 7a; mains 8-15zł; ◷ lunch & dinner) This evocatively named pizza place on Chełm's main shopping street has a lengthy menu of the usual pizza and pasta dishes.

Restauracja Gęsia Szyja (☎ 565 23 21; ul Lubelska 27; mains 10-20zł; ◷ lunch & dinner) Set in three vaulted cellars, Gęsia Szyja is cosy, quiet and pleasant, and serves up a decent range of traditional Polish dishes and a variety of pizzas.

Restauracja Pod Paragrafem (☎ 564 06 10; ul Gdańska 13; mains 15-20zł; ◷ 10am-11pm Mon-Fri, 2-11pm Sat & Sun) This is another agreeable outlet for hearty and good-quality Polish standards of the meat-and-cabbage kind.

Getting There & Away

BUS

The bus terminal is on ul Lwowska, 300m south of the Rynek. PKS buses to Lublin (10zł, 1½ hours) go roughly every two hours, and there are also faster, and more frequent, private minibuses departing from just outside the terminal (9zł, one hour). Half a dozen buses a day run to Zamość (10zł, 1½ hours), plus several private minibuses (9zł, 1½ hours). Two fast buses go straight to Warsaw daily (229km).

TRAIN

The town has two train stations: Chełm Miasto 1km west of the Old Town, and Chełm Główny 2km to the northeast. Both are serviced by urban buses. Trains to Lublin (18zł, two hours) run every hour or two, and there are three fast trains per day to Warsaw; all these trains stop at both stations.

ZAMOŚĆ

☎ 84 / pop 65,000

The Pearl of the Renaissance, the Padua of the North, the Town of Arcades – these are just some of the grandiose titles bestowed upon Zamość (*zah*-moshch) by overexcited tourist-brochure copywriters. Despite the hyperbole, this is truly a unique town. Designed in its entirety in the late 16th century by Italian architect Bernardo Morando, Zamość was built in one go in the middle of the Lublin Upland, and it stands relatively unchanged today. With more than 100 architectural monuments of historical and artistic value, Zamość's Old Town was included on the World Heritage List by Unesco in 1992.

History

Zamość was the brain child of Jan Zamoyski (1542–1605), who was the chancellor of Poland and the commander-in-chief of the armed forces. A Renaissance man, Zamoyski intended to create a perfect city, which would at the same time be a great cultural and trading centre and an impregnable fortress.

Having studied in Padua, Zamoyski – like virtually all the Polish aristocracy of the period – was looking for artistic inspiration and models in Italy, not in neighbouring Russia. For his great plan,

he commissioned an Italian architect from Padua, Bernardo Morando, who followed the best Italian theories of urban planning of the day in putting Zamoyski's ideas into practice.

The whole project started in 1580, and within 11 years there were already 217 houses built and only 26 plots still empty. Soon afterwards most of the public buildings, including the palace, church, town hall and university, were completed, and the city was encircled with a formidable system of fortifications.

The experiment proved as successful as its founder hoped. The location of the town on the crossroads of the Lublin–Lviv and Kraków–Kyiv trading routes attracted foreign merchants including Armenians, Jews, Greeks, Germans, Scots and Italians, who came to settle here. The Zamoyski Academy, founded in 1594 as the third institution of higher education in Poland, after Kraków and Vilnius, soon became one of the main centres of learning.

The first military test of the fortress came in 1648, when Cossacks raided – the city had no problems defending itself. The town's defensive capabilities were confirmed during the Swedish invasion of 1656, when Zamość was one of only three Polish cities to withstand the Swedish siege (Częstochowa and Gdańsk were the other survivors).

During the partitions, Zamość fell first to Austria but later came under tsarist rule. In the 1820s the Russians further fortified the town, at considerable aesthetic cost. It was then that many of the previously splendid buildings (the palace, academy and the town hall among others) were adapted for military purposes and accordingly were given a uniform, barracks-like appearance. The defences were abandoned in 1866 and partly dismantled soon afterwards.

During WWII Zamość, renamed Himmlerstadt by the Germans, became the centre of Nazi colonisation, and the first of its kind on Polish territory. After the brutal expulsion of the Polish population, Germans settled in their place to create what Hitler planned would become the eastern bulwark of the Third Reich. They had to flee the Red Army, however, and fortunately didn't manage to destroy the city.

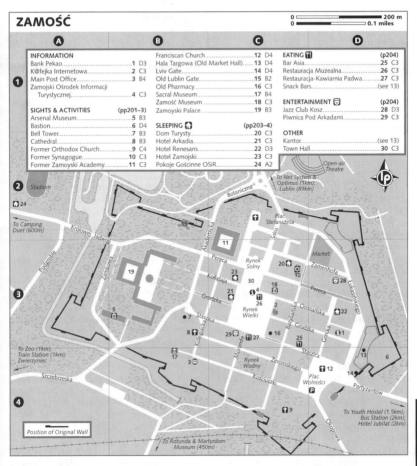

ZAMOŚĆ

Information

In the Old Town, you can use the computer at the public library in the former synagogue. Internet cafés are generally open from 10am to 9pm and charge 2zł to 3zł per hour. There are *kantors* inside the old market hall.

Bank Pekao (ul Grodzka 2) Changes travellers cheques, has an ATM and gives advances on Visa and MasterCard. It also changes cash, as do several central *kantors*, but rates may be lower than in large cities.

K@fejka Internetowa (☎ 639 29 32; Rynek Wielki 10) Internet access.

NetSystem (☎ 639 34 75; ul Peowiaków 9) Internet access.

Optimus (☎ 639 20 56; ul Peowiaków 6) Internet access.

Zamojski Ośrodek Informacji Turystycznej (☎ /fax 627 08 13; Rynek Wielki 13; ☽ 8am-6pm Mon-Fri, 10am-4pm Sat, 10am-3pm Sun May-Sep, 8am-4pm Mon-Fri Oct-Apr) Located in the town hall, with helpful and knowledgeable staff, and a range of maps and booklets.

Sights

Zamość is one of those towns in which strolling aimlessly is more fun than walking map in hand from one sight to the next. The Old Town is partly a car-free area and only 600m long by 400m wide. It's centred on the square, which is likely to be your starting point.

The original fortifications were altered beyond recognition by the Russians; those on the eastern side of town survived in part, including one of the bastions, and the position of the rest can still be traced by the mound surrounding the Old Town.

OLD TOWN SQUARE

Measuring 100m by 100m, the spectacular Italianate Renaissance Rynek Wielki is lined with old arcaded burghers' houses, and dominated by a lofty, pink **town hall**, built into the northern side of the square. Constructed soon after the town's foundation, it was extended around the mid-17th century and got its curving exterior stairway in 1768.

Each side of the Rynek has eight houses (except for the northern one where half the space is taken by the town hall) and each is bisected by streets designed as the two main axes of the town: one running west–east from the palace to the most important bastion, and the other one oriented north–south, linking three market squares. The town's founder, Jan Zamoyski didn't want the town hall to compete with his palace and interrupt the view, and that's why it doesn't sit, as is usual, in the middle of the square.

Originally, all the houses had decorative parapets on their tops but these were removed in the 1820s; only those on the northern side have been restored. These are the most beautiful houses in the square, and probably always were. As they once belonged to Armenian merchants, you will find some Oriental motifs on their façades. Two of these houses now shelter the **Zamość Museum** (Muzeum Zamojskie; ☎ 638 64 94; Rynek 24/26; admission 4zł; ☉ 9am-4pm Tue-Sun). The intriguing displays here include a scale model of the 16th-century town and a letter to Jan Zamoyski from his architect, Bernardo Morando, with a hand-drawn plan of the square, complete with the names of the first occupants of each building. Portraits of the Zamoyski family, folk costumes and archaeological finds are also on show. Note too the original wooden ceilings and decoration around the windows and doors.

Walk through the arcades around the square to see some fine doorways, such as those at Nos 21 and 25, and the stucco work on the vaults in the vestibules, as at No 10. The old pharmacy at No 2, dating from 1609, is also worth a look.

AROUND THE OLD TOWN

The **cathedral**, just southwest of the Rynek, took about 40 years, from 1587 to 1628, to complete. The outside form was largely changed in the early 19th century, but the interior has preserved many original features. Note the authentic Lublin-Renaissance-style vault, some good stone and stucco work, and the unusual arcaded organ loft. In the high altar is the rococo silver tabernacle of 1745. The Zamoyski chapel at the head of the right-hand aisle shelters the tomb of the founder. The stairs next to the chapel will take you down to the family crypt (for a nominal entry fee).

Back outside the church, you can go up to the top of the freestanding **bell tower** (admission 1zł; ☉ 10am-4pm Mon-Sat May-Sep) for a panoramic view, though the terrace is not high enough to provide a good vista over the Old Town and the Rynek. The original tower was made of timber and went up in flames. The present one was built from 1755 to 1775. There are three bells inside, of which the largest, named Jan after the founder, weighs 4300kg and is over three centuries old.

Behind the church is the former vicarage from the 1610s, known as the Infułatka, with its splendid ornate doorway. It leads to the **Sacral Museum** (Muzeum Sakralne; ul Kolegiacka 2; admission 3zł; ☉ 10am-4pm Mon-Fri, 10am-1pm Sat & Sun May-Sep, 10am-1pm Sat & Sun only Oct-Apr), which features a collection of religious art accumulated by the church.

West from the collegiate church is the old arsenal, which now houses the **Arsenal Museum** (Muzeum Arsenał; ☎ 638 40 76; ul Zamkowa 2; adult/concession 4/2.50zł; ☉ 9am-4pm Mon-Fri). There's a small and undistinguished collection of cannons, swords, muskets and other military hardware on show, and occasional temporary exhibitions. To the north is the **Zamoyski Palace** (Pałac Zamoyskich), which was reputedly a splendid residence until it was turned into a military hospital in the 1830s. It now houses government offices, and is not open to the public.

A partly ruined brick structure, just north across ul Królowej Jadwigi, is the **Old Lublin Gate** (Stara Brama Lubelska). Just after its construction in 1588 it was walled up to commemorate the victorious battle at Byczyna, in which the Austrian Archduke Maximilian, a claimant to the Polish throne, was taken prisoner and triumphantly led under guard into the town through the gate. He was the last person to walk through.

To the east of the gate is the famous **Academy** (Akademia), which, again, lost its style in tsarist times. Behind it you'll find the Rynek Solny, the Salt Market Sq. You are now at the back of the town hall. Have a look at the symbol of justice over the gate; there was once a jail inside.

One block east from the Rynek Solny is the Renaissance **synagogue** built from 1610 to 1618, complete with its reconstructed decorative parapets. Today it's a public library; go inside to see the partly surviving stucco decoration and some fragments of wall paintings on the vault.

The area around the Rynek Solny and ul Zamenhofa was once the heart of the Jewish quarter. The Jews were granted permission to settle in Zamość in 1588, and by the mid-19th century they accounted for about 60% of the town's population of 4000. By the eve of WWII their numbers had grown to 12,000 (45% of the total population). In 1941 they were moved to the ghetto that was formed to the west of the Old Town, and by the following year most had been murdered in death camps.

On the eastern edge of the Old Town is the **Hala Targowa**, the old Market Hall, which is home to numerous little shops, a *kantor* and a few simple cafés. The market is adjacent to the best surviving **bastion** of the seven the town originally had. Guided tours, in Polish, take you along the **walls** (☎ 627 07 48; adult/concession 2/1.5zł; ☽ 9am-5pm Mon-Sat May-Sep), and the entrance is beside the **Lviv Gate** (Brama Lwowska). This was one of three gateways to the city and, despite later changes, it has kept some of its original decoration, including an inscription about the foundation of the town (from its eastern side).

Opposite the gate is the massive **Franciscan Church** (Kościół Franciszkanów; Plac Wolności). When built (from 1637 to 1665), it was reputedly the largest and one of the most beautiful baroque churches in Poland, yet virtually nothing of its splendour is left. After the Partitions, the Austrians turned it into a hospital; then the Russians used it as an arms depot until 1840, when they remodelled it for barracks, pulling down its magnificent twin baroque towers in the process. Between the wars, the building housed a

museum and a cinema, and after WWII an art college moved in as soon as the museum found a new location. It wasn't until 1994 that the Franciscans eventually reclaimed the building and made it a church again.

Further south is the former **Orthodox Church**, built in the 1620s by Greek merchants, and complemented with a fortified tower half a century later. The church was rebuilt several times but the original stucco decoration of the vault has been preserved.

OTHER ATTRACTIONS
Roughly 450m southwest of the Old Town is the **Rotunda**, a ring-shaped fort built in the 1820s as part of the city's defence. During WWII it was used by the Nazis for executions (8000 local residents were executed here), and now it is the **Martyrdom Museum** (Muzeum Martyrologii; ul Męczenników Rotundy; admission free; ☽ 9am-6pm May-Oct). It's more a shrine than a museum.

Zamość has a small **zoo** (Ogród Zoologiczny; ☎ 639 34 70; ul Szczebrzeska 8; adult/concession 4/2zł; ☽ 9am-7pm Apr-Sep, 7am-3pm Oct-Mar), which features popular local species and some exotic attractions, including monkeys and tigers. It's opposite the train station.

Festivals & Events
Zamość hosts three annual jazz festivals: the **Jazz on the Borderlands** in July, the **International Meeting of Jazz Vocalists** in September, and the **Zamość Blues Festival** in early December. All three events are organised by, and take place at, **Jazz Club Kosz** (☎ 638 60 41; ul Zamenhofa 3).

The **Zamość Theatre Summer** takes place from mid-June to mid-July with open-air performances on the Rynek Wielki in front of the town hall.

Sleeping
Zamość has a fair supply of places to lay your head at night, though most are pretty uninspiring affairs, which is surprising given the town's unique artistic merit. The Old Town has the best collection of hotels.

BUDGET
Dom Turysty (☎ 639 26 39; ul Zamenhofa 11; s & d 45zł) This very small hotel has neat and simple rooms with shared facilities. It's a basic affair, but it's in a very central location and the price is hard to beat.

Youth hostel (☎ 627 91 25; ul Zamoyskiego 4; dm 12-16zł; 🕑 Jul & Aug) This place is pretty simple but functional, and very cheap. It's in a school, 1.5km east of the Old Town, and not far from the bus terminal.

Pokoje Gościnne OSiR (☎ /fax 638 60 11; www .osir.zamosc.pl in Polish; ul Królowej Jadwigi 8; dm/s/d/tr/q incl breakfast 23.50/90/125/150/180zł; P) Another budget place within walking distance of the Old Town, OSiR is a sports hostel and is sometimes full with sports groups.

Camping Duet (☎ 639 24 99; ul Królowej Jadwigi 14; s/d/tr 65/75/95zł; P 🏊) This conveniently located campsite is only about 1.5km west of the Old Town. It has neat bungalows, tennis courts, and a restaurant, a sauna and a Jacuzzi. Larger bungalows sleep up to six.

MID-RANGE & TOP END
Prices at all of the following places to sleep include breakfast.

Hotel Zamojski (☎ 639 25 16; zamojski@orbis.pl; ul Kołłątaja 2/4/6; s/d Mon-Fri 202/285zł, Sat & Sun 160/190zł; P ✗) This agreeable Orbis-run hotel is by far the best in town, and set up in three, thoroughly modernised, connecting old houses leading off the square. The rooms are pleasingly plush and tastefully furnished, and all come with minibars. There are two good on-site restaurants that are open to nonguests, and there's a fitness centre.

Hotel Renesans (☎ 639 20 01; hotelrenesans@hoga. pl; ul Grecka 6; s/d Mon-Fri 128/183zł, Sat & Sun 105/152zł; P) This eye-wateringly ugly concrete box certainly wasn't inspired by the Renaissance, though on the plus side it's very central and rooms are comfortable enough, if you can ignore the brown-patterned carpets. The weekend rates are great value.

Hotel Arkadia (☎ 638 65 07; makben@wp.pl; Rynek Wielki 9; d/tr 150/180zł; P) Arkadia has just six rooms, two of which overlook the main square. It's a grand old place in a great location, and has lots of charm, but it has seen better days.

Hotel Jubilat (☎ 638 64 01; hoteljubilat@hoga.pl; ul Kardynała Wyszyńskiego 52; s/d Mon-Fri 126/166zł, Sat & Sun 104/138zł; P) The Jubilat is an acceptable, if rather characterless place to spend the night, right beside the bus station. It couldn't be handier for late arrivals or early departures, but it's a long way from anywhere else and not in the most scenic of locations. It's under the same management as the Renesans.

Eating
There are a few eateries scattered around the Old Town, though there's not a great variety on offer. The hotel restaurants are the best options, while if you're just looking for cheap eats, there are some takeaway counters inside the old indoor market.

Restauracja Muzealna (☎ 638 64 94; ul Ormiańska 30; mains 10-25zł; 🕑 lunch & dinner) Housed in an atmospheric, mural-bedecked cellar below the main square, Muzealana serves a better class of Polish cuisine, and has a well-stocked bar. The entrance is via steps leading down from the square.

Restauracja-Kawiarnia Padwa (☎ 638 62 56; ul Staszica 23; mains 7-14zł; 🕑 lunch & dinner) Another deep-cellar establishment, located opposite the town hall, Padwa is a decent place for hearty and reasonably priced Polish food.

Bar Asia (☎ 639 23 04; ul Staszica 10; mains from 8zł; 🕑 8am-5pm Mon-Fri, 8am-3.30pm Sat) This old-style milk bar serves cheap and filling Polish food, of the soup-dumplings-and-cabbage variety.

Entertainment
Piwnica Pod Arkadami (☎ 627 14 43; ul Staszica 25) One of the first pubs in Zamość, this cellar watering hole with pool tables continues to be a popular haunt that's often full with all the locals.

Jazz Club Kosz (☎ 638 60 41; ul Zamenhofa 3) Apart from the jazz festivals (p203), Kosz stages unscheduled jazz concerts and jam sessions when somebody turns up in town. Entrance is from the back of the building.

Getting There & Away
BUS
The bus terminal is 2km east of the town centre; frequent city buses link it with the Old Town. Buses to Lublin (11.50zł, two hours), either fast or ordinary ones, run roughly every half-hour till about 6pm, and there are also plenty of private minibuses, which are cheaper and faster (10zł, 1½ hours). There are two morning buses to Rzeszów (16zł, three hours), passing Łańcut on the way, and one to Przemyśl (17zł, 3½ hours). One morning fast bus goes directly to Kraków (21zł, four hours), and four go to Warsaw (247km). Private minibuses leave for several destinations from the stand right opposite the bus terminal; check the timetable there for details of departures.

TRAIN

The train station is about 1km southwest of the Old Town; walk or take the city bus. There are several slow trains to Lublin (20zł, 3½ hours) but give them a miss – they take a long, roundabout route. It's much faster to go by bus.

Three ordinary trains go directly to Warsaw (45zł), but they take over six hours to get there. Go by bus direct to Warsaw or to Lublin and there change to train travel. Inquire at the tourist office for timetables.

ZWIERZYNIEC

☎ 84 / pop 3800

Zwierzyniec (zvyeh-*zhi*-nyets), 32km southwest of Zamość, developed at the end of the 16th century, when Jan Zamoyski created a game reserve in the area (see p206). Soon afterwards the family's summer residence, complete with a palatial larch-wood villa and a spacious park, was established here. Later a chapel was built on an island on the lake opposite the palace. Meanwhile, a hamlet grew around the residence, eventually developing into a small town. The palace itself was pulled down in 1833.

Information

There is a small **tourist office** (☎ 687 26 60; zokir@poczta.oneta.pl; ul Słowackiego 2; ☼ 8am-7pm Mon-Sat May & Sep, 8am-7pm Mon-Sat, 9am-5pm Sun Jul & Aug, 8am-4pm Mon-Fri Oct-Apr), located in the centre of town.

Sights

Today Zwierzyniec is essentially the gateway to the Roztocze National Park, housing the park's headquarters and the **Natural History Museum** (Muzeum Przyrodnicze; ☎ 687 20 66; ul Plażowa 3; adult/concession 3/2zł; ☼ 9am-5pm Tue-Sun May-Oct, 9am-4pm Tue-Sun Nov-Apr) related to the park. It's on the southern edge of the town, roughly 1km from the bus stop.

The only significant structure left of Zamoyski's residential complex is the little chapel. Known as the **Chapel upon the Water** (Kaplica na Wodzie), this charming, small baroque church enjoys a spectacular location: it sits on one of the four tiny islets on the small lake named the Staw Kościelny (Church Pond), and is linked to the mainland by a bridge. The lake is situated halfway between the bus stop and the museum.

Near the church is the **Zwierzyniec Brewery**, established here in 1806 and producing an excellent beer named – yes, you've guessed it – Zwierzyniec. You probably won't be allowed to visit the facility, but you can at least try their brew, which is served in the bar at the entrance to the brewery. Don't miss it, as it's almost impossible to find it elsewhere (virtually all the production goes for export).

Sleeping & Eating

Apart from the places listed here, the town has several holiday centres and plenty of locals rent rooms in their homes – ask at the tourist office.

Camping Echo (☎ 687 23 14; ul Biłgorajska 3; camp sites/per person 6.50/6.50zł, cabins per person 12-17zł; ☼ May-Sep; **P**) Echo camping ground has very basic cabins with three and six-bed rooms and a snack bar serving simple meals.

Youth hostel (☎ 687 21 75; ul Partyzantów 3B; dm 30zł; ☼ Jul & Aug) The 40-bed summer hostel, in the local school, is basic but cheap.

Hotel Jodła (☎ 687 20 12; fax 687 21 24; ul Parkowa 3A; d/tr 57.78/86.67zł) Jodła is near the bus stop, in a large timber villa, with two side buildings. It's a simple but pleasant place and has a café. Meals are available only if requested in advance, while room rates are cheaper after the first night.

Karczma Młyn (☎ 687 25 27; ul Wachniewskiej 1A; s/d 60/80zł) Pleasant and inexpensive, Karczma has just five well-kept rooms, while its restaurant is possibly the best place around for a lunch or dinner.

Ośrodek Wypoczynkowy Anna (☎ 687 25 90; ul Dębowa 1; d 70-80zł, tr 120-140zł; **P**) Anna is a good, central place offering neat and cosy rooms, though only the pricier ones come with private bathrooms.

Getting There & Away

The bus stop is on ul Zamojska, in the town centre. There's a large town map posted beside it, which has the tourist attractions and facilities marked on it. Buses to Zamość (32km) pass pretty regularly, and there are infrequent buses to more-distant destinations, including Sandomierz and Rzeszów. The train station is about 1km east of town.

ROZTOCZE NATIONAL PARK
☎ 84
Decreed in 1974, the **Roztocze National Park**
(Roztoczański Park Narodowy; park's office in Zwierzyniec
☎ 687 20 70; roztoczepn@pro.onet.pl; ul Plażowa 2, Zwierzyniec; admission 2zł) covers an area of 79 sq km
to the south and east of Zwierzyniec. The
site was a nature reserve for over 350 years
as part of the estates owned by the Zamoyski
family. Following the purchase of a vast
stretch of land, complete with six towns,
149 villages and about 1600 sq km of forest
in 1589, Jan Zamoyski created an enclosed
game reserve named Zwierzyniec (hence
the name of the town). It was a remarkable
achievement at that time, as this was not a
hunting ground but a protected area where
various species of animals roamed in relative freedom. It was here that the world's
last specimens of the original tarpan (see
p122) were kept in the 19th century, until
they were given away to the locals when the
estate fell into disarray under tsarist rule.

Today's national park includes much of
Zamoyski's original reserve. Occupying undulating terrain, 93% of which is covered
with forest, the park retains much of its
primeval character, with rich and varied
flora and fauna. The park is crossed from
east to west by the Wieprz, one of the least
polluted rivers in the region.

The forest features an interesting mix of
plant species typical of the valley as well as
of the mountain. A product of different soil
types, topography, climate and water sources,
it contains a wide variety of trees, including
fir, spruce, pine, beech, sycamore, hornbeam,
oak, elm and lime. Fir trees in the park reach
heights of up to 50m – the tallest in Poland –
and beech trees are not much shorter.

The park's fauna is just as diverse. Almost all species of forest animals, including
stag, roe deer, boar, fox, marten and badger,
live here, and elk, wolves and lynxes show
up from time to time. In 1969 beavers were
reintroduced, and in 1982 a refuge for tarpans was created.

There are about 190 bird species –
including the spotted eagle, black stork
and honey buzzard – about 130 of which
nest regularly in the park. There is also a
rich world of insects, with the beetles alone
numbering approximately 2000 different
species.

Walking Trails
The normal starting point for walks in the
park is the town of Zwierzyniec, or, more
specifically, the museum (p205). Here you
can buy booklets and maps on the park,
and the staff can provide further information. Tarpans can be seen beyond the museum – ask the staff to point out where
they are.

The most popular walking path begins
from the museum and goes south up to the
top of the Bukowa Góra (Beech Mountain)
at 306m (a 75m ascent). Just 1.5km long,
the path (which is actually a former palace's
park lane) gives a good idea of the park's
different forest habitats, passing from pine
to fir to beech woods at 500m intervals.

There are some side paths branching off
from the main one and allowing for a return by a different way. There are also some
longer trails, called tourist trails, crossing
various parts of the park and providing access to selected areas; they are marked on
tourist maps. Inquire at the museum information desk for advice and information.

The Carpathian Mountains

The Carpathian Mountains (Karpaty in Polish) are the highest and largest mountain system in Central Europe, and form one of the most scenic regions in Poland, stretching along the southern border with Slovakia towards the Ukraine. This is a wild, rugged area, still largely unspoilt, and its wooded hills and snowy mountains make it hugely popular with hikers, skiers and cyclists from Poland and other counties. Its remoteness and relative inaccessibility over the centuries have preserved its strong regional culture and, even today, this is one of the most traditional parts of Poland; travelling around you'll still see plenty of picturesque timber houses and rustic shingled churches as well as hundreds of tiny roadside chapels and shrines.

The region's biggest city is the vast urban sprawl of Rzeszów, which has excellent transport links but few real attractions in itself. The most popular destination by far is the ever-busy resort town of Zakopane, which sits at the heart of the Tatra Mountains (Tatry), the highest section of the Polish Carpathians, on the Slovakian border to the far south. This area offers the best winter sports and mountain walks in Poland. Elsewhere, a mosaic of small, modest towns provide jumping-off points for some of Poland's wildest national parks and most rewarding walking trails, laid-back spa resorts present a chance to unwind, and historic regional towns such as Przemyśl, Tarnów and Sanok offer unique and fascinating sights of their own.

This is a rural corner of Poland that relatively few foreign tourists explore in any depth, and unless you have your own set of wheels, trying to see more than a fraction of it on just one visit will be a challenge, to say the least. Instead, adopt the local pace of life and amble at your leisure through some of the country's most stunning scenery.

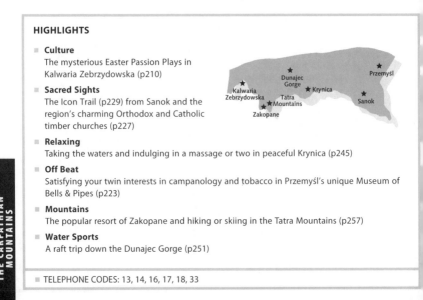

HIGHLIGHTS

- **Culture**
  The mysterious Easter Passion Plays in Kalwaria Zebrzydowska (p210)

- **Sacred Sights**
  The Icon Trail (p229) from Sanok and the region's charming Orthodox and Catholic timber churches (p227)

- **Relaxing**
  Taking the waters and indulging in a massage or two in peaceful Krynica (p245)

- **Off Beat**
  Satisfying your twin interests in campanology and tobacco in Przemyśl's unique Museum of Bells & Pipes (p223)

- **Mountains**
  The popular resort of Zakopane and hiking or skiing in the Tatra Mountains (p257)

- **Water Sports**
  A raft trip down the Dunajec Gorge (p251)

■ TELEPHONE CODES: 13, 14, 16, 17, 18, 33

THE CARPATHIAN MOUNTAINS

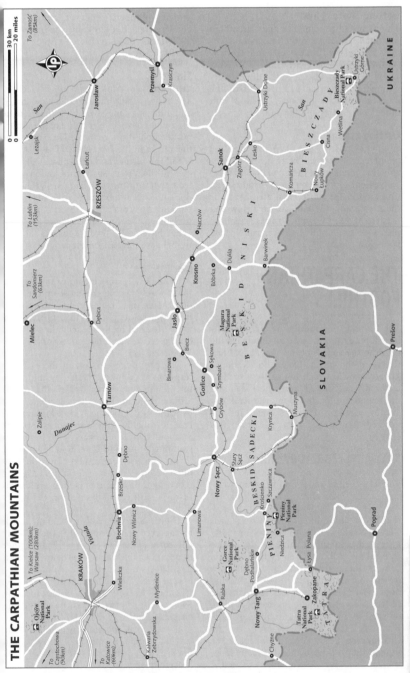

Getting There & Away

The main entry points for the Carpathian Mountains region are the major transport hubs of Kraków (in the west) and Rzeszów (in the east). Both have air links with Warsaw, and Kraków also has a few direct international flights (see p159). Most of the larger towns have bus or train links with other Polish cities and beyond.

Getting Around

Although most of the main towns in the region can be reached by train, you'll probably find buses to be the quickest and most convenient mode of public transport. Getting around the more rural areas, such as the Bieszczady, though, can be a slow and frustrating exercise, and unless you have plenty of time, and patience, you'll need your own transport.

THE CARPATHIAN FOOTHILLS

The Carpathian Foothills are a green, hilly belt sloping from the true mountains in the south to the valleys of the Vistula and San Rivers to the north. Except for Kalwaria Zebrzydowska, which is usually visited in a round trip from Kraków, most sights in the region are located along the Kraków–Tarnów–Rzeszów–Przemyśl road (and are ordered accordingly, west to east, in this chapter).

KALWARIA ZEBRZYDOWSKA

☎ 33 / pop 4800

Poland's second most important pilgrimage centre (after Częstochowa), Kalwaria Zebrzydowska (kahl-*vah*-ryah zeb-zhi-*dof*-skah) is set amid hills about 30km southwest of Kraków. The town owes its existence and subsequent fame to the squire of Kraków, Mikołaj Zebrzydowski, who commissioned the church and monastery for the Bernardine order in 1600. Having noticed a resemblance in the area to the site of Jerusalem, he set about creating a place of worship similar to that in the Holy City. By 1617, 24 chapels were built over the surrounding hills, some of which looked as though they'd been brought directly from the mother city. As the place attracted

growing numbers of pilgrims, more chapels were erected, eventually totalling 40. In 1999 it was added to Unesco's list of World Heritage Sites.

Sights
CHURCH

The original **church** was gradually enlarged and today it's a massive edifice. Its baroque high altar boasts a silver figure of the Virgin, but the holiest image inside is a painting of the Virgin in the **Zebrzydowski Chapel**, to the left of the high altar. Legend has it that the eyes of the Virgin shed tears in 1641, and from that time miracles happened. Pilgrims flock to Kalwaria on all Marian holy days, particularly from 13 to 15 August, when processions around the chapels are held. What have really made Kalwaria famous, though, are the Passion Plays.

PASSION PLAYS

A blend of religious ceremony and popular theatre, re-enacting the most crucial days of Christ's life, the plays have been held in Kalwaria since the 17th century. They are performed by locals, including monks, during a two-day-long procession in Holy Week (Easter).

The procession sets off in the early afternoon of Maundy Thursday and goes on till dusk, covering half of the circuit around the chapels. It starts again at about 6am the next morning (Good Friday) and ends at roughly 2pm. The procession calls at about two dozen chapels, with various stopping times and a sermon in most of them. The play performed along the way often becomes such a realistic spectacle that more-vigorous pilgrims have been known to rush in to rescue Jesus from the hands of his oppressors.

The time of year adds a dramatic touch to the ceremony, especially when Easter falls early, at the end of winter. The weather is unpredictable then, with snow or rain possible at any time and mud almost guaranteed over large stretches of the route. It sometimes gets bitterly cold, especially when you are moving slowly around the chapels for most of the day.

If your visit coincides with one of the two big religious events you'll find Kalwaria flooded with people; at other times it's a peaceful place.

Sleeping

All hotel prices given in this chapter are for rooms with private bathroom and breakfast, unless otherwise stated.

Dom Wycieczkowy Indra (☎ 876 62 54; www.indra.com.pl in Polish; ul Zebrzydowice 10; d/tr/q from 40/60/80zł; P) Indra is a charming, homy place with simple, cosy rooms. Those with private bathroom cost roughly double, but it's one of the better choices in town.

Hotel Merkury Tatarscy (☎ /fax 867 62 77; ul Zadowa 11; s/d/tr from 99/108/162zł; P) Merkury is a good central option and has a range of comfortable rooms.

Hotel Kalwarianka (☎ /fax 876 64 92; ul Mickiewicza 16; s/d/tr from 33/45/52zł; P) Located next to the stadium, Kalwarianka is basic but is about the cheapest place around; rooms with private facilities cost slightly more. There's also a tennis court on site.

Getting There & Away

There are several buses a day from Kraków to Kalwaria (5.60zł, one hour). Trains also pass Kalwaria on their way to Zakopane.

NOWY WIŚNICZ
☎ 14 / pop 2500

The little town of Nowy Wiśnicz (*no-vi veesh*-neech), situated just south of Bochnia, has reached the pages of travel guidebooks thanks mostly to its castle. This well-proportioned, early-baroque building was designed by Italian architect Matteo Trapola for one of the most powerful men in Poland at the time, Stanisław Lubomirski (1583–1649).

As soon as the castle was completed, Lubomirski commissioned the same architect to build the monastery for the Discalced Carmelites. Equally splendid and similarly fortified, the monastery was erected between 1622 and 1635, about 500m up the hill from the castle, and the two structures were connected by an underground passage. By the time of the monastery's completion, the energetic Lubomirski was already rebuilding his newly acquired possession, the castle in Łańcut.

After the Carmelites were expelled in the 1780s, the monastery was turned into a prison and remains so to this day. It's designed for particularly dangerous criminals and is among the best guarded in the country.

Sights

The **castle** (☎ 612 83 41; adult/concession 3/2zł; ☽ 9am-2pm Mon-Fri Oct-Apr, 9am-2pm Mon, 9am-4pm Tue-Thu, 9am-5pm Fri, 10am-5pm Sat, 10am-6pm Sun & public holidays May-Sep) is around 1.5km uphill from the town's centre. It was built between 1615 and 1621 using the foundations and parts of the walls of a 14th-century stronghold that previously stood on this site. The new castle was reputedly very well prepared to defend itself from enemies – it had food and ammunition to withstand a three-year siege. Despite its enviable defences, the castle surrendered to the Swedes in 1655 in exchange for the promise that they would not destroy it. They indeed kept their word, but nonetheless thoroughly plundered the interior, taking away some 150 wagonloads of treasure. The castle suffered a series of further misfortunes, including a fire in 1831, which left it in ruins. Only after WWII was restoration undertaken, and this is ongoing. The exterior has already been renovated, but there is still a long way to go on the inside.

All visitors are guided around in groups, so you may have to wait a while for the next tour to depart. The 45-minute tour covers the courtyard and rooms on the two upper floors including the domed chapel, a large hall with a splendid ornate ceiling, and a huge ballroom measuring 30m by 9m and 9m high. There's also the sarcophagus of Stanisław Lubomirski, a small exhibition displaying three models of the castle from different periods and photographic documentation of postwar reconstruction.

The road up the hill from the castle goes to the prison. Halfway along you'll find a fine wooden house called Korzynówka in which Jan Matejko was once a frequent guest. Today it's a modest **museum** (☎ 612 83 47; admission 2zł; ☽ 10am-2pm Wed-Sun), which features some memorabilia of this most famous Polish history painter.

In the town centre, near the Rynek, you can visit the **parish church**, also the work of Trapola.

Sleeping & Eating

Nowy Wiśnicz has a couple of places to stay, though there's a much wider choice in nearby Bochnia.

Hotel Cold (☎ 612 28 02; www.hotel.cold.pl; ul Storynka 5, Bochnia; s/tw/apt 95/135/160zł; P) This unfortunately named place in Bochnia is actually a very smart, modern hotel that represents value for money. It has a restaurant, tennis court and tenpin bowling alley, and is right in the heart of town.

Hotel Kmita (☎ /fax 612 88 25; d/ste 240/440zł; P) Installed in the reconstructed building on the castle's defensive walls, the Kmita offers 22 beds in comfortable rooms and suites. It has its own restaurant, but meals have to be requested in advance.

Hotel Restauracja Hetmańska (☎ 685 54 10; ul Grunwaldzka 2; s/tw 20/60zł; P) The cheapest place in town, the 20-bed Hetmańska has fairly basic but acceptable rooms, above a decent restaurant. Single rooms do not have private bathrooms.

Hotel Atlas (☎ 685 59 30; Stary Wiśnicz 410; s/d/ste 107/150/185zł; P) The small Atlas offers 10 neat rooms and also has its own restaurant. Breakfast is an optional extra. It's 2.5km from Nowy Wiśnicz (3km from the castle), on the road to Bochnia.

There are a few simple eating outlets in the town centre, on and around the Rynek.

Getting There & Away

Nowy Wiśnicz is well serviced from Bochnia (2.40zł, 15 minutes) by either the hourly suburban Bochnia bus 12, or the PKS buses running every quarter of an hour or so. Bochnia is on the main Kraków–Tarnów route and has frequent buses and trains to both destinations.

DĘBNO
☎ 14 / pop 1200
Halfway between Bochnia and Tarnów is the small village of Dębno. Though little known and rarely visited, the **castle** here is a good example of a small defensive residence. It was built in the 1470s on the foundations of a previous knights' stronghold, and was gradually extended until the 1630s. It was plundered several times since, but the structure survived without major damage. Postwar restoration took more than three decades and the result is admirable – the castle looks much as it would have done 350 years ago.

The castle consists of four two-storey buildings joined at the corners to form a small rectangular courtyard, all surrounded by a moat and ponds, now dry. The structure is adorned with fine corner towers, oriels, bay windows and doorways, which have survived almost intact.

The castle is now a **museum** (☎ 665 80 35; adult/concession 4/3zł; ☺ 10am-5pm Tue, 9am-3pm Wed & Fri, 9am-5pm Thu, 11am-3pm Sat & Sun). You can visit a good part of the interior including the cellars. The rooms have been refurnished and have exhibitions of paintings and weaponry. Its small size gives you the refreshing feeling that you are visiting a modest private home, the only two larger rooms being the knights' room and the concert room, the latter hosting occasional piano recitals.

Sleeping & Eating

Restauracja Agawa (☎ 665 83 17; Wola Dębińska 278; d 70zł), 1km down the highway toward Tarnów, offers budget food and has 10 rooms upstairs. Very basic rooms are also available at **Klub Sportowy Jadowniczanka** (☎ 686 70 19; ul Sportowa 24, Brzesko; beds in tw/tr 15zł; P), around 3km west, on the road to Bochnia.

Getting There & Away

The castle is an easy stopover on the Kraków–Tarnów highway. There are regular buses on this road that will let you off at the village centre, from which the castle is just 500m or so.

TARNÓW
☎ 14 / pop 125,000
Tarnów (*tar*-noof) is an important regional industrial centre, yet you wouldn't notice this while strolling about its pleasant, finely restored Old Town. The city has some attractions and can be a worthwhile stop if you are travelling around the region.

The city map reveals a familiar layout – an oval centre with a large square in its middle – suggesting that the town was planned in medieval times. Tarnów is indeed an old city, its municipal charter was granted in 1330. Developing as a trade centre on the busy Kraków–Kyiv route, the town enjoyed good times in the Renaissance period, and a branch of the Kraków Academy was opened here.

Not uncommonly for the region, Tarnów had a sizable Jewish community, which by the 19th century accounted for half the city's population. Of 20,000 Jews living here in 1939, only a handful survived the war. Today the city is considered to be one of the major centres for Poland's relatively small Roma population.

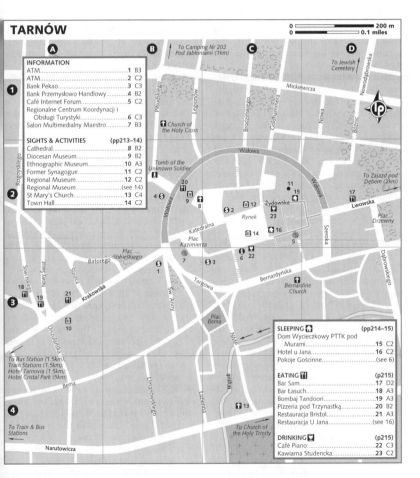

TARNÓW

INFORMATION
ATM..1 B3
ATM..2 C2
Bank Pekao...3 C3
Bank Przemysłowo Handlowy......4 B2
Café Internet Forum........................5 C2
Regionalne Centrum Koordynacji i
   Obsługi Turystyki.........................6 C3
Salon Multimedialny Maestro.......7 B3

SIGHTS & ACTIVITIES   (pp213–14)
Cathedral..8 B2
Diocesan Museum............................9 B2
Ethnographic Museum..................10 A3
Former Synagogue.........................11 C2
Regional Museum...........................12 C2
Regional Museum....................(see 14)
St Mary's Church.............................13 C4
Town Hall..14 C2

SLEEPING   (pp214–15)
Dom Wycieczkowy PTTK pod
   Murami..15 C2
Hotel u Jana.....................................16 C2
Pokoje Gościnne.......................(see 6)

EATING   (p215)
Bar Sam...17 D2
Bar Łasuch..18 A3
Bombaj Tandoori............................19 A3
Pizzeria pod Trzynastką................20 B2
Restauracja Bristol.........................21 A3
Restauracja U Jana...................(see 16)

DRINKING   (p215)
Café Piano..22 C3
Kawiarna Studencka......................23 C2

Information
INTERNET ACCESS
Some central facilities:
Café Internet Forum (☎ 627 43 46; ul Wekslarska 9)
Salon Multimedialny Maestro (Plac Kazimierza Wielkiego 5)

MONEY
If you need to get some money, convenient central ATMs include those on Plac Katedralny and Plac Sobieskiego. Travellers cheques can be cashed at **Bank Przemysłowo Handlowy** (ul Wałowa 10) – take note of the ornate façade of the building – or **Bank Pekao** (Plac Kazimierza Wielkiego 4). *Kantors* (private currency-exchange offices) are easy to find in the central area.

TOURIST INFORMATION
Tarnowskie Regionalne Centrum Koordynacji i Obsługi Turystyki (☎ 637 87 35; www.it.tarnow.pl; Rynek 7; 8am-6pm Mon-Fri year-round, 9am-5pm Sat May-Sep)

Sights
The **Rynek** retains much of its former appearance. The **town hall** in the middle is a familiar combination of Gothic walls and a tower, with Renaissance parapets topping the roof. The Renaissance doorway at the southern side leads to the **Regional Museum** (Muzeum Okręgowe; ☎ 621 21 49; Rynek 1; adult/concession 4/3zł; 10am-5pm Tue & Thu, 9am-3pm Wed & Fri, 10am-2pm Sat & Sun), which features a collection of historic paintings, armoury, furniture,

glass and ceramics. The museum's **extension** (Rynek 20/21), in the arcaded houses on the northern side of the square, holds temporary exhibitions.

The **cathedral**, just off the Rynek, dates from the 14th century but was thoroughly remodelled in the 1890s, eventually mutating into a neo-Gothic edifice. The interior shelters several Renaissance and baroque tombs, of which two in the chancel are among the largest in the country. Also of interest are the 15th-century stalls under the choir loft and two original stone portals – at the southern and western porches – both dating from the early 16th century.

Right behind the cathedral, in a 1524 house, is the **Diocesan Museum** (Muzeum Diecezjalne; ☎ 621 99 93; Plac Katedralny 6; admission free; ⊙ 10am-noon & 1-3pm Tue-Sat, 9am-noon & 1-2pm Sun & public holidays). It has a good collection of Gothic sacred art, including some marvellous Madonnas and altarpieces, and an extensive display of folk and religious painting on glass, reputedly the best in the country.

The area east of the Rynek was traditionally inhabited by Jews, but little original architecture has survived. Of the 17th-century **synagogue** off ul Żydowska, only the brick almemar is left. A more moving sign of the Jewish legacy is the **Jewish Cemetery** (Cmentarz Żydowski), which is a short walk north along ul Nowodąbrowska, then to the right into ul Słoneczna. The cemetery dates from the 17th century and boasts about 3000 tombstones (the oldest surviving one is from 1734), many fallen or leaning perilously. The original cemetery gate is now on display at the United States Holocaust Memorial Museum in Washington. The cemetery is locked but you can look over the fence from ul Słoneczna. For a closer inspection, ask for the key at the guard desk of the Regional Museum at Rynek 20/21.

Back in the Old Town, stroll along the restored **ul Wałowa**, which is lined with fine neoclassical buildings. Closed to traffic, it's a popular rendezvous among the locals. Its curved course follows the line where the medieval moat once was.

The **Ethnographic Museum** (Muzeum Etnograficzne; ☎ 622 06 25; ul Krakowska 10; adult/concession 4/3zł; ⊙ 10am-5pm Tue & Thu, 9am-3pm Wed & Fri, 10am-2pm Sat & Sun) has a collection of exhibits relating to Roma culture. Six Roma caravans can be seen at the back of the museum.

There are two beautiful, small wooden churches south of the Old Town. The shingled **St Mary's Church** (Kościół NMP; ul Konarskiego) dates from the 1440s, making it one of the oldest surviving wooden churches in Poland. The interior has charming folk decoration including a fine rococo high altar.

About 500m further south, behind the cemetery (take ul Tuchowska to get there), is the **Church of the Holy Trinity** (Kościół Św Trójcy), built in 1562, with a similar naively charming rustic interior including an early-baroque high altar.

Sleeping

Hotel U Jana (☎ 626 05 64; www.hotelujana.pl; Rynek 14; s/d/tr from 150/200/280zł) U Jana is the classiest hotel in the Old Town, conveniently located on the main square. The range of stylish rooms all have modern bathrooms, and there's a very good restaurant (opposite).

Hotel Tarnovia (☎ 621 26 71; www.hotel.tarnovia .pl; ul Kościuszki 10; s/d/ste from 90/144/370zł; P) The three-star Tarnovia, in a modern suburb near the bus and train stations, is one of the best places to stay in the city. Rooms are bright and spacious and there's a gym and solarium, as well as a modern art gallery.

Hotel Cristal Park (☎ 633 12 25; www.hotel.cristal park.pl; ul Traugutta 5; s/d/tr from 135/200/328zł; P ✗ ⚏) Cristal Park, located around 5km west of town, is an upscale, modern place offering an appropriately high standard of comfort. It's a little out of the way if you don't have your own transport, but nearby public facilities include a swimming pool, tennis courts and ice rink.

Zajazd Pod Dębem (☎ 626 96 20; www.zajazd.pod debem.tarnow.pl; ul Marusarz 9B; s/d/tr from 77/105/125zł; P) This spotless, modern motel is roughly 2km east of town, and offers excellent value, with its cheerful, fresh-looking rooms and a good restaurant. Breakfast is 11zł extra.

Dom Wycieczkowy PTTK Pod Murami (☎ /fax 621 05 00; ul Żydowska 16; s/d/tr 50/80/90zł) This simple but acceptable place has basic rooms with shared facilities, in a convenient spot just off the Rynek.

Pokoje Gościnne (☎ 627 87 35; fax 627 87 38; Rynek 7; s/tw/tr 60/85/100zł; P) Rented out by the tourist office, all four rooms are on the top floor and are great value. You can book in at reception, which is open 24 hours.

Camping Nr 202 Pod Jabłoniami (☎ 621 51 24; www.camping.tarnow.pl; ul Piłsudskiego 28A; beds in s/d/q bungalows 15zł; ☷ Apr-Nov; Ⓟ) Tarnów's camping ground is 1km north of the Old Town. It has simple, cheap cabins without private bathrooms.

Eating

Restauracja U Jana (☎ 626 46 36; Rynek 14; mains 15-50zł; ☷ lunch & dinner) In the hotel of the same name, this is one of Tarnów's more upmarket restaurants, serving a higher class of traditional Polish cuisine.

Bombaj Tandoori (☎ 627 07 60; ul Nowy Świat 2; mains 20-40zł; ☷ lunch & dinner) An interesting addition to the local culinary picture, this fine restaurant offers Indian and Asian cuisine in elegant surroundings.

Restauracja Bristol (☎ 621 22 79; ul Krakowska 9; mains 15-49zł; ☷ lunch & dinner) This intact survivor of the communist era, with its old-fashioned décor and atmosphere, serves the usual range of hearty Polish specialities.

Bar Łasuch (☎ 627 71 23; ul Sowińskiego 4; mains 5-15zł; ☷ 8am-7pm Mon-Fri, 8am-3pm Sat) Łasuch is a modernised milk bar that is nothing particularly special but the food is cheap and filling.

Bar Sam (☎ 627 71 19; ul Lwowska 12; mains 5-10zł; ☷ 7am-7pm) Another refurbished milk bar, Sam serves up basic budget fare and is close to the Old Town.

Pizzeria Pod Trzynastką (☎ 621 97 35; ul Wałowa 13; mains 5-10zł; ☷ lunch & dinner) This is a simple little place offering a menu of cheap pizzas and salads.

Drinking

Café Piano (☎ 621 92 48; Rynek 9) Set in beautifully decorated cellars, this charming place offers plenty of drinks, a few budget dishes and live jazz on some Friday nights.

Kawiarna Studencka (☎ 0600 693 323; ul Żydowska 3) The Studencka is a cosy traditional pub, which has regular live music.

Getting There & Away

The train and bus stations are next to each other, southwest of the centre, just over 1km from the Old Town. It's an easy walk, or you can take buses 2, 9, 30, 32, 35, 37 or 41.

BUS

There are frequent buses west to Kraków (10zł, two hours) and regular departures southeast to both Jasło (7.60zł, 1½ hours) and Krosno (9.80zł, two hours). For Sandomierz

(11.80zł, 2½ hours), take any of the Tarnobrzeg buses, which depart every two hours, and then change; there is frequent transport between Tarnobrzeg and Sandomierz.

TRAIN

Trains to Kraków (20zł, two hours) run every hour or so; get off in Bochnia if you plan on visiting Nowy Wiśnicz castle. There are regular departures to Rzeszów (22zł, 2½ hours) and Nowy Sącz (24zł, three hours), and several trains to Warsaw (39zł, 4½ hours).

ZALIPIE

☎ 14 / pop 800

The village of Zalipie has been known as a centre for folk painting for almost a century, since its inhabitants started to decorate their houses with colourful floral designs. Actually, they used to adorn almost everything possible: cottages, barns, wells, stoves, tools and furniture.

The best-known painter was Felicja Curyłowa (1904–74), and since her death her farm has been open to the public as a **museum** (☎ 641 19 12; admission 2zł; ☷ 10am-4pm Tue-Sun). If you find it locked, ask for the keys at the house across the road.

In order to help maintain the tradition, the 'Painted Cottage' contest for the best decorated house has been held annually since 1948. It takes place just after Corpus Christi (Friday to Sunday), but it's not a tourist event. It's better to visit Zalipie after the contest rather than before, as you'll see fresh paintings.

The **House of Women Painters** (Dom Malarek; ☎ 641 19 38) was opened in 1978 to serve as a centre for the village's artists. A large board in front of the house features a map of the village showing the location of the decorated houses and the so-called 'trail of the painted farms'. Obviously, don't expect every house to be painted over – there are perhaps a dozen decorated cottages in the whole village.

There are only a few buses daily from Tarnów (5.60zł, 1½ hours), and the village spreads over a large area. It's very useful to have your own transport, instead of having to walk around the place. Before setting off, inquire at Tarnów's tourist office and Ethnographic Museum for current information about Zalipie.

RZESZÓW

☎ 17 / pop 155,000

The chief city of southeastern Poland, Rzeszów (*zheh*-shoof) is a huge, cluttered concrete sprawl, which on first sight may seem to offer little immediate inducement to stay any longer than it takes to get the next bus out again. Nevertheless, the town does have a few interesting museums that are worth a browse through, and several historic buildings of note. Rzeszów is also an important university town and a major regional transport hub, and makes a handy base for exploring the surrounding countryside.

Rzeszów started life in the 13th century as an obscure Ruthenian settlement. When Kazimierz Wielki captured vast territories of Ruthenia in the mid-14th century, the town became Polish and acquired its present name. It grew rapidly in the 16th century when Mikołaj Spytek Ligęza, the local ruler, commissioned a castle and a church, and built fortifications. It later fell into the hands of the powerful Lubomirski clan but this couldn't save the town from the subsequent gradual decline experienced throughout Poland.

Rapid postwar development increased the size of Rzeszów, but with little aesthetic consideration, and the layout of much of the town is confusing. Fortunately, enough of its historic core survived the bulldozers of the communist era to make a stopover worth while.

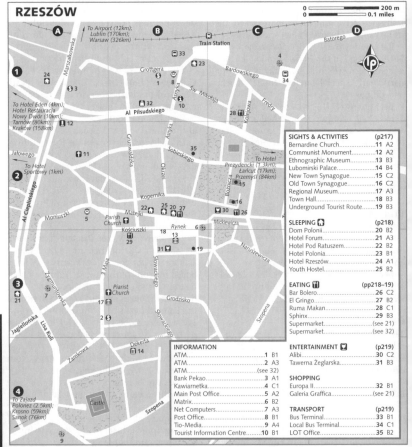

RZESZÓW

0 —— 200 m
0 —— 0.1 miles

SIGHTS & ACTIVITIES	(p217)
Bernardine Church	11 A2
Communist Monument	12 A2
Ethnographic Museum	13 B3
Lubomirski Palace	14 B4
New Town Synagogue	15 C2
Old Town Synagogue	16 C2
Regional Museum	17 A3
Town Hall	18 B3
Underground Tourist Route	19 B3

SLEEPING	(p218)
Dom Polonii	20 B2
Hotel Forum	21 A3
Hotel Pod Ratuszem	22 B2
Hotel Polonia	23 B1
Hotel Rzeszów	24 A1
Youth Hostel	25 B2

EATING	(pp218–19)
Bar Bolero	26 C2
El Gringo	27 B2
Ruma Makan	28 C1
Sphinx	29 B3
Supermarket	(see 21)
Supermarket	(see 32)

INFORMATION	
ATM	1 B1
ATM	2 A3
ATM	(see 32)
Bank Pekao	3 A1
Kawiarnetka	4 C1
Main Post Office	5 A2
Matrix	6 B2
Net Computers	7 A3
Post Office	8 B1
Tio-Media	9 A4
Tourist Information Centre	10 B1

ENTERTAINMENT	(p219)
Alibi	30 C2
Tawerna Żeglarska	31 B3

SHOPPING	
Europa II	32 B1
Galeria Graffica	(see 21)

TRANSPORT	(p219)
Bus Terminal	33 B1
Local Bus Terminal	34 C1
LOT Office	35 B2

To Airport (12km); Lublin (170km); Warsaw (326km)

Train Station

To Hotel Eden (4km); Hotel Restauracja Nowy Dwór (10km); Tarnów (80km); Kraków (158km)

To Hotel Sportowy (1km)

To Hotel Prezydencki (1.3km); Łańcut (17km); Przemyśl (84km)

To Zajazd Polonez (2.5km); Krosno (59km); Sanok (76km)

Information

INTERNET ACCESS

Internet access is cheap in Rzeszów (around 3zł to 4zł an hour). Some central facilities:
Kawiarnetka (☎ 852 69 14; ul Bardowskiego 5; 🕑 24 hr)
Matrix (☎ 853 70 70; ul Mickiewicza 4)
Net Computers (☎ 852 99 11; ul Zygmuntowska 7)
Tio Media (☎ 852 71 08; Plac Śreniawitów 6)

MONEY

Bank Pekao (Al Cieplińskiego 1), opposite Hotel Rzeszów, cashes travellers cheques, gives advances on Visa and MasterCard and also has an ATM. There are plenty of ATMs around the centre, including ones at the huge Europa II shopping mall at Al Piłsudskiego 34, in the Galleria Graffica complex, and at ul 3 Maja 21 and 23. Cash can be exchanged in *kantors*, which are also plentiful in the centre.

TOURIST INFORMATION

Tourist office (☎ 852 46 11; www.rcit.res.pl in Polish; ul Asnyka 6; 🕑 9am-6pm Mon-Fri, 10am-4pm Sat) Tiny but very helpful. Sells a good range of maps of the town and the wider region.

Sights

Most of the **Rynek** has been restored over recent years, though some work is still ongoing. In the middle of the square is a monument to Tadeusz Kościuszko, while the 16th-century **town hall**, in the corner of the Rynek, was wholly remodelled a century ago in pseudo-Gothic style and looks a little overelaborate in this setting.

The city's most recent attraction is the **Underground Tourist Route** (Podziemna Trasa Turystyczna; ☎ 875 41 99; Rynek 12, entrance from ul Króla Kazimierza; admission 4zł; 🕑 10am-5pm Tue & Fri, 9am-5pm Wed-Thu, noon-5pm Sun). It took 17 years to link 34 old cellars into a 213m-long route, which opened in 2001. The cellars date from various periods (from the 15th to 20th centuries) and are on different levels (the deepest one is nearly 10m below the Rynek's surface). Visits are by half-hour-long guided tours.

The **Ethnographic Museum** (Muzeum Etnograficzne; ☎ 862 02 17; Rynek 6; adult/concession 5/3zł; 🕑 9am-2pm Tue-Thu & Sun, 9am-5pm Fri) has traditional folk costumes and old woodcarvings from the region on permanent display and puts on occasional temporary exhibitions.

The Ethnographic Museum is part of the **Regional Museum** (Muzeum Okręgowe; ☎ 853 52 78; ul 3 Maja 19; adult/concession 6/4zł, free Sun; 🕑 10am-5pm Tue & Fri, 10am-3pm Wed & Thu, 9am-2pm Sun). Housed in the former Piarist monastery, the museum has permanent exhibitions featuring Polish painting from the 18th to 20th centuries, European painting from the 16th to 19th centuries, glass, faïence, and furniture. A bonus attraction is the surviving 17th-century frescoed vaults.

A short walk south is the early-18th-century baroque **Lubomirski Palace** (ul Dekerta), the work of Tylman van Gameren, today home to the Academy of Music.

Nearby, to the southwest, stands the **castle**. Begun at the end of the 16th century, the building has changed a lot since then but the entrance tower and the bastions have retained their original shape. From the 19th century until 1981 the castle served as a jail; among its inmates were several political prisoners. It was solidly renovated in the 1990s and houses the law court.

Return north to the **Bernardine Church** (Kościół Bernardynów; ul Sobieskiego), with its opulent furnishing and decoration. It was built for Ligęza as his mausoleum, and there are life-size alabaster effigies of his family in the side walls of the chancel. In the gilded chapel to the right is the early-16th-century statue of the Virgin Mary to whom numerous miracles have been attributed; intriguing wall paintings on both sides depict 100 people who were cured.

Close by, you can't miss the overblown **Communist Monument** (Al Cieplińskiego), erected 'in memory of the heroes of the revolutionary struggles'. It towers over a rather arid square facing the Hotel Rzeszów and is a rare survivor from the old regime. These days it's a magnet for skateboarders.

Go eastwards towards ul Bożnicza where two synagogues stand close to each other. Though less attractive from the outside, the 18th-century **New Town Synagogue** (Synagoga Nowomiejska; ☎ 853 38 11; ul Sobieskiego 18) has more to offer on the inside as it holds an art gallery. Note the entrance to its café on the 1st floor – it's the work of the contemporary sculptor Marian Kruczek. The 17th-century **Old Town Synagogue** (Synagoga Staromiejska; ul Bożnicza 4) now houses the city's registry and is also a centre for studies on the history of local Jews.

Sleeping

Rzeszów is amply supplied with budget and mid-range accommodation options, although most are fairly ordinary, functional affairs. On the plus side, prices remain quite reasonable.

BUDGET

Hotel Sportowy (☎ /fax 853 49 97; ul Jałowego 23A; s/d 70/100zł; P ☢) Located in a sports complex, roughly 1km west of the Rynek, Sportowy is a great budget choice, with good facilities on site. It also has cheaper doubles without bathrooms or washbasins (from 50zł).

Youth hostel (☎ 853 44 30; Rynek 25; dm/d/tr from 15/50/75zł) This is the cheapest and most central option – right on the main square. It has some doubles and triples but most spaces are in nine- to 18-bed dorms. Bedclothes cost 5zł extra.

Hotel Eden (☎ 852 56 83; www.hotel.eden.prv.pl; ul Krakowska 150; s/d/tr/q from 30/60/90/120zł) Eden is a student hostel that offers reasonable standards, but it's a long way – just over 4km – northwest of the centre. Rooms with washbasins or en suite bathrooms cost slightly more. Westbound bus 1 or 22 from Al Piłsudskiego will bring you here.

Hotel Polonia (☎ 852 03 12; ul Grottgera 16; s/d 65/80zł) Polonia has been revamped and is just about OK for the price, though its location right opposite the train station is not the most picturesque or quiet.

MID-RANGE

Hotel Restauracja Nowy Dwór (☎ 856 09 90; www .hotelnowydwor.pl in Polish; Świlcza 146; d/ste from 140/450zł; P) Around 10km west of town, on the E4 motorway towards Kraków, Nowy Dwór is one of the more stylish hotels in the area. It has a range of attractive, well-equipped rooms and a good restaurant. It's only practical, however, if you have your own car.

Hotel Forum (☎ 859 40 38; www.hotelforum.pl in Polish; ul Lisa Kuli 19; s/d/apt 140/180/300zł; P) In the same block as the Galeria Graffica shopping centre, this modernised high-rise offers the best facilities in the city centre, with light and spacious rooms and big bathrooms. It's also quite handy having a supermarket, cafés and a bank right on your doorstep.

Zajazd Polonez (☎ 860 54 50; www.polonez.rzeszow .pl; ul Graniczna 21; s/d/ste 100/160/250zł; P) Around 2.5km south of the centre, in the suburb of Drabinianka, the Polonez is an attractive, modern place in a quiet, but perhaps not too convenient, location. All rooms have bathrooms and modem connections, and it has its own restaurant.

Hotel Rzeszów (☎ 875 00 00; www.hotelesemako .com.pl; Al Cieplińskiego 2; s/d/apt from 95/220/250zł; P) Although pretty drab and dated, with a functional décor scheme recalling all the glamour of the Eastern Bloc circa 1980, this hulking concrete high-rise is very central and convenient, and the price is reasonable too. The cheaper single rooms are tiny but still perfectly adequate, and the restaurant offers a big menu of decent Polish cuisine.

Dom Polonii (☎ /fax 862 14 52; Rynek 19; s/d 130/220zł) Another very central option, Dom Polonii has just two single rooms and two double suites (the suites overlook the Rynek). It's good value, though it's not easy to find a vacancy here.

Hotel Pod Ratuszem (☎ 852 97 80; fax 852 97 70; www.hotelpodratuszem.rzeszow.pl in Polish; ul Matejki 8; s/d 100/160zł) This modern, perfectly central hotel offers 13 neat, if rather small, rooms. Again, it's a fair choice but the décor's somewhat dated and it's nothing special.

TOP END

Hotel Prezydencki (☎ 862 68 35; www.hoteleprezy denckie.com.pl; ul Podwisłocze 48; s/d/ste 230/320/490zł; P) Located around 1km southeast of the city centre, on the opposite side of the Wisłok River, the Prezydencki is a big, contemporary place geared towards business travellers. Consequently, it's fairly bland, but it's bright and clean, and has a sauna, solarium and restaurant.

Eating

Ruma Makan (☎ 0603 795 794; ul Kolejowa 9; mains 6.50-12.50zł; ☽ lunch & dinner) Rzeszów may seem an incongruous place to find an Indonesian restaurant, but this friendly little place is about as authentic as they come. It offers cheap buffet meals, with plenty of vegetarian options, plus traditional fish and chicken dishes. You pay for your plate, then fill it with what you like. The Indonesian chef will be happy to explain what's on offer.

El Gringo (☎ 864 21 18; Rynek 17; mains 12-20zł; ☽ lunch & dinner) Burritos, tacos and other Mexican favourites are on the menu at this colourful, cactus- and sombrero-bedecked place, and it's also a pleasant spot for a drink.

Bar Bolero (☎ 852 02 49; ul Mickiewicza 19; mains 5-10zł; ☽ lunch & dinner) One of the best addresses for a tasty budget meal in the centre, Bolero is a pleasant place offering an extensive menu including salads, and has a nonsmoking area downstairs in a vaulted cellar.

Sphinx (☎ 853 45 98; ul Kościuszki 9; mains 8.90-40.90zł; ☽ lunch & dinner) Another branch of the ubiquitous, nationwide Egyptian-themed restaurant chain, serving lots of variations on kebabs, cabbage and grilled meat dishes. It's dependable, if not particularly exciting, but it's always busy and the quasi kasbah décor is certainly striking.

Self-caterers will find well-stocked supermarkets in the **Europa II** (Al Piłsudskiego 34) and **Galeria Graffica** (ul Lisa Kuli 19) shopping centres. Both also house several snack bars, cafés and bigger restaurants.

Entertainment

Alibi (☎ 852 93 33; ul Mickiewicza 13) This modern restaurant-cum-nightclub has discos on most nights.

Tawerna Żeglarska (☎ 862 02 39; Rynek 6, entrance from ul Króla Kazimierza) Frequented by students, this 'Sailors' Tavern' often hosts musical evenings.

Getting There & Around

The train and bus stations are next to each other and only about 500m from the Rynek. Rzeszów is an important transport hub and there are plenty of buses and trains in all directions. The airport is in Jasionka, 11km north of the city, accessible by bus 14 from Al Piłsudskiego.

AIR

There are daily flights to Warsaw year-round, Rzeszów's only direct air link. The **LOT office** (☎ 862 03 47; Plac Ofiar Getta 6) will book and sell tickets.

BUS

PKS buses leave regularly throughout the day to Sanok (10.60zł, two hours), Krosno (8.60zł, 1½ hours), Przemyśl (10.20zł, two hours) and Lublin (24zł, 3½ hours). Buses go to Ustrzyki Dolne (13.50zł, 2½ hours, six daily) and Ustrzyki Górne (25zł, 3½ hours, four daily). Buses also go to Zamość (26.90zł, three hours, two daily) and Nowy Sącz (25zł, three hours, two daily). Buses to Łańcut (4zł, 30 minutes) run roughly every half-hour and are more convenient than trains, as they deposit you near the palace. Eurolines also operates numerous international services from the station. There are information boards detailing destinations, which include London, Paris, Prague and Lviv, and you can make inquiries at the **Centrum Eurobus office** (☎ 852 64 98) here.

TRAIN

There are about 20 trains daily to Przemyśl (21zł, 1½ hours) and the same number to Tarnów (20zł, 1½ hours). A dozen trains a day leave for Kraków (33zł, three hours). To Warsaw (40zł, 4½ hours), there are two morning express trains and one evening fast train. There's also one train to Lviv, which continues to Kyiv.

ŁAŃCUT

☎ 17 / pop 18,000

Łańcut (*wine*-tsoot) is famous for its castle, which is arguably the best-known aristocratic home to be found anywhere in Poland. It's one of the largest residences of its kind and holds an extensive and diverse collection of art.

The building started life in the 15th century, but it was Stanisław Lubomirski who made it a great residence, a palace rather than a castle. Soon after he had successfully completed his beautiful Nowy Wiśnicz castle, he came into possession of the large property of Łańcut and commissioned Matteo Trapola to design a new home even more spectacular than the old one. It was built between 1629 and 1641 and surrounded with a system of fortifications laid out in the shape of a five-pointed star, modelled on the latest Italian theories of the day.

Some 150 years later the fortifications were partly demolished while the castle was reshaped in rococo and neoclassical style. The last important alteration, executed at the end of the 19th century, gave the building its neo-baroque façades, basically the form which survives today.

A fabulous collection of art was accumulated in the castle over the centuries. The last private owner, Alfred Potocki, was regarded as one of the richest men in prewar Poland. Shortly before the arrival of the Red Army in July 1944, he loaded 11 railway carriages with the most valuable objects and fled with the collection to Liechtenstein.

THE CARPATHIAN MOUNTAINS

Sights

Just after WWII, the castle was taken over by the state and opened as a **castle museum** (☎ 225 20 08; ul Zamkowa 1; adult/concession 18/11zł; 9am-4pm), which suggests that there must have been enough works of art left to put on display. The collection has systematically been enlarged and supplemented, and today it conveys the impression of being bigger than before the war. In fact the rooms are so crammed that it's virtually impossible to take it all in on one visit.

The castle is visited in groups accompanied by a guide, and the tour takes from 1½ to two hours. The last tours depart one hour before closing time, but try to avoid them as they tend to rush at breakneck speed to visit the complex in an hour. Guides speaking English, French and German are available for 180zł per group (plus tickets). Book your guide a day or two in advance by calling ☎ 225 29 23. In summer, there are many individual foreign visitors and package bus excursions, and you can often tag along with one of these groups and share costs.

You'll be shown around the whole 1st floor and the western side of the ground floor, altogether about 50 castle rooms. In the carefully restored original interiors – representing various styles and periods – you will find heaps of paintings, sculptures and *objets d'art* of all descriptions. The 18th-century theatre (reshaped later), the ballroom, and the dining room with a table that seats 80 people are among the highlights. Brochures in English are available.

After viewing the castle's rooms, you'll be shown around the **orangery** adjoining the castle, and then will go to see Potocki's collection of 55 **carriages** in the coach house, south of the castle. A further 75 old, horse-drawn vehicles have been acquired by the museum since WWII, making this one of the largest collections of its kind. Both the orangery and carriages are visited on the same ticket as the castle, with the same guided tour.

You can then individually visit a **collection of icons** (adult/concession 6/3.50zł; 9am-4pm). There are over 1000 icons here, from the 15th century onwards, but this is essentially a storage facility and only a small portion is on display.

The castle is surrounded by a well-kept **park** (admission free; 7am-sunset).

Just outside the park to the west is the **synagogue** (adult/concession 7/4zł; 10.30am-4.30pm Tue-Sun 15 Jun-30 Sep). Built in the 1760s, the synagogue has retained much of its original decoration. It can be visited in other months but you will need to request this a few days in advance by faxing 225 20 12.

Festivals & Events

In May, the **Old Music Festival** is held in Łańcut for about 10 days, with chamber music concerts performed in the castle ballroom. The festival has gained a high reputation and, given the limited capacity of the auditorium, tickets sell out fast. The castle is closed to visitors during the festival.

Sleeping & Eating

Hotel Zamkowy (☎ 225 26 71; fax 225 26 72; ul Zamkowa 1; d 60-165zł, tr 90-180zł) Located in the castle, the hotel is quite simple but OK and cheap, unless you need a room with a private bathroom, which are quite a bit dearer. It may be hard to find a vacancy here in summer. The hotel's Restauracja Zamkowa, across the small courtyard, has acceptable food at reasonable prices.

Dom Wycieczkowy PTTK (☎ 225 45 12; fax 225 31 84; ul Dominikańska 1; beds in d/tr/q 15-25zł; P) This 50-bed hostel, in the former Dominican monastery just off the Rynek, offers simple rooms with shared bathrooms that sleep from two to 10. It has its own restaurant.

Pensjonat-Restauracja Pałacyk (☎ /fax 225 20 43; www.palacyk.lancut.pl; ul Paderewskiego 18; d/apt 120/150zł) About 200m south of the synagogue, the Pałacyk (literally 'small palace') is set in a diminutive palacelike mansion and is a pleasant place to stay. It has six doubles and a suite, plus its own restaurant.

Hotel Szwadron (☎ 225 60 42; ul Mickiewicza 16; d/tr from €30/45; P) About 300m beyond the Pałacyk and housed in another historic mansion (from 1784), the Szwadron has 26 beds and a restaurant – another agreeable family-run place for the night.

Getting There & Away

The bus terminal is 500m northeast of the castle while the train station is about 2km north; it's therefore more convenient to arrive and depart by bus.

Buses to Rzeszów (4zł, 30 minutes) run roughly every half-hour, and to Przemyśl (8.70zł, 1½ hours) every hour or two.

PRZEMYŚL

☎ 16 / pop 70,000

Przemyśl (*psheh*-mishl) is a small, sleepy town located close to the Ukrainian border and some way off the usual tourist route. It's an agreeable little place though, with an attractive main square, a couple of worthwhile museums to explore and plenty of places to sit and relax with a cold drink on a warm day.

Founded in the 10th century on terrain long fought over by Poland and Ruthenia, Przemyśl changed hands several times before being annexed by the Polish Crown in 1340. It experienced its golden period in the 16th century, and declined afterwards. During the Partitions it fell under Austrian administration.

In around 1850 the Austrians began to fortify Przemyśl. This work continued right up until the outbreak of WWI, and was responsible for producing one of the largest fortresses in Europe, perhaps the second-biggest after Verdun in France. It consisted of a double ring of earth ramparts, including a 15km-long inner circle and an outer girdle three times longer, with over 60 forts placed at strategic points. This formidable system played an important role during WWI but nevertheless the garrison surrendered to the Russians in 1915 due to a lack of provisions.

At the end of WWII, only 60% of Przemyśl's buildings were left. The major historic monuments in the Old Town were restored, while new districts sprang up on the opposite (northern) side of the San River.

Orientation

MAPS

The 1:15,000 *Przemyśl Plus 6* map is widely available and, usefully, also features maps of Sanok, Łańcut and Ustrzyki Dolne.

Information

INTERNET ACCESS

The **Internet Game Cafe** (☎ 676 92 60; ul Ratuszowa 8) is the most central, though it seems mainly to function as a noisy gaming centre for local kids. Alternatively, check the Internet service in the **Miejska Biblioteka Publiczna** (City Public Library; ul Słowackiego 15), located in the old synagogue, or **Blue Net** (☎ 678 55 62; ul Słowackiego 14) next door.

MONEY

Bank Pekao branches at ul Jagiellońska 7 and ul Mickiewicza 6 handle travellers cheque transactions and have useful ATMs, and you'll find more ATMs around the Old Town. There are several *kantors* in the town centre, some of which may offer poor exchange rates; shop around.

TOURIST INFORMATION

Centrum Informacji Turystycznej (☎ 675 16 64; oitinform@wp.pl; Rynek 26; ☙ 8am-6pm Mon-Fri, 9am-3pm Sat May-Aug, 8am-4pm Mon-Fri Sep-Apr) Just off the northern side of the square, has friendly, English-speaking staff and plenty of maps. It can arrange accommodation too.

Sights

Perched on a hillside and dominated by four mighty churches, the **Old Town** is a picturesque place, pleasant for leisurely strolls. The sloping **Rynek** has preserved some of its old arcaded houses, mostly on its southern and northern sides.

The **Franciscan Church** (Kościół Franciszkański), just off the Rynek, was built between 1754 and 1778 in late-baroque style, but its monumental façade was remade later. The church has a beautiful interior with florid baroque decoration of both the altars and vault.

Just up the hill behind it stands the former **Jesuit Church** (Kościół Pojezuicki). Built between 1627 and 1659, it's also a baroque construction, and it has its original façade. The church now serves the Uniat congregation. All the Catholic fittings have been removed and replaced with decoration related to the Eastern rite, principally the heavily gilded iconostasis.

The adjacent former Jesuit college shelters the **Archdiocesan Museum** (Muzeum Archidiecezjalne; ☎ 678 27 92; Plac Czackiego 2; admission free; ☙ 10am-3pm May-Oct), which contains religious art.

Up the hill is one more house of worship, the **Carmelite Church** (Kościół Karmelitów). Designed by Italian architect Galeazzo Appiani (who also built Krasiczyn castle, see p224), the church has preserved some of its original features, including the main doorway and stucco work on the vaulting. Note the large wooden pulpit in the shape of a boat complete with mast, sail and rigging.

A few steps down from the church is the **Regional Museum** (Muzeum Ziemi Przemyskiej;

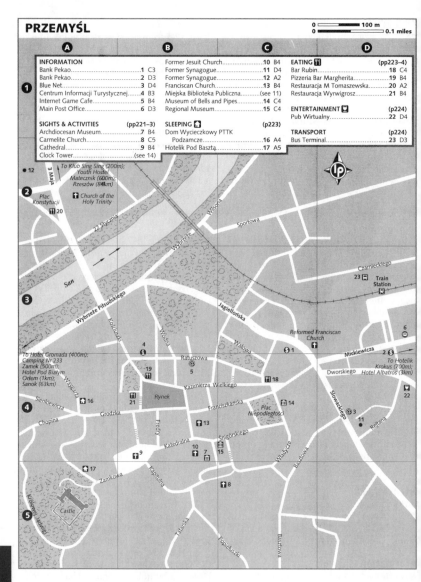

PRZEMYŚL

0 — 100 m
0 — 0.1 miles

INFORMATION		Former Jesuit Church	10 B4	EATING	(pp223–4)
Bank Pekao	1 C3	Former Synagogue	11 D4	Bar Rubin	18 C4
Bank Pekao	2 D3	Former Synagogue	12 A2	Pizzeria Bar Margherita	19 B4
Blue Net	3 D4	Franciscan Church	13 B4	Restauracja M Tomaszewska	20 A2
Centrum Informacji Turystycznej	4 B3	Miejska Biblioteka Publiczna	(see 11)	Restauracja Wyrwigrosz	21 B4
Internet Game Cafe	5 B4	Museum of Bells and Pipes	14 C4		
Main Post Office	6 D3	Regional Museum	15 C4	ENTERTAINMENT	(p224)
				Pub Wirtualny	22 D4
SIGHTS & ACTIVITIES	(pp221–3)	SLEEPING	(p223)		
Archdiocesan Museum	7 B4	Dom Wycieczkowy PTTK		TRANSPORT	(p224)
Carmelite Church	8 C5	Podzamcze	16 A4	Bus Terminal	23 D3
Cathedral	9 B4	Hotelik Pod Basztą	17 A5		
Clock Tower	(see 14)				

Former Jesuit Church........................10 B4
Former Synagogue............................11 D4
Former Synagogue............................12 A2
Franciscan Church.............................13 B4
Miejska Biblioteka Publiczna.........(see 11)
Museum of Bells and Pipes.............14 C4
Regional Museum.............................15 C4

To Klub Sing Sing (200m);
Youth Hostel
Matecznik (600m);
Rzeszów (84km)

3 Maja

12

Plac
Konstytucji

Church of the
Holy Trinity

20

22 Stycznia

Wybrzeże

Wiocha

Sportowa

San

Czarnieckiego

Wybrzeże Piłsudskiego

Kokocha

Jagiellońska

23 Train
Station

6

Reformed Franciscan
Church

Walowa

Mickiewicza

2

To Hotel Gromada (400m);
Camping Nr 233
Zamek (500m);
Hotel Pod Białym
Orłem (1km);
Sanok (63km)

4

Wodna

Ratuszowa
5

19

18

To Hotelik
Krokus (700m);
Hotel Albatros (3km)

Dworskiego

Słowackiego

3

11

22

Sienkiewicza

16

Grodzka

21

Fredry

Rynek

Kazimierza Wielkiego

Franciszkańska

13

Plac
Niepodległości

14

Słowackiego

Reitana

Chopina

Katedralna

10

Śnigórskiego

Wałowa

9

7
15

Wybrzeże

Basztowa

Kapitulna

17

Zamkowa

8

Kościuszki Leśnika

Castle

Tatarska

Popiełuszki

Basztowa

☎ 678 33 25; Plac Czackiego 3; adult/concession 4/2zł; ⏱ 10.30am-5.30pm Tue & Fri; 10am-2pm Wed, Thu, Sat & Sun). On the ground floor, there's a dry assortment of local archaeological finds, while upstairs you'll find a small collection of Ruthenian icons and other religious art dating back to the 15th century, as well as liturgical items recalling the town's Jew-ish heritage. Also here is an exhibition on the history of the Przemyśl fortress, with photographs, postcards, weapons and com-memorative mementos. Other rooms are taken up by temporary displays.

A short walk west along ul Katedralna is the **cathedral** with its 71m-high freestand-ing bell tower. Originally a Gothic building (still visible in the vault in the chancel), the church was remodelled on various occasions and is now predominantly baroque.

Continue up the same street to the **castle**, or rather what is left of it. Built by Kazimierz Wielki in the 1340s, it mutated into a Renaissance building two centuries later when it got its four corner towers. Two of them have been repaired along with one side of the castle. A local theatre, Teatr Fredreum, and a café now occupy the restored rooms. One of the towers is open to visitors in summer, but the view over the Old Town is obscured by trees.

Together at last, Przemyśl's oddest assemblage of artefacts is on show at the **Museum of Bells & Pipes** (Muzeum Dzwonów i Fajek; ☎ 678 96 66; ul Władycze 3; adult/concession 4/2zł; ⏰ 10.30am-5.30pm Tue, Fri & Sat, 10am-2pm Wed & Thu, 11am-7pm Sun), housed in an 18th-century baroque Clock Tower. Here you can cast an eye over several floors of antique bells and elaborately carved pipes. It's anybody's guess what the connection is, though it's the pipes, which include some fantastically ornate examples, as well as lots of workaday ones, which are the more engaging. Unfortunately, labelling is only in Polish. There's also a case of cigar cutters for a touch of variety, while the rooftop affords a panoramic view of the town.

Those very interested in military matters may be drawn to the famous Austro-Hungarian **fortifications**. As these were mostly earth ramparts, however, they are now seriously overgrown with grass and bushes and resemble natural rather than artificial bulwarks. If you want to see what's left anyway, perhaps the best places to go are **Siedliska** (Fort I), **Łętownia** (Fort VIII) and **Bolestraszyce** (Fort XIII). The tourist office can give you information about these sites and transport details.

The only significant relics of the Jewish legacy are two **synagogues** (of four existing before WWII), both dating from the end of the 19th and beginning of the 20th centuries, renovated after the war and given other uses. One is off Plac Konstytucji, on the northern side of the San River; the other (now the city public library) is on ul Słowackiego.

Sleeping

Przemyśl has no shortage of beds in modest budget-range hotels, plus a few good mid-range options.

BUDGET
Dom Wycieczkowy PTTK Podzamcze (☎ 678 53 74, ☎ /fax 678 32 74; ul Waygarta 3; dm/d 17.50/53zł; [P]) Conveniently located just one block from the Rynek, the PTTK hostel has the usual basic but clean rooms, and shared kitchens.

Youth Hostel Matecznik (☎ /fax 670 61 45; ul Lelewela 6; dm 16-20zł; [P]) This big PTSM hostel is across the River San, just over 1km north of the Old Town. It's on a quiet side street off the main thoroughfare, ul 3 Maja.

Camping Nr 233 Zamek (☎ /fax 675 02 65; Wybrzeże Piłsudskiego 8A; d/tr/q 34/50/65zł; [P]) This camping ground has fairly simple rooms in year-round cabins and is quite close to the centre. Seasonal cabins are open from May to September.

MID-RANGE
Hotel Gromada (☎ 676 11 11; www.hotels.gromada .pl; Wybrzeże Piłsudskiego 4; s/d Mon-Thu 159/199zł, Fri-Sun 139/185zł; [P] [X]) Offering the expected high standards and range of facilities of the countrywide Gromada chain, this modern, central hotel has 116 comfortable rooms and its own restaurant. The weekend rates are excellent value.

Hotel Pod Białym Orłem (☎ /fax 678 61 07; ul Sanocka 13; d/tr/apt 120/145/250zł; [P]) Located about 1km west of the Old Town, this 16-room hotel is an affordable option with private facilities and is within easy walking distance of the Old Town.

Hotel Albatros (☎ 678 08 70; www.albatros.c-net.pl; ul Ofiar Katynia 26; s/d/tr/q 119/149/179/199zł; [P]) The Albatros is an outwardly anonymous, concrete box affair some 3km east of the town centre, but it's a big, bright place with a wide range of rooms and a good restaurant. It also has its own travel agency.

Hotelik Pod Basztą (☎ 678 82 68; ul Królowej Jadwigi 4; s/d/tr 39/59/89zł) Enjoying a quiet, central location, this small hotel offers one single, five doubles and one triple. Rooms don't have private facilities.

Hotelik Krokus (☎ /fax 678 51 27; ul Mickiewicza 47; s/d 60/100zł) About 1.3km east of the Rynek, the Krokus provides adequate standards in rooms with private facilities. It's not far from the train station.

Eating & Drinking
Restauracja M Tomaszewska (☎ 670 72 40; Plac Konstytucji 3 Maja 6; mains 12-45zł; ⏰ 9am-9pm) Just north of the river, Tomaszewska is an

elegant and surprisingly inexpensive place serving good-quality Polish cuisine in attractive surrounds reminiscent of a *belle époque* salon, complete with ferns, swags, old photographs and regal portraits.

Pizzeria Bar Margherita (☎ 678 98 98; Rynek 4; mains 5.50-20zł; ☯ lunch & dinner) This inviting place has a long list of pizzas, plus risotto, pasta and fast food such as hot dogs. One of the cheapest eateries around.

Bar Rubin (☎ 678 25 78; ul Kazimierza Wielkiego 19; mains 8-20zł; ☯ lunch & dinner) This small and friendly family restaurant is one of the best places to grab a bite to eat in the Old Town, with tasty Polish food at very affordable prices. There are only seven tables, so you may well have to wait a few minutes in the midafternoon.

Restauracja Wyrwigrosz (☎ 678 58 58; Rynek 20; mains 7-20zł; ☯ lunch & dinner) For a break from Polish cuisine, this restaurant-cum-pub offers budget Asian-style food. It has a pleasant outdoor eating/drinking area in summer, with comfortable wicker chairs and a view over the Rynek.

The Restauracja Wyrwigrosz is a good place for a drink. Alternatively, you can try the modern **Pub Wirtualny** (☎ 676 04 70; ul Dworskiego 12), which also has an outdoor section.

Entertainment

Klub Sing Sing (☎ 677 05 00; ul 3 Maja 19) Occupying a spacious basement of the Dom Handlowy Szpak, a shopping centre 200m past Plac Konstytucji, Sing Sing has a restaurant, bar, pizzeria, pool tables and one of the trendiest discos in town.

Getting There & Away

The train and bus stations are next to each other, on the northeastern edge of the town centre.

BUS

At least five buses run daily to Sanok (8.70zł, 1½ hours). Buses also go to Ustrzyki Dolne (9.60zł, two hours, three to four daily) and Rzeszów (11zł, two hours, 10 daily).

TRAIN

Trains to Rzeszów (21zł, 1½ hours) depart regularly throughout the day. There are half a dozen fast trains and two express trains a day to Kraków (41zł, three to four hours). One express and two fast trains go daily to

Warsaw (50zł, four to five hours), and one fast train runs to Lublin (40zł, three hours). International trains to Lviv, Odesa and Kyiv pass via Przemyśl.

Have a look at the station building, a neobaroque piece of architecture, now an historic monument. Built in 1895, it retains some of its decoration, both inside and out.

KRASICZYN
☎ 16 / pop 1000

No-one would notice the small village of Krasiczyn (krah-*shee*-chin) if not for its **castle** (☎ 671 83 16; adult/concession 5.50/3.50zł; ☯ for tours only), a late-Renaissance construction acclaimed as one of the finest of its kind in the country. It's in a spacious landscaped **park** (tours adult/concession 1/0.50zł; ☯ dawn-dusk) abounding with a variety of trees and shrubs.

The castle was designed by an Italian, Galleazzo Appiani, and built between 1592 and 1618 for the wealthy Krasicki family. Despite numerous wars and fires it has somehow retained most of its original features though it is not in good shape. It has been partly restored over recent decades.

The castle is more or less square, built around a spacious, partly arcaded courtyard, with four different cylindrical corner towers. They were supposed to reflect the social order of the period and were named (clockwise from the southwestern corner) after God, the pope, the king and the nobility. The God tower, topped with a dome, houses a chapel. The fifth, square tower, in the middle of the western side, served as the main entrance to the castle and is accessible by a long arcaded bridge over a wide moat. The king (Royal) tower houses the enticingly titled **Gallery of the Industrial Development Agency**, which showcases works by contemporary local artists. Admission is included in the main castle ticket.

Tourists can visit the courtyard and three of the corner towers in summer. Visits are in groups with a guide, which depart on the hour between 10am and 4pm.

Sleeping & Eating

Hotel Zamkowy (☎ 671 83 21; www.krasiczyn.motronik .com.pl; Krasiczyn 179; s/d/tr/ste from 130/210/270/330zł; Ⓟ ☒) The Hotel Zamkowy, in the castle's former coach house, must be one of the most attractive and evocative places to stay n the whole of Poland, offering elegant, comfortable modern rooms in a unique and historic setting. The suites come in blue, pink or green and there's a gym, sauna, solarium and restaurant. Even better, you can also stay in wonderfully restored rooms in the castle itself (doubles/suites cost 210zł/ 400zł). Other accommodation options include the self-contained five-bed Hunter's Pavilion (800zł), which has its own kitchen and garden, and the charming 17th-century Swiss Pavilion (doubles/suites cost 180zł/ 270zł), which reputedly comes with its own resident ghost. Bikes and fishing equipment can be rented, while you can also take a boat out on the pond (15zł per hour). Package deals are available.

Getting There & Away

The castle is a short round trip from Przemyśl (2.80zł, 20 minutes) on one of the PKS buses or the regular suburban bus 40. You can continue from Krasiczyn to Sanok (7.80zł, one hour, four daily) or Ustrzyki Dolne (8.70zł, 1½ hours, three daily).

THE BIESZCZADY

The Bieszczady (byesh-*chah*-di) is a wild, scantily populated mountain region of thick forests and open meadows. It's in the far southeastern corner of Poland, sandwiched between the Ukrainian and Slovakian borders. Largely unspoilt and unpolluted, it's one of the most attractive areas in the country. As tourist facilities are modest, roads sparse and public transport limited, the Bieszczady retains its relative isolation and makes for an off-the-beaten-track destination. It's popular with nature-lovers and hikers. Large-scale tourism hasn't yet arrived.

In geographical terms, the Bieszczady is a mountain system running east–west for some 60km along Poland's southern frontier, with lower hills to the north, referred to as the Przedgórze Bieszczadzkie. In practical terms, the Bieszczady is the whole area to the southeast of the Nowy Łupków–Zagórz–Ustrzyki Dolne railway line, up to the national borders: approximately 2100 sq km, about 60% of which is forest, largely fir and beech. Trees survive only to an altitude of about 1200m, above

which you find the *połoniny*, steppelike pastures that are particularly lush in the month of June.

The highest and most spectacular part has been decreed the Bieszczady National Park (Bieszczadzki Park Narodowy), and at 271 sq km it's Poland's third-largest national park after Biebrza and Kampinos. The highest peak is Mt Tarnica (1346m).

The region was once much more densely populated than it is today – and not by Poles, but by ethnic groups known as Boyks and Lemks. See the boxed text on p227 for more about them. You can visit the skansen (open-air museum of traditional architecture) in Sanok, which has some good examples of Boyk and Lemk architecture.

SANOK

☎ 13 / pop 40,000

For most Poles, Sanok probably brings to mind the Autosan – the locally produced bus, used in intercity and urban transportation throughout the country. The bus factory, along with several other plants, makes the town an important regional industrial centre. More interestingly, Sanok is also the starting point for the fascinating Icon Trail (p229), a signposted walking route taking in the surrounding countryside's wealth of churches. The small town centre is pleasant enough, and there are a number of important attractions in the vicinity, including the excellent Museum of Folk Architecture, said to be one of the finest open-air museums in Europe.

Information

MONEY

Bank Pekao's branches at ul Mickiewicza 29 and ul Kościuszki 4 change travellers cheques and have ATMs. There are half a dozen *kantors* on ul Kościuszki in the vicinity of the latter Pekao branch, and more in the centre.

TOURIST INFORMATION

In the absence of a municipal tourist office, the helpful **PTTK office** (☎ 463 21 71; www .sanok.pl; ul 3 Maja 2; 8am-4pm Mon-Fri) performs this role. More brochures and information can be had at the tourist information desk inside **Orbis Travel** (☎ 463 28 59; ul Grzegorza 4; 8am-5pm Mon-Fri, 9am-1pm Sat). Both can also arrange accommodation.

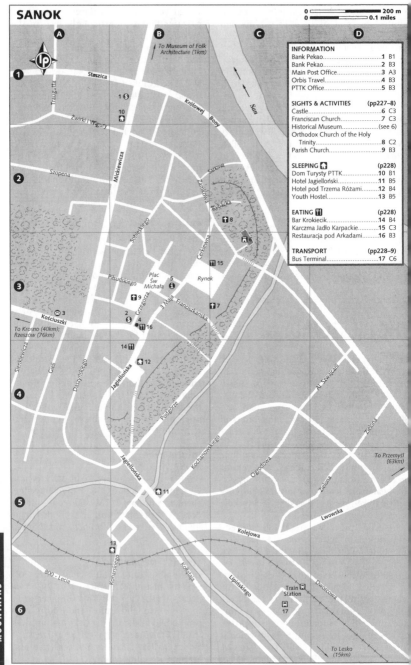

SANOK

0 — 200 m
0 — 0.1 miles

To Museum of Folk
Architecture (1km)

To Krosno (40km);
Rzeszów (76km)

To Przemyśl
(63km)

Train
Station

To Lesko
(15km)

THE CARPATHIAN
MOUNTAINS

THE BOYKS & THE LEMKS – VARIATIONS ON A THEME

The Bieszczady, as well as the Beskid Niski and Beskid Sądecki further west, were settled from about the 13th century by various nomadic groups migrating from the south and east. Most notable among them were the Wołosi from the Balkans and the Rusini from Ruthenia. Living in the same areas and intermarrying for centuries, they slowly developed into distinct ethnic groups known as the Bojkowie and Łemkowie.

The Bojkowie (Boyks) inhabited the eastern part of the Bieszczady, roughly east of Cisna, while the Łemkowie (Lemks) populated mountainous regions stretching from western Bieszczady up to the Beskid Sądecki. The two groups had much in common culturally, though there were noticeable differences in dialects, dress and architecture. They shared the Orthodox creed with their Ukrainian neighbours.

After the Union of Brest in 1596, most Lemks and Boyks turned to the Uniat Church, which accepted the supremacy of Rome but retained old Eastern rites and religious practices. From the end of the 19th century, however, the Roman Catholic hierarchy slowly but systematically imposed Latin rites. In response, many locals opted for a return to the Orthodox Church. By WWII both creeds were practised in the region, coexisting with varying degrees of harmony and conflict. By that time the total population of Boyks and Lemks was estimated at 200,000 to 300,000. Ethnic Poles were a minority in the region and consequently the Roman Catholic Church was insignificant.

All this changed dramatically in the aftermath of WWII when the borders were moved and the new government was installed. Not everyone was satisfied with the new status quo and some of its opponents didn't lay down their arms. One such armed faction was the Ukrainian Resistance Army, which operated in the Bieszczady. Civil war continued in the region for almost two years.

In order to destroy the rebel base, the government decided to expel the inhabitants of all the villages in the region and resettle the entire area. In the so-called Operation Vistula (Operacja Wisła) in 1947, most of the population was brutally deported either to the Soviet Union or to the northern and western Polish territories just regained from Germany. Ironically, the main victims of the action were the Boyks and the Lemks, who had little to do with the conflict apart from the fact that they happened to live there. Moreover, Lemks were also deported from areas further west where there was no partisan activity. Their villages were abandoned or destroyed, and those that survived were resettled with new inhabitants from other regions. Only some 20,000 Lemks were left in the whole region, and very few Boyks.

Today, the most evident survivors of their tragic history are the Orthodox or Uniat churches. These dilapidated wooden buildings still dot the countryside and add to the region's natural beauty. When hiking on remote trails, especially along the Ukrainian border, you'll find traces of destroyed villages, including ruined houses and orchards.

Sights

One of Sanok's star attractions is the **Historical Museum** (Muzeum Historyczne; ☎ 464 13 66; ul Zamkowa 2; admission 10zł; ⊙ noon-3pm Mon, 9am-5pm Tue-Sun 16 Jun-15 Sep, noon-3pm Mon, 9am-5pm Tue & Wed, 9am-3pm Thu-Sun 16 Sep-15 Jun). Housed in a 16th-century castle, thoroughly refurbished over recent years, the museum has several sections, of which the highlight is a 700-piece collection of Ruthenian icons, the best in Poland. The selection on display consists of about 450 pieces, dating from the 15th to 18th centuries. They are displayed in roughly chronological order, so you can study the evolution of the style: the pure, somewhat unreal early images gradually giving way to the greater realism of later icons, which show the Roman Catholic influence. Most icons were acquired after WWII from abandoned Uniat churches. If you are particularly interested in icons, note that there are also collections in Przemyśl, Łańcut, Nowy Sącz and in Sanok's skansen.

The museum's other treasure is the collection of paintings by Zdzisław Beksiński, presented on the castle's top floor. Beksiński is one of Poland's most remarkable contemporary painters, who was born and lived in Sanok. The exhibition features 90-odd paintings, including some of his best works.

Another place you shouldn't miss is the local skansen, the **Museum of Folk Architecture** (Muzeum Budownictwa Ludowego; ☎ 463 16 72; ul Rybickiego 3; adult/concession 9/6zł; ✆ 8am-6pm May-Oct, 8am-4pm Nov-Apr), 1.5km north of the centre. Poland's largest open-air museum, it has gathered about 120 traditional buildings from the southeast of the country and provides an insight into the culture of the Boyks and Lemks. Among the buildings, there are four beautiful timber churches (one Catholic and three Orthodox/Uniat ones), an inn, a school and even a fire brigade station. The interiors of many cottages are furnished and decorated as they once were, while some buildings house exhibitions; one of these features a collection of 200 icons.

Visits are in guided groups of up to 20 people (in Polish), and the tour takes about two hours. In summer, there may be some English-speaking guides – inquire at the ticket office, or preferably call in advance on ☎ 463 16 72. Tours cost 30zł per group, in addition to the entry ticket. You can buy a leaflet in English or German with a short description of selected objects. There's a café at the entrance serving the usual fare of snacks and light dishes. Bus 1 or 3 from the Rynek will let you off by the bridge leading across the San River to the skansen.

Of the town's churches, the oldest (built in the 1630s) is the **Franciscan Church** (ul Franciszkanska), but it was reshaped several times after its construction. In the left altar is the venerated painting of the Virgin Mary. The neo-Romanesque **parish church** (ul Grzegorza), dating from 1874 to 1886, has Art Nouveau wall paintings. The neoclassical **Orthodox Church of the Holy Trinity** (ul Zamkowa) was built in 1784 and initially served the Uniat congregation; it's open at 10.30am and 5pm for Sunday Mass, but can be opened on request for visitors – inquire at the building next door.

Sleeping

Hotel Jagielloński (☎ /fax 463 12 08; ul Jagiellońska 49; s/d/tr from 90/110/130zł; **P**) Jagielloński is the best place to stay in town, and is excellent value. Rooms are spacious and have private facilities. It has its own restaurant, which, like the hotel itself, is probably the best eatery in town (mains 16zł to 32zł; open for lunch and dinner).

Hotel Pod Trzema Różami (☎ /fax 463 09 22; ul Jagiellońska 13; s/d 75/95zł; **P**) About 200m south of the main square, Under Three Roses is a small place that offers rather plain but perfectly clean and acceptable rooms and a convenient city centre location. It also has a pizzeria in the basement.

Youth hostel (☎ /fax 463 09 25; ul Konarskiego 10; dm 12-15zł; ✆ Jul & Aug) One of the very cheapest places to stay in town, the local youth hostel is a modest 60-bed establishment between the bus terminal and the centre.

Dom Turysty PTTK (☎ 463 10 13, ☎ /fax 463 14 39; ul Mickiewicza 29; dm/d/tr 18/50/75zł) This large year-round PTTK hostel offers plenty of beds. Private bathrooms and low prices may seem an attractive option, but some rooms are on the shabby side. Make sure to inspect the room before you decide. The hostel has its own restaurant, which is basic but very cheap.

Eating

Most of the places to stay have their own eating facilities. Other eating options worthy of mention:

Bar Krokiecik (ul Jagiellońska 2; mains 5-10zł; ✆ lunch & dinner) Krokiecik is one of the cheapest acceptable options for a meal.

Restauracja Pod Arkadami (☎ 464 44 54; ul Grzegorza 2; mains 10-20zł; ✆ lunch & dinner) This basement restaurant is not particularly memorable, but it provides some solid Polish food.

Karczma Jadło Karpackie (☎ 464 67 00; Rynek 12; mains 12-25zł; ✆ 9am-10pm) This is an amenable, folksy bar and restaurant on the main square, serving up the usual range of Polish dishes and beer.

Getting There & Away

The train and bus stations are next to each other, a bit over 1km southeast of the centre.

Two fast trains run to Warsaw daily (55zł, five hours) and two to Kraków (35zł, 3½ hours). A dozen ordinary trains go to Jasło (18zł, two hours) via Krosno.

There's regular bus transport to Rzeszów (10.60zł, 1½ hours) and Lesko (3.80zł, 20 minutes). Buses also run to Ustrzyki Dolne (6.20zł, one hour, about 10 daily) and Ustrzyki Górne (10.50zł, 1½ hours, six daily). There are several buses to Cisna (7.80zł, one hour) and Wetlina (8.90zł, 1½ hours) plus additional buses in summer. A couple of buses go to Komańcza (6.20zł, one hour). Five fast buses go directly to Kraków (31zł, three hours) and two to Warsaw (40zł, four to five hours).

AROUND SANOK
Icon Trail

The environs of Sanok are sprinkled with small villages, many of which still boast old Orthodox or Uniat **churches**, a reminder of the prewar ethnic and religious fabric of the region. You can see many of these churches on a marked walking trail, called the Szlak Ikon (Icon Trail). The first, and most popular, route is a 70km loop path that begins and ends in Sanok and winds along the San River valley north of the city. The net walking time is about 15 hours, and it's also suitable for bicycles.

The route covers about a dozen churches, most of which are charming small timber structures typical of the region. Most date from the 18th and 19th centuries, but the route also includes the oldest Orthodox timber church in Poland, in **Ulucz**, built in 1510. You can visit all the churches on the way; arrangements have been made with each of the churches' hosts to let visitors in and show them around. A small donation is appreciated.

A longer route follows the Osława River valley south of Sanok into the Bieszcady, and almost up to the Slovak border, although it's not marked in the same way as most of the churches here are close to the main road. One of the more interesting churches on this trail is the wooden Orthodox church at Turzańsk, built in 1803 (see p234).

A large board in front of Sanok's castle has the first route's sketch map and general description (in Polish). Inquire at Sanok's PTTK office or Orbis Travel for further information and brochures with the trails' descriptions (published in Polish and English). They include details of where to ask to have the church opened for you. Also inquire at the office about accommodation and eating options along the routes.

Czerteż

Czerteż is a small village 5km northwest of Sanok on the Rzeszów road. It has a beautiful wooden Uniat church, dating from 1772, still fitted out the original iconostasis.

It's not included in the Icon Trail, but it's one of the best churches in the region and is worth a short trip. Sanok urban buses will drop you nearby. The church is hidden in the cluster of tall trees behind an agricultural cooperative. It can be visited under the same arrangements as churches on the Icon Trail. The PTTK office may provide further information.

LESKO
☎ 13 / pop 6200

Founded in 1470, Lesko had a mixed Polish-Ruthenian population, a reflection of the region's history. From the 16th century onwards, many Jews arrived, initially from Spain, trying to escape the Inquisition. Their migration continued to such an extent that by the 18th century, Jews made up half of the town's population.

WWII and the years that followed changed the ethnic picture altogether. The Jews were slaughtered by the Nazis, the Ukrainians were defeated by the Polish military and the Lemks were deported. The town was rebuilt, and without having developed any significant industry, is now a small tourist centre, a stopover on the way south into the Bieszczady.

Information
TOURIST INFORMATION
Bieszczadzkie Centrum Informacji Turystycznej
(☎ 469 66 95; 🕑 8am-4pm Mon-Fri) Located in a pavilion next to the town hall on the Rynek. A large town map, posted on a board next to the office, is useful for orientation.

Sights

Lesko is notable for its Jewish heritage. The 17th-century **synagogue** (ul Joselewicza), just off the Rynek, has a Spanish flavour and its tower is a sure sign that it was once part of the town's defensive system. The interior houses an art gallery but little of its original decoration has survived. At the front is what looks like a row of small houses built on to the main structure; these served as a prayer hall for women.

Follow ul Moniuszki downhill from the synagogue and you'll see stairs on the right leading up to the old **Jewish cemetery**. More than 1000 gravestones, the oldest ones dating back to the mid-16th century, are scattered amid trees and high grass. Some of them have amazingly rich decoration.

Left in total isolation, in different stages of decay, they're a very impressive sight.

Go back to the Rynek, passing the 19th-century **town hall** in the middle, and head 200m north to the **parish church** (ul Kościuszki). It was built in 1539 and its exterior still retains many Gothic features. The freestanding baroque bell tower was added in 1725. At that time the church's interior got its baroque overlay, including the high altar and ornate pulpit.

Lesko has a **castle** – it's on the Sanok road, 200m downhill from the Rynek. Built at the beginning of the 16th century, it lost most of its original form with extensive neoclassical alterations. Postwar restoration converted it into a hotel.

Sleeping & Eating

Hotelik Ratuszowa (☎ 469 86 32; ratuszowa@ooh.pl; Rynek 12; s/d/tr 50/70/125zł) This cosy place has small, plain rooms in the centre of town. It's one of the better places to stay.

Motel Fux (☎ 469 67 81; ul Bieszczadzka 4; s/d/tr 20/40/60zł; P) Fux, just behind the petrol station, is a fairly unprepossessing place offering basic but clean rooms. The price is hard to beat though.

Pensjonat Zamek (☎ 469 62 68; fax 469 68 78; ul Piłsudskiego 7; s/d/tr 90/110/138zł) Located in the castle (but don't expect stylish castle chambers), Pensjonat Zamek was once a holiday centre for miners. It's now a regular hotel with 100 beds and a gym. It also hires out mountain bikes.

Camping Nad Sanem (☎ 469 66 89; ul Turystyczna 1; beds per person 18zł, half board 36zł; ☼ May-Sep) The camping ground is on the riverside beneath the castle. It has a dozen bungalows with rooms of different sizes, an area where you can pitch your tent and a restaurant.

There are half a dozen basic eateries on or near the Rynek.

Getting There & Away

There's no railway in Lesko. The bus terminal is on ul Piłsudskiego (the road to Sanok), about 1km from the Rynek. It's convenient to all the hotels reviewed.

There are plenty of buses to Sanok (3.80zł, 20 minutes), a dozen of which continue to Krosno (7.80zł, one hour). About 10 buses run to Rzeszów daily (11.50zł, two hours) and one goes directly to Kraków (30zł, three hours).

For the Bieszczady, there are several buses to Cisna daily (6.50zł, one hour) and some wind up as far as Wetlina (7.80zł, 1½ hours). Three or four buses to Ustrzyki Górne (10.20zł, two hours;) go via Ustrzyki Dolne. In summer, there are a couple of extra buses to each of these destinations.

USTRZYKI DOLNE

☎ 13 / pop 8800

An uninspiring town in the southeastern corner of Poland, Ustrzyki Dolne (oost-*shi*-kee *dol*-neh) is really only an overnight stop for those heading south into the Bieszczady. There's not much to see here except for the **Natural History Museum** (Muzeum Przyrodnicze; ☎ 461 10 91; ul Bełska 7; adult/concession 3/2zł; ☼ 9am-5pm Tue-Sat year-round, 9am-2pm Sun Jul & Aug), just off the Rynek, which is a good introduction to the geology, flora and fauna of the Bieszczady National Park.

If you plan on trekking up to the mountains independently, Ustrzyki Dolne is the last reliable place to stock up on a decent range of provisions and to exchange money. Further south, food supplies will be more limited.

Information

MONEY

There are a few *kantors*, including one in the tourist office. **Bank Pekao** (Rynek 17) is next door and has an ATM in the Dom Handlowy Halicz, a shopping centre just east of the Rynek. There's another ATM opposite the museum.

TOURIST INFORMATION

Bieszczadzkie Centrum Informacji i Promocji (☎ 471 11 30; Rynek 16; ☼ 8am-5pm Mon-Fri)

Information desk (☼ 9am-5pm Tue-Sat year-round, 9am-2pm Sun Jul & Aug) At the museum. Has information on Bieszczady National Park.

Sleeping & Eating

There are half a dozen regular places to stay in town and many locals rent out rooms in their homes.

Willa Stasia (☎ 461 11 11; willa_stasia@op.pl; ul Ustjanowa Górna 58; d/tr/apt 100/135/180zł; P) Stasia is a traditional, wooden chalet-style hotel with attractive, pine-clad rooms and bright modern bathrooms. The apartments are large and very comfortable.

Dom Wyczasowy Laworta (☎ 461 11 78; www
lwlaworta.com.pl in Polish; ul Nadgórna 107; s/d/tr/
ot 95/140/180/380zł; P ☂) To the north of
own, high on the mountain slope, around
.5km uphill from the train and bus sta-
ions, Laworta is a big, peaceful place set
n its own parkland. It has good facilities,
ncluding tennis courts and a sauna, and its
wn restaurant.

Hotelik Bieszczadzki (☎ 461 10 71; fax 461 10
4; Rynek 19; s/d/tr/q from 30/50/70/90zł) The most
entral place, the Bieszczadzki is quite sim-
le and has a similarly simple budget res-
aurant. Rooms with en suite facilities cost
lightly more.

Getting There & Away

The train and bus stations are in one build-
ng. You won't get far by train (trains to
rzemyśl and on to Warsaw no longer op-
rate, and there are only a few to Zagórz
nd Jasło), but bus traffic is reasonable. Two
lozen buses run daily to Sanok (6.20zł, one
our) and pass Lesko (5zł, 30 minutes) on
he way. Five buses (several more in sum-
ner) go daily to Ustrzyki Górne (7.20zł, 1½
ours). Most come through from Przemyśl
r Sanok. There are also bus services to fur-
her destinations, including Przemyśl (9.60zł,
wo hours, five daily), Rzeszów (13.50zł, 2½
ours, five daily) and Kraków (34zł, four
ours, one daily).

USTRZYKI GÓRNE

☎ 13 / pop 500

Ustrzyki Górne is just a string of houses
oosely scattered along the road, rather than
village in the proper sense of the word.
Yet, it's the Bieszczady's major hiking base.

Thanks to its location in the heart of these
beautiful mountains (now a national park),
the place has long attracted trekkers curious
for something new and prepared for basic
facilities.

Since the Bieszczady loop road was built
between 1955 and 1962, the mountains
have become more accessible and fashionable. The region is changing but the process
is slow. It's still remote country and Ustrzyki Górne is a good example – there are
a few mostly rudimentary places to stay and
eat, a shop and not much else. The village
springs to life in summer, then sinks into a
deep sleep for most of the rest of the year,
only stirring a little in winter when cross-
country skiers arrive.

Sleeping & Eating

Apart from the places listed here, many
locals rent out rooms in their homes, and
even the priest provides beds for tourists
in a large house next to the church. Tiny
villages such as this one often don't have
street names, but general directions should
get you there.

Hotel Górski (☎ 461 06 04; fax 461 06 20; s/d from
€18/36; P ☂) This PTTK-run hotel, at the
end of the village, on the Ustrzyki Dolne
road, is significantly better and larger than
anything else around. It has 64 rooms – singles, doubles, triples, quads and suites – all
clean, comfortable and modern, and all
have their own bathrooms. The hotel has
a gym and sauna, and its own reasonably
priced restaurant.

Hotelik Biały (☎ 461 06 41; beds in 4- or 5-bed dm
25zł) This 63-bed hostel is run by the management of the Bieszczady National Park.

HIKING IN THE BIESZCZADY

The Bieszczady is one of the best places in Poland to go hiking. The region is beautiful and easy to
walk around, and you don't need a tent or cooking equipment as hostels and mountain hostels are
a day's walk apart and provide food. The main area for trekking is the national park, with Ustrzyki
Górne and Wetlina being the most popular starting points. You can also use Cisna as a base.

Once in the mountains, things become easier than you may expect. There are plenty of well-
marked trails giving a good choice of shorter and longer walks. All three jumping-off points have
PTTK hostels and friendly staff can give you information. All have boards depicting marked trails
complete with walking times, uphill and downhill, on all routes. The mountain hostels will put you
up for the night and feed you regardless of how crowded they get. In July and August the floor
will most likely be your bed, as these places are pretty small. Take a sleeping bag with you.

Get a copy of the *Bieszczady* map (scale 1:50,000) which covers the whole region, not just the
national park. The map is also helpful if you plan to explore the region using private transport.

THE CARPATHIAN MOUNTAINS

It's on a side road, about 500m from the turn-off next to the shop. It has slightly better standards than the Kremenaros.

Schronisko PTTK Kremenaros (☎ 0502 234 501; dm 19zł, beds in d/tr 22/20zł; ☻ Apr-Oct) Kremenaros is in the last house of the village on the Cisna road. It's old and basic, but staff is friendly and the atmosphere is good. The Gospoda Kremenaros has a very short menu but the food is cheap and acceptable.

Camping Nr 150 PTTK (☎ 461 06 17; tent sites/per person 6/6zł, beds in cabins from 38zł; ☻ May-Sep) The camping ground is in the northern part of the village. It has some old triple cabins without bathrooms and newer double cabins with bathrooms.

Apart from the two year-round PTTK eateries listed above, more places open in summer along the main road.

Getting There & Away
There are four buses daily to Ustrzyki Dolne (7zł, 1½ hours), two to Krosno (13.50zł, 2½ hours) and one bus to Rzeszów (25zł, 3½ hours). A couple more buses run in July and August to the above destinations, as well as several buses to Wetlina (3.80zł, 25 minutes) and Cisna (6.50zł, 45 minutes).

WETLINA
☎ 13 / pop 400
Wetlina is another popular jumping-off spot for hiking in the Bieszczady. In many ways it's similar to Ustrzyki Górne and has a limited choice of simple places to sleep and eat.

Sleeping & Eating
Zajazd Pod Połoniną (☎ 468 46 11; beds in d/tr/q 20-80zł) The 48-bed Zajazd has rooms with and without bathrooms and a budget restaurant. It may have bikes for hire.

Dom Wycieczkowy PTTK (☎ 463 22 04; dm/beds in d/tr 12/20-25zł) This old and basic hostel offers beds year-round in doubles/triples and larger dorms. In summer you can also stay in cabins and pitch your tent on the grounds. There's a straightforward restaurant here.

Pensjonat U Rumcajsa (☎ 468 46 33; s/d/tr 20/40/60zł; P) This small pension has basic but serviceable rooms for a night or two.

Locals also offer private rooms for rent. In summer, a number of places to eat open along the main road.

Getting There & Away
The village of Wetlina is accessible from both Sanok (8.90zł, 1½ hours) and Lesko (7.80zł, 1½ hours) by a few buses per day year-round. Several buses a day also run in summer east to Ustrzyki Górne (3.80zł, 25 minutes).

CISNA
☎ 13 / pop 700
Cisna sits on the borderland between the territories once inhabited by the Boyks to the east and the Lemks to the west. The region was quite densely populated before the events of WWII. Today Cisna and its environs have no more than 1000 inhabitants, yet it's still the largest village in the central part of the Bieszczady. The village is not attractive in itself but it has a choice of accommodation and can therefore be used as a base for hiking. It is also the place from which to catch the narrow-gauge tourist train.

Sleeping & Eating
Ośrodek Wczasowy Perełka (☎ /fax 468 63 25; bed 60zł; P ☻) Possibly the best place to stay in Cisna, the Perełka has 34 beds in singles and doubles plus seasonal cabins. Meals are served on request.

Bacówka PTTK Pod Honem (☎ 0503 137 279; www.podhonem.home.pl in Polish; beds in dm/d/tr/ 19/22/21/20zł) The 44-bed PTTK mountain hostel is beautifully located high on the mountain slope above Cisna (around 2km up the hill from the centre along a steep dirt track). It's basic and friendly and you'll be allowed to sleep on the floor if all the rooms are taken. It also serves uncomplicated meals.

Villa Helena (☎ 0502 573 061; s/d 20/35zł; ☒) This pleasant little guesthouse has 11 neat old-fashioned rooms. It's fairly simple, but comfortable and homy.

Noclegi Okrąglik (☎ 468 63 49; beds in d/tr/q 20-60zł) Centrally located on the crossroads the Okrąglik operates as long as there's demand. It has plain rooms with shared facilities.

Pokoje Noclegowe Centrum (☎ 468 63 90; Cisna 51; beds 15-50zł) Another central, no-frills establishment offering a choice of private rooms with shared facilities.

Half a dozen budget eateries open in summer near the crossroads.

Getting There & Away

BUS

Several buses run daily to Sanok (7.80zł, one hour) and Wetlina (4zł, 25 minutes). There are more seasonal buses in summer, including a few to Ustrzyki Górne.

TRAIN

The narrow-gauge train known as **Bieszcza-dzka Kolejka Leśna** (Bieszczady Forest Train) was built for transporting timber and had its main station in Majdan, 2km west of Cisna. The first stretch of the railway between Maj-dan and Nowy Łupków was built at the end of the 19th century and subsequently extended north to Rzepedź and east to Moc-zarne beyond Wetlina. The train on the Majdan–Rzepedź route was used until 1993 for the transport of timber. Additionally, a tourist train was put into operation on this line in summer. Though the trip lost some charm in 1980 after steam was replaced by diesel, it was still a spectacular ride.

Both the freight and tourist trains were suspended in 1993 due to the dangerous condition of the railway. After several seasons out of operation, the tourist train now operates the 12km stretch from Majdan to Przysłup (midway between Cisna and Wetlina), and in the opposite direction, the 18km stretch from Majdan to Wola Michowa. Check at **Majdan station** (☎ 468 63 35; fax 468 63 01) or a regional tourist office for periods of operation, schedules and fares.

KOMAŃCZA

☎ 13 / pop 600

A village nestled in the valley between the Bieszczady and Beskid Niski, Komańcza is yet another base for hikers. Though not as popular as Ustrzyki Górne, Wetlina or Cisna, it offers something different. As it somehow escaped Operation Vistula in 1947, there's more of an ethnic and religious mix here than elsewhere in the region. There's a sizable community of Lemks living in and around the village, and old Uniat and Orthodox rites have not been pushed out by Catholicism.

One of the area's more recent attractions is the so-called **Trans-bordering Bicycle Route** (Transgraniczna Trasa Rowerowa), a signposted cycling route into Slovakia; the tourist office will have maps, brochures and other practical details.

Information

TOURIST INFORMATION

Centrum Informacji Turystycznej (☎ 467 70 76; www.komancza.regiony.pl; ☒ 7am-3pm Mon-Fri) Located in the village's municipal office.

Sights

Small as Komańcza is, it boasts three churches – Uniat, Orthodox and Roman Catholic – and all three are in use. The oldest is a beautiful wooden **Orthodox church** dating from 1805, tucked away on the outskirts of the village, on the Dukla road. It's only open for Sunday morning Mass and attracts a small congregation. If you can't make it at that time, the local **Orthodox priest** (☎ 467 72 24; Komańcza 216) may open it for you.

The Uniats make up a significant part of the village's population. In the late 1980s, they built a fair-sized **Uniat church** in the centre of the village. In the basement of the church is the **Lemk Museum** featuring a small collection of objects (household items, tools, crafts) referring to the Lemk culture. The museum is normally locked – you need to go to the **Plebania** (☎ 467 72 24) and ask to have it open.

The **Roman Catholic church**, a modest wooden structure, was built in the early 1950s for newly settled worshippers of the creed, which was virtually nonexistent in the region before WWII. The church is opposite the train station on the road to Sanok.

Continuing north along this road for about 1km and taking a narrow track that branches off to the left under the railway bridge, you'll get to the **Convent of the Nazarene Sisters**. Known to Poles as the site of the house arrest (from 1955 to 1956) of Cardinal Stefan Wyszyński, primate of Poland until 1981, this fine timber mansion is now a sort of shrine, though there's nothing special to look at inside.

Sleeping & Eating

Schronisko PTTK (☎ 467 70 13; dm 16zł, beds in cabins 25-30zł; ☒) Fully refurbished, the year-round 20-bed Schronisko, close to the convent, offers good standards. It serves simple hot meals. In summer it also operates cabins.

There's also a summer youth hostel, a camping ground, and a dozen agrotourist farms – look out for 'Agroturystyka' boards along the main road.

Getting There & Away

The standard-gauge railway links Komańcza with Zagórz via Rzepedź, with four trains daily in each direction. From Zagórz, there's frequent bus transport to Sanok and Lesko.

There are half a dozen daily buses to Sanok (7zł, one hour). One bus goes daily to Cisna (5zł, 45 minutes) and there is also sporadic transport to Dukla (6.80zł, one hour).

AROUND KOMAŃCZA

Avid church visitors will not want to miss some fine Uniat and Orthodox churches scattered around the Komańcza region. You'll find the first good specimen in the village of **Rzepedź**, 5km north of Komańcza. It's 750m west of the main road. Extensively restored over recent years, this wooden structure, dating from 1824, with a bell tower in front of the entrance, is today the Uniat church. The key is kept by Mr Sławomir Jurkowski, Rzepedź 26, about 500m from the church.

A bit different in shape, and perhaps even more attractive, is the church in **Turzańsk**, 1.5km east of Rzepedź. Topped with graceful onion domes and a free-standing belfry, the church was built in 1803 and has preserved its internal decoration, complete with rococo iconostasis. Today the church serves the Orthodox community and holds Mass at 10am every second Sunday. If you want to visit at other times, the keys are kept at the house of Mr Teodor Tchoryk, Turzańsk 63, at the opposite end of the village, about 2km from the church.

One more *cerkiew* (an Orthodox or Uniat church), also following the Orthodox rite, is in the village of **Szczawne**, 3km north of Rzepedź by the main road, just before crossing the railway track. Watch out to the left as it's well hidden in a cluster of trees. Masses are held every second Sunday. The keys are kept by Mr Jan Walorny, Szczawne 20, in the large white house near the train station, 2km from the church.

THE BESKID NISKI

The Beskid Niski (literally 'Low Beskid') is a mountain range that runs for about 85km west–east along the Slovakian frontier. It's bordered on the west by the Beskid Sądecki and on the east by the Bieszczady. As its name suggests, it is not a high outcrop, its highest point not exceeding 1000m. Made up of gently undulating and densely forested hills, the Beskid Niski is easier for walking than its taller neighbours. It perhaps offers less-spectacular vistas than the Bieszczady, but dozens of small Orthodox and Uniat churches add to its charm. Most of them are in the western half of the region.

HIKING IN THE BESKID NISKI

Two main trails wind through the whole length of the range. The trail marked blue originates in Grybów, goes southeast to the border and winds eastwards all along the frontier to bring you eventually to Nowy Łupków near Komańcza. The red trail begins in Krynica, crosses the blue trail around Hańczowa, continues east along the northern slopes of the Beskid, and arrives at Komańcza. Both these trails head further east into the Bieszczady.

You need four to six days to do the whole of the Beskid Niski on either of these routes, but there are other trails as well as a number of rough roads that link the two main trails.

A dozen youth hostels scattered in small villages throughout the region provide shelter but most are open only in July and August. There are also a number of agrotourist farms, and these are open longer or even year-round. If you plan on more ambitious trekking, camping gear may be useful. You can buy some elementary supplies in the villages you pass but you're better off stocking up on essentials before you start.

The major starting points for the Beskid Niski are Krynica, Grybów and Gorlice from the west; Komańcza and Sanok from the east; and Krosno, Dukla and Barwinek for the central part.

The *Beskid Niski i Pogórze* map (scale 1:125,000) will give you all the information you need for hiking. It's usually available in larger cities, but not always in the region itself. The map is also very useful for those exploring the region using private transport.

KROSNO

☎ 13 / pop 49,000

Founded in the 14th century and prospering during the Renaissance – even referred to as 'little Kraków' – Krosno, like the rest of Poland, slid into decay later on. It revived in the mid-19th century with the development of the oil industry in the region and since then has slowly grown to become a regional petroleum centre. Krosno is also well known for its glassworks.

Today it is a rather ordinary town except for its tiny historic core perched on a hill, a remnant of its glorious past. There are some interesting sights nearby, notably the church in Haczów and the skansen in Bóbrka.

Information

INTERNET ACCESS

Some central facilities:

Internet Expo (Rynek 10)

Kafejka Internetowa (ul Piłsudskiego 10)

MONEY

Bank Pekao (ul Bieszczadzka 5) is pretty far from the centre, but **PKO Bank** (ul Słowackiego 4) is just off the Rynek and has an ATM. There are several *kantors* around the Old Town.

TOURIST INFORMATION

Tourist office (☎ /fax 432 77 07; www.krosno.pl in Polish; Rynek 5; ☯ 9am-5pm Mon-Fri, 9am-2pm Sat) On the main square.

Sights

The **Old Town** is the focal point for visitors. The spacious **Rynek** has retained some of its former appearance, notably in the houses fronted by wide arcaded passageways that line the south and half of the north side of the square.

A few steps east of the Rynek is the large 15th-century **Franciscan Church** (Kościół Franciszkanów), today filled with neo-Gothic furnishings. The showpiece here is the **Oświęcim Family Chapel** (Kaplica Oświęcimów), just to the left as you enter the church. Built in 1647 by Italian architect Vincenti Petroni, and embellished with stucco work by another Italian master Jan Falconi, the chapel has been preserved with virtually no changes and is considered one of the best early-baroque chapels in Poland.

Another huge brick structure, the **parish church** is 50m northwest of the Rynek. Founded in 1402, it was almost entirely consumed by fire in 1638 (only the chancel survived) and reconstructed in an altered style. In contrast to its sober exterior, the church's interior is exuberant. The powerful gilded high altar is 350 years old, as is the elaborate pulpit. The organ looks a bit more modest, yet it's acclaimed for its excellent sound, reputedly the best in the region. The freestanding onion-domed belltower was erected in the 17th century and houses three bells, named Urban, Jan and Marian. Urban, with a perimeter of 490cm, is said to be one of the largest in Poland.

One block northwest of the church is the **Regional Museum** (Muzeum Podkarpackie; ☎ 432 43 01; ul Piłsudskiego 16; adult/concession 4/3zł, free Sun; ☯ 10am-4pm Tue-Sun May-Oct, 10am-2pm Tue-Sun Nov-Apr). Installed in the 15th-century former Bishops' Palace, the museum has the usual historical, archaeological and art sections but the highlight is an extensive collection of decorative old kerosene lamps, reputedly the largest in Europe. Also worth seeing is the collection of contemporary artistic glass from regional glassworks.

Directly opposite is the **Craft Museum** (Muzeum Rzemiosła; ☎ 432 41 88; ul Piłsudskiego 17; adult/concession 4/3zł; ☯ 8am-3pm Mon-Fri, 10am-2pm Sat), featuring displays recalling a wide range of local crafts, including clockmaking, weaving, saddlery and even hairdressing.

Roughly 1km north of town is the very famous **Krosno glassworks** (☎ 432 80 00; www.krosno.com.pl; ul Tysiąclecia 13). There's a factory shop on site selling a range of its products, though prices aren't much different to those in regular crystalware shops around the country.

Sleeping

Hotel Krosno-Nafta (☎ 436 62 12; www.hotel.nafta.pl; ul Lwowska 21; s/d/q 230/360/500zł; ℗) The city's top-end accommodation, this large, modern hotel, a little over 1km from the centre on the Sanok road, has been refurbished and offers satisfactory conditions and its own upmarket restaurant. It may have discount rates on weekends.

Hotelik Restauracja Śnieżka (☎ 432 34 49; sniezka1@polbox.com; ul Lewakowskiego 22; s/d/tr 80/100/120zł; ℗) This attractive little place, very close to the bus and train stations, has just six cosy rooms, all sparklingly modern, with polished wood floors and big bathrooms. As the name suggests, there is also a restaurant.

Hotel Bengol (☎ 436 04 78; www.bengol.rze.pl; ul Długa 15D; s/d/ste 150/200/280zł; **P**) This converted house, in a quiet residential area west of the centre, has just eight spacious and stylish rooms. It's also the unexpected venue for a decent Indian restaurant.

Reshotel (☎ 432 19 54; ul Okulickiego 13A; s/d 30/50zł) This former workers' hostel, in an industrial suburb 1km west of the train station, now welcomes everybody and is one of the cheapest year-round places to stay in Krosno.

Eating

Piwnica Wójtowska (☎ 432 15 32; Rynek 7; mains 10-30zł; ☽ lunch & dinner) Located in a pleasant vaulted cellar on the Rynek, the Piwnica offers a variety of Polish dishes as well as international fare of the chicken-and-chips variety.

Marhaba Bar (☎ 420 24 92; ul Sienkiewicza 2; mains 5-10zł; ☽ lunch & dinner) Marhaba offers some cheap Middle Eastern standards such as kebab, felafel, kofta and the like.

La Piazza (☎ 436 82 22; Rynek 6; mains 12-20zł; ☽ 9am-midnight) This vaguely Italian-style place serves the usual round of pizzas and pasta.

Cukierna Santos (☎ 431 51 27; ul Staszica 16; pastries 3-6zł; ☽ breakfast, lunch & dinner) This very popular little bakery sells a wide range of pastries, cakes and other sweet and savoury snacks. There are a few seats in the corner.

Getting There & Away

The train and bus stations are next to each other, 1.5km west of the Old Town; it's a 15-minute walk to the centre, or you can take the urban bus.

Most trains cover the Zagórz–Jasło route, which can be used for Sanok but not much else. There are trains to Warsaw (55zł, six hours, three daily) and Kraków (29zł, three hours, four daily).

Bus traffic is busier and will take you all around the region. There are a dozen buses eastwards to Sanok (6.90zł, 1½ hours), of which four continue to Ustrzyki Dolne (10zł, two hours) and two go as far as Ustrzyki Górne (15zł, three hours). A dozen fast buses depart daily to Kraków (26zł, three hours), and hourly buses go to

Rzeszów (8.60zł, 1½ hours). To the south, there are around seven buses a day to Dukla (4.80zł, 45 minutes) and regular buses to Bóbrka (3.20zł, 30 minutes). There are at least five buses daily to Haczów (3.60zł, 40 minutes); on the timetable, look out for Brzozów buses via Haczów.

HACZÓW

The village of Haczów (*hah*-choof), 13km east of Krosno, boasts what is considered the largest timber Gothic **church** in Europe. Built around the mid-15th century on the site of a previous church founded by Władysław Jagiełło in 1388, it is also one of Europe's oldest timber churches. What's more, it has beautiful interior wall paintings, dating from approximately 1494, discovered in 1955 and restored in the 1990s. There are also five baroque side altars, but the main altar, complete with its singularly impressive original pietà from around 1400, is now in the new church, built between 1935 and 1939 right next to the old one.

Both churches are open during the day, but if you find them locked, the priest, who lives in the house next to the churches, may let you have a look inside. There's another excellent old timber church in **Blizne**, 5km north of Brzozów.

Getting There & Away

You shouldn't wait more than an hour for a bus to Krosno. They go either via Krościenko Wyżne or Miejsce Piastowe. Buses to Brzozów (3.20zł, 25 minutes) run regularly throughout the day.

BÓBRKA

☎ 13 / pop 800

The small village of Bóbrka, 10km south of Krosno, was the cradle of the oil industry. It was here that the world's first oil well was sunk by Ignacy Łukasiewicz in 1854.

Skansen

Today the site where the oil business was born is a skansen, the **Museum of the Oil Industry** (Muzeum Przemysłu Naftowego; ☎ 433 34 89; 38-458 Chorkówka; adult/concession 4/3zł; ☽ 9am-5pm Tue-Sun May-Sep, 7am-3pm Tue-Sun Oct-Apr).

Established in 1961, this interesting open-air museum is unique – it doesn't feature old peasant architecture, but old oil machinery. It's based on a group of early oil wells, complemented by their old drilling derricks and other machinery collected elsewhere. The first surviving oil shaft from 1860, Franek, can be seen with oil still bubbling inside. The other shaft nearby, Janina, is over 100 years old and still used commercially.

The building, which was at one time Łukasiewicz' office, now houses a small museum. The collection of kerosene lamps includes decorative and industrial examples. Note the original map of the Bóbrka oil field with the shafts marked on it; the deepest went down as far as 319m. A copy of the lamp invented by Łukasiewicz can also be seen. Łukasiewicz also invented a method of refining oil.

Sleeping & Eating

Gospodarstwo Agroturystyczne Bazyl (☎ 469 19 30; www.bobrka.com; Bóbrka 60; d/tr 105/125zł; P) This charming modern guesthouse is the only reliable place to stay in Bóbrka. It offers spotless, well-kept rooms and a restful, friendly atmosphere. All meals can be provided, using home-grown produce, and there are also craft classes and pony rides for kids. If you're staying more than one night, the price decreases, while if you can do without an en suite bathroom, beds cost 40zł per person.

There are plenty of homes offering private rooms in Bóbrka but availability is sporadic; the tourist office in Krosno should be able to help.

Getting There & Away

The usual jumping-off point for Bóbrka is Krosno. There are about 10 buses daily (fewer on weekends) to the village of Bóbrka. The skansen is 2km away, linked by road but not by bus. This road leads through the forest and is a pleasant walk. Alternatively, take a bus from Krosno to Kobylany or Makowiska (at least a dozen daily), get off in Równe Skrzyżowanie and walk 600m uphill to the skansen. One or two buses from Równe run south to Dukla, or you can walk 1.5km east to the main road where buses to Dukla pass by every hour.

DUKLA

☎ 13 / pop 2200

Dukla is close to the **Dukla Pass** (Przełęcz Dukielska), the lowest and most easily accessible passage over the Western Carpathians. In the 16th century this strategic location brought prosperity to the town, which became a centre of the wine trade on the route from Hungary. In autumn 1944, however, the town's position led to its

---

BÓBRKA'S BLACK GOLD

Natural oil was known in the Krosno region for centuries. It oozed to the earth's surface out of crannies in the rock and was used by locals for domestic and medicinal purposes. But it was in 1854 in Bóbrka that Ignacy Łukasiewicz sank what is thought to be the world's first oil well, giving birth to commercial oil exploitation.

Łukasiewicz, a pharmacy graduate from universities in Lviv, Kraków and Vienna, studied the properties of crude oil, and he was the first to obtain paraffin oil from petroleum. In 1853 he constructed the world's first kerosene lamp, which was first used in the Lviv hospital to light a surgical operation that had to be carried out urgently at night. A year later in Gorlice, the world's first kerosene streetlamp was lit by Łukasiewicz. It was then that a local landlord pointed out a site in the Bóbrka forest, where substantial amounts of oil accumulated in natural hollows in the land.

The first approach to get oil out of the soil was by means of a ditch. A 120m-long, 1.2m-deep ditch was dug and oil was collected by bucket, but there was not that much to collect. This led to experiments with vertical shafts, which proved to be much more effective. By 1858, four years after initial trials, the new Małgorzata shaft yielded about 4000L of oil a day, a milestone that fostered further exploitation.

More shafts were immediately sunk all over the place, followed by the opening of primitive refineries. The region prospered, reaching its peak before WWI. Later on, when larger deposits were discovered elsewhere, the importance of the local oil fields diminished. Rudimentary exploitation continues, and even though output today is insignificant, the site preserves the memory of what happened here 150 years ago, introducing a product that changed the world.

destruction. One of the fiercest mountain battles of WWII was fought nearby, in which the combined Soviet and Czechoslovakian armies crushed the German defence, leaving more than 100,000 soldiers deceased.

Sights

Dukla's large **Rynek** boasts a squat town hall in the middle. Across the Krosno road is the mighty **parish church**, built from 1764 to 1765, a good example of late-baroque architecture.

Diagonally opposite the church is the **Historical Museum** (Muzeum Historyczne; ☎ 433 00 85; Trakt Węgierski 5; adult/concession 4/3zł; ☉ 10am-6pm Tue-Sun May-Sep, 10am-3.30pm Tue-Sun Oct-Apr). Accommodated in an 18th-century palace, it has a permanent display on the battle of 1944 and some temporary exhibitions. In the palace park there are some heavy weapons from WWII.

Sleeping & Eating

Dom Wycieczkowy PTTK (☎ 433 00 46; Rynek 18; dm 17-20zł, beds in s/tr 30/25zł) The local PTTK offers the usual simple and unremarkable rooms and facilities, and it also has a cheap restaurant.

Schonisko Młodzieżowe youth hostel (☎ 433 08 86; Rynek 9; dm 16-20zł) Another basic option on the Rynek, this year-round youth hostel has 40 beds.

Getting There & Away

There are regular buses north to Krosno (4.80zł, 45 minutes) and several buses south to Barwinek (3.80zł, 40 minutes), near the border. Crossing the border is fast and easy, but get rid of any currency you have in złoty in Barwinek's *kantor* – it will be hard to trade them in Svidnik or Bardejov in Slovakia.

One seasonal bus runs the backwoods route from Dukla to Komańcza (6.80zł, one hour) and on to Cisna (8.90zł, two hours), which is a short cut to the Bieszczady.

BIECZ

☎ 13 / pop 5100

One of the oldest settlements in Poland, Biecz (pronounced byech) was for a long time a busy commercial centre benefiting from the trading route heading south over the Carpathians to Hungary. In the

17th century its prosperity came to an end and Biecz found itself in the doldrums, left only with its memories. This sleepy atmosphere seems to have remained to this day, however, some important historic monuments and a good museum make the town a worthwhile stop on your route.

Sights

The town's landmark is the **town hall** or the Rynek or, more precisely, its huge 66m-high octagonal **tower**, looking a bit like a lighthouse. It was built between 1569 and 1581, except for the top, which is a later, baroque addition. It was recently thoroughly restored, including its original Renaissance decoration and the unusual 24-hour clock face on its eastern side. The town hall now houses the local municipal office – inquire there during office hours and you may be let up to the top of the tower.

West of the Rynek is a monumental **parish church**. This mighty Gothic brick structure, evidence of former wealth but now looking too large for the town's needs, dates from the late 15th/early 16th centuries. Inside, the chancel holds most of the church's treasures, most notably the late-Renaissance Flemish high altar and massive stalls, all from the early 17th century. Less conspicuous but worthy of attention is a gilded woodcarving depicting the genealogical tree of the Virgin Mary, standing to the side of the high altar. Further up is an impressive crucifix from 1639.

The church is only open for visits immediately before or after Mass. There are several Masses on Sunday, but on weekdays they are only held early in the morning and late in the afternoon.

Biecz has a good **Regional Museum** (☎ 447 10 93; ul Węgierska & ul Kromera 3; adult/concession 2/1zł, ☉ 8am-3pm Tue-Sat Oct-Apr year-round, 9am-2pm Sun May-Sep). It's housed in two 16th-century buildings, both close to the church. The one at ul Węgierska holds the complete contents of an ancient pharmacy including its laboratory, as well as musical instruments, traditional household utensils and equipment from old craft workshops. The other part of the museum, at ul Kromera, has more historical exhibits on the town's past, plus archaeological and numismatic collections.

Sleeping & Eating

Hotel Centennial (☎ /fax 447 15 76; www.centennial
.com.pl/en/welcome.html; Rynek 6; s/d 182/235zł; P)
The upscale Centennial offers the best facilities in town, including suites of different
size and design in two historic burghers'
houses. The hotel has three restaurants, one
of which, Restauracja Ogród, serves excellent and reasonably priced Polish food.
There are often big reductions at weekends.

Youth hostel (☎ /fax 447 10 14; ul Parkowa 1;
dm 25-30zł) The 60-bed youth hostel is in a
large school building around 1km from the
Rynek. The hostel is on the top floor and
only has doubles and quads, so it provides
more privacy than most.

Hotel Restauracja Grodzki (☎ /fax 447 11 21; ul
Kazimierza Wielkiego 35; s/d 55/75zł) This is an acceptable budget option, close to the youth
hostel. It's nothing out of the ordinary, but
it does have its own restaurant.

Getting There & Away

The train station, 1km west of the centre,
handles 10 trains a day to Jasło (9zł, 25 minutes), two to Nowy Sącz (18zł, 1½ hours),
two to Kraków (27zł, 2½ hours) and one to
Warsaw (50zł, five hours).

There's no bus terminal in Biecz; all buses
pass through and stop on the Rynek. Buses
to Jasło (5zł, 35 minutes) run regularly
but only a few buses continue to Krosno
(6.90zł, one hour). Plenty of buses, both the
PKS and No 1 suburban buses, run to Gorlice (3.80zł, 25 minutes). A couple of buses
go daily to Nowy Sącz (7.80zł, 1½ hours),
Nowy Targ (16zł, 2½ hours) and Zakopane
(19zł, 3½ hours).

BINAROWA

The village of Binarowa, about 5km northwest of Biecz, has a beautiful wooden Catholic **church**. Built in around 1500, its interior
is entirely covered with paintings that have
remained in remarkably good shape. Those
on the ceiling were produced shortly after
the church's construction, while the wall
decoration, in quite a different style, dates
from the mid-17th century. Though the
church is open only for Mass (early in the
morning on weekdays, all morning till
noon on Sunday) the priest who lives in
the house behind it will probably open it
for you.

Binarowa is accessible by buses from
Gorlice via Biecz. They go every hour or so
on weekdays, less frequently on weekends.

GORLICE

☎ 18 / pop 31,000
Gorlice's name was made, along with
Bóbrka's, with the beginnings of the Polish
oil industry. In 1853, in the local chemist
shop in Gorlice, Ignacy Łukasiewicz obtained paraffin from crude oil. Gorlice was
also the site of a great 1915 battle, fought for
126 days, which ended with the Austrians
breaking through the Russian Carpathian
front, leaving 20,000 dead.

Gorlice has little to entice tourists but
the region to the south was once Lemk
land and still shelters some amazing old
Orthodox and Uniat churches. The town is
a major transportation hub for the region,
and the helpful tourist office can provide
information.

Gorlice can be used as a starting point for
hiking into the Beskid Niski. Two marked
trails, blue and green, wind southeast from
the town up the mountains, joining the main
west–east red trail that crosses the range.

Information

INTERNET ACCESS
Toxic Internet café (☎ 353 67 00; ul Piekarska 5; per
hr 2-3zł)

MONEY
Bank Pekao is at ul Legionów 12, and there
are a few *kantors* and ATMs in the centre.

TOURIST INFORMATION
Gorlickie Centrum Informacji (☎ 353 50 91; www.it
.gorlice.pl in Polish; ul Legionów 3; ☼ 8am-6pm Mon-Fri,
9am-3pm Sat)

Sights

The **Regional Museum** (☎ 352 26 15; ul Wąska 7/9;
adult/concession 3/2zł; ☼ 9am-4pm Tue-Fri, 10am-2pm
Sat year-round, 10am-2pm Sun May-Sep), just off the
Rynek, has exhibitions on Lemk ethnography, the oil industry and the Gorlice battle of 1915.

Gorlice claims to have the world's first
kerosene **streetlamp**. It's attached to the
chapel topped by a figure of a contemplat-
ing Christ, on the corner of ul Kościuszki
and ul Węgierska, a short walk south from
the centre.

THE CARPATHIAN MOUNTAINS

Sleeping & Eating

Dwór Karwacjanów (☎ 353 56 18; fax 353 56 01; ul Wróblewskiego 10A; d 80zł) Next door to the Dom Nauczyciela, the Dwór is an attractive fortified mansion whose roots reputedly go back to 1417. Extensively renovated, the building now houses an art gallery, a pub, and eight double rooms.

Hotelik Dark Pub (☎ 352 02 38; www.hotelik gorlice.pl; ul Wąska 11; s/d 85/120zł) This amenable little place, near the museum, has just three double rooms, all with bright modern bathrooms. There's a restaurant and a Britishstyle pub downstairs.

Hotel Max (☎ /fax 353 61 73; ul Legionów 6D; d 100zł) Max is yet another small, central hotel, with six neat rooms. Discount rates may be on offer at weekends.

Dom Nauczyciela (☎ 353 52 31; fax 353 56 32; ul Wróblewskiego 10; s/d from 50/100zł) The cheapest of the central places, offering simple, acceptable facilities. It's 100m from the Rynek.

Getting There & Away

BUS

Travelling by bus is the more convenient option. Six fast buses go to Kraków (16zł, 2½ hours) and double that number to Nowy Sącz (6.80zł, one hour). Buses also go to Nowy Targ (13.50zł, two hours, five daily), Krosno (7.80zł, 1½ hours, five daily). For Biecz (3.20zł, 30 minutes), buses run every half-hour or so.

There's also a reasonable service southwards to Łosie, Ujście Gorlickie, Hańczowa and Wysowa, plus occasional buses to Izby, Kwiatoń, Smerekowiec and Gładyszów.

The bus terminal is next to the shuttle train station, around 1.5km from the Rynek.

TRAIN

Gorlice has no train station as such. The main railway track is 5km north, through the village of Zagórzany, which is linked with Gorlice by a shuttle train, running back and forth every two or three hours. From Zagórzany, there's transport to Jasło, and two trains a day to Kraków.

SĘKOWA

Sitting in the prewar ethnic borderland between the Poles and the Lemks, Sękowa was one of the southernmost outposts of Roman Catholicism. Further south, the Orthodox and Uniat faith predominated and you won't find old Catholic churches beyond this point.

The small wooden **church** in Sękowa is an exquisite example of timber architecture. The main part of the building dates back to the 1520s, though the bell tower and *soboty*, which look like verandas around the church, were added in the 17th century. The *soboty* – the word means 'Saturdays' – were built to shelter churchgoers from distant villages arriving late on Saturday night in time for early Sunday morning Mass. You will see many *soboty* on churches in the region.

The church passed through particularly hard times during WWI when the Austro-Hungarian army took part of it away to reinforce the trenches and for firewood, but careful reconstruction has restored its gracious outline. The interior lacks some furnishings but it's worth seeing anyway – the nuns who live in the house next to the church will give you the key.

Getting There & Away

The church is 5km southeast of Gorlice. To get there, take the suburban bus 6 (to Ropica), 7 (to Owczary) or 17 (to Sękowa), get off in Siary and continue in the same direction for 50m until the road divides. Take the left-hand fork, cross the bridge 300m ahead and you'll see the church to your right.

SZYMBARK

☎ 18 / pop 2800

Szymbark is just a scattering of houses that spreads along the Gorlice–Grybów road for over 3km. You'd hardly notice you were passing through it if not for the road signs with the village's name. Roughly halfway through is a large modern church and it's here that the buses stop.

The old peasant cottages in the orchard next to the church constitute a skansen, the **Centre of Folk Architecture** (Ośrodek Budownictwa Ludowego; ☎ 351 31 14; adult/concession 3/2zł; ☼ 9am-4pm Tue-Fri, 10am-2pm Sat & Sun May-Sep, 9am-3pm Mon-Fri Oct-Apr). The skansen is pretty small but nonetheless has some curiosities, the biggest being a fortified castlelike manor house from the 16th century, adorned with characteristic Renaissance parapets. It's being renovated and is off-limits to visitors. Of a dozen old timber cottages in the grounds, some have been furnished and decorated and can be visited.

Sleeping & Eating

Pensjonat Perełka (☎ 351 30 11; beds in d/tr/q 20-25zł) This simple guesthouse, in an 80-year-old timber villa, is across the road from the skansen. Meals can be provided if requested in advance.

Hotel Restauracja Watra (☎ 801 00 14; d 50zł) Watra, 500m from the skansen towards Gorlice, is a roadside restaurant that serves reasonable food and has six double rooms with private bathrooms for rent.

Getting There & Away

Buses on the main east–west road run regularly throughout the day to both Gorlice (2.80zł, 20 minutes) and Nowy Sącz (5.90zł, 50 minutes).

THE BESKID SĄDECKI

Lying south of Nowy Sącz, the Beskid Sądecki (*bes*-keed son-*dets*-kee) is yet another attractive mountain range where you can hike, sightsee or simply have a rest in one of the mountain spas, the most popular being Krynica. The mountains are easily accessible from Nowy Sącz by two roads that head south along the river valleys, joining up to form a convenient loop; public transport is good on this route.

The Beskid Sądecki consists of two ranges, the Pasmo Jaworzyny and the Pasmo Radziejowej, separated by the valley of the Poprad River. There are a number of peaks over 1000m, the highest being Mt Radziejowa (1262m). It's good hiking country and you don't need a tent or cooking gear as mountain hostels dot the trails.

The Beskid Sądecki was the westernmost territory populated by the Lemks, and a dozen of their charming rustic churches survive, particularly around Krynica and Muszyna. The *Beskid Sądecki* map (scale 1:75,000) is helpful for both hikers and *cerkiew* seekers.

NOWY SĄCZ

☎ 18 / pop 81,000

Nowy Sącz (*no*-vi sonch) is a small, sleepy town with an attractive main square and a few decent attractions, most notably the Ethnographic Park. It's hardly the most happening of places, but it can be a good base for further exploration of the surrounding countryside.

Founded in 1292 and fortified in the 1350s by King Kazimierz Wielki, Nowy Sącz developed rapidly until the 16th century thanks to its strategic position on trading crossroads. Between 1430 and 1480 the town was the centre of the renowned Sącz School (Szkoła Sądecka) of painting. The works of art created here in that period now adorn a number of collections, including that of the royal seat of Wawel in Kraków.

As elsewhere, the 17th-century decline gave way to a partial revival at the close of the 19th century. Nowy Sącz grew considerably after WWII, and its historic district has been largely restored over recent years.

Information

BOOKSHOPS

EMPiK (☎ 443 72 41; Rynek 17) Has a small selection of maps, plus a few English-language books.

INTERNET ACCESS

Some central Internet facilities:
C@ffe Internet (☎ 443 84 33; ul Kościuszki 22)
Kawiarnia Cechowa (☎ 443 88 47; Rynek 11)

MONEY

Bank Pekao (ul Jagiellońska 50A) changes travellers cheques and gives advances on Visa and MasterCard. It's outside the centre, but has a useful ATM at ul Jagiellońska 15, near the Rynek. Even more central is an ATM on the western wall of the town hall.

TOURIST INFORMATION

Centrum Informacji Turystycznej (☎ /fax 443 55 97; www.nowy-sacz.info in Polish; ul Piotra Skargi 2; ☼ 8am-6pm Mon-Fri, 9am-2pm Sat) Located just off the Rynek, has a few brochures and maps, but staff only speaks Polish.

Sights

At 160m by 120m, the **Rynek** is one of the largest in Poland and is lined on all sides by a harmonious collection of historic houses. The **town hall**, erected in the middle in 1897, is quite large but it fortunately doesn't look oversized on this spacious square. It was designed in a mix of styles, with a fair dose of Art Nouveau.

St Margaret's Church (Kościół Św Małgorzaty), a block east of the Rynek, is the oldest in town, dating from the 17th century, yet it has undergone many additions and changes. The eclectic interior goes from Gothic to contemporary. A large Renaissance high

THE CARPATHIAN MOUNTAINS

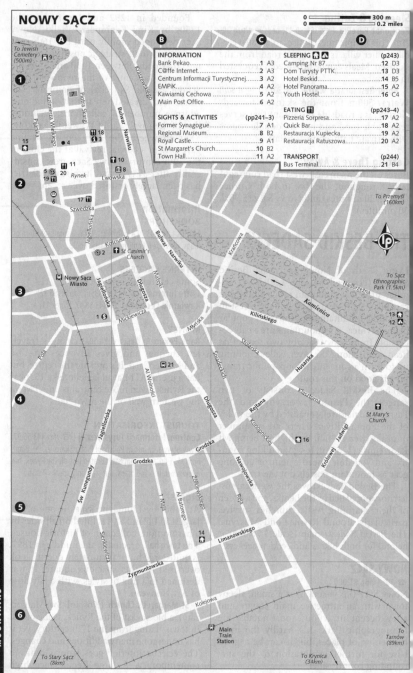

NOWY SĄCZ

| 0 | 300 m |
| 0 | 0.2 miles |

INFORMATION
Bank Pekao.............................1 A3
C@ffe Internet.........................2 A3
Centrum Informacji Turystycznej......3 A2
EMPiK....................................4 A2
Kawiarnia Cechowa....................5 A2
Main Post Office.......................6 A2

SIGHTS & ACTIVITIES (pp241–3)
Former Synagogue.....................7 A1
Regional Museum.......................8 B2
Royal Castle............................9 A1
St Margaret's Church..................10 B2
Town Hall...............................11 A2

SLEEPING (p243)
Camping Nr 87.........................12 D3
Dom Turysty PTTK.....................13 D3
Hotel Beskid...........................14 B5
Hotel Panorama.......................15 A2
Youth Hostel..........................16 C4

EATING (pp243–4)
Pizzeria Sorpresa......................17 A2
Quick Bar..............................18 A2
Restauracja Kupiecka..................19 A2
Restauracja Ratuszowa................20 A2

TRANSPORT (p244)
Bus Terminal..........................21 B4

THE CARPATHIAN MOUNTAINS

altar has a small 15th-century image of Christ, recalling the Byzantine influence.

The building to the south of the church houses the **Regional Museum** (Muzeum Okręgowe; ☎ 443 77 08; ul Lwowska 3; adult/concession 3/2zł; 🕑 10am-3pm Tue-Thu, 10am-5.30pm Fri, 9am-2.30pm Sat & Sun). The museum is dedicated to religious art, with naive religious paintings and crude folk-art woodcarvings collected from rural churches, domestic altars and roadside chapels throughout the region. A higher level of craftsmanship is apparent in the collection of Ruthenian Orthodox icons, which includes a splendid iconostasis of the 17th century. There's little labelling in anything other than Polish though.

Two blocks north of the Rynek is the former **synagogue** (☎ 444 23 70; ul Joselewicza 12; adult/concession 3/2zł; 🕑 10am-2.30pm Wed & Thu, 10am-5.30pm Fri, 9am-2.30pm Sat & Sun), built in the first half of the 18th century in baroque style but remodelled in the 1920s. Partly destroyed in WWII, it was restored and now houses an art gallery, which presents changing exhibitions, plus a small permanent display of Jewish memorabilia.

The remains of the **Royal Castle** (Zamek Królewski), built by King Kazimierz Wielki in the 1350s, are 100m further north. The castle often hosted Polish kings but after a fire in 1616 and subsequent misfortunes of nature it never revived, and there's little left here today, save for a few crumbling walls.

A further 500m north on ul Rybacka is the **Jewish cemetery**. It's a moving sight: a couple of hundred destroyed tombstones amid overgrown grass. This can be seen from over the fence but if you want a closer inspection, the keys to the cemetery gate are kept in the house at ul Rybacka 3, directly opposite the gate.

The **Sącz Ethnographic Park** (Sądecki Park Etnograficzny; ☎ 441 44 12; ul Długoszowskiego 83B; adult/concession 4/3zł; 🕑 10am-5pm Tue-Sun May-Sep, 10am-2pm Mon-Fri Oct-Apr) is one of the best skansens in the country. It's about 3.5km southeast of the centre (1.5km beyond the camping ground). Infrequent urban buses 14 and 15 go there from the train station, passing the bus terminal on their way and skirting the edge of the central area.

The skansen gives an insight into typical rural architecture of the region. The buildings of several ethnic cultures from the Carpathian Mountains and the foothills are displayed in groups. About 55 buildings have been assembled, of which a dozen can be visited. The interiors have all been carefully decorated, furnished and filled with household implements. Visits are in groups guided in Polish. You can buy a booklet in English or German that describes the skansen's contents.

Sleeping

Hotel Beskid (☎ 443 57 70; beskid@orbis.pl; ul Limanowskiego 1; s/d 180/212zł; **P** 🗶) This Orbisrun hotel is at the top of the price scale. It's 300m from the train station but a long walk to the centre (take a bus or taxi). Discount weekend rates may be available.

Hotel Panorama (☎ 443 71 10; fax 442 36 00; ul Romanowskiego 4A; s/d/tr from 92/140/165zł) The slightly dated Panorama is the only place to stay in the Old Town, and is handily situated just off the Rynek. Rooms are large, clean and comfortable, and come with satellite TV and modern bathrooms. Breakfast is 13zł extra, though it's barely worth the bother.

Youth hostel (☎ /fax 442 38 97; ul Reytana 18; dm 16-20zł) The 50-bed youth hostel is about the cheapest place to stay. It has two triples but most beds are in larger dorms (six to 10 beds). It's a bit hard to find – take the small ul Konopnickiej and follow the signs.

Dom Turysty PTTK (☎ 441 50 12; ul Jamnicka 2; d/tr 30/50zł) This basic, year-round PTTK hostel operates a camping ground, Camping Nr 87, from May to September.

Eating

Restauracja Kupiecka (☎ 442 08 31; Rynek 10; mains 15-45zł; 🕑 lunch & dinner) Another vaulted cellar affair, the Kupiecka offers Polish and European cuisine. It's one of the better places in town.

Restauracja Ratuszowa (☎ 443 56 15; Rynek 1; mains 10-20zł; 🕑 lunch & dinner) Located in the cellar vaults of the town hall, the Ratuszowa has the expected range of filling Polish food, including lots of dumplings. There's no English menu though.

Pizzeria Sorpresa (☎ 443 41 89; ul Jagiellońska 14; mains 6-20zł; 🕑 lunch & dinner) No Polish town seems complete without a pizzeria or two and this is where the locals come for their *quattro stagioni*. Besides the usual lengthy list of pizzas there's a selection of other dishes including steaks and salads, though service is pretty indifferent.

Quick Bar (☎ 442 14 48; ul Piotra Skargi 4; mains 5-15zł; ⏲ lunch & dinner) Next to the tourist office just off the Rynek, this small café offers simple Polish standards.

Getting There & Away

BUS

The bus terminal is midway between the city centre and the train station. Buses to Kraków (10zł, 2½ hours) and Krynica (4.50zł, 1½ hours) depart every half-hour or so and are much faster than the trains. There's a regular service to Gorlice (6.50zł, two hours), Szczawnica (7zł, two hours) and Zakopane (15zł, three hours). Frequent PKS and urban buses run to Stary Sącz (2.60zł, 20 minutes).

TRAIN

The main train station is 2km south of the Old Town but urban buses run frequently between the two. There are some trains to Kraków (30zł, three hours) but buses are more useful. Trains run to Krynica (18zł, 2½ hours) regularly throughout the day and pass Stary Sącz on their way. There's a reasonable service to Tarnów (17zł, two hours), with trains departing every hour or two, and three trains a day to Warsaw.

The Nowy Sącz Miasto station is close to the centre but trains (six a day) only go from here to Chabówka (halfway along the Kraków–Zakopane route).

STARY SĄCZ

☎ 18 / pop 8500

The oldest town in the region, Stary Sącz (stah-ri sonch) owes its existence to Princess Kinga (1234–92), the wife of King Bolesław Wstydliwy (Bolesław the Shy), who in the 1270s founded the convent of the Poor Clares (Klasztor Klarysek) here. After the king's death, Kinga entered the convent, where she lived for the last 13 years of her life, becoming its first abbess. This, together with various charitable acts and donations she made to the town, gave birth to the cult of the Blessed Kinga, which spread through the region. The name Kinga is ubiquitous in the town.

On the secular front, the town's position on the trade route between Kraków and Buda (modern-day Budapest) made it a busy commercial centre, though it gradually lost out to its younger but more pro-gressive sister, Nowy Sącz. Today there's no comparison between the two – Stary Sącz is just a small satellite town. It has , however, preserved much of its old atmosphere and architecture.

Sights

There are not many genuine cobbled market squares left in Poland but the **Rynek** in Stary Sącz is definitely one of them. A solitary cluster of trees in its centre shades an old well. The town hall that was once here burnt down in 1795. The neat houses lining the square are almost all one-storey buildings. The oldest, No 6, dates from the 17th century and now holds the **Regional Museum** (☎ 446 00 94; Rynek 6; admission 2zł; ⏲ 10am-1pm Tue-Sun, closes later in summer). Its collection of objects relating to the town is reminiscent of a charming antique shop.

Enter the gate at Rynek 21 and have a look at the decoration on the vault above your head. Then walk to the back yard to see a dilapidated **house** guarded by folksy figures. Until 1990 this was a centre for local naive artists, complete with a folk-art gallery. It was run by Józef Raczek, an amateur painter, sculptor and writer, but since his death the house has gradually fallen into ruin. Hopefully, you'll still be able to see some of the decoration left in this unique place.

The **parish church**, one block south of the Rynek, dates from the town's beginnings but has been changed considerably and is now a textbook example of unbridled baroque, with its five large florid altars that are fitted into the small interior. The elaborate pulpit, organ and, particularly, the unique stalls under the choir loft, complete the decoration.

Equally splendid is the **Church of the Poor Clares** (Kościół Klarysek), a short walk east. Surrounded by a high defensive wall, this was the birthplace of the town. Originally a Gothic building completed in 1332, this church also ended up with opulent baroque fittings. The traces of its creator are clearly visible: the baroque frescoes in the nave depict scenes from the life of the Blessed Kinga, and her chapel (in front of you as you enter the church) boasts a 1470 statue of her on the altar. On the opposite wall, the pulpit from 1671 is an extraordinary piece of art.

Sleeping & Eating

Zajazd Szałas (☎ 446 00 77; ul Jana Pawła II 77; d 35zł) The only year-round accommodation in the area, the Zajazd is 1.5km outside the town on the Nowy Sącz road. It has only a few rooms, and its restaurant serves inexpensive meals. Breakfast costs extra.

Restauracja Marysieńka (☎ 446 00 72; Rynek 12; mains 10-20zł; ☺ lunch & dinner) Established on the 1st floor of the tallest house in the square, the Marysieńka is probably the most pleasant place to eat in town. If the weather is fine, the balcony is the right place to grab a table and enjoy the vista over the square.

Getting There & Away

BUS

Buses stop in the Rynek. A continuous service to Nowy Sącz (2.60zł, 20 minutes) is provided by both the PKS and several lines of urban buses (8, 9, 10, 11, 24 and 43).

TRAIN

The train station is around 2km east of the centre and has a regular service south to Krynica (15zł, 1½ hours) and north to Nowy Sącz (9zł, 15 minutes). Several daily trains to Kraków and Tarnów depart mostly in the afternoon and evening.

KRYNICA

☎ 18 / pop 13,500

Set in attractive countryside amid the wooded hills of the Beskid Sądecki, Krynica (kri-*nee*-tsah), often known as Krynica-Zdrój (Krynica Spa), is possibly Poland's most popular mountain health resort. Though the healing properties of the local mineral springs had been known for centuries, the town only really began to develop in the 1850s. By the end of the nineteenth century it was a fashionable hang-out for the artistic and intellectual elite, and continued to be so right up till WWII. Splendid villas and pensions were constructed in that period, blending into the wooded landscape. Development continued after the war but priorities shifted towards cheap mass tourism, and massive concrete holiday homes and sanatoriums came to occupy the slopes of surrounding hills, some of them less than sympathetic to their environment. Nevertheless, Krynica has retained much of its laid-back, refined atmosphere and is still a pleasant place to unwind.

Information

MONEY

You'll find useful ATMs at ul Piłsudskiego 3 and 19; ul Zdrojowa 35 and ul Kraszewskiego 1. There are also some *kantors*, including ones at ul Piłsudskiego 9 and in the **post office** (ul Zdrojowa 1).

TOURIST INFORMATION

Tourist office (☎ 471 61 05; www.kot.org.pl in Polish; ul Piłsudskiego 8; ☺ 10am-6pm Mon-Fri, 10am-2pm Sat) Has lots of brochures and can book accommodation in town and around.

Sights & Activities

About 20 mineral springs are exploited and roughly half of them feed the public pump rooms where, for 1zł, the waters can be tried by anybody. The largest of all is the **Main Pump Room** (Pijalnia Główna; ☎ 471 22 23; Al Nowotarskiego 9; ☺ 6.30am-6pm). It's in a large modern building in the middle of Al Nowotarskiego, the central pedestrian promenade (called *deptak*) where the life of the town is concentrated.

There are a number of different waters to choose from in the Pijalnia and displays list the chemical composition of each. By far the heaviest, as you'll notice, is the Zuber, which has over 21g of soluble solid components per litre – a record for all liquids of that type in Europe. It's a sulphurous brew that won't be to everyone's liking.

You'll need your own drinking vessel; a bottle or a plastic cup will do, but if you want to follow local style, buy one of the kitsch porcelain tankards from the water 'bars' themselves, or from the shops downstairs in the Pijalnia. Local practice is to drink the water slowly while walking up and down the promenade. Otherwise, you can simply sit inside the tropical plant–filled building, quietly sipping from your porcelain pussycat or flowery tankard.

On a more cultural front, there's the interesting **Nikifor Museum** (Muzeum Nikifora; ☎ 471 53 03; Bulwary Dietla 19; admission 5zł; ☺ 10am-1pm & 2-5pm Tue-Sun). Located just west of the promenade, the museum displays about 50 works by Nikifor (1895–1968), possibly the best-known Polish naive painter. Lemk by origin, he produced hundreds of watercolours and drawings and is referred to as the Matejko of Krynica, the town of his birth. There are also various temporary exhibitions.

THE CARPATHIAN MOUNTAINS

You can take a short trip on the **Funicular to Góra Parkowa** (Kolej Linowa na Górę Parkową; ☎ 471 22 62; ul Nowotarskiego 1; one-way/return 15/17zł). The bottom station is near the northern end of the promenade. The car departs every half-hour (more often in the high season) till 9pm or 10pm, depending on the season and the demand. The ascent of 142m takes less than three minutes. You can walk down or take the funicular back.

A longer trip can be taken by the modern **Cable Car to Mt Jaworzyna** (Kolej Gondolowa na Jaworzynę; ☎ 471 38 68; ul Czarny Potok 75; adult/concession one-way 15/12zł, return 17/13zł). Finished in 1997, the Austrian-made cable car system consists of 55 six-person cars that run from the bottom station in the Czarny Potok Valley (about 5km from Krynica's centre) up to the top of Mt Jaworzyna (1114m). The route is 2210m long and the cable car climbs 465m in seven minutes.

Sleeping & Eating

Krynica has lots of holiday homes, hotels and pensions – approximately 120 in all – and there are also plenty of private rooms waiting for visitors. Like all resorts of this sort, the supply of accommodation changes notably throughout the year, peaking in summer, particularly in July and August, and in winter, mostly in January and February. Prices fluctuate depending on the season, weather, annual events etc, and are sometimes negotiable in the low season.

Many places – particularly holiday homes, but also some pensions – will offer you full board, not just a bed, which can be convenient.

The tourist office also arranges private rooms (around 35zł per person), though in the high season few owners will be interested in travellers intending to stay just a night or two (it's less hassle in the low season). There aren't many other budget options around.

BUDGET

Dom Wypoczynkowy PTTK Rzymianka (☎ 471 22 27; ul Dąbrowskiego 17; beds 35zł) The PTTK only offers shared facilities. It's pretty central, just 300m from the tourist office.

MID-RANGE & TOP END

Małopolanka (☎ 477 73 25; www.malopolanka .pl; ul Bulwary Dietla 13; s/d/apt from 80/120/180zł; [P] [X]) Right in the centre of town, the

Małopolanka is an elegant, old-fashioned pension and spa dating from the 1930s. Rooms are very modern and various spa treatments and comprehensive health and fitness programmes are available. There's also a yoga studio, restaurant and bar.

Hotel Saol (☎ 471 58 58; ul Zdrojowa 16; www.hotel .saol.com.pl in Polish; s/d/tr 100/200/270zł; [P] [💻]) This is one of Krynica's more modern hotels, not far from the centre. It offers bright, clean rooms and good facilities, including a sauna, solarium and restaurant.

Pensjonat Witolodówka (☎ 471 55 77; www.witol dowka.com.pl; ul Bulwary Dietla 10; s/d 105/120zł) This big wooden hotel looks like a grand Gothic lodge on the outside, while inside 1970s décor seems to be in favour. It's in a great central location, close to the pump room, and rooms are comfortable enough, if a little dated. There's also a bar and restaurant.

Ośrodek Panorama (☎ 471 28 85; fax 471 54 15; www.panorama.krynica.pl in Polish; ul Wysoka 15; s/d from 90/160zł) This large 140-bed holiday home, high up the wooded slope, offers OK standards, though it's lacking in ambience.

Hotel Rapsodia (☎ /fax 471 27 85; ul Ebersa 5; s/d/tr 135/160/195zł) This is a typical mid-range option, with private facilities and a fine level of comfort, plus its own restaurant. Rapsodia is close to the train and bus stations, convenient for late arrivals.

Hotel Wysoka (☎ 471 58 93; www.wysoka.com in Polish; ul Polna 2; s/d/apt 120/160/340zł; [P]) Wysoka is a big, chalet-style hotel offering a range of facilities and reasonable accommodation, though it's not the most atmospheric place around.

Like accommodation, the culinary scene is also heavily influenced by the seasons. In the high season heaps of eating establishments open, including dining rooms and cafés in holiday homes and pensions, and small bistros and snack bars along the central streets.

Getting There & Away

The train and bus stations are next to each other on ul Dr Henryka Ebersa in the southern part of town; it's roughly 1km to the promenade from there.

BUS

Buses to Nowy Sącz (4.50zł, 1½ hours) take a different, much shorter route to the train and run every half-hour to hour. The buses to Grybów (4.40zł, 50 minutes, six daily) pass through Berest and Polany. There are plenty of buses (both PKS and suburban) south to Muszyna (2.80zł, 25 minutes) via Powroźnik, and a fairly regular service to Mochnaczka, Tylicz and Muszyna.

TRAIN
There's a regular train service going to Nowy Sącz (14zł, 2½ hours) by a roundabout but pleasant route via Muszyna and Stary Sącz. Ten trains continue to Tarnów (20zł, three hours) and several of these go up to Kraków (29zł, four hours).

AROUND KRYNICA
☎ 18

Krynica is a good base for hiking into the surrounding countryside, with its beautiful wooded valleys, hills and charming small villages. Some of these, once populated by the Lemks, have their old churches preserved to this day. An essential aid for exploring the region (whether you're interested in hiking or in churches) is the *Beskid Sądecki* map (scale 1:75,000), which is readily available.

Sights & Activities
Most of the churches are accessible by bus. All churches listed here were originally the Uniat churches of the Lemks, but were taken over by the Roman Catholics after WWII. All are wooden structures, characteristic of the region.

To the north of Krynica, on the road to Grybów, there are good *cerkwie* in **Berest** and **Polany**, both retaining some of the old interior fittings including the iconostasis. Buses ply this route every hour or so and you shouldn't have problems coming back to Krynica or continuing to Grybów, from where there's frequent transport west to Nowy Sącz or east to Szymbark and Gorlice.

The loop via Mochnaczka, Tylicz and Powroźnik is an interesting trip. The 1846 church in **Mochnaczka Niżna** still has its old iconostasis, although it's disfigured by a central altar. You can also see the old small *cerkiew*, 600m down the road towards Tylicz on the other side. Built in 1787 it holds a beautiful tiny iconostasis complete with original icons. If you find the church locked, ask the nuns living in the nearby house to open it. There are several buses

from Krynica to Mochnaczka daily but take an early one if you want to continue along the route.

The next village, **Tylicz**, boasts two churches, a Catholic one and the Uniat *cerkiew*. The latter is only used for funerals. The priest is not eager to open the churches for visitors but in July and August he runs a guided tour around their interiors.

From Tylicz, a spectacular road skirts the Muszyna River valley to **Powroźnik**, which features yet another *cerkiew*. This one is the oldest in the region (1643) and the best known. The exterior is beautiful, and inside is an 18th-century iconostasis and several older icons on the side walls. The church can only be visited just before or after Mass, which is held at 7am and 11am on Sunday, and once a day on weekdays: at 6pm on Wednesday and Friday, at 6.30am on remaining days.

If you have your own means of transport, you can include the area around Muszyna and **Wojkowa** in your loop, both of which have old churches (bus transport is infrequent on these side roads). St Mary's Church in Krynica (the town's main church) displays the times of religious services in all churches in the region, which could help you plan your trip.

HIKING
Two marked trails, green and red, head westward from Krynica up to the top of Mt Jaworzyna (1114m). It takes two to three hours to walk there by either trail (or you can get there faster by cable car). At the top, you'll get some good views, and may even spot the Tatras on clear days. There's a **PTTK mountain hostel** (☎ 471 54 09) just below the summit where you can stay overnight (in good doubles or cheap dorms) and eat, or you can go back down to Krynica the same day. You can also continue on the red trail west to Hala Łabowska (2½ hours from Mt Jaworzyna) where you'll find another **PTTK mountain hostel** (☎ 442 07 80) providing cheap beds and food. The red trail continues west to Rytro (five hours). This route, leading mostly through the forest along the ridge of the main chain of the Beskid Sądecki, is spectacular and easy, and because of the accommodation on the way you can travel light. From Rytro, you can go back to Krynica by train or bus.

MUSZYNA

☎ 18 / pop 4900

Much smaller in size than Krynica, Muszyna is also geared to tourism. Here, too, mineral springs have been discovered and exploited and a number of sanatoriums have sprung up in the area. There's a small **Regional Museum** (☎ 471 41 40; ul Kity 26; admission 2zł; ☷ 9am-4pm Wed-Fri, 9am-1.30pm Sat & Sun) in the old inn, which displays artefacts and old household implements collected from the region. Otherwise, Muszyna has no remarkable sights, though it can be a convenient starting point for trips into the surrounding region (see right), which is every bit as interesting as the area around Krynica.

Information

The **tourist office** (☎ /fax 477 79 22; Rynek 31; ☷ 8.30am-3.30pm Mon-Fri) is in the centre of town. The **Vector travel agency** (☎ 471 80 03; info@btvector.com; ul Kity 24; ☷ 8am-6pm Mon-Sat year-round, 8am-3pm Sun Jun-Aug) can also provide tourist information, help in finding accommodation, organise a tour and find a guide who speaks English.

Sleeping

There are perhaps as many as 30 holiday homes in the area and plenty of private rooms; the Vector travel agency will be able to help you with these. There are also lots of places offering spa and other health treatments.

Ośrodek Sanatoryjno-Wczasowy Geovita (☎ / fax 471 41 83; www.geovita.pl; Złockie 80; s/d/ste from 48/62/102zł; P ⊠ ☣) Located in Złockie, around 3km north of Muszyna, this is one of the best places around, with a variety of hydrotherapy programmes and its own sauna and tennis courts. Full-board options are also available.

Ośrodek Wypoczynkowy Mimoza (☎ 471 40 23; www.mimoza.pl; ul Nowa 4; d 20-30zł, with meals 35-50zł; P) This central 'holiday centre' is one of the most inexpensive places in town. Rooms are fairly plain but they're clean; some have balconies and there are fabulous views. It also has a range of facilities available including a playground and basketball court.

Pensjonat Jaworzyna (☎ 471 47 33; www.sabtur yst.republika.pl in Polish; ul Polna 24; d/tr 50/90zł) Jaworzyna is a neat little chalet-style place

with cosy modern rooms. It offers very good standards for the price.

Sanatorium Uzdrowiskowe Korona (☎ 471 43 90; www.sanatoriumkorona.pl in Polish; ul Mściwujewskiego 2; s/d/apt 55/80/120zł; P ☣) Another modern hotel-cum-hydrotherapy centre, the Uzdrowiskowe Korona has bright, well-maintained rooms and a good choice of spa treatments.

Getting There & Away

Muszyna is on the Nowy Sącz–Krynica railway line and trains go regularly to either destination. Buses to Krynica (2.80zł, 25 minutes) run frequently, and there's also an adequate service to Nowy Sącz (7.50zł, 1½ hours).

AROUND MUSZYNA

Having belonged to the bishops of Kraków for nearly 500 years (from 1288 to 1772), Muszyna was traditionally a Polish town so, not surprisingly, it has a Catholic church but not a *cerkiew*. But the surrounding villages were populated predominantly by Lemks, whose wooden Uniat churches still dot the region, and there are at least five within 5km of Muszyna.

Three of them are north of the town, in **Szczawnik**, **Złockie** and **Jastrzębik**. All three were built in the 19th century – the one in Złockie, built in the 1860s, being the youngest and different in style – and each boasts the original iconostasis. Krynica suburban buses go via Muszyna to these villages several times a day and can shorten the walk.

Two more wooden churches, in **Milik** and **Andrzejówka**, are west of Muszyna, and have their original iconostases; you can get there by the regular buses or trains heading for Nowy Sącz. In Andrzejówka, ask for the key in the mustard-coloured house 50m down the road from the church; in Milik, the priest lives in the house at the foot of the *cerkiew*.

Two **hiking trails** originate in Muszyna and wind north up the mountains. The green one will take you to **Mt Jaworzyna** (1114m), while the yellow one goes to the peak of **Mt Pusta Wielka** (1061m). You can get to either in three to four hours, then continue to Krynica, Żegiestów or Rytro – the *Beskid Sądecki* map (see p241) has all the details.

THE PIENINY

The Pieniny, the mountain range between the Beskid Sądecki and the Tatras, is famous for the raft trip down the spectacular Dunajec Gorge, which has become one of Poland's major tourist highlights. Yet there's much more to see and do here. Walkers won't be disappointed with the hiking paths, which offer more-dramatic vistas than the Beskid Sądecki or Bieszczady, while lovers of architecture will find some amazing old wooden Catholic churches here. There's also a picturesque mountain castle in Niedzica, or you can just take it easy in the pleasant spa resort of Szczawnica.

The Pieniny consists of three separate ranges divided by the Dunajec River, the whole chain stretching east–west for about 35km. The highest and most popular is the central range topped by Mt Trzy Korony (Three Crowns; 982m), overlooking the Dunajec Gorge. Almost all this area is now the Pieniny National Park (Pieniński Park Narodowy). To the east, behind the Dunajec River, lies the Małe Pieniny (Small Pieniny), while to the west extends the Pie-

niny Spiskie. The latter outcrop is the lowest and the least spectacular, though the region around it, known as the Spisz, has an interesting blend of Polish and Slovakian cultures.

SZCZAWNICA

☎ 18 / pop 6800

Szczawnica (shchahv-*nee*-tsah) is the major tourist hub in the region. Picturesquely located along the Grajcarek River, the town has developed into a popular summer resort, while its mineral springs have made it an important spa. It's also the finishing point for Dunajec Gorge raft trips.

The town spreads over 4km along the main road, ul Główna, and is divided into two suburbs, the Niżna (Lower) to the west and Wyżna (Upper) to the east, with the bus terminal between the two. A good part of the tourist and spa facilities are in the upper part, which also boasts most of the fine old timber houses.

Szczawnica is a good starting point for hiking in the Pieniny or the Beskid Sądecki. Three trails originate from the town and two more begin from Jaworki, 8km east.

HIKING IN THE PIENINY

Almost all hiking concentrates on the central Pieniny range, a compact area of 40 sq km that has been decreed a national park. Trails are well marked and short and no trekking equipment is necessary. There are three starting points on the outskirts of the park, all providing accommodation and food. The most popular is Krościenko at the northern edge, then Szczawnica on the eastern rim and Sromowce Niżne to the south. Buy the *Pieniński Park Narodowy* map, which shows all hiking routes.

Most walkers start from Krościenko. They follow the yellow trail as far as the pass, the **Przełęcz Szopka**, then switch to the blue trail branching off to the left and head up to the top of **Mt Trzy Korony** (982m), the highest summit of the central range. The reward for this two-hour walk is a breathtaking panorama that includes the Tatras, 35km to the southwest, if the weather is clear. You are now about 520m above the level of the Dunajec River.

Another excellent view is from **Mt Sokolica** (747m), 2km east as the crow flies from Mt Trzy Korony, or a 1½-hour walk along the blue trail. From Mt Sokolica, you can go back down to Krościenko by the green trail, or to Szczawnica by the blue one, in less than an hour to either.

If you plan on taking the raft trip through the Dunajec Gorge, you can hike all the way to Kąty. There are several ways of getting there and the *Pieniński Park Narodowy* map shows them all. The shortest way is to take the blue trail heading west from the Przełęcz Szopka and winding up along the ridge. After 30 to 40 minutes, watch for the red trail branching off to the left (south) and leading downhill. It will take you directly to the wharf in about half an hour.

Alternatively, take the yellow trail descending south from the Przełęcz Szopka into a gorge. In half an hour or so you'll get to the beautifully located PTTK hostel. You can stay here for the night, or continue 1km downhill to the village of Sromowce Niżne (where there is a basic camping ground and some private rooms for rent) and go by bus (nine daily) or foot to Kąty (5km).

Sleeping & Eating

Accommodation in Szczawnica is the same as in many other mountain resorts: plentiful, inexpensive and highly varied depending on the season. There are few regular year-round hotels as well as a number of small pensions and holiday homes (most only open in summer). Plenty of locals also rent out rooms.

Travel agencies that arrange accommodation include **Orbis Travel** (☎ 262 22 57, ☎ /fax 262 22 37; ul Główna 32), 150m east of the bus terminal; **Podhale Tour** (☎ 262 23 70, ☎ /fax 262 27 27; ul Główna 20), 150m further east; and **PTTK** (☎ 262 23 32, ☎ /fax 262 22 95; ul Główna 1), another 150m further east along the same road. One more agency, the **Pieniny** (☎ 262 14 79, ☎ /fax 262 21 74; ul Skotnicka 8), is 400m west of the bus terminal.

All the offices tend to close around 4pm or 5pm, but don't panic if you arrive later – just ask for a bed where you spot the signs '*noclegi*', '*pokoje*' or '*kwatery*', indicating private rooms. There are plenty of these signs along ul Główna and the side streets. Expect to pay from 20zł to 30zł a bed.

There are plenty of small eateries on or just off ul Główna, most of which only open in the tourist season.

Getting There & Away

Buses to Nowy Targ (6.20zł, 1½ hours) depart roughly every hour. There are also regular buses to Nowy Sącz (7zł, two hours) which pass via Stary Sącz (6.50zł, 1½ hours). Six fast buses run daily straight to Kraków (13.50zł, 2½ hours).

For the Dunajec Gorge, take a bus (four daily in the high season) to Sromowce Niżne and get off in Kąty (4.50zł, 40 minutes) – the driver will set you down at the right place. There are also private minibuses that depart when full. Also, check the PTTK, which organises tours if it can assemble 10 or more people; this may work out to be much the same price that you'd pay if doing the trip on your own.

KROŚCIENKO

☎ 18 / pop 4500

A small town, founded in 1348 at the northern foot of the Pieniny, Krościenko is today a local holiday resort that fills with tourists in summer. Rich mineral springs were discovered here in the 19th century, but the town didn't exploit them and the title of spa

went to nearby Szczawnica, which did take advantage of the curative waters. With time Szczawnica overshadowed Krościenko in popularity, yet Krościenko remains number one as a hiking base for the Pieniny.

While in town, you can drop into the local **church** to see the surviving fragments of 15th-century frescoes depicting scenes from the life of Christ, and look over the pleasant **Rynek** in front of the church.

Information

TOURIST INFORMATION

Tourist office (☎ 262 33 04; Rynek 32; ☼ 8am-4pm Mon-Fri)

Sleeping & Eating

Willa Maria (☎ 262 61 51; www.kroscienko.info; ul Św Kingi 75a; beds in s/d/tr 25zł; [P]) is one of the more attractive small hotels, with a variety of rooms, most with balconies overlooking the Dunajec River. Meals are available for an extra charge.

Restauracja U Walusia (☎ 262 30 95; ul Jagiellońska; mains 10-30zł; ☼ lunch & dinner) is the best of Krościenko's restaurants. It's 800m from the Rynek along the Nowy Targ road. Specialities include the *placki po góralsku* (potato pancakes with goulash).

There are half a dozen small pensions including **Pensjonat Granit** (☎ 262 57 07; ul Jagiellońska 70), **Pensjonat Leśnik** (☎ 262 30 22; ul Jagiellońska 102), **Pensjonat Hanka** (☎ 262 55 28, ul Jagiellońska 55) and **Pensjonat U Gerwazego** (☎ 262 34 52; ul Zdrojowa 23). They all are simple but acceptable and will set you back about 25zł to 35zł per bed.

The **PTTK office** (☎ 262 30 59; ul Jagiellońska 28), right in the centre, has a list of private rooms for rent. Otherwise, just look for signs that read '*noclegi*' or '*kwatery*' outside the houses.

Getting There & Away

Lying on the Nowy Sącz–Nowy Targ route, Krościenko has a regular bus service to both these destinations. To Szczawnica (2.40zł, 15 minutes), buses run every 20 minutes or so. Four buses go to Sromowce Niżne daily (4.40zł, 25 minutes), which is the way to the raft wharf in Kąty (16km), and there are also private minibuses to Kąty in summer. You can also walk to Kąty (see p251). Five fast buses run directly to Zakopane. Krościenko's main bus stop is at the Rynek.

DUNAJEC GORGE

☎ 18

The **Dunajec Gorge** (Przełom Dunajca) is a spectacular stretch of the Dunajec (doo-nah-yets) River, which snakes for about 8km between steep cliffs, some of which are over 300m high. The river is narrow, in one instance funnelling through a 12m-wide bottleneck, and changes constantly from majestically quiet, deep stretches to shallow mountain rapids.

The place has been a tourist attraction since the mid-19th century, when primitive rafts did the honours for guests of the Szczawnica spa. Today the raft trip through the gorge attracts some 200,000 people annually, not counting those in their own kayaks. Take note though that this is not a white-water experience but a leisurely pleasure trip; the rapids are gentle and you won't get wet.

The raft itself is a set of five narrow, 6m-long, coffinlike canoes lashed together with rope. Until the 1960s they were genuine dugouts but now they are made of spruce planks. The raft takes 10 passengers and is steered by two raftsmen, each decked out in embroidered folk costume and armed with a long pole used to navigate.

The raft trip begins in the small village of **Kąty**, at the **Raft Landing Place** (Przystań Flisacka; ☎ 262 97 21, ☎ /fax 262 97 93; ⏱ 8.30am-5pm May-Aug, 8.30am-4pm Sep, 9am-2pm Oct). You'll take a 17km trip and disembark in Szczawnica. The journey takes two to three hours, depending on the level of the river. Some rafts go further downstream to Krościenko, but there's not much to see on that stretch of the river.

You can organise a trip at any travel agency in Zakopane or at the tourist office. The cost is around 35zł to 43zł per person, and includes transport, equipment and guides.

There are about 250 rafts in operation and they depart as soon as 10 passengers are ready to go. In general you won't have to wait long to get on the raft.

Rafts normally operate from 1 May to 31 Oct though both dates can change if it snows. There may also be some trips in late April and early November if the weather is fine. The trips may be suspended occasionally for a day or two when the river level is high.

Getting There & Away

Kąty is serviced by five buses daily from Nowy Targ (5.60zł, 45 minutes) and four from Szczawnica (4.40zł, 30 minutes). There's also a seasonal private minibus service from Szczawnica and Krościenko, and two PKS buses a day from Zakopane. Another way of getting to Kąty is to hike from Krościenko or Szczawnica. Travel agencies in Kraków, Zakopane, Szczawnica, Krynica and other touristy places in the region organise tours.

If you have private transport, you either have to leave your vehicle in Kąty and come back for it after completing the raft trip in Szczawnica, or you can drive to Szczawnica and leave your vehicle there, so you'll have it as soon as you complete the trip. There are car parks in both Kąty and Szczawnica, and the raft operator provides a bus service between the two locations.

NIEDZICA

☎ 18 / pop 3000

Niedzica, 5km west of Kąty, is known for its **castle**. Perched on a rocky hill above the Dunajec reservoir, the castle was built in the first half of the 14th century as one of the Hungarian border strongholds and was extended in the early 1600s. Since then it has altered little and has retained its graceful Renaissance shape.

The castle shelters a **museum** (☎ 262 94 89; adult/concession 5/2zł; ⏱ 9am-5pm May-Sep, 9am-4pm Tue-Sun Oct-Apr) featuring small collections on the archaeology and history of the region. You'll also get fine views over the surrounding area, including the reservoir of a hydroelectric project, just at the foot of the castle. An ethnographic section of the museum is presented (in summer only) in an old timber granary, 150m from the castle.

Sleeping & Eating

Zespół Zamkowy (☎ 262 94 89; fax 262 94 80; s/d/apt €52/67/104) Part of the castle has been adapted for hotel needs, providing 32 beds, some of which are in the historic castle chambers. The castle management also offers cheaper rooms (some without private bathroom) in the Celnica, a fine timber house built in the local style, 200m up the road from the castle. The castle restaurant provides meals. Some snack bars open in the tourist season near the castle entrance.

Hotel Lokis (☎ 262 85 40; www.lokis.com.pl; Zamek 76; d/apt 90/360zł) Situated in a wonderful spot overlooking the Czorsztyn Lake, around 500m from the castle, the Lokis is one of the more attractive hotels in the area. It has 21 doubles and two spacious apartments, and there's a big balcony with lake views.

Pensjonat Pieniny (☎ /fax 262 94 08; pieniny@ noclegi.com; ul 3 Maja 12; beds in r/cabins with shared bathroom 30-40zł) This large pension is in Niedzica, about 2km south of the castle. It offers 100 budget beds year-round, plus another 50 beds in basic seasonal cabins. Meals are available.

Hotel Pieniny (☎ 262 93 83; hotel.pieniny@ niedzica.pl; ul Kanada 38; s/d/tr 65/120/160zł; ℗ 💻) Located halfway between Niedzica village and the castle, this hotel is a reasonably priced option with its plain but comfortable rooms. It also has a tennis court and a sauna.

Getting There & Away

There are half a dozen buses a day from Nowy Targ (4.40zł, 40 minutes) to Niedzica castle. The village of Niedzica is better serviced from Nowy Targ, with about 10 buses per day, but not all go via the castle. When buying your ticket, make sure to specify 'Niedzica-Zamek' (castle). Bus links between the castle and other towns in the region are sporadic.

CZORSZTYN
☎ 18 / pop 2500

The village of Czorsztyn (*chor*-shtin), across the Dunajec from Niedzica, boasts another **castle** (admission 2.50zł; ☯ 9am-5pm May-Sep, 10am-3pm Tue-Sun Oct-Apr). It was built as the Polish counterpart to the Hungarian Niedzica stronghold. It's now just a ruin, but a picturesque one, and provides some fine views over the Dunajec valley and the Tatras. There's a small exhibition featuring the castle's history.

The castle is 2km west of the new village of Czorsztyn (no public transport). The village was built in the 1990s to accommodate residents of old Czorsztyn, further west, which is now flooded by the waters of the hydroelectric scheme. The village is just off the Krośnica–Katy road, accessible by the same buses you take for the Dunajec raft trip at Kąty.

DĘBNO PODHALAŃSKIE
☎ 18 / pop 3000

This small village boasts one of the oldest and most highly rated timber churches in Poland. The **church** was built in the 1490s on the site of a former church and, like most others, the larch-wood construction was put together without a single nail. The paintings that cover the ceiling and most of the walls date from around 1500 and have not been renovated since; despite that, the colours are still brilliant.

A triptych from the late 15th century adorns the high altar, whereas the crucifix that stands on the rood beam dates from 1380 and was probably transferred from the previous church. There are some antique objects on the side walls, including a wooden tabernacle from the 14th century.

Another curiosity is a small musical instrument, a sort of primitive dulcimer from the 15th century, which is used during Mass instead of the bell. The seemingly illogical thing about it is that the thicker the bars, the higher the notes they produce.

The priest living just across the road takes visitors through the church. He expects tourists from 8.30am to noon and from 2pm to 4.30pm weekdays (until 3.30pm in autumn and winter). He will wait until about 10 people turn up, so you may have to wait as well.

THE TATRAS

The Tatras are the highest range of the Carpathians and the only alpine type, with towering peaks and steep rocky sides dropping hundreds of metres to icy lakes. There are no glaciers in the Tatras but patches of snow remain all year. Winters are long, summers short and the weather erratic.

The vegetation changes with altitude, from mixed forest in the lower parts (below 1200m) to evergreen spruce woods higher up (to 1500m), then to dwarf mountain shrubs and highland pastures (up to 2300m) and finally moss. The wildlife is similarly stratified, with deer, roe deer and wildcat living in the lower forests, and marmot and chamois in the upper parts.

The whole range, roughly 60km long and 15km wide, stretches across the Polish-Slovakian border. A quarter of it is Polish

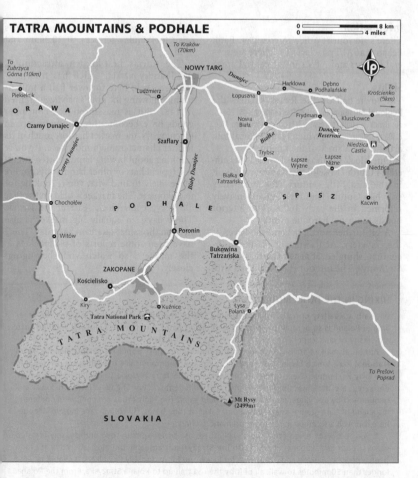

TATRA MOUNTAINS & PODHALE

territory and is now the Tatra National Park (Tatrzański Park Narodowy), encompassing 212 sq km. The Polish Tatras boast two dozen peaks exceeding 2000m, the highest of which is **Mt Rysy** (2499m).

At the northern foot of the Tatras lies the Podhale region, which spreads from Zakopane to Nowy Targ. The Podhale, dotted with small villages populated by the *górale* ('literally 'highlanders'), is one of the few Polish regions where old folk traditions are still observed in everyday life.

NOWY TARG
☎ 18 / pop 34,000

One of the oldest settlements at the foot of the Tatras, Nowy Targ started life around the 13th century, but in 1784 it was almost entirely consumed by fire and little of its old architecture has survived. Comfortably sitting in the fork of the Czarny (Black) and Biały (White) Dunajec Rivers, today it is a busy commercial town and a transport hub on the crossroads between the Tatras, Gorce, Pieniny, Spisz and Orawa. Nowy Targ is also known as a gliding centre; the airfield is on the southeastern outskirts of the town.

The town is a possible jumping-off point for travellers wanting to get to the surrounding countryside, though accommodation offerings are poor. You'll find a better selection of lodging options in Zakopane and Szczawnica.

Information

There's no tourist office to speak of. Bank Pekao is at Al Tysiąclecia 44. There are several *kantors* and ATMs in the central area.

Sights

The town hall on the Rynek shelters the **Regional Museum** (Muzeum Podhalańskie; ☎ 266 77 76; Rynek 1; adult/concession 3/1zł; ☑ 10am-6pm Mon, 8.30am-3.30pm Tue-Fri), which features local folk art and the history of the region.

One block north of the Rynek is **St Catherine's Church** (Kościół Św Katarzyny), built in the mid-14th century (the presbytery still has Gothic features) but extensively reformed in the early 1600s. The interior boasts the usual baroque overlay.

A bit further north, beyond the River, is the cemetery. At its entrance is the 16th-century shingled **St Anne's Church** (Kościół Św Anny). The interior is embellished with wall paintings from 1866. The church is open for Sunday services, at 10.30am and 4pm.

The town's best-known attraction is the **Thursday market**, which has traditionally been held here for over half a millennium, following the king's privilege granted in 1487. But as mass-produced consumer goods have become the dominant fare in recent years, the market has lost much of its former character and atmosphere. If you're thinking about buying hand-knitted sweaters, typical hats or other handicrafts, you're more likely to find what you're looking for in Zakopane. The market is held on the Plac Targowy, a few blocks east of the Rynek. These days, an equally big market is also held on the same square on Saturday. There have been some reports of pickpockets at the markets, so watch your belongings closely.

HIKING IN THE TATRA MOUNTAINS

With a huge variety of trails, totalling around 250km, the Tatras are ideal for walking. No other area of Poland is so densely crisscrossed with hiking paths, and nowhere else will you find such a diversity of landscapes.

Although marked trails go all across the region, the most popular area for hiking is **Tatra National Park**, which begins just south of Zakopane. Geographically, the Tatras are divided into the Tatry Zachodnie (West Tatras) to the west and the Tatry Wysokie (High Tatras) to the east. Both areas are attractive, though they offer quite different scenery. The West Tatras are lower and gentler and by and large are easier to walk and safer. The High Tatras are completely different; it's a land of bare granite peaks with alpine lakes at their bases. Hikers will face more challenges here, but will also enjoy much more dramatic scenery.

If you just want to go for a short walk, there are several picturesque and densely forested valleys south of Zakopane, of which **Dolina Strążyska** is arguably the most attractive. It's long been a popular walking and picnic area for locals and for reasonably fit walkers, it should take no longer than 50 minutes to walk all of it by the red trail up to Polana Strążyska. From the Polana, you can come back the same way or transfer by the black trail to either of the neighbouring valleys, the **Dolina Białego** to the east being the usual way. It takes around an hour to get to this charming valley and another hour to go all the way down to Zakopane.

The most popular mountain top climbed on foot in the Tatras, **Mt Giewont** (1894m), is the symbol of Zakopane. Part of the drawing power seems to be due to the huge cross on top, erected there in 1901, which has made the site a shrine. A reasonable level of fitness is required to attempt this climb.

Before you do any walking or climbing, you should get hold of the 1:25,000 scale *Tatrzański Park Narodowy* map, published by Sygnatura. It shows all the trails in the area, complete with walking times both uphill and downhill.

You normally won't need a guide for hiking in the Tatras, as trails are well marked, but if you do require this service, the **Centrum Przewodnictwa Tatrzańskiego** (Tatra Guide Centre; ☎ 206 37 99; ul Chałubińskiego 42/44; ☑ 9am-3pm) in Zakopane is able to arrange English- and German-speaking mountain guides.

Camping is not allowed in the park, but there are several basic PTTK mountain hostels dotted around; the tourist office in Zakopane will have details.

If you happen to be in the area on 15 August (the Assumption), try not to miss visiting the small village of **Ludźmierz**, only 5km from Nowy Targ, where the holy statue of the Virgin Mary in the local church attracts large numbers of pilgrims, most of them dressed up in their traditional costumes.

Sleeping

Hotel Limba (☎ 266 70 64; fax 266 89 43; ul Sokoła 8; s/d/tr from 35/60/80zł) Just one block off the Rynek, the Limba is convenient but basic. Rooms with private bathrooms cost slightly more.

Klub Sportowy Gorce (☎ /fax 266 26 61; Al Tysiąclecia 74; beds in d/tr 20-30zł) This place, a few blocks south of the Rynek, has hotel rooms plus three heated cabins. Conditions aren't exactly plush but rates aren't high.

Dom Turysty PTTK (☎ 441 50 12; ul Nadbrzeżna 40; d/tr 60/70zł; P) The PTTK offers the usual basic facilities, which are clean and adequate, though again, hardly luxurious.

Getting There & Away

The bus terminal is on the western edge of the central area of Nowy Targ, around 1.5km from the Rynek; the train station is 1km southwest of the bus station, on the town's outskirts.

All the Kraków–Zakopane traffic passes through town and the route is pretty busy. Buses to Zakopane (6zł, 45 minutes) run frequently. To Kraków, it's faster to go by bus (9.60zł, two hours) as the trains take the long way around (14zł, three hours).

Buses to Szczawnica (6.20zł, 50 minutes) run roughly every hour. There are three morning buses to Niedzica castle, going via the village of Niedzica. Three buses go daily to the border crossing at Łysa Polana (6zł, 45 minutes), and five to Kąty (5.50zł, 40 minutes), where the raft trips through the Dunajec Gorge begin.

ZAKOPANE

☎ 18 / pop 30,000

Nestled at the foot of the Tatras, Zakopane is the most famous mountain resort in Poland and the winter sports capital. The town attracts a couple of million tourists a year, with peaks in summer and winter. Although Zakopane is essentially a base for either skiing or hiking in the Tatras, the town itself is an enjoyable enough place to hang about for a while, and it has lots of facilities.

Zakopane came to life in the 17th century, but only in the second half of the 19th century did it become something more than a mountain post, attracting visitors and artists alike. When the Young Poland artistic movement developed in Kraków in the 1890s, Zakopane became popular with artists, many of whom came to settle and work here. The best known of these are the composer Karol Szymanowski and the writer and painter Witkacy. The father of the latter, Stanisław Witkiewicz (1851–1915), was inspired by the traditional local architecture and created the so-called 'Zakopane style'; some of the buildings he designed stand to this day.

The town grew at a faster pace in the interwar period, and shortly before WWII the cableway and funicular railway were built, today the prime attractions. Development continued after the war but it's still reasonably small and hasn't been marred by the concrete blocks typical of most Polish urban centres. Apart from a few central streets, Zakopane feels more like a large village rather than a town, its mainly villa-type houses set informally in their own gardens.

Orientation

Zakopane sits at an altitude of 800m to 1000m at the foot of Mt Giewont. The bus and train stations are adjacent in the northeast part of town. It's just less than 1km down ul Kościuszki to the town's heart, the pedestrian mall of Krupówki, which is always jammed with tourists.

The funicular to Mt Gubałówka is off the northwestern end of Krupówki. The cable car to Mt Kasprowy Wierch is at Kuźnice, 3km to the southeast.

MAPS

The 1:13,000 *Zakopane Falk* map, published by Pascal, is widely available.

Information

BOOKSHOPS

Księgarnia Górska (☎ 201 24 81) Located in the Dom Turysty PTTK, with the best choice of maps and guidebooks on the Tatras and other mountain regions.

INTERNET ACCESS

Internet facilities:

Internet Club Mikrokomputery (☎ 201 33 10; ul Krupówki 54)

Top Net (☎ 206 42 31; ul Krupówki 2)

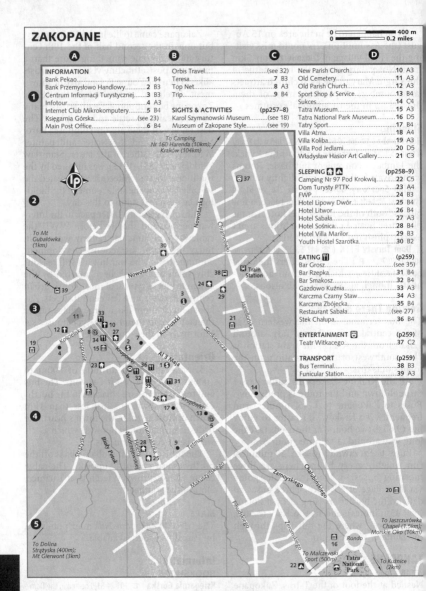

ZAKOPANE

0 _____ 400 m
0 _____ 0.2 miles

INFORMATION
Bank Pekao.................................**1** B4
Bank Przemysłowo Handlowy......**2** B3
Centrum Informacji Turystycznej..**3** B3
Infotour.....................................**4** A3
Internet Club Mikrokomputery.....**5** B4
Księgarnia Górska...................(see 23)
Main Post Office........................**6** B4

Orbis Travel............................(see 32)
Teresa......................................**7** B3
Top Net....................................**8** A3
Trip..**9** B4

SIGHTS & ACTIVITIES   (pp257–8)
Karol Szymanowski Museum.......(see 18)
Museum of Zakopane Style........(see 19)

New Parish Church....................**10** A3
Old Cemetery...........................**11** A3
Old Parish Church.....................**12** A3
Sport Shop & Service.................**13** B4
Sukces....................................**14** C4
Tatra Museum..........................**15** A3
Tatra National Park Museum.......**16** D5
Tatry Sport..............................**17** B4
Villa Atma...............................**18** A4
Villa Koliba.............................**19** A3
Villa Pod Jedlami.....................**20** D5
Władysław Hasior Art Gallery.....**21** C3

SLEEPING   (pp258–9)
Camping Nr 97 Pod Krokwią.......**22** C5
Dom Turysty PTTK....................**23** A4
FWP.......................................**24** B3
Hotel Lipowy Dwór...................**25** B4
Hotel Litwor............................**26** B4
Hotel Sabała............................**27** A3
Hotel Sośnica...........................**28** B4
Hotel Villa Marilor....................**29** B3
Youth Hostel Szarotka...............**30** B2

EATING   (p259)
Bar Grosz...............................(see 35)
Bar Rzepka..............................**31** B4
Bar Smakosz............................**32** B4
Gazdowo Kuźnia.......................**33** A3
Karczma Czarny Staw.................**34** A3
Karczma Zbójecka.....................**35** B4
Restaurant Sabała....................(see 27)
Stek Chałupa............................**36** B4

ENTERTAINMENT   (p259)
Teatr Witkacego.......................**37** C2

TRANSPORT   (p259)
Bus Terminal............................**38** B3
Funicular Station.......................**39** A3

To Camping
Nr 160 Harenda (10km);
Kraków (104km)

To Mt
Gubałówka
(1km)

To Dolina
Strążyska (400m);
Mt Giewont (3km)

To Jaszczurówka
Chapel (1.5km);
Morskie Oko (10km)

To Malczewski
Sport (500m)

To Kuźnice
(2km)

Tatra
National
Park

Rondo

Train
Station

MONEY

Bank Pekao (Al 3 Maja 5) changes most major brands of travellers cheques and pays advances on Visa and MasterCard. **Bank Przemysłowo Handlowy** (ul Krupówki 19) will change cheques and accepts Visa card. *Kantors* dot ul Krupówki every 50m or so, and there are also a number of ATMs.

TOURIST INFORMATION

Centrum Informacji Turystycznej (☎ 201 22 11; www.zakopane.pl; ul Kościuszki 17; ❤ 8am-8pm in season both summer & winter, 9am-5pm at other times)

TRAVEL AGENCIES

Orbis Travel (☎ 201 48 12; ul Krupówki 22) organises accommodation in private homes.

Other useful travel agencies are **Trip** (☎ 202 02 00; ul Tetmajera 18); **Teresa** (☎ 201 43 01; ul Kościuszki 7); and **Infotour** (☎ 206 42 64; ul Kościeliska 11B). They arrange accommodation in private rooms, sell transportation tickets and may have tours to popular regional destinations, including the Dunajec Gorge (see p251).

Sights

You'll probably start your sightseeing at Krupówki, the trendy central mall that's lined with restaurants, cafés, boutiques and souvenir shops. After wandering up and down you should have a good feel for the local atmosphere. Krupówki is the place to be, and some visitors seem to do nothing but parade in this mall for days on end.

The **Tatra Museum** (Muzeum Tatrzańskie; ☎ 201 52 05; ul Krupówki 10; admission 4zł; ☽ 9am-4pm Tue-Sun) has sections on history, ethnography, geology and flora and fauna and is a good introduction to the region.

At the lower end of Krupówki is the neo-Romanesque **parish church**, which looks as though it has been imported from a completely different culture. It was built at the end of the 19th century when the smaller **old parish church** couldn't cope any longer with the numbers of worshippers. The latter, 100m away on ul Kościeliska, is a rustic wooden construction dating from 1847. It has charming folksy decorations inside.

The **stone chapel** standing beside it is about 30 years older and is in fact the first place of worship and the oldest surviving building in Zakopane. Just behind it is the **old cemetery** with a number of amazing wooden tombs.

West on ul Kościeliska is the **Villa Koliba**, the first design (1892) of Witkiewicz in the Zakopane style. It's now home to the **Museum of Zakopane Style** (Muzeum Stylu Zakopiańskiego; ☎ 201 36 02; ul Kościeliska 18; admission 4zł; ☽ 9am-4pm Wed-Sun).

About 500m southeast is **Villa Atma**, once the home of Karol Szymanowski. Today it's a **museum** (☎ 206 31 50; ul Kasprusie 19; admission 2zł; ☽ 10am-4pm Tue-Sun) dedicated to the composer. Summer piano recitals are held here.

Don't miss the **Władysław Hasior Art Gallery** (☎ 206 68 71; ul Jagiellońska 18C; admission 4zł; ☽ 11am-5pm Wed-Sat, 9am-3pm Sun), displaying striking assemblages by the late artist, who was also closely associated with Zakopane.

A little under 2km south of here, next to the roundabout called Rondo, is the **Tatra National Park Museum** (Muzeum TPN; ☎ 201 41 92; ul Chałubińskiego 42a; admission 4zł; ☽ 9am-2pm Mon-Sat) featuring an exhibition on the natural history of the park.

A short walk east up the hill takes you to **Villa Pod Jedlami**, another splendid Zakopane-style house (the interior cannot be visited). Perhaps Witkiewicz' greatest achievement is the **Jaszczurówka Chapel**, about 1.5km further east on the road to Morskie Oko.

Activities

CYCLING

Cycling can be a pleasant and convenient means of getting around the Zakopane region, including some of the less-steep parts of the Tatras. Bikes are permitted in certain areas of Tatra National Park, but only on designated routes. These include the Dolina Chochołowska and Dolina Suchej Wody, both picturesque and attractive for biking. Droga Pod Reglami, the service road that marks the northern boundary of the park, also offers some good rides. Check when you arrive which routes are open for bikes, because this tends to change. Note that the access road to Lake Morskie Oko is no longer open for bikes. They can go only as far as the car park at Polana Palenica.

Bicycles are available for hire from a number of companies in Zakopane, including **Sukces** (☎ 206 41 97; ul Sienkiewicza 39); **Sport Shop & Service** (☎ 201 58 71; ul Krupówki 52A); **Tatry Sport** (☎ 201 44 23; ul Piłsudskiego 4); and **Malczewski Sport** (☎ 201 20 05; ul Bronisława Czecha).

SKIING

Zakopane is known as Poland's winter sports capital. The town's environs have a number of ski areas, ranging from flat surfaces to steep slopes – suitable for everyone from beginners to ski masters – dotted with about 50 ski lifts in all.

Mt Kasprowy Wierch offers some of the most challenging ski slopes in the area, as well as the best conditions, with the ski season extending right up until early May. You can get to the top by **cable car** (return 29zł; ☽ 7.30am-8pm summer, 7.30am-3.30pm winter) then stay up the mountains and use the two chairlifts, in the Goryczkowa and Gąsienicowa valleys, on both sides of Mt Kasprowy Wierch.

Mt Gubałówka is another popular skiing area and it too, offers some steep slopes and good conditions. It's easily accessible by the funicular from central Zakopane, and there are some T-bar lifts up there. The **funicular** (one-way/return 8/14zł) covers the 1388m-long route in less than five minutes and climbs 300m from the funicular station, just north of ul Krupówki. It operates between 9am and 9pm from 1 May to 30 September, but at other times it only runs on weekends. An all-day pass for skiers costs 70zł; a one-day pass at other times for 10 rides costs 50zł.

Nearby, 2km to the west, is **Mt Butorowski Wierch**, with its 1.6km-long chairlift, making it yet another good skiing area.

One more major ski area is at the slopes of **Mt Nosal**, on the southeastern outskirts of Zakopane. Facilities include a chairlift and a dozen T-bars. Mt Nosal is also very popular for paragliding.

Ski-equipment hire is available at most facilities and from a number of hire companies in Zakopane. The bicycle-hire companies also hire out ski equipment in winter.

Festivals & Events
The **International Festival of Mountain Folklore** is held in late August and is the town's leading cultural event. In July, a series of **concerts** presenting music by Karol Szymanowski and other composers is held in the Villa Atma.

Sleeping
Zakopane has no shortage of places to stay and, except for occasional peaks, finding a bed is no problem. Even if hotels and hostels are full, there will generally be private rooms around, which provide some of the most reasonable and best accommodation in town. Check at the tourist office for details (double rooms should cost roughly 40zł to 50zł) or look for signs reading '*pokoje*', '*noclegi*' or '*zimmer frei*' outside private homes. There are plenty of them in town.

There are many holiday homes in Zakopane and most of them are open to the general public, renting rooms either directly or through travel agencies. The major agent is **FWP** (☎ 201 27 63; ul Kościuszki 19; ⊙ 8am-5pm Mon-Fri year-round, 8am-5pm Sat in high season), located in the DW Podhale. The office rents out rooms in nine FWP holiday homes around the town. Rooms range from doubles to quads, some with private bathrooms. You can take just a room or room with board (three meals).

As with all seasonal resorts, accommodation prices in Zakopane fluctuate (sometimes considerably) between the high and low seasons, peaking in late December, January and February, and then in July and August. Prices given are for the high season.

BUDGET
Youth Hostel Szarotka (☎ 201 36 18; ul Nowotarska 45; dm/d 35/50zł) This friendly and homy place gets packed (and untidy) in the high season, but rates are negotiable at other times.

Dom Turysty PTTK (☎ /fax 206 32 81; ul Zaruskiego 5; dm/s/d/tr from 16/50/60/84zł; P) The very central PTTK hostel has 470 beds in lots of rooms of different sizes, mostly dormitories. Rooms with private facilities cost more. This place can often be swamped with school excursion groups.

Camping Nr 97 Pod Krokwią (☎ 201 22 56; ul Żeromskiego 34; camping per person/tent 10/7zł, beds in bungalows 20-35zł; P) The camping ground has large heated bungalows, each containing several double and triple rooms. They are often full in the July/August period. To get to the camping grounds from the bus/train stations, take any bus to Kuźnice or Jaszczurówka and get off at Rondo.

Camping Nr 160 Harenda (☎ 201 47 00; ul Harenda 51B; camping per person/tent 10/8zł, beds in cabins 20-35zł; P) Around 10km out of town on the Kraków road, Harenda offers neat and cosy cabins that are great value, and space to pitch your tent or park your campervan. It also boasts a sauna.

MID-RANGE & TOP END
As with the cheaper options, there's a wide range of more upscale hotels around town. They don't always represent good value, but there are some decent options from which to choose.

Hotel Villa Marilor (☎ 206 44 11; www.hotelmarilor.com; ul Kościuszki 18; s/d/ste 450/550/1100zł; P ✗) The Marilor is an elegant, upmarket hotel, dating from 1912. It's one of the very best places in town, with suitably stylish rooms and top-end facilities, including a tennis court and a superb restaurant.

Hotel Sabała (☎ 201 50 92; www.sabala.zakopane.pl; ul Krupówki 11; s/d from 195/260zł) Situated in a beautiful, typically local villa from 1894, which has been meticulously restored over recent years, Sabała provides some of the best and most atmospheric accommodation in town. It enjoys a superb location overlooking the picturesque pedestrian thoroughfare and has cosy, attic-style rooms. Half-board options are also available.

Hotel Litwor (☎ 201 27 39; www.litwor.pl; ul Krupówki 40; s/d €119/157; P ✗ ⊋) A sumptuous four-star place, with large, restful rooms and all the usual top-end facilities, including a gym and sauna. It has an excellent restaurant serving traditional game dishes.

Lipowy Dwór (☎ 206 67 96; fax 201 43 36; ul Heleny Modrzejewskiej 7; s/d 94/128zł; P) On a quiet street south of the centre, this charming wooden chalet-style hotel offers good-value accommodation, with small, well-maintained rooms. Guests may use the facilities at its sister establishment, the Sośnica.

Hotel Sośnica (☎ 206 67 99; sosnica@gat.pl; ul Heleny Modrzejewskiej 7; s/d 94/128zł; P ⊋) Right opposite the Lipowy Dwór, and also under the same management, the Sośnica is a larger place, with 93 beds. Many rooms have balconies with mountain views, and although it's a little dated, it's still fine value for the location.

Eating

The main street, ul Krupówki, has plenty of cafés and restaurants. Eating cheaply is not a problem in Zakopane – the proliferation of small fast-food outlets around town is astonishing, and there are also plenty of informal places in private homes in back streets, displaying boards saying '*obiady domowe*' (home-cooked lunches). Don't miss trying the smoked sheep's-milk cheese sold at street stands all along ul Krupówki.

Bar Rzepka (☎ 201 54 16; ul Krupówki 43; mains 10-15zł; ☽ lunch & dinner) Rzepka serves tasty typical Polish fare at very reasonable prices.

Gazdowo Kuźnia (☎ 201 72 01; ul Krupówki 1; mains 10-15zł; ☽ lunch & dinner) A small menu of characteristic local cuisine is on offer here.

Karczma Zbójecka (☎ 201 38 56; ul Krupówki 28; mains 18-30zł; ☽ lunch & dinner) An attractive basement eatery, the Karczma offers standard regional food and a good atmosphere, plus local folk music on some evenings.

Stek Chałupa (☎ 201 59 18; ul Krupówki 33; mains 15-25zł; ☽ lunch & dinner) With a Wild West theme and rustic timber furniture, Chałupa is a pleasant place for grilled sausages, steaks, baked potatoes and local specialities.

Karczma Czarny Staw (☎ 201 38 56; ul Krupówki 2; mains 10-25zł; ☽ lunch & dinner) With the same management as Zbójecka, this is similar but more upmarket. It offers tasty Polish dishes and there's live music nightly.

Restaurant Sabała (☎ 201 50 92; ul Krupówki 11; mains 15-25zł; ☽ lunch & dinner) A lively, friendly place serving a wide range of traditional local specialities, again with live music.

Among the cheapest places to eat are the basic **Bar Grosz** (Krupówki 28) and **Bar Smakosz** (ul Krupówki 22). You can expect to pay around 10zł for a simple meal in any of them.

Entertainment

Teatr Witkacego (Witkacy Theatre; ☎ 206 82 97; www .witkacy.zakopane.pl; ul Chramcówki 15) This is one of the best theatres in Poland, with a full programme of plays (in Polish) by the likes of Pirandello, Christopher Marlowe and Arthur Miller.

Getting There & Away

Most regional routes are covered by bus, while train is better for long-distance travel, eg to bigger cities such as Warsaw.

BUS

The PKS fast buses run to Kraków (9zł, two hours) every 30 to 40 minutes or so. There are also two private companies, Trans Frej and Szwagropol, that run services roughly hourly to Kraków (10zł, 1¾ hours), departing from the front of DW Podhale at ul Kościuszki 19. There are several daily PKS buses to Nowy Sącz (15zł, three hours) and daily buses to Tarnów (24zł, four hours), Przemyśl (26zł, 4½ hours) and Rzeszów (25zł, 4½ hours). PKS has two direct buses travelling to Kąty (for the Dunajec raft trip) in summer.

In the region around Zakopane, bus transport is relatively frequent. PKS buses can take you to the foot of the Kościeliska and Chochołowska valleys as well as to Polana Palenica, the gateway to Lake Morskie Oko. There are also private minibuses that ply the most popular tourist routes, departing across the road from the PKS terminal.

There are a few international departures each week; check the website www .eurolinespolska.pl for current destinations, times and prices.

TRAIN

There are a number of trains to Kraków (25zł, 3½ hours), but buses are faster and more frequent. One train (a few more in the high season) runs daily to Warsaw (58zł, six hours). Tickets are available from the station or from **Orbis Travel** (☎ 201 48 12; ul Krupówki 22).

THE CARPATHIAN MOUNTAINS

Silesia

CONTENTS

Of all Poland's regions, Silesia has the most distinct identity, comparable with German Saxony or Czech Bohemia and closely related to both. The area was defined long before the modern-day Polish state, and parts now fall within the borders of the Czech Republic.

This culture is not the result of a continuous development, but rather the last vestiges of a stronger regional tradition largely destroyed by forced population shifts after WWII. This area had a German majority for much of its existence, and many towns here have spent more time within Prussian, Saxon and Bohemian borders than they ever have as part of Poland. Memories of the mass 'repatriation' of Silesia's German communities still linger in certain quarters, and the whole region is marked by their influence. Luckily you'll encounter little rancour here, and the province as a whole is open and receptive to all visitors. The principal city, Wrocław, is an historical gem, but the real draw is the Sudeten Mountains, a perfect strip of natural beauty, and holiday towns stretching along the Czech border. Hikers, bikers and spa fans alike won't find much to complain about here.

The rich history of the region underpins its charm, with architecture ranging from medieval fortresses to baroque cathedrals. Most importantly, this is the site of Auschwitz concentration camp, preserved as a grim memorial that should be compulsory viewing. Silesia may afford plenty of opportunities for fun and relaxation, but it takes a glimpse of the dark side to really appreciate the significance of this once-turbulent piece of Europe.

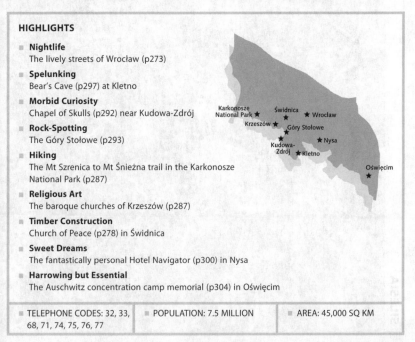

HIGHLIGHTS

- **Nightlife**
  The lively streets of Wrocław (p273)

- **Spelunking**
  Bear's Cave (p297) at Kletno

- **Morbid Curiosity**
  Chapel of Skulls (p292) near Kudowa-Zdrój

- **Rock-Spotting**
  The Góry Stołowe (p293)

- **Hiking**
  The Mt Szrenica to Mt Śnieżna trail in the Karkonosze National Park (p287)

- **Religious Art**
  The baroque churches of Krzeszów (p287)

- **Timber Construction**
  Church of Peace (p278) in Świdnica

- **Sweet Dreams**
  The fantastically personal Hotel Navigator (p300) in Nysa

- **Harrowing but Essential**
  The Auschwitz concentration camp memorial (p304) in Oświęcim

Map labels: Karkonosze National Park ★ · Świdnica ★ · Wrocław ★ · Krzeszów ★ · Góry Stołowe ★ · Nysa ★ · Kudowa-Zdrój ★ · Kletno ★ · Oświęcim ★

- TELEPHONE CODES: 32, 33, 68, 71, 74, 75, 76, 77
- POPULATION: 7.5 MILLION
- AREA: 45,000 SQ KM

SILESIA

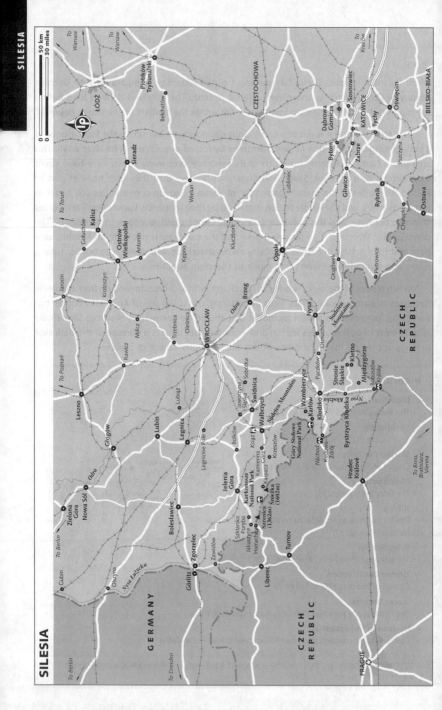

WROCŁAW

☎ 71 / pop 675,000

Poland's fourth-largest city, on the Odra River in the middle of Lower Silesia, Wrocław (*vrots*-wahf) is the major industrial, commercial, educational and cultural centre for the whole of southwestern Poland. After six centuries in foreign hands – Bohemian, Austrian and Prussian – the city has a unique architectural and cultural make-up, best seen in its magnificent old market square. The Odra location, with its 12 islands, 112 bridges and riverside parks, has prompted the inevitable comparisons with Venice, and the beautifully preserved ecclesiastical district is a treat for Gothic groupies.

Wrocław is also a lively cultural centre, with several theatres, some major festivals, rampant nightlife and a large student community. It's a hugely appealing city with a character all its own, embracing everything modern Poland has to offer, and there's really no excuse for missing out.

HISTORY

Wrocław was originally founded on the island of Ostrów Tumski. The first recorded Polish ruler, Duke Mieszko I, brought the town, together with most of Silesia, into the Polish state. It must have already been a fair-sized stronghold by the year 1000, as it was chosen as one of Piast Poland's three bishoprics, along with Kraków and Kołobrzeg.

During the period of division in the 12th and 13th centuries, Wrocław was the capital of one of the principalities of the Silesian Piasts. Like most settlements in southern Poland, Wrocław was burned down by the Tatars. The town centre was then moved to the left bank of the river and laid out on the chessboard plan that survives to this day.

Wrocław continued to grow under Bohemian administration (1335–1526), reaching perhaps the height of its prosperity in the 15th century, and maintaining trade and cultural links with the Polish Crown. This speedy development led to the construction of new fortifications at the beginning of the 16th century, and the wide moat of the Fosa Miejska shows where they were once positioned.

The Habsburgs, who ruled the city for the next two centuries, were less tolerant of the Polish and Czech communities, and things got even worse for the Slavic populations after 1741, when Wrocław fell to Prussia. For the next two centuries the city was increasingly Germanised, changing its name to Breslau, and by the 1930s the whole area was very much a German principality.

As one of the major eastern outposts of the Reich, Hitler gave Breslau a key defensive role in the last stages of WWII, converting the whole city into a fortified compound sealed off from the outside world. Besieged by the Red Army for nearly three months, the Nazis defended their last bastion to the end, executing anyone who refused to fight. During the battle, 70% of the city was razed to the ground.

Of the prewar population of more than 600,000, an estimated 30% died (10 times more than the number of soldiers killed on both sides), mostly as a result of the fighting and the botched evacuation that preceded it. The handful of Germans who remained were expelled to Germany, and the ruined city was resettled with people from Poland's prewar eastern regions, mostly from Lviv, which had been lost to the Soviet Union.

The reconstruction was painful and difficult, and continued well into the 1980s. There's a lot of postwar concrete, but the most important historic buildings have been faithfully reconstructed. Only in the late 1980s did the city surpass its prewar population level.

ORIENTATION

The train and bus stations are near each other, 1km south of the ring road surrounding the roughly oval Old Town. Almost all major sights are within walking distance in the central area.

INFORMATION
Bookshops

Columbus (☎ 342 41 74; ul Kuźnicza 57/58)
EMPiK Plac Kościuszki (☎ 341 70 15; Plac Kościuszki 21/23); Rynek (☎ 343 39 72; Rynek 50)
Podróżnika (☎ 346 00 71; www.mapy.wroclaw.pl; ul Wita Stwosza 19/20)
PolAnglo Rynek (☎ 341 79 60; Rynek 7); ul Kuźnicza (☎ 341 97 60; ul Kuźnicza 49a)
Vademecum (☎ 351 78 12; www.bookworld.com.pl; ul Kuźnicza 22)

Discount Cards

Wrocław Tourist Pass (in Warsaw ☎ 22-615 83 30; www.wroclaw.pl; 1/3 days 39/79zł) Unlimited public transport and free or discounted entry to museums and attractions, plus hotel, restaurant and leisure discounts.

Internet Access

Adan (☎ 781 86 69; ul Ruska 60/61; per hr 3.50zł)
Cyber Tea Tavern (☎ 372 35 71; ul Kuźnicza 29a; per hr 3-6zł; ☉ 10am-10pm Mon-Sat, 4-10pm Sun)
Galaxy (☎ 374 61 14; ul Kazimierza Wielkiego 55; per hr 4zł; ☉ from 9am)
Korbank (☎ 781 76 30; ul Psie Budy Szajnochy; per hr 4zł; ☉ 24hr)
W Sercu Miasta (☎ 342 46 76; Przejście Żelażnicze 8, Rynek-Ratusz; per hr 4zł; ☉ 24hr)

Money

Bank Pekao (☎ 344 44 54; ul Oławska 2)

Post

Post office Rynek (☎ 347 19 38; Rynek 28); ul Piłsudskiego (☎ 343 09 06; ul Piłsudskiego 12)

Tourist Information

Cultural Information Centre (Osrodek Kultury i Sztuki; ☎ 344 28 64; www.okis.pl; Rynek-Ratusz 24; ☉ 10am-6pm Mon-Sat)
Tourist office (☎ 344 31 11; www.wroclaw.pl; Rynek 14; ☉ 10am-9pm)

Travel Agencies

Almatur (☎ 343 41 35; ul Kościuszki 34)
PTTK (Polskie Towarzystwo Turystyczno-Krajoznawcze, Polish Tourist & Countryside Association; ☎ 343 83 31; Rynek-Ratusz 11/12)
Orbis Travel (☎ 344 44 08; Rynek 29)

SIGHTS
Rynek

Wrocław's old market square is the second largest in the country, surpassed only by that in Kraków. The central town hall complex is so big that it incorporates three internal streets. Fully renovated over recent years, the Rynek is lively and architecturally mixed. In summer especially it's the focal point of city life, circled by buskers and street performers exploiting the captive audience spilling out from the many restaurant terraces.

TOWN HALL

This is certainly one of the most beautiful historic town halls in Poland. The main structure took almost two centuries (1327–

1504) to complete, and work on the tower and decoration continued for another century. Since then, it hasn't changed much; amazingly, it came through WWII without major damage.

The eastern façade reflects the stages of the town hall's development, split into three distinct elements. The northern segment, with its austere early Gothic features, is the oldest, while the southern part is the most recent and shows elements of the early Renaissance style. The central and most impressive section is topped by an ornamented triangular roof adorned with pinnacles – a favourite cover picture for local tourist brochures. The astronomical clock, made of larch wood, was incorporated in 1580.

The southern façade, dating from the early 16th century, is the most elaborate, with bay windows, carved stone figures and two elaborate friezes. The cellar on this side holds a popular pub-restaurant.

The western elevation is the most austere, apart from the early-baroque doorway from 1615, which leads to the **Museum of Burgher Art** (Muzeum Sztuki Mieszczańskiej; ☎ 344 14 34; Rynek-Ratusz; adult/concession 4/2zł, free Wed; ☉ 11am-5pm Wed-Sat, 10am-6pm Sun). The museum's period interiors are every bit as magnificent as the building's exterior. The most amazing is probably the huge Knights' Hall (Sala Rycerska) on the 1st floor, with the original carved decorations from the end of the 15th century. Next to it is the Princes' Room (Sala Książęca), which was originally a chapel. The historic rooms house exhibitions, including a collection of gold and silverware, but they're virtually eclipsed by the surroundings.

The decorative post in front of the façade is the **whipping post** (pręgierz), marking the site where public floggings were carried out in medieval times. It's an exact replica of the 1492 original, which stood here until WWII, and is now generally used as a seat or meeting point by locals and underage drinkers.

AROUND THE RYNEK

The Rynek was laid out in the 1240s and lined with timber houses, which were later replaced with brick structures. They gradually changed over the centuries; some adopted the architectural style of the day, while others kept closer to tradition. After the wartime destruction, they were rebuilt as they had been before the war, so they now offer an amalgam of architectural styles from Gothic onwards, an appealing sight whatever the weather. Take a stroll right the way round to get the full effect.

One of the buildings houses the **Museum of Medal Art** (Muzeum Sztuki Medalierskiej; ☎ 344 39 83; Rynek 6; adult/concession 7/5zł; ☼ 10am-5pm Wed & Fri, 11am-5pm Thu & Sat, 10am-6pm Sun), a collection of old badges and military decorations from throughout Wrocław's history.

Set in the northwestern corner of the Rynek are two charming houses called **Jaś i Małgosia** (Hansel and Gretel) linked by a baroque gate from 1728, which once led to the church cemetery. Just behind them is the monumental brick **St Elizabeth's Church** (Kościół Św Elżbiety), with its 83m-high **tower** (admission 2zł; ☼ 9am-6pm Mon-Fri, 11am-6pm Sat, 1-6pm Sun); you can go to the top for a good view. This Gothic church went up in flames in 1975 in suspicious circumstances, and much of the furnishings, including the organ, were lost. It was declared a Basilica Minor in 2003.

The southwestern corner of the Rynek gives onto **Plac Solny** (Salt Sq). As its name suggests, the square was the site of the city's salt trade, a business that was carried on for over five centuries until 1815, when the last stalls were closed down. Nowadays it's occupied by 24-hour flower stalls and an overspill of restaurants from the main square.

Old Town

Wrocław's extensive Old Town is so full of historic buildings that you could wander round for weeks and still feel like you've barely scratched the surface. For the best selection, concentrate on the area north and east of the Rynek.

RACŁAWICE PANORAMA

Wrocław's most visited sight is the **Racławice Panorama** (Panorama Racławicka; ☎ 344 23 44; ul Purkyniego 11; adult/concession 20/15zł; ☼ 9.30am-5pm Tue-Sun). Accommodated in a cylindrical building in the park behind the Museum of Architecture (p269), it's a cyclorama, a giant canvas painting (15m high and 114m long) wrapped around the internal walls of the rotunda in the form of an unbroken circle and viewed from an elevated central balcony.

The picture depicts the battle of Racławice (a village about 40km northeast of Kraków), fought on 4 April 1794 between the Polish insurrectionist peasant army, led by Tadeusz Kościuszko, and Russian troops. One of the last attempts to defend Poland's independence, the battle was won by the Poles, but some months later the nationwide insurrection was crushed by the tsarist army and the Third Partition was effected. Poland formally ceased to exist until WWI, yet the battle lived in the hearts of Poles as the most glorious engagement of the rebellion.

One hundred years after the battle, a group of patriots in Lviv set about commemorating the event and the idea of the panorama emerged. The painting is essentially the work of two artists, Jan Styka and Wojciech Kossak, with the help of seven painters commissioned for background scenes and details. They completed the monumental canvas in an amazingly short time – nine months and two days – while a specially designed rotunda was erected. The picture became one of Lviv's favourite attractions and was on display until 1944 when a bomb damaged the canvas.

After the war, the painting, along with most of Lviv's legacy, was moved to Wrocław, but since it depicted a defeat of the Russians, Poland's official friend and liberator, the communist authorities were reluctant to put it on display. Only in 1980, after the Solidarity movement had brought the beginnings of democracy, was the decision taken to renovate the canvas and put it on public view.

Visits are by tours, which depart every half-hour and take just that. You move around the balcony to inspect each scene in turn while a recorded commentary provides you with explanations. Foreign-language versions including English, German and French are available. Tickets are also valid for same-day admission to the National Museum.

Buy your ticket early, as the place tends to be overrun by tourists (the 10.30am, 1pm and 3.30pm tours are so popular they have to be booked a week in advance!). You can kill any spare time in the waiting room, where videos of the painting's restoration are shown, or visit the exhibition in the 'small rotunda', just behind the ticket office, which features a model of the battlefield and the uniforms of forces engaged in the battle.

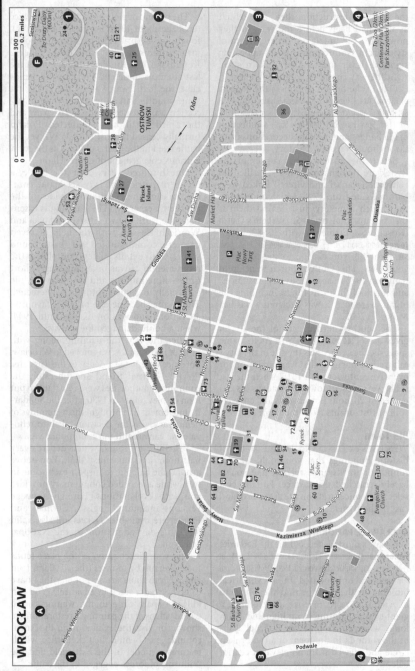

WROCŁAW

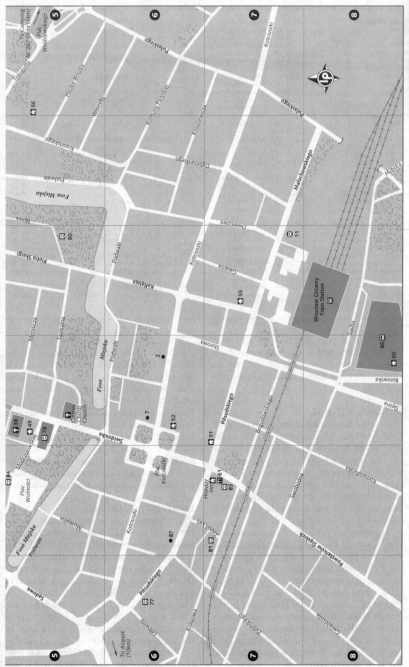

On your way in or out, have a look at the **Katyń Monument** in the park behind the rotunda, a striking memorial to the victims of the infamous Soviet massacres (see p24 and p76).

NATIONAL MUSEUM

Wrocław's **Muzeum Narodowe** (☎ 343 88 39; Plac Powstańców Warszawy 5; adult/concession 15/10zł, free Sat; ☺ 10am-4pm Wed, Fri & Sun, 9am-4pm Thu, 10am-6pm Sat) is a treasure-trove of fine art, with extensive permanent collections and a stunning skylit atrium displaying sculpture and temporary modern art exhibits. It's a lot to take in, but the top-floor café is good for alleviating culture fatigue!

The museum's medieval Silesian art section is one of the highlights of the collection. Medieval stone sculpture is displayed on the ground floor, and exhibits include the Romanesque tympanum from the portal of the Church of St Mary Magdalene (opposite), depicting the Dormition of the Virgin Mary. Medieval wooden sculpture is on the 1st floor and features some powerful Gothic triptychs and statues of saints. Also on this floor are European paintings from the 15th to 19th centuries.

The 2nd floor holds Polish art, mainly paintings, from the 17th century to the present. The collection covers most of Poland's big names, including Jacek Malczewski, Stanisław Wyspiański, Witkacy and Jan Matejko. Wrocław's collection of modern Polish painting is considered one of the best in the country, with plenty of very individual installations alongside the usual abstract shapes. For ironic, humorous takes on Polish religion, Władysław Hasior and Eugeniusz Stankiewicz-Get are names to look out for – the latter's DIY crucifix is a neat example.

UNIVERSITY QUARTER

The university district occupies the northern part of the Old Town, between the riverfront and ul Uniwersytecka. Coming from the museum, the first important historic building you see is the Gothic **St Vincent's Church** (Kościół Św Wincentego), originally a Romanesque basilica founded before 1240. The largest church in the city after the cathedral, it was burned out in 1945 and only reconstructed in the 1990s. It's now used by the Uniat congregation as their cathedral.

The baroque **Church of the Holy Name of Jesus** (Kościół Najświętszego Imienia Jezus) was built in the 1690s on the site of the former Piast castle. Its spacious interior, crammed with ornate fittings and adorned with fine illusionist frescoes on its vaulting, is quite spectacular.

The monumental building adjoining the church is the main **university** itself. It was founded by Emperor Leopold I in 1702 as the Jesuit Academy and was built between 1728 and 1742. Enter the central gate and go up to the 1st floor to see the **Aula Leopoldinum** (☎ 375 22 45; Plac Uniwersytecki; adult/concession 3/1.50zł; ☼ 10am-3.30pm Mon-Fri). Embellished with elaborate stucco work, sculptures, paintings and a trompe l'œil ceiling fresco, it's the best baroque interior in the city. Classical music concerts are occasionally held here, but it's often closed for special university ceremonies. The slightly more modest **Oratorium Marianum**, on the ground floor, is open the same hours.

OTHER SIGHTS
One block east of the Rynek is the **Church of St Mary Magdalene** (Kościół Św Marii Magdaleny), a mighty Gothic brick building constructed during the city's heyday in the 14th century. Its showpiece is a Romanesque portal from around 1280, which originally adorned the Benedictine Abbey in Ołbin, but was moved here in 1546 after the abbey was demolished. The original tympanum is on display in Wrocław's National Museum.

A little further east you'll find the excellent **Awangarda Art Gallery** (☎ 344 10 56; ul Wita Stwosza 32; adult/concession 8/4zł; ☼ 11am-6pm Tue-Sun), housed in a palatial historic building, which has temporary exhibitions of contemporary art and a quirky café-pub frequented by suitably arty types. Ceramics and design displays are held in its two annexes.

A former Bernardine church and monastery provides a splendid setting for the **Museum of Architecture** (Muzeum Architektury; ☎ 344 82 79; www.ma.wroc.pl; ul Bernardyńska 5; adult/concession 7/5zł, free Wed; ☼ 10am-4pm Tue, Wed, Fri & Sat, noon-6pm Thu, 11am-7pm Sun). The collection features stone sculptures and stained-glass windows from various historic buildings of the region. The oldest exhibit, a Romanesque tympanum, dates from 1165. The museum also has the oldest Jewish tombstone in Poland, salvaged from the town's original 12th-century Jewish cemetery.

The church just to the west, opposite the massive Galeria Dominikańska shopping centre and hotel complex, is the single-naved Dominican **St Adalbert's Church** (Kościół Św Wojciecha), another largish Gothic structure. The highlight of its interior is the baroque chapel adjoining the southern transept, with its alabaster sarcophagus of the Blessed Czesław, founder of the original monastery here.

Ostrów Tumski & Piasek Island
The island of Ostrów Tumski was the cradle of Wrocław. It was here that the Ślężanie constructed their stronghold in the 7th or 8th century. After the town was incorporated into the Polish state and a bishopric established in 1000, Wrocław's first church was built here and was followed by other ecclesiastical buildings. Towards the 13th century the centre of town moved to the left bank of the Odra, but Ostrów retained its role as the seat of the church authorities.

Over time a number of churches, monasteries and other religious buildings were constructed, and many of them are still standing today, giving a distinctive, markedly ecclesiastical character to the district. With the cobbled streets and lack of urban intrusion, walking through the church quarter is genuinely like skipping back a couple of centuries, and the island is a compulsory stop for tour groups.

The centrepiece of the island is the mammoth two-towered **cathedral**. This three-aisled Gothic basilica was built between the 13th and 15th centuries and is the fourth church on this site. Seriously damaged during WWII, it was reconstructed in its previous Gothic form, dragon guttering and all, and its dim interior was refurbished with works of art collected from other churches. The high altar boasts a triptych from 1522 depicting the Dormition of the Virgin Mary, attributed to the school of Veit Stoss. For once you don't need strong thighs to climb the tower – this is the only historic church in Poland that has a lift. Try to be a little sensitive about when you enter, as the church is still in use and many tour guides let their groups heedlessly barge in on anything from solemn mass to summer weddings.

In complete contrast to the huge cathedral, **St Giles' Church** (Kościół Św Idziego) is barely a cubby hole. Built between 1218 and 1230, this is the oldest surviving church in Wrocław, and has an original Romanesque doorway at the entrance.

The small 15th-century **Church of SS Peter and Paul** (Kościół Św Piotra i Pawła) has a fine Gothic vault supported by a single central column. It's open only for Mass in the morning and evening. The entrance is through the adjoining building, a former orphanage.

A few steps east is the **Archdiocesan Museum** (Muzeum Archidiecezjalne; ☎ 327 11 78; Plac Katedralny 16; adult/concession 3/2zł; ☯ 9am-3pm Tue-Sun). It has a large collection of Silesian sacred art, including some exquisite Gothic altarpieces.

Adjoining the quarter is Piasek Island, connected to the Old Town by the Most Piaskowy (Piasek Bridge). The main monument here is the **Church of St Mary on the Sand** (Kościół NMP na Piasku), a lofty 14th-century building that dominates this tiny islet. The church was badly damaged during WWII but carefully reconstructed, including its magnificent ribbed vaulting. Almost all the prewar fittings were burned out and the old triptychs you see inside have been collected from other Silesian churches. The Romanesque tympanum in the right-hand aisle is the only remnant of the original 12th-century church. There's a mechanised *szopka* (Nativity scene) in the first chapel to the right.

If you've had enough of bricks and mortar, Ostrów Tumski also holds the city's **Botanical Gardens** (Ogród Botaniczny; ☎ 322 59 57; ul Sienkiewicza 23; adult/concession 5/3zł; ☯ 8am-6pm Apr-Oct, 10am-6pm Nov-Mar), a charming patch of greenery.

West & South of the Old Town

Just outside the ring road, the **Arsenal** (Arsenał) is the most significant remnant of the 15th-century fortifications. It now houses the **Military Museum** (Muzeum Militariów; ☎ 344 15 71; ul Cieszyńskiego 9; adult/concession 7/5zł, free Wed; ☯ 11am-5pm Wed-Sat, 10am-6pm Sun) featuring old weapons, uniforms and one of Europe's largest collections of helmets and tin hats.

The arsenal is also home to the **Archaeological Museum** (Muzeum Archeologiczne; ☎ 344 28 29; ul Cieszyńskiego 9; adult/concession 5/3zł, free Wed; ☯ 11am-5pm Wed-Sat, 10am-6pm Sun), which displays the usual collection of archaeological

finds, emphasising the Polish and Slavic roots of the region.

A short walk southeast will take you to the **Ethnographic Museum** (☎ 344 33 13; ul Kazimierza Wielkiego 34). Part of the collection features old artefacts brought from the east by postwar settlers. It's currently closed for restoration.

The massive Gothic affair located just south of the Old Town is **St Dorothy's Church** (Kościół Św Doroty), founded in 1351 to commemorate the meeting between Polish King Kazimierz Wielki and his Bohemian counterpart, Charles IV, at which it was agreed to leave Silesia in Bohemia's hands. The lofty, whitewashed interior is filled with large baroque altars, and there's a sizable rococo tomb in the right-hand (southern) aisle.

Eastern Suburbs

There are some attractions in the eastern districts. Take tram 2 or 10 from Plac Dominikański (2zł) to reach the **zoo** (Ogród Zoologiczny; ☎ 348 30 24; ul Wróblewskiego 1; adult/concession 10/4zł; ☯ 9am-6pm summer, 9am-4pm winter). With about 4000 animals representing over 500 species, this is Poland's largest zoo and supposedly the best. It's also the country's oldest zoo, founded in 1865.

Across the street is the **Centenary Hall** (Hala Ludowa), a huge, round auditorium capable of accommodating 6000 people. It was designed by German architect Max Berg, and built in 1913 to commemorate Napoleon's defeat in 1813. The hall is topped with a huge dome, 65m in diameter, regarded as a great achievement in its day. The 96m-high steel **spire** *(iglica)* in front of the entrance was built in 1948, on the occasion of the Exhibition of the Regained Territories. Today the hall is a venue for large-scale performances, exhibitions and sporting events. At other times it's usually locked, but the guards may let you in to have a look.

Behind the Centenary Hall is **Park Szczytnicki**, Wrocław's oldest and largest wooded area, encompassing 112 hectares. A short walk north along the pergola will bring you to a small Japanese Garden, while further east is a fine 16th-century larch church, brought here from the Opole region and reassembled in 1914. Temporary exhibitions are held in the church in summer.

FESTIVALS & EVENTS

Some of Wrocław's major annual events:

Musica Polonica Nova Contemporary Music Festival (☎ 0601 552 334; www.musicapolonicanova.pl in Polish) Held in February.

Jazz on the Odra (☎ 348 18 21) Held in May.

Arsenal Chamber Music Festival (☎ 788 80 99; www.wieczory-w-arsenale.pl) Held in July.

Wratislavia Cantans International Festival (☎ 342 72 57; www.wratislavia.art.pl) Wrocław's top music and fine-arts festival, held in September.

SLEEPING
Budget

Finding a cheap bed isn't usually a problem, with plenty of places around the station district; posters in the station itself advertise various seasonal options and private accommodation. All budget places listed here have rooms with shared bathrooms and don't offer breakfast.

HOSTELS & HOTELS

Bursa Nauczycielska (☎ 344 37 81; ul Kotlarska 42; s/d/tr/q 50/90/90/105zł) With a location this good it could probably get away with murder – luckily the management of the town's most central teachers' dorm likes to maintain a certain minimum standard, and regular hostel-dwellers should find nothing to jade them here.

Dizzy Daisy (☎ 321 00 14; www.hostel.pl; ul Górnickiego 22; s/d/tr/q 45/80/105/120zł; ☺ Jul-Sep; 💻) On Ostrów Tumski, northeast of the historic quarter, this is your typical backpacker-oriented hostel, occupying a student accommodation block for the summer hiatus. The station stand hands out information and offers free transfers to the hostel.

MDK Youth Hostel (☎ 343 88 56; ul Kołłątaja 20; dm 16-22zł, d 60zł) Located within sneezing distance of the main train station, the main HI hostel is often full due to its convenient position. More than 50 beds are available, mostly in dorms for five to seven people.

Pokoje U Szermierzy (☎ 343 49 89; ul Krasińskiego 30b; s 50-75zł, d 70zł, tr 75-90zł, q 100zł) Not as good or central as the Bursa but cheaper, this sports dorm has 29 beds within easy walking distance of the Old Town. The hostel is in a detached building off the street itself – enter gate No 30 and you'll see it in front of you.

Another option is the hostel at Hotel Tumski (see right).

CAMPING

Camping Nr 267 Ślęża (☎ 343 44 42; ul Na Grobli 16/18; camping per person 14zł, cabins 60-150zł) Wrocław's all-year camping ground occupies a good spot on the bank of the Odra, 2km east of the Old Town. There's no transport all the way there; go to Plac Wróblewskiego (tram 4 from the train station) and walk 1km east.

Mid-Range

Wrocław's accommodation supply lets it down slightly in the intermediate category, with a disappointing paucity of reasonably priced hotels in the centre of town. If all of these options are full, you may have to consider staying further out or paying a little more/less than you'd planned.

Hotel Tumski (☎ 322 60 99; www.hotel-tumski.com .pl; Wyspa Słodowa 10; s/d/f 199/270/310zł, ste 380-480zł; P 🐾) Located on one of the islands on the Odra River, within easy walking distance of both the Old Town and Ostrów Tumski, this small, neat hotel has a nice riverside setting (if you can ignore the busy road). For the more budget-conscious, part of the hotel is an official HI youth hostel (dorm beds cost 30zł to 40zł per person).

Hotel Savoy (☎ 340 32 19; www.savoy.wroc.pl; Plac Kościuszki 19; s 90-100zł, d 110-130zł, tr 141zł, ste 150-180zł) It may not look like much but the Savoy is one of your best shots at a bargain. Pot plants, half-decent furniture and town views liven up the best rooms, and even solo travellers may find themselves unexpectedly spoilt by the largest singles.

Hotel Monopol (☎ 343 70 41; ul Modrzejewskiej 2; s 115-170zł, d 150-260zł, tr 290zł, ste 380-430zł) Wrocław's oldest hotel has seen quite a few famous faces in its century-plus lifetime, not least a certain Herr Hitler, who used to rant from the balcony during the German occupation. It's not the top choice it once was, but the public areas retain a grandeur you don't often find in this class, and the mostly en suite rooms are thoroughly acceptable.

Hotel Europeum (☎ 371 45 00; www.europeum.pl; ul Kazimierza Wielkiego 27a; s/d 230/270zł; P) Prices might just edge the Europeum out of the comfortable mid-range bracket, but it's one of the few places of its type that may actually cut its rates in summer. An initiative of the Krzyżowa Foundation, a Silesian NGO promoting youth exchange programmes, you can expect conference-class accommodation with a social conscience.

SILESIA

Hotel Zaułek (☎ 341 00 46; www.hotel.uni.wroc.pl; ul Garbary 11; s/d/tr 240/290/350zł; **P**) Run by the university, this is a very personal guesthouse at the upper end of the scale, accommodating just 18 visitors in quaintly homy rooms. The late check-out's a boon for heavy sleepers, and weekend prices are a snip.

Hotel Podróżnik (☎ 373 28 45; ul Sucha 1; s 60-88zł, d/tr/q/ste 130/162/196/160zł; **P**) Staying at the bus station isn't just a last resort for tired coach-goers – this skylit establishment is light, clean and quite comfortable enough for a night or two. There are a couple of cheap, basic singles, essentially box rooms without so much as a washbasin. Student discounts are available.

Hotel Polonia (☎ 343 10 21; www.odratourist.pl; ul Piłsudskiego 66; s 148-198zł, d 178-218zł; **P**) There's little spectacular about this place, but it's close to the station, and frequent weekend and summer promotions can make it decent value. Rooms are divided into two categories, depending on size and quality. Students get the best deal: from around 42zł per person.

Top End

Wrocław has one of the largest selections of top-flight hotels outside Warsaw and Krakow, dominated by the international chains, with a particular concentration around St Elizabeth's Church. All the hotels listed here have weekend discounts, dataports and at least one restaurant, and most offer specially adapted rooms for physically disabled clients.

Dwór Polski (☎ 372 34 15; www.dworpolski.wroclaw .pl; ul Kiełbaśnicza 2; s/d 240/290zł, ste 400-470zł; **P** **X**) You can't ask for much more character than this – a restored house right on the Rynek, complete with idiosyncratic rooms and original dark-wood fittings throughout. Overblown competition nearby keeps the price right, and the atmospheric internal courtyard's a real selling point.

Hotel Dorint (☎ 358 83 00; www.dorint.com/wroclaw; ul Św Mikołaja 67; s/d €114/130, ste €150-500; **P**) The complete opposite of the Dwór Polski's historic slant, the Dorint is so modern that you might have to check what year it is. Chrome, glass, concept furniture and every conceivable comfort make this one of the most desirable expense-account establishments in town, though frankly the superb hi-fi systems are wasted on business travellers.

Art Hotel (☎ 787 71 00; www.arthotel.pl; ul Kiełbaśnicza 20; s 275-315zł, d 315-355zł, ste 335-395zł; **P** **X** **□**) What's art got to do with it? Apparently not a lot, so it's better to concentrate on the comfortable fittings and the fine restaurants occupying the cellar and conservatory. Overall it's a good independent establishment in a popular location.

Qubus Hotel (☎ 341 08 98; www.qubushotel.pl; ul Św Marii Magdaleny 2; s €89, d €105-132, ste €153-297; **P** **X** **□**) Another vast chain hotel in the heart of the old town, right opposite the Church of Mary Magdalene. For this price you might expect a bit more from the standard rooms, but the comprehensive facilities are top class.

EATING

You don't need to walk far to find a meal in the Old Town – the Rynek is lined with restaurants on every side, not to mention in the middle, and in summer the whole square is clogged with beer gardens and streetside seating. Venture out into the side streets to encounter further fleets of eateries just waiting to fill your guts.

Restauracja Vincent (☎ 341 05 20; ul Ruska 39; mains 35-85zł; ✿ breakfast, lunch & dinner Mon-Sat, lunch & dinner Sun; **X**) Situated in a historic building with tenuous Freudian associations, Vincent's beautiful interiors conjure up a charming atmosphere, highly conducive to feasting on the perfectly presented international cuisine. Anything from wild boar to live accordion music can pop up on the menu, and there's a selection of Moroccan-style *tajines* for the well-travelled palate.

Złoty Pies (☎ 372 37 60; Rynek 41; mains 14-55zł; ✿ lunch & dinner) The Golden Dog descends into fabulous vaulted cellars via a series of stepped nooks, serving up solid Polish and European food to consistent crowds. The chef seems particularly good at stuffing massive amounts of filling into things.

Restauracja JaDka (☎ 343 64 61; ul Rzeźnicza 24/25; mains 18-72zł; ✿ lunch & dinner) If, like most non-Poles, you've never heard of Magda Gessler, come here to find out exactly what you've been missing. The country's top female chef knocks out impeccable modern versions of Polish classics in impeccable surroundings, and the service is, well, impeccable.

Bar Wegetariański Vega (☎ 344 39 34; Sukiennice 1/2; mains 3.40-4.20zł; ✿ breakfast, lunch & dinner Mon-Fri, breakfast & lunch Sat & Sun) Vegetarians rejoice: not only is there a place for you in Wrocław, but it's cheap, central and quite unfeasibly good value. As usual, flyers for t'ai chi classes and homeopathy stores paper the porch.

Kuchnia Marché (☎ 343 95 55; ul Świdnicka 53; dishes 3.80-18.30zł; ☯ breakfast, lunch & dinner) Taking its cue from the Mövenpick chain of buffet restaurants, the covered market experience comes in restaurant form at this imaginative eatery; browse the counters for a range of tasty treats, then mix and match at will.

Restauracja St Petersburg (☎ 341 80 84; ul Igielna 14/15; mains 26-82zł; ☯ lunch & dinner) Russian haute cuisine? Yes, it does exist, and if your experience of Russia's great culinary traditions is limited to stroganoff and vodka then this slightly haughty restaurant will be a revelation. Meat, fish and game prop up the high-powered menu, along with sweet and savoury *blinis* (wholewheat pancakes).

Mercado (☎ 344 40 40; ul Więzienna 30; mains 8-29zł; ☯ lunch & dinner) Part of the prodigious Sphinx chain, this new offering has a more earthy, rustic feel to it, with rough-hewn walls and handmade ceramics. The menu's a familiar mix of Middle Eastern and Italian platters, plus a smattering of Greek, Chinese and even Indian efforts.

Pastabar (ul Św Antoniego 15; mains 3.50-6.80zł; ☯ lunch & dinner) With its jarring yellow colour scheme and retro styling this could be a hip bar in some European capital, but in fact it's a cut-price Italian doing big plates of pasta fast-food style for the nearby pub clientele. Open till 2am at weekends.

Blue Bar Café (Plac Solny 8/9; mains 6-28zł; ☯ breakfast, lunch & dinner) The small, quiet square occupied by Wrocław's flower market has a few streetside eating options, not least of which is this smart café-bar. Dine out on hefty salads, snacks and sandwiches, or while away the evening in front of strange cable TV on the huge screen inside.

Bar Mleczny Miś (☎ 343 49 63; ul Kuźnicza 48; mains 1-5.30zł; ☯ breakfast & lunch Mon-Sat) Frequented by students from the nearby university quarter, Miś is a classic old-school milk bar ideal for anyone on a micro-budget.

DRINKING

As ever, the Rynek is the obvious place to start a night on the tiles, and when the patio furniture comes out in summer you can't beat the atmosphere. Elsewhere in the Old Town you'll find scores of more idiosyncratic places catering for students and locals, and if your tastes run to the seamy side of life, the row of drinking dens under the arches of the railway track are dependably dodgy.

Spiż (☎ 344 72 25; Rynek-Ratusz 2) Poland's first microbrewery bar-restaurant is buried in a basement under the town hall, with harassed staff scurrying around the copper vats to serve the voracious clientele. The summer beer garden is the busiest on the Rynek.

Pub 4 Podkowy (☎ 0697 100 831; ul Więzienna; ☯ from 10am) The 4 Horseshoes is part of the new Galeria Italiana centre, though there's not much noticeably Italian about it. An unobtrusive balcony overhangs the streets outside, and the Sunday chill-out sessions are perfect for maxin' and relaxin'.

Kalogródek (ul Kuźnicza 29b; ☯ 10am-midnight) Hidden behind some rough-looking wooden hoardings, the big stepped terrace here is like a playground for students; table football, darts and cheap beer make sure it's generally crawling with them, even when the weather's uncooperative.

Więzienna (☎ 344 16 08; ul Więzienna 6; ☯ 4pm-1am) Look out for the small sign above head height – it's almost the only indicator that a lively drinking space lurks behind this blank brick façade. The discreet doorway opens onto Wrocław's best concealed courtyard.

Café Uni (☎ 375 28 38; Plac Uniwersytecki 11) As the name suggests, this is student central, a traffic-cone's throw from the main university buildings. Semislick décor, patient staff and decidedly noncheesy music set it apart from lesser institutions.

Pożegnanie z Afryką (☎ 341 77 32; ul Kiełbaśnicza 24; ☯ 8am-10pm Mon-Sat, 10am-10pm Sun; ☒) A growing concern in Poland, this remarkable private coffee franchise blows its big-business rivals out of the (hot) water with a superb selection of imported beans and grounds. The name means 'Out of Africa', hinting at its fair trade credentials.

ENTERTAINMENT

Wrocław is an important cultural and nightlife centre, and there's a lot of activity all year round. Local papers have listings, or pick up either of the free monthlies, *Co Jest Grane* and *Aktivist*. Both are in Polish only, but the what's-on sections can be deciphered easily enough. For a detailed rundown of local bars, clubs etc, seek out the reliably forthright *Wrocław in Your Pocket* (5zł).

Theatre

Wrocław is internationally known for the avant-garde Teatr Laboratorium (Laboratory Theatre) created by radical director Jerzy Grotowski. He started out in 1959 in Opole's Theatre of 13 Rows, but moved to Wrocław in 1965 and directed the Laboratorium until 1984. The theatre was dissolved after Grotowski moved to Italy and established a theatre research centre in Pontedera. He died in 1999.

Centre of Studies on Jerzy Grotowski's Work (☎ 343 42 67; www.grotcenter.art.pl; Rynek-Ratusz 27) Founded in 1990 in the theatre's former home, the Grotowski centre has documentaries on the Laboratory Theatre and can present them on request. It also invites various experimental groups, often from abroad, to give performances in its small theatre.

Wrocławski Teatr Pantomimy (☎ 337 21 03; www.pantomima.wroc.pl in Polish) Wrocław's principal ambassador for contemporary theatre, created by impresario Henryk Tomaszewski. It's usually on tour – check with the tourist office to see when it's in town.

Teatr Polski (☎ 316 07 00; www.teatrpolski.wroc.pl in Polish; ul Zapolskiej 3) This is the major mainstream city venue, staging classic Polish and foreign drama. Two smaller stages take on diverse repertory duties.

Teatr Współczesny (☎ 358 89 00; ul Rzeźnicza 12) Near the centre of town, Teatr Współczesny tends more towards contemporary productions from modern Polish and international playwrights.

Clubs

Entry charges for all these venues vary depending on the night, the time you arrive, your gender and anything else that the promoters can think of. The usual range is between zero and 15zł.

Radio Bar (☎ 372 50 13; www.radiobar.neostrada .pl; Rynek 48) Ask locals where to go out in Wrocław and this will probably be the first name off their lips. Loud, proud and central, the Radio Bar is an essential stop for first-timers and anyone aiming to dig the scene.

Dziwne Dni (☎ 788 91 07; ul Kazimierza Wielkiego 39) An unusual combination of bar-club and Internet café. The Bomber Clock nights showcase some of the best electronica in the city, and you'll also find some quality drum 'n bass going down.

VuleVu (☎ 0601 667 144; www.vulevu.pl; ul Świdnicka 53; ☉ Wed-Sat) Behind the large Holiday Inn, lashings of house, garage and black music bring regular designer-casual crowds to the boil in true clubland style.

Wagon Club (☎ 341 29 48; Plac Lwowskich 20a; ☉ from 10am Mon-Sat, from 7am Sun) One of several venues near this ring road location, the Wagon is strictly for those who like their beats hard and their bass in their face. Techno, drum 'n' bass and industrial dominate the soundscape.

W-Z (☎ 790 00 33; www.wzklub.pl in Polish; Plac Wolności 7; ☉ from 11am Tue-Fri, from 6pm Sat) If you're not sure what you like, you'll probably find it here – eclectic is the name of the game, and you'll seldom hear the same sound two nights running.

Scena (☎ 342 11 82; www.scenaclub.com in Polish; ul Piotra Skargi 18; ☉ Wed-Sat) One of Poland's oldest gay clubs, Scena welcomes an upfront crowd for high-energy dance nights and more-camp mixed midweek events.

Jazz

Express Jazz Club (☎ 344 91 81; ul Ruska 34) Finally plugging Wrocław into the Western jazz craze, the Express Jazz Club has live gigs of different flavours every night in summer, with a varying programme outside the season.

Opera & Classical Music

Filharmonia (Philharmonic Hall; ☎ 342 20 01; www .filharmonia.wroclaw.pl; ul Piłsudskiego 19) Fridays and Saturdays are the usual slots for concerts here, with the hard-working Wrocław Philharmonic turning out for all kinds of classical engagements.

Opera House (☎ 341 07 38; www.opera.wroclaw.pl; ul Świdnicka 35) Opposite the Hotel Monopol, the venerable opera house is the traditional venue for opera and ballet performances. At the time of research it was closed for restoration.

GETTING THERE & AWAY
Air

The small **airport** (☎ 358 13 10; www.airport .wroclaw.pl) in Strachowice, 10km west of the city centre, is accessible by buses 406 and 117 from the main train station (2.60zł, 20 minutes). A taxi to the airport should cost no more than 75zł. There are currently direct connections with Warsaw (up to six times daily), Frankfurt am Main (daily), Copenhagen (six weekly), Munich (twice daily), Paris (twice weekly) and Cologne (five weekly).

LOT (☎ 0801 300 952; ul Piłsudskiego 36) has an office near the train station.

Bus

The **bus terminal** (ul Sucha) is positioned just south of the train station. You probably won't need a bus to get out of Wrocław, except to go to Trzebnica (8.60zł, 40 minutes), Sobótka (6.40zł, one hour), Świdnica (8.90zł, 1½ hours) and Nysa (13.50zł, two hours), where there are no direct trains. Note that some regional buses arriving from the north terminate at **Wrocław Nadodrze** (Ostrów Tumski) instead of at the main PKS station.

There are a number of international bus routes to places including Prague and plenty of cities in Western Europe. Tickets are available from local travel agencies.

Train

Fast trains going to Katowice (34.03zł, three hours) depart every two hours or so and pass via Opole (21.62zł, 1¼ hours) on their way. Most continue to Kraków (41.24zł, 4½ hours). There are at least half a dozen fast trains plus three express trains to Warsaw (48.13zł, five to six hours); some call at Łódź (39.66zł, 3¾ hours) en route. Wrocław also has regular train links with Poznań (31.85zł, two hours, roughly hourly), Wałbrzych (10.50zł, two hours, every two hours), Jelenia Góra (17.20zł, 3½ hours, every two hours), Legnica (10.50zł, 1½ hours, roughly hourly) and Kłodzko (14.50zł, 1¾ hours, every two hours).

International destinations serviced by train include Berlin, Budapest, Dresden, Hamburg and Prague.

GETTING AROUND

Wrocław has an efficient network of trams and buses covering the city centre and suburbs. Journeys within the centre cost 2zł, longer trips 2.60zł; night buses and fast services cost 2.80zł. Useful routes include trams 8, 9 and 32, which link the bus and train stations, Ostrów Tumski and the Botanical Gardens. Numerous lines circle the Old Town, though only four tram routes actually pass through it.

AROUND WROCŁAW

TRZEBNICA

☎ 71 / pop 12,000

A small town 24km north of Wrocław, Trzebnica (tsheb-*nee*-tsah) is noted for its former Cistercian Abbey (Opactwo Cysterskie). The order was brought to Poland in 1140 and established its first monastery in Jędrzejów, from where it swiftly expanded and set up nearly 40 abbeys all over the country.

Trzebnica was also the site of the first Cistercian convent in Poland, founded in 1202 by Princess Jadwiga (Hedwig), the wife of the Duke of Wrocław, Henryk Brodaty (Henry the Bearded). After the hirsute duke's death, she entered the abbey and lived an ascetic life to the end of her days; just 24 years later, in 1267, she was canonised. She is regarded as the patron saint of Silesia, and the abbey church where she was buried has become a destination for pilgrims. Even if you're not one of the faithful, it's an impressive site and a pleasant half-day trip from Wrocław.

Sights

The **church** is thought to be one of the first brick buildings of its kind in Poland. Though it was rebuilt in later periods, the structure has preserved much of its initial austere Romanesque shape and, more importantly, still boasts two original **portals**. The one next to the main entrance, unfortunately partly hidden behind the baroque tower added in the 1780s, is particularly fine thanks to its tympanum from the 1220s, which depicts King David on his throne playing the harp to Queen Bathsheba.

Once inside, you are surrounded by ornate baroque decoration, including a marble pulpit and a lavishly ornamented high altar. At its foot is the very modest tomb of Henryk Brodaty.

The showpiece of the interior is **St Hedwig's Chapel** (Kaplica Św Jadwigi), to the right of the chancel. It was built soon after the canonisation of the princess, and the graceful, ribbed Gothic vaulting has been preserved unchanged, though the decoration dates from a later epoch. Its central feature is the large tomb of St Hedwig, an elaborate work in black marble and alabaster created in stages between 1680 and 1750. Beside the sarcophagus is the entrance to the three-naved crypt, the oldest part of the church.

The rest of the chapel is full of gilded and marbled altars, many with scenes somehow resembling classical mythology more than traditional religious art. The glowering black organ also strikes a sharp contrast with the white walls and pastel colours of the ornamentation. If you have some loose change, you can get extra lighting on Hedwig's tomb or illuminate some electric 'flickering' candles – all to support the church, of course.

Getting There & Away

Buses to Wrocław PKS station (8.60zł, 40 minutes) run once or twice an hour. There are also extra services and hourly private minibuses to Wrocław Nadodrze (4zł, 30 minutes).

LUBIĄŻ

☎ 71 / pop 1000

The small village of Lubiąż (*loo*-byonsh), about 50km northwest of Wrocław, also owes its fame to the Cistercians. It boasts a gigantic **Cistercian Abbey** (Opactwo Cystersów), one of Europe's largest monastic complexes. Founded in 1175, the modest original abbey was gradually extended as the order grew. After the Thirty Years' War the monastery entered a period of prosperity, and it was then that the magnificent baroque complex here was built – the work took almost a century, finishing in 1739. It has a 223m-wide façade and 365 rooms. A team of distinguished artists, including the famous painter Michael Willmann, was commissioned for the monumental project.

In 1810 the abbey was closed down, and the buildings were subsequently occupied, used and abused by a bizarre range of tenants: at various times the complex was a horse stud, a mental hospital, an arsenal, a Nazi military plant (during WWII), a Soviet army hospital (1945–48), and finally a storehouse for the state book publisher. Postwar renovation was minimal and a large part of the complex is still unused.

It wasn't until 1991 that a Polish-German foundation took things in hand in order to restore the abbey. A few rooms have already been renovated and are open to the public as a small **museum** (☎ 389 71 66; adult/concession 4/2zł; ☯ 9am-6pm May-Sep, 10am-3pm Oct-Apr). The showpiece is the huge hall with its 15m-high ceiling and opulent baroque decoration from the 1730s.

The work on further interiors, including the refectory and library, is in progress, but the mighty church and adjoining chapel will probably take longer to be restored. As yet they have no decoration apart from some surviving portals and fragments of frescoes by Willmann. The crypt beneath the church reputedly holds 98 mummified bodies, including that of Willmann himself, but cannot be visited.

Lubiąż lies off the main roads and transport is infrequent, with only one bus to/from Legnica daily (5.80zł, 45 minutes) and several to/from Wrocław (8.90zł, 1½ hours).

SOBÓTKA & MT ŚLĘŻA

☎ 71 / pop 6800

About 35km southwest of Wrocław, the solitary forested cone of Mt Ślęża rises from an open plain to a height of 718m, about 500m above the surrounding plain. Mt Ślęża was one of the holy places of an ancient pagan tribe, which (as in many other places around the world) used to set up its cult sites atop mountains. It's not known for sure who they were, though we do know that a centre of worship existed here from at least the 5th century BC till the 11th century AD, when it was overtaken (and duly stamped out) by Christianity. The summit was circled by a stone wall marking off the sanctuary where rituals were held, and the remains of these ramparts survive to this day. Mysterious votive statues were carved crudely out of granite, and several of them are still scattered over the mountain's slopes.

At the northern foot of the mountain is the small town of Sobótka, a starting point for the hike to the top. The town's Rynek is dominated by the massive **St Jacob's Church**, originally Romanesque but repeatedly remodelled over the years. Nearby, to the northwest on Plac Wolności, is **St Anne's Church**, and beside it one of the stone statues, known as the Mushroom (*grzyb*).

About 200m south of the Rynek is the small **Regional Museum** (Muzeum Ślężańskie; ☎ 316 26 22; ul Św Jakuba 18; admission 2zł; ☯ 9am-4pm Tue-Sun), recognisable by a fine Renaissance doorway from 1568. The museum displays some of the finds of archaeological excavations in the region.

Proceed south along the same street for another 300m and take ul Garncarska to the right (west), heading uphill. After crossing the main road you can turn left and take the red route up **Mt Ślęża**, a hike that should take you about an hour. You'll find two more statues on the way, plus a tall TV mast and a 19th-century church at the top. Grab a snack and enjoy the scene from the viewpoint.

Coming down, you can take the steeper yellow route directly to the youth hostel (see below), about 800m west of your starting point. There's a **viewing tower** about halfway down, and on the road back into town you'll pass another stone statue, called the Monk (*mnich*), the finest and best preserved of all.

Sleeping & Eating

Dom Turysty Góra Ślęży (☎ 342 61 42; dm 22-24zł, d 55-69zł) Opposite the church, on the summit of Mt Ślęża itself, this basic lodging house provides accommodation with or without en suite in case you don't feel like going down in a hurry. The snack bar sells the only food on the mountain.

Dom Turysty Pod Wieżycą (☎ 316 28 57; ul Armii Krajowej 13; r 55-90zł) The PTTK youth hostel, at the foot of Mt Ślęża, is very simple but pleasant enough, and also has a restaurant, with surprising items such as kangaroo steak on the menu. The yellow mountain trail starts here.

Zajazd Pod Misiem (☎ 316 20 34; ul Mickiewicza 7/9; d/tr 60/75zł, ste 140zł) The Zajazd is a reasonable hotel block, just off Sobótka's Rynek, and it, too, has its own restaurant.

Getting There & Away

Sobótka is easily accessible by bus from Wrocław (6.40zł, one hour, twice hourly) and Świdnica (5.60zł, 40 minutes, 18 daily). Buses drop you in the town centre next to St Anne's Church.

THE SUDETEN MOUNTAINS

Anyone who's studied WWII history should have heard of the Sudetenland. The Sudeten Mountains (Sudety) are the northernmost part of this area, running for over 250km along the Czech-Polish border. The highest part of this old and eroded chain of mountains is the Karkonosze, reaching a maximum height of 1602m at Mt Śnieżka. Though the Sudetes don't offer much alpine scenery, they are amazingly varied and heavily cloaked in forest, with spectacular geological formations such as the Góry Stołowe adding some real drama for the many visitors.

To the north, the Sudetes gradually decline into a belt of gently rolling foothills known as the Przedgórze Sudeckie. This area is more densely populated, and many of the towns and villages in the region still boast some of their centuries-old buildings. Combining visits to these historic settlements with hikes into the mountains and the surrounding countryside is the best way to explore the region, and keen walkers certainly won't regret setting aside a few days to road-test the slopes.

ŚWIDNICA

☎ 74 / pop 65,000

One of the wealthiest towns in Silesia in medieval times, Świdnica (shfeed-*nee*-tsah) was founded in the 12th century, and in 1290 became the capital of one of the myriad Silesian Piast principalities, the Duchy of Świdnica-Jawor. The Duchy was one of the most powerful of the Piast dynasties, thanks essentially to its two gifted rulers: Bolko I, who founded it, and his grandson Bolko II, who significantly extended it.

The capital itself was a flourishing commercial centre, well known for its beer, which was served on the tables of Prague, Buda and Kraków. Until the Thirteen Years' War (1454–66) it was one of the largest Polish towns, with 6000 inhabitants. By 1648, however, the population had dropped to 200, and Świdnica has never managed to become a city, remaining way behind its former rival Wrocław.

Modern Świdnica is maybe best known as the birthplace of Manfred von Richthofen, the German WWI flying ace known and feared as the Red Baron. Perhaps inspired by his miraculous survival powers, Świdnica escaped major damage in WWII and has kept some important historic buildings. It's an amenable place for a stopover, a convenient jumping-off point for Książ castle (p280), and you can still get a decent beer here.

SILESIA

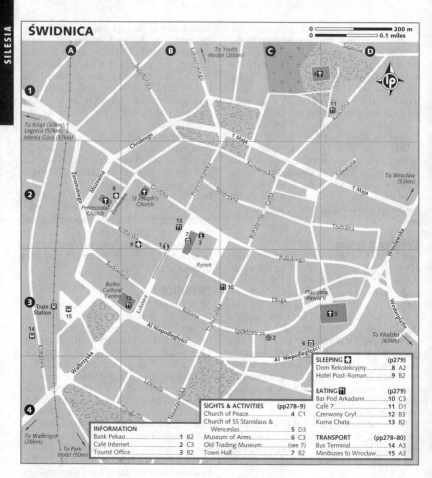

ŚWIDNICA

0 _____ 200 m
0 _____ 0.1 miles

Information

Bank Pekao (☎ 852 03 43; Rynek 30)
Café Internet (☎ 852 04 63; ul Spółdzielcza 14; per hr 3zł; ☼ 10am-8pm Mon-Sat, noon-8pm Sun)
Tourist office (☎ 852 02 90; www.um.swidnica.pl; ul Wewnętrzna 2, Rynek; ☼ 9am-5pm Mon-Fri, 8am-4pm Sat)

Sights

The unique **Church of Peace** (Kościół Pokoju; ☎ 852 28 14; Plac Pokoju 6; adult/concession 4/2zł; ☼ 9am-1pm & 3-5pm Mon-Sat, 3-5pm Sun), a short walk north of the centre, was erected between 1656 and 1657 in just 10 months as a Protestant church following the Peace of Westphalia of 1648 (hence its name). It's a wood-and-clay shingled structure laid out in the form of a cross, reputedly constructed without a

single nail, and has no fewer than 28 doors. The 17th-century baroque decoration, with paintings covering the walls and ceiling, has been preserved intact. The large organ proved unreliable so another one was added above the high altar. Along the walls, two storeys of galleries and several small balconies were installed, reminiscent of an old-fashioned theatre. Arranged this way, the interior was able to seat 3500 people in comfort, plus another 4000 standing; these days, however, you're unlikely to find more than 50 worshippers. The church was added to the Unesco World Heritage List in 2001.

Świdnica's **Rynek** has everything from baroque to postwar architecture, the cumulative effect of rebuilding after successive fires and the damage caused by Austrian, Prussian and Napoleonic sieges. Most of the façades have been thoroughly revamped over recent years and are lit up at night, giving the square an attractive appearance, though peering through some of the doorways and iron grilles might give you an entirely different impression.

The well-kept **town hall** dates from the 1710s, and looks a bit squat without its tower, which collapsed in 1967. Inside is the **Old Trading Museum** (Muzeum Dawnego Kupiectwa; ☎ 852 12 91; Rynek 37; adult/concession 3/2zł; 10am-3pm Tue-Fri, 11am-5pm Sat & Sun), which features re-creations of an old-time inn, pharmacy and grocery, and a collection of historic scales and balances.

The parish **Church of SS Stanislaus & Wenceslas** (Kościół Św Stanisława i Wacława; ☎ 852 27 29; Plac Jana Pawła II 1), east of the Rynek, is a massive Gothic stone building whose façade is adorned with four elegant 15th-century doorways and an 18m-high window. The tower, completed in 1565, is 103m high, making it Poland's tallest historic church tower after that of the basilica in Częstochowa (106m). The spacious interior has the familiar Gothic structure and ornate baroque decoration and furnishings. Six huge paintings that hang high up in the nave seem thoroughly at home in this lofty interior. The original church was accidentally burnt down in 1532 by unfortunate *voit* (mayor) Franz Glogisch, who duly fled from the angry townspeople but was hunted down in Nysa and beaten to death. Guided visits are available between 10am and 4pm Tuesday to Friday.

The **Museum of Arms** (Muzeum Broni; ☎ 852 52 34; ul Niepodległości 21; admission 3zł; 11am-2pm Tue-Sun), practically a fortified compound in itself, displays arms, artillery and weapons from the 19th and 20th centuries.

Sleeping

Dom Rekolekcyjny (☎ 853 52 60; ul Muzealna 1; s/d/tr 45/75/95, apt 110-170zł; P) Conveniently positioned just one block off the Rynek, this Pentecostal Church facility is excellent value and nowhere near as monastic as you might expect, although there's no breakfast, and bibles take the place of TVs. Atheists can relax here too – no participation is required. Enter from ul Zamkowa 6.

Hotel Piast-Roman (☎ 852 13 93; www.hotel-piast-roman.pl; ul Kotlarska 11; s/d 120/160zł; P) The award-winning Piast-Roman, just off the Rynek, isn't quite as swish as the ground-floor restaurant might lead you to believe, but it's a good three-star nevertheless and you can't top the location.

Park Hotel (☎ 853 70 98; www.park-hotel.com.pl; ul Pionierów 20; s/d/tr 150/220/280zł, ste 300-350zł; P) A modern faux-castle hotel within easy walking distance of the Old Town, the Park is a slightly smarter alternative to its more central rival and offers some good big suites.

Youth Hostel (☎ 852 26 45; ul Kanonierska 3; dm 22-24zł) This hostel, 700m north of the Rynek, offers acceptable HI-standard accommodation in three- to seven-bed dorms.

Eating

Kurna Chata (☎ 856 94 94; Rynek 35; mains 6-16zł; lunch & dinner) Tucked away within the Rynek's main pub, this charming sunken restaurant is modelled on a rustic hut, with handmade crockery, hefty home cooking and a hanging menu written on sackcloth (English and German versions come in rather more modern laminated form).

Café 7 (☎ 640 63 64; Plac Pokoju 7; mains 5-22zł; breakfast, lunch & dinner) In summer the 7 is hands-down the most attractive place for a drink or light meal in town, occupying a lovely walled garden right by the Church of Peace. The timbered building itself is hardly ugly either.

Czerwony Gryf (☎ 853 36 93; Plac Grunwaldzki 11; mains 6-17zł; dinner) The Red Gryphon, part of the Bolko Cultural Centre, theoretically offers more good pub grub, though on a quiet night you may find you're stuck with a limited choice from the adjacent all-day cafeteria. Most people are here for the beer anyway.

Bar Pod Arkadami (☎ 853 49 02; ul Trybunalska 2; mains 3-10.80zł; breakfast & lunch Mon-Sat) This tiny snack bar is the place to get your lips round some proper *barszcz* (beetroot broth) and a *pasztecik* (hot pastry filled with meat, cheese, or cabbage with mushrooms).

Getting There & Away

The train station is a very convenient five-minute walk from the Rynek; the PKS bus station is just behind it, though you have to go the long way round via the level crossing to get there.

Direct train services are to Legnica (9.30zł, 1½ hours, twice daily); change at Jaworzyna

Śląska or Kamieniec Ząbkowicki (departures every two hours) for Wrocław, Jelenia Góra and other regional destinations.

Hourly buses run to Wrocław (8.90zł, 1½ hours), while 10 buses a day depart for Kłodzko (10zł, 1¾ hours) and five for Legnica (8.90zł, 1½ hours). Private minibuses to Wrocław depart from the front of the train station. Private buses on the 31 route to Wałbrzych leave every 20 minutes (less often on Sunday), travelling via Książ castle (3.30zł, 30 minutes).

KSIĄŻ
☎ 74

With its 415 rooms, Książ (pronounced kshonsh) **castle** is the largest in Silesia. It was built in the late 13th century by the Silesian Piast Prince Bolko I of Świdnica and continuously enlarged and remodelled until well into the 20th century. It's thus an amalgam of styles from Romanesque onwards; the central portion, with three massive arcades, is the oldest. The eastern part (to the right) is an 18th-century baroque addition, while the western segment was built between 1908 and 1923, in neo-Renaissance style.

During WWII Hitler planned to use the castle as a shelter and a huge bunker was hewn out of the rock directly beneath the courtyard. The castle itself was stripped of its valuable art collection. The Soviets used it as a barracks until 1949, after which it was more or less abandoned for 20 years. Finally, the authorities set about restoring the whole building and turned it into a **museum** (☎ 840 58 62; www.zamekksiaz.pl; ul Piastów Śląskich 1; adult/concession 9/6zł; ☻ 10am-5pm May-Sep, 10am-4pm Tue-Sun Apr & Oct, 10am-3pm Tue-Sun Nov-Mar).

The castle's showpiece is the **Maximilian Hall**, built in the first half of the 18th century. It's the largest room in the castle and the only one restored to its original lavish form, including the painted ceiling (1733) that depicts mythological scenes. As well as the main rooms, there are all kinds of temporary, rotating and hobby exhibits squirrelled away in the many smaller chambers, most with separate admission charges. The corridors often hold displays of historical paintings and photos – look out for the castle's last owners, Duke Bolko VI and his wife Daisy von Pless, who apparently featured in *Country Life* magazine on a regular basis in the 1920s.

The 12 terraced **gardens** on the slopes around the castle were laid out gradually as the medieval fortifications were dismantled from the 17th century onwards. You can walk around the terraces, looking straight into the dense forest that surrounds the walls.

Approaching the castle from the car park, you will pass near the **viewpoint**; it's just to the left past a large, decorative, freestanding gate. Seen from the lookout, the castle, majestically perched on a steep hill amid lush woods, looks just as impressive as from close up.

A five-minute walk east of the castle is a **stud farm** (Stadnina Koni; ☎ 840 58 60; ul Jeżdziecka 3; admission 3zł; ☻ 10am-5pm Tue-Sun), once the castle stables. It can be visited, and also offers riding lessons and has horses for hire.

Sleeping & Eating
Hotel Książ (☎ 664 38 90; ul Piastów Śląskich 1; s/d/tr 170/260/360zł, ste 360-480zł; **P**) The hotel occupies several outbuildings in the castle complex, providing varied standards and facilities, though sadly little of the historical character seems to have rubbed off on the rooms. There are also two restaurants and a café on the site.

Getting There & Away
The castle is on the northern administrative boundaries of Wałbrzych, about 8km from the centre. You can get to it from Wałbrzych by the No 8 city bus (1.80zł, 15 minutes), which runs every 30 to 50 minutes and will take you to the entrance. Alternatively, private buses ply the No 31 Wałbrzych–Świdnica route every 20 minutes or so (3.30zł, 30 minutes), and will let you off on the main road, a 10-minute walk from the castle.

JELENIA GÓRA
☎ 75 / pop 96,000

Set in a valley surrounded by mountain ranges, Jelenia Góra is a deceptively quiet place with a fair bit of historic character. Founded in 1108 by King Bolesław Krzywousty (Boleslaus the Wry-Mouthed) as one of his fortified border strongholds, the town came under the rule of the powerful Duchy of Świdnica-Jawor. Gold mining in the region gave way to glass production around the 15th century, but weaving gave the town a solid economic base, and its high-quality linen was exported all over Europe.

SILESIA

JELENIA GÓRA

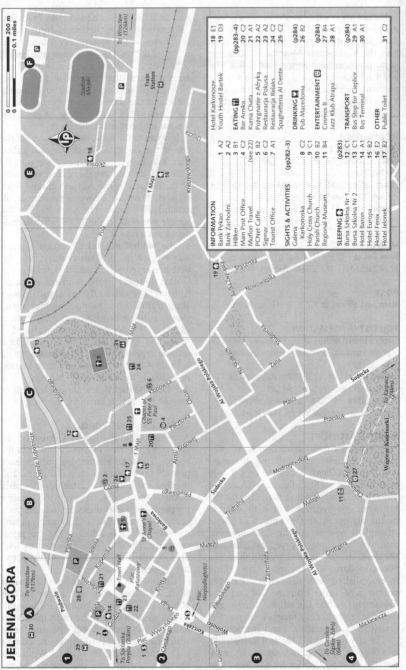

0   200 m
0   0.1 miles

To Wrocław (126km)

To Wrocław (117km)

To Szklarska Poręba (20km)

To Cieplice Śląskie-Zdrój (6km)

To Cieplice Śląskie-Zdrój (6km)

To kalpacz (21km)

Stadion Miejski

Train Station

Town Hall

Chapel of SS Peter & Paul

St Anne's Chapel

Podwale

Złotnicza

1 Maja

Pola

Kraszewskiego

Nowowiejska

Różcka Zawiłecka

Snycerska

Na Skałkach

Al Wojska Polskiego

Oacza

Pocztowa

Konopnicka

Amil Krajowej

1 Maja

Osiedle Robotnicze

Kilińskiego

Piłsudskiego

Górna

Bankowa

Kopernika

Jelenia

Piłarska

Chrobrego

Pocztowa

Plac Ratuszowy

Krótka

Długa

Plac Niepodległości

Korzeniówa

Wolności

Plausckiego

Grunowa

Wolności

Matejki

Teatralna

Sudecka

Ptasia

Zana

Na Skałkach

Studencka

Al Wojska Polskiego

Modrzejewskiej

Zamenhofa

Grottgera

Mickiewicza

Al Wojska Polskiego

Chojnika

Wzgórze Kościuszki

Sudecka

Przeskok

Matejki

INFORMATION	
Bank Pekao	1 A2
Bank Zachodni	2 A2
HiB(ker.	3 B1
Main Post Office	4 C2
Muflon Travel	(see 22)
PCNet Caffe	5 B2
Sigmar	6 C2
Tourist Office	7 A1

SIGHTS & ACTIVITIES	(pp282-3)
Galeria Karkonoska	8 C2
Holy Cross Church	9 C1
Parish Church	10 B2
Regional Museum	11 B4

SLEEPING	(p283)
Bursa Szkolna Nr 1	12 C1
Bursa Szkolna Nr 2	13 C1
Hotel Baron	14 A1
Hotel Europa	15 B2
Hotel Fenix	16 E2
Hotel Jelonek	17 B2

Hotel Karkonosze	18 E1
Youth Hostel Bartek	19 D3

EATING	(pp283-4)
Bar Anika	20 C2
Kurna Chata	21 A1
Pożegnanie z Afryką	22 A2
Restauracja Pokusa	23 A2
Restauracja Relaks	24 C2
Spaghetteria Al Dente	25 C2

DRINKING	(p284)
Pub Macedonia	26 B2

ENTERTAINMENT	(p284)
Cosmos II	27 B4
Jazz Klub Atrapa	28 A1

TRANSPORT	(p284)
Bus Stop for Cieplice	29 A1
Bus Terminal	30 A1

OTHER	
Public Toilet	31 C2

Unlike many other towns in Silesia, Jelenia Góra survived WWII pretty much undamaged, and makes a great base for trips into the Karkonosze Mountains. Relaxing is no problem here either – as well as the laid-back historic centre, the town has the pleasant Cieplice spa at its southern end. You couldn't ask for a better introduction to the Sudety strip.

Information

INTERNET ACCESS

H@ker (☎ 0506 996 365; ul Górna 3; per hr 2zł; 🕒 from 11am)

PCNet Caffe (☎ 642 94 40; ul Bankowa 20; per hr 2-3zł; 🕒 9am-10pm Mon-Sat, noon-9pm Sun)

Sigmar (☎ 752 53 04; ul Klonowica 3; per hr 3zł; 🕒 10am-6pm Mon-Fri, 10am-2pm Sat)

MONEY

Bank Pekao (☎ 764 72 17; Plac Wyszyńskiego 35)

Bank Zachodni (☎ 752 54 07; Plac Niepodległości 4)

POST

Main post office (☎ 752 35 30; ul Pocztowa 9/10)

TOURIST INFORMATION

Cieplice tourist office (☎ 755 88 44; www.karkonosze .it.pl; Plac Piastowski 36, Cieplice; 🕒 9am-5pm Mon-Fri, 10am-2pm Sat)

Muflon Travel (☎ 752 31 63; Plac Ratuszowy 2/3; 🕒 10am-5pm Mon-Fri, 10am-1pm Sat)

Tourist office (☎ 767 69 25; www.jeleniagora.pl; ul Grodzka 16; 🕒 9am-6pm Mon-Fri, 10am-2pm Sat)

Sights & Activities

Jelenia Góra's main attraction is an outstanding ecclesiastical building, the massive **Holy Cross Church**. Designed by a Swede and modelled on St Catherine's Church in Stockholm, it was built in the 1710s for the Lutheran congregation and is thought to be the biggest Protestant church in Silesia (though it now serves the Catholic community). The three-storeyed galleries plus the dark, densely packed ground floor can accommodate 4000 people. The ceiling is embellished with illusionistic baroque paintings of scenes from the Old and New Testaments, while the ornate 1720 organ over the high altar is a magnificent piece of craftwork and sounds as good as it looks.

The city has a good **Regional Museum** (Muzeum Okręgowe; ☎ 752 34 65; ul Matejki 28; adult/concession 5/3zł; 🕒 9am-3.30pm Tue, Thu & Fri, 9am-4.30pm

Wed, Sat & Sun), renowned for its extensive collection of glass that dates from medieval times to the present day. About 1200 pieces of the total of 7000 items (the largest collection in Poland) are on display. There are some amazing exhibits, including Art Nouveau pieces from the late 19th and early 20th centuries. The museum also has a large collection of old folk paintings on glass, but it's not on permanent display.

In terms of town life, the centrepiece of the city is the elongated **Rynek**, formally called Plac Ratuszowy, lined with a harmonious group of historic burghers' houses. Much of their charm is due to their ground-floor arcades, providing a covered passageway all around the square. The town hall on the square was built in the 1740s, after its predecessor collapsed.

The **parish church**, off the central square, was erected in the 15th century, and the best-preserved relic from that time is the Gothic doorway in the southern entrance. The interior, with its theatrical rococo high altar crafted from orange marble, boasts mostly baroque furnishing and decoration.

As you wander down the main street between the Rynek and Holy Cross, take a minute to peek into **Galeria Karkonoska** (☎ 752 32 93; ul 1 Maja 27), a department store housed in a lovely restored 1905 building. The Art Deco skylights are almost impressive enough to warrant buying something.

CIEPLICE ŚLĄSKIE-ZDRÓJ

As its suffix 'Zdrój' suggests, Cieplice (cheh-plee-tseh) is a spa – one of the oldest in the region. The local sulphur hot springs have probably been used for a millennium, and the first spa house was established as early as the 13th century, however, the curative properties of the springs were only properly recognised in the late 18th century, paving the way for the building of the spa infrastructure. The town was absorbed by Jelenia Góra in 1976, but retains its distinctive leisure-zone atmosphere.

The town's core is made up by a **Spa Park** (Park Zdrojowy) with an outdoor **Spa Theatre** (Teatr Zdrojowy) built on its grounds. At the western end of the main mall is the 18th-century **parish church**, the interior of which has baroque furnishings, including a high altar painting by Michael Willmann. Should you wish to try the local waters, the

pump room *(pijalnia)* is near the church on ul Ściegiennego and serves water from four of the eight springs that the town exploits.

South of the spa park is the Norwegian Park and the delightful timbered **Natural History Museum** (Muzeum Przyrodnicze; ☎ 755 15 06; ul Wolności 268; adult/concession 3.50/2.50zł; 9am-6pm Tue-Fri, 9am-5pm Sat & Sun May-Sep, 9am-4pm Tue-Sun Oct-Apr). Its display of birds and butterflies from all over the world stems from the collection of the prominent Schaffgotsch family, local nobles who established the museum in 1876.

To get to Cieplice, take any of the frequent urban buses (2.10zł, 15 minutes) from the stop near the bus station. Nos 4, 6, 7, 9, 14, 17, 18, 26 and 29 all go here.

Sleeping

Hotel Baron (☎ 752 53 91; ul Grodzka 4; s/d 165/220zł; P) Even the most demanding traveller should consider the Baron's individual, spacious rooms a bargain. More of a guesthouse than a hotel, the personable owners contribute to an unforced atmosphere both sides of the reception desk. Breakfast is served in the smarter of the two ground-floor restaurants.

Hotel Jelonek (☎ 764 65 41; www.hotel-jelonek .com.pl in Polish; ul 1 Maja 5; s/d 155/195zł, ste 295-450zł) Situated in a fine historic burgher's house, this is a perfectly smart and appealing *hotel garni*, as long as you can turn a blind eye to the Pizza Hut downstairs. The suites are ideal for self-pampering.

Hotel Fenix (☎ 641 66 00; www.hotelefenix.pl; ul 1 Maja 88; s/d 189/249zł; P ✕) More convenient for the station than the centre, Jelenia's flashest new hotel offers good modern facilities, including bar, sauna, Jacuzzi and gym. The Excellent Restaurant (mains from 12zł to 68zł) blows its own trumpet with theme weeks and specials such as crocodile tail.

Hotel Europa (☎ 764 72 31; ul 1 Maja 16/18; s/d 120/170zł, ste 250zł; P) The large block opposite the Jelonek can't compete in terms of ambience and charm, but you do get some good big rooms, a house disco, McDonald's (!) and 20% off at weekends. Rear views are better.

Youth Hostel Bartek (☎ 752 57 46; ul Bartka Zwycięzcy 10; dm 15-22zł; P) Modest but pleasant, the youth hostel provides about 50 beds distributed in doubles, triples, quads, and six- and 10-bed dorms.

Bursa Szkolna Nr 1 (☎ 752 68 48; ul Kilińskiego 5/7; dm 15-20zł; Jul & Aug) Bursa is a basic school dorm that rents out its 130 beds during the holidays. There's a second facility further up the road, and some space may be available in term time as well, mostly on weekends.

Hotel Karkonosze (☎ 752 67 56; ul Złotnica 12; d/ tr/q 100/110/120zł; P) Out towards the station, this is one of the better sports dorms you'll come across in Poland, despite the tartan carpets. Sadly you can't quite see into the adjacent stadium from the rooms, but that just gives you more time to investigate the Chinese restaurant.

Hotel Pod Różami (☎ 755 14 53; www.podrozami .pl; Plac Piastowski 26, Cieplice; s/d 120/170zł, ste 200-250zł; P) If you want to stay in Cieplice and make the most of the spa facilities, Under the Roses is a sophisticated option with sizeable doubles and plenty of wood around the place. It's set directly opposite the former Schaffgotsch Palace (now a high school).

Ośrodek Wczasowo-Sanatoryjny Śnieżka (☎ 755 16 73; Plac Piastowski 28, Cieplice; s/d 53.50/64.20zł) Just next door, the Śnieżka offers 30 simple but perfectly acceptable budget rooms. The bathrooms are shared and breakfast is not included.

Eating

Restauracja Relaks (☎ 753 30 85; ul 1 Maja 60; mains 4-18zł; breakfast, lunch & dinner) Part of the small municipal cultural centre, Relaks is a restaurant of the old school, catering for traditional tastes in every regard. As it's opposite Holy Cross it tends to be popular with tour groups at lunchtime.

Restauracja Pokusa (☎ 752 53 47; Plac Ratuszowy 12; mains 5-20zł; lunch & dinner) With outdoor tables in the arcaded passageway circling the Rynek, Pokusa is an agreeable place; the repertoire is mostly based on Polish food, much like its neighbours.

Kurna Chata (☎ 642 58 50; Plac Ratuszowy 23/24; mains 6-19zł; lunch & dinner) A small cosy café with a pub feel and folksy décor (think gnomes bedded in straw), Kurna Chata has good food and an inventive menu.

Spaghetteria Al Dente (ul 1 Maja 31; mains 5.50-22zł; lunch & dinner) Nestled in the foyer of the local cinema, Spaghetteria offers competent versions of all the Italian standards, great for any gangster-movie marathons that come along.

Bar Arnika (☎ 767 61 24; ul Pocztowa 8; mains 5-15.50zł; ⏱ breakfast & lunch Mon-Fri, lunch Sat) One of the cheapest central options, Arnika is a tiny cafeteria that serves basic Polish food.

Café Sonata (☎ 755 72 12; Plac Piastowski 13, Cieplice; dishes 6-12zł; ⏱ lunch & dinner) The nicest of Cieplice's relatively limited eating options, Sonata fills a traditional detached house with suitably refined interiors and home-made cakes, plus weekly piano recitals.

Drinking & Entertainment

Pub Macedonia (☎ 753 53 55; ul 1 Maja 3) A smoky basement bar off the main street with live music from time to time, Macedonia is a popular central watering hole among local folks, and has a large outdoor terrace in summer. There's nothing vaguely Greek or Yugoslavian about it.

Pożegnanie z Afryką (☎ 755 03 76; Plac Ratuszowy 4; ⏱ 10am-6pm Mon-Fri, 10am-5pm Sat, 11am-5pm Sun) Another branch of the serious independent coffeehouse, peddling such imported delights as Papua New Guinea Peaberry, Yemen Matań and, um, espresso. Sip, savour and stock up your grinder.

Jazz Klub Atrapa (☎ 642 47 84; ul Forteczna 1; ⏱ 6pm-4am) One of the most attractive haunts in the centre, Atrapa is a charming club with a dance floor, cheap beer and occasional live music. Note that jazz isn't always high on the programme.

Cosmos II (☎ 0606 621 583; www.cosmos.jelenia .pl in Polish; ul Chełmonskiego; ⏱ 8pm-6am Thu-Sat) Trance, dance and techno batter the weekend crowds at JG's top party palace.

Getting There & Away

The train station is about 1km east of the Old Town, a 15-minute walk from the Rynek, while the bus terminal is the opposite side of town, just northwest of the ring road.

Trains cover Szklarska Poręba (6.80zł, one hour, six daily) and Wrocław (17.20zł, 3½ hours, 13 daily), with one daily service each to Kraków (27.50zł, 7½ hours), Warsaw (31.50zł, 10¼ hours) and Gdynia (33.50zł, 12½ hours). There are no trains to Karpacz.

Buses to Karpacz (5.30zł, one hour) and Szklarska Poręba (5.30zł, 40 minutes) run every hour or so, with departures from the train station as well as the PKS terminal. There's also regular bus transport from the terminal to Kamienna Góra (7zł, one hour), Legnica

(13.80zł, 2½ hours) and Wrocław (16zł, 3½ hours). In summer there are buses to Prague and Berlin; contact local travel agents or the bus terminal for more information.

SZKLARSKA PORĘBA
☎ 75 / pop 8700

At the foot of Mt Szrenica (1362m), on the western side of the Karkonosze National Park, Szklarska Poręba (*shklahr*-skah po-*rem*-bah) is one of the two major resorts catering for visitors to this inviting part of the mountains, the other one being Karpacz on the eastern side. The main street, ul Jedności Narodowej, skirts the Kamienna River on its way up into the hills; at the lower end is the bus terminal, while the train station is off the upper end. It's a lively little town, full of walkers, skiers and strange souvenir cudgels most of the year, and makes a good base for the region's many outdoor activities.

Information

Bank Zachodni (☎ 753 81 90; ul Jedności Narodowej 16)
BT WNW (☎ 717 21 00; www.szklarska.com.pl; ul Wzgórze Paderewskiego 4) Travel agency.
Mountain Rescue (GOPR; ☎ 985)
Sudety IT (☎ 717 29 39; www.sudetyit.com.pl in Polish; ul Turystyczna 26; ⏱ 9am-4pm Mon-Sat, 9am-1pm Sun) Travel agency.
Tourist office (☎ 717 24 49; www.szklarskaporeba.pl; ul Pstrowskiego 1; ⏱ 8am-6pm Mon-Fri, 10am-6pm Sat & Sun)

Sights & Activities

The town has a few small museums (the tourist office has details), but it's the natural beauty of the region and its activities that attract most visitors. There's a **chairlift to Mt Szrenica** (Kolej Linowa na Szrenicę; ☎ 717 30 35; www .sudetylift.com.pl; ul Turystyczna 25a; one-way/return 22/25zł; ⏱ 9am-4.30pm May-Oct), which takes you up 603m in two stages, and deposits you at the top in about 25 minutes. The lower chairlift station is about 1km south of the centre, uphill along ul Turystyczna; note that you'll be charged the national park entry fee (see p287) to go to the summit. Different lift prices and times apply during the ski season.

There are some attractions within easy walking distance of Szklarska Poręba. The road to Jelenia Góra winds east in a beautiful valley along the Kamienna River. Some 3km down the road (or along the green trail on the opposite side of the river) is the 13m-high **Szklarka Waterfall** (Wodospad Szklarki). From here the blue trail heads up to the mountains and you can walk it to Mt Szrenica in two to three hours.

The road that goes west from Szklarska Poręba to the Czech border in Jakuszyce passes the rocky cliffs called Krucze Skały (Ravens' Rocks). About 500m further on, a red trail branches off to the left. It's a 1.5km walk along this trail to the **Kamieńczyk Waterfall** (Wodospad Kamieńczyka), the highest (27m) and one of the prettiest falls in the Polish part of the Sudetes. Continue for about 1½ hours along the same trail to get to Mt Szrenica.

Sleeping & Eating

There are plenty of accommodation options here, including 10 hotels, 90 holiday homes, 50 pensions and 60 registered private-room owners. The tourist office has all the listings, and local travel agencies also handle bookings.

Husarz (☎ 717 33 63; www.husarz.wczasy.net.pl; ul Kilińskiego 18; r per person 120zł; **P**) A discreet 19th-century villa near the centre holds one of the most individual hotels in the mountains, with varied rooms and a magnificent restored dining hall – you eat at a table inherited from Kłodzko castle.

Scots British Pub (ul Kilińskiego 11a; r per person 65zł) The annexe to Husarz – possibly the most incongruous slice of UK nostalgia ever to grace Poland.

Schronisko Hala Szrenicka (☎ 717 24 21; dm 16-30zł, d/ste 90/180zł; 🖳) Perched on the summit of Mt Szrenica itself, this ageing wooden hostel is often full of school groups hiding from the weather. The basic two- to 12-bed dorms are perfectly serviceable, and there are a couple of en suite rooms if you prefer privacy. The top choice for serious walkers.

OSSiR Mauritius (☎ 717 20 83; ul Dworcowa 6; s/d 77.50/134zł; **P** 🖳) At the northern end of town, 100m from the station, the tropically misnomered Mauritius is a surprisingly good facility run by the post office. Neat, comfortable rooms, balconies, gym and café-bar all contribute to the value.

Hotel Las (☎ 717 52 52; www.hotel-las.pl; ul Turystyczna 8; s/d 160/220zł, ste 300-600zł; **P** 🖳 🕊) Occupying its own forest clearing about 4km from the centre, the Las isn't the most unobtrusive structure in the woods, but the range

of facilities is quite astounding – as well as all the usual fitness stuff you get volleyball, basketball and even a winter ice rink.

Camping Pod Klonem (☎ 717 35 25; ul Armii Krajowej 2; per person 9zł) One of several camping grounds in the area, this is a fairly sparse facility but it's just 500m from the centre of town.

Getting There & Away

Trains (five daily) and buses (at least hourly) run to Jelenia Góra (5.30zł, 40 minutes). There are also three trains (18.60zł, 4½ hours) and five buses (24zł, three hours) daily to Wrocław.

For the Czech Republic, take the bus to Jakuszyce (2.20zł, 15 minutes) and cross the border to Harrachov, the first Czech village, from where there are buses onwards.

KARPACZ

☎ 75 / pop 5400

Karpacz sits on the slopes of Mt Śnieżka (1602m), the highest peak of the Sudetes. It's one of the most popular mountain resorts in Poland, as much for skiers in winter as for walkers in summer – its reliable snow cover makes Mt Śnieżka one of the country's top winter sports centres.

Orientation

Karpacz is essentially a large village spread over 3km along a winding road, ul Konstytucji 3 Maja, without any obvious central area. The eastern part, known as Karpacz Dolny or Lower Karpacz, has most of the places to stay and eat. The western part, Karpacz Górny or Upper Karpacz, is just a collection of holiday homes. In the middle of the two districts is the main bus terminal and the sadly defunct Hotel Biały Jar. About 1km uphill from here is the lower station of the chairlift to Mt Kopa (1375m).

Information

Bank Zachodni (☎ 753 81 20; ul Konstytucji 3 Maja 43)

BT Karpacz (☎ 761 95 47; www.btkarpacz.com.pl; ul Konstytucji 3 Maja 50) Travel agency.

BT Sudety (☎ 761 63 92; www.btsudety.com.pl; ul Konstytucji 3 Maja 55) Travel agency.

Hoteli.pl (☎ 761 92 65; www.hoteli.pl; ul Konstytucji 3 Maja 72B) Accommodation agency.

Tourist office (☎ 761 97 16; www.karpacz.pl; ul Konstytucji 3 Maja 25a, Lower Karpacz; 🕐 9am-5pm Mon-Sat, 10am-2pm Sun)

SILESIA

Sights & Activities

Amid all the holiday villas and hotels, Karpacz just happens to have a curious architectural gem – the **Wang Chapel** (Świątynia Wang; ☎ 752 82 99; ul Na Śnieżkę 8; adult/concession 4/3zł; ☺ 9am-6pm Mon-Sat, 11.30am-6pm Sun Apr-Oct, to 5pm Nov-Mar) in Upper Karpacz, the only Nordic Romanesque building in Poland.

The remarkable wooden chapel was originally built at the turn of the 12th century on the bank of Lake Wang in southern Norway as one of about 400 of its kind (just 23 survive today). By the 19th century it became too small for the local congregation, and was offered for sale, to make way for a larger and better building. It was bought in 1841 by the Prussian King Friedrich Wilhelm IV, carefully dismantled piece by piece and brought to Berlin. It was then transported to Karpacz, meticulously reassembled over a period of two years and consecrated in the presence of the king himself. Not only is it the oldest church in the Sudetes, it's also the most elevated, sitting at an altitude of 886m.

The church is made of hard Norwegian pine and put together without a single nail. It's surrounded by a cloister that helps to keep it warm. Part of the woodcarving is original and preserved in excellent shape, particularly the carved doorways and the capitals of the pillars. The freestanding stone belfry was added later. There is a taped commentary with German and English versions available, and regular German-language services are held inside.

Karpacz is an ideal starting point for **hiking**, bordered on the south by Karkonosze National Park. Most tourists aim for Mt Śnieżka, and there are half a dozen different trails leading there. The most popular routes originate from Hotel Biały Jar, taking you to the top in three to four hours. When planning a trip to Mt Śnieżka, try to include in your route two picturesque postglacial lakes, Wielki Staw and Mały Staw, both bordered by rocky cliffs. A couple of trails pass near the lakes.

If you don't want to walk all the way, the **chairlift to Mt Kopa** (Kolej Linowa na Kopę; ☎ 761 92 84; ul Turystyczna 4; one-way/return 17/22zł; ☺ 8.30am-5pm) takes you up 528m in 17 minutes. From Mt Kopa, you can get to the top of Mt Śnieżka in less than an hour by the trail signposted in black.

Sleeping & Eating

It's easy to find a room in Karpacz, even in high season – about 12,000 beds are available, more than twice the number of inhabitants! At peak times (summer or winter), most holiday homes and private houses will cost around 20zł to 40zł per person without bathroom (30zł to 70zł with). The tourist office has a full list of accommodation and will provide details and advice. Rooms in private houses and holiday homes can also be arranged through local travel agencies.

Hotel Vivaldi (☎ 761 99 33; www.vivaldi.pl; ul Olimpijska 4; s 220zł, d 250-290zł, ste 340zł; P 🖳 🐛) A pale yellow building in the midst of the trees, the Vivaldi is a classy proposition on the winding road up to the chairlift and national park entrance. Smart modern rooms continue the yellow theme, while model planes dogfight on the bar ceiling.

Hotel Kolorowa (☎ 761 95 03; ul Konstytucji 3 Maja 58; s/d 120/180zł, ste 200-250zł) This multilingual German-run hotel-guesthouse in the centre of Lower Karpacz offers good standards, the all-important welcome chocolates on pillows and some rooms with views. There's a restaurant on site.

Schronisko PTTK Strzecha Akademicka (☎ 753 52 75; www.strzecha-akademicka.com.pl in Polish; dm/s/d 25/35/60zł) Karpacz' own rugged mountaintop hostel sits snugly in a shallow valley atop Mt Złotówka (1258m), next to Mt Kopa and reached by a separate chairlift. The accommodation's strictly basic budget stuff, but you should see it when it snows. Heating and sheets cost extra.

Hotel Karolinka (☎ 761 98 66; www.karolinka.karpacz.pl; ul Linowa 3b; r per person 70zł; P) The best thing about staying in this large modern hotel is that if you stay inside, you don't have to look at the outside. Luckily the sweeping views from the front rooms make some amends for this hilltop eyesore of a building, and facilities include its own ski-lift.

Camping Nr 211 Pod Brzozami (☎ 761 88 67; ul Obrońców Pokoju 4; adult/child 6/4zł; ☺ Jun-Sep) One of Karpacz' two camping grounds, both administered by the same operator. It's on the left, 1km up the road from the old train station.

Getting There & Away

Trains no longer call at Karpacz, but buses run regularly to Jelenia Góra (5.30zł, one hour, up to twice hourly). They go along

Karpacz' main road, and you can pick them up at any of eight different points, though fewer go right the way to the Upper Karpacz stop. In summer there are two buses a day to Szklarska Poręba (5.80zł, 50 minutes).

KARKONOSZE NATIONAL PARK

The **Karkonosze National Park** (Karkonoski Park Narodowy; ☎ 75-755 33 48; www.karkonosze.it.pl; adult/concession 4/2zł), just south of Karpacz and Szklarska Poręba, stretches up to the Czech border (which follows all the highest peaks of the Karkonosze). The 56-sq-km park is a narrow belt that runs along the frontier for some 25km. On the other side, its Czech counterpart protects the southern part of the outcrop.

The range is divided by the Przełęcz Karkonoska (Karkonosze Pass; 1198m). The highest summit of the eastern section is Mt Śnieżka (1602m), while the western portion is crowned by Mt Wielki Szyszak (1509m). Up to an altitude of about 1250m the park is predominantly spruce forest; higher up are dwarf mountain pines and alpine vegetation, which fade away to leave only mosses on the highest peaks.

The characteristic features of the Karkonosze landscape are **kotły** (cirques): huge hollows carved by glaciers during the ice age and bordered with steep cliffs. There are six cirques on the Polish side of the range; the most spectacular are Kocioł Małego Stawu and Kocioł Wielkiego Stawu near Mt Śnieżka, and Śnieżne Kotły at the foot of Mt Wielki Szyszak.

The Karkonosze is known for its harsh climate, with heavy rainfall (snow in winter) and highly variable weather – strong winds and mists are possible at any time of year. Statistically, the best chances of good weather are in January, February, May and September. Higher up, there's snow on the ground for six months of the year.

The national park is the most popular **hiking** territory in the Sudetes. The two main gateways are Karpacz and Szklarska Poręba, from where most tourists ascend Mt Śnieżka and Mt Szrenica, respectively. For longer walks, the red trail runs right along the ridge between the two peaks, with excellent views on both sides. The trail also passes along the upper edges of the *kotły*. You can walk the whole stretch in six to seven hours. If you start early enough,

it's possible to do the Karpacz–Szklarska Poręba (or vice versa) trip within a day, preferably by using the chairlift to speed up the initial ascent.

You can break the walk by taking any of the trails that branch off from the main route, or by stopping at one of the half-dozen mountain hostels. The **Odrodzenie mountain hostel** (☎ 752 25 46; dm 13zł) is roughly halfway between the two peaks, while the **Samotnia hostel** (☎ 761 93 76; www.samotnia.com.pl; dm 19-26zł, s/d/tr 31/58/87zł) at Kocioł Małego Stawu has the best views in the park. Advance reservations are required for both.

Walking, cycling, downhill and cross-country skiing, snowboarding, carving and sledding are all popular activities here. Local tourist offices and travel agencies will dole out all you need in the way of route information and the like, and every town has stacks of equipment to rent in the relevant seasons. Whatever you're into, get a detailed map of the area and take warm, waterproof clothes to deal with the unpredictable weather.

KRZESZÓW

☎ 75 / pop 1000

If you plan on visiting just a few of Poland's best baroque churches, Krzeszów (*ksheh-shoof*) should be included on your list. This obscure village near the Czech border, well off the main roads and tourist routes, has not one but two extraordinary churches.

Founded in 1242, Krzeszów was granted to the Cistercian order by Prince Bolko I of the newly created Duchy of Świdnica-Jawor. The resulting monastery church became the mausoleum of the Świdnica-Jawor dukes until the line died out in the late 14th century. Despite repeatedly being destroyed by various invaders, from the Hussites to the Swedes, the monastery was systematically rebuilt and extended over the centuries. At the end of the 17th century a fair-sized church was raised, followed some 40 years later by another one, twice the size and even more splendid.

Despite the fact that the Cistercian order was secularised in 1810 and the abbey was abandoned for over a century, the two churches survive today virtually unchanged, and were finally Unesco-listed in 2004. If you're even vaguely interested in religious architecture you won't regret making the effort to come here.

Sights

The older building, **St Joseph's Church** (Kościół Św Józefa), was built between 1690 and 1696. From the outside, the building looks a bit plain, largely because its towers collapsed soon after they were built and were never reconstructed. The interior, by contrast, is more than impressive, with frescoes covering the whole of the vault, the chancel and 10 side chapels. These wall paintings are the work of Michael Willmann and are considered to be among his greatest achievements, portraying the life of St Joseph in some 50 scenes, with the Holy Trinity on the vault of the chancel. Painted at the end of the 17th century, some of the frescoes are unusually free in their composition and execution, strangely evocative of the Impressionist style of two centuries later. In proper Hitchcock style, Willmann left his own image on the walls – he is standing at the door of an inn painted on the wall in the right-hand chapel just before the chancel. Also note the elaborate rococo pulpit and a tiny organ.

The **Church of the Assumption** (Kościół Wniebowzięcia NMP; 1728–35) is much more developed architecturally than St Joseph's, and at 118m in length is much bigger. Its twin-towered façade (70m high) is elaborately decorated from top to bottom and rich in detail. You can go up one of the towers for a view.

The lofty interior is exceptionally coherent stylistically, as the church was built from scratch and not adapted from an earlier structure. Furthermore, all the decoration and furnishings date from the short period of the church's construction, and hardly anything here was added later. The high altar, with the huge background painting by Peter Brandl depicting the Assumption of the Virgin Mary, displays a miraculous icon of the Madonna, while at the opposite end of the church, the organ is regarded as the most splendid instrument in Silesia. The frescoes on the vault are the bravura work of George Wilhelm Neunhertz, the grandson and pupil of Willmann.

Behind the high altar is the **mausoleum** of the Świdnica Piasts, built as an integral part of the church (but accessed from the outside via a separate entrance). It's in the form of two circular chambers, each topped with a frescoed cupola and linked with a decorative arcade. The mausoleum holds the 14th-century tombstones of Prince Bolko I and his grandson Prince Bolko II, while the ashes of the two dukes and other rulers of the line have been deposited in the pillar in between. The frescoes, like those in the church, were executed by Neunhertz and show scenes from the abbey's history.

The abbey occupies the centre of the village, with the main church sitting in the middle of the grounds and the other one just 50m to the north. Between the two churches is an information office, which sells brochures and tickets to the tower and mausoleum. The churches can be visited free of charge from 9am to 6pm (till dusk in winter) except during Mass.

Getting There & Away

The usual jumping-off point for Krzeszów is the town of Kamienna Góra, 8km to the north; buses run every hour or two on weekdays, but the service is poorer at weekends. Kamienna Góra has regular bus links with Jelenia Góra (7zł, one hour) and Wałbrzych (4.50zł, 40 minutes).

KŁODZKO

☎ 74 / pop 32,000

One of the oldest towns in Silesia, Kłodzko (*kwots*-ko) started out as a major trade centre thanks to its desirable river location. Like most settlements in the region, it changed ownership every century or so, with Bohemia, Austria and Prussia all having a crack, and only after WWII did the town revert to Poland.

Kłodzko's Old Town sits on a hillside, and its steep winding streets, sloping main square and overhanging houses give it a unique and special charm. Strolling about the place is an interesting up-and-down affair through a rich architectural mix accumulated throughout the town's long history.

Thanks to its strategic position, the town has a long tradition of fortification. The early castles were replaced by a monstrous brick fortress, started by the Austrians in 1662 and only completed two centuries later by the Prussians. Today it's the dominant, somewhat apocalyptic, landmark of the town and the best reason to pay Kłodzko a visit.

KŁODZKO

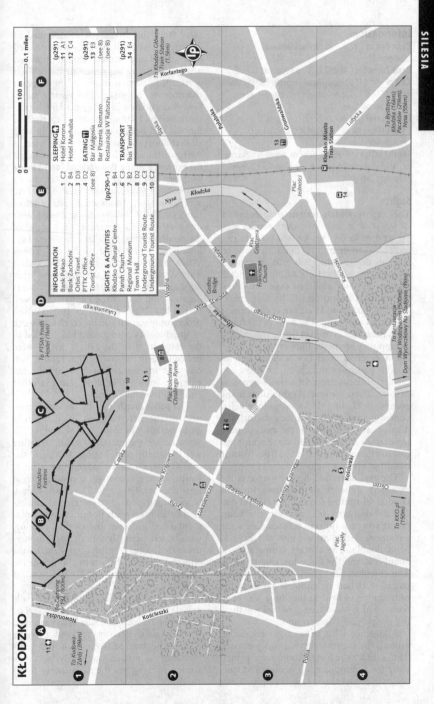

0   100 m
0   0.1 miles

INFORMATION
Bank Pekao..........................1 C2
Bank Zachodni.....................2 B4
Orbis Travel.........................3 D3
PTTK Office.........................4 D2
Tourist Office......................(see 8)

SIGHTS & ACTIVITIES   (pp290–1)
Kłodzko Cultural Centre.........5 B4
Parish Church.......................6 C3
Regional Museum..................7 B2
Town Hall.............................8 D2
Underground Tourist Route....9 C3
Underground Tourist Route...10 C2

SLEEPING   (p291)
Hotel Korona......................11 A1
Hotel Marhaba....................12 C4

EATING   (p291)
Bar Małgosia.......................13 E3
Bar Pizzeria Romano............(see 8)
Restauracja W Ratuszu..........(see 8)

TRANSPORT   (p291)
Bus Terminal.......................14 E4

Information

Bank Pekao (☎ 867 41 10; Plac Bolesława Chrobrego 20)

Bank Zachodni (☎ 867 22 52; ul Kościuszki 7)

KKO.pl (☎ 647 60 45; ul Okrzei 17; per hr 3zł; ☯ 10am-midnight Mon-Sat, 3pm-midnight Sun) Internet access, south of the old town.

Orbis Travel (☎ 867 27 75; Plac Grottgera 1)

PTTK office (☎ 867 37 40; ul Wita Stwosza 1; ☯ 8am-4pm Mon-Fri)

Tourist office (☎ 865 89 70; www.ziemia-klodzka.org .pl; Plac Bolesława Chrobrego 1; ☯ 10am-6pm Mon-Fri, 10am-4pm Sat)

Sights

The mighty **Kłodzko Fortress** (Twierdza Kłodzka; ☎ 867 34 68; ul Grodzisko 1; adult/concession 6/4zł; ☯ 9am-6pm Apr-Oct, 9am-4pm Nov-Mar), begun under Austrian rule in the 17th century, takes its design principally from the medieval Dutch school of fortification. Extended, modernised and modified over 200 years, the complex now covers 17 hectares, making it the largest and best preserved fortress of its kind in Poland. The walls in the lower parts measure up to 11m thick, and even at the top they are never thinner than 4m.

On entering, you can wander around various pathways and chambers and go to the top of the fortress for a bird's-eye view of town. There are several exhibitions in the grounds, including old fire-brigade vehicles, contemporary glass from local factories, a display on the history of the castle, and a lapidarium containing old stone sculptures (mostly tombstones) collected from historic buildings around the region.

The real attraction here, though, is the extensive network of defensive tunnels. Guided 40-minute tours of the **labirynt** (tunnels; adult/concession 6/4zł) begin on the hour, taking you on a 1km circuit including some passageways that are so low you have to bend double. The average temperature is about 8°C and the humidity almost 100%. The corridors are now lit but the soldiers had to work here in complete darkness; the only source of light at that time was open flame, which was a teensy bit risky with all the gunpowder lying around.

Altogether 40km of tunnels were drilled around the fortress, serving two purposes. Those under the fortifications were principally for communication, shelter and storage, while the others, running up to 500m

away from the fortress, were designed to destroy enemy artillery. They were divided into sectors and stuffed with gunpowder; when the enemy happened to move their guns into a particular sector, the relevant chamber was blown up. This bizarre minefield was initiated in 1743 by a Dutch engineer, and by 1807 an immense labyrinth of tunnels had been built, though sadly after all that effort the system was never used.

Down the steps from the fortress hill is the entrance to the **Underground Tourist Route** (Podziemna Trasa Turystyczna; ☎ 867 30 48; ul Zawiszy Czarnego 3; adult/concession 7/5zł; ☯ 9am-5pm Apr-Oct, 10am-3pm Nov-Mar), another interesting set of tunnels. The 600m route, scattered with dungeon-type implements, uses some of the medieval storage cellars that were hollowed out under most of the Old Town. When trade slumped, most of the cellars were abandoned and the town was only reminded of their existence when houses began falling down for no apparent reason. In the late 1950s a complex conservation programme started and the combined work of speleologists, miners and builders led to the restoration of the cellars, which were linked to form the underground route. You can walk the whole length in 10 minutes, entering from either direction; the other end is in the Old Town.

The **parish church**, just by the lower tunnel entrance, is the most imposing religious building in town. It took almost 150 years before the massive Gothic structure was eventually completed in 1490, and the overall shape hasn't changed much since. Inside, however, changes continued for at least another 250 years. The altars, pulpit, pews, organ and 11 monumental confessionals all blaze with florid baroque ornamentation, and even the Gothic vaulting, usually left plain, has been sumptuously decorated. Organ recitals are held in the church – inquire at the tourist office or the **Kłodzko Cultural Centre** (☎ 867 33 64; www.kok .ng.pl; Plac Jagiełły 1).

A short walk uphill is the **Rynek**, officially called Plac Bolesława Chrobrego. Several houses on its southern side have preserved their original Renaissance and baroque décor. The **town hall** was built 100 years ago after its predecessor had gone up in flames; nothing but the Renaissance tower survived.

The **Regional Museum** (Muzeum Ziemi Kłodzkiej; ☎ 867 35 70; ul Łukasiewicza 4; adult/concession 5/3zł; ☙ 10am-5pm Tue-Fri, 11am-5pm Sat & Sun) has a display relating to the history of the town and the region, and a collection of contemporary glass by local artists (the region is noted for its glass production), plus varying temporary exhibitions.

Sleeping

Hotel Marhaba (☎ 865 99 33; ul Daszyńskiego 16; s 90-100zł, d 100-130zł, tr/ste 135/190zł; P) Bedsit-style rooms with shower or full en suite are the mainstay of this unfussy two-storey establishment on the south side of town, a convenient walk from the bus station. Breakfast, served in the house restaurant, is extra.

Hotel Korona (☎ 867 37 37; ul Noworudzka 1; s/d 125/150zł, ste 170-200zł; P) Freshly refurbished and looking all the better for it, the Korona accommodates up to 40 people in a modern building just across the ring road from the fortress and the old town.

PTSM Youth Hostel (☎ 867 25 24; ul Nadrzeczna 5; dm 16.37-21.94zł) Kłodzko's PTSM Youth Hostel, 1km north of the Rynek, offers 53 beds in doubles, triples, quads and larger dorms. The reception closes at 9pm.

Dom Wycieczkowy Na Stadionie (☎ 867 24 25; www.noclegi.pop.pl; ul Kusocińskiego 1; d/tr/q 60/80/100zł; P) The sports centre by the city stadium, 500m south of the Old Town, offers simple accommodation and access to a variety of sports facilities. Most rooms have private showers; there's a cafeteria, a handy barbecue spot and a children's playground.

Camping Nr 132 (☎ 867 30 31; ul Nowy Świat 57; camp site adult/child 12/6zł, d/tr/q 60/75/100zł, cabins 80zł) This place, 1km north of the centre, offers 45 all-year rooms, plus 30 beds in summer cabins. It has tent space and a cafeteria.

Eating

Restauracja w Ratuszu (☎ 865 81 45; Plac Bolesława Chrobrego 3; mains 7-25zł; ☙ lunch & dinner) In an elegant dining room within the town hall, Kłodzko's smartest restaurant has a good range of well-done regional food, a tree-shaded summer terrace and staff just deferential enough to make you feel important.

Bar Pizzeria Romano (☎ 867 09 35; Plac Bolesława Chrobrego 1; mains 8-22zł; ☙ lunch & dinner) Also in the town hall, Romano intersperses the usual Italian treats with the usual Polish grub, and doesn't do a bad job of either.

Bar Małgosia (☎ 867 36 40; ul Połabska 2; mains 4-15zł; ☙ breakfast, lunch & dinner Mon-Fri, breakfast & lunch Sat & Sun) A simple self-service bar that serves hearty Polish meals until the early evening.

Restauracja Nad Wodospadem (☎ 867 61 45; ul Malczewskiego 7a; mains 9-18zł; ☙ lunch & dinner) Out on the south side of town, the Waterfall is a good traditional pub-restaurant turning out respectable dollops of Polish home cooking.

Getting There & Away

BUS

The bus terminal, next to Kłodzko Miasto train station, is the transport hub of the region. Buses to Kudowa-Zdrój (6zł, 50 minutes) and Bystrzyca Kłodzka (4zł, 30 minutes) run roughly every hour. There's also a regular service to Wrocław (17.40zł, 1¾ hours). There are no direct buses to Kletno; take the bus to Stronie Śląskie (see p297) and change or walk from there.

The Czech Republic

There are two road border crossings in the region, both open 24 hours for pedestrians and vehicles. One is at Kudowa-Zdrój/ Náchod, 37km west of Kłodzko on the way to Prague. The other one is at Boboszów/ Králíky, 40km south of Kłodzko on the Brno road.

One daily bus goes across the border from Kłodzko to Náchod (9.90zł, 1½ hours), leaving around 7am or 8am and travelling via Kudowa-Zdrój.

There are no buses direct to the Czech Republic via Boboszów. Take the bus to Boboszów (9.90zł, 1½ hours, 6am weekdays only) and walk across the border 2km to Králíky, from where you have onward transport. There are more frequent buses to Boboszów from Bystrzyca Kłodzka.

TRAIN

Kłodzko has two train stations. The centrally located Kłodzko Miasto station handles regional services, including trains to Bystrzyca Kłodzka (4.60zł, 20 minutes, nine daily), to Kudowa-Zdrój (6.80zł, one hour, nine daily) and to Wrocław (14.50zł, 1¾ hours, 11 daily), and most (but not all) long-distance trains. There are more long-distance trains from the main Kłodzko Główne station, 2km north.

KUDOWA-ZDRÓJ

☎ 74 / pop 11,000

There are three popular spas west of Kłodzko: Polanica-Zdrój, Duszniki-Zdrój and Kudowa-Zdrój. Kudowa is possibly the most attractive, favoured by a mild climate and several mineral springs, and it's also the usual jumping-off point for the marvellous Góry Stołowe.

Kudowa-Zdrój is the biggest spa in the Kłodzko area, with well-preserved spa architecture and a pleasant park lining the single main road. It's also one of the oldest, having celebrated its 650th anniversary in 2004, and provides an ideal atmosphere for chilling out in between the more strenuous activities the region has to offer.

Information

Góry Stołowe National Park Headquarters (Dyrekcja PNGS; ☎ 866 14 36; ul Słoneczna 31)

Raj Internet (☎ 866 41 36; Park Zdrojowy; per hr 3zł; ☺ 10am-10pm)

Tourist office (☎ 866 13 87; www.kudowa.pl; ul Zdrojowa 44; ☺ 8am-8pm Mon-Fri, 8am-6pm Sat, 9am-5pm Sun May-Sep, 9am-5pm Mon-Fri, 9am-2pm Sat Oct-Apr)

Sights & Activities

The only compulsory activity here is a visit to Czermna, 1km north of the centre, to see the macabre **Chapel of Skulls** (Kaplica Czaszek; ☎ 866 14 33; adult/concession 3/2zł; ☺ 9.30am-1pm & 2-5.30pm Tue-Sun) in the grounds of St Bartholemew's church. Inside, the whole length of its walls and ceiling are covered with human skulls and bones – about 3000 of them, with another 21,000 filling the crypt below. A guardian waits within to play a recording explaining the contents, so far only available in Polish, Czech or German. The overall effect is stunning, and should certainly provide a reality check.

For a more relaxed experience, Kudowa has an attractive **Spa Park** (Park Zdrojowy), which occupies 17 hectares, a substantial part of the town. The **pump room** (Pijalnia; ☺ 7am-6pm Mon-Fri, 9am-6pm Sat & Sun) is in the southeastern corner of the park and serves several local waters. If you feel in need of a more thorough 'cure', the **Galos salt caves** (☎ 868 04 81; www.galos.pl in Polish) claim to relieve all your ills with their remarkable artificial sea-salt chambers. The **Aqua Park** (☎ 866 45 02; ul Św Moniuszki 2a; admission 7.50-11zł; ☺ 9am-9pm Mon-Fri, 10am-9pm Sat & Sun), on the edge of the park, has active watery fun.

Fans of the bizarre should hop on over to the Góry Stołowe park headquarters and check out the first ever **Polish Frog Museum** (Muzeum Żaby; ul Słoneczna 31; admission free; ☺ 9am-5pm Mon-Fri, 9am-1pm Sat & Sun). With a collection of everyday objects with an amphibian theme (think newt-shaped soap holders), it's probably the only museum in the world where you can bring your own frog-related items to add to the collection. The stated aim is to raise awareness of frog conservation issues.

HEAD CASES

The Chapel of Skulls in Czermna was built in 1776 and looks pretty modest from the outside. Inside, however, it's a different story: thousands of neatly arranged skulls and bones plaster the walls, with more suspended from the ceiling. It's the only chapel of its kind in Poland and reputedly one of just three in Europe.

The creator of this unusual 'Sanctuary of Silence' was Václav Tomášek, a Czech parish priest (Czermna belonged to the Prague Archdiocese at that time). He and the local grave-digger spent two decades collecting human skeletons, perhaps as many as 30,000 of them, which they then cleaned and conserved. The 'decoration' of the chapel wasn't completed until 1804. Skulls and bones that didn't fit on the walls and the ceiling were deposited in a 4m-deep crypt.

Since the region was the borderland of the Polish, Czech and German cultures, and Catholic, Hussite and Protestant traditions, many of the bones belonged to victims of nationalist and religious conflicts. The skeletons came mostly from numerous mass graves, the result of two Silesian wars (1740–42 and 1744–45) and the Seven Years' War (1756–63). The cholera epidemic that plagued the region also contributed to such an impressive quantity of material.

Several anatomically interesting skulls are displayed on the main altar, including those of a Tatar warrior, a giant and a victim of syphilis. Alongside them are the skulls of the masterminds of the enterprise – the priest and the grave-digger, finally at one with their work.

Sleeping & Eating

Like most resorts of this kind, Kudowa has an extensive accommodation array, providing more than 3000 beds in all. The tourist office can inform you about the options and their rates.

Willa Sanssouci (☎ 866 13 50; www.sanssouci.info .pl; ul Buczka 3; s/d/tr/ste 90/120/140/180zł; **P**) Located in one of the loveliest historic villas in town, the 48-bed Sanssouci has comfortable, ample rooms and good service. If you're feeling lucky, it also has its own wishing well in the garden.

Pensjonat Akacja (☎ 866 27 12; www.akacja.info.pl; ul Kombatantów 5; s/d/tr 95/140/165zł; **P** **⌨**) A modern house impersonating the classic spa villa style, this is an excellent family-run guesthouse in a quiet spot with plenty of space and some balconies on the upper floors.

Recepcja FWP (☎ 866 12 61; ul Zdrojowa 36; dm 18-22zł, s 58-86zł, d 112-160zł; ☽ 7am-7pm) This handy organisation will book a room in any of its seven budget holiday homes, providing 580 beds altogether.

Pensjonat Sudety (☎ 866 37 56; www.kudowa.net .pl in Polish; ul Zdrojowa 32; s 26-30zł, d 44-80zł, tr 60-105zł, q 80-92zł; **P**) The two buildings making up the Sudety's holdings could do with more than a touch of external renovation, but inside you'll find perfectly acceptable budget accommodation, plus a couple of en suite doubles and triples.

Recepja ZUK (☎ 868 04 01; www.zuk-sa.pl; ul Moniuszki 2; dm 26-33zł, s 34-88zł, d 60-130zł, tr 77-155zł, q 136-176zł, ste 153-242zł; **P** **✕**) The ZUK (Kłodzko Health Resort Company) administers some of the finest old villa sanatoriums in the centre of town, providing an unparalleled range of rooms. The emphasis is on medical treatment but they will accept casual guests; disabled visitors in particular may appreciate the extra facilities.

Pod Palmani (☎ 866 38 33; Park Zdrojowy; mains 7-17zł; ☽ breakfast, lunch & dinner; ⌨) Also run by the ZUK, this brick-lined parkside restaurant is one of the best places in town to grab a bite, and stays open till 1am on weekends for a bit of music-bar action.

Getting There & Away

BUS

Buses depart in the town centre from ul 1 Maja . There's frequent transport to Kłodzko (6zł, 50 minutes, hourly) and Wrocław (18zł, three hours, 10 daily).

For the Góry Stołowe, there are half a dozen buses a day to Karłów (4.20zł, 25 minutes), which pass by the turn-off to Błędne Skały. In the high season there are also private minibuses.

One morning bus (except Sunday) comes through from Kłodzko and goes across the Czech border to Náchod (see p291). Alternatively, go to the border (3km) and cross it on foot to Náchod, 2km behind the frontier, from where there are onward buses and trains.

TRAIN

The train station is a long way south of the town and isn't much use unless you want to go to Warsaw (49.80zł, 9½ hours, one train daily). To Kłodzko and Wrocław it's better to go by bus.

GÓRY STOŁOWE

☎ 74

The Góry Stołowe (goo-ri sto-wo-veh; Table Mountains) are among the most spectacular ranges of all the Sudetes. Lying roughly 10km northeast of Kudowa-Zdrój, they are almost as flat-topped as their name suggests. That said, the main plateau is punctuated by remnants of an eroded upper layer, forming secondary 'islands' scattered with fantastic rock formations. This magical landscape was created when the main strata of soft sandstone were eroded, leaving harder rocks behind. Lush vegetation adds colour to the rocks.

In 1994 the whole area became the Góry Stołowe National Park (Park Narodowy Gór Stołowych), which covers 63 sq km. The highlights of the park are the Szczeliniec Wielki and the Błędne Skały.

Information

The park's headquarters in Kudowa-Zdrój can provide all the information you need. Whether you hike in the mountains or explore them by car, the PPWK Góry Stołowe map is a great help. It has all the walking routes and the important rocks individually marked, as well as plans of the Szczeliniec and the Błędne Skały.

Sights

SZCZELINIEC WIELKI

Szczeliniec Wielki (adult/concession 5/2.50zł) is the highest outcrop of the whole range (919m), and has been a magnet for visitors since forever – in 1790 the great German writer and walking enthusiast Goethe was one of the first trail tourists to pass through here, and a plaque commemorates his visit. From a distance, the plateau looks like a high ridge adorned with pinnacles, rising abruptly from the surrounding fields. The most popular way to the top is from Karłów, a small village about 1km south of the plateau, from where a short road leads to the foothills. You then ascend 682 stone steps (built in 1790) to a PTTK snack bar on the top – it takes about half an hour to get there.

The trail around the summit skirts the cliff edge (giving excellent views) before turning inland. The 'Long Steps' take you down to the 'Devils' Kitchen' from where, after passing through the chasm of 'Hell' and 'Purgatory', you can climb the narrow rocky steps to 'Heaven', another viewpoint. Less pious travellers may find the scenery reminds them rather more of wandering through some lost ancient civilisation, the gigantic rocks resembling building blocks scattered and abandoned in the ruins of a monolithic citadel. Either way, it's an experience you'll not forget in a hurry.

The trail continues to two more viewpoints on the opposite side of the plateau and winds back to the starting point, passing a string of rocks carved into a wild array of shapes by time and erosion. Signs tell you the names given to each formation; it takes more than a little imagination to see where some of these came from, but others, such as the Camel and the Horse, will raise a smile when you get them. Don't miss the great Ape overlooking the plains – as an act of random chance it's truly remarkable.

The whole loop takes about an hour, including scenic stops. You can visit at any time; outside the summer period there may be no one to collect the admission fee.

BŁĘDNE SKAŁY

About 4km west as the crow flies, the Błędne Skały (Erratic Boulders) are another impressive sight. Hundreds of monstrous boulders were deposited here by glaciers in vaguely geometric shapes, forming a vast stone labyrinth. A trail runs between the rocks, which are so close together in places that you have to squeeze through sideways.

An hour is enough to do the loop, stopping to take pictures. As in Szczeliniec, you can visit the place whenever you wish; some adventurous trekkers come here in the middle of winter and dig their way through chest-deep snow! Admission is 4zł for adults and 2zł concession in summer, plus an extra charge for vehicles. Cars are only allowed in and out within set 15-minute windows every hour, but you can stay as long as you like once you're parked.

The Błędne Skały are about 3.5km from the Kudowa–Karłów road, linked to it by a narrow, paved road (no public transport). The turn-off is 7km from Kudowa (6km from Karłów). There's a red hiking trail between Szczeliniec and the Błędne Skały.

Getting There & Away

The Góry Stołowe cover a fairly small area, and a day trip generally gives enough time to cover the two highlights. There are half a dozen buses a day from Kudowa-Zdrój to Karłów (4.20zł, 25 minutes), though some of these buses run in summer only and not on weekends. They go along the Road of the Hundred Bends, which snakes spectacularly through the forest and has virtually no straight sections. There are also private minibuses from Kudowa. Cyclists can take advantage of a cycle path leading right the way through to the Czech Republic.

WAMBIERZYCE

☎ 74 / pop 1200

A small village at the northeastern foot of the Table Mountains, Wambierzyce (vahm-byeh-*zhi*-tseh) is an important pilgrimage site, and one of the oldest in Poland. Legend has it that in 1218 a blind peasant recovered his sight after praying to a statue of the Virgin Mary, which had been placed in a hollow lime-tree trunk. A wooden chapel was constructed on the site of the miracle and was later replaced with a church. The fame of the place spread, and a large, two-towered basilica was subsequently built between 1695 and 1711. When this collapsed shortly after its completion, a new sanctuary was built using the surviving Renaissance façade, creating the church that stands here to this day, more or less unchanged.

The largest numbers of pilgrims arrive on 8 July, 15 August and 8 September, and on the nearest Sunday to those dates.

Sights

A flight of 33 steps (symbolising Christ's age when he was crucified) leads to the 50m-wide façade of the **church** (☼ 7.30am-6pm), its palatial appearance emphasised by the absence of towers. The side entrance takes you into the square cloister running around the church, lined with chapels and Stations of the Cross; the walls densely adorned with Tyrolean paintings of Mary and old votive pictures. You'll also find a relic of one of Poland's modern saints, Zygmunt Gorazdowski (1845–1920), a native of Polish Lvov who fought in the 1863 Uprising, despite severe pulmonary problems, and went on to become a pioneering priest, author and educator. He was beatified by the pope in 2001.

The church proper, in the centre of the complex, is much smaller than you'd think from the outside, due to the size of the cloister. It's laid out on two ellipses, with the main one being the nave and the other the chancel, each topped with a painted dome. The baroque décor includes an unusually elaborate pulpit. In the presbytery behind an ornamental grille of 1725, the florid high altar displays the miraculous miniature figure (only 28cm high) of the Virgin Mary with Child. The paintings packed in here include works by master artists Bonoro and Willman.

Every weekend evening in summer the church illuminations take place, lighting up the façade dramatically with some serious technical wizardry. If you happen to be staying in town it's a good time to stroll down to the steps.

The hill opposite the church is dotted with a motley collection of chapels, gates, grottoes, sculptures etc, all representing the **Stations of the Cross**. Known as the Calvary, it was established in the late 17th century to mirror the one in Jerusalem, and was subsequently developed to include 79 stations, with extra additions springing up all over town.

East of the church you'll find the **Szopka** (☎ 871 91 97; ul Objazdowa; admission 3zł; ☼ 9am-4pm May-Sep, 10am-4pm Oct-Apr), a set of mechanised Nativity scenes. The main scene, representing Jesus' birth in Bethlehem, includes 800 tiny figurines (all carved of lime wood), 300 of which can move. Other scenes portray the Crucifixion, the Last Supper and the Massacre of the Innocents. The Szopka was made by local artist Longinus Wittig (1824–95); it took him 28 years.

About 2.5km west of the church is the town's private **skansen** (☎ 871 91 84; ul Wiejska 52; ☼ 9am-sunset). The result of 10 years' work by the eccentric owner, this is a museum featuring just about everything you could think about, including antiques, old household implements, minerals, stuffed birds and miners' uniforms, plus a mini zoo. It's free, but donations are appreciated. The skansen also offers budget accommodation and food.

Sleeping & Eating

Hotel Wambierzyce (☎ 871 91 86; www.hotel-wambierzyce.pl in Polish; Plac NMP 1; s/d/tr/ste 150/240/280/600zł; P) Everything you need in one convenient package, no more than a one-minute pilgrimage from the church. Rooms have some nice old-style trappings (including a couple of tiled heating stoves), the restaurant's the best in town, and the pool table, bar, disco and mini-gym should dispose of an evening one way or another.

For cheaper options, locals rent out rooms in their homes. The priests, too, offer budget accommodation – follow the signs to the Dom Pielgrzyma Nazaret or Betlejam. There are a few simple places to eat around the main square.

Getting There & Away

There are regular buses to Kłodzko (6.40zł, one hour) via Polanica-Zdrój, but only three services go direct to Kudowa-Zdrój (6.10zł, 55 minutes). Wambierzyce is not on a railway line.

BYSTRZYCA KŁODZKA

☎ 74 / pop 14,000

Bystrzyca Kłodzka (bist-*shi*-tsah *kwots*-kah) is the second-largest town in the region after Kłodzko, perched on a similar hilltop setting above the Nysa Kłodzka River. Since the 13th century, when it was founded, the town has been destroyed and rebuilt several times, though ironically it survived WWII virtually unmolested. The few attractions here don't really add up to much, but it's convenient if you're trying to get to the southern Kłodzko region.

Information

Tourist office (☎ 811 37 31; www.bystrzycaklodzka.dolnyslask.pl; Baszta Rycerska, ul Rycerska 20; ☼ 8am-5pm Mon-Fri, 10am-4pm Sat)

Sights

The grubby houses lining the **Rynek** (Plac Wolności) are a blend of styles of different epochs. The octagonal Renaissance tower of the **town hall**, in the middle of the square, gives the place an unusual, almost southern European feel. The tower, built in 1567, is the only really old part of the building, which assumed its current appearance in the 19th century. Next to the town hall is the elaborate baroque votive **Monument of the Holy Trinity**.

In the 14th century the town was surrounded by fortified walls, some of which are still in place. The most substantial structures include the **Water Gate** (Brama Wodna) just south of the Rynek, and the **Kłodzko Tower** (Baszta Kłodzka) on the opposite side of the Old Town.

The nearby **Knights' Tower** (Baszta Rycerska) was reshaped in the 19th century and turned into the belfry of a Protestant church that had been built alongside. After WWII the church was occupied by a **Philumenistic Museum** (Muzeum Filumenistyczne; ☎ 811 06 37; Mały Rynek; admission 3zł; ☼ 8am-4pm Tue-Sun) related to the match industry. A display of old cigarette lighters and matchbox labels from various countries forms the core of the museum's collection. On the square in front of the museum stands the old **whipping post** *(pręgierz)* from 1556; the Latin inscription on its top reads 'God punishes the impious'.

The **parish church** sits at the highest point of the Old Town, one block northwest of the Rynek. It has an unusual double-naved interior with a row of six Gothic columns running right across the middle.

Sleeping & Eating

Hotel Piast (☎ 811 03 22; ul Okrzei 26; s 35-60zł, d 50-80zł) On the edge of the Old Town, this is a basic hotel with a mixture of rooms with and without en suite. The TVs are next to useless and the shower curtains nonexistent, but it still gets quite a few German youth groups.

Bistro Bałuszek (ul Sienkiewicza; mains 4-10zł; ☼ breakfast, lunch & dinner) Unfancy pub grub in a fairly traditional style, with a couple of nice patios for summer drinking.

Getting There & Away

The train station is just east of the Old Town; trains go from here to Kłodzko daily (4.60zł, nine daily), Międzylesie (4.60zł, 10 daily) and Wrocław (15.90zł, eight daily).

You can also get to Kłodzko by bus (4zł, 30 minutes); it goes at least once an hour from the terminal, 200m north of the parish church. There are also reasonable bus connections to Międzygórze (4zł, 40 minutes, hourly) and a few buses to Stronie Śląskie (6.80zł, one hour) and Boboszów (5zł, 50 minutes). Note that most of the bus stands serving local destinations are on the other side of ul Sienkiewicza from the main stop, down a short track between buildings.

MIĘDZYGÓRZE

☎ 74 / pop 700

Międzygórze (myen-dzi-*goo*-zheh) is the epitome of mountain living, a small, charming village beautifully set in a deep valley surrounded by forest. The town was an exclusive German mountain resort in the late 19th and early 20th centuries, and still has some splendid (albeit run-down) historic villas that look as if they have been dropped straight in from the Tyrol.

Information

Library (ul Santoryjna 2; per hr 4zł) Internet access.
PTTK office (☎ 813 51 95; www.pttkmiedzygorze .ta.pl; ul Wojska Polskiego 2; ☼ 8am-4pm Mon-Fri, plus 8am-2pm Sat Jun-Sep) Tourist information.

Sights & Activities

Międzygórze's countryside is a gold mine for strollers, hikers and the outdoors-inclined. Northwest of the village is **Mt Igliczna** (845m), with a small baroque church on top. You can get there by any of three different routes – waymarked red, green or yellow – in about an hour.

About halfway up the yellow trail you'll find the **Ogród Bajek** (Fairy-Tale Garden; adult/concession 3.50/2zł; ☼ 10am-6pm May-Sep, 10am-4pm Oct-Apr), a little hillside plot of models and huts based on Polish fairy stories originally assembled in the 1920s and completely restored in the 1970s and late 1980s. It's not always obvious which legends the scenes refer to (Roadrunner and Wile E Coyote provide a rather incongruous exception), but the bizarre constructions of wood, pine cones and other materials certainly catch the eye.

There are at least five longer trails originating in or passing through the village. The most popular is the hike to the top of **Mt Śnieżnik** (1425m), the highest peak in the region. It will take about three hours to get there by the red trail. If you plan on hiking in the area, get a copy of the *Ziemia Kłodzka* map (scale 1:90,000).

A little further away is Czarna Góra, the Black Mountain, which has an excellent modern **ski centre** (☎ 814 12 45; www.czarnagora .pl in Polish) and reliable snow coverage.

Międzygórze itself boasts the lovely 21m-high **Wilczki Waterfall**, just off the road on the western edge of the village. Shrouded in forest, there are paths all around the falls so you can see and snap them from various angles, including from a bridge right above the drop.

Sleeping & Eating

Pensjonat Millennium (☎ 813 52 87; www.millen nium.maxi.pl; ul Wojska Polskiego 9; s 75zł, d 95-99zł, ste 135zł; **P** ✗) Central alpine-style accommodation at bargain prices. The name may be a couple of years behind the times, but it's still excellent value, with its own restaurant and a charming communal balcony.

Centralna Recepcja FWP (☎ 813 51 09; www.fwp .pl; ul Sanatoryjna 2; r per person 20-35zł, ste 125-150zł; ✆ 7am-9pm) The FWP runs nine of the better holiday homes in town, offering everything from shared-bathroom singles to full-board suites. The office does all the paperwork, charges the room fee and then gives you the keys to the door.

Dom Wczasowy Nad Wodospadem (☎ 813 51 20; www.miedzygorze.net; ul Wojska Polskiego 12; d 65-90zł, tr/q/ste 80/90/150zł; **P**) At the western end of the village, right next to the waterfall, Nad Wodospadem offers reasonable rooms more or less on a par with the Millennium, and also has its own restaurant.

Schronisko Na Śnieżniku (☎ 813 51 30; dm 15-20zł) If you're doing the Mt Śnieżnik climb and don't want to come back the same day, this 58-bed PTTK hostel awaits you half an hour before the summit. Take candles – there's no electricity there.

Getting There & Away

All outbound buses go via Bystrzyca Kłodzka (5.50zł, 40 minutes), with services every couple of hours or so. Six buses continue to Kłodzko (7.40zł, one hour).

To walk to the Bear's Cave at Kletno (right), take the ski trail marked black that goes east from the village along a rough road, and switch to the yellow one leading north. You should get to the cave in two hours.

KLETNO

☎ 74 / pop 300

Kletno is an elongated hamlet stretching along its one road for over 3km. It's not the smattering of cottages that bring visitors here, however – Poland's most beautiful cave is hidden in the trees beyond the village, making it an essential stop for the curious. Bones belonging to a cave bear, which lived here during the last ice age, were found and gave the place its name, the **Bear's Cave** (Jaskinia Niedźwiedzia; ☎ 814 12 50; adult/concession 18/13zł; ✆ 10am-5.40pm Feb-Apr, 9am-4.40pm May-Aug, 10am-5.40pm Sep-Nov, closed Mon & Thu).

The cave was discovered accidentally during marble quarrying in 1966, and a small 400m section of the 3km labyrinth was opened to the public in 1977. You enter through a protective pavilion that houses a snack bar and a small exhibition focusing on the cave's history, then proceed through into the spectacular corridors and chambers, festooned with stalactites and stalagmites. The humidity inside the cave is nearly 100% and the temperature is 6°C all year, so bring something warm.

Visits are by 40-minute tours (Polish only) in groups of up to 15 people, starting every 20 minutes. The cave is very popular and may be swamped with school excursions and individual visitors, especially in the late spring and summer. It's worth calling the management in advance to check the situation and book if necessary.

If you miss a bus or decide to stick around for any reason, you'll find the whole stretch of the Kletno road lined with pensions, camping grounds and agrotourist accommodation.

Getting There & Away

Kletno is best reached via Stronie Śląskie, which has regular bus connections with Kłodzko (7.40zł, 1¼ hours, 15 daily) and Bystrzyca Kłodzka (6.80zł, one hour, 10 daily). From here it's a 9km walk to the cave by the yellow trail (2½ hours). If this is too much for you, take the bus to Bolesławów (twelve daily), get off at Stara Morawa and walk the remaining 5km. There's one afternoon bus to Kletno from Stronie Śląskie (3.30zł, 15 minutes), but as it returns straight away you'll either have to walk back or leave in time to get the last bus from Stara Morawa (around 5pm).

You can also get to the cave by walking from Międzygórze.

PACZKÓW
☎ 77 / pop 8600

A sleepy town midway between Nysa and Kłodzko, 750 years of history have left Paczków (*patch*-koof) with one of the most complete sets of medieval fortifications in the country. Within the walls, the tiny Old Town has hung onto some of its old appearance, not to mention much of its charm.

Information
Bank Zachodni (☎ 431 65 55; Rynek 11)
Tourist office (☎ 431 67 90; www.paczkow.pl; ul Słowackiego 4; 7am-8pm Mon-Fri, 9am-5pm Sat)

Sights
The oval ring of Paczków's **defensive walls** was built around 1350 and surrounded by a moat. This system protected the town for a time, but when firearms arrived in the 15th century, an additional, external ring of defences was erected outside the moat (it was pulled down in the 19th century). The original walls were fortunately retained and, as the town escaped major destruction during WWII, they still encircle the historic quarter. They were initially about 9m high for the whole of their 1200m length and had a wooden gallery for sentries below the top.

Four gateways were built, complete with towers and drawbridges (three towers are still in place), and there were 24 semicircular towers built into the walls themselves (19 have survived, though most are incomplete). The best way to see the system is to walk along the walls, inside or outside. The oldest of the three main towers, the 14th-century **Wrocław Tower** (admission 3zł; 10am-5pm May-Sep), can be climbed.

The **Rynek** occupies a good part of the Old Town. The **town hall** was built in the mid-16th century but only its tower is original; the main building was largely modernised in the 1820s. You can climb to the top of the **tower** (admission 3zł; 10am-5pm May-Sep), which provides much better views than the Wrocław Tower.

The **parish church** of St John the Evangelist, just south of the Rynek, is a squat Gothic cube built in the second half of the 14th century, perhaps taking the idea of defending the faith too literally. Even the

Renaissance parapets are heavy and rather unattractive, though the Gothic doorway is some compensation. Inside, the church now has predominantly neo-Gothic furnishings, and only a few fittings from earlier times remain. The most unusual feature is the well in the right-hand aisle, which provided water in times of siege.

A short walk north of the Rynek is the interesting **Museum of Gas Industry** (Muzeum Gazownictwa; ☎ 431 68 34; ul Pocztowa 6; admission free; 8am-2pm Mon-Fri), installed in an old red-brick gas works that operated from 1902 to 1977. The museum gives an insight into the gas production process, featuring the machinery and various related products such as heaters, irons, lamps and stoves, as well as Europe's largest collection of gas meters (over 500 items).

Sleeping
Hotel Korona (☎ 431 62 77; ul Wojska Polskiego 31; d/tr/q 80/95/115zł; P) Korona is a small 10-room hotel just southeast of the historic quarter. Decent rooms, friendly owner-staff and a homely atmosphere are capped off by a lovely garden and patio.

PTSM Hostel Pod Basztą (☎ 431 64 41; ul Kołłątaja 9; dm 20-30zł; Jul & Aug) The hostel is on the 3rd floor of the school, well located on the west side of the walled town; the entrance is at the back of the building. Most beds are in large dorms.

Camping Nr 258 (☎ 431 65 09; ul Jagiellońska 8; site/cabin/apt 5/45/90zł; Jun-Sep) This camping ground to the south of the old town has a collection of rustic cabins and a tent area. It's in the local sports centre, which has a swimming pool.

Getting There & Away
The bus terminal, on the edge of the Old Town, has services to Nysa (6zł, 45 minutes) and Otmuchów (4.80zł, 30 minutes) at least twice an hour, with some splendid mountain views along the way. In the opposite direction, buses run to Kłodzko (6.80zł, 50 minutes) every two to three hours.

OTMUCHÓW
☎ 77 / pop 5500

If you are travelling the Kłodzko–Nysa route, you may want to stop in Otmuchów (ot-*moo*-hoof). The town was the property of the Wrocław bishops for over 500 years and came to be an important ecclesiastical centre. Set between two lakes – Lake Otmuchowskie to the west and Lake Nyskie to the east – Otmuchów has now become a local holiday spot, and is well worth a quick stop.

Sights

The sloping Rynek retains little of its former character apart from the 16th-century **town hall**, which has a Renaissance tower and a lovely double **sundial** built in 1575 around the corner of two walls. The baroque **parish church**, overlooking the Rynek, was built at the end of the 17th century and most of its internal decoration, including frescoes by Dankwart and paintings by Willmann, dates from that period.

Just south of the church, atop the hill, is a massive **castle**, erected in the 13th century but much extended and remodelled later. It's now a hotel, but you can climb the tower in summer, and **tours** (per person 3-4zł) of the rest of the building are available for groups. You can also wander around the front terrace and the park area surrounding the hill.

Sleeping & Eating

Gościniec Zamek (☎ 431 46 91; www.zamek.otmu chow.pl; ul Zamkowa 4; s/d/tr/ste 130/160/190/200zł; **P**) If you're going to stick around it would really be criminal to stay anywhere else. The castle has no end of character, with a vine-covered restaurant, lots of greenery, the odd cannon and farming artefacts all over the place. Breakfast is not included.

Getting There & Away

Otmuchów lies on the Nysa–Paczków road and buses ply this route regularly, stopping at the bus terminal, which is just south of the castle hill.

NYSA

☎ 77 / pop 48,000

For centuries Nysa (*ni*-sah) was one of the most important religious centres in Silesia. In the 17th century it became a seat of the Catholic bishops, who were in flight from newly Protestant Wrocław. The bishops soon made Nysa a bastion of the Counter-Reformation, so strong that it came to be known as the Silesian Rome. A number of churches were built in that time, some of which still survive.

Around 80% of Nysa's buildings were destroyed during the fierce battles of 1945, and the postwar reconstruction leaves a lot to be desired in aesthetic terms, though some historical elements persist. Come for the dramatic cathedral, the little-big town vibe and one rather nice hotel.

Information

JTR (☎ 448 10 00; ul Bracka 1; per hr 3zł) Internet access.
Post office (☎ 433 22 25; ul Krzywoustego 21)
PTTK office (☎ 433 41 71; ul Bracka 4; ◐ 9am-4pm Mon-Fri) Tourist information.

Sights

There's no mistaking Nysa's powerful brick **cathedral**, with its imposing blackened bulk and fine stone double doorway. Built in the 1420s, it was remodelled after a fire in 1542, but hasn't changed much since then. The cathedral's 4000-sq-metre roof is one of the steepest church roofs in Europe.

The vast interior is not crammed with the usual baroque furnishings and looks distinctly sober and noble, its loftiness being the most arresting feature. On closer inspection, however, you'll see that its side chapels (18 in all) boast some glowing stained glass and a wealth of tombstones, funeral monuments and epitaphs, making up the largest collection of funerary sculpture in any Silesian church.

The freestanding block next to the cathedral is its **bell tower**, begun 50 years after the church and originally intended to be over 100m high. Despite 40 years' work it only reached half that height, and consequently looks quite odd, especially with the silly turret tacked on as an afterthought.

To the east of the cathedral is the 17th-century Bishops' Palace (Pałac Biskupi), a spacious former residence now occupied by the **Nysa Museum** (☎ 433 20 83; ul Jarosława 11; adult/concession 4/2zł, free Sat; ◐ 9am-5pm Tue, 9am-3pm Wed-Fri, 10am-3pm Sat & Sun). The collection relates to the town's history and includes exhibits ranging from archaeological finds to photos documenting war damage, plus a model of the town in its heyday. The museum also features European paintings from the 15th to the 19th centuries, mostly from the Flemish and Dutch schools.

Stretching out from the foot of the cathedral, the vast **Rynek** shows the extent of the war damage. Only the southern side of the

SILESIA

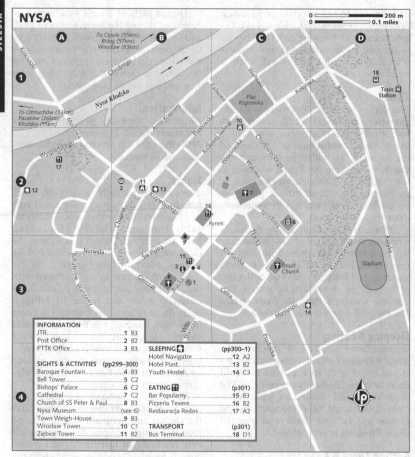

NYSA

0 — 200 m
0 — 0.1 miles

To Opole (55km);
Brzeg (57km);
Wrocław (83km)

Plac
Kopernika

Train
Station

To Otmuchów (13km);
Paczków (26km);
Kłodzko (55km)

Nysa Kłodzka

Rynek

Jesuit
Church

Stadium

INFORMATION	
JTR	1 B3
Post Office	2 B2
PTTK Office	3 B3

SIGHTS & ACTIVITIES	(pp299–300)
Baroque Fountain	4 B3
Bell Tower	5 C2
Bishops' Palace	6 C2
Cathedral	7 C2
Church of SS Peter & Paul	8 B3
Nysa Museum	(see 6)
Town Weigh-House	9 B3
Wrocław Tower	10 C1
Ziębice Tower	11 B2

SLEEPING	(pp300–1)
Hotel Navigator	12 A2
Hotel Piast	13 B2
Youth Hostel	14 C3

EATING	(p301)
Bar Popularny	15 B3
Pizzeria Tevere	16 B2
Restauracja Redos	17 A2

TRANSPORT	(p301)
Bus Terminal	18 D1

square is anything like it used to be, with its restored houses originally dating from the 16th century. The detached building facing them, the 1604 **Town Weigh-House** (Dom Wagi Miejskiej), retains fragments of 19th-century wall painting on a side wall. Just round the corner, on ul Bracka, there are more historic houses and a 1701 baroque **fountain**.

Just past the fountain is the twin-towered **Church of SS Peter & Paul**, built in the 1720s for the Hospitallers of the Holy Sepulchre. It has one of Silesia's best baroque interiors, complete with an opulent high altar, organ and trompe l'œil wall paintings. The church is locked except for services (8am or 6pm weekdays and 10am Sunday).

The only significant traces of the medieval defences are two 14th-century brick towers: the **Ziębice Tower** (Wieża Ziębicka; ul Krzywoustego) and the **Wrocław Tower** (Wieża Wrocławska; ul Wrocławska).

Sleeping

Hotel Navigator (☎ 433 41 70; www.aro.pl/navigator; ul Wyspiańskiego 11; s 80-150zł, d 100-180zł; **P**) Why aren't there more places like this in Poland? This charming establishment is exactly what a guesthouse should be, from the antique furniture to the sociable breakfasts in the family kitchen. Top-floor rooms are smaller and simpler, but still thoroughly serviceable; for real class, ask for the Danzig room. All in all, highly recommended.

Hotel Piast (☎ 433 40 84; ul Krzywoustego 14; s/d/tr/ste 135/170/255/230zł) Good tourist-class standards, a fridge in every room and small balconies go a long way towards distracting clients from the odd hole in the wall (hopefully the building work should be finished by now). The Piast also has its own restaurant, a useful facet of Nysa's eating scene.

Youth Hostel (☎ 433 37 31; ul Moniuszki 9; dm 15-25zł) Conveniently set just a few short blocks from the Rynek, the 54-bed youth hostel has small dorms of two to four beds, providing a little more privacy than many other hostels.

Eating

Restauracja Redos (☎ 433 49 72; ul Wyspańskiego 1a; mains 8-18zł; lunch & dinner) A seemingly innocent pavilion near the river holds this lively bar-restaurant, whipping out pizza and other modern staples for a youngish public. Occasional club nights tear up the sound system.

Pizzeria Tevere (☎ 433 30 03; Rynek 36b; mains 7-25zł; lunch & dinner) Drinkers and diners alike congregate in this brick-clad subterranean den of pasta, pizza, steak and schnitzel, relishing the loud music, perforated bar and random photo art.

Bar Popularny (☎ 433 30 15; Rynek 23/24; mains 3-8.70zł; breakfast & lunch Mon-Sat) This unreformed milk bar-cafeteria looks drab and basic, but the food is never less than acceptable.

Getting There & Away

The bus and train stations face each other, a convenient 600m walk from the Rynek. Getting around the area is easiest by bus – there are services to Paczków (6zł, 45 minutes, nine daily), Kłodzko (8.90zł, 1¾ hours, nine daily), Opole (8.90zł, 1¾ hours, hourly) and Wrocław (13zł, two hours, 15 daily). Trains are less frequent but may be useful when travelling to Opole (9.80zł, 1½ hours, seven daily).

UPPER SILESIA

After the unfettered nature and spa-town pace of the Sudetes, Upper Silesia may come as a bit of a shock. Heavily developed and industrialised, the area occupies just 2% of Poland's territory, yet it's home to over 10% of the country's population. Thanks to large deposits of coal it's become the nation's main centre of heavy industry and the most densely urbanised area in Central Europe, not to mention the most polluted.

Of course, few people come to Upper Silesia for the views. Whatever your feelings on urban sprawl, there are some important sights in the region, including the unmissable Auschwitz concentration camp museum, and it's an easy port of call if you're heading to Kraków or the Czech Republic.

KATOWICE

☎ **32 / pop 385,000**

Katowice (kah-to-*vee*-tseh) is the centre of the so-called Upper Silesian Industrial District (Górnośląski Okręg Przemysłowy). The GOP contains 14 cities and a number of neighbouring towns, forming one vast conurbation with a population of over three million. It's one of the biggest industrial centres in Europe, and one of the most outdated – it's hoped that the new EU money will fund substantial modernisation work.

Historically, Katowice is a product of the 19th-century industrial boom, but it only became a city in the interwar period. After WWII, at the height of the Stalinist craze, the city was renamed Stalinogród, but reverted to its old name soon after Comrade Joseph died. Katowice has few significant historical monuments, but like any big city it's a major commercial and cultural centre, with no shortage of activity, international transport links and some very smart accommodation.

Information

INTERNET ACCESS

Café Kontakt (☎ 781 59 08; http://cafekontakt.pl in Polish; ul Stawowa 3; per hr 3.50zł; 8am-11pm)

Café Net.Pl (www.cafe.net.pl in Polish; ul Kochanowskiego 16; per hr 3zł; 10am-1am Mon-Sat, 2pm-1am Sun) Free access with drink orders.

Eurocafé (☎ 257 53 61; www.cafe.katowice.pl in Polish; train station; per hr 3zł; 24hr)

Internet Bob Café (☎ 0501 406 567; ul Chopina 8; per 15 min 1zł; 10am-midnight Mon-Thu, 10am-2am Fri & Sat, 2-10pm Sun)

MONEY

Bank Pekao ul Św Jana (☎ 253 90 51; ul Św Jana 5); ul Warszawska (☎ 259 60 41; ul Warszawska 8)

PKO Bank (☎ 357 90 61; ul Chopina 1)

TOURIST INFORMATION

Orbis Travel (☎ 355 99 60; ul Staromiejska 21)

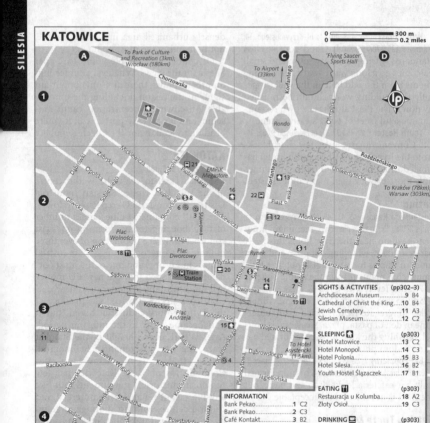

KATOWICE

0 _____ 300 m
0 _____ 0.2 miles

TRAVEL AGENCIES

Orbis Travel (☎ 355 99 60; ul Staromiejska 21)

Sights

Katowice has Silesia's best-preserved **Jewish Cemetery** (Cmentarz Żydowski; ☎ 251 28 26; ul Kozielska 16; ⏰ 8am-5pm Sun-Thu, 8am-noon Fri). Established in 1869, it's divided into two parts, of which the front one is older. Amid trees and thick undergrowth are several hundred tombstones, many of which are in remarkably good shape. Inscriptions on the older tombstones are in Hebrew and German, while those on the more recent ones are in Hebrew and Polish – a small but significant reflection of the region's chequered history.

The **Park of Culture and Recreation** (Wojewódzki Park Kultury i Wypoczynku) is possibly Katowice's most popular attraction (though administratively it belongs to the neighbouring city of Chorzów). This vast park, over 5 sq km, is the conurbation's major recreation area. It includes a stadium, zoo, amusement grounds, planetarium and a skansen, the Upper Silesian Ethnographic Park (Górnośląski Park Etnograficzny). The park is about 3km northwest of Katowice's centre; bus and tram lines going to Chorzów will take you there.

Back in the centre of Katowice, the **Silesian Museum** (Muzeum Śląskie; ☎ 258 56 61; www .muzeumslaskie.art.pl; Al Korfantego 3; adult/concession 6/3.50zł, free Sat; ⏰ 10am-5pm Tue-Fri, 11am-5pm Sat

& Sun) features a permanent exhibition of Polish paintings from 1800 to 1939, plus various temporary and rotating displays from its vast collections. The imposing building was once the city's premier hotel, built in the 19th century.

An 800m walk south from the Rynek is the **Cathedral of Christ the King** (Katedra Chrystusa Króla; ul Powstancow), a massive sandstone structure erected between 1927 and 1955. It's one of the biggest churches built in modern Poland. The spacious interior is topped with a large dome, but apart from colourful stained-glass windows and an unusual 'wheel' crucifix it's fairly plain.

Right behind the cathedral is the **Archdiocesan Museum** (☎ 608 14 52; ul Jordana 39, enter from ul Wita Stwosza 16; admission 4zł; 🕑 2-6pm Tue & Thu, 2-5pm Sun). It has a collection of sacral art from the late 14th century, including some beautiful Gothic altarpieces and Madonnas.

About 1.5km further to the southwest, in Park Kościuszki, is the lovely, timber-shingled **St Michael's Church** (Kościół Św Michała), dating from 1510. It was brought here from the Upper Silesian village of Syrynia and reassembled in 1939.

Sadly, Katowice's central **Rynek** is lined not with historic burghers' houses but with drab postwar blocks. It's a showpiece of the early Gierek style – the term Poles sarcastically give to architecture spawned during the fleeting period of apparent prosperity in the early 1970s, when Edward Gierek's government took out hefty loans from the West to make Poland a 'second Japan'. EU accession has also prompted some foreign-funded development, but so far nothing quite so crass has sprung up.

Sleeping

Hotel Monopol (☎ 782 82 82; www.hotel.com.pl; ul Dworcowa 5; s/d 490/560zł, ste 650-790zł; 🔣) A reincarnation of Katowice's most prestigious prewar hotel: brand new, modern and full of stylish walnut and chrome, this is the way top-end should be done, contrasting sharply with the mediocre options further down the price scale. Genuinely friendly staff, huge shower heads, two restaurants, a fitness centre and a mosaic in the lobby count among the highlights. Go for a corner room if you can get one.

Hotel Polonia (☎ 251 40 51; hotelpolonia@o2.pl; ul Kochanowskiego 3; s/d/tr 120/190/270zł) Back in the real world, this convenient hotel is just a five-minute walk south of the train station. It's nothing special, but probably the best value in the centre. Rooms without bathroom are only marginally cheaper.

Hotel Asystencki (☎ 255 44 33; ul Paderewskiego 32; s 56-70zł, d/tr/studio 105/135/200zł) Run by the University of Silesia, this residential facility, 1.5km east of the town centre, is unusually comfortable for its class. Some even cheaper beds are available from July to mid-September.

Hotel Katowice (☎ 258 82 81; www.hotel-katowice .com.pl; Al Korfantego 9; s/d/tr 180/224/298zł, ste 272-292zł; 🅿) A typical communist-era product, this 308-bed block has little character and some downright nasty rugs, but standards are acceptable, it's not short on amenities (who can resist a cake shop?) and the town centre's a light stroll away.

Youth Hostel Ślązaczek (☎ 259 68 49; zowptsm@ wp.pl; ul Sokolska 26; dm 22-40zł) This 50-bed HI hostel is an 800m walk north of the train station, offering the usual basic accommodation in dorms of up to eight people.

Hotel Silesia (☎ 259 62 11; silesia@orbis.pl; ul Piotra Skargi 2; s/d 230/260zł; 🅿) An uninspiring upmarket facility, this large Orbis-run hotel is roughly similar to the Katowice, but more central and more expensive.

Eating & Drinking

Two pedestrian strips hold Katowice's highest concentrations of eateries: ul Stawowa, just north of the train station, has plenty of snack bars and unfancy restaurants, while the area around ul Staromiejska, east of the train station, is a bit more cosmopolitan and upmarket.

Złoty Osioł (☎ 203 50 05; ul Mariacka 1; mains 3.50-8zł; 🕑 breakfast, lunch & dinner Mon-Sat, lunch & dinner Sun) A cheerful, popular vegetarian café of the kind you'd expect in health-conscious Western Europe, with fast-growing pot plants and a slightly hippy décor.

Restauracja U Kolumba (☎ 253 08 64; Plac Wolności 12a; mains 25-50zł; 🕑 lunch & dinner) On the western side of town, this elegant and historic basement restaurant offers a long menu of Polish and European dishes.

Gaudi Café (☎ 206 98 11; ul Wawelska 2) In tribute to the acclaimed Spanish architect, this is the coolest café on the centre's coolest side street. The coffee and cakes are good, but it's the out-there interior that'll leave you in awe.

Getting There & Away

AIR

The **airport** (☎ 392 73 85; www.gtl.com.pl) is in Pyrzowice, 33km north of Katowice. Domestic flights currently cover Warsaw (four daily), Poznań and Wrocław (both twice weekly), with international services to a dozen or so European destinations, including Frankfurt (up to three daily), London (up to seven daily), Paris (10 weekly) and Stockholm (daily).

BUS

The PKS **bus terminal** (ul Piotra Skargi), 500m north of the train station, handles a couple of buses a day to most destinations around the region, with plenty of long-distance and international services.

Polski Express buses depart from Al Korfantego, opposite Hotel Katowice. There are two buses a day to Kraków (80 minutes) and two to Warsaw (54zł, 6½ hours) via Częstochowa and Łódź.

TRAIN

Trains are the main means of transport in the region and beyond. The train station is in the city centre and trains depart frequently in all directions, including Oświęcim (6.80zł, one hour), Pszczyna (6.80zł, 45 minutes), Kraków (19.47zł, 1½ hours), Opole (23.93zł, 1¾ hours), Wrocław (34.03zł, three hours), Poznan (44.65zł, 5½ hours), Częstochowa (13.10zł, 80 minutes) and Warsaw (43.04zł, 2¾ hours). International destinations include Berlin, Bratislava, Budapest, Hamburg, Prague and Vienna.

OŚWIĘCIM

☎ 33 / pop 48,000

Oświęcim (osh-*fyen*-cheem) is a medium-sized, quiet industrial town on the borderline between Silesia and Małopolska, about 30km south of Katowice and 60km west of Kraków. The Polish name may be unfamiliar to outsiders, but the German one – Auschwitz – is certainly not.

The Auschwitz concentration camp was established in April 1940 in the prewar Polish army barracks on the outskirts of Oświęcim, and came to be the largest experiment in genocide in the history of humankind. Originally intended to hold Polish political prisoners, the camp was 'repurposed' as a dedicated centre for the extermination of European Jews. For this purpose, the much larger Birkenau (Brzezinka) camp, also referred to as Auschwitz II, was built 2km west of the original site in 1941 and 1942, followed by another one in Monowitz (Monowice), several kilometres to the west. About 40 smaller camps were subsequently established all over the region.

It's estimated that in total this death factory eliminated some 1.5 million people of 27 nationalities, including 1.1 million Jews, 10,000 Russians, 145,000 Poles and 20,000 Roma. It's now considered the largest mass cemetery in the world.

The name Auschwitz is commonly used for the whole Auschwitz-Birkenau complex, both of which are open to the public as the **State Museum Auschwitz-Birkenau** (☎ 843 20 22; www.auschwitz-muzeum.oswiecim.pl; ul Więźniów Oświęcimia 20; ⊙ 8am-7pm Jun-Aug, 8am-6pm May & Sep, 8am-5pm Apr & Oct, 8am-4pm Mar & Nov, 8am-3pm Dec-Feb).

Auschwitz

Auschwitz was only partially destroyed by the fleeing Nazis, and many of the original buildings stand to this day as a bleak testament to the camp's history. A dozen of the 30 surviving prison blocks now house museum exhibitions, either general or dedicated to victims from particular countries that lost citizens at Auschwitz.

During the communist era, the museum was conceived as an antifascist exhibition – the fact that most of the victims were Jewish was played down, and undue prominence was given to the Poles killed here. This approach has changed; block No 27, dedicated to the 'suffering and struggle of the Jews', now presents Auschwitz more correctly as a place of martyrdom of European Jewry.

From the visitors centre in the entrance building, you enter the barbed-wire encampment through the infamous gate, still displaying the grimly cynical legend '*Arbeit Macht Frei*' (Work Sets You Free). The logical order is to visit as many of the exhibitions as you want in the prison blocks, then finish up with the gas chamber and crematorium.

You don't need much imagination to take in what happened here (in fact you'll

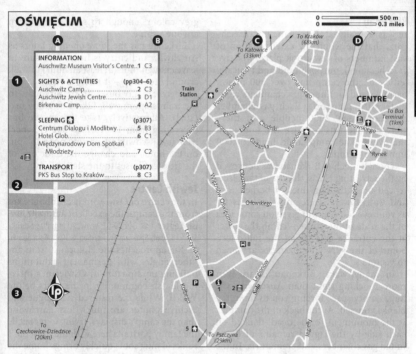

OŚWIĘCIM

0 ——— 500 m
0 ——— 0.3 miles

INFORMATION
Auschwitz Museum Visitor's Centre..1 C3

SIGHTS & ACTIVITIES (pp304–6)
Auschwitz Camp...................................2 C3
Auschwitz Jewish Centre................3 D1
Birkenau Camp..................................4 A2

SLEEPING
Centrum Dialogu i Modlitwy..........5 B3
Hotel Glob..6 C1
Międzynarodowy Dom Spotkań
Młodzieży.......................................7 C2

TRANSPORT (p307)
PKS Bus Stop to Kraków...................8 C3

To Katowice (33km)
To Kraków (68km)
Train Station
CENTRE
To Bus Terminal (1km)
Rynek
Orłowskiego
To Czechowice-Dziedzice (20km)
To Pszczyna (29km)

probably wish you had less imagination altogether). The things that really stand out are the little touches that bring home the sheer gall of the SS administration – the prisoners' orchestra playing to calm arriving inmates and the fake shower heads in the gas chamber are two particularly biting reminders of the detached efficiency with which the camp was run.

A 15-minute **documentary** (adult/concession 3.50/2.50zł) about the liberation of the camp by Soviet troops on 27 January 1945 is screened in the visitors centre every half-hour, with a foreign-language soundtrack a few times a day (the English version is normally at 11am and 1pm). Check with the information desk at the visitors centre for screening times of the different language versions – although the film's message is clear in any language.

Photography, filming and videoing are all permitted throughout the camp, though obviously, few people stand around posing for snapshots. Anyone under the age of 14 is advised by the museum management not to visit the camp, but the final decision is left to the accompanying adults. There's a cheap, self-service snack bar by the entrance, facing the car park. There's also a *kantor* (private currency-exchange office), a free left-luggage room and several bookshops stocked with publications about the place.

Get a copy of the small museum guidebook (4zł; available in 17 languages, including Polish, English, French and German), which has plans of both Auschwitz and Birkenau camps and is quite enough to get you round the grounds. In summer, English-language tours of both camps are organised daily at 11am (40zł per person, 3½ hours), and sometimes also at 1pm if there's enough demand. Otherwise you can hire a foreign-language guide for your party at the information desk (192zł to 224zł per group).

From 15 April to late October, there is a special bus from Auschwitz to Birkenau (2zł). It departs hourly, 11.30am to 4.30pm, from outside the entrance to the visitors centre. Alternatively, you can walk (2km) or take a taxi (10zł).

Birkenau

It was actually at Birkenau, not Auschwitz, that the wholesale extermination of vast numbers of Jews took place. Massive (175 hectares), purpose-built and typically 'efficient', the camp had over 300 prison barracks and four huge gas chambers complete with crematoria. Each gas chamber accommodated 2000 people and there were electric lifts to raise the bodies to the ovens. The camp could hold 200,000 inmates at a time.

Though much of Birkenau was destroyed by the retreating Nazis, the size of the place, fenced off with long lines of barbed wire and watchtowers stretching almost as far as your eye can see, will give you some idea of the scale of the crime – climb the tower at the entrance gate to get the full effect. Some of the surviving barracks are open to visitors.

In many ways, Birkenau is an even more shocking sight than Auschwitz, the huge empty space forcing you to fill in the blanks yourself. At the back of the complex is the monument to the dead, flanked on each side by the jagged remains of dynamited gas chambers and crematoria. In the far northwestern corner of the compound is a pond into which the ashes of the victims were dumped. It is still a distinctive grey colour; enough to send chills down anyone's spine.

Birkenau has the same opening hours as Auschwitz and entry is free. Make sure to leave enough time (at least an hour) to walk around the camp – it really is vast.

There are no buses from Birkenau to the train station; walk (2km) or go by taxi (10zł). Alternatively, take the shuttle bus (operating from 15 April to late October) back to Auschwitz (departing noon to 5pm on the hour) and change there for one of the frequent buses to the station.

Jewish Centre

In the centre of Oświęcim itself, about 3km from the camps, the excellent **Auschwitz Jewish Center** (☎ 844 70 02; www.ajcf.org; Plac Skarbka 5; 🕑 8.30am-8pm Sun-Fri Apr-Sep, 8.30am-6pm Sun-Fri Oct-Mar) approaches the Holocaust from another angle, with permanent exhibitions building up a picture of Oświęcim's thriving Jewish community in the years before WWII. While the restored synagogue and archive photos are much less harrowing than the camp's displays, trying to reconcile the family portraits here with the museum's ranks of mug shots quickly brings home the realities of what happened, and it's hard to forget you're looking at the last remnants of an exterminated culture.

ST MAXIMILIAN

Maximilian Kolbe is a prophet and a sign of the new era, the civilization of love.

Pope John Paul II

One of Auschwitz' most famous Polish victims was Father Maximilian Kolbe, born Raymond Kolbe, a Catholic priest who founded the evangelistic Marian movement the Militia of the Immaculata. Kolbe was sent to Auschwitz for publishing religious periodicals from his friary near Warsaw; in the camp he continued to work clandestinely as a priest, and finally swapped his own life for that of another prisoner. He was executed by lethal injection in 1941 after surviving two weeks in a starvation cell.

In 1982 Father Kolbe was declared a saint by the pope, and his picture now appears in many Polish churches, revered as a patron saint for journalists, families, prisoners, the pro-life movement and victims of addiction. But his beatification was not without controversy – allegations emerged that he had printed anti-Semitic material in his various periodicals before WWII, casting doubt on his saintly character. Conversely, it was also reported that the Warsaw friary sheltered several thousand Polish and Jewish fugitives from the Nazis. With continued debate over the role of the Catholic Church in the Holocaust, it's unlikely these issues will ever be fully resolved.

Whatever the truth, St Maximilian has become one of the best-loved modern saints and martyrs in Poland, representing for millions a strain of humanity amid the horrors of Auschwitz. He may not have performed three miracles, but the example of his death has certainly earned him a place in history.

Sleeping & Eating

For most visitors, the Auschwitz-Birkenau camp is a day trip, in most cases from Kraków, and the visitors centre probably has all you need to keep you going. If you do decide to stay, however, Oświęcim has a choice of places to stay and eat.

Centrum Dialogu i Modlitwy (Centre for Dialogue & Prayer; ☎ 843 10 00; www.centrum-dialogu.oswiecim .pl; ul Kolbego 1; camping per adult/student €6/5, bed per adult/student €22/17; **P**) The 45-bed centre is a Catholic facility 700m southwest of the museum, providing comfortable and quiet accommodation in rooms of two to 10 beds (most en suite) and a restaurant.

Międzynarodowy Dom Spotkań Młodzieży (International Meeting House for Youth; ☎ 843 21 07; www.mdsm .pl; ul Legionów 11; camping 15zł, s/d/tr 100/135/150zł; **P**) The German-built MDSM, 1km east of the train station, essentially exists to house longer-term groups, but will take anyone if there are vacancies. Meals and cheaper rooms with shared bathroom are available.

Hotel Glob (☎ 843 06 43; ul Powstańców Śląskich 16; s/d/tr 70/100/120zł; **P**) Looking like an air-traffic control tower, the Globe gives the impression it's barely been touched since communism, but it's very handy for the train station. Breakfast is not included.

Getting There & Around

For most tourists, the jumping-off point for Oświęcim is Kraków. Buses (8zł, 1½ hours, up to 15 daily) can be a more convenient option than trains, as they drop you off on ul Więźniów Oświęcimia, right by the Auschwitz museum. Don't miss the stop, otherwise you'll have to backtrack 4km from the terminal. You can return to Kraków by bus, but take note that the last one leaves around 6pm, so if you want to return later you'll need to take a train.

Many tours to the camp are also organised from Kraków (p149), though even the cheapest tour will cost you much more than you'd spend taking public transport.

If Katowice is your starting point, there are eight daily trains (6.80zł, one hour) and about 10 buses (5.40zł, 1½ hours), though only one goes to the museum stop.

If you want to go to Pszczyna (5.70zł, one hour) from Oświęcim, take the train to Czechowice-Dziedzice (14 daily) and change there. The whole journey should take around an hour.

To get from the train station to the museum, take any of the southbound city buses. Taxis will take you to either camp for a fixed price of 10zł.

PSZCZYNA

☎ 32 / pop 38,000

In heavily industrialised Upper Silesia, Pszczyna (*pshchi-nah*) is not so much a surprise as a shock – it's the kind of small market town you'd expect to find in rural Pomerania, with a perfectly restored palace that could have jumped straight out of Germany. Coming from Katowice you're likely to find this place incongruous to say the least, but you'll certainly appreciate the contrast.

Pszczyna is one of the oldest towns in Silesia, its origins going back to the 11th century. In 1847, after centuries of changing ownership, it became the property of the powerful Hochberg family of Prussia.

In the last months of WWI, Pszczyna was the cradle of the first of three consecutive Silesian uprisings, in which Polish peasants took up arms and demanded that the region be incorporated into Poland. Their wishes were granted in 1921, following a plebiscite held by the League of Nations.

Information

Bit tourist office (☎ 212 99 99; Brama Wybranców 1; ☉ 8am-4pm Mon-Fri, 10am-4pm Sat & Sun) In the castle gate.

ING Bank Śląski (☎ 327 94 00; ul Bankowa 1)

PTTK office (☎ 210 35 30; www.pttk-pszczyna.slask.pl in Polish; Rynek 16; ☉ 8am-5pm Mon-Fri, 9am-1pm Sat)

Sights

On the western side of town, Pszczyna's grandiose **castle** dates back to the 12th century when the Opole dukes built a hunting lodge here, but the building has been enlarged and redesigned several times, most recently at the end of the 19th century. The simple medieval castle gradually became a magnificent palace, incorporating various styles from Gothic to neoclassical.

The Hochbergs, who owned the castle until 1945, furnished their home according to their status – they were among the richest families in Europe, ruling vast swathes of land from their Silesian family seat, Książ castle (p280). Numerous priceless works of art completed the opulent scene, but sadly most were lost during WWII.

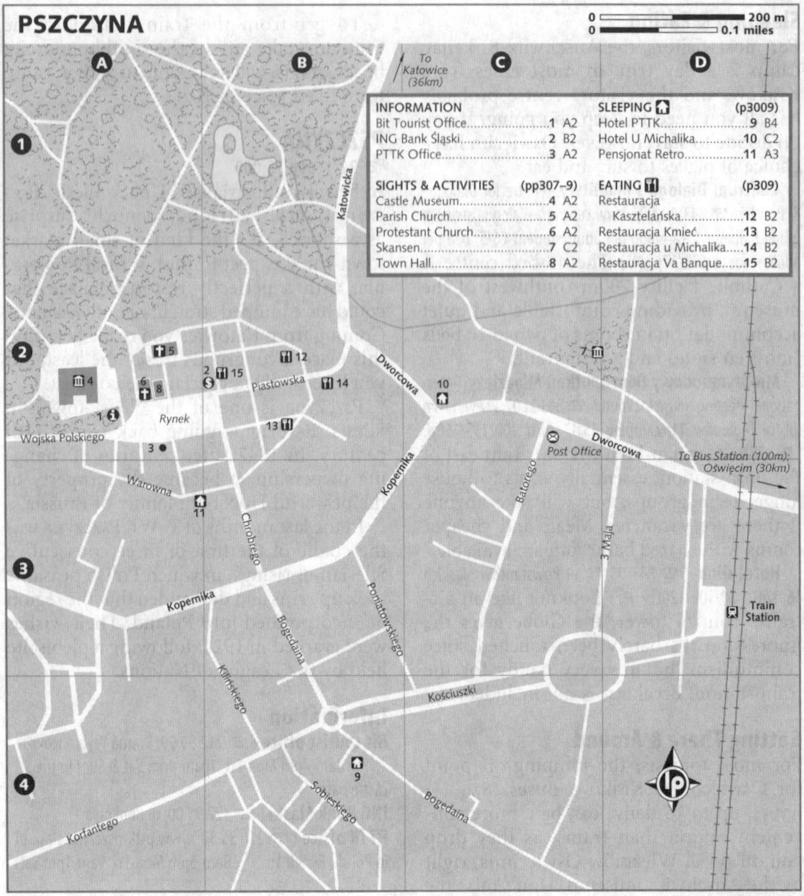
PSZCZYNA
0 200 m
0 0.1 miles
A
B
C
D
1
2
3
4
To Katowice (36km)
INFORMATION
Bit Tourist Office 1 A2
ING Bank Śląski 2 B2
PTTK Office 3 A2
SIGHTS & ACTIVITIES (pp307–9)
Castle Museum 4 A2
Parish Church 5 A2
Protestant Church 6 A2
Skansen 7 C2
Town Hall 8 A2
SLEEPING (p3009)
Hotel PTTK 9 B4
Hotel U Michalika 10 C2
Pensjonat Retro 11 A3
EATING (p309)
Restauracja Kasztelańska 12 B2
Restauracja Kmieć 13 B2
Restauracja u Michalika 14 B2
Restauracja Va Banque 15 B2
Katowicka
Dworcowa
Piastowska
Rynek
Wojska Polskiego
Warowna
Kopernika
Chrobrego
Post Office
Batorego
3 Maja
To Bus Station (100m); Oświęcim (30km)
Poniatowskiego
Bogedaina
Kilińskiego
Kościuszki
Sobieskiego
Korfantego
Train Station

After the war the palace – which had been plundered but not destroyed – was taken over by the state, restored and turned into the **Castle Museum** (Muzeum Zamkowe; ☎ 210 30 37; www.zamek-pszczyna.pl; adult/concession 11/6zł; 🕑 10am-3pm Tue, 9am-4pm Wed, 9am-3pm Thu & Fri, 10am-6pm Sat & Sun; also 11am-3pm Mon Apr-Oct). Last entry is one hour before closing time, with shorter weekend hours in winter. You can buy a guidebook (in English and German) on the castle's history and the museum's contents.

The furnished and decorated interiors, representing different periods of the castle's existence, feature some splendid rooms, such as the Mirror Hall, which hosts occasional chamber music concerts. Some of the palace's rooms also shelter themed exhibitions, including a collection of armour on the ground floor and hunting trophies on the 2nd floor. There's also a café-restaurant in the courtyard, named after 18th-century composer Georg Philipp Telemann, who lived here for four years in his twenties.

Right behind the castle is an extensive, 84-hectare English-style **park**. With its lakes, streams, arched bridges, pavilions and a variety of exotic trees and shrubs, it's regarded as the most picturesque landscape park in Silesia, and should tempt even the most recalcitrant couch potato into their strolling shoes.

From the entrance gate, the castle fronts onto the elongated **Rynek**, lined with old burghers' houses dating mostly from the

18th and 19th centuries. On its northern side is the **Protestant church** and, next to it, the **town hall**, both remodelled early this century. Behind the town hall is the 14th-century **parish church**, extensively rebuilt over the years, with a typically lavish interior featuring a ceiling painting of the Ascension.

A five-minute walk east of the Rynek is a small but interesting **skansen** (Zagroda Wsi Pszczyńskiej; ☎ 0603 131 186; ul Parkowa; admission 4zł; ☺ 10am-3pm Tue-Sat Apr-Nov), which features half a dozen old timber houses collected from the region. Most of the buildings are about 200 years old and feature ethnographic exhibitions.

Sleeping
Hotel U Michalika (☎ 210 13 55; www.umichalika.com .pl; ul Dworcowa 11; s/d 95/130zł; **P**) The latest venture from local chef-turned-entrepreneur Stefan Michalika provides the best tourist-class standards in town. The house restaurant (mains 7zł to 29zł) is a smart clone of its boss' original eatery in the town centre.

Hotel PTTK (☎ 210 38 33; ul Bogedaina 16; dm 26zł, s 45-70zł, d 80-100zł; **P**) The PTTK hotel, south of the Rynek, is charmingly situated in a former prison building, though the last inmate left in 1975. There's nothing cell-like about the rooms now, and while you can choose to share a bathroom you'll never have to go in a bucket. Breakfast is not included.

Pensjonat Retro (☎ 210 12 63; www.retro.of.pl; ul Warowna 31; s/d/tr 99/140/160zł) Named (and decorated) long before retro became a byword for cool, this is a small, friendly central guesthouse with 44 beds and its own restaurant.

Eating
Restauracja Va Banque (☎ 210 34 72; ul Bankowa 2; mains 10-21zł; ☺ breakfast, lunch & dinner) Classic basement dining just off the Rynek, with a French-tinged menu and dancing on Fridays. Expect high standards and a demanding clientele.

Restauracja Kmieć (☎ 210 36 38; www.kmiec.pna .pl; ul Piekarska 10; mains 10-30zł; ☺ lunch & dinner) Set in a historic townhouse dating from 1756, this long-established family restaurant has a solid range of traditional Polish food.

Restauracja Kasztelańska (☎ 210 52 78; ul Bednarska 3; mains 8-19zł; ☺ lunch & dinner) This new pub-restaurant is a bit more relaxed than the Rynek places, and makes a good spot for a leisurely beer as well as a meal.

Getting There & Away
The bus and train stations are to the east of the centre, 200m apart. Trains to Katowice (6.80zł, 45 minutes) run roughly every hour. To Oświęcim (5.70zł, one hour), take any of the frequent trains to Czechowice-Dziedzice and change there. There are only two buses to Oświęcim (6.60zł, 40 minutes), both continuing to Kraków (15.30zł, 2¼ hours). If you want to get to Kraków and there's no bus due, go by train to Katowice, from where trains leave every hour or so.

LOWER SILESIA

A fertile lowland extending along the upper and middle course of the Odra River, Lower Silesia (Dolny Śląsk) was settled relatively early on, and is full of old towns and villages. Architecture buffs will have a field day with the wide assortment of castles and churches preserved in some unlikely spots, and the area's larger towns have more than enough to tempt the party-minded.

OPOLE
☎ 77 / pop 132,000
Halfway between Katowice and Wrocław, Opole lies on the border of Upper and Lower Silesia, but generally considers itself part of its own Opolan Silesia (Śląsk Opolski). The region is known for an active German minority, one of the few communities of its kind to survive the war, which is still well represented in local government.

It may not look it, but Opole already has 1000 years on the clock. The first stronghold was built in the 9th century; in the 13th century it became the capital of its principality and was ruled by a line of Silesian Piasts until 1532, even though it was part of Bohemia from 1327. Later, Opole fell to Austria, then to Prussia, and after significant destruction in WWII returned to Poland in 1945.

Today it's a fairly large regional industrial centre best known for its **Festival of Polish Song**, which has taken place annually in June since 1963 and is broadcast nationwide on TV. On these days the city sees crowds of visitors; the rest of the year few tourists bother to come here. If you're looking for a slice of city life without the tourist hordes of Wrocław, Opole can be a good alternative, offering plenty of opportunities to grab a bit of culture.

Information

INTERNET ACCESS
HMS Computers (☎ 453 12 00; ul Krakowska 26; per hr 3zł; ☺ 9am-5pm Mon, 8am-6pm Tue-Fri, 8am-3pm Sat)
Kafka Pub (☎ 453 60 70; ul Kołłątaja 9; per hr 4zł; ☺ noon-11pm)

MONEY
Bank Pekao (☎ 453 02 12; ul Osmańczyka 15)
Bank Zachodni (☎ 451 68 00; ul Ozimska 6)

TOURIST INFORMATION
Orbis Travel (☎ 453 97 30; www.orbis.opole.pl; ul Krakowska 31)
PTTK office (☎ 454 51 13; ul Krakowska 15/17; ☺ 9am-6pm Mon-Fri, 9am-2pm Sat)
Tourist office (☎ 451 19 87; www.opole.pl; ul Krakowska 15; ☺ 10am-6pm Mon-Fri, 10am-1pm Sat)

Sights

The **Rynek** was badly damaged during WWII but remarkably rebuilt, and is once again the focal point of the city, lined with baroque-rococo houses. The oversized **town hall** in the middle looks as if it has been imported from another cultural sphere entirely. Its 64m-tall tower (1864) was patterned on the Palazzo Vecchio in Florence and looks a little out of place in the typically Eastern European surroundings. It collapsed in 1934 but was rebuilt in the same style.

The **Franciscan Church** (Kościół Franciszkanów), off the southern corner of the Rynek, was built around 1330, but the interior was reshaped later on various occasions. It boasts an ornate high altar, 18th-century organ, and domed Renaissance chapel in the left-hand aisle, separated by a fine late-16th-century wrought-iron grille.

The highlight of the church is the **Piast Chapel**, which is accessible from the right-hand aisle through a doorway with a tympanum. The Gothic-vaulted chapel houses a pair of massive double tombs (interring the local dukes) carved in sandstone in the 1380s. They were originally painted but the colour has almost disappeared.

Two blocks east of the Rynek, a former Jesuit college (1698) houses the **Regional Museum** (Muzeum Śląska Opolskiego; ☎ 453 66 77; Mały Rynek 7; adult/concession 4/2zł, free Sat; ☺ 10am-4pm Tue-Fri, 10am-3pm Sat, noon-5pm Sun). The permanent display features the prehistory and history of the surrounding area and city, and there are always temporary exhibitions.

The Gothic **cathedral**, a short walk north of the Rynek, now features mostly baroque furnishing. The chapel in the right-hand aisle shelters the red-marble tombstone of the last of the Opole dukes, who popped his ducal clogs here in 1532. A Gothic triptych, the last survivor from the church's original collection of 26 pieces, is also displayed in this chapel.

The only remaining vestige of the dukes' castle is the 51m-tall **Piast Tower** (Wieża Piastowska; ☎ 452 42 24; ul Piastowska 14; adult/concession 4/2zł; ☺ 10am-12.30pm & 2-6pm Tue-Fri, 10am-12.30pm & 2-7pm Sat & Sun), a sturdy watchtower with 3m walls and foundations 6m deep. Built in the 14th century, the castle was pulled down in the 1920s to make room for office buildings. The tower, which miraculously escaped 'modernisation', sticks up oddly from behind the drab blocks. You can climb to the top for a panoramic view over the city.

Opole also has a good skansen, the **Opolan Village Museum** (Muzeum Wsi Opolskiej; ☎ 474 30 21; ul Wrocławska 174; adult/student 6/4zł, free Sat; ☺ 10am-6pm Tue-Sun 16 Apr-15 Oct, 9am-2pm Mon-Fri 16 Oct-15 Apr). Located in the Bierkowice suburb, 5km west of the centre and accessible by urban bus 5, the skansen has a variety of rural architecture from the region. The shingled church of 1613, the water mill of 1832 and a couple of large granaries are among the showpieces. Several houses are fully furnished and decorated, and can be visited. From mid-October to mid-April the buildings stay locked.

Sleeping

Hotel Piast (☎ 454 97 10; www.hotelpiast.com.pl; ul Piastowska 1; s/d 240/288zł; **P**) Commanding the best location in the centre, the Piast sits on the northern tip of Pasieka Island, a short trot away from the old town. As you'd expect for these prices, rooms are classy and comfortable, and the house restaurant and bar do good business. Traffic noise detracts slightly from the quality.

Dom Wycieczkowy Toropol (☎ 453 78 83; ul Barlickiego 13; dm 30zł; **P**) This good budget bet is well located next to the open-air amphitheatre on quiet Pasieka Island. Unfortunately, its 13 triples can often be filled up with groups.

Hotel Weneda (☎ 456 44 99; www.hotel-weneda.opole.pl; ul 1 Maja 77; s/d/ste 220/270/320zł; **P**) Don't be put off by the slightly shabby block – this is a decent mid-category hotel offering

SILESIA

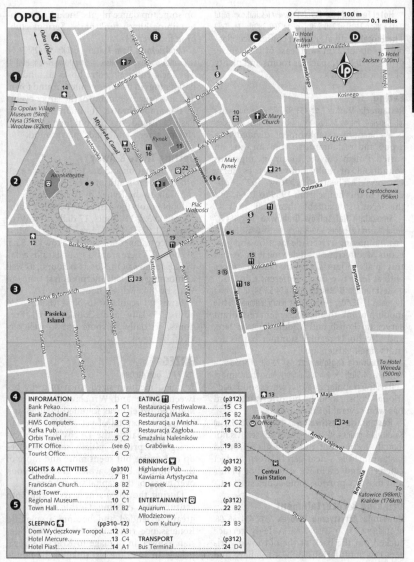

OPOLE

0 ——————— 100 m
0 ——————— 0.1 miles

INFORMATION		EATING 🍴	(p312)
Bank Pekao...................................**1** C1		Restauracja Festiwalowa....**15** C3	
Bank Zachodni............................**2** C2		Restauracja Maska.............**16** B2	
HMS Computers..........................**3** C3		Restauracja u Mnicha........**17** C2	
Kafka Pub..................................**4** C3		Restauracja Zagłoba..........**18** C3	
Orbis Travel................................**5** C2		Smażalnia Naleśników	
PTTK Office...........................(see **6**)		Grabówka......................**19** B3	
Tourist Office.............................**6** C2			
		DRINKING 🍸	(p312)
		Highlander Pub................**20** B2	
SIGHTS & ACTIVITIES	(p310)	Kawiarnia Artystyczna	
Cathedral.....................................**7** B1		Dworek............................**21** C2	
Franciscan Church.......................**8** B2			
Piast Tower..................................**9** A2		ENTERTAINMENT 🎭	(p312)
Regional Museum.......................**10** C1		Aquarium.........................**22** B2	
Town Hall..................................**11** B2		Młodzieżowy	
		Dom Kultury..................**23** B3	
SLEEPING 🛏	(pp310–12)		
Dom Wycieczkowy Toropol.....**12** A3		TRANSPORT	(p312)
Hotel Mercure.........................**13** C4		Bus Terminal....................**24** D4	
Hotel Piast...............................**14** A1			

substantial weekend discounts. Unusually, the restaurant serves Greek as well as Polish food. It's a 1km walk from the station, with plenty of city buses going past.

Hotel Zacisze (☎ 453 95 53; ul Grunwaldzka 28; s 65zł, d 100-130zł, tr 120zł, s/d with private bathroom 110/200zł; P) Located within a reasonable walking distance of the Rynek (10 minutes),

the Zacisze has a range of small but acceptable rooms in a leafy residential area.

Hotel Mercure (☎ 451 81 00; mer.opole@orbis.pl; ul Krakowska 57-59; s/d 299/325zł; P 🖳) This big strategically sited chain hotel faces the train station, luring new arrivals with full mod cons. You can knock about 100zł off the price at weekends (Friday to Monday).

Hotel Festival (☎ 455 60 11; www.festival.com.pl; ul Oleska 86; s 240zł, d 250-270zł, q/ste 360/380zł; P Ⓔ) The Hotel Festival, a smart conference-class option about 2km northeast of the centre, provides decent, spacious rooms and plenty of extra amenities.

Eating

Restauracja Maska (☎ 453 92 67; www.pubmaska .pl; Rynek 4; mains 8-28zł; ☯ lunch & dinner) Maska is a charming establishment divided into a pub and restaurant, so you can dine on varied Polish cuisine to an incongruous soundtrack of funky house classics. Jerzy Grotowski's Theatre of 13 Rows (p274) operated in this house from 1959 to 1964, and the décor's still suitably theatrical.

Smażalnia Naleśników Grabówka (☎ 454 17 96; ul Mozarta 2; crêpes 3.50-8.50zł; ☯ breakfast, lunch & dinner) Enjoying a riverside location and gorgeous Mediterranean-style vine terrace, this tiny place offers authentic-tasting crêpes with at least two dozen different fillings.

Restauracja U Mnicha (☎ 454 52 34; ul Ozimska 10; mains 12-18.50zł; ☯ breakfast, lunch & dinner) This modern monk-themed basement restaurant serves up Polish and Middle Eastern fare, and also holds regular summer barbecues in its small garden area.

Restauracja Zagłoba (☎ 441 78 60; ul Krakowska 39; mains 14-30zł; ☯ lunch & dinner) Another smart cellar, the popular Zagłoba serves solid traditional Polish food in historic vaults, and has won several local awards.

Restauracja Festiwalowa (☎ 441 78 55; ul Kościuszki 3; mains 4.50-16zł; ☯ lunch & dinner) It's not exactly festive, but this long glass-fronted restaurant fills a neat gap between budget cafeteria and exclusive eatery. Pot plants and mosaics provide some added interest.

Drinking & Entertainment

Kawiarnia Artystyczna Dworek (☎ 454 36 06; ul Studzienna 1; ☯ 11am-2am) A leafy terrace tucked out the back of the old town shelters this multifarious pub, art gallery and music club, associated with the Easy Radio station. Live jazz is a regular occurrence.

Highlander Pub (☎ 465 55 28; ul Szpitalna 3) A good central place for a beer and a bop, the not-very-Scottish Highlander hosts DJs playing anything from tribal house to Latin and dancehall.

Aquarium (ul Franciszkańska 1; ☯ 5pm-4am) Soaked in UV light, the basement Aquarium brings on some top dance nights, including an entertaining kitsch funk party. Serious clubbing for over-21s.

Młodzieżowy Dom Kultury (MDK; ☎ 425 27 14; www.mdk.opole.pl in Polish; ul Strzelców Bytomskich 1) The local cultural centre hosts all kinds of happenings in its three venues around town, and also organises many of the larger events in the amphitheatre. Its main branch, on Pasieka Island, has an outdoor stage and cinema screen and a kids' playground.

Getting There & Away

The train station and bus terminal face each other, not far south of the Old Town; you can walk to the Rynek in 10 minutes.

Opole is on the main line between Katowice (23.93zł, 1¾ hours, 17 daily) and Wrocław (21.62zł, 1¼ hours, hourly). Most Katowice trains continue to Kraków (31.85zł, 3½ hours). There are also several trains a day to Częstochowa (14.50zł, two hours), as well as morning and late afternoon fast trains to Warsaw (44.65zł, 4¾ hours).

Buses go regularly to Nysa (8.90zł, 1½ hours, 15 daily) and Kłodzko (15zł, three hours, six daily), a route not so well serviced by trains.

BRZEG

☎ 77 / pop 40,000

A quiet, medium-sized town midway between Opole and Wrocław, Brzeg (pronounced bzhek) was founded in 1248 and became the capital of yet another Silesian Piast principality, the Duchy of Legnica-Brzeg. The princes initially set themselves up in Legnica but spent more and more of their time in Brzeg, which gradually took over many of the capital's functions.

During the town's heyday in the 16th century the existing Gothic castle was greatly extended and became a splendid Renaissance residence, dubbed the 'Silesian Wawel' in homage to Kraków's royal palace. In 1675 the last duke of the family died, marking the end of the Piast dynasty in Poland, and the town came under direct Habsburg rule. Subsequent Prussian and Napoleonic fortifications were eventually replaced with a ring of parks, which now surrounds the historic core of the town.

The town, like the whole region, was defended fiercely by the Germans in 1945, and half of its buildings were destroyed.

The most important monuments have been reconstructed, and it's worth breaking your journey for a couple of hours just to have a look at the castle.

Information

Bank Pekao (☎ 416 30 99; Rynek 9)
Spider Café Internet (☎ 416 88 34; ul Mleczna 5; per hr 3zł; ☺ 9am-10pm Mon-Fri, noon-midnight Sat & Sun)

Sights

At the northwest corner of the oval Old Town, the ancient Piast **castle** is the town's best feature. It started as a stronghold built in the 13th century, but it was turned into a large Renaissance palace by Duke Jerzy II (George II). The richly decorated façade of the central three-storey gateway gives some idea of the palace's former splendour. Immediately above the archway are the stone figures of Duke Jerzy and his wife Barbara. Further up, the two-tier frieze depicts 24 busts of the Piast kings and princes, from the first legendary Piast to the father of Jerzy II, Duke Fryderyk II (Frederick II). In the middle of the balustrade at the top is the coat of arms of King Zygmunt August, with the Jagiellonian eagle at the centre.

The gate leads to a spacious arcaded courtyard, vaguely reminiscent of that of the Wawel except that one of the sides is missing. Note the Renaissance portals; the one at the main gate is particularly elaborate.

Part of the interior houses the **Museum of Silesian Piasts** (Muzeum Piastów Śląskich; ☎ 416 32 57; Plac Zamkowy 1; adult/concession 5/3zł; ☺ 10am-4pm Tue & Thu-Sun, 10am-6pm Wed), which traces the history of Silesia under the dynasty. The rooms upstairs shelter a collection of Silesian art from the 15th to 18th centuries, including some extraordinary altarpieces, retables and statues. The adjacent **St Hedwig's Church** (Kościół Św Jadwigi), formerly the castle's chapel, is sometimes opened for guided tours. It's also open to the faithful for Sunday mass.

Two churches complete Brzeg's trinity of major sights. The monumental 14th-century Gothic **St Nicholas' Church** (Kościół Św Mikołaja) was partially burned during WWII and the twin towers were reconstructed – you can tell from the different colour of the brick. The plain-walled interior has some impressive stained glass and burghers' epitaphs on the walls.

The much more extravagant **Holy Cross Church**, in front of the castle, was built in the 1730s for the Jesuits. Its ample, single-naved interior is decorated in exuberant baroque style throughout, including the trompe l'œil painted vault, which seems to extend the altar up to the ceiling.

Sleeping & Eating

Hotel Piast (☎ 416 20 27; piast@piast.strefa.pl; ul Piastowska 14; s/d/tr/ste 120/160/200/230zł; **P**) At the southern end of town, near the bus and train stations, the predictably named Hotel Piast is not great value but provides everything you'll need, including some half-price rooms with shared bathroom, and one surprisingly stylish suite. There's a restaurant on site.

Restauracja Ratuszowa (☎ 416 52 67; Rynek-Ratusz; mains 15-30zł; ☺ breakfast, lunch & dinner) The Ratuszowa, in the basement of the town hall, not only does the best food in town but also stays open longer than anywhere else, clocking off as late as 3am on Saturday.

Getting There & Away

The train and bus stations are opposite each other, 1km south of the Old Town. All trains go via Wrocław (fast/slow 14zł/8.20zł, 45 minutes) or Opole (11.80zł/6.80zł, 35 minutes). A dozen fast trains continue east as far as Kraków (36.12zł, four hours). Eight daily buses go south to Nysa (8.90zł, 1½ hours).

LEGNICA

☎ 76 / pop 105,000

To the west of Wrocław, Legnica's origins go back to the 10th century, but it wasn't until the 13th century that its real development began when it became the co-capital of the Duchy of Legnica-Brzeg. In the 16th century the town saw good times under Bohemian rule as an active centre of culture, establishing the first university in Silesia. After the last Piast duke died in 1675 the town fell to the Habsburgs, and in 1741 to the Prussians.

Badly damaged during WWII, Legnica has revived as an industrial centre following the discovery of copper deposits in the region. Much of the city is drab and unspectacular, but the few surviving historic buildings in the centre make for an interesting diversion.

Information

Bank Pekao (☎ 852 52 63; ul Wrocławska 26/28)
Bank Zachodni (☎ 852 26 44; ul Gwarna 4A)
Strefa X Internet (☎ 856 58 75; ul Złotoryjska 95; per hr 4zł; ⏰ 10am-9.30pm Mon-Thu, 10am-11pm Fri & Sat, 2-9.30pm Sun)
Tourist office (☎ 851 22 80; Rynek 29; ⏰ 9am-5pm Mon-Fri, 9am-1pm Sat)

Sights

The brick **castle** on the northern edge of the old town should be your first port of call. Built in the 13th century, it was rebuilt in Gothic style (two towers from that period survive), then thoroughly modernised in the 1530s as a Renaissance residence, and again in 1835 when the noted German architect Karl Friedrich Schinkel gave it a neoclassical look. Enter through the main gate, which is embellished with a Renaissance portal, the only significant remnant of the 16th-century renovation. A pavilion in the middle of the courtyard shelters the foundations of the 13th-century Romanesque **chapel** (admission 2.50zł; ⏰ 9.30am-5pm Tue-Sat) built here along with the original brick-and-stone castle by Henryk Brodaty. The castle is now part of the city university, full of student types who would doubtless leave a few Piasts rolling in their graves.

The baroque **St John's Church** (Kościół Św Jana), southwest of the castle and north of the Rynek, is Legnica's most important church, though it's being restored and isn't always open. The chapel off the right-hand wall is actually the presbytery of the former Gothic church, set at right angles to the current one. Richly decorated, with a spectacular painted ceiling, it's also the mausoleum of the Legnica Piasts and houses their extravagant tombs – essential viewing for history buffs. Inquire at the **Museum of Copper** (Muzeum Miedzi; ☎ 862 49 49; ul Partyzantów 3; ⏰ 11am-5pm Tue-Sat) nearby and they will open the chapel for you and show you around.

On the Rynek itself, the **Church of SS Peter and Paul** impresses more than any other building in town thanks to a splendid tiled roof and a fine restoration job. Two original Gothic doorways survive; the one on the northern side (facing the Rynek) has a splendid tympanum depicting the Adoration of the Magi. The interior has the usual hotchpotch of furnishings, of which the old-

est piece, the bas-reliefed bronze baptismal font (in the chapel off the left aisle), dates from the late 13th century and is reputedly the oldest metal font in Poland.

St Mary's Church (Kościół Mariacki) is another notable building, one of the oldest churches in Silesia but refurbished in mock-Gothic style in the 19th century. It's used today by the small Protestant community for infrequent services (Sunday only), and doubles as a stage for cultural events, such as organ and chamber music concerts.

Sleeping & Eating

Hotel Kamieniczka (☎ 723 73 92; ul Młnarska 15/16; s 80-140zł, d 120-205zł, tr/q/ste 270/360/400zł; **P**) New, central and impeccably modernised, this 17th-century townhouse hotel is the pick of Legnica's scant accommodation offerings. Rooms are smart but not overdone, there are four spacious suites, and the house restaurant consolidates the touch of class.

Hotel Tramp (☎ 862 00 10; ul Kominka 7; s 76-106zł, d 105-145zł, tr 157.50-210zł) This small hotel looks better from outside than inside, but it's still not a bad place for the price, as long as you don't mind creaky beds and shared facilities. The location and breakfast are plus points.

Qubus Hotel (☎ 866 21 00; legnica@qubushotel.com; ul Skarbowa 2; s/d €64/84; **P**) Believe it or not, the Tramp is part of the same chain as this towering business hotel, a massive modern edifice that seems totally overblown for Legnica's modest needs. Still, if it's comfort you want you won't be complaining, and some hefty discounts are available.

PTSM Youth Hostel (☎ 862 54 12; ul Jordana 17; dm/d/tr 23/55/78zł) The youth hostel, an 800m walk east of the centre and about the same distance from the train station, offers 55 beds, most of which are in five- to 10-bed dorms.

Restauracja Tivoli (☎ 862 23 04; ul Złotoryjska 21; mains 15-30zł; ⏰ breakfast, lunch & dinner) This low-key traditional restaurant has been serving hearty Polish fare since 1957, with scant regard for the innate Italianness of its name. You'll find it about 200m west of the Rynek.

Snac Bar Gusto (☎ 852 35 33; Rynek 9; mains 4-7zł; ⏰ breakfast, lunch & dinner Mon-Sat, lunch & dinner Sun) Swift, central and popular with da kidz, the tragically misspelt Gusto is the place to go for fast food.

Getting There & Away
The train and bus stations are next to each other on the northeastern edge of the city centre; both offer regular services to Wrocław (trains 10.50zł, 1½ hours, roughly hourly). Take the bus to other regional destinations such as Jelenia Góra (13.50zł, 2½ hours, 11 daily), Świdnica (8.90zł, 1½ hours, five daily) and Kłodzko (17zł, three hours, two daily). There are two trains to Warsaw daily (46.54zł, 7½ hours).

LEGNICKIE POLE
☎ 76 / pop 2000
The small village of Legnickie Pole (leg-neets-kyeh po-leh; Legnica Field) holds its place in folk history due to a great battle in 1241, in which Silesian troops under the command of Duke Henryk Pobożny (Henry the Pious) were defeated by the Tatars. The duke himself was killed and beheaded; the Tatars stuck his head on a spear and proceeded to Legnica, but failed to take the town. In the absence of his head, the duke's wife, Princess Anna, identified his body by the six toes on his left foot.

Henryk's mother, Princess Hedwig (Księżna Jadwiga; see p275), built a small commemorative chapel on the site of his decapitation, later replaced by a Gothic church. The church now shelters the **Museum of the Battle of Legnica** (Muzeum Bitwy Legnickiej; ☎ 858 23 98; adult/concession 4/2zł; ☉ 11am-5pm Wed-Sun). The modest exhibition features a hypothetical model of the battle (commentary in English and German available) and some related objects, including a copy of the duke's tomb (the original is in the National Museum in Wrocław).

Across the road from the museum is the former Benedictine Abbey. Its central part is occupied by **St Hedwig's Church**, a masterpiece of baroque art designed by Austrian architect Kilian Ignaz Dientzenhofer and built in the 1730s. Past the elaborate doorway you'll find yourself in a beautifully proportioned, bright and harmonious interior, with splendid frescoes on the vault, the work of Bavarian painter Cosmas Damian Asam. The fresco over the organ loft shows Princess Anna with the body of her husband after the battle, as does the painting on the high altar.

The church is locked except for religious services (it still serves as a parish church). A visit is included in the price of the museum admission ticket, though you'll probably have to wait for a group to gather.

Sleeping & Eating
Jurta Motel (☎ 858 20 94; ul Kossak-Szczuckiej 7; s 55-70zł, d 65-90zł, tr/ste 90/140zł; **P**) The only year-round place to stay in Legnickie Pole. Rooms come with or without bathroom, and there's a simple restaurant to keep you from starving.

Camping Nr 234 (☎ 858 23 97; ul Henryka Brodatego 7; camping/cabin 9/70zł; ☉ May-Sep; ☀) This basic camping ground has 10 triangular cabins and a tent area. Nonguests can pay a pittance to cool off in the pool, should it ever be necessary.

Getting There & Away
Sixteen daily PKS services run to Legnica (3.70zł, 30 minutes), though most leave in the morning. There are also a number of private minibuses (3zł).

ZIELONA GÓRA
☎ 68 / pop 118,000
Like the majority of its regional neighbours, Zielona Góra was founded by the Silesian Piasts. It was part of the Głogów Duchy, one of the numerous regional principalities, before it passed to the Habsburgs in the 16th century and to Prussia two centuries later. Unlike most other Silesian towns, however, Zielona Góra came through the 1945 offensive with minimal damage, which is why prewar architecture is well represented, giving the town a refreshingly stylish appearance.

The town also stands out as Poland's only wine producer. The tradition goes back to the 14th century, but the climate is less than ideal and business was never very profitable. Today's output is merely symbolic, yet the city still holds the **Feast of the Grape Harvest** (Święto Winobrania) at the end of September, as it has for almost 150 years.

If you are coming overland from Germany, Zielona Góra is a good first stop and an easy introduction to modern Poland. History nuts won't look twice at the place, but it's an inviting, forward-looking town with a pleasant pedestrianised centre and plenty of accommodation. Grab a drink and settle into the rhythm of real Polish life.

Information

Bank Pekao ul Chopina (☎ 327 26 34; ul Chopina 21); ul Pieniężnego (☎ 327 00 51; ul Pieniężnego 24)

Bank Zachodni ul Bohaterów Westerplatte (☎ 324 05 00; ul Bohaterów Westerplatte); ul Sikorskiego (☎ 325 46 21; ul Sikorskiego 9)

Internet Pub (☎ 324 63 69; www.ipub.pl; ul Kupiecka 28; per hr 5zł; ☯ 9am-9pm Mon-Fri, 10am-8pm Sat, noon-8pm Sun)

Main post office (☎ 322 10 80; ul Bohaterów Westerplatte 21)

Tourist office (☎ 327 03 23; www.zielonagora.pl; ul Kupiecka 17; ☯ 9am-5pm Mon-Fri, plus 10am-2pm Sat & Sun 15 Jun-15 Sep)

Sights

The renovated **Rynek** (formally called Stary Rynek), lined with brightly painted houses, is a pleasant and harmonious place, the culmination of the long pedestrian stretch of Al Niepodległości and ul Żeromskiego. The 17th-century **town hall**, complete with its slim 54m tower, has managed to escape being over-modernised in spite of changes over the years, and fits nicely on the square. Look closely at the dome and you'll see it's slightly uneven, the result of some seemingly minor errors during its construction.

The **Regional Museum** (Muzeum Ziemi Lubuskiej; ☎ 320 26 78; www.zgora.pl/muzeum; Al Niepodległości 15; adult/concession 6/4zł, free Sat; ☯ 11am-5pm Tue, Thu & Fri, 10am-3pm Sat, 10am-4pm Sun) illustrates the history of wine-making in the region, and also has a permanent exhibition of works by Marian Kruczek (1927–83). Kruczek used everyday objects – anything from buttons to spark plugs – to create some striking assemblages, and this is the largest collection of his work in Poland. Temporary displays rotate items from the museum's stored collections of Art Nouveau and modern art.

Next door to the museum is the **BWA Art Gallery** (☎ 325 37 26; Al Niepodległości 19; admission 4zł; ☯ 11am-5pm Tue, Thu, Fri & Sun, 10am-3pm Wed, noon-6pm Sat), which hosts changing exhibitions of contemporary art.

There's a **skansen** (☎ 321 15 91; adult/concession 6/4zł; ☯ 10am-5pm Tue-Sun) in Ochla, 7km south of the city, serviced by the regular bus 27 (get off before arriving at the village; ask the driver to let you off near the entrance). Of about 20 traditional buildings reassembled on the grounds, about half a dozen are furnished and decorated and can be visited.

Sleeping

Hotel Śródmiejski (☎ 325 44 71; hotel11@wp.pl; ul Żeromskiego 23; s 90-135zł, d 140-300zł, tr 180zł) You can't argue with anything this central, and anyway, the staff here are too well trained to talk back. Slightly institutional corridors don't detract from the comfortable rooms, which come with or without en suite. Weekend discounts.

Hotel Pod Lwem (☎ 324 10 55; ul Dworcowa 14; s/d 135/190zł) Convenience of a different kind – the house Under the Lion sits neatly opposite the bus station, looking like a rural guesthouse that somehow woke up between a main road and a train line. Cosy furnishings expand on the homy theme, and there are a couple of no-frills budget rooms if you just want to catch a bus.

Hotel Senator (☎ 324 04 36; ul Chopina 23a; s 256-296zł, d 296-384; **P**) Prices may seem a little steep here, but that's mainly because they include half board and drinks; if you're not that flush, you can knock a whopping 50% off these rates at weekends (room only). Either way it's a great little establishment, with eager service, nice rooms and lots of wicker.

Hotelik Przy Kinie Wenus (☎ 327 13 29; Al Konstytucji 3 Maja 6; s/d 70/120zł, with private bathroom 100/150zł) This family house on the southern ring road has been converted somewhat haphazardly into a small guesthouse. Amazingly, some of the resulting accommodation is unexpectedly inviting – sofas and dark wood go a long way.

Hotel Pod Wieżą (☎ 327 10 91; ul Kopernika 2; s 75-130zł, d 120-190zł, tr 154-199zł, ste 240zł) Second fiddle to the Śródmiejski, the Pod Wieżą also enjoys a very central setting and a range of rooms, but the plastic bathroom fittings let it down. There's 25% off at weekends.

Hotel Polan (☎ 327 00 91; polan@orbis.pl; ul Staszica 9a; s/d/ste 235/324/460zł; ✗) Batting slightly out of its weight, the Polan doesn't have much style or a great location but does provides relative tourist-class comfort and a bit of peace and quiet. It's also a good bet for disabled travellers.

Hotel Relaks (☎ 320 21 97; ul Wyspańskiego 15b; r per person 27-100zł) One of two workers' dorms in the area east of the station. Plain, clean rooms cater for a clientele mainly consisting of school groups and Polish families, with varying standards available.

PTSM Youth Hostel (☎ 320 22 37; www.cku.zgora .pl; ul Długa 13; dm 20-35zł, s/d 100/140zł) This new hostel, off the ring road 700m west of the Rynek, can sleep up to 70 tired bodies, mostly in good six-bed dorms.

Eating
Restauracja Nieboska Komedia (☎ 327 20 59; Al Niepodległości 3/5; mains 18-35zł; ☒ lunch & dinner) This pleasantly arty place in the theatre build-

ing has a good choice of tasty Polish dishes to accompany the modern repertoire, and stays open late enough to permit at least a couple of post-performance nightcaps.

TK Restauracja (☎ 325 00 68; ul Bolesława Chrobrego 35/41; mains 12-30zł; ☒ lunch & dinner Mon-Sat, lunch Sun) Discreetly removed from the centre, TK's is so unobtrusive you barely

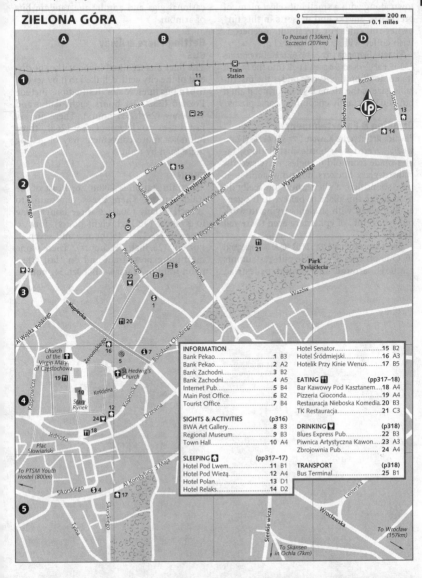

ZIELONA GÓRA

INFORMATION	
Bank Pekao	**1** B3
Bank Pekao	**2** A2
Bank Zachodni	**3** B2
Bank Zachodni	**4** A5
Internet Pub	**5** B4
Main Post Office	**6** B2
Tourist Office	**7** B4

SIGHTS & ACTIVITIES	(p316)
BWA Art Gallery	**8** B3
Regional Museum	**9** B3
Town Hall	**10** A4

SLEEPING	(pp317–17)
Hotel Pod Lwem	**11** B1
Hotel Pod Wieżą	**12** A4
Hotel Polan	**13** D1
Hotel Relaks	**14** D2

Hotel Senator	**15** B2
Hotel Śródmiejski	**16** A3
Hotelik Przy Kinie Wenus	**17** B5

EATING	(pp317–18)
Bar Kawowy Pod Kasztanem	**18** A4
Pizzeria Gioconda	**19** A4
Restauracja Nieboska Komedia	**20** B3
TK Restauracja	**21** C3

DRINKING	(p318)
Blues Express Pub	**22** B3
Piwnica Artystyczna Kawon	**23** A3
Zbrojownia Pub	**24** A4

TRANSPORT	(p318)
Bus Terminal	**25** B1

notice it's there – quite an achievement for a 20-foot glass-fronted restaurant. Inside are four smart themed dining rooms, often hired out for events, banquets and the like; the varied menu's strong on fish.

Bar Kawowy Pod Kasztanem (☎ 327 29 08; Plac Pocztowy 15; dishes 1.50-8zł; ☽ breakfast, lunch & dinner) Sup the best coffee and milkshakes in town along with a small but select menu of breakfasts, snacks and desserts in this tiny owner-run café. For a real jolt, a generous Irish coffee will set you back 11zł.

Pizzeria Gioconda (☎ 324 65 65; ul Mariacka 5; mains 6.40-15.30zł; ☽ lunch & dinner) Tuck into the fastest Italian food on the Rynek under the inscrutable gaze of the Mona Lisa. Gourmet it ain't, but you'll certainly encounter worse pizzas.

Drinking & Entertainment

Piwnica Artystyczna Kawon (☎ 324 43 86; ul Zamkowa 5) Weird beer-bottle installations, tables made from old mangles, rusty swords, stained-glass boozers downing steins – it may sound like a cliché, but you really do need to see this place to believe it. It's generally packed with students trying to work out which bits of ephemera aren't screwed down.

Blues Express Pub (☎ 328 03 40; Al Niepodległości 10) One of several versatile pub-restaurants scattered around the central pedestrian zone, the Blues Express has a reasonable menu, plenty of drinks, and regular live jazz and blues in the basement.

Zbrojownia Pub (☎ 454 93 57; ul Krawiecka 7/9; ☽ noon-4am Mon-Sat, 4pm-1am Sun) Yet another basement bar, boasting the best opening hours in town. Insomniacs, barflies and plenty of part-timers gather to take in occasional gigs and admire the random bits of armour.

Getting There & Away
BUS
The busy bus terminal is about 1km northeast of the city centre, linked to it by several urban bus lines. Major destinations include Poznań (25zł, 2¾ hours, eight daily) and Wrocław (28zł, 3½ hours). There are six fast buses to Jelenia Góra (26zł, three hours), a more convenient way of getting there than by train.

TRAIN
The train station is 200m northeast of the train station. There are seven trains to Wrocław daily (30.03zł, three hours), one to Kraków (48.13zł, eight hours), four to Szczecin (36.12zł, 4¼ hours) and seven to Poznań (28.38zł, 2½ hours). There's one morning express train and one fast afternoon train to Warsaw (49.80zł, 5½ hours).

Wielkopolska

CONTENTS

WIELKOPOLSKA

WIELKOPOLSKA

Wielkopolska means Great Poland, and it's not just a random name. This is the land at the root of it all, where the warring Slavic tribes first merged to form the original Poles and where the Polish nation itself was forged in the crucible of the Middle Ages. Wherever you go in the region, you'll find a firm, almost stubborn conviction that this is the real heart of Poland, a seat of historical significance and national pride.

Despite this acute self-belief, Wielkopolska is little known outside Poland, as it lacks the distinct character of Silesia and the holiday infrastructure of Pomerania. Its provincial capital, Poznań, may get a flicker of recognition from Eastern European travellers and business types, but on the whole the region escapes the foreign hordes that converge on Kraków, Warsaw and Gdańsk.

For those visitors who do come here, this is clearly no bad thing, as it makes looking around the many varied historical and natural sights far less frenetic. Once you've had your fill of Poznań's discreet charms, head out into the country to discover Iron-Age settlements, family castles, palaces, churches and nature reserves. And whatever you do, call in at the great cathedral in Gniezno – this really was the birthplace of modern Catholic Poland.

Above all, when travelling around keep an eye open for traces of the past. Every town has its own treasured site, relic or fragment from a previous era, and a lot of store is set by them. Wielkopolskans may seem obsessed with history, but with so much to look back on, they surely have just cause.

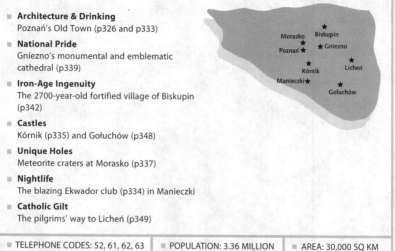

HIGHLIGHTS

- **Architecture & Drinking**
  Poznań's Old Town (p326 and p333)

- **National Pride**
  Gniezno's monumental and emblematic cathedral (p339)

- **Iron-Age Ingenuity**
  The 2700-year-old fortified village of Biskupin (p342)

- **Castles**
  Kórnik (p335) and Gołuchów (p348)

- **Unique Holes**
  Meteorite craters at Morasko (p337)

- **Nightlife**
  The blazing Ekwador club (p334) in Manieczki

- **Catholic Gilt**
  The pilgrims' way to Licheń (p349)

| ■ TELEPHONE CODES: 52, 61, 62, 63 | ■ POPULATION: 3.36 MILLION | ■ AREA: 30,000 SQ KM |

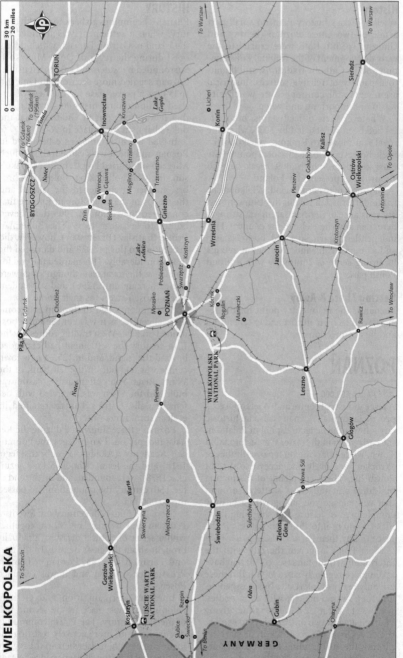

History

Wielkopolska's history is in no small part a tale of two cities: Poznań (below) and Gniezno (p338). Both were crucial to the early development of the original Polish nation and its Catholic traditions, and thanks to a paucity of reliable sources, historical arguments still continue over which city was more important, and when.

Whatever their official status, both cities had been superseded by 1038, when the royal seat moved to Kraków. Wielkopolska itself, however, remained a focal point of the Piast kingdom, which at its peak covered almost all of present-day Poland.

Like most of eastern Poland, Wielkopolska fell under Prussian rule in the 19th century, but resistance to Germanisation was stronger here than anywhere else in the country. This independent spirit survived both Nazism and communism, and the region retains its strong sense of continuity with a proud Polish past.

Getting There & Away

Poznań is the main entry point for the region, with its own airport and excellent rail and bus connections.

POZNAŃ

☎ 61 / pop 580,000

A large industrial centre and Wielkopolska's provincial capital, Poznań is also an historic city – it was the de facto capital of Poland in the early years of the state. The restored Old Town, while not quite on a par with that of Wrocław, is a lively and accessible slice of Polish life. There are plenty of fascinating buildings and museums scattered around that will engage you, along with a healthy complement of leisure and shopping facilities (if you're into Puma shoes, this is the place to buy them).

Most Poles associate the city with the international trade fairs (see p330) that have taken place regularly since WWI. But these are only really of interest to businesspeople, and they swamp the city with extra bodies. It's best to come at a quieter time, giving yourself at least two or three days to explore the city. Once you get stuck in or start exploring the surrounding area, chances are you'll stay longer than you thought.

HISTORY

Poznań's beginnings go back to the 9th century, when a settlement was founded on the island of Ostrów Tumski, which developed during the reign of Duke Mieszko I. Surrounded by water and easily defensible, Poznań seemed more secure than Gniezno (p339) as a power base for the newly baptised nation. Some historians even claim that it was here, not in Gniezno, that the duke's baptism took place in 966.

In 968 the bishopric was established in Poznań and the town's cathedral, in which Mieszko was buried in 992, built. Mieszko's son, the first Polish king, Bolesław Chrobry, further strengthened the island, and the troops of the Holy Roman Empire that conquered the region in 1005 didn't even bother to lay siege to it. The Bohemian Prince Bratislav (Brzetysław), however, did get around to this in 1038 and damaged the town considerably. This marked the end for Poznań as the royal seat (though kings were buried here up until 1296), and subsequent rulers chose Kraków as their home.

Poznań continued to develop as a commercial centre, as it was conveniently positioned on East–West trading routes. By the 12th century the settlement had expanded beyond the island, and in 1253 a new town centre was laid out on the left bank of the Warta River. Soon afterwards a castle was built and the town was encircled with defensive walls. Ostrów Tumski retained its ecclesiastical functions.

Poznań's trade flourished during the Renaissance period. Two colleges, the Lubrański Academy (Akademia Lubrańskiego; 1518) and the Jesuit School (Szkoła Jezuicka; 1578), were founded, and by the end of the 16th century the population had passed the 20,000 mark.

From the mid-17th century on, Swedish, Prussian and Russian invasions, together with a series of natural disasters, gradually brought about the city's demise. In the Second Partition of 1793, Poznań fell under Prussian occupation and it was renamed Posen.

Intensive Germanisation and German colonisation took place in the second half of the 19th century. The Polish community dug its heels in, more actively resisting the incursion here than elsewhere in the region. During that time the city experienced steady

STRIKING OUT

The June 1956 industrial strike in Poznań was the first mass protest in the Soviet bloc. Breaking out just three years after Stalin's death, it became the first milestone on Eastern Europe's road to democracy, and in some ways it served as an example for the chain of revolts that broke out in Poland, Hungary and Czechoslovakia over the following decades.

Poznań's protest originated in the city's largest industrial plant, the Cegielski metalworks (then named after Stalin), which produced railway stock. When the workers demanded the refund of an unfairly charged tax, the factory management refused and simply threw the workers' delegates out of the meeting room. This sparked a spontaneous strike the next day, in which the metalworkers, joined by workers from other local industrial plants, headed for Plac Mickiewicz (then named Plac Stalin).

The 100,000-strong crowd that gathered (a quarter of the city's total population) demanded 'bread and freedom', insisting that changes had to be introduced to improve working conditions, and requested that authorities come and discuss the issue. The demonstration was disregarded by city officials.

Matters soon got out of hand. The angry crowd stormed police headquarters and the Communist Party building, and released 257 prisoners from the local jail after disarming the guards. Shortly after, a battle for the secret-police headquarters broke out, and it was there that the bloodshed began, when police started firing at people surrounding the building. Tanks were introduced into the action, and troops were hastily brought from Wrocław and told they were there to pacify a German riot.

Fierce street battles continued for the whole night and part of the next day, resulting in a total of at least 76 dead and 900 wounded. More than 300 people were arrested, 58 of whom were indicted.

These figures make the protest the most tragic in communist Poland, yet it was underreported and for a long time underestimated. The historic importance of the revolt has only recently been appreciated and given the status it deserves, as an event on a par with the internationally famous shipyard strikes in Gdańsk.

industrial growth and by the outbreak of WWI its population had reached 150,000.

The Wielkopolska Insurrection, which broke out in Poznań in December 1918, liberated the city from German occupation and led to its return to the new Polish state. Poznań's long trading traditions were given new life with the establishment of the trade fairs in 1921, and four years later these were given international status.

The city fell into German hands once more during WWII, a particularly galling fate for such a staunchly Polish community. The battle for its liberation in 1945 took a month and did a huge amount of damage, some of which was never fully made good.

In the postwar era, Poznań was one of the first cities to feel the forceful hand of the communist regime, during a massive workers strike in June 1956 (see the boxed text above). The spontaneous demonstration, cruelly crushed by tanks, left about 76 dead and 900 wounded; it turned out to be the first of a wave of popular protests on

the long and painful road to overcoming communist rule.

ORIENTATION

Poznań Główny train station is about 2km southwest of the Old Town, which is the main tourist destination. Between the two spreads the modern city centre, where most businesses and many hotels are located.

Most tourist sights are either on or near the medieval marketplace, the Stary Rynek. The other important area for visitors is the birthplace of the city, Ostrów Tumski island, 1km east of the Old Town, beyond the Warta River.

Maps

All of Poland's major publishers produce good, detailed maps of Poznań, which are readily available in the city. The tourist offices can provide free plans of the Old Town and central area, but generally charge a fair bit more than normal bookshops for full-size maps.

WIELKOPOLSKA

POZNAŃ

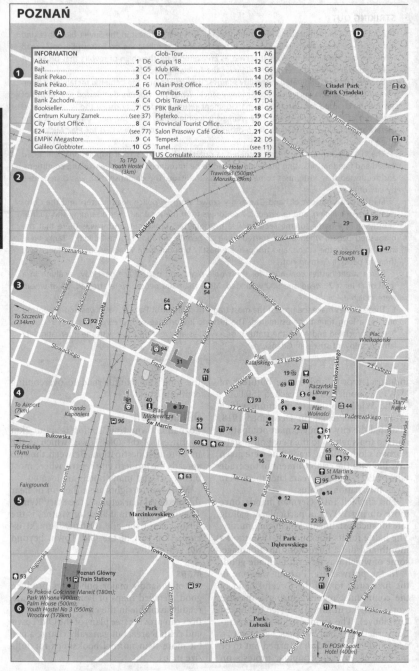

INFORMATION	
Adax	**1** D6
Bajt	**2** G5
Bank Pekao	**3** C4
Bank Pekao	**4** F6
Bank Pekao	**5** G4
Bank Zachodni	**6** C4
Bookseller	**7** C5
Centrum Kultury Zamek	(see 37)
City Tourist Office	**8** C4
E24	(see 77)
EMPiK Megastore	**9** C4
Galileo Globtroter	**10** G5
Glob-Tour	**11** A6
Grupa 18	**12** C5
Klub Klik	**13** G6
LOT	**14** D5
Main Post Office	**15** B5
Omnibus	**16** C5
Orbis Travel	**17** D4
PBK Bank	**18** G5
Pięterko	**19** C4
Provincial Tourist Office	**20** G6
Salon Prasowy Café Głos	**21** C4
Tempest	**22** D5
Tunel	(see 11)
US Consulate	**23** F5

Map labels (selected):

To TPD Youth Hostel (3km)

To Hotel Trawiński (500m); Morasko (8km)

Citadel Park (Park Cytadela)

42
43

Przepadek

Al Armii Poznań

Kutrzeby

29
39
47

Pułaskiego

Poznańska

Al Niepodległości   Kościuszki

St Joseph's Church

Św Wojciech

Solna

Nowowiejskiego

Wolnica

To Szczecin (234km)

Kochanowskiego   Mickiewicza   Roosevelta   Dąbrowskiego   92

Słowackiego

Wełniana   Al Niepodległości   Kościuszki   Libelta

54
64

Plac Wielkopolski

Młyńska

To Airport (7km)

Rondo Kaponiera

94
31
76
Fredry
Mielżyńskiego

Plac Ratajskiego   23 Lutego

Al Marcinkowskiego

23 Lutego

Stary Rynek

Raczyński Library

19
69
80
6
8
9
44

91
40
37
Plac Mickiewicza
Św Marcin

59
93
74

27 Grudnia

Plac Wolności

21
72
61
17

Paderewskiego

Szkolna   Wrocławska

96

Bukowska

To Eskulap (1km)

60
62
15
3
16

Św Marcin

65
57

63
Taczaka
Kościuszki

Podgórna

Ratajczaka

St Martin's Church
95

Fairgrounds

Park Marcinkowskiego

Al Niepodległości

7
12
14

Ogrodowa

22

Park Dąbrowskiego

Składowa

Towarowa

Kościuszki

Rybaki

Łąkowa

Krakowska

77
71

Park Lubuski

53
11   Poznań Główny Train Station

To Pokoje Gościnne Marwit (180m);
Park Wilsona (200m);
Palm House (500m);
Youth Hostel No 3 (550m);
Wrocław (178km)

Głogowska

Przemysłowa

Spichrzowa

97

Niedziałkowskiego

Królowej Jadwigi

Górna Wilda

To POSiR Sport Hotel (400m)

WIELKOPOLSKA

SIGHTS & ACTIVITIES	(pp326–30)
Archaeological Museum	24 G6
Archdiocesan Museum	25 G3
Arsenal City Art Gallery	26 G5
Castle	27 F5
Cathedral	28 G3
Cemetery of the Meritorious	29 D2
Church of St John of Jerusalem	30 H4
Collegium Maius	31 B4
Collegium Minus	(see 91)
Dominican Church	32 E4
Ethnographic Museum	33 F5
Fish Sellers' Houses	34 G5
Franciscan Church	35 F5
Górka Palace	(see 24)
Historical Museum of Poznań	(see 50)
Jesuit School	36 G6
Kaiserhaus	37 B4
Lubrański Academy	38 G3
Monument to the Poznań Army	39 D2
Monument to the Victims of June 1956	40 B4
Museum of Decorative Arts	(see 27)
Museum of Musical Instruments	41 G5
Museum of the Poznań Army	42 D1
Museum of Weapons	43 D2
National Museum	44 D4
Parish Church	45 G6
Psalteria	46 G3
St Adalbert's Church	47 D3

St Margaret's Church	48 H3
St Mary's Church	49 G3
Town Hall	50 G5
Weigh House	51 G5
Wielkopolska Military Museum	52 G5

SLEEPING	(pp330–2)
Biuro Zakwaterowania Przemysław	53 A6
Dizzy Daisy	54 B3
Dom Polonii	55 G5
Dom Turysty	56 G5
Domina Prestige	57 D5
Hotel Ibis	58 F6
Hotel Lech	59 B4
Hotel Royal	60 B4
Hotel Rzymski	61 D4
Hotel Wielkopolska	62 C4
Mini Hotelik	63 B5
Pokoje Gościnne PAN	64 B3

EATING	(p332)
Bar Mamamija	65 D5
Bar Mleczny Apetyt	66 G6
Bar Wegetariański	67 G6
Brovaria	68 G5
Café Pravda	69 C4
Café Pravda	70 H6
Pancake Square	71 D6
Restauracja Delicja	72 C4
Restauracja Orfeusz	73 G6

Restauracja Sphinx	74 C4
Restauracja Sphinx	75 G5
Restauracja W-Z	76 B4
Stary Browar	77 D6
Trattoria Valpolicella	78 G6

DRINKING	(p333)
Alter Ego	79 G6
Bars	80 C4
Czarna Owca	81 G6
Galeria i Scena Anny Kareńskiej	82 H5
Muchos Patatos	83 H5
Nargila Klub	84 G6
Piwnica 21	85 H5
Pole Café	86 G6
Proletaryat	87 G6

ENTERTAINMENT	(pp333–4)
Blue Note Jazz Club	(see 37)
Charyzma	88 H5
Czerwony Fortepian	89 G4
Deep	90 G6
Filharmonia	91 B4
Teatr Nowy	92 A3
Teatr Ósmego Dnia	(see 8)
Teatr Polski	93 C4
Teatr Wielki	94 B4
Trendy	95 D5

TRANSPORT	(pp334–5)
Bus stop for Kórnik	96 B4
PKP Office	(see 63)
PKS Bus Terminal	97 B6

INFORMATION

Bookshops

Bookseller (☎ 856 02 79; ul Powstańców Wielkopolskich; ☿ 9am-5pm)

EMPiK Megastore (☎ 852 66 90; ul Ratajczaka 44; ☿ 10am-10pm Mon-Sat, 11am-5pm Sun)

Galileo Globtroter (☎ 853 29 15; Stary Rynek 98/100; ☿ 10am-6pm Mon-Fri, 10am-2pm Sat) Enter from ul Żydowska.

Grupa 18 (☎ 855 10 85; ul Ratajczaka 18)

Omnibus (☎ 853 61 82; ul Św Marcin 39; ☿ 10am-7pm Mon-Fri, 10am-2pm Sat)

Salon Prasowy Café Głos (☎ 852 26 12; ul Ratajczaka 39)

Cultural Centres

Centrum Kultury Zamek (Zamek Cultural Centre; ☎ 852 32 38; www.zamek.poznan.pl in Polish; ul Św Marcin 80/82) Located in the Kaiserhaus, this is an active cultural centre that encompasses an art-house cinema and several galleries as well as hosting music and other events. In summer, concerts are staged in the building's courtyard.

Internet Access

Adax (☎ 850 11 00; ul Półwiejska 28; per hr 2.5zł)

Bajt (☎ 853 18 08; ul Zamkowa 5/2; per hr 3zł; ☿ 24hr)

E24 (☎ 859 63 04; Stary Browar; per hr 3zł; ☿ 24hr)

Klub Klik (☎ 0609 276 072; ul Szkolna 15/3; per hr 3-4zł)

Pięterko (☎ 662 38 45; ul Nowowiejskiego 7; per hr 2-2.25zł)

Tempest (☎ 663 94 26; ul Piekary 13B; per hr 2zł; ☿ 24hr)

Tunel (Poznań Główny, ul Dworcowa 1; per hr 3zł; ☿ 24hr)

Money

Bank Pekao ul Maszatlarska (☎ 855 24 11; ul Maszatlarska 8A); ul Paderewskiego (☎ 852 26 72; ul Paderewskiego 3); ul Św Marcin (☎ 855 81 05; ul Św Marcin 52/56)

Bank Zachodni (☎ 856 49 00; Plac Wolności 16)

PBK Bank (☎ 856 78 00; Stary Rynek 97/98)

Post

Main post office (☎ 869 73 00; ul Kościuszki 77; ☿ 7am-9pm Mon-Fri, 9am-5pm Sat, 10am-4pm Sun)

Tourist Information

City tourist office (CIM; ☎ 851 96 45; www.cim .poznan.pl; ul Ratajczaka 44; ☿ 10am-7pm Mon-Fri, 10am-5pm Sat)

Glob-Tour (☎ 866 06 67; Poznań Główny, ul Dworcowa 1; ☿ 24hr)

Provincial tourist office (☎ 852 61 56; www.city .poznan.pl; Stary Rynek 59/60; ☿ 9am-6pm Mon-Fri, 10am-4pm Sat Jun-Sep, 9am-5pm Mon-Fri, 10am-2pm Sat Oct-May)

Travel Agencies

Atut Tourist (☎ 853 06 49; Plac Wolności 8; ☿ 10am-5pm Mon-Fri, 10am-1pm Sat) Eurolines agent.

LOT (☎ 858 55 00; ul Piekary 6)

Orbis Travel (☎ 852 49 94; Al Marcinkowskiego 21; ☿ 9am-6pm Mon-Fri, 10am-2pm Sat)

SIGHTS

Old Town Square

Unchallenged as the heart of the city, the **Stary Rynek** was laid out in 1253 along with the rest of the Old Town. The early timber buildings lining the square later gave way to brick burghers' houses, and in the 18th-century two palaces were erected (Nos 78 and 91). The middle of the square has gradually changed over time too, and the buildings that you see today make up a haphazard collection dating from different periods.

TOWN HALL

The unquestioned architectural pearl of Poznań is the Renaissance town hall, topped with a 61m-high tower. What you see is the second building on this site; it replaced the 13th-century Gothic town hall, which was entirely consumed by fire in the early 16th century, along with much of the town. Designed by Italian architect Giovanni Battista Quadro and constructed from 1550 to 1560, only the tower is a later addition, built in the 1780s after its predecessor collapsed. The crowned eagle on top of the spire, with an impressive wingspan of 2m, adds some Polish symbolism.

The main eastern façade is embellished with a three-storey **arcade**. Above it, the painted frieze depicts kings of the Jagiellonian dynasty. In the middle of the decorative parapet, above the clock, there's a pair of small doors; every day at noon two metal goats appear through them and butt their horns together 12 times, in reference to an old story about the unveiling of the clock. Apparently two stolen goats intended for the celebratory banquet escaped and ended up clashing horns above the clock itself, much to the amusement of the assembled dignitaries. The clockmaker was duly ordered to add the errant animals' images to his piece.

The **Historical Museum of Poznań** (Muzeum Historii Miasta Poznania; ☎ 852 56 13; Stary Rynek 1; adult/concession 5.50/3.50zł, free Fri; ☿ 10am-4pm Mon, Tue & Fri, noon-6pm Wed, 10am-3pm Sun) is inside the town hall. There's an interesting and well-presented exhibition on the town's history, and the building's original interiors are worth the entry price on their own.

The Gothic vaulted **cellars** are the only remains of the first town hall. They were initially used for trade but later became a jail. Today they house exhibits on medieval Poznań, including fragments of Romanesque and Gothic sculpture and a model of the town as it was 1000 years ago. You will also find some coffin portraits, a Polish art form particularly common in Wielkopolska.

The 1st floor is home to three splendid rooms. The largest, the richly ornamented **Renaissance Hall** (Sala Renesansowa), is a real gem, with its original stucco work and paintings from 1555. The 2nd floor contains more-recent exhibits, including artefacts from the Prussian period, documents illustrating city life in the 1920s and '30s, and a collection of photos showing the devastation of the city in WWII.

In front of the building, near the main entrance, is the **whipping post** *(pręgierz)*, once the site of public floggings – and of more serious penalties, as the dinky model executioner on top suggests. The original, dating from 1535, is on display in the museum.

AROUND THE SQUARE

Behind the town hall is the **Weigh House** (Waga Miejska), a postwar replica of the 16th-century building designed by Quadro, which was dismantled in the 19th century. South of it are two large, modern structures, strikingly out of harmony with the rest of the old Rynek. Unfortunately, the postwar authorities built these ugly blocks on the site of the old arsenal and cloth hall, ruining the architectural harmony of the square and obstructing most views of the original surviving buildings.

The arsenal site now houses the **Arsenal City Art Gallery** (Galeria Miejska Arsenał; ☎ 852 95 01; www.arsenal.art.pl in Polish; Stary Rynek 3; adult/concession 3/2zł; 🕑 11am-6pm Tue-Sat, 10am-3pm Sun), which goes some way towards atoning for its design sins with temporary exhibitions of modern art, plus a restaurant and bookshop. Its neighbour is the **Wielkopolska Military Museum** (Wielkopolskie Muzeum Wojskowe; ☎ 852 67 39; Stary Rynek 9), which was closed at the time of writing for major refurbishment.

On the east side of the two monstrosities is a much more endearing row of small, arcaded buildings, known as the **Fish Sellers' Houses** (Domki Budnicze). They were built in the 16th century on the site of the fish stalls but were largely destroyed in WWII and reconstructed later.

Directly opposite is the **Museum of Musical Instruments** (Muzeum Instrumentów Muzycznych; ☎ 856 81 78; Stary Rynek 45; adult/concession 5.50/3.50zł, free Sat; 🕑 11am-5pm Tue-Sat, 11am-3pm Sun). It houses hundreds of instruments, from whistles to concert pianos from Europe and beyond, dating from the 15th to 20th centuries, and includes some intriguing folk specimens. A separate exhibition is dedicated to composer Frédéric Chopin.

Southeastern Old Town

Off the southeastern corner of the Rynek, inside the 16th-century **Górka Palace** (Pałac Górków), is the **Archaeological Museum** (Muzeum Archeologiczne; ☎ 852 82 51; ul Wodna 27; adult/concession 5/2zł, free Sat; 🕑 10am-4pm Tue-Fri, 10am-6pm Sat, 10am-3pm Sun). Before going in, stop and have a look at the fine Renaissance doorway on the building's eastern façade. The museum itself presents the prehistory of the region, from the Stone Age to the early medieval period, as well as an extensive Egyptian collection. You'll also find a replica of the famous bronze doors from Gniezno cathedral (p339).

A few steps south of the museum is the **Parish Church** (Kościół Farny; ul Gołębia), originally built for the Jesuits by architects from Italy. After more than 80 years of work (1651–1732), an impressive baroque church was created, with an ornamented façade and a lofty interior supported on massive columns and crammed with monumental altars.

Facing the church is the former **Jesuit School** (Szkoła Jezuicka), which was granted a college charter by King Zygmunt Waza, later annulled by the pope when the Kraków Academy protested. Today it's the Ballet School; in summer, plays are occasionally performed in the arcaded courtyard.

A five-minute walk east from here is the **Ethnographic Museum** (Muzeum Etnograficzne; ☎ 852 30 06; ul Grobla 25; adult/concession 5.50/3.50zł, free Sat; 🕑 10am-4pm Tue, Wed, Fri & Sat, 10am-3pm Sun). It has a good collection of folk woodcarving – of note are the large roadside posts and crosses – and traditional costumes of the region. Confusingly, you enter from ul Mostowa 7, not ul Grobla.

Western Old Town

The western edge of the Old Town is de-marcated by **Plac Wolności**, one of the main squares of contemporary Poznań. Its chief attraction is the **National Museum** (Muzeum Narodowe; ☎ 856 80 00; Al Marcinkowskiego 9; adult/concession 10/6zł, free Sat; ⓧ 10am-6pm Tue, 9am-5pm Wed, 10am-4pm Thu & Sun, 10am-5pm Fri & Sat), where an extensive collection of Polish and European art is displayed in countless rooms. The unappealing building was erected in the early years of the 20th century to serve as a Prussian museum, sadly with far less attention paid to the aesthetics of the architecture than that of the contents.

Polish painting of the last two centuries is represented by almost all the big names, including Jan Matejko, Stanisław Wyspiański and Jacek Malczewski. The museum also has a reasonable selection of Italian, Spanish, Flemish and Dutch painting. A range of heavyweight temporary exhibitions often take centre stage.

A curiosity worth noticing is the collection of coffin portraits. Medieval church woodcarving and painting are displayed in the basement, and various small displays showcase posters, design and old coins.

Between Plac Wolności and the Rynek stands Poznań's **castle**, or what's left of it. The original 13th-century castle was repeatedly destroyed and rebuilt, and the residence you see today is the postwar reconstruction of a late-18th-century building, hardly looking like a castle at all. It now houses the **Museum of Decorative Arts** (Muzeum Sztuk Użytkowych; ☎ 852 20 35; Góra Przemysława 1; adult/concession 5.50/3.50zł, free Sat; ⓧ 10am-4pm Tue, Wed, Fri & Sat, 10am-3pm Sun). The collection includes furniture, gold and silverware, glass, ceramics, weapons, clocks, watches and sundials from Europe and the Far East. Exhibits date from the 13th century to the present.

Just south of the castle is the **Franciscan Church** (Kościół Franciszkanów; ul Franciszkańska 2). Built from 1674 to 1728, it has a complete baroque interior adorned with wall paintings and rich stucco work. The **Chapel of the Virgin Mary** (Kaplica NMP), in the left transept, has an altar carved in oak and a tiny, miraculous image of St Mary.

Ostrów Tumski

The island of Ostrów Tumski is where Poznań, and with it the Polish state, took its first steps. The original 9th-century settlement was gradually transformed into an oval stronghold surrounded by wood-and-earth ramparts, and an early stone palace was built. Mieszko I added a cathedral and further fortified the township, and by the end of the 10th century Poznań was the most powerful stronghold in the country.

A couple of centuries later, the settlement spread beyond the island, first to the right, then to the left bank of the river. In the 13th century, when the newly designed town was laid out, Ostrów lost its trade and administrative importance, but remained the residence of the Church authorities, which it still is.

Today it's a tiny, quiet ecclesiastical quarter, radiating an air of history and dominated by Poznań's monumental, double-towered **cathedral**. Basically Gothic with additions from later periods, most notably the baroque tops of the towers, the cathedral was badly damaged in 1945 and its reconstruction took 11 years. Since little of the internal furnishing survived, the present-day decoration has been collected from other churches, mostly from Silesia.

The aisles and the ambulatory are ringed by a dozen chapels containing numerous tombstones. The most famous of these is the **Golden Chapel** (Złota Kaplica), behind the high altar. Dating from the 15th century, it was completely rebuilt in the 1830s as the mausoleum of the first two Polish rulers, Mieszko I and Bolesław Chrobry. Enveloped in Byzantine-style decoration are the double tomb of the two monarchs on the one side and their bronze statues on the other.

The rulers' original burial site was the **crypt**, accessible from the back of the left-hand aisle. Apart from the fragments of what are thought to have been their tombs, you can see the relics of the first pre-Romanesque cathedral dating from 968 and of the subsequent Romanesque building from the second half of the 11th century.

Opposite the cathedral is **St Mary's Church** (Kościół NMP; ul Panny Marii), built in the mid-15th century and virtually unaltered since then. Its internal decoration, though, is modern. Just behind the church is the early-16th-century **Psałteria**, which was home to the choristers.

North of the cathedral is **Lubrański Academy** (Akademia Lubrańskiego), also known as the Collegium Lubranscianum, the first

View of cable-car and chairlift stations, Mt Kasprowy Wierch (p255), Tatra Mountains

Lines of barbed wire, Auschwitz-Birkenau extermination camp (p304), Oświęcim

Spruce forest, Tatra Mountains (p252)

Burghers' houses, Plac Solny (p265), Wrocław

Cathedral (p339), Gniezno

Former Bernardine Church (p346), Kalisz

Way of the Cross, Golgotha (p349), Licheń

Fish Sellers' Houses (p327), Old Town Sq, Poznań

high school in Poznań (1518). Across the street from it is the **Archdiocesan Museum** (Muzeum Archidiecezjalne; ☎ 852 61 95; ul Posadzego 2; adult/concession 3/2zł; ☻ 9am-3pm Mon-Sat), which has a collection of sacred art dating from the 12th century onwards.

North of the Old Town

Before WWII, the area north of the Rynek was populated mainly by Jews, though there's little trace of their community any more. Even the old synagogue has long since been converted – into a swimming pool, of all things.

The oldest surviving monument on this side of the river is the former **Dominican Church** (Kościół Podominikański), now belonging to the Jesuits. Built in the mid-13th century, it was repeatedly reshaped and redecorated in later periods, but the fine early-Gothic doorway at the main entrance is still in place.

Further north, outside the boundaries of the Old Town, is the 15th-century **St Adalbert's Church** (Kościół Św Wojciecha). Its 16th-century, freestanding wooden belfry is the only substantial historic wooden building in Poznań. Inside the church, the Gothic vaulting is decorated with striking Art Nouveau wall paintings. The crypt beneath, open to visitors, has become a mausoleum for the most eminent Poles from Wielkopolska, among them Józef Wybicki, who wrote the lyrics of the national anthem.

During the Christmas period, the mechanised *szopka* (Nativity scene) is open in the church. It includes several dozen movable figures that depict the history of the region, from Mieszko I to the present day.

Not far from the church you'll find the stark, modern **Monument to the Poznań Army** (Pomnik Armii Poznań), dedicated to the local armed force that resisted the German invasion of 1939 for almost two weeks. It's just opposite the sloping **Cemetery of the Meritorious** (Cmentarz Zasłużonych), the oldest existing graveyard in the city (1810).

Further north is the large **Citadel Park** (Wzgórze Cytadela), laid out on what was once a massive fortress known as the **Citadel** (Cytadela). It was built by the Prussians in the 1830s on a hill once occupied by vineyards (a tragic waste given the scarcity of good Polish wine). The fortress was involved in one major battle, when the Ger-

mans defended themselves for four weeks in 1945. It was completely destroyed and only a few fragments have survived, replaced instead with extensive parklands.

Today the park incorporates two museums: the **Museum of Weapons** (Muzeum Cytadeli Poznańskiej; ☎ 820 45 03; adult/concession 4/2zł, free Fri; ☻ 9am-4pm Tue-Sat, 10am-4pm Sun) and the **Museum of the Poznań Army** (Muzeum Armii Poznań; ☎ 820 45 03; adult/concession 4/2zł, free Fri; ☻ 9am-4pm Tue-Sat, 10am-4pm Sun). There are also cemeteries for Polish, Soviet, British and Commonwealth soldiers, all on the southern slopes of the hill.

Station Area

On **Plac Mickiewicza**, west of the Old Town, at the station end of ul Św Marcin, you'll find one of Poznań's most significant memorials, the **Monument to the Victims of June 1956** (Pomnik Poznańskiego Czerwca 1956), which commemorates the ill-fated workers' protest (see the boxed text on p323). The monument, consisting of two 20m-tall crosses bound together, was unveiled on 28 June 1981, the 25th anniversary of the strike, at a ceremony attended by over 100,000 people. It's a huge, evocative landmark, similar to the Monument to the Fallen Shipyard Workers (p366) in Gdańsk.

There are also copious examples of Prussian architecture grouped around this area. Notable specimens include the **Teatr Wielki** (Grand Theatre), the **Collegium Maius**, the **Collegium Minus** and, largest of all, the neo-Romanesque **Kaiserhaus**, built from 1904 to 1910 for Emperor Wilhelm II. The sombre, blackened building is today the Centrum Kultury Zamek (p326), which houses several major venues and galleries.

A little further south, a five-minute walk from the main train station along ul Głogowska, is the large **Park Wilsona**. Enter it and walk to the northern end to visit the **Palm House** (Palmiarnia; ☎ 865 89 07; ul Matejki 18; adult/concession 5.50/3.50zł; ☻ 9am-5pm Tue-Sun). Constructed in 1910 and occupying a large area of 4600 sq metres and a volume of 46,000 cu metres, this is one of the biggest greenhouses on the continent. Inside, 19,000 species of tropical and subtropical plants are housed, including the continent's largest cactus collection and tallest bamboo trees. The adjacent aquarium is home to exotic fish.

Outer Suburbs

If you venture east from Ostrów Tumski, past the bridge that stretches over the Cybina River, you'll encounter several small and little-visited historical suburbs. The microscopic Śródka district was the main trade centre of Poznań in the 13th century, but lost its significance when the town was moved to its present site. **St Margaret's Church** (Kościół Św Małgorzaty; Rynek Środecki), originally a 14th-century structure but much altered later, is one of the few remainders of the area's heyday.

More interesting is the **Church of St John of Jerusalem** (Kościół Św Jana Jerozolimskiego; ul Świetojańska 1), in the suburb of Komandoria, a five-minute walk further east, behind the Rondo Śródka. The late-12th-century building (one of the oldest brick churches in the country) was extended in the Gothic period and later acquired a baroque chapel. The interior is an unusual combination of a nave with a single aisle to one side (both with beautiful Gothic star vaults) plus a chapel on the opposite side. The Romanesque doorway in the main western entrance is magnificent.

Southeast of the church is the 70-hectare artificial **Lake Malta** (Jezioro Maltańskie), a favourite summer spot for families, picnickers and boating enthusiasts. During the Malta International Theatre Festival (below) in June, the banks are used for outdoor theatre productions and other events, creating a lively and, well, festive atmosphere.

FESTIVALS & EVENTS

Poznań's trade fairs are its pride and joy, though few are of interest to casual visitors. The main ones take place in January, June, September and October, with two dozen other fairs throughout the year. July, August and December are fair-free months.

Major cultural events:

Poznań Jazz Festival (☎ 813 25 66; www.jazz.pl)
Held in March.

St John's Fair (Jarmark Świętojański; ☎ 853 60 81) A handicraft and antiques fair, held on the Stary Rynek in June.

Malta International Theatre Festival (☎ 646 52 43; www.malta-festival.pl) Fringe and alternative theatre, held in late June.

Wieniawski International Violin Competition (☎ 852 26 42; www.wieniawski.pl) Held every five years in October (next due in 2006).

SLEEPING

Trade fairs wreak havoc on Poznań's accommodation range – prices tend to double across the board, and during major fairs you won't find anything anywhere near the centre. Prices given here are standard weekday rates for 'off-fair' periods. Unless otherwise specified, prices are for rooms with private bathrooms and include breakfast. The tourist offices and Glob-Tour (p326) are knowledgeable about lodging options and should be able to help you find a bed.

Budget

HOSTELS & HOTELS

Dizzy Daisy (☎ 829 39 02; www.hostel.pl; Al Niepodległości 26; dm 40zł, d 100zł; ☼ Jul & Aug; ⓟ 🖳) A sociable summer backpacker haunt within easy reach of the centre. The standards won't amaze but it's got everything you need, the atmosphere's spot on and there's even a piano in case you're feeling talented.

Mini Hotelik (☎ 863 14 16; Al Niepodległości 8; s 53.50zł, d 107-135zł; ⓟ) Round the back of the PKP (Polish State Railways) ticket office, this is a step up from hostel accommodation and still within budget range if you plump for a room without en suite. Little extras such as TV and kettle add to the comfort factor.

Youth Hostel No 3 (☎ 866 40 40; ul Berwińskiego 2/3; dm 20-35zł) This is the closest hostel to the city centre, a 550m walk southwest from the train station along ul Głogowska. It's the smallest and most basic of the lot and fills up fast. Most of the 52 beds here are in eight- to 10-bed dorms.

TPD Youth Hostel (☎ 848 58 36; www.schroniskotpd .ta.pl; ul Drzymały 3; dm 16.50-25zł; ⓟ) Pine bunks, bright carpets and the occasional overgrown pot plant give the TPD hostel a bit of individuality often lacking in these institutions. It's near Lake Solacki, 3km from the station and the Old Town; tram Nos 9 and 11 stop nearby.

PRIVATE ROOMS

Biuro Zakwaterowania Przemysław (☎ 866 35 60; www.przemyslaw.com.pl; ul Głogowska 16; s 40-65zł, d 60-90zł; ☼ 8am-6pm Mon-Fri, 10am-2pm Sat) The largest of Poznań's private-accommodation agencies is opposite the train station. It has its own *kantor* (private currency-exchange office), bookshop and mobile-phone dealer to boot. Rooms are almost always available, but at fair times prices double and there may be less choice.

CAMPING
Camping Nr 155 Malta (☎ 876 62 03; www.posir .poznan.pl; ul Krańcowa 98; camping per person 7zł, bungalows 150-400zł) Malta is the best of Poznań's three camping grounds, and the closest to the centre – it's on the northeastern shore of Lake Malta, 3km east of the Old Town. Sixty-six heated bungalows, including five specially adapted for disabled guests, provide good all-year shelter.

Mid-Range
Dom Polonii (☎ 852 71 21; Stary Rynek 51; s/d 117/181zł) Dating from 1488, the Dom Polonii occupies one corner of Poznań's market square, offering just two double rooms to anyone who's organised enough to book sufficiently in advance. The only way you could get more central would be tunnelling under the town hall.

Hotel Rzymski (☎ 852 81 21; www.rzymskihotel .com.pl; Al Marcinkowskiego 22; s/d/tr 195/250/300zł, ste 280-430zł; P) An historic and sophisticated hotel that just tucks itself into the mid-range category, though the two restaurants help it keep in touch with the top end. It's got nothing to do with rhythm, incidentally – Rzymski is the Polish for Rome and a translation of its original German name.

Hotel Lech (☎ 853 08 80; www.hotel-lech.poznan .pl; ul Św Marcin 74; s/d/tr 150/220/300zł) A comfortable, good, standard three-star, set in a convenient location, midway between the train station and the Old Town. Accommodating staff are well drilled in dealing with a mainly tourist clientele.

Hotel Wielkopolska (☎ 852 76 31; ul Św Marcin 67; s 140-160zł, d 180-200zł; P) Just opposite the Lech, this venerable building is gradually being refurbished to meet the same tourist-class standards. The newer rooms are considerably better, but you can still get a cheap bed without bathroom if you prefer.

POSiR Sport Hotel (☎ 833 05 91; www.posir.poznan .pl; ul Chwiałkowskiego 34; s/d/tr 150/180/260zł; P 🏋) You don't often get use of one swimming pool for these prices, let alone two. Run by the municipal sports body, the Sport Hotel is a handy all-rounder, next to the city stadium and directly above a public pool. An outdoor pool opens in summer, perfect for swim fans and chlorine junkies.

Pokoje Gościnne Marwit (☎ 661 10 44; ul Śniadeckich 12A; s/d/tr 117.70/160.50/171.20zł) Family guesthouses are few and far between in Poznań, which is a shame if this is anything to go by. Eccentric colour schemes, homy fittings and a breakfast room swamped in faux-tropical greenery should bat a few eyelids. Some cheaper shared-bathroom rooms are available.

Pokoje Gościnne PAN (☎ 851 68 41; zpg@man .poznan.pl; ul Wieniawskiego 17/19; s/d/ste 120/195/240zł; P) Don't be confused by the signs – this is indeed part of the Poznań Supercomputing and Networking Center, occupying part of the large office behind the Grand Theatre. Thankfully you don't have to be even vaguely computer literate to stay here.

Hotel Ibis (☎ 858 44 00; ul Kazimierza Wielkiego 23; r 235zł; P ✗) A typical entry in this reliable business chain, Poznań's Ibis offers 146 air-conditioned rooms within an easy walk of the historic centre. If you don't like surprises, this is a good place to hang your hat.

Dom Turysty (☎ 852 88 93; Stary Rynek 91; dm 56-70zł, s/d 130/200zł) Like the Dom Polonii, this former palace has an enviable location on the Rynek, though the interior is nowhere near as grand as the outside may suggest. There are plenty of better places around town, but if you want to be where the action is, this'll do the job. Enter the hotel from ul Wroniecka.

Top End
Domina Prestige (☎ 859 05 90; www.dominahotels.com; ul Św Marcin 2; apt €175-240; P) Some hotels try to make you feel like you're at home – the Domina makes you wish your home was a bit more like this. The luxury serviced apartments come with stylish interiors, fully featured kitchens and more mod cons than a New York penthouse. And just to round it off there's a clutch of hotel facilities downstairs.

Hotel Royal (☎ 858 23 00; www.hotel-royal.com.pl; ul Św Marcin 71; s/d 320/395zł, studio 435zł; P ✗) Tasteful terracotta tones predominate in this smart, refined hotel, situated on the main road leading into the centre. Spring for the spacious studio room and you can put in some work on the ski machine, or just hang around the lobby perusing the photos of famous Polish guests.

Hotel Trawiński (☎ 827 58 00; www.hoteltrawinski .com.pl; ul Żniwna 2; s/d 365/490zł, ste 590-1200zł; P ✗) Perhaps not the most attractive building in Park Cytadela, but nonetheless offering impeccable accommodation, Poznań's Best Western contribution ranks up there with the many other conference-class places scattered around the outer reaches of town. The park is 2.5km north of the centre.

EATING

As ever, the Old Town is the place to start a culinary field trip – munching your way around the Rynek alone would take a fair while. And Poznań has reams of restaurants further afield as well, with notable concentrations around ul Św Marcin and ul 27 Grudnia.

Restauracja W-Z (☎ 665 88 01; ul Fredry 12; mains 12-29.50zł; ☺ lunch & dinner) Short for Wielkopolska Zagroda (Wielkopolskan Farm), the W-Z takes its rustic theme to the limit – the building contains a re-creation of a country cabin, complete with timber roof, allowing diners to feast on excellent Polish cooking either inside or round the edge. If it's all too confusing you can sit outside the restaurant itself and be baffled by silly art instead.

Restauracja Delicja (☎ 852 11 28; www.delicja.com .pl; Plac Wolności 5; mains 28-49zł; ☺ lunch & dinner) One of Poznań's top restaurants, tucked away off Plac Wolności, the Delicja has its own miniature courtyard and an intimidating reputation for top-notch international cuisine along French-Italian lines. Refinement and elegance come as standard.

Bar Mamamija (ul Św Marcin 12; mains 2-6.50zł; ☺ lunch & dinner) Dragging the traditional milk bar firmly into the, um, 1970s, students and snackers alike dig this deeply retro joint's rainbow paint job and kidney-shaped tables. Pasta, stroganoff and other fads join the usual suspects on the budget menu.

Brovaria (☎ 858 68 68; www.brovaria.pl; Stary Rynek 73/74; mains 18-34zł; ☺ lunch & dinner; ✗) A good Rynek option with an imaginative menu, covering wider territory than your average tourist eatery. There are even hotel rooms upstairs (priced from 230zł for a single and 290zł for a double). It's also great for avid beer hunters – Brovaria is one of a handful of microbreweries springing up around Poland. While the basic lager isn't up to much, it's worth trying the unusual honey beer.

Pancake Square (☎ 0506 184 605; ul Półwiejska 45; mains 4-8.50zł; ☺ breakfast, lunch & dinner) No prizes for guessing which dish takes centre stage here. The modern café ambience suits the lightness of the raw materials, and with variations such as waffles and breakfast deals, this is really the *crème de la crêpe*.

Café Pravda (☎ 853 19 30; ul Wodna 3/4; mains 14.50-26.90zł; ☺ breakfast, lunch & dinner) The second of its kind to open, this Pravda is much brighter than its deliberately downbeat sister at ul Nowowiejskiego 7. It doubles as a gallery and showcase for local artists and is a great place to look thoughtful over a coffee, cake or light meal.

Trattoria Valpolicella (☎ 855 71 91; ul Wrocławska 7; mains 25-58zł; ☺ lunch & dinner) It's all in the name: Valpolicella serves up a wide variety of pasta and other Italian specialities, well suited to a glass of the eponymous vino, in convincingly rustic Mediterranean surroundings.

Stary Browar (☎ 850 10 76; www.starybrowar.pl in Polish; ul Półwiejska 42; ☺ 9am-9pm) The food court in Poznań's latest contribution to contemporary shopping chic offers a fine cross section of the kind of food you don't often find elsewhere, from proper Ottoman Turkish cuisine to wine sold by serious merchants. If you're not hungry you can grab a drink amid the artwork on the roof.

Restauracja Orfeusz (☎ 851 98 44; ul Świętosławska 12; mains 32-65zł; ☺ lunch & dinner) Orfeusz brings a faint whiff of Victorian severity to town with its air of staid elegance and green-striped wallpaper. Polish and European cuisine make up a heavyweight menu, but the real challenge is to sit for an entire meal without mentioning the wicker giraffes outside.

Bar Wegetariański (☎ 852 12 55; ul Wrocławska 21; mains 1.30-4.80zł; ☺ breakfast & lunch Mon-Sat; ✗) This simple, tiny place is virtually the only purely vegetarian eatery in town and follows the customary canteen formula. Thanks to the bargain prices it attracts some pretty mixed crowds.

Restauracja Sphinx (mains 8.90-35.90zł; ☺ lunch & dinner) Stary Rynek (☎ 852 80 25; Stary Rynek 77); ul Św Marcin (☎ 852 07 02; ul Św Marcin 66/72) Firmly installed on the Poznań food map, the all-conquering kebab chain pushes its mounds of meat amid dangling lanterns. The big-screen TV ensures even denser crowds on football nights.

Bar Mleczny Apetyt (☎ 852 13 39; ul Szkolna 4; mains 2.91-6.16zł; ☺ breakfast, lunch & dinner) The latest-closing milk bar in town enjoys a good, central location. The food is exactly what you'd expect, and none the worse for that.

DRINKING

Once you've done the rounds of the beer gardens on the Rynek, there are plenty of places elsewhere in town worth seeking out for a drink or several. Ul Woźna and ul Nowowiejskiego have plenty of student-oriented bars, while ul Żydowska caters for a more mature audience and the southern Old Town has a bit of everything.

Alter Ego (☎ 851 80 35; Stary Rynek 63; ☿ 11pm-1am) The basement of the Powszechna bookshop conceals an intriguing narrow bar, run by the Deep club, which has a dance-music policy. Look closely at the portholes separating the seating booths – you may find something alive inside…

Proletaryat (☎ 0508 173 608; ul Wrocławska 9; ☿ 1pm-2am) It didn't take long after 1989 for communism to become a design trend, though you wouldn't exactly call the tongue-in-cheek décor at this café-club nostalgic. Lenin oversees the rowdy proceedings with suitably patriarchal disdain, swamped by a frenzy of predemocracy tat.

Muchos Patatos (☎ 851 91 73; ul Szewska 2; ☿ 4pm-2am Mon-Sat) We're not sure where the potatoes come into it, but within these red-yellow walls the Latin craze has never gone away, making it a firm favourite with a lively crowd of cocktail-drinking, hip-shaking *chicas* and *chicos*.

Czarna Owca (☎ 855 32 40; ul Jaskółcza 13; ☿ from noon Mon-Fri, from 7pm Sat & Sun) Calling your pub the 'Black Sheep' hardly encourages good behaviour, and sipping a quiet half is seldom on the agenda here. When you've finished boozing in the dark, intimate bar (baa?), join the herd on the downstairs dance floor.

Piwnica 21 (☎ 855 18 27; ul Wielka 21; ☿ from 5pm) On the good nights this brick basement bar is packed with music fans taking in DJs, or classic live pub gigs in a jazz-blues vein, helped on by table football and draft stout. On the quiet nights it's empty and distinctly chilly. If you'd rather have the former, weekends are a good bet.

Pole Café (☎ 853 28 37; ul Jaskółcza 16; ☿ 1-10pm Mon-Sat, 4-10pm Sun) This tiny, dimly lit café never seems to have anyone in it, but if you don't mind being first through the door you'll find a great little coffeehouse with allegedly some of the best cheesecake around.

Galeria i Scena Anny Kareńskiej (☎ 852 08 85; ul Kramarska 15; ☿ 11am-10pm) Dresden china, chintz armchairs, antique watercolours – this gallery-café looks purpose-built to pump high tea into old ladies who probably used to lunch. If you're a fan of quaint English tearooms you'll love it.

Nargila Klub (☎ 855 10 26; ul Kozia 5/4; ☿ 2pm-midnight) If you don't know what a narghile is, one look at the generic Turkish-Arabic décor here should give you a clue. Whether you call it a sheesha, hookah, hubble-bubble or water pipe, you can bung in some flavoured tobacco and puff away on the snug cushions and carpets. Unlike the real Muslim versions, however, you can buy alcohol too.

ENTERTAINMENT

Poznań's comprehensive what's-on monthly *iks* (4zł) contains listings and comments on everything from museums to outdoor activities. It's in Polish, but has a short summary of the most important events in English. It's available from Ruch kiosks and the tourist offices (p326). The free monthlies *Aktivist* and *City Magazine Poznań* can also be helpful, especially for nightlife.

Clubs

Eskulap (☎ 869 44 29; www.eskulapklub.pl in Polish; ul Przybyszewskiego 39; admission 15-30zł; ☿ Tue-Sat) Part of the student cultural centre at Poznań's University of Medical Sciences, Eskulap consistently hosts the biggest and brightest dance nights in town, bringing in as many serious clubbers as wasted medics.

Trendy (☎ 663 61 98; ul Piekary 5; ☿ from 8am) Ignore the terrible name – this chic bar-club does actually have some quite funky metallic décor going on, and the music policy favours electronic dance beats that bring out as much partying as posing.

Czerwony Fortepian (☎ 852 01 74; www.czerwony-fortepian.pl; ul Wroniecka 18; ☿ from 5pm Mon-Sat, 2-10pm Sun) A smart bar-restaurant and jazz joint for upscale aficionados who know their swing from their scat and their cigars from their elbows.

Charyzma (☎ 851 79 48; ul Ślusarska 6; ☿ from 3pm) No overbearing personality here, just an intelligent, low-key sense of cool and some well-chosen, left-field dance music. People come to Charyzma because they actually like the place, which is high praise indeed.

Deep (☎ 855 73 02; ul Wrocławska 5; ☿ from 8pm) One for the townies, this underground den is a hotbed of sportswear, short skirts

---

GET OUT OF TOWN!

Poznań has a reasonable selection of dance venues, but for dedicated clubbers around the country there's only one place to go for a real weekender: Manieczki. Never heard of it? Hardly surprising – you'll have trouble finding it on any large-scale map. And when you do eventually track it down, you'll have even more trouble believing that this tiny town south of the Wielkopolska National Park could ever be a nightlife mecca.

Roll up at the weekend, however, and you will quickly be persuaded otherwise. Manieczki is home to **Ekwador** (☎ 282 08 50; www.ekwador.com.pl in Polish; ul Wybickiego; ☽ Fri & Sat), possibly the most famous club in Poland and a consistent ambassador for dance music at home and abroad. The list of visiting DJs is stellar; it's the only Polish club to be represented at the Berlin Love Parade; and the massive special events here are legendary. The Amsterdam Dance Mission in May is the country's biggest technofest, kicking off on the shores of Lake Malta.

If you can't make it to the club itself, parties are held in more accessible venues around the country; look out for the summer Sunrise event (the location changes every year). If you are near Poznań on the weekend, though, this place is as essential as Fabric or the Ministry in London and Twilo in New York. Turn up, tune in and reach for the lasers.

It's easiest to get here with your own transport, but there are a few buses each day from Poznań (7zł, 1¼ hours).

---

and bumpin' black music. Good for rowdy nights out with your mates.

Live Music

As well as the Dubliner, Balzac and Bogota pubs, the Centrum Kultury Zamek is also home to the **Blue Note Jazz Club** (☎ 851 04 08; www.bluenote.poznan.pl; ul Św Marcin 80/82), a major live jazz spot and occasional dance club, which holds regular concerts and jam sessions by local groups and occasional big-name gigs.

Classical Music, Opera & Ballet

Filharmonia (Philharmonic Hall; ☎ 852 47 08; info@filhar monia.poznan.pl; ul Św Marcin 81) Under the direction of Spanish conductor José Maria Florêncio, the Poznań Philharmonic Hall holds concerts at least weekly, performed by the house symphony orchestra, often featuring visiting artists. Poznań also has Poland's best boys choir, the Polskie Słowiki (Polish Nightingales), who can be heard here.

Teatr Wielki (Grand Theatre; ☎ 659 02 00; www .opera.poznan.pl; ul Fredry 9) The Grand Theatre is the usual stage for opera, ballet and various visiting performances. The annual Verdi festival is a particular highlight, and you should also look out for productions by the renowned Polski Teatr Tańca dance group.

Theatre

Teatr Polski (Polish Theatre; ☎ 852 56 27; www.teatr -polski.pl; ul 27 Grudnia 8/10) The Polish Theatre is Poznań's main repertory stage, with a sound reputation and plenty of classics such as Chekhov and Kafka on the programme, alongside newer Polish works.

Teatr Nowy (New Theatre; ☎ 847 24 40; www.teatr nowy.pl; ul Dąbrowskiego 5) Another important city theatre, this one tends towards more contemporary productions, spread over several stages. Adaptations of US plays and films are particularly popular, covering everything from David Mamet and Woody Allen to Elizabeth Taylor.

Teatr Ósmego Dnia (Theatre of the Eighth Day; ☎ 855 20 86; osmego.dnia.info.poznan.pl; ul Ratajczaka 44) One of Poland's best alternative theatre groups, founded in the 1960s as an avant-garde, politically involved student troupe. It's still impressive and creative, performing more outdoors than indoors and playing with a lot of group improvisation.

Teatr Biuro Podróży (Travel Agency Theatre; ☎ 0605 217 668; www.teatrbiuropodrozy.ipoznan.pl) The Travel Agency Theatre is also an excellent street theatre group that's gaining countrywide acclaim for its spectacular productions and collaborating with various international projects.

GETTING THERE & AWAY
Air

Poznań's **airport** (☎ 849 23 43; www.airport-poznan .com.pl) is in the western suburb of Ławica, 7km from the centre. There are flights from Poznań to Warsaw (four daily), Brussels (two weekly), Copenhagen (up to three daily), Munich (up to three daily), Frankfurt (daily) and London (three weekly).

Bus

The **PKS bus terminal** (☎ 664 25 25; www.pks.poznan .pl in Polish; ul Towarowa 19) is about 750m east of the train station. Buses run half-hourly to Kórnik (5.40zł, 40 minutes) and every couple of hours to Rogalin (6.40zł, one hour). You can also get to Kórnik by hourly suburban bus NB from ul Św Marcin. Buses to Gniezno (9.80zł, 1½ hours) depart at least hourly and go via either Kostrzyn or Pobiedziska; the latter pass Lake Lednica (6.40zł). On longer routes, you could use buses to get to Kalisz (18zł, 2½ hours, nine daily) and Zielona Góra (22zł, 2¾ hours, eight daily), as they run more frequently than trains.

Train

Poznań is a busy railway hub. From **Poznań Główny train station** (☎ 866 12 12; ul Dworcowa 1) there are about 20 trains to Warsaw daily (InterCity/fast 88.50zł/43zł, three to 3½ hours), including luxury InterCity and Euro-City trains. Equally frequent services run to Wrocław (InterCity/fast/slow 67.40zł/ 31.85zł/19.70zł, two to three hours) and Szczecin (InterCity/fast 55.80zł/36.12zł, 2½ to three hours), and there are also six direct trains to Kraków (express/fast 80zł/49zł, six to seven hours).

Trains to Gdańsk (43.04zł, 4¾ hours, seven daily) and Toruń (fast/slow 30.03zł/ 18.60zł, 142km, four daily) all pass via Gniezno (fast/slow 15.90zł/9.30zł, 45 minutes). Seven trains depart for Zielona Góra daily (28.38zł, 2¼ hours).

Six international trains run to Berlin daily (145zł, 261km), including four Euro-City services taking just three hours. There are also direct trains to Brussels, Budapest, Cologne, Kyiv and Moscow.

Tickets and couchette reservations are handled by the train station, travel agencies and **PKP office** (☎ 863 12 90; Al Niepodległości 8A).

GETTING AROUND
To/From the Airport

Poznań's airport is accessible by several bus lines (2.40zł, 25 minutes), Nos 59, 77 and 78, which all run into town as far as Rondo Kaponiera, near the train station (the stop's called Bałtyk). A taxi should cost around 20zł (10 minutes).

Public Transport

Poznań's public transport system uses both timed and distance-based tickets. Timed tickets cost 1.20zł for a 10-minute ride, 2.40zł for half an hour, 3.60zł for up to one hour, and 4.80zł for 1½ hours. Approximate journey times are posted at stops. Distance-based tickets cost 1.80zł for a ride of up to 10 stops and 3zł for any longer trip. A day ticket costs 10.20zł (and is far less complicated to work out!).

AROUND POZNAŃ

KÓRNIK
☎ 61 / pop 6000

The village of Kórnik, 20km southeast of Poznań, wouldn't attract much attention if it wasn't for its squat, sturdy **castle**. Built by the powerful Górka family in the 15th century, it changed hands several times and was much altered in later periods. Its present-day appearance dates from the mid-19th century, when its owner, Tytus Działyński, gave the castle a somewhat eccentric mock-Gothic character, partly based on a design by German architect Karl Friedrich Schinkel. The building now looks as though two halves of completely different castles were spliced together, perhaps by force, and provides some interesting photos from varying angles.

The interior, too, was extensively (though more consistently) remodelled to provide a plush family home and accommodate the owner's vast art collection. On the 1st floor a spectacular Moorish hall was created (clearly influenced by the Alhambra in Granada) as a memorable setting for the display of armour and military accessories. The collection was expanded by Działyński's son Jan and his nephew Władysław Zamoyski; the latter donated the castle and its contents to the state in 1924.

The castle luckily survived the war and, miraculously, so did its contents. Part of it is now open as a **museum** (☎ 817 00 81; ul Zamkowa 5; adult/concession 8/4zł; ⏱ 9am-5.30pm Mon-Fri, 10am-5pm Sat & Sun). You can wander through its fully furnished and decorated 19th-century interiors, some of which have family collections on display. Make sure you don the

WIELKOPOLSKA

slippers handed out at the entrance – the amazing wooden floors are original and the result of an intensive restoration process, so scuff marks are not appreciated.

Behind the castle is a large, English-style park known as the **Arboretum** (☎ 817 01 55; adult/concession 3/2zł; ⏰ 9am-5pm May-Sep, 9am-3pm Oct-Apr), which was laid out during the castle's reconstruction. Numerous exotic species of trees and shrubs were imported from leading European nurseries, and Kórnik was considered to be the best-stocked park in the country. Many species were later transplanted to Gołuchów, where Jan Działyński was creating his new residence. Today the Arboretum is run by a scientific research institute and has some 2500 plant species and varieties; the best times to visit are May to June and September to October, when the greatest number of specimens come into flower.

Some of the castle's outbuildings are also used for exhibitions. **Galeria Klaudynowka** (adult/concession 2/1zł; ⏰ 10am-4pm Tue-Sun), a servants' house from 1791, displays contemporary paintings, while the **powozownia** (coach house; admission free), on the opposite side of the road, holds three London coaches, brought from Paris by Jan Działyński in 1856.

Getting There & Away

There's frequent bus transport from Poznań to Kórnik (5.40zł, 40 minutes). You can either take the PKS bus from the central bus terminal (departing every half hour or so) or go by suburban bus NB from ul Św Marcin (hourly). Both deposit you at the Rynek in Kórnik, a three-minute walk to the castle.

If you plan to continue on to Rogalin (3.70zł, 25 minutes), there are approximately two buses daily (check the timetable before visiting the castle).

ROGALIN

☎ 61 / pop 800

The tiny village of Rogalin, 13km west of Kórnik, was the seat of yet another Polish aristocratic clan, the Raczyński family, who built a **palace** here in the closing decades of the 18th century, and lived in it until WWII. Typical of such country residences of the period, the complex included a garden, park and some outbuildings complete with stables and coach house. Plundered but not damaged during WWII, the palace was taken over by the state and is today a branch of Poznań's **National Museum** (☎ 813 80 30; adult/concession 8/5.50zł, free Wed; ⏰ 10am-4pm Tue-Sun). It's an excellent place to visit, despite the overzealous staff members, who tend to follow you around the collections like suspicious store detectives.

Less visited than Kórnik's castle and much more Germanic in its appearance, the Rogalin palace consists of a massive, two-storey, baroque central structure and two modest symmetrical wings linked to the main body by curving galleries, forming a giant horseshoe around a vast forecourt. The main house was closed at the time of writing due to snail-paced restoration, but the wings were open and used for temporary displays of some of the Raczyński collection. Don't miss the delightful orangery downstairs in the historic (left-hand) wing.

Just beyond the left wing is the **Gallery of Painting** (Galeria Obrazów), an adapted greenhouse displaying Polish and European canvases from the 19th and early 20th centuries. The Polish collection includes some first-class work, with Jacek Malczewski best represented. The side room with portraits by lesser-known artists is particularly interesting, stylistically. The dominant work, though, is Jan Matejko's *Joan of Arc*.

In the **coach house**, near the front courtyard, are a dozen old coaches, including Poznań's last horse-drawn cab.

Opposite the main house is a small French garden, which leads into the larger **English landscaped park**, originally laid out in primeval oak forest. Not much of the park's design can be deciphered today, but the ancient oak trees are still here. The three most imposing specimens have been fenced off and baptised with the names Lech, Czech and Rus, after the legendary founders of the Polish, Czech and Russian nations. Rus is the largest at 9m in circumference, and also seems to be in the best health – interpret that as you will.

One more place to see is the **chapel**, on the eastern outskirts of the village. It was built in the 1820s to serve as a mausoleum for the Raczyński family and is a replica of the Roman temple known as the Maison Carrée in Nîmes, southern France. The vaulted crypt beneath the church houses several dilapidated tombstones. The priest living in the house behind the church may open it for you.

If you're particularly smitten with the palace, or just miss the last bus, you can stay in the row of former servants' **cottages** (s/d 80/92zł) in the French garden.

Getting There & Away

There are several buses from Poznań to Rogalin (6.40zł, one hour), going by various routes. Buses back to Poznań pass through every couple of hours till late afternoon, but at the time of writing no timetable was displayed – ask the palace staff, or just hang around and grab the first thing going towards Kórnik.

WIELKOPOLSKA NATIONAL PARK

☎ 61

The 76-sq-km **Wielkopolska National Park** (Wielkopolski Park Narodowy; ☎ 813 22 06; wpnarod@optimus .poznan.pl) is just a few kilometres southwest of Poznań's administrative boundaries. About 80% of the park is forest – pine and oak being the dominant species – and its postglacial lakes give it a certain charm. It's reputedly one of the most interesting stretches of land in Wielkopolska, for its diversity and for the variety of flora and fauna concentrated in its small area. It can be a pleasant day away from the city rush.

The best way to see the park is on foot – **hiking** is the main attraction here, and there are walking trails leading into it from different sides. If you plan on a day trip, a good point to start is the town of Mosina (21km from Poznań), which is served regularly by both train and bus from Poznań. From Mosina, follow the blue-marked trail heading northwest to Osowa Góra (3km). Once you reach small Lake Kociołek, switch to the red trail which winds southwestwards. After passing another miniature lake, the trail reaches Lake Góreckie, the most beautiful body of water in the park. The trail then skirts the eastern part of the lake and turns northeast to bring you to the town of Puszczykowo, from where trains and buses can take you back to Poznań. It's about a 17km walk altogether, through what's probably the most attractive area of the park.

If you want to do more walking, there are four more trails to choose from. They cover most of the park and cross each other at several points. Get a copy of the TopMapa *Wielkopolski Park Narodowy* map (scale 1:35,000), which has all the details.

Accommodation is available in Puszczykowo and Mosina, in case you decide on a longer stay. The two towns sit conveniently on the eastern edge of the park, just 4km apart on the Poznań–Wrocław railway line. There's regular transport in both directions to/from Mosina (4.60zł, 20 minutes) and to/from Puszczykowo (3.80zł, 15 minutes).

MORASKO

☎ 61

Now here's something you don't see everyday – just 10km from the centre of Poznań, a small patch of ground near the Góra Moraska hill has been designated a natural reserve, not for its rare flora but for the massive **meteorite craters** that pepper the area. The Reserwat Meteoryt Morasko is one of just two registered impact sites in Europe, a real thrill for geologists and researchers. The idea of great balls of flaming space rock crash-landing in the peaceful forest here may seem bizarre, but that's exactly what happened roughly 10,000 years ago, and eight craters are still clearly visible, some filled with water. The largest is over 100m across and 13m in depth, and while it's overgrown enough not to look like the surface of the moon, the extent of the dent is still pretty impressive.

To get here you can catch tram 12, 14 or 15 from the train station and either go to Sobieskiego and walk 4km or change at Szymanowskiego for bus 88 to Morasko village.

THE PIAST ROUTE

The Piast Route (Szlak Piastowski) is a popular tourist route, winding from Poznań to Kruszwica, that is followed by many tour buses and private vehicles. It covers places related to the early centuries of the Polish state, and other historic monuments, including the Iron-Age village of Biskupin. Anyone with an interest in premedieval history will be in their element, and even nonenthusiasts should appreciate the insights into the formative years of a much-evolved nation.

LAKE LEDNICA

☎ 61

Lake Lednica, 30km east of Poznań, is the first important point on the Piast Route. The 7km-long elongated postglacial lake has four islands, the largest of which, Ostrów Lednicki, was an important defensive and administrative outpost of the early Polish state.

Excavations have shown that Ostrów Lednicki was one of the major settlements of the first Piasts in the late 10th and early 11th centuries, rivalling Poznań and Gniezno. It was settled as early as the Stone Age, and in the 10th century a stronghold was built here, along with a stone palace and a church. Two wooden bridges were constructed to link the island to the lake's western and eastern shores, and it was over these bridges that the route between Poznań and Gniezno ran. The western bridge was 428m long and its foundations were nearly 12m under water at the deepest point.

The settlement was overrun by the Bohemians and destroyed in 1038, and though the church and the defensive ramparts were rebuilt, the island never regained its importance. Between the 12th and 14th centuries a large part of it was used as a graveyard. Some 2000 tombs have been found here, making the site the largest cemetery from that period discovered in Central Europe.

Some of the finds of the excavations are on display in the museum established opposite the island, and there's also an interesting skansen (open-air museum of traditional architecture) nearby. If that all sounds a bit dry for you, try to visit during the annual Archaeological Gala, when the costumes and axes come out for a panoply of historically themed events.

Sights

MUSEUM OF THE FIRST PIASTS

On the lakeshore facing the island of Ostrów Lednicki is the **Museum of the First Piasts** (Muzeum Pierwszych Piastów; ☎ 427 50 10; www .lednicamuzeum.pl in Polish; Lednogóra; adult/concession 5/3zł; ☑ 9am-5pm Tue-Sun 14 Feb-31 Oct). Among the buildings in the grounds is the oldest windmill in Poland (built in 1585), and an 18th-century granary, which has a display of human remains excavated on the island and at the cemetery behind the museum.

The main exhibition is in the church-like building, which has two floors of finds from excavations on and around the island. Among the exhibits, most of which date from the 10th and 11th centuries, are weapons, household items and implements, pottery, ornaments, and a dugout canoe, which is one of the very few wooden objects to have survived for almost a millennium.

A small boat takes visitors (between mid-April and October) from the museum's jetty to the island of Ostrów Lednicki, 175m away, where you can see what's left of the palace and the church. The foundations and lower parts of the walls are still in place and give a rough idea of how big the complex was. There are some helpful drawings in the museum of what the buildings might have looked like.

WIELKOPOLSKA ETHNOGRAPHIC PARK

Two kilometres south of the museum, also on the lakeshore, is the **Wielkopolska Ethnographic Park** (Wielkopolski Park Etnograficzny; ☎ 427 50 40; Dziekanowice; adult/concession 5/3zł; ☑ 9am-3pm Tue-Sun 15 Feb-14 Apr & 1-15 Nov, 9am-5pm Tue-Sun 15-30 Apr & 1 Jul-31 Oct, 10am-6pm Tue-Sun 1 May-30 Jun, closed 16 Nov-14 Feb). It's on the eastern side of the lake, 500m north of the Poznań–Gniezno road.

The skansen features a good selection of 19th-century rural architecture from Wielkopolska. About half of a typical village has been re-created so far and several houses can be visited. Just to the south is a manor house and its outbuildings, but they're occupied by the administration and can only be seen from the outside.

A combined ticket covering entry to the museum and the skansen costs 8zł for adults and 5zł concession.

Getting There & Away

The lake lies on the Poznań–Gniezno road and there's a regular bus service between the two cities – up to 12 daily to/from Poznań (6.40zł) and to/from Gniezno (4.50zł). From whichever end you start, take the bus via Pobiedziska, not via Kostrzyn. Coming from Poznań, you'll see three old windmills on the hill to the left of the road; stay on the bus for another 2.5km and get off at the turn-off to Komorowo (the bus stop is just by the turn-off). From here it's a five-minute walk to the skansen, then another 2km walk on a sealed road will bring you to the museum.

GNIEZNO

☎ 61 / pop 73,000

Looking at Gniezno (*gnyez*-no) today you'd never think of it as a political hot spot, but history would have it otherwise – the town has been both a royal and religious seat in its time, and is commonly considered to be the cradle of the Polish state, for it was here that the dispersed tribes of the region were first unified in the 10th century.

The present-day town shows little sign of its former influence, leading an unremarkable existence as a typical modern piece of urban fabric. The old town has some charm, however, and sees a bit of life at times, and visitors can still admire the great cathedral that once put Gniezno on the map.

History

Legend has it that Gniezno was founded by the mythical Lech, the grandson of the original legendary Piast and the grandfather of Mieszko I. While hunting in the area, young Lech found the *gniazdo* (nest) of a white eagle, giving the town its name and the nation its emblem. (The man himself had to settle for having a beer named after him.)

In historical terms, the settlement most likely existed since the 7th or 8th century, and was initially the centre of a pagan cult. Archaeological excavations have shown that by the end of the 8th century, Gniezno was already fortified with wood and earth ramparts, and had regular trade links with commercial centres far outside the region.

This early development contributed to the key role that the town played. Duke Mieszko I is thought to have been baptised here in 966, thus raising the autonomous region of Wielkopolska from obscurity to the rank of Christianised nations.

Despite this, Mieszko seems to have favoured Poznań as a city, and as records are scarce some historians have argued that Gniezno was never officially Wielkopolska's capital – the first cathedral was, after all, built in Poznań, and the ruler was buried there.

Gniezno came to the fore again in the year 1000, when the archbishopric was established here, and its position was further strengthened in 1025 when Bolesław Chrobry was crowned in the local cathedral as the first Polish king. Only 13 years later, the Bohemians invaded, devastating the entire region, and prompting the Poles to shift their seat of power to the more secure Kraków.

This inevitably deprived the town of its importance, though kings were crowned in Gniezno until the end of the 13th century. The town retained its status as the seat of the Church of Poland and is still the formal ecclesiastical capital, even if the archbishops are only occasional guests these days.

Information

Bank Pekao (☎ 424 19 81; ul Dąbrówki 14)
Interngniezno (☎ 424 19 96; ul Bolesława Chrobrego 32; per hr 2-2.50zł; ☼ 8am-10pm Mon-Fri, 9am-10pm Sat, 10am-10pm Sun) Internet access.
Internet Pub Małpa (☎ 424 55 59; ul Tumska 15; per hr 3zł; ☼ 8.30am-11pm Mon-Fri, noon-midnight Sat, 2-11pm Sun)
Post office (☎ 426 12 26; ul Bolesława Chrobrego 36)
Tourist office (☎ 428 41 00; ul Tumska 12; ☼ 9am-5pm Mon-Fri, 9am-3pm Sat, 10am-2pm Sun)

Sights
CATHEDRAL

Understandably, Gniezno's heart and soul is rooted in its **cathedral** (☎ 0602 708 231; ☼ 9am-5pm May-Sep, 9am-4pm Mar, Apr & Oct, by appointment Nov-Feb), an imposing, double-towered, brick Gothic structure, which looks pretty similar to the one in Poznań. The present church is already the third or fourth building on this site (the first was built in the 970s), and was constructed in the second half of the 14th century after the destruction of the Romanesque cathedral by the Teutonic Knights in 1331. It changed a lot in later periods: chapels sprouted all around it, and the interior was redecorated in successive styles. After considerable damage in WWII, it was rebuilt according to the original Gothic structure.

Inside, the focal point is the elaborate silver **sarcophagus of St Adalbert**, which is in the chancel. The baroque coffin was the work of Peter van der Rennen and was made in 1662 in Gdańsk. It's topped with the semireclining figure of the saint, who looks remarkably lively considering his unfortunate demise.

Adalbert was a Bohemian bishop who passed through Gniezno in 997, on a missionary trip to convert the Prussians, a heathen Baltic tribe inhabiting what is now Masuria in northeastern Poland. The pagans were less than enthusiastic about accepting the new faith and terminated the bishop's efforts by cutting off his head.

Bolesław Chrobry recovered the bishop's body, paying its weight in gold, then buried it in Gniezno's cathedral in 999. In the same year, Pope Sylvester canonised the martyr. This contributed to Gniezno's elevation to an archbishopric a year later, and also led to the placing of several important memorials to the saint in the church.

One of these is the red marble **tombstone of St Adalbert**, made in around 1480 by Hans Brandt. Unfortunately, it has been moved from the middle of the church to behind the high altar and it's impossible to get close enough to see it.

Easier to appreciate are two carved tombstones on the back wall of the church. To the left is the red marble **tomb of Primate Zbig-**

niew Oleśnicki, attributed to Veit Stoss; and to the right, the late-15th-century bronze **tomb of Archbishop Jakub** from Sienna. Also note an expressive wooden crucifix from around 1440, placed high on the rood beam at the entrance to the chancel.

The most precious possession of the church is the pair of Romanesque **bronze doors** from about 1175, in the back of the right-hand (southern) aisle, at the entrance from the porch. Undeniably one of the best examples of Romanesque art in Europe, the doors depict, in bas-relief, 18 scenes from the life of St Adalbert. They are ordered chronologically from the bottom side of the left-hand door – where the birth of the saint is portrayed – up to its top and then

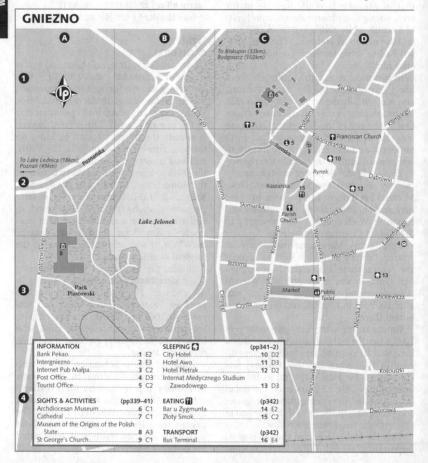

GNIEZNO

INFORMATION
Bank Pekao	**1** E2
Intergniezno	**2** E3
Internet Pub Małpa	**3** C2
Post Office	**4** D3
Tourist Office	**5** C2

SIGHTS & ACTIVITIES (pp339–41)
Archdiocesan Museum	**6** C1
Cathedral	**7** C1
Museum of the Origins of the Polish State	**8** A3
St George's Church	**9** C1

SLEEPING (pp341–2)
City Hotel	**10** D2
Hotel Awo	**11** D3
Hotel Pietrak	**12** D2
Internat Medycznego Studium Zawodowego	**13** D3

EATING (p342)
Bar u Zygmunta	**14** E2
Złoty Smok	**15** C2

TRANSPORT (p342)
Bus Terminal	**16** E4

WIELKOPOLSKA

down the other door to the final scene of the burial in the cathedral.

Framing the doors is the exquisite 15th-century **Gothic portal** with the scene of the Last Judgment in its tympanum. In the opposite porch, right across the nave, is another elaborate **Gothic portal**, dating from the same period, this one with the scene of the Crucifixion in its tympanum.

The nearby entrance in the back wall of the church leads downstairs to the **basement**, where the relics of the previous Romanesque cathedral can be seen, along with the Gothic tombstones of the bishops.

All along the aisles and the ambulatory are **chapels**, built from the 15th to 18th centuries, and separated from the aisles by decorative wrought-iron screens. There are 17 screens in all, ranging in style from Gothic via Renaissance to baroque, and comprising one of the most beautiful collections of its kind to be gathered in a single church in Poland. Inside the chapels, there are some fine tombstones, altarpieces, paintings and wall decorations – well worth a closer look.

One interesting modern artwork sits in the body of the church: a **statue of Cardinal Stefan Wyszyński**, the Polish primate credited with persuading the Soviets to relax their antireligious stance during the communist era. The panelled piece shows various scenes from the cardinal's eventful life and career.

You can look around the interior free of charge, except for the **bronze doors and basement** (adult/concession 5/2zł; 9-11.45am & 1-5pm May-Sep, to 4pm Mar, Apr & Oct), both of which are visited with a guide. English- or German-speaking guides may be available for 45-minute cathedral tours at around 80zł per group – inquire at the office in the porch opposite the doors.

MUSEUMS

The **Museum of the Origins of the Polish State** (Muzeum Początków Państwa Polskiego; ☎ 426 46 41; ul Kostrzewskiego 1; adult/concession 5.50/3.50zł; 9.30am-5.30pm Tue-Sun), on the far side of Lake Jelonek, illustrates Gniezno's pivotal role in Polish history. The permanent collection contains archaeological finds, architectural details, documents and works of art, all relating to the development of the Polish nation from pre-Slavic times to the end of the Piast dynasty. The museum also runs an audiovisual presentation about Poland under the Piasts (English soundtrack available) and hosts temporary displays on tangential themes.

Near the cathedral and behind St George's Church (Kościół Św Jerzego), the **Archdiocesan Museum** (Muzeum Archidiecezji Gnieźnieńskiej; ☎ 426 37 78; ul Kolegiaty 2; admission 3zł; 10am-4pm Tue-Sun Apr-Oct, 9am-3pm Tue-Sat Nov-Mar) holds a collection of sacral sculpture and painting, liturgical fabrics, coffin portraits and votive offerings. The building is one of several houses built in the 18th and 19th centuries as homes for the canons and priests.

Sleeping

Hotel Pietrak (☎ 426 14 97; www.pietrak.pl; ul Bolesława Chrobrego 3; s/d 160/190zł; P) Located in two 18th-century burghers' houses, just shy of

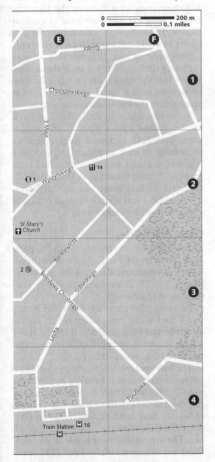

WIELKOPOLSKA

the Rynek, the Pietrak provides the best facilities in town, with minibars, data ports, a fitness centre with spa and dedicated disabled access. The restaurant (mains from 9zł to 35zł) is also a quality choice.

Hotel Awo (☎ 426 11 97; www.hotel-awo.pl; ul Warszawska 32; s/d/tr/q 150/170/210/250zł) This midrange place is no match for the Pietrak but is still perfectly comfortable, and the staff here act less like the hotel's doing you a favour by existing. It's right by the city market; potentially noisy for south-facing rooms.

City Hotel (☎ 425 35 35; Rynek 15; r 65-90zł, ste 100zł) The City doesn't really make the most of a potentially prestigious position right on the Rynek – the sofa beds and dodgy green-brown colours aren't what you'd call classy. That said, the price is right, the rooms and the café look out onto the square, and you really can't get much closer to the cathedral.

Internat Medycznego Studium Zawodowego (☎ 426 34 09; ul Mieszka I 27; d 65zł; ℗) Gniezno's medical college rents out 24 double rooms to the general public. The rooms are quiet, neat and ample – excellent value. One bathroom is shared between four adjacent rooms. The Internat is at the back Medical School (Zespół Szkół Medycznych) compound; enter by the gate from ul Mieszka I.

Eating

Złoty Smok (☎ 426 74 08; ul Kaszarska 1; mains 8-32zł; ☺ lunch & dinner) The Golden Dragon is a pretty standard Chinese restaurant in general terms, but stands out as about the only adventurous eating choice in the town centre. It's popular with locals and the staff's relatives seem to eat here too – always a good sign.

Bar U Zygmunta (☎ 426 37 74; ul Wyszyńskiego 20; mains 0.60-5.10zł; ☺ breakfast & lunch) Out in the more modern part of town, this self-service cafeteria has a good claim to being the cheapest budget eatery in the central area, and has a fine grasp of milk-bar standards.

Getting There & Away
BUS
Buses travel to Poznań (9.80zł, 1½ hours) from the **bus terminal** (☎ 426 38 93; ul Dworcowa) at least once hourly; if you want to stop at Lake Lednica (4.50zł, 35 minutes), take one that goes via Pobiedziska (up to 13 daily).

There are nine daily buses running to Żnin (6.40zł, one hour), where you can

change for the narrow-gauge train going to Biskupin or you can just walk the 2km.

TRAIN
Trains run regularly throughout the day to Poznań (fast/slow 15.90zł/9.30zł, 45 minutes/one hour), and in the opposite direction to Inowrocław (9.10zł, 55 minutes). There are also departures to Bydgoszcz (26.24zł, 1¾ hours, 13 daily), to Toruń (14.50zł, 1¾ hours, five daily), to Gdańsk (41.24zł, four hours, six daily) and to Wrocław (36.12zł, 3½ hours, six daily).

BISKUPIN
☎ 52
Biskupin is a fortified lake town built about 2730 years ago by a tribe of the Lusatian culture, which at that time lived in Central Europe. The settlement was accidentally discovered in 1933 and unearthed from beneath a thick layer of turf. It is the only known surviving Iron-Age town in Poland, and proves that the region was already inhabited by well-organised social groups over 1600 years before the Polish state was born.

Today the site is an intriguing flashback to the distant past – parts of the settlement have been recreated to give visitors something to look at amid the forest and lakeland, and the distinctive thatched huts are meticulously maintained. With so much of Polish culture rooted in the medieval, it would be a real shame to miss out on a glimpse of what came before.

Sights & Activities
The Iron-Age town, together with the park lying between the road and the lake shore, form the **Archaeological Reserve** (Rezerwat Archeologiczny; ☎ 302 50 25; adult/concession 6/4zł; ☺ 9am-6pm, closes at dusk in winter).

Entering the complex from the road, you'll find a car park, ticket office, half a dozen budget food outlets and several stalls selling souvenirs and publications about the site (including some in English).

The **Iron-Age town** lies on the peninsula in the northern end of the park, a five-minute walk from the entrance. The gateway, a fragment of the defensive wall and two rows of houses have been reconstructed to give some idea of what the town once looked like. The interiors of a few houses have been fitted out as they may have been 2700 years ago. From the wharf near the gateway, a **pleasure boat** (trips 4zł) departs several times a day for a short trip around the lake.

The **museum**, halfway between the peninsula and the park's entrance, shows finds excavated on and around the island, together with background information (there's some English signage) about the place and the people. There's also a model of the town as it once looked.

Getting There & Away
BUS
From the bus stop at the entrance to the Archaeological Reserve, buses run every hour or two north to Żnin (2.40zł, 20 minutes) and south to Gąsawa (2.20zł, 10 minutes). For Gniezno, go to Żnin (7zł, 1¼ hours) and change.

TRAIN
The narrow-gauge tourist train operates from May to September between Żnin (40 minutes) and Gąsawa (10 minutes), passing Biskupin on the way. There are five trains daily (six in July and August) in either direction between 9am and 4pm. In Żnin, the station is alongside the standard-gauge train station; in Gąsawa it's 700m

southwest of the Rynek on the Gniezno road. In Biskupin, it's right by the entrance to the reserve. Tickets cost 6zł one way, 11zł return.

STRZELNO
☎ 52 / pop 6000
Strzelno (*stshel*-no) boasts two of the best Romanesque churches in the region and a museum. It's a good side trip for architecture buffs and church-art fans.

Sights
Strzelno's attractions are all next to each other, 200m east of the Rynek. The churches are usually locked, but a local guide **Damian Rybak** (☎ 318 33 30; churches 2zł, museum 2zł; ☯ 9am-5pm Mon-Sat, 1.30-5pm Sun) runs tours.

ST PROCOPIUS' CHURCH
Built of red stone in around 1150, **St Procopius' Church** (Kościół Św Prokopa; Plac Św Wojciecha) has preserved its austere Romanesque form remarkably well, even though its upper part was rebuilt in brick after damage in the 18th century. It has a circular nave, with a square chancel on one side and a tower on the other, the whole adorned with typical semicircular apses on the northern side of

WIELKOPOLSKA

IRON LIFE

The Iron-Age settlement of Biskupin was built around 740–730 BC, taking just a few years to be constructed in its entirety. Following a complicated and highly organised plan, the island was encircled by a 6m-high barricade consisting of a wooden framework filled with earth and sand. The island's shores were reinforced with a palisade of about 20,000 oak stakes driven into the lake bottom, which served as a breakwater and an obstacle for potential invaders. The only access to the town was through a gateway topped with a watchtower and connected to the lake shore by a 250m-long bridge.

Within the defensive walls, 13 parallel rows of houses were laid out with streets between them, the whole encircled by a street running inside the ramparts. Over 100 houses were built, each inhabited by one family of seven to 10 members. The total population of the settlement was about 800 to 1000 people, which probably constituted a big city for its inhabitants. The town was essentially self-sufficient, but also benefited from nearby trade routes.

Around 400 BC the town was destroyed, most likely by the Scythians, and was never rebuilt. This was essentially because of climatic changes, which caused the lake's level to rise, making the island uninhabitable. The remains of the wooden structure were preserved in mud and silt for 2300 years. Early in the 20th century the water level began to drop and the island re-emerged, eventually turning into a peninsula, as it is today.

A lot of effort was put into reconstructing the houses and ramparts when the town was rediscovered, and the results haven't just impressed the steady trickle of tourists who come here. The authenticity and location of the site have made it a favourite with Polish filmmakers, and Biskupin has already appeared in Jerzy Hoffman's historical epics *Stara Baśń* (2003) and *Ogniem i Mieczem* (1999), as well as the TV series *Sagala*. In some small way, the Iron Age is back.

the nave. The interior, almost free of decoration, looks admirably authentic. By the entrance is the original 12th-century font.

CHURCH OF THE HOLY TRINITY

Built a decade or two after its neighbour, the larger **Church of the Holy Trinity** (Kościół Św Trójcy; Plac Św Wojciecha) was later changed significantly. It acquired a Gothic vault in the 14th century and a baroque façade four centuries later. The interior has mainly baroque furnishings, including the high altar and a decorative rood beam, which form a remarkably harmonious composition with Gothic vaulting supported on four original Romanesque columns. These columns, revealed only during postwar restoration, are the most precious treasure of the church, particularly the two with elaborate figurative designs. There are 18 figures carved in each column; those on the left-hand column personify vices while those on the right are virtues.

The door at the head of the right-hand aisle leads to St Barbara's Chapel; its fine palmlike vault resting on yet another delicately carved Romanesque pillar.

MUSEUM

Located in the building adjacent to the larger church, the **museum** (Plac Św Wojciecha) presents some architectural remains (including a Romanesque portal with a tympanum depicting the scene of the Teaching of Christ) and archaeological finds.

Getting There & Away

The bus terminal is at the western end of town, and has regular services to Gniezno (7.70zł, 50 minutes) and to Inowrocław (4.50zł, 30 minutes).

KRUSZWICA

☎ 52 / pop 9000

Set on the northern end of Lake Gopło, Kruszwica (kroosh-*fee*-tsah) existed from at least the 8th century as a fortified village of the Goplanie, one of the Slav tribes living in the area. The Goplanie were eventually wiped out by the Polanie, forerunners of the medieval Poles, who made considerably more of a mark on history.

Today Kruszwica is an undistinguished, small industrial town notable for its remnants of the Piast legacy and a few strange legends about the region's early days (see the boxed text below).

Sights & Activities

The 32m-high, octagonal **Mouse Tower** (Mysia Wieża; adult/concession 3.60/2.90zł; ☉ 9am-6pm May-Sep), near the Rynek, is the only remainder of the 14th-century castle built by King Kazimierz III Wielki (Casimir III the Great). The name derives from a legend about the evil ruler of the Goplanie, Duke Popiel, who was supposedly eaten here by mice. You can go to the top for a view over the town and lake. From the foot of the tower, a **tourist boat** (trips 7.20zł) sails several times a day in summer for an hour-long trip around Lake Gopło.

THE LEGEND OF DUKE POPIEL

Once upon a time, a duke named Popiel lived in the castle of Kruszwica and ruled a vast country named Poland. The duke was a cruel and despotic ruler, and greedy for power. Like most tyrants, he was terrified that he could be overthrown, even by someone from his own family, and replaced by a more worthy person. In order to ensure there were no competitors to the throne he decided to kill all his relatives and other distinctive members of the community.

To put his diabolical plan into effect, the duke organised a great party in the castle, inviting his family and other distinguished persons. Once the initial toasts had relaxed the guests, a poisonous wine was discreetly served to selected invitees, all of whom died in a great deal of pain. Popiel then threw the dead bodies out of the castle and refused to bury them, as an example to others.

As weeks passed, the decomposing bodies attracted thousands of mice that rushed to the castle. Popiel sought refuge high up in the castle's tower but the mice cornered him and devoured him. Since then the tower has been known as the Mouse Tower.

Following Popiel's death, a modest peasant named Piast was chosen by the people and proclaimed the new ruler. He was the first leader of the Piast dynasty, which ruled Poland for many years and made it great and prosperous. As for the mice, nobody has seen them since…

The early-12th-century stone Roman-esque **collegiate church** (ul Kolegiacka) was altered in later periods but returned more or less to its original form during postwar restoration. The interior fittings include the 12th-century baptismal font. The church is on the northeastern outskirts of town, an 800m walk from the Rynek.

Getting There & Away

The main bus stop is on the Rynek. Buses to Strzelno (3.70zł, 10 minutes) depart every other hour or so. Take a bus to Inowrocław (3.70zł, 20 minutes) for transport further afield.

SOUTHEASTERN WIELKOPOLSKA

KALISZ

☎ 62 / pop 108,000

The main population centre of southeastern Wielkopolska, Kalisz (*kah*-leesh) is hardly a major tourist destination, but can be a place to break your journey if you're travelling in the area. The old centre, ringed by parks, still has the feel of a small market town despite the gradual incursion of modern life, and it's easy to forget the urban stresses while taking full advantage of the city's facilities.

History

Kalisz has the longest documented history of any town in Poland: it was mentioned by Claudius Ptolemy in his renowned *Geography* of the 2nd century AD as Kalisia, a trading settlement on the Amber Route between the Roman Empire and the Baltic Sea. In the 9th century a stronghold was built in the present-day suburb of Zawodzie, where the town continued to develop until the 13th century. Burnt down in 1233, it was rebuilt further to the north, in its present location.

During the reign of Kazimierz III Wielki the town acquired defensive walls with 15 watchtowers and a castle. It continued to grow steadily until the 16th century, from which point it began to decline. A huge fire in 1792 left only the churches standing, and almost all the fortifications were taken down in the early 19th century.

The greatest blow to civic pride, sometimes compared to Warsaw's annihilation in 1944, came in WWI – in August 1914 Kalisz was razed to the ground by the invading Germans. Within a month, the population dropped from 70,000 to 5000 and most buildings were reduced to ruins, though the churches once again miraculously escaped destruction. The town was rebuilt on the old street plan, but in a new architectural style. Most of the buildings survived WWII without much damage, but the subsequent renovation and modernisation process appears to be rather slow.

Information

Bank Pekao ul Grodzka (☎ 767 73 81; ul Grodzka 7); ul Śródmiejska (☎ 768 23 33; ul Śródmiejska 29)
City Jungle (☎ 767 67 00; Al Wolności 6; per hr 3zł; ☽ 9am-10pm Mon-Sat, 10am-10pm Sun) Internet access.
Main post office (☎ 767 74 00; ul Zamkowa 18/20)
Połanglo (☎ 502 98 98; ul Złota 1) Bookshop.
Tourist office (☎ 764 21 84; ul Garbarska 2; ☽ 10am-5pm Mon-Fri, 10am-2pm Sat)

Sights

The Old Town sits in the angle between the Prosna and Bernardynka Rivers, with a dozen small bridges and **Park Miejski** (City Park) stretching to the southeast. The best point to begin your sightseeing is possibly the tower of the **town hall** (admission 2zł; ☽ 10am-2pm Mon-Fri, 10am-1pm Sat & Sun), on the low-key central Rynek. Apart from fine views from the top, there's an exhibition inside relating the history of Kalisz and of the town hall itself.

For a more in-depth examination of these themes, the **Regional Museum** (Muzeum Ziemi Kaliskiej; ☎ 757 16 08; www.muzeum.kalisz.pl; ul Kościuszki 12; adult/concession 4/2zł; ☽ 10am-2.30pm Tue, Thu, Sat & Sun, noon-5.30pm Wed & Fri) features archaeological and historical exhibits from Kalisz and surrounding areas. The museum has an annexe in the Jesuit college, the **Centre of Drawing & Graphic Arts** (Centrum Rysunku i Grafiki; ☎ 757 29 99; ul Kolegialna 4; adult/concession 4/2zł; ☽ noon-5.30pm Thu, 10am-2pm Wed, Fri & Sat). It displays temporary exhibits of drawings and graphic arts, including works by Tadeusz Kulisiewicz (1899–1988), a Kalisz-born artist known mainly for his drawings. Enter from ul Łazienna.

Kalisz also has some fine religious buildings. The oldest, **St Nicholas' Church** (Kościół Św Mikołaja; ul Kanonicka 5), dates from the 13th century and was originally Gothic, but has

WIELKOPOLSKA

been modernised several times. The interior today is mainly baroque with a vault in Renaissance style. The painting of the Descent from the Cross over the high altar is a copy. The original, painted in Rubens' workshop in about 1617 and donated to the church, was burnt or stolen during a mysterious fire in 1973.

The 1607 former **Bernardine Church** (Kościół Pobernardyński; ul Stawiszyńska 2), now owned by the Jesuits, has a spectacular interior. The church is unprepossessing from the outside, but its wide nave glows with sumptuous baroque decoration. Both the altars and the wall paintings on the vault date from around the mid-18th century.

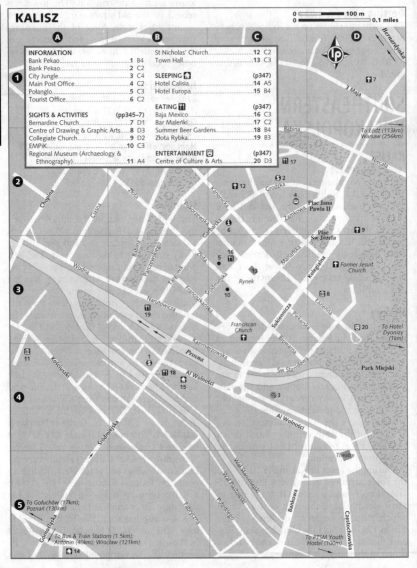

KALISZ

0 — 100 m
0 — 0.1 miles

INFORMATION
Bank Pekao..1 B4
Bank Pekao..2 C2
City Jungle...3 C4
Main Post Office...............................4 C2
Polanglo..5 C3
Tourist Office....................................6 C2

SIGHTS & ACTIVITIES (pp345–7)
Bernardine Church...........................7 D1
Centre of Drawing & Graphic Arts....8 D3
Collegiate Church..............................9 D2
EMPiK..10 C3
Regional Museum (Archaeology & Ethnography)..............................11 A4

St Nicholas' Church..........................12 C2
Town Hall...13 C3

SLEEPING (p347)
Hotel Calisia....................................14 A5
Hotel Europa...................................15 B4

EATING (p347)
Baja Mexico.....................................16 C3
Bar Maleński....................................17 C2
Summer Beer Gardens.....................18 B4
Złota Rybka......................................19 B3

ENTERTAINMENT (p347)
Centre of Culture & Arts..................20 D3

To Łódź (113km);
Warsaw (256km)

Former Jesuit Church

Rynek

Franciscan Church

Park Miejski

To Hotel Dyonizy (1km)

Theatre

To Gołuchów (17km);
Poznań (130km)

To Bus & Train Stations (1.5km);
Antonin (40km); Wrocław (121km)

To PTSM Youth Hostel (100m)

Finally, the **Collegiate Church** (Sanctuary of St Joseph; Plac Jana Pawła II 3) is a typical example of a lavish Catholic church, built in 1353 and rebuilt in the 18th century. It boasts a baroque interior flooded with gilt and glitter and is a popular pilgrimage site thanks to a miraculous picture of the Holy Family, dating from the 17th century.

Festivals & Events

Kalisz Theatre Meetings (☎ 502 32 22) Held at the beginning of May.

International Piano Jazz Festival (☎ 765 25 00) Held in late November.

Sleeping

Hotel Europa (☎ 767 20 32; www.hotel-europa.pl; Al Wolności 5; s 55-125zł, d 80-150zł, tr 130-170zł, q 165zł; P) The only really convenient central hotel has had a major makeover and punches far beyond its weight in most respects, from the friendly, unflappable staff to the shiny new en suites. Rooms come in three categories: standard, deluxe (with air-con, fridge and hydro-massage bath) and lower standard (with shared bathrooms). Student and weekend deals are available.

Hotel Calisia (☎ 767 91 00; www.hotel-calisia.pl; ul Nowy Świat 1-3; s/d/tr 160/220/260zł, apt 400zł; P) The swamp-green wicker isn't the nicest touch, but in all other respects this is a thoroughly commendable, service-oriented hotel. Weekend discounts can save you a bit of cash as well.

PTSM Youth Hostel (☎ 757 24 04; Wał Piastowski 3; dm 20-26zł) The 52-bed youth hostel is pleasantly set in a park on the riverbank, 200m off ul Częstochowska. Check in before 9pm.

Hotel Dyonizy (☎ /fax 757 46 50; ul Łódzka 29; d/tr 119/130zł) Run by the PTTK (Polish Tourist & Countryside Association), this former hostel is the least convenient option in town but can be useful as a fallback plan, with a choice of en suite and shared bathrooms. It's 1km east of the centre; you can walk there through Park Miejski in 15 minutes.

Eating

As usual, there are plenty of eating options on the Rynek and the streets around it. In summer a gaggle of beer gardens and snack stalls (each with their own TV set) spring up around the top end of Al Wolności, just by the Hotel Europa.

Złota Rybka (☎ 501 86 74; ul Narutowicza 4; mains 8-21zł; ☺ lunch & dinner Mon-Sat) The Golden Fish is indeed a gem of a seafood restaurant, somewhat unusually for landlocked Wielkopolska. Dig into some fine fish dishes behind the aquatic-themed stained glass.

Baja Mexico (☎ 767 55 04; Główny Rynek 3; mains 10-20zł; ☺ breakfast, lunch & dinner) There's not much authenticity about this Tex-Mex theme bar, but fajitas and enchiladas do make a change from the usual rounds of cutlets and *pierogi*, and you shouldn't have any problems understanding the menu.

Bar Maleńki (☎ 501 93 03; ul Parczewskiego 2-3; mains 5-9.50zł; ☺ breakfast & lunch Mon-Sat) *Maleńki* means tiny, and this diminutive cafeteria certainly lives up to that. If you can find room, it's arguably the best place in town for an ultrabudget meal.

Entertainment

For more active cultural pursuits, the **Centre of Culture & Arts** (Centrum Kultury i Sztuki; ☎ 765 25 00; www.ckis.kalisz.pl in Polish; ul Łazienna 6) holds a variety of events, and also has its own pub.

Getting There & Around

The bus and train stations are close to each other, about 2km southwest of the Old Town. To get to the centre, take bus 11, 18, 19 or 12 from the main road (2zł).

BUS

There are nine buses to Poznań daily (18zł, 2½ hours) via Gołuchów (6.60zł, 25 minutes), and six to Wrocław (17zł, 2½ hours) via Antonin (9zł, one hour). The hourly suburban bus 12A to Kowalew also passes through Gołuchów; it stops in Kalisz centre on Plac Jana Pawła II.

TRAIN

Trains to Łódź (15.90zł, 2½ hours) run regularly throughout the day. There are fast trains to Warsaw (39.66zł, 4¼ hours, four daily) and Wrocław (28.38zł, two hours, five daily). There's just one daily direct service to Poznań (17.20zł, 2½ hours).

GOŁUCHÓW

☎ 62 / pop 1200

The small village of Gołuchów (go-*woo*-hoof) boasts a castle nearer those in the Loire Valley than the sturdy brick creations found elsewhere in Poland. Set in extensive

WIELKOPOLSKA

landscaped gardens popular with wedding photographers, you don't really need another reason to stop off here for a look around.

Sights

CASTLE

Gołuchów's castle began life around 1560 as a small fortified mansion with four octagonal towers at the corners, built by the Leszczyński family. Some 50 years later it was enlarged and reshaped into a palatial residence in late-Renaissance style. Abandoned at the end of the 17th century, it gradually fell into ruins until the Działyński family, the owners of Kórnik castle (p335), bought it in 1856. It was completely rebuilt between 1872 and 1885, and it was then that it acquired its French appearance.

The castle's stylistic mutation was essentially the brainchild of Izabela Czartoryska, daughter of Prince Adam Czartoryski and wife of Jan Działyński. She commissioned the French architect Viollet le Duc to reinvent the residence; under his supervision many architectural bits and pieces were brought from abroad, mainly from France and Italy, and incorporated into the building.

Having acquired large numbers of works of art, Izabela crammed them into her new palace, which became one of the largest private museums in Europe. During WWII the Nazis stole the works of art but the building itself survived relatively undamaged. Part of the collection was recovered and is now once more on display in its rightful home.

Wander around and you'll notice the castle looks different from various sides; the best view is from the northern side. Inside the building is the **museum** (☎ 761 50 90; ul Działyńskich 2; adult/concession 8/5.50zł; ☯ 10am-4pm Tue-Sun). In its numerous rooms, a wealth of furniture, paintings, sculptures, weapons, tapestries, rugs and the like have been collected from Europe and beyond. One of the highlights is a collection of Greek vases from the 5th century BC. You enter the castle through a decorative 17th-century doorway, which leads into a graceful arcaded courtyard; admission is strictly limited, with tours running for a set number of visitors every half hour.

CASTLE PARK

The vast 160-hectare, English-style **park** (admission free; ☯ 8am-8pm) surrounding the castle was laid out during the last quarter of the 19th century and holds several hundred species of trees and shrubs. Its oldest part is the 350m-long lime-tree alley, planted in 1856. Various other bits and bobs around the grounds are open to visitors.

To the south of the castle is the **oficyna**, which looks like a small palace. Initially a distillery, it was considerably extended in 1874 and adapted as a residence. It was here that the owners lived after the castle was turned into a museum. Today the building accommodates the **Museum of Forestry** (Muzeum Leśnictwa; ☎ 761 50 36; ul Działyńskich 2; adult/concession 3.50/2zł; ☯ 10am-3pm Tue-Fri, 10am-4pm Sat & Sun), which focuses on the history of Polish forestry and the timber industry. There's also a collection of contemporary art connected to forestry, either in subject matter or by means of the material used. The building has its original interior decoration. You can have a cup of coffee or lunch in the café in the adjoining building before taking a stroll through the park. There's also an **annexe** (☯ 10am-4pm Tue-Fri, 10am-4.30pm Sat & Sun) of ecological displays in an old coach house.

The **Museum of Forest Techniques** (Muzeum Techniki Leśnej; ☎ 761 50 10; admission 1zł; ☯ 10am-4pm Tue-Sun), in the far north of the park, 750m beyond the castle, is another outpost of the main museum, featuring tools and machinery used in forestry.

A dozen bison live relatively freely in a large, fenced-off **bison enclosure** (☯ 7am-sunset), west of the park, 500m beyond the forestry techniques museum (follow the Żubr signs).

Sleeping & Eating

If you're taken enough with the estate to want to stay over, **Dom Pracy Twórczej** (☎ 761 50 44; ul Borowskiego 2; d 100zł; P), set in a historic building, offers a neat selection of double rooms inside the park, just a short amble from the castle. The house **restaurant** (mains 4-30zł) does a good line in Polish specialities and event catering (including whole roast piglet), and has its own semipermanent summer marquee.

Getting There & Away

Suburban bus 12A goes roughly hourly to/from Kalisz (6.60zł, 25 minutes). About six PKS buses run to Poznań daily (15zł, 2¼ hours).

ANTONIN
☎ 62 / pop 500

Today a small lakeside resort, before WWII Antonin was the summer residence of the Radziwiłł family, one of the richest and best-known aristocratic clans in Poland. It's a pleasant, relaxing place, ideal for a quick stopover or a slightly longer break.

Sights & Activities

Antonin is named after Prince Antoni Radziwiłł, who put this spot on the map by building his **Hunting Palace** (Pałac Myśliwski) here from 1822 to 1824. This handsome wooden structure is still the town's showpiece; it was designed by Karl Friedrich Schinkel, one of the outstanding German architects of the period, who was also responsible for numerous monumental buildings in Berlin and Prussia.

The palace has an unusual structure. The main part is a large, octagonal, three-storey hall, called the Chimney Room, with a column in the middle supporting the roof and also functioning as a chimney for the central fireplace. There are four side wings, originally designed as living rooms for the owner and his guests. One such guest, Frédéric Chopin, stayed here a couple of times, performing concerts and composing.

The Centre of Culture & Arts in Kalisz now runs the palace as a hotel, and there is also a small museum and 'creative work centre' for casual visitors. Regular piano recitals are held here, with special buses laid on from Ostrów Wielkopolski and Kalisz.

The palace is surrounded by a 46-hectare **nature reserve**, which offers some pleasant **walks** of up to 25km. You can also go **fishing**, **boating** or take up any number of activities on the lake, which borders the main road.

Festivals & Events

Chopin Festival A prestigious four-day festival held at the Hunting Palace in September/October.

Sleeping & Eating

Hunting Palace (Pałac Myśliwski; ☎ 734 81 14; s 140zł, d 180-260zł; P) How could you stay anywhere else? This is the most romantic option for miles, even if you're just grabbing a bite in its stylish restaurant in the Chimney Room. Advance booking is recommended; it's invariably swamped with wedding parties on Saturday in summer.

Motel Lido (☎ 734 81 91; ul Wrocławska 6; camping per person 7-10zł, cabins 24-55zł, d 60-65zł, tr 80zł; P) If you can't quite stretch to the palace (or are beaten to it by a bride), the Lido has decent rooms and a range of camping, cabin and leisure facilities, all on the lakeside site next door.

Getting There & Away

The train station is about 1km from the palace, beyond the lake. Four trains run to Poznań daily (17.20zł, two hours). There are no direct trains to Kalisz – change in Ostrów Wielkopolski.

There are seven daily buses to Wrocław (13zł, two hours) and five to Kalisz (9zł, one hour). About 10 buses go to Ostrów Wielkopolski (4.50zł, 30 minutes), from where suburban buses run regularly to Kalisz.

LICHEŃ
☎ 63 / pop 1500

Licheń (*lee*-hen) is reputedly Poland's second most visited pilgrimage site after Częstochowa. The pilgrims' destination, a sizable **ecclesiastical complex**, occupies the village's centre and includes two churches, a fairy-tale stone fortress (Golgotha) depicting the Way of the Cross in model tableaux, chapels, grottoes and statues scattered all over the grounds, and more images of the Virgin Mary than you can swing a censer at. About 1.5 million pilgrims pass through here annually, coming to pay tribute to a miraculous icon of Mary in the main church. (It's tucked away in the high altar if you're interested – follow the queue of people shuffling on all fours.)

In the last 10 years, however, the face of the site has changed dramatically. Energetic local priest Eugeniusz Makulski decided to build a third church as a 'votive offering of the nation for the year 2000', to celebrate two millennia of Christianity. Construction began in 1994, and the monumental building, next to the main gardens, was finally officially consecrated in 2004.

You'll see straight away that this is not your average church. The gigantic **Bazilika Licheńska** (Church of Our Lady of Licheń) is Poland's largest place of worship, exceeding anything that was built in the country over the past 1000 years, and the golden dome can be spotted from miles away in the flat countryside. The interior is resplendent with

LICHEŃ: BREAKING RECORDS

Licheń's basilica is enough to give Guinness a headache. It's Poland's longest church (120m), the seventh longest in Europe and 11th longest in the world. It's also Poland's widest (77m) and highest (97m) church, and has the country's greatest volume (268,800 cu metres), floor area (8290 sq metres) and capacity (17,000 worshippers). More than 250,000 people can easily gather on the square in front of the church.

The tower is Poland's highest at 128m, well ahead of the second tallest, the Jasna Góra Monastery of Częstochowa (106m). Licheń also has Poland's largest bell (third largest in Europe), the 14,770kg Maryja Bogurodzica, leaving the 11,000kg Zygmunt in Kraków's Wawel Royal Cathedral trailing. In front of the church is the largest monument to Pope John Paul II ever built – a 9m-tall, 8-tonne bronze statue designed by Kraków sculptor Marian Konieczny.

The basilica may hold yet another record: the cost of its construction. The total has to be astronomical, as the doors and windows alone cost US$3 million. Father Makulski, however, won't give an exact amount, saying that one shouldn't look into God's pockets. You can't blame him for his reticence – the project was financed exclusively by donations from the faithful, collected over 20 years. God's pockets may run deep, but He shows no sign of dipping into them Himself.

gilded ornamentation, chandeliers, paintings, two massive triptychs and no fewer than 50 confessionals.

Beneath the main hall is an underground level containing the round **Golden Chapel**, which is a good-sized church in itself. Completed in 1996, it's crammed full with crystal chandeliers and golden stucco, and the walls outside are tiled with plaques giving the names of the many donors to the project (sized according to the amount given, of course). The floor is of marble, imported from all over the world, to form a multicoloured design. The side rooms down on this level are used for exhibitions on themes ranging from the pope to the Turin Shroud.

Give yourself sufficient time for a visit here, at least half a day. There's a lot to see in the basilica and the gardens, and the constant crowds of pilgrims really add to the atmosphere. Local guidebooks (some in English) are sold at various locations and have full details of the diverse attractions.

Sleeping

Dom Pielgrzyma Arka (☎ 270 81 62; www.lichen.pl; ul Klasztorna 4; r 70-140zł) The main lodging facility, operated by the church. Simple, immaculate rooms for one to 10 people are available to pilgrims and anyone else wanting to sleep over. The complex has its own chapel, café, restaurant, video room and bookshop.

DP Betania (r 64-100zł) This identical accommodation, also within the sanctuary, has more beds, and a third annexe is currently under construction.

Getting There & Away

To get to Licheń you'll need to go via Konin, a fair-sized town, 13km to the southwest, which sits on the busy Poznań–Warsaw rail line. There are seven or so daily buses between Konin and Licheń (6.90zł, one hour).

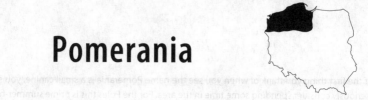

Pomerania

CONTENTS

If the first thing you think of when you see the name Pomerania is a small canine, you should seriously consider spending some time in the area. For the Poles this is prime summer-holiday territory, from the sandy beaches that line the Baltic shores to the lake-strewn lowlands of the south, and the easy border crossings mean that more Germans are coming to agree.

The German connection isn't arbitrary – Pomerania has switched hands between the two nations dozens of times, and if you go straight from one to the other you may have trouble spotting the difference, especially in the coastal resorts. Head east, though, and a distinctly Polish character asserts itself, tinged with influences from Swedes, Danes and other past invaders. It all culminates in the amazing historic city of Gdańsk. History is the main draw in central Pomerania, too, where the legacy of medieval conquerors still looms large amid the well-worn towns and cities. Castles, churches and ancient granaries provide enough red brick to wall in the world, and every name on the map seems to have its own architectural keepsake. Picking and choosing what to see is just one of the pleasures the region affords, and its areas of natural beauty provide yet another facet to its attractions.

Whether you explore by land or water, from border to border or no further than the coast, Pomerania will make you seriously rethink your preconceptions of Poland, and that in itself makes it worth an extended stay.

HIGHLIGHTS

■ **Café Culture**
Shopping and sipping on ul Mariacka, the hidden heart of historic Gdańsk (p361)

■ **Street Life**
Chełmno's walled town (p392)

■ **Resort Life**
Sopot (p374), holiday heaven in the Tri-City

■ **Knight Life**
Malbork's remarkable Teutonic castle (p396)

■ **Gothic Relics**
The mighty brick buildings of Toruń (p387)

■ **Beach**
Sand meets sea at Świnoujście (p415)

■ **Stargazing**
Frombork (p400), home of Nicolaus Copernicus

■ **Unique View**
The shifting dunes of Słowiński National Park (p404)

■ **Annual Event**
The Dominican Fair (p368) in Gdańsk

| ■ TELEPHONE CODES: 52, 55, 56, 58, 59, 91, 92, 94 | ■ POPULATION: 7 MILLION | ■ AREA: 59,000 SQ KM |

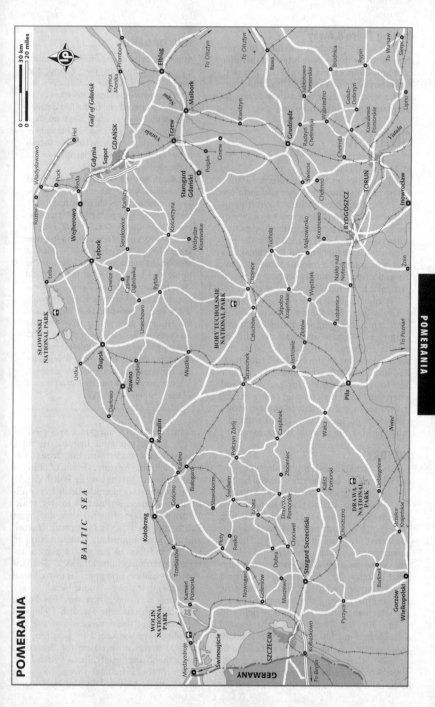

POMERANIA

Getting There & Away

Gdańsk is the principal transport hub for the region, with its own international airport and connections to other Polish and European cities by road, rail, bus and boat. In the west, Szczecin offers easy access to Germany and southern Poland.

GDAŃSK

☎ 58 / pop 475,000

Of all the cities on the Baltic coast, Gdańsk has perhaps the most character and certainly the most chequered history. Centuries of independence asserted the port as a city in charge of its own destiny, and while its fortunes have waxed and waned with the political developments around it, Gdańsk has always maintained a resolute sense of identity and pride. Twentieth-century events in particular have marked the city as an evocative symbol of modern-day Poland.

Today Gdańsk is the showpiece of Polish Pomerania, bringing in almost as many visitors as Warsaw and Kraków with its painstakingly reconstructed Old Town and perfect location at the heart of the coast. Buildings, boats, beaches and bars do their best to offer something for everyone, and when you tire of the compact centre there's still the rest of the Tri-City to explore. However long you spend here, try to make the most of this truly unique environment.

HISTORY

Gdańsk started life as a tiny fishing village in the 9th century, but the city's official history is counted from the year 997, when the Bohemian Bishop Adalbert arrived here from Gniezno and baptised the inhabitants before setting off eastwards on his ill-fated mission to convert the Prussians (see p339). The settlement developed as a port over the following centuries, expanding northwards onto what is today the Old Town. The German community arrived from Lübeck in the early 13th century, giving the town the cosmopolitan character that has come to define it.

In 1308 the Teutonic Knights seized Gdańsk and quickly turned it into a major trade centre, joining the Hanseatic League in 1361. Ongoing wars with the Polish stretched the inhabitants' patience with the order, and in 1454 a local uprising razed the

SONS OF DANZIG

As a lively cultural and intellectual centre, it's hardly surprising that Gdańsk has spawned some famous names over the years. Astronomer Johannes Hevelius (1611–87), who produced one of the first detailed maps of the moon's surface, was born, lived and worked here, and now has a tasty beer named after him. Also born here was Gabriel Daniel Fahrenheit (1686–1736), the inventor of the mercury thermometer.

Gdańsk was the birthplace of pessimist philosopher Arthur Schopenhauer (1788–1860), notable for his unconventional view that will is the primary creative factor. German author Günter Grass (b 1927) is perhaps Gdańsk's most famous living son, best known for his first novel *The Tin Drum*. A novelist, dramatist and poet, Grass won the Nobel prize for literature in 1999, and still visits his home town regularly.

Gdańsk's most prominent Polish inhabitant is former president Lech Wałęsa, and the city maintains strong links with the Solidarity trade union, born here in 1980. Wałęsa can be seen sometimes, popping in and out of his office in the Green Gate. Current president Aleksander Kwaśniewski is also no stranger to the city, having studied economics here in the 1970s.

knights' castle, and allegiance was pledged to the Polish monarch instead. In turn, Gdańsk was rewarded with numerous privileges, including a greater degree of political independence than any other Polish city.

By the mid-16th century, Gdańsk controlled three-quarters of Poland's foreign trade. With a population of 40,000 it was the largest Polish city, even bigger than royal Kraków, and the most important trading centre in Central and Eastern Europe. Legions of international traders joined the local German-Polish population, bringing their own cultural influences to the city's unique blend.

Gdańsk was one of the very few Polish cities to withstand the Swedish Deluge of the 1650s, but the devastation of the surrounding area weakened its position, and by 1793 it was no problem for Prussia to annex the shrinking city. Just 14 years later, however, the Prussians themselves were under attack, besieged by the Napoleonic

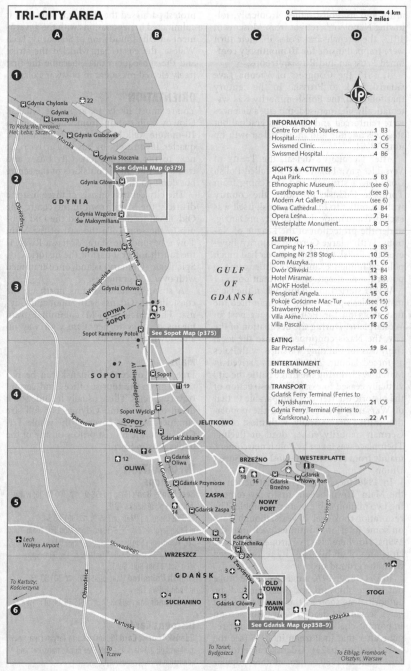

TRI-CITY AREA

0 — 4 km
0 — 2 miles

A **B** **C** **D**

1

Gdynia Chylonia
Gdynia Leszczynki
22
Gdynia Grabówek
To Reda; Wejherowo; Hel; Łeba; Szczecin
Morska
Gdynia Stocznia

See Gdynia Map (p379)

2

Gdynia Główna

G D Y N I A

Gdynia Wzgórze
Św Maksymiliana

Al Zwycięstwa

Obwodnica

Gdynia Redłowo

3

Wielkopolska

Gdynia Orłowo
5
13
9

**GDYNIA
SOPOT**

Sopot Kamienny Potok
1

See Sopot Map (p375)

**GULF
OF
GDAŃSK**

7

S O P O T

Sopot
19

4

Spacerowa

Al Niepodległości

Sopot Wyścigi

JELITKOWO

**SOPOT
GDAŃSK**

Gdańsk Żabianka

12
6
Gdańsk Oliwa

OLIWA

BRZEŹNO

21

WESTERPLATTE
8
Gdańsk
Nowy Port

Al Grunwaldzka

Gdańsk Przymorze

ZASPA

18
16
Gdańsk
Brzeźno

To Kartuzy; Kościerzyna

5

Lech Wałęsa Airport

14
Gdańsk Zaspa

**NOWY
PORT**

Słowackiego

Gdańsk Wrzeszcz

Gdańsk
Politechnika
20

Al Hallera

WRZESZCZ

Al Zwycięstwa

3

**OLD
TOWN**

STOGI

10

Obwodnica

G D A Ń S K

4
SUCHANINO

15
Gdańsk Główny

2

**MAIN
TOWN**

11
Elbląska

Kartuska

17

See Gdańsk Map (pp358–9)

6

To Tczew

To Toruń; Bydgoszcz

To Elbląg; Frombork; Olsztyn; Warsaw

POMERANIA

INFORMATION
Centre for Polish Studies.....................1 B3
Hospital...2 C6
Swissmed Clinic.................................3 C5
Swissmed Hospital.............................4 B6

SIGHTS & ACTIVITIES
Aqua Park...5 B3
Ethnographic Museum....................(see 6)
Guardhouse No 1...........................(see 8)
Modern Art Gallery........................(see 6)
Oliwa Cathedral.................................6 B4
Opera Leśna......................................7 B4
Westerplatte Monument......................8 D5

SLEEPING
Camping Nr 19...................................9 B3
Camping Nr 218 Stogi.......................10 D5
Dom Muzyka....................................11 C6
Dwór Oliwski....................................12 B4
Hotel Miramar..................................13 B3
MOKF Hostel....................................14 B5
Pensjonat Angela.............................15 C6
Pokoje Gościnne Mac-Tur...............(see 15)
Strawberry Hostel.............................16 C5
Villa Akme..17 C6
Villa Pascal......................................18 C5

EATING
Bar Przystań....................................19 B4

ENTERTAINMENT
State Baltic Opera...........................20 C5

TRANSPORT
Gdańsk Ferry Terminal (Ferries to
 Nynäshamn)..................................21 C5
Gdynia Ferry Terminal (Ferries to
 Karlskrona)....................................22 A1

army and its Polish allies. Ironically, following Napoleon's retreat from Moscow in 1813, the French and Poles in their turn were trapped inside for 10 months by combined Prussian and Russian troops.

In 1815 the Congress of Vienna gave Gdańsk back to Prussia. In the century that followed, the Polish minority was systematically Germanised, the city's defences were reinforced and there was gradual but steady economic and industrial growth up until WWI.

After Germany's defeat, the Treaty of Versailles gave Poland the so-called Polish Corridor, a strip of land stretching from Toruń to Gdańsk, providing the country with an outlet to the sea. Gdańsk itself was excluded and made the Free City of Danzig, under the protection of the League of Nations. With a large German majority, however, the Polish population never had much political influence, and once Hitler came to power it was effectively a German port.

WWII started in Gdańsk when the German battleship *Schleswig-Holstein* fired the first shots on the Polish military post in Westerplatte. During the occupation of the city, the Nazis continued to use the local shipyards for building warships, with Poles as forced labour. The Russians arrived in March 1945; during the fierce battle the city virtually ceased to exist. The destruction of the historic quarter was comparable to that of Warsaw's Old Town, and the population shifted dramatically, with most of the German majority either dead or fleeing. Their place was taken by Polish newcomers, mainly from the territories lost to the Soviet Union.

In 1949 the complex reconstruction of the Main Town began, firstly by removing two million cubic metres of rubble. The restoration took over 20 years, though work on some interiors continued well into the 1990s. Nowhere else in Europe was such a large area of an historic city reconstructed from the ground up.

In December 1970 a massive strike broke out in the shipyard and was 'pacified' by authorities as soon as the workers left the gates, leaving 44 dead. This was the second important challenge to the communist regime after that in Poznań in 1956 (see the boxed text on p323). Gdańsk came to the fore again in 1980, when another popular protest paralysed the shipyard. This time it culminated in negotiations with the government and the foundation of Solidarity. Lech Wałęsa, the electrician who led the strike and the subsequent talks, became the first freely elected president in postwar Poland.

ORIENTATION

You're most likely to arrive at Gdańsk Główny train station, from where it's just a 10-minute walk to the core of the historic quarter. If you come by bus, you arrive right next to the train station. City buses and trams operate on the outskirts of the centre but don't go through it.

The city centre consists of three historic districts: the Main Town in the centre, the Old Town to the north, and the Old Suburb to the south. To the east of the Main Town, beyond the Stara Motława River, is the fourth integral part of the historic city, Spichlerze (Granary) Island, once crammed with over 300 granaries.

A string of suburbs runs north up the coast, linking Gdańsk with Sopot and Gdynia. The efficient SKM commuter train means it's easy to negotiate your way up and down the Tri-City.

Maps

Free maps of central Gdańsk can be obtained from the tourist offices and certain travel agencies. These usually include some detail on Sopot and Gdynia. For full-size commercial maps covering the whole Tri-City, go to the tourist offices or any of the bookshops in town.

INFORMATION
Bookshops

Best Books Bank (Map pp358-9; ☎ 300 08 36; www
.bbb.com.pl; ul Rajska 4D/E)
EMPiK Długi Targ (Map pp358-9; ☎ 301 40 34;
ul Długi Targ 28/29; 🕑 9.30am-8pm Mon-Fri, 10am-7pm
Sat, 10am-6pm Sun); ul Podwale Grodzkie (Map pp358-9;
☎ 301 72 44; ul Podwale Grodzkie 8; 🕑 9am-9pm
Mon-Sat, 11am-8pm Sun)
English Unlimited (Map pp358-9; ☎ 301 33 73;
ul Podmłyńska 10)
Libri Mundi (Map pp358-9; ☎ 305 15 74; ul Rajska 1)

Discount Cards

Gdańsk Tourist Card (Gdańska Karta Turystyczna; www
.polkarta.pl; 2/3 days 45/70zł) Free public transport and
admission to major museums.

Tri-City Tourist Card (Karta Turystyczna Trójmiasta; www.touristcard.pl; 3 days 16zł) Five to 50% discounts on attractions, restaurants and boat trips.

Internet Access
Flisak (Map pp358-9; ☎ 301 85 62; ul Chlebnicka 9/10; per hr 4zł) Pub-restaurant.
Jazz'n'Java (Map pp358-9; ☎ 305 36 16; www.cafe.jnj.pl in Polish; ul Tkacka 17/18; per hr 5zł; ⏰ 10am-10pm)
Kawiarnia Internetowa (Map pp358-9; ☎ 320 92 30; Cinema City, ul Karmelicka 1; per hr 5zł; ⏰ 9am-1am Mon-Sat, 9.30am-1am Sun)
Spacja (Map pp358-9; ☎ 301 62 12; ul Motławska 14; per hr 4zł; ⏰ 11am-8pm) On Spichlerze Island.
Telekomunikacja Polska (Map pp358-9; ☎ 320 10 33; ul Długa 22/27; free; ⏰ 10am-6pm Mon-Fri) Has a 30-minute limit.
Wojewódzka Biblioteka Publiczna (Map pp358-9; ☎ 301 48 11; Targ Rakowy 5/6; per hr 4zł; ⏰ 11am-8pm Mon, Tue, Thu & Fri) County library.

Internet Resources
gdansk.naszemiasto.pl Information, listings and news (Polish only).
guide.trojmiasto.pl Detailed Tri-City tourist guide.
roots.gdansk.pl Interesting and unusual history/trivia site.
www.gdansk.pl Excellent city information site.

Medical Services
Hospital (Map p355; ☎ 302 30 31; ul Nowe Ogrody 1/6)
Swissmed (☎ 0603 344 999) clinic (Map p355; ul Swłodowskiej-Curie 5); hospital (Map p355; ul Wileńska 44) Private medical care.

Money
Bank Millennium Długi Targ (Map pp358-9; Długi Targ 14/16); Wały Jagiellońskie (Map pp358-9; ☎ 0801 121 000; Wały Jagiellońskie 14/16)
Bank Pekao (Map pp358-9; ☎ 346 37 22; ul Garncarska 23)
PBK Bank (Map pp358-9; ☎ 323 14 00; ul Ogarna 116)

Post
Main post office (Map pp358-9; ☎ 301 80 49; ul Długa 23/28)

Tourist Information
PTTK Tourist Office (Map pp358-9; ☎ 301 91 51; www.pttk-gdansk.pl; ul Długa 45; ⏰ 9am-5pm Mon-Fri Oct-Apr, 10am-6pm daily May-Sep)
Regional Tourist Information Point (Map pp358-9; ☎ 766 74 66; info@prot.gda.pl; Madison Centre, ul Rajska 10; ⏰ 9am-9pm Mon-Sat, 10am-9pm Sun)
Regional Tourist Office (Stowarzyszenie Turystyczne Pomorze Gdańskie; Map pp358-9; ☎ 301 43 55; ul Heweliusza 27; ⏰ 9am-6pm Mon-Fri)

Tourist information booth (Map pp358-9; ul Podwale Grodzkie; ⏰ 9am-6pm Mon-Fri, 10am-6pm Sat & Sun) Outside Gdańsk Główny train station.

Travel Agencies
Almatur (Map pp358-9; ☎ 301 29 31; Długi Targ 11)
Biuro Turystyki Lauer (Map pp358-9; ☎ 301 16 19; ul Piwna 22/23) Organises trips to Kaliningrad in Russia.
Feniks Travel (Map pp358-9; ☎ 763 44 52) At Gdańsk Główny train station.
Orbis Travel ul Heweliusza (Map pp358-9; ☎ 301 21 32; Hotel Mercure Hevelius, ul Heweliusza 22); ul Podwale Staromiejskie (Map pp358-9; ☎ 301 44 25; ul Podwale Staromiejskie 96/97)
PTTK (Map pp358-9; ☎ 301 60 96; ul Długa 45) Above the tourist office; arranges foreign-language tours and other excursions.

DANGERS & ANNOYANCES
In general Gdańsk is perfectly safe, though the crowded streets are a gift for pickpockets at busy times. Beware of the moneychangers who hang around Długi Targ and Długie Pobrzeże offering foreigners attractive rates; you may not get what you expect! During the peak tourist season there's a noticeable police presence around the Main Town, with regular random ID checks.

SIGHTS
Main Town
Gdańsk's Main Town (Główne Miasto; Map pp358-9) is the largest of the three historic quarters. It was always the richest architecturally, and after WWII was the most carefully restored. It now looks much as it did some 300 to 400 years ago, during the times of its greatest prosperity. Prussian accretions of the Partition period were not restored.

The town was laid out in the mid-14th century along a central axis consisting of ul Długa (Long St) and Długi Targ (Long Market). The latter was designed for trading, which would have taken place in the Rynek or central market square. The axis came to be known as the Royal Way, for it was the thoroughfare through which the Polish kings traditionally paraded during their periodic visits.

ROYAL WAY
Of the three Royal Ways in Poland (Warsaw, Kraków and Gdańsk), the Gdańsk one is the shortest – only 500m long – but it's architecturally perhaps the most refined.

POMERANIA

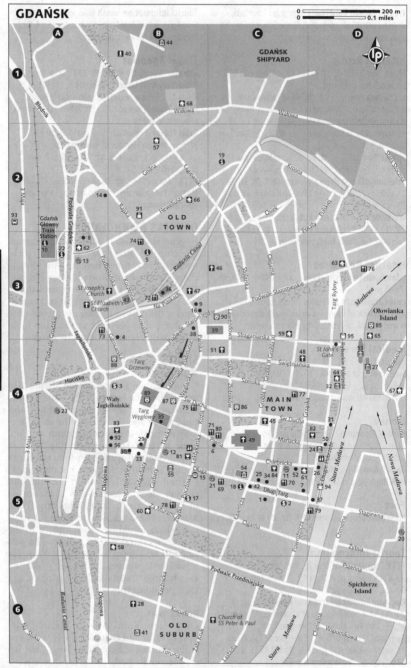

GDAŃSK

The traditional entry point for kings was the **Upland Gate** (Brama Wyżynna; Map left), at the western end of the Royal Way. The gate was built in 1574 as part of the city's new fortifications, which were constructed outside the medieval walls to strengthen the system. The authorities weren't happy with the original structure, so in 1586 they commissioned a Flemish artist, Willem van den Block, to embellish it. It was covered with sandstone slabs and ornamented with three coats of arms: Prussia (with unicorns), Poland (with angels) and Gdańsk (with lions). You'll find Gdańsk's shield, invariably featuring heraldic lions, on countless public buildings throughout the city.

Just behind the Upland Gate is a large 15th-century construction known as the **Foregate** (Przedbramie; Map left). It consists of the **Torture House** (Katownia) to the west and a high **Prison Tower** (Wieża Więzienna) to the east, linked to one another by two walls.

When the Upland Gate was built, the Foregate lost its defensive function and was turned into a jail. The Torture House then had an extra storey added as a court room and was topped with decorative Renaissance parapets. A gallows was built on the square to the north, where public executions of condemned foreigners were held (locals had the 'privilege' of being hanged on Długi Targ). The Foregate was used as a jail till the mid-19th century. It was damaged during WWII and the restoration that began in 1951 has not yet been completed.

Further to the east is the **Golden Gate** (Złota Brama; Map left). Its function was not defensive but symbolic. Designed by Abraham van den Block, son of the decorator of the Upland Gate, and built in 1612, it's a sort of triumphal arch ornamented with a double-storey colonnade and topped with eight allegorical statues. The four figures on the side of the Prison Tower represent Peace, Liberty, Wealth and Fame, for which Gdańsk was always struggling to achieve against foreign powers, the Polish kings included. The sculptures on the opposite side symbolise the burghers' virtues: Wisdom, Piety, Justice and Concord. Today's figures are postwar copies of the 1648 originals.

POMERANIA

Adjoining the gate to the north is the **Court of the Fraternity of St George** (Dwór Bractwa Św Jerzego; Map pp358–9), a good example of late-Gothic secular architecture, dating from the 1490s. The roof is topped with a 16th-century octagonal tower, with St George and the Dragon on the spire (the 1556 original is in Gdańsk's National Museum).

Once you pass the Golden Gate, you are on the gently curving **ul Długa**, one of the loveliest streets in Poland, which, despite its name, is only 300m long. In 1945 it was just a heap of smoking rubble. Stop at the **Uphagens' House** (Dom Uphagena; Map pp358–9; ☎ 301 23 71; ul Długa 12; adult/concession 6/3zł; free Mon; ☽ 10am-3pm Mon, 10am-6pm Tue-Sat, 11am-6pm Sun) to see the restored historic interior, now a branch of the History Museum.

TOWN HALL

At the eastern end of ul Długa is the **town hall** (Map pp358–9), with its tall slim tower, the highest in Gdańsk (81.5m). Look at the pinnacle; there's a life-sized gilded figure of King Zygmunt II August on top – he was particularly generous in granting privileges to the city.

The town hall has both Gothic and Renaissance elements. The first building was reputedly put up in the 1330s, but it grew and changed until the end of the 16th century. In 1945 it was almost completely burnt out and the authorities were on the point of demolishing the ruin, which was eventually saved thanks to local protests.

After serving as a municipal seat for over half a millennium, today it houses the **Historical Museum of Gdańsk** (Muzeum Historii Miasta Gdańska; Map pp358–9; ☎ 301 48 71; ul Długa 47; adult/concession 8/3zł; ☽ 10am-4pm Tue-Sun, to 5pm in summer). Enter the building by twin flights of balustraded stairs and go through an ornate baroque doorway (1766), which is topped by the city's coat of arms guarded by two lions that, unusually, are both looking towards the Golden Gate, supposedly awaiting the arrival of the king. The doorway was the final addition to the external decoration of the building.

Inside are several rooms decked out in period decoration, either original or recreated from old drawings, engravings and photographs. The showpiece is the **Red Room** (Sala Czerwona), done up in Dutch mannerist style from the end of the 16th century,

which was once the setting for the town council's debates. There's a large, richly carved fireplace (1593) and a marvellous portal (1596), but your eyes will immediately be attracted to the ornamented ceiling – 25 paintings dominated by the oval centrepiece entitled *The Glorification of the Unity of Gdańsk with Poland*. The painter, Isaac van den Block, yet another member of the Flemish family of artists, incorporated various themes in the painting, from everyday scenes to the panorama of Gdańsk on the top of the triumphal arch. All the room's decoration is authentic; it was dismantled in 1942 and hidden outside Gdańsk.

The 2nd floor houses exhibitions related to Gdańsk's history, including photos of the destruction of 1945. From here you can enter the **tower** (admission 3zł; ☽ closed Mon) for great views across the city.

Combined tickets including entrance to Artus Court and the Uphagens' House cost 15zł.

DŁUGI TARG

The Long Market, Długi Targ, was once the main city market and is now the major focus for visitors, brimming with buskers, street stalls and restaurants.

Next to the town hall is the **Neptune Fountain** (Fontana Neptuna; Map pp358–9). The bronze statue was the work of another Flemish artist, Peter Husen; it was made between 1606 and 1613 and is the oldest secular monument in Poland. In 1634 the fountain was fenced off with a wrought-iron barrier. This is linked to a legend that the Gdańsk vodka, Goldwasser, spurted out of the trident one merry night and Neptune found himself endangered by crowds of drunken locals. A menagerie of stone sea creatures was added in the 1750s during the restoration of the fountain.

The nearby 1618 **Golden House** (Złota Kamienica; Map pp358–9), designed by Johan Voigt, has the richest façade in the city. In the friezes between storeys are 12 elaborately carved scenes interspersed with busts of famous historical figures, including two Polish kings. The four statues waving to you from the balustrade at the top are Cleopatra, Oedipus, Achilles and Antigone.

The Long Market is flanked from the east by the **Green Gate** (Zielona Brama; Map pp358–9), marking the end of the Royal

Neptune Fountain and town hall (p360), Gdańsk

Teutonic castle (p396), Malbork

Old Town (p365), Gdańsk

Słowiński National Park (p403)

Yachting, the Great Masurian Lakes (p438)

Organ, Church of Our Lady (p437),
Święta Lipka

Castle, Reszel (p436)

Slipways, Elbląg-Ostróda Canal (p434)

Way. It was built in the 1560s on the site of a medieval defensive gate and was supposed to be the residence of the kings. But they never stayed in what turned out to be a cold and uncomfortable lodge; they preferred the houses nearby, particularly those opposite the Artus Court.

ARTUS COURT

Behind the Neptune fountain, the **Artus Court** (Dwór Artusa; Map pp358-9; ☎ 346 33 58; Długi Targ 43/44; adult/concession 8/3zł; ☟ 10am-5.30pm Mon-Sat, 11am-5.30pm Sun) is perhaps the single best-known house in Gdańsk – it even has a brand of vodka named after it. The court has been an essential stop for passing luminaries ever since its earliest days, and a photo display in the entrance shows an enviable selection of famous visitors, from King Henry IV of England right through to a host of contemporary presidents.

Built at the end of the 15th century, the court was given its monumental façade by Abraham van den Block in the 1610s. Inside there's a huge hall, topped by a Gothic vault supported on four slim granite columns, decorated with hunting murals and dominated by a vast painting depicting the Battle of Grunwald. Wealthy local merchants used the building as a communal guildhall, holding meetings, banquets and general revelries in the lavishly decorated interior.

Like most of the centre, the court was comprehensively destroyed in WWII, but has been painstakingly restored from old photographs and historical records, recapturing at least a glimpse of its remarkable past. The hall is still the undisputed centrepiece, but the adjoining chambers hold historical artefacts and some exquisite pieces of classic Danzig furniture in the dark-wood style synonymous with the city's golden age.

The plainly renovated upper floors hold a selection of historical exhibits, including a photographic 'simulacrum' of how the great hall would have looked at its peak – even in two dimensions it's a breathtaking space, filled from top to bottom with paintings, models and stuffed animals.

One unique feature of the interior is its giant Renaissance **tiled stove**, standing in the corner of the hall and almost touching the ceiling. It's reputedly the highest tiled stove in Europe. Looking like a five-tier tower, 10.65m high, the stove is also lavishly or-

namented, with a wealth of decoration portraying, among other things, rulers, allegorical figures and coats of arms. Built in 1546 by Georg Stelzener, the stove survived virtually unchanged until 1943, when local conservators dismantled the upper part and hid it outside the city. The lower tiers were badly damaged during fighting in 1945. All fragments were collected after the war, and after a long and complex restoration, the stove was eventually put together and revealed to the public in 1995. It contains 520 tiles, 437 of which are original.

WATERFRONT

Just behind the Green Gate is the Motława River. There once was a busy quay along here, crowded with hundreds of sailing ships loading and unloading their cargo, which was stored either in the cellars of the burghers' houses in town or in the granaries on the other side of the river, on Spichlerze Island. Today it's a popular tourist promenade lined with cafés, art galleries and souvenir shops.

In medieval times, the parallel east–west streets of the Main Town all had defensive gates at their riverfront ends. Some of them still exist, though most were altered in later periods. Walking north along the Długie Pobrzeże (literally, Long Waterfront), you first get to the **Bread Gate** (Brama Chlebnicka; Map pp358-9), at the end of ul Chlebnicka. It was built around 1450, still under the Teutonic order, as shown by the original city coat of arms consisting of two crosses. The crown was added by King Kazimierz Jagiellończyk in 1457, when Gdańsk was incorporated into the kingdom.

Enter the gate and walk a few steps to see the palatial **House Under the Angels** (Dom Pod Aniołami; Map pp358-9), which is also known as the English House (Dom Angielski) after the nationality of the merchants who owned it in the 17th century. At that time it was the largest burgher's house in Gdańsk. Today it's a student dorm, which says a lot about changing standards!

At No 14 stands the late-Gothic **Schlieff House** (Map pp358-9) of 1520. It's a replica built after the emperor of Prussia, Friedrich Wilhelm III, fell in love with its predecessor in the 1820s and had it taken apart brick by brick and rebuilt in Brandenburg. The original is in Potsdam, near Berlin.

The tiny ul Grząska will take you to **ul Mariacka**, the most atmospheric of all the streets in Gdańsk and unique in Poland. It was reconstructed after the war, almost from the ground up, with the utmost piety on the basis of old documents and illustrations, and every detail found in the rubble was incorporated. It looks amazingly authentic. It's the only street with a complete row of terraces, which gives it enormous charm, and is a trendy place lined with shops selling amber jewellery. You'll also find some of the best stalls here during the Dominican Fair (p368).

The street ends at **St Mary's Gate** (Brama Mariacka; Map pp358–9), similar to the Bread Gate but constructed later, as you'll see from its coats of arms. Next to it is the fair-sized Renaissance **House of the Naturalists' Society** (Dom Towarzystwa Przyrodniczego; Map pp358–9), which has a tower and a five-storey oriel, unusual in Gdańsk. It houses the **Archaeological Museum** (Muzeum Archeologiczne; Map pp358-9; ☎ 301 50 31; ul Mariacka 25/26; adult/concession 4/3zł, free Sat; ⊙ 10am-5pm Tue-Sun). The extensive collection stresses the Polish cultural and ethnic roots of the region; if you haven't had your fill of views elsewhere, you can also go to the top of the **tower** (admission 2zł; ⊙ 8am-4pm Mon, 10am-5pm Tue-Sun).

GDAŃSK CRANE & CENTRAL MARITIME MUSEUM

Back on the waterfront, just beyond the modest **Gate of the Holy Spirit** (Brama Św Ducha; Map pp358–9), is the conspicuous and world-renowned **Gdańsk Crane** (Żuraw Gdański; Map pp358-9; ☎ 301 53 11; ul Szeroka 67/68; adult/concession 6/4zł; ⊙ 10am-6pm May-Sep, 9.30am-4pm Tue-Fri, 10am-4pm Sat & Sun Oct-Apr). Built in the mid-15th century as the biggest double-towered gate on the waterfront, it also served to move heavy cargoes directly onto or off the vessels. For this purpose two large wheels – 5m in diameter – were installed as a hoist with a rope wound around the axle; it was put in motion by people 'walking' along the inner circumference of the wheels as a treadmill. It could hoist loads of up to 2000kg, making it the biggest crane in medieval Europe. At the beginning of the 17th century another set of wheels was added higher up, for installing masts.

The crane suffered considerable damage in 1945 but was carefully rebuilt; it's the only fully restored relic of its kind in the world, administered by the Central Maritime Museum. The interior has exhibits relating to the history of shipping, plus a collection of shells, corals and other marine life. You can also have a closer look at the hoisting gear.

Next door to the crane, the main annexe of the **Central Maritime Museum** (Centralne Muzeum Morskie; Map pp358-9; ☎ 320 33 58; www.cmm.pl; ul Szeroka 67/68; adult/concession 6/4zł; ⊙ 10am-6pm May-Sep, 10am-4pm Tue-Sun Oct-Apr) is a featureless modern building displaying traditional rowing and sailing boats from various non-European countries.

The museum continues in three reconstructed **granaries** (Map pp358-9; ☎ 301 86 11; ul Ołowianka 9/13; adult/concession 6/4zł) just across the Motława, on Ołowianka Island. The museum's own ferry service shuttles between the crane and the island; otherwise it's a 15-minute walk around via the bridge facing the Green Gate. The exhibits, displayed in nine large halls within the granaries, illustrate the history of Polish seafaring from the earliest times to the present and include models of old sailing warships and ports, a 9th-century dugout, navigation instruments, ships' artillery, flags and the like.

Finally, there's the **MS Sołdek** (Map pp358-9; adult/concession 6/4zł), a museum ship moored in front of the granaries. It was the first freighter built in Gdańsk after WWII (1948); it has now been withdrawn from service and is open to visitors.

Set aside three hours to visit all the sites – there's really a lot to see. Combined tickets for all four sections, including the crane, cost 14zł; tours in English or Russian cost 20zł to 40zł, depending on numbers.

ST MARY'S CHURCH

Set right in the middle of the Main Town, the **Kościół Mariacki** (Kościół NMP; Map pp358–9) is believed to be the largest old brick church in the world. It's 105m long and 66m wide at the transept, and its massive squat tower is 78m high. About 25,000 people can be easily accommodated in its half-hectare (5000-sq-metre) interior.

The church was begun in 1343 and reached its present gigantic size in 1502. It served as the parish church for the Catholic congregation until the Reformation gale blew into Gdańsk, and it passed to the Protestants in 1572, to be used by them until WWII.

The church didn't escape the destruction of 1945; half of the vault collapsed and the interior was largely burnt out. Fortunately, the most valuable works of art had been removed and hidden before the battle front arrived. They were brought back after a long and complex reconstruction.

The church's elephantine size is arresting and you feel even more antlike when you enter the building. Illuminated with natural light passing through 37 large windows (the biggest is 127 sq metres in area) the three-naved, whitewashed interior, topped by an intricate Gothic vault, is astonishingly bright and spacious. It was originally covered with frescoes, the sparse remains of which are visible in the far right corner. Imagine the impact the church must have made on medieval worshippers.

On first sight, the church looks almost empty, but walk around its 30-odd chapels to discover how many outstanding works of art have been accumulated. In the floor alone, there are about 300 tombstones. In the chapel at the back of the left (northern) aisle is a replica of Memling's *The Last Judgment* – the original is in the National Museum. Note the extraordinary baroque organ.

The high altar boasts a Gothic polyptych from the 1510s, with the Coronation of the Virgin depicted in its central panel. Large as it is, it's a miniature in this vast space. The same applies to the 4m crucifix high up on the rood beam. Directly below it is a lofty wooden sacrarium from 1482, elaborately carved in the shape of a tower.

One object that does stand out, in terms both of its size and rarity, is the 15th-century **astronomical clock** (see the boxed text on below), placed in the northern transept. Another great attraction of the church is its **tower** (adult/concession 3/1.50zł), or rather the sweeping bird's-eye view you get if you can climb the 405 steps to the tiny viewing platform. The guttering directly below the platform has been adopted as an impromptu wishing well – it's probably best not to ask what happens to all those coins when it rains.

ROYAL CHAPEL

Just to the north of St Mary's Church, and completely overshadowed by the massive monster, sits the small **Royal Chapel** (Kaplica Królewska; Map pp358–9), which is squeezed between two houses. The only baroque church in old Gdańsk, it was built between 1678 and 1681 to fulfil the last will of the primate of Poland of the time, Andrzej Olszowski, who set aside funds for a Catholic house of worship in what was by then a predominantly Lutheran city. The local clergy felt obliged to respect the primate's bequest and reluctantly allocated part of the upper floor of St Mary's vicarage to the chapel.

POMERANIA

CLOCKING ON

The huge astronomical clock in St Mary's Church was constructed in the 1460s by Hans Düringer from Toruń and functioned until 1553. It's claimed that during that time it lost only three minutes. When made, it was the largest clock in the world, 14m tall. Legend has it that Düringer was blinded to prevent him creating another clock that may have competed with this one. He was probably buried under his own masterpiece.

Not only did the clock show the hour, day, month and year but also the phases of the moon, the positions of the sun and moon in the zodiac cycle and the calendar of the saints. It had six devices allowing figures of saints and the apostles to appear and disappear at certain times, chased by the grim reaper. Adam and Eve rang the bells every hour.

The clock was neglected for centuries but stayed in its place until WWII. As the eastern front advanced in the late stage of the war, the clock was dismantled and stored outside Gdańsk in fear of its safety. In the mid-1980s a long and costly reconstruction began, largely financed by sponsorship and donations from private citizens.

About 70% of the clock's original housing survived to be restored and complemented with missing elements and new mechanisms. It was mounted in its place and put back to work in 1990, after 437 years of quiescence. There are still some figures missing, but the clock shows the right time and displays some modest puppet-theatre abilities. Join the crowds at noon to see it in action.

The chapel was designed by famous royal architect Tylman van Gameren. It was built on the 1st floor, though the façade was extended over the whole of the elevation to make the building look bigger and more impressive. Parts of the two adjoining houses were adapted as the chancel and the vestibule, and the nave was topped with a dome, typical of the baroque style and particularly of Gameren's style. The façade is more attractive than the bare interior. It has the coats of arms of Poland, Lithuania and King Jan III Sobieski (the founder of the chapel) but, significantly, not that of Gdańsk.

GREAT ARSENAL

To the west of St Mary's Church, ul Piwna (Beer St) ends at the **Great Arsenal** (Wielka Zbrojownia; Map pp358–9). This being Gdańsk, even such an apparently prosaic building as an armoury has evolved into an architectural gem. It's the work of Antoon van Opberghen, built at the beginning of the 17th century and, like most of Gdańsk's architecture, clearly shows the influence of the Low Countries. The main eastern façade, framed within two side towers, is floridly decorated (if a little blackened) and guarded by figures of soldiers on the top. Military motifs predominate, and the city's coat of arms guards the doorways. A small stone structure rather like a well, in the middle of the façade, is the lift that was used for hoisting heavy ammunition from the basement. Above it stands Athena, goddess of warfare.

The armoury is now home to a supermarket, not exactly what its creators intended. Walk through to the square on the opposite side, Targ Węglowy (Coal Market), to see the western façade – though not as heavily ornamented as the eastern one, it's a fine composition that looks like four burghers' houses.

NORTHERN MAIN TOWN

The main attraction of this sector is **St Nicholas' Church** (Map pp358–9), one of the oldest in town. It was built by the Dominican order on its arrival from Kraków in 1227, but only reached its final shape at the end of the 15th century. Unlike most of the other Gothic churches in the city, the interior of St Nick's is very richly decorated. The magnificent late-Renaissance high altar of 1647 first catches the eye, followed by the imposing

baroque organ made a century later. Among other highlights are the stalls in the chancel and an ornate baptismal chapel in the right-hand aisle, just as you enter the church. And don't miss the bronze rosary chandelier (1617), which features the Virgin and Child carved in wood, hanging in the nave in front of the entrance to the chancel.

Just behind the church is the large **Market Hall** (Hala Targowa; Map pp358–9), constructed in the late 19th century after the Dominicans were expelled by the Prussian authorities and their monastery standing on this site was pulled down. At the time of writing the market was closed for extensive renovations, and looks unlikely to reopen in the near future.

In front of the market hall is the tall octagonal **Hyacinthus' Tower** (Baszta Jacek; Map pp358–9), one of the remnants of the medieval fortifications. It was built around 1400 and, apart from its defensive role, it also served as a watchtower. Today it houses a florist's shop and photo lab.

About 200m east towards the river is the massive Gothic **St John's Church** (Kościół Św Jana; Map pp358–9). It was built during the 14th and 15th centuries on marshy ground and buttresses had to be added to support it. Damaged but not destroyed during the war, the church was locked for four decades. The internal decorations were removed and distributed around the parishes; the organ and the pulpit, for instance, now adorn St Mary's Church. Only the monumental stone high altar was left inside, simply because it was too large and heavy to be moved elsewhere. The interior has been partly restored and is now used as an exhibition space and auditorium, showcasing everything from National Geographic photography to gospel choirs and Ray Charles tributes.

Old Town

Despite its name, Gdańsk's Old Town (Map pp358–9) was not the cradle of the city. The earliest inhabited site, according to archaeologists, was in what is now the Main Town area. Nonetheless, a settlement existed in the Old Town from the late 10th century and developed in parallel to the Main Town.

Under the Teutonic order, the two parts merged into a single urban entity, but the Old Town was always poorer and had no defensive system of its own. One other difference was that the Main Town was more 'German' while the Old Town had a larger Polish population. During WWII it suffered as much as its wealthier cousin but, apart from a handful of buildings (mainly churches) it was not rebuilt in its previous shape. Today it's little more than an average postwar town, garnished here and there with reconstructed relics. The most interesting area is along the Radunia Canal, between ul Garncarska and ul Stolarska.

The largest monument of the Old Town is **St Catherine's Church** (Kościół Św Katarzyny; Map pp358–9), the oldest church in Gdańsk, which was begun in the 1220s. It was the parish church for the whole town until St Mary's was completed. As is common, the church evolved over centuries and only reached its final shape in the mid-15th century (save for the baroque top to the tower, added in 1634); since then it has remained unchanged.

The vaulted Gothic interior was originally covered with frescoes, fragments of which were discovered under a layer of plaster. Note the huge painting (11m long) depicting the entry of Christ to Jerusalem, placed under the organ loft in the left-hand aisle, and the richly carved enclosure of the baptismal font (1585) in the opposite aisle. The astronomer Johannes Hevelius was buried in the church's chancel and there is an 18th-century epitaph above the grave.

The church is home to the **Tower Clocks Museum** (Muzeum Zegarów Wieżowych; Map pp358-9; ☎ 305 64 92; ul Wielkie Młyny; adult/concession 4/2zł; 10am-5pm Tue-Sun), which features a collection of old tower clocks from the 15th century onwards. You can also go up the tower to see the **carillon** (admission 3zł), a set of 49 bells that plays a selection of familiar melodies every hour.

Set immediately behind St Catherine's is **St Bridget's Church** (Kościół Św Brygidy; Map pp358–9). Founded 700 years ago, the building was almost completely destroyed in 1945, and until 1970 only the walls were left standing. Once the authorities set about rebuilding it, it took five years for the whole structure, complete with a perfect Gothic vault and tacked-on Renaissance tower, to be returned to its original state. There's almost nothing left of the prewar furnishing and the interior has unusual, striking modern fittings, with lots of wrought iron and a

sparkling altarpiece that mimics the organ pipes. Amber also plays a big part – there's a spectacular 174cm-high amber monstrance depicting the tree of life and the monumental high altar, a recent construction, using a record-breaking 6500kg of the stuff.

Lech Wałęsa attended Mass here when he was an unknown electrician in the nearby shipyard. With the wave of strikes in 1980 the church became a strong supporter of the dockyard workers and its priest, Henryk Jankowski, took every opportunity to express their views in his sermons. The church remains a record of the Solidarity period, with several contemporary craftworks related to the trade union and to modern Polish history in general. You'll find the tombstone of murdered priest Jerzy Popiełuszko, the Katyń epitaph, a collection of crosses from the 1980 and '88 strikes and a door covered with bas-reliefs of scenes from Solidarity's history – all in the right-hand (northern) aisle.

The peculiar seven-storey building opposite St Catherine's Church is the **Great Mill** (Wielki Młyn; Map pp358–9). Built in around 1350 by the Teutonic Knights, it was the largest mill in medieval Europe, over 40m long and 26m high, and equipped with a set of 18 millstones, each 5m in diameter. The mill operated until 1945 and just before WWII produced 200 tonnes of flour per day. It might still be working today if not for the war damage. The building was reconstructed, but its machinery wasn't, and it now houses a modern shopping mall.

Behind the mill, across a small park, is the **Old Town Hall** (Ratusz Staromiejski; Map pp358–9), once the seat of the Old Town council. A well-proportioned Renaissance building crowned with a high central tower typical of its Flemish provenance, it was designed at the end of the 16th century by Antoon van Opberghen, the architect later responsible for the Great Arsenal. The brick structure is delicately ornamented in stone, including the central doorway and a frieze with the shields of Poland, Prussia and Gdańsk.

The Old Town Hall now houses the Baltic Cultural Centre and an exhibition hall. Go upstairs to see the foyer, notable for its rich decoration, partly assembled from old burghers' houses. Note the arcaded stone wall (1560) with three Roman gods in bas-relief. This composition, older than the town hall itself, was moved here from one of the houses in the Main Town. One of the doors leads to the Great Hall, which can also be visited. Concerts are held here – check the programme for details.

SHIPYARD

Gdańsk's **shipyard** (Map pp358–9) is not just an industrial zone, it's a piece of history. It was here that discontent with the communist regime boiled over into strikes and dissent, and here that the first signs of resistance were stamped out by Soviet forces in 1970; 10 years later it was here that an electrician named Lech Wałęsa sprang up to address the crowds of strikers, leading to the formation of the Solidarity movement and ultimately to democracy for Poland.

Since the heady times of Wałęsa's presidency, however, the yard has largely lost its protected status. While it had always been a major local employer, business under the free market was never good enough for the site to be anything but an economic liability, and once the postcommunists came to power the shipyard was finally declared bankrupt.

Just in front of the gates, on Solidarity Sq, the **Monument to the Fallen Shipyard Workers** (Pomnik Poległych Stoczniowców; Map pp358–9) commemorates the workers killed in the riots of 1970. Unveiled on 16 December 1980, 10 years after the massacre, the monument is a set of three 42m-tall steel crosses, with a series of bronze bas-reliefs in their bases. One of the plates contains a fragment of a poem by late Nobel laureate Czesław Miłosz: 'You who wronged a simple man / Do not feel safe. A poet remembers. / You can kill one, but another is born.'

The first monument in a communist regime to commemorate the regime's victims, it immediately became a symbol and landmark of Gdańsk and a must see for every visitor.

On the grounds of the yard itself is the **Roads to Freedom exhibition** (Droga do Wolności; ☎ 769 29 20; www.fcs.org.pl; ul Doki 1; adult/concession 5/3zł; ☒ 10am-5pm Tue-Sun), a collection of multimedia displays and artefacts illustrating Poland's turbulent path to democracy, from the 1956 uprisings to martial law and the collapse of communism. Outdoor art installations offer a more unusual perspective, reflecting Solidarity's views on the moral and social responsibility of the artist.

The whole thing is a poignant reminder of just how much has changed over the last 50 years, and of just how much dedication and sacrifice went into achieving that change.

Old Suburb

The Old Suburb (Stare Przedmieście; Map pp358–9), south of the Main Town, was the product of the expansion of the city between the 15th and 17th centuries. Reduced to rubble in 1945 and rebuilt in the familiar bland postwar fashion, the suburb has little charm but boasts some important sights.

The most significant of these is the **National Museum** (Muzeum Narodowe; Map pp358–9; ☎ 301 70 61; www.muzeum.narodowe.gda.pl; ul Toruńska 1; adult/concession 15/9zł; ☒ 10am-8pm), located in the vaulted interiors of the former Franciscan monastery. Among the best museums in the country, it covers the broad spectrum of Polish and international art and crafts, boasting extensive collections of paintings, woodcarvings, gold and silverware, embroidery, fabrics, porcelain, faience, wrought iron and furniture. It has the original figure of St George from the spire of the Court of the Fraternity of St George, an assortment of huge, elaborately carved Danzig-style wardrobes (typical of the city, from where they were sent all over the country) and several beautiful ceramic tiled stoves.

The 1st floor is given over to paintings, with a section devoted to Dutch and Flemish work. The jewel of the collection is Hans Memling's (1435–94) triptych of the *Last Judgment,* one of the earlier works of the artist, dating from 1472 to 1473. You'll also find works by the younger Brueghel and Van Dyck, and the beautifully macabre *Hell* by Jacob Swanenburgh, who was the master of the young Rembrandt.

Adjoining the museum from the north, and formerly belonging to the Franciscan monastery, is the **Church of the Holy Trinity** (Kościół Św Trójcy; Map pp358–9), which was built at the end of the 15th century, when the Gothic style had already reached its late decorative stage. This style is best seen in the elaborate top of the western façade. After St Mary's Church it's the largest in town, with a spacious and lofty whitewashed interior topped with a superb, netlike vault. The chancel was badly damaged during the war and was separated from the nave by a wall.

The high altar has an assembly of panels from triptychs of different origins, while the filigree late-Gothic pulpit from 1541 is topped with a Renaissance canopy. Note the floor paved almost entirely with old tombstones and the spidery baroque chandeliers of the mid-17th century.

Westerplatte

Westerplatte (Map p355) is a long peninsula at the entrance to the harbour, 7km north of the historic town. When Gdańsk became a free city after WWI, Westerplatte was the Polish tip of the port. It served both trading and military purposes and had a garrison to protect it.

WWII broke out here at dawn on 1 September 1939, when the German battleship *Schleswig-Holstein* began shelling the Polish guard post. The garrison, which numbered just 182 men, held out for seven days before surrendering, earning immense respect from their attackers and even from Hitler himself. The site is now a memorial, with some of the ruins left as they were after the bombardment, plus a massive **monument** (Map p355) put up in memory of the defenders. The surviving **Guardhouse No 1** (Wartownia Nr 1; Map p355; ☎ 343 69 72; ul Sucharskiego; adult/concession 3/1.50zł; ☻ 8am-7pm May-Oct) houses a small exhibition related to the event, including a model of the battle labelled in English.

Buses 106 and 158 go to Westerplatte from the main train station, but a more attractive way to get here is by boat. Boats depart several times daily from the wharf next to the Green Gate. You can take the boat that includes a visit to the port en route.

Oliwa

Oliwa (Map p355), a desirable suburb about 9km from the historic centre, boasts a fine cathedral set in a quiet park, and provides an enjoyable half-day break from the dense attractions of the Main Town. To get here, take the commuter train from central Gdańsk and get off at Gdańsk Oliwa station, from where it's a 10-minute walk.

The beginnings of Oliwa go back over 800 years, when the Pomeranian dukes who then ruled Gdańsk invited the Cistercians to settle here in 1186 and granted them land together with privileges, including the revenues of the port of Gdańsk.

The abbey didn't have an easy life. The original church from around 1200 was burnt out by the pagan Baltic Prussians, then by the Teutonic Knights. A new Gothic church, built in the mid-14th century, was surrounded by defensive walls, but that didn't save it from further misfortunes. When in 1577 the abbots supported King Stefan Batory in his attempts to reduce the city's independence, the citizens of Gdańsk burned the church down in revenge. The monks rebuilt their holy home once more, but then the Swedish wars began and the church fell prey to repeated looting, losing its organ and pulpit among other things. The monks' troubles came to an end in 1831, when the Prussian government decided to expel them from the city. The church was given to the local parish and, in 1925, raised to the rank of **cathedral** (Map p355). It came through the war almost unscathed, and is an important, and unusual, example of ecclesiastical architecture.

The first surprise is its façade, a striking composition of two slim octagonal Gothic towers with a central baroque portion squeezed between them. You enter the church by going downstairs, for its floor is more than 1m below the external ground level. The interior looks extraordinarily long, mainly because of the unusual proportions of the building – the nave and chancel together are 90m long but only 8.3m wide. At the far end of this 'tunnel' is a baroque high altar (1688), while the previous oak-carved Renaissance altar (from 1606) is now in the left-hand transept. Opposite, in the right transept, is the marble tombstone of the Pomeranian dukes (1613).

The showpiece of the church is the **organ**. The instrument, begun in 1763 and completed 30 years later, is noted for its fine tone and the mechanised angels that blow trumpets and ring bells when the organ is played. In July and August, recitals take place on Tuesday and Friday evenings, but 20-minute performances are held daily every hour or two between 10am and 3pm or 4pm (afternoon only on Sunday). Check the schedule with the tourist offices before setting off.

Behind the cathedral is the 18th-century abbots' palace that now accommodates the **Modern Art Gallery** (Wystawa Sztuki Współczesnej; Map p355; ☎ 552 12 71; ul Cystersów 18; adult/concession 8/4zł; ☻ 9am-4pm Tue-Sun), which is a branch of the National Museum of Gdańsk. The old granary opposite the palace houses the **Ethnographic Museum** (Muzeum Etnograficzne; Map p355; ☎ 552 41 39; ul Cystersów 19; adult/concession 6/3zł; ☒ 9am-4pm Tue-Sun) and its interesting collection of rural household implements and crafts from the region. The 18th-century **park**, with its lakes, old exotic trees, a palm house, a greenhouse and a small formal French garden, supplies a fine natural setting for the historic complex.

FESTIVALS & EVENTS

The oldest and most important event that takes place in the city is the **Dominican Fair** (Jarmark Dominikański; ☎ 554 93 34; www.mtgsa.pl), which dates back to 1260, when the local Dominican monks received the papal privilege of holding a fair on the feast day of their saint. The fair was initially held on Plac Dominikański, the square next to St Nicholas' Church, but today it's spread out, taking up 6000 sq metres of the Main Town for three weeks every August. There's no shortage of tacky crap on offer, but you'll still find plenty of antiques, bric-a-brac and craft stalls; fans of old militaria and Art Deco objects, in particular, will be in their element. The fair is accompanied by various cultural events, including street theatre, concerts, races and parades.

Other major events:

International Organ Music Festival (☎ 305 20 40; www.filharmonia.gda.pl in Polish) Held in the Oliwa cathedral, with twice-weekly organ recitals from mid-June till the end of August.

International Festival of Open-Air & Street Theatre (FETA; ☎ 557 42 47; www.feta.pl) Held in July.

International Organ, Choir & Chamber Music Festival (☎ 620 76 33) Held on Friday in July and August in St Mary's Church.

International Shakespeare Festival (☎ 305 68 00; www.teatr-szekspir.gda.pl) Held in August.

Sounds of the North Festival (www.nck.org.pl) Held in August, featuring folklore-inspired music from such exotic locations as Greenland and Kamchatka.

World Amber Trawling Championship (☎ 247 82 93) Unusual all-comers contest held in August in the seaside village of Jantar, 20km east of Gdańsk.

SLEEPING
Budget

Prices listed under this budget category do not include breakfast; bathrooms are shared unless otherwise indicated.

HOSTELS

Hostel Przy Targu Rybnym (Map pp358-9; ☎ 301 56 27; www.gdanskhostel.com; ul Grodzka 21; dm 40zł, r per person 60zł; P ☒) This excellent private place is the kind of travellers' den that attracts the unswerving loyalty of both its volunteer staff and its mixed clientele. A sardine-tin dorm and five more-spacious private rooms take up the quaint little house by the waterfront; just about any service you can think of is thrown in free. No reservations are taken, as people tend to forget to leave.

Dizzy Daisy (Map pp358-9; ☎ 301 39 19; www.hostel .pl; ul Gnilna 3; dm/s/d/tr 35/110/120/165zł; ☒ Jul & Aug; P ☒) Look out for the booth at the station; as elsewhere, 'greeters' are employed to round up likely looking arrivals and shepherd them to these unfancy student rooms. The location's good and staff friendly.

Dizzy Daisy Hilton (Map pp358-9; ☎ 301 68 01; ul Podwale Przedmiejskie 20; d/tr/q 140/150/160zł) A second branch of the Dizzy Daisy chain, the ironically named Hilton offers much the same in a larger block just south of the Main Town.

Strawberry Hostel (Map p355; ☎ 342 94 79; www .strawberryhostels.com; ul Krasickiego 9/9a; s/d/tr/q €18/ 24/30/40; ☒ Jul & Aug; P) Another good summer hostel targeting the backpacker market. The nearby seafront more than makes up for the slight trek out to Brzeźno, with regular beach parties cementing the social side. There's a free shuttle service, or you can take tram 13. Pets are welcome, so feel free to stick your cat in your suitcase.

Dom Studenta ASP (Map pp358-9; ☎ 301 28 16; ul Chlebnicka 13/16; dm adult/student 30/26zł; ☒ Jul–mid-Sep) This is the dorm of the Academy of Fine Arts, ideally located in the historic House Under the Angels in the Main Town. It's basic (prices don't even include sheets) and there's an inconvenient four-night minimum, but look at the house and location!

MOKF Hostel Al Grunwaldzka (Map p355; ☎ 341 16 60; www.mokf.com.pl; Al Grunwaldzka 240/244; s 50.29zł, d 72.76-100.58zł, q 94.16zł; ☒); ul Wałowa (Map pp358-9; ☎ 301 23 13) Arguably the best of Gdańsk's two year-round HI hostels, though the restrictive rules make it a poor alternative to the independent places. The 208 beds are mainly in doubles (some with private bathroom) and quads. It's in a sports complex 6km northwest of the centre; take the SKM to Gdańsk Zaspa and walk northwest. The other branch is at ul Wałowa 21.

PRIVATE ROOMS

Grand-Tourist (Map pp358-9; ☎ 301 26 34; www.gt .com.pl; ul Podwale Grodzkie 8; s 50-60zł, d 80-100zł; ☷ office 10am-6pm Mon-Fri, 10am-2pm Sat) Opposite the train station, this is the main agency handling private rooms. You can book by phone or email, but you must then go to the office in person to do the paperwork and pay. When making your choice, don't worry too much about the distance from the centre – work out how close the place is to the SKM commuter train.

CAMPING

Camping Nr 218 Stogi (Map p355; ☎ 307 39 15; www .kemping-gdansk.pl; ul Wydmy 9; camp site per adult 10zł, child 5-9zł, cabins 40-100zł; ☷ May-Sep) Located in the suburb of Stogi, about 5.5km northeast of the centre, this is the most convenient of Gdańsk's three camping grounds. Just 200m away is one of the city's best beaches, with the cleanest water you'll find for miles. Tram 8 from the main train station passes here.

Mid-Range

Gdańsk seems to have a mysterious lack of mid-priced accommodation in the old centre, but you don't have to go far into the suburbs to find a room – Suchanino, a short bus ride from the main station, has a particularly handy cluster of private guesthouses, and there are plenty of other options not too much further afield.

Dom Muzyka (Map p355; ☎ 300 92 60; ul Łąkowa 1/2; s 150zł, d 210-230zł; ⓟ) Gdańsk isn't famed for its musical associations, but the Academy of Music seems to have high hopes for the future, putting up weary travellers to help fund the tinklings and tootlings of its talented charges. Once all the instruments are locked up for the night, this is actually an endearingly quiet, comfortable place, and within walking distance of the centre to boot.

Pensjonat Angela (Map p355; ☎ 302 23 15; ul Beethovena 12; s/d 160/180zł; ⓟ) One of the most convenient Suchanino choices, Angela is a friendly family home turned upscale guesthouse, with smart hotel-standard rooms, big beds, sun-catching balconies and good buffet breakfasts. To get here take bus 184, or alternatively grab a taxi (12zł to 15zł) – it's copiously signed, so you should have no problem knowing when to get off.

Pokoje Gościnne Mac-Tur (Map p355; ☎ 302 41 70; www.mactur.gda.pl; ul Beethovena 8; s/d/tr €30/40/50; ⓟ ☱) Just next door to Angela, Mac-Tur offers broadly similar accommodation in small but individual bedrooms, plus all the usual comforts and table tennis for the energetic. On the other side is its sister hotel, the Abak.

Villa Akme (Map p355; ☎ 302 40 21; www.akme.gda .pl;ul Drwęcka 1; s/d/tr 110/150/210zł; ⓟ) Guess what? It's another small family-run suburban pension. About 2km southwest of the train station, Akme has 11 newly furnished rooms and is easily accessible by bus 118, 208 or 295 from the station. It may not be original, but you won't be disappointed either.

Villa Pascal (Map p355; ☎ 342 75 92; www.villa-pascal .com.pl; ul Łamana 5; s 160-190zł, d 250zł, ste 280-400zł; ⓟ) Out in Brzeźno, just a short distance from the beach, this sturdy red-tiled guesthouse falls more into the hotel category. Unpretentious rooms are decked out in a range of colours, and the house restaurant has some good lunch deals.

Dom Aktora (Map pp358-9; ☎ 301 59 01; www.dom aktora.pl; ul Straganiarska 55/56; s/d/apt 200/250/300zł; ⓟ) Self-catering accommodation doesn't come any more central than the small apartments here, each with its own kitchenette. The appealingly unaffected style is supposedly Italian, in much the same way that Polish pizza is. You're paying for the location, but it's money well spent.

Dom Harcerza (Map pp358-9; ☎ 301 36 21; www .domharcerza.prv.pl; ul Za Murami 2/10; r 104-300zł) Occupying a venerable theatre building just shy of ul Długa, there's not much that's dramatic about this simple workers' hotel, which offers rooms to accommodate between one and 12 people as well as a couple of en suite doubles and triples.

Old Town Apartments (☎ 22-887 98 00; www.war sawshotel.com; apt €60-150) This Warsaw-based firm arranges apartments in four Main Town locations for a relatively inoffensive mark-up. Long-term lets are also available.

Top End

In keeping with the restored splendour of the Main Town, Gdańsk has some unique and truly superb accommodation options for those who can afford the finer things in life. Look out for serious discounting at weekends and out of season.

Hotel Królewski (Map pp358-9; ☎ 326 11 11; www .hotelkrolewski.pl; ul Ołowianka 1; s 290zł, d 340-390zł, ste 510-650zł; ☒) They say luxury comes at a price, but if this is all it costs you won't hear many complaints. The latest addition to Gdańsk's top flight has an unbeatable location right on the waterfront (it's an old granary), genuinely charming staff and some absolutely stunning modern suites, all at prices that would make most Western hoteliers choke. Book well in advance.

Hotel Podewils (Map pp358-9; ☎ 300 95 60; www .podewils-hotel.pl; ul Szafarnia 2; s €166-181, d €203-246, ste €447-653; ✗) Right on the marina, refinement and elegance ooze from every pore at the Podewils, bestowing a certain intimate charm on the antique lounge and individually decorated 18th-century bedrooms. Personal service and extras such as DVD players and spa baths set it apart from even the most ambitious competition.

Hotel Hanza (Map pp358-9; ☎ 305 34 27; www .hanza-hotel.com.pl; ul Tokarska 6; s/d 665/695zł, ste 885-1090zł; P ✗ 💻) Comfortably situated at the top of its game, the Hanza makes the most of an exclusive location next to the Gdańsk Crane, wooing guests with modern styling and warm, muted orange tones. The inevitable fitness centre and a waterfront terrace complete the picture.

Dwór Oliwski (Map p355; ☎ 554 70 00; www.dwor -oliwski.com.pl; ul Bytowska 4; s/d €105/126, ste €158-232; P ✗ 🐾) Oliwa may not seem the most convenient place to stay in the Tri-City, but this magnificent manor house provides a compelling reason to get out of town. Set in extensive grounds with a variety of traditional buildings, the rooms are sophistication incarnate, and the restaurant has a fantastic reputation for French cuisine.

Hotel Mercure Hevelius (Map pp358-9; ☎ 321 00 00; mer.hevelius@orbis.pl; ul Heweliusza 22; s 380zł, d 420-440zł, ste 872-970zł; P ✗ 💻) The 17-storey Hevelius is not exactly the best feature of the city skyline; luckily the standards and amenities make it one of Orbis' better efforts. For views over old Gdańsk, demand a room facing south.

EATING

There are plenty of eateries throughout the centre catering to every budget – just walking down ul Długa is an exercise in decision making. As you may expect, fish is plentiful, though mainly in more expensive establishments. Oddly enough for such an important port and cosmopolitan city, ethnic cuisines are poorly represented, and

you'll have to look around to find anything more exotic than sweet 'n sour pork or a doner kebab.

Restauracja Gdańska (Map pp358-9; ☎ 305 76 71; ul Św Ducha 16; mains 19-100zł) Eating here is as much an experience as anything else: the five banquet rooms and salons are crammed to the rafters with antique furniture, paintings, model ships, random *objets d'art* and nimble waiters in epaulettes, giving a pretty good idea what the Artus Court might have looked like in its heyday. The upper-end traditional cooking makes a visit doubly worthwhile.

Gospoda Pod Wielkem Młynem (Map pp358-9; ☎ 305 30 69; ul Na Piaskach 1; mains 12-40zł; ✷ lunch & dinner) A sure-fire tip for summer, this charming half-timbered building behind the Great Mill has the city's best garden, effectively an island on the Radunia Canal. Romantics in particular will lap up the secluded atmosphere, surrounded by shady trees and rustic hay wains. Hevelius beer and Hungarian wine help the food down nicely.

Restauracja Pod Łososiem (Map pp358-9; ☎ 301 76 52; www.podlososiem.com.pl in Polish; ul Szeroka 54; mains 45-90zł; ✷ lunch & dinner) Gdańsk's classiest and most famous restaurant, rivalled only by the pricier but emptier Tawerna (see opposite), off Długi Targ. Founded in 1598, its strong point is fish, particularly the salmon after which the place is named, but it also has a list of meat dishes. The speciality drink here is Goldwasser, a thick, sweet vodka with flakes of gold floating in it, invented and produced in its cellars from the end of the 16th century till the outbreak of WWII. Any VIP who ever visited Gdańsk has probably eaten here.

Pesca Bar (Map pp358-9; ☎ 783 72 31; ul Rajska 4C; mains 4.50-29zł; ✷ lunch & dinner) Seafood comes in more affordable form here, one of the few places in town where you can get a decent fish supper without worrying about weight or unseen extras. A range of snacks and sandwiches supplements the proper meals.

Bar Pod Rybą (Map pp358-9; ☎ 305 13 07; Długi Targ 35/38; mains 6-17zł; ✷ lunch & dinner) You wouldn't normally expect much from a budget eatery at the heart of the tourist trail, but cynics should be pleasantly surprised by the standards at this neat central bar. Baked potatoes are particularly good, and old photos of Gdańsk give you something to look at.

Towarzystwo Gastronomiczne (Map pp358-9; ☎ 305 29 64; ul Korzenna 33/35; mains 21-49zł; ✷ lunch

& dinner) The 'Friends of Gastronomy' provide a more modern take on Polish cuisine, using their artsily decorated cellar under the Old Town Hall to experiment on innocent fish, fowl and mammals. Staff is knowledgeable, attentive and unfazed by large groups.

Restauracja Kubicki (Map pp358-9; ☎ 301 00 50; ul Wartka 5; mains 25-45zł; ⚘ lunch & dinner; ✗) This family firm has served solid, tasty Polish food from its waterfront location since 1918, making it Gdańsk's oldest continuously operated restaurant. The lively bar is a more recent addition.

Czerwone Drzwi (Map pp358-9; ☎ 301 57 64; www .reddoor.gd.pl; ul Piwna 52/53; mains 17-45zł; ⚘ lunch & dinner) Red in name and nature, a relaxed, refined café atmosphere helps you digest the small but interesting menu of Polish-international meals. Multilingual staff coax a varied clientele into constant consumption (not that they meet much resistance). It claims to stay open until the last guest wants to leave.

Green Way (Map pp358-9; ☎ 301 41 21; ul Garncarska 4/6; mains 4.90-8.50zł; ⚘ lunch & dinner; ✗) Part of the fast-growing national chain, this is a typically simple, modern place serving tasty vegetarian and organic food. As the ultimate accolade, even nonveggies come to eat here.

Restauracja Wileńska (Map pp358-9; ☎ 301 66 53; ul Ogarna 11; mains 20-60zł; ⚘ breakfast, lunch & dinner; ✗) Aficionados of Eastern European cooking shouldn't miss the chance to tick off another underrated nation: keeping up the great traditions of the region, the hearty Lithuanian food here should leave you itching for a trip around the Baltic states.

Bar Mleczny Neptun (Map pp358-9; ☎ 301 49 88; ul Długa 33/34; mains 1-8zł; ⚘ breakfast, lunch & dinner Mon-Fri, breakfast & lunch Sat & Sun) Ultrabudget dining in original communist milk-bar style.

Also recommended:

Kuchnia Rosyjska (Map pp358-9; ☎ 301 27 35; Długi Targ 11; mains 9-35zł; ⚘ lunch & dinner)

Tawerna (Map pp358-9; ☎ 301 41 14; www.tawerna.pl; ul Powroźnicza 19/20; mains 50-120zł; ⚘ lunch & dinner)

Złota Rybka (Map pp358-9; ☎ 301 39 24; ul Piwna 50/51; mains 9.90-17.90zł; ⚘ 11am-2am)

DRINKING

The photogenic ul Mariacka has several romantic little café-bars, which put tables on their charming front terraces. You'll find plenty of open-air summer bars amid the fancy restaurants on the waterfront, Długie Pobrzeże, especially at the Targ Rybny end.

Latający Holender (Map pp358-9; ☎ 802 03 63; Wały Jagiellońskie 2/4) Buried in the basement round the back of the nasty prefab LOT building, the Flying Dutchman is one of the strangest places you'll encounter in Poland. The eponymous airman hanging grimly above the door sets the tone perfectly, ushering you into an interior populated by weird creatures and gothic contraptions.

Kamienica (Map pp358-9; ☎ 301 12 30; ul Mariacka 37/39; ⚘ 9am-11pm) The pick of the bunch on Mariacka is this excellent two-level café with a calm, sophisticated atmosphere and the best patio on the block. It's as popular for daytime coffee and cakes as it is for a sociable evening beverage.

Punkt (Map pp358-9; ☎ 0503 373 956; ul Chlebnicka 2; ⚘ from 4pm) Popular with a hipper brand of student, the murky stained glass here conceals a den of wannabe urban chic, complete with cutting-edge music and fashionable ennui. Look for the permanent gaggle of people on the steps outside.

Irish Pub (Map pp358-9; ☎ 320 24 74; www.irish.pl in Polish; ul Korzenna 33/35) Set in the vast vaulted cellars of the Old Town Hall, this is not exactly an Irish pub, but it does adhere to the great tradition of shamelessly naff nights and cheap booze. There's some kind of music most nights, and (very) late closing at weekends – see the suitably tasteless website for details.

Celtic Pub (Map pp358-9; ☎ 301 29 99; ul Lektykarska 3; ⚘ from 5pm) Another cellar bar with late-night parties, the Celtic Pub is exactly the kind of messy, crowded, chaotic dive you need to round off a hard day's drinking. For even more fun, you can inform people that the building used to be a public toilet.

Pub U Filipa (Map pp358-9; ☎ 320 23 23; ul Długa 45) Overbright lights dazzle what could be intimate tables and the walk-in clientele's pretty much what you'd expect from a place this central, but somehow Filipa gets away with it – if you get a corner seat it's almost cosy. Spontaneous dancing occasionally obstructs the way to the bar.

ENTERTAINMENT

Check the local press for up-to-date cultural and entertainment listings. *Gdańsk in Your Pocket* provides comprehensive and usefully opinionated reviews of the city's nightlife options. But, as anyone in town will tell you, Sopot is the place to go for a serious night out.

Clubs & Live Music

Rudy Kot (Map pp358-9; ☎ 301 86 49; www.rudykot.pl; ul Garncarska 18/20; parties 10zł; ☺ from 10am) Combining a bar-club with an Internet café isn't exactly the most obvious idea, but the Ginger Cat makes it seem inspired. The weekend club nights range from dance to metal; the big windows give you an idea of what's going on before you enter.

Parlament (Map pp358-9; ☎ 320 13 65; ul Św Ducha 2; admission 5-10zł; ☺ from 9pm Thu-Sat) Altogether more serious, this is the centre's highest-profile club, playing host to big dance events punctuated by anything from industrial to Asian beats. Oh, and karaoke on Thursday.

Yesterday (Map pp358-9; ☎ 301 39 24; ul Piwna 50/51) Looking at the pop-art windows outside gives you a good idea of what to expect from Yesterday – whoever decorated this basement space didn't miss a single cliché. Still, free entry, plentiful beer and a totally random music policy will quickly ease you into tomorrow.

Cotton Club (Map pp358-9; ☎ 301 88 13; ul Złotników 25/29) One of the very few places in town where you have a chance of finding regular live jazz, with some highly variable weekday jam sessions. If you don't catch the vibe, then at least there are three pool tables to while away the evening.

Leisure Activities

U7 (Map pp358-9; ☎ 305 55 77; www.u7.pl; Plac Dominikański 7; ☺ 9am-1am) Taking the American under-one-roof concept to extremes, U7 offers much more than your average bowling alley: a snack bar, gym, sauna, solarium, pool tables, darts, Internet café and even a shooting range are packed into the subterranean space by the market hall. Unsurprisingly, the heady combination of tenpin and live ammo is a magnet for Gdańsk yoof.

Opera, Classical Music & Theatre

Baltic Philharmonic Hall (Map pp358-9; ☎ 305 20 40; www.filharmonia.gda.pl in Polish; ul Ołowianka 1) This is the usual home of chamber music concerts, and also organises many of the major music festivals throughout the year.

State Baltic Opera (Map p355; ☎ 341 05 63; www.operabaltycka.pl; Al Zwycięstwa 15) The opera house

is in Gdańsk Wrzeszcz, just off the Gdańsk Politechnika train station. Alongside the usual classical repertoire, you'll get the occasional novelty such as adaptations of *Star Wars*. Symphonic concerts are also held here.

Teatr Wybrzeże (Map pp358-9; ☎ 301 70 21; Targ Węglowy 1) The main city stage, next to the Arsenal in the Main Town, Wybrzeże features mostly mainstream fare, including some top productions of great Polish and foreign classics. There's also a good nightclub in the basement.

SHOPPING

Gdańsk is widely known for its amber (see the boxed text opposite). It's sold either unset or in silver jewellery, some of which is high quality. Although a selection of amber can also be found in Warsaw, Kraków and other major cities, Gdańsk has perhaps the best choice; shops are concentrated around ul Mariacka, Długi Targ and Długie Pobrzeże, with dozens more stalls springing up around the Dominican Fair in August. Beware of overpriced jewellery and souvenir shops preying on clueless Western visitors.

Gdańsk is also a good place for Western-style multiplex shopping, with several massive malls around town – the centre in the **Great Mill** (see p365) is worth a look just for the building, while the modern **Madison Centre** (Map pp358-9; ☎ 766 75 41; www.madison.gda.pl; ul Rajska 10) provides four floors of international brands, food and a gym, not to mention free public toilets.

GETTING THERE & AWAY
Air

Lech Wałęsa airport (Map p355; ☎ 348 11 54; www.airport.gdansk.pl) is in Rębiechowo, 14km west of Gdańsk. Bus B goes to the airport up to twice hourly from Gdańsk Główny station (35 minutes; check timetables carefully), or you can take bus 110 from Gdańsk Wrzeszcz (23 minutes). The **LOT office** (Map pp358-9; ☎ 301 11 61; Wały Jagiellońskie 2/4) is next to the Upland Gate.

The only domestic flights are to Warsaw (at least five times daily), but the small terminal is becoming an increasingly important base for low-cost European airlines. International flights currently serve Copenhagen (up to four times daily), Malmö (three times

BALTIC GOLD

If there's a typically Polish precious stone, it's amber – or it would be if amber was actually a precious stone at all. In fact it's an organic substance, a fossilised tree resin. Different kinds of amber have been found all over the world, from Canada to New Zealand, but the largest deposits are along the Baltic shores.

Baltic amber was formed roughly 40 to 60 million years ago. The vast subtropical forests of the region produced thousands of tonnes of resin; later the climate cooled and the forests were buried under a thick layer of ice. They surfaced again in a fossilised form with the climatic warming millions of years later. The melting ice also formed the Baltic Sea itself, which only reached its present size in around 6000 BC.

The majority of amber is found on the Baltic's southeastern shores, particularly on the Samland Peninsula in the Kaliningrad Region (between Lithuania and Poland). Smaller deposits are along the Polish, Lithuanian and Latvian coasts, and still smaller ones in other countries bordering the Baltic.

Baltic amber was collected and traded for at least 12,000 years, but it wasn't until the 1860s that commercial exploitation, by dredging and mining, started. Until then amber was simply collected as it washed up on the beaches. Over recent years, amber has become one of the most popular 'stones' used in Polish jewellery. Manufacturers use 220 to 250 tonnes a year, but only 10% to 20% is collected in Poland (mainly on the shores of the Gulf of Gdańsk); the rest comes from the Kaliningrad Region. About 85% of Polish amber jewellery is exported, earning roughly US$300 million annually. Not bad for a little lump of tree…

weekly), Frankfurt (twice daily), Hamburg (daily), Munich (daily) and London (once or twice daily). With several further carriers interested, the number of both international and domestic services should grow considerably over the next few years.

Bus

Gdańsk's PKS terminal (Map pp358–9) is right behind the central train station, linked by an underground passageway. Buses are handy for several regional destinations which seldom, or never, have trains.

There is one morning bus directly to Frombork (14.50zł, three hours); alternatively, you can take any of the frequent buses to Elbląg (fast/slow 13zł/11zł, 1½ hours) and change there. Four fast buses go to Olsztyn daily (23zł, four hours) and two to Lidzbark Warmiński (23zł, 4¼ hours). For Łeba, head for Lębork (9.50zł, 2¼ hours, five daily) and change there.

For the Kaszuby region, there are hourly buses travelling to Kartuzy (6.90zł, one hour) and 15 daily services to Kościerzyna (9.50zł, 1¾ hours).

There are plenty of connections from Gdańsk to Western European cities; travel agencies (including Almatur and Orbis, p357) have information and sell tickets. Daily PKS buses travel to Kaliningrad (28zł,

five hours, not Sunday) and Vilnius (125zł, 16 hours) via Olsztyn.

Ferry

Polferries (☎ 343 18 87; www.polferries.pl) operates car ferries from Gdańsk Nowy Port (Map p355) to Nynäshamn in Sweden (adult/concession Skr610/Skr510, 18 hours, up to four times weekly). Information, bookings and tickets can be obtained from Orbis and other travel agents. See also p479.

Train

The main train station, Gdańsk Główny (Map pp358–9), on the western outskirts of the Old Town, handles all incoming and outgoing traffic. Note the station building itself; it's another historic monument that has been restored to its former glory.

Almost all long-distance trains to/from the south originate and terminate in Gdynia. On the other hand, most trains running along the coast to western destinations such as Szczecin start in Gdańsk and stop at Gdynia en route. Timetables show departure times from all the main Tri-City stations – ensure you look at the correct column.

Gdańsk is a busy railway junction, with 22 trains to Warsaw daily (44.65zł, four hours). All these trains go via Malbork (15.90zł, 40 minutes), but InterCity trains don't stop there. There are seven fast trains daily to Olsztyn (31.85zł, 2¾ hours), also via Malbork. If you're travelling these routes and don't plan on stopping in Malbork, make sure your camera is ready as you pass the castle.

There are three fast trains to Wrocław (49.80zł, seven hours); they all go through Bydgoszcz (30.03zł, two hours) and Poznań (43.04zł, 4¼ hours). There are also five fast trains each to Toruń (36.12zł, 3½ hours) and Szczecin (44.65zł, 5½ hours). For Łeba, take one of the frequent trains to Lębork (11.80zł, 1¼ hours) and change there.

GETTING AROUND
Boat

From May until September **Żegluga Gdańska** (Map pp358-9; ☎ 302 72 31; www.zegluga.gda.pl) runs pleasure boats and hydrofoils from Gdańsk's wharf, near the Green Gate, to Sopot (one-way/return 35zł/48zł), Gdynia (41zł/56zł) and across the Gulf of Gdańsk to the fishing village of Hel (48zł/61zł). Concession tickets cost about two-thirds of the normal fare, but none are available on the hydrofoils. The trip to Hel is a nice way to get in a sailing mood and do some sightseeing and beach bathing (see p381).

Both Żegluga Gdańska and paddle-steamer company **Żegluga Pomeranka** (Map pp358-9; ☎ 301 13 00), further up the wharf, run regular boats to Westerplatte from April to October, usually including a visit to the port.

Commuter Train

A commuter train, known as the SKM (Szybka Kolej Miejska; Fast City Train), runs constantly between Gdańsk Główny and Gdynia Główna (4zł, 35 minutes), stopping at a dozen intermediate stations, including Sopot (2.80zł). The trains run every five to 10 minutes at peak times and every hour or so late at night. You buy tickets at the stations or some Ruch kiosks and validate them in the big yellow boxes at the platform entrance (not in the train itself).

Tram & Bus

These are a slower means of transport than the SKM but cover more ground, running from 5am until around 11pm, when a handful of night lines take over. Fares depend on the duration of the journey: 1.20zł for up to 10 minutes, 2.40zł for 30 minutes

and 3.60zł for one hour. A day ticket costs 7.80zł. Remember to validate your ticket in the vehicle; it's stamped with the date and time you get on.

AROUND GDAŃSK

SOPOT
☎ 58 / pop 43,000

Sopot, immediately north of Gdańsk, has been one of Poland's most fashionable seaside resorts for almost 200 years. A fishing village belonging to the Cistercians of Oliwa has existed here since the 13th century, yet Sopot was really 'discovered' by Jean Georges Haffner, a former doctor of the Napoleonic armies, who established sea bathing here in 1823. When the town was attached to the Free City of Danzig after WWI it quickly boomed, becoming a place where the filthy rich of the day rubbed shoulders. By the outbreak of WWII, it was a vibrant resort with 30,000 residents.

Recovering quickly in the postwar period, Sopot received a generous injection of 'new' architecture, which happily hasn't managed to overpower what was built earlier. Today it's given over almost entirely to tourism, attracting huge numbers of visitors with its long, sandy beach and tumultuous nightlife. Stay in any of the swish hotels here and you can still feel some of the glamour of the past, even if the guest lists are a bit more democratic these days.

Information
Centre for Polish Studies (Map p355; ☎ 550 68 59; www.learnpolish.edu.pl; ul Podgórna 8) Polish-language courses.

Monciak Internet (Map opposite; Centrum Rezydent, ul Haffnera 6; per hr 6zł; ☽ 11am-10pm)

NetCave (Map opposite; ☎ 551 11 83; www.netcave.coco .pl; ul Pułaskiego 7A; per hr 4zł; ☽ 10am-10pm) Internet access.

Tourist office (Map opposite; ☎ 550 37 83; www .sopot.pl; ul Dworcowa 4; ☽ 9am-8pm)

www.c@fe (Map opposite; ☎ 555 14 24; ul Chmielewskiego 5A; per hr 4zł; ☽ 8am-midnight) Internet access.

Sights & Activities

All roads in Sopot lead to **ul Bohaterów Monte Cassino**, the town's attractive and invariably crowded pedestrian mall. In summer particularly, the length of this restaurant-lined strip becomes almost impassable, crammed with tourists, locals, buskers, street artists, ice-cream vendors and costumed flyer girls. On your way down the street, you can't fail to notice the warped modern **Centrum Rezydent shopping centre** (Map below; ☎ 555 51 23; ul Haffnera 6), which is well worth investigating. Concealed within its twin-level innards are no fewer than six restaurants and a handful of shops, including a regular Kashubian market.

At the end of Monte Cassino, beyond Plac Zdrojowy, is the famous **Molo** (Map below; ☎ 551 00 02; www.molo.sopot.pl; adult/concession Mon-Fri 2.50/1.20zł, Sat & Sun 3.30/1.70zł), Poland's longest pier, built in 1928 and jutting 515m out

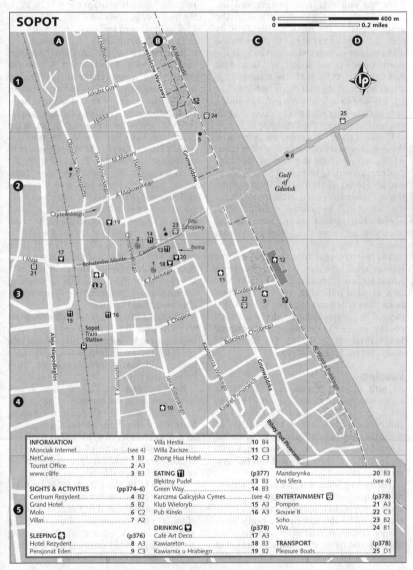

POMERANIA

into the Gulf of Gdańsk. Various attractions along its length come and go with the seasons – sea-lion shows, 'pirate' cruises and waxworks seem to make regular appearances. It's also the longest wooden pier in the whole of Europe.

North of the pier is the old-fashioned 1927 **Grand Hotel**, adjoining the long waterfront **spa park** that first popularised the town. The park backs directly onto the **beach**, arguably the finest in the Tri-City area and Sopot's main *raison d'être* in the all-too-short summer season. Towards the northern end of the stretch is a large **Aqua Park** (Map p355; ☎ 555 85 55; www.aquaparksopot.pl; ul Zamkowa Góra 3/5; day ticket 29zł; ⏰ 8am-11pm May-Sep, 8am-10pm Oct-Apr), which has tubes, slides, spas and the only wild river ride in Poland, guaranteed to keep the kids happy.

If you wander about the backstreets in the centre, you'll find some fine **villas** (Map p375), dating from the end of the 19th century; according to insiders the best examples are on ul Obrońców Westerplatte, though many have been left unrestored. Either way, you'll be amazed at the peaceful, undisturbed suburban atmosphere you find once you get more than 50m away from Monte Cassino.

The western part of Sopot, behind the railway track, consists of newer suburbs, which ascend gradually, finally giving way to a wooded hilly area. Here is the **Opera Leśna** (Opera in the Woods; Map p355; ☎ 555 84 00; ul Moniuszki 12), an amphitheatre that seats 5000 people, where the prestigious **International Song Festival** (☎ 22-647 76 05) has been held every August for over 40 years.

Sleeping

As with all such resorts, accommodation varies hugely in price and quantity between the high and low seasons. Year-round facilities are supplemented by a variety of pensions and holiday homes in summer. Prices listed are for the high season, which peaks in July and August and can be very, very busy.

The tourist office keeps track of accommodation options, from private rooms and student dorms to holiday homes and villas, and should be able to help you find a place to stay. Locals often hang around the office offering rooms in their own houses, but watch yourself – competition can be fierce,

and some of the old ladies, in particular, market their lodgings very forcefully!

Zhong Hua Hotel (Map p375; ☎ 550 20 20; www .zhonghua.com.pl; Al Wojska Polskiego 1; r 300zł, apt 400-500zł) An absolutely extraordinary wooden long house-pagoda building houses this Chinese hotel, kitted out in Oriental trappings that stop just short of kitsch. Naturally the house restaurant (☎ 550 20 19) is the best spot in town for Asian food (mains 17zł to 99zł), and includes a range of Eastern cuisines beyond the basic Sichuan.

Hotel Miramar (Map p355; ☎ 550 00 11; www.hotel miramarsopot.com.pl; ul Zamkowa Góra 25; s/d/tr 190/265/330zł; P) A respectable all-year budget hotel, Hotel Miramar has plenty of rooms of different classes, with and without bathroom; off-season weekends are the cheapest times. If you're too impatient to get to the beach, the Aqua Park is just 20m away.

Willa Zacisze (Map p375; ☎ 551 78 68; www.aparta menty.gda.pl; ul Grunwaldzka 22; apt 200zł; P ✗) Ideal for self-caterers and late risers, these funky modern apartments give a taste of real Sopot life. You pay for your own electricity use in summer, and there's a 40zł cleaning charge per stay. In the high season longer-term rentals cost 4000zł a week.

Pensjonat Eden (Map p375; ☎ 551 15 03; ul Kordeckiego 4/6; r 100-320zł) It's not exactly paradise, but Eden's central location makes it a tempting proposition, with its range of decent-value rooms tucked away in a venerable townhouse setting.

Villa Hestia (Map p375; ☎ 550 21 00; ul Władysława IV 3/5; r 225-650zł; P) Ultra top end of the scale, this stunningly restored 19th-century villa provides full-on indulgence for just nine guests, and has its own equally exclusive conservatory restaurant.

Hotel Rezydent (Map p375; ☎ 555 58 00; www .hotelrezydent.com.pl; Plac Konstytucji 3 Maja 3; s 490zł, d 610-890zł, ste 960zł; P) Opposite the station, a stone's throw from Monte Cassino, the Rezydent has everything it needs to dominate the affluent end of the market. The atmosphere of discreet luxury is redolent of Sopot's fashionable heyday.

Camping Nr 19 (Map p355; ☎ 550 04 45; ul Zamkowa Góra 25; camp site adult/child 11/6zł, bungalows 80-90zł; ⏰ May-Sep) Located in the northern end of town (a five-minute walk from the Sopot Kamienny Potok train station), Camping Nr 19 is a good big camping ground right by the Aqua Park and the beach.

Eating

Much of Sopot's cuisine scene is seasonal, particularly in the beach area, but there is no shortage of good options that stay open all year.

Bar Przystań (Map p355; ☎ 555 06 61; www.bar przystan.pl; Al Wojska Polskiego 11; mains per 100g 3.80-6.50zł; ☺ lunch & dinner) Tipped by locals as the best spot in town for fresh-cooked fish, the Przystań enjoys a superb location right on the beach, about 1km south of the centre. The fantastic roof terrace makes it even more popular. Look out for the 'mini museum' of old fishing gear just up the beach.

Karczma Galicyjska Cymes (Map p375; ☎ 555 52 21; Centrum Rezydent, ul Haffnera 6; mains 12-30zł; ☺ lunch & dinner) Our pick of the Rezydent Centre's bunch would probably be this charming and unusual restaurant, which showcases the distinctive Spanish influences of Galician cooking, from the southern Polish region near Kraków.

Pub Kinski (Map p375; ☎ 802 56 38; ul Kościuszki 10; mains 8.50-28zł; ☺ lunch & dinner) The house and birthplace of legendary German actor and psychopath Klaus Kinski (see the boxed text below) has been converted into a suitably offbeat bar-restaurant, with plenty of film posters and decadent-looking drapery. The man himself probably would have trashed the place, but it can take that as a compliment.

Klub Wieloryb (Map p375; ☎ 551 57 22; www.klub -wieloryb.com.pl; ul Podjazd 2; mains 24-60zł; ☺ lunch & dinner) Another pub-cum-restaurant, the characterful Whale offers an ambitious mix of French-influenced cuisine plus plenty of drinks. The eye-popping décor was once described as 'mystifying aquatic nonsense', which seems to fit the bill nicely and could also apply to the entertaining website.

Błękitny Pudel (Map p375; ☎ 551 16 72; ul Bohaterów Monte Cassino 44; mains 15-36zł) A cosy, wilfully arty place in the middle of the main drag, the popular Blue Poodle holds a strangely familiar assortment of random objects. As an added plus it serves German Paulaner wheat beer, making it as good for a drink as it is for dinner.

Green Way (Map p375; ☎ 661 88 88; ul Bohaterów Monte Cassino 67; mains 4.90-8.50zł; ☺ lunch & dinner; ☒) Similar to its franchise siblings in Gdańsk and the rest of Poland, Green Way is a simple place trading on its excellent budget vegetarian food.

FEELING KINSKI

If you've ever seen a Klaus Kinski film, you won't have any difficulty believing the many outlandish stories about the legendarily lunatic actor. Kinski's wild, piercing eyes and unruly blonde hair gave him the look of an Aryan angel gone bad, and the manic intensity he brought to his roles was less an exaggeration than a muted version of his off-screen persona. He was arguably the ultimate Method actor, seeing his body as a conduit for the souls of the characters he portrayed.

It's generally accepted that the actor's finest work came in his collaborations with equally idiosyncratic German New Wave director Werner Herzog. The two met while sharing an apartment in Munich in the 1950s, when 13-year-old Herzog watched Kinski destroying everything around him in a spectacular outburst of rage. Their working relationship preserved much the same volatility – one classic archive photo shows Kinski attacking the director with a machete, while on another occasion Herzog had to put a gun to his star's head to 'persuade' him to keep working.

Despite the acclaim for his independent film work, Kinski refused to distinguish between art-house and commercial projects, accepting work regardless of its audience or quality. He memorably described his chosen profession as 'prostitution', basing decisions purely on who he was selling himself to, and for how much – busking French poetry in a Berlin bar for pfennigs was the same to him as performing *Hamlet* for a lucrative private client.

Alongside acting and money, Kinski's main obsession was women. Considering himself a reincarnation of the legendary 'devil violinist', composer and philanderer Niccolò Paganini, Kinski threw himself into the constant pursuit of sexual conquests, with quite frightening success. Towards the end of his life the great actor finally completed his 20-year ambition to make a film biography of Paganini; the end product was cut to shreds by distributors and censors due to its highly explicit content, but remains a unique, fragmented, glorious chaos, saying as much about Kinski as it does about his idol. Of all his films, this is perhaps the greatest tribute to a truly tortured genius.

POMERANIA

Drinking

Vini Sfera (Map p375; ☎ 555 51 23; Centrum Rezydent, ul Haffnera 6) Wine-lovers shouldn't miss out on this excellent little specialist store, which has a delectable range of fine international vintages at up to 20zł a glass and some real top-end stock (Dom Perignon is 840zł a bottle). There's a token food menu to help soak up your chosen tipple.

Mandarynka (Map p375; ☎ 550 45 63; www.manda rynka.pl; ul Bema 6) The latest hip spot to create a buzz in Sopot and beyond, Mandarynka marks the arrival of the lounge bar in Poland, wooing the trendsetters with deeply fashionable ochre shades, sofas and chilled-out electronica. Some posing is obligatory.

Kawiareton (Map p375; ☎ 555 07 21; ul Pułaskiego 15) Jazz fiends, rejoice: this is one of the few places anywhere near Gdańsk where you can find quality live jazz on a regular basis. The ground-floor café, done up in 1920s living room style, makes a good holding area for the upstairs gig space.

Café Art Deco (Map p375; ☎ 555 01 60; ul Bohaterów Monte Cassino; ☽ 11am-10pm; ☒) Tucked away at the quiet western end of Monte Cassino, the tiny Art Deco serves some alcohol, but it's the coffee that makes it special. It's hard not to linger here on a peaceful afternoon.

Kawiarnia u Hrabiego (Map p375; ☎ 550 19 97; ul Czyżewskiego 12; ☽ 10am-10pm) The oldest family home in Sopot now houses a charming little café and art gallery, far from the madd(en)ing summer crowds. The quaint interior is perfect for cake and conversation.

Entertainment

ViVa (Map p375; ☎ 551 62 68; www.vivaclub.pl; Al Mamuszki 2; admission 5-25zł; ☽ from 9pm; ℗) The self-proclaimed 'No 1 in the Tri-City' is certainly the top spot around for all-out spectacle, hosting vast beachfront dance nights with all the eye candy and hi-tech wizardry it can muster. The varied special events programme is also legendary.

Soho (Map p375; ☎ 0605 255 270; ul Bohaterów Monte Cassino 61; ☽ from noon) Currently the haunt of choice for Sopot's scenesters, celebs and fashionistas, Soho goes for a surprisingly rough-cut retro style: brown walls, pink and yellow stripes and square poufs surround the glamorous crowds.

Pompon (Map p375; www.pompon.glt.pl; ul 1 Maja 3i) One of the few openly gay clubs in conservative Catholic Poland, Pompon puts on fabulous dance and retro parties in its converted house, off ul 1 Maja. It's down a dirt track and can be hard to find in the dark – if you don't want to out yourself to passers-by, ask for directions to Klubowa, next door.

Siouxie 8 (Map p375; ☎ 551 74 76; ul Grunwaldzka 11; ☽ from 9am) This rather appealing timbered villa near the beach has quite a reputation – locals say it's a hotbed of drink, drugs and wild wild women, with a core clientele of teenage technoheads and plenty of bodybuilders in shiny sportswear to add that mafia vibe. It's chaotic, messy and great fun.

Getting There & Away

All trains that service Gdańsk go to Gdynia and stop in Sopot – see p373. Commuter trains to Gdańsk and Gdynia (2.80zł) run every five to 10 minutes at peak times.

Pleasure boats (Map p375) and hydrofoils, which operate from May to September, go to Gdańsk (one-way/return 35zł/48zł), to Gdynia (20zł/35zł), to Westerplatte (24zł/35zł) and to Hel (37zł/50zł). The landing site is at the pier.

GDYNIA

☎ 58 / pop 260,000

North of Sopot is the third component of the Tri-City, Gdynia. Though a fishing village existed here as early as the 14th century, it had hardly more than 1000 inhabitants by the outbreak of WWI. In the aftermath of that war, when Gdańsk became autonomous and no longer represented Polish interests, the Polish government decided to build a new port to give Poland an outlet to the sea. By 1933 Gdynia was the largest and most modern port on the Baltic.

The port was badly damaged during WWII, but was rebuilt and modernised and is now the base for much of Poland's merchant and fishing fleet. Sadly the town itself lacks much style or character, but it has a good beach and a few attractions down by the water.

Information

Baltic Information Point (Map right; ☎ 620 77 11; Molo Południowe; ☽ 9am-6pm Mon-Fri, 10am-5pm Sat, 10am-4pm Sun)

Crist@l Internet (Map right; ☎ 0504 666 993; ul Armii Krajowej 13; per hr 4zł; ☽ 10am-10pm Mon-Fri & Sun, 10am-11pm Sat)

Orbis Travel (Map right; ☎ 620 48 44; ul 10 Lutego 2)

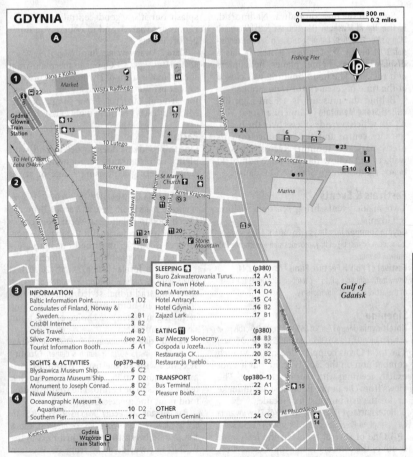

GDYNIA

0 — 300 m
0 — 0.2 miles

Fishing Pier

Gulf of Gdańsk

INFORMATION	
Baltic Information Point	**1** D2
Consulates of Finland, Norway &	
Sweden	**2** B1
Crist@l Internet	**3** B1
Orbis Travel	**4** B2
Silver Zone	(see 24)
Tourist Information Booth	**5** A1

SIGHTS & ACTIVITIES	(pp379–80)
Błyskawica Museum Ship	**6** C2
Dar Pomorza Museum Ship	**7** D2
Monument to Joseph Conrad	**8** D2
Naval Museum	**9** C2
Oceanographic Museum &	
Aquarium	**10** D2
Southern Pier	**11** C2

SLEEPING	(p380)
Biuro Zakwaterowania Turus	**12** A1
China Town Hotel	**13** A2
Dom Marynarza	**14** D4
Hotel Antracyt	**15** C4
Hotel Gdynia	**16** B2
Zajazd Lark	**17** B1

EATING	(p380)
Bar Mleczny Słoneczny	**18** B3
Gospoda u Józefa	**19** B2
Restauracja CK	**20** B2
Restauracja Pueblo	**21** B2

TRANSPORT	(pp380–1)
Bus Terminal	**22** A1
Pleasure Boats	**23** D2

OTHER	
Centrum Gemini	**24** C2

Silver Zone (Map right; ☎ 628 18 00; Centrum Gemini, ul Waszyngtona 21; per hr 6zł; ⏰ 1-10pm) Internet access, part of the Silver Screen cinema.

Tourist information booth (Map above; ☎ 628 54 66; www.gdynia.pl; Gdynia Główna train station; ⏰ 8am-6pm Mon-Fri, 9am-4pm Sat, 9am-3pm Sun May-Sep, 10am-5pm Mon-Fri, 10am-3pm Sat Oct-Apr)

Sights & Activities

The **Southern Pier** (Molo Południowe; Map above) is the focal point of Gdynia's tourist zone. Moored on the northern side are two museum ships, a definite highlight for visitors. The beautiful three-masted frigate **Dar Pomorza** (Map above; ☎ 620 23 71; adult/concession 5/3zł; ⏰ 9am-6pm daily Jun-Sep, 10am-4pm Tue-Sun Oct-May) is a real treat, built in Hamburg in 1909

and used as a training ship for German sailors. Much more functional, the battle-hardened destroyer **Błyskawica** (Map above; ☎ 626 36 58; adult/concession 4/2zł; ⏰ 10.10am-1pm & 2-5pm Tue-Sun May-Sep) is the last surviving Polish ship built before WWII.

Near the tip of the pier is the **Oceanographic Museum & Aquarium** (Muzeum Oceanograficzne i Akwarium Morskie; Map above; ☎ 621 70 21; www.akwarium.gdynia.pl; Al Zjednoczenia 1; adult/concession 10/6zł; ⏰ 9am-7pm daily May-Aug, 10am-5pm Tue-Sun Sep-Apr), a predictable but nonetheless interesting collection of all things fishy and sea-dwelling. Beyond it is a large **monument** (Map above) to Józef Konrad Korzeniowski, better known to the English-speaking world as author Joseph Conrad.

South of the pier, on Bulwar Nadmorski, is the **Naval Museum** (Muzeum Marynarki Wojennej; Map p379; ☎ 626 39 84; ul Sędzickiego 3; adult/concession 2/1zł, free Fri; ⏲ 10am-4pm Tue-Sun). It has a display of guns, fighter planes, helicopters and rockets. The main building was closed at the time of research for renovations.

Behind the museum is a 52m-high hill called **Stone Mountain** (Kamienna Góra; Map p379), which provides views over the beach, the city centre and the harbour from its pretty parkland summit. Keen cyclists or walkers can follow the Bulwar Nadmorski beach road down to Sopot and Gdańsk.

Festivals & Events

Two major events bring seasonal visitors to Gdynia:

Gdynia Summer Jazz Days (☎ 0501 154 485; www .colosseum.gdynia.pl) In July, provides some much-needed musical flavour.

Festival of Polish Feature Films (☎ 301 52 44; www.festiwalfilmow.pl) In September, highlights the best of the active national film industry.

Sleeping

Hotel Gdynia (Map p379; ☎ 666 30 40; gdynia@orbis.pl; ul Armii Krajowej 22; s/d 305/365zł, ste 670-755zł; P ☒ ☎) The local Orbis complex doesn't face much competition on the facility front, but it's not exactly teeming with flair or character. The views from the upper floors just about make up for the grim multistorey façade.

Hotel Antracyt (Map p379; ☎ 620 65 71; www.antra cyt.home.pl; ul Korzeniowskiego 19; s/d/tr 170/250/320zł; P) One of several hotels in the leafy area south of the centre, the hill-top Antracyt offers comfortable accommodation with views over the sea, just a stagger from the beach.

China Town Hotel (Map p379; ☎ 620 92 21; ul Dworcowa 11a; s/d/tr 90/120/220zł; P) Stacked above a mediocre Chinese restaurant, rooms here are basic but nowhere near as scabby as you'd expect, and being right opposite the station and SKM platform does have its advantages. Breakfast not included.

Dom Marynarza (Map p379; ☎ 622 00 25; Al Piłsudskiego 1; s/d/tr 150/190/235zł) Another beachside place on the centre's south edge, with reasonable rooms and a bracing whiff of sea air.

Zajazd Lark (Map p379; ☎ 621 80 47; ul Starowiejska 1; s/d/tr 80/115/130zł) One of the cheapest options outside seasonal student dorms, it's being charitable to say that the Lark is basic, but if you want to crash out rather than splash out it's a good central spot. Bathrooms are shared, and of course you don't get breakfast.

Biuro Zakwaterowania Turus (Map p379; ☎ 621 82 65; ul Starowiejska 47) Opposite the main train station (enter from ul Dworcowa), Turus arranges private rooms, mostly in the centre, for around 60zł/100zł per single/double. Minimum stays of three nights are required.

Eating

One thing Gdynia does do well is food, with plenty of restaurants throughout the city centre offering a pleasing range of styles and cuisines.

Restauracja CK (Map p379; ☎ 699 05 51; ul Świętojańska 49; mains 8-55zł; ⏲ lunch & dinner) Bringing Czech food to Poland may seem like a coals-to-Newcastle scenario, but the massive portions of quality grub dished out here are a great excuse to play 'spot the difference'.

Gospoda u Józefa (Map p379; ☎ 620 3051; ul Świętojańska 49; mains 6.50-16zł; ⏲ lunch & dinner) A charming traditional-styled café offering a good line in home-made Polish cooking, including an extensive choice of sweet and savoury pancakes.

Restauracja Pueblo (Map p379; ☎ 621 60 07; ul Abrahama 56; mains 15-40zł; ⏲ lunch & dinner) Quality Tex-Mex with all the usual trappings: primary colours, funky lamps and music that really wants to be Latino. The well-executed food is an unexpected bonus.

Bar Mleczny Słoneczny (Map p379; ☎ 620 53 16; ul Władysława IV; mains 1.52-6.76zł; ⏲ breakfast, lunch & dinner Mon-Fri, breakfast & lunch Sat) Just next to the Pueblo but worlds away from its Western excesses, this is a genuine commie-era milk bar with exclusively vegetarian dishes that cost next to nothing. Efficient, clean and tasty, it's deservedly popular among locals.

Getting There & Away

BOAT

Stena Line (☎ 660 92 00; www.stenaline.pl) operates ferries to/from Karlskrona, Sweden (adult 150zł to 240zł, concession 115zł to 190zł, 10½ to 12 hours, one or two daily). Services depart from the **Terminal Promowy** (Map p355; ul Kwiatkowskiego 60), 5km northwest of central Gdynia. Information, bookings and tickets can be obtained from Orbis and other travel agents. See also p479.

There are pleasure boats/hydrofoils to Gdańsk (one-way/return 41zł/56zł), Sopot

(35zł/20zł) and Hel (48zł/35zł) from May to September, departing from the southern pier. The hydrofoils to Hel are actually considerably faster than taking the train. One-hour boat excursions to Gdynia harbour go several times daily from April to October (15zł to 23zł).

BUS

The bus terminal (Map p379) is next to the train station. Regional routes include Hel (11.20zł, 2½ hours, hourly) and Łeba (13.20zł, three hours, three daily).

TRAIN

For long-distance trains, see p373. There are several trains daily to Hel (11.80zł, two hours, hourly in summer). Roughly hourly trains run to Lębork (9.30zł, one hour), where you can change for Łeba.

HEL PENINSULA

☎ 58

The Hel Peninsula (Mierzeja Helska) is a 34km-long, crescent-shaped sandbank to the north of the Tri-City. The peninsula is only 300m wide at the base and no wider than 500m for most of its length. Only close to the end does it expand out, reaching a breadth of about 3km. The highest point of the peninsula is 23m above sea level. Much of the landscape is covered with trees – picturesque, wind-deformed pines predominate – and there's also a number of typical coastal plant varieties including sand sedge and dune thistle.

The peninsula was formed over the course of about 8000 years by sea currents and winds, which gradually created an uninterrupted belt of sand. At the end of the 17th century, as old maps show, the sand bar was still cut by six inlets making it a chain of islands. In the last century the peninsula was cut several times by storms. The edges have been strengthened and the movement of the sand has been reduced by vegetation, but the sand bar continues to grow.

The peninsula is enclosed by two fishing ports: Hel at its tip and Władysławowo at its base. Between them is a third port, Jastarnia, and three villages: Chałupy, Kuźnica and Jurata. All are tourist resorts during the short summer season (July and August). There's a railway and a good road running the whole length of the peninsula.

All along the northern shore stretch beautiful sandy beaches and, except for small areas around the resorts (which are usually packed with holiday-makers), they are clean and deserted.

The Hel Peninsula is easily accessible from the Tri-City by train, bus and boat. The bus and train can take you anywhere you want, while boats and hydrofoils sail from Gdańsk, Sopot and Gdynia to Hel. A boat trip is the most popular way of getting a feel for the peninsula.

Hel

Hel is a fishing port whose history is buried in the obscurity of the 9th century. The original village was founded 2km to the northwest from where it is today, not much later than Gdańsk, and benefited from its strategic location at the gateway of the developing port. By the 14th century Hel had a population of over 1200 and was a prosperous fishing port and trading centre.

The town never grew much bigger, however, as it was constantly threatened by storms and the shifting coastline, and was relatively isolated from the mainland because of the lack of overland links. Long belonging to Gdańsk, Hel followed the changes in power and religion of the big city, and, like Gdańsk, declined in the 18th century.

During the Nazi invasion of 1939, Hel was the last place in Poland to surrender; a garrison of some 3000 Polish soldiers defended the town until 2 October. The peninsula became a battlefield once more in 1945, when about 60,000 Germans were caught in a bottleneck by the Red Army and didn't lay down their arms until 9 May; it was the last piece of Polish territory to be liberated.

SIGHTS

The **Fokarium** (☎ 675 08 36; www.fokarium.com; ul Morska 2; admission 2zł; ☒ 8.30am-dusk) is Hel's signature attraction, and the place to see the region's grey seals. It has three large tanks housing half a dozen seals, and a museum is also being built. Feeding takes place at 9am and 3pm. The grey seal is the largest and most populous seal species in the Baltic, numbering about 6500, but it's under threat from development and pollution. Even in the Fokarium itself, the seals have been endangered by the superstitious Polish habit of throwing coins into any body of water;

one of the older animals actually died in 2001 after eating massive amounts of small change over several years. Grisly posters warn visitors against repeating the incident.

Elsewhere in town, a dozen 19th-century, half-timbered **fishing houses** on the main street, ul Wiejska, managed to survive the various battles. The oldest building in town is the Gothic church dating from the 1420s, which is now the **Museum of Fishery** (Muzeum Rybołówstwa; ☎ 675 05 52; Bulwar Nadmorski 2; adult/concession 5/3zł; ☒ 10am-6pm daily Jul & Aug, 10am-4pm Tue-Sun Sep-Jun). It features exhibits on fishing and boat-building techniques, plus a collection of old fishing boats. Go up to the **tower** (admission 2zł) for good views over the town, the peninsula and the Gulf of Gdańsk.

There's a beautiful 100m-wide beach on the sea coast, 1km north of town, and a 42m-high brick **lighthouse**, which is open to visitors in summer.

SLEEPING & EATING

The town has a reasonable array of places to stay and eat, most of which only open in summer. Many locals rent out rooms in their homes – just ask around. The usual price is about 65zł per double room, but you'll probably find that few locals will want to rent out a room for just one night.

Many of the tourist restaurants on ul Wiejska also offer rooms. Try **Tawerna Helska** (☎ 675 12 05; ul Wiejska 82), **Captain Morgan Pub Hotel** (☎ 675 00 91; ul Wiejska 21) or **Pensjonat Nelson** (☎ 675 11 55; ul Wiejska 62) – a double room should cost around 100zł to 140zł in any of them.

GETTING THERE & AWAY

Hel can be reached by road and rail (there are fairly regular services by train and bus from Gdynia) and by pleasure boat/hydrofoil from May to September from Gdańsk (see p374), Sopot (p378) and Gdynia (p380). Note that a return ticket is considerably cheaper than two singles, so buy one if you plan on returning by boat – you can mix and match ship and hydrofoil services for your outward and return journeys. The boat schedule allows for up to eight hours at Hel.

Around Hel

Instead of hanging around in Hel, you may like to walk along the beach to **Jurata** (12km) or 2km further to **Jastarnia** and take the train

back from there, or stay for the night. Both are lively holiday resorts and have camping grounds, places to eat, some nightlife and a range of holiday homes.

Further northwest are two tiny ports, **Kuźnica** and **Chałupy**, which have retained their old atmosphere more than other places on the peninsula. Finally you get back to the base of the peninsula at **Władysławowo**, the largest fishing port and a town of some 13,000 people, which has a good wide beach. The town has a number of accommodation options and an array of restaurants.

Between Chałupy and Władysławowo, there are eight camping grounds that have windsurfing centres, providing equipment and instructors. This is one of the most popular **windsurfing** areas in Poland, especially recommended for beginners. The centres organise courses of different lengths and levels, and hire out equipment. Some also offer **kitesurfing**.

Around 8km west along the coast from Władysławowo is the **Rozewie Cape** (Przylądek Rozewie), the northernmost tip of Poland. Its 33m-high cliff-top lighthouse has a small museum dedicated to the lighthouse business; you can go to the top for sweeping views.

KASHUBIA
☎ 58

According to legend, the region of Kashubia (Kaszuby in Polish) was created by giants, whose footprints account for the many hills and lakes that characterise the landscape. Stretching for 100km southwest of Gdańsk, it's a picturesque area garnished with small villages where people still live in touch with their surroundings. There are no cities, towns are few and far between, and large-scale industry hasn't arrived, leaving the waterways virtually unpolluted.

The original inhabitants, the Kashubians, were Slavs, once closely related to the Pomeranians. In contrast to most of the other groups who gradually merged to form one big family of Poles, the Kashubians have managed to retain some of their early ethnic identity, expressed in their distinctive culture, dress, crafts, architecture and language. Interestingly, they were not displaced in the aftermath of WWII by the communist regime, which removed most other groups that didn't fit the standard ethnic picture.

The Kashubian language, still spoken by some of the old generation, is the most distinct dialect of Polish; other Poles have a hard time understanding it. It's thought to derive from the ancient Pomeranian language, which survived in its archaic form but which has assimilated words of foreign origin – mostly German during the Germanisation imposed by the Prussians.

The region between Kartuzy and Kościerzyna is the most topographically diverse and the highest point of Kashubia, Mt Wieżyca (329m), is here. This is also the most touristy area of Kashubia; an array of facilities have already been built and others are in progress. Public transport between Kartuzy and Kościerzyna is fairly regular, with buses running every hour or two.

Unless you have your own transport – which is particularly useful for exploring Kashubia – you miss out on some of the region by being limited to the major routes. Public transport becomes less frequent the further off the track you go. The two regional destinations detailed below will give a taste of the culture of Kashubia, though less of its natural beauty.

Kartuzy
☎ 58 / pop 16,000

The town of Kartuzy, 30km west of Gdańsk, owes its birth and its name to the Carthusians, a religious order that was brought here from Bohemia in 1380. Originally founded in 1084 near Grenoble in France, the order was known for its austere monastic rules, its monks living an ascetic life in hermitages and, like the equally morbid Camaldolese (see p145), passing their days in the contemplation of death, following the motto 'Memento Mori' (remember you must die).

When they arrived in Kartuzy the monks built a church and, beside it, 18 hermitages laid out in the shape of a horseshoe. The order was dissolved by the Prussians in 1826 and the church is now a parish church. Of the hermitages, only one survives, still standing beside the church. The church is a 10-minute walk west of the bus and train stations across the town centre.

The **church** (☎ 681 20 85; ul Klasztorna 5) seems to be a declaration of the monks' philosophy; the original Gothic brick structure was topped in the 1730s with a baroque roof that looks like a huge coffin. On the outer wall of the chancel there's a sundial and, just beneath it, a skull with the 'Memento Mori' inscription.

The maxim is also tangibly manifested inside, on the clock on the balustrade of the organ loft. Its pendulum is in the form of the angel of death armed with a scythe. The clock is tactfully stopped if there's an unusual number of funerals in town.

The interior fittings are mainly baroque, and the richly carved stalls deserve a closer look. There's some unusual cordovan (painting on goat leather) decoration (1685) in the chancel, while the church's oldest artefact, an extraordinary panel from a 15th-century Gothic triptych, is in the right-hand chapel.

Another attraction is the **Kashubian Museum** (Muzeum Kaszubskie; ☎ 681 14 42; www.muzeum-kaszubskie.gda.pl; ul Kościerska 1; adult/concession 8/6zł; ⏲ 8am-4pm Tue-Fri, 8am-3pm Sat year-round, 10am-2pm Sun May-Sep), south of the train station near the railway track. It depicts the traditional culture of the region, with everything from curious folk instruments to typical household implements and furniture. German Tours are available for about 60zł per group.

There's only one hotel in town, but you can easily leave on one of the hourly buses to Gdańsk (6.90zł, 50 minutes).

Wdzydze Kiszewskie
☎ 58 / pop 1000

The small village of Wdzydze Kiszewskie, 16km south of Kościerzyna, boasts an interesting **skansen** (Kaszubski Park Etnograficzny; ☎ 686 12 88; adult/concession 8/6zł; ⏲ 9am-6pm Jul & Aug, 9am-4pm Tue-Sun May-Jun & Sep, 10am-3pm Tue-Sun Oct-Apr) featuring typical Kashubian architecture. Established in 1906 by the local schoolmaster, this was Poland's first skansen (open-air museum of traditional architecture). Pleasantly positioned on the lakeside, it now contains a score of buildings collected from central and southern Kashubia, including cottages, barns, a school, a windmill and an 18th-century church used for Sunday Mass. Some of the interiors are fitted with authentic furnishings, implements and decorations, showing how the Kashubians lived a century or two ago.

There are a few budget pensions in the village, which provide around 100 beds in all. Wdzydze is linked to Kościerzyna by several buses daily.

POMERANIA

THE LOWER VISTULA

The valley of the lower Vistula is a fertile land bisected by the wide, leisurely river. Flat, open and largely occupied by farms, the region shelters a rich cultural inheritance, even though much of it was lost in WWII.

The Vistula was an important waterway through which goods were shipped to the Baltic and abroad. In the 13th and 14th centuries many trading ports were established along its banks, all the way from Toruń to Gdańsk. Most of these towns were founded by the Teutonic order, the powerful league of Germanic knights who by then occupied much of the valley. Remnants of the order now comprise some of the most important sights in the region.

BYDGOSZCZ

☎ 52 / pop 390,000

Sitting on the border of Wielkopolska and Pomerania, Bydgoszcz (*bid*-goshch) was outside the territory of the Teutonic order, and developed unhurriedly as a trading centre, beer producer and military base. Subjugated by the Prussians in the First Partition of 1773, Bydgoszcz returned to Poland in 1920 and underwent intensive industrial development. It's now Poland's eighth-largest city.

Despite all this, the city ranks low on travel itineraries; the Old Town shows little trace of its historic character, while the rest of the city is essentially a postwar industrial zone. That said, the haphazard development around the river and the lively central square are somehow typical of the emerging 'new' Poland, and local authorities are making the effort to appeal to travellers with a range of exhibitions, parks and services. It's not worth skipping Toruń for, but if you find yourself with some time to kill there are worse places to spend an afternoon.

Information

Bank Pekao (☎ 321 53 53; ul Dworcowa 6)
Tourist office (☎ 348 23 73; www.it.byd.pl; Stary Rynek 15; ◔ 9am-6pm Mon-Fri, 9am-2pm Sat)

Sights & Activities

The Old Town is on the southern bank of the Brda River, a 20-minute walk from the train station. Its heart, the **Stary Rynek**, is dominated by the palatial town hall and a large Soviet-style monument to the victims of fascism. The riverside area around the Old Town bridge is also rapidly becoming a focal point for city life; some very noticeable modern prestige buildings rub shoulders with restored granaries, and the nearby cafés do a roaring trade.

The 16th-century brick **parish church**, just off the square, has preserved its Gothic form pretty well. The gilded baroque high altar boasts a 1466 painting of the Virgin Mary, and the stained-glass windows on both sides are fine replicas of medieval originals. The blue and purple vaulting and the 1920s motifs on the walls also make for a striking interior, while the metal front door shows scenes from the town's 1000-year history.

The Regional Museum has branches in several interesting buildings around town. The most important of these is the 18th-century **Biały Spichrz** (White Granary; ☎ 327 03 93; ul Mennica 1; adult/concession 4/2zł; ◔ 10am-6pm Tue-Fri, noon-4pm Sat & Sun), west of the Rynek on a small island known as Wyspa Młyńska (Mill Island). Displays here outline the region's history and illustrate traditional arts and crafts; a neighbouring warehouse currently contains an interactive technology exhibit.

For a more relaxing perspective on the city, **boat tours** (☎ 323 32 31; adult/concession 10/8zł) run from the Old Town waterfront up to eight times daily in summer.

Sleeping & Eating

Hotel Pod Orłem (☎ 583 05 30; www.hotelpodorlem .pl; ul Gdańska 14; s/d 399/478zł, ste 585-669zł; Ⓟ ✗) If you are going to stay in Bydgoszcz, this is the place to do it. Under the Eagle has been the city's most prestigious inn ever since it opened in 1898, hosting Prussian and Polish VIPs alike. It's also the regional base for Orbis Travel, which restored the building to its prewar Art Nouveau elegance towards the end of the communist period. Bizarrely, prices actually go down in high summer.

Youth hostel (☎ 322 75 70; ul Sowińskiego 5; dm 25-50zł) At the opposite end of the price (and comfort) scale, the 100-bed youth hostel, just five minutes' walk from the station, has everything from singles to 10-bed dorms available all year.

Hotel Ratuszowy (☎ 3228861; www.hotelratuszowy .com.pl; ul Długa 37; s 160-200zł, d 230-280zł) Visitors wishing to stay in the Old Town will probably find this is still the only option. Luckily it's a nice, low-key place in a quiet, central location, and the rooms are just homy enough to be welcoming.

Hotel Brda (☎ 585 01 00; www.hotelbrda.com.pl; ul Dworcowa 94; s 180-280zł, d 260-350zł; P ☒) Less interesting than the Pod Orłem but substantially less costly, the Brda is a standard conference-class block near the station with neat rooms and a good range of facilities. Weekend rates are cheaper.

Hotel Centralny (☎ 322 88 76; ul Dworcowa 85; s 138zł, d 218-260zł, tr 315zł, q 308zł) Just one block from the station, the Centralny is pretty poor value but may be useful if you need a mid-priced bed near the trains. Cheaper rooms with shared facilities are available; breakfast is extra.

Restauracja Kaskada (☎ 324 93 32; ul Mostowa 2; mains 8-16zł; ☽ lunch & dinner) A big modern multilevel eatery, dominating one corner of the Rynek. Indecisive diners can ponder their options inside, outside or in the adjoining snack bar; if all else fails, at least the kiosk here is open 24 hours.

Gallery Restaurant (☎ 322 60 23; Stary Rynek 15/21; mains 10-28zł; ☽ lunch & dinner) Fine food is the watchword in the two themed dining rooms occupying Gallery's cellar, with a bar, cigars and weekend dancing to aid the digestion. The street-level café provides a more relaxed alternative. Despite the name, you won't find much contemporary art here.

Getting There & Away

The train station is 1.5km northwest of the Old Town, while the bus terminal is 1km east; city buses 77 and 104 link the two stations, passing through the centre.

Both trains and PKS buses go frequently to Toruń (train 15.90zł, bus 8.40zł) and to Inowrocław (train 8.20zł, bus 8.40zł). There are about 20 trains daily to Gdańsk (30.03zł, two hours) and six to Warsaw (43.04zł, four hours). Polski Express has buses roughly hourly to Warsaw (52zł, 4½ hours) via Toruń and Płock.

TORUŃ

☎ 56 / pop 208,000

Famed for its rich history and wealth of Gothic architecture, the former Hanseatic port of Toruń has one of the best-preserved old towns in Pomerania, packed with monumental red-brick edifices, baroque façades and vaulted roofs. Local authorities have taken a highly proactive approach to the conservation, restoration and exhibition of the town's treasures, transforming the town centre into a veritable hotbed of culture.

Toruń is also the birthplace of Nicolaus Copernicus (1473–1543). Though the famous astronomer only spent his youth here, the city is very proud of the man who 'stopped the sun and moved the earth', and his name (Mikołaj Kopernik in Polish) is all over town.

In 1997 Toruń's Old Town was included on Unesco's World Heritage List, further sealing its reputation as an essential stop on any discerning traveller's itinerary. You certainly won't regret joining the gingerbread-munching tourists for a couple of days at the heart of historical Poland.

History

A Slav settlement is known to have existed on this site as early as the 11th century, but Toruń really came to life in 1233, when the Teutonic Knights set about transforming it into one of their early outposts. The knights surrounded the town, then known as Thorn, with a ring of walls and built a castle; this, and a strategic position on the Vistula, accelerated its growth. Rapid expansion meant that newly arriving merchants and craftspeople had to settle outside the city walls and soon built what became known as the New Town. In the 1280s Toruń joined the Hanseatic League, giving further impetus to its development.

Toruń was a focal point of the conflict between Poland and the Teutonic order, and when the Thirteen Years' War finally ended in 1466, it was the Treaty of Toruń that finalised the peace. The treaty returned a large area of land to Poland, stretching from Toruń to Gdańsk.

The period of prosperity that followed ended with the Swedish wars, and since then the town's fortunes have been erratic. Following the Second Partition in 1793 the city fell under Prussian domination and didn't return to Poland until the Treaty of Versailles in the aftermath of WWI.

After WWII, which fortunately did relatively little damage to the city, Toruń expanded significantly, with vast new suburbs and industries. But the medieval quarter was almost unaffected and largely retains its old appearance. A lot of money and effort has

POMERANIA

been poured into restoration works over recent decades, and there are still a lot of projects in the offing.

Orientation

The historic sector of Toruń sits on the northern bank of the Vistula. It is made up of the Old Town (Stare Miasto) to the west and the New Town (Nowe Miasto) to the east. Both towns, originally separated by walls and a moat, developed around their market squares, but gradually merged after the walls were taken down in the 15th century. All the major attractions are in this area.

The bus terminal is a five-minute walk north of the historic quarter, while the main train station is south across the river, a short bus ride away. When coming from the station over the bridge, you'll get a fine view of the historic district, the silhouette of the cathedral being the dominant landmark.

Information

INTERNET ACCESS

Klub Intertnetowy Jeremi (☎ 633 51 00; www.jeremi .pl; Rynek Staromiejski 33; per hr 4zł; ☒ 24hr)

Space Café (☎ 621 01 91; ul Szewska 6; per hr 4zł; ☒ 10am-10pm Mon-Sat, 2-10pm Sun)

MONEY

Bank Pekao (☎ 652 14 06; ul Wielkie Garbary 11)

POST

Main post office (☎ 619 43 00; Rynek Staromiejski 15)

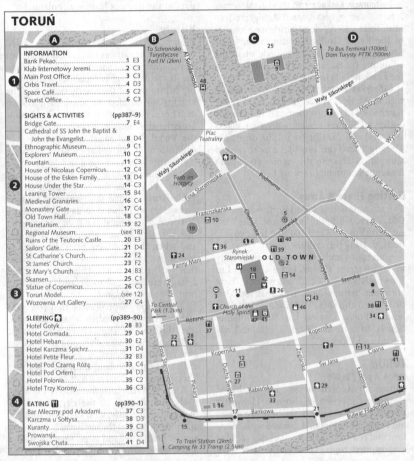

TORUŃ

INFORMATION
Bank Pekao	1 E3
Klub Internetowy Jeremi	2 C3
Main Post Office	3 C3
Orbis Travel	4 D3
Space Café	5 C2
Tourist Office	6 C3

SIGHTS & ACTIVITIES (pp387-9)
Bridge Gate	7 E4
Cathedral of SS John the Baptist & John the Evangelist	8 D4
Ethnographic Museum	9 C1
Explorers' Museum	10 C2
Fountain	11 C3
House of Nicolaus Copernicus	12 C4
House of the Esken Family	13 D4
House Under the Star	14 C3
Leaning Tower	15 B4
Medieval Granaries	16 C4
Monastery Gate	17 C4
Old Town Hall	18 C3
Planetarium	19 B2
Regional Museum	(see 18)
Ruins of the Teutonic Castle	20 E3
Sailors' Gate	21 D4
St Catharine's Church	22 F2
St James' Church	23 F2
St Mary's Church	24 B3
Skansen	25 C1
Statue of Copernicus	26 C3
Toruń Model	(see 12)
Wozownia Art Gallery	27 C4

SLEEPING (pp389-90)
Hotel Gotyk	28 B3
Hotel Gromada	29 D4
Hotel Heban	30 E2
Hotel Karczma Spichrz	31 D4
Hotel Petite Fleur	32 B3
Hotel Pod Czarną Różą	33 C4
Hotel Pod Orłem	34 D3
Hotel Polonia	35 C2
Hotel Trzy Korony	36 C3

EATING (pp390-1)
Bar Mleczny pod Arkadami	37 C3
Karczma u Sołtysa	38 D3
Kuranty	39 C3
Prowansja	40 C3
Swojska Chata	41 D4

To Schronisko Turystyczne Fort IV (2km)

To Bus Terminal (100m); Dom Turysty PTTK (500m)

Plac Teatralny

Plac Teatralny

OLD TOWN

Rynek Staromiejski

Church of the Holy Spirit

To Central Park (1.2km)

To Train Station (2km); Camping Nr 33 Tramp (2.5km)

Bulwar Filadelfijski

POMERANIA

TOURIST INFORMATION
Orbis Travel (☎ 658 42 21; ul Mostowa 7)
Tourist office (☎ 621 09 31; www.it.torun.pl; Rynek Staromiejski 25; ⏱ 9am-4pm Mon & Sat, 9am-6pm Tue-Fri year-round, 9am-1pm Sun May-Aug)

Sights
OLD TOWN
The **Old Town Sq** (Rynek Staromiejski) is the usual starting point for the visitor, dominated by the massive red-brick town hall and lined with fine restored houses, most graced by intricate decorative façades. The concentration of shops and restaurants here makes it a natural centre for town life.

The **Old Town Hall** (Ratusz Staromiejski) was built at the end of the 14th century and

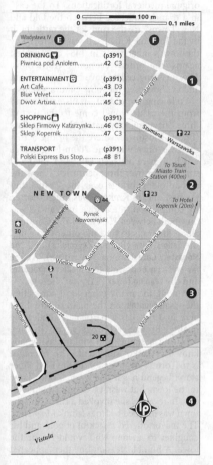

DRINKING 🍷	(p391)
Piwnica pod Aniołem...........42 C3	
ENTERTAINMENT 🎭	(p391)
Art Café.......................43 D3	
Blue Velvet...................44 E2	
Dwór Artusa..................45 C3	
SHOPPING 🛍	(p391)
Sklep Firmowy Katarzynka......46 C3	
Sklep Kopernik................47 C3	
TRANSPORT	(p391)
Polski Express Bus Stop..........48 B1	

hasn't changed that much, though some Renaissance additions have given an ornamental touch to the sober Gothic structure. Besides serving as the municipal seat, the town hall used to provide market facilities, but lost them in the course of internal remodelling in the 19th century. After WWII it also lost its administrative functions, and today most of the building is occupied by the main branch of the **Regional Museum** (Muzeum Okręgowe; ☎ 622 70 38; www.muzeum.torun.pl;Rynek Staromiejski 1; adult/concession 7.49/5.35zł; ⏱ noon-6pm Tue & Thu, 10am-4pm Wed & Fri-Sun).

In the original interiors, there are several sections, including a collection of Gothic art (painting, woodcarving and stained glass), a display of local 17th- and 18th-century crafts, and a gallery of Polish paintings from around 1800 to the present. You can go up the **tower** (adult/concession 6.42/4.28zł; ⏱ 10am-6pm Tue-Sun May-Sep) for a fine panoramic view. A few steps from the entrance towards the museum is a **Statue of Copernicus**, one of the oldest monuments dedicated to the stargazer and a regular feature in holiday snaps.

Copernicus pops up again in the Regional Museum's second big attraction, the brick Gothic **House of Nicolaus Copernicus** (Dom Mikołaja Kopernika; ☎ 622 67 48; ul Kopernika 15/17; adult/concession 7.49/5.35zł; ⏱ 10am-4pm Tue, Thu & Sun, noon-6pm Wed, Fri & Sat). The astronomer was born here in 1473; today it houses a biographical exhibition, including replicas of his original astronomical instruments. The museum also runs a short **audiovisual presentation** (adult/concession 8.56/5.35zł) regarding Copernicus' times in Toruń, with a **model** of the town during that period. There are soundtracks in several languages, English included; a combined ticket with the main house costs 12.84zł/8.56zł.

As if that wasn't enough, the Regional Museum also owns several of the more interesting old houses in town, using them as satellite venues for a range of exhibitions.

The **House Under the Star** (Kamienica Pod Gwiazdą; ☎ 622 70 38; Rynek Staromiejski 35; adult/concession 5.35/3.21zł; ⏱ 10am-4pm Tue-Sun), the most richly decorated house on the main square, hosts all kinds of interesting temporary displays. Its ornate baroque appearance is the result of the extensive modernisation of an original Gothic structure.

The Gothic **House of the Esken Family** (Dom Eskenów; ☎ 622 86 80; ul Łazienna 16; adult/concession

5.35/3.21zł; ☺ 10am-4pm Tue-Sun), set behind the cathedral, was converted into a granary in the 19th century and now features a collection of historic exhibits relating to the city, a small display of old weapons and an archaeological section.

Finally, the **Explorers' Museum** (Muzeum Podróżników; ☎ 622 70 38; ul Franciszkańska 11; adult/concession 6.42/4.28zł; ☺ 10am-4pm Tue-Sun) offers an exotic alternative to Gothic brick and historical artefacts, displaying photographs and ethnographic items from shores as distant as Vanuatu. If escapism's your thing, you'll love it.

Of the historical buildings outside the museum's remit, the largest and most impressive is the giant Gothic **Cathedral of SS John the Baptist & John the Evangelist** (Katedra Św Janów; ul Św Jana; donation adult/child 2/1zł, tower 6/4zł). Work started around 1260 and was only completed at the end of the 15th century, by which time the church dominated the town's skyline, as it does today. Its massive tower houses Poland's second-largest historic bell (after the one in the Wawel Royal Cathedral of Kraków), the Tuba Dei (God's Trumpet). Cast in 1530, it weighs 7238kg and is rung for significant religious and national events. On the southern side of the tower, facing the Vistula, is a large 15th-century clock; its original face and single hand are still in working order.

The elements within the church are being restored one by one, but the overall effect is still of a dusty antiquity, with the fading ornaments of elaborate altars resting beneath the whitewashed vaulting. The original, brightly coloured medieval wall paintings were covered over by the Protestants, who used the church during the Reformation era. Small fragments have been uncovered and can be seen in the chancel and the aisles. The most striking murals are the monochrome paintings set high at the back of each aisle, which depict a monk and a devil or plague figure; created by an unknown artist, the black-and-white style is highly unusual for this kind of church art.

The high altar, adorned with a Gothic triptych and topped with a crucifix, has as a background a superb stained-glass window in the best medieval style. The last chapel in the right-hand aisle holds the oldest object in the church, the font where Copernicus was baptised. To one side is his epitaph.

The third great Gothic structure in the old town is **St Mary's Church** (Kościół NMP; ul Panny Marii), erected by the Franciscans at the end of the 13th century. Austere and plain from the outside, it has a lofty interior with tall, intricate stained-glass windows and a prominent golden altarpiece, framed by a wooden archway depicting a complete crucifixion scene. The surviving fragments of late-14th-century frescoes can be seen in the right-hand nave, and the impressive early-15th-century stalls in the chancel contrast with the simple wooden pews. The organ, placed unusually on a side wall, was added two centuries later.

History buffs should also take the opportunity to check out the remnants of the town's original medieval fortifications. To the east, in a triangle squeezed between the Old and New Towns, are the ruins of the **castle**, built by the Teutonic Knights. It was destroyed by the town's inhabitants in 1454 as a protest against the order's economic restrictions. The surviving cellars have been cleared out and are now used for some cultural events.

Following the old city walls east around from the castle, you'll come to the first of three surviving city gates, the **Bridge Gate** (Brama Mostowa), where the bridge across the river once was. The 700m-long bridge was built here between 1497 and 1500 and survived for over three centuries. It was the second-oldest bridge over the Vistula, but the first one, in Kraków, was much shorter. By comparison, the bridge in Warsaw was only built between 1568 and 1573. Continue along the walls to find the other two gates, the **Sailors' Gate** (Brama Żeglarska) and the **Monastery Gate** (Brama Klasztorna). At the far western end are a few **medieval granaries** and the **Leaning Tower** (Krzywa Wieża).

Among the many other local curiosities, the small **fountain** on the main square, built here in 1914, has a particularly endearing quality. Bronze-cast frogs sit on its rim, admiring a statue of a violin-playing boy known as Janko Muzykant. The reference is to Toruń's own version of the Pied Piper story. Legend has it that a witch once came to the town, but wasn't welcomed by the locals. In revenge, she invoked a curse, and the town was invaded by frogs (think *Magnolia*). The mayor offered a sackful of gold and his daughter to anyone who would rescue the town. A humble peasant boy then appeared and began to play his rustic fiddle. The frogs, enchanted by the melodies, followed him to the woods and the town was saved.

Amid all the history, Toruń's not short of more-modern pursuits either. The **Wozownia Art Gallery** (☎ 622 63 39; ul Rabiańska 20; admission 5zł, free Tue; ☼ 10am-6pm Tue-Fri, 11am-6pm Sat & Sun) has changing displays of contemporary art, while aspiring astronomers can see what Copernicus was on about at the **Planetarium** (☎ 622 60 66; www.planetarium.torun.pl in Polish; ul Franciszkańska 15/21; adult/concession 9.50/7.50zł). Installed in an old gas tank, the high-tech auditorium can seat 160 spectators, and usually has a couple of daily shows in English.

NEW TOWN

North of the castle lies the New Town, centred on the **New Town Sq** (Rynek Nowomiejski). Grubby and scrappily modernised, it's not as spectacular as its older counterpart, nor does it have a town hall – the building in the middle is the former Protestant church, erected in the 19th century after the town hall was pulled down. It's currently home to the Blue Velvet club (see p391). Among the houses that line the Rynek, the best two are at opposite ends of the southwestern side of the square.

St James' Church (Kościół Św Jakuba; ul Św Jakuba), just off the eastern corner of the square, dates from the same period as its Old Town counterparts. It's also huge, though it's shaped like a basilica and is more elaborate from the outside, thanks to architectural details including a series of pinnacles adorning the rim of the roof. Its interior is filled with mostly baroque furnishings, but Gothic wall paintings have been uncovered in various places, notably under the organ loft. The high altar and the decorative rood arch both date from the 1730s.

A block behind St James' is **St Catharine's Church** (Kościół Garnizonowy; Plac Św Katarzyny), the local garrison church and another prominent feature of the Toruń skyline. Built around the end of the 19th century, it's an impressive chunk of neo-Gothic brickwork with a pretty amazing white altarpiece of Christ.

OTHER SIGHTS

In a park just to the north of the Old Town is the **Ethnographic Museum** (Muzeum Etnograficzne; ☎ 622 80 91; Wały Sikorskiego 19; adult/concession 8/5zł; ☼ 9am-4pm Mon, Wed & Fri, 10am-6pm Tue, Thu, Sat & Sun May-Sep, 9am-4pm Tue-Fri, 10am-4pm Sat & Sun Oct-Apr). It focuses on traditional fishery, with all sorts of implements, boats and nets. Admission also lets you visit the small but good **skansen** in the grounds, which contains examples of the traditional rural architecture of the region and beyond, including two farms, a blacksmith's shop, windmill and water mill. Access to the permanent collection is free on Monday (Sunday in winter).

Festivals & Events

Probaltica Music & Art Festival of Baltic States
Held in May.
Contact International Theatre Festival Held in May/June.
Music & Architecture International Summer Festival Held in July and August.

Sleeping

Toruń has plenty of central places to stay and finding a room isn't usually difficult; weekdays are busiest, and many places offer substantial weekend discounts. The tourist office keeps an eye on local accommodation and seasonal options such as student dorms, and should be able to help you track down a bed.

BUDGET

Schronisko Turystyczne Fort IV (☎ 655 82 36; www .fort.torun.pl in Polish; ul Chrobrego 86; dm 18-28zł; ☼ year-round) Located in a characterful old Prussian fort, this 110-bed hostel has dorms ranging from two beds to a military-style 18 beds. There's a budget cafeteria. It's some way out of town, but bus 14 runs to both the centre and the train station.

Dom Turysty PTTK (☎ 622 38 55; ul Legionów 24; s/d/tr/q 60/70/90/100zł) The 65-bed PTTK hostel is in a residential house, a 10-minute walk north of the Old Town (five minutes from the bus terminal). It has a 24-hour reception and a snack bar on site.

Hotel Trzy Korony (☎ 622 60 31; www.hotel3korony .pl; Rynek Staromiejski 21; s with/without bathroom 150/ 90zł, d 190/110zł) Prices here seem a little inflated for the unfancy rooms, but with views onto the Old Town Sq it's easy to see why. Whatever its flaws, the Three Crowns has an impeccable pedigree and a distinguished history to go with its prime location.

Hotel Kopernik (☎ 652 25 73; ul Wola Zamkowa 16; s 105-145zł, d 130-185zł; **P**) Located in the New Town, just two blocks off the main square, this former army hostel shows little trace of

POMERANIA

its military roots. Rooms come with wash-basin, toilet or full en suite.

Camping Nr 33 Tramp (☎ 654 71 87; www.tramp
.mosir.torun.pl; ul Kujawska 14; camp site per adult/child 7/
4zł, d 60zł, tr 75-80zł, cabins 30-100zł; ☷ mid-May–mid-
Sep) This camping ground, a five-minute
walk from the main train station, has basic
hotel-style rooms, a collection of dilapidated
cabins, and a tent/caravan area. Some triple
rooms have their own bathrooms.

MID-RANGE

Apparently Toruń appeals to a very specific
class of traveller – the number of three-star
hotels in the centre of town is staggering,
and the competition keeps standards grati-
fyingly high, though tour groups take up
much of the space at peak times.

Hotel Pod Czarną Różą (☎ 621 96 37; www.hotel
czarnaroza.pl; ul Rabiańska 11; s/d/tr 170/210/250zł)
The Black Rose is a real gem, providing
15 stately rooms in an historic burgher's
house. Pile carpets and proper rugs line the
floors, antique furniture decks the halls, the
staff is friendly and pets are welcome.

Hotel Petite Fleur (☎ 663 44 00; www.hotel.torun
.com.pl; ul Piekary 25; s 180-270zł, d 240-290zł) Equally
historic and even more central, the Petite
Fleur offers smart quarters in two comfort
categories, with a sedate lounge for perusing
the papers. The excellent restaurant (mains
from 10zł to 49zł) specialises in French cuisine, making fine use of the Gothic cellar.

Hotel Gotyk (☎ 658 40 00; www.hotel-gotyk.com.pl;
ul Piekary 20; s 150zł, d 250-300zł) Yet another restored townhouse hotel is this relatively
new arrival, just opposite the Petite Fleur.
Like its more established rivals, you can
expect individually decorated rooms, classic furniture and decent service.

Hotel Pod Orłem (☎ 622 50 24; www.hotel.torun.pl;
ul Mostowa 17; s 110zł, d 140-180zł; P ☐) The Pod
Orłem is one of Toruń's oldest hotels, with
a history going back more than 100 years.
Leather-padded doors hide some pretty spacious rooms; the cheaper ones are strangely
like staying at your grandma's. Breakfast is
an extra 15zł.

Hotel Polonia (☎ 657 18 00; www.polonia.torun.pl;
Plac Teatralny 5; s 150zł, d 190-220zł, tr 245zł, q 280zł)
Smart if compact rooms feature faux-
antique furniture in a handy location on the
boundary of the Old Town. Confusingly,
the house restaurant is in the basement,
accessible by lift.

Hotel Gromada (☎ 622 60 60; ul Żeglarska 10/14;
s 180-190zł, d 245-350zł) Another straightforward
tourist hotel in the same class as the Polonia, this 14th-century townhouse offers
comfortable accommodation with a slightly
disappointing lack of character inside.

TOP END

Hotel Karczma Spichrz (☎ 657 11 40; www.spichrz.pl;
ul Mostowa 1; s/d 190/250zł, ste 300-350zł; P) An old
granary right by the Bridge Gate is the setting for this unique wood-saturated hotel;
standard rooms are unspectacularly pleasant, but the split-level studios are great and
the luxury suites are downright amazing.
With an atmospheric restaurant and charming courtyard, grain never had it so good.

Hotel Heban (☎ 652 15 55; www.hotel-heban.com.pl;
ul Małe Garbary 7; s 190-250zł, d 300-350zł, ste 350-500zł)
Toruń's most luxurious central option, the
Heban is a meticulously restored townhouse
with a veneer of old-school sophistication.
The tastefully decorated rooms provide all
the usual comforts, and the elegant restaurant has a good reputation.

Eating

Karczma U Sołtysa (☎ 622 66 74; ul Mostowa 17;
mains 9.90-35zł; ☷ lunch & dinner) Styled as an
old Polish inn, complete with besmocked
kitchen staff, U Sołtysa serves solid traditional Polish fare. Gargantuan roasts for
four or more people start at 69zł.

Prowansja (☎ 622 21 11; ul Szewska 19; mains 8-
15zł; ☷ lunch & dinner) The quirky setup of this
charming café does a convincing imper-
sonation of a Provence patio – but inside
rather than outside (just as well with the
Central European climate). Quiche, crepes
and salads add to the Frenchness of it all,
but it's the wine list that's the highlight.

Swojska Chata (☎ 621 12 87; ul Mostowa 7; mains
8-20zł; ☷ lunch & dinner) Swojska stands out
from the competition on busy ul Mostowa
by offering food modelled on classic Teutonic dishes, such as 'gizzards in cream
sauce', with rustic thatching to complement
the medieval menu.

Kuranty (☎ 662 52 52; Rynek Staromiejski 29; mains
9-18.50zł; ☷ 11am-2am) The menu here pitches
at a younger crowd, based on the three Ps:
pizza, pasta and Polish. Random photos,
extraordinary Art Deco lights and a clearly
stolen pub sign add to the atmosphere. It
hosts regular DJs and live music.

POMERANIA

Bar Mleczny Pod Arkadami (☎ 622 24 28; ul Różana 1; mains 2-6.50zł; ❤ breakfast & lunch Mon-Sat) Toruń's most central milk bar is just off the Old Town Sq, and offers plenty of sturdy bites at silly prices.

Drinking

Piwnica Pod Aniołem (☎ 622 70 39; Rynek Staromiejski 1) This splendid, spacious cellar in the town hall is one of the old quarter's most popular drinking haunts. Live music can be enjoyed here from time to time, along with more offbeat activities such as tarot reading. Free wireless Internet access.

Entertainment

Dwór Artusa (☎ 622 88 05; Rynek Staromiejski 6) The Artus Court, one of the most impressive mansions on the main square, is now a major cultural centre and has an auditorium used for musical events, including concerts and recitals. The refined café also gets consistent praise from visitors.

Art Café (☎ 652 20 76; ul Szeroka 35) The insider's address for everything new and cool in electronic music, from house to hardcore, with occasional hip-hop nights thrown in. Art Café is a pretty good spot for a drink as well.

Central Park (☎ 622 67 63; www.centralpark.torun .com.pl in Polish; Szosa Bydgoska 3) One of Poland's largest dance spaces, Central Park is Toruń's prime venue for serious clubbing, hosting occasional international names alongside the national talent.

Blue Velvet (Rynek Nowomiejski 28) Seldom packed but always interesting, the cavernous hall of the New Town's former church hosts art exhibitions, film nights, bands and DJs, as well as dishing out cheap beer and kebabs.

Shopping

Toruń is famous for its *pierniki* (gingerbread), which has been produced here since the town was founded; the Kopernik factory is one of the town's major employers. The confection comes in a variety of shapes, including (of course) figures of Copernicus, though some of the more decorative designs aren't actually meant to be eaten. Good places to buy it are **Sklep Firmowy Katarzynka** (☎ 622 37 12; ul Żeglarska 25) and **Sklep Kopernik** (☎ 622 88 32; Rynek Staromiejski 6), in the Dwór Artusa.

Getting There & Away

BUS
The PKS terminal, close to the northern edge of the Old Town, handles regular bus services to Chełmno (9.30zł, 1½ hours), Golub-Dobrzyń (7.80zł, 1½ hours) and Bydgoszcz (8.40zł, one hour). Polski Express runs hourly departures from Al Solidarności to Bydgoszcz and Warsaw (48zł, 3¾ hours).

TRAIN
The Toruń Główny main train station is about 2km south of the Old Town, on the opposite side of the Vistula. Buses 22 and 27 (1.80zł) link the two. There's also the Toruń Miasto train station, 500m east of the New Town, but not all trains call in here.

It's easy to get around the region as trains to Grudziądz (10.50zł, 1½ hours), to Bydgoszcz (fast/slow 15.90zł/9.30zł, 50 minutes), to Inowrocław (11.80zł/6.80zł, 1¾ hours) and to Włocławek (9.30zł, 50 minutes) leave at least every other hour. As for longer routes, there are departures to Malbork (17.20zł, 3½ hours, three daily), Gdańsk (36.12zł, 3½ hours, seven daily), Olsztyn (fast/slow 31.85zł/19.70zł, 2¼ to 2¾ hours, eight daily) and Poznań (18.60zł, 2¾ hours, five daily). One express and four fast trains go to Warsaw (37.64zł, 3½ hours).

GOLUB-DOBRZYŃ
☎ 56 / pop 12,500

The town of Golub-Dobrzyń, about 40km east of Toruń, was created in 1951 by unifying two settlements on opposite sides of the Drwęca River. Dobrzyń, on the southern bank, is newish and not worth a mention, but Golub was founded in the 13th century as a border outpost of the Teutonic Knights, who left behind a castle.

Castle
It's hard to miss Golub's sturdy, square **castle**, which looms over the town from its position on a central hill. The structure consists of a massive Gothic brick base topped with a slightly more refined Renaissance cornice, which was added in the 17th century. The whole building was extensively restored after WWII. The small **museum** (☎ 683 24 55; adult/concession 7/3.50zł; ❤ 9am-4pm) inside is interesting more for the original Gothic interiors than for its modest ethnographic collection.

POMERANIA

Festivals & Events

Every July the castle hosts the **International Knights' Tournament**, a big mock-medieval jamboree including jousting, music and lots of costumes.

Sleeping & Eating

Dom Wycieczkowy PTTK (☎ 683 24 55; fax 683 26 66; dm/d 40/90zł) The castle's upper floor houses some of the cheapest 'castle accommodation' in Poland. A pleasant café in the vaulted cellar serves snacks and drinks.

Getting There & Away

The town has a regular bus service to Toruń (7.80zł, 1½ hours) and four daily buses to Grudziądz (9.50zł, two hours). There's a bus stop at the foot of the castle, but not all incoming services stop there – you may have to walk 1.5km from the bus station in Dobrzyń.

CHEŁMNO

☎ 56 / pop 22,000

Chełmno (heum-no), around 41km north of Toruń, is no ordinary provincial town. Not only has it retained almost its entire ring of medieval fortified walls – perhaps the most complete in Poland – but it also boasts half a dozen red-brick Gothic churches and a beautiful town hall. The sights and atmosphere here somehow totally transcend the town's small size and make it an appealing stopover.

Chełmno was a Polish settlement existing from the late 10th century, but it really began to develop as the first seat of the Teutonic Knights, who originally planned to make it their capital. They arrived in the late 1220s and immediately began to build a castle, which they completed by 1265. Chełmno also profited from its position on the Vistula trade route, fostering a lucrative affiliation to the Hanseatic League.

After the Treaty of Toruń, Chełmno returned to Poland, but despite its royal privileges the glory days were gone. The Swedish invasion did considerable damage and a series of wars in the 18th century left the town an unimportant place with some 1600 inhabitants. Though it survived WWII without major damage, it never really revived. Today it's a relaxed, drama-free town sealed within its own walls, much as it was six centuries ago.

Information

Bank Gdański (☎ 686 16 20; ul Dworcowa 3)
Kredyt Bank (☎ 676 11 95; ul Dworcowa 24A)
Netclub (ul Wodna 9; per hr 0.50zł; ⏰ 9am-11pm) Internet access.
Tourist office (☎ 686 21 04; Ratusz, Rynek; ⏰ 8am-3pm Mon & Sat, 8am-4pm Tue-Fri)

Sights

Coming from the bus terminal, you'll enter the Old Town through the **Grudziądz Gate** (Brama Grudziądzka), the only surviving medieval gateway. It was remodelled in the 17th century to incorporate a chapel. Note an expressive pietà in the niche in the gate's eastern façade.

Past the gate, you'll find yourself on a chessboard of streets, with the Rynek at its heart. In the middle stands the graceful Renaissance **town hall**, built around 1570 on the site of the previous Gothic structure and now home to the **Regional Museum** (Muzeum Ziemi Chełmińskiej; ☎ 686 16 41; admission 5zł; ⏰ 10am-4pm Tue-Fri, 10am-3pm Sat, 11am-2pm Sun). The collection relating to the town is exhibited in the original interiors, including a spectacular courtroom.

On the back wall of the town hall is the old Chełmno measure, the 4.35m-long pręt chełmiński. The entire town was laid out according to this measure, setting all the streets exactly the same width apart. It is divided into 'feet' a little smaller than an English foot. This unique system was used until the 19th century, and the town also had its own weights.

Just off the Rynek is the massive, late-13th-century Gothic **parish church**. The magnificent interior is crammed with ornate baroque and rococo furnishings, including the 1710 high altar, the shell-shaped pulpit, the elaborate three-part organ from 1690 and numerous altarpieces scattered throughout the nave and aisles. There are also some remnants from previous periods, notably the Romanesque stone baptismal font and fragments of Gothic frescoes.

The **Church of SS John the Baptist & John the Evangelist** (Kościół Św Jana Chrzciciela i Jana Ewangelisty), in the western end of the Old Town, was built between 1266 and 1325 next to the castle (which hasn't survived) as part of the Cistercian convent. Unusual for its two-level nave, it has a richly gilded high altar and an ornate organ to the side.

Underneath the organ is a black-marble tombstone from 1275, one of the oldest in the region. The church is usually closed; enter the gate at ul Dominikańska 40 and ask to be let in.

The town's other churches are less spectacular and most are unused (even in Catholic Poland, a town of this size just doesn't need six houses of worship). Nevertheless you can have a look at them just for their original Gothic structures, all dating from the 13th and 14th centuries.

Finally, you may want to inspect the 2.2km-long **fortified walls**, which are, together with those in Paczków in Silesia, the only examples in Poland to have survived almost in their entirety. There once were 23 defensive towers in the walls and some still exist, though they're not all in good shape.

Sleeping & Eating

Karczma Chełminska (☎ 679 06 05; www.karczma chelminska.pl; ul 22 Stycznia 1b; s/d 120/160zł; **P**) Playing to the tourist market, this timber-styled courtyard hotel, in the southwestern corner of the Old Town, is a little cheesy at times (see the big wooden figure outside) but offers spanking-new rooms with great stone-effect bathrooms. Reception will happily sell you maps and other information.

Hotelik (☎ 676 20 30; ul Podmurna 3; s/d 120/140zł) Located in a quiet corner of the Old Town, right near the Grudziądz Gate, the half-timbered Hotelik offers good value for money and a late-opening restaurant.

Hotel Centralny (☎ 686 02 12; ul Dworcowa 23; s/d/tr/q 90/120/150/180zł) Outside the city walls, the Centralny is simple but perfectly pleasant, with weekend discounts and some budget shared-facility rooms. It's very convenient for the bus station, and also has a good restaurant (mains 5.50zł to 16zł).

Ośrodek Wypoczynkowy (☎ 686 12 56; d/q cabins 40/70zł; ☺ May-Sep) On Lake Starogrodzkie, 2km west of the walled town, the Ośrodek has a colony of basic cabins and a camping ground.

Restauracja Spichlerz (☎ 686 99 12; ul Biskupia 3; mains 6-15zł; ☺ lunch & dinner) Full of farmhouse beams and fantasy murals, the combination of pub-restaurant and youth hang-out makes for an interesting atmosphere. Cocktails, pool tables, English menus and an extensive MP3 jukebox add to the appeal. It's just off the Rynek.

Getting There & Away

Trains no longer come to town but buses leave roughly hourly to Bydgoszcz (8.40zł, 1½ hours), Toruń (13zł, one hour) and Grudziądz (6.20zł, 50 minutes). There are also two buses a day direct to Gdańsk.

GRUDZIĄDZ

☎ 56 / pop 100,000

Approximately 30km down the Vistula River from Chełmno, Grudziądz (*groo-*dzy-onts) is a large industrial town that started life as an early Piast settlement. Repeatedly destroyed by the Prussians, it came under the rule of the Teutonic Knights as Graudenz in the 1230s, returning to the Crown in 1454 after an anti-Prussian rebellion. In the First Partition of 1773 it was swallowed up by Prussia, returning to Poland once more in the aftermath of WWI.

Grudziądz was badly damaged in 1945 but the new authorities decided to make it an important regional industrial centre, as it had been before the war. Today it's an active, if fairly unremarkable, modern town distinguished only by its few historical attractions, most notably the line of gigantic granaries.

Information

Bank Millennium (☎ 0801 125 000; ul Sienkiewicza 19)

Bank Pekao (☎ 465 82 88; ul Chełmińska 68)

Café Internet (ul Pańska 6; per hr 3.50zł; ☺ 10am-10pm)

Tourist office (☎ 461 23 18; www.it.gdz.pl; ul M Skłodowskiej-Curie 19; ☺ 9am-5pm Mon-Fri, 9am-2pm Sat, 10am-2pm Sun)

Sights

The extraordinary row of crumbling **granaries** *(spichrze)* is the best reason to stop off in Grudziądz. Built along the whole length of the town's waterfront to provide storage and protect the town from invaders, their size and location make them unique in Poland. Begun in the 14th century, they were gradually rebuilt and extended until the 18th century, and some were later turned into housing blocks by cutting windows in the walls. Decayed as they are, these massive buttressed brick buildings – most of them six storeys high – are an impressive sight. The best view is from the opposite bank of the Vistula but it's a long walk

POMERANIA

south and then over the bridge; if you're arriving by bus from Chełmno, you can sit on the left-hand side to get the full effect with much less effort.

The town's other principal attraction is the regional **museum** (☎ 465 90 63; ul Wodna 3/5; adult/concession 6/3zł; ☀ 10am-4pm Tue, 10am-3pm Wed-Sat, 10am-2pm Sun), based in a former Benedictine convent at the southern end of the old quarter. The main building houses contemporary paintings from the region and temporary exhibitions, with further sections on local archaeology and history in two old granaries just to the west.

A few other buildings in the centre retain their historical significance. The Gothic **parish church**, set behind the granaries, is a well-preserved original structure in red-brick style. Next to it is the **town hall**, originally a Jesuitic college, and the former **Jesuit Church** (Kościół Pojezuicki), built in 1715. Most of the chapel's small space is taken up by a beautiful baroque high altar, and the surrounding ornamentation includes some unusual chinoiserie (particularly visible beneath the organ loft), a decorative style almost unused in Polish churches.

At the top of the hill that slopes up from the granaries, you'll find the remnants of the Teutonic order's 13th-century **castle**. There's practically nothing left apart from a few walls and a well, and the park area is mainly used by delinquent drinkers at night (watch out for broken glass), but you do get some good Vistula views from the edge.

Sleeping & Eating

Hotelik (☎ 462 61 41; ul Kwiatowa 28; d 50-75zł, tr 75zł) A converted residential house halfway between the train station and the Old Town, this is a decent budget option in the 'basic but serviceable' category. The extra furniture makes it almost homy.

Hotel Karolewicz (☎ 462 60 37; ul Toruńska 28; s 60-80zł, d 90-105zł; P) Recommended as much for its convenient location as its unspectacular two-star facilities, the Karolewicz is handily equipped with its own restaurant and *kantor* (private currency-exchange office). Prices depend on whether you want a TV or not.

Youth hostel (☎ 643 55 40; ul Hallera 37; dm 17-20zł; ☀ year-round) The 150-bed hostel is in a large, nondescript, 11-storey block, part of the Bursa Szkolna (School Dorm), 1.5km

south of the Old Town. It has doubles and triples only, so provides more privacy than many similar hostels.

Ośrodek Wypoczynkowy Rudnik (MORiW; ☎ 462 25 81; ul Zaleśna 1; bungalows 45-100zł) This highly rated two-star camping ground, on a lake 5km south of town, has an enviable selection of facilities, including restaurants, sports equipment, boats, children's playground, paddling pool, summer bus service and its own police post. Best of all, it's specially adapted to accommodate disabled visitors.

Getting There & Away

The train station is about 1km southeast of the Old Town, a 15-minute walk. The bus terminal is a short walk north of the station. Seven or eight trains run daily to Toruń (10.50zł, 1½ hours) and Kwidzyn (6.80zł, one hour); most of the latter continue further north to Malbork (10.50zł, 1¾ hours), with two services running as far as Gdynia. Buses to Bydgoszcz (10.50zł, 1¾ hours) and Chełmno (6.20zł, 50 minutes) leave roughly hourly. There are also eight buses to Kwidzyn (fast service 10zł, 45 minutes).

KWIDZYN

☎ 55 / pop 40,000

About 30km downriver from Grudziądz is Kwidzyn, another medieval Teutonic stronghold noted for its castle and cathedral. Like much of the region, the town only became Polish after 1945, and was formerly known as Marienwerder.

Sights

The square **castle** and its central courtyard was built in the first half of the 14th century. It experienced many ups and downs in subsequent periods and suffered a serious loss in 1798 when the Prussians pulled down two sides (eastern and southern) and the main tower. It passed unscathed through WWII.

After the war, the Polish authorities treated the castle with more respect than their predecessors had, carefully restoring what was left. Most of the building is now the **Kwidzyn Museum** (☎ 279 38 89; ul Katedralna 1; adult/concession 7/5zł; ☀ 9am-5pm Tue-Sun), which has several sections including displays on medieval sacred art, regional folk crafts and plenty of farming implements, as well as a display in the cellar detailing the German-funded archaeological excavations around the site. You won't find any English labelling, but the fine original interiors justify a visit.

The most curious feature of the castle is the two unusual towers standing some distance away from the western and southern sides, linked to the main building by arcaded bridges. The smaller tower held a well, while the western one was the *gdanisko* (knights' toilet), and later also served as the execution ground. You can visit both while wandering around the interior, but it's also worth walking around the outside.

The **cathedral** attached to the castle is the familiar Gothic brick blockbuster, which has a suitably defensive appearance, thanks to its 19th-century tower. Look for the interesting ceramic mosaic (from around 1380) in the external wall above the southern porch. The spacious interior, supported on massive columns, has fragments of 14th-century frescoes while the furnishings are a combination of Gothic and neo-Gothic elements.

Sleeping & Eating

Hotel Kaskada (☎ 279 37 31; ul Chopina 42; s/d 130/150zł) Right opposite the train station, the Kaskada has been recently redone in bright colours and also has a simple restaurant, making it a good option if you decide to stay over.

Pensjonat Miłosna (☎ 279 40 52; ul Miłosna 2; d/tr 180/230zł; **P**) Miłosna is a stylish villa set in the woods off the Grudziądz road; about 4km from Kwidzyn, it's basically only a proposition for motorists. Rooms are cosy and comfortable, and there's also a good restaurant.

Getting There & Away

The bus and train stations are set 200m apart, around a 10-minute walk to the castle. Trains to Malbork (6.80zł, 45 minutes) and Grudziądz (6.80zł, one hour) go fairly regularly throughout the day. Three direct trains run to Toruń (14.50zł, 2½ hours) and two to Gdańsk (13.10zł, 2¼ hours). There are 15 buses daily to Malbork (6.30zł, 50 minutes), six to Elbląg (9.50zł, 1½ hours) and four to Gdańsk (12zł, two hours).

GNIEW

☎ 58 / pop 7200

Less known and visited than Kwidzyn, the small town of Gniew (pronounced gnyef), on the other side of the Vistula, has an equally prominent and remarkably well-maintained castle. The town has also re-

tained its original medieval layout in the tiny old centre. With few interruptions from modern life, it's a charming place to visit for a couple of hours.

Sights

The first stronghold of the Teutonic order on the left bank of the Vistula, the **castle** was built in the late 13th century and is a massive multistorey brick structure with a deep courtyard. In 1464 it came under Polish rule and remained so until the First Partition of 1773. The Prussians remodelled it to accommodate a barracks, jail and ammunition depot. It was seriously burnt out in 1921, but the 2m-thick walls survived. Restoration work began in 1976 and is still in progress.

The castle now houses the **Archaeological Museum** (☎ 535 21 62; www.zamek-gniew.pl; Plac Zamkowy 2; adult/concession 8/5zł; ☉ 9am-5pm Tue-Sun). The archaeological exhibition is in two rooms, but you will also get to see the chapel and temporary exhibitions in other rooms, and wander through most of the castle. All visits are guided and the tour takes up to 1½ hours; unless you pay 50zł for a foreign-language guide, this will mean tagging along with a Polish group and hanging around through some fairly lengthy explanations of each display (including a dramatic account of the Battle of Grunwald). At weekends historical performances are held twice a day.

Sleeping & Eating

Pałac Marysieński (☎ 535 49 49; www.hotelmarysienki .pl; Plac Zamkowe 3; s 95-125zł, d 155-195zł, q 240zł, ste 250-350zł; **P**) The Pałac is a large, imposing building set next to the castle, fully renovated and offering a fine range of comfortable accommodation. The house restaurant is of equally good value.

Dormitorium (☎ /fax 535 21 62; dm 35zł; ☉ year-round) In part of the castle, the 90-bed Dormitorium offers bunk accommodation in spacious vaulted dorms, which are heated in winter. It's simple but clean and has character, and you'll hardly find a cheaper castle bed in Poland. The castle's vaulted cellars provide a great setting for the Piwnica Rycerska, which serves drinks and budget meals.

Getting There & Away

Gniew's bus terminal is about 200m north-west of the Rynek. There are roughly hourly services to Tczew (5.60zł, 45 minutes),

POMERANIA

nine to Gdańsk (10.50zł, 1½ hours), three to Grudziądz (9zł, one hour) and three to Toruń (12zł, 2½ hours).

MALBORK

☎ 55 / pop 42,000

Malbork is famous for one thing: this small, quiet town boasts what is reputedly Europe's largest Gothic castle, a splendid Unesco-listed example of the classic medieval fortress style. In summer hordes of tourists, holidaymakers and coach parties descend on the site, making it quite deservedly one of the region's most popular attractions. You could easily come here as a day trip from Gdańsk, but it's worth taking more time to dodge the crowds and appreciate the castle fully.

Information

Bank Pekao (☎ 272 81 62; ul Piłsudskiego 9)
Tourist office (☎ 273 49 90; ul Piastowska 15; ⏱ 10am-6pm Mon-Fri, 10am-2pm Sat & Sun)

Sights

Malbork's pride and joy is the castle that sits on the bank of the Nogat River, an eastern arm of the Vistula, which was once the main bed of the river. Built by the Teutonic Knights, the **Marienburg** (Fortress of Mary), was the main seat of the order for almost 150 years, and its vast bulk reflects the weight of its long history.

The immense castle took shape in stages. First was the so-called High Castle, the formidable central bastion, which was begun around 1276 and finished within three decades. When Malbork became the capital of the order in 1309, the fortress was expanded considerably, both to cope with its newly acquired functions and to provide adequate security. The Middle Castle was built to the side of the high one, followed by the Lower Castle still further along. The whole complex was encircled by three rings of defensive walls and strengthened with dungeons and towers. The castle eventually spread over 21 hectares, making it the largest fortress built in the Middle Ages.

The castle was only seized in 1457, during the Thirteen Years' War, when the military power of the knights had already been eroded. Malbork then became the residence

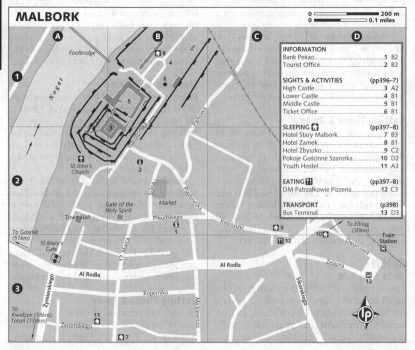

MALBORK

INFORMATION	
Bank Pekao	1 B2
Tourist Office	2 B2

SIGHTS & ACTIVITIES	(pp396–7)
High Castle	3 A2
Lower Castle	4 B1
Middle Castle	5 B1
Ticket Office	6 B1

SLEEPING	(pp397–8)
Hotel Stary Malbork	7 B3
Hotel Zamek	8 B1
Hotel Zbyszko	9 C2
Pokoje Gościnne Szarotka	10 D2
Youth Hostel	11 A3

EATING	(pp397–8)
DM Patrzałkowie Pizzeria	12 C3

TRANSPORT	(p398)
Bus Terminal	13 D3

of Polish kings visiting Pomerania, but from the Swedish invasions onwards it gradually went into decline. After the First Partition, the Prussians turned it into barracks, destroying much of the decoration and dismantling parts that were of no military use.

In the 19th century the Marienburg was one of the first historic buildings taken under government protection to become a symbol of the glory of medieval Germany. It underwent thorough restoration right up until the outbreak of WWI, regaining a shape close to the original. During WWII, however, the eastern part of the fortress was shelled and the whole process had to start again, this time with Polish restorers. The bulk of the work was finished by the 1970s and the castle looks much as it did six centuries ago, dominating the town and the surrounding countryside.

The castle's enormous size is what hits you first – almost the entire complex has been preserved, complete with the multiple defensive walls, towers and dense internal layout. The best view is from the opposite side of the river (you can get there by footbridge), especially in the late afternoon when the brick turns an intense red-brown in the setting sun.

The fortress is now run as the **Castle Museum** (Muzeum Zamkowe; ☎ 647 08 02; www.zamek .malbork.pl; ul Starościńska 1; tours adult/concession 23/14zł; ☽ 9am-8pm Tue-Sun May-Sep, 10am-3pm Tue-Sun Oct-Apr) and access is strictly controlled. Most of the rooms and chambers are open to visitors, housing a total of 23 exhibitions on various historical and archaeological topics.

The entrance to the complex is from the northern side, through what used to be the only way in. From the main gate, you walk over the drawbridge, then go through five iron-barred doors to the vast courtyard of the **Middle Castle** (Zamek Średni). On the western side (to your right) is the **Grand Masters' Palace** (Pałac Wielkich Mistrzów), which has some splendid interiors. Alongside is the **Knights' Hall** (Sala Rycerska), which is the largest chamber in the castle at 450 sq metres. The remarkable ceiling has its original palm vaulting preserved, but the foundations of the building are subsiding and rescue work is in progress. The building on the opposite side of the courtyard houses a collection of armour and an excellent display of amber.

The tour proceeds to the **High Castle** (Zamek Wysoki), over another drawbridge and through a gate (note the ornamented 1280 doorway) to a spectacular arcaded courtyard that has a reconstructed well in the middle. You'll then be taken around the rooms on three storeys, including the knights' dormitories, kitchen, bakery, chapterhouse and refectory. The entrance to the **castle church** is through a beautiful Gothic doorway, known as the Golden Gate. Underneath the church's presbytery is St Anne's Chapel, with the grand masters' crypt below its floor.

Finally, you can climb the castle's main square **tower** for an excellent view over the whole complex and the flat countryside around, and visit the terraces that run around the High Castle between the main buildings and the fortified walls.

Visitors must join a tour to enter the castle. Costumed Polish guides pick up groups every half-hour, taking up to three hours to go around; in summer there are three daily tours each in English and German, with a small charge added to the ticket price. Late tours (adult/concession 14zł/9zł), which leave shortly before closing time, run at breakneck speed and miss some exhibitions. Access to the grounds on Monday, when all the buildings and exhibition rooms are closed, costs just 4.50zł.

If you miss the relevant slot or visit out of season, German- and English-speaking guides are available on request for 150zł per group (plus the standard entrance fee). Otherwise, you have two options: wait until a foreign tour group arrives and ask the tour guide/driver if you can join; or get in with a Polish group, then 'lose' it and lurk behind a foreign-language tour.

Sleeping & Eating

Hotel Zamek (☎ /fax 272 33 67; ul Starościńska 14; s/d 250/300zł; ℗) Nestled in a restored medieval building in the Lower Castle, the 42-room Hotel Zamek isn't quite as palatial as you may expect, but the prime location, darkwood surrounds and excellent restaurant make it unarguably Malbork's top choice.

Hotel Stary Malbork (☎ 647 24 00; www.hotelstary malbork.com.pl; ul 17 Marca 26/27; s 210zł, d 300-360zł, ste 550-650zł; ℗ ☐) While it can't compete in terms of location, this new townhouse hotel equals or exceeds the Zamek in every other respect, targeting the international visitor market with its well-drilled staff, comprehensive amenities and impeccable rooms.

Hotel Zbyszko (☎ 272 26 40; ul Kościuszki 43; s/d 140/190zł, tr 250-280zł; **P**) Refurbished over recent years, the 50-bed Zbyszko is well located and reasonable value. The hotel has its own restaurant, with a good spacious dining room. Some cheaper but scrappier shared-facility rooms are also available.

Pokoje Gościnne Szarotka (☎ /fax 612 14 44; ul Dworcowa 1A; s/d/tr/q 25/45/65/80zł) This handy 56-bed workers' dorm, just round the corner from the train station, offers basic but inoffensive rooms with shared bathroom.

Youth hostel (☎ 272 24 08; ul Żeromskiego 45; bed 20-35zł; ☒ year-round) Housed in the local school, the hostel has a few doubles, but most beds are in dorms sleeping eight or more people. It's a few minutes' walk south of the castle.

DM Patrzałkowie Pizzeria (☎ 272 39 91; ul Kościuszki 25; mains 5.90-15.50zł; ☒ lunch & dinner) At the station end of town, friendly staff dishes up pizza, pasta, *pierogi* (dumplings) and other staples to a mixed crowd of locals and tourists.

Getting There & Away

The train station and bus terminal are at the eastern end of the town centre, 1km from the castle. Malbork sits on the busy Gdańsk–Warsaw railway route, so there are plenty of trains to Gdańsk (express/fast 21.40zł/15.90zł, 40 minutes) and Warsaw (60.60zł/41.24zł, 3½ hours). There are also frequent links with Elbląg (5.70zł, 30 minutes) and up to nine daily services to Kwidzyn (6.80zł, 45 minutes), Grudziądz (10.50zł, 1¾ hours) and Olsztyn (28.38zł, two hours). PKS buses also serve most regional destinations.

Coming from Gdańsk by train, you'll catch a splendid view of the castle; watch out to your right when crossing the river.

ELBLĄG

☎ 55 / pop 130,000

Elbląg (*el*-blonk) isn't the first place most Poles would think of going on holiday: WWII turned the historical town into a heap of rubble, and these days its main significance is as an important industrial zone. That said, you'll still find a few coach parties coming through to look at the new centre, an innovative attempt to create a modern 'old town'.

Historically, Elbląg was one of the earliest strongholds of the Teutonic Knights and became their first port. At that time the Vistula Lagoon (Zalew Wiślany) extended further south than it does today, allowing the town to develop for several centuries as a maritime port. When Elbląg came under Polish rule after the Treaty of Toruń, it became one of the Crown's main gateways to the sea, taking much of the trade from the increasingly independent Gdańsk. Later, Swedish invasions and the gradual silting up of the waterways eclipsed the town's prosperity, and a partial revival came only with industrial development in the late 19th century.

The port may have gone, but the city still enjoys favourable geography – it's a gateway to Frombork, the starting/finishing point of the Elbląg-Ostróda Canal (see p434), and a jumping-off point for the Russian region of Kaliningrad.

Information

INTERNET ACCESS

Inferno (ul Czerwonego Krzyża 6; per hr 3zł; ☒ 10am-10pm)
Meteor (Plac Dworcowy 1; per hr 3zł; ☒ 8am-8pm)

MONEY

Bank Pekao Stary Rynek (☎ 232 80 17; Stary Rynek 18A); ul Hetmańska (☎ 235 47 00; ul Hetmańska 3)
Kredyt Bank (☎ 236 57 45; ul 1 Maja 16)

TOURIST INFORMATION

PTTK (☎ 232 64 69; ul Krótka 5; ☒ 9am-3pm Mon-Wed & Fri, 10am-6pm Thu)
Tourist office (☎ 232 42 34; www.it.elblag.com.pl; ul Czerwonego Krzyża 2; ☒ 9am-5pm Mon-Fri, 10am-2pm Sat)

TRAVEL AGENCIES

Elzam (☎ 230 61 91; Elzam Hotel, Plac Słowiański 2)
Lobos (☎ 642 19 52; ul Nitschmana 20/22)
Orbis Travel (☎ 236 85 55; ul Hetmańska 24)
Watur (☎ 232 40 90; ul Garbary 7)

Sights

For a long time after WWII, the old town area was not much more than a patch of waste ground scattered with the remains of old buildings. With democracy and reform, however, came a drive for restoration, and in the early 1990s work started on a project combining modern and traditional elements, creating a stylised **New Old Town** harking back to the merchants' quarters of the great Hanseatic cities. The results so far are patchy to say the least, and construction is ongoing, but amid the jumble of styles and façades, the area has acquired a distinctive character, aided by the flurry of new restaurants, bars and hotels cashing in on what is really a unique address.

One blast from the past still dominates this evolving site: **St Nicholas' Church** (Kościół Św Mikołaja) is a sturdy, red-brick concoction, noted for its 95m-high, carefully reconstructed tower. Sadly less care was taken with the interior, and what was once a Gothic vault is now a flat concrete ceiling. At least part of the original woodcarving, including several triptychs, escaped war destruction.

Some 200m to the north is the **Galeria El** (☎ 232 53 86; ul Kuśnierska 6; adult/concession 4/2zł; 10am-6pm Mon-Sat, 10am-5pm Sun), formerly St Mary's Church. Another massive Gothic brick structure, the original church was gutted and now houses a gallery of contemporary art, with occasional concerts and events. It's worth a look just to see the imposing, lofty interior. A few steps from here is the only surviving gate of the medieval fortifications, the **Market Gate** (Brama Targowa).

A five-minute walk south along the river bank is the **Elbląg Museum** (☎ 232 72 73; Bulwar Zygmunta Augusta 11; adult/concession 7/5zł; 10am-4pm Tue, Wed, Fri & Sat, 10am-6pm Thu & Sun). Occupying two large buildings, the museum has sections on archaeology and the city's history, plus a photographic record of the town from the 19th century to WWII.

Sleeping

Pensjonat Boss (☎ 239 37 28; boss@elblag.com.pl; ul Św Ducha 30; s/d/tr/ste 150/220/300/300zł) One of several small hotels springing up in the Old Town, Pensjonat Boss offers 13 comfortable rooms above its own café and restaurant. The building is a nicer example of the new-look architecture, especially when the window boxes kick in.

Hotel Sowa (☎ 233 74 22; ul Grunwaldzka 49; s 125-165zł, d 165-225zł; P) The centre's a bit of a walk from this smart new two-star, but the bus station is right across the road, making it ideal if you want an early start out of town. Friendly staff and a range of rooms are an added plus.

Hotel Viwaldi (☎ 236 25 42; www.viwaldi.m.walentynowicz.pl; Stary Rynek 16; s/d/ste 230/300/385zł) Despite some trouble with other Vivaldi hotels over naming issues, the Old Town's

top top-end tip has no problem satisfying its demanding target market. Restaurant, nightclub and 10% discount at weekends.

MOSiR Hotel (☎ 642 11 81; ul Związku Jaszczurczego 17; dm/s/d 40/75/110zł; P) Within moderate walking distance of the Old Town, the local sports hotel provides above-average budget rooms, some with TV.

Camping Nr 61 (☎ 232 43 07; www.camping-elblag.alpha.pl; ul Panieńska 14; camp site per adult/child 12/6zł, d/q 60/80zł; May-Sep) Elbląg's pleasantly shaded camping ground occupies an unusually convenient spot on the Elbląg River, close to the Old Town and about 1km west of the train and bus stations.

Eating & Drinking

Café Carillon (☎ 232 52 95; ul Mostowa 22; mains 9-18zł; breakfast & lunch) Probably the best design in the Old Town: the small patio overlooks a quiet, undeveloped spot within sight of the Market Gate, while the interior is an amazing pastiche of Art Deco–style stained glass on a musical theme. The extensive drinks menu is more enticing than the token selection of light meals.

Restauracja Pod Aniołami (☎ 236 17 26; www.pod-aniolami.w.interia.pl; ul Rybacka 23/24B; mains 12-29.90zł; lunch & dinner) Tempting tourists and hip locals alike, the Latin American menu here brings a welcome touch of chilli to a country where spice still seems exotic. It's hard not to say *olé*.

Green Way (☎ 641 90 19; ul 1 Maja 9; mains 2.50-11zł; breakfast, lunch & dinner Mon-Sat, lunch & dinner Sun) The successful vegetarian-oriented chain scores another hit, packing in the usual crowds of sensitive types at its handy central location.

Złoty Żuraw (☎ 642 22 33; Stary Rynek 35C; mains 8-19zł; lunch & dinner) One of two Chinese restaurants facing off across ul Św Ducha, the Golden Crane wins out on value if not on ambition. The Buddha statue outside tells you everything you need to know.

Bar Słoneczny (☎ 641 66 16; ul Hetmańska 16/22; mains 4-9zł; breakfast, lunch & dinner Mon-Fri, lunch & dinner Sat & Sun) One of the cheapest places to eat in the centre, the Słoneczny has standard, acceptable cafeteria food.

Getting There & Away
BOAT
Boats heading for the Elbląg-Ostróda Canal depart from the quay next to the Old Town.

Information and tickets are available at Camping Nr 61 (p399).

The neighbouring wharf is the departure point for hydrofoils to Kaliningrad in Russia, operated by **Żegluga Gdańska** (☎ 232 73 19; www.zegluga.gda.pl; same-day return adult/child €42/32). They depart at 7.30am daily from May to September, calling in at Krynica Morska and Frombork en route, and return at 6pm Russian time, leaving about five hours for visiting the city. Information and bookings are available from most travel agencies in town, or the tourist office organises group day trips for around €85 per person.

BUS

The bus terminal is next to the train station; PKS buses to Gdańsk (fast/slow 13zł/11zł, 1½ hours) and Braniewo, for Frombork (7.30zł, 40 minutes), operate at least hourly. Private minibuses serve the same Braniewo via Frombork route.

TRAIN

The train station is 1km southeast of the centre. There are regular trains to Malbork (5.70zł, 30 minutes, roughly hourly), Gdańsk (11.80zł, 1½ hours, 14 daily) and Olsztyn (14.50zł, 1½ hours, 11 daily), but only three to Frombork (6.80zł, one hour).

FROMBORK

☎ 55 / pop 2600

Frombork, like Malbork, owes the 'bork' in its name to the fortified complex at the heart of its history. Frombork's distinctive hilltop castle is, in fact, a cathedral, established by the Warmian bishops (see p428) in the 13th century after a forced departure from nearby Braniewo. The resulting ecclesiastical township sadly lacked the formidable defences of its centrepiece and was sacked on numerous occasions, most damagingly by Swedes in the 17th century. WWII continued the pattern, destroying almost the entire town, but the cathedral somehow survived, giving its already imposing presence another evocative layer of history.

While the complex on its own could be enough to bring in visitors, it's the site's association with Nicolaus Copernicus that has ensured it a place on every travel itinerary. Although Kraków, Toruń and Olsztyn can all claim close links with the astronomer, it was actually here that he spent the latter half of his life and conducted most of the observations and research for his heliocentric theory. Copernicus was buried in the cathedral (where else?), though his precise whereabouts are unknown.

Sights

CATHEDRAL HILL

The Cathedral Hill complex (Wzgórze Katedralne) is today the **Nicolaus Copernicus Museum** (Muzeum Mikołaja Kopernika; ☎ 243 72 18; www.frombork .art.pl). It covers several sights within the fortified complex, each visited on a separate ticket. The entrance is from the southern side through the massive **Main Gate** (Brama Główna), where you'll find the ticket office.

The **cathedral** (adult/concession 3/2zł; ♥ 9.30am-5pm Mon-Sat May-Sep, 9am-4pm Mon-Sat Oct-Apr), in the middle of the courtyard, is a huge brick Gothic construction embellished with a decorated western façade and a slim octagonal tower at each corner. Built from 1329 to 1388, it was the largest church ever built by the Warmian bishops, and became a model for most of the subsequent churches they founded throughout the region.

Inside, the nave and chancel (95m long altogether) are topped with a Gothic star vault and crammed with predominantly baroque altars. The large marble high altar was made in around 1750. Up to that year, a 1504 polyptych was here, which is now in the left-hand (northern) aisle.

The baroque organ, dating from 1683, is a replacement for the one looted by the Swedes in 1626. The instrument is noted for its rich tone, best appreciated during the Sunday recitals held annually in July and August. Ask about these at a tourist office before you set off for Frombork.

Note the large number of tombstones (97 in all), some of which are still set in the floor while others have been lifted and placed in the walls to preserve their carvings. There's a particularly fine example (from around 1416) at the entrance to the chancel. Also look for the two intriguing baroque marble epitaphs, each with the image of a skeleton and a skull: one is on the first northern column (near the chancel), the other on the fifth southern column.

In the southeastern corner of the courtyard is the **Old Bishops' Palace** (Stary Pałac Biskupi; adult/concession 3/2zł; ♥ 9am-4.30pm Tue-Sun May-Sep, 9am-4pm Tue-Sun Oct-Apr), now the museum's main exhibition space. On the ground floor are objects discovered during postwar archaeological excavations, while the other levels are largely devoted to the life and work of Copernicus, along with temporary displays and a collection of old telescopes.

Though Copernicus is essentially remembered for his astronomical achievements, supplanting the old geocentric Ptolemaic system with his revelation that the earth revolves around the sun, his interests extended to many other fields, including medicine, economy and the law. Apart from the early edition of his famous *De Revolutionibus Orbium Coelestium* (On the Revolutions of the Celestial Spheres), there are copies of his treatises and manuscripts on a range of subjects, together with astronomical instruments and a copy of Jan Matejko's painting depicting the astronomer at work – British visitors may be unaccountably reminded of TV fop Lawrence Llewellyn-Bowen.

The high tower at the southwestern corner of the defensive walls is the former cathedral **belfry** (dzwonnica; adult/concession 4/2zł; 9.30am-5pm May-Sep, 9am-4pm Oct-Apr), which has a **planetarium** at its base presenting half-hour shows in Polish. Go to the top of the tower for views of the cathedral and the town. Beyond the marina is the Vistula Lagoon, a vast but shallow lagoon separated from the sea by a narrow sandy belt, which extends for some 90km to its only outlet, near Kaliningrad.

At the northwestern corner of the complex is the 14th-century **Copernicus Tower** (Wieża Kopernika; adult/concession 4/2zł; 9.30am-5pm Tue-Sat May-Sep, on request Tue-Sat Oct-Apr). It's believed that the astronomer took some of his observations from here, and the top floor is set up to re-create his study; if he'd looked down he could also have seen his own house, which was just across the road.

OTHER SIGHTS

The 15th-century **Hospital of the Holy Ghost** (243 75 62; ul Stara; adult/concession 4/2zł; 10am-6pm Tue-Sat May-Sep, 9am-4pm Tue-Sat Oct-Apr), formerly St Anne's Chapel, still boasts late-15th-century wall paintings depicting the Last Judgment, plus exhibitions of religious art and old medicine. Note the giant stork's nest on the roof, one of the oldest documented in Poland. The hospital's a short walk east of the cathedral.

The **Water Tower** (Wieża Wodna; 243 75 00; ul Elbląska 2; admission 2zł; 8am-6pm May-Aug, 8am-3pm Sep-Apr), across the main road from the cathedral, was built in 1571 as part of one of the first water-supply systems in Europe and was used for two centuries to provide Cathedral Hill with water through oak pipes. The water was taken from the Bauda River by a 5km-long canal built for this purpose. The admission fee lets you climb to the top of the tower, though the views aren't as good as from the hill.

Sleeping & Eating

Dom Familijny Rheticus (243 78 00; dom familijny@gabo.pl; ul Kopernika 10; s/d/tr 88/120/150zł, apt 120-240zł) It's not just the fine family villa that makes Rheticus the best deal in town: the 10 spacious apartments offer various configurations, sleeping up to five people, and the on-site solarium, hairdresser and florist all add to the informal character of the place. If you don't feel like using your kitchen, breakfast is an extra 7zł.

Pensjonat Natalia (243 74 24; ul Rybacka 12; s/d 70/140zł; P) This freestanding old warehouse by the marina has been converted into a hotel by a Polish-Russian cultural foundation and offers neat, sparingly furnished rooms with some lagoon views. Staff may be able to help with Russian visas.

Hotel Kopernik (243 72 85; hotel.kopernik@wp .pl; ul Kościelna 2; s/d 120/160zł; P) The modern Hotel Kopernik has 32 reasonable rooms, its own budget restaurant and the only *kantor* in town. The motel look doesn't sit well with Frombork's more traditional buildings, but you can't find much fault with the interior.

Kwatery Prywatne Koczergo (243 73 57; ul Kapelańska 5; r per person 40zł; P) Convenient, nicely turned-out lodgings in a residential house just off the Rynek. Several other private homes around town rent rooms to visitors at similar prices – look out for the *kwatery prywatne* signs.

Camping Nr 12 (243 73 83; ul Braniewska 14; d/tr 40/65zł; mid-May–mid-Sep) The PTTK camping ground is at the eastern end of town, on the Braniewo road. It has basic cabins and a snack bar on the grounds.

Restauracja Akcent (243 72 75; ul Rybacka 4; mains 5-12zł; breakfast, lunch & dinner;) An alternative to the hotel eateries listed above, this is a decent place with a sightline to the castle and a menu that goes beyond the basics.

Self-caterers can stock up on all the usual provisions and perishables at the large **Rojalmarket** (☎ 58-343 03 90; ul Mickiewicza 3), on the Rynek.

Getting There & Away

The train and bus stations are next to each other, near the waterfront. Buses run to Elbląg (7.30zł, 40 minutes) roughly hourly, and four fast buses continue daily to Gdańsk (18zł, 2½ hours). Trains are of less interest – there are just two departures a day to Elbląg (6.80zł, one hour).

Just north of the stations is the marina; pleasure boats go to Krynica Morska (25zł, 1½ hours) several times daily in summer, with one service continuing to Kaliningrad (return 150zł; see p399).

NORTHERN & WESTERN POMERANIA

Heading northwest from Gdańsk, you'll quickly hit the Baltic coast, Poland's key summer holiday strip. The coastline is predominantly flat and straight, but its dunes, woods and coastal lakes give it a lot of charm, and the dozens of resort towns are just small enough to be engaging without lacking life. Sandy beaches stretch almost all the way from Hel to Świnoujście, and two particularly interesting portions of the coast have been made into national parks.

In case you hadn't guessed, the Baltic is considerably colder than the Mediterranean, and the sea-bathing season is limited to a few weeks in July and August, depending on the weather. On the whole, summers are not as hot on the coast as in central Poland; on the plus side, winters are not as cold.

If you venture south from the shoreline, the lakes and forests take over again, only thinning out as you descend to the Szczecin Lowland (Nizina Szczecińska), around the Odra River and the border with Germany. Northern and central Pomerania is essentially rural and sparsely populated, with only occasional towns and very little industry. Whether you're travelling by public transport, car, bicycle or kayak, it's a lovely region to explore.

ŁEBA

☎ 59 / pop 4100

Łeba (*weh*-bah) is a small, old fishing port that now leads a dual existence as a popular seaside resort. The original settlement was founded on the western side of the Łeba River, but moved to the opposite bank after a disastrous storm in 1558. Even in the new location shifting dunes played havoc with both maritime trade and agriculture; at the end of the 19th century a new port was built and the dunes were forested, slowing down the movement of the sands. This, together with the construction of road and railway links, brought modest economic growth.

Today Łeba is still a large village rather than a town, but summer visitors swell the population by a factor of 10, turning it into a buzzing resort zone. The wide sandy beach stretches in both directions as far as the eye can see and the water is reputedly the cleanest on the Polish coast. The town is also an ideal base for trips to the nearby Słowiński National Park (right). If you're looking to soak up some Baltic beach life, Łeba is a great introduction to the Polish summer.

Orientation

The train and bus stations are next to each other in the southwestern part of Łeba, two blocks west of ul Kościuszki, the town's main drag. This shopping street runs north to the port, set on a brief stretch of the Łeba River that joins Lake Łebsko to the sea. The river divides Łeba's beach in two. The town is nestled behind the eastern beach, and this is also the main resort area. The beach on the western side of the river is less crowded and the broad white sands stretch back 75m to the dunes, making up some of the best stretches of beach on the Baltic coast.

Information

Bank Pekao (☎ 866 29 03; ul Kościuszki 87)
Biuro Wczasów Przymorze (☎ 866 13 60; ul Dworcowa 1) Information and accommodation.
Café Internet (☎ 0604 221 375; ul Morska 1; per hr 6zł; ⌚ from 10am)
Centrum Turystyczne Łeba (☎ 866 22 77; ul Kościuszki 64) Information and accommodation.
Net & Games (☎ 864 48 65; ul Chełmońskiego; per hr 5zł; ⌚ 24hr) Internet access.
Post office (☎ 866 15 62; ul Kościuszki 23) Postal services, *kantor* and Internet access.

Tourist office (☎ 866 25 65; www.leba.pl; ul 11 Listopada 5A; ✆ 8am-8pm Mon-Fri, 8am-6pm Sat, 10am-4pm Sun Jun-Aug, 8am-4pm Mon-Fri Sep-May)

Sleeping & Eating

As in most seaside resorts, the lodging and culinary picture varies widely between the high season and the rest of the year. In July and August it's hard to find a building that *doesn't* offer accommodation, with everything from old train carriages to alpine huts being called into service for the tourist hordes. Most places have their own eating facilities, and countless fish stalls and snack bars spring up all around town in season.

If you've turned up without booking, the tourist office and various other agencies around town will show you what's available and advise on where to go. All prices given here are for the peak season.

Arkun (☎ 866 24 19; arkun@ta.pl; ul Wróbleskiego 11; s/d 100/190zł; **P**) The modern-traditional building by the fishing wharf looks like it ought to be pretty fancy, but in fact rooms here are a reasonable lower mid-range standard. Prices come down if you stay for more than one night, though breakfast always costs extra. Popular with French speakers.

Hotel Gołąbek (☎ 866 29 45; www.hotel-golabek .leb.pl; ul Wybrzeże 10; s 240zł, d 280-330zł; **P** ✗) The impeccably stylish Gołąbek sits on the opposite side of the wharf, with charming old fishing boats and port life to view from your window or the upstairs terrace. The sauna, solarium and waterfront restaurant all add to the value.

Hotel Neptun (☎ 866 23 57; www.neptunhotel.pl; ul Sosnowa 1; s 405zł, d 425-605zł, tr 645-725zł, ste 805-1020zł; **P** ✆) Łeba's hotel heavyweight, this spectacular historic villa, right on the seashore, sets the standard for class and refinement. It has a terrace pool area overlooking the beach and great views of the sunset. Prices practically halve out of season.

Mazowsze (☎ 866 18 70; www.zwmazowsze.pl; ul Nadmorska 15; s/d/tr 140/160/230zł; **P**) A stiff walk east of the centre, but just 150m from the beach, the Mazowsze complex accommodates up to 250 people in comfortable rooms. As its main function is as a health resort, all kinds of interesting treatments and fitness activities are available, and it has no problem catering for disabled visitors.

Dom Turysty PTTK (☎ 866 13 24; ul Kościuszki 66; dm 40zł) A surprisingly good entry in the ultrabudget category, the PTTK is often virtually empty between groups, so you may even get a room to yourself. The shared bathrooms are showing the strain, but when this price includes breakfast you can't really quibble.

Camping Nr 41 Ambré (☎ 866 24 72; www.ambre .leba.pl; ul Nadmorska 9A; camp site per adult/child 12/6zł, bungalows 150-320zł) Of the dozen or so camping grounds in Łeba, this is among the better options, with a handy range of rooms and facilities. It's open for caravans all year.

Relaks (☎ 866 12 50; ul Nadmorska 13; cabins 210-390zł, r 255-475zł; **P** ✆) At the far eastern end of town, Relaks is that rarest of things, an upmarket camping ground. Full amenities, beach access, charming wooden Toblerone cabins (sleeping up to six people) and some more-spacious rooms make this a worthwhile treat, and the swimming pool is a miracle.

Getting There & Away

The usual transit point to/from Łeba is Lębork, a town 29km to the south, offering good connections with Gdańsk, Gdynia and some other destinations. Trains to Lębork (6.80zł, 50 minutes) depart up to 18 times daily in summer, but only twice daily the rest of the year. Buses (4zł, 35 minutes) ply the route at least every hour, supplemented by private minibuses. There are three direct buses between Łeba and Gdynia (13.20zł, three hours).

SŁOWIŃSKI NATIONAL PARK

☎ 59

The 186-sq-km **Słowiński National Park** (Słowiński Park Narodowy; ☎ 811 72 04; adult/concession 4/2zł; ✆ 7am-9pm May-Sep, 8am-4pm Oct-Apr) takes up the 33km stretch of coast between Łeba and the fishing tourist village of **Rowy**, complete with two large lakes, the Łebsko and the Gardno, and their surrounding belts of peat bog, meadows and woods. The park is named after the Slav tribe of the Slovincians (Słowińcy), a western branch of the Kashubians whose descendants inhabited this part of the coast right up until the 19th century.

The park contains a diversity of habitats, including forests, lakes, bogs, beaches and dunes. There's also a skansen and a natural history museum, and the lake wildlife is remarkably rich, particularly in birds. The park was included on Unesco's 1977 list of World Biosphere Reserves.

Sights

SHIFTING DUNES

The most unusual feature of the national park are the **shifting dunes** (wydmy ruchome), which create a genuine desert landscape. They're on the sand bar separating the sea from Lake Łebsko, about 8km west of Łeba. It's actually a vast ridge of sand 40m high and…it's moving. Rommel's Afrika Korps trained in this desert during WWII, and the site was also a secret missile testing ground from 1940 to 1945.

The dunes are easily reached from Łeba: take the road west to the hamlet of **Rąbka** (2.5km), where there's a car park and the gate to the national park. Private minibuses (4zł) and motorised trains (5zł) ply this road in summer, or you can just walk. The sealed road continues into the park for another 3.5km to the site of the rocket launcher, now an outdoor **museum** (adult/concession 8/5zł). From here a wide path goes on through the forest for another 2km to the southern foot of the dunes, where half-buried trees jut out of the sand. You can then scramble up a vast dune for a sweeping view of desert, lake, beach, sea and forest.

No cars or buses are allowed beyond the car park. You can walk to the dunes (70 minutes), take one of the small electric trolleys (25zł per three people), take a horse-drawn cart (60zł per five people) or rent a bicycle (3zł per hour). There are also large electric trolleys (3zł per person) and boats (10zł), but both only go as far as the launcher, so you'll still have 2km to walk to the dunes. Coming back, you can either retrace your steps or walk to Łeba along the beach (8km), perhaps stopping for a swim – something you certainly can't do in the Sahara.

LAKES

There are four lakes in the park, two large and two small. They are shallow lagoons that started life as bays and were gradually cut off from the sea by the sand bar. With densely overgrown, almost inaccessible marshy shores, they provide a habitat for about 250 species of birds, which live here either permanently or seasonally. They include swans, mallard, gulls, geese and grebes, to list but a few. The white-tailed eagle, Poland's largest bird, nests in the park, though nowadays it's very rare. Large

SHIFTING SANDS

The 'walking' dunes in the Słowiński National Park are reputedly the world's only such phenomenon on this scale. They consist of an accumulation of sand thrown up on the beach by waves. Dried by wind and sun, the grains of sand are then blown away to form dunes that are steadily moving inland. The 'white mountain' walks at a speed of 2m to 10m a year, depending on the particular area, burying everything it meets on its way. The main victim is the forest, which is gradually disappearing under the sand, to reappear several decades later as a field of skeletal trees.

The process started at least 5000 years ago, and so far the dunes have covered an area of about 6 sq km and reached a height of 30m to 40m, the highest peak at 42m. They apparently no longer grow higher but they do continue to spread inland over new areas. It all feels like being in a sort of miniature Sahara-on-the-Sea, a bizarre concept even if you've never seen the real thing!

parts of the lake shores have been made into strict no-access reserves, safe from human interference.

About 16km long and 71 sq km in area, **Lake Łebsko** is the biggest in Pomerania and the third-largest in Poland, after Śniardwy and Mamry in Masuria. It's steadily shrinking as a result of the movement of the dunes, the growth of weeds, and silting.

KLUKI

Set on the southwestern shore of Lake Łebsko, Kluki is a tiny hamlet of perhaps 200 souls. At the end of the 19th century, Kluki's population numbered over 500, mostly descendants of the Slovincians. Isolated from the outside world, this was the last place their local traditions survived, and the little that is left of their material culture can now be seen in the skansen.

Occupying the central part of the village, the **skansen** (Muzeum Wsi Słowińskiej; ☎ 846 30 20; adult/concession 7.50/4.50zł; ☼ 9am-3pm Mon, 9am-6pm Tue-Sun Jun-Aug, 9am-3pm Tue-Sun Sep-May) is modest but authentic, as most of the buildings are in situ and not collected from around the region, as is the case in most other museums of this type. The long, two-family, whitewashed houses are fitted with traditional furniture and decorations.

Bus transport to Kluki is only from Słupsk (8.90zł, one hour). In summer, half a dozen buses run in each direction, but fewer on Sunday; in winter, only a couple of buses ply this route.

During summer there's one daily bus between Kluki and Łeba, though it's not very convenient; you may be able to negotiate hire of a private minibus. Daily summer boat tours go to the skansen (adult/concession 29zł/25zł), making a six-hour round trip. You can also get here by bicycle.

SMOŁDZINO

West of Kluki, outside the park's boundaries, Smołdzino boasts a fine **Natural History Museum** (Muzeum Przyrodnicze; ☎ 811 72 04; adult/concession 3/1.50zł; ✆ 9am-5pm daily May-Sep, 7.30am-3.30pm Mon-Fri Oct-Apr), which feature collections of flora and fauna from the park's various habitats. The park's headquarters are also here.

Just 1km southwest of the village is **Mt Rowokół**, the highest hill in the area at 115m above sea level. On its top is a 20m **observation tower**, providing sweeping views over the forest, the lakes and the sea. The path up the hill begins next to the petrol station and you can get to the top in 15 minutes.

Buses to Słupsk (6.70zł, 45 minutes) go fairly regularly till late afternoon. There's one morning bus to Łeba in the summer holidays.

SŁUPSK

☎ 59 / pop 105,000

A large town 18km from the coast, Słupsk (pronounced swoopsk) has a history every bit as chequered as that of other Pomeranian settlements, though there's not a huge amount left to show for it. After its birth in the 11th century as a Slav stronghold on the Gdańsk–Szczecin trading route, the town came under the rule of the Gdańsk dukes in 1236, passed to the Brandenburg margraves in 1307, and later became part of the West Pomeranian Duchy. In 1648 it reverted to the Brandenburgs and remained under Prussian administration until WWII.

Słupsk is not a particularly obvious tourist destination, but it has some attractions, a pleasant centre and a choice of places to stay and eat. It's equally good as a base for visiting nearby resorts or a more fleeting stopover on the east–west coastal route.

Information

Bank Pekao (☎ 841 20 00; ul 9 Marca 6)
Kawiarnia Internet (☎ 0601 641 003; per hr 4zł; ✆ 10am-10pm) At the train station.
Tourist office Plac Zwycięstwa (summer info booth; Plac Zwycięstwa; ul Sienkiewicza (☎ 842 43 26; www.slupsk.pl; ul Sienkiewicza 19; ✆ 8am-6pm Mon-Fri, 9am-3pm Sat Jun-Sep, 8am-4pm Mon-Fri Oct-May)

Sights

Słupsk's main attraction is the 16th-century **castle**, an unassuming structure containing the **Museum of Central Pomerania** (Muzeum Pomorza Środkowego; ☎ 842 40 81; ul Dominikańska 5; adult/concession 6/4zł; ✆ 10am-3pm Mon, 10am-5pm Tue-Sat, 10am-6pm Sun). Sacral woodcarvings, historic furniture and other exhibits illustrate the town's history, but the highlight is a 200-piece collection (the best in Poland) of portraits by Stanisław Ignacy Witkiewicz, the artist popularly known as Witkacy. A controversial writer, photographer and painter, Witkacy was one of the foremost figures in interwar Polish art.

The building opposite the castle gate is the 14th-century **mill**, used as an annexe to house the museum's ethnographic collection.

Next to the mill, the 15th-century **St Hyacinthus' Church** (Kościół Św Jacka) has had substantial later alterations and contains a late-Renaissance high altar and pulpit, both from 1602. The main body of the church is often closed outside service times, but the anteroom has some poignant memorial plaques and a macabre wooden crucifix, and you can peer through the grille at the rest of the interior. The fine organ can be heard at the regular summer concerts, held midweek in July and August.

Of the 15th-century fortified walls that once encircled the town, only two remnants survive: the **Mill Gate** (Brama Młyńska), beside the mill, and the **Witches' Tower** (Baszta Czarownic), a bit further north. In the 17th century the latter was turned into a jail for women suspected of witchcraft, a common accusation at the time. The last woman condemned to the stake here was burned in 1714, and one of her predecessors, known as Trina Papisten, became a notorious figure in local folklore.

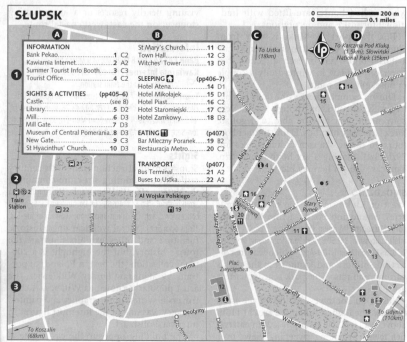

SŁUPSK

0 ━━━━━━━━ 200 m
0 ━━━━━━━━ 0.1 miles

INFORMATION
Bank Pekao.............................1 C2
Kawiarnia Internet..................2 A2
Summer Tourist Info Booth.....3 C3
Tourist Office.........................4 C2

SIGHTS & ACTIVITIES (pp405–6)
Castle...............................(see 8)
Library................................5 D2
Mill....................................6 D3
Mill Gate.............................7 D3
Museum of Central Pomerania..8 D3
New Gate............................9 C3
St Hyacinthus' Church..........10 D3

St Mary's Church...................11 C2
Town Hall.............................12 C3
Witches' Tower......................13 D3

SLEEPING (pp406–7)
Hotel Atena..........................14 D1
Hotel Mikołajek.....................15 D1
Hotel Piast...........................16 C2
Hotel Staromiejski.................17 C2
Hotel Zamkowy......................18 D3

EATING (p407)
Bar Mleczny Poranek..............19 B2
Restauracja Metro..................20 C2

TRANSPORT (p407)
Bus Terminal.........................21 A2
Buses to Ustka......................22 A2

To Ustka (18km)

To Karczma Pod Kluką (1.5km); Słowiński National Park (35km)

To Koszalin (68km)

To Gdynia (110km)

One more enduring element of the fortifications is the **New Gate** (Brama Nowa), facing the elaborate Renaissance-Gothic **town hall**. You can climb the castlelike hall's impressive main **tower** (adult/concession 2/1zł; ⏱ 9am-5pm Mon-Fri, 9am-3pm Sat & Sun) for a full Słupsk panorama. Fans of red brick should also check out the chunky Gothic **St Mary's Church** and the restored city **library** (built between 1276 and 1281), itself formerly a house of God.

Festivals & Events
Polish Piano Festival (☎ 842 64 87) Held in September.
Komeda Jazz Festival (☎ 841 09 29; www.komeda jazzfestival.slupsk.pl) Held in November, dedicated to the father of Polish jazz, Krzysztof Komeda.

Sleeping
Słupsk seems to have just the right number of accommodation options – as it's not on the coast you shouldn't have any problems finding a room, although tour groups may book up the smarter hotels in summer.

Hotel Piast (☎ 842 52 86; ul Jedności Narodowej 3; s 122-263zł; d 139-280zł; tr 240zł; ste 390-490zł; **P**)

With accommodation ranging from bog-standard guesthouse-style rooms to proper luxury suites, you're spoilt for choice at this central townhouse.

Hotel Atena (☎ 842 88 14; www.hotel.atena.prv.pl; ul Kilińskiego 7; s/d/tr 100/155/177zł; **P**) The Greek theme doesn't go much beyond the name, but if there's a goddess of bathrooms then she's surely watching over the hotel's above-average amenities. The rooms themselves sugar the deal further, with a nice line in blue furniture.

Hotel Zamkowy (☎ 842 52 94; ul Dominikańska 4; s 90-150zł; d 160-200zł; **P**) Right next to the castle, this is a good, unfancy option, with rooms ranging from tiny singles to spacious two-room doubles. Choose between the church side (views of St Hyacinthus') and the road side (better than it sounds); upstairs rooms are better either way.

Hotel Mikołajek (☎ 842 50 12; ul Szarych Szeregów 1; s 70zł, d 80-90zł) Run by the PTTK, standards here are not at all bad for the price, with TV in all the rooms, a random selection of duvet covers and a choice of en suite or shared bathrooms.

Hotel Staromiejski (☎ 842 84 64; ul Jedności Narodowej 4; s 130-190zł, d 220-250zł, tr 270zł) Right next door to the Piast, the Staromiejski is sniffier but smarter and a bit more consistent in its standards. The fancy restaurant (mains 15zł to 32zł) dishes up fine Polish food.

Eating

All the hotels listed under Sleeping have their own restaurants. Other options:

Bar Mleczny Poranek (☎ 844 33 97; Al Wojska Polskiego 46; mains 1.45-6.58zł; ☼ breakfast, lunch & dinner Mon-Fri, breakfast & lunch Sat & Sun) Basic milk bar and pizzeria.

Karczma Pod Kluką (☎ 842 34 69; ul Kaszubska 22; mains 16-25zł; ☼ lunch & dinner) Home-made regional cooking.

Restauracja Metro (☎ 842 25 83; ul 9 Marca 3; mains 13.60-38zł; ☼ lunch & dinner) Smart traditional cuisine.

Getting There & Away

BUS

PKS buses serve Łeba (10.50zł, 1½ hours, six daily), Gdynia (14.50zł, three hours, five daily), Koszalin (10.50zł, 1½ hours, 13 daily) and Darłowo (10.50zł, 1½ hours, nine daily). Buses to Smołdzino (6.70zł, 45 minutes) go regularly throughout the day, and some continue as far as Kluki (8.90zł, one hour).

Five different companies operate buses to Ustka (3.60zł, 30 minutes), including PKS and MZK, the local bus company; you can expect several services hourly in summer, departing from Al Wojska Polskiego.

TRAIN

The PKP station has roughly hourly trains east to Gdańsk (28.38zł, two hours) and west to Koszalin (fast/slow 17.50zł/10.50zł, 55 minutes, 67km); five trains continue west to Szczecin (39.66zł, 3½ hours). Three trains go straight to Warsaw (49.80zł, six hours), with three extra services in summer.

USTKA

☎ 59 / pop 17,500

The fishing port of Ustka is also a typical coastal resort, with a long beach backed by a lively promenade and semiwild parkland. It's not the equal of Łeba in any respect, but this doesn't stop vast numbers of visitors descending on the town at the first hint of summer, and the seasonal infrastructure has thrown up some appealing accommodation options for those who do catch the vibe.

Information

Doma Ustka (☎ 814 5623; www.doma.ustka.pl; ul Wilcza 22) Accommodation-finding service.

Post office (☎ 814 44 04; ul Marynarki Polskiej 47) Postal services and Internet access.

Tourist office (☎ 814 71 70; www.ustka.pl; ul Marynarki Polskiej 87; ☼ 8am-8pm Mon-Sat, 10am-6pm Sun Jul & Aug, 7.30am-3.30pm Mon-Fri Sep-Jun)

Sleeping & Eating

The tourist office can help find you a place in a hotel, pension, holiday home or private house. The cheapest summer lodgings shouldn't cost more than 40zł per person.

Baltic Art Gallery (Bałtycka Galeria Sztuki; ☎ 814 60 89; www.hotel.baltic-gallery.art.pl; ul Zaruskiego 1A; s/d/tr 48/64/80zł; ▣) A real find for art-lovers and budget travellers alike, this 19th-century granary, right by the port, has neat pine-filled rooms with shared bathrooms and a communal kitchen. Downstairs is the modern art gallery itself and the Galeria pub, two more excellent reasons to seek the place out.

Pensjonat Oleńka (☎ 814 85 22; ul Zaruskiego 1; d/ste 250/450zł) Just next door, in the middle of the granary row, the elegantly stylish Oleńka has just three rooms and four suites, all of which situate it firmly at the top of the range. Sadly, trees obstruct any potential sea views.

Hotel Rejs (☎ 814 78 50; www.hotelrejs.com in Polish; ul Marynarki Polskiej 51; s 150zł, d 170-195zł, ste 200-280zł; ℗) A new, very central hotel, just minutes from the beach, the 14-room Hotel Rejs offers spiffing modern standards and has an award-winning house restaurant, with full board available.

Villa Red (☎ 814 80 00; www.villa-red.pl; ul Żeromskiego 1; s/d/tr/ste 260/320/330/440zł; ℗ ▣) Built in 1886 for German 'Iron Chancellor' Otto von Bismarck, Ustka's most prominent beachside villa still does the business, crammed with antique furniture and some of the nicest linen on the coast. Despite facing directly onto the promenade, there's no beach access from the front, which is annoying.

Camping Słoneczny (☎ 814 42 10; ul Grunwaldzka 35; cabins per person 30zł) The most convenient of the two seasonal camping grounds, about 1200m away from the beach. Cabin space disappears like snow in summer.

Getting There & Away

The only major transport connections here are with Słupsk, which is 18km to the south

POMERANIA

(see p407). Trains call here roughly every other hour (4.60zł, 20 minutes), but the bus service is much more frequent. Regular buses also go to Rowy, on the edge of Słowiński National Park.

DARŁOWO

☎ 94 / pop 16,000

West of Ustka, the first place on the coast that's larger than a village is Darłowo (dar-*wo*-vo). Once a prosperous medieval Hanseatic port, Darłowo is one of a handful of towns in Western Pomerania that has retained some of its original character. It still has the familiar chessboard of streets, laid out in 1312, and several interesting historic buildings.

Darłowo itself isn't on the coast but 2.5km inland, on the Wieprza River. The town's gateway to the sea is Darłówko, a small fishing port that has developed as a summer resort around its beaches and has a totally different atmosphere to the main town. The two are linked by local buses that run regularly along both sides of the river.

Information

Tourist office (☎ 314 35 72; www.cit.darlowo.pl; ⏰ 10am-6pm Mon-Fri, 10am-4pm Sun & Sat) In the castle's main tower.

Sights

DARŁOWO

South of the central Rynek is the 14th-century **castle**, the oldest and best-preserved Gothic castle in northern and Western Pomerania. It was the residence of the Pomeranian dukes until the Swedes devastated it during the Thirty Years' War, and the Brandenburgs took it following the Treaty of Westphalia. The dethroned King Erik, who ruled Denmark, Norway and Sweden between 1396 and 1438 and became known as the 'last Viking of the Baltic', lived in the castle for the last 10 years of his life. He is believed to have hidden his enormous ill-gotten treasure here; so far it remains undiscovered, at least as far as anyone knows.

The castle is now a **museum** (Muzeum Zamku Książąt Pomorskich; ☎ 314 23 51; www.muzeumdarlowo .pl; ul Zamkowa 4; adult/concession 8/4zł; ⏰ 10am-6pm Mon-Fri, 10am-4pm Sat & Sun). In the well-restored period interiors (an attraction in themselves) you'll find a varied collection including folk woodcarving, portraits of Pomeranian princes, original Danzig fur-

niture, sacred art, armour and even some exhibits from the Far East. The brick torture chamber in the basement and a rather camp 1993 tapestry of the famous Erik make amusing diversions.

Besides the main body of the castle, there is a **Nautineum** (admission 3zł) holding seafaring artefacts, just under the ramparts. Other sections hold temporary exhibitions, including the castle's main **tower** (admission 2zł).

The western side of the Rynek is occupied by the **town hall**, a largish baroque building, lacking a tower and fairly sober in decoration except for its original central doorway. Right behind it rises the massive brick **St Mary's Church**. Begun in the 1320s and enlarged later, it has preserved its Gothic shape pretty well (particularly the beautiful vaults), even though the fittings date from different periods, with lots of crusading cherubs and a modern picture showing stages in the church's history.

Worth special attention are the three **tombs** placed in the chapel under the tower. The one made of sandstone holds the ashes of King Erik, who died in Darłowo in 1459. After his unwilling abdication, the king first went into exile in the castle of Visby on Gotland, from where he commanded corsair raids on Hanseatic ships until forced to flee to Pomerania. His tombstone, commissioned in 1882 by the Prussian Emperor Wilhelm II, isn't as impressive as the two mid-17th-century, richly decorated tin tombs standing on either side of it, which contain the remains of the last West Pomeranian duke Jadwig and his wife Elizabeth.

A few hundred metres north of the Rynek is the marvellous **St Gertrude's Chapel** (Kaplica Św Gertrudy). The most unusual building in town, it is 12-sided and topped with a high, shingled central spire. It's been renovated and looks amazing, but is sadly only open for Mass.

DARŁÓWKO

Darłówko is not a place for historic sights but a pleasant beach resort, packed with tourists in summer. It's cut in two by the Wieprza River, and linked by a pedestrian drawbridge that opens when boats go into or out of the bay, providing a spectacle for tourists. Two breakwaters lead into the sea at the outlet of the river and make for an enjoyable walk.

Sleeping

Accommodation is highly seasonal, with all-year places scarce and summer lodgings operating mainly in Darłówko. There are plenty of private guesthouses, and many locals rent out rooms in their homes. Private rooms start at around 25zł per person.

Róża Wiatrów (☎ 314 21 27; www.rozawiatrow.pl; ul Muchy 2, Darłówko; camp site per adult/child 10/8zł, d/tr 65/58zł, cabins 54-105zł, apt 91-116zł; May-Oct, camping Jun-Aug) This multifaceted holiday complex near the sea has camping space for 100 bodies and plenty of other accommodation.

Klub Plaza (☎ 314 24 07; ul Słowiańska 3, Darłówko; apt 250-1170zł;) Whatever you think about resort hotels, it's hard to turn your nose up at the staggering facilities this complex has to offer. Prices include breakfast (even with self-catering facilities), the huge penthouse apartments sleep up to six people and you get a choice of sea or park views.

Hotel Irena (☎ 314 36 92; Al Wojska Polskiego 64, Darłowo; s/d/tr/q/ste 70/90/110/130/150zł) One of a handful of options in central Darłowo, the Irena is an unexciting but decent enough pension, with easy access to the castle and the bus station.

Getting There & Away

The bus terminal is at the southwestern end of Darłowo, a 10-minute walk from the Rynek; many intercity services also call in at Darłówko. Buses run roughly hourly to Koszalin (7.20zł, 45 minutes) and about a dozen times a day to Ustka (8.20zł, 50 minutes) and Słupsk (10.50zł, 1½ hours).

KOSZALIN

☎ 94 / pop 115,000

Ideally situated halfway between Szczecin and Gdańsk, Koszalin (ko-*shah*-leen) was once a wealthy Hanseatic port competing with Kołobrzeg for sea trade. By the 17th century, however, the town's sea access route had silted up, effectively stifling its economy. Devastated in WWII, Koszalin was rebuilt with little care, and these days it's mainly of interest to visitors as a transport hub and staging post for the coast.

Information

Bank Pekao (☎ 346 61 00; ul Jana z Kolna 11)
BT Turysta (☎ 342 45 11; www.koszalin.pl; ul Andersa 2) Information and travel services.
PTTK (☎ 342 26 52; ul Dworcowa 4)

Sights

The only historic relic of any substance in the centre is the **cathedral**, just off the Rynek, which miraculously survived the 1945 shelling. It has some lofty, finely restored Gothic vaulting but otherwise little remains of the old fittings. The colourful organ is regularly put through its paces in summer concerts – you may also be able to catch the performers practising during the day.

The central branch of the **Regional Museum** (☎ 343 20 11; www.muzeum.koszalin.px.pl; ul Młyńska 37; adult/concession 6/4zł; 10am-4pm Tue-Sun), 300m north of the Rynek, hosts temporary exhibitions on historical topics, plus a small ethnographic display in a 200-year-old cottage beside the main building. The museum's **headquarters** (☎ 343 21 53; ul Piłsudskiego 53), another 1.2km northeast, focuses on the region's archaeology and the history of the city. Admission covers both buildings.

Sleeping & Eating

Hotel Arka (☎ 342 79 11; ul Zwycięstwa 20/24; s 139-245zł, d 175-320zł, ste 190-449zł;) A versatile business hotel perched above its own shopping centre, nightclub and highly salubrious restaurant, Koszalin's entry in the Gromada chain is almost enough to make you want to stick around. We did say almost.

Hotel Posejdon (☎ 342 78 51; ul Zwycięstwa 4; s/d/tr 52/63/88zł;) If you don't feel the need for that much comfort or service, this classic cheap 'n shabby place is right opposite the bus station, perfectly located for quick getaways. Shared bathrooms, no breakfast.

Getting There & Away

The train and bus stations are 800m west of the Rynek. Hourly buses run to the nearest seaside resorts as do regular trains to Szczecin (31.85zł, 2¾ hours) and Gdańsk (34.03zł, three hours). Trains to Kołobrzeg (14zł, 55 minutes) leave every hour or two and there are up to four fast trains to Poznań (39.66zł, four hours). If you're heading to Słupsk, note that buses travelling via Darłowo take almost twice as long as direct services.

KOŁOBRZEG

☎ 94 / pop 48,000

With 1300 years of history, Kołobrzeg (ko-*wob*-zhek) is one of Poland's oldest settlements, going back to the 7th century when salt springs were discovered and it developed

POMERANIA

into a major trading centre. In 1000 it became a seat of the Polish bishopric, putting it on a par with Kraków and Wrocław.

From the Thirty Years' War onward things started to go wrong, and it was occupied successively by Swedes, Brandenburgs, Russians and the Napoleonic army. Once the French left, the ravaged town recovered slowly as a spa and seaside resort, but the worst was yet to come – in March 1945 the two-week battle for the city left it completely devastated.

Rebuilt, Kołobrzeg is once more a lively town and an important port, though it lacks any real sense of history. For visitors, however, it's the beach, spa park and the mass of holiday homes and sanatoriums that make it an essential stop. Bigger than most of its

fellow Baltic resorts, with a smattering of culture to boot, you could do worse than join the busloads of German tourists in soaking up some sea air.

Information

INTERNET ACCESS

M@trix (☎ 354 43 50; ul Armii Krajowej 24/7; per hr 5zł; ⏱ from 11am)

Net Spin (☎ 354 73 66; Giełdowa 7C; per hr 4zł; ⏱ 10am-10pm)

Vobis (☎ 354 08 91; ul Armii Krajowej 20; per hr 4zł; ⏱ 10am-10pm)

MONEY

Bank Pekao (☎ 354 68 50; ul Źródlana 5)

PBK Bank (ul Łopuskiego 6)

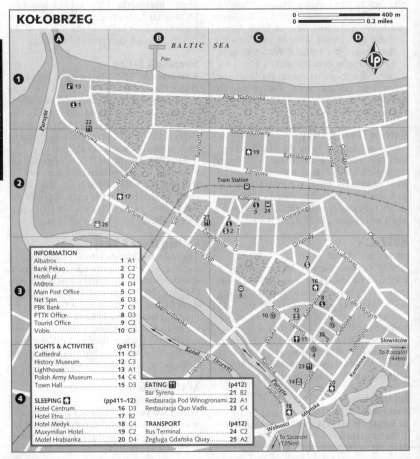

KOŁOBRZEG

INFORMATION	
Albatros	1 A1
Bank Pekao	2 C2
Hoteli.pl	3 C2
M@trix	4 D4
Main Post Office	5 C3
Net Spin	6 D3
PBK Bank	7 C3
PTTK Office	8 D3
Tourist Office	9 C2
Vobis	10 C3

SIGHTS & ACTIVITIES	(p411)
Cathedral	11 C3
History Museum	12 C3
Lighthouse	13 A1
Polish Army Museum	14 C3
Town Hall	15 D3

SLEEPING	(pp411–12)
Hotel Centrum	16 D3
Hotel Etna	17 B2
Hotel Medyk	18 C4
Maxymilian Hotel	19 C2
Motel Hrabianka	20 D4

EATING	(p412)
Bar Syrena	21 B2
Restauracja Pod Winogronami	22 A1
Restauracja Quo Vadis	23 C4

TRANSPORT	(p412)
Bus Terminal	24 C2
Żegluga Gdańska Quay	25 A2

BALTIC SEA

Pier

Aleja Nadmorska

Rodziewiczówny

Rafińskiego

Zdrojowa

Train Station

Kolejowa

Kniewskiego

Okopowa

Drzymały

Unii Lubelskiej

Walki Młodych

Słowińców

To Koszalin (44km)

Kanał Drzewny

Łopuskiego

Zygmuntowska

I Armii WP

Dworcowa

Żwirczewska

Solna

Portowa

Parsęta

Reczna

Spalna

Budowlana

Kamienna

Wolności

Myńska

To Szczecin (135km)

POST

Main post office (☎ 354 50 20; ul Armii Krajowej 1)

TOURIST INFORMATION

Albatros (☎ 354 28 00; www.kwatera.prv.pl; ul Morska 7A; ⏰ 9am-4pm Mon-Fri) Accommodation service.

Hoteli.pl (☎ 354 82 00; www.hoteli.pl; ul Żródlana 5C; ⏰ 8.30am-8pm) Accommodation service.

PTTK (☎ 354 46 93; butpttk@interia.pl; Baszta Prochowa, ul Dubois 20; ⏰ 8am-4pm Mon-Fri) Accommodation and information.

Tourist office (☎ 352 79 39; www.kolobrzeg.pl in Polish; ul Dworcowa 1; ⏰ 7am-1pm & 3-7pm daily Jul & Aug, 7am-3pm Mon-Fri Sep-Jun)

Sights

Not much remains of Kołobrzeg's old quarter, but the area around the central Rynek has been rebuilt as what you might call the **New Old Town** – an interesting blend of old and new that adds some character to the otherwise uninspiring tower blocks surrounding it. Pedestrian streets and a dash of café culture inject some seasonal colour, and the area also holds the town's main nonbeach attractions.

The 14th-century **cathedral** is the most important historic sight in town. Though badly damaged in 1945, it has been rebuilt close to its original form. Its colossal two conjoined towers occupy the whole width of the building, and the façade is a striking composition of windows placed haphazardly – a bizarre folly of its medieval builders and rebuilders.

The five-naved interior is impressively spacious and still retains fragments of old frescoes. The most striking feature, however, is the leaning columns on the right side of the nave, which give the impression that the cathedral is on the point of collapsing. Don't worry – they have been leaning since the 16th century.

Old fittings include three 16th-century triptychs and a unique Gothic wooden chandelier (1523) in the central nave. There are some even older objects such as the bronze baptismal font (1355) featuring scenes of Christ's life, a 4m-high, seven-armed candelabrum (1327) and the stalls in the chancel (1340). Outside is a striking modern monument celebrating 1000 years of Polish Catholicism; the design, a symbolic split cross joined by a peace dove, depicts influential rulers Bolesław Chrobrego and Otto III.

The **town hall**, just east of the cathedral, is a neo-Gothic structure designed by Karl Friedrich Schinkel and erected in the 1830s after the previous 14th-century building was razed by Napoleon's forces in 1807. One of its wings houses a modern **art gallery** (⏰ 10am-6pm Tue-Sun).

If you are interested in military matters, the **Polish Army Museum** (Muzeum Oręża Polskiego; ☎ 352 52 53; ul Gierczak 5; adult/concession 7/4zł; ⏰ 9.30am-5pm Mon, Tue & Thu-Sun, 9am-noon Wed Jun-Aug, 9am-3pm Tue-Sun Sep-May) covers the history of the country's army, with an outdoor display of suitably daunting weapons and vehicles. Its sister institution, the **History Museum** (☎ 352 52 53; ul Armii Krajowej 13; adult/concession 7/4zł; ⏰ 10am-4pm Wed & Fri-Sun, noon-6pm Thu May-Sep, 9am-3pm Tue, Wed & Fri-Sun, 11am-5pm Thu Oct-Apr), has history and archaeology exhibits, including a film about the town and a display of its old weights and measures.

In the seaside sector, there are no real sights; the beach itself is the attraction, supplemented by the usual seasonal stalls, games, novelty boat trips, buskers and other street life. Walk out 200m over the sea on the *molo* (pier), an obligatory trip for holiday-makers. To the west, by the harbour, stands the **lighthouse**, which you can climb for panoramic views over land and sea.

Sleeping

The summer crowds can make a real dent in Kołobrzeg's substantial accommodation range. Private rooms provide some of the cheapest beds, but a minimum stay is often required, and don't even dream about the beach district. Locals often hang around outside the tourist office brandishing *wolne pokoje* (room free) signs – it's a very competitive market in summer, and things can get rather heated!

Many of the holiday homes in the seaside area rent out rooms to the general public if they're not booked up by groups. The tourist office has a full list.

Maximilian Hotel (☎ 354 00 12; www.maximilian -hotel.pl; ul Borzymowskiego 3; s/d/tr 250/320/390zł, ste 500-570zł; Ⓟ Ⓡ) One of the loveliest villas in the seaside area, the splendid Maximilian revels in a quiet location and good-standard three-star rooms, all packaged with a touch of finesse often lacking in resort hotels. The restaurant and spa facilities mean you don't have to go far to relax.

POMERANIA

Motel Hrabianka (☎ 3542868; www.hrabianka.com; ul Budowlana 35A; s/d 115/180zł) The high point of this small, informal place is definitely the exhaustive breakfasts, served in the atmospheric traditional restaurant downstairs.

Hotel Medyk (☎ 352 34 51; www.hotelmedyk.ta.pl; ul Szpitalna 7; s 90-140zł, d 140-190zł, tr 190zł) Ten storeys of varying standards directly overlooking the river, just south of the Old Town. The more basic rooms don't include breakfast, but at least you can always moor your canoe here.

Hotel Centrum (☎ 354 55 60; www.hotelcentrum .ta.pl; ul Katedralna 12; s/d/tr/ste 140/200/240/280zł; **P**) Popular with tour groups, Hotel Centrum provides comfortable accommodation right in the city centre, with its own restaurant, café and nightclub. Satiny counterpanes give a slightly louche feel to the otherwise strait-laced rooms.

Hotel Etna (☎ 355 00 12; www.hoteletna.pl; ul Portowa 18; s/d 190/280zł, ste 350-400zł; **P**) The massive beach-area block isn't much to look at, but the facilities on offer are top-class, with a full range of spa treatments. All rooms have small balconies; go for the west side (sea views) rather than the east (views of building site).

Eating
In the beach district, most holiday homes provide meals for their guests (and often for nonguests); there are seasonal fast-food outlets and cafés everywhere, as well as some good year-round options.

Restauracja Pod Winogronami (☎ 354 73 36; www .winogrona.pl; ul Towarowa 16; mains 24-36zł; ⏱ lunch & dinner) In the harbour area, Under the Grapes has a slight French air, but the hearty menu draws mainly on the Polish and German rulebooks, with a few intriguing specials such as 'diabolic food in bread'.

Restauracja Quo Vadis (☎ 352 89 61; ul Gierczak 26A; mains 15-37zł; ⏱ lunch & dinner) Another smart tourist joint occupying a cosy basement locale in the Old Town, Quo Vadis serves solid, reliable Polish food.

Bar Syrena (☎ 352 31 88; ul Zwycięzców 11; mains 3.50-10zł; ⏱ lunch & dinner) Get back to basics at this simple self-service eatery in the train station area, doling out the usual tasty Polish fare.

Getting There & Away
The train and bus stations are next to each other, halfway between the beach and the historic centre. The harbour is 1km northwest.

Kołobrzeg lies off the main Szczecin–Gdańsk route so there are only a few trains to either destination. A regular service goes to Koszalin (14zł, 55 minutes). Two fast trains go nightly to Warsaw (52.62zł, eight hours).

The most frequent bus connection is with Koszalin (8.90zł, 1½ hours, at least hourly). Three or four fast buses a day go to Świnoujście (18zł, 2½ hours) and Słupsk (18zł, 2¾ hours).

In July and August **Żegluga Gdańska** (☎ 354 24 64; www.zegluga.pl) operates four weekly catamaran cruises to Nexo on Bornholm Island, Denmark (one-way/return 90zł/130zł, five hours). Additional boats depart from Ustka and Darłowo, and the more frequent hydrofoil services should resume in 2005.

KAMIEŃ POMORSKI
☎ 91 / pop 9500
Founded in the 9th century, Kamień Pomorski has been a major religious centre, port and trading centre at various points during its history, and only became part of Poland in the aftermath of WWII. The destruction wreaked on the town in 1945 has left it a relative backwater, but the waterfront location and the venerable 1176 cathedral provide ample motivation for a short visit.

Information
Bank Pekao (☎ 382 03 24; ul Gryfitów 2A)
Post office (☎ 382 01 05; ul Pocztowa 1)

Sights
Begun by the Wolinian bishops in a Romanesque style, Kamień's **cathedral** was thoroughly revamped in the 14th century in the Gothic fashion, which has basically survived to this day. Inside, the chancel has retained some of its old fixtures and fittings, including an impressive triptych on the high altar, thought to derive from the school of Veit Stoss, the maker of the famous pentaptych in St Mary's Church (p137) in Kraków. Oak stalls provide suitable seating, and a large crucifix is suspended from the painted vaulting. Up above the altar some of the original 13th-century wall paintings have survived.

Baroque outfits were added in the second half of the 17th century and include a decorative wrought-iron screen separating the chancel from the nave, the elaborate pulpit and the organ. The latter deserves special attention for its impressive appearance and excellent sound quality. The nationally renowned Festival of Organ & Chamber Music was started here in 1965 and takes place annually from mid-June to late August, with concerts held every Friday evening. If you can't make it on a Friday, short organ performances are held twice daily for the duration of the festival.

While you're in the church, go up the steps from the left transept to the former treasury, now a small museum, and don't miss the cloister **garth** (wirydarz; admission 1zł) – the entrance is through a door from the left-hand aisle. The 1124 baptismal font in the middle is the cathedral's oldest possession. The old tombstones on the walls of the cloister were moved here in 1890 from the church's floor. You can also go to the top of the tower, but as there's almost no view there's not much point.

Going west through the centre of town you'll get to the **Wolin Gate** (Brama Wolińska), part of the 14th-century city walls and the only surviving medieval gate of the original five. It now houses the **Museum of Precious Stones** (Muzeum Kamieni; ☎ 382 42 43; ul Słowackiego 1; adult/child 5/3zł; ☼ 10am-6pm), which features semiprecious rocks and baubles from around Silesia.

Festivals & Events
Festival of Organ & Chamber Music (☎ 382 05 41) Takes place annually from mid-June to late August, with concerts held every Friday evening.

Sleeping & Eating
Hotel Pod Muzami (☎ 382 22 41; www.podmuzami .pl; ul Gryfitów 1; s/d/tr 110/158/218zł) In a beautiful historic timbered house on the corner of the central Rynek, the friendly Pod Muzami has 12 spacious rooms within sight of the water, plus a good house restaurant.

Hotel Staromiejski (☎ 382 26 44; www.hotel-star omiejski.pl; ul Rybacka 3; s/d/tr 125/181/237zł; **P**) Just next door, the Staromiejski is a bit smarter and more service-oriented than its neighbour, but the building is much plainer and lacks charm.

Youth hostel (☎ 382 08 41; Plac Katedralny 5; dm 15-20zł; ☼ Jul & Aug, reception 7-10am & 5-10pm) In a school across the road from the cathedral, the 60-bed hostel has large dorms only, though the impressive red-brick edifice doesn't lack character.

Getting There & Away
The bus terminal, 600m south of the centre, has services every hour or so to Szczecin (18zł, two hours), Międzyzdroje (8.90zł, 1½ hours) and Świnoujście (11.40zł, 1¾ hours). There are also four fast buses daily to Kołobrzeg (13.40zł, 1½ hours) and two to Gdynia (40zł, seven hours) via Koszalin and Słupsk.

MIĘDZYZDROJE
☎ 91 / pop 6000
Blessed with warm seas and clean beaches, Międzyzdroje (myen-dzi-*zdro*-yeh) is one of Poland's most popular seaside resorts. A long sandy shoreline and a picturesque coastal cliff occupy the northeast of town, and the attractive Wolin National Park stretches to the southeast. Międzyzdroje lives almost entirely off summer tourism and is more or less dead for the rest of the year.

Information
Bałtyk Travel (☎ 328 15 18; ul Zwycięstwa 2A)
Danagro Travel (☎ 328 08 70; www.danagro.republika .pl; train station, ul Kolejowa 57)
Internet café (☎ 328 04 21; ul Norwida 17A; per hr 3zł; ☼ from 11am)
Tourist office (☎ 328 27 78; www.miedzyzdroje.pl; MDK, ul Bohaterów Warszawy 20; ☼ 10am-5pm)
Viking Tour (☎ 328 07 68; www.vikingtour.com.pl; ul Niepodległości 2A)

Natural History Museum
The **Natural History Museum** (Muzeum Przyrodnicze; ☎ 328 07 37; ul Niepodległości 3; adult/concession 5/3zł; ☼ 9am-5pm Tue-Sun) features the varied flora and fauna of Wolin National Park. There's a good display of stuffed birds, including the white-tailed eagle, a symbol of the park and reputedly a model for Poland's national emblem. The museum also has an amazing collection of 150 ruffs, each different, which makes it one of the largest collections of this species in Europe.

Two large bird cages can be found on either side of the museum building; one holds two long-eared owls, the other a genuine (if slightly scruffy-looking) white-tailed eagle. The national park's headquarters are just opposite the eagle.

Sleeping & Eating
Międzyzdroje is crammed with holiday homes and pensions, and there are also plenty of private rooms offered by locals.

In all, Międzyzdroje has several thousand beds waiting for holiday-makers. Instead of going room hunting by yourself, it's better to contact one of the specialised local travel agencies (see p413). Private rooms start at 30zł per person in July and August, 20zł in other months. Pensions/holiday homes will cost from 40zł/30zł per person.

Hotel Amber Baltic (☎ 328 10 00; www.hotel-amber-baltic.pl; Promenada Gwiazd 1; s/d €91/128, ste €200-260; P ✗ ⊠) If you fancy a splurge, you're in the right place – the vast Amber Baltic complex is one of the best resort hotels on the coast, with enough amenities to found a small town. Golfers can catch a shuttle bus to the hotel's own course, a short drive away.

FWP Posejdon (☎ 328 05 67; www.fwp.pl; Promenada Gwiazd 4; s/d/tr 100/190/270zł; P) As well as the hotel-standard rooms in its three main buildings, the FWP offers roughly 500 beds spread over 33 budget holiday homes. The central reception at the Posejdon has full details on all the options.

Dom Turysty PTTK (☎ 328 03 82; ul Kolejowa 2; s/d 35/90zł; P) The two PTTK hostels are among the cheapest places to stay in Międzyzdroje, though standards and location aren't exactly stellar. The central branch books beds in other PTTK properties, including the Dąbrówka hostel (singles/doubles 25zł/60zł), nearer the beach, and may also offer private rooms.

Camping Nr 24 Gromada (☎ 328 02 75; ul Polna 10A; tents per person 13-15zł; ☼ Jun-Sep) At the southwestern end of town, Gromada is the largest camping facility here; there are another two camping grounds slightly closer to the beach.

Getting There & Away

The train station is at the southern end of town, with a PKS stop outside. Międzyzdroje is on the Szczecin–Świnoujście railway line and all trains stop here, providing roughly 20 daily trains in each direction. There are also some trains that go further on to Wrocław (49.80zł, 9½ hours) and Warsaw (54.60zł, 9¼ hours).

The main bus stop is on ul Niepodległości, opposite the museum. PKS and private buses run to Świnoujście (3.80zł, 30 minutes) up to six times an hour. Six fast buses go daily to Kołobrzeg (18zł, 2½ hours) and two as far as Gdynia (44zł, eight hours). In summer there are hourly buses to Kamień Pomorski (8.90zł, 1½ hours), fewer during the rest of the year.

WOLIN NATIONAL PARK

Set in the far northwestern corner of the country, Wolin National Park (Woliński Park Narodowy) occupies the central section of Wolin Island, just southeast of Międzyzdroje. With a total area of about 50 sq km, it's one of the smaller Polish parks, yet it's picturesque enough to deserve a day or two's walking.

The park encompasses a coastal moraine left by a glacier, which reaches a maximum height of 115m on its northern edge and drops sharply into the sea, forming an

---

WHERE EAGLES DARE

The most important resident of Wolin National Park is the white-tailed eagle (*Haliaeetus albicilla*), known to Poles by its popular name *bielik*. With a wingspan of up to 2.5m, it's the largest predatory bird species in Europe. It once populated the whole continent, but was pushed eastwards by the shrinking of its natural habitat; by the early 20th century, it was only found in northeastern Europe and northern Asia. The global population is now estimated at 9000 to 11,000 pairs, and thanks to the preservation measures of recent decades, the eagle no longer seems to be threatened with extinction.

An adult bird can weigh up to 6kg and lives for up to 30 years. It usually inhabits areas close to water, building its nests high up among the trees. Nests that have been used for many seasons can reach monumental dimensions – 4m high and 2m in diameter – and can weigh up to 500kg. The bird hunts on open waters and its favourite diet includes fish and water birds, but in winter it doesn't mind carrion.

In Poland, the white-tailed eagle lives in the northern part of the country, mostly in Western Pomerania and Masuria. Its current population is put at roughly 450 pairs, Europe's second largest after Norway. There are four or five pairs living in the Wolin National Park.

11km-long sandy cliff nearly 100m high in places. It's the only cliff of its kind on the Polish coast, apart from a much lower cliff at Rozewie on the opposite, eastern side of the coast. To the south, the moraine descends gradually to the Szczecin Lagoon (Zalew Szczeciński).

The park features a number of lakes. Most are on the remote eastern edge of the park, forming a small lakeland. The most beautiful is the horseshoe-shaped **Lake Czajcze**. Away from the lakeland, there's **Lake Turkusowe** (Turquoise), named after the colour of its water, at the southern end of the park, and the lovely **Lake Gardno** close to the seashore, next to the Międzyzdroje–Dziwnów road. by mixed forest, with beech, oak and pine predominating. The flora and fauna is relatively diverse, with a rich bird life. There's a small **bison reserve** (adult/concession 5/3zł; ⏱ 10am-6pm Tue-Sun) inside the park, 2km east of Międzyzdroje. The bison here were shipped in from Białowieża, and some have already been born in the reserve. The last bison living wild in Pomerania were wiped out in the 14th century; in a bid to raise local awareness, 2004 was declared 'Year of the Bison'.

Activities

The best way to explore the park is by **hiking**, and the small area means a good walk needn't be too taxing. Three marked trails wind into the park from Międzyzdroje. The red trail leads northeast along the shore, then turns inland to **Wisełka** and continues through wooded hills to the small village of **Kołczewo**. The green trail runs east across the middle of the park, skirts the lakeland and also ends in Kołczewo. The blue trail goes to the southern end of the park, passing the Turquoise Lake on the way. It then continues east to the town of **Wolin**.

All the trails are well marked and easy. Get a copy of the detailed *Woliński Park Narodowy* map (scale 1:30,000), and consult the park headquarters in Międzyzdroje for further information.

ŚWINOUJŚCIE

☎ 91 / pop 45,000

The westernmost town on the Polish coast, perched on one of Europe's most arbitrary island borders, Świnoujście (shve-no-*ooysh*-cheh) is a fairly large fishing and trading port and an important naval base. It's also a major resort thanks to its beach strip and salt springs, used for over a century to treat a variety of diseases. Devotees of German literature may be interested to know that novelist and travel writer Theodor Fontane lived here for four years in the 1830s.

The town is a convenient entry/exit point for travel between Poland and Scandinavia, with ferry links with Denmark and Sweden. It also has boat services and an overland border crossing with Germany. While there's little to engage culture buffs, Świnoujście remains a busy seaport and thriving tourist centre, with a lively collection of Poles, Scandinavians and Germans mingling around the waterfronts in summer.

Orientation

Świnoujście sits on two islands at the mouth of the Świna River. The eastern part of town, on Wolin Island, has the port and transport facilities; the main town is across the river on Uznam Island (Usedom in German), linked by a frequent shuttle ferry. Here you'll find the unprepossessing centre and, 1km further north, the beach resort; the two are separated by a belt of parks.

Information

Bank Pekao ul Monte Cassino (☎ 322 05 40; ul Monte Cassino 7); ul Piłsudskiego (☎ 321 57 40; ul Piłsudskiego 4)
Biuro Podróży Partner (☎ 322 43 97; ul Bohaterów Września 83/14) Information and ferry tickets.
J@zz (☎ 321 03 09; ul Monte Cassino 35; per hr 4zł; ⏱ from 10am) Internet access.
Main post office (☎ 321 42 26; ul Piłsudskiego 1)
Morskie Biuro Podróży PŻB (☎ 322 43 96; ul Bema 9/2) Information and ferry tickets.
Tourist office (☎ 322 49 99; www.swinoujscie.pl; Wybrzeże Władysława IV; ⏱ 9am-5pm)

Sights & Activities

The **beach** is, of course, the major tourist attraction – it's apparently the widest and longest in Poland, though environmentalists have persistent concerns about pollution from the river and the port. The waterfront resort district still retains a certain *fin-de-siècle* air in places, with some elegant villas amid the tourist hotels, and the main pedestrian promenade is packed with stalls and amusements in summer.

The town centre is considerably more run-down, but there's a lot of development going on and the marina waterfront is good

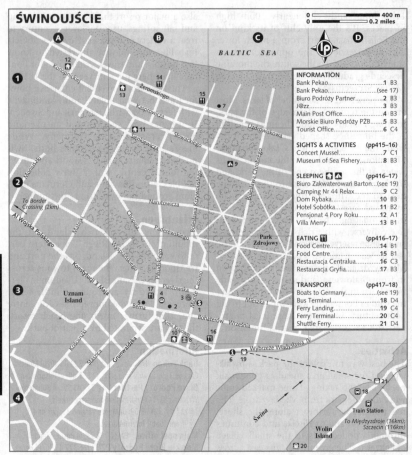

ŚWINOUJŚCIE

BALTIC SEA

0 — 400 m
0 — 0.2 miles

INFORMATION
Bank Pekao...........................**1** B3
Bank Pekao.....................(see 17)
Biuro Podróży Partner........**2** B3
J@zz....................................**3** B3
Main Post Office..................**4** B3
Morskie Biuro Podróży PZB....**5** B3
Tourist Office......................**6** C4

SIGHTS & ACTIVITIES (pp415–16)
Concert Mussel.....................**7** C1
Museum of Sea Fishery.........**8** B3

SLEEPING (pp416–17)
Biuro Zakwaterowań Barton...(see 19)
Camping Nr 44 Relax...........**9** C2
Dom Rybaka.......................**10** B3
Hotel Sobótka....................**11** B2
Pensjonat 4 Pory Roku........**12** A1
Villa Merry..........................**13** B1

EATING (pp416–17)
Food Centre........................**14** B1
Food Centre........................**15** B1
Restauracja Centralna.........**16** C3
Restauracja Gryfia..............**17** B3

TRANSPORT (pp417–18)
Boats to Germany...............(see 19)
Bus Terminal......................**18** D4
Ferry Landing.....................**19** C4
Ferry Terminal....................**20** C4
Shuttle Ferry.....................**21** D4

To Border
Crossing (2km)

Park
Zdrojowy

Uznam
Island

To Międzyzdroje (16km);
Szczecin (116km)

Wolin
Island

Train Station

Świna

---

for a stroll. You can also visit the **Museum of Sea Fishery** (Muzeum Rybołówstwa Morskiego; ☎ 321 23 26; Plac Rybaka 1; adult/concession 5/3zł; ⏰ 10am-6pm Tue-Sun). It has collections of sea fauna, fishing equipment and navigation instruments, plus exhibits relating to the town's history and occasional temporary displays on incongruous topics such as African desert travel.

Festivals & Events
At the end of September, just as the tourist season is waning, Świnoujście takes part in the **Four Corners Culture Week** (☎ 321 37 05; www.cultureweek.org), a series of concerts and exhibitions held in conjunction with similar events on Bornholm (Denmark), Rügen (Germany) and Southeast Skåne (Sweden).

The main stage is the playfully designed open-air Concert Mussel (Muszla Koncertowa), near the beach.

Sleeping & Eating
As in other Baltic beach resorts, the high season is in July and August – at other times prices will be lower and more beds should be vacant. Many of the holiday homes near the beach accept individual tourists, though some will insist on full board. Prices vary according to demand and standards, but count on roughly 80zł to 150zł per bed with three meals. The tourist office keeps an eye on what's available in all categories.

There are a few year-round restaurants, mostly in the centre, but the majority of places are seasonal, with all kinds of bistros, street stalls, bars and nightclubs springing up around the beach area. Two loosely defined food centres on the beach promenade, ul Żeromskiego, have convenient clusters of eating options. There are also plenty of supermarkets around for self-caterers.

Pensjonat 4 Pory Roku (☎ 321 16 94; www .4poryroku.com.pl; ul Ujejskiego 8; d €50-60, tr/q €80/90, ste €70-90; **P** ✗) A touch of rustic style distinguishes this rather fine villa, off the main promenade. It has plenty of pine fittings and chessboard floors. Breakfast is served in the sociable communal kitchen, and it also smokes its own fish.

Hotel Sobótka (☎ 321 49 64; www.sobotka.uznam .net.pl; ul Sienkiewicza 13; d/tr 184/255zł, ste 200-360zł; **P** 💻) The Sobótka is a smart modern sanatorium hotel, opposite the park, and has a playground, volleyball court and all kinds of outlandish treatments available (jonophoresis anyone?). Full board available.

Villa Merry (☎ 321 26 19; www.villa-merry.uznam .net.pl; ul Żeromskiego 16; apt €24-89; **P**) One of the top self-catering options in town, Merry's two swish Secession-period buildings hold a wide selection of multiperson apartments and a café-bistro for when the kitchenettes lose their allure.

Biuro Zakwaterowań Barton (☎ 321 11 55; www .barton.com.pl; Wybrzeże Władysława IV) For private rooms, head to this small office by the ferry landing. Prices average around 30zł to 50zł per person; note that most are in the southwestern suburbs, with almost none in the beach area.

Dom Rybaka (☎ 321 29 43; Wybrzeże Władysława IV 22; s/d 40/80zł) If it wasn't the only option anywhere near the shuttle ferry we'd have trouble recommending this place – sure, it's cheap, but the shared bathrooms need immediate attention and the rooms smell like someone didn't make it further than the sink. Use only if you're catching an early ride out.

Camping Nr 44 Relax (☎ 321 39 12; www.camping -relax.com.pl; ul Słowackiego 5; camp site per adult/ student/child 11/9/6zł, bungalows 85-200zł) This large, popular camping ground is superbly located between the beach and the spa park and has a good selection of year-round bungalows, though you'll need a miracle to get one in July or August. Up to 1200 campers can squeeze in here.

Restauracja Gryfia (☎ 321 25 78; ul Piłsudskiego 10; mains 10-30zł; 🕑 breakfast, lunch & dinner) This traditional Polish place livens up the grim centre of town with hearty food, music and dancing until 5am at weekends.

Restauracja Central'a (☎ 321 26 40; ul Armii Krajowej 3; mains 10-45zł; 🕑 lunch & dinner) Popular with hip young locals and older cigar puffers, the Central'a has a deep red interior, a fantastic rear courtyard and sporadic live jazz. Grab a window seat for marina views.

Getting There & Away

The overland crossing to/from Germany is 2km west of town. The first town on the German side, Ahlbeck, handles transport further into the country. The border is open to pedestrians only (with bicycles if desired).

BOAT

Tickets for all boat services are available at the terminals and from most travel agencies around town.

Germany

The German company **Adler-Schiffe** (☎ 322 42 88; www.adler-schiffe.de) runs boats from Świnoujście to Ahlbeck, Heringsdorf, Bansin and Sassnitz up to seven times daily. A return ticket, including a stopover, costs 20zł for adults and 10zł concession. **Hanse-Schiffe** (☎ 321 87 75) has twice-daily services to Ahlbeck (adult/concession 12zł/8zł, 45 minutes).

Adler-Schiffe and **Reederei Peters** (www .reederei-peters.de) also run daily car ferries to Altwarp (two hours); these depart from the ferry terminal on Wolin Island, across the Świna River.

Scandinavia

Major carrier **Polferries** (☎ 322 61 40; www.pol ferries.pl) operates ferries to Ystad (Sweden; adult/concession Skr535/Skr445, 9½ hours, daily), Rønne (Denmark; 225kr/205kr, six hours, weekly) and Copenhagen (425kr/ 355kr, nine hours, five weekly). **Unity Line** (☎ 359 55 92; www.unityline.pl) runs daily ferries to Ystad (Skr520/Skr430, seven hours).

All ferries depart from the ferry terminal on Wolin Island.

CAR & MOTORCYCLE

If you're arriving with your own transport, you can only use the shuttle ferry at weekends and after 10pm on weekdays; otherwise you'll have to head for the Dźwina River crossing, 7km south of Świnoujście. Expect to wait during the peak season (usually no longer than a couple of hours). Passage for both vehicles and passengers is free.

TRAIN & BUS

The bus and train stations are next to each other on the right bank of the Świna River. Passenger ferries shuttle constantly between the town centre and the stations (free, 10 minutes).

All trains go via Międzyzdroje (fast/slow 6.80zł/3.80zł, 15 minutes) and Szczecin (28.24zł/15.90zł, 2¼ hours), with departures every hour or two. There's one fast sleeper train directly to Warsaw (56.03zł, 9¾ hours) and two fast services to Kraków (61.10zł, 12½ hours) via Poznań (43.04zł, 5½ hours) and Wrocław (49.80zł, eight hours).

Only three daily buses run to Szczecin (20zł, 2½ hours), but plenty of services cover the coast. There are half a dozen buses to Kamień Pomorski (11.40zł, 1¾ hours), and three or four fast buses to Kołobrzeg (18zł, 2½ hours). All routes go via Międzyzdroje, which is also served by half-hourly private buses (3.60zł, 30 minutes).

Europa-Linie buses (€1.70) link the Polish and German sides of the island – while they don't actually cross the border, timetables are coordinated so you can get off one bus, walk through the checkpoint and board an onward service straight away. A day pass valid for six single journeys costs 8zł, or €4 in Germany. City bus 8 also runs to the border (2zł, 10 daily).

SZCZECIN

☎ 91 / pop 425,000

Just 130km away from Berlin (and four times that distance from Warsaw), Western Pomerania's former capital is still the main urban centre of northwestern Poland, a major university town and the largest Polish port in terms of tonnage handled. As you'd expect, Szczecin (*shcheh*-cheen) has a colourful and stormy history; sadly most of the physical reminders were destroyed in WWII, and the city still feels like a work in progress, though there's more than enough life here to keep its half a million urbanites occupied.

History

Szczecin's beginnings go back to the 8th century, when a Slav stronghold was built here.

In 967 Duke Mieszko I annexed the town, together with a large chunk of the coast, for the newborn Polish state, but was unable to hold or Christianise it. It was Bolesław Krzywousty who recaptured the town in 1121 and brought the Catholic faith to the locals.

Krzywousty died in 1138 and the Polish Crown crumbled; Pomerania formally became an independent principality. At that time, the Germans were expanding aggressively, and by 1181 the Pomeranian Duke Bogusław I was paying homage to the Holy Roman Emperor Frederick Barbarossa.

Three years later Denmark attacked and conquered Pomerania, taking control of the Baltic coast as far as Estonia. In 1227 the Danes were finally defeated and forced out again, and Szczecin came back under the rule of the Pomeranian princes, by then strongly dependent on the Brandenburg margraves.

In 1478 Western Pomerania was unified by Duke Bogusław X and Szczecin was chosen as the capital. Since the duke had been brought up at the Polish court and had married the daughter of Polish King Kazimierz Jagiellończyk, he was keen to seek closer relations with Poland. This led to protests from the Brandenburgs, and Pomerania grudgingly acknowledged its allegiance to its western neighbour in 1521.

The next shift in power came in 1630, when the Swedes conquered the city and occupied it until the Treaty of Westphalia of 1648 formally assigned it to them. Once the Peace of Stockholm had ended the Northern War in 1720, Sweden sold Szczecin to the kingdom of Prussia, which held the region until WWII. Under Prussian rule, Szczecin (Stettin in German) grew considerably, becoming the main port for landlocked Berlin. By the outbreak of WWII the city had about 300,000 inhabitants.

In April 1945 the Red Army passed through on its way to Berlin, leaving 60% of the urban area in ruins. Only 6000 souls remained of the former population, most of the others having fled.

With new inhabitants and new rulers, the battered city started a new life in the postwar era. Only a handful of individual buildings were restored, however, the rest replaced with the usual concrete creations. Local authorities are belatedly making amends with the development of the old quarter around the surviving town hall.

Information

INTERNET ACCESS

Bondi (per hr 3zł; ⏲ 9am-11pm) Al Wyzwolenia (Al Wyzwolenia 1-3); ul Jedności Narodowej (☎ 812 20 28; ul Jedności Narodowej 1)

Portal (☎ 488 40 66; ul Kaszubska 52; per hr 5zł; ⏲ 24hr)

MONEY

Bank Pekao Al Wojska Polskiego (☎ 440 61 00; Al Wojska Polskiego 1); Plac Żołnierza Polskiego (☎ 440 06 21; Plac Żołnierza Polskiego 16); ul Grodzka (☎ 434 36 30; ul Grodzka 9); ul Obrońców Stalingradu (☎ 440 62 88; ul Obrońców Stalingradu 10/11)

Deutsche Bank (☎ 431 48 80; Al Wyzwolenia 12)

POST

Post office main post office (☎ 440 11 03; Al Niepodległości 41/42); station branch (☎ 440 12 39; ul Dworcowa 20B)

TOURIST INFORMATION

Orbis Travel (☎ 434 26 18; Plac Zwycięstwa 1)

PTTK (☎ 434 56 24; Al Jedności Narodowej 49A)

Tourist office Al Niepodległości (☎ 434 04 40; Al Niepodległości 1; ⏲ 9am-5pm Mon-Fri year-round, also 10am-2pm Sat Jun-Aug); castle branch (☎ 489 16 30; www.zamek.szczecin.pl; ⏲ 10am-6pm)

Sights & Activities

Szczecin's local authorities seem to have finally picked up on the potential power of the tourist market, and considerable work has been put into new initiatives and infrastructure. One handy innovation is the **Red Tourist Route**, a 7km walking circuit around town covering 42 of the most important sights and buildings; pick up the explanatory map at the tourist offices and look for the red arrows sprayed graffiti-style on the pavement.

The most sizable city monument is the **Castle of the Pomeranian Princes** (Zamek Książąt Pomorskich). A large, relatively plain residence with a square central courtyard, it was originally built in the mid-14th century but only received its current form in 1577. The structure was further enlarged and remodelled on various occasions, and extensive postwar reconstruction has given it a predominantly Renaissance look, based on its late-16th-century incarnation. You can go to the top of the 58.6m **bell tower** (adult/concession 3/2zł) for a view of the town.

The castle now accommodates the opera auditorium, the Western Pomeranian Marshall's office, a restaurant and the **Cas-**

tle Museum (Muzeum Zamkowe; ☎ 434 22 62; www .zamek.szczecin.pl; ul Korsarzy 34; adult/concession 6/3zł; ⏲ 10am-6pm Tue-Sun). The permanent exhibition on the castle's history includes six spectacular sarcophagi of the Pomeranian princes. They are large tin boxes decorated with a fine engraved ornamentation, made between 1606 and 1637 by artists from Königsburg. Following the death of the last Pomeranian duke, Bogusław XIV, the crypt, containing 14 sarcophagi, was walled up and only opened in 1946. The remains of the dukes were deposited in the cathedral, while the best-preserved sarcophagi have been restored and are now the highlight of the display.

Various temporary exhibitions are presented in other rooms of the castle. In summer, concerts are held on Sunday in the courtyard or the former chapel, which occupies nearly half the northern side. As the regional registry office is also here, the castle is hugely popular for weddings, particularly on summer weekends.

A short walk south will bring you to the 15th-century Gothic **town hall**, one of the finest buildings in the city. This is the only relic of the Old Town, which was razed to the ground in 1945 and never rebuilt. The quarter is now undergoing some redevelopment: a line of stylised burghers' houses has been put up right behind the town hall, in striking contrast to the line of communist blocks opposite, and the area is rapidly filling up with fashionable cafés and upscale bars.

The town hall accommodates the interesting **Historical Museum of Szczecin** (Muzeum Historii Miasta Szczecina; ☎ 488 02 49; Plac Rzepichy 1; adult/concession 2/1.50zł; ⏲ 10am-6pm Tue-Fri, 10am-4pm Sat & Sun), which highlights various aspects of the city's long and turbulent past.

There are two historic churches nearby. **St John's Church**, a typical 14th-century Gothic building, somehow managed to escape war destruction. Its interior is refreshingly devoid of decoration and has a perfect vault in the nave, supported on charmingly leaning columns. Vestiges of wall paintings from 1510 can still be seen in the right-hand aisle.

The **cathedral** (Basilica of St James; requested donation €1; ⏲ groups 2-5pm Mon-Sat) is similar in shape to St John's Church, but much larger. It was consecrated in 1187 but only reconstructed in 1972, and the interior is now largely fitted

POMERANIA

SZCZECIN

0 — 400 m
0 — 0.2 miles

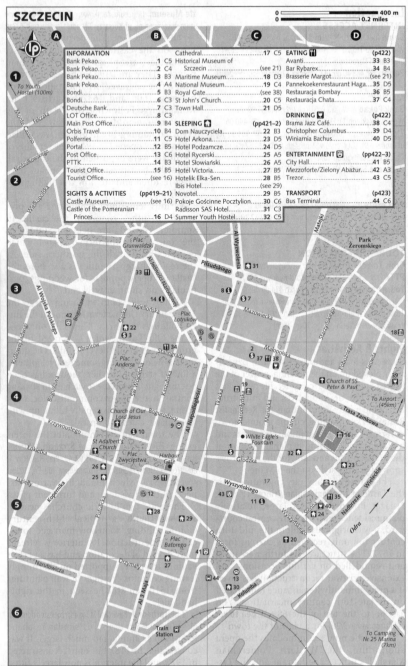

INFORMATION
Bank Pekao..............................1 C5
Bank Pekao..............................2 C4
Bank Pekao..............................3 B3
Bank Pekao..............................4 A4
Bondi.......................................5 B3
Bondi.......................................6 C3
Deutsche Bank..........................7 C3
LOT Office................................8 C3
Main Post Office.......................9 B4
Orbis Travel............................10 B4
Polferries................................11 C5
Portal.....................................12 B5
Post Office..............................13 C6
PTTK.......................................14 B3
Tourist Office..........................15 B5
Tourist Office....................(see 16)

SIGHTS & ACTIVITIES (pp419–21)
Castle Museum.................(see 16)
Castle of the Pomeranian
  Princes.................................16 D4

Cathedral................................17 C5
Historical Museum of
  Szczecin.........................(see 21)
Maritime Museum....................18 D3
National Museum.....................19 C4
Royal Gate......................(see 38)
St John's Church......................20 C5
Town Hall...............................21 D5

SLEEPING (pp421–2)
Dom Nauczyciela.....................22 B3
Hotel Arkona..........................23 D5
Hotel Podzamcze.....................24 D5
Hotel Rycerski........................25 A5
Hotel Słowiański......................26 A5
Hotel Victoria.........................27 B5
Hotelik Elka-Sen.....................28 B5
Ibis Hotel........................(see 29)
Novotel..................................29 B5
Pokoje Gościnne Pocztylion......30 C6
Radisson SAS Hotel.................31 C3
Summer Youth Hostel..............32 C5

EATING (p422)
Avanti....................................33 B3
Bar Rybarex...........................34 B4
Brasserie Margot...............(see 21)
Pannekoekenrestaurant Haga...35 D5
Restauracja Bombay................36 B5
Restauracja Chata...................37 C4

DRINKING (p422)
Brama Jazz Café.....................38 C4
Christopher Columbus.............39 D4
Winiarnia Bachus....................40 D5

ENTERTAINMENT (pp422–3)
City Hall................................41 B5
Mezzoforte/Zielony Abażur......42 A3
Trezor...................................43 C5

TRANSPORT (p423)
Bus Terminal..........................44 C6

out with modern decoration. On one side of the cathedral is the 15th-century vicarage and on the other a huge bell weighing almost 6 tonnes, dating from 1681.

Two blocks north is the **National Museum** (Muzeum Narodowe; ☎ 433 50 66; www.muzeum.sz czecin.pl; ul Staromłyńska 27; adult/concession 2/1.50zł; ☻ 10am-5pm Tue-Fri, 10am-4pm Sat & Sun), located in the 18th-century palace, which formerly served as the Pomeranian parliament. It features a collection of religious art, mostly woodcarving from the 14th to 16th centuries, plus other historical exhibits relating to Szczecin and Pomerania. The museum **annexe**, which is directly across the street, contains changing displays of modern art; the building once housed the 13 Muses Club, a parliamentary watering hole, and still displays the heads of prominent 20th-century Szczecinites (in stone, of course) on its façade.

Also part of the national museum is the imposing **Maritime Museum** (Muzeum Morskie; ☎ 433 60 02; Wały Chrobrego 3; adult/concession 6/3zł; ☻ 10am-5pm Tue-Fri, 10am-4pm Sat & Sun), on the hill above the waterfront. Apart from an exhibition related to maritime matters, the museum has regional archaeology displays and ethnographical artefacts from Africa and Asia.

Sleeping
BUDGET
Pokoje Gościnne Pocztylion (☎ 440 12 09; ul Dworcowa 20B; dm 41.73zł; **P**) Don't let the guarded entrance put you off – this post office facility is surprisingly nice once you get inside, offering spacious rooms, all-new furniture, fridges and TVs with lousy reception. There's also a communal lounge (with pool table) and kitchen.

Hotelik Słowiański (☎ 812 54 61; ul Potulicka 1; s 73-108zł, d 88-120zł, tr 117-135zł) A former police dorm, the Słowiański could never be accused of daylight robbery. Modest but neat rooms provide creaky new pine-effect fittings and a choice of en suite or shared bathrooms.

Youth hostel (☎ 422 47 61; www.ptsm.home.pl; ul Monte Cassino 19A; dm 20-22zł, s/d/q 50/56/96zł; **P** ✗ 🖳) Friendly and well run, with places reasonably distributed in rooms of up to 14 beds. It's 2km northwest of the centre; take tram 3 from the station to Plac Rodła and change for the westbound tram 1.

Summer hostel (☎ 433 29 24; ul Grodzka 22; dm 16-25zł; ☻ Jul & Aug) A more central option.

Camping Nr 25 Marina (☎ 460 11 65; camping .marina@pro.onet.pl; ul Przestrzenna 23; adult/child 12/6zł, cabins 27-100zł; ☻ May-Sep) Szczecin has a good camping ground with cabins on the shore of Lake Dąbie in Szczecin Dąbie, about 7km southeast of the city centre. If you are coming by train, get off in Szczecin Dąbie and continue by urban bus 56 or walk 2km.

MID-RANGE
Hotel Podzamcze (☎ 812 14 04; ul Sienna 1; s/d 175/210zł, ste 230-260zł; **P**) On the corner of the reconstructed Old Town, this small guesthouse offers cosy modern rooms above a traditional restaurant and pub, with suitably personal service. Once the building site opposite is gone this should be one of the most dynamic areas in town.

Hotel Victoria (☎ 434 38 55; Plac Batorego 2; s/d 130/180zł; **P**) Just uphill from the bus terminal and train station, the friendly Victoria lays on the traditional trappings to great effect. Rooms vary in size so it's best to have a look first. Demanding clients take note: a sign in the hall promises 'none of your wishes will remain without consequences'. Nightclub on site.

Hotelik Elka-Sen (☎ 433 56 04; elka-sen@zse2 .szczecin.pl; Al 3 Maja 1A; s/d 110/170zł; **P**) Strange name, strange location: the Elka-Sen has a lift as its front door and occupies a basement space in the School of Economics, itself next door to the local prison. Luckily none of this makes the rooms any less of a good deal.

Hotel Rycerski (☎ 488 81 64; www.hotelrycerski.pl; ul Potulicka 2A; s/d/ste 180/240/360zł; **P**) Any building with its own walled grounds is worthy of attention, and once this red-brick place has grabbed you it aims to earn its keep with a smart restaurant, lots of walnut effect and two very spacious suites. Friendly staff and a central location give the Rycerski bonus brownie points.

Dom Nauczyciela (☎ 433 04 81; domnauczyciela@pf .pl; ul Śląska 4; s 130zł, d 160-190zł, t 210zł) Quiet, neat and central, this is an unpretentious residential establishment with an international bookshop, home-cooked food and massive discounts for students. Rooms come with TV, kettle and phone; the only quibble is the slightly thin beds.

Hotel Arkona (☎ 488 02 61; arkona@orbis.pl; ul Panieńska 10; s/d 160/200zł; **P**) Hotel Arkona's building is such a hideous communist relic that you almost feel guilty sleeping here, but thankfully the interior has been respectably revamped and it's a good spot right by the up-and-coming Old Town area.

TOP END

Radisson SAS Hotel (☎ 359 51 11; info.szczecin@ radissonsas.com; Plac Rodła 10; s €89-109, d €100-120, ste €189-289; **P** ✕ ▣) Szczecin's fanciest option, if not its prettiest, the salmon-pink Radisson comes complete with its own shopping centre, taxi services, wheelchair access, three restaurants, sauna, gym, bars and a surprisingly credible tropical-themed nightclub – in short, exactly what you'd expect from a modern five-star complex.

Novotel (☎ 480 14 00; h3367@accor-hotels.com; Al 3 Maja 31; s/d €71/79; **P** ✕ ▣ ▣) A new addition muscling in on the moneyed market, with lots of rooms and the full complement of facilities. The location is ideal for transport links.

Ibis business chain (☎ 480 18 00; r 185zł) A cheaper option, housed in the Novotel.

Eating

Restauracja Bombay (☎ 488 49 32; www.india.pl; ul Partyzantów 1; mains 10-48zł; ☒ lunch & dinner; ✕) This would be quite a treat even if it wasn't in Poland – quality Indian food, including items such as *thali* plate meals, served in tastefully exotic surrounds by waiters with impeccable English. It's owned by a former Miss India (1973 vintage), a fact that probably raises as many questions as it answers.

Pannekoekenrestaurant Haga (☎ 812 17 59; ul Sienna 10; mains 9-20zł; ☒ lunch & dinner) If you thought pancakes were the domain of the French, think again: Haga specialises in Dutch crepes, 300 varieties in all, proving that the Low Countries are no slouch with batter either. A selection of Dutch and Polish dishes round out the good-value menu.

Restauracja Chata (☎ 488 73 70; Plac Hołdu Pruskiego 8; mains 24-72zł) The Hut (no relation to Jabba) is a charming place serving traditional Polish food in rustic timber surroundings; some interesting specials tempt the curious, like *slivovitz* (plum brandy) coffee, four-person game plates and 'cheese on a plank'. Polish pop oldies shake the dance floor at weekends.

Avanti (☎ 434 31 31; Al Jedności Narodowej 43; mains 14-45zł; ☒ lunch & dinner) Serious and authen-

tic Italian food for people who don't put ketchup on their pizza. The refined, atmospheric interior wouldn't be out of place in any Western European capital.

Brasserie Margot (☎ 488 34 81; Księcia Mściwoja 8; mains 24-33zł; ☒ lunch & dinner) Yet another entry in Szczecin's pantheon of international cuisine, the town hall's vaulted cellar restaurant offers intelligent French-influenced food and menu descriptions in four languages. You can also have a bop here at weekends.

Bar Rybarex (☎ 434 32 22; ul Obrońców Stalingradu 6; mains 3-10zł; ☒ breakfast, lunch & dinner Mon-Fri, breakfast & lunch Sat) Hard-up fish fans can get a taste of the sea here without splashing out (sorry...). Swift and efficient, this budget cafeteria has a reasonable range of fish and a few other dishes to choose from.

Drinking

Szczecin's current hotspots are the burgeoning Old Town area, for sophisticated drinks and conversation, and the funkier pedestrian strip of ul Bogusława, for terrace lounging and decent music.

Winiarnia Bachus (☎ 488 37 21; www.bachus.szin.pl in Polish; ul Sienna 6) Part of the Old Town's attempt to appeal to a more aspirational class of tourist and local, Bachus is an excellent wine merchant, bar and restaurant and a haven for the discerning palate, whatever beverage tickles your tastebuds.

Christopher Columbus (☎ 489 34 01; www.colum buspub.pl; Wały Chrobrego 1; ☒ 10am-1am Sun-Thu, 10am-2am Fri & Sat) An attractive bar-restaurant overlooking the river, Columbus has a bar shaped like a boat, a large balcony above it, and a vast beer garden. Live music crops up from time to time.

Brama Jazz Café (☎ 804 62 95; www.brama.szczecin .pl; Plac Hołdu Pruskiego 1) Housed in the baroque Royal Gate, another fragment of lost history, the unposy Brama café-bar has regular live jazz and a laid-back soundtrack the rest of the time.

Entertainment

Check the local press and flyers for the latest nightlife listings, or log onto www.clubbing .szn.pl (Polish only).

Mezzoforte/Zielony Abażur (☎ 814 41 44; www .abazur.pl in Polish; ul Bogusława 8; mains 6.40zł to 31zł) This Italian restaurant leads a double life as one of Szczecin's hippest bar-clubs, with a different musical flavour on the upstairs stereo everyday and guests including some of Berlin's best electro and downtempo acts laying beats in the basement at night.

City Hall (Czerwony Ratusz, ul Dworcowa; admission 5-10zł; ☻ from 6pm) The basement of the massive Red Town Hall packs in up to 400 mad-for-it clubbers for some of the biggest nights in town, featuring rhythms from soul to house to R&B. The best night is Saturday, when Berlin DJs often hop over the border to play here.

Trezor (☎ 812 55 52; www.trezor-club.com; ul Wyszyńskiego 14; admission 10-15zł; ☻ 9pm-4am Wed-Sat) An unpromising entrance halfway between the Tardis and a Portaloo leads down into three floors of good old reach-for-the-lasers hedonism. Over-20s only.

Getting There & Away

AIR

Szczecin currently has services to Warsaw (up to five daily), Copenhagen (three weekly), Malmö (weekdays) and London (twice weekly). The **airport** (☎ 484 74 00; www .airport.com.pl) is in Goleniów, about 45km northeast of the city; minibuses run from the bus station (6zł), or a taxi should cost around 15zł. With the ongoing low-cost airline boom, you can expect more international services by the end of 2005.

BUS

The bus terminal is uphill from the train station and handles frequent departures to Stargard Szczeciński (6.16zł, 50 minutes, twice hourly) and Kamień Pomorski (18zł, two hours, up to 10 daily). There are regular summer buses to nearby beach resorts, but almost nothing to Świnoujście and Międzyzdroje – go by train.

Evatrans (www.evatrans.pl) and a couple of other companies run daily minibuses to Berlin (one-way/return €19/€29, 2½ hours). Inquire at the bus terminal or the train station for details.

TRAIN

The main train station, Szczecin Główny, is on the bank of the Odra River, 1km south of the centre. There are a dozen fast trains daily to Poznań (35.91zł, 2¾ hours) and five to Gdańsk (44.65zł, 5½ hours). There are three express trains to Warsaw (72zł), including one InterCity (5½ hours). Three

trains leave daily for Kołobrzeg (16.80zł, three hours) and six a day to Zielona Góra (21.50zł, five hours). Trains to Stargard Szczeciński (6.80zł, 25 minutes) depart approximately every 30 minutes, and to Świnoujście (15.50zł, two hours) every hour or so (fewer in winter).

STARGARD SZCZECIŃSKI
☎ 92 / pop 73,000

It's rather hard to believe, but the small town of Stargard Szczeciński was once a flourishing port and commercial centre that was so prosperous that it fought with Szczecin for control of the Odra River trade route. The fierce competition between the two ports even led to a war in 1454, which included regular battles, complete with the ransacking and sinking of the enemy's ships.

The picture today couldn't be more different: Stargard has no port at all, and is little more than a satellite town of its old rival. Over 70% of its buildings were destroyed during WWII, and reconstruction left the town a grey urban sprawl with a fair amount of industry.

The area of the Old Town evokes mixed feelings: parts of the medieval walls, once reputedly the most elaborate system of fortified walls in Pomerania, have been preserved, but the bulk of the area is occupied by a mass of drab and cheerless postwar blocks. The two massive churches that dominate the skyline are worth visiting, but sensitive architecture fans may be more than a little depressed by the thought of what's been lost.

Information
www.mapa.stargard.com.pl Interactive map in Polish only.

Sights
The town's pride and joy is **St Mary's Church**, a mighty brick construction (one of the largest in Western Pomerania) begun in 1292 and extended successively until the end of the 15th century. Remarkably, no major alterations have been made to its structure since then. It has a rich external decoration of glazed bricks and tiles, with three elaborate doorways; inside, you can gaze up at the amazing painted columns and ceiling vault.

POMERANIA

Next to the church is the **Regional Museum** (☎ 577 25 56; Rynek Staromiejski 2/4; adult/concession 5/3zł, free Sat; ⌚ 10am-4pm Tue-Sun), which features exhibits on local history, archaeology, and weights and measures. Adjoining the museum is the **town hall**, a late-Gothic building with a beautifully ornamented Renaissance gable. Try to block out the other buildings on the Rynek, examples of the worst kind of unimaginative postwar modernism.

St John's Church, on the opposite side of the Old Town, was constructed in the 15th century but was later changed significantly; it has the highest tower in Western Pomerania (99m).

The **fortified walls** were begun in the late 13th century and completed at the beginning of the 16th century, by which time they were 2260m long. Roughly half of that length has survived, complete with three gates and four towers; some of these may have exhibitions in summer, administered by the museum, and you can generally climb them for the view.

Sleeping & Eating

Hotel PTTK (☎ 578 31 91; ul Kuśnierzy 5; s 79zł, d 90-150zł, tr 130zł) Just a few minutes' walk from the cathedral, the PTTK occupies one of the few old buildings to have survived in the area, a charming (if crumbling) gabled house overlooking the small canal. The strangely shaped rooms are pretty good for what you pay, though breakfast is not included.

Hotel Staromiejski (☎ 577 22 23; ul Spichrzowa 2; s 55-80zł, d 75-110zł, tr 87zł, ste 150-180zł; P) This large apartment block is geared towards coach parties, offering a greater choice of rooms (shared or en suite) but not much in the way of personality. The granary restaurant, opposite, compensates somewhat.

Getting There & Away

The train and bus stations are close to each other, 1km west of the Old Town. Urban buses ply this route if you feel lazy.

Szczecin is easily reached by bus (6.16zł, 50 minutes) and train (6.80zł, 25 minutes), both running twice hourly. You can pick up most eastbound rail services from Szczecin here.

Warmia & Masuria

CONTENTS

It may not have a coastline, but water defines Warmia and Masuria just as surely as it does the Baltic seafront. This is the Polish lakeland, riven throughout its area with rivers, canals, wetlands, swamps and lakes, and the unique access to the countryside that these waterways afford makes the whole region a magnet for a more-active breed of holiday-maker.

In summer the resort towns are abuzz with life, every harbour and wharf packed with locals and visitors. Even at the peak of the season, however, the bustle doesn't compare to the seaside towns further west, and once you set out it's easy to unwind and just drift along, away from the crowds, on the open waters of the Great Masurian Lakes. Those who like more of a challenge can buff up their shoulder muscles with a kayak trip into the country's most spectacular hinterland, following the quiet Czarna Hańcza route right up to the Belarussian border.

Of course the area is not without its cultural attractions either. The location, right at the junction of Russia and the Baltic states, has seen just as much historical strife as the rest of Poland, and traces of the past, from Gothic castles to Nazi bunkers, litter the countryside, offering plenty to see when you step off the boat, barque or bus.

However you choose to spend your time, you'll quickly realise that this is an engaging area, remote enough to be peaceful and developed enough to be accessible. The historical autonomy of its distinct parts may have gone, but people here still take pride in their region and its chequered past, and it's hard not to be drawn in by the diverse influences and unique atmosphere of Poland's northeastern outposts. Take to the water and see for yourself.

HIGHLIGHTS

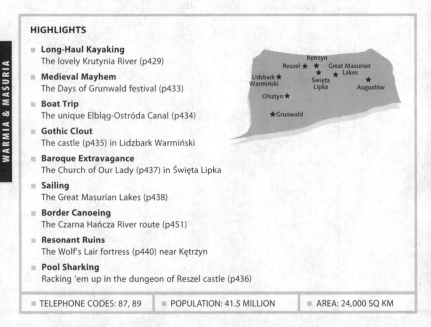

- **Long-Haul Kayaking**
  The lovely Krutynia River (p429)

- **Medieval Mayhem**
  The Days of Grunwald festival (p433)

- **Boat Trip**
  The unique Elbląg-Ostróda Canal (p434)

- **Gothic Clout**
  The castle (p435) in Lidzbark Warmiński

- **Baroque Extravagance**
  The Church of Our Lady (p437) in Święta Lipka

- **Sailing**
  The Great Masurian Lakes (p438)

- **Border Canoeing**
  The Czarna Hańcza River route (p451)

- **Resonant Ruins**
  The Wolf's Lair fortress (p440) near Kętrzyn

- **Pool Sharking**
  Racking 'em up in the dungeon of Reszel castle (p436)

| ■ TELEPHONE CODES: 87, 89 | ■ POPULATION: 41.5 MILLION | ■ AREA: 24,000 SQ KM |

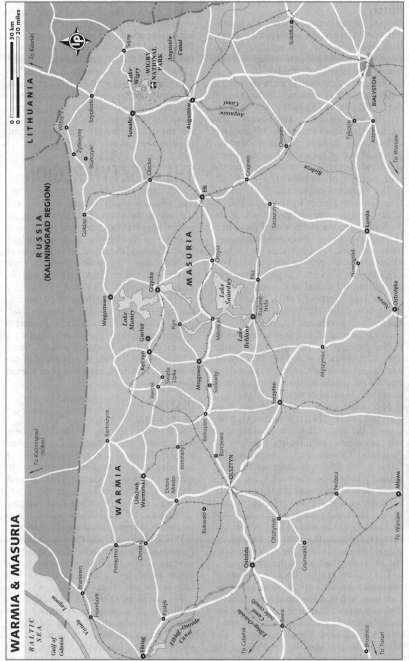

History

Despite being lumped together administratively, Warmia and Masuria have always been separate entities with separate populations, and their histories, though broadly similar, are largely independent.

Warmia's name derives from its original inhabitants, the Warmians, who were wiped out by the Teutonic Knights in the 13th century, in much the same manner as other ethnic communities of the region. What clearly differentiates it from the other Teutonic provinces is that for more than five centuries it was a largely autonomous ecclesiastical state, run by Catholic bishops.

The Warmian diocese was the largest of four that were created by the papal bulls of 1243. Though administratively within the Teutonic state, the bishops used papal protection to achieve a far-reaching autonomy. Their bishopric extended from the north of Olsztyn up to the present-day national border, and from the Vistula Lagoon in the west to the town of Reszel in the east. Following the 1466 Treaty of Toruń, Warmia was incorporated into the kingdom of Poland, but the bishops retained much of their control over internal affairs, answering directly to the pope. When the last grand master adopted Protestantism in 1525, Warmia became a bastion of the Counter-Reformation. In 1773 the region fell under Prussian rule, along with swathes of western Poland.

Meanwhile, Masuria was dealing with its own upheavals. The Jatzvingians (Jaćwingowie), the first inhabitants, belonged to the same ethnic and linguistic family as the Prussians, Latvians and Lithuanians. For farmers they were unusually warlike, and caused plenty of headaches for the Mazovian dukes, as they invaded and ravaged the northern outskirts of the principality on a regular basis and even pressed as far south as Kraków. In the second half of the 13th century, however, the Teutonic Knights expanded eastwards over the region, and by the 1280s they had wiped the tribe out.

The region quickly became a bone of contention between the Teutonic order and Lithuania, and remained in dispute until the 16th century. At that time the territory formally became a Polish dominion, but its colonisation was slow. Development was also hindered by the Swedish invasions of the 1650s and the catastrophic plague of 1710.

In the Third Partition of 1795, the region was swallowed up by Prussia, and in 1815 it became a part of the Congress Kingdom of Poland, only to be grabbed by Russia after the failure of the November Insurrection of 1830. After WWI Poland took over the territory, though not without resistance from Lithuania, but the region remained remote and economically unimportant. Warmia was finally restored to Poland after WWII, and the two halves became a single administrative zone, as they are today.

THE OLSZTYN REGION

The Olsztyn region covers Warmia and the land to the south of Olsztyn. There are several important architectural monuments in this area (notably the castle in Lidzbark Warmiński and the church in Święta Lipka), a good skansen (open-air museum of traditional architecture) in Olsztynek, and the unique Elbląg-Ostróda Canal.

The Teutonic Knights arrived here in the mid-13th century, but it was the Warmian bishops who eventually converted and colonised the region, controlling it for several centuries. Travelling around the region, you'll still come across relics of the bishops' great days, mostly in their former district seats.

OLSZTYN

☎ 89 / pop 170,000

The history of Olsztyn (*ol*-shtin) has been a successive overlapping of Prussian and Polish influences, as in most of the region. Founded in the 14th century as the southernmost outpost of Warmia, Olsztyn came under Polish control following the Treaty of Toruń in 1466. With the First Partition of Poland in 1773, Olsztyn became Prussian (renamed Allenstein) and remained so until WWII. Only in 1945 did the town return to Poland. After massive rebuilding, the city is now the largest and most important urban centre in Warmia and Masuria – though little can be seen of its past.

For travellers, Olsztyn is probably more significant as a jumping-off point for, or stopover between, attractions in the region, rather than a destination in itself. You can see its historic sites in a few hours, but if you're looking for a place to hang out and grab a meal or a few beers, the recon-structed Old Town has more than enough to keep you entertained.

Information

Bank Pekao (☎ 534 90 60; ul 1 Maja 10)

Gex (☎ 0603 454 094; ul Kościuszki 26; per hr 3zł; ☿ 10am-9.30pm Mon-Sat, 11am-8pm Sun) Internet access.

Kawiarnia.net (☎ 527 22 90; ul Okopowa 23; per hr 3-4zł; ☿ noon-midnight Mon-Sat, 4-10pm Sun) Internet access.

Main post office (☎ 527 90 01; ul Pieniężnego 21)

Orbis Travel (☎ 535 16 78; orbis.olsztyn@pbp.com.pl; ul Dąbrowszczaków 1)

PBK Bank (☎ 535 22 74; ul Mickiewicza 2)

Regional tourist office (☎ 535 35 65; www.warmia .mazury.pl; ul Staromiejska 1; ☿ 8am-6pm Mon-Fri year-round, 10am-2pm Sat & Sun Jul & Aug)

Sights

The most important historic building in town is the **castle**, a massive, red-brick, 14th-century structure. As well as an art gallery, a restaurant and an open-air theatre, it now houses the main part of the **Museum of Warmia & Masuria** (Muzeum Warmii i Mazur; ☎ 527 95 96; ul Zamkowa 2; adult/concession 6/4zł; ☿ 9am-5pm Tue-Sun Jun-Aug, 10am-4pm Tue-Sun Sep-May), which features works of art from Warmia, including paintings and silverware. Part of the 1st floor is dedicated to the great astronomer Nicolaus Copernicus, who was the administrator of Warmia and lived in the castle for more than three years (1516–20). He made some of his astronomical observations here, and you can still see the diagram he drew on the cloister wall to record the equinox, and thereby calculate the exact length of the year. Models of the instruments he used are on display in his former living quarters, and various gormless statues are placed around the city for photo opportunities.

The **High Gate**, the historic gateway to the Old Town, is the only remainder of the 14th-century city walls. Just to the west, on the quiet old fish-market square, is the main an-nexe of the **Museum of Warmia & Masuria** (☎ 534 01 19; Targ Rybny 1; adult/concession 6/4zł; ☿ 9am-5pm Tue-Sun Jun-Aug, 10am-4pm Tue-Sun Sep-May), housed in the former *Gazeta Olsztyńska* newspa-per building. The paper was famed for its outspoken politics under occupation, which swiftly led to the arrest and execution of its publisher in 1940 and the destruction of the offices. Reconstructed, the building now has exhibitions related to the city's and region's past, and the political role of journalism.

A block south is the **Rynek** (formally called ul Stare Miasto), which was destroyed dur-ing WWII and rebuilt in a grandiose style only superficially reverting to the past. It's best seen at night, when the town hall is lit up with dazzling spotlights and half the population turns out for an evening drink.

The Gothic **cathedral** on the other side of the Old Town dates from the same period as the castle, though its huge 60m tower was only added in 1596. Here, as in the castle, crystalline vaults can be seen in the aisles, but the nave has netlike arches dating from the 17th century. Among the remarkable works of art are the 16th-century triptych at the head of the left aisle, and a shimmering gold-and-silver altarpiece of the Virgin Mary.

Copernicus fans can get a bit more hands-on at the **astronomical observatory** (☎ 527 67 03; ul Żołnierska 13; adult/concession 6/3.50zł; ☿ Mon-Sat), located in an old water tower out to the east of town. It offers observations of the sun (hourly between 9am and 3pm) and the stars (twice nightly), provided the sky is clear.

For a dramatic look at the heavens, the **planetarium** (☎ 533 49 51; www.planetarium.olsztyn.pl in Polish; Al Piłsudskiego 38; adult/concession 7.50/6zł) has hourly shows and occasional temporary exhibits. Foreign-language soundtracks (in English, German, French and Russian) are generally offered during two shows a day.

Fans of our feathered friends should consider a day trip out to the tiny town of **Bukwałd**, 12km from Olsztyn, where you'll find **Strusiolandia** (☎ 530 57 06; www.strusiolandia .olsztyn.pl in Polish & German), a real working os-trich farm. Similar places have sprung up all over Poland, supplementing the income from the birds' meat by admitting visitors; the ostrich-riding show is one of the strang-est sights you'll ever see.

Activities
KAYAKING

The travel agency **PTTK Mazury** (☎ 527 40 59; www.pttkmazury.pl in Polish; ul Staromiejska 1) runs 10-day kayaking tours along the Krutynia River route (known as Szlak Kajakowy Krutyni). The 103km trip begins at **Stanica Wodna PTTK** (☎ 742 81 24) in Sorkwity, 50km east of Olsztyn, and goes down the Kru-tynia River and Lake Bełdany to Ruciane-Nida (see p447). Tours (€250) depart daily from late June to mid-August. The price includes kayak, food, insurance, lodging in cabins and a Polish-speaking guide; the maximum group size is 19 people.

You can also do the trip on your own, hiring a kayak (25zł to 30zł per day) from the Stanica Wodna PTTK in Sorkwity, but check availability in advance. You can use the same overnight bases as the tours but you can't always count on cabins – be prepared to camp. It's easier to get a kayak and shelter in June or September than in July and August.

Brochures in English and German, with a detailed description and maps of the Krutynia route, are available at the Mazury office. Information in German is also available online (www.masuren-online.de).

Festivals & Events

Summer of Arts (Olsztyńskie Lato Artystyczne, OLA; ☎ 527 09 64; www.mok.olsztyn.pl) Citywide festival of cultural events, held from 15 June to 15 September.
Olsztyn Blues Nights (☎ 527 09 64; www.mok .olsztyn.pl in Polish) One of Poland's oldest blues festivals, held in mid-July.

Sleeping

Prices quoted for accommodation in this chapter are, unless otherwise stated, for rooms with private bathrooms.

Hotel Pod Zamkiem (☎ 535 12 87; www.hotel .olsztyn.com.pl; ul Nowowiejskiego 10; s/d/tr 150/190/230zł; P) Set in a large historic villa, once the home of the influential Sperl family, this is a stylish traditional inn with character in spades.

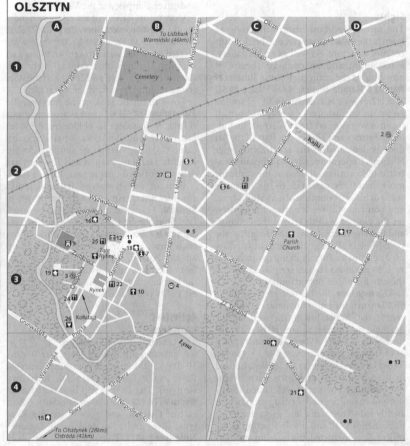

OLSZTYN

Wooden beams, murals and lots of pine provide atmosphere, and the park setting puts you right by the castle and the Old Town.

Hotel Wysoka Brama (☎ 527 36 75; ul Staromiejska 1; dm/s 22/58zł, d 58-100zł) The 70-bed PTTK hotel is superbly located on the edge of the Old Town, actually occupying a section of the High Gate with its mid-sized dorms. The newer annexe has slightly scrappy private rooms and a handful of much nicer en suites. Predictably, it's crammed with backpackers in summer.

Villa Pallas (☎ 535 01 15; www.villapallas.pl in Polish; ul Żołnierska 4; s incl breakfast 199zł, d 249-270zł, ste 370zł; P) The best of several options east of town, this sophisticated villa is named for the Greek goddess Athena, whose statue makes

up part of the mix 'n match décor. Negotiate the maze of stairways to find refined, spotless rooms and some great suites (just ignore the red vinyl sofas). A smart restaurant and small spa centre complete the look.

Polsko-Niemieckie Centrum Młodzieży (☎ 534 07 80; www.pncm.olsztyn.pl in Polish & German; ul Okopowa 25; s/d 150/200zł; P) The Polish-German Youth Centre is ideally located next to the castle; you don't have to be Polish, German or even a youth to stay here, though speaking some *deutsch* would certainly make things easier. Everything is appropriately shipshape and orderly, and there's a good restaurant on the premises.

Hotel Kopernik (☎ 522 99 29; www.kopernik.olsztyn.pl; ul Warszawska 37; s/d 190/230zł, ste 340-380zł; P) Done out in shades of blue you never knew existed, plus a few other cheerful tones, the Copernicus is a sprightly mid-class option to the south of the Old Town, with good wheelchair access and helpful staff.

Hotel Warmiński (☎ 522 14 00; www.hotel-warminski.com.pl; ul Kołobrzeska 1; s/d 230/270zł, ste 320-350zł; P 🖳) A characterless modern block houses the nearest thing you'll get to a full-service hotel in Olsztyn. Prices include full board and use of the 'biological renewal complex'; the restaurant specialises in regional cuisine and the in-house travel agency organises anything from bonfires to hunting trips.

Hotel Gromada (☎ 534 58 64; kormoran@gromada.pl; Plac Konstytucji 3 Maja 4; s/d 152/168zł; P) Right across the road from the PKP and PKS terminals, you won't find much imagination in this business chain but standards are fine and it's fully equipped with a restaurant, ATM and soundproofing. Just what you need if you're aiming for a 4am bus.

PTSM Youth Hostel (☎ 527 66 50; ssmolsztyn@ptsm.pl; ul Kościuszki 72/74; dm 19zł, s 54zł, d with shared bathroom 46zł; P) The youth hostel is well run and tidy, with private rooms and dorms for up to six people. There's a shared kitchen and bike hire for guests.

Eating

Restauracja u Artystów (☎ 527 43 21; ul Kołłątaja 20; mains 8-18zł; ⏰ lunch & dinner) Unlike many so-called 'art pubs', the creative input into this homy restaurant isn't limited to the random clutter strewn around the place – genuine local artists (professional and amateur) have scrawled cartoons and caricatures all around the outside door, with regular additions.

Różana Café (☎ 523 50 39; www.rozanacafe.pl; Targ Rybny 14; mains 16-44zł; ☺ lunch & dinner) A well-translated trilingual menu, with just a dash of humour, introduces you to this refined selection of Polish dishes, while waiters in braces gently woo you with extras. The portions won't blow you away, but it's a good excuse to stick around for dessert or one last drink.

Restauracja Corner Café (☎ 527 57 26; www.restauracje.olsztyn.pl; ul Dąbrowszczaków 8/9; mains 16-46zł; ☺ lunch & dinner) Catering for a young, well-heeled clientele, this is straightforward international cuisine with plenty of salads. Confusingly, the inside looks like it's outside – the place really does impersonate an old street corner, complete with streetlamps and house fronts. The restaurant's outside the Old Town area.

Bar Dziupla (☎ 527 50 83; ul Stare Miasto 9/10; mains 3-8.50zł; ☺ breakfast, lunch & dinner) Dziupla takes on the milk-bar mantle to provide some of the best budget meals in the Old Town, including delicious *pierogi* (dumplings) and *chłodnik* (cold beetroot soup).

Drinking

Bohema Jazz Club (☎ 0604 483 789; Targ Rybny 15) Relocated to swish modern premises on Olsztyn's classy alternative square, the Bohema maintains its reputation for live jazz and now throws cocktails, karaoke and a chill-out area into the mix. It may also be the only basement club in Poland with a lift.

Klub SARP (☎ 535 96 49; ul Kołłątaja 14) The riverside area around the southern end of the Old Town is a hotbed of pubs, clubs and restaurants, and SARP is a top contender, boasting a split-level setup in a former granary. It's run by the local Association of Polish Architects.

Entertainment

Boomtown (☎ 0608 499 839; www.boomtown.net.pl; ul 1 Maja 5A; ☺ 3pm-2am Mon-Thu, 3pm-4am Fri & Sat, 6pm-2am Sun) Olsztyn's premier commercial dance club infests the subterranean space below a theatre and cinema complex, propagating broad-spectrum electronic and black music to a keen public.

Getting There & Away

The busy bus and train stations are both in a big L-shaped building on Plac Konstytucji 3 Maja. You can walk to the Old Town in 15 minutes or take one of the frequent city buses that drop you off in front of the High Gate.

BUS

Buses to Olsztynek (5.60zł, 50 minutes) and Lidzbark Warmiński (8.40zł, one hour) go at least every hour. There are regular departures to Giżycko (16zł, three hours, 10 daily), Kętrzyn (14zł, 2¼ hours, hourly) and Elbląg (21zł, 2¼ hours, seven daily). Half a dozen fast buses run to Warsaw (32zł, four hours).

International buses serve 14 European countries. Among the most frequent are PKS' daily departures to Kaliningrad in Russia (20zł, four hours) and four weekly services to Vilnius in Lithuania (60zł, nine hours).

TRAIN

About five fast trains leave for Gdańsk daily (31.85zł, three hours) via Elbląg (23.93zł, 1¾ hours). One express and two fast trains go to Warsaw (fast train 37.64zł, 3½ hours) all year, and there are a couple more trains in summer. Half a dozen trains run to Toruń (31.85zł, 2¼ hours) daily, a route that is not covered by buses.

OLSZTYNEK
☎ 89 / pop 8000

If you're looking for a half-day break from Olsztyn, the small nearby town of Olsztynek has an interesting skansen, the **Museum of Folk Architecture** (Muzeum Budownictwa Ludowego; ☎ 519 21 64; ul Sportowa 21; adult/concession 6/4zł; ☺ 9am-3pm Tue-Sun Apr & Oct, 9am-5pm daily May, 9am-5.30pm daily Jun & Aug, 9am-4.30pm Tue-Sun Sep, 9am-3pm Mon-Fri Nov-Mar). Tucked away on the northeastern outskirts of town, the skansen features about 40 examples of regional timber architecture from Warmia and Masuria, and also has a cluster of Lithuanian houses. There's a variety of peasant cottages complete with outbuildings, various windmills and a thatch-roofed church. A number of buildings have been furnished and decorated inside, and it's been done really well.

The 14th-century Protestant church, on the pretty Rynek, was rebuilt after suffering damage in WWII and is now an **art gallery** (☎ 519 24 91; Rynek 1; adult/concession 3/2zł; ☺ 9am-5pm Tue-Sun May-Sep, 9am-4pm Tue-Sun Oct-Apr), mostly displaying crafts and visiting exhibitions.

The train station is 1km northeast of the centre, close to the skansen. Nine trains run to Olsztyn (6.80zł, 30 minutes) daily.

The bus terminal is 250m south of the Rynek, but many regional buses call in at the train station. You can travel from either to Olsztyn (5.60zł, 50 minutes, once or twice hourly), Grunwald (5zł, 30 minutes, up to eight daily) and Ostróda (6.30zł, one hour, seven daily). Private minibuses duplicate many of the local lines.

GRUNWALD
☎ 89

Grunwald is hard to find even on detailed maps, yet the name is known to every Pole. Here, on 15 July 1410, the combined Polish and Lithuanian forces (supported by contingents of Ruthenians and Tatars) under King Władysław II Jagiełło defeated the army of the Teutonic Knights. A crucial moment in Polish history, the 10 hours of carnage left the grand master of the Teutonic order, Ulrich von Jungingen, dead and his forces decimated. This was reputedly the largest medieval battle in Europe, with an estimated 70,000 troops aiming to hack each other to bits.

The battlefield is an open, gently rolling meadow adorned with three monuments. Built on the central hill is the **Museum of the Grunwald Battlefield** (Muzeum Bitwy Grunwaldzkiej; ☎ 647 22 28; adult/concession 6/3zł; ⏰ 8am-6pm 1 May–15 Oct). It displays items such as period armour, maps and battle banners and its cinema runs films about the battle. Five hundred metres from the museum are the ruins of a **chapel**, erected by the order a year after the battle, on the spot where the grand master is supposed to have died. All signs are in Polish, but the shop by the entrance to the battlefield sells brochures in English and German.

Frequently visited by Poles, Grunwald is essentially a memorial to this glorious moment in Poland's history, and unpartisan foreigners may find it less interesting. The best time to visit the place is in July during the **Days of Grunwald festival** (☎ 647 20 59; www .republika.pl/grunwald), a medieval extravaganza that has lots of stalls, tournaments, concerts and costumed characters, culminating in a huge re-enactment of the battle itself. Watched by almost as many people as attended the original skirmish, it's one of the biggest and most colourful spectacles of its kind in Poland, which is saying something in a country that's so marked by its Middle Ages.

Year-round at least four or five daily buses go to Olsztynek (5zł, 30 minutes) and Olsztyn (9.50zł, 1½ hours) from the battlefield, with another two or three departures to Ostróda (6.30zł, 45 minutes).

OSTRÓDA
☎ 89 / pop 35,000

In case you couldn't guess, Ostróda is the southern terminus of the Elbląg-Ostróda Canal, and if you take a boat in either direction you're likely to spend a night here. Apparently Napoleon once ruled Europe from this deceptively sleepy lakeside town; he wouldn't look twice at it now, but the leisurely pace of life seems to suit locals and holiday-makers alike.

Sleeping & Eating
Hotel Hindenburg (☎ 646 30 35; ul Mickiewicza 7; d/tr 92/130zł; **P**) Obliging, friendly and convenient, this owner-operated establishment has a good eye for the backpacker market. It's named not for the famous disaster but for the equally ill-fated prewar president of Germany, Paul von Hindenburg, who stayed in room 12 in 1934. There are shared bathrooms, communal lounge.

Hotel Promenada (☎ 642 81 00; www.hotelprom enada.com.pl in Polish; ul Mickiewicza 3; s/d 120/180zł; **P**) The Promenada offers a more upmarket touch, just around the corner from the Hindenburg and the boat quay. At the time of writing it was being extended to increase its capacity.

Getting There & Away
The train and bus stations are next to each other, 500m west of the wharf. Trains to Olsztyn (6.80zł, 39km) and Iława (5.70zł, 30km) run every couple of hours, and there are six daily trains to Toruń (17.20zł, 124km). For Elbląg, Warsaw and Gdańsk, change at Iława.

There's bus transport to Olsztyn (8.80zł, 1¼ hours, 10 daily), Olsztynek (6.30zł, one hour, seven daily), Grunwald (6.30zł, 45 minutes, two or three daily) and Elbląg (11.40zł, 1¾ hours, 11 daily).

From May to September a boat to Elbląg leaves daily at 8am (see p434).

WARMIA & MASURIA

THE ELBLĄG-OSTRÓDA CANAL

The 82km Elbląg-Ostróda Canal is the longest navigable canal still in use in Poland. It's also the most unusual: the canal deals with the 99.5m difference in water levels by means of a unique system of **slipways**, where boats are physically dragged across dry land on rail-mounted trolleys.

The canal follows the course of a chain of six lakes, most of which are now protected conservation areas. The largest is the considerably overgrown **Lake Drużno** near Elbląg, left behind by the Vistula Lagoon, which once extended deep into this region.

The five slipways are on a 10km stretch of the northern part of the canal. Each slipway consists of two trolleys tied to a single looped rope, operating on the same principle as a funicular. They are powered by water.

Boat Excursions

From May to September, pleasure boats operated by **Żegluga Ostródzko-Elbląska** (in Ostróda ☎ 89-646 38 71; www.zegluga.com.pl) sail the main part of the canal between Ostróda and Elbląg. They depart from both towns at 8am and arrive at the opposite end at about 7pm (adult/under-18 80zł/60zł). Bulky luggage costs 16zł extra, and it's 32zł for a bicycle.

If you don't feel like committing to the full 11-hour stretch, take the boat from Elbląg as far as Buczyniec (65zł/45zł, five hours), which covers the most interesting part of the canal, including all five slipways. This is a good solution for motorists leaving their vehicles in Elbląg, and is probably the best way to do the trip on limited time (or patience).

The boats, which have a capacity of 65 passengers, only run when at least 20 passengers turn up. You can expect regular daily services in July and August but outside this period there may be some days off. It's worth ringing the wharf a couple of days in advance to find out about the availability of tickets and the current timetable status. Boats have snack bars on board, which serve some basic snacks, as well as tea, coffee and beer.

If you're not going to take the boat trip, but have your own transport and want to have a look at the slipways, head to **Buczyniec** between noon and 2pm to see the boats pass on their way north and south. There's a small **museum** here and you can see the impressive machinery that powers the trolleys.

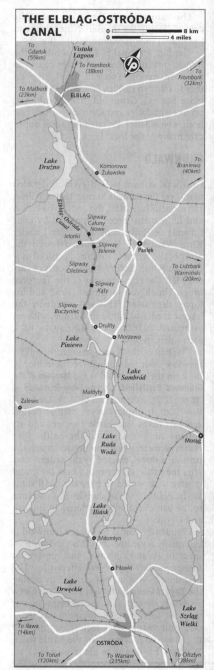

THE ELBLĄG-OSTRÓDA CANAL

BARGING IN

The rich forests of the Ostróda region have attracted merchants from Gdańsk and Elbląg since medieval times, yet until the 19th century, the only way of getting timber down to the Baltic was a long water route along the Drwęca and Vistula Rivers via Toruń. Engineers considered building a canal as a short cut, but quickly found that the terrain was rugged and too steep for conventional locks.

In 1836 Prussian engineer Georg Jakob Steenke (1801–82), from Königsberg, produced a sophisticated design for an Elbląg–Ostróda canal incorporating slipways, but Prussian authorities rejected the project as unrealistic and too costly. Steenke didn't give up, however, and eventually succeeded in getting an audience with the king of Prussia. With typical kingly shrewdness, the monarch approved the plan, not because of its technical or economic aspects but because nobody had ever constructed such a system before.

The part of the canal between Elbląg and Miłomłyn, which included all the slipways, was built between 1848 and 1860, and the remaining leg to Ostróda was completed by 1872. The canal proved to be reliable and profitable, and cut the distance of the original route along the Drwęca and Vistula almost fivefold. Various extensions were planned, including one linking the canal with the Great Masurian Lakes 120km to the east, but none were ever built.

The canal was damaged during the 1945 Red Army offensive but was repaired soon after liberation and opened for timber transport in 1946. A year later, the first tourist boat sailed the route. It remains the only canal of its kind in Europe and continues to operate, though the timber boats have long since faded away.

There are also daily departures on the much less adventurous side canal running from Ostróda to Iława (46zł/34zł, six hours) at 9am.

LIDZBARK WARMIŃSKI
☎ 89 / pop 16,500

Lidzbark Warmiński, 46km north of Olsztyn, is a peaceful if rather ordinary town. Its past is certainly more glorious than its present; it was the capital of the Warmian bishopric for over four centuries. In 1350 the bishops chose it as their main residence; a castle and a church were built and the town swiftly became an important religious and cultural centre. Copernicus lived here between 1503 and 1510, serving as a doctor and adviser to his uncle, Bishop Łukasz Watzenrode.

When the Reformation arrived in the 16th century, Lidzbark, along with most of the province, became a citadel of Catholicism, and it remained so until the First Partition of 1773. Deprived of his office, the last bishop, Ignacy Krasicki, turned to literature, becoming an outstanding satirist and all-round man of letters.

Today there's little trace of the town that was reputedly the richest and most cultured in Warmia, but the castle alone is enough to justify a day trip.

Castle

This mighty square red-brick structure, adorned with turrets on the corners, is the most important sight in Lidzbark and one of Warmia's most-significant cultural gems. Enter from the south through the palatial, horseshoe-shaped building surrounding Plac Zamkowy, which was extensively rebuilt in the 18th century. A wide brick bridge runs up to the main castle gate.

The castle was constructed in the second half of the 14th century on a square plan with a central courtyard, the whole surrounded by a moat and fortified walls. When the bishops' era ended with the Partitions, the castle fell into decline and served a variety of purposes, including as barracks, storage, hospital and orphanage. Restoration was undertaken in the 1920s and within 10 years the building had been more or less returned to its original form. Miraculously, it came through the war unharmed, and today it is easily one of Poland's best-preserved medieval castles.

Most of the interior, from the cellars up to the 2nd floor, now houses the **Warmian Museum** (Muzeum Warmińskie; ☎ 767 21 11; Plac Zamkowy 1; adult/concession 6/3zł; ⏰ 9am-5pm Tue-Sun Jun-Aug, 10am-4pm Tue-Sun Sep-May). The first thing you'll notice is a beautiful courtyard with two-storey arcaded galleries all round it.

It was constructed in the 1380s and has hardly changed since.

The 1st floor boasts the castle's main chambers; the vaulted **Grand Refectory** (Wielki Refektarz) is the most remarkable. The chessboard-style wall paintings date from the end of the 14th century. The exhibition inside features works of medieval art from the region, including some charming Madonnas. The adjoining chapel was redecorated in rococo style in the mid-18th century.

The top floor contains several exhibitions, including 20th-century Polish painting and a collection of icons dating from the 17th century onward. The excellent two-storey vaulted cellars have some old cannons on display. These belonged to the bishops, who had their own small army – an essential ecumenical accessory at that point in time.

Sleeping & Eating

Hotelik Przy Bramie (☎ 767 20 99; ul Konstytucji 3 Maja 18; d 180zł; **P**) A small modern hotel just along from the High Gate, the entrance to Lidzbark's blandly rebuilt old quarter. It's not wildly exciting but provides the best standard you'll get from the modest options here.

Gościniec Myśliwski (☎ 767 52 59; ul Konstytucji 3 Maja 26; d 90zł; **P**) Located in a stylish timbered building with its own restaurant, there's a touch of the hunting lodge about the Myśliwski. Four double rooms are available, with three sharing a bathroom.

Restauracja Happy End (☎ 767 58 21; ul Konstytucji 3 Maja 6; mains 7.60-20.80zł) With a name so evocative of dodgy massage parlours, it comes as quite a relief to find that this is just a pleasant café-restaurant. Good Polish staples in amenable surrounds.

Getting There & Away

The bus terminal occupies the defunct train station, about 500m northwest of the Old Town. Buses to Olsztyn (8.40zł, one hour) depart at least hourly, and are supplemented by private minibuses (6zł). There are five buses a day to Gdańsk (23zł, 2½ hours) and four to Kętrzyn (10.50zł, 1½ hours), passing Reszel and Święta Lipka on the way.

RESZEL

☎ 89 / pop 6000

Reszel (reh-shel) is a little market town that came to life in the 13th century as the easternmost outpost of the Warmian bishopric.

A century later it evolved into a small fortified town, complete with a central square, castle and church, and remained a prosperous craft centre until the wars of the 18th century. The town never really recovered and is now very much a backwater, though its minuscule centre still boasts the original street plan and a fine castle.

Sights

Reszel's tiny Old Town is centred around the Rynek and its low-key town hall. One block east is the 14th-century brick **castle** (☎ 755 02 16; ul Podzamcze 3; adult/concession 1.50/1zł), built at the same time as that in Lidzbark and likewise retaining much of its original form, except for the southern side, which was turned into a Protestant church in the 19th century, with a belfry and a jarring concrete gable added to the top. Today the complex is open to the public and houses a hotel, a restaurant, some function rooms and an **art gallery** (adult/concession 6/3zł; ☼ 10am-4pm Tue-Sun). Go to the top of the castle's massive cylindrical tower for some views over the red-tiled roofs of the Old Town, then head down into the subterranean former dungeon for a rather surreal game of pool.

The other main building in town is the 14th-century **parish church**, a large Gothic brick construction with a tall square tower. It was refurnished and redecorated in the

---

HIGH STAKES

Reszel may have the dubious distinction of being the last place in Europe to sentence a woman to death as a witch. Where most such cases had died out by the early 18th century, massive fires in 1806 and 1807 incensed the townspeople here to such a degree that they accused unfortunate local woman Barbara Zdunk of sorcery and imprisoned her in the castle. The case reached the attention of Prussia's highest authorities and was referred to several courts and even to King Frederick Wilhelm II himself – incredibly, all of them upheld the guilty verdict. In 1811 Zdunk was burned at the stake, though legend has it that the executioner mercifully strangled her before torching the wood. Not what you'd expect from the Age of Enlightenment...

1820s after fires that devastated much of the centre, and has a harmonious though not outstanding interior.

At the entrance to the Old Town from Kętrzyn is the unusually massive brick **Fishing Bridge** (Most Rybacki), also known as the Gothic Bridge (Most Gotycki), built in the 14th century and recently so extensively restored that it looks like new. Don't be fooled by the name – you'd need a long line and a lot more river before you could actually catch anything!

Sleeping & Eating

If you're going to stay anywhere in Reszel, it may as well be the castle. The big suitelike rooms of the **Kreativ Hotel** (☎ 755 01 09; www .zamek-reszel.com in Polish & German; ul Podzamcze 3; s 140-170zł, d 230-250zł, q 360zł; P) are long on atmosphere, if slightly short on luxury, and the vaulted **restaurant** (mains 9-30zł) takes over the central courtyard in warm weather.

Getting There & Away

Trains no longer call in at Reszel, but bus transport is OK. The bus terminal is by the old station, a five-minute walk north of the Old Town. There are plenty of buses east to Kętrzyn (5.40zł, 30 minutes), passing via Święta Lipka (3zł). A dozen buses go to Olsztyn daily (10.50zł, 1½ hours). Two buses run west to Lidzbark Warmiński (8.50zł, one hour), one of them a fast service to Gdańsk (33zł, four hours).

ŚWIĘTA LIPKA

☎ 89

The name of this tiny hamlet means 'Holy Lime Tree', and the origins of Święta Lipka (*shfyen*-tah *leep*-kah) are linked to one of Poland's most-famous miracle stories. Apparently a prisoner in Kętrzyn castle was visited the night before his execution by the Virgin Mary, who presented him with a tree trunk so he could carve an effigy of her. The resulting figure was so beautiful that the judges took it to be a sign from heaven and gave the condemned man his freedom. On his way home he placed the statue on the first lime tree he encountered, which happened to be in Święta Lipka.

Miracles immediately began to occur, and even sheep knelt down while passing the shrine. Pilgrims arrived in increasing numbers, including the last grand master of the Teutonic order, Albrecht von Hohenzollern, who walked here barefoot (ironically he converted to Luthernism six years later). A timber chapel was built to protect the miraculous figure, and was later replaced with the present building. It's perhaps the most magnificent baroque church in northern Poland, a huge attraction and still a major pilgrimage site.

Church of Our Lady

Built between 1687 and 1693, and later surrounded by an ample rectangular cloister, the **church** (☽ 8am-6pm except during Mass) was built around four identical corner towers, all housing chapels. The best artists from Warmia, Königsberg (Kaliningrad) and Vilnius were commissioned for the furnishings and decoration, which were completed by about 1740. Since then the church has hardly changed, either inside or outside, and is regarded as one of the purest examples of a late-baroque church in the country.

The entrance to the complex is through an elaborate wrought-iron **gateway**. Just behind it, the two-towered cream façade holds a stone **sculpture** of the holy lime tree in its central niche, with a statue of the Virgin Mary perched on top.

Once inside, the visitor is enveloped in colourful and florid, but not overwhelming, baroque ornamentation. All the frescoes are the work of Maciej Mayer of Lidzbark, and display trompe l'œil images, which were fashionable at the time. These are clearly visible both on the vault and the columns; the latter look as if they were carved. Of course Mayer also left behind his own image – you can see him in a blue waistcoat with brushes in his hand, in the corner of the vault painting over the organ.

The three-storey, 19m-high **altar**, covering the whole back of the chancel, is carved of walnut and painted to look like marble. Of the three paintings in the altar, the lowest one depicts the Virgin Mary of Święta Lipka with the Christ child.

The pulpit is ornamented with paintings and sculptures. Directly opposite, across the nave, is a **holy lime tree** topped with the figure of the Virgin Mary, supposedly placed on the spot where the legendary tree itself once stood.

The pride of the church is its **organ**, a sumptuously decorated instrument of about

5000 pipes. The work of Johann Jozue Mosengel of Königsberg, it is decorated with mechanical figures of saints and angels that dance around when the organ is played, much like an astronomical clock. Short demonstrations are held several times a day from May to September and irregularly the rest of the year. From June to August, full organ recitals take place every Friday evening.

The cloister surrounding the church is ornamented with frescoes, also masterminded by Mayer. The artist painted the corner chapels and parts of the northern and western cloister, but died before the work was complete. It was continued in the same vein by other artists but, as you can see, without the same success.

Święta Lipka is visited frequently by both tourists and pilgrims. The main religious celebrations fall on the last Sunday of May, and on 11, 14 and 15 August.

Sleeping & Eating

Hotel w Świętej Lipce (☎ 755 37 37; Święta Lipka 16; s/d 180/230zł; P) Big, modern and a pale imitation of a traditional timbered farmhouse, the town's latest tourist venture is instantly redeemed by a leafy setting and perfect views of the church. The rooms are good and staff are eager to please. It's also known as Hotel 500.

Dom Pielgrzyma (☎ 755 14 81; fax 755 14 60; dm 25zł) This simple pilgrims' place, in the monastery complex next to the church, provides 85 beds in rooms for up to five people, but it can often be full in July and August. Budget meals are available if requested in advance.

Getting There & Away

Buses to Kętrzyn (4zł, 20 minutes) and Reszel (3zł, 10 minutes) run every hour or so. There are several to Olsztyn (11.20zł, 1¾ hours) and Mrągowo (4.60zł, 30 minutes), and a couple to Lidzbark Warmiński (8.40zł, 1¼ hours).

THE GREAT MASURIAN LAKES

The Great Masurian Lake District (Kraina Wielkich Jezior Mazurskich), east of Olsztyn, is a verdant land of rolling hills dotted with countless lakes, healthy little farms, scattered tracts of forest and small towns. The district is centred around Lake Śniardwy (114 sq km), Poland's largest lake, and Lake Mamry and its adjacent waters (an additional 104 sq km). Over 15% of the area is covered by water and another 30% by forest.

The lakes are well connected by rivers and canals, to form an extensive system of waterways. The whole area has become a prime destination for yachtspeople and canoeists, and is also popular among anglers, hikers, bikers and nature-lovers. Any boating enthusiast worth their (freshwater) salt should make Masuria their first port of call.

The main lakeside centres are Giżycko and Mikołajki, with two minor ones, Węgorzewo and Ruciane-Nida, at the northern and southern ends of the lakeland, respectively. Visitors arrive in great numbers in July and August, though after 15 August the crowds begin to thin out.

Getting Around

Yachties can sail most of the larger lakes, all the way from Węgorzewo to Ruciane-Nida, which are interconnected and form the district's main waterway system. Kayakers will perhaps prefer more intimate surroundings alongside rivers and smaller lakes. The best established and most popular kayak route in the area originates at Sorkwity and follows the Krutynia River and Lake Bełdany to Ruciane-Nida (see p429). There's also a beautiful kayak route along the Czarna Hańcza River in the Augustów area, further east (see p451).

If you're not up for doing everything yourself, you can enjoy the lakes in comfort from the deck of one of the pleasure boats operated by the **Żegluga Mazurska** (in Giżycko ☎ 87-428 53 32; www.zeglugamazurska.com.pl). These large boats have an open deck above and a coffee shop below, and can carry backpacks and bicycles.

Theoretically, boats run between Giżycko, Mikołajki and Ruciane-Nida daily from May to September, and to Węgorzewo from June to August. In practice, as trips can be cancelled if too few passengers turn up, the service is most reliable from late June to late August. Schedules are clearly posted at the lake ports.

The detailed *Wielkie Jeziora Mazurskie* map (scale 1:100,000) is a great help for anyone exploring the region by boat, kayak,

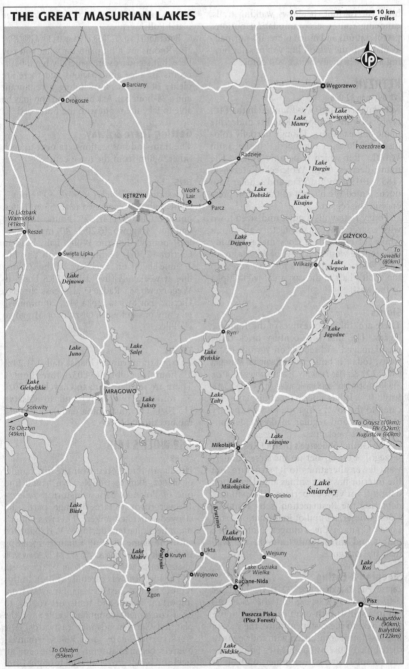

bike, car or foot. It shows walking trails, canoeing routes, accommodation options, petrol stations and much more. It's normally available in the region but you're safer buying a copy in a city before you come.

KĘTRZYN

☎ 89 / pop 32,000

Kętrzyn (*kent*-shin) was founded in the 14th century by the Teutonic Knights under the name of Rastenburg. Though partially colonised by Poles, it remained Prussian until WWII, after which it became Polish. The name derives from Wojciech Kętrzyński (1838–1919), an historian and scholar who documented the history of the Polish presence in the region.

Today Kętrzyn is a quiet mid-sized town with a large mayonnaise factory and not a whole lot else. But it does make a handy base for the western fringes of the Masurian Lake District, and allows for easy access to the Wolf's Lair to the east and Święta Lipka to the west.

Sights

There are still some vestiges of the Teutonic legacy. The mid-14th-century brick **castle** was damaged and rebuilt on various occasions; today it houses the **Regional Museum** (☎ 752 32 82; Plac Zamkowy 1; adult/concession 4/2zł; ⏰ 10am-5pm Jun-Sep, 9am-4pm Tue-Fri, 9am-3pm Sat & Sun Oct-May). It has a permanent display dedicated to the town's history, plus temporary exhibitions and regular medieval demonstrations at weekends.

The Gothic **St George's Church** (Kościół Św Jerzego), a bit further up the street, underwent fewer alterations to its structure, but the interior has furnishings and decoration dating from various periods. The painting depicting the Resurrection is by Heinrich Königswieser, a pupil of Reformation artist Lucas Cranach the Younger. Note a fine pulpit and three tombstones in the wall near the entrance.

Sleeping & Eating

Zajazd Pod Zamkiem (☎ 752 31 17; www.zajazd .ketrzyn.pl; ul Struga 3; s/d/tr/q 100/140/180/240zł; P) Set in a stylish 19th-century country house right next to the castle entrance, the Zajazd has just four rooms, each with four beds to distribute or use as you please. The terrace restaurant is great in summer, and offers a few Chinese dishes as a change from the usual Polish grub.

Hotel Koch (☎ 752 20 58; ul Traugutta 3; s/d 180/250zł; P) Rooms are a bit plain for what you pay here, but standards are generally high, bathrooms are nice and spacious and there are plenty of amenities, including a restaurant and a 24-hour bar. Ask nicely and you may be able to take the room with the water bed.

Getting There & Away

The train and bus stations are next to each other, 600m from the town centre.

BUS

Buses run to Giżycko (6.90zł, 40 minutes, eight daily), Węgorzewo (8zł, 55 minutes, hourly), Olsztyn (14zł, 2¼ hours, 16 daily) and to Mrągowo (6.20zł, 40 minutes, at least hourly). For the Wolf's Lair, head to Gierłoż (2.50zł, 15 minutes) with city bus 1 (nine daily) on weekdays or the Zielona line at weekends (five daily). PKS buses to Węgorzewo via Radzieje also pass through Gierłoż. For Święta Lipka (4zł, 20 minutes), take any bus to Reszel, Olsztyn, or Mrągowo via Pilec.

TRAIN

Two fast trains run to Gdańsk daily (41.24zł, 4½ hours) via Elbląg (34.03zł, three hours). There are regular trains to Giżycko (5.70zł, 35 minutes, five daily) and to Olsztyn (13.10zł, 1¾ hours, nine daily), but check the bus timetable too.

THE WOLF'S LAIR

☎ 89

Hidden in thick forest near the tiny hamlet of **Gierłoż**, 8km east of Kętrzyn, you'll find one of Poland's eeriest historical relics – 18 overgrown hectares of huge, partly destroyed concrete bunkers. This was Hitler's main headquarters during WWII, baptised with the name of Wolfsschanze, meaning **Wolf's Lair** (Wilczy Szaniec; ☎ 752 44 29; www.wolfs schanze.home.pl; adult/concession 8/5zł; ⏰ 8am-sunset).

The location was carefully chosen in this remote part of East Prussia, far away from important towns and transport routes, to be a convenient command centre for the planned German advance eastwards. The work, carried out by some 3000 German labourers, began in autumn 1940; the cement, steel and basalt gravel were all brought from

THE HIT ON HITLER

Hitler used to say that the Wolf's Lair was one of the very few places in Europe where he felt safe. Ironically, it was here that an assassination attempt came closest to succeeding. It was organised by a group of pragmatic, high-ranking German officers who considered the continuation of the war to be suicidal, with no real chance of victory. They planned to negotiate peace with the Allies after eliminating Hitler.

The leader of the plot, Colonel Claus von Stauffenberg, arrived from Berlin on 20 July 1944 under the pretext of informing Hitler about the newly formed reserve army. A frequent guest at the Wolf's Lair, he enjoyed the confidence of the staff and had no problems entering the bunker complex with a bomb in his briefcase. He placed the case beneath the table a few feet from Hitler and left the meeting to take a prearranged phone call. The explosion killed two members of Hitler's staff and wounded half a dozen others, but the Führer himself suffered only minor injuries and was even able to meet Mussolini later the same day. Stauffenberg and some 5000 people involved directly or indirectly in the plot were executed.

Had the outcome been different, it could have radically changed the final course of WWII. A peace treaty between the Germans and the Allies in 1944 might well have saved the lives of some five million people and prevented the devastation of vast parts of Poland and Germany.

Germany. About 80 structures were finally built, including seven heavy bunkers for the top leaders: Bormann (Hitler's adviser and private secretary), Göring (Prussian prime minister and German commissioner for aviation) and Hitler himself were among the residents. Their bunkers had walls and ceilings up to 8m thick.

The whole complex was surrounded by multiple barriers of barbed wire and artillery emplacements, and a sophisticated minefield. An airfield was built 5km away and there was an emergency airstrip within the camp. Apart from the natural camouflage of trees and plants, the bunker site was further disguised with artificial vegetation-like screens suspended on wires and changed according to the season of the year. The Allies did not discover the site until 1945.

Hitler arrived in the Wolf's Lair on 26 June 1941 (four days after the invasion of the Soviet Union) and stayed there until 20 November 1944, with only short trips to the outside world. His longest journey outside the bunker was a four-month stint at the Ukraine headquarters of the Wehrmacht (the armed services of the German Reich) in 1942, overseeing the advancing German front.

As the Red Army approached, Hitler left the Wolf's Lair and the headquarters were evacuated. The army prepared the bunkers to be destroyed, should the enemy have attempted to seize them. About 10 tonnes of explosives were stuffed into each heavy bunker. The complex was eventually blown

up on 24 January 1945 and the Germans retreated. Three days later the Soviets arrived, but the extensive minefield was still efficiently defending the empty ruins. It took 10 years to clear the area of mines; about 55,000 were detected and defused.

Today, the site is a popular attraction with a busy car park area and no more than the natural camouflage. There's a board with a map of the site by the entrance, from which a red-marked trail winds around the bunkers. All structures are identified with numbers and marked with big signs telling you not to enter the ruins, advice that, of course, many people ignore. Of Hitler's bunker (No 13) only one wall survived, but Göring's 'home' (No 16) is in relatively good shape. A memorial plate (placed in 1992) marks the location of Colonel Claus von Stauffenberg's 1944 assassination attempt on Hitler (see the boxed text above), and a small exhibition room houses a scale model of the original camp layout.

English-, German- and Russian-speaking guides are available for 50zł per 1½ hour tour; if that's too much, you may be able to negotiate late in the day, or just buy the detailed information booklet (12zł). It can be worth bringing mosquito repellent in summer.

Sleeping & Eating

Hotel Wilcze Gniazdo (☎ 752 44 29; s 70zł, d 80-90zł, tr 130zł; **P**) The former officers hostel at the entrance to the complex has been fully refurbished to serve as a hotel, and is certainly a

WARMIA & MASURIA

lot more comfortable than the dank remains of the bunkers. There's also a snack bar and a budget restaurant on the site. Hotel guests can enter the bunker complex for free.

Getting There & Away
PKS buses between Kętrzyn (3.30zł, 15 minutes) and Węgorzewo (6.30zł, 45 minutes) stop here several times a day. You can also go to Kętrzyn by suburban bus 1.

WĘGORZEWO
☎ 87 / pop 12,500

The small but busy town of Węgorzewo (ven-go-*zheh*-vo) on Lake Mamry is the northernmost lakeside centre for both excursion boats and independent sailors. The main town itself isn't quite on the lake shore, but is linked to it by a 2km river canal.

Less overrun by tourists than its southern cousins Giżycko and Mikołajki, Węgorzewo is an amenable place to start or end a lake cruise, and offers good transport links east and west. If you turn up on the first weekend of August you'll encounter a large craft fair, which has taken place for 25 years and attracts plenty of artisans from the region and beyond. It's a good way to get the flavour of the whole Masurian culture.

Information
Klub Internetowy (☎ 427 50 74; ul Teatralna 1D; per hr 3zł; ☉ 10am-9pm)
PKO Bank (☎ 427 40 60; Plac Wolności 18)
Tourist office (☎ 427 40 09; www.wegorzewo.pl in Polish; Plac Wolności 11; ☉ 9am-6pm Mon-Fri, 10am-3pm Sat & Sun)

Activities
Masuria isn't normally seen as an extreme-sports destination, but the company **S-Borg** (☎ 427 49 39; www.s-borg.pl in Polish) seems to be aiming to change that – off-roading, climbing, diving, paintballing and bungee are just some of the oddball pastimes on offer, if a boat ride's too stately for you.

Cycling is also a good way to appreciate the picturesque surroundings. Keen peddlers can take advantage of 18 marked routes in the area, with well-planned circuits ranging from 25km to 109km.

Sleeping & Eating
As the focus of activity is on the lake area, you won't find that many places to stay around the centre. There are dozens of pensions and larger leisure facilities spread out in the surrounding area, particularly in the lakeside suburb of Kal, but they can be tricky to get to and usually only open in summer.

Pensjonat Nautic (☎ 427 20 80; www.nautic.pl; ul Słowackiego 14; s 100zł, d 180-210zł, q 400zł, apt 250-580zł; ℗) An excellent and versatile family guesthouse near the canal and the boat wharf. Rooms range from comfortable standard en suites with blue wood fittings to a pair of amazing apartments with their own kitchenettes and terraces. The restaurant here also comes recommended.

Stanica Wodna PTTK (☎ 427 24 43; ul Wańkowicza 3; dm/s/d 35/70/90zł; ℗) The PTTK does its usual good job of covering the budget end of the spectrum, setting up shop in a handy central location. Cheaper shared-bathroom beds are only available in summer.

Pensjonat Pod Dębami (☎ 427 22 18; ul Łuczańska 33; r per person 40zł; ℗) Two kilometres from the centre on the Giżycko road, this decent farmhouse-cottage pension offers accommodation with a touch of traditional rustic style, surrounded by a neat garden (badminton net included).

Camping Nr 175 Rusałka (☎ 427 21 91; www.cmazur elknet.pl in Polish & German; ul Leśna 2; camp site per adult/child 13/8zł, cabins 100-176zł; ☉ May-Sep) With its pleasant wooded grounds, a restaurant, and boats and kayaks for hire, Rusałka is a good place and well run, though most cabins are pretty basic. It's on Lake Święcajty, 4km from Węgorzewo off the Giżycko road. Infrequent PKS buses go there in season; if you don't want to wait, take any bus to Giżycko, get out at the turn-off and walk the last 1km.

Getting There & Away
Trains no longer operate here but the bus terminal, 1km northwest of the centre, provides reasonable transport to Giżycko (6.20zł, 55 minutes, at least hourly) and Kętrzyn (8zł, 55 minutes, hourly); buses to Kętrzyn via Radzieje will drop you at the entrance to the Wolf's Lair. Several buses go to Gołdap (8.40zł, 1½ hours), from where you can continue to Stańczyki and Suwałki. Four fast buses run directly to Warsaw (38zł, 5½ hours); book in advance in the high season.

From July to August, there's an afternoon excursion boat that goes to Giżycko (adult/concession 37zł/27zł, 2½ hours).

GIŻYCKO

☎ 87 / pop 31,000

Positioned on the northern shore of Lake Niegocin, Giżycko (ghee-*zhits*-ko) is the largest sailing centre in the lakes, and the focal point of the seasonal tourist trade here. The town started life under the Teutonic Knights but was destroyed on numerous occasions by Lithuanians, Poles, Swedes, Tatars, Russians and Germans in turn.

Today, Giżycko is a rather ordinary place with more bustle than character. It's essentially a transport hub and provision base for the holiday homes and water-sports centres that have grown up outside the town, and for the hordes of lake-bound holiday-makers who arrive en masse in the short summer season. You'll find it's a useful springboard for the whole of the Masurian lake district, and the mighty fortress is worth a look, if you have some time to kill in town.

Orientation

Giżycko sits on the bank of Lake Niegocin and is split neatly by the Łuczański Canal, which separates the fortress area from the centre of town and the main marina. Motorists should note that the rotary bridge on ul Moniuszki opens six times daily to allow boats through, closing to traffic for between 30 minutes and 1¾ hours each time. Take the long way round via ul Obwodowa if you don't want to wait. Pedestrians can just take the footbridge, 100m to the north of the rotary bridge.

Information

Bank Pekao ATM (ul Olsztyńska 15A)
Main post office (☎ 429 28 34; ul Pocztowa 2)
Orbis Travel (☎ 428 31 12; ul Dąbrowskiego 3)
Romix Internet (☎ 429 29 97; ul Olsztyńska 11B; per hr 3.50zł; ☯ 9am-9pm)
Tourist office (☎ 428 52 65; www.gizycko.turystyka.pl; ul Warszawska 7; ☯ 8am-7pm Mon-Fri, 10am-4pm Sat & Sun Jun-Aug, Mon-Sat only Jun & Sep, Mon-Fri only Oct-Apr)

Sights

BOYEN FORTRESS

Named after the then Prussian minister of war, General Hermann von Boyen, the **Boyen Fortress** (Twierdza Boyen; adult/concession fortress & museum 5/2zł) was built between 1844 and 1855 to protect the kingdom's border with Russia. Since the frontier ran north–south along the 90km string of lakes, the

stronghold was strategically placed in the middle, on the isthmus near Giżycko.

The fortress, which consists of several bastions and defensive towers surrounded by a moat, was continually modified and strengthened, and successfully withstood Russian attacks during WWI. In WWII, it was a defensive outpost of the Wolf's Lair, given up to the Red Army without a fight during the 1945 offensive. The fortifications have survived in pretty good shape, though they're slowly being taken over by bushes. There's an amphitheatre and youth hostel here, while some of the old buildings are used as storage rooms. In the hostel building is a small **museum** (☯ summer only) dedicated to the fortress.

Activities

YACHT CHARTERS

With **yachting** such a huge business here, the boat-charter market is highly volatile and operators often change. The tourist office is likely to have the current list of agents and can provide advice. It's also worth getting a copy of the monthly yachting magazine *Żagle*, in which plenty of firms advertise.

Giżycko has the largest number of yacht-charter agencies in the area, and accordingly offers the widest choice of boats. The town is also a recognised centre for disabled sailors, with regular national regattas, and many companies provide specialist equipment, advice and training.

Finding anything in July and August without advance booking can be difficult. Boats are much easier to find in early June and late September, but shop around, as prices and conditions vary substantially and bargaining is possible with some agents.

In July and August, expect to pay somewhere between 150zł and 900zł per day for a sailing boat large enough to sleep around four to five people, depending on the size of cabins, toilet and kitchen facilities and so on. Prices are significantly lower in June and September – often half of the high-season prices. You pay for your own petrol, though most firms throw in a few litres for free.

Check the state of the boat and its equipment in detail, and report every deficiency and bit of damage in advance to avoid hassles when returning the boat. Come prepared with your own equipment, such as sleeping bag, sturdy rain gear and torch.

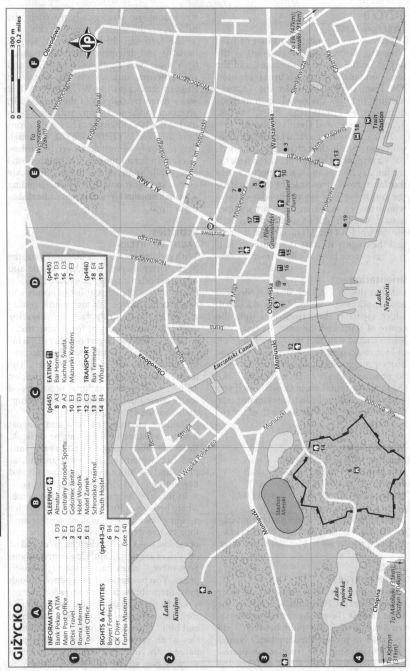

GIŻYCKO

300 m
0.2 miles

Charter operators:

Bełbot (☎ 428 03 85; www.marina.com.pl in Polish)

Grzymała (☎ 428 62 76; http://czarter.mazury.info.pl)

Osmolik Romuald (☎ 428 86 86; www.osmolik.trinet .pl in Polish)

PUH Żeglarz (☎ 428 20 84; www.zeglarz-czartery.pl in Polish)

Sygnet (☎ 89-751 86 77; www.sygnet-czarter.com.pl in Polish)

DIVING

CK Diver (☎ 428 43 62; www.ckdiver.suw.pl in Polish; ul Mickiewicza 9) offers scuba-diving courses for all levels throughout the year, in groups or on an individual basis. Prices start at 100zł for a taster session, going up to 1600zł for advanced tuition.

Festivals & Events

St John's Night (Noc Świętojńska; ☎ 428 43 26) Street festival in honour of the apostle, held in late June.

Giżycko Festival (☎ 428 43 26) Concerts, performances and special events, held in the fortress in July.

St Bruno's Fair (☎ 428 43 26) Held in July.

Sleeping

Like most summer-holiday centres, accommodation rates change notably, peaking in July and August. The rates given here are for this peak season. Many places stay closed for the rest of the year.

Gościniec Jantar (☎ 428 54 15; ul Warszawska 10; s/d 120/180zł; P) Stacked above its own traditional restaurant in the centre of town, this is an excellent little guesthouse with 12 pine-filled rooms, thick rugs and a personable German-speaking owner. Rooms at the rear have balconies, though there's not a whole lot to see.

Hotel Wodnik (☎ 428 38 72; www.cmazur.elknet.pl in Polish & German; ul 3 Maja 2; s/d/ste 180/250/400zł; P) Giżycko's only real upmarket option is more notable for its amenities (currency-exchange office, restaurant, bar, solarium, pool table) than for its rooms (small and confusingly numbered). The comfort level's fine, however, and prices drop by 40% out of season.

Youth hostel (☎ 428 29 59; ul Turystyczna 1; dm 15zł; P) It has to be said, staying inside the brick buttresses of the Boyen Fortress itself is pretty damn cool, even if the large, basic dorms are no better than you'd expect from an average army barracks.

Schronisko Krasnal (☎ 428 22 24; krasnal@ssm krasnal.prv.pl; ul Kolejowa 10; dm 15zł) The Hostelling International–affiliated Krasnal has 30 year-round beds, plus another 20 in July and August. The building is actually a preschool, so it's a lot brighter than most similar hostels and has a playground in the garden.

Centralny Ośrodek Sportu (COS; ☎ 428 23 35; recepcja@gizycko.cos.pl; ul Moniuszki 22; s/d/cabins 110/150/175zł; P) The COS is a typical large activity centre on Lake Kisajno, offering accommodation in a variety of cabins and hotel rooms. It has eating and sports facilities, equipment hire and yacht charters.

Almatur (☎ 428 59 71; www.sail-almatur.pl in Polish; ul Moniuszki 24; d 85zł, cabins 60-360zł; P) Like the COS, Almatur is a large waterside centre with a full spectrum of leisure activities, run by the Almatur student travel agency.

Motel Zamek (☎ 428 24 19; www.cmazur.elknet .pl in Polish; ul Moniuszki 1; camping per person 25zł, d 130-160zł; P) One of a gaggle of options on the fortress peninsula, Zamek follows the American motel model, with a separate parking garage under each room. It's a nice spot, and you can camp next door in summer. Boat, bike and kayak hire available.

Eating

In the high season you only have to wander down to the waterfront to find dozens of temporary cafés, stands and snack bars catering for the holiday crowds. Outside these times you'll have to choose from the hotel restaurants and a handful of other year-round eateries in the centre.

Mazurski Kredens (☎ 428 58 41; Plac Grunwaldzki 1; mains 8.90-39.90zł; lunch & dinner) Mine the rich vein of Masurian regional cooking at this smart little restaurant, tricked out with the usual rustic bits and bobs. Even with a main road outside, the interior exudes a relaxed ambience.

Kuchnia Świata (☎ 429 22 55; ul Olsztyńska 3A; mains 7.90-39.90zł; lunch & dinner) The only bar-restaurant worthy of the name. A varied menu (Polish to Chinese via Italian) and occasional live music bring in consistent crowds, as does the trellised summer terrace.

Bar Hornet (☎ 428 12 67; Plac Grunwaldzki 12; mains 7-21zł; breakfast, lunch & dinner) The enterprising Hornet splits itself into two sections, a self-service cafeteria and a smarter sit-down restaurant. The only difference between them is the waiters, but it's nice to have a choice! The food's respectable value anyway, and the wooden decking is good for warm evenings.

Getting There & Away

BOAT

Żegluga Mazurska boats operate from May to September, with extra services in July and August. There are two daily departures to Mikołajki (adult/concession 48zł/35zł, 4½ hours) via Rydzewo, and one daily trip north to Węgorzewo (37zł/27zł, 2½ hours). If you want to stay around town, you can take a spin around Lake Niegocin (25zł/20zł, 80 minutes) or an evening dancing cruise (48zł, two hours). The wharf is near the train station.

BUS

Next to the train station, the bus terminal offers hourly services to Węgorzewo (6.20zł, 55 minutes) and Mrangowo (8.40zł, 1¼ hours). Regular buses run to Mikołajki (6.90zł, one hour, 10 daily), Kętrzyn (6.90zł, 40 minutes, eight daily) and Olsztyn (16zł, three hours, 11 daily), and Suwałki (16zł, two hours, seven daily). Two buses go to Lidzbark Warmiński (13.20zł, 1¾ hours), and up to seven fast buses serve Warsaw (35zł, five hours).

Heading to the Baltic, an international overnight bus to Vilnius (50zł, eight hours) comes through three times a week.

TRAIN

The train station is on the southern edge of town near the lake. Trains run to Ełk (8.20zł, 50 minutes, 11 daily) and to Olsztyn (15.90zł, two hours, nine daily) via Kętrzyn (5.70zł, 35 minutes), with three fast trains each to Gdańsk (43.04zł, 5¼ hours) and Białystok (30.03zł, 2½ hours). Trains to Warsaw (44.65zł, six hours) take a roundabout route – it's faster to go by bus.

MIKOŁAJKI

☎ 87 / pop 4000

Smaller than Giżycko but at least as popular, Mikołajki (mee-ko-*wahy*-kee) is important as a base for the Great Masurian Lakes. Perched on picturesque narrows crossed by three bridges, the town has a collection of fine red-roofed houses and a lively waterfront packed with hundreds of yachts in summer. Tourism has virtually taken over here, with a strong German presence, and seemingly every other building caters for the seasonal trade one way or another.

Like most resorts of this kind, Mikołajki lives a frenetic life in July and August, takes it easy in June and September, and dies al-

most totally the rest of the year. As it lies on the main waterway linking Giżycko with Ruciane-Nida, and is the gateway to the vast Lake Śniardwy, yacht and pleasure-boat traffic is often gridlocked here in summer. Luckily the energy and charm of the town soothe petty frustrations, and once you're waterborne, you won't regret coming.

Information

Piwnica Internetowa (ul Szkolna 4D; per hr 6zł; ☒ 10am-10pm)
PKO Bank (☎ 421 69 36; Plac Wolności 7)
Tourist office (☎ 421 68 50; www.mikolajki.pl in Polish; Plac Wolności 3; ☒ 9am-8pm)

Activities

BOAT HIRE

As in Giżycko, yacht hire is big business here in summer, and dozens of companies vie for the seasonal trade. The **Wioska Żeglarska** (☎ 421 60 40; ul Kowalska 3), on the waterfront, has sailing boats for hire, or staff may be able to advise you on other companies if they're booked out. See p443 for more information on yacht charters.

For shorter-term excursions, **Port Rybitwa** (☎ 421 61 63; surf@su.onet.pl; ul Okrężna 5) hires out low-powered motorboats (from 70zł per hour, 350zł per day).

Sleeping & Eating

The centre of town is largely reserved for 'proper' hotels. In the outer areas, small pensions do a roaring trade and lots of private rooms become available in summer; the tourist office can provide a full list. On the whole, prices are flexible. Try not to arrive late in the day in midsummer as you could be forced to pay over the odds.

For food, you can amble along the waterfront in summer and take your pick from the competing restaurants, stalls, cafés and bars. There are also enough year-round places to keep you from starving, if you happen by out of season.

Hotel Mazur (☎ 421 69 41; www.hotelmazur.com.pl; Plac Wolności 6; d 200zł; **P**) Stylish and refined, the Mazur dominates Mikołajki's main square – unsurprising considering it used to be the town hall. Luckily you don't have to dabble in politics to enjoy the discreet rooms and ample facilities.

Hotel Król Sielaw (☎ 421 63 23; ul Kajki 5; s/d/tr 80/140/180zł; apt 240-320zł; **P**) Rustic beams

WARMIA & MASURIA

and twee crafts provide the usual touch of colour in these very reasonable rooms, with the country theme continued in the unpretentious fish restaurant downstairs. Staff can be flustered by foreigners but is always friendly.

Pensjonat Mikołajki (☎ 421 64 37; www.pensjonat mikolajki.prv.pl; ul Kajki 18; s 120zł d 160-180zł; ste 340zł) This lovely, timbered modern villa offers some superb lake views to the select few who book earliest. Rooms without en suite are also available.

Pensjonat As (☎ 421 68 89; Osiedle Na Górce 7; s/d/tr 100/130/150zł; ✄) One of a dense collection of pensions just off the road to Ruciane-Nida. The friendly family owners let you choose from a motley range of strangely shaped rooms and are generally eager to please.

Hotel Gołębiewski (☎ 429 07 00; www.golebiewski .pl; ul Mrągowska 34; s 330-395zł, d 385-470zł, ste 700zł; P ᴥ) Full service hits Masuria: this five-star complex leaves nothing to be desired, with three restaurants, a nightclub, bowling, a sauna, tennis courts, a marina and its own indoor aqua park. Prices are surprisingly uninflated for what you get, and there are some cracking special offers.

Camping Nr 2 Wagabunda (☎ 421 60 18; www .wagabunda-mikolajki.pl; ul Leśna 2; camping per person 10zł, cabins 80-250zł; ☼ May-Sep) The Wagabunda is the town's main camping ground. It's across the bridge from the centre and a 600m walk southwest. In addition to the camping area it has plenty of small cabins that vary in standard and price.

Restauracja Prohibicja (☎ 0602 472 27 13; Plac Handlowy 13; mains 14-38zł; P) Of all the gin joints in all the world, Mikołajki is the last place you'd expect to find a gangster-themed bar-restaurant. If you fancy sleeping with the fishes, there's also a fistful of hotel rooms upstairs. Despite the name, alcohol is sold over the counter, and it's all family-friendly, of course. Fittingly, there's an Alcatraz elsewhere in town.

Getting There & Away
BOAT
From May to September, boats ply the main routes from Mikołajki to Giżycko (adult/concession 40zł/32zł, three hours) and Ruciane (36zł/27zł, two hours), the round trip to Lake Śniardwy (25zł/18zł, 1½ hours), and combination routes (eg Mikołajki–Lake Śniardwy–Ruciane; 40zł/32zł, 2½ hours).

BUS
The bus terminal is in the centre, near the Protestant church. Buses to Mrągowo (5.60zł, 40 minutes) run roughly every hour; change there for Olsztyn or Kętrzyn. Ten buses go to Giżycko daily (6.90zł, one hour), and there's one service to Suwałki (15.50zł, 1¾ hours). Six buses depart daily to Warsaw (39zł, five hours) in summer and are much faster than the trains.

TRAIN
The sleepy train station is 1km from the centre, on the Giżycko road. It handles just a few trains a day to Ełk (10.50zł, 1¼ hours), Olsztyn (13.10zł two hours) and Białystok (19.70zł, 3½ hours).

ŁUKNAJNO RESERVE
The shallow 700-hectare **Lake Łuknajno**, 4km east of Mikołajki, shelters Europe's largest surviving community of wild swans (*Cygnus olor*) and is home to many other birds – 128 species have been recorded here. The 1200- to 2000-strong swan population nests in April and May but stays at the lake all summer. A few observation towers beside the lake make swan-viewing possible.

A rough road from Mikołajki goes to the lake but there's no public transport. Walk 3.5km until you get to a sign that reads '*do wieży widokowej*' (to the viewing tower), then continue for 10 minutes along the path to the lake shore. The track can be muddy in spring and after rain, so choose your shoes wisely. Depending on the wind, the swans may be close to the tower or far away on the opposite side of the lake.

RUCIANE-NIDA
☎ 87 / pop 6000
Ruciane-Nida (roo-*chah*-neh *nee*-dah) is the southernmost base for the Great Masurian Lakes. Set on the banks of two lakes, **Lake Guzianka Wielka** and **Lake Nidzkie**, the town is surrounded by forest. As the name suggests, it consists of two parts: Nida, an unremarkable collection of apartment blocks, and the busy main lakeside resort of Ruciane, 2km northeast. The halves are linked by Al Wczasów, which runs through woods and is lined with holiday homes. About 1.5km north of Ruciane is the Śluza Guzianka, the only lock on the Great Masurian Lakes.

WARMIA & MASURIA

Ruciane-Nida is a handy point to stop at on your trans-Masurian journey. From here, excursion boats go north to Mikołajki and south to the beautiful Lake Nidzkie. You can also use the town as a jumping-off point to explore the **Puszcza Piska** (Pisz Forest), a vast area of thick woodland to the southeast. There are no marked trails but dirt tracks and paths crisscross the woods; most are OK for bikes.

Sleeping

Ośrodek Wypoczynkowy NBP Guzianka (☎ 424 06 00; guzianka@infowm.pl; ul Guzianka 7; s/d/tr/cabins 70/130/195/280zł; **P**) The superb new Guzianka complex is associated with the National Bank of Poland, a slightly strange side project for such an august institution. Still, it's modern, comfortable and spacious, and the extensive grounds hold four-bed cabins, tennis courts and its own marina. It's about 2km north of the station, near the Guzianka lock.

Dom Wczasowy Perła Jezior (☎ 423 10 44; ruciane@fwp.pl; Al Wczasów 15; s/d 65/110zł; **P**) A cluster of blocks and one cabin make up this large holiday compound, which offers simple, neat rooms with shared facilities towards the Nida end of town. Full board is available.

PTTK Camping No 7 (☎ 423 10 12; Al Wczasów 17; camping per person 10zł, cabins 80-90zł, d 100-140zł, apt 200-240zł; ☼ May-Sep) Further up the road, the resident PTTK site has just about every type of accommodation you could think of, making the most of its tree-lined setting.

Getting There & Away

BOAT

One daily Żegluga Mazurska excursion boat operates to Mikołajki (adult/concession 34zł/25zł, two hours) in summer, with a second going via Lake Śniardwy (38zł/30zł, 2½ hours). A few boats a day depart for round trips south around Lake Nidzkie (18zł/14zł, one hour). Local rival **Faryj** (☎ 423 10 06; www.faryj.pl in Polish) does similar routes, including a Lake Nidzkie tour (10zł/8zł) and Mikołajki via Guzianka (30zł/25zł), and also serves Pisz (40zł/35zł, three hours).

BUS

There are nine buses to Mrągowo (7.30zł, 45 minutes) daily and five to Mikołajki (7.50zł, 35 minutes). One or two buses go as far east as Suwałki daily.

TRAIN

Two trains each serve Olsztyn (15.90zł, two hours) and Pisz (4.60zł, 45 minutes) daily. There's also a weekend connection to Warsaw (23.80zł, six hours) and Łódź (27.50zł, 8¼ hours).

THE AUGUSTÓW-SUWAŁKI REGION

Known as Suwalszczyzna, the far northeastern corner of Poland is noted for its lakeland, a set of waterways in complete contrast to the Great Masurian Lake District. Here the lakes (about 200 altogether) are smaller but deeper and even more crystal-clear than further west. At 108.5m, Lake Hańcza is the deepest lake in the country, and perhaps in the whole Central European lowland. Forests cover only about 20% of the land area, but the terrain is rugged and dramatic, with steep hills and deep valleys.

To the south, towards Augustów, the terrain becomes flatter and more forested. The area east of Augustów, up to the national border, is an uninterrupted stretch of woodland known as the Augustów Forest (Puszcza Augustowska), which is cut in two by the Augustów Canal (Kanał Augustowski).

The modern population of the region consists predominantly of Poles, but it was for centuries an ethnic and religious mosaic comprising Poles, Lithuanians, Belarusians, Tatars, Germans, Jews and Russians. Traces of this complex cultural mix can still be found, at least in the local cemeteries.

Despite its natural beauty, the region is far less visited than the Great Masurian Lakes, perhaps because it's the coldest part of Poland, with snow on the ground for up to a third of the year. Yachting is restricted, as the lakes are smaller and not connected by channels, but canoeists will be in their element on the local rivers, which are among the best in the country. Walking, cycling and riding are all good alternatives.

There are only two important towns in the region, Augustów and Suwałki, which you may use as a base for further exploration. Though close together, they are notably different from each other and provide access to different parts of the region.

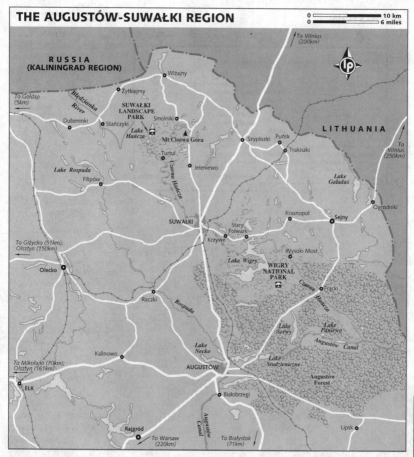

THE AUGUSTÓW-SUWAŁKI REGION

0 — 10 km
0 — 6 miles

RUSSIA
(KALININGRAD REGION)

To Vilnius
(200km)

Wiżajny

To Gołdap
(5km)

Błędzianka
River

Żytkiejmy

SUWAŁKI
LANDSCAPE
PARK

Smolniki

LITHUANIA

Dubeninki

Stańczyki

Lake
Hańcza

Mt Cisowa Góra

Szypliszki

Puńsk

Turtul

Trakiszki

To
Vilnius
(250km)

Lake Rospuda

Czarna Hańcza

Jeleniewo

Lake
Galadś

Filipów

SUWAŁKI

Stary
Folwark

Krasnopol

Sejny

Ogrodniki

To Giżycko (51km);
Olsztyn (150km)

Krzywe

Wysoki Most

Olecko

Lake Wigry

WIGRY
NATIONAL
PARK

Czarna Hańcza

Frącki

Raczki

Rospuda

Lake
Serwy

Lake
Paniewo

Augustów Canal

To Mikołajki (70km);
Olsztyn (161km)

Kalinowo

Lake
Necko

Lake
Studzieniczne

Augustów
Forest

EŁK

AUGUSTÓW

Białobrzegi

Augustów Canal

Rajgród

To Warsaw
(220km)

To Białystok
(71km)

Lipsk

AUGUSTÓW

☎ 87 / pop 30,000

Augustów (aw-*goos*-toof) is a small but sprawling town straddling the River Netta as it enters Lake Necko. It was founded in 1557 by King Zygmunt II August and named after him. Despite the strategic location, its development only really began in the 19th century after the construction of the Augustów Canal (p452), and was further boosted when the Warsaw–St Petersburg railway was completed in 1862.

WWII effectively reset the clock – during the two-month battle in 1944 the town switched hands several times and 70% of it was destroyed. Predictably, there's not much to see of the prewar architecture, which was replaced with residential blocks numbered so confusingly that they have to have their address painted on the side.

Of course, it's not the town that's the attraction but its surroundings. The beautiful Augustów Forest begins just on the eastern outskirts of the town, encompassing the spectacular Czarna Hańcza River and the unusual Augustów Canal. The town is a handy base for these places and has become the most-popular waterside centre in this corner of Poland, even regaining a modicum of charm with its leafy lakeside setting.

Information

Atol tourist office (☎ 643 28 83; www.augustow.pl in Polish; Rynek 44; ◔ 8am-8pm Mon-Fri, 10am-6pm Sat & Sun)

AUGUSTÓW

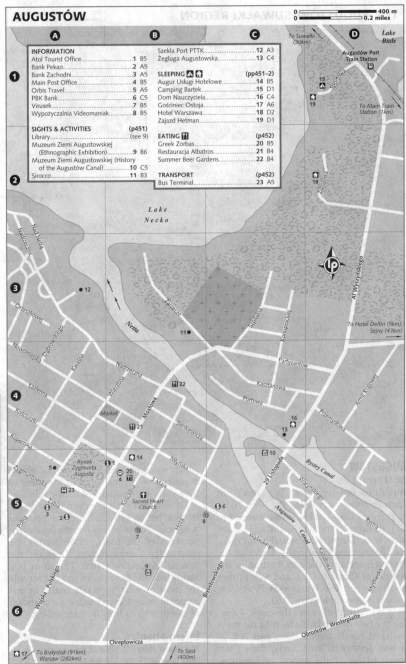

0		400 m
0		0.2 miles

INFORMATION
Atol Tourist Office...................................1 B5
Bank Pekao..2 A5
Bank Zachodni...3 A5
Main Post Office.......................................4 B5
Orbis Travel..5 A5
PBK Bank...6 C5
Virusek...7 B5
Wypożyczalnia Videomaniak....................8 B5

SIGHTS & ACTIVITIES   (p451)
Library..(see 9)
Muzeum Ziemi Augustowskiej
   (Ethnographic Exhibition)......................9 B6
Muzeum Ziemi Augustowskiej (History
   of the Augustów Canal)........................10 C5
Sirocco...11 B3

Szekla Port PTTK....................................12 A3
Żegluga Augustowska..............................13 C4

SLEEPING   (pp451–2)
Augur Usługi Hotelowe............................14 B5
Camping Bartek......................................15 D1
Dom Nauczyciela.....................................16 C4
Gościniec Ostoja......................................17 A6
Hotel Warszawa......................................18 D2
Zajazd Hetman..19 D1

EATING   (p452)
Greek Zorbas...20 B5
Restauracja Albatros................................21 B4
Summer Beer Gardens..............................22 B4

TRANSPORT   (p452)
Bus Terminal..23 A5

To Suwałki (30km)

Lake Białe

Augustów Port Train Station

To Main Train Station (1km)

Lake Necko

To Hotel Delfin (5km); Sejny (43km)

Netta

Zarzecze

Market

Rynek Zygmunta Augusta

Sacred Heart Church

3 Maja

Bystry Canal

Augustów Canal

To Białystok (91km); Warsaw (282km)

Chreptowicza

To Szoł (400m)

Bank Pekao (☎ 643 66 27; ul Żabia 3)
Bank Zachodni (☎ 643 57 30; ul Żabia 9/1)
Main post office (☎ 643 41 12; Rynek 3)
Orbis Travel (☎ 643 26 13; Rynek 22)
PBK Bank (☎ 643 34 06; ul 3 Maja 43)
Virusek (☎ 644 51 28; ul Ks Skorup 10/3; per hr 3zł; ☯ noon-10pm) Internet access.
Wypożyczalnia Videomaniak (☎ 643 53 39; ul 3 Maja 46; per hr 3zł; ☯ 10am-10pm)

Sights

REGIONAL MUSEUM

The most important sight in town, the **Muzeum Ziemi Augustowskiej**, is at two locations. The main section, featuring a small **ethnographic exhibition** (☎ 643 27 54; ul Hoża 7; adult/concession 3/2zł; ☯ 9am-4pm Tue-Sun), is on the 3rd floor of the tatty, modern public library. There is also a more interesting section dedicated to the history of the **Augustów Canal** (☎ 643 23 60; ul 29 Listopada 5A; adult/concession 3/2zł; ☯ 9am-4pm Tue-Sun), housed in a quaint, 19th-century wooden cabin in front of some council offices.

Activities

KAYAKING

Kayak trips are absolutely the best reason to come to Augustów, and while your arms may feel the strain, the scenery is well worth a few aching muscles. Tours are organised by numerous local operators, including several hotels and hostels. They all run various routes on the different rivers in the region, and can create personal itineraries according to your requirements and time availability. Alternatively, kayaks can be hired individually (around 18zł per day), so you can head out on your own tour.

The Czarna Hańcza River is the most popular kayaking destination in the region. The traditional route is designed as a loop, beginning in Augustów and leading along the Augustów Canal as far as Lake Serwy and up to the northern end of this lake. The kayaks are then transported overland to Lake Wigry or the village of Wysoki Most on the Czarna Hańcza, from where canoeists follow the river downstream to the Augustów Canal and return to Augustów. The full loop takes 12 days with stops, and should cost around 800zł all-inclusive (camping accommodation). Various shorter trips are also available: for example, **Szot** (☎ 643 43 99; www.szot.pl; ul Konwaliowa 2) organises one-day trips through arguably the most spectacular bit of the Czarna

Hańcza, the 25km journey from Frącki to Jałowy Róg (130zł/€38 per person).

Other rivers used for kayaking trips by tour operators include the Rospuda (four to six days) and the Biebrza (seven to 10 days); some will even take you right the way into Lithuania (seven days).

Other kayak operators:
Sirocco (☎ 643 31 18; sirocco@formica.pl; ul Zarzecze 5A)
Szekla Port PTTK (☎ 643 38 50; www.szekla.pl in Polish; ul Nadrzeczna 70A)

BOAT EXCURSIONS

From May to September, pleasure boats operated by **Żegluga Augustowska** (☎ 643 28 81; ul 29 Listopada 7) ply the surrounding lakes and a part of the Augustów Canal to the east of town. All trips depart from and return to the **wharf** (ul 29 Listopada).

Boats depart hourly from 10am to 5.15pm in July and August, and twice daily the rest of summer. The shortest trips (15zł, 1½ hours) will take you around the Necko and Białe Lakes but don't go along the canal. More interesting are the cruises further east along the canal system; the longest is currently the trip to Lake Studzieniczne (35zł, 3½ hours).

Festivals & Events

Augustów Theatre Summer Held in July and August.
Polish Sailing in Anything Championships (Mistrzostwa Polski w Pływaniu na Byle Czym; ☎ 643 36 59) Highly bizarre and entertaining open event for home-made vessels, held in August.

Sleeping

There's a range of year-round hotels and hostels scattered throughout the town, which is about 4km long from end to end. Plenty of holiday homes open in summer and accommodate individual tourists whenever they have vacancies.

Gościniec Ostoja (☎ 643 02 22; ul Wojska Polskiego 53A; s/d 60/100zł; Ⓟ ⌨) At the southern end of town, this family house provides excellent homy accommodation in a range of individually furnished rooms. It's spacious, the bathrooms are gleaming and breakfast is substantial, certainly enough to make up for minor niggles such as dodgy TV reception, road noise and a lack of curtains.

Hotel Warszawa (☎ 643 28 05; www.hotelwarszawa.pl; ul Zdrojowa 1; s/d/tr/ste 200/300/370/550zł; Ⓟ) It's not clear why you'd want a taste of Warsaw out in rural Masuria, but luckily this prestige three-star doesn't live up to its name. It hides discreetly amid the trees in a fine lakeside location, and the facilities include a restaurant, a bar, a sauna, bikes, boats and classic-car hire.

Dom Nauczyciela (☎ 643 20 21; www.dn.augustow .pl in Polish; ul 29 Listopada 9; s/d/tr 85/120/140zł; **P**) Right by the pleasure-boat wharf, the DN is a neat and very reasonable option with its own restaurant and a travel agency offering all the usual regional activities. Some cheaper shared-bathroom accommodation is also available.

Augur Usługi Hotelowe (☎ 643 62 17; www.augur .pl in Polish; ul 3 Maja 1; s/d/tr 75/100/120zł, 6-bed r 180zł; **P**) Self-catering accommodation bang in the centre of town. Rooms are plain but have en suite and TV, and share a communal kitchen; character comes in the form of a stone-clad dining/function room and a small paved garden area.

Hotel Delfin (☎ 644 31 12; www.hotel-delfin.com .pl in Polish; ul Turystyczna 81; s/d/tr/ste €62.50/75/ 87.50/107.50; **P** **⊠** **♨**) If you want the full resort experience, this expanding complex, located east of town, really does the business, with comprehensive spa-and-fitness facilities, boat trips, equipment hire and its own water park. Harassed parents can take advantage of a free child-minding service.

Zajazd Hetman (☎ 644 53 45; ul Sportowa 1; d/tr 115/140zł; **P**) Designed in 1939 by Polish architect Maciej Nowicki, later codesigner of the UN building in New York, the Hetman was once hailed as 'a model of tourist investment'. Today it's little more than acceptable, but does offer a range of rooms in a pleasant lakefront setting. The hotel also runs the basic Camping Bartek, just opposite.

Eating

Augustów is fairly light on year-round restaurants. In summer, head to the semi-permanent **beer gardens** (ul Mostowa), by the Netta bridge, for cheap food and drink in a festive atmosphere.

Greek Zorbas (☎ 643 29 39; ul Kościelna 4; mains 9.50-29.50zł; ♥ lunch & dinner) Unaccountably the most popular place in town, Zorbas is about as Greek as Pavarotti, but the meaty maestro would doubtless approve of the pizza- and pasta-based menu, not to mention the token slabs of moussaka.

Restauracja Albatros (☎ 643 21 23; ul Mostowa 3; mains 9-18zł; ♥ lunch & dinner) The Albatros is pitched halfway between a cafeteria and a proper restaurant, offering cut-price lunch deals and dancing in the evenings.

Getting There & Away
BUS
The bus terminal is on the southern side of the Rynek and handles roughly hourly services to Białystok (13.20zł, two hours) and Suwałki (7.50zł, 45 minutes). There are five buses directly to Warsaw (33zł, 4½ hours); all come through from Suwałki and can be full. Four buses a day run to Sejny (8.40zł, one hour), and two international buses head to Vilnius (45zł, 6½ hours) every week.

TRAIN
Augustów has two train stations, but both are a long way from the town centre. Augustów Port train station is convenient for some of the lakeside hotels, but fast trains don't stop there and it doesn't have a ticket office.

There are two fast trains, leaving from the main station, to Warsaw (43.04zł, five hours) daily, going via Sokółka and Białystok. There are also six trains a day to Suwałki (6.80zł, 50 minutes).

AROUND AUGUSTÓW
Augustów Canal
Built in the 1820s, the Augustów Canal (Kanał Augustowski) is a 102km-long waterway connecting the Biebrza and Niemen Rivers. Linking lakes and stretches of river with artificial channels, it's a picturesque route marked with old locks and floodgates. No longer used commercially, it's experiencing a renaissance as a tourist attraction and kayak route.

The canal begins at the confluence of the Netta and Biebrza Rivers and flows for 33km north to Augustów through low and swampy meadows. It then continues eastwards through a chain of wooded lakes to the border with Belarus, where it extends into foreign territory for another 19km. This eastern part is the most spectacular, and should be included in your itinerary however long you plan to spend in the region.

A remarkable achievement of 19th-century hydraulic engineering, the canal was built by the short-lived Congress Kingdom of Poland. It was intended to provide the country with an alternative outlet to the Baltic Sea, since the lower Vistula was in the hands of a hostile Prussia. The project aimed to connect the tributaries of the Vistula with the Niemen River and to reach the Baltic at the port of Ventspils in Latvia. Despite the round about route, this seemed to be the most viable way of getting goods abroad.

The Polish part of the waterway was designed by an army engineer, General Ignacy Prądzyński, and built in just seven years (1824–30), though final works continued until 1839. The Russians were meant to build their part from the town of Kaunas up to Ventspils around the same time, but the work was never completed.

The Augustów Canal ended up as a regional waterway, and though it contributed to local development, it never became an international trade route. Its route includes 28km of lakes, 34km of canalised rivers and 40km of canal proper. There are 18 locks along the way (14 in Poland) whose purpose is to bridge the 55m change in water level. The lock in Augustów itself has an extra twist to its history: badly damaged in WWII, it was rebuilt in 1947 – in a completely different location!

The whole Polish stretch of the canal is navigable, but tourist boats from Augustów only go as far east as Lake Gorczyckie – the locks beyond this point are inoperative. By kayak, you can continue to the border. Contact tour companies (see p451) for information, tour options and kayak-hire conditions.

Augustów Forest

The Augustów Forest (Puszcza Augustowska) stretches east of Augustów, as far as the Lithuanian-Belarussian border. At about 1100 sq km, it's Poland's largest continuous forest after the Bory Dolnośląskie in Lower Silesia. It's a remnant of the vast primeval forest that once covered much of eastern Poland and southern Lithuania.

The forest is made up mainly of pine and spruce, with colourful deciduous species such as birch, oak, elm, lime, maple and aspen. The wildlife is rich and diversified, and includes beavers, wild boars, wolves, deer and even some elks. Birds are also well represented and the lakes abound in fish. There are 55 lakes in the forest.

The forest was virtually unexplored until the 17th century. Today there are paved roads, dirt tracks and paths crisscrossing the woodland, yet large stretches remain almost untouched, and if you want to get firmly off the beaten track then this is a great swathe of nature to do it in.

You can explore part of the forest using private transport; roads will take you along the Augustów Canal almost to the border. Many of the rough tracks are perfectly OK for bikes and horses, and on foot you can get almost everywhere except the swamps. Bikes can be hired out in Augustów; the **Atol tourist office** (in Augustów ☎ 643 28 83; www .augustow.pl in Polish; Rynek 44; ☺ 8am-8pm Mon-Fri, 10am-6pm Sat & Sun) can provide information, including brochures on cycle routes in the forest. The detailed *Puszcza Augustowska* map (scale 1:70,000) shows all the roads, tracks and tourist trails.

SUWAŁKI

☎ 87 / pop 65,000

Suwałki (soo-*vahw*-kee) appeared on the map at the end of the 17th century as one of the villages established by the Camaldolese monks from Wigry. The small multinational community grew slowly; at different times it included Jews, Lithuanians, Tatars, Russians, Germans and Old Believers, a religious group that split off from the Russian Orthodox Church in the 17th century.

Suwałki is the largest town in the region, but lacks the lakes and forests that popularised Augustów and is far less visited. There are no holiday homes, nor much in the way of facilities. It's a gateway to the surrounding countryside rather than a destination in itself, and if you're not getting out and about you won't find much reason to stay.

Information

Bank Pekao (☎ 565 32 41; ul Noniewicza 95)
Internet Café Grand (☎ 565 06 69; ul Korczaka 2A; per hr 3zł)
Post office (☎ 565 17 72; ul Sejneńska 13)
Tourist office (☎ 566 58 72; www.sirt.suwalki.com.pl in Polish; ul Kościuszki 45; ☺ 8am-6pm Mon-Fri, 9am-2pm Sat Jun-Aug, 8am-4pm Mon-Fri Sep-May)

Sights

It might seem a bit grim as an attraction, but the local **cemetery** gives a good picture of the town's ethnic and religious history.

WARMIA & MASURIA

It actually consists of several separate cemeteries for people of the different creeds – the religious tolerance of the community not extending to shared burial grounds.

You'll notice straight away the large size of the **Jewish cemetery** – at the beginning of the 20th century Jews made up half the town's population. Their cemetery was destroyed in WWII and only a memorial stands in the middle, assembled out of fragments of old grave slabs. The tiny **Muslim graveyard** is the last remnant of the Tatars, but the graves are now hardly recognisable.

At the back of the **Orthodox cemetery** is the **Old Believers' graveyard**. A dwindling handful of followers still congregate on Sunday mornings at the **church** (molenna; ul Sejneńska 37A) on the opposite side of town. The simple timber church dates from the beginning of the 20th century, but the icons inside are significantly older. Except for during Mass, you have little chance of seeing them.

The main thoroughfare of the town, ul Kościuszki, retains some 19th-century neoclassical architecture. Here you'll also find the **Regional Museum** (☎ 566 57 50; ul Kościuszki 81; adult/concession 5/3zł; ☽ 8am-4pm Tue-Fri, 9am-5pm Sat & Sun), which presents the little that is known of the Jatzvingians, the first settlers in this area. Its annexe, the **Museum of Maria Konopnicka** (adult/concession combined ticket 7/4zł), is dedicated to one of Poland's best-loved authors and poets.

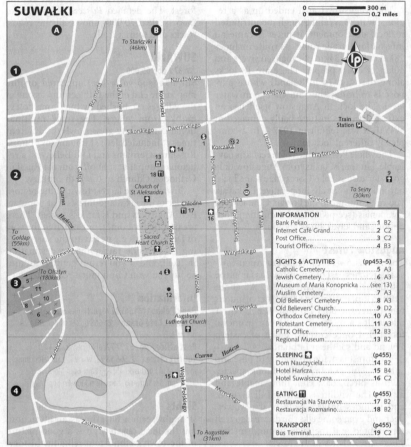

SUWAŁKI

INFORMATION	
Bank Pekao...................................	1 B2
Internet Café Grand.....................	2 C2
Post Office....................................	3 C2
Tourist Office................................	4 B3

SIGHTS & ACTIVITIES	(pp453–5)
Catholic Cemetery.........................	5 A3
Jewish Cemetery............................	6 A3
Museum of Maria Konopnicka ......(see 13)	
Muslim Cemetery...........................	7 A3
Old Believers' Cemetery.................	8 A3
Old Believers' Church....................	9 D2
Orthodox Cemetery.......................	10 A3
Protestant Cemetery.....................	11 A3
PTTK Office...................................	12 B3
Regional Museum..........................	13 B2

SLEEPING 🏠	(p455)
Dom Nauczyciela...........................	14 B2
Hotel Hańcza.................................	15 B4
Hotel Suwalszczyzna.....................	16 C2

EATING 🍴	(p455)
Restauracja Na Starówce................	17 B2
Restauracja Rozmarino..................	18 B2

TRANSPORT	(p455)
Bus Terminal..................................	19 C2

Activities

The **PTTK office** (☎ 566 59 61; ul Kościuszki 37) operates kayak trips down the Czarna Hańcza River (see p451). The office also provides information and hires out kayaks (18zł per day), if you would rather do the trip on your own.

Sleeping & Eating

Suwałki has a decent enough range of accommodation, but don't feel you have to stay in town – this is prime agrotourism territory, and the tourist office and local travel agencies will happily set you up with a rural idyll for a few nights.

Hotel Suwalszczyzna (☎ 565 19 00; www.hotel -suwalszczyzna.suwalki.com.pl in Polish; ul Noniewicza 71A; s/d 140/170zł; **P**) Tucked away behind an unpromising façade, both the hotel and its ground-floor restaurant offer some of the best standards in town. The collection of framed, signed football shirts on the stairway suggests either an abiding passion for soccer or and unusual preponderance of sporting guests.

Dom Nauczyciela (☎ 566 69 00; www.domnauczy ciela.suwalki.pl; ul Kościuszki 120; s 116-148zł, d 148-168zł, tr/q 192/216zł, ste 196-240zł; **P**) This former teachers' dorm has rooms of different sizes and standards; the cheapest ones may be nothing special, but the studio suites are pleasingly plush. The hotel also has a well-rated restaurant – try the 'roast brawn'.

Hotel Hańcza (☎ 566 66 33; www.hotelhancza.com; ul Wojska Polskiego 2; s/d/tr/ste 70/98/145/180zł; **P**) You wouldn't expect much from this huge block in the southern part of town, but actually it's not a bad choice, with lake views and two budget restaurants. It is alarmingly popular with school groups though. Breakfast is 10zł extra.

Restauracja Rozmarino (☎ 566 59 04; ul Kościuszki 75; mains 8.90-24.90zł; ☽ breakfast, lunch & dinner) Never has so much been crammed into so little space with so few negative results. As pizzeria-cum-piano bar-cum-art gallery-cum-restaurants go, this is an amazing place, boasting a two-tiered summer garden for live music, a menu that looks like a newspaper and unusual treats such as crab claws and ostrich balls to shake up the usual Italian suspects. If you do plump for pizza, it comes with a dainty jug of tomato sauce.

Restauracja Na Starówce (☎ 563 02 57; ul Chłodna 2; mains 19.60-31.85zł; ☽ breakfast, lunch & dinner) Trad- itional and sophisticated, the Na Starówce almost seems too ambitious for Suwałki, basing its imaginative menus around regularly changing themes (the French months are highly recommended).

Getting There & Away

The train station is 1.5km northeast of the centre; the bus terminal is closer to the central area. Trains are useful mostly for longer journeys, with several departures a day to Białystok (17.20zł, 2¾ hours) and Warsaw (39.53zł, 5½ hours) and an irregular 2am sleeper to Vilnius (100zł, 6¼ hours).

Buses serve most regional destinations, and also ply intercity routes. Two weekly buses run to Vilnius (4½ to 5½ hours), operated by PKS (20zł) and Biacomex (56zł); local travel agencies also offer regular day trips to Vilnius (60zł).

AROUND SUWAŁKI
Wigry National Park
☎ 87

The Wigry National Park (Wigierski Park Narodowy) covers the whole of Lake Wigry and a wide, predominantly forested belt of land around it that's sprinkled with about 50 small lakes. At 21 sq km, **Lake Wigry** is the largest lake in the region and one of the deepest, reaching 73m at its greatest depth. It's also one of the most beautiful lakes. Its shoreline is richly indented, forming numerous bays and peninsulas, and there are 15 islands on the lake. The Czarna Hańcza River, a favourite among canoeists, flows through the park. The park's wildlife is diverse, including fish, birds and mammals. The beaver is the park's emblem.

There is a **monastery** spectacularly located on a peninsula in Lake Wigry. It was built by the death-obsessed Camaldolese monks (see p145) soon after they were brought to Wigry by King Jan II Kazimierz Waza in 1667. The whole complex, complete with a church and 17 hermitages, was originally on an island, which was later connected to the shore. It has now been turned into a hotel, providing an atmospheric base for exploring the park.

There are marked trails throughout the park, leading to some truly remote corners. You can walk all around the lake (49km by the green trail), provided you have three days. Lakeside camping grounds along the

WARMIA & MASURIA

trail are located within reasonable day-long walking distances. The *Wigierski Park Narodowy* map shows all the necessary detail.

Access is easiest from the Suwałki–Sejny road, which crosses the northern part of the park. The park **headquarters** (☎ 566 63 22) are on this road, in Krzywe, which is 5km from Suwałki.

There's quite a choice of accommodation around the park. The park's headquarters run various lodges and camping grounds in the reserve itself, and there are several agrotourist farms nearby. Suwałki's tourist office will give you details.

The Suwałki–Sejny road is serviced by regular buses. If you want to go directly to the monastery, take the bus to Wigry (four daily buses in summer).

Sejny

☎ 87 / pop 5000

Sejny, 30km east of Suwałki, is the last Polish town before the Ogrodniki border crossing to Lithuania, 12km beyond. The town grew around the Dominican monastery, which had been founded in 1602 by monks from Vilnius. The order was expelled by the Prussian authorities in 1804 and never returned, but the proud two-towered silhouette of their **church** still dominates the town from its northern end. Dating from the 1610s, the façade was thoroughly remodelled 150 years later in the so-called Vilnius baroque style. Its pastel interior has harmonious rococo decoration.

At the opposite, southern end of the town is a large **synagogue**, built by the sizable local Jewish community in the 1880s. During the German occupation it served as a fire station and after the war as a storage room. Today it's an art gallery operated by the **Borderland Foundation** (Fundacja Pogranicze; ☎ 516 27 65), focusing on the arts and culture of different ethnic and religious traditions from the region.

Hourly buses run from Sejny to Suwałki (6.30zł, 45 minutes).

Suwałki Landscape Park

☎ 87

Established in 1976, the 63-sq-km Suwałki Landscape Park (Suwalski Park Krajobrazowy) was the first nature reserve of its kind. It covers some of the most picturesque stretches of land in the region, north of Suwałki, including 26 lakes (totalling 10% of the park's area) and patches of fine forest (another 24%).

The village of **Smolniki**, 20km north of Suwałki, is probably the most convenient base for the park. There are several marked trails passing through the village, and a handful of accommodation options; inquire at the Suwałki **tourist office** (☎ 566 58 72; www.sirt.suwalki.com.pl in Polish; ul Kościuszki 45) for details of these.

The Smolniki neighbourhood is rugged, largely wooded, and dotted with a dozen small lakes, and there are three good viewpoints in the village, which allow you to

---

TROUBLED WATERS?

The two bridges at Stańczyki were designed by the Italians and built by the Germans, in what was then the territory of East Prussia, as part of the Gołdap–Żytkiejmy railway track. The first bridge was constructed between 1912 and 1914; 12 years later the second identical bridge was built parallel to it, just 15m to the south. Construction was interrupted by WWII, but the northern line was used until late 1944, when the Red Army dismantled the tracks and took them to the Soviet Union, leaving the bridges inoperable.

You don't need to be an architect to realise there are a lot of unanswered questions surrounding the bridges – it's unclear why anyone in their right mind would build not just one but two massive structures in such an awkward part of such a remote area, just to prop up an underused railway line (three services a day hardly justifies the massive effort involved). It all seems a far cry from the customary Prussian pragmatism.

Perhaps the authorities were seduced by the monumental classical form of the design itself – the bridges are undeniably attractive. Sadly the structure isn't as solid as it looks, and the increase in tourism threatens to destroy both the bridges and the riverbank on which they stand. Bungee-jumping has already been banned here, but unless a conservation plan is put in place, Stańczyki's bridges may soon be lost once again.

enjoy some of this landscape. One of the numerous walking options is an hour's walk west to **Lake Hańcza**, the deepest lake in the country. With its steep shores, stony bottom and amazing crystal-clear water, it's like being up in the mountains.

If you travel between Smolniki and Suwałki, it's worth stopping in **Gulbieniszki** at the foot of **Mt Cisowa Góra**. This 256m-high hill, just off the road, is cone-shaped like a volcano and provides a fine view over the surrounding lakes.

The 1:50,000 map *Suwalski Park Krajobrazowy i Okolice* is good for exploring the area. It has all the hiking trails marked on it and good sightseeing information in English on the reverse.

Stańczyki
☎ 87 / pop 200
Deep among forested hills close to the northern border, there's a pair of unusual **railway bridges** (see the boxed text opposite)

that rise out of the woods. Linking the steep sides of the valley of the Błędzianka River, 36m above water level, these two identical, 180m-long constructions were built next to each other. With their tall pillars supporting wide, elegant arches, they have the air of a Roman aqueduct. Now unused and without tracks, the bridges look like huge, surreal sculptures in the middle of nowhere.

You can walk on the top of both bridges and go down and look at them from below – it's really a weird sight. For a long time almost unknown and forgotten, they are now becoming an attraction, and a car park with some basic facilities was built and is attended in summer.

There are two daily buses from Suwałki (8.40zł, 70 minutes) in summer. Alternatively, there's access from the Gołdap–Wiżajny road, serviced by about six buses daily. Get off at the Stańczyki turn-off and walk 1.5km, and you'll see the bridges on your left.

DIRECTORY

Directory

CONTENTS

ACCOMMODATION

The choice and availability of accommodation in Poland has grown and diversified considerably over the past decade. Prices have risen as well, though they are still well below those in Western Europe. Budget accommodation can still be very cheap, but the standard is usually low.

In this book, budget listings generally include anything costing less than 150zł for a double room; mid-range covers hotels priced from approximately 150zł to 300zł a double, and anything over 300zł is considered top end. Warsaw and Kraków have higher rates, and the mid-range category in those chapters is between 200zł and 400zł.

Room prices are usually displayed at the reception desk. You are most likely to find listings for *pokój 1-osobowy* (single rooms) and *pokój 2-osobowy* (double rooms), possibly *z łazienką* (with bathroom) or *bez łazienki* (without bathroom), or *z umywalką* (with basin only). Rates normally include value-added tax (VAT), so you will be charged the rate shown, unless indicated otherwise.

Warsaw is the most expensive place to stay, followed by Kraków, Poznań and other major cities. The further away from the big cities you go, the cheaper accommodation gets. The summer resorts, particularly those on the Baltic coast, on the Masurian lakes and in the mountains, have higher prices in the high season (July and August). Similarly, the mountain ski centres put their prices up in winter. The price of accommodation is the same for foreigners as for Poles, except in some youth hostels, which charge foreigners marginally more.

Agrotourist Accommodation

Known as *kwatery agroturystyczne*, agrotourist accommodation refers to accommodation in farms, country houses and cottages, where owners rent some of their rooms to tourists. They can normally provide meals if requested, and sometimes offer other facilities such as horse riding, angling, canoes, bikes etc. In most cases, rooms are simple and rarely have private bathrooms, but prices are reasonable, usually between 20zł and 50zł per bed.

The owners of these places are affiliated with *stowarzyszenia agroturystyczne* (agrotourist associations), which have 30-plus regional offices around the country, and a central office in Warsaw.

Agrotourist lodging can be an interesting option for those who want to relax for a while, somewhere in the countryside. It's easy to enjoy the slower pace of life, local folklore and traditions, and healthy regional food – all for a reasonable price. It can also be an accommodation alternative for those who have their own means of transport and can easily roam along the back roads and rural areas.

This accommodation type is not included in this book, but information is pretty easy to get from tourist offices, which will either give you the relevant information or direct you to the regional agrotourist-association office.

Camping

Poland has over 500 camping and bivouac sites registered at the **Polish Federation of Camping & Caravanning** (www.pfcc.info). They are distributed throughout the country, and can be found in all the major cities (usually on the outskirts), in many towns and in the countryside, particularly in attractive tourist areas.

About 40% of them are camping grounds with full facilities, including lighting, electricity, running water, showers, kitchen and caravan pitches. Many also have wooden cabins for rent, which are like very basic hotel rooms.

The remaining 60% of sites are bivouac sites, which are very basic campsites, usually equipped with toilets but not much else. The *Campingi w Polsce* map, available from bookshops, has details of registered camping and bivouac sites.

In recent years, a number of private camping grounds have sprung up all over Poland. They range from small back gardens with a bathroom in the owner's house to large grounds with bungalows, cafés, shops, bike and boat hire, and so on. These private sites are not included on the camping map.

Most camping grounds are open from May to September, but some run only from June to August. The opening and closing dates given here are a rough guide only: they may open and close earlier or later in the season, depending on the weather, flow of tourists, an owner's whim etc.

Fees are usually charged per tent site, plus an extra fee per person and per car.

Holiday Homes

In popular holiday areas, such as the mountains or the coast, you'll come across workers' holiday homes, known to Poles as *domy wczasowe* or *domy wypoczynkowe*. In communist times, these large establishments either served the employees of a company or were directed centrally by the Fundusz Wczasów Pracowniczych (FWP; Workers' Holiday Fund), but were off limits to individual tourists. Nowadays they welcome everybody. Most are open in summer only, but some run year-round. They tend to be full in July and August, but it's relatively easy to get a room in June or September. Their standards vary but on the whole they're not bad, and prices are usually reasonable. Almost all have their own dining rooms. Full board is usually optional but in some homes it can be compulsory.

Hostels
PTTK & MOUNTAIN HOSTELS
Polskie Towarzystwo Turystyczno-Krajoznawcze (PTTK; Polish Tourist & Countryside Association; ☎ 22-826 22 51; www.pttk.pl; ul Senatorska 11, Warsaw) has built up a network of its own hostels, called *dom turysty* or *dom wycieczkowy*. They are aimed at budget travellers, providing basic accommodation for hikers and backpackers in cities, towns and villages as well as in the countryside.

PTTK hostels rarely have single rooms, but always have a choice of three- and four-bed rooms, usually with shared facilities, where you can often rent just one bed (not the whole room) for around 20zł to 40zł. Some PTTK hostels, particularly those in the cities, are now under private management and cost more.

PTTK also runs a network of *schroniska górskie* (mountain hostels), which are an essential resource for trekkers. They are often wonderfully located and are charming buildings in themselves. Conditions are usually simple but you don't pay much and the atmosphere can be great. They also serve cheap hot meals. The more-isolated mountain hostels are obliged to take in all-comers, regardless of how crowded they get, which means that in the high season (summer and/or winter) it can sometimes be hard to find even a space on the floor. These hostels are open all year, though you'd better check at the nearest regional PTTK office before setting off.

STUDENT HOSTELS

These are hostels set up in student dormitories during the summer school-holiday period (July to late September). Each major university city has at least a few student dorms, some of which are open as student hostels in summer. Some student dorms have a limited number of rooms available year-round. Student hostels charge around 60zł to 120zł for a double room. Facilities are usually shared but some hostels have rooms with private bathrooms.

YOUTH HOSTELS

The *schroniska młodzieżowe* (youth hostels) in Poland are operated by the **Polskie Towarzystwo Schronisk Młodzieżowych** (PTSM; Polish Youth Hostel Association; ☎ 22-849 81 28; www.ptsm.com .pl; Room 20, ul Chocimska 28, Warsaw; ☺ 8am-3pm Mon-Fri), a member of Hostelling International (HI). PTSM has its main office in Warsaw and branch offices in all provincial capitals. Founded in 1926, it was the world's third youth-hostel organisation (after Germany and Switzerland) and managed to operate throughout the period of communist rule as the only such institution in Eastern Europe.

Poland has about 580 hostels, including 130 all-year hostels and 450 seasonal ones, open in July and August only. They are distributed more or less evenly throughout the country, and there's at least one in every major city. PTSM publishes *Informator PTSM*, a guidebook containing the full list of youth hostels in Poland. It's updated every two years and is available from PTSM offices and in some major youth hostels.

The all-year hostels are more reliable and have more facilities, including showers, a place to cook and a dining room. Some hostels are in poor shape, while others have good, modern facilities.

Seasonal hostels are usually located in schools, while pupils are on holidays. These schools are in no way adapted to being hostels – they hardly ever have showers or kitchens, and hot water is rare. Seasonal hostels are highly unreliable; only about 80% of them will actually be open at any one time.

Many previously strict hostel rules have been relaxed or abandoned. Youth hostels are now open to all, members and nonmembers alike, and there is no age limit. Curfew is 10pm, but some hostel staff may be flexible about this. Almost all hostels are closed between 10am and 5pm. Check-in time is usually until 9pm or 10pm, but may be 8pm in some minor seasonal hostels. It's best to check in as soon as possible after 5pm.

A dorm bed in a hostel costs from 15zł to 40zł, depending on the hostel's category. Singles, doubles and triples, if there are any, cost about 20% to 50% more. A hostelling card gives a 10% to 25% discount off these prices for nationals and, in some places, for foreigners. If you think you'll be using youth hostels regularly, bring along a membership card or buy one at any PTSM office in Poland. If you don't have your own bed sheets, the staff will hire out sheets for 4zł to 6zł (not available in some seasonal hostels).

Youth hostels are the cheapest form of accommodation after camping, but do be prepared for basic conditions. Given the low prices, hostels are popular with travellers and are often full. A particularly busy time is between early May and mid-June, when hostels are crowded with Polish school groups.

Youth hostels are marked with a sign, featuring a green triangle with the PTSM logo inside, placed over the entrance.

Hotels

This is the most voluminous category of accommodation and is growing fast. It is also the most diverse group, encompassing an immense variety of old and new places ranging from ultrabasic to extraplush.

The old generation of hotels, dating from before the Berlin Wall came down, was graded from one to five stars, intended to reflect the quality and price. The rudimentary one-stars are mostly confined to the smaller provincial towns, whereas the upmarket five-star establishments, now monopolised by Orbis, dot the central areas of big cities.

The arrival of the market economy has changed the picture altogether. On the one hand, plenty of small, mostly private hotels have sprung up. Many of them cater to the middle-priced market, thus nicely filling the gap between PTTK and Orbis. On the other hand, various international hotel chains have arrived to provide luxury for those who were not satisfied with Orbis' services. Lastly, various state-run lodging networks, previously accessible to only a few, have now opened to all. The latter category includes the sports and workers' hotels, both of which fall into the bottom price bracket.

Most hotels provide single and double rooms, and some also offer triples. A double usually costs only 20% to 40% more than a single. A triple often costs only slightly more than a double. Rooms with private bathrooms can be considerably more expensive than those with shared facilities.

If possible, check the room before accepting. Don't be fooled by the hotel reception areas, which may look great in contrast to the rest of the establishment. If you ask to see a room, you can be pretty sure that they won't give you the worst one, which may happen otherwise.

ORBIS & OTHER UPMARKET HOTELS
Orbis (www.orbis.pl) runs the largest hotel chain in Poland – 55 hotels with a total of more than 10,000 rooms. They are found in most major cities and travel destinations. Focusing on moneyed tourists and businesspeople from abroad, as well as more-affluent Poles, Orbis hotels keep their prices high – about 160zł to 350zł a single and 250zł to 500zł a double, or even more in some establishments in Warsaw, Kraków and Wrocław.

Until recently a monopolist of hotel luxury, Orbis now faces increasing competition from various joint ventures with international hotel chains, which have moved in to

build some even ritzier venues, mostly in the bigger cities. In these, guests can enjoy most of the luxuries found in top-class hotels in the West.

SPORTS HOTELS
Sports hotels were built in sports centres in order to create facilities for local and visiting teams. For a long time most of them accepted athletes only but now almost all are open to the public. In many aspects they are similar to the PTTK hostels and workers' hotels: they seldom have singles, offer mostly shared facilities and you can usually pay just for your bed, not the whole room. Expect to pay 20zł to 50zł per head. They are usually located next to the local sports stadium, often well away from the town or city centre. Most commonly, they are called *hotel sportowy*, *hotel OSiR* or *hotel MOSiR*, and some offer camping grounds in summer.

WORKERS' HOTELS
During the postwar period of industrial development, large factories and other enterprises had to provide lodging facilities for their workers, many of whom came from other regions. An extensive network of workers' dormitories was built up during the communist period, each dorm exclusively for the employees of a given company. Most of these places are now open to the general public.

These hotels are generally found in the cities, particularly industrial ones. They are almost always large, drab apartment blocks, often a long way from the city centre. They are called *hotel pracowniczy* or *hotel robotniczy*, though most have disguised themselves under a proper name. Their standards are usually low, but so is the price (20zł to 40zł per bed in a double, triple or quad). Singles are rare, as are private bathrooms. They are just about the cheapest hotels you can find and, judging by their facilities, they may as well be classified as hostels.

Pensions
Also concentrated in the attractive summertime resorts, *pensjonaty* (pensions) are small, privately run guesthouses that provide bed and half- or full board. By and large, pensions are clean, comfortable, friendly, and good value: singles/doubles cost around 80zł/120zł. Some of them are aimed specifically at

Western tourists, particularly Germans, and may have higher prices.

Private Rooms

These are rooms in private homes rented out to tourists. They are available in some major cities and many smaller tourist places. They are arranged through specialist agencies or directly with the owners.

In the large cities (such as Warsaw or Kraków), rooms cost from 60zł to 80zł for singles and from 100zł to 120zł for doubles. The staff in the agency will show you what's available, you then decide, pay and go to the address given to you. The most important thing is to choose the right location, taking into consideration both distance and transport. Some places are a long way from the centre and you'd do better paying more for a central hotel and saving hours travelling on public transport.

Private rooms are a lottery: you don't know what sort of room you'll get or who your hosts will be. It's therefore a good idea to take the room for a night or two and then extend if you decide to stay longer.

In popular holiday resorts, you'll find plenty of signs saying 'pokoje' (rooms) or 'noclegi' (lodging) at the entrances to private homes. They are usually cheaper than in the cities – 25zł to 50zł a head in most cases.

ACTIVITIES
Bird-Watching

Poland offers good bird-watching opportunities, particularly around the lakes and wetlands in the northeastern part of the country. **Bird Service** (☎ 292 14 60; www.bird.pl; ul Św Krzyża 17), in Kraków, is one of the country's best specialist agencies for organising bird-watching tours.

Caving

There are over 1000 caves of various kinds in Poland, most of which are found in the Kraków-Częstochowa Upland and in the Tatra Mountains. But only a handful of caves are adapted for tourists and open to the public. The most spectacular of these are the Bear's Cave (p297), in Kletno, and Paradise Cave (p173), near Kielce.

Cycling

Having your own two wheels gives you an opportunity to explore remote areas rarely visited by tourists. Don't worry about the state of the roads – most are in acceptable shape – and most of the country is comfortably flat for biking. Inquire at local tourist offices about where to hire a bike.

Hang-Gliding & Paragliding

Both hang-gliding and paragliding are popular in Poland, especially in the mountains of the south; one of the most popular take-off sites is Mt Nosal, above Zakopane. There are several schools and agencies in Zakopane that offer training and/or tandem flights – contact Zakopane's tourist office (p256) for more information.

Hiking

This is probably the most popular outdoor activity in Poland. There are thousands of kilometres of marked trails running through the most attractive areas of the countryside, particularly in the mountains. Trails are usually well marked and easy to follow and don't present great difficulties even for beginners. The most popular hiking routes are those in the Tatra Mountains (see the boxed text on p254) but there are many other amazing trails in the Pieniny, the Bieszczady and the Karkonosze, to list just a few. Hiking is generally a summer activity, with the season starting in May.

Horse Riding

Horse riding is popular in Poland and there are plenty of stud farms. Many of them have riding courses for beginners and will hire horses to experienced riders.

Kayaking

There are some almost virgin regions that offer fabulous conditions for kayakers. The Krutynia and Czarna Hańcza Rivers, both in Masuria, have some of the best kayaking in the country (see p429 and p451 for details).

Rafting

Probably the only rafting trip you will be able to find is the well-organised run through the Dunajec Gorge (p251).

Sailing

The Masurian lakes are ideal for sailing and get crowded with hundreds of boats in summer. It's possible to hire sailing boats in Giżycko (p443), in Mikołajki (p446) and several other Masurian resorts. Some travel agencies organise sailing holidays.

Skiing

Skiing is fairly popular and is mostly concentrated in the Carpathian Mountains. Zakopane (p255), at the foot of the Tatra Mountains, is Poland's number one ski centre, and the second is probably Szczyrk in the Beskid Śląski. There are plenty of other, smaller ski resorts though their facilities are usually more modest.

Windsurfing

Windsurfing is popular along the Baltic coast, with the main centre in the Gulf of Gdańsk, between Władysławowo and Chałupy (see p382).

BUSINESS HOURS

Consider the following as a rough guide only; hours can vary considerably from shop to shop (or office to office) and from the city to the village.

Most grocery shops are open from 7am or 8am to 6pm or 7pm on weekdays and till around 2pm on Saturday. Delicatessens and supermarkets usually stay open longer, until 8pm or 9pm (and are often open on Sunday from 9am till 7pm), and there's at least one food shop in every major town and every district of the city that is open 24 hours. All such night shops have a section selling beer, wine and spirits, which is what keeps them going. Shops normally open at 10am or 11am and close at 6pm or 7pm (at 2pm or 3pm on Saturday). The office working day is theoretically eight hours long, Monday to Friday, and there's usually no lunch break.

The opening hours of museums and other attractions vary greatly. Most museums are closed on Monday; some of them also stay closed on the day following a public holiday. Many museums close one or two hours earlier in the low season. Museums usually stop selling tickets half an hour (sometimes even one hour) before their official closing time.

Churches are a bigger puzzle. The major churches in the main cities are often open all day long. On the other hand, rural churches in small villages will almost always be locked except during Mass, which may be only on Sunday morning.

CHILDREN

If you plan on taking your offspring on a trip to Poland, you shouldn't encounter any specific problems. Children enjoy privileges on local transport, accommodation and entertainment. Age limits for particular freebies or discounts vary from place to place, but are not often rigidly enforced. Basic supplies are easily available in the cities. There are quite a few shops devoted to kids' clothes, shoes and toys, and you can buy disposable nappies (diapers) and baby food in supermarkets and pharmacies. For general suggestions on how to make a trip with kids easier, pick up a copy of Lonely Planet's *Travel with Children*, by Cathy Lanigan.

CLIMATE CHARTS

Poland's climate is influenced by a continental climate from the east and a maritime climate from the west. As a result, the weather is changeable, with significant differences from

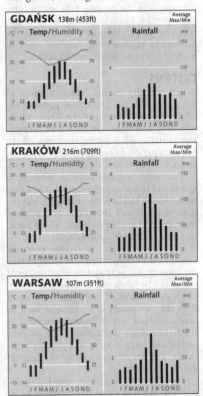

day to day and from year to year. Winter one year can be almost without snow, whereas another year very heavy snows can paralyse transport for days on end. Summer can occasionally be cold, wet and disappointing.

The seasons are clearly differentiated. Spring starts in March and is initially cold and windy, later becoming pleasantly warm and often sunny. Summer, which begins in June, is predominantly warm but hot at times, with plenty of sunshine interlaced with heavy rains. July is the hottest month. Autumn comes in September and is at first warm and usually sunny, turning cold, damp and foggy in November. Winter lasts from December to March and includes shorter or longer periods of snow. High up in the mountains, snow stays well into May. January and February are the coldest months. The temperature sometimes drops below -15°C or even -20°C.

The average annual rainfall is around 600mm, with the greatest falls in the summer months. Central Poland is the driest, receiving about 450mm a year, while the mountains receive more rain (or snow in winter) – around 1000mm annually.

CUSTOMS

When entering Poland, you're allowed to bring duty-free articles for your personal use while you travel and stay there. They include still, cine and video cameras plus accessories; portable, self-powered electronic goods, such as a personal computer, video recorder, radio, CD player and the like, together with accessories; a portable musical instrument; sports and tourist equipment, such as a sailboard, kayak (up to 5.5m in length), bicycle, tent, skis etc; and medicines and medical instruments for your own use. You'll rarely be asked to declare these things.

Unlimited amounts of foreign currency and travellers cheques can be brought into the country, but only up to the equivalent of €5000 can be taken out by a foreigner without a declaration. If you enter with more than the equivalent of €5000 and want to take it all back out of Poland, you need to fill in a currency-declaration form on your arrival and have it stamped by customs officials. You are allowed to import or export Polish currency.

Travellers arriving from non-EU countries can bring in up to 200 cigarettes or 50 cigars or 250g of pipe tobacco, up to 2L of nonsparkling wine, and up to 1L of spirits. If you're arriving from an EU member state, the allowances are 800 cigarettes or 200 cigars or 1kg of pipe tobacco, and up to 110L of beer, 90L of wine and 10L of spirits.

When leaving the country, you may take out gifts and souvenirs of a total value not exceeding €90, free of duty. The export of items manufactured before 9 May 1945 is strictly prohibited, unless you first get an *pozwolenie eksportowe* (export permit). Official antique dealers – such as **Desa Unicum** (Map pp64-5; ☎ 621 66 15; Rynek Starego Miasta 4/6; ☷ 11am-7pm Mon-Fri, 11am-4pm Sat & Sun) in Warsaw – may offer to help you out with the paperwork, but the procedure is time-consuming and bureaucratic, and involves paying a fee equivalent to 25% of the item's value. Beware of dealers who tell you that the law has changed since Poland's accession to the EU – it has not.

DANGERS & ANNOYANCES

Poland is a relatively safe country to travel in, even though there has been a steady increase in crime since the fall of communism. Always keep your eyes open and use common sense. Problems mostly occur in big cities, with Warsaw being perhaps the least-safe place in Poland. Take care when walking alone at night, particularly in the centre and the suburb of Praga, and be alert at Warszawa Centralna (Warsaw Central) train station, the favourite playground for thieves and pickpockets. Other large cities appear to be quieter, but keep your wits about you. By and large, the smaller the town, the safer it is.

Don't venture into any run-down areas, dubious-looking suburbs and desolate parks, especially after dark. Use taxis if you feel uncertain about an area. Try to stay away from groups of suspicious-looking male characters hanging around markets, shady bars and bus and train stations. Stay at a safe distance from dogs. Poles are keen on big dogs, many of which roam without leads, and not all are muzzled. Some are bigger and uglier than others.

Keep a sharp eye on your pockets and your bag in crowded places such as markets or city buses and trams. Beware of short-changing at train stations, taxis, restaurants etc. Always have some smaller bills in order to make change more easily. Hotels are generally safe, though it's better not to leave valuables in your room; in most places you can deposit them at the reception desk.

Theft from cars has become widespread. 'Pirate' or 'mafia' taxis can be a problem in Warsaw (see p92) and some other large cities, and robbery in trains has also been on the increase.

If your passport, valuables and/or other belongings are lost or stolen, report it to the police. They will give you a copy of the statement, which serves as a temporary identity document; if you have insurance, you'll need to present the statement to your insurer in order to make a claim. English-speaking police are rare, so it's best to take along an interpreter if you can. Don't hold out high hopes of having your possessions returned to you, for the police earn next to nothing and can be rather cynical about a 'rich' foreigner complaining about losing a few dollars.

Heavy drinking is a way of life in Poland and drunks may at times be disturbing. Poles smoke a lot and so far there has been little serious antitobacco campaigning. Polish cigarettes are of low quality and the smoke they produce is barely tolerable for anyone not used to them, let alone a nonsmoker.

Slow and impolite service in shops, offices and restaurants is slowly being eradicated, though you can still occasionally experience it. Cheating is not common but there are some areas, especially those connected with foreign tourism, where you should be alert. By the way, if a couple of young boys offer to bag your shopping at a supermarket, they're not begging or scamming – they're boy scouts collecting for charity.

Since WWII Poland has been ethnically an almost entirely homogeneous nation, and Poles, particularly those living in rural areas, have had little contact with foreigners. That's why travellers looking racially different may attract some stares from the locals. In most cases, this is just a curiosity, without any hostility in mind. On the other hand, there have been some acts of racism in the cities, though it's still not a social problem by any definition.

DISABLED TRAVELLERS

Poland is not well set up for people with disabilities, even though there has been a significant improvement over recent years.

Wheelchair ramps are available only at some upmarket hotels and restaurants, and public transport will be a challenge for anyone with mobility problems. Few offices, museums or banks provide special facilities for the disabled traveller, and wheelchair-accessible toilets are few and far between.

Disabled travellers in the USA may like to contact the **Society for Accessible Travel & Hospitality** (☎ 212-447 SATH; www.sath.org; Suite 610, 347 Fifth Ave, New York, NY 10016). In the UK, a useful contact is the **Royal Association for Disability & Rehabilitation** (☎ 020-7242 3882; www.radar.org .uk; 25 Mortimer St, London W1N 8AB).

DISCOUNT CARDS

See p61 for information about the Warsaw Tourist Card.

Hostel Cards

An HI membership card can gain you 10% to 25% discount on youth hostel prices, though some hostels don't give discounts to foreigners. Bring the card with you, or get one issued in Poland at the provincial branch offices of the PTSM in the main cities.

Student Cards

If you are a student, bring along your International Student Identity Card (ISIC card). You can also get one in Poland if you have your local student card or any document stating that you're a full-time student. The Almatur Student Bureau (which has offices in most major cities) issues ISIC cards for around 30zł (bring a photo). The card gives reductions on museum admissions (normally by 50%), Polferry ferries (20%), LOT domestic flights (10%) and urban transport in Warsaw (50%), plus discounts on international transport tickets. There are no ISIC discounts on domestic trains and buses.

EMBASSIES & CONSULATES
Polish Embassies & Consulates

Poland has embassies in the capitals of about 90 countries. The consulates are usually at the same address as the embassy. In some countries there are additional consulates in other cities.

Australia Canberra (☎ 02-6273 1208; 7 Turrana St, Yarralumla, Canberra ACT 2600); Sydney (☎ 02-9363 9816; 10 Trelawney St, Woollahra NSW 2025)
Belarus Minsk (☎ 017-213 43 13; ul Rumiancewa 6, Minsk 220034)

Canada Montréal (☎ 514-937 9481; 1500 Ave des Pins Ouest, PQ H3G 1B4); Ottawa (☎ 613-789 0468; 443 Daly Av, Ont K1N 6H3); Toronto (☎ 416-252 5471; 2603 Lakeshore Blvd W, Ont M8V 1G5); Vancouver (☎ 604-688 3530; Ste 1600, 1177 W Hastings St, BC V6E 2K3)

Czech Republic Ostrava (☎ 69-611 80 74; ul Blahoslavová 4, 70100); Prague (☎ 2-257 530 388; Valdštejnská 8, Malá Strana)

France Lille (☎ 03 20 06 50 30; 45 Boulevard Carnot, 59800); Lyons (☎ 04 78 93 14 85; 79 rue Crillon, 69006); Paris (☎ 01 43 17 34 22; 5 rue de Talleyrand, 75007)

Germany Berlin (☎ 30-22 31 30; Lassenstrasse 19-21, 14193); Cologne (☎ 221-93 73 00; Lindenalle 7, 50968); Hamburg (☎ 040-631 20 91; Gründgensstrasse 20, 22309)

Ireland Dublin (☎ 01-283 0855; 5 Ailesbury Rd, Ballsbridge, Dublin 4)

Japan Tokyo (☎ 3-5794 7020; 2-13-5 Mita, Meguro-ku)

Latvia Riga (☎ 2-703 15 00; Mednieku iela 6b, 1010 Riga)

Lithuania Vilnius (☎ 27-09 001; Smelio gatve 20 A)

Netherlands The Hague (☎ 70-360 28 06; Alexanderstraat 25, 2514 JM)

Russia Kaliningrad (☎ 0112-27 35 77; ulitsa Kashtanova 51, 236000); Moscow (☎ 095-231 15 00; ulitsa Klimashkina 4, 123557); St Petersburg (☎ 812-274 41 70; ulitsa 5 Sovietskaya 12/14, 193130)

Slovakia Bratislava (☎ 7-544 13 175; ul Hummelova 4, 81491)

UK Edinburgh (☎ 0131-552 0301; 2 Kinnear Rd, Edinburgh E3H 5PE); London (☎ 0870 774 2800; 73 New Cavendish St, London W1N 7RB)

Ukraine Kyiv (☎ 44-224 80 40; vulitsya Yaroslaviv 12, 252034); Lviv (☎ 322-97 08 61; vulitsya Ivana Franko 110, 290000)

USA Chicago (☎ 312-337 8166; 1530 North Lake Shore Dr, IL 60610); Los Angeles (☎ 310-442 8500; Ste 555, 12400 Wilshire Blvd, CA 90025); New York (☎ 212-237 2100; 233 Madison Ave, NY 10016); Washington DC (☎ 202-234 3800; 2640 16th St NW, 20009)

Embassies & Consulates in Poland

The closest New Zealand embassy is in Berlin, Germany.

Australia Warsaw (Map pp62-3; ☎ 22-521 34 44; www.australia.pl; 3rd fl, ul Nowogrodzka 11, Warsaw)

Belarus Białystock (Map p113; ☎ 85-744 55 01; ul Elektryczna 9, Białystok); Gdańsk (☎ 58-341 00 26; Room 905, ul Wały Piastowskie 1, Gdańsk); Warsaw (☎ 22-742 09 90; ul Wiertnicza 58, Warsaw)

Canada Warsaw (Map pp62-3; ☎ 22-584 31 00; wsaw@dfait-maeci.gc.ca; ul Matejki 1/5, Warsaw)

Czech Republic Katowice (☎ 32-609 99 52; ul Stalmacha 21, Katowice); Warsaw (Map pp62-3;

☎ 22-628 72 21; www.mfa.cz/warsaw; ul Koszykowa 18, Warsaw); Wrocław (☎ 71-782 60 60; Rynek 13, Wrocław)

France Kraków (☎ 12-424 53 00; ul Stolarska 15, Kraków); Poznań (☎ 61-851 61 40; ul Miełżyńskiego 27, Poznań); Sopot (☎ 58-550 32 49; ul Kościuszki 16, Sopot); Warsaw (Map p58; ☎ 22-529 30 00; www.ambafrance -pl.org; ul Puławska 17, Warsaw); Wrocław (☎ 71-780 51 31; ul Powstańców Śląskich 95, Wrocław)

Germany Gdańsk (☎ 58-340 65 00; Al Zwycięstwa 23, Gdańsk); Kraków (☎ 12-424 30 00; ul Stolarska 7, Kraków); Warsaw (Map p58; ☎ 22-584 17 00; www.amb asadaniemiec.pl; ul Dąbrowiecka 30, Warsaw); Wrocław (☎ 71-377 27 00; ul Podwale 76, Wrocław)

Ireland Warsaw (Map p58; ☎ 22-849 66 55; www .irlandia.pl; ul Humańska 10, Warsaw)

Japan Warsaw (Map p58; ☎ 22-696 50 00; www.emb -japan.pl; ul Szwoleżerów 8, Warsaw)

Latvia Warsaw (Map p58; ☎ 22-617 43 89; embassy .poland@mfa.gov.lv; ul Królowej Aldony 19, Warsaw)

Lithuania Sejny (☎ 87-516 22 73; ul 22 Lipca 9, Sejny); Warsaw (Map p58; ☎ 22-625 34 10; litwa_amb@waw .pdi.net; Al Szucha 5, Warsaw)

Netherlands Warsaw (Map p58; ☎ 22-559 12 00; nlgovwar@ikp.pl; ul Kawalerii 10, Warsaw)

Russia Gdańsk (☎ 58-341 10 88; ul Batorego 15, Gdańsk); Kraków (☎ 12-422 26 47; ul Biskupia 7, Kraków); Poznań (☎ 61-841 75 23; ul Bukowska 53a, Poznań); Warsaw (Map p58; ☎ 22-621 34 53; www.poland.mid .ru; ul Belwederska 49, Warsaw)

Slovakia Warsaw (Map p58; ☎ 22-525 81 10; www .ambasada-slowacji.pl; ul Litewska 6, Warsaw)

South Africa Warsaw (Map pp62-3; ☎ 625 62 28; saem bassy@supermedia.pl; 6th fl, ul Koszykowa 54, Warsaw)

UK Gdańsk (☎ 58-341 43 65; ul Grunwaldzka 100/102, Gdańsk); Katowice (☎ 32-206 98 01; ul PCK 10, Katowice); Kraków (☎ 12-421 70 30; ul Św Anny 9, Kraków); Warsaw (Map pp62-3; ☎ 22-311 00 00; www.britishembassy.pl; Al Róż 1, Warsaw); Wrocław (☎ 71-344 89 61; ul Oławska 2, Wrocław)

Ukraine Warsaw (Map p58; ☎ 22-629 34 46; www .ukraine-emb.pl; Al Szucha 7, Warsaw)

USA Kraków (☎ 12-424 51 00; ul Stolarska 9, Kraków); Poznań (Map pp324-5; ☎ 61-851 85 16; ul Paderewskiego 8, Poznań); Warsaw (Map pp62-3; ☎ 22-504 20 00; www .usinfo.pl; Al Ujazdowskie 29/31, Warsaw)

FESTIVALS & EVENTS

Apart from some well-established national or international festivals of film, theatre and music, there are plenty of small local feasts, fairs, contests, meetings and competitions, some of which involve local folklore. Add to this a lot of religious celebrations. The following are some of Poland's biggest festivals and events.

Festivals

JANUARY

Festival of Theatre Festivals (www.teatrdramatyczny
.pl; Warsaw) International programme of performances by
the masters of modern theatre.

FEBRUARY

Shanties (www.shanties.pl in Polish; Kraków) Celebration
of old sailors' songs, accompanied by copious quantities
of beer.

Musica Polonica Nova (www.musicapolonicanova.pl
in Polish; Wrocław) International festival of contemporary
music.

MARCH

Poznań Jazz Festival (www.jazz.pl in Polish; Poznań)
Week-long line-up of local and international jazz stars.

MAY

Juvenalia (www.juvenalia.krakow.pl in Polish; Kraków)
Student carnival with fancy dress, masquerades and
dancing in the street.

Gaude Mater (www.gaudemater.pl; Częstochowa)
Week-long international festival of religious music.

JUNE/JULY

Jewish Culture Festival (www.jewishfestival.pl;
Kraków) Biggest festival of its kind in Europe.

Mozart Festival (www.wok.pol.pl; Warsaw) Performances of all 26 of Mozart's stage productions.

Summer Jazz Festival (www.cracjazz.com in Polish;
Kraków) Best of modern Polish jazz.

Warsaw Summer Jazz Days (www.adamiakjazz.pl in
Polish; Warsaw) Series of concerts spread throughout July
and August.

AUGUST

International Festival of Mountain Folklore (www
.zakopane.pl/festiwal; Zakopane) Poland's oldest and
biggest festival of folk culture.

SEPTEMBER

Warsaw Autumn (www.warsaw-autumn.art.pl; Warsaw)
Ten-day international festival of contemporary music.

OCTOBER

Warsaw International Film Festival (www.wff.pl;
Warsaw) A packed programme of art-house film premieres,
lectures and screen-writing workshops.

Religious Events

Given the strong Roman Catholic character of the nation, religious feasts are much
celebrated in Poland, especially in the
more conservative countryside areas. The
Church calendar is marked by two major
cycles, which culminate in Boże Narodzenie
(Christmas) and Wielkanoc (Easter). There
are also a number of feast days devoted to
particular saints, of whom the Virgin Mary
is the most widely celebrated.

CHRISTMAS

The Christmas cycle begins with Adwent
(Advent), a four-week period that precedes
Christmas, and is characterised by the pre-
paration of Nativity scenes in churches.
Kraków is particularly notable for this, hold-
ing a competition for the best examples.

As for Christmas itself, Wigilia (Christmas Eve) is the day most celebrated in
Polish homes, culminating in a solemn supper that begins when the first star appears
in the evening sky. Before the meal the
family shares *opłatek* (holy bread), wishing
each other all the best for the future. Then
the supper, which traditionally consists of
12 courses, including some of the best of
traditional Polish cuisine, begins. An extra
seat and place setting are left prepared for
an unexpected guest. Kids will find their
gifts under the *choinka* (Christmas tree),
or sometimes they will be handed out by
Święty Mikołaj (Santa Claus) himself.

In the more traditional rural homes, there
will still be much magic and witchcraft involved in the ceremony, the forms differ-
ing from region to region. It's believed, for
example, that animals speak with human
voices on that one night, and that at midnight the water in wells turns into wine.

After the supper is finished, the family will set off for church for the specially
celebrated Pasterka (Christmas Mass) at
midnight. The service is held by almost all
churches, and all are packed.

Christmas Day is, like the previous day,
essentially a family day, featuring Mass, eating and relaxing. The holiday atmosphere
continues for the remaining days of the year
up until Sylwester (New Year's Eve), when
the action starts with a variety of formal
balls and private parties, held principally
among urban communities.

On 6 January comes Dzień Trzech Króli
(Epiphany), marked by carol singers, usually armed with a small portable crib or
other religious images, who go in groups
from door to door. On this day people have
a piece of chalk consecrated in church, then

use it to write 'K+M+B' (the initials of the three Magi) on their front doors, to ensure Heaven's care over the home.

EASTER

Easter is a moveable feast falling on the first Sunday following the first full moon after 21 March (which can be any day between 22 March and 25 April). It's preceded by Wielki Post (Lent), the season of fasting and penitence, which begins on Środa Popielcowa (Ash Wednesday), 40 weekdays prior to Easter.

Wielki Tydzień (Holy Week) commences with Niedziela Palmowa (Palm Sunday), a reminder of the triumphal entry of Christ into Jerusalem, where he was welcomed with date-palm branches. Today the most common substitutes are willow branches overspread with white catkins, though there are still some villages, notably Rabka, Tokarnia (near Rabka) and Łyse (in the Kurpie region), where the tradition is taken quite seriously: the 'palms' made there are elaborate works of art stretching up to 10m in height.

Palm Sunday also marks the beginning of the famous ceremony in Kalwaria Zebrzydowska (p210) near Kraków, which reaches its zenith on Wielki Czwartek (Maundy Thursday) and Wielki Piątek (Good Friday), when a Passion play is performed, re-enacting the last days of the life of Christ. In a blend of religious rite and popular theatre, local amateur actors take the roles of Roman soldiers, apostles, Jewish priests and Christ himself, and circle 20-odd Calvary chapels, representing the stages of the Way of the Cross, accompanied by a crowd of pilgrims and spectators.

On Good Friday people visit the Holy Sepulchres set up in churches, while on Wielka Sobota (Holy Saturday) the faithful go to church with baskets filled with food, such as bread, sausage, cake and eggs, to have them blessed. The eggs are decoratively painted, sometimes with elaborate patterns. Inspired by this tradition, eggs made of wood are painted and sold as souvenirs.

Niedziela Wielkanocna (Easter Day) begins with Mass, which is usually accompanied by a procession. After that the faithful return home to have a solemn breakfast, at which the consecrated food is eaten. Before breakfast, family members share eggs while wishing each other the best.

Lany Poniedziałek (Easter Monday) is when people sprinkle each other with water, which can be anything from a symbolic drop of perfumed water to a bucket of water over the head, or even a dousing from a fire engine.

Zielone Święta (Pentecost) falls on the 50th day after Easter Day (hence its name), and 10 days later comes Boże Ciało (Corpus Christi). The latter is characterised by processions held all over the country, of which the best known is that in Łowicz (p103).

OTHER FEASTS

Among the Marian feasts, the most important is the Święto Wniebowzięcia NMP (Assumption) on 15 August, celebrated in many places throughout Poland, but nowhere as elaborately as in the Monastery of Jasna Góra in Częstochowa (p168), where pilgrims from all corners of the country arrive on that very day, sometimes after a journey of several days on foot.

Dzień Wszystkich Świętych (All Saints' Day) on 1 November is a time of remembrance and prayers for the souls of the dead. On no other day do cemeteries witness so many people leaving flowers, wreaths and candles on the graves of their relatives, and they look most spectacular at night. The celebrations continue to a lesser extent on the following day.

FOOD

The eating listings in this book are organised by budget in the larger towns, based on the average price of a main course. This is less than 15zł (20zł in Warsaw) for budget places; from 15zł to 30zł (20zł to 40zł in Warsaw) for mid-range; and more than 30zł (40zł in Warsaw) for top end. For more on Polish food and drink see p49.

GAY & LESBIAN TRAVELLERS

Homosexuality is legal in Poland; the age of consent is 15, which is the same as for heterosexual sex. Despite the fairly liberal legal situation, Polish society is overwhelmingly conservative and for the most part deeply hostile towards homosexuality.

The Polish gay and lesbian scene is fairly discreet; Warsaw and Kraków are the best places to find bars, clubs and gay-friendly accommodation. The free tourist brochure the *Visitor* lists a few gay nightspots.

The best source of information in Warsaw is the **Pride Society** (☎ 0604 883 554; www.pridesociety.org; ◷ 7-9pm). Other websites worth checking out include http://warsaw.gayguide.net and www.innastrona.pl.

HOLIDAYS

The following are public holidays in Poland:

New Year's Day 1 January
Easter Monday March or April
Labour Day 1 May
Constitution Day 3 May
Corpus Christi A Thursday in May or June
Assumption Day 15 August
All Saints' Day 1 November
Independence Day 11 November
Christmas 25 and 26 December

INSURANCE

This not only covers you for medical expenses, theft or loss, but also for cancellation of, or delays in, any of your travel arrangements. There's a variety of policies and your travel agent can provide recommendations.

Make sure the policy includes health care and medication in Poland. See p489 for information on health insurance and p484 for car insurance.

Always read the small print carefully. Some policies specifically exclude 'dangerous activities' such as scuba diving, motorcycling, skiing, mountaineering and even trekking.

Not all policies cover ambulances, helicopter rescue or emergency flights home. Most policies exclude cover for pre-existing illnesses.

INTERNET ACCESS

If you're travelling with a laptop, you should be able to log on via a hotel room phone socket for the cost of a local call by registering with an Internet roaming service such as **MaGlobe** (www.maglobe.com), which has access numbers for Poland. Or you can try Telekomunikacja Poska's Internet service for the price of a local call: set your modem to dial ☎ 020 21 22, and use the username 'ppp' and password 'ppp'. Note that download speeds are glacially slow. Most newer midrange and top-end hotels have telephone jacks (usually US-standard RJ-11), which you can plug your modem cable into.

Buy a line tester (a gadget that goes between your computer and the phone jack)

so that you don't inadvertently fry your modem. Get on and off quickly, as calls from hotels are expensive. There are also an increasing number of hot spots in Polish cities where you can access the Internet with a WiFi-enabled laptop; search for hot spots on http://intel.jiwire.com. For more information on travelling with a laptop see www.kropla.com.

Major Internet-service providers, such as **AOL** (www.aol.com), **CompuServe** (www.compuserve.com) and **AT&T** (www.attbusiness.net), have dial-in nodes in Poland. If you have an account with one of these ISPs, you can download a list of local dial-in numbers before you leave home.

If you access your account at home through a different ISP or your office or school network, your best option is to open a webmail account such as Yahoo or Hotmail before you leave, and either give your new webmail address to your friends and family, or use the account's 'Check Other Mail' option to download mail from your home account (this may not work for work-based accounts).

For a list of useful Polish Internet resources, see p11.

LEGAL MATTERS

Foreigners in Poland, as elsewhere, are subject to the laws of the host country. While your embassy or consulate is the best stop in any emergency, bear in mind that there are some things it can't do for you, like getting local laws or regulations waived because you're a foreigner, investigating a crime, providing legal advice or representation in civil or criminal cases, getting you out of jail, and lending you money.

A consul can, however, issue emergency passports, contact relatives and friends,

WHEN YOU'RE LEGAL
In Poland the following are the minimum legal ages:
▪ drinking alcohol: 18
▪ driving: 17
▪ heterosexual/homosexual sex: 15
▪ marriage: 18
▪ voting: 18

DIRECTORY

advise on how to transfer funds, provide lists of reliable local doctors, lawyers and interpreters, and visit you if you've been arrested or jailed.

MAPS

Poland produces plenty of maps, and they are generally of good quality, inexpensive and easily available. Apart from the state-run map producer, the **PPWK** (www.ppwk.pl), there are also a number of private map publishers.

There's a wide range of general maps of Poland to choose from. You can buy either a single map covering the whole country or a set of four or eight sheets (sold separately) that feature fragments of the country on a larger scale and provide greater detail. The book-format *Atlas Samochodowy* (Road Atlas) is also available, including sketch maps of major cities, Polish road signs and a full index.

All cities and most large towns have their own city maps; the Demart city plans, with the orange cover, are excellent. These maps have a lot of useful information including tram and bus routes, alphabetical lists of streets, post offices, hotels, hospitals, pharmacies and the like.

Other very useful maps are the large-scale tourist maps (usually between 1:50,000 and 1:75,000) of the most popular destinations. They cover a relatively small sector, a single mountain range or a group of lakes, and are very detailed. These maps show marked hiking routes and practically everything else you may be interested in when hiking, driving, biking etc. They are a must if you plan on doing any serious walking.

All the maps mentioned previously are easy to find in the larger urban centres; buy them there (at bookshops and/or tourist offices), as they may be hard to come by in the smaller towns. Maps (including city maps) cost somewhere between 5zł and 15zł each. Polish maps are easy to decipher. Most symbols are based on international standards, and they are explained in the key in three foreign languages, English included.

On the city maps, the word for street, ulica or its abbreviated version ul, is usually omitted, but Aleje or Aleja, more often shortened to Al, is placed before the names of avenues to distinguish them from streets.

MONEY

Following its accession to the EU, Poland declared its intention to adopt the euro as its currency as soon as possible. The poor state of the economy, however, means that it is unlikely that this will happen before 2008 at the earliest. The official Polish currency is the złoty (literally, 'golden'), abbreviated to zł and pronounced *zwo*-ti. It is divided into 100 groszy, which are abbreviated to gr. Banknotes come in denominations of 10zł, 20zł, 50zł, 100zł and 200zł, and coins in 1gr, 2gr, 5gr, 10gr, 20gr and 50gr, and 1zł, 2zł and 5zł. The banknotes feature Polish kings, come in different sizes and are easily distinguishable.

Try to keep some small-denomination notes for shops, cafés and restaurants – getting change for the 100zł notes that ATMs often spit out can be a problem.

For an indication of costs in Poland, see p9. For exchange rates, see the inside front cover of this book.

ATMs

There is a good network of *bankomaty* (ATMs) all over Poland. Most accept Visa, MasterCard, Cirrus and Maestro cards.

The easiest and cheapest way to carry money is in the form of a debit card, with which you can withdraw cash either over the counter in a bank or from an ATM. Charges are minimal at major Polish banks (typically from zero to about 2%) and some home banks charge nothing at all for the use of their cards overseas. Provided you make withdrawals of at least 500zł at a time, you'll pay less than the assorted commissions on the same amount in travellers cheques. Make sure you know your personal identification number (PIN; four to six digits, numbers only), and check with your bank about transaction fees and withdrawal limits.

Cash

The place to exchange cash is the ubiquitous *kantor* (private currency-exchange office), which you'll find on almost every city street corner. They are either self-contained offices or just desks in travel agencies, train stations, post offices, department stores and the more upmarket hotels. The further out from the cities you go, the less numerous they are, but you can be pretty sure that every medium-sized town will have at least a few of them. *Kantors* are usually open between 9am and 6pm on weekdays and till around 2pm on Saturday, but some open longer and a few stay open 24 hours.

Kantors change cash only (no travellers cheques) and accept major world currencies. The most common and thus the most easily changed are US dollars and euros. Australian dollars and Japanese yen are somewhat exotic to Poles and not all *kantors* will change them. There's no commission on transactions – the rate you get is what is written on the board (every *kantor* has a board displaying its exchange rates). The whole operation takes a few seconds and there's no paperwork involved. You don't need to present your passport or fill out any forms.

Kantors buy and sell foreign currencies, and the difference between the buying and selling rates is usually not larger than 2%. Exchange rates differ slightly from city to city and from *kantor* to *kantor* (about 1%). Smaller towns may offer up to 2% less, so it's better to change money in large urban centres if you can.

To avoid hassles when exchanging currency, one important thing to remember before you set off from home is that any banknotes you take to Poland must be in good condition, without any marks or seals. *Kantors* can refuse to accept banknotes that have numbers written on them (a common practice of bank cashiers totalling bundles of notes) even if they are in an otherwise perfect condition.

Credit Cards
Credit cards are increasingly widely accepted for buying goods and services, though their use is still limited to upmarket establishments, mainly in major cities. Among the most popular cards accepted in Poland are Visa, MasterCard, Amex, Diners Club, Eurocard and Access.

Credit cards can also be used for getting cash advances in banks, and the procedure is faster than changing travellers cheques. The best card to bring is Visa, because it's honoured by the largest number of banks, including the Bank Pekao, which will also give cash advances on MasterCard.

International Transfers
You can have money sent to you through the Western Union money transfer service.

You'll receive your money within 15 minutes of the sender transferring it (along with the transaction fee) at any of the 30,000 Western Union agents scattered worldwide. Western Union outlets can be found in all Polish cities and most large towns. Information on locations and conditions can be obtained toll-free on ☎ 0800 120 224.

Taxes
Poland's VAT is calculated at three levels: zero (books, press, some basic food products); 7% (most food); and 22% (fine food, hotels, restaurants, petrol, luxury items). The tax is normally included in the advertised price of goods and services.

Tipping & Bargaining
In restaurants, service is included in the price so you just pay what's on the bill. Tipping is up to you and there don't seem to be any hard and fast rules about it. In low-priced eateries guests rarely leave a tip; they may, at most, round the total up to the nearest whole figure. In upmarket establishments it's customary to tip up to 10% of the bill.

Tipping in hotels is essentially restricted to the top-end establishments, which usually have decent room service and porters, who all expect to be tipped. Taxi drivers are normally not tipped, unless you want to reward someone for their effort.

Bargaining is not common in Poland, and is limited to some informal places such as flea markets, fruit bazaars and street stalls.

Travellers Cheques
Changing travellers cheques is not quite as straightforward as changing cash, and is more time-consuming. The usual place to change travellers cheques is a bank, but not all banks handle these transactions. The main bank that offers this facility is the Bank Pekao, which has a dozen offices in Warsaw and branches in all major cities. They change most major brands of cheque, of which Amex is the most widely known and accepted.

Several other banks, including Bank Gdański, Bank Zachodni, Bank Śląski, Powszechny Bank Kredytowy and Powszechny Bank Gospodarczy, also provide this service, and they too have many regional branches.

The exchange rate is roughly similar to, or marginally lower than, that for cash in *kantors*, but banks charge *prowizja* (commission) on transactions, which varies from bank to bank (somewhere between 1% to 2.5%). Banks also have a set minimum charge of between US$2 and US$3. For example, the Bank Pekao commission on cashing cheques is 1.5% with a minimum charge of US$2.50.

Banks can be crowded and inefficient; you'll probably have to queue a while and then wait until they complete the paperwork. It may take anything from 10 minutes to an hour. You'll need to produce your passport. Some provincial banks may insist on seeing the original receipt from the purchase of your travellers cheques.

You can also cash travellers cheques in an Amex office, but there are only two offices in Warsaw (p61). They are efficient, their staff speak English, they change most major brands of cheque, and their rates are a bit lower than those of the banks.

In case of theft or loss of Amex cheques, call toll-free ☎ 00 800 44 11 200. You will be asked for the missing cheque numbers, and the date and place of their purchase, and will be given a code that you have to present at one of the Amex offices in Warsaw to get your refund.

PHOTOGRAPHY & VIDEO

Print and slide film are widely available in cities and larger towns; EMPiK stores sell film and offer express processing services, as do countless mini photo labs. A 36-exposure print film costs about 10zł, and slide film of 36 exposures is about 24zł, both excluding processing. A three-pack of 60-minute DV-Mini cassettes costs about 55zł.

Except for the usual restrictions on photographing military, industrial, transport and telecommunications installations, you can take pictures or video of just about anything. You can take photos in most churches, but keep in mind that the interiors are usually pretty dim and a tripod or a flash may be necessary. Many museums don't allow photography inside, or will charge extra (sometimes a lot) for the permit.

Skansens are good places for photographing the traditional rural architecture. As for people shots, the best places are regional folk festivals and religious feasts. It's here that you're most likely to see locals decked out in their traditional costumes. Markets, on the other hand, are usually colourless and dull. Needless to say, you should be very discreet and respectful when photographing people.

If you want to buy video tapes to play back home, make sure they have been recorded using the same format as your video player back home. The French Secam used to be the standard image registration system in communist Poland, but it has been replaced by PAL, which is the same as in most of Western Europe but different from the NTSC format used in the USA.

POST

Postal services are provided by Poczta Polska. In large cities there will be a dozen or more post offices, of which the *poczta główna* (main post office) will usually have the widest range of facilities, including poste restante and fax. Larger city post offices are normally open from 8am to 8pm weekdays, and one will usually stay open 24 hours. They are often open on Saturday from 8am to 2pm. In the smaller localities business hours may only be till 4pm on weekdays.

Letters and postcards sent by air from Poland take about one week to reach a European destination and up to two weeks if sent to anywhere else. The cost of sending a normal-sized letter (up to 20g) or a postcard to other European countries is 2.10zł, rising to 2.50zł for North America and 3.30zł for Australia. Packages and parcels are reasonably cheap if sent by surface mail but they can take up to three months to reach their destination. The cost of sending airmail packages is comparable to that in Western Europe.

You can receive mail care of poste restante in large cities such as Warsaw, Kraków and Gdańsk. Mail is held for 14 working days, then returned to the sender. Amex customers can receive poste restante mail via the Warsaw Amex offices (p61).

SHOPPING

The Cepelia chain of shops, with branches in all large cities, specialise in local handicrafts. Common Polish crafts include paper cutouts, woodcarving, tapestries, embroidery, paintings on glass, pottery and hand-painted wooden boxes and chests.

Amber is typically Polish. It's the fossil resin of ancient pine trees, and occurs as translucent nuggets in earthy hues ranging from pale yellow to reddish brown. You can buy amber necklaces in Cepelia shops, but if you want a designer look, check out specialist jewellery shops or commercial art galleries. Prices vary with the quality of the amber and the level of craftwork. You'll find the best choice of amber jewellery in Gdańsk.

Polish contemporary painting, original prints and sculpture are renowned internationally and sold by commercial art galleries. Galleries in Warsaw and Kraków have the biggest and the most representative choice. Polish posters are among the world's finest (a tempting souvenir). The best selection is, again, in Warsaw and Kraków.

The main seller of art and antiques is a state-owned chain of shops called Desa Unicum. These shops often have an amazing variety of old jewellery, watches, furniture and whatever else you can imagine. Remember that it's officially forbidden to export any item manufactured before 9 May 1945, works of art and books included, unless you've got a permit (see p464).

Poland publishes an assortment of well-edited and lavishly illustrated coffee-table books about the country, many of which are also available in English and German. Polish music (pop, folk, jazz, classical and contemporary) is easily available on CD.

SOLO TRAVELLERS

Travelling by yourself in Poland is easy and fairly hassle-free. Note, though, that solo hitching anywhere in Poland isn't wise. The biggest nuisance for solo travellers is the extra cost of single rooms in hotels and pensions compared to sharing a double. The easiest places to meet other people, be it English-speaking locals or other travellers, is in hostels and Internet cafés.

Women travelling by themselves should encounter no extra difficulties, as long as sensible precautions, as observed in most Western countries, are adhered to – see p475 for more information.

TELEPHONE

The state telecommunications provider is Telekomunikacja Polska (TP), which usually has a telephone centre near or inside the main post office. Card-operated public phones can be found pretty much everywhere. All land-line numbers throughout

the country have seven digits, preceded by a two-digit area code when calling long-distance.

International Calls

To call Poland from abroad, dial your country's international access code (usually ☎ 00), then Poland's country code (☎ 48), then the two-digit area code, and then the seven-digit local number.

To call abroad from Poland, dial the international access code (☎ 00), then the country code, then the area code (minus any initial zero) and number. There are no cheap-rate periods for international calls.

You can also use the Home Country Direct service to make reverse charge (collect) calls or credit- or charge-card calls, or to connect to an operator in your home country. Inquire at any TP office for the toll-free number for the country you want to call, then call from any public or private telephone (you'll still need a phone card, though it will only be charged one unit). Note the following Home Country Direct numbers:

Australia (☎ 00 800 61 111 61)
France (☎ 00 800 33 111 33)
Germany (☎ 00 800 49 111 49)
UK (☎ 00 800 44 111 44)
USA (AT&T; ☎ 00 800 1 1111 11)

Local & National Calls

To make a local call, you simply dial the seven-digit subscriber number. When calling long-distance, you first dial 0, then the two-digit area code and the subscriber number. Cheap rates on long-distance calls operate from 6pm to 8am daily.

Mobile Phones

Codes for mobile phones usually begin with ☎ 05, ☎ 06 or ☎ 09. Poland uses the GSM 900/1800 network, which covers the rest of Europe, Australia and New Zealand, but isn't compatible with the North American GSM 1900 or the totally different system in Japan (though some North Americans have GSM 1900/900 phones that will work in Poland). If you have a GSM phone, check with your service provider about using it in Poland, and beware of calls being routed internationally (very expensive for a 'local' call). You can also buy a Polish SIM card for as little as 59zł.

Network coverage can be a bit patchy in remote rural areas.

Phonecards

There are no coin-operated public phones in Poland; all of them work using a phonecard, which you can buy from post offices, newspaper kiosks and some tourist offices and hotel reception desks. TP cards cost 9zł/15zł/24zł for a 15-/30-/60-*impuls* (unit) card. A 60-*impuls* card is enough for an 11-minute call to the UK, or an eight-minute call to the USA.

Alternatively, you can buy a calling card from a private telephone service provider, such as **Intrafon** (www.intrafon.pl), whose international rates are much cheaper – 0.67zł a minute to both the UK and USA. Just follow the instructions that come with the calling card.

TIME

All of Poland lies within the same time zone, GMT/UTC+1, the same as most of continental Europe (see the World Time Zones map on p492). Poland observes Daylight Saving Time (DST), and puts the clock forward one hour at 2am on the last Sunday in March, and back again at 3am on the last Sunday in October.

The 24-hour clock is used for official purposes, including all transport schedules. In everyday conversation, however, people commonly use the 12-hour clock.

When it is noon in Warsaw (in summer, during DST), the time in other cities around the world is as follows:

Auckland 10pm
Berlin noon
Hong Kong 6pm
London 11am
Los Angeles 3am
Moscow 2pm
New York 6am
Paris noon
Prague noon
San Francisco 3am
Stockholm noon
Sydney 8pm
Tokyo 7pm
Toronto 6am
Vancouver 3am

TOILETS

Public toilets in Poland are few and far between, and when you do find one the stink can be staggering. If you're really desperate, do as the Poles do and nip into the near-est McDonald's fast-food restaurant and use its toilets. Hotels, museums and train stations are other emergency options, but don't expect pristine facilities. Toilets are labelled '*toaleta*' or simply 'WC'. The gents will be labelled '*dla panów*' or '*męski*' and/or marked with a triangle, and the ladies will be labelled '*dla pań*' or '*damski*' and/or marked with a circle.

The use of a public toilet (including those in restaurants and train stations) is almost never free. The fee – usually 1zł – is collected by a toilet attendant sitting at the door, who will give you a piece of toilet paper. It's a good idea to bring your own toilet paper, just in case.

TOURIST INFORMATION
Local Tourist Offices

Most larger cities have local tourist offices, which are usually good sources of information; most also sell maps and tourist publications. Most staff members speak English and/or German.

In smaller localities, where there are no genuine tourist offices, look for a PTTK office (see p459). PTTK was once a helpful organisation, focusing on outdoor activities such as hiking, sailing, cycling and camping. Today it's just another travel agency, but many of its offices are well stocked with maps and trekking brochures, and can arrange guides and accommodation and provide tourist information.

Tourist Offices Abroad

Polish tourist offices abroad include the following:

France (☎ 01 42 44 19 00; www.tourisme.pologne.net; 9 rue de la Paix, 75002 Paris)
Germany (☎ 30-210 09 2-0; www.polen-info.de; Kurfürstendamm 71, 10709 Berlin)
Netherlands (☎ 20-625 35 70; www.members.tripod .com/~poleninfo; Leidsestraat 64, 1017 PD Amsterdam)
UK (☎ 0870 067 5010; www.visitpoland.org; Level 3, Westec House, West Gate, London W5 1YY)
USA (☎ 201-490 99 10; www.polandtour.org; 5 Marine View Plaza, Hoboken NJ 07030)

VISAS

Citizens of EU countries do not need visas to visit Poland and can stay indefinitely. Citizens of the USA, Canada, Australia, New Zealand, Israel and Japan can stay in Poland for up to 90 days without a visa.

Other nationals should check current visa requirements with the Polish embassy or consulate in their home country, or on the **Ministry of Foreign Affairs** (www.mfa.gov.pl) website.

WOMEN TRAVELLERS

Women are unlikely to have any problems travelling in Poland, although common-sense caution should always be observed, especially in towns and cities. Women can enter most pubs alone, but there are still a few places where this may attract undesirable attention. Cosmopolitan city pubs are fine – you'll get a pretty good idea as soon as you enter. Sticking to pubs frequented by travellers is always a safe bet. Many parts of central Warsaw are best avoided late at night.

On the other hand, a woman travelling alone, especially in remote rural areas, may expect to receive more help, hospitality and generosity from the locals than would a man on his own.

Transapport

GETTING THERE & AWAY

ENTERING THE COUNTRY
Passport

A valid passport is essential for entry into Poland, and your passport must be stamped with a visa if you require one (see p474 for information). Theoretically, the expiry date of your passport should not be less than three months after the date of your departure from Poland.

AIR
Airports & Airlines

The vast majority of international flights to Poland arrive at **Warsaw-Frédéric Chopin Airport** (Port Lotniczy im F Chopina, WAW; Map p58; ☎ 22-650 41 00; www.lotnisko-chopina.pl).

The following are also international airports in Poland:

Gdańsk – Lech Wałęsa (GDN; ☎ 58-348 11 54; www.airport.gdansk.pl)

Katowice (KTW; ☎ 32-392 72 85; www.gtl.com.pl)

Kraków–Balice (KRK; ☎ 12-639 30 00; www.lotnisko-balice.pl)

Wrocław (WRO; ☎ 71-358 13 10; www.airport.wroclaw.pl)

THINGS CHANGE

The information in this chapter is particularly vulnerable to change. Check directly with the airline or a travel agent to make sure you understand how a fare (and ticket you may buy) works and be aware of the security requirements for international travel. Shop carefully. The details given in this chapter should be regarded as pointers and are not a substitute for your own careful, up-to-date research.

Poland's national carrier **LOT** (LO; ☎ 0801 300 952, from mobile phones ☎ 22-9572; www.lot.com) flies to all major European cities, as well as most major cities in Germany. Outside Europe it has direct flights to/from Chicago, Istanbul, New York, Tel Aviv and Toronto.

A wave of budget airlines, including EasyJet, GermanWings, SkyEurope and Wizz Air, has moved in on the Polish market, offering very cheap flights both to Warsaw and to various regional airports.

Fares vary greatly depending on what route you're flying and what time of year it is. Poland's high season (and that of Europe in general) is in summer (June to August) and a short period around Christmas. The rest of the year is quieter and cheaper.

These airlines fly to and from Poland:

Aeroflot (airline code SU; in Warsaw ☎ 22-628 25 57; www.aeroflot.com; hub Moscow)

Air France (airline code AF; in Warsaw ☎ 22-556 64 00; www.airfrance.com; hub Paris)

Alitalia (airline code AZ; in Warsaw ☎ 22-826 28 01; www.alitalia.it; hub Rome)

British Airways (airline code BA; in Warsaw ☎ 22-529 90 00; www.ba.com; hub London)

EasyJet (airline code EZY; www.easyjet.com; hub London)

GermanWings (airline code 4U; www.germanwings.com; hub Cologne/Bonn)

KLM (airline code KL; in Warsaw ☎ 22-862 70 00; www.klm.com; hub Amsterdam)

Lufthansa (airline code LH; in Warsaw ☎ 22-338 13 00; www.lufthansa.com; hub Frankfurt)

Malev (airline code MA; in Warsaw ☎ 22-697 74 72; www.malev.hu; hub Budapest)

SAS (airline code SK; in Warsaw ☎ 22-850 05 00; www.scandinavian.net; hub Stockholm)

SkyEurope (airline code NE; www.skyeurope.com; hub Vienna)

WizzAir (airline code WZZ; in Warsaw ☎ 22-500 94 99; www.wizzair.com; hub Katowice)

Tickets

Fierce competition on most European routes has resulted in price wars between no-frills carriers and full-service airlines. Discounted Web fares offer the best deals, and one-way tickets make it easy to fly into one city and out of another. Note that if you're booking on short notice (that is, less than around three or four weeks before departure), national carriers often offer better prices than the budget airlines.

On transatlantic and long-haul flights your travel agent is probably still the best source of cheap tickets, although there is an increasing number of online booking agencies. Be sure to check the terms and conditions of the cheapest fares before booking.

Australia

There are no direct scheduled flights between Australia and Poland; generally it's cheapest to fly into London, Frankfurt or Amsterdam and continue to Warsaw from there. Round-the-world (RTW) tickets are another good bet and are often better value than standard return fares. For online bookings, try www.travel.com.au.

The following are well-known agencies for cheap fares:

Flight Centre (Australia-wide ☎ 133 133; www.flight centre.com.au)

STA Travel (Australia-wide ☎ 1300 733 035; www.sta travel.com.au)

Continental Europe

There are flights to Warsaw from all major European capitals, with both LOT and other carriers.

GermanWings flies from Cologne/Bonn and Stuttgart to both Warsaw and Kraków, while WizzAir flies into Katowice from Athens, Dortmund, Milan, Paris, Rome and Stockholm, and into Warsaw from Brussels, Dortmund and Malmö.

DEPARTURE TAX

There is no departure tax to be paid when flying out of Poland.

The following are recommended travel and ticket agencies:

FRANCE

Anyway (☎ 0892 893 892; www.anyway.fr)

Lastminute.com (☎ 0892 705 000; www.fr.lastminute .com)

Nouvelles Frontières (☎ 0825 000 747; www.nouvel les-frontieres.fr)

OTU Voyages (☎ 01 40 29 12 22; www.otu.fr) Specialises in student and youth travellers.

Voyageurs du Monde (☎ 01 40 15 11 15; www.vdm .com)

GERMANY

Expedia (www.expedia.de)

Just Travel (☎ 089 747 3330; www.justtravel.de)

Lastminute.com (☎ 01805 284 366; www.de.last minute.com)

STA Travel (☎ 01805 456 422; www.statravel.de) For travellers under the age of 26.

ITALY

CTS Viaggi (☎ 06 462 0431; www.cts.it)

THE NETHERLANDS

Airfair (☎ 020 620 5121; www.airfair.nl)

SPAIN

Barcelo Viajes (☎ 902 11 62 26; www.barceloviajes.com)

Nouvelles Frontiéres (☎ 902 17 09 79; www.nouvel les-frontieres.es)

The UK & Ireland

Flights on the London Heathrow–Warsaw route are offered daily by both LOT and British Airways. LOT also has daily direct flights from Manchester to Warsaw, London Heathrow to Kraków, and Dublin to Warsaw.

Budget airline EasyJet flies from London Luton to Warsaw and Kraków. WizzAir has flights from London Luton to Warsaw, Gdańsk and Katowice, and from Liverpool to Warsaw and Katowice.

Discount air travel is big business in London. Advertisements for many travel agencies appear in the travel pages of the weekend broadsheet newspapers, in *Time Out*, the *Evening Standard* and in the free magazine *TNT*.

The following are recommended travel agencies:

Bridge the World (☎ 0870 444 7474; www.b-t-w.co.uk)

Flight Centre (☎ 0870 890 8099; www.flightcentre.co.uk)

Flightbookers (☎ 0870 010 7000; www.ebookers.com)

North-South Travel (☎ 01245 608 291; www.north southtravel.co.uk) Donates part of its profit to projects in the developing world.
Quest Travel (☎ 0870 442 3542; www.questtravel.com)
STA Travel (☎ 0870 160 0599; www.statravel.co.uk) For travellers under the age of 26.
Trailfinders (www.trailfinders.co.uk)
Travel Bag (☎ 0870 890 1456; www.travelbag.co.uk)

The USA & Canada

LOT (in both the USA & Canada ☎ 1-800-223 0593) has direct flights from New York, Chicago and Toronto to Warsaw.

Agents often use indirect connections with other carriers such as British Airways, Lufthansa, KLM or Air France. Not only may these work out cheaper, but they can also let you break the journey in Western Europe for the same price or a little extra – a bonus if you want to stop en route in London, Paris or Amsterdam.

Travel Cuts (☎ 800-667 2887; www.travelcuts.com) is Canada's national student travel agency. For online bookings try www.expedia.ca and www.travelocity.ca.

In the USA, a reputable discount travel agency is **STA Travel** (☎ 800-777 0112; www.sta .com). The following agencies are recommended for online bookings:

American Express (www.itn.net)
CheapTickets (www.cheaptickets.com)
Expedia (www.expedia.com)
Lowestfare.com (www.lowestfare.com)
Orbitz (www.orbitz.com)
Travelocity (www.travelocity.com)

LAND
Border Crossings

Sitting in the middle of Europe and sharing its borders with seven countries, Poland has plenty of rail and road crossings with its neighbours. Border crossings are more numerous with Germany to the west, and the Czech and Slovak republics to the south, than they are with the Ukraine, Belarus, Lithuania and Russia to the east and northeast.

Remember that Poland's eastern border is now one of the external borders of the EU. If you're travelling overland to Russia, be aware that you may need a Belarusian transit visa, which must be obtained in advance. Following is a list of 24-hour border crossings for heading east out of Poland by road.

Belarusian border (south to north): Terespol, Kuźnica Białostocka
Lithuanian border (east to west): Ogrodniki, Budzisko
Russian border (east to west): Bezledy, Gronowo
Ukrainian border (south to north): Medyka, Hrebenne, Dorohusk

Belarus, Lithuania & the Ukraine
BUS

The Polish-owned Eurolines partner **PKS** (www.pekaesbus.com.pl) has daily buses to Warsaw from Lviv (85 hv, 10 hours) in the Ukraine, Minsk (65zł, 12 hours) in Belarus, and Vilnius (110 Lt, 12 hours) in Lithuania. There are also regular buses between Przemyśl and Lviv, and one bus a week between Suwałki and Vilnius.

TRAIN

Warsaw has direct rail links with Kyiv in the Ukraine, Minsk and Hrodna in Belarus, and Vilnius in Lithuania. These trains are sleeper only, and you'll be automatically sold a sleeping berth when buying your ticket.

Remember that the main Warsaw to Vilnius railway line passes through Hrodna in Belarus, and you may need a transit visa

---

TRAIN THEFT WARNING

Theft on international trains is becoming a problem, mainly on the Berlin–Warsaw trains, which are notorious for gangs of thieves who break into compartments and steal the valuables of sleeping passengers. There have been some recent reports of armed assaults in these trains. Most cases of theft occur between the German-Polish border and Poznań. You should also be on your guard on Berlin–Kraków and Prague–Warsaw trains.

Some travellers have been robbed at knifepoint in slow local trains while sitting by themselves in a compartment. Don't sit in a cabin alone; join other passengers.

Watch your luggage and your pockets closely when you are getting on or off the train, as these are the most convenient moments for pickpockets to distract your attention. Warsaw's central train station is a favourite playground for thieves; take particular care when passing through.

even if you have no intention of leaving the train until Vilnius. Belarusian border guards take pleasure in turning visa-less tourists around and putting them on the next train back to Warsaw.

The alternative is to take a train from Warsaw to Kaunas via Suwałki (avoiding Belarus), and then catching a local train from Kaunas to Vilnius.

The Czech Republic
BUS
Eurolines-Sodeli CZ (☎ 02-224 239 318; www.euro lines.cz; Senovážné nám 6, Nové Město, Prague) runs buses from Prague to Warsaw (800Kà, 10½ hours) via Wrocław (670Kà, 4¾ hours).

TRAIN
There are daily express trains from Prague to Warsaw (1140Kà, 9½ hours) via Wrocław or Katowice, and to Kraków (885Kà, 8½ hours).

The UK
BUS
Eurolines (☎ 08705 143219; www.eurolines.co.uk) runs buses from London to Warsaw (one way UK£60, 28 hours) via Ostend, Brussels and Poznań, and to Kraków (UK£60, 27 hours; using the same route as far as Poznań, and then via Wrocław and Katowice). The frequency of the service varies depending on the season: it's as often as daily in summer and slows down to twice weekly the rest of the year. Tickets can be bought from any National Express office and from a number of travel agencies.

TRAIN
You can travel from London to Warsaw via the Channel Tunnel, with a single change of train at Brussels (20 hours). The ordinary return fare in high season is around UK£300.

Western Europe
BUS
Eurolines (www.eurolines.com) operates an extensive network of bus routes all over Western Europe. Standards, reliability and comfort may vary from bus to bus, but on the whole are not too bad. Most buses are from the modern generation, and come equipped with air-conditioning, toilet facilities and a video.

As a rough guide only, average one-way fares and journey times between some Western cities and Warsaw are as follows:

To	One way	Time
Amsterdam	€90	21hr
Brussels	€90	22hr
Cologne	€65	20hr
Frankfurt	€60	19hr
Hamburg	€50	16hr
Munich	€60	20hr
Paris	€70	27hr
Rome	€100	27hr

TRAIN
A number of German cities are linked by train (direct or indirect) with major Polish cities. Direct connections with Warsaw include Berlin, Cologne, Dresden and Leipzig. There are also direct trains between Berlin and Kraków (via Wrocław; €50, 9½ hours).

The Warsaw–Berlin route (via Frankfurt/Oder and Poznań; €36, 6½ hours) is serviced by six trains a day in each direction, including three EuroCity express trains that cover the distance in 6½ hours.

There are direct trains from Brussels (Bruxelles-Nord) to Warsaw (14½ hours), and you can get from Paris to Warsaw in 16½ hours, with a single change of trains at Brussels.

SEA
Poland has regular car-ferry services plying the routes from Denmark and Sweden to Gdańsk and Świnoujście on the coast of Poland. The fares quoted here are for a foot passenger/small car with driver in the summer.

Denmark
Polferries (www.polferries.pl) From Copenhagen to Świnoujście (425/595kr, 10 hours, five times a week).

Sweden
Polferries (www.polferries.pl) Operates the Ystad–Świnoujście (Skr535/805, nine hours, daily) and Nynäshamn-Gdańsk (Skr610/1005, 18 hours, daily) routes.
Stena Line (www.stenaline.com) From Karlskrona to Gdynia (from Skr290/575, 11 hours, daily).
Unity Line (www.unityline.pl) From Ystad to Świnoujście (Skr375/1240, eight hours, daily).

TRANSPORT

GETTING AROUND

AIR

LOT (www.lot.com) operates a comprehensive network of domestic routes. There are daily flights between Warsaw and Bydgoszcz, Gdańsk, Katowice, Kraków, Łódź, Poznań, Rzeszów, Szczecin, Wrocław and Zielona Góra. All flights between regional cities travel via Warsaw, and connections aren't always convenient.

The regular one-way fare on any of the direct flights to/from Warsaw is around 140zł. Any combined flight via Warsaw (eg Szczecin–Kraków or Gdańsk–Wrocław) will cost around 285zł. Tickets can be booked and bought at any LOT or Orbis office, and from some other travel agencies.

Senior citizens over 60 years of age pay 80% of the full fare on all domestic flights. Foreign students holding an ISIC card get a 10% discount. There are attractive stand-by fares (about 25% of the regular fare) for young people aged under 20 and students under 26; tickets have to be bought right before scheduled departure. There are also some promotional fares on selected flights in certain periods (eg early or late flights, selected weekend flights); they can be just a third of the ordinary fares and are applicable to everybody.

Most airports are a manageable distance – between 10km and 20km – from city centres and are linked to them by public transport. Only Szczecin and Katowice airports are further out. You must check in at least 30 minutes before departure. Have your passport at hand – you'll be asked to show it as ID. There's no departure tax on domestic flights.

BICYCLE

Poland is not a bad place for cycling. Most of the country is fairly flat, so riding is easy and any ordinary bike is OK. Camping equipment isn't essential, as hotels and hostels are usually no more than an easy day's ride apart, but carrying your own camping gear will give you more flexibility.

Major roads carry pretty heavy traffic and are best avoided. Instead, you can easily plan your route along minor roads, which are usually much less crowded and in reasonable shape. Stock up on detailed tourist maps, which feature all minor roads, specifying which are sealed and which are not, and also show marked walking trails. Some of these trails are easily travelled by bike, giving you still more options.

On a less-optimistic note, the standard of driving in Poland may not be quite what you've been used to at home. Some vehicles may drive along the middle of the road and fail to move over for you. Some drivers seem compelled to overtake anything in their path – particularly cyclists – regardless of oncoming traffic. Note that in Poland cyclists are not allowed to ride two abreast.

Cities are not pleasant for cyclists either, as dedicated cycle tracks are few and far between, and some drivers are not particularly polite to cyclists. Furthermore, city roads are often in poor shape, and cobbled streets are not uncommon.

Hotel staff will usually let you put your bike indoors for the night, sometimes in your room; it's often better to leave it in the hotel during the day as well, and get around city sights on foot or by public transport. Bikes, especially Western ones, are attractive to thieves, so it's a good idea to carry a solid lock and chain (for the frame and both wheels), and always use them when you leave the bike outdoors, even if only for a moment.

You can take your bike on the train. Some long-distance trains have a baggage car. If this is the case, you should normally take your bike to the railway luggage office, fill out a tag and pay a small fee. They will then load the bike and drop it off at your destination. It's a good idea to strip the bike of anything easily removable and keep an eye out to be sure it has actually been loaded on the train. You can also take your bike straight to the baggage car (which is usually at the front or the rear of the train), but this can be difficult at intermediate stations where the train may only stop for a few minutes.

Bikes are not allowed on express trains or on those that take reservations, since these trains don't have baggage cars. Many ordinary trains don't have baggage cars either, but you can try to take the bike into the passenger car with you as some Poles do. Check at the baggage window in the station before you do so. Buses don't normally take bikes.

Cycling shops and repair centres are popping up in large cities, and in some of the major tourist resorts. You can now buy various makes of Western bikes and some popular spare parts. For rural riding, you should carry all essential spare parts, for it's unlikely there'll be a bike shop close at hand. In particular, spare nuts and bolts should be carried.

Bike-hire outlets are still few and far between. They seldom offer anything other than ordinary Polish bikes, and their condition may leave little to be desired.

BOAT

Poland has a long coastline and lots of rivers and canals, but passenger-boat services are pretty limited and operate only in summer. There are no regular boats running along the main rivers or along the coast. Several cities, including Szczecin, Gdańsk, Toruń, Wrocław and Kraków, have local river cruises during the summer, and a few coastal ports (Kołobrzeg and Gdańsk) offer sea excursions.

On the Masurian lakes (p438), excursion boats run in summer between Giżycko, Mikołajki, Węgorzewo and Ruciane-Nida. Tourist boats are also available in the Augustów area where they ply part of the Augustów Canal (p452). The most unusual canal trip is the full-day cruise along the Elbląg-Ostróda Canal (p434).

BUS

Buses are often more convenient than trains over a short distance. On longer routes, too, you may sometimes find a bus to be better and faster when, for instance, the train route involves a long detour. You'll often travel by bus in the mountains, where trains are slow and few. Ordinary buses on short routes are cheaper than the 2nd class of ordinary trains.

Most of Poland's bus transport is operated by the former state bus company, PKS (Państwowa Komunikacja Samochodowa), which has split up into dozens of smaller, regional spin-off enterprises. These regional bus companies are gradually being snapped up by private operators, so Poland's domestic bus services are likely to be in a state of flux for the next few years until the new regime settles in.

You can find details of their services online at their various websites, which mostly take the form www.pks.xxxx.pl, where the 'xxxx' is the name of the town, eg www.pks .warszawa.pl and www.pks.krakow.pl. Most are in Polish only, but some have English versions.

The bus network is much more comprehensive than the rail network, and buses go to most villages that are accessible by road. The frequency of service varies a great deal: on the main routes there may be a bus leaving every quarter of an hour or so, whereas some small, remote villages may get only one bus a day. Almost all buses run during the daytime, sometimes starting very early in the morning.

PKS' main competitor is **Polski Express** (www.polskiexpress.pl), a joint venture with Eurolines National Express based in the UK. It runs several long-distance routes out of Warsaw, serving Białystok, Gdańsk (via Ostróda and Elbląg), Kraków (via Łódź and Katowice), Rzeszów (via Puławy and Lublin) and Bydgoszcz (via Płock and Toruń). Its buses are faster and more comfortable than PKS ones, but cost much the same.

The local PKS bus station (*dworzec autobusowy* PKS) is usually found alongside the train station. Save for the large terminals in the major cities, bus stations don't normally provide a left-luggage service and have few other facilities. They are closed at night.

Costs

The approximate fares for intercity bus journeys are as follows:

Distance	Fare
20km	5zł
40km	8zł
60km	10zł
80km	12zł
100km	14zł
150km	18zł
200km	23zł
250km	28zł
300km	33zł

Tickets

The only place to buy PKS tickets is at the bus station itself. Tickets on long routes serviced by fast buses can be bought up to 30 days in advance but those for short, local routes are only available the same day.

Tickets are numbered, and buying one at the counter at the terminal assures you of a seat. If you get on the bus somewhere along the route, you buy the ticket directly from the driver and you won't necessarily have a seat.

Tickets for Polski Express buses can be bought at the bus stations and from some Orbis Travel offices.

Timetables

Timetables are posted on boards either inside or outside PKS bus terminal buildings. There are also notice boards on all bus stops along the route (if vandals haven't damaged or removed them). The timetable of departures (*odjazdy*) lists destinations (*kierunek*), the places passed en route (*przez*) and departure times.

Keep in mind that there may be more buses to the particular town you want to go to than those that are mentioned in the destination column of the timetable under the town's name. You therefore need to check whether your town appears in the *przez* column on the way to more-distant destinations.

Also check any additional symbols that accompany the departure time, which can mean that the bus runs only on certain days or in certain seasons. They're explained in the key at the end of the timetable.

You can find online bus timetables at www.polskibus.pl.

Types of Bus

There are two types of PKS bus service: ordinary and fast. The ordinary or local buses (*autobusy zwykłe*) stop at all stops en route and their average speed barely exceeds 35km/h. The standard of these buses leaves a little to be desired. Their departure and arrival times appear in black on timetable boards. The fast buses (*autobusy pospieszne*), marked in red, cover mainly long-distance routes and manage an average speed of 45km/h to 55km/h. As a rule, they take only as many passengers as they have seats, and the standards tend to be better than that of the ordinary buses.

CAR & MOTORCYCLE
Automobile Associations

The **Polski Związek Motorowy** (PZM, Polish Automobile & Motorcycle Federation; ☎ 22-849 93 61; www .pzm.pl; ul Kazimierzowska 66, 02-518 Warsaw) is Poland's national motoring organisation. It is affiliated with the Alliance Internationale de Tourisme and the Fédération Internationale de l'Automobile, and provides a 24-hour national **roadside assistance** (☎ 9637) service. If you are a member of an affiliated automobile association, PZM will help you on roughly the same terms as your own organisation would. If not, you must pay for all services.

Bring Your Own Vehicle

Many Western tourists, particularly Germans, bring their own vehicles into Poland. There are no special formalities: all you need at the border is your passport (with a valid visa if necessary), your driving licence, vehicle registration document and third-party insurance (Green Card). If your insurance isn't valid for Poland, you can buy an additional policy at the border (depending on the size of the engine, this costs from 67zł/95zł for 15 days/one month). A nationality plate or sticker must be displayed on the back of the car.

If you do decide to bring your own vehicle to Poland, remember that life will be easier for you if it's not brand-new. Expensive recent models are favourite targets for gangs of organised car thieves in large cities. The shabbier your car looks, the better. Don't wash it too often.

There's a widespread network of garages that specialise in fixing Western cars (though not many for motorcycles), but they mostly deal with older, traditional models with mechanical technology. The more electronic and computer-controlled bits your car has, the more problems you'll face having something fixed if it goes wrong. These parts can be ordered for you, but they'll usually take a while to arrive.

Driving Licence

If you plan on driving in Poland, make sure you bring your driving licence. Foreign driving licences are valid in Poland for up to 90 days. Strictly speaking, licences that do not include a photo ID need an international driving permit as well, although this rule is rarely enforced – ordinary UK licences without a photograph are normally accepted without comment.

Fuel & Spare Parts

Petrol (*benzyna*) is readily available at hundreds of petrol stations, which have mushroomed throughout the country. There are

Road Distances (km)

	Białystok	Bydgoszcz	Częstochowa	Gdańsk	Katowice	Kielce	Kraków	Łódź	Lublin	Olsztyn	Opole	Poznań	Rzeszów	Szczecin	Toruń	Warsaw	Wrocław	Zielona Góra
Białystok	---																	
Bydgoszcz	389	---																
Częstochowa	410	316	---															
Gdańsk	379	167	470	---														
Katowice	485	391	75	545	---													
Kielce	363	348	124	483	156	---												
Kraków	477	430	114	565	75	114	---											
Łódź	322	205	121	340	196	143	220	---										
Lublin	260	421	288	500	323	167	269	242	---									
Olsztyn	223	217	404	156	479	394	500	281	370	---								
Opole	507	318	98	485	113	220	182	244	382	452	---							
Poznań	491	129	289	296	335	354	403	212	465	323	261	---						
Rzeszów	430	516	272	642	244	163	165	306	170	516	347	517	---					
Szczecin	656	267	520	348	561	585	634	446	683	484	459	234	751	---				
Toruń	347	46	289	181	364	307	384	159	375	172	312	151	470	313	---			
Warsaw	188	255	222	339	297	181	295	134	161	213	319	310	303	524	209	---		
Wrocław	532	265	176	432	199	221	268	204	428	442	86	178	433	371	279	344	---	
Zielona Góra	601	259	328	411	356	422	427	303	542	453	245	130	585	214	281	413	157	---

several different kinds and grades of petrol; most hire cars run on 98-octane unleaded (*bezołowiowa*) or diesel (*diesel*). The price of fuel can differ between petrol stations by up to 10%. An increasing number of petrol stations accept credit cards.

Virtually all petrol stations have adopted a self-service system. Air and water are usually available, as well as oil, lubricants and basic spare parts such as light bulbs, fuses etc. An increasing number of new stations also offer food and drink. Many stations located along main roads and in the large cities are open round the clock.

Hire

Car-hire agencies will require you to produce your passport, a driving licence held for at least one year, and a credit card. You need to be at least 21 or 23 years of age (depending on the company) to hire a car, although hiring some cars, particularly luxury models and 4WDs, may require a higher age.

One-way hire within Poland is possible with most companies (usually for an additional fee), but most will insist on keeping the car within Poland. In any case, no company is likely to allow you to take its car beyond the eastern border.

High insurance premiums mean that car hire in Poland is not cheap, and there are seldom any promotional discounts. As a rough guide only, economy models offered by reputable local companies begin at around 135zł/990zł per day/week (including insurance and unlimited mileage). Rates at the big international agencies start at around 470zł/1800zł. It's usually cheaper to book your car from abroad.

When hiring a car, read the contract carefully before signing. Pay close attention to any theft clause, as it may load a large percentage of any loss onto the hirer. Check the car carefully before you drive off.

LOCAL & INTERNATIONAL CAR-HIRE AGENCIES
Avis (toll-free ☎ 0801 120 010; www.avis.pl)
Budget (in Warsaw ☎ 22-650 40 62; www.budget.pl)
E-car (toll-free ☎ 0801 332 232; www.e-car.pl)
Europcar (in Warsaw ☎ 22-650 25 64; www.europcar.com.pl)

Hertz (toll-free ☎ 0800 143 789; www.hertz.com)
Local Rent-a-Car (in Warsaw ☎ 22-826 71 00; www
.lrc.com.pl)

Insurance

Bring along a good insurance policy from a
reliable company for both the car and your
possessions. Car theft is a major problem
in Poland, with organised gangs operating
in the large cities. Some of them cooperate
with Russians in smuggling stolen vehicles
across the eastern border, never to be seen
again.

Even if the car itself doesn't get stolen,
you may lose some of its accessories, most
likely the radio/cassette player, as well as any
personal belongings you've left inside. Hide
your gear, if you must leave it inside; try to
make the car look empty. If possible, always
park your car in a guarded car park (*parking
strzeżony*). If your hotel doesn't have its own,
the staff will tell you where the nearest one is,
probably within walking distance.

In the cities, it may be more convenient
and safer to leave your vehicle in a secure
place (eg your hotel car park), and get
around by taxi or public transport.

Road Conditions

The massive increase in traffic over recent
years, along with a lack of maintenance, has
led to a deterioration in road surfaces, with
some in better shape than others.

Poland has only a few motorways in the
proper sense of the word, but an array of
two- and four-lane highways crisscross the
country. Secondary roads are narrower but
they usually carry less traffic and are OK
for leisurely travel. The sealed minor roads,
which are even narrower, are also often in
acceptable condition, though driving is
harder work as they tend to twist and turn,
are not so well signposted and pass through
every single village along the way.

Road Hazards

Drive carefully on country roads, particularly at night. There are still a lot of horse-
drawn carts on Polish roads, and the further
off the main routes you wander, the more
carts, elderly cyclists, tractors and other agricultural machinery you'll encounter. They
are often lit poorly or not at all. The same
applies to bicycles – you'll hardly ever see a
properly lit bike.

Road Rules

Road rules are the same as in the rest of
Europe. A vehicle must be equipped with
a first-aid kit, a red-and-white warning triangle and a nationality sticker on the rear;
the use of seat belts is compulsory. Drinking and driving is strictly forbidden – the
legal blood alcohol level is 0.02%. Police can
hit you with on-the-spot fines for speeding
and other traffic offences (be sure to insist
on a receipt).

Polish speed limits are 20km/h or 60km/h
in built-up areas, 90km/h on open roads,
110km/h on dual carriageways and 130km/h
on motorways; motorcycles are limited to
80km/h. At level crossings over rail lines the
speed limit is 30km/h. Beware of speed
traps. From October to February, car and
motorcycle lights must be on at all times
while driving, even during a sunny day.
Motorcyclists should remember that both
rider and passenger must wear helmets.

Unless signs state otherwise, cars and
motorcycles can be parked on pavements,
as long as a minimum 1.5m-wide walkway is
left for pedestrians. Parking in the opposite
direction to the flow of traffic is allowed.

The following are traffic signs that may
be unfamiliar to Britons and non-European
visitors:

Blue disc with red border and red slash No parking
on the road, but you still can park on the footpath; if
the sign is accompanied by a white board below saying
'*dotyczy również chodnika*' or '*dotyczy także chodnika*'
(meaning 'it also refers to the footpath'), you can't park
on either the road or the footpath.
Yellow diamond with white border You have right
of way; a black slash through it means you no longer have
right of way.
Yellow triangle (point down) with red border
Give way.

When driving in cities be aware of trams.
You may overtake a tram only on the right,
and only if it's in motion. You must stop behind any tram taking on or letting off passengers where there's no passenger island.
If there's a pedestrian island, you don't have
to stop. A tram has right of way when making any signalled turn across your path.

HITCHING

Hitching (*autostop*) is never entirely safe
anywhere in the world. Travellers who decide to hitch should understand that they

are taking a small but potentially serious risk. Those who choose to hitch will be safer travelling in pairs, and letting someone know where they are planning to go.

That said, hitching does take place in Poland, though it's not very popular. Car drivers rarely stop to pick up hitchers, and large commercial vehicles (which are easier to wave down) expect to be paid the equivalent of a bus fare.

LOCAL TRANSPORT
Bus, Tram & Trolleybus

Most cities have both buses (autobus) and trams (tramwaj), and some also have trolleybuses (trolejbus). Public transport operates from around 5am to 11pm and may be crowded during the rush hours (7am till 9am and 4.30pm till 6.30pm Monday to Friday). The largest cities also have night-time services, on either buses or trams. Timetables are usually posted at stops, but don't rely too much on their accuracy.

In many cities there's a flat-rate fare for local transport so the duration of the ride and the distance make no difference. If you change vehicles, however, you need another ticket. The ordinary fare is usually around 2.40zł. In some cities the fare depends on how long you travel, with the ticket valid for a certain period of time, such as 30 minutes or one hour. Night services are more expensive than daytime fares.

There are no conductors on board; you buy tickets beforehand and punch or stamp them in one of the little machines installed near the doors. You can buy tickets from Ruch or Relay newspaper kiosks or, in some cities, from street stalls around the central stops, recognisable by the bilety (tickets) boards they display. Buy a bunch of them at once if you are going to use public transport. Buy enough tickets on Saturday morning to last you until Monday, as few kiosks are open on Sunday. Tickets purchased in one city cannot be used in another.

Plain-clothed ticket inspectors are always on the prowl and foreign backpackers are their favourite targets. These inspectors tend to be officious, dogged and singularly unpleasant to deal with.

If you are caught without a ticket, it's best to pay the fine straight away. Never give an inspector your passport, even if they threaten you with police intervention if you don't.

Taxi

Taxis are easily available and not too expensive. As a rough guide, a 5km taxi trip will cost around 12zł, and a 10km ride shouldn't cost more than 20zł. Taxi fares are 50% higher at night (10pm to 6am), on Sunday and outside the city limits. The number of passengers (usually up to four) and the amount of luggage doesn't affect the fare.

There are plenty of taxi companies, including the once monopolist state-run **Radio Taxi** (☎ 919), which is the largest and operates in most cities. Taxis are recognisable by large signs on the roof with the company's name and phone number. There are also pirate taxis (called 'mafia' taxis by Poles), which usually have just a small 'taxi' sign on the roof with no name or phone number. These are best avoided.

Taxis can be waved down on the street, but it's easier to go to a taxi stand (postój taksówek), where you'll almost always find a line of them. There are plenty of stands and everybody will tell you where the nearest is. Taxis can also be ordered by phone, and there's usually no extra charge for this.

When you get into a taxi, make sure the driver turns on the meter. Also check whether the meter has been switched to the proper rate: '1' identifies the daytime rate, and '2' is the night-time rate. A typical scam against foreigners is to drop the flag to the higher night-time rate during the daytime.

Remember to carry small bills, so you'll be able to pay the exact fare. If you don't, it's virtually impossible to get change from a driver who's intent on charging you more. It's always a good idea to find out before how much the right fare should be by asking hotel staff or an attendant at the airport.

TOURS

The following Polish agencies offer organised tours in Poland:

Bird Service (Map pp132-3; ☎ 12-292 14 60; www .bird.pl; ul Św Krzyża 17, Kraków) Offers nature tours (bird-watching, kayaking, biking etc) in out-of-the-way areas, and week-long cycle tours along the Dunajec River.

Jarden Tourist Agency (Map p141; ☎ 12-421 71 66; www.jarden.pl; ul Szeroka 2, Kraków) A Jewish-interest agency that organises tours of Auschwitz-Birkenau.

Kampio (Map p58; ☎ 22-823 70 70; www.kampio.com .pl; ul Maszynowa 9/2, Warsaw) Focuses on ecotourism, organising biking tours in Masuria, bird-watching in Białowieża and kayaking in Biebrza National Park.

Our Roots (Map pp62-3; ☎ /fax 22-620 05 56; ul Twarda 6, Warsaw) Specialises in tours of Jewish sites in Warsaw, and trips to Holocaust sites such as Treblinka.
PTTK Mazury (Map pp430-1; ☎ /fax 89-527 40 59; www .pttkmazury.pl in Polish; ul Staromiejska 1, Olsztyn) Runs 10-day kayak tours along the Krutynia River from late June to mid-August.

TRAIN

Trains will be your main means of transport, especially when travelling long distances – they are relatively inexpensive, fairly reliable and usually run on time. They are normally not overcrowded, except for peak holiday periods in July and August.

The railways are administered by the Polskie Koleje Państwowe (Polish State Railways), commonly known by the abbreviation PKP. With over 27,000km of lines, the railway network is fairly extensive and covers most places you might wish to go to. Predictably, the network covers less of the mountainous parts of southern Poland, and trains are slower there.

Costs

Tickets for fast trains (see p488 for information on types of trains) are about 60% more expensive than those for ordinary trains, and an express train costs 50% more than a fast train. First class is 50% more expensive than 2nd class. Fares are dependent on distance; fares in the following table are approximate prices for 2nd-class tickets.

Distance	Ordinary	Fast
50km	8zł	14zł
100km	15zł	24zł
150km	19zł	30zł
200km	21zł	34zł
250km	24zł	40zł
300km	26zł	43zł
350km	27zł	45zł
400km	28zł	47zł
450km	30zł	50zł
500km	31zł	52zł

A reservation costs an additional 8zł (12zł on InterCity trains) regardless of distance. A 2nd-/1st-class couchette costs an additional 50zł/60zł, while a sleeper costs an additional 90zł/130zł.

The approximate fares on InterCity trains (including the compulsory seat reservation)

from Warsaw to Gdańsk, to Katowice, to Kraków or to Poznań are 80zł/120zł in 2nd/1st class.

There are no discounts for ISIC card holders on domestic trains, even though there are reduced fares for Polish students.

Tickets

Since most train-station ticket offices have been computerised, buying tickets is now less of a hassle than it used to be, but queuing is still a way of life. Be at the station at least half an hour before the departure time of your train and make sure you are queuing at the right ticket window. As cashiers rarely speak English, the easiest way of buying a ticket is to have all the relevant details written down on a piece of paper. These should include the destination, the departure time and the class – *pierwsza klasa* (first) or *druga klasa* (second). If seat reservation is compulsory on your train, you'll automatically be sold a reserved-seat ticket (*miejscówka*); if it's optional, you must state whether you want a *miejscówka* or not.

If you are forced to get on a train without a ticket, you can buy one directly from the conductor for a small supplement, but you should find him or her right away. If the conductor finds you first, you'll be fined for travelling without a ticket.

Couchettes and sleepers can be booked at special counters at larger stations; it's advisable to reserve them in advance. Advance tickets for journeys of over 100km and couchette and sleeper tickets can also be bought at any Orbis Travel office and some other agencies – perhaps a quicker option.

Timetables

Train timetables (*rozkład jazdy*) are displayed in all stations, with departures on yellow boards and arrivals (*przyjazdy*) on white ones.

Ordinary trains are marked in black print, fast trains in red, and if you spot an additional 'Ex', this means an express train. InterCity trains are identified by the letters 'IC'. The letter 'R' in a square indicates a train with compulsory seat reservation. There will be some letters and/or numbers following the departure time; always check them in the key below. They usually say that the train runs (*kursuje*) or doesn't run (*nie kursuje*) in particular periods or days.

POLISH RAILWAYS

The timetables also indicate which platform (*peron*) the train departs from.

You can check train timetables online at http://rozklad.pkpik.pl.

Train Passes

Eurodomino Passes are available for three to eight days of rail travel in Poland in a one-month period, and are priced in three bands: youth (under 26), adult (26 to 59) and senior (60 and over). You must be a resident of a European country, and you have to buy the pass before you arrive in Poland. A youth/adult Eurodomino Pass purchased in the UK costs UK£36/UK£55 for three days and UK£73/UK£86 for eight days, travelling second class.

For full details, see www.raileurope.co.uk and www.railchoice.co.uk.

Train Stations

Most larger train stations have a range of facilities, including waiting rooms, snack bars, newsagents, left-luggage and toilets. The biggest stations in the major cities may also have a restaurant, a *kantor* (currency-exchange office) and a post office. In some small villages, on the other hand, the station may be no more than a shed with just a ticket window, which will be open for a short time before a train arrives. If there's more than one train station in a city, the main one is identified by the name 'Główny' or 'Centralny'.

Some train stations – even major ones – are poorly marked, and, unless you're familiar with the route, it's easy to miss your stop. If in doubt, asking fellow passengers is probably the best plan of action.

All large stations have left-luggage rooms (*przechowalnia bagażu*), which are usually open round the clock. You can store your luggage there for up to 10 days. There's a low basic daily-storage charge per item (3zł), plus 1% of the declared value of the luggage as insurance. One thing to remember is that they usually close once or twice a day for an hour or so. The times of these breaks are displayed over the counter. If you've put your baggage in storage, be sure to arrive at least half an hour before your departure time to allow time for some queuing and paperwork. You pay the charge when you pick up your luggage, not when you deposit it.

Types of Train

There are three main types of train: express, fast and ordinary. The express train (*pociąg ekspresowy* or *ekspres*) is the fastest and the most comfortable, operating on long intercity routes and only stopping at major cities en route. They carry only bookable seats; you can't travel standing if all the seats are sold out. Express trains tend to run during the daytime, rather than overnight. Their average speed is from 80km/h to 100km/h.

A more luxurious version of the express train, the InterCity train, began operating in the early 1990s. InterCity trains are even faster and more comfortable than regular express trains, and a light snack is included in the price (EuroCity trains are international InterCity trains). These trains run on some major routes out of Warsaw and they don't stop en route at all. The main destinations (along with distances and approximate travelling times) include: Gdańsk (three hours and 20 minutes, 333km); Katowice (two hours and 40 minutes, 303km); Kraków (two hours and 35 minutes, 297km); Poznań (three hours and 10 minutes, 311km); and Szczecin (five hours and 40 minutes, 525km).

Fast trains (*pociąg pospieszny*) stop at more intermediate stations. Usually not all carriages require booking; some will take passengers regardless of how crowded they are. At an average speed of between 60km/h and 80km/h, they are still a convenient way to get around the country and are one-third cheaper than express trains. They often travel at night, and if the distance justifies it they carry couchettes (*kuszetki*) or sleepers (*miejsca sypialne*) – a good way to avoid hotel costs and reach your destination early in the morning. Book as soon as you decide to go, as there are usually only a couple of sleeping cars and beds may sell out fast.

An ordinary or local train (*pociąg osobowy*) is far slower as it stops at all stations along the way. These trains mostly cover shorter distances, but they also run on longer routes. You can assume that their average speed will be between 30km/h and 40km/h. They are less comfortable than express or fast trains and don't require reservations. They are OK for short distances, but a longer journey can be tiring.

Almost all trains have two classes of carriage: 2nd class and 1st class. The carriages of long-distance trains are usually divided into compartments: the 1st-class compartments have six seats, while the 2nd-class ones contain eight seats. Smoking is allowed in some compartments and the part of the corridor facing them, but many Poles are chain smokers and a journey in such company can be almost unbearable. It's better to book a seat in a nonsmoking compartment and go into the smoking corridor if you wish to smoke.

The 2nd-class couchette compartments have six beds, with three to a side; the 1st-class compartments have four beds, two to a side. Sleepers come in both 2nd and 1st class; the former sleep three to a compartment, the latter only two, and both have a washbasin, sheets and blankets.

Health
Dr Caroline Evans

Travel health depends on your predeparture preparations, your daily health care while travelling and how you handle any medical problem that does develop. There's a popular Polish saying: 'To be ill in Poland, it helps to be healthy'. It's a wryly humorous reference to the poor state of health care in the country; political mismanagement and lack of investment have seen the health service decline in the last five years. Fortunately, there are private hospitals and clinics in the main cities where the level of care is the same as you'll find in the West (see Medical Services p60 and p129).

BEFORE YOU GO

Prevention is the key to staying healthy while you are abroad. A little planning before your departure, particularly for pre-existing illnesses, will save trouble later: see your dentist before a long trip, carry a spare pair of contact lenses and glasses, and take your optical prescription with you. Bring medications in their original, clearly labelled containers. A signed and dated letter from your physician describing your medical conditions and medications, including generic names, is also a good idea. If carrying syringes or needles, be sure to have a physician's letter documenting their medical necessity.

INSURANCE

If you're an EU citizen, an E111 form, which is available from health centres (or, in the UK, from post offices), covers you for most medical care. E111 will not, however, cover you for nonemergencies or emergency repatriation home. Citizens from other countries should find out if there is a reciprocal arrangement for free medical care between their country and the country they plan to visit. If you do need health insurance, strongly consider a policy that covers you for the worst possible scenario, such as an accident requiring an emergency flight home. Find out in advance if your insurance plan will make payments directly to providers or if they'll reimburse you later for overseas health expenditures. The former option is generally preferable, as it doesn't require you to pay for services in a foreign country.

RECOMMENDED VACCINATIONS

The World Health Organization (WHO) recommends that all travellers should be covered for diphtheria, tetanus, measles, mumps, rubella and polio, regardless of their intended destination. Since most vaccines don't produce immunity until at least two weeks after they're given, visit a physician at least six weeks before your departure.

INTERNET RESOURCES

International Travel and Health, a publication of the WHO, is revised annually and is available online at www.who.int/ith. Other useful websites include www.mdtravelhealth.com (travel health recommendations for every country, which are updated daily), www.fitfortravel.scot.nhs.uk (general travel advice for the layperson), www.ageconcern.org.uk (advice on travel for the elderly) and www.mariestopes.org.uk (information on women's health and contraception).

It's also a good idea to consult your government's travel health website before departure:

Australia (www.dfat.gov.au/travel/)
Canada (www.travelhealth.gc.ca)
United Kingdom (www.doh.gov.uk/traveladvice)
United States (www.cdc.gov/travel)

IN TRANSIT

DEEP VEIN THROMBOSIS (DVT)

Blood clots may form in the legs during plane flights, chiefly because of prolonged immobility. The longer the flight, the greater the risk. The chief symptom of DVT is swelling or pain of the foot, ankle or calf, usually but not always on just one side. When a blood clot travels to the lungs, it may cause chest pain and breathing difficulties. Travellers with any of these symptoms should immediately seek medical attention.

To prevent the development of DVT on long flights you should walk about the cabin, contract the leg muscles while sitting, drink plenty of fluids and avoid alcohol and tobacco.

JET LAG & MOTION SICKNESS

To avoid jet lag (common when crossing more than five time zones) try drinking plenty of nonalchoholic fluids and eating light meals. Upon arrival, get exposure to natural sunlight and readjust your schedule (for meals, sleep and so on) as soon as possible.

Antihistamines such as dimenhydrinate (Dramamine) and meclizine (Antivert, Bonine) are usually the first choice for treating motion sickness. A herbal alternative is ginger.

IN POLAND

AVAILABILITY & COST OF HEALTH CARE

High-quality medical care is not always readily available outside of major cities, but embassies, consulates and five-star hotels can usually recommend doctors or clinics. In some cases, medical supplies required in hospital may need to be bought from a pharmacy and nursing care may be limited.

Note that there can be an increased risk of hepatitis B and HIV transmission via poorly sterilised equipment.

INFECTIOUS DISEASES

Tick-borne encephalitis is spread by tick bites. It is a serious infection of the brain and vaccination is advised for those in risk areas who are unable to avoid tick bites (such as campers, forestry workers and walkers). Two doses of vaccine will give a year's protection, and three doses will cover you for up to three years.

TRAVELLER'S DIARRHOEA

To prevent diarrhoea, avoid tap water unless it has been boiled, filtered or chemically disinfected (with iodine tablets) and steer clear of ice. Only eat fresh fruits or vegetables if cooked or peeled, and be wary of dairy products that may contain unpasteurised milk. Eat food that is hot through and avoid buffet-style meals. If a restaurant is full of locals the food is probably safe.

If you develop diarrhoea, be sure to drink plenty of fluids, preferably an oral rehydration solution (eg dioralyte). A few loose stools don't require treatment, but if you start having more than four or five stools a day, you should start taking an antibiotic (usually a quinolone drug) and an antidiarrhoeal agent (such as loperamide). If diarrhoea is bloody, persists for more than 72 hours or is accompanied by fever, shaking, chills or severe abdominal pain you should seek medical attention.

ENVIRONMENTAL HAZARDS
Insect Bites & Stings

Mosquitoes are found in most parts of Europe. They are a particular pest around the region of the Great Masurian Lakes. They may not carry malaria but can cause irritation and infected bites. Use a DEET-based insect repellent.

Bees and wasps cause real problems only to those with a severe allergy (anaphylaxis). If you have a severe allergy to bee or wasp stings carry an 'epipen' or similar adrenaline injection.

Bed bugs lead to very itchy, lumpy bites. Spraying the mattress with crawling insect killer after changing bedding will get rid of them.

Scabies are tiny mites that live in the skin, particularly between the fingers. They cause an intensely itchy rash. Scabies are easily treated with lotion from a pharmacy; other members of the household also need treating to avoid spreading scabies between asymptomatic carriers.

TRAVELLING WITH CHILDREN

All travellers with children should know how to treat minor ailments and when to seek medical treatment. Make sure the children are up to date with routine vaccinations, and discuss possible travel vaccines well before departure, as some vaccines are not suitable for children under one year of age.

In hot moist climates any wound or break in the skin is likely to let in infection. The area should be cleaned and kept dry.

Remember to avoid contaminated food and water. If your child has vomiting or diarrhoea, lost fluid and salts must be replaced. It may be helpful to take rehydration powders for reconstituting with boiled water.

Children should be encouraged to avoid and mistrust any dogs or other mammals because of the risk of rabies and other diseases. Any bite, scratch or lick from a warm-blooded, furry animal should immediately be thoroughly cleaned. If there is any possibility that the animal is infected with rabies, immediate medical assistance should be sought.

WOMEN'S HEALTH

Travelling during pregnancy is usually possible but always consult your doctor before planning your trip. The most risky times for travel are during the first 12 weeks of pregnancy and after 30 weeks.

SEXUAL HEALTH

Emergency contraception is most effective if taken within 24 hours after unprotected sex. The **International Planned Parent Federation** (www.ippf.org) can advise about the availability of contraception in different countries.

When buying condoms, look for a European CE mark, which means that they have been rigorously tested, and then keep them in a cool dry place or they may crack and perish.

HEALTH

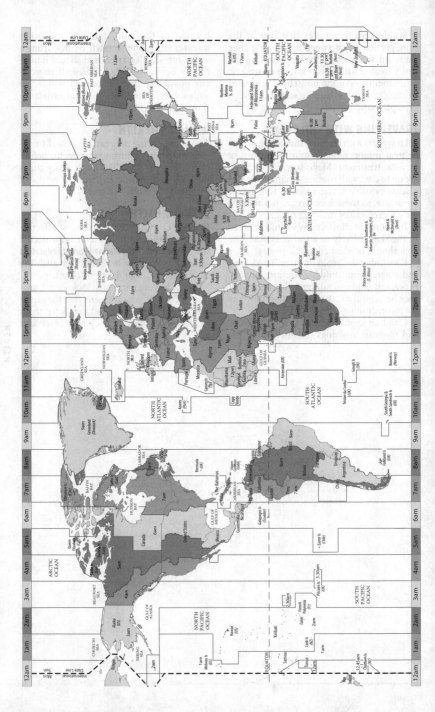

Language

CONTENTS

Polish is a western variety of the Slavonic languages found in Central and Eastern Europe, such as Croatian, Czech, Russian, Serbian, Slovak and Slovene.

Ideally, everyone who wants to travel in Poland should know some basic Polish – the more you know the easier your travel is likely to be and the more you'll get out of your time in the country. For a more comprehensive guide to the language, get a copy of Lonely Planet's *Polish Phrasebook*.

THE POLISH ALPHABET

Polish letters with diacritical marks are treated as separate letters, and the order of the Polish alphabet is as follows:

a ą b c ć d e ę f g h i j k l ł m n ń o ó p (q) r s ś t u (v) w (x) y z ź ż

The letters **q**, **v** and **x** appear only in words of foreign origin.

PRONUNCIATION

Written Polish is phonetically consistent, which means that the pronunciation of letters or clusters of letters doesn't vary from word to word. The stress almost always falls on the second-last syllable.

Vowels

Polish vowels are pure, consisting of one sound only, and are of roughly even length. Their approximate pronunciations are as follows:

a	as the 'u' in 'cut'
ą	a highly nasalised vowel; a cross between the 'awn' in 'lawn' and the 'ong' in 'long'
e	'e' in 'ten'
ę	also highly nasalised; like the 'eng' in 'engage' (where the 'ng' is one sound, not 'n' followed by 'g'); pronounced as **e** when word-final
i	as in 'police' but shorter
o	as in 'not'
ó	the same as Polish **u**
u	as in 'put'
y	as the in 'i' in 'bit'

Consonants

Most Polish consonants are pronounced as in English. However, there are some very fine distinctions between certain consonants in Polish, which English speakers may find difficult to produce. The following guide only gives approximations of the correct pronunciation – your best bet is to listen to and learn from native speakers:

c	as the 'ts' in 'its'
ch	as the 'ch' in Scottish *loch*
cz	as the 'ch' in 'church'
ć	similar to **c** but pronounced with the tongue a little further back on the roof of the mouth; pronounced as 'tsi' before vowels
dz	as the 'ds' in 'adds up'
dź	similar to **dz** but pronounced with the tongue a little further back on the roof of the mouth; pronounced as 'dzi' before vowels
dż	as the 'j' in 'jam'
g	as in 'get'
h	the same as **ch**
j	as the 'y' in 'yet'
ł	as the 'w' in 'wine'
ń	as the 'ni' in 'onion'; written as 'ni' before vowels

r	always trilled
rz	as the 's' in 'pleasure'
s	as in 'set'
sz	as the 'sh' in 'show'
ś	similar to **s** but not as strident; written as 'si' before vowels
w	'v' in 'van'
ź	similar to **z** but not as strident; written as 'zi' before vowels
ż	the same as **rz**
szcz	the most obtuse-looking consonant cluster; pronounced as the 'shch' in 'fresh cheese'

The following consonants are unvoiced when they are word-final: **b** is pronounced as 'p', **d** as 't', **g** as 'k', **w** as 'f', **z** as 's' and **rz** as 'sz'.

Finally, here's the favourite Polish tongue-twister for you to test your pronunciation skills on:

Chrząszcz brzmi w trzcinie.
The cockchafer buzzes in the weeds.

ACCOMMODATION

Where can I find a ...?
Gdzie mogę znaleźć ...?   gdje *mo*·ge zna·leshch ...

camping ground
camping   kam·peenk
guesthouse
pensjonat   pen·*syo*·nat
hotel
hotel   *ho*·tel
youth hostel
schronisko młodzieżowe   sro·*nees*·ko mwo·dje·*zho*·ve

Where is a cheap hotel?
Gdzie jest tani hotel?   gdje yest *ta*·nee *ho*·tel
What is the address?
Jaki jest adres?   *ya*·kee yest *a*·dres
Please write down the address.
Proszę to napisać.   *pro*·she to na·*pee*·sach
Do you have any rooms available?
Czy są wolne pokoje?   chi som *vol*·ne po·*ko*·ye

I'd like (a) ...
Poproszę o ...   po·*pro*·she o ...
bed
łóżko   *woosh*·ko
single room
pokój jednoosobowy   *po*·kooy yed·no·o·so·*bo*·vi
double bed
podwójnym łóżkiem   pod·*vooy*·nim *woosh*·kyem
room
pokój   *po*·kooy

twin room with two beds
pokój dwuosobowy   *po*·kooy dvoo·o·so·*bo*·vi
room with a bathroom
pokój z łazienką   *po*·kooy s wa·*zhen*·kom
to share a dorm
łóżko w sali zbiorowej   *woosh*·ko *fsa*·lee zbyo·*ro*·vey

MAKING A RESERVATION
(for written and phone inquiries)

from ...	*od ...*
to ...	*do ...*
date	*data*
surname	*nazwisko*
I'd like to book ...	*Chcę zarezerwować ...*
price	*cena*
credit card	*karta kredytowa*
number	*numer*
expiry date	*data ważności*

How much is it per night?
Ile kosztuje za noc?   ee·le kosh·*too*·ye za nots
May I see it?
Czy mogę go zobaczyć?   chi *mo*·ge go zo·*ba*·chich
Where is the bathroom?
Gdzie jest łazienka?   gdje yest wa·*zhen*·ka
Where is the toilet?
Gdzie są toalety?   gdje som to·a·*le*·ti
I'm leaving today.
Wyjeżdżam dziś.   vi·*yesh*·djam djeesh

CONVERSATION & ESSENTIALS

Hello.	*Dzień dobry.*	djen *do*·bri
Goodbye.	*Do widzenia.*	do vee·*dze*·nya
Yes.	*Tak.*	tak
No.	*Nie.*	nye
Please.	*Proszę.*	*pro*·she
Thank you.	*Dziękuję.*	djen·*koo*·ye
You're welcome.	*Proszę.*	*pro*·she
Excuse me.	*Przepraszam.*	pshe·*pra*·sham
Sorry.	*Przepraszam.*	pshe·*pra*·sham
I like ...	*Lubię ...*	*loo*·bye ...
I don't like ...	*Nie lubię ...*	nye *loo*·bye ...
Just a minute.	*Chwileczkę.*	hfee·*lech*·ke

What's your name?
Jak masz na imię?   yak mash na *ee*·mye
My name is ...
Mam na imię ...   mam na *ee*·mye ...
I'm from ...
Jestem z ...   *yes*·tem s ...
Where are you from?
Skąd pan/pani jest?   skont pan/*pa*·nee yest (pol, m/f)
Skąd jesteś?   skont *yes*·tesh (inf)

DIRECTIONS

Where is ...?
Gdzie jest ...? gdje yest ...
Go straight ahead.
Proszę iść prosto. pro-she eeshch pros-to
Turn left.
Proszę skręcić w lewo. pro-she skren-cheech fle-vo.
Turn right.
Proszę skręcić w prawo. pro-she skren-cheech fpra-vo.
at the corner
na rogu na ro-goo
at the traffic lights
na światłach na shfya-twah

SIGNS

Wejście	Entrance
Wyjście	Exit
Informacja	Information
Otwarte	Open
Zamknięte	Closed
Wzbroniony	Prohibited
Posterunek Policji	Police Station
Toalety	Toilets/WC
Panowie	Men
Panie	Women

---

behind	za	za
in front of	przed	pshet
opposite	naprzeciwko	na-pshe-cheef-ko
far (from)	daleko	da-le-ko
near (to)	blisko	blees-ko

beach	plaża	pla-zha
bridge	most	most
castle	zamek	za-mek
cathedral	katedra	ka-te-dra
church	kościół	kosh-choow
island	wyspa	vis-pa
lake	jezioro	ye-zho-ro
main square	plac główny	plats gwoov-ni
market	targ	tark
old city (town)	stare miasto	sta-re mya-sto
palace	pałac	pa-wats
ruins	ruiny	roo-ee-ni
sea	morze	mo-zhe
square	plac	plats
tower	wieża	vye-zha

HEALTH

I'm ill.
Jestem chory/a. yes-tem ho-ri/a (m/f)
It hurts here.
Tutaj mnie boli. too-tay mnye bo-lee

EMERGENCIES

Help!
Na pomoc! na po-mots
It's an emergency.
To jest nagły przypadek. to yest na-gwi pshi-pa-dek
I'm lost.
Zgubiłem się. zgoo-bee-wem she (m)
Zgubiłam się. zgoo-bee-wam she (f)
Leave me alone!
Proszę odejść! pro-she o-deyshch

Call ...! Proszę wezwać ...! pro-she vez-vach ...
 a doctor lekarza le-ka-zha
 the police policję po-lee-tsye

I'm asthmatic/epileptic.
Mam astmę/epilepsję. mam as-tme/e-pee-lep-sye
I'm diabetic.
Jestem diabetykiem. yes-tem dya-be-ti-kyem

I'm allergic to ...
Mam uczulenie na ...
mam oo-choo-le-nye na ...
 antibiotics antybiotyki an-ti-byo-ti-kee
 penicillin penicylinę pe-nee-tsi-lee-ne
 bees pszczoły pshcho-wi

 antiseptic antyseptyczny an-ti-sep-tich-ni
 aspirin aspiryna as-pee-ri-na
 condoms kondomy kon-do-mi
 contraceptive środek anty- shro-dek an-ti-
  koncepcyjny kon-tsep-tsiy-ni
 diarrhoea biegunka bye-goon-ka
 medicine lek lek
 nausea mdłości mdwosh-chee
 sunblock cream krem do opalania krem do o-pa-la-nya
 tampons tampony tam-po-ni

LANGUAGE DIFFICULTIES

Do you speak English?
Czy pan/pani mówi chi pan/pa-nee moo-vee
 po angielsku? po an-gyel-skoo (m/f)
Does anyone here speak English?
Czy ktoś tu mówi chi ktosh too moo-vee
 po angielsku? po an-gyel-skoo
How do you say ...?
Jak się mówi ...? yak she moo-vee ...
What does it mean?
Co to znaczy? tso to zna-chi
I understand.
rozumiem. ro-zoo-myem
I don't understand.
Nie rozumiem. nye ro-zoo-myem

Could you write it down, please?
Proszę to napisać. pro·she to na·*pee*·sach
Can you show me (on the map)?
Proszę mi pokazać pro·she mee po·*ka*·zach
(na mapie). (na *ma*·pye)

NUMBERS

0	zero	ze·ro
1	jeden	ye·den
2	dwa	dva
3	trzy	tshi
4	cztery	chte·ri
5	pięć	pyench
6	sześć	sheshch
7	siedem	she·dem
8	osiem	o·shem
9	dziewięć	dje·vyench
10	dziesięć	dje·shench
11	jedenaście	ye·de·*nash*·che
12	dwanaście	dva·*nash*·che
13	trzynaście	tshi·*nash*·che
14	czternaście	chter·*nash*·che
15	piętnaście	pyent·*nash*·che
16	szesnaście	shes·*nash*·che
17	siedemnaście	she·dem·*nash*·che
18	osiemnaście	o·shem·*nash*·che
19	dziewiętnaście	dje·vyet·*nash*·che
20	dwadzieścia	dva·*djesh*·cha
21	dwadzieścia jeden	dva·*djesh*·cha ye·den
22	dwadzieścia dwa	dva·*djesh*·cha dva
30	trzydzieści	tshi·*djesh*·chee
40	czterdzieści	chter·*djesh*·chee
50	pięćdziesiąt	pyen·*dje*·shont
60	sześćdziesiąt	shesh·*dje*·shont
70	siedemdziesiąt	she·dem·*dje*·shont
80	osiemdziesiąt	o·shem·*dje*·shont
90	dziewięćdziesiąt	dje·vyen·*dje*·shont
100	sto	sto
1000	tysiąc	*ti*·shonts

PAPERWORK

given names	imiona	ee·*myo*·na
surname	nazwisko	naz·*vees*·ko
nationality	narodowość	na·ro·do·*voshch*
date of birth	data urodzenia	da·ta oo·ro·*dze*·nya
place of birth	miejsce	*myey*·stse
	urodzenia	oo·ro·*dze*·nya
sex/gender	płeć	pwech
passport	paszport	*pash*·port
visa	wiza	*vee*·za

QUESTION WORDS

Who?	Kto?	kto
What?	Co?	tso
What is it?	Co to jest?	tso to yest
When?	Kiedy?	*kye*·di
Where?	Gdzie?	gdje
Which?	Który?	*ktoo*·ri
Why?	Dlaczego?	dla·*che*·go
How?	Jak?	yak

SHOPPING & SERVICES

I'd like to buy ...
Chcę kupić ... htse *koo*·peech ...
How much is it?
Ile to kosztuje? ee·le to kosh·*too*·ye
I don't like it.
Nie podoba mi się. nye po·*do*·ba mee she
May I look at it?
Czy mogę to zobaczyć? chi *mo*·ge to zo·*ba*·chich
I'm just looking.
Tylko oglądam. *til*·ko o·*glon*·dam
It's expensive.
To jest drogie. to yest *dro*·gye
I'll take it.
Wezmę to. *vez*·me to
Can I pay by credit card?
Czy mogę zapłacić chi *mo*·ge za·*pwa*·cheech
kartą kredytową? *kar*·tom kre·di·*to*·vom

more	więcej	*vyen*·tsey
less	mniej	mnyey
smaller	mniejszy	*mnyey*·shi
bigger	większy	*vyenk*·shi

Where's ...?
Gdzie jest ...? gdje yest ...

a bank
bank bank
the church
kościół *kosh*·choow
the city centre
centrum *tsen*·troom
the ... embassy
ambasada ... am·ba·*sa*·da ...
the hospital
szpital *shpee*·tal
the hotel
hotel *ho*·tel
an Internet café
kawiarnia internetowa ka·*vyar*·nya een·ter·ne·*to*·va
the market
targ tark
the museum
muzeum moo·ze·oom
the police station
posterunek policji pos·te·*roo*·nek po·*lee*·tsyee
the post office
poczta *poch*·ta
a public phone
automat telefoniczny aw·*to*·mat te·le·fo·*neech*·ni

a public toilet
toaleta publiczna   to·a·*le*·ta poo·*bleech*·na
the tourist information office
biuro informacji   *byoo*·ro een·for·*ma*·tsyee
  turystycznej   too·ris·*tich*·ney

POLISH COMPUTER JARGON

If you surf the Web at a Polish Internet café you may
have to do it in Polish. The following is a bit of useful
Polish cyberspeak:

Bookmark	*Zakładka*
Close	*Zamknij*
Copy	*Kopiuj*
Cut	*Wytnij*
Delete	*Usuń*
Edit	*Edycja*
Exit	*Zakończ*
File	*Plik*
Help	*Pomoc*
Insert	*Wstaw*
New	*Nowy*
Open	*Otwórz*
Paste	*Wklej*
Print	*Drukuj*
Save	*Zapisz*
Save As	*Zapisz Jako*
Search	*Szukaj*
View	*Widok*

TIME & DATES
What time is it?
  Która jest godzina?   *ktoo*·ra yest go·*djee*·na
It's 10 o'clock.
  Jest dziesiąta.   yest dje·*shon*·ta

in the morning	*rano*	*ra*·no
in the afternoon	*po południu*	po po·*wood*·nyoo
in the evening	*wieczorem*	vye·*cho*·rem
today	*dziś/dzisiaj*	djeesh/*djee*·shay
tomorrow	*jutro*	*yoo*·tro
yesterday	*wczoraj*	*fcho*·ray

Monday	*poniedziałek*	po·nye·*dja*·wek
Tuesday	*wtorek*	*fto*·rek
Wednesday	*środa*	*shro*·da
Thursday	*czwartek*	*chfar*·tek
Friday	*piątek*	*pyon*·tek
Saturday	*sobota*	so·*bo*·ta
Sunday	*niedziela*	nye·*dje*·la

January	*styczeń*	*sti*·chen
February	*luty*	*loo*·ti
March	*marzec*	*ma*·zhets

April	*kwiecień*	*kfye*·chen
May	*maj*	may
June	*czerwiec*	*cher*·vyets
July	*lipiec*	*lee*·pyets
August	*sierpień*	*sher*·pyen
September	*wrzesień*	*vzhe*·shen
October	*październik*	pazh·*djer*·neek
November	*listopad*	lees·*to*·pat
December	*grudzień*	*groo*·djen

TRANSPORT
Public Transport
What time does the ... leave/arrive?
O której odchodzi/przychodzi ...?
o *ktoo*·rey ot·*ho*·djee/pshi·*ho*·djee ...

boat	
łódź	wooch
bus	
autobus	aw·*to*·boos
plane	
samolot	sa·*mo*·lot
train	
pociąg	*po*·chonk
tram	
tramwaj	*tram*·vay

I'd like a ... ticket.
Poproszę bilet ...
po·*pro*·she *bee*·let ...

one-way	
w jedną stronę	*fyed*·nom *stro*·ne
return	
powrotny	po·*vrot*·ni

I want to go to ...
  Chcę jechać do ...   htse *ye*·hach do ...

1st class	*pierwszą klasę*	*pyer*·fshom *kla*·se
2nd class	*drugą klasę*	*droo*·gom *kla*·se
cancel	*odwołać*	ot·*vo*·wach
delay	*opóźnienie*	o·poozh·*nye*·nye
the first	*pierwszy*	*pyer*·fshi
the last	*ostatni*	os·*tat*·ni
platform	*peron*	*pe*·ron
ticket office	*kasa biletowa*	*ka*·sa bee·le·*to*·va
timetable	*rozkład jazdy*	*ros*·kwat *yaz*·di
train station	*dworzec kolejowy*	*dvo*·zhets ko·le·*yo*·vi

Private Transport
I'd like to hire a ...
Chcę wypożyczyć ...
htse vi·po·*zhi*·chich ...

bicycle	
rower	*ro*·ver

car

samochód	sa·*mo*·hoot
motorbike	
motocykl	mo·*to*·tsikl

Where's the nearest petrol station?
Gdzie jest najbliższa — gdje yest nay·*bleesh*·sha
stacja benzynowa? — *sta*·tsya ben·zi·*no*·va
Please fill it up.
Proszę napełnić bak. — *pro*·she na·*peoo*·neech bak
I'd like ... litres.
Poproszę ... litrów. — po·*pro*·she ... *leet*·roof

petrol	*benzyna*	ben·*zi*·na
regular	*zwykła*	*zvik*·wa
leaded	*ołowiowa*	o·wo·*vyo*·va
unleaded	*bezołowiowa*	be·so·wo·*vyo*·va

ROAD SIGNS

Objazd	Detour
Parkowanie Wzbronione	No Parking
Uwaga	Caution
Wjazd	Entry
Wjazd Wzbroniony	No Entry
Wyjazd	Exit

Is this the road to ...?
Czy ta droga prowadzi — chi ta *dro*·ga pro·*va*·djee
do ...? — do ...
Can I park here?
Czy można tu parkować? — chi *mozh*·na too par·*ko*·vach
How long can I park here?
Jak długo można — yak *dwoo*·go *mozh*·na
tu parkować? — too par·*ko*·vach
I need a mechanic.
Potrzebuję mechanika. — pot·she·*boo*·ye me·ha·*nee*·ka
The car has broken down.
Samochód się zepsuł. — sa·*mo*·hoot she *zep*·soow
It won't start.
Nie zapala. — nye za·*pa*·la
I have a flat tyre.
Złapałem gumę. — zwa·*pa*·wem *goo*·me (m)
Złapałam gumę. — zwa·*pa*·wam *goo*·me (f)
I've run out of petrol.
Zabrakło mi benzyny. — za·*brak*·wo mee ben·*zi*·ni

TRAVEL WITH CHILDREN
Where can I find a baby-sitter?
Gdzie można znaleźć opiekunkę do dziecka?
gdje *mozh*·na *zna*·leshch o·pye·*koon*·ke do *djets*·ka
Can you put an extra bed in the room?
Poproszę o dodatkowe łóżko w pokoju.
po·*pro*·she o do·dat·*ko*·we *woosh*·ko fpo·*ko*·yoo

I need a car with a child seat.
Potrzebuję samochód z fotelikiem dla dziecka.
pot·she·*boo*·ye sa·*mo*·hoot sfo·te·*lee*·kyem dla *djets*·ka
Do you have a children's menu?
Czy są jakieś dania dla dzieci?
chi som *ya*·kyesh *da*·nya dla *dje*·chee
Could you make it a child's portion?
Czy mogę prosić o porcję dla dziecka?
chi *mo*·ge pro·*sheech* o *por*·tsye dla *djets*·ka
Are children allowed to enter?
Czy dzieci mogą wejść?
chi *dje*·chee *mo*·gom veyshch
Are there any facilities for children?
Czy są jakieś udogodnienia dla dzieci?
chi som *ya*·kyesh oo·do·go·*dnye*·nya dla dje·chee

Glossary

The following is a list of terms and abbreviations you're likely to come across in your travels through Poland. For food and drink terms see p53.

Aleja or Aleje – avenue, main city street; abbreviated to Al in addresses and on maps
apteka – pharmacy

bankomat – ATM
bar mleczny – milk bar; a sort of basic self-service soup kitchen that serves very cheap, mostly vegetarian dishes
basen – swimming pool
bez łazienki – room without bathroom
bilet – ticket
biuro turystyczne – travel agency
biuro zakwaterowania – office that arranges private accommodation

Cepelia – a network of shops that sell artefacts made by local artisans
cerkiew (cerkwie) – Orthodox or Uniat church(es)
ciągnąć – push (on door)
cocktail bar – a café that serves cakes, pastries, milk shakes, ice creams and other sweets
cukiernia – cake shop

Desa – chain of old art and antique sellers
dom kultury – cultural centre
dom wycieczkowy – term applied to PTTK-run hostels; also called dom turysty
domek campingowy – cabin, bungalow, chalet

grosz – unit of Polish currency, abbreviated to gr; plural groszy; see also *złoty*

kantor(s) – private currency-exchange office(s)
kasa – ticket office
kawiarnia – café
kino – cinema
kiosk Ruch – newsagency
kolegiata – collegiate church
komórka – literally, 'cell'; commonly used for cellular (mobile) phone
kościół – church
kościół farny – parish church
księgarnia – bookshop
kwatery agroturystyczne – agrotourist accommodation
kwatery prywatne – rooms in private houses rented out to tourists

miejscówka – reserved-seat ticket
na zdrowie! – cheers!; literally, 'to the health'
noclegi – accommodation

odjazdy – departures (on transport schedules)
ogródek – literally, 'small garden', but also commonly used for any outdoor area of a café, restaurant or bar
otwarte – open

park narodowy – national park
parking strzeżony – guarded car park
pchać – pull (on door)
pensjonat(y) – pension or private guesthouse(s)
peron – railway platform
piekarnia – bakery
PKS – Państwowa Komunikacja Samochodowa; former state-run company that runs most of Poland's bus transport
plac – town square
poczta – post office
poczta główna – main post office
pokój 1-osobowy – single room
pokój 2-osobowy – double room
prowizja – commission banks charge on transactions
przechowalnia bagażu – left-luggage room
przez – via, en route (on transport timetables)
przyjazdy – arrivals (as seen on transport schedules)
PTSM – Polskie Towarzystwo Schronisk Młodzieżowych; Polish Youth Hostel Association
PTTK – Polskie Towarzystwo Turystyczno-Krajoznawcze; Polish Tourist & Countryside Association

rachunek – bill or check
rozkład jazdy – transport timetable
Rynek – Old Town Sq

schronisko górskie – mountain hostel, providing basic accommodation and meals, usually run by the *PTTK*
schronisko młodzieżowe – youth hostel
Sejm – the lower house of parliament
skansen – open-air museum of traditional architecture
sklep – shop
specjalność zakładu – on a menu, speciality of the house
stanica wodna – waterside hostel, usually with boats, kayaks and other water-related facilities
stołówka – canteen; restaurant or cafeteria of a holiday home, hostel etc

Święty/a – saint; abbreviated to Św (St)

toalety – toilet

ulgowy (bilet) – reduced or discounted (ticket)
ulica – street; abbreviated to ul in addresses (and placed before the actual name); usually omitted on maps

wejście – entrance; also called wjzad
wódka – vodka; the number one Polish spirit
wyście – exit; also called wyjazd

z łazienka – room with bathroom
zakaz parkowanie – no parking
zakaz wstępu – no entry
zamek – castle
zamknięte – closed
zdrój – spa
złoty – unit of Polish currency; abbreviated to zł; divided into 100 units called *grosz*
zniżka studencka – student discount

Behind the Scenes

THIS BOOK
The first four editions of Lonely Planet's *Poland* were written by Krzysztof Dydyński. The research and writing of this edition was coordinated by Neil Wilson with assistance from Tom Parkinson and Richard Watkins. Dr Caroline Evans wrote the Health chapter.

THANKS from the Authors
Neil Wilson *Dzękuję bardzo* to the helpful staff at tourist information desks around Poland, and to the curator of Warsaw's Mauzoleum Walki i Męczeństwa for his moving reminiscence of WWII. Thanks also to Lonely Planet's hard-working editors and cartographers for their patience and encouragement.

Tom Parkinson As ever, this book would have been far less fun without the random folk who joined me for a drink (or dozen) and fed me info: a cheery *chuj ci w dupe* to Lukasz, Ania and friends at the Czerwony Gryf; Judd and Erica at the Wolf's Lair; Thomas, Erik, Tobias, Magda and the hostel folk in Gdańsk; Jenni, for some quality time out; Kathryn Hanks, for invaluable assistance in Gdańsk and light relief in Sopot; and Nina K, for a whole load of stuff I don't deserve. Extra special thanks to Bartek Lisek of Euro-26, who gave me an expert tour of Sopot purely because he knows Neil's girlfriend's best mate.

Thanks also to the various people who looked after my baggage en route, the bus drivers who told me where to get off and the lady hoteliers in Grudziądz who very kindly complimented me on my six words of Polish. Finally, cheers to Neil W and Fiona C, for making this whole thing a nice smooth process.

Richard Watkins Many thanks are due to the helpful and professional staff at the tourist offices in Lublin, Przemyśl, Sanok, Rzeszów, Chełm, Zamość and Krynica. I would also like to thank Adam Bogaczewicz in Rzeszów, and Jan Piotrowski, Gosia Graczyk and staff at the Polish embassy in London for their kind assistance with my research.

CREDITS
This title was commissioned and developed in Lonely Planet's London office by Fiona Christie and Imogen Franks with the help of Stefanie Di Trocchio. Cartography for this guide was developed by Mark Griffiths.

Sarah Sloane coordinated the cartography and Helen Christinis the editing. Eoin Dunlevy managed this project. The book was laid out by Sally Darmody, and Margie Jung selected the colour images. Jane Hart designed the cover, and Sonya Brooke did on the artwork. Quentin Frayne coordinated the editing of the language content.

A talented team of editors, proofers, cartographers and designers assisted on this project: Katie Lynch, Victoria Harrison, Monique Choy, Anne Mulvaney, Peter Cruttenden, Evan Jones, Kate McLeod, Suzannah Shwer, Laura Jane, Jenny Jones, Michael Ruff, Katherine Marsh, Jacqueline McLeod, Nina Rousseau, Bonnie Wintle, Jovan Djukanovic, Piotr Czajkowski and Wayne Murphy.

THE LONELY PLANET STORY
The story begins with a classic travel adventure: Tony and Maureen Wheeler's 1972 journey across Europe and Asia to Australia. There was no useful information about the overland trail then, so Tony and Maureen published the first Lonely Planet guidebook to meet a growing need.

From a kitchen table, Lonely Planet has grown to become the largest independent travel publisher in the world, with offices in Melbourne (Australia), Oakland (USA) and London (UK). Today Lonely Planet guidebooks cover the globe. There is an ever-growing list of books and information in a variety of media. Some things haven't changed. The main aim is still to make it possible for adventurous travellers to get out there – to explore and better understand the world.

At Lonely Planet we believe travellers can make a positive contribution to the countries they visit – if they respect their host communities and spend their money wisely. Every year 5% of company profit is donated to charities around the world.

THANKS from Lonely Planet

Many thanks to the hundreds of travellers who used the last edition and wrote to us with helpful hints, useful advice and interesting anecdotes:

A Rene Allen, Andrew Ambrosius, Brian & Mary Ashmore, Bev & Joe Atiyah, Olivier Auber **B** Steve Barnett, Janice Barrett, Marta Ewa Bartoszek, Tim J Bertram, Sander Bots, Kees Botschuijver, Andy Bramwell, Michelle Brazier, Tomas Brisuda, Dr John D Brunton, Grzegorz Brzezicki, David Bugden, John T Burke **C** Mairead & Edel Callanan, Alexandre Campanella, Alexander Cellmer, Cass Chan, Paul Church, Mark Cooper, Kevin Cullinane, Pat Culliton, Bryan Cumner **D** Cor Dam, Steve Davies, Nicolas Delerue, Mike Dickens, Nelson Duarte, Jane Duffy **E** Michael J Eatroff, Elizabeth Elizabeth **F** Mario Falzon, Coralie Farlee, Stephen Fenech, Tim Finn **G** John Geddes, David Goldberg, Sam Golledge, Alessandro Grimaldi, Rafal Guzewicz **H** Beata Haber, Tim Hall, Lynn Halliday, Mariska Hansen, Adrian Holloway, Chris Howard, Kevin Hubbard, Denis Hughes, Gareth Hughes, Marcin Hunderuk **I** Gabrielle A Iwanow **J** Arne Jansen, Mark Jitlal, Andrew Joseph, Maritta Jumppanen **K** Edward Kellow, Colin Kirk, Danielle Kriz, Agata Krynicka, Noriko Kumagai **L** Joerg Lehnert, Maria Loebig,

Siria Lopez **M** Slava Madorsky, Gian Carlo Marciano, Mirek Marut, Howard Mathers, Jacek Matwiejczyk, Carol McGillivray, Dr J S McLintock, Sarah Merrit, Tomasz Migdal, Jan Misiewicz, Richard Moriarty, Tracey Murphy **N** Jacques Noel, L E Nowosielska **O** Lucy Openshaw, Chris Owen **P** Duncan Paisley, Gregory A Palermo, Alison Parfitt, Roger Parris, Michael Parsons, Agata Pietrzykowska, Jacek Pliszka, Adrian Pritchard **R** Peter Ratcliffe, Rachel Reeson, Wilfried Rekowski, Ronald Jan Rieger, Danyo Romijn, Jack Rush **S** Michal S, Marcin Sadurski, Eva Schrom, Larry Schwarz, Kerstin Seja, Aneta Singh, Jacek Sosnowski, Barry Stiefel, Rita Swiecilo **T** Julie Tabor, Wojciech Tyszlewicz **V** Dewy Van Hoogmoed, Muntsa Vilamitjana **W** Diana Weinert, Kate Wierciak, John Wilks, Mark Wilson, Joseph & Elaine Wojtowicz **Y** Pete Yates **Z** Mathieu Zagrodzki, Daniela Zambaldi, Paul Zoglin

ACKNOWLEDGMENTS

Many thanks to the following for the use of their content:

Globe on back cover © Mountain High Maps 1993 Digital Wisdom, Inc.

SEND US YOUR FEEDBACK

We love to hear from travellers – your comments keep us on our toes and help make our books better. Our well-travelled team reads every word on what you loved or loathed about this book. Although we cannot reply individually to postal submissions, we always guarantee that your feedback goes straight to the appropriate authors, in time for the next edition. Each person who sends us information is thanked in the next edition – and the most useful submissions are rewarded with a free book.

To send us your updates and find out about Lonely Planet events, newsletters and travel news visit our award-winning website: **www.lonelyplanet.com/feedback**

Note: We may edit, reproduce and incorporate your comments in Lonely Planet products such as guidebooks, websites and digital products, so let us know if you don't want your comments reproduced or your name acknowledged. For a copy of our privacy policy visit www.lonelyplanet.com/privacy.

Index

INDEX

000 Map pages
000 Location of colour photographs

INDEX

INDEX

000 Map pages
000 Location of colour photographs

INDEX

INDEX

INDEX

INDEX

000 Map pages
000 Location of colour photographs

INDEX

MAP LEGEND

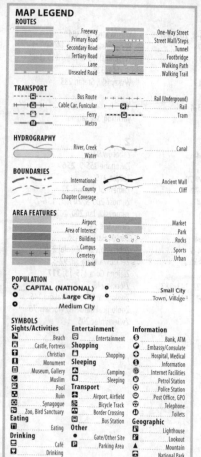

ROUTES

Freeway	One-Way Street
Primary Road	Street Mall/Steps
Secondary Road	Tunnel
Tertiary Road	Footbridge
Lane	Walking Path
Unsealed Road	Walking Trail

TRANSPORT

Bus Route	Rail (Underground)
Cable Car, Funicular	Rail
Ferry	Tram
Metro	

HYDROGRAPHY

River, Creek	Canal
Water	

BOUNDARIES

International	Ancient Wall
County	Cliff
Chapter Coverage	

AREA FEATURES

Airport	Market
Area of Interest	Park
Building	Rocks
Campus	Sports
Cemetery	Urban
Land	

POPULATION

○ CAPITAL (NATIONAL)	● Small City
● Large City	● Town, Village
● Medium City	

SYMBOLS

Sights/Activities
- Beach
- Castle, Fortress
- Christian
- Monument
- Museum, Gallery
- Muslim
- Pool
- Ruin
- Synagogue
- Zoo, Bird Sanctuary

Eating
- Eating

Drinking
- Café
- Drinking

Entertainment
- Entertainment

Shopping
- Shopping

Sleeping
- Camping
- Sleeping

Transport
- Airport, Airfield
- Bicycle Track
- Border Crossing
- Bus Station

Other
- Gate/Other Site
- Parking Area

Information
- Bank, ATM
- Embassy/Consulate
- Hospital, Medical
- Information
- Internet Facilities
- Petrol Station
- Police Station
- Post Office, GPO
- Telephone
- Toilets

Geographic
- Lighthouse
- Lookout
- Mountain
- National Park
- River Flow

LONELY PLANET OFFICES

Australia
Head Office
Locked Bag 1, Footscray, Victoria 3011
☎ 03 8379 8000, fax 03 8379 8111
talk2us@lonelyplanet.com.au

USA
150 Linden St, Oakland, CA 94607
☎ 510 893 8555, toll free 800 275 8555
fax 510 893 8572, info@lonelyplanet.com

UK
72–82 Rosebery Ave,
Clerkenwell, London EC1R 4RW
☎ 020 7841 9000, fax 020 7841 9001
go@lonelyplanet.co.uk

Published by Lonely Planet Publications Pty Ltd
ABN 36 005 607 983

© Lonely Planet 2005

© photographers as indicated 2005

Cover photographs: Royal Palace, Warsaw, Jon Arnold/Photolibrary
.com (front); Beach life on Baltic the coast, Krzysztof Dydyński/
Lonely Planet Images (back). Many of the images in this guide are
available for licensing from Lonely Planet Images: www.lonely
planetimages.com.

Printed through Colorcraft Ltd, Hong Kong
Printed in China